HANDBOOK OF PSYCHOLOGICAL CHANGE

HANDBOOK OF
PSYCHOLOGICAL
CHANGE

Psychotherapy Processes & Practices for the
21st Century

edited by

C. R. Snyder
&
Rick E. Ingram

John Wiley & Sons, Inc.
New York • Chichester • Weinheim • Brisbane • Singapore • Toronto

ACQUISITIONS EDITOR   Ellen Schatz
MARKETING MANAGER   Sue Lyons
PRODUCTION EDITOR   Sarah Wiley
SENIOR DESIGNER   Harry Nolan
ILLUSTRATION EDITOR   Anna Melhorn

This book was set in 9.5/11.5 Janson Text by PRD Group and printed and bound by Hamilton Printing. The cover was printed by Phoenix Color Corp.

This book is printed on acid free paper. ∞

ISBN 0-471-24191-1

Printed in the United States of America

10 9 8 7 6 5 4 3 2

To the prospect of a 21st century,
where psychotherapy will be available for the many,
rather than just the few . . .

It remains a reasonably well-accepted contention that it is undesirable for a therapist to be *a*theoretical when designing, implementing, or evaluating treatment programs. Theory guides intervention: Although it is true that no one theory accounts for or explains all human emotion, thought, and action, theory nevertheless provides proper guidance for clinical endeavors.

Yet the clear majority of psychological treatises have more to do with describing individuals or social systems than with the specific processes of *change*. Not surprisingly, for clinical work, the most direct and useful theories are those that propose to explain the processes of psychological change. For the first time, Snyder and Ingram have collected all-star authors to provide current conclusions and clues to the future on the various topics related to psychological change. Indeed, a welcome feature of almost all of the chapters in Snyder and Ingram's *Handbook of Psychological Change* is the direct attention given to the future. The authors—a group of valued contributors and promising pioneers—not only provide rich descriptions of what is known from various areas of scholarly inquiry but also set their sights on the as-yet unknown. This forward-looking feature is a decided strength that empowers the book to be not only a summary of past travels but also a blueprint for forthcoming journeys.

Reading the handbook is akin to taking a train ride from coast to coast along the central continua of the psychotherapeutic enterprise. One gets to see all of the sights while also getting to stop at all of the key stations along "Psychotherapy Central." One travels through long-term and short-term therapy, efficacy and effectiveness, prevention and therapy, health care and managed care, practice reform and practice standards, empirically-supported treatment (EST) and manual-based intervention, methodological issues and practice concerns, psychological and physical health, drugs and diagnostics, hope and perceived control, society and political matters, and therapist training and therapy evaluation. One also gets to look at the various participants in change (e.g., the client, the therapist) and their features (e.g., race, gender) and to visit the dominant theoretical orientations (e.g., behavioral, cognitive, cognitive-behavioral, interpersonal, psychodynamic) as practiced with individual adults, children, and the aged, and with marital couples and groups.

Although the authors represent a collection of scholars with firm roots in clinical science, the work is quite broadly conceived, and includes a wide range of topics that touch upon psychological change. Even within chapters there is evidence of breadth—citations to the influential and informative randomized clinical trials evaluating approaches to therapy are juxtaposed with occasional references to Bob Dylan, religious thinkers, or Chinese philosophy. Not unlike the recent but more circumscribed centennial celebration of clinical psychology (Routh & DeRubeis, 1998), the present handbook applauds our accomplishments and offers future directions. *Bon voyage!*

Philip C. Kendall, Ph.D., ABPP
Temple University

Routh, D.K., & DeRubeis, R.J. (Eds.) (1998). *The science of clinical psychology: Accomplishments and future directions.* Washington, DC: American Psychological Association.

This volume truly is an intergenerational effort. The senior editor recruited "his" former graduate student turned colleague as a co-editor. We have worked together on this project in a virtually seamless manner, sharing remarkably similar views about all matters pertaining to the present and future of the psychotherapy field. So too do many of the chapter authors have intergenerational relationships. As editors, we have invited our former and present graduate students to help on various chapters. Likewise, the individual chapter authors have blended their efforts with persons sharing common academic lineages. In this sense, there is a "passing on" of psychotherapy knowledge from one generation to the next in this volume. Although we reflect differing generations of writers, all involved in this project have set their gazes toward that string of tomorrows in the psychotherapy field. Indeed, this volume will be published in the first year of the second millennium, with the authors offering a collective vision about what lies ahead.

The reason for launching this project and our goal for the completed volume are one and the same—we perceived that there was a need for a year 2000 volume in which the authors traced not only how far we have come but provided some visions about what lies ahead for the psychotherapy field. We wanted to give a multifaceted look to the psychotherapy enterprise that could be read and used by seasoned practitioners, academicians, researchers, and students who were first embracing a possible career in the field. Again, therefore, this book is intergenerational because the authors wrote not only for those readers who already have completed their various graduate educations but also for the students who are presently in the throes of their psychotherapy training. We have tried to capture within the covers of this volume chapters that were at once authoritative, thoroughly up-to-date, evocative, and lucidly written. You will find that our scholars often share perspectives, but they also sometimes disagree, quite strongly, about future happenings in the field. Through this diversity of ideas, we want to promote a continued dialogue about the difficult issues that lie ahead for the psychotherapy field.

In this volume, we want to provide readers with in-depth information about the important research, practice, and viability issues that are (and sometimes are not) being faced in the psychotherapy field. As we considered the enormity of the psychotherapy field, it became obvious that we had limited space and would need to apportion sections according to our perceptions of their relative importance. Thus, in comparing the first section, Part I: Psychotherapeutic Change in Perspective, to the last section, Part VI: Psychotherapy into the 21st Century, you will notice that we have allotted only one chapter to the former and six to the latter. This reflects our view that we should be attending more to where we are going than where we have been. We also had the luxury of allocating only one chapter to history because of our confidence in the particular author's ability to describe it succinctly. Thus, in an approach to viewing our heritage that is unique from other historical coverages, in Chapter 1 A Changing History of Efforts to Understand and Control Change: The Case of Psychotherapy, Michael Mahoney traces the progression of our collective psychotherapy history as if it were a person who has come to us for help.

We view the effectiveness of psychotherapy as being important and in Part II we have devoted two chapters to the topic of Effectiveness of Psychotherapeutic Change. To dissect the effectiveness area, two teams of scholars take somewhat different and yet complementary approaches to this important topic. In Chapter 2 Randomized Clinical Trials in Psychotherapy Research: Methodology, Design, and Evaluation, David Haaga and William Stiles critique our previous methodologies aimed at exploring the reliability of the change process. Even more important, however, they provide new and workable suggestions for increasing the rigor of how we design, run, and interpret studies aimed at helping people. In Chapter 3 Empirically Supported Treatments: A Critical Analysis by Rick Ingram, Adele Hayes, and Walter Scott, we see just how far we have come in helping our clients to improve. Tracing the development of the empirically supported treatments area, Ingram and his colleagues describe the benefits of psychotherapy, along with an important caveat—it is better to make prudent statements about the small but growing list of treatments that do work than it is to take too much pride in the simplistic and oversold maxim that "psychotherapy works." The authors of the chapters in Part II remind us of the centerpiece role of empirical support in the viability of our various psychotherapy interventions. These authors also share the view that effective psychotherapy starts with a sense of humility for what we know about psychological change as well as a respect for what we do *not* know at this point in time.

As we thought about the next logical partition of the psychotherapy field, we concluded that we needed a sizable section, Part III: Components of Psychotherapeutic Change, to cover the heuristic elements found in most all psychotherapies (i.e., those factors believed to be fundamental to understanding what makes these interventions "work"). Accordingly, there are six chapters in this "How does it work?" Part III. At the beginning of Part III in Chapter 4 Therapist Variables, Edward Teyber and Faith McClure give us a glimpse of effective therapists, those who realize that psychotherapy is a relational enterprise, who can place personal views in the background so as to focus on the clients' worldviews, and who are flexible. Next, Nancy Petry, Howard Tennen, and Glenn Affleck in their Chapter 5 Stalking the Elusive Client Variable in Psychotherapy Research undertake a detectivelike search for the effective psychotherapy client variables. We will not expose their conclusions here, but we will comment that, based on the thoroughness of their scholarly search, any such client variable would be found.

"Change at Differing Stages" is the title of Chapter 6, written by James Prochaska. His latest views about the impactful roles of stages help us to understand some of the seemingly inexplicable happenings along the psychotherapy road. In the ensuing Chapter 7 Hope Theory: Updating a Common Process for Psychological Change by C. R. Snyder, Stephen Ilardi, Scott Michael, and Jen Cheavens, as well as Chapter 8 The Long and Short of Psychological Change: Toward a Goal-Centered Understanding of Treatment Durability and Adaptive Success by Paul Karoly and Cindy Wheeler Anderson, these two sets of authors offer carefully reasoned analyses about goal-guided self-regulation as a positive common factor in various intervention strategies. In Chapter 9 Enhancing Perceived Control in Psychotherapy, Suzanne Thompson and Michelle Wierson provide a compelling case for the underlying power and potential use of perceived control as a common process in guiding psychotherapy.

In Part IV: Psychotherapeutic Approaches, we include the latest theory, research, and applications pertaining to the most prominent systems of psychotherapy. We have made Part IV the largest one in the handbook, containing thirteen chapters on different therapeutic approaches. An additional aspect that we have inserted into Part IV is that the chapter authors include case histories to vivify and clarify their particular psychotherapeutic approaches. This latter aspect of the handbook reflects our desire to blend psychotherapy theories and applications in the spirit of their mutual benefit—this theme runs throughout the volume.

To launch Part IV, we open with the first major psychotherapy approach to impact the field and society more generally with its appealing ideas and concepts. We speak, of course, of the psychodynamic approach, which is the centerpiece of Chapter 10 Psychodynamic Approaches to Psychotherapy: Philosophical and Theoretical Foundations of Effective Practice by Doug Vakoch and Hans Strupp. Although the authors of this chapter cover the usual psychodynamic concepts, we believe that the reader will be surprised at the proposed new directions within a psychodynamic framework—

this chapter reflects turn-of-the-century thinking, and we do not mean the 20th but rather the 21st century. As a companion to Chapter 10, we next have Drew Westen's Chapter 11 Integrative Psychotherapy: Integrating Psychodynamic and Cognitive-Behavioral Theory and Technique. Westen provides a lens for clearly seeing how the psychodynamic principles lend themselves to more recent cognitive-behavior theories and psychotherapy research. His treatment of the topic is both integrative and extremely creative in blending these two important approaches.

We follow the psychodynamic-related chapters with another approach that has a fairly long history. Specifically, in Chapter 12 Existential Approaches to Psychotherapy, Constance Fischer, Brian McElwain, and J. Todd DuBoise show how clients, through existential psychotherapy approaches, can find meaning and solutions to their life problems by means of strong therapeutic relationships. This interpersonal theme is continued in the context of another approach that is based on relationships. More specifically, in Chapter 13 Interpersonal Psychotherapy, Ian Gotlib and Pamela Schraedley reveal the potential power of the therapeutic relationship in promoting positive change. Perhaps the very prototype of matters interpersonal is explored next in Chapter 14 Marital Therapy: Theory, Practice, and Empirical Status by Donald H. Baucom, Norman Epstein, and Kristina Coop Gordon. We certainly know that there will be many potential clients for this approach given the extremely high divorce rate. The importance of the interpersonal context for psychological change also is the focus of Chapter 15 Groups as Change Agents by Donelson Forsyth and John Corazzini. Taken together, the authors of chapters 12, 13, 14, and 15 use differing psychotherapy approaches to show how our human connection can promote positive psychological change.

Next is Chapter 16 Constructivist and Narrative Psychotherapies, where Robert Neimeyer and Alan Stewart advance the constructivist view that reality is a perceptual, contextual matter rather than some objective, veridical one. It is this perspective that lends itself beautifully to the various narrative approaches that help people to adjust their guiding, self-theories so as to become happier and more productive in their environmental settings. In the next Chapter 17 Feminist Therapy, Laura Brown shows how constructivist perspectives are empowering to people amidst constraining societal conditions; moreover, she speaks to the issue of clients changing those societal forces. By bringing to light the implicit assumptions that we make about the change process as contextualized in our society, Brown is at once revolutionary in thought and practical in linking feminist therapy to other treatments.

The next chapters in this section on psychotherapeutic approaches form a trilogy of sorts. In order, the authors focus initially (Chapter 18) on behavior therapy (which came first temporally), followed immediately by cognitive behavioral treatment approaches (Chapter

19), an evolution of behavior therapies, and then brief therapies (Chapter 20), most of which are cognitive behavioral in content. The advocates of modern behavior therapy, based on its early and classic research on stimulus-response principle, have staked out a well articulated theoretical and practice position. William Follette and Steven Hayes provide a lucid rationale and the related applications in their Chapter 18 Contemporary Behavior Therapy. These proponents of "traditional" behavioral therapy may have advanced it to a point beyond what you may have envisioned. In the next essay, Chapter 19 Cognitive and Cognitive Behavioral Therapies, Keith Dobson, Barbara Backs-Dermott, and David Dozois help the reader to understand why these cognitive-behavioral approaches have gained tremendous popularity among present-day therapists. In describing the present and future evolution of these approaches, the reader can discern how cognitive-behavioral psychotherapy is based on the fertile intellectual soil of cognitive approaches psychology more generally. Bernard Bloom, in his Chapter 20 Planned Short-Term Psychotherapies, thoroughly describes short-term treatments. His case, and it is a forceful one, is that with careful planning, we can quickly and effectively provide sufficient problem-focused help so that a large portion of people attain higher levels of functioning. The advocates of these short-term approaches typically use some variant of cognitive behavioral approaches and, as such, these brief approaches arguably will represent a numerical majority of future psychological interventions.

In Chapter 21, Long-Term Psychotherapy, of Paul Crits-Christoph and Jacques Barber address the issue of effectiveness in elongated treatment protocols, as well as how we may best understand change in this context. In the final Chapter 22 Psychopharmacology in Conjunction with Psychotherapy in Part IV, Michael Thase dissects the change process so as to illustrate when "talking" approaches are equally or perhaps even more effective than pharmaceutical ones. More importantly, he describes those instances when the outcomes achieved by non-pharmaceutical interventions are surpassed with the addition of suitable psychiatric drugs. Furthermore, in some instances, psychiatric medication per se may be the most efficacious mode of change. After reading this chapter, you should be more informed about the appropriate use of psychiatric medications.

We strongly believe that diversity issues and special samples are extremely important in psychotherapy at this point in time, and they will become even more crucial in the coming years. As such, in Part V: Psychotherapy with Special Samples, we have six chapters focusing on such issues. As with chapters in Part IV, those in Part V are brought to life by case historylike examples. We begin with children, where Michael C. Roberts, Eric M. Vernberg, and Yo Jackson in their Chapter 23 Psychotherapy with Children and Families provide an overarching framework for understanding the psychological change process in children. In our al-

beit biased view, they have produced the clearest available chapter-length presentation of the many important issues that we must face to provide better psychological care for our children. We thought it would be informative in our handbook to also take an in-depth look at two problems that originate in childhood. Accordingly, Alan J. Litrownik and Idalia Castillo-Cañez in their Chapter 24 Childhood Maltreatment: Treatment of Abuse/Incest Survivors tackle problems—abuse and incest—that reflect a national disgrace regarding parenthood. They review how difficult it can be to unravel these "trails of misery" and, equally important, suggest interventions to stop this tragic intergenerational cycle.

Along with the abuse and incest psychotherapy topic, we see another problem of almost epidemic proportions. We speak of persons who have undergone a traumatic stress of some sort and how to help them in psychotherapy. Addressing this point, Mardi Horowitz details the etiologies and the related effective treatment approaches in his Chapter 25 Brief Cognitive-Dynamic Treatment of Stress Response Syndromes. If you thought that persons with such stress reactions were virtually unreachable via treatment, Horowitz may change your views in this chapter.

In Chapter 26 Health Psychology by Timothy W. Smith, Jill B. Nealy, and Heidi A. Hamann, we are given an overview of perhaps the fastest growing approach to the change process. In this chapter, we see how psychologists can use diverse treatments in an equally diverse number of arenas where patients are treated for with physical problems. Through this chapter, we can begin to appreciate how much more we can do in this area in the 21st century. As such, professional health psychologists at the turn of this century may influence how we construe psychological change to the same degree that psychodynamic psychotherapists impacted the field at the turn of the last century.

The United States will be a truly multicultural society as we move deeper into the 21st century. Our psychotherapies that are aimed and tested largely on Caucasian, middle-class people still will work for this group whose relative population percentage is shrinking. But what do we know about psychological treatments for different racial and ethnic groups, the very ones who will increasingly be approaching a majority in subsequent decades? The usual answer to this latter question is "Very little." But you will find in Chapter 27 Race and Ethnicity in Psychotherapy Research that Bernadette Gray-Little and Danielle Kaplan provide an agenda that may change that answer.

To close Part V, perhaps it is fitting to address what we can do to deliver more effective and more widespread psychotherapy services. One need only look at the enormous cohort of baby boomers who with the march of time soon will make the numbers of seniors swell to unheard heights. At the risk of stating the obvious, unlike other "minority" groups, the elderly is one that, in time, most of us will join. Dolores Gallagher-Thompson, Christine McKibbin, Darrelle Koonce-

Volwiler, Ana Menendez, Douglas Stewart, and Larry W. Thompson in their Chapter 28 Psychotherapy with Older Adults make cogent suggestions about how we can vastly improve our psychotherapy efforts with the elderly.

This brings us to the final six chapters in Part VI: Psychotherapy into the 21st Century. C. R. Snyder, Diane McDermott, Ruth Leibowitz, and Jen Cheavens lead off with their Chapter 29 The Roles of Female Clinical Psychologists in Changing the Field of Psychotherapy. Based on the enormous numbers of female as compared to male graduate students who are obtaining their doctorates in clinical psychology, they speculate about a 21st century psychotherapy field in which females will play the leadership roles—some predictions are positive, some more negative, and all may prove provocative.

Next is Chapter 30 Future Directions for Prevention Science: From Research to Adoption by Kenneth Heller, Mary Wyman, and Sean M. Allen. Their compelling case is that those of us in the psychotherapy field could greatly help people if we engaged in more preventative activities rather than the psychotherapy applied after problems have formed.

In the next pair of chapters, based on current trends in the psychotherapy field, two renowned psychologists each foresee serious problems. For example, in Charles Kiesler's Chapter 31 National Mental Health Issues, he presents a sobering view that we had best change our mental health care policies to provide better and more widespread care to our population. Without such changes, he suggests that psychotherapists will not be reimbursed by insurers, thereby necessitating a massive downsizing in the educational psychotherapist training structure in the 21st century. Taking a somewhat different, albeit still critical, tact in Chapter 32 Critique of Psychotherapy in American Society, George Albee argues that we already have the psychological knowledge to affect positive changes in the lives of people, but we have done a poor job of making such help available to a wide range of people of differing ages, socioeconomic backgrounds, and race. He also decries the drift that he observes in the psychotherapy field toward an ever more biological and medication-oriented bias.

In Chapter 33 Psychotherapy: Questions for an Evolving Field, we, the editors, pose many thorny questions and provide our best answers to each. We will present a sample of roughly a fourth of our questions so that you get a sense of the psychotherapy landscape that we cover. Do we know the characteristics of good psychotherapists, and can we educate students so as to facilitate these characteristics? Do we really have a solid understanding of the interplay of people's needs for stability and their needs for change? Should our psychotherapy theories be aimed at just "troubled people" or be based on principles that are applicable to all people? Will biological or environmental change factors predominate in the 21st century? What role will com-

puters play in psychotherapy? How can those in the science and practitioner camps begin to think and behave in "us" terms? How will psychotherapy be viewed in the 21st century? Can we really do a better job of getting psychotherapy to more people?

Michael Mahoney provides an inspiring end to our handbook in his Chapter 34 Training Future Psychotherapists. To frame his thoughts, Mahoney uses seven themes that characterize a good psychotherapist: self-knowledge, human relatedness, compassion, philosophy, survival and coping skills, values, and lifespan development. Mahoney, in his succinct and powerful style, concludes that we would be wise to place the respect for the lifelong learning process and the human context at the top of our agendas for 21st century psychotherapists.

Having given you a tour of the handbook, we pose a final question: What benefits can be derived from reading this volume? These may vary depending upon the reader. For the student, we believe that the chapter authors not only provide outstanding essays on the basic topics in the psychotherapy field, but, more generally, they invite the reader to learn more about their particular topics. For the academician, the chapter authors of this book deliver the most current, comprehensive exploration of the field that is available; moreover, scholars can use it both as a reference and as a catalyst for their convergent and divergent thoughts about psychotherapy. For the researcher, there are theoretical, design, and methodological suggestions for the field in general and particular psychotherapeutic approaches. Likewise, psychotherapy researchers are aided by clear understandings of what actuallyt ranspires in the applications of treatments. We also firmly believe that advances in psychotherapy research rest upon a growing cohort of experimenters who are informed of general and specific change processes. Finally, for practitioners, the chapter authors supply informative syntheses of what has happened as well as what may happen in the future of our field. Likewise, in about half of the chapters, the authors have included one or more case studies that help to illustrate their approaches.

In the pages that follow, we believe that these forward-looking scholars embark on a trilogy aimed at informing, reassuring, and stimulating you the reader. They have delivered handsomely, we believe, in weaving a collective tale of where we will be going in the psychotherapy field as the 21st century unfolds. Perhaps our belief that our volume has "a little something" for everyone will not be completely fulfilled, but we wanted to aim high. On this count, you will be the final judge.

And now, for some specific praise. Our handbook did not become a reality until we had recruited the leaders in their respective areas. We thought long and hard about our "dream team" of authors, and what role they would play in this volume. Fortunately, as journal editors and by the mere virtue of having been around for many years, we knew most of the people whom we wanted for this new psychotherapy handbook. In recruiting the authors for this handbook, we typically were able to get commitments from the very people—a mixture of seasoned authors and outstanding young scholars—whom we wanted for particular chapters. These are busy people with more offers to write book chapters than they probably ever needed or wanted; as such, we are extremely thankful to them for sharing their visions about our field. Additionally, the chapter authors deserve kudos for delivering their chapters in a timely manner. May all editors have similar positive experiences with their authors.

Beyond the authors, we also would like to turn a duel spotlight of gratitude and praise upon our superb editors at Wiley—first Chris Rogers and then Ellen Schatz—who offered support at every stage of this project. To Chris, who somehow knew enough to keep asking (for several years) the senior editor about doing this book, and to Ellen, who gave us trust and the freedom that goes with it, we could not ask for better editorial support. Sarah Wiley and Eman Hudson also offered cheerful, prompt, and understanding help in the production stage of this large project. We also must thank two "carriers of information" without which we would have been woefully unable to communicate—the express mail companies and e-mail. Lastly, to our families, who have understood that love is the ultimate form of help, we lack sufficient words to convey our profound appreciation. We are humbled by their giving.

C. R. Snyder
Lawrence, Kansas

Rick E. Ingram
Dallas, Texas

GLENN AFFLECK
Professor, Department of Psychiatry, University of Connecticut Health Center, Farmington

GEORGE W. ALBEE
Professor Emeritus, Department of Psychology, University of Vermont

SEAN M. ALLEN
Doctoral Student, Clinical Psychology Program, Department of Psychology, Indiana University

CINDY WHEELER ANDERSON
Doctoral Student, Clinical Psychology Program, Department of Psychology, Arizona State University

BARBARA J. BACKS-DERMOTT
Doctoral Student, Department of Psychology, University of Calgary

JACQUES P. BARBER
Associate Professor of Psychology in Psychiatry, Department of Psychiatry, University of Pennsylvania

DONALD H. BAUCOM
Professor and Director, Graduate Training Program in Clinical Psychology, Department of Psychology, University of North Carolina, Chapel Hill

BERNARD L. BLOOM
Professor Emeritus, Department of Psychology, University of Colorado, Boulder

LAURA S. BROWN
Private Practice, Seattle

IDALIA CASTILLO-CAÑEZ
Doctoral Student, University of California, San Diego, and San Diego State University Doctoral Program in Clinical Psychology

JEN CHEAVENS
Doctoral Student, Graduate Training Program in Clinical Psychology, Department of Psychology, The University of Kansas, Lawrence

JOHN G. CORAZZINI
Professor and Director of University Counseling Services, Department of Psychology, Virginia Commonwealth University

PAUL CRITS-CHRISTOPH
Professor of Psychology in Psychiatry, Department of Psychiatry, University of Pennsylvania

KEITH S. DOBSON
Professor, Director of Clinical Training, and Associate Head, Department of Psychology, University of Calgary

DAVID J. A. DOZOIS
Assistant Professor, Department of Psychology, University of Western Ontario

J. TODD DUBOISE
Department of Psychology, Duquesne University

NORMAN EPSTEIN
Department of Psychology, University of North Carolina, Chapel Hill

CONSTANCE T. FISCHER
Professor, Department of Psychology, Duquesne University

WILLIAM C. FOLLETTE
Professor, Department of Psychology, University of Nevada, Reno

DONELSON R. FORSYTH
Professor, Department of Psychology, Virginia Commonwealth University

DOLORES GALLAGHER-THOMPSON
Older Adult & Family Research and Resource Center, VA Palo Alto Health Care System, and Associate Professor, Department of Psychiatry and Behavioral Sciences, Stanford University School of Medicine

KRISTINA COOP GORDON
Department of Psychology, University of North Carolina, Chapel Hill

IAN H. GOTLIB
Professor, Department of Psychology, Stanford University

BERNADETTE GRAY-LITTLE
Professor, Department of Psychology, and Associate Dean, College of Arts and Sciences, University of North Carolina, Chapel Hill

DAVID A. F. HAAGA
Professor, Department of Psychology, American University

HEIDI A. HAMANN
Doctoral Student, Department of Psychology, University of Utah

ADELE HAYES
Department of Psychology, University of Miami

STEVEN C. HAYES
Professor, Department of Psychology, University of Nevada, Reno

KENNETH HELLER
Professor, Department of Psychology, Indiana University

MARDI HOROWITZ
Professor and Director of Center on Stress and Personality, Department of Psychiatry, Langley Porter Institute, University of California, San Francisco

STEPHEN ILARDI
Wright Scholar Assistant Professor, Graduate Training Program in Clinical Psychology, Department of Psychology, The University of Kansas, Lawrence

RICK E. INGRAM
Professor, Department of Psychology, Southern Methodist University

YO JACKSON
Assistant Professor, Clinical Child Psychology Program, The University of Kansas, Lawrence

DANIELLE KAPLAN
Doctoral Student, Department of Psychology, University of North Carolina, Chapel Hill

PAUL KAROLY
Professor, Clinical Psychology Program, Department of Psychology, Arizona State University

CHARLES A. KIESLER
Former Chancellor, University of Missouri, Columbia

DARRELLE KOONCE-VOLWILER
Postdoctoral Fellow, Stanford University School of Medicine

RUTH Q. LEIBOWITZ
Doctoral Student, Graduate Training Program in Clinical Psychology, Department of Psychology, The University of Kansas, Lawrence

ALAN J. LITROWNIK
Child and Family Research Group, and Professor, Department of Psychology, San Diego State University

MICHAEL J. MAHONEY
Professor, Clinical Psychology Program, Department of Psychology, University of North Texas

FAITH MCCLURE
Professor, Department of Psychology, California State University, San Bernadino

DIANE S. MCDERMOTT
Associate Professor, Psychology and Research in Education Department, University of Kansas, Lawrence

BRIAN MCELWAIN
Department of Psychology, Duquesne University

CHRISTINE MCKIBBIN
Older Adult and Family Research and Resource Center, Geriatric Research, Education, and Clinical Center, VA Palo Alto Health Care System

ANA MENENDEZ
Older Adult and Family Research and Resource Center, Geriatric Research, Education, and Clinical Center, VA Palo Alto Health Care System

SCOTT T. MICHAEL
Doctoral Student, Graduate Training Program in Clinical Psychology, Department of Psychology, The University of Kansas, Lawrence

JILL B. NEALY
Doctoral Student, Department of Psychology, University of Utah

ROBERT A. NEIMEYER
Professor, Clinical Psychology Program, Department of Psychology, University of Memphis

NANCY M. PETRY
Assistant Professor, Department of Psychiatry, University of Connecticut Health Center, Farmington

JAMES O. PROCHASKA
Cancer Prevention Research Center and Professor, Department of Psychology, University of Rhode Island

MICHAEL C. ROBERTS
Professor and Director, Clinical Child Psychology Program, The University of Kansas, Lawrence

PAMELA K. SCHRAEDLEY
Department of Psychology, Stanford University

WALTER SCOTT
Assistant Professor, Department of Psychology, University of Wyoming

TIMOTHY W. SMITH
Professor and Chairperson, Department of Psychology, University of Utah

C. R. SNYDER
Professor and Director, Graduate Training Program in Clinical Psychology, Department of Psychology, University of Kansas, Lawrence

ALAN E. STEWART
Assistant Professor, Clinical Psychology Program, Department of Psychology, University of Florida, Gainesville

DOUGLAS STEWART
Psychology Intern, VA Palo Alto Health Care System

WILLIAM B. STILES
Professor, Department of Psychology, Miami University

HANS H. STRUPP
Distinguished Professor, Clinical Psychology Program, Department of Psychology, Vanderbilt University

HOWARD TENNEN
Professor, Department of Psychiatry, University of Connecticut Health Center, Farmington

EDWARD C. TEYBER
Professor and Director of Community Counseling Center, Department of Psychology, California State University, San Bernadino

MICHAEL E. THASE
Professor, Department of Psychiatry, School of Medicine, University of Pittsburgh

LARRY W. THOMPSON
Professor, Pacific Graduate School of Psychology, Palo Alto, California

SUZANNE C. THOMPSON
Professor, Department of Psychology, Pomona College

DOUGLAS A. VAKOCH
Postdoctoral Research Fellow, Clinical Psychology Program, Department of Psychology, Vanderbilt University

ERIC M. VERNBERG
Associate Professor and Clinic Coordinator, Clinical Child Psychology Program, The University of Kansas, Lawrence

DREW WESTEN
Associate Professor, Department of Psychiatry, Harvard Medical School and the Cambridge Hospital

MICHELLE WIERSON
Associate Professor, Department of Psychology, Pomona College

MARY F. WYMAN
Doctoral Student, Clinical Psychology Program, Department of Psychology, Indiana University

CONTENTS

PART I

PSYCHOTHERAPEUTIC CHANGE IN PERSPECTIVE

•

A CHANGING HISTORY OF EFFORTS TO UNDERSTAND AND CONTROL CHANGE: THE CASE OF PSYCHOTHERAPY[1]

MICHAEL J. MAHONEY
University of North Texas

THE IMPORTANCE OF CHANGE

We humans have been obsessed with change, as well as with its regularities or "laws." As Boorstin (1983) and others have noted, the earliest records of human communication have converged on issues of change and exchange (from cycles and seasons to markets and reasons). We are inherently historical and yet fundamentally future-oriented beings. We want to understand the past in part so that we can understand and perhaps change the future.

Documentations of change are readily accessible. One need only look at political, economic, and geophysical realms. The planet is changing. And if change in general is not strikingly obvious, one has only to go home. Families, relationships, and our senses of ourselves are in transition. Like it or not, we are changing. We now live in the most rapidly changing era of human history (Anderson, 1997; Braudel, 1979; Gergen, 1991; Tarnas, 1991).

Current estimates suggest that the average citizen of the 19th century was born, lived a life of 50–60 years, and died—all within a radius of less than 8 miles (a leisurely jog for many moderns). Poignantly, it has been predicted that the average citizen of the 21st century will interact (directly or indirectly) with more people in one day than average citizens of the 19th century ever met in their entire lifetimes. These figures remind us that not only are we participant-observers in a rapidly changing world but also the present rate of change is so dizzyingly exponential that we have no reasonable hope of knowing our proximal and distal futures.

How are we changing? And what does such change mean? Do we have a voice—a warranted sense of agency—in the process? Questions like these have shaped major developments in philosophy for millennia. The *I Ching* is China's central book of wisdom, and it opens with the assertion, "If we know the laws of change, we can precalculate in regard to them, and freedom of action thereupon becomes possible." Life should be so simple: to know the laws of change, to translate those laws into concrete predictions, and then to act consciously in ways that make such knowledge serve our needs.

Many of us do seem to live as if life were that simple—or that it could be. Many of us believe, for example, in the *myth of arrival*. This is the myth that someday, after hard work and survived crises, life will be what we always wanted. We will have our "self" and our "life" together, living in the relationship for which we have longed, in the house of our dreams, in the job (and at the salary) we have wanted, and so on. The big life crises will be behind us, and from that point on it will be smooth sailing. Arrival is what our childhood stories promised with their theme of "living happily ever after." But, as

---

[1]This chapter is based on material in M. J. Mahoney, *Constructive Psychotherapy: Exploring Principles and Practices* (New York: Guilford, in press).

the child who learned the truth about Santa Claus, there comes a time when the myth of arrival no longer serves our journeying. *The next problem is always in the mail*—if not literally in our mailbox, then in our daily life. We may seek other myths and learn to believe in (and be) Santa Claus at preciously metaphoric levels, but there are no paths without pain. Rather than encourage our children and clients to seek painless paths, it may be more valuable to teach them to explore the lessons and meanings of their pain and to honor their hope and their strength in pursuing their journey (Snyder, McDermott, Cook, & Rapoff, 1997).

Beyond the arrival myth, we psychotherapists are prone to believe what I call the *Secret Manual of Helping*. We all have copies, right? It is the manual—never publicly seen, of course, because it is confidential—that tells us exactly what to think, say, and do in every conceivable situation with a client. It is the manual that our teachers had and their teachers before them. The right thing to do, or to have done, is always in the manual. Of course, the problem is that the manual does not exist. Indeed, it cannot and *never* will exist. No one, no committee of experts, no matter how brilliant, can claim such omniscience. Like our teachers, we are on our own with our clients, and as any seasoned clinician will testify, one has never seen it all.

If we are honest about it, we admit that we are flying by the seats of our being. No one knows, for sure; not really. People may speak and act with great authority, cite scientific scripture and gigabytes of empirical evidence, but they cannot really *know* what will happen if you do (or do not) use a particular intervention with your client in the next session. That is an elegant secret. It is part of the ongoing mystery whenever we assume the role of professional helper in someone else's life. Our clients often assume that we do know. After all, isn't that the essence of professional expertise? We are supposed to know for sure what to do, and those who lobby on our behalf stess that we do.

That we professionals, even the most skilled of us, are amateurs at helping may not be a welcome message, but I believe it. Life is very complex. So, too, are we and our clients, and so are our interactions. We often desperately cling to theories and scientific evidence because they spare us from the existential meat hook of responsibility in the face of the unknowns and unknowables. This insight, if it penetrates, moves us into new realms of questions. What should we do? I remember how personally heartened I felt as a student when I read Immanuel Kant's simple

and questioning intentions at the beginning of his revolutionary *Critique of Pure Reason*: "What can I know?" "What may I hope?" and "What should I do?" Such simple questions; such complex answers. This chapter is a respectful genuflection to these and related questions.

THE CONCEPT OF CHANGE IN THE HISTORY OF IDEAS

In our current cultural contexts, change is the coin of the realm. Viewed from the perspective of recorded (written) history, the nature and mysteries of change have been perennially central to cultural quests that situate the person in the world. Among the pre-Socratic philosophers of ancient Greece, there was debate about the very *possibility* of change. Parmenides (539–469 B.C.) argued that "all change is illusion," with reality being fixed and timeless. His contemporary Heraclitus (540–475 B.C.) held the opposite view, asserting that nothing ever stays the same. Indeed, Heraclitus held that "all is becoming" was the basic statement of a process philosophy. Thus, in his famous koan, he reasoned, "One cannot step into the same river twice." In postmodern language, this translates to "One cannot awaken twice in the same life."

Heraclitus also was the first Western thinker to acknowledge the generative power of "opposite tensions." He anticipated Hegel by more than two thousand years in suggesting that the interaction of contrasts lies at the heart of development. A similar idea was expressed by his Chinese contemporary Lao Tzu, who thereby founded the wisdom tradition known as Taoism. These convergent insights remain apparent in a spectrum of modern discussions, ranging from the opponent process of sensation, perception, and motivation to the developmental generativity of dialectical and dialogical processes. Heraclitus and Lao Tzu argued that we and our paths are always changing and are expressive of tensions that are essential not only to each other's existence but also and more importantly to the forms and expressions emerging out of such tensions.

But Heraclitus and Lao Tzu were faint voices in comparison to the larger traditions that they challenged. Lao Tzu and his students sometimes were perceived as threats by Mahayana Buddhists and later by Confucianists (Batchelor, 1994; Smith, 1988). Heraclitus was writing in the formidable shadow of Pythagoras, who would establish rationalism and mathematics as the royal dyad leading to "knowing." Rationalism presumed a single and harmonic reality, best expressed in mathematical terms. For more than two thousand years, rationalism has dominated Western attempts at knowing. Since the Renaissance and the scientific revolution, however, the nature of both reality and knowing have been reconsidered. The European Enlightenment and British empiricism converged on a logical positivism of science as the best possible coupling of reason and (public) experience. It was "logical" because it insisted on consistency and "positive" because it appealed to public demonstration. The romance of logic and publicity has fueled more than three centuries of technolatry, quantophilia, and undeniable revolutions in a wide range of specialties. Our planet has been changed forever, as satellite photos readily document. Indeed, change is the postmodern norm: hairstyles, clothing, jobs, residences, partners, self-concepts, religions, and so on. The changing being is in vogue.

In Western civilizations (a planetary population minority), the possibility and positivity of change were ushered in with the Renaissance that began in the 15th and 16th centuries in Europe. It is no accident of history that the European Renaissance gave birth to humanism, modern rationalism, romanticism, constructivism, and empiricism (the scientific revolution). Francis Bacon became the legendary hero of natural philosophy (later called science), which emphasized careful observation, cautious induction (versus Aristotelian deduction), and eventually, systematic experimentation.[2] For Galileo and Newton, the world as we know it was made up of matter (mass) and energy (force). The central point here is that Galileo and Newton, as well as their devout followers through more than three centuries of science, believed that change is a linear, causal sequence in which an *exter-*

nal force impacts on an *isolated* body that responds (like a projectile or billiard ball) by being moved in a predictable trajectory. Motion *was* change, and discovering the laws of motion (including gravitation) resulted in technological advances that were unprecedented in human history.

But life is more complex than a billiard table. Indeed, even nonliving systems are more complex than either Galileo or Newton ever imagined. Newtonian physics is brilliantly practical for its simple systems with a limited number of variables and parameters. As the system becomes more complex, greatly accelerated, and more open to interactions with other systems, however, the limitations of the laws of mechanics become increasingly apparent. Meteorology is the classic example in the physical sciences, and economics, politics, and psychology are favorite choices in the social sciences. Human beings are not inert objects that remain at rest until forced to move by an external energy. The essence of living systems is self-organizing activity, of which humans are the most complex examples on this planet.[3] Charles Darwin's "dangerous idea" was revolutionary not simply because it challenged religious creationism but also because it suggested that we, like all life forms, have been, are, and always will be changing. We exist in process, always under construction. Being is becoming. This idea was dangerous because it implied that an idea itself is a living process—and it is.[4]

It is hardly coincidental that existentialism flourished in the wake of evolutionary theory. Søren Kierkegaard (1813–1855) died four years before the publication of Darwin's revolutionary treatise, but Kierkegaard was a precocious exception. Friedrich Nietzsche (1844–1900) was an adolescent when Darwin was suddenly "forced" to publish his dangerous idea.[5] Sigmund Freud

---

[2]It is noteworthy that some of the pioneering figures in science, including Bacon, Copernicus, Kepler, and Hobbes, and some of the most influential scientists of all time, such as Charles Darwin and Albert Einstein, conducted little (if any) experimentation in their lifetimes. Indeed, Bacon died as a result of one of his first experiments. Curious about the capacity of cold to forestall the spoilage of animal flesh, he instructed his carriage driver to stop and shoot a game bird so that he could test his idea. Old and already failing in health, Bacon developed pneumonia soon after this experiment, and he died shortly thereafter. In contemporary use, the term *empirical* has come to connote *experimental*—implying an intentional and systematically arranged intervention into the course of events. Originally and most enduringly, however, *empirical* means *experiential* (based in experience).

[3]I shall not here belabor the distinction between living and nonliving systems.

[4] Richard Dawkins would later formalize this statement in the context of evolutionary biology as a *meme* (see Brockman, 1995).

[5]The "force," in Darwin's case, came in a letter from a young colleague, Alfred Russel Wallace, who, in the delirium of malaria, chanced on the idea that Darwin had been meticulously cultivating for more than two decades. Darwin handled the prospect of being scooped with admirable dignity, and he generously shared the honors of discovery with his unsuspecting junior colleague at a meeting of the Linnean Society on July 1, 1858. Darwin wrote *On the Origin of Species* in the next eight months, and it was published in 1859.

(1856–1940) was a young child at this time, but he would be deeply influenced by Darwin's evolutionary theory, Nietzsche's existentialism, and the romanticist works of writers like Goethe and Schopenhauer. Why should existentialism follow upon evolutionary theory? There are numerous speculations, some of which include radically postmodern spins on the negative ramifications of human beings as just another expression of life's longing after itself. Personally, I incline toward renditions that emphasize a resonance between chances and choices, each bearing an existential responsibility. Jean-Paul Sartre (1905–1980) emphasized the fact that we are our choices. Even when we choose not to choose, that is a choice. Life is filled with options, with choice points. We are thrown, to be sure, into our unique circumstances of embodiment, family, social class, culture, time, and so on. The options that come our way thereby are influenced, but we *do* choose, for better or for worse, in each of those moments of opportunity.

The essence of Charles Darwin's theory can be reduced to three basic principles: variation, selection, and retention (or perpetuation). For evolution to occur, and it turns out that evolution appears to be a macroprocess akin to all learning and development, there must be (1) variability (in form or function), (2) a selectivity process that "chooses" or otherwise evaluates among the apparent alternatives, and (3) some means of projecting this choice and its spatiotemporal correlates (what behaviorists call antecedents and consequences) into the near and possibly distant future. Contemporary constructivists, in ideological garbs that now include behaviorists, cognitivists, complexity scientists, dynamic systems specialists, existentialists, humanists, psychoanalysts, and transpersonalists,[6] seem to concur on these three basic principles. For change to occur, that is, for learning, development, or evolution to take place, there must first be some variability in patterns of activity. Within that variability, I would argue, there must be occasional novelty. It cannot be just the same old "reruns" of one's life experiences. There must be at least some occasional forays, including "mis-takes," into new experiential territory. Without novel variability in experiencing, what statisticians often lament as individual variance or error variance, there is nothing from which to choose. Change requires itself, at least at the level of microvariations. Most of those variations are ignored or forgiven, but some are nursed and nurtured. They are selected, so to speak, but the nature and sufficiency of Darwin's version of natural selection processes merits being explored and elaborated.

However, old realities earn tenure much more easily than do most academicians. And, unlike emeriti professors, old realities never go away. Once they have served a person's life survival, no matter how poorly or expensively, they remain privileged and accessible for the life of their progeny.[7] Hence, I believe that it is ethically irresponsible for any form of psychotherapy to promise that it can permanently *eliminate* anything, especially old patterns of coping with life's ambiguities and challenges. Functionally and structurally,[8] the human being (nervous system and all) is very reluctant to let go of old patterns of activity. We are aware superficially of this tendency to conserve (to preserve and protect our past families of action), especially in previous centuries when "leading" (technological) cultures openly encouraged change, liberation, and "progress." On this point, I hope that I am not the only psychologist who is dismayed by coclassification of psychology with "self-help" or "self-improvement" in bookstores. The cult of progress is a seductive one. It promises positive and desired change, not just any change—hence the caricature that "progressives" are always pressing for change whereas "conservatives" are always protecting tradition (Campbell, 1975). Like most therapists, most psychotherapy clients are complex and individually expressed reflections of such tensions. We all are trying to change and to stay the same—to hold on to what we trust, while exploring what we don't know.

WHAT IS CHANGING IN OUR THEORIES OF CHANGE?

Donald O. Hebb (1975) once suggested that the half-life of knowledge in psychology is approxi-

---

[6] See such periodicals as the *Journal of Constructivist Psychology* and *Constructivism in the Human Sciences* or books like Mahoney (1991, in press b) and Neimeyer & Mahoney (1995).

[7] This is, I believe, among the brilliant insights of Carl G. Jung. He construed and packaged it differently, but the fundamental insight is the same.

[8] The difference between function and structure that is so central to the history of differentiation in 20th-century psychology turns out to be the relative time scale (Thelen & Smith, 1984).

mately five years; as such, "facts" in our field have averaged a conceptual life of about that duration. Every five years, approximately half the facts (accepted knowledge) of psychology have been revised or replaced. Hebb used this conjecture to recommend that graduate students in psychology be trained in thinking and questioning skills rather than in rotely memorized facts. Whether Hebb's quantitative estimate was accurate is less provocative than his apt observation that psychological knowledge is rapidly changing. Although we may (expensively) pride ourselves on having moved beyond the James-Lange theory of emotion or Clark L. Hull's Herculean efforts to systematize the principles of learning, it is extremely important to recognize that our relatively young field of inquiry is moving at a pace that may be appreciated adequately only by future historians. What has changed or is changing? I feel self-conscious in my attempt to respond to that question. I honestly don't know. But I am an academician, and we are trained to say something even when we are unsure. So I have created a list—this week's list—of half a dozen responses to such a question. See what you think about them.

Abandoning Simplicity

Now this is an easy one, but it would not have been at midcentury. From its beginnings in the 19th century through almost half of the 20th, psychology was dominated by prime mover (first cause) arguments that artificially separated each person into categories of behavior, cognition, and affect. When their contrasts were even honored as real phenomena (rather than epiphenomena), they were deemed secondary to the chosen cause. In the heyday of behaviorism, for example, behavior was the cue ball on life's billiard table (never mind the agent with the stick). Change behavior and you changed life. Behavioral change was the key to cognitive and emotional change.

When the cognitive revolution hit just after midcentury, the popular cause shifted from behavior to cognition. How and what a person thinks was considered central to his or her actions, emotions, and overall well-being. The behaviorists faced off against the cognitivists (as they had earlier against psychoanalysts), and each mustered considerable theory and evidence for their cause. The emotionalists (bless their hearts!) kept getting emotional about it, but they really never got organized (other than clustering on the western coast of North America). The psychoan-

alysts were protoemotionalists, of course, but they kept splitting on issues of interpretation and practice. Its nucleus of orthodoxy has become more and more seclusive and fragile, and psychoanalysis will not soon regain the power and popularity it had enjoyed in the first half of the 20th century (see, however, Chapter 10 in this volume, for a more optimistic possible evolution of this "classic").

But wait, the century and the millennium have just come to a close, and what we see are strong signs of movement toward conceptualizations of human experience that are decidedly more holistic, complex, and coalitional, with multiple models of embeddedness and reciprocity (Bandura, 1986, 1997; Mahoney, 1991; Masterpasqua & Perna, 1995; Wilber, 1998). Future observers may read the record differently than those of us who are still in our present conceptual canoes, trying to remain upright and off the rocks of these postmodern rapids. Perspective is precious, but it seems to come more easily with distances of space and time. Ironically, those very distances are what appear to be disappearing at our point in history. The various parts of the planet have never been so connected as they are now. People are in greater contact than ever before (for better and for worse, which is, of course, a matter of perspective). Our economies and local environments and health are intricately codependent. And the further we go in our observations and the further we go into the space and time of universal cosmology or the "ultimate" mysteries of biochemistry and genetics, the more interconnected we appear.

If the 20th century is remembered for anything other than its exponential development of the technologies of communication, transportation, and massive biodestruction, it probably will be recognized for its beginning attempts to abandon simplistic models and its efforts to embrace complexity. In the physical sciences, relativism became an impetus to even deeper questions about important mysteries. In the social and behavioral sciences, relativism got translated into "postmodernism." There are, of course, two kinds of postmodernism: the good and the bad (never mind the ugly). Bad postmodernism came to be associated with deconstructionism, the destruction of all messages and texts. It created an "anything goes" sense of both freedom and despair, arguing that all perspectives are equally viable. The result was negativity and a negative form of self-focus: "The Postmodernists, unanchored in any conception of truth, had nothing left but their own dispositions: narcissism and nihilism as a postmodern tag team from hell" (Wilber, 1998, p. 140). The "good" postmodernists turned out to be a diverse and uninformed crew who labeled themselves activists, Buddhists, existentialists, feminists, humanists, eclectics, integrationists, and transpersonalists—a diversity that many are beginning to call constructivists (Franklin & Nurius, 1998; Guidano, 1987, 1991; Mahoney, 1991, in press b; Neimeyer & Mahoney, 1995; Neimeyer & Raskin, in press; Sexton & Griffin, 1997; see Chapter 16 in this volume; see also below).

The (Re)Turn of the Body in Psychology

Another noteworthy development in contemporary psychology is a rather ironic one. The body has come back. We lost most of it to medicine in a turf war that dominated the economics of health care in the first half of the 20th century. Until recently, the mind was the domain of psychology, and the body/brain/nervous system was the domain of medicine and psychiatry. The problem with this arrangement was its untenable dualism. Body, brain, and being are integral—hence the economic fights in contemporary health care, including managed care, prescription privileges, and alternative therapies. Whose turf is defined by what? (Talk about postmodern ambiguities!)

The embodiment of psychology has been multiply expressed. For example, we have witnessed the maturation of health psychology (sometimes called behavioral medicine), the growing popularity of exercise and sports psychology, and the emergence of embodied mind theories in cognitive psychology (Johnson, 1987; Mahoney, 1991, in press a). The latter are theories of knowledge development and representation that move beyond traditional notions of symbols stored in the head. According to embodied mind theories, all human knowledge (including abstract thought and language) is based on protocols, prototypes, and differentiations of bodily experience (Johnson, 1987; Leder, 1990; Zaner, 1971). The conceptual and practical gap that remains between the head and the body in psychology is formidable. Contrary to the revealing meditations of Descartes (Leder, 1990) and the foreboding warnings of Skinner (1990), it is time that psychology bring body and mind back to-

gether in a more complex fashion than either of these two thinkers ever imagined. The writings of Johnson (1987), Lakoff (1987), Leder (1990), Merleau-Ponty (1962), Sperry (1988, 1993), and Zaner (1971) on this topic are noteworthy in their appeal to a dialectical emergence that transcends the long-standing dualism that has shackled theoretical psychology. I shall not presume here to offer a crystalline aggregate of that emergence, but I do believe that it represents a promising path for our field.

Cultures, Contexts, Feminism, and Human Rights

Another theme in the development of our theories of change has been a growing appreciation for what some contemporary feminists call our positionality (Goldberger, Tarule, Clinchy, & Belenky, 1996), which is related to culture and gender. This is more than the relativism of generic postmodernism. It has become manifest in a diverse maturation of ethical consciousness, for example, in social movements to prevent and address child and elder abuse; to protect the rights of homosexuals; to promote responsible care of animals and ecosystems; to reduce violence of any form; to protect the rights of handicapped or otherwise "challenged" individuals; and to foster respect for cultural, ethnic, and individual diversity. In the process of many of these developments, we have come to recognize that the history of so-called Western civilization[9] has been a history of the politics of power that has maintained and protected a predominantly male, Caucasian, western European–North American view of psychological life (see Chapter 17 in this volume). The dominating leadership of this first world, male, Anglo-American thinking is a major challenge facing the development of 21st-century psychology (Fisher, 1989; see also Chapter 29 in this volume on the feminizing of psychotherapy).

---

[9]Relevant here is an anecdote in which the late Mahatma Ghandi, while his train was leaving the station in London, was hurriedly asked by a young journalist to make some statement for the press. Ghandi responded, "But what is your question?" At a loss for a specific topic, the young journalist returned, "Well . . . Mr. Ghandi . . . what is your opinion of Western civilization?" With his gentle voice and well-known smile, Ghandi is reported to have replied, "Well . . . I think it is a good idea."

Feminist perspectives have contributed to truly revolutionary developments in both our knowledge and our ethical consciousness, as has been aptly summarized by Tarnas (1991):

> Considered as a whole, the feminist perspective and impulse has brought forth perhaps the most vigorous, subtle, and radically critical analysis of conventional intellectual and cultural assumptions in all of contemporary scholarship. No academic discipline or area of human experience has been left untouched by the feminist reexamination of how meanings are created and preserved, how evidence is selectively interpreted and theory molded with mutually reinforcing circularity, how particular rhetorical strategies and behavioral styles have sustained male hegemony, how women's voices remained unheard through centuries of social and intellectual male dominance, how deeply problematic consequences have ensued from masculine assumptions about reality, knowledge, nature, society, the divine. Such analyses in turn have helped illuminate parallel patterns and structures of domination that have marked the experience of other oppressed peoples and forms of life. (p. 408)

Feminism has many faces, of course, and its continuing differentiation reflects some of the most challenging issues facing our profession and our planet (Tobias, 1997). Many of those issues relate to values, human rights, the inherent connectedness of our being, and the need to nurture personal and social responsibility.

Spirituality, Values, and Wisdom

Late 20th-century psychology not only has become value conscious but also has softened its traditional aversion to questions of spirituality, values, and the wisdom traditions. The signs of this development are increasingly evident in general psychology (Campbell, 1975; Sperry, 1988), and they are even more apparent in the literatures of counseling and psychotherapy and their increasing interaction with the humanities (Claus, 1981; Kelly & Strupp, 1992; Kovel, 1991; Payne, Bergin, & Loftus, 1992; Vaughan, 1991). In a survey of therapists' responses to clients' reports of mystical experiences, responses were attributed to pathological causes according to the therapists' theoretical orientations (Allman, de La Rocha,

Elkins, & Weathers, 1992). It is interesting that the incidence of such experiences was approximately ten times more common among the therapists than it was among their clients. Also, repeated surveys of psychotherapists rarely have found them to be "religious" (i.e., a member of an organized church community), but they are commonly self-described as "spiritual." This trend is paralleled (and almost overshadowed) by trends in the general population toward a new and more visible kind of spirituality. Although some religious organizations and churches reported declines in the third quarter of this century, many reported increases in the fourth quarter. Moreover, a "transtheological" spirituality has grown exponentially in recent decades, with less emphasis on God, scripture, and afterlife and more emphasis on community (connectedness), compassion, forgiveness, hope, love, peace, responsibility, trust, and service. I believe that such spiritual themes should and will form a central role in 21st-century psychotherapy.

One of the debates that surfaced during the 20th-century quest for dominance in psychotherapy was whether it could or should be value-free. Without belaboring the nuances of this debate, it can be said that most theorists and researchers now concede that values are unavoidable in any form of psychological testing, diagnosis, and counseling. No matter how liberal, enlightened, or accepting psychotherapists may be, they necessarily are embedded in a system of personal, historical, familial, cultural, ethnic, and spiritual values that significantly influences the life counsel they offer.

The meaning of the term spiritual is itself a living example of protean evolution. Once nearly synonymous with the term religious (at least in Western civilizations), spirituality is beginning to mean something much more abstract, value-defined, and acceptable within scientific and literary cultures. It contains an ethics of constraints ("thou shalt not's") elaborated into a larger system of virtues and wisdom (hence the recent discussion of wisdom as a central element of multicultural spiritual traditions).

Like it or not, we must acknowledge that spiritual and value issues are central to what it means to be a psychological service provider. We counsel the abused and the abandoned, the violated and the violent, the suffering and the dying. We are asked for counsel on guilt, shame, and sin. Our clients offer confessions that they have not shared with their clergy, their family, or their friends. Whether we wish it to be so, we become the sole confidantes of their private traumas; their wildest fantasies; and their real and imagined violations of personal, community, and moral statutes. What are we to do? Can or should we be totally accepting, empathic, nondirective, and client-centered? I think not. Should we offer moralizing expressions of the status quo? I think not. Then where and how do we establish the parameters of our counsel? This, I believe, is a live question that only now is being addressed by psychotherapy researchers and practitioners. We are faced with issues that the clergy have addressed for millennia: the meaning of life, the right or wrong things to do, the power of love and forgiveness, the foundations of self-esteem, and so on. These are not simple issues with equally simple answers. Nor are the answers likely to be found in manuals in straightforward algorithms of what (not) to do as a professional psychological service provider. These issues, and more to come, are the existential questions that will stretch our profession toward more adequate understanding of what it means to be human (here and now, as well as in unknown futures) and—even more pertinent to our collective endeavor—what it means to strive toward an understanding and facilitation of human lives in process.

The Return of the Person: Therapist and Client

The fifth emerging theme involves the role of the person in the process. Studies of psychotherapy outcome have yielded observations that are open to many interpretations. A consistent pattern of findings has shown, however, that the most powerful predictors of outcome cluster into three broad groupings: (1) client variables, (2) therapist variables, and (3) theory and technique variables. The vast majority of existing research has focused on client variables and techniques. Only recently has the therapist been appreciated as an active ingredient in the change process (see Chapter 4 in this volume). Let us not forget that the client is the most important variable in our analyses, although the present methods and results that explore client variables have not yielded coherent results (see Chapter 5 in this volume).

People are unique. Once you have seen one person with agoraphobia, you have seen one person with agoraphobia. It is the same with all other persons on whom we have applied one of our diagnostic labels. We must, I believe, move toward conceptualizations that acknowledge phenomenological uniqueness, but we must learn to treasure that uniqueness rather than trying to "partial it out" with statistical maneuvers that beg the very questions they are said to answer. The experience of life and the phenomenology of change can be enriched by searching for collective patterns, but the patterns themselves must be honored as sacredly unique—never before, never again (even with the genetic wonders of cloning). It is this life, in this body, in these times and in these contexts. Every client is a universe unto oneself. It is the same with therapists and the unique relationships that emerge in the process of working together.

To focus my desired point, I want to emphasize that clients are agents of their own experiencing. Therapists are potentially important facilitators of that development. Relative to the contribution of psychotherapy theories and techniques, the therapist as a person is six to ten times more important. Some therapists are better (more helpful) than others. Some therapists learn and develop more quickly and differently than others. I have some hunches about the themes in their development, and I will return to these in the concluding chapter of this handbook. For the moment, let me simply say that the person of the therapist is beginning to be appreciated in contemporary psychotherapy research. Furthermore, one cannot appreciate the person of the client and the person of the therapist without sensing the importance of their relationship in the processes of either's development (see Chapter 4 in this volume).

Measures, Methods, and Models: Promises from Complexity Studies, Constructivism, and Dynamic Systems Theories

The sixth and final theme I address here comes back to the first. In abandoning simplicity, psychology has begun to embrace complexity. We are making peace with our conceptual loss of Galilean and Newtonian mechanics. It is not the case that they were completely wrong, however, but only that they were limited in their usefulness for understanding complex, multivariate, open, self-organizing systems with self-reflective and symbolic capacities (i.e., ourselves). This is my construction, of course, but I like to say that constructivists believe that there are two kinds of people in the world: (1) those who believe that there are two kinds of people in the world and (2) those who do not. This koan emphasizes the active categorical processes that pervade human knowing—our tendency to organize our experience by means of enhancing contrasts and then to navigate by our enhancements (see Wright, 1991). This tendency is readily apparent in philosophy and psychology, and it has been an increasingly frequent observation in all open systems.

Chaos theory and the sciences of complexity (dynamics systems theory) are the new kids on the conceptual block, and they are nothing short of awesome (Bonner, 1988; Ford, 1987; Gleick, 1987; Hayles, 1991; Jantsch, 1980; Kauffman, 1993, 1995; Kelso, 1995; Lewin, 1992; Mahoney, 1991; Masterpasqua & Perna, 1995; Mingers, 1995; Mittenthal & Baskin, 1992; Robertson & Combs, 1995; Salthe, 1993; Thelen & Smith, 1994; Waldrop, 1992). *Holons* is a term invented by Arthur Koestler and used by many contemporary theorists. It refers to nested systems in which each part is simultaneously made up of subunits and also a part of something larger. Concepts such as hierarchy have been around since humans have imagined angels; hierarchy refers to a vertical ordering process. The idea of heterarchy is more recent and much more ambiguous. It refers not only to the ongoing interaction of multiple hierarchies but also to the multiplex levels at which such interactions must occur (at least three dimensions of space and another of time).

My translation is this: the older simplicities no longer work as well as the newer complexities. Beginning questions are well put in binaries (dichotomies), and they deserve to be explored as dualities as long as that exploration yields productive crops of new questions. But human experience—albeit filled with binaries and dichoomies—cannot be enveloped conceptually without creating a more complex fabric. Systems of either/or are essential in path generation. Systems of both/neither/and become essential at later points in the journey. I think we are beginning to enter those points in the field of psychology more generally, and psychotherapy in particular.

Concluding Introductory Remarks

With T. H. Huxley, I hold that it is necessary to believe something, even—or perhaps especially—when one is haunted by doubts about the warrant for such a belief. As I am an academic educator, a practitioner, a psychotherapy supervisor, and a scientist, it may not be surprising that my first personal inclination with regard to commitment is to the process of inquiry—especially to a style of inquiry that does not first enshrine any method, master, or model. This kind of commitment does not necessarily leave us floating in an ethereal realm of endless openness so much as it requires us to be conscious of the fact that our teachings—whether as academicians, practitioners, or research scientists—are fundamentally "reachings," that is, quests for better questions. In other words, we teach and counsel best when we model in vivo that the processes of living, adapting, and learning are fundamentally processes of dialogue, exploration, and experimentation with possibilities. This is particularly apparent in the symbiosis of psychological science and service, where a coalition of conscience is of utmost importance.

Not only are the times changing, as Bob Dylan's cutting voice placed in our awareness, but the planet and its inhabitants are now engaged in a veritable torrent—a rapids of movement—whose directions and outcomes are very difficult to discern, let alone predict or control. We are participant-observers not only of the developments at the end of one century and the beginning of the next but also of changes that represent truly (r)evolutionary changes in our profession. Ours is an age of more than transition; it is truly an age of transformation. The words of Carl Jung (1970) are pertinent here:

> We are living in what the Greeks called the *kairos*—the right moment—for a "metamorphosis of the gods," of the fundamental principles and symbols. This peculiarity of our time, which is certainly not of our conscious choosing, is the expression of the unconscious human within us who is changing. Coming generations will have to take account of this momentous transformation if humanity is not to destroy itself through the might of its own technology and science. . . . So much is at stake and so much depends on the psychological constitution of modern humans. . . . Does the individual know that *she* or *he* is the makeweight that tips the scales? (pp. 585–586).

With all of its problems and politics, psychology and one of its crown jewels—psychotherapy—form a most viable and promising alliance for enhancing our understanding and facilitation of the future developments of uniquely individual selves in increasingly complex social systems.

REFERENCES

Allman, L. S., de La Rocha, O., Elkins, D. N., & Weathers, R. S. (1992). Psychotherapists' attitudes toward clients reporting mystical experiences. *Psychotherapy, 29*, 564–569.

Anderson, W. T. (1997). *The future of the self: Inventing the postmodern person.* New York: Tarcher/Putnam.

Bandura, A. (1986). *Social foundations of thought and action.* Upper Saddle River, NJ: Prentice Hall.

Bandura, A. (1997). *Self-efficacy: The exercise of control.* Upper Saddle River, NJ: Prentice Hall.

Batchelor, S. (1994). *The awakening of the West: The encounter of Buddhism and Western culture.* Berkeley, CA: Parallax Press.

Bonner, J. T. (1988). *The evolution of complexity by means of natural selection.* Princeton, NJ: Princeton University Press.

Boorstin, D. J. (1983). *The discoverers: A history of man's search to know his world and himself.* New York: Random House.

Braudel, F. (1979). *The structures of everyday life* (3 vols.). New York: Harper & Row.

Brockman, J. (1995). *The third culture: Beyond the scientific revolution.* New York: Simon & Schuster.

Campbell, D. T. (1975). On the conflicts between biological and social evolution and between psychology and moral tradition. *American Psychologist, 30*, 1103–1126.

Claus, D. B. (1981). *Toward the soul: An inquiry into the meaning of such before Plato.* New Haven, CT: Yale University Press.

Fisher, D. (1989). Boundary work: A model of the relation between power and knowledge. *Knowledge: Creation, Diffusion, Utilization, 10*, 156–176.

Ford, D. H. (1987). *Humans as self-constructing living systems: A developmental perspective on behavior and personality.* Hillsdale, NJ: Erlbaum.

Franklin, C., & Nurius, P. (Eds.). (1998). *Constructivism in practice.* Milwaukee, WI: Families International.

Gergen, K. J. (1991). *The saturated self: Dilemmas of identity in contemporary life.* New York: Basic Books.

Gleick, J. (1987). *Chaos: Making a new science.* New York: Viking.

Goldberger, N., Tarule, J., Clinchy, B., & Belenky, M. (Eds.). (1996). *Knowledge, difference, and power: Essays inspired by* Women's Ways of Knowing. New York: Basic Books.

Guidano, V. F. (1987). *Complexity of the self: A developmental approach to psychopathology and therapy.* New York: Guilford.

Guidano, V. F. (1991). *The self in process: Toward a post-rationalist cognitive therapy.* New York: Guilford.

Hayles, N. K. (Ed.). (1991). *Chaos and order: Complex dynamics in literature and science.* Chicago: University of Chicago Press.

Hebb, D. O. (1975). Science and the world of imagination. *Canadian Psychology, 16*, 4–11.

Jantsch, E. (1980). *The self-organizing universe: Scientific and human implications of the emerging paradigm of evolution.* New York: Pergamon.

Johnson, M. (1987). *The body in the mind: The bodily basis of meaning, imagination, and reason.* Chicago: University of Chicago Press.

Jung, C. G. (1970). The undiscovered self. In R. F. C. Hull (Trans.), *The collected works of C. G. Jung* (Vol. 10, pp. 585–586). Princeton, NJ: Princeton University Press.

Kauffman, S. A. (1993). *The origins of order: Self-organization and selection in evolution.* Oxford: Oxford University Press.

Kauffman, S. A. (1995). *At home in the universe.* Oxford: Oxford University Press.

Kelly, T. A., & Strupp, H. H. (1992). Patient and therapist values in psychotherapy: Perceived changes, assimilation, similarity, and outcome. *Journal of Consulting and Clinical Psychology, 60*, 34–40.

Kelso, J. A. S. (1995). *Dynamic patterns: The self-organization of brain and behavior.* Cambridge, MA: MIT Press.

Kovel, J. (1991). *History and spirit.* Boston: Beacon Press.

Lakoff, G. (1987). *Women, fire, and dangerous things: What categories reveal about the mind.* Chicago: University of Chicago Press.

Leder, D. (1990). *The absent body.* Chicago: University of Chicago Press.

Lewin, R. (1992). *Complexity at the edge of chaos.* New York: Macmillan.

Mahoney, M. J. (1991). *Human change processes: The scientific foundations of psychotherapy.* New York: Basic Books.

Mahoney, M. J. (in press a). *The body in psychotherapy.* New York: Guilford.

Mahoney, M. J. (in press b). *Constructive psychotherapy: Explorations in principles and practices.* New York: Guilford.

Masterpasqua, F., & Perna, P. A. (Eds.). (1995). *The psychological meaning of chaos.* Washington, DC: American Psychological Association.

Merleau-Ponty, M. (1962). *Phenomenology of perception.* C. Smith (Trans.). London: Routledge & Kegan Paul.

Mingers, J. (1995). *Self-producing systems.* New York: Plenum.

Mittenthal, J. E., & Baskin, A. B. (Eds.). (1992). *The principles of organization in organisms.* Reading, MA: Addison-Wesley.

Neimeyer, R. A., & Mahoney, M. J. (Eds.). (1995). *Constructivism in psychotherapy.* Washington, DC: American Psychological Association.

Neimeyer, R. A., & Raskin, J. D. (Eds.). (in press). *Constructions of disorder.* Washington, DC: American Psychological Association.

Payne, I. R., Bergin, A. E., & Loftus, P. E. (1992). A review of attempts to integrate spiritual and standard psychotherapy techniques. *Journal of Psychotherapy Integration, 2,* 171–192.

Robertson, R., & Combs, A. (Eds.). (1995). *Chaos theory and psychology in the life sciences.* Mahwah, NJ: Erlbaum.

Salthe, S. N. (1993). *Development and evolution: Complexity and change in biology.* Cambridge, MA: MIT Press.

Sexton, T. L., & Griffin, B. L. (Eds.). (1997). *Constructivist thinking in counseling practice, research, and training.* New York: Teachers College Press.

Skinner, B. F. (1990). Can psychology be a science of mind? *American Psychologist, 45,* 1206–1210.

Smith, S. G. (1988). *The concept of the spiritual.* Philadelphia: University of Pennsylvania Press.

Snyder, C. R., McDermott, D., Cook, W., & Rapoff, M. A. (1997). *Hope for the journey: Helping children through good times and bad.* Boulder, CO: Westview Press.

Sperry, R. W. (1988). Psychology's mentalist paradigm and the religion/science tension. *American Psychologist, 43,* 607–613.

Sperry, R. W. (1993). The impact and promise of the cognitive revolution. *American Psychologist, 48,* 878–885.

Tarnas, R. (1991). *The passion of the Western mind.* New York: Ballantine.

Thelen, E., & Smith, L. B. (1994). *A dynamic systems approach to the development of cognition and action.* Cambridge, MA: MIT Press.

Tobias, S. (1997). *Feminism: An activist's reflections on the women's movement.* New York: HarperCollins.

Vaughan, F. (1991). Spiritual issues in psychotherapy. *The Journal of Transpersonal Psychology, 23,* 105–119.

Waldrop, M. M. (1992). *Complexity: The emerging science at the edge of order and chaos.* New York: Simon & Schuster.

Wilber, K. (1998). *The marriage of sense and soul: Integrating science and religion.* New York: Random House.

Wright, B. A. (1991). Labeling: The need for greater person-environment individuation. In C. R. Snyder & D. R. Forsyth (Eds.), *Handbook of social and clinical psychology: The health perspective* (pp. 469–487). Elmsford, NY: Pergamon.

Zaner, R. M. (1971). *The problem of embodiment.* The Hague: Nijhoff.

PART II

EFFECTIVENESS
OF
PSYCHOTHERAPEUTIC
CHANGE

CHAPTER 2

RANDOMIZED CLINICAL TRIALS IN PSYCHOTHERAPY RESEARCH: METHODOLOGY, DESIGN, AND EVALUATION

DAVID A. F. HAAGA
American University
WILLIAM B. STILES
Miami University

This chapter addresses principles and practices useful in designing and evaluating studies aimed at determining how well a particular psychotherapy method works. Our focus is on controlled research designs. Uncontrolled studies such as simple pre-post, single-group comparisons are subject to fundamental concerns about internal validity. Confounds such as history, maturation, regression to the mean, and measurement reactivity serve as viable rival hypotheses for any apparent treatment effects. Chambless and Hollon (1998) and the Task Force on Promotion and Dissemination of Psychological Procedures (1995) have argued that randomized clinical trials (RCTs), in which participants are randomly assigned to the treatment under investigation or to a comparison condition, can yield the most convincing evidence of the efficacy of a psychotherapy. As we discuss throughout the chapter, however, actually executing an RCT in such a way as to generate conclusive evidence about a psychotherapy's effects is not simple, and many potential pitfalls to valid interpretation require attention from investigators and from research consumers.

Randomized clinical trials are an adaptation of the experimental method, which is the closest science has come to a means for demonstrating causality. This justifies the effort put into RCTs, despite the difficulties. The logic of the experi-

mental method is that if all prior conditions except one (the independent variable) are held constant (controlled), then any differences in the outcome (the dependent variable) must have been caused by the one condition that varied. For example, if one patient is given psychotherapy and another identical patient is not but is treated identically in all other respects, then any differences in their outcomes must have been caused by the therapy.

Difficulties arise because no two people are identical and because it is impossible to treat two people identically in all respects except one (i.e., except for the theoretically specified treatment, the independent variable). Most of this chapter is devoted to describing these difficulties and ways investigators have sought to address them.

Randomized clinical trials address the differences among patients statistically. Rather than comparing single patients, investigators randomly assign patients to groups that are to receive the different treatments, on the assumption that any prior differences that might affect the outcomes will be more or less evenly distributed across the groups. Even though individuals' outcomes might vary within groups (because patients are not identical), any mean differences between groups beyond those due to chance should be attributable to the different treatments.

In this chapter we focus on experimental

group designs. Many of the issues we examine, such as considerations in the measurement of independent and dependent variables, generalize to other designs. The technical issues associated with single-case experimental designs are detailed by Kazdin (1998, Chap. 9). We focus on methods for assessing psychotherapy's outcomes rather than its processes; treatment process research methods have been described elsewhere (e.g., Lambert & Hill, 1994; Stiles, Honos-Webb, & Knobloch, in press). We focus on individual studies rather than meta-analyses. Meta-analytic procedures for synthesizing research findings and guidelines for reporting meta-analyses have also been described elsewhere (e.g., Hunter & Schmidt, 1990; Rosenthal, 1995).

Many of the difficulties associated with conducting RCTs of psychotherapies can be understood as manifestations of *responsiveness*—behavior that is affected by emerging context, including others' characteristics and behavior (Stiles, Honos-Webb, & Surko, in press). For example, therapists are being responsive when they make a treatment assignment based on a patient's presenting problems or design homework assignments that take into account a patient's abilities and circumstances or rephrase an explanation that a patient seemed not to understand the first time. Responsiveness may be contrasted with *ballistic* action, which is determined at its inception and carries through regardless of external events. Giving all patients the same treatment or identical homework assignments or identically worded explanations would be ballistic.

Therapists and patients are responsive to each other and to their context in many ways and on time scales that range from months to milliseconds (Stiles, Honos-Webb, & Surko, in press). Though far from perfect, their responsiveness usually aims to be appropriate; that is, they try to respond to emerging requirements in ways that promote desired outcomes, such as reduction in symptoms or improvement in life functioning. In this way the (anticipated) outcome (the dependent variable) feeds back to influence the delivery of the treatment (the independent variable). To the extent that the participants are appropriately responsive, they may confound research designs and distort results in a variety of ways, as we illustrate throughout this chapter.

CHOICE OF COMPARISON CONDITIONS

Perhaps the first issue confronted by an investigator planning to evaluate the impact of a specific form of psychotherapy is the choice of a comparison condition. No one choice is right for all projects. The best choice for a particular project depends on the goals of the study, the state of existing research on the therapy, and the resources available to the investigator.

Wait-list or No-treatment Comparisons

Wait-list or *no-treatment control* conditions involve random assignment of some patients to the group that receives no psychotherapy intervention. Often, the intervention is offered to wait-listed patients after a posttreatment assessment has been completed, which can serve as an incentive to remain in the investigation. This comparison condition provides many more methodological advantages than an uncontrolled study. If there were no wait-list group and we found, say, lower depression symptom scores after a three-month course of person-centered therapy than before treatment, we would be uncertain whether person-centered therapy contributed to the effect or if the reduction was caused entirely by such artifacts as history (e.g., change of season may be relevant for some depressed patients), repeated testing (e.g., seeing in black and white one's level of depression motivates self-help activities outside of the treatment context), or measurement unreliability. Participants in treatment studies are generally selected in the first place on the basis of having unusually high symptom scores; therefore, any regression to the mean attributable to measurement unreliability is likely to be in the form of declining scores over time.

Wait-list comparison conditions are particularly useful when little is known about the effectiveness of a treatment. For example, if the utility of person-centered therapy for treating depression is unknown, then the first order of business is to find out if it is more helpful than no treatment at all.

Wait-list comparisons have limitations, however. For quite a few common psychological disorders there is already substantial evidence that at least one effective psychosocial treatment exists (DeRubeis & Crits-Christoph, 1998). In these cases, demonstration of superiority to no treatment has no clear pragmatic implication for choice of therapy. In any circumstance, demonstration of superiority to no treatment is uninformative with respect to what in particular is helpful about the therapy or whether the associated theory of change is valid. Also, it is generally considered ethically problematic to continue to withhold treatment from people in need of it. Accordingly, wait-list comparisons usually remain intact only through posttreatment evaluation rather than follow-up and then cannot inform us about long-term effects.

Moreover, it may be difficult to sustain a pure "no-treatment" condition because people identified as wanting and needing help but not receiving it in the research project may avail themselves of other forms of assistance (e.g., books, friends, videos, computer programs, World Wide Web sites, and religious leaders). From the patients' perspective, such help-seeking activities outside the research protocol may represent appropriate responsiveness to their own requirements, speeding their own psychological improvement. The effect on the research, however, is to make the study inadvertently a comparison of active treatment vs. an unspecified amalgam of other forms of help rather than of active treatment vs. nothing. Complicating matters further, treated participants are also responsive to their own requirements and may also engage in extra-project help seeking, perhaps as much as or even more than do untreated participants (Cross, Sheehan, & Khan, 1980).

Finally, patients' responsiveness to wait-list assignment could inflate the apparent treatment efficacy. Basham (1986) argued that the wait-list comparison has problematic demand characteristics: wait-list conditions entail professional ratification (based on intake assessment) that the prospective patient indeed needs help but is not going to receive treatment. This could create a negative expectancy of improvement, thereby leading to an exaggeration of treatment efficacy if one simply compares the outcome of the treatment with the wait-list condition.

Treatment-as-Usual Comparisons

An alternative to the no-treatment comparison condition is the *treatment-as-usual* comparison condition, in which patients are free to seek whatever other treatment is available in the community. Such a condition was used in evaluating dialectical behavior therapy for parasuicidal women with borderline personality disorder (Linehan, Armstrong, Suarez, Allmon, & Heard, 1991). The treatment-as-usual condition has advantages over wait-list in that it is ethically reasonable to sustain such a condition through follow-up evaluation and for severe disorders. Patients assigned to this condition receive the same services they would have received in the absence of the study. This design also addresses a very practical question: does the investigated therapy yield better outcomes than are obtainable in the same com-

munity by patients with the same disorder but no access to the investigated treatment? Pragmatically, treatment-as-usual seems to represent more adequately the actual alternative, which would rarely be no treatment.

The main disadvantage of treatment-as-usual comparisons is the variability of treatment-as-usual. We do not really know to what treatment the investigated therapy has been shown to be equivalent, superior, or inferior. Treatment-as-usual is temporally and geographically specific and fluid, reducing the generality of the findings.

Placebo Comparisons

Concerns about expectancies and other non-specifics of therapy (e.g., contact with another individual, getting a chance to talk about one's problems, and taking time from usual routines to focus on oneself and on psychological issues) motivate another alternative to the wait-list comparison, the *placebo treatment* comparison condition. The idea here is to identify the specific impact of a theory-driven psychotherapy by comparing it to a quasi therapy that mobilizes positive expectancies on the part of patients but does not contain the theory-specified elements of the therapy under investigation. This design relies on an analogy to drug research in which the specific chemical effects of an investigated drug are studied in comparison to the impact of a chemically inert pill designed to control for the patient's expectancy of benefiting from taking a drug.

There is substantial evidence that patients' positive expectancies for benefiting from a treatment predict a positive outcome (e.g., Safren, Heimberg, & Juster, 1997). Psychotherapy placebos have the potential benefit of isolating therapy effects due to credibility and mobilization of expectancy from other theory-specified mechanisms of action. However, there are ambiguities with this comparison condition as well (Parloff, 1986). First, for the logic of the design to follow, one must devise a "treatment" having none of the theoretically useful properties of the active treatment yet equivalent in its credibility throughout the course of therapy. A placebo condition that sounds reasonable when described in five minutes at an intake interview but that is unimpressive after three sessions of treatment relative to the active therapy is not in fact equivalent in nonspecifics and would fail to control for them.

Second, in drug research, placebo effects are usually considered to reflect the psychological aspects of the treatment, not the drug's biologically active ingredients. Transferring the placebo concept to psychotherapy research, therefore, requires some adjustment and tends to be problematic. For one thing, theories of psychotherapy differ about which components are therapeutically important. The neat segregation of plausibly-chemically-active vs. surely-chemically-inert drug ingredients does not seem to be matched by an equally consensual definition of what psychotherapy process components should or should not have a specific effect. Psychological placebos have historically included treatment methods that were thought to be inert or nonspecific from the point of view of the investigator but that, from other defensible points of view, were viable treatments (e.g., relaxation training or nondirective therapy). Such placebo comparison designs in effect devolve into alternative treatment comparison designs. In such cases, it seems misleading to use the "placebo" designation and thereby invoke the metaphorical connection to placebo controls in drug research.

Finally, in psychotherapy research, the placebo condition is typically not a subcomponent of the main treatment under investigation but rather an alternative intervention altogether. As such, it fails to follow the componential logic of using the placebo treatment to estimate the impact of nonspecifics in the active treatment. In drug or other medical intervention research, the placebo shares superficial features with the active intervention (e.g., taking a pill, a sham injection, or sham surgery), so that the specific benefit of the drug or procedure can be estimated by subtraction. With a psychotherapy placebo that utilizes different interventions, this logic is strained. If one uses, for example, nondirective therapy as a placebo comparison in a study of in vivo exposure for specific phobia, the nondirective therapy is not equivalent to a "nonspecific" aspect of the in vivo exposure program that can be peeled off from exposure therapy to quantify its nonspecific impact.

Component Control Designs (Dismantling)

The concern that placebo controls do not necessarily represent a dissociable subset of the active intervention being studied leads to consideration of *component control* designs, also called *dismantling* studies. The idea behind such studies is that we can learn about the effective components of treatment protocols experimentally by using as comparison conditions a portion of the treatment. For example, Jacobson et al. (1996) attempted to isolate the impact of cognitive techniques in cognitive behavior therapy of depression by comparing the full treatment (which they analyzed in terms of three major com-

ponents: behavioral activation strategies, automatic thoughts modification, and schema work) to protocols consisting of just the first two components or of just the first component. Similarly, a study of the utility of progressive muscle relaxation training as part of a comprehensive psychosocial treatment program for men with borderline essential hypertension compared relaxation plus education (e.g., advice to lower salt intake and engage in regular exercise) to education alone (Davison, Williams, Nezami, Bice, & DeQuattro, 1991). The impact of the isolated components is estimated in this design by the difference in effectiveness between conditions including them and conditions excluding them.

As a more detailed example, consider the nonaversive behavioral treatment for cigarette smoking that involves nicotine fading and self-monitoring (Foxx & Brown, 1979). The two major components of the program are (1) nicotine fading, in which one smokes progressively lower-nicotine cigarettes each week for the three weeks before quitting altogether, and (2) self-monitoring, in which the smoker records situational variables, thoughts, and feelings associated with each instance of smoking during a baseline phase, with an eye toward learning about one's personal smoking habit and devising useful alternative coping tactics for personally relevant high-risk situations after cessation. If one found this treatment more useful than nothing, a further question would be whether both components contribute to the effect.

A dismantling study could address this issue by randomly assigning smokers to four groups: (A) nicotine fading plus self-monitoring, (B) nicotine fading alone, (C) self-monitoring alone, and (D) wait-list. The contribution of self-monitoring is estimated in two ways in this design (C vs. D and A vs. B), as is the utility of nicotine fading (B vs. D and A vs. C). The two estimates need not yield the same result, and the discrepancy could itself be informative. For example, if group A does better than B, but C is no better than D, this would suggest that self-monitoring is helpful, but only in the context of nicotine fading; thus, there is a synergistic interaction of treatment components rather than a constant main effect of self-monitoring.

A major question in designing dismantling studies is whether to equate the conditions for the total amount of therapy time, in which case the ostensibly "common" component equated across conditions may actually be delivered better or more completely when it is the only component, or to let the multicomponent treatment programs run longer, in which case the greater duration would be a possible explanation of any superior efficacy of the program.

Letting treatment length vary across conditions can show whether the effectiveness of a full treatment protocol can be maintained while reducing costs and improving disseminability by abbreviating treatment. For example, a cognitive-behavioral protocol for panic disorder was as effective at a six-month follow-up when delivered in 4 sessions with the adjunctive use of a palmtop computer program as when delivered in 12 sessions (Newman, Kenardy, Herman, & Taylor, 1997). A complication in interpreting this sort of study, however, is that the desired outcome is a null result (brief, low-cost treatment that is nonsignificantly different in outcome from full treatment). Therefore, method flaws (inadequate statistical power, poor implementation of intended treatments, and unreliable outcome measures) actually increase the likelihood of obtaining the desired result. It is therefore critical in such studies to provide assurance that such flaws do not characterize the study and cannot account for the findings.

Combination Treatment Designs; Parametric Variation

The opposite of the dismantling design, in a sense, is the *combination treatment* design, in which one studies whether the effectiveness of a standard treatment can be enhanced by adding a further treatment. Frequently the motive for such an investigation is the perception that different treatments target different, complementary aspects of the syndrome. For example, in the treatment of depression, antidepressant medication may achieve rapid symptom suppression and address vegetative symptoms, whereas psychotherapies may teach rehabilitative coping skills and address cognitive, behavioral, and emotional symptoms.

A variant of studies that contrast long vs. brief versions of treatments or full treatments vs. component controls would be *parametric variation* studies that utilize comparison conditions identical to the main treatment except for altering one specific parameter of the treatment format to determine whether it has an impact on outcome. Many such studies have been conducted with respect to behavior therapy for anxiety disorders, contrasting, for instance, the effectiveness of massed (short intersession interval) vs. spaced (longer intersession interval) exposure schedules, long vs. short exposure sessions, in vivo vs. imaginal exposure, therapist-directed vs. self-directed exposure, and so on (Bouman & Emmelkamp, 1996).

Parametric variation experiments ideally could and should be applied to a long list of features of psychotherapy practice (Does the common custom of weekly appointments make sense? Let us randomly assign patients to conditions in which sessions are held weekly, biweekly, or semiweekly and compare results. Is regular monitoring of symptom scores reactive in the sense of improving treatment? Randomly assign patients to engage in regular assessment vs. not. . . .) Realistically, only parameters perceived to be especially crucial and of particularly high impact will lend themselves to isolated study in this sense. It is difficult enough, as we discuss later in the chapter, to execute experiments powerful enough to detect the difference between a complete treatment protocol and a much more minimalistic effort. In view of all the many influences on treatment outcome, including patient and therapist variables, it is probably unrealistic to expect the most-likely-subtle impact of minor parametric variations to be detectable in modest-sized samples typical of therapy studies.[1]

Dismantling, combination, and parametric

---

[1]What might seem to be an obvious correlational strategy for identifying the "active ingredients" of a psychotherapy is also blocked, for reasons that trace to responsiveness. One might think that by coding for the frequency or intensity of a therapy process component (e.g., therapist's provision of accurately empathic reflections of feeling) and correlating this with outcome, one could determine whether the process component is helpful, harmful, or inert by observing whether the correlation was positive, negative, or null, respectively. Unfortunately, this logic implicitly assumes that the process component is delivered ballistically, or at least randomly, with respect to patients' requirements. Such a conversation would be absurd. If therapists respond more or less appropriately to clients' requirements for a particular process component, then each client will tend to get about the optimum amount at the optimum time. If a component were always delivered at an optimum level, then outcome would tend to be the same across clients insofar as it depended on that component. The level of the process component might vary across clients, but it would not predict outcome unless, by coincidence, clients' requirements happened to predict outcome. Therapists are not perfectly responsive, of course, but any appropriate responsiveness tends to defeat the process-outcome correlation logic and may even reverse it (Stiles, 1988; Stiles, Honos-Webb, & Surko, in press; Stiles & Shapiro, 1994).

To highlight the problem, assume that *focus on negative self-image* really is an important component in cognitive therapy for depression. However, clients' requirements for this component vary. Some clients variation studies assume that treatment components are self-contained modules that can be added and removed independently. However, therapists and patients may compensate for restrictions by responsively making different or more extensive use of the tools they are allowed, thus confounding experimental manipulations. For example, a therapist told to decrease question asking may compensate by using more evocative reflections or remaining silent, giving patients more space to talk, a manifestation of responsiveness. Cox, Holbrook, and Rutter (1981; Cox, Rutter, & Holbrook, 1981) observed such compensation when they experimentally manipulated interviewers' styles in diagnostic interviews. Interviewers using four contrasting styles (directive vs. nondirective crossed with active vs. passive) elicited very similar levels of information and feeling but by different paths, as participants responsively adjusted to the experimental manipulations.

Comparisons with Bona Fide Alternatives

Finally, a treatment can be compared to another *bona fide alternative psychotherapy* in a comparative outcome experiment. Wampold, Mondin, Moody, Stich, Benson, and Ahn (1997) defined bona fide alternatives as those based on psychological principles and offered to the public as plausible treatments for the condition being studied. This definition contrasts bona fide alternative therapies with weaker comparison conditions designed to control for expectancy effects or treatment time but not really expected to be effective therapies. Such comparative RCTs are of great intrinsic interest, holding out the promise of identifying the most effective among the available treatments.

Given the small effects it is reasonable to expect in comparisons of bona fide psychotherapies

---

respond quickly to such a focus and require very little, whereas others require a great deal of this focus, perhaps because their self-image was more negative or more resistant to change. Suppose that therapists are appropriately responsive but imperfectly. That is, the needier clients tend to get more of this focus but not quite enough, so their outcomes are relatively worse. As a consequence, focus on negative self-image will be *negatively* correlated with outcome across clients, even though, as we assumed, it is an important component in the therapy. Reviewers seeing reports of such negative correlations are likely to conclude, mistakenly, that focus on negative self-image is useless or harmful.

(Wampold et al., 1997), it is important to ensure adequate statistical power. It is also important to include a minimal treatment or wait-list comparison in the design so that if null results are obtained in the main comparison one can determine whether this occurred because the treatments were equally effective or equally ineffective.

In the special case of comparisons of psychotherapy with medication, Klein (1996) argued that a pill placebo condition is necessary, to ensure via internal calibration that the sample was medication-responsive and therefore apt for a comparison of psychotherapy with medication. McNally (1996) has countered, however, that this requirement makes the efficacy of medications nonfalsifiable (only if medications prove effective is the sample a fair one in which to test the efficacy of medications) and sets a double standard for comparative efficacy studies (i.e., there is no symmetric requirement that only psychotherapy-responsive samples can be used to study whether medications are as effective as psychotherapies).

A particular concern in comparative studies is the investigator's allegiance to one of the therapies being compared. Evidence from reviews and meta-analyses suggests that allegiance effects may account for a larger proportion of outcome variance than differences between therapeutic approaches and that when allegiance effects are statistically controlled, outcome differences between treatments may be negligible (Luborsky et al., in press; Robinson, Berman, & Neimeyer, 1990). This need not imply that investigators are misrepresenting their results. Designing, implementing, and analyzing a comparative psychotherapy study is complex, and there are hundreds of points at which an investigator's differential expertise and allegiance could influence choices in ways that favor one treatment over another (recruiting, inclusion or exclusion criteria, setting and context, instructions to therapists, measures, etc.). Indeed, it would be surprising if an investigator's grasp of his or her own preferred therapy were not more subtle, differentiated, and thorough than of a nonpreferred alternative.

One unfortunate implication of the investigator allegiance effect is that aggregate outcome results for various therapies are confounded with the inclination among their proponents to conduct outcome studies. This inclination is certainly not equal across theoretical orientations. For example, a meta-analysis of RCTs on family and marital therapy covering a 25-year span included 40 studies of behavioral treatments and only 1 of psychodynamic treatment (Shadish, Montgomery, Wilson, Wilson, Bright, & Okwumabua, 1993).

SAMPLING ISSUES

Deciding how to select prospective participants for a therapy study is a complicated process involving judgment and tradeoffs. There is no one right way. Issues include the homogeneity of the sample, the criteria for selection, the method of recruitment, and the size of the sample.

Homogeneity of Sample

One issue requiring careful consideration is the extent and nature of sample homogeneity. To the degree that the investigator precisely specifies the target population (e.g., Caucasian women between the age of 25 and 40 with a Diagnostic and Statistical Manual of Mental Disorders, 4th Edition (DSM-IV) diagnosis of panic disorder but no comorbid Axis I or Axis II diagnoses, at least two years of college, married, with children under the age of 8, living in rural areas, and employed outside the home), homogeneity is increased, within-group variability is probably decreased, and research consumers have a clearer idea of the sorts of patients to whom the findings can be applied.

There are also disadvantages of such detailed specification, however. Restriction of the range on client variables prevents us from finding out empirically which ones predict the treatment response. In an analogous way, historically a very high percentage of medical research used homogeneous samples of men, giving inadequate attention to whether findings could be generalized to women. Also, each exclusion criterion decreases the size of the population to which the study results pertain. In extreme cases, clinicians might find that most of their caseloads do not correspond to the samples studied in clinical trials. Finally, from a practical point of view, narrower definitions of the target sample increase the costs and difficulties associated with recruiting a sufficiently large sample of patients to complete the project in a timely manner.

Diagnoses and Alternative Means of Defining Eligibility

Probably the most common basis for selecting homogeneous samples in contemporary psychotherapy research is the DSM-IV Axis I principal diagnosis, such that all the participants are believed, based on structured diagnostic interviewing, to have a diagnosable disorder (a dysthymic disorder, generalized anxiety disorder, etc.). Age range is usually also homogeneous, at least within the child vs. adult distinction. Often some minimum symptom-severity standard is set as well, based on scores on widely used measures. Beyond these points of similarity, samples are usually allowed to vary widely, with patient variables that are considered potentially influential measured and later examined in secondary analyses concerning whether they affected response. Ideally, theory and prior research are used to select in advance a manageable number of predictor variables that will be allowed to fluctuate in the sample, and sampling is planned to allow for a statistically powerful examination of the relevance of these variables (Kazdin, 1998).

As indicated by Chambless and Hollon (1998), however, DSM diagnoses need not be the only means of defining homogeneous samples; indeed, Beutler (1991) has argued that diagnoses are not the most relevant individual-difference variables to consider. For example, Coyle and Enright (1997) recruited a sample of men who indicated that they felt emotionally hurt by a partner's decision to obtain an abortion, a selection based on nondiagnostic psychological variables. Another possibility is to use diagnosis as a predictor but not as an inclusion requirement. A recent study of eye movement desensitization and reprocessing defined the sample in terms of having had a traumatic experience, but the diagnosis of posttraumatic stress disorder (PTSD) was not a requirement and characterized only about one-half of the participants, permitting empirical examination of whether this variable moderated treatment efficacy (Wilson, Becker, & Tinker, 1997).

Solicited Volunteers and Treatment Seekers

Increasingly, investigators have turned to media advertisements to recruit potentially eligible participants, as opposed to recruiting solely from among those who seek treatment on their own. This practice was at one time considered controversial (Krupnick, Shea, & Elkin, 1986). One can readily imagine that the solicited patients may be more passive, less motivated, and less severely symptomatic in that they did not initiate treatment until becoming aware of the advertisements. The acceptability of soliciting patients for therapy studies from outside treatment settings appears to have increased, however. In an informal review of the 1997 volume of the *Journal of*

Consulting and Clinical Psychology for the outcome studies in which the recruitment method was identifiable, 11 utilized solicited patients, 14 regular clinic referrals, and 7 from both sources. The studies involving multiple sources did not report comparative outcome analyses and typically did not even report how many participants were recruited in which manner.

Controversial or not, the question remains of whether the treatment outcome is similar across recruitment methods. A qualitative review of studies directly addressing the comparability of solicited and traditionally referred patients reported that the treatment response was similar, though too few studies were available to support strong conclusions on this point (Krupnick et al., 1986). More recently, Shadish et al. (1997) conducted a secondary analysis of investigations reported in previously published meta-analyses of therapy outcomes and found effect sizes very similar to overall average effects for a subset of studies that met multiple criteria for clinical representativeness, including "patients that were referred through usual clinical routes rather than solicited by the experimenter" (p. 358). In sum, there are fewer directly relevant data than would be desirable for such a basic sampling issue, but what is available tends to bolster the inference that results are similar whether or not the patients are recruited by advertisements.

Sample Size
Statistical Power

For any given alpha level, effect size, and choice of one- versus two-tailed statistical testing, the higher the sample size the greater the statistical power, or the probability of rejecting a false null hypothesis. By convention, many investigators choose two-tailed tests with the alpha set at .05, and many investigators appear to find Cohen's (1988) suggested convention of a desired power of .8 reasonable. Based on these specifications, one can consult printed tables or computer programs to identify the necessary sample size to be obtained, given various projected population effect sizes. The results can be sobering. For instance, if a "medium" (per Cohen's conventions) effect size of $d = .50$ (half a standard deviation difference in means) is expected between two groups on a primary outcome measure, the needed sample size is 64 per group (Cohen, 1992). For a "large" effect of $d = .80$, the needed sample size is 26 per group, which may seem feasible. However, an effect size of .8 is more char-

acteristic of treatment vs. no-treatment comparisons than of comparisons among active treatments, for which small to medium effects are more plausible (Kazdin & Bass, 1989). Moreover, even the standard of 26 per group may be difficult to achieve; a survey of 1984–1986 published outcome studies from major journals revealed a median sample size of 12 per group, with 25th and 75th percentile values of 10 and 19, respectively (Kazdin & Bass, 1989).

It seems widely appreciated that low power complicates the interpretation of nonsignificant results—is there really no difference in effectiveness between these treatments, or was the study too small to detect the difference that really exists? Less generally understood is that low power also complicates the interpretation of studies with significant results. Rossi (1990) found an average power for small effects of just .17 in a survey of studies in major personality and clinical journals. If one is working in an area characterized by small effects, "the probability of rejecting a true null hypothesis may be only slightly smaller than the probability of rejecting the null hypothesis when the alternative is true. That is, the ratio of Type I errors to power may be uncomfortably large, indicating that a substantial proportion of all significant results may be due to false rejections of valid null hypotheses" (p. 652).

However, there is hope that the situation may improve gradually. First, the use of meta-analysis has increased sensitivity to the importance of reporting effect size magnitudes and therefore awareness of what effect sizes are typical. Also, grant proposals are routinely evaluated in part with respect to the adequacy of power and sample size planning, and this affects the published literature downstream, albeit imperfectly (Kraemer, Gardner, Brooks, & Yesavage, 1998).

Post Hoc Power Analysis

Less attention has been devoted in the published literature to post hoc uses of power analysis. Once a study has been completed, sample size becomes a fixed point rather than an unknown to solve. However, statistical power remains relevant in evaluating and reporting the study.

Consider a comparative therapy experiment that obtains nonsignificant differences on major outcome variables between two alternative treatments. The question arises about whether (1) the treatments really were about equally effective (in the population studied, therapists given this amount of training, etc.) or (2) the treatments were differentially effective, but the study was too small and underpowered to detect this at a conventional level of statistical significance. A null result may be a laudable outcome if, for example, the researcher is comparing a briefer, less costly, novel treatment to a longer, more intensive, established one. Even when there are no cost or efficiency advantages with one treatment, null results in comparative therapy studies are interesting, and some investigators consider that they are to be routinely expected in such studies. However, as stated by Hallahan and Rosenthal (1996),

> It is crucially important that power be considered when interpreting the results of research in which the null is a research hypothesis. With low power, one would be unlikely to reject the null even if it were false, but this failure to reject does not mean that the null is true. . . . It is a serious error to infer that the null is true on the basis of a test that has little chance of rejecting a genuinely false null. (p. 493)

We note two questionable approaches to post hoc power analysis that seem to be gaining currency. First, some authors hypothesize the actual effect size obtained in the study and indicate what power for detecting that effect size was at the number (n) available in the study. This approach strikes us as uninformative because it essentially guarantees that no nonsignificant result can be found convincing. If there were 50,000 participants in each condition and nonsignificant group differences, then there must be a tiny sample effect size (ES), and hypothesizing that this ES is the parameter will lead us to detect low power.

A second approach appears to be excessively liberal in interpreting null results as indicators of equal efficacy. Authors comment on the implications of their null results by indicating how many participants would have been needed to detect the sample ES as significant. For example, Vollmer and Blanchard (1998) found no significant differences in outcome between group cognitive therapy (GCT) and individual cognitive therapy (ICT) in the treatment of irritable bowel syndrome. As there were only 11 participants per treatment condition, the authors acknowledged low statistical power as a methodological limitation of the research. However, on the basis of the very small difference in average effects across conditions, they argued, "With statistical power of .80 and a significance level of .05, 1,158 subjects would be needed to obtain a significant difference between GCT and ICT. It thus seems apparent that the two active treatments were equivalent in efficacy for all practical purposes" (p. 26).

This approach to post hoc power analysis also seems suboptimal. First, its result is stated in terms relevant to the research planner (how many subjects?) rather than to the therapist, patient, third-party payer, and so on (how large is this effect?). Second, it treats the sample ES as an equally good guess at the parameter, regardless of the n, whereas the estimate actually gets more precise the larger the n is. To take an extreme example, by the "how many subjects would it take to find significance if this ES is the parameter?" logic, a study with $n = 3$ per cell that happened to find identical mean scores in the two groups would be completely convincing evidence of equal efficacy since an infinite n would be needed to detect this ES of 0 as significant.

We believe it would make more sense to report either (1) what the power was to detect conventionally defined effect sizes (e.g., for what Cohen, 1992, labels a "small" effect, the study had power of XX, for a "medium" effect YY, and for a "large" effect ZZ) or (2) the smallest ES for which the study had adequate power, and then characterize for readers in everyday terms the implications of that ES [e.g., what it corresponds to in the binomial effect size display (Rosenthal & Rubin, 1982), what other interventions are characterized by that ES, etc]. Either of these approaches has the commonsensical feature of resulting in a more convincing null result the larger the study was.

Nonequivalence of Groups and the Reversal Paradox

In addition to low statistical power and the corresponding danger of Type II errors, the use of small samples in therapy research increases the probability that random assignment will fail to yield subsamples equivalent in all important respects at pretreatment. The idea behind random assignment is that the groups will start out alike with respect to all nuisance variables that could otherwise confound our interpretation of treatment effects, whether we know in advance what these nuisance variables are or not. This is assured, however, only with large samples. Hsu (1989) analyzed this problem by calculating probabilities of nonequivalence on nuisance variables across two groups divided according to simple random assignment. For an n of 24 assigned to two groups of 12 each (a median psychotherapy outcome study sample size according to the review by Kazdin & Bass, 1989), if there are three relevant nuisance variables, the probability of nonequivalence is greater than one-half (53%). Hsu defined nonequivalence for this purpose as a twofold or greater difference between groups in the proportion of participants belonging to one category of a dichotomous (or dichotomized) nuisance variable. Nonequivalence could in turn lead to inaccurate estimates of treatment effects, or in an extreme case to a reversal or "Simpson's" paradox (Messick & Van de Geer, 1981; Simpson, 1951) in which the relative standing of two treatment conditions on an outcome variable in the total sample could be the reverse of what it is at every level of a nuisance variable.

Table 2.1 illustrates such a reversal. It shows the results of a hypothetical study in which cognitive therapy (CT) is more effective at every level of the nuisance variable, marital status (married or unmarried), but worse overall than interpersonal therapy (IPT). This reversal reflects the nonequivalence of the two groups (CT and IPT) on the nuisance variable. Married patients, who fared better in either treatment than their unmarried counterparts, were overrepresented in IPT.

IMPLEMENTATION OF THE INDEPENDENT VARIABLE

Meaningful interpretation of any experiment requires assurance that the independent variable was successfully manipulated. In RCTs of psychotherapy, each patient must receive the treatment specified for his or her group for the results to be interpretable. Because psychotherapy therapists and patients are responsive to emerging conditions, however, studies of psychotherapy cannot realistically aspire to precise standardization in the delivery of the independent variable. Credible therapy interactions will be unscripted, with the therapist's utterances (let alone nonverbal communications) variable and responsive to the patient's statements.

Accordingly, therapy as delivered will vary with respect to degree of fidelity to therapy as intended, and the differences between therapy conditions may vary from the investigator's intentions. In the limiting case, the treatments may differ only on paper and not in practice. Clearly, if the therapies did not differ as intended, then the interpretation of outcome similarities or differences is impossible.

Investigators, therefore, try to impose a degree of standardization on treatments, most notably by the use of treatment manuals, and they routinely report evaluations of the independent variable in therapy research. At least four major aspects of the latter issue can be distinguished (Haaga, Dryden, & Dancey, 1991): positive adherence, negative adherence, differentiability, and quality.

Treatment Manualization

Although psychotherapy interactions can never be completely standardized and scripted to the extent that, say, audiotaped instructions in a laboratory experiment might be, a treatment manual fleshes out the investigator's concept of the treatment and appears to reduce variability in the therapist's success (Crits-Christoph et al., 1991).

TABLE 2.1   Illustration of a Reversal Paradox in a Hypothetical Small *n* Comparative Outcome Study with Nonequivalent Nuisance Variable of Marital Status

Dependent variable = posttreatment Beck Anxiety Inventory scores (lower scores reflecting better outcome)

	Cognitive Therapy	**Interpersonal Therapy**
Married Patients	M = 4, *n* = 4	M = 5, *n* = 8
Unmarried Patients	M = 13, *n* = 8	M = 14, *n* = 4
Total Sample	M = 10, *n* = 12	M = 8, *n* = 12

Cognitive therapy is better (results in lower mean scores) for married patients and for unmarried patients but worse overall because (1) marital status is strongly related to outcome and (2) marital status is—despite random assignment—nonequivalent across treatment conditions.

In addition to a broad overview of the principles underlying the treatment, it is common to include detailed session-by-session road maps of suggested techniques, as well as troubleshooting guidelines. The availability of a written manual facilitates the training of therapists for the study itself, guides the development of measures of the integrity and quality of the therapy, and makes replication efforts possible.

Codification of the treatment in a manual is now generally regarded as desirable in psychotherapy outcome research and indeed has been advanced as a requirement for studies to count toward the evaluation of a treatment as empirically supported (Chambless & Hollon, 1998) or empirically validated (Chambless et al., 1998). It also seems likely that manuals are helpful in the dissemination of treatments found in research to be effective (Addis, 1997).

Nevertheless, there are dangers. In the short and medium term, introducing manuals risks interfering with therapists' responsiveness, as therapists try to implement interventions described in the manual without attending to the client's current condition or requirements. This may impair their effectiveness, at least until they have mastered the new approach (Anderson & Strupp, 1996; Henry, Strupp, Butler, Schacht, & Binder, 1993).

Adherence

Adherence, also referred to as fidelity or integrity (Yeaton & Sechrest, 1981), refers to the extent to which therapists conformed to the techniques (or nontechnical stylistics) of the intended therapy condition. Adherence is typically assessed by rating scales that translate the treatment manual's principles into behaviors observable in session tape recordings (e.g., Shapiro & Startup, 1992; Startup & Shapiro, 1993). Positive adherence is the extent to which the therapist performed behaviors prescribed by the intended therapy, whereas negative adherence is the extent to which the therapist refrained from performing behaviors proscribed by the intended therapy. Both prescribed and proscribed therapy actions should be specified in rating scales, and independent raters (masked to the intended treatment) should rate each aspect of adherence on the basis of audio- or videotapes (randomly sampled) of therapy sessions, with interrater reliability evaluated. If only positive adherence is evaluated, misleading conclusions could result. For instance, suppose that exposure plus response prevention (ERP) is found to be superior to progressive muscle relaxation training in the treatment of obsessive-compulsive disorder. If therapists in the ERP condition indeed conducted prolonged exposure with prevention of compulsive rituals (i.e., positive adherence was high) but also encouraged patients to engage in frequent primal scream rituals (an unintended feature of ERP; i.e., negative adherence was low), we would not know whether the ERP tactics or the primal scream rituals or both were responsible for superior outcome, and this ambiguity would be missed altogether if only positive adherence were measured.

Differentiability

Differentiability refers to the degree to which masked raters can tell, based on descriptions of the intended therapy conditions, which one is being conducted in video- or audiotapes to which they are exposed. If adherence ratings for each condition are high, and the therapies were indeed specified to have meaningful differences, then differentiability should be high; however, it is important to verify this assumption. For example, one comparative study of four cognitive-behavioral and one behavioral treatment for social anxiety found that raters could correctly classify 93% of 15-minute tape segments (DiGiuseppe, McGowan, Sutton Simon, & Gardner, 1990). This type of finding provides reassurance that the psychotherapies under investigation differed noticeably in practice, not solely in name or intent.

Quality

Quality or competence refers to how well therapists implemented the intended treatments. In contrast to adherence, quality or competence involves appropriate and skillful application of abstract treatment principles (Hoffart, 1997). Thus, competence demands responsiveness to the patient's emerging requirements, and judging competence involves evaluating whether the responsiveness was appropriate. A therapist who delivered treatment components mechanically (unresponsively) could be evaluated as high in adherence but low in competence.

One example of a scale designed to assess quality is the Cognitive Therapy Scale (Young & Beck, 1980). On the item relating to setting an agenda, for example, a fairly low score is given if the rater's judgment is that the "Therapist set agenda that was vague or incomplete," whereas the maximum score requires that the "Therapist worked with patient to set an appropriate agenda with target problems, suitable for the available time. Established priorities and then followed the agenda." Clearly, in each case the therapist is adhering to the cognitive therapy technique of setting an agenda for the session, but the one receiving a higher score is doing so more skillfully. The Cognitive Therapy Scale has shown adequate interrater reliability, convergent validity with experts' global ratings of quality (Vallis, Shaw, & Dobson, 1986), and specificity in the sense that ratings are not consistently related to quality ratings on a general measure of therapists' competence (Vallis, Shaw, & McCabe, 1988).

Developing competence measures for specific psychotherapy protocols is a high priority, for if a therapy appears ineffective it is important to know whether that was the result of unskillful use. Moreover, it is important to evaluate competence in a way that is discriminantly valid vis-à-vis intervention effectiveness (Shaw, 1984), lest poor outcome always be attributed to the therapist's incompetence so that we can never actually determine that a therapy protocol—even done well— has failed. A special concern in comparative outcome experiments is the issue of whether the alternative psychotherapies were conducted with equivalent competence. Indeed, Borkovec (1993) depicted this as the "greatest threat to internal validity" in comparative outcome studies, arguing that "if differences between conditions exist in how well the therapies are conducted, comparison of the conditions is meaningless" (p. 261). To take a simple example, if a clinical research team with very high competence in time-limited dynamic psychotherapy (TLDP) but absolutely no expertise in interpersonal therapy (IPT) found TLDP more effective than IPT, we would have no way of knowing if this result reflects the general superiority of TLDP or simply the differential expertise of the therapy team.

Measuring therapy quality is complex and requires expertise and subjective inference; thus, less progress has been made in this regard than in the evaluation of adherence and differentiability (Waltz, Addis, Koerner, & Jacobson, 1993). One possible compromise—if modality-specific, validated competence measures are unavailable—is to use general therapist skillfulness measures that are not unique to a particular therapy. In the Project MATCH (Matching Alcoholism Treatments to Client Heterogeneity) study of cognitive behavior therapy, 12-step facilitation, and motivational enhancement therapy for alcohol-dependent people, Carroll et al. (1998) showed that the three treatments, besides being discriminable and adherent, were conducted with roughly equal levels of general competence (e.g., empathy and maintaining boundaries).

MEASURING THE DEPENDENT VARIABLES OR OUTCOMES

Selection of Measures

The first priority in any outcome measurement battery is the evaluation of change on the target problems or symptoms. For example, a study of treatment for generalized anxiety disorder (GAD) would certainly need to evaluate reduction in the frequency and/or intensity of GAD symptoms such as worrying. Couples therapy programs would need measures of relationship distress, depression treatments, depressive symptoms, and so on. Such assessments may yield an *incomplete* picture of the effects of treatment, but it is difficult to envision a credible treatment evaluation that does not include them.

Measures of core treatment targets should have high reliability and validity. Investigators bear the burden of reporting this evidence for established measures or of collecting it if novel measures must be used. It also makes sense to report the obtained interrater reliability of any subjectively evaluated measures (e.g., structured interviews and behavioral observations). It is one thing to say, for example, that a particular role-play test of social skills has been scored with high reliability in past research, but that is no guarantee that the coders involved in one's current project did so.

Outcome measures should be sensitive to change. A measure could have been validated by differentiating between known groups (e.g., an extraversion test that yields higher scores for successful salespeople than for psychology teachers) and showing apt correlational patterns (e.g., the extraversion test is more strongly correlated with another extraversion measure than with an indicator of conscientiousness) yet not be sensitive to even powerful manipulations (e.g., if childhood events or long-lasting perceptions and behavioral trends are the content focus of the test). Such a measure would probably be insensitive to changes effected by short-term psychotherapy.

Howard (1982) suggested that investigators should consider "response-shift biases" in self-report outcome measures. Treatment may produce changes in participants' understanding of the phenomenon being measured, altering the basis of their self-ratings and obscuring or exaggerating actual change. For example, consider the concept of "irrational beliefs" in rational emotive behavior therapy—beliefs demanding that the world, the self, or the people around you must be a certain way (Kendall, Haaga, Ellis, Bernard, DiGiuseppe, & Kassinove, 1995). Theoretically, such irrational beliefs are preconscious, and indeed part of the job of the rational emotive behavior therapist is calling patients' attention to them. If irrationality were scaled on a 0–100 scale, perhaps a pretreatment self-rating of 45 would be an underestimate of the patient's "real" irrationality level of 65. If treatment then increased awareness while decreasing irrationality, we might find the patient giving an accurate, insightful rating of 45 at posttreatment, which would give the misleading impression that no change was made. Howard (1982) advocated the use of "then-post" ratings (posttreatment ratings, taking into account new self-understanding, of what one had been like at pretreatment) to illuminate this possibility.

One straightforward reporting requirement is that researchers should routinely report descriptive statistics for each treatment condition for all dependent measures. Quantitative reviewers routinely report that such data are not universally available in published articles, no doubt as a result of space pressures typifying psychological journals (e.g., Wampold et al., 1997). This sort of omission, sometimes selectively characteristic of nonsignificant results, is unfortunate in that it dictates the use of inexact estimates with various biasing effects when such studies are incorporated in meta-analytic reviews.

Utility of Multimethod Measurement

Treatment outcome evaluations are maximally informative if multiple methods of measurement are employed in evaluating the variables expected to change. These can include measures of overt behavior, emotion, cognition, and psychophysiology, for example. Multiple measures may directly target the same reality; for instance, self-reports of whether one has smoked a cigarette in the past week and carbon monoxide levels in expired air can be thought of as corroborating or disconfirming each other. If they are in disagreement one has to be wrong.

In other circumstances, multiple methods may target different aspects of the phenomenon. In treatment studies of anxiety disorders (Lang, 1968), for example, if avoidance behavior is unchanged by treatment but heart rate reactivity to imaginal exposure to the feared stimulus is, this desynchrony is itself substantively interesting and informative about the nature of the disorder and some limitations of the treatment protocol, but neither result invalidates the other.

Side Effects

In addition to focal symptoms of the target disorder, it is valuable to round out the picture by examining positive and negative side effects of treatment. The distinction between a core, targeted effect and a side effect is blurry, but a treatment involving, say, the scheduling of pleasant events to increase contact with response-contingent positive reinforcers and thereby reduce a depressed mood could be evaluated in terms of changes in depression (core target), as well as changes in absenteeism at one's place of employment, medical care utilization, and alcohol consumption (side effects not directly targeted but plausibly associated with changes in depression).

There has been considerable interest in side effects of psychotherapy that can be linked closely to dollar costs (e.g., work productivity, absenteeism, need for inpatient services, health-care utilization), and a recent review of such studies found that most of them revealed a significant favorable economic impact of psychotherapy interventions such as dialectical behavior therapy for borderline personality disorder and family therapy for families of persons with schizophrenia (Gabbard, Lazar, Hornberger, & Spiegel, 1997).

Considering Multiple Points of View

Comprehensive therapy outcome evaluation should include the perspectives of the patient, the therapist, and independent evaluators who were masked to the treatment condition in which the patient participated. These independent evaluators are presumably less influenced than either the patient or the therapist by demand characteristics calling for evidence of improvement to justify the expense and effort involved in the treatment.

Besides being masked to the treatment condition, it is ideal if independent evaluators can be masked even to which participants have completed treatment, as some evidence suggests that this information alone can create expectancies that bias ratings of behavior (Ernst, Bornstein, & Weltzien, 1984). To be sure, depending on the nature of the measure, this can be difficult to arrange. If the evaluation is based on interview ratings, for instance, it is difficult to stop the patient from saying something that would reveal to the interviewer that treatment has already occurred or has not.

Follow-up Measurement

Follow-up assessments conducted after posttreatment evaluations permit an assessment of the durability of gains. Maintenance of change may be a particularly revealing issue in comparative evaluations of psychotherapy and medication. There is evidence that cognitive therapy's immediate effects on depressive symptoms may be roughly equivalent to those of standard antidepressant medications, yet cognitive therapy's maintenance of these effects is superior (e.g., Evans et al., 1992). Other studies have shown enhanced psychotherapy effects at follow-up evaluations (Carroll, Rounsaville, Nich, Gordon, Wirtz, & Gawin, 1994). This pattern could occur if a psychotherapy method teaches coping skills that foster improved adjustment but require extended practice in vivo to show a noticeable effect.

Follow-up assessments are useful also for estimating absolute results and describing realistic trajectories of symptom levels for clinicians and patients to consider in deciding on a course of treatment. In the treatment of addictive behaviors, absolute abstinence is often the treatment goal, and this is readily described in terms of percentages of patients achieving success vs. failure. If a particular cigarette smoking cessation program, for example, yielded superior outcomes to those of a control condition at both posttreatment and one-year follow-up, the consistently superior comparative results are qualified if the absolute percentages of abstinent patients are 80% vs. 65% at posttreatment but 25% vs. 15% at one-year follow-up. The one-year follow-up evaluation has clearly added information useful to investigators, therapists, and patients.

There are, however, numerous complications associated with follow-up evaluations. First, it is rarely feasible, and often considered unethical, to maintain a no-treatment control group through extended follow-up; accordingly, treatment vs. no-treatment comparisons are almost always based solely on evaluations through the end of active treatment.

Second, it is difficult, and again arguably unethical, to prevent patients from returning to treatment during the follow-up interval. This re-

sponsiveness by patients to their own requirements has ambiguous implications for evaluating effects of the original treatment. It is possible to consider this the equivalent of a relapse, but it is also possible to consider it as active coping. Assuming that it represents relapse may lead to an underestimate of long-term treatment effects. Conversely, if return to treatment is ignored, then symptom evaluations at follow-up may exaggerate long-term treatment effects to the extent that the treatment during the follow-up interval was helpful. Chambless and Hollon (1998) discuss the advisability of conducting multiple analyses involving various inferences about the meaning of return to treatment in order to provide a range of perspectives on long-term outcome.

Third, cross-sectional symptom evaluations at follow-up points may miss much of the complexity of the course of symptoms during the follow-up interval. Clients can be asked to give retrospective reports of their symptoms during the interval, however, and it is therefore preferable to assess participants often enough that credible retrospective judgments of symptoms since the prior follow-up can be rendered. A complicating factor in this strategy is that prospective research using computer-assisted real-time self-monitoring in the field does not support high confidence in the accuracy of retrospective evaluations (e.g., Stone et al., 1998).

Fourth, if treatments are differentially effective with patients who differ in relapse vulnerability, this nonequivalence will confound comparisons of a long-term course or maintenance of change (Klein, 1996). Relapse is calculated on the basis of patients who show remission of symptoms after treatment, and patients successfully treated with different treatments may differ in unknown ways. Suppose, for example, that therapy A is much more effective than therapy B with an unidentified, vulnerable subgroup of patients whose symptoms are particularly likely to recur. Then, patients who received therapy A may misleadingly show higher overall rates of relapse (because more of the vulnerable patients enter the pool of patients who show remission), even though therapy A might actually be more effective than therapy B in the long term with any given patient. That is, differential relapse rates may reflect differences in the samples that achieve initial change with respect to their ability to maintain that change, rather than to an enduring quality of the changes achieved by therapy A or B. These issues can in principle be sorted out, but only if investigators have indicators of relapse vulnerability.

Finally, attrition subsequent to random assignment detracts from the presumption of equivalence of groups and therefore the internal validity of comparative follow-up evaluations. In practice, this issue becomes even more problematic in follow-up intervals than it is during treatment because it is more difficult to retain participants through lengthy follow-up intervals.

Contextualizing "Average Outcome" to Inform Interpretation

Thus far, we have been considering design and measurement features useful in determining with precision in an RCT which treatment condition yields superior outcomes on average. Differences in average outcome are not sufficient, however, as a description of the overall impact of treatments. In this section we consider several ways in which investigators can supplement group average comparisons to bolster the interpretability of their studies.

Treatment Acceptability

The best therapy imaginable will not have much impact on public health if prospective patients refuse to avail themselves of it. The extent to which a therapy is acceptable is an important issue that is potentially distinguishable from treatment efficacy. To take a simple example, a rigorous, daily, hour-long exercise program might be highly effective for treating obesity or mild hypertension, but it might be difficult to disseminate in clinical practice and have little impact because it is unacceptably difficult for patients to adhere to consistently.

Evaluating the acceptability of treatments on the basis of detailed descriptions of them to prospective consumers (as opposed to patients who have already completed the therapy and therefore represent a select, possibly biased, sample) can shed light on this important issue. One study of behavioral parent training indicated that lower-income parents evaluated the technique of time out as no more acceptable than spanking. Middle- or upper-income parents, by contrast, considered time out more acceptable than spanking (Heffer & Kelley, 1987). Given the centrality of time out as a punishment strategy in behavioral parent training, the authors proposed that these acceptability findings might help account for the lesser success of behavioral parent training with

lower socioeconomic status (SES) samples in some studies.

Attrition

Even if a treatment is acceptable and attractive to prospective patients, not all will complete treatment and comply with posttreatment evaluations. Suppose, for instance, that treatment A leads to complete abstinence from cigarette smoking of 100 patients, continued smoking of 50 who complete follow-up, and attrition of 50, whereas treatment B leads to abstinence of 120, continued smoking of 80, and no attrition. If attrition is ignored and only treatment completers are included in the outcome analyses, treatment A is the "winner" (67% abstinence vs. 60% for treatment B). If attrition is taken to represent treatment failure (i.e., assuming that anyone who failed to complete treatment did not benefit) in an "intent-to-treat" analysis, then treatment B is the winner (60% success vs. 50% for treatment A).

Common procedures for handling attrition include (1) conducting an inferential statistical test of whether the frequency of attrition differs significantly across treatment conditions and (2) statistically comparing treatment completers with attriters on variables collected for both at baseline. If attrition rates are nonsignificantly different across conditions and attriters are nonsignificantly different from completers at baseline, then investigators often conclude that attrition can be ignored in the remainder of the analyses. According to Flick (1988), though, this is not sufficient. First, it involves accepting a null result as proof of equivalence, which is hazardous—more likely if one has small n's and weak baseline measures. It would seem preferable to use equivalency testing to show affirmative evidence of equivalence, not just insufficient evidence of differential attrition rates (Rogers, Howard, & Vessey, 1993). Second, attrition could lead to bias even if it occurs at the same rate across groups and is not associated with pretreatment measures. For example, suppose that motivation to get better was not formally measured at baseline, and 25% of participants dropped out of both a treatment condition and a wait-list condition. If the treatment-condition dropouts were less motivated, and the wait-list conditions dropouts more motivated (because they want to seek off-study treatment), this would not be detected by the usual methods but would seriously bias the outcome analyses.

A range of statistical strategies has been devised for handling attrition (see Flick, 1988; Shadish, Hu, Glaser, Kownacki, & Wong, 1998). In general, the notion behind these methods is to report a range of possible outcomes based on differing assumptions about the clinical status of dropouts (e.g., all dropouts are failures; all dropouts would show the same symptom levels as at pretreatment; all dropouts would show the same symptom levels as at the last assessment they completed).

Variability of Response

Even if all prospective patients accept and complete treatment, finding one treatment significantly superior statistically to nothing or to an alternative treatment does not necessarily mean that this is the treatment of choice for all subsequent patients with the same disorder. For one thing, not all viable treatments will have been included in the investigation. For another, there may not be a local practitioner expert in the administration of the successful treatment. And even an effective treatment may have a variable impact across different subgroups of patients. Within-group variability is treated statistically as "error" in the conventional analysis-of-variance framework, but if reliable dependent measures were utilized, then at least some of the within-group variability in response reflects real individual differences in the impact of the treatment. If we could identify what types of patients are particularly likely not to benefit from a treatment (even an on-average effective treatment), we might be able to find alternative treatments that are more effective than the index treatment for this subgroup. This is the promise of aptitude-treatment interaction research as a basis for patient-treatment matching, taken up later in the chapter.

Post hoc analyses of the variability of response can be productive in generating ideas for subsequent confirmatory replication studies of possible interactions of patient and treatment variables. Lyons and Howard (1991) provided detailed guidelines for statistical procedures useful in analyzing such effects.

Clinical Significance

Finding that a treatment had a significantly greater impact statistically on key dependent variables than a comparison condition does not directly tell us whether the treatment had a large impact on a high proportion of patients. A very small degree of improvement, leaving consider-able residual distress and dysfunction at posttreatment, could be associated with statistically significant between-group comparisons if the n is large, within-group variability small, or both (Jacobson & Truax, 1991).

Most investigators, therefore, consider it important to supplement statistical significance testing with evaluations of the practical importance or clinical significance of therapy effects. Various means of operationalizing this concept have been proposed. In behavioral medicine, it has been proposed that the association of a measure with physical health be considered the paramount practical consideration (Blanchard & Schwarz, 1988). Thus, lowering systolic blood pressure an average of five points would be evaluated according to the extent to which it improves health and reduces the risk of disease outcomes and ultimately mortality. In psychological health, the practical value of therapy-induced gains may be judged according to the extent to which patients achieve normative levels of functioning (Kendall & Grove, 1988).

Another perspective on the practical importance of therapy effects is afforded by the concept of social validation. Here the idea is that a change is of practical importance if peers and significant others can notice the change and judge it favorably (Kazdin, 1977). Thus, if coworkers note that someone is easier to get along with and more agreeable after treatment, this would provide social validation for the results of a role-play or self-report test suggesting decreases in the expression of explosive anger.

Finally, perhaps the most widely used method to judge clinical significance in contemporary research is the approach described by Jacobson and his colleagues (Jacobson, Follette, & Revenstorf, 1984; Jacobson & Truax, 1991), which suggests that to be considered as having shown a clinically significant benefit, the patient's end-of-treatment score (1) must be statistically more likely to come from the distribution of scores characterizing a healthy population than from the distribution of scores characterizing the population with the disorder in question and (2) must have achieved statistically reliable improvement across treatment, as indicated by a reliable change index (Jacobson and Truax suggested the pre-post difference divided by the standard error of the difference on the outcome measure).

The requirement that after treatment patients must statistically resemble healthy people to be judged successful raises a number of issues. First, there is often inadequate normative research on clinical outcome measures. Second, for some disorders it might be unrealistic to anticipate complete normalization. Third, the assumption that there are two different normal distributions, one for a functional and one for a dysfunctional population, might not hold for all disorders (Wampold & Jenson, 1986). Fourth, selecting the representative, healthy population to which the patient should be compared is complicated (Hayes & Haas, 1988). For example, there was an inverse relation between income and social anxiety symptoms in a normative study by Gillis, Haaga, and Ford (1995); should a low-income, socially phobic patient's posttreatment score be compared to overall averages or to the average of the low-income subsample from the normative study? Similar considerations arise when there are age, sex, or ethnic differences in symptom scores in normative studies. What about geographical differences, as in the finding that anxiety disorders are more prevalent in the northeastern region of the United States (Kessler et al., 1994)?

Cost Effectiveness

It can be difficult to attach a precise monetary value to every benefit derived from psychotherapy (what is the dollar value of a decrease of two panic attacks per week?) or to every cost associated with the provision of psychotherapy (what is the dollar value of the inconvenience associated with the patient's need to tie up the family car each Tuesday morning for five months to get to a therapy session?). Nevertheless, it is possible to evaluate cost effectiveness in much more detail than just by making coarse overall evaluations, such as 20 sessions cost more than 15, individual therapy costs more than group, or professional services cost more than paraprofessional. For instance, a framework for examining direct costs borne by the patient or a third-party payer (e.g., therapist's fees and lost wages), direct costs to the community (e.g., reduced taxes because of lost wages), and indirect costs to society (e.g., lost productivity during treatment) was described by Yates (1995). One application of cost effectiveness analysis, based on data derived from meta-analyses of treatment effects and a series of explicit assumptions (e.g., about average hours of volunteer community service provided each year by well adults, travel costs for transportation to therapy sessions, and many more), concluded that cogni-

tive behavior therapy was more cost-effective in the treatment of major depression than fluoxetine (Antonuccio, Thomas, & Danton, 1997). This study may serve as a helpful point of departure for future studies, which might profitably focus on refining the assumptions used in valuing costs and benefits, as well as in updating the outcome literature to arrive at better estimates of the probability and frequency of occurrence of the various favorable and unfavorable outcomes for each treatment.

PATIENT VARIABLES

It is well known to all clinicians and researchers that no psychotherapy is universally effective. It is therefore of interest to identify patient variables that predict response to a given treatment.

Predictive or Prognostic Studies

Knowing which patient variables predict response to treatment can suggest indications for and limitations of the treatment. If, for instance, a treatment program for panic disorder with agoraphobia were to yield poorer results for those with especially severe pretreatment agoraphobic avoidance, it would suggest the advisability of modifying the treatment to meet the needs of such patients. Predictive data could even aid classification of psychopathology. A consistent predictor could reveal a subgroup previously considered indistinct from others with the same disorder.

Predictive data do not, however, typically have direct implications for treatment selection (Hollon & Najavits, 1988). That is, the question addressed by predictive studies (What patients are helped most by this treatment?) is distinct from the treatment selection question (What treatment would be most helpful for this patient?). Table 2.2 illustrates these ambiguities by depicting some alternative outcomes of a hypothetical study of general intelligence as a predictor of response to cognitive therapy (CT) and interpersonal therapy (IPT). The first example shows the intuitively clearest result: high intelligence predicts favorable response to CT, and the overall pattern of results favors assigning high-IQ patients to CT. In Example 2, however, IQ is unrelated to the response to CT, but because of its strong association with the response to the alternative treatment, it is useful for guiding treatment selection. Example 3 shows an even more counterintuitive possibility, in which high intelli-

TABLE 2.2 Prediction of Response Does Not Entail Prescription of Optimal Treatment

Dependent variable = average 0–100 rating of improvement during therapy, 100 being the maximum improvement.
Predictor variable = full-scale intelligence, dichotomized at IQ = 100.
Treatment under investigation = cognitive therapy (CT).
Alternative treatment available = interpersonal therapy (IPT).

Example 1: High IQ predicts good response to CT and is a favorable indicator for prescribing CT.

	CT	IPT
IQ > 100	70	60
IQ < 100	50	60

Example 2: IQ does not predict response to CT but is useful for treatment selection.

	CT	IPT
IQ > 100	60	80
IQ < 100	60	40

Example 3: High IQ predicts good response to CT but is a negative indicator for prescribing CT.

	CT	IPT
IQ > 100	70	80
IQ < 100	50	40

gence is associated with the favorable response to CT, but the pattern of results suggests that CT should be reserved for low-IQ patients.

PRESCRIPTIVE STUDIES: APTITUDE BY TREATMENT INTERACTIONS

Studies that can guide treatment selection on the basis of patient variables are those that reveal interactions of the treatment condition with a patient variable (usually generically called an *aptitude* in this literature, hence an aptitude-treatment interaction, or ATI; Cronbach, 1975) in predicting outcome. The patient aptitude thus serves as a moderator, qualifying the impact of the treatment variable. For example, if time-limited dynamic psychotherapy is more effective than in vivo exposure for men with specific phobias, whereas the opposite is true for women, then this would represent an ATI with specific and obvious prescriptive implications (select time-limited dy-

namic therapy for men and in vivo exposure for women with specific phobias).

Conceptually, some ATIs follow a "compensation" model, in which the characteristic of the treatment compensates for an existing deficit in the patient. For instance, Michelson (1986) found superior efficacy for agoraphobic patients assigned to a treatment matching the modality of their most severe anxiety response (gradual exposure for those whose prominent reaction was avoidance behavior, paradoxical intention for cognitive reactors, and progressive muscle relaxation for physiological reactors). Alternatively, other ATIs follow a "capitalization" model, which takes advantage of existing patient strengths. There is some evidence that capitalization strategies are useful for depressed patients, perhaps resulting from remoralization associated with utilizing one's relative strengths, for example, social skills training for patients with intact social skills (Rude & Rehm, 1991).

On the whole, there have been few robust,

replicable instances of ATIs capable of guiding treatment prescription. This may reflect inadequate statistical power. As noted earlier, sample sizes of RCTs have commonly been insufficient even for detecting moderate-sized main effects. Interactions of patients' characteristics with treatment conditions are presumably even more difficult to detect. Reviewers have suggested that the search for interactions may prove more fruitful if guided by theory-driven hypotheses and clearly differentiated treatments rather than ad hoc selection of aptitudes and treatments and statistical fishing expeditions (Shoham-Salomon, 1991).

A recent example of theory-guided ATI research is a study in which a heterogeneous patient sample (diagnosed most commonly with mood or anxiety disorders) was randomly assigned to either an interpretive or a supportive version of short-term individual dynamic psychotherapy. Patients assessed at pretreatment as scoring high on quality of object relations, or QOR (i.e., showing a high level of maturity in long-standing relationship patterns), were especially likely to benefit from interpretive therapy, whereas this relation was not evident in supportive therapy (Piper, Joyce, McCallum, & Azim, 1998). This interactive effect of object relations and treatment type had been predicted according to the theory that people with high quality of object relations "are better able to tolerate, work with, and benefit from the more demanding aspects of interpretive therapy and, conversely, patients with lower levels of QOR are better able to work with and benefit from the more gratifying aspects of supportive therapy" (p. 559).

Therapists' responsiveness to clients' characteristics may help account for the failure to find ATIs for seemingly important characteristics. For example, Hardy, Stiles, Barkham, and Startup (1998) found that therapists' mix of interventions differed systematically depending on the client's interpersonal style in a comparative clinical trial of cognitive-behavioral and psychodynamic-interpersonal therapies for depression. The therapists tended to use more affective and relationship-oriented interventions with clients who had an overinvolved interpersonal style, particularly in the psychodynamic-interpersonal therapy, whereas in the cognitive-behavioral therapy, therapists tended to use more cognitive and behavioral interventions with clients who had an underinvolved interpersonal style. Despite—or perhaps because of—receiving different mixes of interventions, clients with these different inter-

personal styles had approximately equivalent outcomes in the two treatments.

Mediational Analyses

Some patient variables can be considered as mediating mechanisms that intervene between independent (treatment) and dependent (outcome) variables and account for the relations between the two. For example, a study by DeRubeis, Evans, Hollon, Garvey, Grove, and Tuason (1990) suggested that changes in dysfunctional attitudes and in depressotypic attributional style mediated the impact of cognitive therapy on depressive symptoms. Mediating variables are conceptually distinct from active ingredients of the therapy; in this study, the dysfunctional attitude shifts are not interventions but rather an intervening process accounting for the overall impact of treatment. By analogy, reduction in body fat percentage is not a form of exercise, but one can imagine a positive impact of exercise on longevity causally mediated by reduction in body fat percentage.

Guidelines for the identification of causal mediators, notably the statistical requirements for demonstrating such effects in multiple regression or structural equation modeling designs, have been elaborated by Baron and Kenny (1986) and Holmbeck (1997) and, with specific reference to treatment-induced change, by Hollon, DeRubeis, and Evans (1987). Noteworthy aspects of these guidelines include (1) compelling evidence that causal mediation requires a treatment main effect on the dependent variable, which is one argument for the utility of comparison conditions expected to be less effective than the main treatment(s) under study, and (2) the timing of assessments may be critical.

THERAPIST VARIABLES

Most psychotherapy researchers have been interested in how or how well a particular treatment protocol works, expecting or hoping that the answers to these questions may be generalized across therapists. For example, the goal is to find out if panic control treatment is effective for patients with panic disorder, not panic control treatment as implemented by Dr. X. Accordingly, specific focus on differences among therapists in effectiveness has been rare.

Evidence indicates, however, that the individual therapist is at times a potent predictor of outcome (Lambert, 1989). Perhaps surprisingly, this variation in effectiveness is not closely associated with professional credentials (Christensen & Jacobson, 1994) or with the amount of experience as a therapist. Of 15 psychotherapy meta-analyses reviewed by Matt and Navarro (1997), just 1 obtained a statistically significant correlation between years of experience and intervention effect size. Chambless and Hollon (1998) argued that these null results do not necessarily mean that therapists' training and experience are irrelevant, and they hypothesized that the benefits of training and experience may be more likely to be found if we focus on specific credentials and experience relating to the therapy under investigation (e.g., therapists trained to criterion in behavioral couples therapy who have been using this approach for at least five years) rather than to psychotherapy credentials, degrees, or licenses and years of experience in general.

Therapist effects can be considerable, and ignoring them can bias comparative outcome results (Crits-Christoph & Mintz, 1991). Use of a treatment manual for therapy standardization does seem to reduce the size of these effects. Because therapists' competence cannot safely be inferred from the level of training or experience, it is important to measure competence directly in treatment studies to ensure that all therapists are performing the intended treatments competently and equivalently, thus providing a fair test of the efficacy of the specified treatments. Another possibility for handling therapist effects is to cross therapists with treatment conditions, that is, have each therapist perform each of the treatments being compared (e.g., Shapiro, Barkham, Rees, Hardy, Reynolds, & Startup, 1994). This strategy requires that all therapists be trained to conduct all the treatments (Kazdin, 1994) and, in any event, only equates therapists' competence across conditions if we assume that competence is a general characteristic (main effect) rather than something that might be protocol-specific (i.e., if therapist and therapy interact).

SETTING AND CONTEXT VARIABLES

Serious concerns have been raised about the external validity of the conventional psychotherapy RCTs we have been discussing throughout this chapter. These concerns are not new, but two recent treatments of them provide a helpful point of departure in introducing the relevant issues. Weisz and colleagues, in reviews of child psychotherapy, have called attention to the many differences between what they labeled "research therapy" and "ordinary clinic therapy" (e.g., Weisz, Weiss, & Donenberg, 1992). For example, in an outcome research protocol, the patient is generally randomly assigned to a treatment condition and therapist, whereas in ordinary practice a patient can in principle seek out voluntarily a practitioner whose methods and orientation are perceived as personally suitable. In an outcome study, the therapist is generally following the plan embedded in the treatment manual, whereas in ordinary practice the therapist is free to devise an idiosyncratic, customized intervention plan in response to perceived idiosyncratic requirements of a specific patient—and for that matter, to deviate responsively from the plan at any time as feedback or observations suggest or patients' preferences and progress suggest. In an outcome study, there is usually a definite ending time for the therapy (e.g., four months), whereas in ordinary practice therapy is often of indefinite duration.

Morever, in an outcome study, the therapist is usually specifically trained in the methods to be used in the study just before its start and then receives ongoing supervision aimed at maximizing adherence and competence, whereas in routine clinical practice such features are generally absent. Sessions are routinely taped in outcome studies to promote adherence assessment but not in ordinary practice. Quantitative measurements are taken at regular intervals in outcome studies but not necessarily in routine practice. Extensive diagnostic and other intake assessments are conducted in outcome studies, pure-form rather than eclectic therapies are utilized, fees are waived or greatly reduced, extensive inclusion and exclusion criteria are implemented to facilitate focusing on a homogeneous sample without extensive comorbidity or other complications, and therapists are often relatively inexperienced trainees affiliated with universities; none of these conditions typifies ordinary clinical practice.

All told, the concern voiced by Weisz et al. (1992) and by others is that efforts to maximize internal validity in RCTs by standardizing treatment and using random assignment to control confounding variables may inadvertently diminish the external validity of the studies, limiting generalizability of the findings. In particular, according to their critique, the findings may not generalize to naturalistic settings in which therapists might hope to apply them.

One way to address these issues is to take advantage of the variation that exists among RCTs in the "nonrepresentative" features just noted. That is, although the prototype of research therapy is certainly recognizable, not all RCTs use inexperienced therapists or exclude all complicating co-morbid conditions or deal with very short-term treatment approaches, and so forth. Therefore, one might estimate the relevance of these methods by comparing findings across studies, differing levels of the methods in question. Moreover, one can examine subsets of experiments that appear relatively representative of ordinary clinical practice. This approach, taken by Shadish et al. (1997) in a secondary analysis of earlier psychotherapy meta-analyses, yielded the conclusion that at least the broadbrush finding of psychotherapy outcome studies (that therapy in general is effective) is replicable under more naturalistic conditions.

On the other hand, if there are gulfs between research practice and routine practice, perhaps routine practice is what needs to change. For example, it is possible that the eclecticism and flexibility characterizing ordinary practice detract from the efficacy of following pure-form therapies embedded in manuals somewhat more tenaciously (Wilson, 1996). Some such specific issues can be addressed in naturalistic studies that mimic some aspects of RCTs while letting others vary. For example, Wade, Treat, and Stuart (1998) evaluated the exportability of panic control treatment (Barlow & Craske, 1994) to a community mental health center by utilizing the same measures employed in earlier RCTs of the method, but now in a non-random-assignment naturalistic study with fewer exclusion criteria than in the RCTs.

A further departure from conventional methodological wisdom is the "effectiveness" study conducted as a large-scale reader survey by *Consumer Reports* and described by Seligman (1995) as a viable alternative to RCT's. Such studies may be interesting in their own right, but they can also be considered as a source of hypotheses for better-controlled research (Chambless & Hollon, 1998; Jacobson & Christensen, 1996). That is, many of the issues highlighted by Seligman could actually be addressed in RCTs (e.g., flexible vs. manualized treatment; random assignment to condition vs. patient's choice of therapist; longer-term vs. shorter-term treatment), and the internal validity advantages of doing so would be substantial.

CONCLUSION

As summarized in this chapter and elaborated in numerous other publications, there are many com-plications in psychotherapy research and many points of ambiguity in interpreting such studies. It would be easy, and understandable, to throw up one's hands (figuratively) and conclude that psychotherapy practice is necessarily an art and that it cannot be placed on solid scientific footing on the basis of treatment research. However, we believe this would be an overreaction to the complexities of psychotherapy research methodology. No one study is perfect or unassailable, but over time the application by multiple investigators of increasingly stringent research methods can yield greater confidence in findings than would be possible from any one investigation alone.

Critiques calling attention to specific design flaws have at times had a demonstrable positive impact on research on important questions. Consider, for example, the well-known outcome study comparing cognitive therapy of depression and imipramine by Rush, Beck, Kovacs, and Hollon (1977). This investigation conducted "posttreatment" evaluation only after a couple of weeks of drug withdrawal for the medication patients and found cognitive therapy superior at posttreatment. Several subsequent studies, implementing posttreatment evaluation more immediately, instead found equivalence of short-term results and superiority for cognitive therapy at follow-up. The implication was that Rush et al.'s posttreatment evaluation had confounded immediate outcome with incipient relapse among some medication patients and therefore yielded somewhat misleading conclusions (Hollon, Shelton, & Davis, 1993). This seems to be a clear case in which improvements in the research method led directly to different and sounder conclusions based on subsequent studies. Such examples belie the complaint that research in psychology is just a sort of wheel-spinning, fad-following evolution of points of view or topical interests (Meehl, 1978). The questions, criticisms, suggestions, and issues raised in this chapter are offered in the optimistic sense that such improvements in understanding, abetted by methodological refinements, can become the rule rather than an exception.

REFERENCES

Addis, M. E. (1997). Evaluating the treatment manual as a means of disseminating empirically validated psychotherapies. *Clinical Psychology: Science and Practice, 4,* 1–11.

Anderson, T., & Strupp, H. H. (1996). The ecology of

psychotherapy research. *Journal of Consulting and Clinical Psychology, 64,* 776–782.

Antonuccio, D. O., Thomas, M., & Danton, W. G. (1997). A cost-effectiveness analysis of cognitive behavior therapy and fluoxetine (Prozac) in the treatment of depression. *Behavior Therapy, 28,* 187–210.

Barlow, D. H., & Craske, M. G. (1994). *Mastery of your anxiety and panic II.* Albany, NY: Graywind.

Baron, R. M., & Kenny, D. A. (1986). The moderator-mediator variable distinction in social psychological research: Conceptual, strategic, and statistical considerations. *Journal of Personality and Social Psychology, 51,* 1173–1182.

Basham, R. B. (1986). Scientific and practical advantages of comparative design in psychotherapy outcome research. *Journal of Consulting and Clinical Psychology, 54,* 88–94.

Beutler, L. E. (1991). Have all won and must all have prizes? Revisiting Luborsky et al.'s verdict. *Journal of Consulting and Clinical Psychology, 59,* 226–232.

Blanchard, E. B., & Schwarz, S. P. (1988). Clinically significant changes in behavioral medicine. *Behavioral Assessment, 10,* 171–188.

Borkovec, T. D. (1993). Between-group therapy outcome research: Design and methodology. In L. S. Onken, J. D. Blaine, & J. J. Boren (Eds.), *Behavioral treatments for drug abuse and dependence* (pp. 249–289). NIDA Research Monograph 137. Rockville, MD: National Institute on Drug Abuse.

Bouman, T. K., & Emmelkamp, P. M. G. (1996). Panic disorder and agoraphobia. In V. B. Van Hasselt & M. Hersen (Eds.), *Sourcebook of psychological treatment manuals for adult disorders* (pp. 23–63). New York: Plenum.

Carroll, K. M., Connors, G. J., Cooney, N. L., DiClemente, C. C., Donovan, D. M., Kadden, R. R., Longabaugh, R. L., Rounsaville, B. J., Wirtz, P. W., & Zweben, A. (1998). Internal validity of Project MATCH treatments: Discriminability and integrity. *Journal of Consulting and Clinical Psychology, 66,* 290–303.

Carroll, K. M., Rounsaville, B. J., Nich, C., Gordon, L. T., Wirtz, P. W., & Gawin, F. H. (1994). One-year follow-up of psychotherapy and pharmacotherapy for cocaine dependence: Delayed emergence of psychotherapy effects. *Archives of General Psychiatry, 51,* 989–997.

Chambless, D. L., Baker, M. J., Baucom, D. H., Beutler, L. E., Calhoun, K. S., Crits-Christoph, P., Daiuto, A., DeRubeis, R., Detweiler, J., Haaga, D. A. F., Johnson, S. B., McCurry, S., Mueser, K. T., Pope, K. S., Sanderson, W. C., Shoham, V., Stickle, T., Williams, D. A., & Woody, S. R. (1998). Update on empirically validated therapies, II. *The Clinical Psychologist, 51,* 3–16.

Chambless, D. L., & Hollon, S. D. (1998). Defining empirically supported therapies. *Journal of Consulting and Clinical Psychology, 66,* 7–18.

Christensen, A., & Jacobson, N. S. (1994). Who (or what) can do psychotherapy: The status and challenge of nonprofessional therapies. *Psychological Science, 5,* 8–14.

Cohen, J. (1988). *Statistical power analysis for the behavioral sciences* (2nd ed.). Hillsdale, NJ: Erlbaum.

Cohen, J. (1992). A power primer. *Psychological Bulletin, 112,* 155–159.

Cox, A., Holbrook, D., & Rutter, M. (1981). Psychiatric interviewing techniques VI. Experimental study: Eliciting feelings. *British Journal of Psychiatry, 139,* 144–152.

Cox, A., Rutter, M., & Holbrook, D. (1981). Psychiatric interviewing techniques V. Experimental study: Eliciting factual information. *British Journal of Psychiatry, 139,* 29–37.

Coyle, C. T., & Enright, R. D. (1997). Forgiveness intervention with postabortion men. *Journal of Consulting and Clinical Psychology, 65,* 1042–1046.

Crits-Christoph, P., Baranackie, K., Kurcias, J. S., Beck, A. T., Carroll, K., Perry, K., Luborsky, L., McLellan, A. T., Woody, G. E., Thompson, L., Gallagher, D., & Zitrin, C. (1991). Meta-analysis of therapist effects in psychotherapy outcome studies. *Psychotherapy Research, 1,* 81–91.

Crits-Christoph, P., & Mintz, J. (1991). Implications of therapist effects for the design and analysis of comparative studies of psychotherapies. *Journal of Consulting and Clinical Psychology, 59,* 20–26.

Cronbach, L. J. (1975). Beyond the two disciplines of scientific psychology. *American Psychologist, 30,* 116–127.

Cross, D. G., Sheehan, P. W., & Khan, J. A. (1980). Alternative advice and counsel in psychotherapy. *Journal of Consulting and Clinical Psychology, 48,* 615–625.

Davison, G. C., Williams, M. E., Nezami, E., Bice, T. L., & DeQuattro, V. L. (1991). Relaxation, reduction in angry articulated thoughts, and improvements in borderline hypertension and heart rate. *Journal of Behavioral Medicine, 14,* 453–468.

DeRubeis, R. J., & Crits-Christoph, P. (1998). Empirically supported individual and group psychological treatments for adult mental disorders. *Journal of Consulting and Clinical Psychology, 66,* 37–52.

DeRubeis, R. J., Evans, M. D., Hollon, S. D., Garvey, M. J., Grove, W. M., & Tuason, V. B. (1990). How does cognitive therapy work? Cognitive change and symptom change in cognitive therapy and pharmacotherapy for depression. *Journal of Consulting and Clinical Psychology, 58,* 862–869.

DiGiuseppe, R., McGowan, L., Sutton Simon, K., & Gardner, F. (1990). A comparative outcome study of four cognitive therapies in the treatment of social anxiety. *Journal of Rational-Emotive & Cognitive Behavior Therapy, 8,* 129–146.

Ernst, J., Bornstein, P. H., & Weltzien, R. T. (1984). Initial considerations in subjective evaluation research: Does knowledge of treatment affect performance ratings? *Behavioral Assessment, 6,* 121–128.

Evans, M. D., Hollon, S. D., DeRubeis, R. J., Piasecki, J. M., Grove, W. M., Garvey, M. J., & Tuason, V. B. (1992). Differential relapse following cognitive therapy and pharmacotherapy for depression. *Archives of General Psychiatry, 49,* 802–808.

Flick, S. N. (1988). Managing attrition in clinical research. *Clinical Psychology Review, 8,* 499–515.

Foxx, R. M., & Brown, R. A. (1979). Nicotine fading and self-monitoring for cigarette abstinence or controlled smoking. *Journal of Applied Behavior Analysis, 12,* 111–125.

Gabbard, G. O., Lazar, S. G., Hornberger, J., & Spiegel, D. (1997). The economic impact of psychotherapy: A review. *American Journal of Psychiatry, 154,* 147–155.

Gillis, M. M., Haaga, D. A. F., & Ford, G. T. (1995). Normative values for the Beck Anxiety Inventory, Fear Questionnaire, Penn State Worry Questionnaire, and Social Phobia and Anxiety Inventory. *Psychological Assessment, 7,* 450–455.

Haaga, D. A. F., Dryden, W., & Dancey, C. P. (1991). Measurement of rational-emotive therapy in outcome studies. *Journal of Rational-Emotive & Cognitive-Behavior Therapy, 9,* 73–93.

Hallahan, M., & Rosenthal, R. (1996). Statistical power: Concepts, procedures, and applications. *Behaviour Research and Therapy, 34,* 489–499.

Hardy, G. E., Stiles, W. B., Barkham, M., & Startup, M. (1998). Therapist responsiveness to client interpersonal styles during time-limited treatments for depression. *Journal of Consulting and Clinical Psychology, 66,* 304–312.

Hayes, S. C., & Haas, J. R. (1988). A reevaluation of the concept of clinical significance: Goals, methods, and methodology. *Behavioral Assessment, 10,* 189–196.

Heffer, R. W., & Kelley, M. L. (1987). Acceptance of behavioral interventions for children: The influence of parent race and income. *Behavior Therapy, 18,* 153–163.

Henry, W. P., Strupp, H. H., Butler, S. F., Schacht, T. E., & Binder, J. L. (1993). Effects of training in time-limited dynamic psychotherapy: Changes in therapist behavior. *Journal of Consulting and Clinical Psychology, 61,* 434–440.

Hoffart, A. (1997). A schema model for examining the integrity of psychotherapy: A theoretical contribution. *Psychotherapy Research, 7,* 127–143.

Hollon, S. D., DeRubeis, R. J., & Evans, M. D. (1987). Causal mediation of change in treatment for depression: Discriminating between nonspecificity and noncausality. *Psychological Bulletin, 102,* 139–149.

Hollon, S. D., & Najavits, L. (1988). Review of empirical studies of cognitive therapy. In A. J. Frances & R. E. Hales (Eds.), *American Psychiatric Press review of psychiatry* (Vol. 7, pp. 643–666). Washington, DC: American Psychiatric Press.

Hollon, S. D., Shelton, R. C., & Davis, D. D. (1993). Cognitive therapy for depression: Conceptual issues and clinical efficacy. *Journal of Consulting and Clinical Psychology, 61,* 270–275.

Holmbeck, G. N. (1997). Toward terminological, conceptual, and statistical clarity in the study of mediators and moderators: Examples from the child-clinical and pediatric psychology literatures. *Journal of Consulting and Clinical Psychology, 65,* 599–610.

Howard, G. S. (1982). Improving methodology via research on research methods. *Journal of Counseling Psychology, 29,* 318–326.

Hsu, L. M. (1989). Random sampling, randomization, and equivalence of contrasted groups in psychotherapy outcome research. *Journal of Consulting and Clinical Psychology, 57,* 131–137.

Hunter, J. E., & Schmidt, F. L. (1990). *Methods of meta-analysis: Correcting error and bias in research findings.* Newbury Park, CA: Sage.

Jacobson, N. S., & Christensen, A. (1996). Studying the effectiveness of psychotherapy: How well can clinical trials do the job? *American Psychologist, 51,* 1031–1039.

Jacobson, N. S., Dobson, K. S., Truax, P. A., Addis, M. E., Koerner, K., Gollan, J. K., Gortner, E., & Prince, S. E. (1996). A component analysis of cognitive-behavioral treatment for depression. *Journal of Consulting and Clinical Psychology, 64,* 295–304.

Jacobson, N. S., Follette, W. C., & Revenstorf, D. (1984). Psychotherapy outcome research: Methods for reporting variability and evaluating clinical significance. *Behavior Therapy, 15,* 336–352.

Jacobson, N. S., & Truax, P. (1991). Clinical significance: A statistical approach to defining meaningful change in psychotherapy research. *Journal of Consulting and Clinical Psychology, 59,* 12–19.

Kazdin, A. E. (1977). Assessing the clinical or applied importance of behavior change through social validation. *Behavior Modification, 1,* 427–452.

Kazdin, A. E. (1994). Methodology, design, and evaluation in psychotherapy research. In A. E. Bergin & S. L. Garfield (Eds.), *Handbook of psychotherapy and behavior change* (4th ed., pp. 19–71). New York: Wiley.

Kazdin, A. E. (1998). *Research design in clinical psychology* (3rd ed.). Boston: Allyn & Bacon.

Kazdin, A. E., & Bass, D. (1989). Power to detect

differences between alternative treatments in comparative psychotherapy outcome research. *Journal of Consulting and Clinical Psychology, 57,* 138–147.

Kendall, P. C., & Grove, W. (1988). Normative comparisons in therapy outcome research. *Behavioral Assessment, 10,* 147–158.

Kendall, P. C., Haaga, D. A. F., Ellis, A., Bernard, M., DiGiuseppe, R., & Kassinove, H. (1995). Rational-emotive therapy in the 1990's and beyond: Current status, recent revisions, and research questions. *Clinical Psychology Review, 15,* 169–185.

Kessler, R. C., McGonagle, K. A., Zhao, S., Nelson, C. B., Hughes, M., Eshleman, S., Wittchen, H.-U., & Kendler, K. S. (1994). Lifetime and 12-month prevalence of DSM-III-R psychiatric disorders in the United States: Results from the National Comorbidity Survey. *Archives of General Psychiatry, 51,* 8–19.

Klein, D. F. (1996). Preventing hung juries about therapy studies. *Journal of Consulting and Clinical Psychology, 64,* 81–87.

Kraemer, H. C., Gardner, C., Brooks, J. O., & Yesavage, J. A. (1998). Advantages of excluding underpowered studies in meta-analysis: Inclusionist versus exclusionist viewpoints. *Psychological Methods, 3,* 23–31.

Krupnick, J., Shea, T., & Elkin, I. (1986). Generalizability of treatment studies utilizing solicited patients. *Journal of Consulting and Clinical Psychology, 54,* 68–78.

Lambert, M. J. (1989). The individual therapist's contribution to psychotherapy process and outcome. *Clinical Psychology Review, 9,* 469–485.

Lambert, M. J., & Hill, C. E. (1994). Methodological issues in studying psychotherapy process and outcome. In A. E. Bergin and S. L. Garfield (Eds.), *Handbook of psychotherapy and behavior change* (4th ed., pp. 72–113). New York: Wiley.

Lang, P. J. (1968). Fear reduction and fear behavior: Problems in treating a construct. *Research in Psychotherapy, 3,* 90–102.

Linehan, M. M., Armstrong, H. E., Suarez, A., Allmon, D., & Heard, H. L. (1991). Cognitive-behavioral treatment of chronically parasuicidal borderline patients. *Archives of General Psychiatry, 48,* 1060–1064.

Luborsky, L., Digeur, L., Seligman, D. A., Rosenthal, R., Krause, E. D., Johnson, S., Halperin, G., Bishop, M., Berman, J. S., & Schweizer, E. (in press). The researcher's own therapeutic allegiance—A "wild card" in comparisons of treatment efficacy. *Clinical Psychology: Science and Practice.*

Lyons, J. S., & Howard, K. I. (1991). Main effects analysis in clinical research: Statistical guidelines for disaggregating treatment groups. *Journal of Consulting and Clinical Psychology, 59,* 745–748.

Matt, G. E., & Navarro, A. M. (1997). What meta-analyses have and have not taught us about psychotherapy effects: A review and future directions. *Clinical Psychology Review, 17,* 1–32.

McNally, R. J. (1996). Methodological controversies in the treatment of panic disorder. *Journal of Consulting and Clinical Psychology, 64,* 88–91.

Meehl, P. E. (1978). Theoretical risks and tabular asterisks: Sir Karl, Sir Ronald, and the slow progress of soft psychology. *Journal of Consulting and Clinical Psychology, 46,* 806–834.

Messick, D. M., & Van de Geer, J. P. (1981). A reversal paradox. *Psychological Bulletin, 90,* 582–593.

Michelson, L. (1986). Treatment consonance and response profiles in agoraphobia: The role of individual differences in cognitive behavioral and physiological treatments. *Behaviour Research and Therapy, 24,* 263–275.

Newman, M. G., Kenardy, J., Herman, S., & Taylor, C. B. (1997). Comparison of palmtop-computer-assisted brief cognitive-behavioral treatment to cognitive-behavioral treatment for panic disorder. *Journal of Consulting and Clinical Psychology, 65,* 178–183.

Parloff, M. B. (1986). Placebo controls in psychotherapy research: A sine qua non or a placebo for research problems? *Journal of Consulting and Clinical Psychology, 54,* 79–87.

Piper, W. E., Joyce, A. S., McCallum, M., & Azim, H. F. (1998). Interpretive and supportive forms of psychotherapy and patient personality variables. *Journal of Consulting and Clinical Psychology, 66,* 558–567.

Robinson, L. A., Berman, J. S., & Neimeyer, R. A. (1990). Psychotherapy for the treatment of depression: A comprehensive review of controlled outcome research. *Psychological Bulletin, 108,* 30–49.

Rogers, J. L., Howard, K. I., & Vessey, J. T. (1993). Using significance tests to evaluate equivalence between two experimental groups. *Psychological Bulletin, 113,* 553–565.

Rosenthal, R. (1995). Writing meta-analytic reviews. *Psychological Bulletin, 118,* 183–192.

Rosenthal, R., & Rubin, D. B. (1982). A simple, general purpose display of magnitude of experimental effect. *Journal of Educational Psychology, 74,* 166–169.

Rossi, J. S. (1990). Statistical power of psychological research: What have we gained in 20 years? *Journal of Consulting and Clinical Psychology, 58,* 646–656.

Rude, S. S., & Rehm, L. P. (1991). Response to treatments for depression: The role of initial status on targeted cognitive and behavioral skills. *Clinical Psychology Review, 11,* 493–514.

Rush, A. J., Beck, A. T., Kovacs, M., & Hollon, S. D. (1977). Comparative efficacy of cognitive therapy and pharmacotherapy in the treatment of depressed outpatients. *Cognitive Therapy and Research, 1*, 17–37.

Safren, S. A., Heimberg, R. G., & Juster, H. R. (1997). Clients' expectancies and their relationship to pretreatment symptomatology and outcome of cognitive-behavioral group treatment for social phobia. *Journal of Consulting and Clinical Psychology, 65*, 694–698.

Seligman, M. E. P. (1995). The effectiveness of psychotherapy: The *Consumer Reports* study. *American Psychologist, 50*, 965–974.

Shadish, W. R., Hu, X., Glaser, R. R., Kownacki, R., & Wong, S. (1998). A method for exploring the effects of attrition in randomized experiments with dichotomous outcomes. *Psychological Methods, 3*, 3–22.

Shadish, W. R., Matt, G. E., Navarro, A. M., Siegle, G., Crits-Christoph, P., Hazelrigg, M. D., Jorm, A. F., Lyons, L. C., Nietzel, M. T., Prout, H. T., Robinson, L., Smith, M. L., Svartberg, M., & Weiss, B. (1997). Evidence that therapy works in clinically representative conditions. *Journal of Consulting and Clinical Psychology, 65*, 355–365.

Shadish, W. R., Montgomery, L. M., Wilson, P., Wilson, M. R., Bright, I., & Okwumabua, T. (1993). Effects of family and marital psychotherapies: A meta-analysis. *Journal of Consulting and Clinical Psychology, 61*, 992–1002.

Shapiro, D. A., Barkham, M., Rees, A., Hardy, G. E., Reynolds, S., & Startup, M. (1994). Effects of treatment duration and severity of depression on the effectiveness of cognitive/behavioral and psychodynamic/interpersonal psychotherapy. *Journal of Consulting and Clinical Psychology, 62*, 522–534.

Shapiro, D. A., & Startup, M. (1992). Measuring therapist adherence in exploratory psychotherapy. *Psychotherapy Research, 2*, 193–203.

Shaw, B. F. (1984). Specification of the training and evaluation of cognitive therapists for outcome studies. In J. B. W. Williams & R. L. Spitzer (Eds.), *Psychotherapy research: Where are we and where should we go?* (pp. 173–188). New York: Guilford.

Shoham-Salomon, V. (1991). Introduction to special section on client-therapy interaction research. *Journal of Consulting and Clinical Psychology, 59*, 203–204.

Simpson, E. H. (1951). The interpretation of interaction in contingency tables. *Journal of the Royal Statistical Society, 13*, 238–241.

Startup, M., & Shapiro, D. A. (1993). Dimensions of cognitive therapy for depression: A confirmatory analysis of session ratings. *Cognitive Therapy and Research, 17*, 139–151.

Stiles, W. B. (1988). Psychotherapy process-outcome correlations may be misleading. *Psychotherapy, 25*, 27–35.

Stiles, W. B., Honos-Webb, L., & Knobloch, L. M. (in press). Treatment process research methods. In P. C. Kendall, J. N. Butcher, & G. N. Holmbeck (Eds.), *Handbook of research methods in clinical psychology.* New York: Wiley.

Stiles, W. B., Honos-Webb, L., & Surko, M. (in press). Responsiveness in psychotherapy. *Clinical psychology: Science and practice.*

Stiles, W. B., & Shapiro, D. A. (1994). Disabuse of the drug metaphor: Psychotherapy process-outcome correlations. *Journal of Consulting and Clinical Psychology, 62*, 942–948.

Stone, A. A., Schwartz, J. E., Neale, J. M., Shiffman, S., Marco, C. A., Hickcox, M., Paty, J., Porter, L. S., & Cruise, L. J. (1998). A comparison of coping assessed by ecological momentary assessment and retrospective recall. *Journal of Personality and Social Psychology, 74*, 1670–1680.

Task Force on Promotion and Dissemination of Psychological Procedures (1995). Training in and dissemination of empirically-validated psychological treatments: Report and recommendations. *Clinical Psychologist, 48*, 3–23.

Vallis, T. M., Shaw, B. F., & Dobson, K. S. (1986). The Cognitive Therapy Scale: Psychometric properties. *Journal of Consulting and Clinical Psychology, 54*, 381–385.

Vallis, T. M., Shaw, B. F., & McCabe, S. B. (1988). The relationship between therapist competency in cognitive therapy and general therapy skill. *Journal of Cognitive Psychotherapy: An International Quarterly, 2*, 237–249.

Vollmer, A., & Blanchard, E. B. (1998). Controlled comparison of individual versus group cognitive therapy for irritable bowel syndrome. *Behavior Therapy, 29*, 19–33.

Wade, W. A., Treat, T. A., & Stuart, G. L. (1998). Transporting an empirically supported treatment for panic disorder to a service clinic setting: A benchmarking strategy. *Journal of Consulting and Clinical Psychology, 66*, 231–239.

Waltz, J., Addis, M. E., Koerner, K., & Jacobson, N. S. (1993). Testing the integrity of a psychotherapy protocol: Assessment of adherence and competence. *Journal of Consulting and Clinical Psychology, 61*, 620–630.

Wampold, B. E., & Jenson, W. R. (1986). Clinical significance revisited. *Behavior Therapy, 17*, 302–305.

Wampold, B. E., Mondin, G. W., Moody, M., Stich, F., Benson, K., & Ahn, H. (1997). A meta-analysis of outcome studies comparing bona fide psychotherapies: Empirically, "All must have prizes." *Psychological Bulletin, 122*, 203–215.

Weisz, J. R., Weiss, B., & Donenberg, G. R. (1992). The lab versus the clinic: Effects of child and adolescent psychotherapy. *American Psychologist, 47*, 1578–1585.

Wilson, G. T. (1996). Manual-based treatments: The clinical application of research findings. *Behaviour Research and Therapy, 34,* 295–314.

Wilson, S. A., Becker, L. A., & Tinker, R. H. (1997). Fifteen-month follow-up of eye movement desensitization and reprocessing (EMDR) treatment for posttraumatic stress disorder and psychological trauma. *Journal of Consulting and Clinical Psychology, 65,* 1047–1056.

Yates, B. (1995). Cost-effectiveness analysis, cost-benefit analysis, and beyond: Evolving models for the scientist-manager-practitioner. *Clinical Psychology: Science and Practice, 2,* 385–398.

Yeaton, W. H., & Sechrest, L. (1981). Critical dimensions in the choice and maintenance of successful treatments: Strength, integrity, and effectiveness. *Journal of Consulting and Clinical Psychology, 49,* 156–167.

Young, J. E., & Beck, A. T. (1980). *Cognitive Therapy Scale: Rating manual.* Unpublished manuscript, Center for Cognitive Therapy, University of Pennsylvania, Philadelphia.

CHAPTER 3

EMPIRICALLY SUPPORTED TREATMENTS:
A CRITICAL ANALYSIS

RICK E. INGRAM
Southern Methodist University

ADELE HAYES
University of Miami

WALTER SCOTT
University of Wyoming

Psychotherapy textbooks inevitably contain chapters that examine the effectiveness of therapy (e.g., Lambert & Bergin, 1994). Such appraisals have traditionally posed the question "does psychotherapy work," and although not always the case (e.g., Eysenck, 1952, 1961), they have typically answered in the affirmative. In the earliest days of psychotherapy research, when there were only a handful of studies that empirically evaluated psychotherapy, such broad questions about therapy efficacy were not only appropriate but also essential. Although the examination of questions concerning the overall efficacy of therapy is still worthwhile in a very broad sense, a different set of questions has begun to dominate the discussion of therapy outcomes. We refer specifically to a rapidly emerging professional interest in classifying specific treatments according to their empirically demonstrated efficacy for a relatively well-defined and specific set of psychological problems. Indeed, there is a variety of social, economic, and political forces that has spurred an energetic pursuit of developing and identifying empirically supported treatments (ESTs).

The principles and philosophical issues that underlie the goals of developing and implementing empirically supported treatments are fundamentally sound. Nevertheless, we also believe that substantial concerns arise when one is attempting to translate these principles into the practice of psychotherapy. We believe that any credible discussion of the issues surrounding empirically supported treatment must address these concerns.

In some sense, information and perspectives on empirically supported treatments are expanding so rapidly in journal articles and books, and perhaps most rapidly on the Internet, that commenting on the issues associated with empirically supported treatments is a bit like shoveling one's walk during a blizzard. Such problems not withstanding, in this chapter we briefly trace the origins of the EST movement; examine issues of accountability in the practice of psychotherapy, ethical issues, and issues concerning the public trust; and review the economic, political, and social considerations of the EST movement. We next turn to an examination of the issues raised by the implementation and practice of ESTs. These issues focus on the conceptual foundations of ESTs, specifically the assumptions that underlie clinical trials. We then discuss sources of error variance when findings from clinical trials are applied in actual clinical settings. These sources of variance include therapist variability, therapy variability, and client variability. We assess some of the conceptual and practical foundations of ESTs and focus on the roles of techniques and empirically based principles of therapeutic change. We end with some ideas that focus on graduate training and ESTs.

WHAT IS EMPIRICALLY SUPPORTED THERAPY? HISTORY AND DEFINITIONS

History

The possibility of developing and identifying empirically supported psychological treatments for human dysfunction has been a recent historical development. The scientist-practitioner model for clinical psychology was officially endorsed at the Boulder Conference in 1949. Although the practice of psychotherapy by psychologists had increased significantly by the early 1950s, and indeed had gained some measure of public credibility, the state of the field was such that Hans Eysenck (1952) was able to levy a devastating charge that there was not a shred of evidence supporting the effectiveness of psychotherapy. It was not until the early 1960s, when controlled experimentation identified several behavioral procedures that worked for a few specific problems, that psychologists were finally able to point to examples of empirically supported psychotherapy. With the proliferation of behavioral therapies for a wider variety of human problems, the identification of several therapist variables that appeared to be associated with productive client change, and the empirical investigation of cognitive interventions as effective treatments for affective disorders, the empirical footing of psychotherapy seemed to rest on firmer ground by the 1970s.

Throughout the 1980s and 1990s, research on the effectiveness of various psychotherapies was promulgated (Bergin & Garfield, 1994). Whereas in 1952 Eysenck could find only 24 outcome studies of psychotherapy to evaluate, by the 1980s psychotherapy researchers were able to conduct meta-analyses of outcome studies that numbered in the several hundreds. For example, Smith, Glass, and Miller (1980) reported a meta-analytic study in which the results of 475 investigations were considered. Comparing treated and untreated groups, the authors found, in short, that psychotherapy appeared to "work," showing an average effect size of 0.85 standard deviation units. This size of an effect indicated that the average person who received psychotherapy was in better mental health than 80% of the people who had not received psychotherapy. Similar conclusions were reached by other meta-analytic reviews. In a review of meta-analytic reviews summarizing over a thousand outcome studies and representing a diversity of both psychological treatments and human problems, Lambert and Bergin (1994) reported an overall average effect size that approached a full standard deviation. This indicated that psychotherapy accounted for about 10 percent of the total variation in outcome among clients randomly assigned to treatment and control conditions.

Knowing that psychotherapy "works," however, does not address a variety of other very important questions, including which treatments are the most effective for which kinds of specific problems. Yet, in an era in which government agencies and managed health-care companies are increasingly interested in documenting the "best practices" for specific problems, this is exactly the type of knowledge that is required. Consequently, there has been increasing pressure to develop psychotherapy clinical practice guidelines that specify the preferred modes of treatment for specific problems. In 1989, the Agency for Health Care Policy and Research (AHCPR) was created in the United States to identify the most effective treatments for specific disorders and to disseminate this information as appropriate treatment guidelines. This act, coupled with other trends occurring both inside and outside of psychology, served notice to the field.

In 1993 notice was taken. David Barlow, the president of the Clinical Psychology Division (Division 12) of the American Psychological Association (APA), established the Task Force on Promotion and Dissemination of Psychological Procedures (1995). After this task force widely circulated an initial draft that was heavily debated and discussed, a final report was produced that both specified criteria for evaluating the efficacy of psychotherapy treatments and identified existing psychotherapeutic treatments that appeared to meet the evaluative criteria. Subsequently, this task force report has been updated twice, once in 1996 and again in 1998 (Chambless et al., 1996; Chambless & Hollon, 1998), and updates are expected annually. Guidelines for training students in ESTs have also been suggested by Calhoun, Moras, Pilkonis, and Rehm (1998). We now discuss the evolution of these Division 12 Task Force reports and related materials and specifically focus on how the most recent report (Chambless & Hollon, 1998) defines empirically supported treatment.

Defining Empirically Supported Treatment

The definition of empirically supported therapies has evolved with the successive revisions of the original APA Division 12 Task Force report. In fact, although we use the term *empirically supported therapies* in this chapter, the term officially used by the most recent report remains *empirically validated therapies*. However, the chair of the report committee has agreed with others that the term *empirically validated* is less preferred, as it suggests that the process of verification is complete and that future scientific investigation of an "empirically validated treatment" is unnecessary (Chambless & Hollon, 1998; also see Garfield, 1996, 1998). The task force also expressed concern that although probably more accurate, changing the term to *supported* rather than *validated* might create confusion (Chambless, 1996). Readers interested in the history of these and other developments are referred to the original task force reports (Chambless et al., 1996, 1998; Task Force, 1995) and to several series of journal articles that appeared in the *Journal of Consulting and Clinical Psychology*, Vol. 66, No. 1 (1998), and *Clinical Psychology: Science and Practice*, Vol. 3, No. 3 (1996).

The Division 12 Task Force is very clear in noting what empirical validation criteria do and do not evaluate. The task force is explicit in acknowledging that the criteria are designed to evaluate *treatment efficacy*. The term efficacy refers to the internal validity of outcome research, and it is best demonstrated when a therapy is shown to work in a well-controlled study. For example, treatment efficacy would be demonstrated if patients randomly assigned to the treatment condition did better than patients randomly assigned to a control condition. However, these criteria do not evaluate *treatment effectiveness*, which refers to the external validity of a therapy or to evidence that a therapy works outside of the controlled experimental context. Treatment effectiveness would be demonstrated when an efficacious therapy was also shown to be successful when it was applied in nonresearch settings involving different patients, therapists with different training experiences and backgrounds, and different circumstances. Establishing treatment effectiveness is critical, as ultimately the goal is to disseminate efficacious psychotherapy treatments for use in applied settings, such as community mental health clinics. Although the Division 12 Task Force does not currently include criteria for determining treatment effectiveness, it will be examined in future treatment efficacy studies that have been more thoroughly reviewed (Chambless & Hollon, 1998).

The current Division 12 criteria also do not evaluate treatment feasibility, which concerns such issues as whether clients like or dislike treatments, whether they comply with treatment procedures or not, and the ease with which therapists can be trained in the treatment procedures. These feasibility issues concern how well such psychotherapies can actually be implemented. Finally, the Division 12 Task Force criteria also fail to evaluate treatment efficiency, which refers to the overall cost effectiveness of a treatment procedure (Chambless & Hollon, 1998).

ACCOUNTABILITY IN THE PRACTICE OF PSYCHOTHERAPY

Issues of accountably have received increasing attention among enterprises that operate within the public trust, and there is little reason to believe that this scrutiny will diminish markedly in the future (Barlow, 1996; Kendall, 1998). Although accountably is a responsibility of any psychologist, this is particularly true for clinical psychologists. Although there are certainly psychological scientists who engage only in pure or basic research with few or no implications for understanding, assessing, or changing dysfunctional behavior, a considerable majority of psychologists spend at least some portion of their time engaged in clinical pursuits. These include individuals who are full- or part-time practicing clinicians, those who do not practice but who do research on clinical problems, and those who train clinical psychologists. Of course, it is not only doctoral-level psychologists who do psychotherapy. Many, perhaps most, psychiatrists practice psychotherapy, as do clinical psychologists in training (under supervision). Similarly, psychotherapy is practiced by clinical social workers, many psychiatric nurses, master's-level psychologists, marriage and family counselors, many priests and pastors, numerous bartenders, and a few hair stylists.

Although there are some notable exceptions—for example, therapies developed by psychiatrists such as Beck (Beck, Rush, Shaw, & Emery, 1979) and Klerman (Klerman, Weissman, Rounsaville, & Chevron, 1984)—for the most part it has been psychologists who have developed and disseminated psychotherapy (Vanden-Bos, 1996). We thus focus our discussion on the issues of empirically supported therapy as they affect psychologists, although we note explicitly that issues of accountability are relevant for anyone who practices psychotherapy or counseling.

Accountability is a complex concept with numerous facets. We focus here on three interrelated issues that affect the core of applied clinical psychology as a scientific discipline. They include the implications of the scientific verification of treatment efficacy, the ethical obligations of psychotherapy practitioners and researchers, and the current (and most likely future) economic and political forces that affect decisions concerning the availability, quality, and quantity of psychotherapy.

Scientific Accountability

The roots of clinical psychology can be traced back nearly one hundred years (see Routh & DeRubeis, 1998). However, clinical psychology did not establish scientific credentials until somewhat more recently. The behaviorist era of the 1950s and 1960s witnessed some of the first attempts to empirically verify treatment procedures. Contemporary clinical psychology is widely (although perhaps not universally) recognized as a science. To most, such a statement is patently obvious. Nevertheless, this straightforward statement warrants discussion in the context of psychotherapy research and practice. In particular, it is essential that the basic elements of applied psychology, particularly in the treatment arena, be built on a solid scientific foundation that is represented by sound empirical data.

In this context, we can elaborate on the basic goal of scientific verification; in short, the scientific status of psychology dictates that we must determine empirically whether therapy "works." Indeed, as scientists and practitioners, psychologists have a scientific responsibility and obligation to verify that their applied efforts are both worthwhile and efficacious. In principle, there is no reason to believe that any type of psychotherapy cannot (nor should not) be subjected to empirical verification. In verifying efficacy, however, it is critical to examine the conceptual and methodological details.

Investigators have commented on the criteria used to judge a treatment efficacious. For example, Chambless and Hollon (1998) summarize five criteria for judging that a treatment has been empirically supported. They note that the treatment must be compared to an adequate control group and must be found to be superior to a control group or equivalent to an already established treatment. The study must employ a manual for the specific treatment of individuals with well-specified problems. To be considered efficacious, they argue that the treatment has to be demon-

strated as effective in at least two different studies, or, to be designated as possibly efficacious, the treatment must be shown to be effective in at least one study. Finally, to be classified as both efficacious and specific, the treatment must be shown to be superior to a placebo or to an alternative established treatment in at least two different research settings.

These criteria are, of course, extremely important. We also believe that it is important to comment at some length about methodological issues that are typically not encompassed in more broadly defined definitions of whether a therapy can be judged efficacious. Certainly, the quantity of work detailing the methodological requirements for psychotherapy outcome research is enormous; for some time, volumes have been devoted largely to psychotherapy evaluation methodologies (Kazdin, 1998; Kendall & Butcher, 1983), as have countless articles, special journal issues, portions of books describing psychotherapy (Kendall & Hollon, 1979), and descriptions of clinical assessment (Kendall & Hollon, 1981). Indeed, and more recently, this volume contains a chapter on clinical methodology (Chapter 2 by Haaga & Stiles) that partially addresses the issue surrounding therapy outcome assessment. Clearly there is no shortage of information on how to evaluate the efficacy of psychotherapy, a fact that we believe attests to how central psychotherapy outcome research is to scientific clinical psychology. Because a comprehensive examination of all of these relevant methodological issues would take at least an entire volume, we thus limit our discussion to what we believe are perhaps the most crucial aspects of empirical verification: the definition and measurement of therapeutic outcomes.

Dimensions of Outcome Assessment

As a first step in demonstrating efficacy, any outcome assessment must define and rely on the appropriate dependent variables. There are several dependent variables that are crucial to understanding the efficacy of a treatment: (1) the *magnitude* of the change (the amount of reduction in targeted symptoms), (2) the *generality* of the change (how much change takes place across a range of different symptoms or across a range of situations, e.g., occupational or interpersonal, that the person may face), (3) the *universality* of change (what percentage of people show positive change vs. no change, negative change, or deterioration), (4) *acceptability* (how likely people are to complete treatment vs. dropping out prematurely), (5) *safety* (the likelihood of undesirable complications such as side effects), and (6) *stability* (how long treatment gains are maintained). Finally, statistical significance must be differentiated from clinical significance. Results must be statistically significant before clinical significance can be established, but statistical significance alone does not ensure that results are meaningful in any clinical or practical sense (Jacobson & Truax, 1991; Kendall, 1998). Good faith conclusions about the efficacy of a treatment must include reference to these types of outcomes. Indeed, the public would be ill served by concluding that a treatment "works," because it reduces targeted symptoms, when it is also associated with substantial dropout rates and undesirable complications for those who do complete treatment.

Constructs Assessed

In addition to the dimensions of outcome, an important consideration in determining the efficacy of treatment is reflected in which constructs are assessed. The possibilities in this regard are quite numerous. For example, patients' satisfaction with treatment is an important dimension, as are reports of symptom change, interpersonal functioning and occupational functioning, and change in more broadly defined constructs like quality of life, self-esteem, and so on. For some types of therapies targeted toward very specific problems, other outcome variables also may be applicable. For example, a psychological treatment targeted toward weight loss would obviously assess weight change after treatment, but it also might include an assessment of eating habits and exercise patterns. Variables believed to be important to a particular kind of treatment would also be assessed. In the case of cognitive therapy, constructs reflective of schemas and automatic thoughts would be natural constructs to be assessed. To facilitate comparisons between clinical trials, researchers are developing standardized batteries of outcome measures for specific disorders. To begin this process, researchers in the fields of psychotherapy, personality assessment, and methodology convened at the 1994 Core Battery Conference to try to reach a consensus on measures of outcome for the study of mood, anxiety, and personality disorders (see Strupp, Horowitz, & Lambert, 1997, for a review of the recommendations of this conference).

Sources of Outcome Data

The complexity of dependent variables does not end with the variety of different possible outcome dimensions or the constructs that are assessed. In many respects, the source of data for these dimensions underlies all other outcome considerations. Although most outcome measures ultimately rely on patient self-reports, four major categories of data sources for assessing outcome are common: others' reports, clinician judgments, diagnostic considerations, and psychometric measurement. Although these sources are probably correlated to some degree, the correlation is not perfect. Thus, for example, patients may improve in their verbal reports and, when assessed, improve psychometrically, yet their therapists may see little meaningful improvement in what are perceived as the underlying causes of the problem. Or a group of patients in a study may no longer receive the disorder diagnosis with which they started, but many might still experience significant psychological symptoms as assessed psychometrically and by verbal reports. The most informative studies are those that employ a multitrait, multimethod approach that, by definition, relies on different sources of outcome data.

Outcome Dimension by Construct by Source of Data Interactions

To complicate matters further, each of the classes of dependent variables may interact to reflect improvements on some variables and not on others, producing something akin to having to interpret multiple higher order interactions. Moreover, some variables may be regarded as more important than other variables by various investigators. This issue can be succinctly seen in the context of the public's perception of the scientific study of psychotherapy outcome by a relatively recent *Consumer Reports* (1995) article on the effectiveness of psychotherapy and the debate among researchers concerning its meaning and significance. As part of their annual members survey, *Consumer Reports* included a number of questions that inquired about the use of and satisfaction with mental health services. Of the 7000 respondents to these questions, approximately 2900 respondents had sought the services of a mental health professional (other respondents talked to friends, family, or clergy about their problems).

As noted by Seligman (1995) in an article that comprehensively described the study, as well as noted its strengths and limitations, the *Consumer Reports* article focused largely on patients' reports of therapy satisfaction. Certainly patient satisfaction is an important variable, but it is insufficient in and of itself to draw conclusions about the effectiveness of therapy. Instead, the kinds of data, the sources of data, and the possible interactions that we noted must be evaluated. Doing so, however, makes it impossible to render the straightforward and simple conclusions that the public tends to demand. On the other hand, because of the complexity of what psychologists study, the different views on what is important, the likely interactions among variables, and the inherent limitations in any study, psychologists are well aware of the need to qualify their conclusions about any study. Although such qualifications could have appeared in this article, they would almost assuredly preclude broad conclusions about whether therapy "works." In this vein, it is difficult to imagine a *Consumer Reports* article that accurately attempts to summarize all of these issues. One could imagine the letters to the editor in the next issue if it did.

Ethical Issues and the Public Trust

Because psychology is synonymous with psychotherapy to the overwhelming majority of the public, the availability of empirical data on the efficacy of psychotherapy helps to shape the public's perception of the scientific stature of psychology. Such perceptions are not merely a matter of seeking good press or a way to justify the legitimacy of psychology. Rather, to the extent that psychology can offer services that will genuinely help improve quality of life, the enhanced perception that what is offered is based on fundamentally sound science is likely to increase willingness to seek what may be the needed professional services. As Barlow (1996) has noted in this regard, psychologists can help alleviate the suffering of innumerable individuals if we can present effective treatments to the public. As such, psychology has an implied social contract to contribute to the public welfare (Fox, 1996).

Accountability to the public touches squarely on ethical issues. Statements relative to the ethical obligation of psychologists in the provision of effective treatment are scattered throughout the American Psychological Association's Ethical Principles for Psychologists. Although no single statement speaks directly to this issue, statements such as "Psychologists respect the integrity and

protect the welfare of the people and groups with whom they work" (Principle 6, emphasis added), make it clear that psychologists, at least those who are members of APA, have certain ethical obligations. We believe that nowhere is this issue more clear-cut than when it is applied to the practice of psychotherapy; any reasonable interpretation of the APA code makes it clear that psychologists have an ethical obligation to ensure that, as much as possible, they offer fundamentally sound psychotherapy.

Although a comprehensive ethics code such as that developed by the APA is necessary, it is important to recognize that this code encompasses aspirational goals rather than a compendium of prescribed and prohibited behaviors for each situation. We believe that it is important to look beyond any institutionalized code of ethical conduct to the principles that underlie it, specifically, to the basic issue of the public trust, which should be a matter of concern to all psychologists in general and to all psychotherapists in particular. There are two reasons for this. First, only psychologists who are members of APA are technically bound by this ethics code. Second, but more important, the ethical code tends to speak somewhat more to individual practitioners than it does to those who develop, assess, disseminate, and render judgments about the efficacy of psychotherapy. We thus believe that the most fundamental understanding of the principles that underlie the ethics code places an equal obligation on practitioners to use empirically supported treatments to guide their work (Meehl, 1997; Persons & Silberschatz, 1998) and on researchers to guide their evaluation of psychotherapy outcomes. Both of these are necessary to help ensure the public trust in clinical psychology.

The flip side to provision of empirically supported treatments to the public is the acknowledgment of their limitations. It is not feasible, nor within the purview of this chapter, to describe the specific limitations of various treatment approaches. Researchers have already done a thorough job in this regard. Instead, we note two general categories of psychotherapy limitations. The first concerns the limitations of various treatment options themselves. At the current stage of treatment evaluation, even the most well-validated treatment is limited in terms of for whom and for what kinds of problems it has been validated. Thus, a treatment found to be effective for adults with a particular kind of disorder cannot be assumed to be effective for children with different problems.[1] The second concern is the limits of our current scientific methods. We believe that some of the best psychological science has emanated from treatment studies (e.g., Hollon, Evans, & DeRubeis, 1990). Yet, even these studies are not prefect. Thus, we must acknowledge the limitations of empirically supported treatment by virtue of the fact that all studies used as the basis for determining support have both flaws and error variance.

Potential pitfalls lie not in the acknowledgment that studies and treatments have limitations as much as in ignoring those limitations. Of course, this is a problem that encompasses more than just psychotherapy; the Diagnostic and Statistical Manual (DSM) of the American Psychiatric Association is a case in point. The limitations of the DSM are clearly spelled out in its introduction of the manual, yet few of these limitations are ever acknowledged by researchers who rely on this manual to diagnose and define study groups (Ingram, Miranda, & Segal, 1998). Nor are they apparently heeded by insurance companies, who base reimbursement decisions solely on DSM categories. The listing of empirically supported treatments faces similar problems. Although for the most part those who develop and disseminate these treatments have been exemplary in identifying and acknowledging limitations, those who are apt to market and use these approaches may not share the same level of enthusiasm for this acknowledgment. Consider the marketing program of the Psychological Corporation, which offers a TherapyWorks program for psychotherapists (e.g., videotapes and therapy manuals). It states in one of its mass-mailed promotional announcements that they are "proud to offer our TherapyWorks line of Empirically Supported treatments. Based on years of research comparing the effectiveness of various psychotherapies, TherapyWorks programs are recognized in several American Psychological Association Clinical Division Task Force Reports as effective forms of treatment for specific disorders." It is noted that these programs were developed to allow clinicians to use them in the same manner in which they were shown to be effective in the research literature. Additionally, the

TherapyWorks promotion comes complete with recommended ages and numbers of sessions for the various programs and materials offered, as well as value pricing on some products for special savings.

We believe that there is much worth in making treatment materials widely available to psychotherapists. But there are also obvious sources of concern with a corporate marketing approach to psychotherapy, such as the implied endorsement of the APA Division 12 Task Force and the lack of mention of any limitations (and indeed the implicit suggestion that there are no limitations: "years of research"; "effective forms of treatment"). It is fortunate that psychologists tend to be well equipped to judge the limits of therapy marketing, but other practitioners may not be, and certainly the public as a whole is quite likely very ill equipped to judge the limits of any given therapy approach or the science on which statements of effectiveness are based. Thus, principles of ethical accountability and the need for psychologists to protect the public trust dictate that we must strive not only to promote what works, but also to make clear the limits of effectiveness; we cannot leave the shortcomings of our work to the fine print.

Economic, Political, and Social Considerations

A subset of ethical considerations can be seen in the issues that have developed around the provision of psychotherapy in the context of larger political and social forces. These issues can be seen in controversies surrounding reimbursement for psychotherapy through managed care or third-party payments. They can also be seen in guidelines that are being promulgated by federal agencies, which may literally dictate what kinds of therapies may or may not be practiced. For example, provision of an approved therapy may shield therapists from malpractice, whereas practicing therapies not on the approved list may leave therapists vulnerable to litigation (Barlow, 1996). Indeed, lawyers see an untapped but enormous potential for lawsuits in a variety of issues surrounding the training in and practice of psychotherapy (e.g., Saccuzo, 1997), and they seek to "impose liability" where they can do so (Smith, 1997).

Such forces thus affect not only how much will be reimbursed but also decisions about the extent and quality of overall coverage. For instance, in many cases, coverage is provided only

---

[1]If a clinician has no other options, such a treatment might still be used, but in this context it would no longer constitute an empirically supported treatment.

for DSM-derived diagnoses, but not for other significant problems (e.g., marital dysfunction), and even then, not all DSM diagnoses are covered (e.g., personality disorders). In addition to limits on what is covered, limits are also frequently placed on the length of treatment; many health maintenance organizations (HMOs) permit a very limited number of sessions. Moreover, many HMOs rely on therapists who are trained only as high as the master's level (and in some case even lower) to make these important decisions. Each of these factors affects the accessibility, quantity, and quality of psychotherapy provided.

The boundaries placed on psychotherapy coverage (and on psychotherapists) raise serious and compelling concerns. Despite these quite legitimate concerns, it is also important to ask the corresponding question of whether psychotherapists should be reimbursed or held liable for providing treatment that has not been empirically supported. We believe that adherence to a principle of public accountably makes the answer to this question clear; it thus necessitates that what service is provided through managed care or is reimbursed must be based on a solid scientific foundation. Of course, this does not mean that only treatments that have been shown to be empirically verified can be used; in most cases therapists cannot ethically turn away individuals whose problems do not conform to those that have been sufficiently studied with a specified therapeutic approach. Rather, the treatment decisions made by therapists must be based on the best science that is available, even when this science may be in short supply for a specific problem. This is certainly the case for pharmacological approaches, many of which are commonly accepted as effective yet lack data to demonstrate their effectiveness as applied in clinical settings (Barlow, 1996). In the case of psychological interventions, however, we believe that much of the relevant science is embodied in the general principles that underlie psychological change, which we discuss later.

Much as with ethical issues in general, even in the context of managed care, psychotherapists must guard against the desire to promote scientifically sound treatment at the expense of acknowledging its limits. This can be a difficult task when psychology is experiencing pressure from all sides and must increasingly justify its existence as both a science and a source of qualified psychotherapists. Nevertheless, because psychologists must be scientifically, ethically, and socially accountable, statements about the empirically determined efficacy of psychological treatment should always be linked to qualifications and cautions about their limits as well.

FROM THEORY TO PRACTICE: CRITICAL ISSUES IN THE IMPLEMENTATION AND PRACTICE OF EMPIRICALLY SUPPORTED TREATMENTS

Meta-models: Assumptions That Guide the Conceptual Foundations of Empirically Supported Treatment

In this section, we comment on the assumptions that underlie the models used to conceptually define and empirically determine treatment efficacy. We label these meta-models because they establish the framework for both gathering and interpreting data and for deciding what conclusions can be drawn about treatment validity.

Reliance on the Medical Model

As with all psychological models, a number of assumptions underlie the current movement to identify, train for, and apply effective treatments. We think it is worthwhile to examine at least one of the major assumptions that serves as the foundation of the EST movement. We refer specifically to a reliance on a medical model approach to the treatment of psychological disorders. This approach to ESTs is evident in two important respects.

The Conceptual Assumptions of Clinical Trials: Design

The randomized clinical trial (RCT) is the standard means by which the efficacy of psychotherapies is evaluated (Chambless & Hollon, 1998). Reviewing the history of the RCT, Goldfried and Wolfe (1998) noted that during the 1970s the National Institute of Mental Health (the primary source of funding for psychotherapy research) determined that this research design was so successful in pharmacotherapy research that it would serve as a model for the study of psychotherapy. In this design, homogeneous patient samples are randomly assigned to the treatment or to one or more comparison conditions, and the outcomes of the groups are compared. Therapists' adherence and competence are measured and are conceptualized as akin to "dosage," and patients' compliance and adherence are measured to evaluate "absorption." In addition, as Stiles and Shapiro

(1994) argue, the assumptions of the medical model pervade the study of the process of change in psychotherapy. Here, researchers try to identify the "active ingredients" of change. Maling, Gurtman, and Howard (1995) even map out and study "dose-response" curves in psychotherapy.

Although the medical model has taken the field far, there are a number of issues that need to be considered when applying it to psychotherapy rather than to pharmacotherapy. Specifically, how well suited is the RCT approach for the clinical realities experienced by the practicing psychotherapists? Much of the answer to this question resides in the external validity, or generality, of the RCT approach and the conceptual assumptions that must guide any efforts to generalize. As Ingram and Scott (1990) have previously argued, in assuming a medical model, RCTs also assume a *prescriptive* approach to psychotherapy. In using an analogy to pharmacotherapy research, RCTs presuppose the psychotherapists will "deliver" treatment to their clients in the same way in which it was delivered in a clinical trial. In pharmacological research, doses of a medication used in a study can be prescribed in a virtually identical fashion to those prescribed in the actual treatment setting. Can the same be said for psychotherapy? Not likely. We comment on some sources of error variance in the next section, but note here that using the same clinical trial–proven methods for the same disorder, practicing psychotherapists will behave quite differently by virtue of their past training, their particular personal attributes and backgrounds, and the vicissitudes of clients' circumstances and behaviors. Even moving to "manualization" of treatments, although perhaps helping to standardize treatment somewhat, is unlikely to ensure that psychotherapy will be delivered in clinical situations in the same way in which it was tested (with therapists specifically trained and regularly supervised in certain therapeutic methods, tested with homogeneous patient samples, etc.). Manualization is a positive development in many ways, particularly in providing guidelines for practicing therapists, but not one that will create unity between the behaviors of study therapists and practicing therapists.

The Conceptual Assumptions of Clinical Trials: Study Patients

The current version of the Diagnostic and Statistical Manual of Mental Disorders, DSM-IV, embodies the decision-making rules governing the current status of psychiatric taxonomy. Taxonomy is, of course, essential to any scientific endeavor; no branch of science could exist without a way to differentiate and classify different phenomena. As Ingram et al. (1998) point out, natural science offers the most complete taxonomy; animals are classified according to their order, family, genus, species, and in some cases subspecies and race. In comparison to natural science, psychiatric taxonomy is quite crude but has nevertheless produced an extensive differentiation and then classification of different disorders, each with its own inclusion and exclusion criteria. No taxonomic system is fixed, however. Just as natural science evolves as species are further differentiated (or in some cases combined, as when two species are recognized as being, in fact, different variants of the same species), so too does psychiatric classification; DSM has undergone four extensive revisions since 1952 and will certainly be revised again in the future.

As a medical, disease-based model, DSM-IV presents a categorical framework for conceptualizing psychological disorders, a framework that works well for physical diseases. Some have argued that psychological disorders are in fact medical disorders that reveal themselves through psychological symptoms (e.g., Spitzer & Endicott, 1978), but many psychologists recognize that the categories imposed by DSM are not as distinct as the categorical classification system used by this manual implies. This recognition notwithstanding, psychosocial interventions are standardized and evaluated in terms of their efficacy in reducing the symptoms of a specific DSM mental disorder (Goldfried & Wolfe, 1998); the homogenous samples that form the basis for testing the efficacy of a given therapy are derived from well-defined groups of individuals who have received a DSM diagnosis. Accordingly, the underlying disease model results in an overemphasis on symptoms and symptom reduction.

Selecting DSM-diagnosed samples to participate in clinical trials is an appropriate research strategy in many respects, but the relatively high level of diagnostic precision also brings about some serious limitations. To recruit a homogeneous sample, many people are potentially screened out by failing to meet DSM inclusion and exclusion criteria. However, generalization limits require that treatments demonstrated to be efficacious in these trials are only informative about treating individuals with the same DSM diagnosis. Although this procedure achieves a well-defined sample, most people with psychological problems do not meet all inclusion and exclusion criteria. Therapists must nonetheless treat these patients. The medical model that guides the standard evaluation of many treatments imposes a framework that may not correspond to the clinical realities experienced by many therapists. There is always a balance to be achieved between internal and external validity, but inasmuch as the final goal must always be external validity, it is easy to become concerned that it has not been sufficiently emphasized by the current EST movement.

Sources of Error Variance

A variety of sources of variance affects the degree to which treatments can be considered effective in actual settings. We describe three interacting sources of variance that may significantly affect the extent to which treatments found effective in research can be generalized to clinical settings.

Therapist Variability

We have alluded to issues concerning therapist variability. Therapies are *entirely* dependent on the therapists who practice them, and as with many issues surrounding ESTs, questions concerning therapist variability have been the subject of vigorous debate. Garfield (1996), for example, notes that "one can reasonably ask whether all therapists perform at the same level or comparable levels of efficacy even if they supposedly have had similar manualized training. In most pursuits—professional, scientific, technical, or artistic—the participants do vary despite what may be viewed as similar training" (p. 221). Such statements can be interpreted to reflect a belief that individuals who are sufficiently therapeutically talented need not be overly concerned with whether the treatments they practice are sufficiently validated: "talent is not enough. . . . If this were so, we could give up on training programs and just learn to select talented therapists when they apply for licensure" (Chambless, 1996, p. 234).

Few would disagree that the outcome of any psychotherapy represents an interaction between the therapist's competence and fundamentally sound therapy. We wish to raise a somewhat different point that bears on the issue of error variance specifically from the perspective of external validity, which is by definition ultimately related to whether ESTs are effective. In particular, we

believe that equally competent therapists will practice the same empirically supported therapy in different ways, even though both will be faithful to the specific therapy procedures and the more general therapy protocol. If we assume for a moment that therapists have received precisely equivalent training in an EST, because they differ on a virtually infinite number of other variables (e.g., intelligence, insightfulness, temperament, educational experiences, personal and professional backgrounds, general psychological and physical health, current mood states, etc.), they will make different decisions at different times that will affect the course and outcome of treatment, perhaps dramatically. Indeed, at the extreme but not unimaginable level, the application of the same, faithfully executed EST might result in significant improvement in one client and no improvement in another.

Of course, the assumption of equal training and equal learning is unfounded; even individuals exposed to identical manualized training will differ in their proficiency, which might reasonably be expected to lead to significant differences in outcome. In 1986, Ingram and Hollon commented on the possible mechanisms of change achieved by cognitive therapy for depression; they noted that although the theory underlying the treatment emphasized that effective treatment was due to changing patients' problematic schemas, a different possibility was that schemas were deactivated rather than changed in any meaningful fashion. Certainly both possibilities are true; even though practicing the same therapy, cognitive therapy in the hands of an extremely insightful therapist might change schemas, but in the hands of a somewhat less insightful therapist, schemas might be deactivated rather than changed.

As we have noted, the criteria used to establish efficacy in a clinical trial do not pertain to treatment *effectiveness*, which refers to the external validity, or to evidence that a therapy works outside of the controlled experimental context. We further noted that arguments for the inclusion of ESTs in practice guidelines require that a given therapy be shown to be effective in clinical settings. It is just the sort of therapist variability that we have discussed here that creates significant difficulties for such requirements; because *all* of the variance in psychological interventions must be attributable to therapist behaviors, the variance in these behaviors from one therapist to another creates a substantial obstacle to demonstrating effectiveness. As Barlow (1996) has correctly argued, even pharmacological approaches that have been shown to be efficacious generally have not been studied adequately with regard to effectiveness in clinical settings. Yet, these approaches do not suffer from the inherent therapist variability that confronts psychotherapies. Although there may be significant variability in how, when, and for how long medications are administered, a given dosage of a drug used in an efficacy trial can be measured in precisely the same way in a clinical setting. Unfortunately, the same simply cannot be said for the various components of a psychological intervention.

Therapy Variability

Variance between a therapy used in a treatment trial and that which is employed in practice is largely a subset of therapist variability. That is, the fact that therapy will vary from research to clinical settings is a function of how the therapy is implemented by different therapists. As we have noted, different therapists can stay faithful to a given theory in its implementation but will conduct the therapy in significantly different ways. There can be a significant advantage in this because therapies are developed and typically manualized in ways that permit a substantial amount of flexibility. Such flexibility is, of course, absolutely essential in clinical practice but is severely problematic if the goal is to empirically demonstrate that research psychotherapies are effective in clinical settings. Thus, the very flexibility that most ESTs embody makes it difficult to take them to the next necessary step of demonstrated effectiveness with the patients who are treated by practicing psychotherapists.

Client Variability

Davison (1998) has noted that the "gold standard" for empirically examining treatments has resulted in the explicit linkage between treatment manuals and the DSM; "appropriate" clients are defined according to prevailing diagnostic criteria. Despite the use of standardized diagnoses, there are at least three basic issues involved in the variance that is attributable to individual clients. The first deals with diagnostic status and coexisting disorders. Clinical trials rely on studying relatively homogeneous groups of individuals, most frequently those who have received a DSM diagnosis. Despite their diagnostic homogeneity, rarely are such samples free of comorbid diagnoses (Chambless, 1996), with personality disorders being recognized as the most common coexisting condition. Sanderson, Wetzler, Beck, and Betz (1992), for example, noted that 50% of patients with major depressive disorder also had at least one diagnosable personality disorder, 52% of dysthymic patients also had a personality disorder, and 69% of individuals with both major depression and dysthymia also had a personality disorder. The potential problem in generalizability to clinical settings lies in the variability that may be a function of such coexisting problems. For example, it is unclear how a treatment that is found to be efficacious for a given disorder may be affected by the fact that other disorders or problems coexist with the target disorder. A client in a clinical setting with one constellation of personality problems in addition to the presenting problems may be affected very differently than another client with similar presenting problems and a different constellation of personality issues. This is the case even if we assume that the empirically supported treatment is the same, which, as we have noted, is a questionable assumption.

Even when clients in a clinical trial are relatively homogeneous diagnostically, the level of homogeneity in the primary diagnosis can be misleading. As Ingram et al. (1998), Ingram and Hamilton (1999), and Kendall and Brady (1995) have pointed out, even clients with the same diagnosis can differ dramatically in the presentation and timing of symptom profiles. In the case of depression, for example, two "homogeneous" and diagnostically depressed clients can, in theory, experience very little symptom overlap; these symptoms are so diverse that two people who are both diagnosed as depressed may actually have few, or even only one, symptom(s) in common. Thus, a sample of individuals with the same "homogeneous" diagnosis may in fact represent an extremely heterogeneous group.

A number of investigators have pointed out in this regard the limitations of the syndrome approach to the study of psychological problems with current diagnostic systems (e.g., Costello, 1992, 1993; Persons, 1986). Many of these limitations stem from the fact that this approach implicitly assumes uniformity among individuals with the same syndrome, specifically that they are alike in all important psychological ways. This assumption is clearly incorrect. Persons has argued that relying solely on the concept of a syndrome to define and then study psychological problems may miss important information. If, for example, negative affect is a variable that is important to treat, then it is important to realize that depressed (with major depressive episode and dysthymia) and anxious (general anxiety states, as well as more specific anxious states like phobia and obsessive-compulsive problems) people experience negative affect, which could be the focus of treatments to be empirically verified. Hence, a specific therapeutic focus on negative affect rather than on syndromes allows for the study of the treatment individuals who share this state and are similar in important respects.

It is thus unclear from clinical trials that have demonstrated the efficacy of a treatment for a given diagnosis how much variability may be represented in the disorder itself. Correspondingly, it is uncertain to what degree such treatments can be generalized to treatment settings. For example, an efficacious treatment for depression may be more or less effective for the client with cognitive difficulties versus those with motivational difficulties, versus those with suicidal ideation, each of which are symptom patterns of depression but few of which are differentially assessed in treatment outcome research. Thus, the variability in clients is much greater than has perhaps been assumed by therapy outcome studies, even those that fastidiously assess their clients diagnostically.

A final problem in client variability lies in the actual presenting problems and life situations of clients. Diagnostic efforts are intended to describe important similarities among clients, but individual differences from one client to the next that are not accounted for in the diagnosis can be remarkably large. For instance, the specific problems presented by an anxious, middle-aged, well-educated, affluent, intelligent woman with a husband, children, and extended family may be radically different from those presented by an anxious man who is young, is not well educated or particularly intelligent, is poor, and has no family. The differential treatment implications of these issues, as well as the day-to-day problems that are presented in therapy, may have huge differential implications for treatments that have been empirically supported. To the extent that these individual differences are represented in treatment groups for empirical validation studies, this problem may be minimized and generalizability enhanced. Unfortunately, it is difficult to determine how much variance in individual differences is represented in these studies. Even the best treatment studies can assess and report on only a limited number of variables in individual differences.

Conceptual and Practical Foundations of Effective Treatment
The Roles of Technique and Empirically Based Principles of Therapeutic Change

Empirically supported treatments and their manuals provide an array of techniques that have been examined in the context of research. As we have discussed, these techniques have been developed and tested in the context of homogeneous study populations, yet the people excluded from these studies make up much of the population seen in clinical settings. In addition, there are a number of problems for which no empirically supported treatments have been identified (e.g., the somatoform and dissociative disorders). Furthermore, the possible combinations of clinical problems and presentations are numerous; thus as emphasized in the discussions of ESTs in the issue of the *Journal of Consulting and Clinical Psychology* to which we previously referred, flexibility must be built into the application of the empirically supported treatments.

What is meant by flexibility and how to apply it, however, has not been as clearly articulated. We contend that the foundation of flexible thinking is principle-based rather than technique-based thinking. More generally, we argue that clinical psychology is a conceptual science rather than a prescriptive science, a science that views psychotherapists as applied scientists who bring to bear their empirically derived knowledge of psychopathology and human change principles to particular scientific (client) problems (Stricker & Trierweiler, 1995). Thus, these scientist-practitioners are characterized by the flexibility to apply their scientific knowledge in a manner that best fits their personalities, background, and training to client's problems, personalities, and backgrounds and to the multitude of problems that clients bring to treatment.

In line with a conceptual- or principle-based approach, Goldfried and Padawer (1982) articulated different levels of abstraction of clinical understanding well before the empirically supported treatment movement was underway. At the lowest level of abstraction is a concrete understanding of therapeutic techniques, that is, understanding the form of the interventions and how to implement them rather than focusing on their function. At the middle level of abstraction is an understanding of principles of therapeutic change, that is, understanding the function or the change mechanisms mobilized by interventions rather than focusing on differences in their form. At the highest level of abstraction is the level of theoretical understanding. This is the overarching theory of psychopathology and change, often one's theoretical orientation (e.g., behavioral, cognitive, psychodynamic, gestalt, and client-centered). Goldfried and Padawer advocated a focus on the mid-level of abstraction to advance knowledge of how different psychotherapies work and to develop new treatments. This level of abstraction, they argue, provides a middle ground that offers freedom from narrow adherence to technique or to theoretical orientation.

The EST movement can turn into an emphasis on the level of therapeutic technique if we are not careful. We argue that Goldfried and Padawer's (1982) call to the mid-level of principles of change needs to be revived. At this level, the flexibility that is so important when implementing the ESTs is natural. Principles of change are derived from empirically grounded theory and can be used to guide the selection and flexible application of the EST techniques. Each of the levels of abstraction articulated by Goldfried and Padawer has a place, and we argue that the balance of these levels is the key to flexible, evidence-based practice.

Because of an emphasis on documenting the efficacy of our therapies, the field has not yet developed a consensus on empirically grounded principles of therapeutic change. It is premature to offer a list of established principles of change, but we offer a few examples of possible candidates and describe how such principles can guide both the selection of intervention strategies and treatment innovation. In addition, we describe a related approach, which is to identify common factors of therapy that are associated with positive outcomes.

Examples of Principle-based Thinking

A principle emerging from the anxiety disorders and trauma literature is that exposure to corrective information without avoidance is a potent way to facilitate change (Barlow & Lehman, 1996; Foa, 1997; Foa & Kozak, 1986). Techniques to facilitate exposure can take a variety of forms and can be applied across a variety of different clinical problems. The exposure-based therapies are among the most efficacious that our field has to offer (Barlow & Lehman, 1996), and they grew out of a sound empirical base. Exposure-based therapies have their roots in the-

ory and research on habituation and extinction (Foa & Kozak, 1986). The principles of exposure are also consistent with research on emotional and information processing (Foa, 1997; Litrell, 1998; Pennebaker, 1997a, 1997b) and with the research on the negative and rebound effects of thought suppression (Beevers, Wenzlaff, Hayes, & Scott, in press; Purdon, in press) and experiential avoidance (Hayes, Wilson, Gifford, Follette, & Strosahl, 1996), the conceptual opposites of exposure. Both exposure and corrective experiences have been proposed as common factors of therapy by several authors (e.g., Arkowitz & Hannah, 1989; Goldfried, 1991; Grencavage & Norcross, 1990; Weinberger, 1993). Thus, at the level of change principles, a relative consensus is emerging across areas on the importance of exposure to corrective information to facilitate change in avoidance-based problems. The form of this exposure can vary and can be tailored to the problem at hand.

Operating from this level of abstraction, a therapist can apply in principle the techniques that have been demonstrated to be efficacious in carefully controlled clinical trials. If one views a number of DSM-IV disorders as problems of experiential avoidance (Hayes et al., 1996), the exposure-based interventions can be applied and tailored to other problems of avoidance that are conceptually similar to the anxiety disorders, such as substance abuse, eating disorders, and the somotoform and dissociative disorders.

Salkovskis and Clark (1993) provide an excellent example of principle-level thinking that is leading to exciting developments in the treatment of hypochondriasis, a disorder for which there is no empirically supported therapy. They view hypochondriasis as conceptually similar to panic disorder in that both are based on misinterpretations of somatic functioning. Thus, they are tailoring the empirically supported therapy for panic disorder to a different but conceptually similar problem.

Similarly, if dissociative identity disorder is viewed as an extreme form of posttraumatic stress disorder, as a coping response to a catastrophic event, then gradual exposure might be an approach to facilitate the processing and integration of the fragmented and blocked memory network (Foa & Hearst-Ikeda, 1996). At present, there is no empirically supported treatment for either hypochondriasis or for dissociative identity disorder. Clinical intervention that is based on extrapolation from empirically sound theory and research may break new ground and help those who are suffering, as we await the years of treatment development, manualization, and clinical research that is required for a treatment to be deemed empirically supported.

Another possible principle of therapeutic change suggested by research is the importance of activating the multiple domains (cognitive, affective, behavioral, and somatic) of the memory networks and introducing corrective information from multiple data streams (Foa, 1997; Hayes & Strauss, 1998; Ingram, 1984; Ingram et al., 1998; Teasdale & Barnard, 1993). Foa (1997) recommends that exposure exercises for anxiety disorders involve cognitive, affective, behavioral, and somatic components of the fear network. Similar recommendations have been made in the cognitively-based therapies for depression (Beck, 1995; Hayes & Strauss, 1998; Teasdale & Barnard, 1993; Young, Beck, & Weinberger, 1993). This multimodal recommendation encourages an integration of strategies from a variety of theoretical orientations.

Principle-based Treatment Innovation

Linehan's (1993) dialectical behavior therapy, Young's (1994) schema-focused approach for personality disorders, and Hayes and Harris's (in press) integrative therapy for depression are excellent examples of approaches that integrate a variety of techniques and are based on a solid foundation of empirically grounded change principles. These approaches are flexible, meet the needs of the individual client, and can be manualized and examined in clinical trials. They exemplify the blending of empirically based theory, principle, and technique, as well as the dynamic process of clinical innovation and treatment development.

Calhoun et al. (1998) remind us that when one looks beyond acute symptom reduction, which is the primary outcome measure of most clinical trials, the clinically significant effects of most therapies are promising but modest (cf. Jacobson & Truax, 1991; Tingey, Lambert, Burlingame, & Hansen, 1996). Thus, the challenge is "to produce a creative tension among those things currently accepted as state of the art, a recognition of their shortcomings, and novel efforts to operationalize new approaches in ways that are scientifically acceptable" (Calhoun et al., 1998, p. 154). Goldfried and Wolfe (1998) also encourage another healthy and essential tension—that between practicing clinicians and clin-

ical researchers. With mutual respect rather than antagonism, they encourage a liaison between clinician and researcher in the design and implementation of a new generation of outcome research. As in most dynamic systems, tensions, variability, and destabilization can be viewed as natural and healthy processes that provide opportunities for growth and adaptation (Hayes & Strauss, 1998; Mahoney, 1991). From this perspective, the list of empirically supported therapies is constantly a work in progress.

The Role of Common Factors in Change

Common factors refer to elements shared by all or most forms of psychotherapy. This terminology is preferred because it avoids several negative conations of the term *nonspecific* and because it allows for the opportunity to eventually specify the effective but ill-defined elements of therapy (see Castonguay, 1993). In fact, there are several such lists of specified common factors (e.g., Grencavage & Norcross, 1990; Karasu, 1986; Lambert & Bergin, 1994; Weinberger, 1993), the most well known being Jerome Frank's (see Frank & Frank, 1991). Frank argued that all healing procedures, including those in non-Western and primitive societies, contain a number of critical common elements, including (1) an emotionally charged, confiding therapeutic relationship; (2) a designated healing setting; (3) a rationale, which explains the client's symptoms and the treatment procedure; and (4) a treatment procedure that is believed by both therapist and client to be the route to achieving mental health. Frank argued that the effectiveness of these common factors was due to helping clients combat demoralization. Lambert and Bergin provide one of the most comprehensive lists of common factors, which they put into three general categories: support factors, learning factors, and action factors. They review considerable evidence that these common factors account for a significant amount of psychotherapy's efficacy.

The identification of such common factors of therapy again suggests that we look beyond the different forms of techniques and their associated theoretical orientations and to the function of the different interventions or the mechanisms of change that they mobilize. It is very likely that principles of change will be identified by looking for the common factors among the lists. These factors are very important to keep in mind, as they remind us of very important contextual and relationship variables (e.g., the therapist's empathy, the therapeutic alliance, and engendering hope) in the change process, which can easily be ignored by an overemphasis on technique.

Graduate Training and Empirically Supported Treatments

A recent special section of the *Journal of Consulting and Clinical Psychology* was devoted to the EST movement and related issues. Calhoun et al. (1998) provide a preliminary set of guidelines for training in ESTs at the predoctoral, internship, postdoctoral, and continuing education levels. At the level of graduate education, they recommend training in the general skills common to all forms of treatment (e.g., forming a therapeutic relationship), knowledge of psychopathology and the theoretical underpinnings of ESTs, basic-level skills in ESTs, and experience leading to basic competence in at least one EST. These authors, as well as Davison (1998), underscore the importance of teaching the psychological principles that underlie the ESTs.

Calhoun et al. (1998) have argued for appropriate caution in the use of manuals for training in ESTs. Similarly, Davison (1998) has discussed some of the pitfalls associated with training in ESTs, which he has referred to as the juggernaut of EST advocacy. Davison notes, for example, that the use of manualized instruction presents a structure that is rarely if ever found in clinical situations. It may also convey a false sense of security about the scientific status of ESTs. Davison reminds us that training in ESTs "should not lead us to lose sight of the limits of our knowledge and of the need to remain open to new ideas, some of which may well come from domains outside the boundary conditions defined by our ESTs" (p. 165). We are reminded in this regard of one of our (Rick Ingram's) trainees several years ago who was so eager to learn cognitive therapy—because of its efficacy data—that he had to be told to stop "doing" cognitive therapy until he learned how to form an alliance with the client and how to genuinely listen to her problems. Therapeutic alliances are always a core of any EST, but it is easy for students in training to be so seduced by the procedures and methods of an "effective" psychological treatment that they fail to attend to the principles that underlie it. Seen in this context, learning an EST may close off trainees to broader, and more important issues that may fall outside its scope.

It is also important to note that if science is viewed as a dynamic process, what students learn in graduate school is likely to change and evolve. Therefore, it is particularly important to teach students how to think critically and innovatively, how to continue to learn, and how to generate new knowledge. These skills will allow them to adapt to the ever-changing landscape of applied clinical science and, perhaps, to contribute to it. Thus, in addition to learning the methods of ESTs, we believe that students must also be taught to think critically about the limitations of specific ESTs, as well as about the limitations of the movement toward ESTs in general. Many students are in graduate school to learn how to be effective therapists, and we suspect that for many there may be a natural tendency not to want to think about the limits of what they are doing, particularly when they are faced with a flesh-and-blood client who is sitting in front of them for the first time. Nevertheless, critical thinking is an important concern in all aspects of graduate training, and it is particularly important in an area that is rife with the social, economic, and political issues that accompany ESTs. This requires a faculty who can keep the ideas and applications of ESTs in perspective.

Before turning to a discussion of ESTs in graduate training, we raise one last issue that we believe is important in the context of the EST movement. Recommendations for training in ESTs almost always advocate that their methods be taught by the available graduate faculty. A number of assumptions accompany this recommendation. For example, it assumes that somewhere among a given faculty group, there is the expertise in one or more ESTs. This may or may not be the case. A perhaps more implicit assumption is that those who might claim some expertise do in fact have it. It is not clear, however, how this is to be determined. Earlier we commented on the considerable variability within and between therapists; this is no less true among faculty supervisors.

One alternative might be to develop continuing education (CE) programs for therapists, and thus some faculty members, to become certified in an EST. Certainly such workshops and programs exist, but we believe that they may be fraught with problems. As Davison (1998) has noted, "The clearest outcome of the push for CE is, I believe, that a small number of people are making a great deal of money for giving 1- or 2-day workshops . . . although many offerings are science based . . . the substance of others is, I would suggest, driven more by theoretical and professional allegiances than by a critical evaluation of controlled research efforts . . . quality control, in my view, is nonexistent" (p. 166).

Even participants in a high-quality, science-based program may or may not gain sufficient expertise in an EST to train students in a way that approaches how the therapy was validated. We have no easy answers for this problem and thus argue that any suggestions for student training in any EST must confront the issues of who will do the training and how closely it models the procedures used in clinical trials with certain types of clients. The EST researchers have reasonably suggested that flexibility in the training and delivery of EST is needed. We agree, but one can question whether the flexibility needed to adapt ESTs to diverse clinical situations invalidates the procedures of an EST as they were tested. The question again is one of external validity, this time in terms of how an EST is taught by faculty and learned by students.

The issue of the ability of instructors to faithfully teach ESTs is strongly, but not exclusively, linked to the types of clients student trainees are taught to treat. There are at least two approaches to this problem. One is to teach students through specialty clinics that treat the types of clients for whom an EST has been shown to be effective. Although these clinics may have a higher degree of faithfulness to an EST as it was developed and validated, they also run the risk of seeing very different types of clients than those who will be seen in the actual clinical settings by most of the graduates of these training programs. On the other hand, more general training clinics that try to treat the problems of most of the clients who walk through the training clinic door will provide a greater degree of flexibility in the application of ESTs. The problem again, however, is that such flexibility brings training further away from the ESTs as they were validated. Again, the problem is external validity. With these issues in mind, we now turn to a discussion of some possible strategies for training in ESTs.

Coursework in ESTs

Before being exposed to the principles that underlie ESTs, students need a basic foundation in empirically grounded theories of human development, personality, and psychopathology. Coursework specifically on ESTs should present the history of the EST movement, why it is important, and the research methodologies used to determine whether treatments are empirically supported. As we previously mentioned, it is essential to examine both the explicit and implicit assumptions that underlie this movement, as well as the limitations of the drive toward ESTs. Research and theory on the common factors of therapy and change processes also provide an essential foundation for learning ESTs, which can be provided in prepracticum or pretherapy courses or as part of the introduction in a course on ESTs.

Books such as Barlow's (1993) *Clinical Handbook of Psychological Disorders* present many of the ESTs for a variety of disorders. Leading scientist-practitioners present the psychopathology research relevant to a particular disorder, the theoretical underpinnings of the treatment approach, and existing outcome data, and they then provide sample session transcripts and discussion throughout the course of therapy. Similar videos are now becoming available for a number of disorders. Several new journals, such as *Cognitive and Behavioral Practice*, *Clinical Psychology: Science and Practice*, and *In-session: Psychotherapy in Practice*, provide excellent training material and readings. These tools provide a structure for learning the techniques of a range of ESTs, and more importantly in our estimation, the basic principles of human change that guide these treatments. In addition, they attempt to model how to integrate theory and research in psychopathology and psychotherapy. Ideally, instructors should also provide strong role models of scientist-practitioners, an ideal we often espouse but less often achieve.

Of course, it is important for students to apply the principles that they learn. This is a very useful exercise because the complexities of the case and the limits of pure-form ESTs can and should be experienced. These limitations help students realize that they must think creatively, given the client in front of them, and that they also must apply general principles by adapting techniques to be congruent with their training experiences, their personality and style, and the variability in the problems presented by their client. In role-playing situations in which the instructor is the client, instructors can introduce various challenges and get a feel for students' delivery and technique, as well as their understanding of the principles of the therapy. These experiential role-playing exercises allow for flexible on-line learning and feedback. Such exercises make particularly apparent how essential a good therapeutic rationale and case conceptualization are. Experiencing the difficulty of translating the psychological jargon embodied in the principles of human change to a layperson is humbling indeed. We spend a significant amount of time teaching students to apply knowledge from psychopathology, psychotherapy, and even basic research to a given case. As in teaching, when they have to explain it concisely and in plain English, they learn and can use the information in a new way. Case conceptualization skills also can be practiced extensively because, as a number of investigators have argued, these skills are fundamental to the application of therapeutic interventions of any sort (Persons & Silberschatz, 1998).

To further facilitate creative and adaptive thinking, examples of problems for which there is not yet an established EST can be brought into the training. For example, students could be presented with a case of body dysmorphic disorder and then together conceptualize the case and generate a treatment plan from their EST knowledge base. Bringing clinical reality into learning can also help students to practice generalizing what they learn from ESTs to the messy world of comorbidity and complex cases. For instance, one former student in an internship in a Veterans Administration inpatient substance abuse unit reported back from the field in despair: "With all of the research that we do, we don't know anything! Everything I learned is useless!" In one week, one of her patients died of a heroin overdose shortly after discharge from a prestigious research hospital, another tried to kill himself after hearing the news, and a former patient was readmitted. This young clinician's questions of how our knowledge base fares in the real world made for thought-provoking discussions on the nature and limits of change, how we conceptualize outcome, and how empirically supported treatments fit into this picture. Again, having students practice applying the principles that they have learned to novel and unfamiliar situations will help them to develop skills to adapt to a changing environment and, it is hoped, to generate new knowledge.

Practicum Training

The practicum site is a place to learn the principles of ESTs firsthand, with clients instead of out of a manual. As Calhoun et al. (1998) suggest, it is important for graduate students to learn the basic foundations of therapy, such as empathy skills and how to develop and maintain a solid therapeutic alliance. We believe that to the extent that the practicum focuses on an EST, students need to continually attend to the principles underlying

the treatment, in addition to the specific therapeutic techniques. They should gain broad exposure to these principles in the classroom and in the hands-on practicum training. As part of the training in the EST principles, students should also learn empirically grounded assessment and measurement of process and outcome. During such training, intensive observation of the process of therapy (e.g., audio- or videotapes or direct observation) is particularly important. Relying solely on students' retrospective self-reports is as unreliable in this setting as it is in research.

As we have noted, this type of training requires faculty supervisors to receive training in the ESTs and to be familiar with the theory, research, and principles that underlie them. Such a system models for students the true blend of science and practice and may help to inspire more to pursue a career that involves research, rather than only practice. We have noted some of the conceptual problems with faculty expertise in ESTs, but there are practical issues as well. For example, a significant problem is that clinical supervision often is not treated by psychology faculty as constituting an entire course, and thus it receives less credit even though it is quite time consuming. As a result, supervision may be farmed out to practitioners in the community, who may have less familiarity with ESTs and may not keep abreast of current literature. In some cases, outside supervisors may rely on methods that have received no scientific support. Thus, the EST movement pulls for more in-house attention to the clinical training of students and faculty who are current on the psychotherapy literature.

SUMMARY AND CONCLUSIONS

In this chapter we have attempted to point out a number of significant issues in the EST movement. In doing so, we have examined the history of the EST movement, as well as some of the assumptions that underlie continuing efforts to develop, categorize, and implement ESTs. We have also addressed issues of accountability, sources of error variance that affect the practice of psychotherapy in clinical settings, and some implications of the EST movement for graduate training. We have also examined some of the ideas that underlie principle-based psychological interventions.

We believe that consideration of these issues is crucial to the desire within clinical psychology to widely promulgate ESTs to the public as effective treatment options. Some may view our perspectives as suggesting that even when they are empirically supported, procedures evaluated in research settings are of little use in actual clinical practice and that we are therefore critical of the idea that psychology can produce therapies that are both sufficiently distinct from one another and effective in the types of settings in which clinicians must work. Nothing could be further from the truth. We believe that much of the outcome data generated from testing various clinical interventions offer exciting possibilities for the professional practice of psychotherapy. Rather, the theme that underlies our discussion is that despite the promise of ESTs, promoting these psychotherapies must nevertheless be approached with a significant degree of caution. As Davison (1998) has noted, although the EST movement has become something of a juggernaut, clinical scientists are nevertheless obliged to approach this movement with the skepticism that must underlie all scientific endeavors.

As we hope is evident from our comments throughout this chapter, our call for caution stems from several sources. Perhaps foremost, and worth reemphasizing, is our argument that clinical psychological science is currently a conceptual science rather than a prescriptive science. Hence, the interventions that we develop and empirically validate in research must always be applied in clinical settings with the goal of implementing the principles of change that constitute the conceptual foundations of these interventions. Ultimately, it is the application of such principles in the context of a number of other sources of variance (therapist variables, client variables, etc.) that will determine whether they are effective in any given case. Techniques and procedures can aid in implementing these principles but only insofar as they represent a vehicle for operationalizing and thus implementing psychological concepts.

In a corresponding fashion, we would view it as a significant step forward if empirical validation efforts shifted from evaluating techniques to evaluating principles or, at a minimum, paid at least as much attention to the principles that underlie the techniques as to the techniques themselves. Conversely, approaches to the evaluation and practice of psychotherapy that mimic the medical model of a prescriptive science will, we believe, ultimately ill serve both psychology and the public.

The history of the EST movement is brief but extremely significant. One of the things that this history shows us is that we no longer need to answer the question of whether psychotherapy works—it does. We believe that one of the most important tasks that faces us now is to ensure that what we evaluate in our clinical research and practice does so in a way that respects the psychology that forms the foundations of our science.

REFERENCES

Arkowitz, H., & Hannah, M. T. (1989). Cognitive, behavioral, and psychodynamic therapies: Converging or diverging pathways to change. In A. Freeman, K. M. Simon, L. E. Beutler, & H. Arkowitz (Eds.), *Comprehensive handbook of cognitive therapy* (pp. 143–167). New York: Plenum.

Barlow, D. H. (1993). *Clinical handbook of psychological disorders: A step-by-step treatment manual* (2nd ed.). New York: Guilford.

Barlow, D. H. (1996). The effectiveness of psychotherapy: Science and policy. *Clinical Psychology: Science and Practice, 3,* 236–240.

Barlow, D. H., & Lehman, C. L. (1996). Advances in the psychosocial treatment of anxiety disorders: Implications for national health care. *Archives of General Psychiatry, 53,* 727–735.

Beck, A. T., Rush, A. J., Shaw, B. F., & Emery, G. (1979). *Cognitive therapy of depression.* New York: Guilford.

Beck, J. S. (1995). *Cognitive therapy: Basics and beyond.* New York: Guilford.

Beevers, C. G., Wenzlaff, R. M., Hayes, A. M., & Scott, W. D. (in press). Depression and the ironic effects of thought suppression: Therapeutic strategies for improving mental control. *Clinical Psychology: Science and Practice.*

Calhoun, K. S., Moras, K., Pilkonis, P. A., & Rehm, L. P. (1998). Empirically supported treatments: Implications for training. *Journal of Consulting and Clinical Psychology, 66,* 151–162.

Castonguay, L. G. (1993). "Common factors" and "nonspecific variables": Clarification of the two concepts and recommendations for research. *Journal of Psychotherapy Integration, 3,* 267–286.

Chambless, D. L. (1996). In defense of dissemination of empirically supported psychological interventions. *Clinical Psychology: Science and Practice, 3,* 230–235.

Chambless, D. L., Baker, M. J., Baucom, D. H., Beutler, L. E., Calhoun, K. S., Crits-Christoph, P., Daiuto, A., DeRubeis, R., Detweiler, J., Haaga, D. A. F., Johnson, S., McCurry, S., Mueser, K. T., Pope, K. S., Sanderson, W. C., Shoham, V., Stickle, T., Williams, D. A., & Woody, S. R. (1998). Update on empirically validated therapies: II. *The Clinical Psychologist, 51*, 3–16.

Chambless, D. L., & Hollon, S. D. (1998). Defining empirically supported therapies. *Journal of Consulting and Clinical Psychology, 66*, 7–18.

Chambless, D. L., Sanderson, W. C., Shoham, V., Bennett Johnson, S., Pope, K. S., Crits-Christoph, P., Baker, M., Johnson, B., Woody, S. R., Sue, S., Beutler, L., Williams, D. A., & McCurry, S. (1996). An update on empirically validated therapies. *Clinical Psychologist, 49*, 5–18.

Consumer Reports. (1995, November). Mental health: Does therapy help?, pp. 734–739.

Costello, C. G. (1992). Conceptual problems in current research in cognitive vulnerability to psychopathology. *Cognitive Therapy and Research, 16*, 379–390.

Costello, C. G. (1993). From symptoms of depression to syndromes of depression. In C. G. Costello (Ed.), *Symptoms of depression* (pp. 291–300). New York: Wiley.

Davison, G. C. (1998). Being bolder with the Boulder model: The challenge of education and training in empirically supported treatments. *Journal of Consulting and Clinical Psychology, 66*, 163–167.

Eysenck, H. J. (1952). The effects of psychotherapy: An evaluation. *Journal of Consulting Psychology, 16*, 319–324.

Eysenck, H. J. (1961). The effects of psychotherapy. In H. J. Eysenck (Ed.), *Handbook of abnormal psychology* (pp. 697–725). New York: Basic Books.

Foa, E. B. (1997). Psychological processes related to recovery from a trauma and an effective treatment for PTSD. In R. Yehuda, & A. C. McFarlane (Eds.), *Psychobiology of posttraumatic stress disorder* (pp. 410–424). Annuls of the New York Academy of Sciences. New York: New York Academy of Sciences.

Foa, E. B., & Hearst-Ikeda, D. (1996). Emotional dissociation in response to trauma: An information processing approach. In L. K. Michelson & W. J. Ray (Eds.), *Handbook of dissociation: Theoretical, empirical, and clinical perspectives* (pp. 207–222). New York: Plenum.

Foa, E. B., & Kozak, M. J. (1986). Emotional processing of fear: Exposure to corrective information. *Psychological Bulletin, 99*, 20–35.

Fox, R. E. (1996). Charlatanism, scientism, and psychology's social contract. *American Psychologist, 51*, 777–784.

Frank, J. D., & Frank, J. B. (1991). *Persuasion and healing: A comparative study of psychotherapy* (3rd ed.). Baltimore: Johns Hopkins University Press.

Garfield, S. L. (1996). Some problems associated with "validated" forms of psychotherapy. *Clinical Psychology, Science and Practice, 3*, 218–229.

Garfield, S. L. (1998). Some comments of empirically supported treatments. *Journal of Consulting and Clinical Psychology, 66*, 121–125.

Goldfried, M. R. (1991). Transtheoretical ingredients in therapeutic change. In R. C. Curtis & G. Striker (Eds.), *How people change: Inside and outside of therapy* (pp. 29–37). New York: Plenum.

Goldfried, M. R., & Padawer, W. (1982). Current status and future directions in psychotherapy. In M. R. Goldfried (Ed.), *Converging themes in psychotherapy: Trends in psychodynamic, humanistic, and behavioral practice* (pp. 3–49). New York: Springer.

Goldfried, M. R., & Wolfe, B. E. (1998). Toward a more clinically valid approach to therapy research. *Journal of Consulting and Clinical Psychology, 66*, 143–150.

Grencavage, L. M., & Norcross, J. C. (1990). What are the commonalities among the therapeutic common factors? *Professional Psychology: Research and Practice, 21*, 372–378.

Hayes, A. M., & Harris, M. S. (in press). The development of an integrative treatment for depression. In S. Johnson, A. M. Hayes, N. Schneiderman, P. McCabe, & T. Fields (Eds.), *Fifteenth Annual Stress and Coping Conference: Depression.* New York: Guilford.

Hayes, A. M., & Strauss, J. (1998). Dynamic systems theory as a paradigm for the study of change in psychotherapy: An application to cognitive therapy for depression. *Journal of Consulting and Clinical Psychology, 66*(6), 939–947.

Hayes, S. C., Wilson, K. G., Gifford, E. V., Follette, V. M., & Strosahl, K. (1996). Experiential avoidance and behavioral disorders: A functional dimensional approach to diagnosis and treatment. *Journal of Consulting and Clinical Psychology, 64*, 1152–1168.

Hollon, S. D., Evans, M .D., & DeRubeis, R. J. (1990). Cognitive mediation of relapse prevention following treatment for depression: Implications of differential risk. In R. E. Ingram (Ed.), *Contemporary psychological approaches to depression: Theory, research, and practice* (pp. 117–136). New York: Plenum.

Ingram, R. E. (1984). Toward an information processing analysis of depression. *Cognitive Therapy and Research, 8*, 443–477.

Ingram, R. E., & Hamilton, N. A. (1999). Evaluating precision in the social psychological assessment of depression: Methodological considerations, issues, and recommendations. *Journal of Social and Clinical Psychology, 18*, 160–180.

Ingram, R. E., & Hollon, S. D. (1986). Cognitive therapy of depression from an information processing perspective. In R. E. Ingram (Ed.), *Information processing approaches to clinical psychology* (pp. 259–281). Orlando, FL: Academic Press.

Ingram, R. E., Miranda, J., & Segal, Z. V. (1998). *Cognitive vulnerability to depression.* New York: Guilford.

Ingram, R. E., & Scott, W. (1990). Foundations of

cognitive-behavioral approaches to treatment. In A. S. Bellack, M. Hersen, & A. E. Kazdin (Eds.), *International handbook of behavior modification and therapy* (2nd ed., pp. 53–65). New York: Plenum.

Jacobson, N. S., & Truax, P. (1991). Clinical significance: A statistical approach to defining meaningful change in psychotherapy research. *Journal of Consulting and Clinical Psychology, 59,* 12–19.

Karasu, T. B. (1986). The specificity versus nonspecificity dilemma: Toward identifying therapeutic change agents. *American Journal of Psychiatry, 143,* 687–695.

Kazdin, A. E. (Ed). (1998). *Methodological issues and strategies in clinical research* (2nd ed.). Washington, DC: American Psychological Association.

Kendall, P. C. (1998). Empirically supported psychological therapies. *Journal of Consulting and Clinical Psychology, 66,* 3–6.

Kendall, P. C., & Brady, E. U. (1995). Comorbidity in the anxiety disorders of childhood: Implications for validity and clinical significance. In K. D. Craig & K. S. Dobson (Eds.), *Anxiety and depression in adults and children* (pp. 3–35). Thousand Oaks, CA: Sage.

Kendall, P. C., & Butcher, J. (1983). *Research methods in clinical psychology.* New York: Wiley.

Kendall, P. C., & Hollon, S. D. (1979). *Cognitive-behavioral interventions: Theory, research, and procedures.* New York: Academic Press.

Kendall, P. C., & Hollon, S. D. (1981). *Assessment strategies for cognitive-behavioral interventions.* New York: Academic Press.

Klerman, G. L., Weissman, M., Rounsaville, B., & Chevron, E. (1984). *Interpersonal psychotherapy of depression.* New York: Basic Books.

Lambert, M. J., & Bergin, A. E. (1994). The effectiveness of psychotherapy. In A. Bergin & S. L. Garfield (Eds.), *Handbook of psychotherapy and behavior change* (4th ed., pp. 143–189). New York: Wiley.

Linehan, M. M. (1993). *Cognitive-behavioral treatment of borderline personality disorder.* New York: Guilford Press.

Litrell, J. (1998). Is the reexperience of painful emotion therapeutic? *Clinical Psychology Review, 18,* 71–102.

Mahoney, M. J. (1991). *Human change processes: The scientific foundations of psychotherapy.* New York: Basic Books.

Maling, M. S., Gurtman, M. B., & Howard, K. I. (1995). The response of interpersonal problems to varying doses of psychotherapy. *Psychotherapy Research, 5,* 63–75.

Meehl, P. (1997). Credentialed persons, credentialed knowledge. *Clinical Psychology: Science and Practice, 3,* 91–98.

Pennebaker, J. W. (1997a). *Opening up: The healing power of expressed emotions* (rev. ed.). New York: Guilford.

Pennebaker, J. W. (1997b). Writing about emotional experience as a therapeutic process. *Psychological Science, 8,* 162–166.

Persons, J. B. (1986). The advantages of studying psychological phenomena rather than psychiatric diagnoses. *American Psychologist, 41,* 1252–1260.

Persons, J. B., & Silberschatz, G. (1998). Are results of randomized controlled trials useful to psychotherapists? *Journal of Consulting and Clinical Psychology, 66,* 126–135.

Purdon, C. (in press). Thought suppression and psychopathology. *Behaviour Research and Therapy.*

Routh, J., & DeRubeis, R. J. (Eds.). (1998). *The science of clinical psychology: Accomplishments and future directions.* Washington, DC: American Psychological Association.

Saccuzo, D. P. (1997). Liability for failure to supervise adequately mental health assistants, unlicensed practitioners, and students. *California Western Law Review, 34,* 115–150.

Salkovskis, P. M., & Clark, D. M. (1993). Panic disorder and hypochondriasis. *Advances in Behavioral Research and Therapy, 15,* 23–48.

Sanderson, W. C., Wetzler, C., Beck, A. T., & Betz, F. (1992). Prevalence of personality disorders in patients with major depression and dysthymia. *Psychiatry Research, 42,* 93–99.

Seligman, M. E. P. (1995). The effectiveness of psychotherapy: The *Consumer Reports* study. *American Psychologist, 50,* 965–974.

Smith, M. L., Glass, G. V., & Miller, T. I. (1980). *The benefits of psychotherapy.* Baltimore: Johns Hopkins University Press.

Smith, S. (1997). From law and bananas to real law: A celebration of scholarship in mental health law. *California Western law Review, 34,* 1–14.

Spitzer, R. L., & Endicott, J. (1978). Medical and mental disorder: Proposed definition and criteria. In R. L. Spitzer & D. F. Klein (Eds.), *Critical issues in psychiatric diagnosis* (pp. 32–47). New York: Raven Press.

Stiles, W. B., & Shapiro, D. A. (1994). Disabuse of the drug metaphor: Psychotherapy process-outcome correlations. *Journal of Consulting and Clinical Psychology, 62,* 942–948.

Stricker G., & Trierweiler, S. J. (1995). The local clinical scientist: A bridge between science and practice. *American Psychologist, 50,* 995–1002.

Strupp, H. H., Horowitz, L. M., & Lambert, M. J. (Eds.). (1997). *Measuring patient changes in mood, anxiety, and personality disorders: Toward a core battery.* Washington, DC: American Psychological Association.

Task Force on Promotion and Dissemination of Psychological Procedures. (1995). Training in and dissemination of empirically-validated psychological treatments: Report and recommendations. *Clinical Psychologist, 48,* 3–23.

Teasdale, J. D., & Barnard, P. J. (1993). Psychological

treatment for depression—The ICS [Interacting Cognitive Subsystems] perspective. In J. D. Teasdale and P. J. Barnard (Eds.), *Affect, cognition, and change* (pp. 225–245). Hove, Eng.: Erlbaum.

Tingey, R. C., Lambert, M. J., Burlingame, G. M., & Hansen, N. B. (1996). Assessing clinical significance: Proposed extensions to method. *Psychotherapy Research, 6,* 109–123.

VandenBos, G. R. (1996). Outcome assessment of psychotherapy. *American Psychologist, 51,* 1005–1006.

Weinberger, J. (1993). Common factors in psychotherapy. In J. Gold & G. Stricker (Eds.), *Handbook of psychotherapy integration* (pp. 43–56). New York: Plenum.

Young, J. E. (1994). *Cognitive therapy for personality disorders* (pp. 19–49). Sarasota, FL: Professional Resource Press.

Young, J. E., Beck, A. T., & Weinberger, A. (1993). Depression. In D. H. Barlow (Ed.). *Clinical handbook of psychological disorders: A step-by-step treatment manual* (2nd ed., pp. 240–277). New York: Guilford.

PART III

COMPONENTS OF PSYCHOTHERAPEUTIC CHANGE

•

CHAPTER 4

THERAPIST VARIABLES

EDWARD TEYBER AND FAITH McCLURE
California State University, San Bernardino

CONCEPTUAL OVERVIEW AND CHAPTER ORGANIZATION

Experienced and expressed differently by each individual, psychological difficulties vary in complexity from discrete behavioral symptoms to clinical syndromes to more multifaceted comorbid disorders. Striving to alleviate the pain of psychological disorders, beginning and experienced therapists alike grapple with the personal and professional challenges posed by clients' diverse experiences, needs, and clinical presentations. One of the ways in which individual therapists seek to help their clients is by understanding the therapeutic process and the role that it plays in effecting change. With parallel goals, researchers have employed an empirical approach to discern the personal qualities of therapists and what they do that helps clients to change. A large but often inconsistent literature on the role of the therapist in the change process has grown since the 1950s as a result of recognizing the critical importance of therapist characteristics in determining a treatment process and outcome (Garfield, 1997). Although much has been learned in these decades of research, it is disappointing to note that eminent leaders who originally pioneered research on the effectiveness of psychotherapy have concluded that "the amount of variance we have accounted for in the change process or in therapeutic outcomes is rather paltry compared with what is left unexplained" (Bergin, 1997, p. 87). As is noted later in this chapter, this lack is probably due to the historical research emphasis on discrete therapist variables and on comparing treatment types and orientations, with insufficient attention to relational factors and therapist variability *within* any discrete grouping such as ethnicity and theoretical orientation.

This chapter is divided into three major sections. The first summarizes existing research findings on *discrete* therapist variables, following the traditional emphasis of focusing on therapist variables as discrete or isolated dimensions that affect treatment outcome. In the second section, therapist variables are seen as embedded in an interpersonal or *relational context*. This section highlights the mutual impact of therapists and clients. For example, the variability in the effectiveness of individual therapists is most evident when they are faced with clients' negativity such as anger, criticism, and disapproval. Because these features are routinely observed in the most commonly occurring disorders (e.g., mood, anxiety, and personality disorders), identifying therapists' characteristics and training models that are most effective with these characteristics becomes especially important. Thus, this more complex approach helps us understand and conceptualize the contributions of the therapist in more meaningful ways and offers promising directions for clinical training and future research.

The third section, on *therapist variability*, highlights the contributions and shortcomings of current psychotherapy research and training paradigms (e.g., manualized treatment approaches, empirically validated treatments, and randomized clinical trials). This section focuses on how these often fail to take into account the individual therapist's contributions to treatment effectiveness. Assessing variability in the effectiveness of individual therapists within treatment modalities is a sensitive issue that only recently has begun to receive attention.

Throughout this chapter, we emphasize that future research and training must give greater attention to individual differences in therapists' effectiveness and to the relational context in which therapists and clients influence each other. Three orienting constructs are utilized throughout this chapter. The first, client response specificity, refers to the therapist's ability to conceptualize the differing therapeutic experiences that therapists need to provide for each varying client. The second, subjective worldview, refers to the therapist's ability to be accurately empathic with diverse clients. This concept highlights therapists' ability to cognitively de-center and enter accurately and respectfully the client's internal working models or cognitive schemas. The third, reparative relational experiences, challenges the therapist's interpersonal range and ability to respond *flexibly* to clients and provide in vivo or experiential relearning in the current interaction with the therapist.

Before turning to the first section, however, we consider Bergin's (1997) sober evaluation that the primary facilitators of therapeutic change remain largely unexplained. To help improve our current state of knowledge, we also consider factors that may have limited the fruitfulness of past research. Two important concepts serve as overarching guidelines for assessing current theoretical paradigms, research strategies, and findings. These two guidelines are (1) the uniformity myth, suggesting that therapists within a given theoretical perspective do not differ in their level of skill or effectiveness with clients, and (2) a relational context that emphasizes that therapists and clients influence and shape reciprocal responses to each other so fundamentally that therapist and client variables cannot be considered usefully in isolation. These two themes provide a metaperspective, or lens, for understanding this challenging research literature and Bergin's sober evaluation. They also suggest directions for future research and training on treatment effectiveness.

Although approximately 30 years have passed since Kiesler (1966, 1971) tried to orient researchers to the uniformity myth in psychotherapy outcome research, the major focus in the field has continued to compare the effectiveness of various theoretical and technical approaches (Lambert, 1989; Luborsky et al., 1986; Robinson, Berman, & Neimeyer, 1990). For example, the preeminent research trends at the turn of this century include randomized clinical trial studies, manualized treatments, and the search for empirically validated treatments (see Ingram, Hayes, and Scott, Chapter 3). Much has been gained from these frameworks—including greater treatment specificity and support for the efficacy of

psychotherapy in general. However, all of these designs regard therapists homogeneously, and the *variability* in the personal qualities of therapists that affect their interventions skills is (theoretically) controlled for or partialed out and seemingly eliminated. As a result, too little attention has been given to the wide variability that exists in the skills and personal qualities of the therapists working within each theoretical orientation, as well as the impact of such variability on treatment outcome.

In addition to therapist variability, the relational context must be incorporated more significantly into psychotherapy research and training. Social and developmental psychologists were among the first to highlight the notion that behavior does not occur in isolation. Rather, parents and children, as well as therapists and clients, share reciprocal influences. In a tour de force research review, Bell (1968) changed the game in child development research by illuminating how children's behavior and characteristics profoundly influenced parental responses; this, in turn, altered children's responses to the parent, and so forth. In this article, Bell virtually ended decades of unidirectional research on how parents influenced children. Others, such as Stolorow, also have noted the "isolated mind" fallacy (Stolorow & Atwood, 1992). Because these interactional processes are more challenging to measure, however, bidirectional or reciprocal effects often have not been included in psychotherapy research (Jones, Cumming, & Horowitz, 1988). Instead, unidirectional and main effect hypotheses have continued to dominate research on therapist variables as related to treatment outcome. Although these relational constructs already had been highlighted by clinicians and researchers decades ago (e.g., Kell & Mueller, 1966; Kiesler, 1966; Leary, 1957), they failed to capture the attention of the major treatment outcome researchers. Examples include the focus on discrete therapist variables such as race (e.g., Yeh, Eastman, & Cheung, 1994), gender (e.g., Flaskerud & Liu, 1991), experience (e.g., Clementel-Jones, Malan, & Trauer, 1990), and so forth, which will be critiqued subsequently.

Although the focus of much research has been on discrete therapist variables, a meaningful body of literature has been developed to examine therapist variables in a relational or interpersonal context. Long ago, for example, Kell and Mueller (1966) elucidated the "reciprocal impact" that clients and therapists exert on each other and how this shapes the content and meaning of each successive verbal interchange. In more contemporary terms, Beutler (1997) argues that the contributions of therapists and clients "are so intrinsically bound together that revealing the contributions of one member of the dyad should invoke a need to consider the compatibility and moderating effects of the other member on measures of clinical outcome" (p. 44). We resonate with this interpersonal perspective and believe that far more meaning is derived when we look at the therapist-in-relationship as opposed to examining therapist variables in isolation or as discrete variables. Thus, the second lens we employ throughout this chapter is the interpersonal or relational context in which therapist and client interact. We examine research studies that consider how therapists and clients influence each other and together shape the meaning of what occurs between them.

DISCRETE THERAPIST VARIABLES

In a recent review of the literature on therapist variables in treatment outcome, Beutler, Machado, and Neufeldt (1994) noted that some therapists consistently produce positive outcomes and others consistently produce negative outcomes. Distilling those therapist qualities that enhance treatment effectiveness has been a major focus of the field. Although the more recent research has focused on the relational or dyadic aspects of therapy, in particular the working alliance (e.g., Raue & Goldfried, 1994), some attention continues to be given to discrete therapist variables such as age, experience and training, ethnicity, and gender. In this section, the literature on these discrete therapist variables as they relate to treatment outcome is reviewed.

Ethnicity

The impact of the therapist's ethnic background and the therapist-client ethnic match on client satisfaction, dropout rate, change in functioning level, and attitudes toward therapists has been investigated in several studies (e.g., Atkinson & Matsushita, 1991; Flaskerud & Liu, 1991; Jones, 1978, 1982; Sue, Fujino, Hu, Tadeuchi, & Zane, 1991; Terrell & Terrell, 1984; Yeh, Eastman, & Cheung, 1994; Yeh, Takeuchi, & Sue, 1994). The data suggest that ethnic match predicts dropout rates (Flaskerud & Liu, 1991; Sue et al., 1991; Yeh, Eastman, & Cheung, 1997; Yeh, Takeuchi,

& Sue, 1994). For example, Sue et al. (1991), in a large community study that included African-, Asian-, and Mexican-American clients, found that when therapists and clients were matched ethnically, there were significantly decreased attrition rates for all three groups. This particular effect seems to be the most robust finding in the race and ethnicity literature as related to treatment outcome and is further documented in literature reviews (Atkinson, 1985; Atkinson & Schein, 1986).

The impact of therapist-client ethnic match is especially evident when dropout rates after one session are assessed. It is likely that in the initial part of therapy, much of the therapist's credibility is based on ascribed characteristics like ethnicity. That is, clients are likely to ascribe greater empathy to therapists who have similar external characteristics such as ethnic background. Sue and Zane (1987) have written eloquently about the importance of therapists' credibility in therapy. *Achieved credibility* refers to the therapist's skill, such as the therapist's sensitivity to the client's particular needs based on culture and other factors. In contrast to competence or what the therapist actually does, *ascribed credibility* refers to initial trust or positive expectations of understanding and help based on therapist-client similarity in ethnicity, religion, gender, and so forth. Ascribed credibility or matching may be more important for client attrition early in treatment, whereas achieved credibility may have more impact on eventual treatment outcome (McClure & Teyber, 1996).

Unfortunately, the research evaluating other outcome criteria based on therapist-client ethnic match is inconclusive (Hill & Corbett, 1993). For example, some studies report that discharge functioning scores based on the Global Assessment Scale (GAS), which is similar to the GAF scale on the DSM-IV, are higher for clients who were ethnically matched with their therapists (Yeh, Eastman, & Cheung, 1994), whereas others fail to find significant admission to discharge changes based on client-therapist ethnic match (Flaskerud & Liu, 1991). Furthermore, some studies (Sue et al., 1991) report that ethnic matches do affect GAS ratings for some ethnic groups (e.g., Hispanics), but not for others (e.g., African Americans).

Overall, several reviews of this literature suggest that the effect of client-therapist match is equivocal, sometimes with positive effects noted and frequently with none (Atkinson, 1983, 1985;

Atkinson & Schein, 1986; Sexton & Whiston, 1991, 1994). Jones (1982), for example, did a retrospective study of white and African-American clients and therapists and concluded that neither therapist ethnicity nor therapist-client match significantly affected treatment outcome.

One major problem with this literature is that it does not specifically evaluate whether common ethnic membership does indeed imply similar cultural values, attitudes, and perceptions or greater empathy for clients' values, attitudes, and perceptions. Indeed, ethnic membership may be moderated by socioeconomic status and other factors that may affect the therapist's ability to enter the client's subjective worldview, convey empathy, and establish a strong working alliance. It is likely that the ethnic or cultural *sensitivity* of the therapist (McClure & Teyber, 1996) is the more salient characteristic that needs to be more systematically evaluated in future studies on ethnicity and treatment effectiveness (Lefley, 1985; Sue, 1990; Wade & Bernstein, 1991).

Gender

Gender socialization processes affect the ways in which men and women structure and view their worlds, and gender is a key feature of how society is organized (Cook, 1990; Eagly, 1994; Geis, 1993). Thus, gender becomes an important potential moderator of therapists' preferred therapy style (e.g., directive/nondirective, problem solving/exploratory, and cognitive/emotive) and of clients' responses. The effect of gender, male/female power differences, and gender-driven interventions has stimulated much interest (Cook & Kipnis, 1986). There has been the concern that the field of psychotherapy may have had or still has a male-oriented bias that would negatively affect or disempower female clients. Other therapists, however, have noted that transference and countertransference issues that may negatively influence the treatment outcome also occur when female therapists treat female clients (Eastwood, Spielvogel, & Wile, 1990). Unfortunately, the lack of well-controlled studies on this topic limits the possible conclusions. Most of the studies have been naturalistic in nature and have yielded inconsistent findings. Nelson (1993), in a review of the literature on gender differences in the treatment process and outcome, concluded that whereas some studies suggest that female clients may do better with female therapists, most studies were inconclusive. The varied findings on gender effects were summarized by Bowman

(1993) as providing some, but inconclusive, support for each of the following three competing perspectives: (1) that female therapists are more effective than male therapists with clients of both genders; (2) that client-therapist gender matching yields the most therapeutic benefit; and (3) that therapist gender is not a good predictor of treatment outcome.

Other research also suggests that gender may be a poor predictor of treatment outcome. For example, in a study with 1746 Asian clients being served in several mental health facilities, Flaskerud and Liu (1991) found no consistent impact of gender match on the number of sessions attended, dropout rate, or GAS scores. Similarly, studies evaluating changes in short-term counseling and counseling with psychiatric outpatients found no outcome differences based on gender (Berry & Sipps, 1991; Hunt, Carr, Dagadakis, & Walker, 1995; Wiggins & Giles, 1984).

In contrast to the above findings, Jones, Krupnick, and Kerig (1987), in a quasi-experimental study with female clients and male and female therapists, reported greater symptomatic improvement in clients who saw female therapists. Unlike the other studies, this one used a manualized brief therapy approach, included therapists who had equivalent training and experience, and randomly assigned the clients to the therapists. This process reduced the impact of confounding variables such as differences in therapists' training, experience, and skill levels and in client severity. Experience has been reported in other studies to be a moderator of gender effects. For example, Fullerton, Yates, and Goodrich (1990) reported that hospitalized adolescents showed the greatest improvement when they saw same-gender therapists who had less than 10 years of experience or opposite-gender therapists who had 10 or more years of experience. The authors suggested that clients' identification with therapists of similar gender and age can be helpful. Furthermore, therapists' ability to deal with sexual countertransference effectively when treating opposite-gender clients is also important. It is likely that the problems the clients are addressing, and perhaps their phase in the life cycle, moderates the impact of the therapists' gender.

Age

The therapists' age and similarity in therapist-client age have both been evaluated as possible moderators of treatment effectiveness. Several reviews of this literature suggest that neither of these factors is related significantly to treatment outcome or effectiveness (Atkinson & Schein, 1986; Beutler, Crago, & Arizmendi, 1986; Sexton & Whiston, 1994). For example, Greenspan and Kulish (1985) found no significant relationship between therapist-client age similarity and client satisfaction or the strength of the therapeutic relationship.

In contrast, other studies suggest that there is a moderately positive relationship between therapist-client age similarity and treatment outcome (Dembo, Ikle, & Ciarlo, 1983; Luborsky et al., 1980; Morgan, Luborsky, Crits-Christoph, Curtis, & Solomon, 1982). For example, Dembo et al. found that young adult clients were less distressed and less socially isolated after treatment when they had seen therapists of similar age than those who had seen therapists 10 or more years younger or older. Unfortunately, it is not clear whether the age similarity might reflect other therapist-client cohort factors such as similarity of developmental experiences and greater understanding of generational values, each of which may contribute to increased empathy. In addition, age similarity might increase clients' perceptions of therapists' credibility, the clients attributing greater understanding of their issues to someone of similar age. Because clients' perceptions of the therapist affect engagement and dropout rate (Garfield, 1994), this might be the more salient factor in outcome.

Other studies suggest that older therapists are judged as more empathic and competent (Chevron, Rounsavillke, Rothblum, & Weissman, 1983). This, too, may be an aspect of ascribed credibility (see Sue & Zane, 1987), wherein age is seen as contributing to greater knowledge, experience, and skill. Indeed, one of the major confounds in using age as a discrete, independent variable is that it is often related to therapists' training and experience, which also are purported to influence outcome (Beutler et al., 1994).

Although some researchers suggest that outcomes are worse when clients see therapists who are 10 or more years younger (e.g., Beck, 1988), other studies report that these efffects are not observed when therapists are using manualized approaches (Beutler et al., 1987; Thompson, Gallagher, & Breckenridge, 1987). It may be that manualized approaches mute the impact of prior experience, training, values, and other factors that may vary with age. As with the other discrete variables reviewed above, a useful direction for future research would be to evaluate the extent to which therapists' age affects clients' perceptions of therapists' credibility, in particular their expectations of empathy, understanding, or the ability to establish a strong working alliance. Doing so may help explain these seemingly disparate findings: (1) therapist-client age similarity is moderately related positively; (2) older therapists are more effective; and (3) the relationship between therapists' and clients' ages with regard to treatment effectiveness is insignificant.

Training and Experience

There has been considerable interest in whether and how professional training, type of degree (e.g., M.S., M.S.W., Ph.D., M.D.) and experience (e.g., number of years of clinical practice and types of clients seen) affect the treatment outcomes. Problematically, training and experience are often confounded and are complicated further by therapists' specific training experiences (e.g., supervision experiences and manualized training).

The effects of various training experiences of therapists have been evaluated. Manualized training, which has gained popularity in recent decades, has been found to improve skills and increase positive outcomes on selected clinical dimensions (Henry, Schacht, Strupp, Butler, & Binder, 1993; Henry, Strupp, Butler, Schacht, & Binder, 1993). As noted by the last study, however, one unexpected change in therapists' use of manualized treatment approaches is an *increase* in certain negative exchanges between the therapist and the client (i.e., mutually expressed frustration, anger, and criticism), prompting them to conclude that "although the treatment was delivered, the *therapy* (at least as envisioned) did not always occur" (p. 438). These important findings suggest that as therapists feel more technically confident or strictly bound to employ a prescribed or uniform approach, they may be less attentive to "nonspecific" therapist skills, which can lead to poorer therapist-client working alliances and poorer outcomes on certain client dimensions, such as satisfaction (e.g., Stolk & Perlesz, 1990). It is possible that the clients may find interventions "too technical"; that is, they address the symptoms but fail to fully see "the person," who may at times need a response not specified in the manual (e.g., affirmation or humor). Future research must attend to the complexities of clinical reality; eschew attempts to find single, direct associations of process with outcome; and examine *simultaneously* the more complex interactions of specific intervention techniques and approaches and nonspecific relational factors like working alliances.

Training in relational skills (e.g., Lambert & Arnold, 1987; Matarazzo & Patterson, 1986), as well as the length and type of training (e.g., professional vs. paraprofessional), has been reported to enhance treatment outcomes (see Baker & Daniels, 1989; Lyons & Woods, 1991). In many studies, however, training and experience are not clearly distinguished. The importance of evaluating each component becomes evident when both are the focus in the same study. For example, in a study evaluating the impact of training (none, self-instructional, and intensive) on outcome, Burlingame, Fuhriman, Paul, and Ogles (1989) reported that experienced therapists produced better outcomes than did less experienced therapists. Furthermore, intensively trained therapists, regardless of experience levels, produced superior outcomes. Other studies suggest, however, that training experience, level, and type of professional degree have no appreciable effect on treatment outcome (Clementel-Jones et al., 1990; Crits-Christoph et al., 1991; Wierbicki & Pekarik, 1993). To further complicate this picture, some studies report that therapists' training interacts with the clients' age (i.e., trained professionals are effective with all ages, whereas graduate students and paraprofessionals are effective primarily with young clients) and type of problem (i.e., the superiority of trained professionals is evident only with overcontrolled rather than undercontrolled problems) (Weisz, Weiss, Alicke, & Klotz, 1987).

Some researchers report little effect from therapists' experience levels (Crits-Christoph et al., 1991; Smith & Glass, 1977), others an inverse relationship (Shapiro & Shapiro, 1982), and still others moderately positive effects (Dush, Hirt, & Schroeder, 1983; Sanchez-Craig, Spivak, & Davila, 1991). In their review, Stein and Lambert (1995) concluded that training and experience produce moderately positive effects on a variety of measures such as clients' satisfaction, change in symptom severity, and dropout rates. They also note that less trained and less experienced therapists have proportionally less success than more trained and more experienced therapists; when the former are successful, it is for a limited range of clients.

Unfortunately, this research on the impact of training and experience is limited by the lack of consistent definitions, confounding therapists' training and experience with age and theoretical orientation (which would be influenced by which theories were more popular at the time of training), the place of training (because desirable trainee qualities are likely to vary in the selection process for different programs), and the interaction among training, experience, and type of presenting problems and issues. Furthermore, training and experience may affect therapists' confidence levels, which reduce their defensiveness, facilitate their ability to enter the clients' subjective worldview, and encourage them to be flexible in their interventions. Clearly, further research on therapists' training and experience on self-perception, self-confidence, and therapeutic flexibility would be useful. In particular, the impact of this training on clients' perceptions of therapists' credibility would enhance our understanding of how these factors may influence treatment effectiveness.

RELATIONAL THERAPIST VARIABLES

To better understand the therapists' contribution to the change process, we must shift our focus from an emphasis on their discrete characteristics to how they influence the therapeutic relationship, as well as to the interaction between the therapist and client. In their comprehensive research review, Sexton and Whiston (1994) conclude that the counseling relationship consistently contributes more to treatment success than techniques, procedures, clients' characteristics, and especially counselors' characteristics. In a comprehensive review of 378 studies, Luborsky, Crits-Cristoph, and Auerbach (1988) found that a "helpful relationship with the counselor" was the most significant factor in successful outcomes. Similarly, Orlinsky and Howard (1986) found a strong relationship between the quality of the therapeutic relationship and positive client outcome in 80% of their reviewed studies. Lambert's (1989) review also concluded that one of the major factors in discriminating helpful from less helpful therapists was the quality of the therapist-client relationship. Together, these findings suggest that the interpersonal skill of the therapist in joining with clients and fostering a strong therapeutic relationship is more important than any discrete quality (Kahn, 1997). That is, conceptually desirable qualities of "good therapists" such as psychological mindedness, intelligence, supportiveness, and other features suggested by experts as important variables have not independently correlated as well with treatment outcomes (Beutler et al., 1994; Parloff, Waskow, & Wolfe, 1978). Thus, elucidating factors that enhance the therapist-client relationship may be the most appropriate focus for future research.

The comprehensive reviews of the counseling literature all suggest that researchers must focus on the interactional dimension of the counseling relationship (Gelso & Carter, 1994; Sexton & Whiston, 1994) rather than studying characteristics of therapists in isolation. We cannot regard "therapists" as an independent variable applied to a uniform or homogeneous client—as in a surgical procedure or other task that is more purely skill-based. Instead, Luborsky (1994) offers a far better conceptualization of the therapeutic process: the personal and technical influence of the therapist is mediated through the relationship formed with the client, which in turn stimulates the client's commitment to treatment and activates the client's resources on behalf of change. In this conceptual shift to the relational context, we should not say that "therapy works" but that the therapist and the client work. The therapist does not change the client in a linear or unidirectional trajectory; rather, each collaboratively influences the other (Bandura, 1986). Following the current emphasis of postmodernist writers, we argue for improving the investigation of the change process by bringing the person of the therapist back into the equation and conceptualizing the relational context in which the therapist and the client influence each other (Atwood & Stolorow, 1984; Goldfried & Wolfe, 1996; Orange, 1995; Russell, 1994; Orange, Atwood, & Stolorow, 1998). We examine below several promising research domains to highlight how therapist variables can be better understood within a relational context.

The Therapist's Use of Self: Self-involving vs. Self-disclosing Comments

One promising focus of current research has been the therapist's use of self to facilitate treatment change. Over the past 15 years, a number of studies have explored the differential effectiveness of therapists' comments that are self-involving vs. self-disclosing. These studies illustrate how more can be learned by examining the activities of therapists in a relational context than by focusing on intervention techniques per se. Self-disclosing statements refer to counselors' personal statements about their past experiences that relate in some way to clients' experiences or reflections

(Therapist: "My parents divorced when I was a teenager, too"). In contrast, self-involving statements refer to a direct, present expression by the counselor about the client's current behavior or how the client is affecting the counselor right now (Therapist: "It's exciting for me to see how well you are putting things together right now"). Researchers have clarified that, in general, self-involving statements create more immediacy, leave the focus of treatment with the client, and are viewed more favorably by clients than self-disclosing statements (McCarthy, 1982; Reynolds & Fischer, 1983).

Self-involving comments can be positive or negative. Positive comments can be reassuring feedback that supports, reinforces, or legitimizes the client's perspective and way of thinking, feeling, or behaving (Therapist: "I appreciate the risk you are taking with me right now"). In contrast, negative self-involving comments can challenge the client's perspective and way of thinking or behaving (Therapist: "I feel as though you are not really with me right now"). Reassuring disclosures were rated as more helpful by clients and therapists than challenging disclosures, especially in the initial sessions. Negative self-involving statements can be misperceived as judgmental or threatening if they are employed before the counseling relationship has been established and before the clients trust the counselors' good intentions in discussing their immediate experience of each other and their current interaction (Anderson & Anderson, 1985; Remer, Roffery, & Buckholtz, 1983). Positive self-involving comments that are reassuring seem to make therapists and clients more equal, perhaps making clients feel safer in exploring further aspects of themselves (Hill, Mahalik, & Thompson, 1989). In this way, self-involving statements facilitate a greater engagement and strengthen the client-therapist relationship.

None of these interesting studies on the counselor's use of self in the therapeutic relationship, however, assesses the context in which these response modes are expressed and the idiographic nature of each therapeutic relationship. That is, on the one hand, a negative self-involving statement may always be problematic for a client who grew up being unfairly or excessively criticized and now chronically expects others to be critical. On the other hand, the same challenging response may be experienced as helpfully caring, authentic, or involved by another client, who was never responded to honestly by an indulgent or uninvolved caregiver. Furthermore, the therapist's judicious willingness to risk sharing a negative self-involving comment ("I'm feeling that you're not with me right now, that you're not as present as you were when we began") may be productive feedback, especially if this emotional withdrawal or interpersonal disengagement is a common coping strategy for the client. Of course, this feedback would be given later in treatment, once trust and safety have become securely established. In addition, if the counselor metacommunicates and provides a context for this type of challenging comment ("I'm concerned that you may misunderstand my feedback as criticism, but I want to risk speaking forthrightly with you, and share my concern that . . ."), the client may be more receptive to the input and understand that the counselor is not being critical or responding as others have in the past. Future research on therapist variables and therapists' use of self to facilitate change needs to include an evaluation of their abilities to utilize their conceptualizations of client dynamics to respond *flexibly* to differing clients' needs (i.e., clients' response specificity).

Extending this important issue beyond the specific research domain of self-involving vs. self-disclosing comments, Strupp (1980a) found that therapists liked clients better who approved of their technical approach, and in turn these clients improved more. Aptly, Strupp questioned why more therapists in his sample did not demonstrate greater flexibility in their technical approach to the client and have the flexibility or interpersonal range to modify their interventions and provide the responses that each client could utilize best. Casting this in familiar but still unheeded terms, we note that psychotherapy is a highly idiographic enterprise. Although organizing patterns and clarifying themes certainly can be discerned in the therapeutic process, our understanding will not progress far if we rely exclusively on nomothetic treatment and research approaches.

Empathy, Core Conditions, and Common Factors

The lack of consistent differences in the overall success rates of differing treatments and techniques has fostered research on common factors across therapies that may be accounting for clients' change (Lambert & Bergin, 1994). Historically, the common factors most frequently studied are the client-centered core conditions of empathy, positive regard or warmth, and genuineness (Weinberger, 1995). Early reviews suggested that these facilitative conditions, and empathy in particular, were positively associated with therapeutic effectiveness (Patterson, 1984). For example, Lafferty, Beutler, and Crago (1991) summed results across groups of more and less effective therapists from 11 different studies based on the extent of clients' symptom change. They found that clients of less effective therapists felt less understood by their therapists, whereas more effective therapists were seen as more empathic by their clients. These findings notwithstanding, however, the strong initial support for facilitative conditions has waned as more recent reviews have found that empathy and other facilitative conditions are more modestly and inconsistently related to successful treatment outcome (Beutler et al., 1986). Clarifying how empathy is operationalized and implemented would be useful. For example, some therapists may be able to cognitively de-center and enter the client's subjective worldview. However, they may not be able to go the extra step of articulating their understanding or using it to provide their clients with the experiences they need for enduring change.

In addition to the distinction between understanding and understanding plus response, empathy and other select therapist variables such as warmth and respect have too often been regarded problematically as enduring traits of a given counselor that are exhibited in a consistent manner across diverse clients and throughout the course of each individual's therapy. Instead of this overgeneralized therapist trait approach, we wish to highlight the interpersonal context and interactional nature of empathy and other facilitative conditions. That is, empathy is contextually bound, and therapists may be more or less empathic depending on the client and his or her presentation. In an important study that clarifies the nature of empathy and how it facilitates therapeutic progress, Barkham and Shapiro (1986) distinguished between the technical content of varying interventions and the therapeutic process. They found that advice by cognitive therapists, reflections by client-centered therapists, and interpretations by dynamic therapists were all negatively related to clients' ratings of the counselors' empathy. They also found that counselors attempts to reduce clients' anxiety through reassurances detracted from the clients' experience of being understood or evidenced failure in the empathic task. Instead of these widely employed interventions, effective empathy came from attempts to *collaboratively* understand the client's experience within an emerging, shared frame of reference. That is, *the therapeutic mode of mutual exploration—characterized by active negotiation between counselor and client—was crucial to the client's experience of being understood.* This collaborative effort to discern shared meaning had significantly more impact than the more traditionally emphasized modes of reflection or interpretation (Hardy & Shapiro, 1987; Hobson, 1985; Shapiro, Barkham, & Irving, 1984).

Our orienting concept of client response specificity may help elucidate the increased complexity and qualified support found in treatment outcome studies for the role of empathy and other facilitative conditions. Client-centered therapists originally conceptualized empathy as a stable or enduring characteristic of the therapist. In contrast, a relational perspective would emphasize that therapists will vary greatly in their abilities to remain *consistently* empathic, warm, accepting, or personally accessible to a client, depending on the topic the client is currently presenting or the interpersonal process between them. For example, a therapist who has just suffered a miscarriage may not be able to remain empathic or nonjudgmental toward a client who is contemplating an abortion. Or a therapist who needs to be liked or is overreactive to being criticized may not be able to remain emotionally present, empathic, respectful, or simply nondefensive when the client expresses reality-based frustrations with how the therapist has been responding. Or in line with the distortions that repeatedly derive from the client's cognitive schemas or internal working models, the therapist may become defensive or have difficulty when the client distorts the therapist's personality and responds angrily to the therapist as controlling, witholding, judgmental, and so forth (McClure & Teyber, in press; Teyber, 2000).

Future research needs to examine facilitative conditions in a more interactional context and assess qualities and activities of therapists who are able to remain *consistently* empathic and accepting with a wide range of clients across the course of treatment. With the helpful concepts of "hot cognitions" and "alliance ruptures," it is essential to focus on therapists' abilities to remain empathic or at least nondefensive enough to be able to sustain the therapeutic stance of trying to explore and understand the client's negative sentiments. That is, therapists need to be able to *sustain* collaborative efforts with the clients at those critical junctures when (1) the therapists' own personal countertransference issues have been activated and (2) the clients' negativities have emerged. Training programs can focus more programmatically on helping supervisees identify their own countertransference propensities and automatic response tendencies when faced with angry, critical, and other unwanted reactions from clients (Teyber, McClure, & Robertson, 2000). That is, through Kagan's (1998) interpersonal process recall, Ivey and Authier's (1978) microskills training, and other role-playing instruction, supervisors can systematically help trainees identify their reflexive or initial response tendencies to angry, critical, distrustful, disappointed, and controlling communications from clients. Such challenging behaviors occur, at least briefly, with virtually every client and are core features or characteristics of many clients. As we see later in this chapter, however, there are extensive research reports that therapists are highly *ineffective* in responding to such negativity. It thus appears that empathy, warmth, congruence, respect, and other facilitative conditions cannot be fully understood as discrete therapist variables. Instead, they must be examined within the idiographic context of a particular therapist-client interaction. The important but often eschewed issues of clients' negativities, as well as the contexts in which they are embedded, can change our conception of therapist variables (empathy being but one obvious example). Further work is needed on this topic.

The Working Alliance

The working (helping and therapeutic) alliance has emerged as perhaps the most important variable in predicting effective treatment outcomes (Hovarth & Greenberg, 1994). In many studies, what therapists say and do in the therapy hour that promotes a good working alliance has proven to be the single most important contributor to change and positive treatment outcomes (Beutler, 1997; Henry, Strupp, Schacht, & Gaston, 1994). A robust and effective ingredient common to all psychotherapies, the working alliance is correlated with successful outcomes across a wide range of clients' symptoms and problems, therapists' characteristics, and therapeutic approaches (Bordin, 1979, 1985; Gelso & Carter, 1994; Horvath, Gaston, & Luborsky, 1993; Kiesler & Watkins, 1989). The term *working alliance* was formulated by Greenson (1967), and it reflects the extent to which the therapist and the client agree on the goals of their work, agree on the tasks that facilitate attainment of these goals, and experience an emotional bond with each other (Bordin, 1979; Hovarth & Greenberg, 1994).

We believe the working alliance construct has become the most fruitful topic in contemporary psychotherapy research because it employs a relational context. Discrete therapist variables such as empathy and other core conditions that have been far more limited in accounting for change were based on the premise that it is the *therapist's* ability to be empathic, warm, accepting, and congruent that facilitates clients' change. In contrast, the working alliance is a relational construct that emphasizes mutuality and collaboration. Both the therapist and the client make important contributions to the formation of an effective therapeutic partnership, and the client's contribution to the alliance is as important as the therapist's (Hovarth & Symonds, 1991). By adopting this relational focus and identifying the positive collaboration between client and therapist as one of the most essential components for success in treatment, the working alliance has also bridged the long-standing dichotomy between process and outcome (Greenberg, 1987; Safran, Crocker, McMain, & Murray, 1990).

Greenson's (1967) original formulation of the therapeutic relationship did not focus just on the working alliance, however, but also included the real relationship and the transference/countertransference dimensions as well. Although the working alliance has received the most empirical and theoretical attention (Hovarth & Symonds, 1991), the real relationship may be the most important component in all therapies, and it needs to become a focus of future research. For some researchers, the real relationship has been operationally defined as *genuineness*—the willingness to be mutually authentic, open, and honest—and as having *realistic perceptions* that are not distorted (Gelso & Carter, 1994). In one of the few studies examining this neglected component of the therapeutic relationship, Gelso and Johnson (1983) found that in both short- and long-term therapies, the stronger the real relationship, the more effective the therapy. These researchers suggest that the deepening relationship that develops over the course of treatment allows transference distortions to be resolved and clients to develop more realistic perceptions of the therapist, themselves, and others. Reflecting a circular causality among these three relational dimensions that have yet to be fully understood and articulated, the genuine caring and respect that may develop between the therapist and client also may serve as

a moderating variable that affects the client's commitment to the working alliance. In this regard, Gelso and Carter suggest that the more positive the real relationship, the stronger the working alliance.

Following Lambert and Okishi (1997) and the *Consumer Report* study (Seligman, 1995), future research should include naturalistic studies that identify effective therapists within each theoretical orientation. Indeed, studies that distinguish therapists on the basis of effectiveness and then evaluate factors contributing to effectiveness note that significant results are almost entirely relationship-oriented (Najavits & Strupp, 1994). Researchers will benefit from studying how the working alliance, the real relationship, and the transference/countertransference component of the therapeutic relationship interact with one another and are utilized by effective therapists to facilitate change. To understand the complexities of therapeutic change, however, researchers ultimately will have to investigate the interaction of these important nonspecific relational factors with specific treatment plans and intervention techniques that are flexibly tailored to meet the varying needs of individual clients.

Alliance Ruptures and Clients' Negativity

To facilitate the working alliance, Binder and Strupp (1997) suggest that the therapist's role is to sustain an empathic, respectful, warm, and interested attitude toward the patient. This alliance-fostering therapeutic stance is not provided consistently, however, as recurrent "ruptures" in the therapeutic alliance inevitably occur during the course of a treatment (Safran, Muran, & Samstang, 1994; Stolorow, Brandchaft, & Atwood, 1994). Alliance ruptures represent episodes of covert or overt hostile sentiments and often interpersonal patterns or scenarios that entangle, ensnare, or embroil both therapists and clients. For therapy to be effective, the therapeutic alliance must be resilient enough to withstand or recover from these expectable ruptures (Hovarth, 1995). That is, the therapist must have the evenness and flexibility to generate ways of successfully managing these ruptures or empathic failures (Safran & Muran, 1995). Although the general assumption is that therapists manage these alliance ruptures well, Binder and Strupp provide empirical support and argue compellingly that most therapists actually fail to address and resolve these crises effectively. In other words, most people, including highly trained therapists, simply don't deal well with interpersonal conflicts *in which they are participants.*

Clinical training in general, even with manualized treatment guidelines, fails to prepare therapists to cope with negative processes (i.e., angry, critical, demanding, distrustful, and controlling responses) that they will experience, at least on occasion, with most clients. As clients enact or reexperience their conflicts *with the therapist* in the therapeutic relationship, clients will become at times overtly or covertly angry, critical, suspicious, demanding, and so forth. In the face of this negative process from the client, therapists commonly fail to respond appropriately with neutral, empathic, or exploratory therapeutic stances that support the therapeutic alliance. Instead, as noted in Binder and Strupp's (1997) review, therapists of every theoretical orientation routinely respond to the clients' negativity personally, with their own emotional reactions, which commonly include anger, emotional withdrawal, subtle rejections, and most frequently a pejorative attitude toward the client! This long-recognized but still unaddressed finding accounts for much of the treatment failures noted across every modality. It remains one of the most important variables for study in treatment outcome research. Focusing more specifically on therapists' differential responses to clients' negativity will help clarify the factors that differentiate effective vs. ineffective treatment processes.

In an illuminating series of eight analogue studies with psychiatrists and clinical psychologists conducted between 1955 and 1965, Strupp and his coworkers found that therapists frequently had negative personal reactions (i.e., were more pessimistic about clients' diagnoses and prognoses, were pejorative in discussing clients, and commonly behaved in overtly hostile ways toward clients) when clients were acting passively, continually pressed the therapist for advice, expressed dissatisfaction with the treatment, or complained about the therapist in some way. These studies were differentiating a "ubiquitous, continuous, and infinitely more subtle form of countertransference than the gross and relatively enduring countertransference reactions usually associated with disrupting the therapeutic alliance" (Strupp, 1962, p. 131). These early observations and recommendations need to be brought back into the clinical discussion today. Clearly, therapists need to be trained more specifically to be able to *consistently* maintain their composure

and adhere to an empathic, respectful stance toward their clients when faced with negativity (Binder & Strupp, 1997).

Irritability is a defining diagnostic feature of most clients who are anxious and depressed; demandingness and hostility are defining diagnostic features of most clients with histrionic, borderline, and narcissistic disorders; and so forth. In other words, these negative features are core defining characteristics of the majority of DSM-IV disorders. Despite their pervasive occurrence, neither clinical training programs nor psychotherapy process researchers have attended to the disquieting issue of therapists' ineffective or reciprocal responses to clients' negativity. Although many clients are going to pull therapists into hostile, critical, or other types of conflictual exchanges, researchers consistently find that most therapists do not deal with client hostility or negativity in a therapeutic manner. Numerous studies, utilizing Benjamin's (1974) SASB (structural analysis of social behavior) interpersonal coding system, find high levels of negative complementarity in which both clients and therapists continue responding to each other in kind, both conveying their own hostility to the other (Henry, Schacht, & Strupp, 1986, 1990; Kiesler & Watkins, 1989; Strupp, 1980b; Tasca & McMullen, 1992; Wiseman, Shefler, Caneti, & Ronen, 1993). In their large-scale clinical study, for example, Safran and Muran (1995) observed that therapists were prone to respond with counter-hostility when faced with overt patient hostility, and they were prone to respond with complementary overbearing or dominant reactions when faced with tacit patient hostility in the form of compliant or avoidant behavior.

Training programs can better prepare trainees to expect negativity from clients, formulate what these eliciting behaviors may mean for each particular client, and conceptualize how the behavior may be linked to the client's presenting problems and maladaptive relational patterns (Teyber, 1997). Without such understanding, it will be hard for most therapists to refrain from responding in kind when clients are angry, critical, or demanding. Training in how to mediate their complementary responses to clients by understanding the origins of clients' negativity, and appreciating the fact that it often represents the clients' (albeit ineffective) attempt to cope, can be incorporated more fully into many training and research programs (Kiesler & Watkins, 1989). Kahn (1997) has refined the concept of nondefensiveness and clarified how counselors can learn much about their clients' symptoms and problems by attending more fully to their own personal (and often unwanted) reactions to their clients.

A negative process and its detrimental effects on treatment effectiveness have been best documented in the Vanderbilt II series of psychotherapy studies, especially by Najavits and Strupp (1994). In this study, more effective therapists (as measured by successful treatment outcomes) showed significantly fewer SASB codings of hostile behavior (e.g., blaming, belittling, ignoring, and rejecting) than less effective therapists. In other words, more effective therapists engaged in more self-reflections, suggesting that their capacity for self-monitoring helped prevent them from becoming embroiled in a negative process with clients. Perhaps most telling was the finding that *every* therapist in the study expressed anger, judgmentalism, and criticism toward the client at some point in treatment. Clearly, all therapists are affected by clients' negativity at times and, understandably, become overreactive or embroiled in it. Too often, however, trainees have not been prepared adequately for this eventuality or been taught how to recover (e.g., metacommunicate and talk with the client about the issue or conflict between them). Similarly, within each theoretical approach and treatment modality, treatment outcome studies often could broaden their focus to include individual differences in the effectiveness of therapists' responses to alliance ruptures and negative processes. By moving beyond the historically narrow conception of countertransference, we could address more clearly the subtle but pervasive issues of negative process and alliance rupture to ameliorate treatment failures.

Researchers have found that clients have negative reactions to the treatment and/or the therapist, and clients do not address these negative sentiments with their therapists (Hill, Thompson, Cogar, & Denman, 1993; Hill, Thompson, & Corbett, 1992). Illustrating this important problem, Rennie (1985, 1992) reported that clients hid negative feelings from their therapists because they believed that their feelings were unjustified or irrational and because they feared that their therapists would disapprove of them for being dissatisfied. In two retrospective studies of "resolved and unresolved misunderstandings" in therapy, Rhodes, Hill, Thompson, and Elliot (1994) found that clients' fears and

expectations about therapists' negative reactions to dissatisfaction were realistic. That is, when misunderstandings between therapists and clients were unresolved at the end of treatment, the clients never communicated their concerns to the therapists, and the therapists did not detect their negative sentiments. Furthermore, when some clients did risk voicing their frustration or dissatisfaction directly to the therapist, they felt that the therapist either dismissed their concerns or, in some instances, became overtly critical of them. These conflicts were not brought up again by therapists or clients, and from the clients' point of view, the therapies tended to be ineffective and have poor outcomes.

Similarly, Johnson, Taylor, D'elia, Tzanetos, Rhodes, and Geller (1995) found that unresolved misunderstandings between client and therapist had serious detrimental effects on the therapeutic alliance. Studying termination sessions with clients at college counseling centers, Quintana and Holahan (1992) also found that clients' negative sentiments about their therapies were rarely addressed. Also, there was significantly less discussion of the therapy process in poor outcome cases than in good ones. They concluded that clients and counselors tended to focus only on positive aspects of the treatment at termination and suggested that "unsuccessful cases may result from counselors and clients limiting discussions of unpleasant material" (p. 301).

These findings thus suggest that tactfully but directly addressing the relational problems that arise between the therapist and client yields better treatment outcomes than when these interpersonal problems are avoided or when the responsibility for them is placed on the client (Foreman & Marmar, 1985; Kivlighan & Schmitz, 1992). It seems that clinical supervisors could target this issue more specifically and do more to help trainees anticipate, recognize, and manage effectively their own personal discomfort arising from conflict with the client or critical feedback from the client. Trainees need to know that this unwanted feedback will at times be distorted or transferential. However, the counselor must strive to remain open to the fact that this feedback indeed may be realistic and, in most cases, *the impasse or conflict involves partial responsibility of both client and therapist.* That is, even if the client's feedback is transferential, its presence in the therapy relationship makes it a therapeutic issue to be addressed and resolved in a reparative way for the client. Thus, to respond effectively to this need, clinical supervisors can help trainees to be more alert and receptive to the unwanted feedback, to inquire about it nondefensively, and to invite clients to clarify and elaborate their concerns. The client and therapist can then work together collaboratively to find ways to resolve the client's negative reactions toward treatment and toward the therapist. Therapists who can remain nondefensive and committed to their therapeutic stance, even in the midst of such anxiety-arousing interactions, provide clients with new levels of interpersonal safety, in vivo relearning, and enactive mastery experiences. This also provides an opportunity for therapists to affirm clients' authenticity and to help them generalize this new coping style of approaching conflicts and addressing misunderstandings with others.

Binder and Strupp (1997) argue that previous attempts to understand negative process have confounded two competing definitions of transference. The traditional dynamic viewpoint emphasizes that the client's displeasure or disappointment with the therapist is an expression of the client's historical relationships with parental figures—a unidirectional model. Typically, this approach leaves clients feeling dismissed, misunderstood, or criticized (Piper, Azim, Joyce, McCallum, Nixon, & Segal, 1991; Safran et al., 1994; Wiley, 1984). In contrast, many contemporary, interpersonal, cognitive-behavioral, and short-term dynamic therapies conceptualize the therapeutic relationship as a dyadic system, with both participants influencing how the therapeutic process unfolds. This bidirectional model attempts to understand how the client's maladaptive interpersonal patterns are being enacted in the immediacy of the therapeutic relationship, with both the client and the therapist participating in the distortions, enactments, and ruptures that inevitably occur in the therapeutic alliance. That is, the therapist will become ensnared by the feelings and reactions the client evokes and commonly will be enlisted to play a complementary role in the client's problematic patterns of relating (Gill, 1982; Kiesler, 1996; Safran & Segal, 1990; Stolorow & Atwood, 1992; Stolorow, Brandchaft, & Atwood, 1987; Strupp & Binder, 1984).

To respond effectively, the therapists' task is not to interpret how clients' current hostility toward them actually reflects the clients' anger toward parental or historical figures or to ignore or avoid this important conflict that is occurring between them. Instead, the therapist's task is to use

process comments, metacommunicative feedback, or therapeutic impact disclosure (Binder & Strupp, 1997; Cashdan, 1988; Kiesler, 1996; Teyber, 2000). In these interventions, the therapist neutrally observes or wonders aloud about what may be occurring between the therapist and client right now in their real-life interaction (Therapist: "Right now, it feels to me as though you are angry with me. What do you see going on between us?" "Right now, it feels to me as though we are engaged in a disagreement, with each of us feeling misunderstood by the other. What do you think might be happening here?" "I am wondering if you experienced my last comment as critical or judgmental? Can we talk about that?"). Making their current interaction overt by inquiring in an open-ended way about what it might mean and inviting a dialogue about what may be occurring between them, the therapist facilitates a collaborative process of mutually naming, exploring, understanding, and changing maladaptive patterns of relating. As many have lamented, however, most therapeutic modalities have failed to emphasize this metacommunicative approach in their technical interventions, and many therapists have not been prepared to utilize this metacommunicative response (Kiesler & VanDenberg, 1993). Too often, therapists have not had the training they need to observe the interpersonal process they are currently participating in, nor have they had instruction in reflecting on such processes, as well as giving the client an open-ended invitation to explore together what may be occurring in the therapeutic relationship (Binder, 1993; Schon, 1987; Teyber, 2000).

To work effectively with the therapeutic process, researchers must examine the broader interactional context in which these or any other interventions are employed. To illustrate, researchers have found that effective transference interpretations tend to *follow* a series of supportive interventions. In contrast, transference interpretations that did not have this supportive prelude lead to decrements in clients' collaboration with the therapist (Gabbard et al., 1994; Kiesler, 1996; Piper, Joyce, McCallum, & Azim, 1993). In parallel, process comments will be effective when therapists are offering genuine bids to understand, talk forthrightly, and explore together. In contrast, these and other interventions will be ineffective when they are employed in the interpersonal context of therapists' own frustrations, impatience, and so forth. Following important research exemplars, such as the informative work on therapists' "intentions" (Hill & O'Grady, 1985), researchers must grapple with the challenge of exploring therapist variables in a relational context rather than as discrete variables whose meaning is not fully understood outside of the interpersonal context in which it is mediated.

In sum, the negative therapeutic process is a pervasive feature of therapeutic relationships that has not been addressed by clinical training programs or psychotherapy process researchers. Although clinical trainees are often poorly prepared for this inevitability, clients routinely present therapists with overtly and covertly expressed hostility, criticism, demandingness, and control. Counselors do not respond well to these expectable interpersonal conflicts, usually because they feel they are not to blame for the conflict or that nothing they have done warrants the clients' negative reactions. In particular, it seems that therapists at every level of training and experience commonly fail to maintain their own appropriate emotional neutrality and nonblaming and nonjudgmental stance toward clients while in the midst of these conflicts. By their fight-or-flight inclinations, it seems that therapists often respond to clients' negativity with their own complementary hostility or emotional withdrawal. Also, many therapists simply *avoid* addressing the negative sentiments directed toward them, as if they were not occurring. Thus, therapists miss an opportunity to empower their clients. Clients need therapists who will take their concerns seriously and demonstrate that relationships can be resilient enough to tolerate, address, and resolve conflicts—which most clients have not experienced in other significant relationships.

Elucidating the characteristics and interventions of therapists who respond effectively to negative processes and are willing to risk exploring and resolving clients' conflicts with them will advance our understanding and yield more consistently positive treatment outcomes. This may be done, for example, by studying sequences of interactions in which the negative therapeutic process is responded to effectively, in contrast to cases in which it is not addressed or resolved, and then evaluating outcomes. This focus will be more effective in helping us to understand treatment success vs. failure than the current focus on differences in outcome based simply on treatment modalities. We believe the most important therapist variables to be explored are those personal qualities that permit some therapists to talk *nondefensively* with clients about their relationship;

address rather than avoid the conflicts that inevitably develop between them; and find ways to resolve these issues occurring between them, which reflect the same relational patterns that are being disruptive with others.

THE NEGLECTED ROLE OF THERAPIST VARIABILITY IN TREATMENT EFFECTIVENESS

Although therapists giving a referral to a friend or family member usually believe strongly that therapists vary greatly in their effectiveness with clients, the highly sensitive issue of differential effectiveness has received little professional attention. In his extensive review of the treatment outcome literature, Lambert (1989) found that the largest amount of variation in therapeutic outcome was attributable to differences in clients' characteristics, with the second largest amount accounted for by therapists' differences. Variations in theory and technique, the most frequently evaluated component believed to have an impact on treatment effectiveness, came in a distant third. Despite repeated findings such as these, the majority of the treatment effectiveness literature has focused on the impact of different theoretical and technical approaches rather than on the differential effectiveness of therapists *within* treatment modalities (Bergin, 1997; Garfield, 1997). For many reasons, the field has been reluctant to examine the personal qualities of effective therapists and has continued to focus instead on the safer topics of theory and technique. Inserting the human element back into the therapeutic enterprise may make it seem less scientific, which could be eschewed in this period of managed care, when skill-based, standardized procedures are more highly valued. Furthermore, the reputations and self-esteem of individual practitioners also might be brought into question when therapists' characteristics are being addressed. Focusing on therapists' personal qualities and differential effectiveness would also provoke those who provide clinical training into giving more systematic evaluative feedback to supervisees, which would probably engender distress and conflict for supervisors and supervisees alike. Although the personal discomfort and professional problems evoked by recognizing more fully the therapist's contribution to therapeutic outcome are evident, so are the possibilities for more effective clinical practice. Let's examine this long-avoided issue.

Although there has been a growing body of research on client and therapist traits, the dominant research bias on the theoretical and technical aspects of treatment has a long history. For example, the tendency *away* from the personal or human contributions of the therapist has increased with more National Institute of Mental Health (NIMH) funding for comparative treatment studies that follow the assumptions of clinical drug trials (Lambert & Okishi, 1997). The randomized clinical trials (RCT) methodology is the preeminent psychotherapy research paradigm at the turn of this century. It attempts to control for, or partial out, the differential effectiveness of individual therapists by having experts (e.g., Aaron Beck or Hans Strupp) train experienced therapists to comply strictly with a carefully defined intervention format such as cognitive-behavioral or interpersonal therapy. Emulating a medical or pharmocological model, therapists follow carefully delineated treatment manuals to provide a "pure dose" of the treatment. Therapists are intensively trained to deliver the specific therapy as described in the manual and are monitored to ensure that they don't "drift" from the prescribed procedures. The aim of this research strategy is to *eliminate* the individual therapist as a variable that might account for clients' improvement. This gold standard for research methodologies as we enter the 21st century is meant to "purify" interventions so that the effects of specific therapies on specific problems can be investigated—theoretically standardizing the treatment (Talley, Strupp, & Butler, 1994).

At least conceptually, client variablility is also controlled in RCT studies by carefully selecting diagnostically homogeneous samples that do not include a variety of disorders. Clients are screened to meet certain criteria for specific disorders or types of psychopathology, such as depression, panic, or other anxiety disorders, without confounding comorbidity. Thus, the studies of clinical trials select patients who are atypical of the multiple-diagnosis patients seen in routine clinical practice or those in effectiveness studies such as the *Consumer Reports* study (Seligman, 1995). Unfortunately, as noted in various studies of clients' contributions to treatment outcome, there is much variance among clients with the same clinical diagnosis (Blatt, Sanislow, Zuroff, & Pilkonis, 1996; Strupp & Binder, 1984). Thus, the current enthusiasm for the RCT research design, wherein the two most important sources of error variance in evaluating treatment effectiveness (i.e., therapist and client variability) are controlled, loses meaningfulness from a clinical perspective.

Without question, the RCT paradigm has been a powerful methodology that has produced important information. Intervention programs have been delineated far more specifically through manualized treatment formats—resolving the long-standing problem in psychotherapy outcome research of vagueness and noncomparability of clinical treatments. The internal validity of the therapies compared in treatment studies has now improved greatly and, serendipitously, the efficacy of psychotherapy in general has been further demonstrated (Beutler, 1997; Garfield, 1997). Despite these important contributions and the scientific appeal of this rigorous methodology, much has been lost by programmatically removing therapist characteristics from outcome research. Indeed, we believe that among the most significant variables affecting positive client outcomes are therapist variables, such as sustained respect for the client, interpersonal and cognitive flexibility, ability to establish—and restore when ruptured—an authentic relationship with the client, among others (see Gelso & Carter, 1994).

Furthermore, even though the role of the therapist in the change process has typically been excluded, empirically validated treatments have also become the focus of training in clinical programs and internships (Sanderson & Woods, 1995). In most cases, these treatments include clearly delineated cognitive behavioral procedures for specific, circumscribed disorders—usually anxiety disorders. However, anxiety symptoms are commonly embedded in complex disorders that include problems in interpersonal relationships and are highly comorbid with both mood disorders and Axis 2 disorders, which readily diminishes the precision of empirically validated treatments in real clinical settings. In a high-profile report, however, the American Psychological Association (Division of Clinical Psychology) Task Force on the Promotion and Dissemination of Psychological Procedures (1995) endorsed empirically validated treatments for clinical training. Although it emphasized the *type* of therapy, there was little or no attention to the role of the individual provider or to variability among therapists. As noted by Garfield (1998), focusing on different forms of empirically supported treatments diminishes the importance of therapist and client characteristics in producing good treatment outcomes.

Early psychotherapy researchers emphasized the role of the therapist as a person who contributes to the change process above and beyond technical competence (Bordin, 1975, 1979; Rogers, 1961). The most fundamental questions about the effectiveness of psychotherapy today, however, are framed in a comparative treatments context. As noted, the predominant research methodologies currently in vogue attempt to remove or ignore variability in the skill and performance of individual therapists as a variable in effecting client change. The random, controlled clinical trial and comparative treatment interventions reached their apex in the large-scale NIMH Treatment of Depression Collaborative Research Program (TDCRP). In this, as in most major psychotherapy outcome studies, the basic focus of the research was to compare the effectiveness of cognitive-behavioral or interpersonal therapy, or psychodynamic, behavioral, or client-centered treatment in other studies (Elkin, 1994).

Kiesler's (1966) uniformity myth was again revealed in the NIMH depression study, the best psychological adaption to date of the highly regarded RCT paradigm. However, Elkin (1994) reports that even though the NIMH therapists had equivalent levels of prior professional experience and were systematically instructed to use criteria-based methods over a two-year period, *therapists varied widely* both in the levels of specific therapeutic skills achieved and in their rates of effectiveness with clients. In a subsequent reanalysis of the NIMH study, Blatt et al. (1996) further demonstrated a wide range of mean improvements within treatment modalities for the 28 therapists studied.

Following this vanguard of interest in techniques and theories over individual therapists, the Second Sheffield Psychotherapy Project compared cognitive-behavioral to interpersonal-psychodynamic treatment (Shapiro & Firth, 1987). Four therapists each saw 6 to 18 clients in a crossover design intended to hold constant individual differences of clients and therapists while maximizing treatment differences. Characteristic of many such studies, the researchers focused on different therapy types and their effects and found a slight advantage for cognitive-behavioral therapy. As in the NIMH study, however, they also reported in a follow-up article that one of their therapists had much better results than the other three and that this particular therapist was responsible for most of the success obtained, even though all four therapists were following the same treatment manual (Shapiro, Firth-Cozens, & Stiles, 1989). This demonstrates, as reported by Henry et al. (1993) and Beutler (1997), that systematic, manual-guided training in specific models of psychotherapy (e.g., cognitive therapy and psychodynamic therapy) does improve levels of efficacy and performance, but it does *not* eliminate the presence of significant variability among individual therapists' rates of efficacy. This cardinal research finding needs to shape the focus and guide the design of future research. It also needs to be incorporated into clinical training programs. Far more could be learned about effective psychotherapy if we broadened our focus beyond theoretical orientation *and* attended to the effectiveness of individual therapists.

Sometimes, richly informative studies are lost in the literature and fail to stimulate follow-up studies that would extend their important findings. For example, Ricks' (1974) illuminating descriptive study brings us experientially close to the issue of differential effectiveness. Unfortunately, it failed to stimulate much direct empirical study of therapists' individual effectiveness. Ricks' study provides a dramatic comparison of two therapists who saw the same caseload of anxious, depressed, vulnerable, and often dissociative teenage boys in an outpatient clinic. In a 20-year follow-up, Ricks found "staggering" differences in the long-term outcomes for these two therapists, especially for their more disturbed clients. As in other studies, similar but less dramatic differences were found for better-functioning clients (Carkhuff, 1969). What did the more effective therapist in Ricks' study do? He invested more time in his clients, made use of resources in the community on the boys' behalf, was firm and direct with the boys' parents, encouraged movement toward autonomy, and facilitated problem-solving skills in the boys' everyday lives. All of these interventions were carried out in the interpersonal context of what we would call a strong therapeutic alliance. In stark contrast, each of these techniques was utilized far less often by the ineffective therapist. Perhaps more informative, the less effective therapist seemed to be frightened by the boys' more serious symptoms of dissociation, and he often withdrew emotionally from them. Unable to continue working toward change, he was therapeutically immobilized by the boys' more serious episodes of depression and, sadly, conveyed to them hopelessness about their futures.

It continues to be informative to read descriptions of what Ricks' highly effective therapist did and compelling to learn about the personality, countertransference, and interpersonal responses of the therapist who produced negative therapeutic outcomes in the majority of his cases (84 percent ended up with a schizophrenic diagnosis in adulthood vs. 27 percent for the effective therapist). Although few clinical studies such as this are published, they are highly informative. Future research should identify and evaluate, using empirical and qualitative designs, what effective therapists are doing with their clients and what distinguishes them from less effective therapists.

As in other reviews, Beutler (1997) reports that the variability among outcomes *within* any type of therapy is usually at least as high as that *between* types of treatments. For example, analyzing outcomes in four treatment studies, Luborsky et al. (1986) compared the amount of variance attributed to therapeutic techniques to the amount attributed to the therapist. They concluded that "the size of therapists' effects generally overshadowed any differences between different forms of treatment in these investigations" (p. 509). Similarly, Lyon and Howard (1991) found in their meta-analyses that treatment outcomes attributable to different therapists are almost always greater than the differences attributable to treatment type. Many studies have been designed to sum across differences in effectiveness between therapists. This is probably the reason for the frequent inability of outcome studies to find significant differences between different treatment modalities and between treatment and control groups. Therapist variability so strongly influences the effectiveness of therapeutic outcomes that this Type II error is likely to permeate the field and prevent researchers from detecting real differences in effectiveness between various treatment approaches.

Researchers find that some therapists are *consistently effective* and others are quite *consistently ineffective*, regardless of the type of treatment practiced (Luborsky et al., 1986; Orlinsky & Howard, 1980). To illustrate, Garfield, Affleck, and Muffly (1963) reported long ago that three judges reliably ranked six therapists on their overall effectiveness as therapists: "The two most favorably rated therapists each kept three out of four of their patients, whereas the two least favorably rated therapists each kept only one out of four assigned patients. The two remaining therapists each had two remainers and two terminators" (p.

477). More recently, Lafferty, Beutler, and Crago (1989) found that fully one-third of their therapists who were working with outpatient clients produced as many negative therapeutic effects as positive ones, independent of the type of therapy utilized. In contrast, other therapists in this study were uniformly effective with most patients. This high degree of variability in the effectiveness of individual therapists again suggests that therapist variables need to be included in research designs and given at least as much attention as treatment models. Although researchers can fruitfully continue to utilize treatment manuals and establish empirically validated treatments, they must attend to Kiesler's (1966) uniformity myth and assess therapists' variability within each treatment modality as well. Our understanding of the therapeutic process has been impeded by bifurcating the field into scientifically hard approaches (e.g., techniques) vs. humanly soft approaches (e.g., therapist variables, individual differences, and personal qualities.) Substituting interaction effects for simple main effects hypotheses would bridge both domains and substantially improve our understanding of the factors that enhance treatment effectiveness.

In this regard, Lambert (1995) argues for a new research strategy that measures the outcomes of each individual therapist's caseload. As already noted, several studies have demonstrated differences in each therapist's general level of helpfulness to clients (Crits-Cristoph & Mintz 1991; Crits-Christoph et al., 1991; Luborsky, McLellan, Woody, O'Brien & Auerback, 1985; Luborsky et al., 1986, 1988; Najavits & Strupp, 1994; Orlinsky & Howard 1980). Studies using the design principles of (1) focusing on each therapist's performance as measured by caseload outcomes (e.g., Seligman, 1995) and (2) examining the therapy and therapist qualities associated with that performance would clarify how therapist variables are related to treatment outcomes. For example, Luborsky, McLellan, Diguer, Woody, and Seligman (1997) studied 22 therapists' caseloads with samples of drug-addicted and depressed clients. They found important differences in the improvement levels and posttreatment outcomes of patient caseloads among the therapists sampled. The differences in improvement were not due to differences in patients' backgrounds or severity. That is, the therapists were seeing similar clients (diagnoses), clients were randomly assigned, therapists had been selected for their competence in their particular form of therapy, and therapists were regularly supervised and guided by treatment manuals. Despite extensive steps to maximize therapists' skill and minimize their differences, the range of improvement for the clients of the 22 therapists varied widely from a slightly negative therapeutic impact to more than 80% improvement. Some therapists were shown to be highly effective across different client populations, some were modestly effective, and others showed no or negative impact at seven-month follow-up evaluations. Therapists' qualities, as judged by their peers, showed that interest in helping patients (.44) and the therapist's psychological health and skill (.41) correlated best with client outcome. Those therapists who adhered to a treatment manual also had better outcomes, probably because it enhanced skill levels. In addition, therapists whose caseloads showed the most improvement were those who were able to engage and retain the largest proportion of assigned patients—suggesting a greater ability to establish a working alliance and provide clients with the reparative experiences they needed.

The therapists in this study who excelled with depressed clients also excelled with drug-addicted clients. Although there were differences for each therapist within their individual caseloads, it was the therapist's capacities or skills that were responsible for change rather than differences in clients' characteristics or diagnoses. In other words, better therapists did better with most of the patients they treated. Revealing the complexity of the therapeutic enterprise, however, and the risk of focusing solely on treatments and techniques, these researchers found that *the two best therapists in their study were very different.* One used mostly supportive techniques, whereas the other used mostly expressive techniques. Clearly, there are different routes to successful performance. However, even though the technical routes differed for these two highly effective therapists, they both showed one common trait— a strong working alliance with their clients.

This focus on therapists' contribution to effective treatments should be extended in future research. For example, groups of effective therapists, within different theoretical orientations, could be evaluated on their personal qualities, interpersonal skills, and therapeutic interventions. In an important exemplar of this promising design, Najavits and Strupp (1994) evaluated 16 therapists who had been recommended by their supervisors as "caring empathetic clinicians." Each therapist was assigned five cases of similar difficulty, and client outcomes were evaluated after 25 sessions. As we have seen, these outcome evaluations revealed wide variability in individual therapist's effectiveness. Based on objective outcome assessments, therapists were divided into two groups of "most effective" and "least effective." Although training and specific technical skills were not related to outcome, nonspecific qualities did distinguish the two groups. As a group, the more effective therapists demonstrated significantly more warmth and understanding, and they had *fewer* recorded instances of ignoring, neglecting, attacking, and rejecting their clients than less effective therapists (see also Strupp & Hadley, 1979). More effective therapists were also less defensive. They were more willing to look at themselves critically and to admit when they had made mistakes than the less effective therapists. We emphasize, however, that some of these negative behaviors were found in every therapist in both groups. These findings suggest that effective therapists are able to cognitively and emotionally de-center and enter the clients' subjective worldview while still being authentic.

In considering explorations of these more effective therapists, however, we must continue to remind ourselves of the broader sociocultural context in which any treatment is provided. At the turn of this century, the propensity for unwarranted litigation against responsible clinicians is pronounced, and in the present era of managed care we are experiencing a profound loss of psychological resources. In subtle but pervasive ways, these two factors have engendered feelings of anxiety and inefficacy in many practitioners. Threats of litigation, especially for practitioners who work with borderline, manic depressive, and other clients with acting-out potential, and the press for "quick fixes" affect therapists' ability to establish strong working alliances and to commit deeply to the real relationship with clients. This context has helped move the field toward prescriptive, manualized, and technique-based approaches that minimize the personal qualities, relational capacities, and differential effectiveness of therapists. Partialing out these features, which researchers have found are most consistently related to successful outcome, is unfortunate indeed. Never has the need been greater for researchers to distill and highlight those features of effective therapists that contribute to successful outcome.

CONCLUSION

In sum, it is time to drop the uniformity myth and better address the contribution of the individual therapist to treatment outcome. Comparative studies of psychotherapy outcome consistently find that therapy modalities are relatively equivalent in effecting client change (Lipsey & Wilson, 1993; Luborsky, Singer, & Luborsky, 1975; Shapiro & Shapiro, 1982; Smith, Glass, & Miller, 1980). In contrast, there is considerable support for the view that the individual therapist's attributes, attitudes, and actions (e.g., interpersonal skills, countertransference propensities, and personality) match or override the effects of particular techniques (Beutler, Machado, & Neufeldt, 1994; Crits-Christoph & Mintz, 1991; Crits-Critsoph et al., 1991; Lafferty et al., 1991; Orlinsky, Grawe, & Parks, 1994). Despite this, therapeutic techniques and their underlying theoretical explanations of change continue to be emphasized almost exclusively in graduate training, in professional and graduate-level textbooks, and in clinical research, with only minimal attention to therapists' personal qualities and their impact on effectiveness (Lambert & Okishi, 1997). Studies that extend these attempts to differentiate the personal qualities *and* technical interventions of more and less effective therapists within each theoretical orientation provide the most promising directions for future research (Lafferty, Beutler, & Crago, 1991; Luborsky et al., 1985; Strupp, 1980a).

To grasp the complexity of the change process, however, we must bridge the false dichotomy between specific and nonspecific factors. Well-defined therapists' actions and techniques and qualities of the therapeutic relationship both interact and contribute to client change (Jones et al., 1988). General relational skills, such as the capacity to engender a strong working alliance with a diverse range of clients, is closely tied to the skillful selection and application of specific therapeutic interventions (Docherty, 1985). Thus, we need to assess the differential effectiveness of individual therapists in their ability to establish productive therapeutic relationships. Simultaneously, we need to differentiate therapists who employ specific skills and techniques *flexibly* to match each particular client's need. That is, research and

training have not attended sufficiently to clients' response specificities and addressed how any specific intervention (e.g., helping clients understand the behavior of others in their lives, questioning pathogenic or distorted beliefs, containing shame-related affects, and assisting in problem solving) will be helpful to one client but irrelevant or even problematic for the next. It is important to remember that therapy is a relational enterprise and that the more effective therapists are probably those who can (1) de-center and conceptualize clients' dynamics and needs based on their individual, subjective worldviews and experiences and (2) be sufficiently cognitively, emotionally, and interpersonally flexible to provide the specific, often varying, reparative relational experiences needed by individual clients. Thus, the challenge before us is to extend research and training models to honor more fully the complexity of the therapeutic relationship and the change process.

REFERENCES

American Psychological Association Task Force on Promotion and Dissemination of Psychological Procedures. (1995). Training in and dissemination of empirically-validated psychological treatments: Report and recommendations. *The Clinical Psychologist, 48*, 3–23.

Anderson, B., & Anderson, W. (1985). Client perceptions of counselors using positive and negative self-involving statements. *Journal of Counseling Psychology, 32*, 462–465.

Arlow, J. A. (1985). Some technical problems of countertransference. *Psychoanalytic Quarterly, 54*(2), 161–174.

Atkinson, D. (1983). Ethnic similarity in counseling psychology: A review of research. *The Counseling Psychologist, 11*, 79–92.

Atkinson, D. R. (1985). A meta-review of research on cross-cultural counseling and psychotherapy. *Journal of Multicultural Counseling and Development, 13*, 138–153.

Atkinson, D., & Matsushita, Y. (1991). Japanese-American acculturation, counseling style, counselor ethnicity, and perceived counselor credibility. *Journal of Counseling Psychology, 38*, 473–478.

Atkinson, D. R., & Schein, S. (1986). Similarity in counseling. *The Counseling Psychologist, 14*, 319–354.

Atwood, G. E., & Stolorow, R. D. (1984). *Structures of subjectivity: Explorations in psychoanalytic phenomenology*. Hillsdale, NJ: Analytic Press.

Atwood, G. E., & Stolorow, R. D. (1993). *Faces in a cloud: Intersubjectivity in personality theory.* Northvale, NJ: Jason Aronson.

Bachelor, A. (1988). How clients perceive therapist empathy: A content analysis of "received" empathy. *Psychotherapy, 25*(2), 227–240.

Baker, S., & Daniels, T. (1989). Integrating research on the microcounseling program: A meta-analysis. *Journal of Counseling Psychology, 36,* 213–222.

Bandura, A. (1986). *Social foundations of thought and action: A social-cognitive theory.* Upper Saddle River, NJ: Prentice Hall.

Barkham, M., & Shapiro, D. (1986). Counselor verbal response modes and experienced empathy. *Journal of Counseling Psychology, 33*(1), 3–10.

Beck, D. (1988). *Counselor characteristics: How they affect outcomes.* Milwaukee, WI: Family Service America.

Bell, R. Q. (1968). Direction of effects revisited. *Psychological Review, 75,* 81–95.

Benjamin, L. S. (1974). Structural analysis of social behavior. *Psychological Review, 81,* 392–425.

Bergin, A. E. (1997). Neglect of the therapist and the human dimensions of change: A commentary. *Clinical Psychology: Science and Practice, 4,* 83–89.

Berry, G., & Sipps, G. (1991). Interactive effects of counselor-client similarity and client self-esteem on termination type and number of sessions. *Journal of Counseling Psychology, 38,* 120–125.

Beutler, L. E. (1997). The psychotherapist as a neglected variable in psychotherapy: An illustration by reference to the role of therapist experience and training. *Clinical Psychology: Science and Practice, 4,* 44–52.

Beutler, L. E., & Clarkin, J. (1991). *Systematic treatment selection: Toward targeted therapeutic interventions.* New York: Brunner/Mazel.

Beutler, L. E., Clarkin, J., Crago, M., & Bergan, J. (1991). Client-therapist matching. In C. R. Snyder & D. R. Forsyth (Eds.), *Handbook of social and clinical psychology: The health perspective* (pp. 699–716). Elmsford, NY: Pergamon.

Beutler, L., Crago, M., & Arizmendi, T. G. (1986). Research on therapist variables in psychotherapy. In S. L. Garfield & A. E., Bergin (Eds.), *Handbook of psychotherapy and behavior change* (pp. 257–310). New York: Wiley.

Beutler, L. E., Engle, D., Mohr, D., Dalrup, R. J., Bergan, J., Meredith, K., & Merry, W. (1991). Predictors of differential and self directed psychotherapeutic procedures. *Journal of Consulting and Clinical Psychology, 59,* 333–340.

Beutler, L. E., Machado, P. P., & Neufeldt, S. (1994). Therapist variables. In A. E. Bergin and S. L. Garfield (Eds.), *Handbook of psychotherapy and behavior change* (4th ed., pp. 229–269). New York: Wiley.

Beutler, L. E., Scogin, F., Kirkish, P. K., Schretlen, D., Corbishley, M. A., Hamblin, D., Meredith, K., Potter, R., Bamford, C. R., & Levenson, A. I. (1987). Group cognitive therapy and Alprazolam in the treatment of depression in older adults. *Journal of Consulting and Clinical Psychology, 55,* 550–556.

Binder, J. (1993). Is it time to improve psychotherapy training? *Clinical Psychology Review, 13,* 301–318.

Binder, J., & Strupp, H. (1997). Negative process: A recurrently discovered and underestimated facet of therapeutic process and outcome in the individual psychotherapy of adults. *Clinical Psychology: Science and Practice, 4,* 121–139.

Blatt, S. J., Sanislow, C. A., Zuroff, D., & Pilkonis, P. (1996). Characteristics of the effective therapist: Further analysis of the data from the NIMH TDCRP. *Journal of Consulting and Clinical Psychology, 64,* 1276–1284.

Bordin, E. S. (1975, August). *The working alliance: Basis for a general theory of psychotherapy.* Paper presented at the meeting of the Society for Psychotherapy Research, Washington, DC.

Bordin, E. S. (1979). The generalizability of the psychoanalytic concept of the working alliance. *Psychotherapy: Theory, Research and Practice, 16,* 252–260.

Bordin, E. S. (1985, June). *Research on the therapeutic alliance.* Paper presented at the annual meeting of the Society for Research in Psychotherapy, Dallas.

Bowman, D. O. (1993). Effects of therapist sex on the outcome of therapy. *Psychotherapy, 30,* 678–684.

Burlingame, G. M., Fuhriman, A., Paul, S., & Ogles, B. M. (1989). Implementing a time-limited therapy program: Differential effects of training and experience. *Psychotherapy, 26,* 303–313.

Butler, S. F., & Strupp, H. H. (1986). Specific and nonspecific factors in psychotherapy: A problematic paradigm for psychotherapy research. *Psychotherapy, 23,* 30–40.

Carkhuff, R. R. (1969). *Helping and human relations: Practice and research.* New York: Holt, Rinehart & Winston.

Cashdan, S. (1988). *Object relations therapy.* New York: Norton.

Chevron, E. S., Rounsaville, B. J., Rothblum, E., & Weissman, M. M., (1983). Selecting psychotherapists to participate in psychotherapy outcome studies: Relationship between psychotherapy characteristics and assessment of clinical skill. *Journal of Nervous and Mental Disease, 171,* 348–353.

Clementel-Jones, C., Malan, D., & Trauer, T. (1990). A retrospective follow-up study of 84 patients treated with individual psychoanalytic psychotherapy: Outcome and predictive factors. *British Journal of Psychotherapy, 6,* 363–374.

Cook, E. (1990). Gender and psychological distress. *Journal of Counseling and Development, 68,* 371–375.

Cook, M., & Kipnis, D. (1986). Influence factors in psychotherapy. *Journal of Consulting and Clinical Psychology, 54,* 22–26.

Crits-Christoph, P., Baranackie, K., Kurcias, J. S., Beck, A. T., Carroll, K., Perry, K., Luborsky, L., McLellan, A. T., Woody, G. E., Thompson, L., Gallagher, D., & Zitrin, C. (1991). Meta-analysis of therapist effects in psychotherapy outcome studies. *Psychotherapy Research, 2,* 81–91.

Crits-Christoph, P., & Mintz, J. (1991). Implications of therapist effects for the design and analysis of comparative studies of psychotherapies. *Journal of Consulting and Clinical Psychology, 59,* 20–26.

Curtis, J. (1982). The effect of therapist self-disclosure on patients' perceptions of empathy, competence, and trust in an analogue psychotherapeutic interaction. *Psychotherapy: Theory, Research and Practice, 19,* 54–61.

Dembo, R., Ikle, D., & Ciarlo, J. (1983). The influence of client-clinician demographic match on client treatment outcomes. *Journal of Psychiatric Treatment and Evaluation, 5,* 45–53.

Docherty, J. P. (1985). The therapeutic alliance and treatment outcome. In R. E. Hales & A. J. Frances (Eds.), *Psychiatry update. Annual review* (Vol. 4, pp. 527–531). Washington, DC: American Psychiatric Press.

Dush, D., Hirt, M., & Schroeder, H. (1983). Self-statement modification with adults: A meta-analysis. *Journal of Consulting and Clinical Psychology, 94,* 408–422.

Eagly, A. (1994). On comparing men and women. *Feminism and Psychology, 4,* 513–522.

Eastwood, J., Spielvogel, A., & Wile, J. (1990). Countertransference risks when women treat women. *Clinical Social Work Journal, 18,* 273–280.

Elkin, I. (1994). The NIMH treatment of depression collaborative research program: Where we began and where we are. In A. E. Bergin & S. L. Garfield (Eds.), *Handbook of psychotherapy and behavior change* (4th ed., pp. 114–139). New York: Wiley.

Flaskerud, J., & Liu, P. (1991). Effects of an Asian client-therapist language, ethnicity, and gender match on utilization and outcome of therapy. *Community Mental Health Journal, 27,* 31–42.

Foreman, S., & Marmar, C. R. (1985). Therapist actions that address initially poor therapeutic alliances in psychotherapy. *American Journal of Psychiatry, 142,* 922–966.

Fromm-Reichmann, F. (1950). *Principles of intensive psychotherapy.* Chicago: University of Chicago Press.

Fullerton, C., Yates, B., & Goodrich, N. (1990). The sex and experience of the therapist and their effects on intensive psychotherapy of the adolescent inpatient. In S. Feinstein (Ed.) et al., *Adolescent Psychiatry: Developmental & Clinical Studies* (pp. 272–278). Chicago: University of Chicago Press.

Gabbard, G. O., Horwitz, L., Allen, J. G., Frieswyk, S., Newsom, G., Colson, D. B., & Coune, L. (1994). Transference interpretations in the psychotherapy of borderline patients: A high-risk, high-gain phenomenon. *Harvard Review of Psychiatry, 2,* 59–69.

Garfield, S. L. (1994). Research on client variables in psychotherapy. In A. E. Bergin & S. L. Garfield (Eds.). *Handbook of Psychotherapy and behavior change* (pp. 190–228). New York: Wiley.

Garfield, S. L. (1997). The therapist as a neglected variable in psychotherapy research. *Clinical Psychology: Science and Practice, 4,* 40–43.

Garfield, S. L. (1998). Some comments on empirically supported treatments. *Journal of Consulting and Clinical Psychology, 66,* 121–125.

Garfield, S. L., Affleck, D. C., & Muffly, R. (1963). A study of psychotherapy interaction and continuation in psychotherapy. *Journal of Clinical Psychology, 19,* 473–478.

Gaston, L. (1990). The concept of alliance and its role in psychotherapy. In A. E. Bergin & S. L. Garfield (Eds.), *Handbook of psychotherapy and behavior change* (4th ed., pp. 190–228). New York: Wiley.

Geis, F. (1993). Self-fulfilling prophecy: A social psychological view of gender. In A. E. Beall & R. L. Sternberg (Eds.), *The psychology of gender* (pp. 9–54). New York: Guilford.

Gelso, C. J., & Carter, J. (1985). The relationship in counseling and psychotherapy. *The Counseling Psychologist, 13,* 155–244.

Gelso, C. J., & Carter, J. A. (1994). Components of the psychotherapy relationship: Their interaction and unfolding during treatment. *The Journal of Counseling Psychology, 41*(3), 296–306.

Gelso, C. J., & Johnson, D. H. (1983). *Explorations in time-limited counseling and psychotherapy.* New York: Teachers College Press.

Gill, M. M. (1982). *The analysis of transference. Vol. 1: Theory and technique.* New York: International Universities Press.

Goldfried, M. R., & Wolfe, B. E. (1996). Psychotherapy practice and research: Repairing a strained alliance. *American Psychologist, 51,* 1007–1016.

Greenberg, L. S. (1987). Research strategies. In L. S. Greenberg & W. M. Pinsoff (Eds.), *The psychotherapeutic process: A research handbook* (pp. 707–734). New York: Guilford.

Greenson, R. R. (1967). *The technique and practice of psychoanalysis* (Vol. 1). Madison, WI: International Universities Press.

Greenspan, M., & Kulish, N. (1985). Factors in premature termination in long-term psychotherapy, *Psychotherapy, 22,* 75–82.

Hardy, G. E., & Shapiro, D. A. (1987). Therapist verbal response mode in prescriptive vs. exploratory psychotherapy. *British Journal of Clinical Psychology, 24,* 235–245.

Henry, W. P., Schacht, T. E., & Strupp, H. H. (1986). Structural analysis of social behavior: Application to a study of interpersonal process in differential psychotherapeutic outcome. *Journal of Consulting and Clinical Psychology, 54,* 27–31.

Henry, W. P., Schacht, T. E., & Strupp, H. H. (1990). Patient and therapist introject, interpersonal process, and differential psychotherapy outcome. *Journal of Consulting and Clinical Psychology, 58,* 768–774.

Henry, W. P., Schacht, T. E., Strupp, H. H., Butler, S. F., & Binder, J. L. (1993). Effects of training in time-limited dynamic psychotherapy: Mediators of therapists' responses to training. *Journal of Consulting and Clinical Psychology, 61,* 441–447.

Henry, W., Strupp, H., Butler, S., Schacht, T., & Binder, J. (1993). Effects of training in time-limited dynamic psychotherapy: Changes in therapist behavior. *Journal of Consulting and Clinical Psychology, 61,* 434–440.

Henry, W. P., Strupp, H. H., Schacht, T. E., & Gaston, L. (1994). Psychodynamic approaches. In A. E. Bergin & S. L. Garfield (Eds.), *Handbook of psychotherapy and behavior change* (4th ed., pp. 467–508). New York: Wiley.

Hill, C. E., & Corbett, M. M. (1993). A perspective on the history of process and outcome research in counseling psychology. *Journal of Counseling Psychology, 40,* 3–24.

Hill, C. E., Mahalik, J., & Thompson, B. (1989). Therapist self-disclosure. *Psychotherapy, 26*(3), 290–295.

Hill, C. E., & O'Grady, K. (1985). List of therapist intentions illustrated in a case study and with therapists of varying theoretical orientations. *Journal of Counseling Psychology, 32*(1), 3–22.

Hill, C. E., Thompson, B. J., Cogar, M. C., & Denman, D. W. (1993). Beneath the surface of long-term therapy: Therapist and client report of their own and each other's covert processes. *Journal of Counseling Psychology, 40,* 278–287.

Hill, C. E., Thompson, B. J., & Corbett, M. (1992). The impact of therapist ability to perceive displayed and hidden client reactions on immediate outcome in first sessions of brief therapy. *Psychotherapy Research, 2,* 143–155.

Hobson, R. F. (1985). *Forms of feeling: The heart of psychotherapy.* London: Tavistock.

Hovarth, A. O. (1995). The therapeutic relationship: From transference to alliance. *Psychotherapy in Practice, 1,* 7–17.

Hovarth, A., Gaston, L., & Luborsky, L. (1993). The therapeutic alliance and its measures. In N. E. Miles, L. Luborsky, J. P. Barber, & J. P. Docherty (Eds.), *Psychodynamic treatment research* (pp. 247–273). New York: Basic Books.

Hovarth, A. O., & Greenberg, L. S. (1989). The development and validation of the Working Alliance Inventory. *Journal of Counseling Psychology, 36,* 223–244.

Hovarth, A. O., & Greenberg, L. S. (1994). *The working alliance. Theory, research, and practice.* New York: Wiley.

Hovarth, A. O., & Symonds, B. D. (1991). Relation between working alliance and outcome in psychotherapy: A meta-analysis. *Journal of Counseling Psychology, 38,* 139–149.

Hunt, D., Carr, J., Dagadakis, C., & Walker, E. (1995). Cognitive match as a predictor of psychotherapy outcome. *Psychotherapy, 22,* 718–721.

Ivey, A., & Authier, J. (1978). *Microcounseling.* Springfield, IL: Thomas.

Johnson, B., Taylor, E., D'elia, J., Tzanetos, T., Rhodes, R., & Geller J. D. (1995). The emotional consequences of therapeutic misunderstandings. *Psychotherapy Bulletin, 30,* 139–149.

Jones, E., Krupnick, J., & Kerig, P. (1987). Some gender effects in brief psychotherapy. *Psychotherapy, 24,* 336–352.

Jones, E. E. (1978). Effects of race on psychotherapy process and outcome: An exploratory investigation. *Psychotherapy: Theory, Research, and Practice, 15,* 226–236.

Jones, E. E. (1982). Psychotherapists' impressions of treatment outcome as a function of race. *Journal of Clinical Psychology, 38,* 722–731.

Jones, E. E., Cumming, D., & Horowitz, M. J. (1988). Another look at the nonspecific hypothesis of therapeutic effectiveness. *Journal of Consulting and Clinical Psychology, 56*(1), 48–55.

Kagan, N. (1998). *Interpersonal process recall update.* North Amherst, MA: Microtraining.

Kahn, M. (1997). *Between therapist and client.* New York: Freeman.

Kell, B., & Mueller, W. J. (1966). *Impact and change: A study of counseling relationships.* Upper Saddle River, NJ: Prentice Hall.

Kiesler, D. J. (1966). Some myths of psychotherapy research and the search for a paradigm. *Psychological Bulletin, 65,* 110–136.

Kiesler, D. J. (1971). Experimental designs in psychotherapy. In A. E. Bergin & S. L. Garfield (Eds.), *Handbook of psychotherapy and behavior change* (pp. 36–74). New York: Wiley.

Kiesler, D. J. (1996). *Contemporary interpersonal theory and research. Personality, psychopathology, and psychotherapy.* New York: Wiley.

Kiesler, D., & VanDenburg, T. (1993). Therapeutic impact disclosure: A last taboo in psychoanalytic theory and practice. *Clinical Psychology & Psychotherapy, 1*(1), 3–13.

Kiesler, D. J., & Watkins, L. (1989). Interpersonal complementarity and the therapeutic alliance: A study of relationship in psychotherapy. *Psychotherapy, 26*(2), 183–194.

Kivlighan, D. M., Jr., & Schmitz, P. J. (1992). Counselor technical activity in cases with improving working alliances and continuing poor working alliances. *Journal of Counseling Psychology, 39*, 32–38.

Lafferty, P., Beutler, L. E., & Crago, M. (1991). Differences between more and less effective psychotherapists: A study of select therapist variables. *Journal of Consulting and Clinical Psychology, 57*, 76–80.

Lambert, M., & Arnold, R. (1987). Research and the supervisory process. *Professional Psychology: Research and Practice, 18*, 217–224.

Lambert, M. J. (1989). The individual therapist's contribution to psychotherapy process and outcome. *Clinical Psychology Review, 9*, 469–485.

Lambert, M. J. (1995, June). *Profiling therapist performance via outcomes-based case management: A minor revolution in therapeutic practice.* Paper presented at the meeting of the Society for Psychotherapy Research, Vancouver.

Lambert, M. J., & Bergin, A. E. (1994). The effectiveness of psychotherapy. In A. E. Bergin & S. L. Garfield (Eds.), *Handbook of psychotherapy and behavior change* (4th ed., pp. 143–189). New York: Wiley.

Lambert, M. J., & Okishi, J. C. (1997). The effects of the individual psychotherapist and implications for future research. *Clinical Psychology: Science and Practice, 4*, 66–75.

Lazarus, A. A. (1995). Integration and clinical verisimilitude (Review of the book *Comprehensive handbook of psychotherapy integration*). *Clinical Psychology: Science and Practice, 2*, 399–403.

Leary, T. (1957). *Interpersonal diagnosis of personality.* New York: Ronald.

Lefley, H. (1985). Mental health training across cultures. In P. Petersen (Ed.), *Handbook of cross-cultural counseling and therapy* (pp. 259–266). Westport, CT: Greenwood Press.

Lipsey, M., & Wilson, D. (1993). The efficacy of psychological, educational, and behavioral treatment: Confirmation from meta-analysis. *American Psychologist, 48*, 1181–1209.

Luborsky, L. (1994). Therapeutic alliances as predictors of psychotherapy outcomes: Factors explaining the predictive success. In A. Horvath & L. Greenberg (Eds.), *The working alliance: Theory, research and practice* (pp. 38–50). New York: Wiley.

Luborsky, L. (1995, June). The psychotherapist as a less neglected variable: Studies of benefits to each therapist's caseload. In S. L. Garfield (Chair), *The psychotherapist as a negative variable in psychotherapy research.* Symposia at the Meetings of the Society for Psychotherapy Research, Vancouver.

Luborsky, L., Crits-Cristoph, P., & Auerbach, A. (1988). *Who will benefit from psychotherapy? Predicting therapeutic outcomes.* New York: Basic Books.

Luborsky, L., Crits-Christoph, P., McLellan, A. T., Woody, G., Piper, W., Liberman, B., Imber, S., & Pilkonis, P. (1986). Do therapists vary much in their success? Findings from four outcome studies. *American Journal of Orthopsychiatry, 56*, 501–512.

Luborsky, L., McLellan, A., Diguer, L., Woody, G., & Seligman, D. (1997). The psychotherapist matters: Comparison of outcomes across twenty-two therapists and seven patient samples. *Clinical Psychology: Science and Practice, 4*, 53–65.

Luborsky, L., McLellan, A. T., Woody, G. E., O'Brien, C. P., & Auerback, A. (1985). Therapist success and its determinant. *Archives of General Psychiatry, 42*, 602–611.

Luborsky, L., Mintz, J., Auerbach, A., Crits-Christoph, P., Bachrach, H., Todd, T., Johnson, M., Cohen, M., & O'Brien, C. (1980). Predicting the outcome of psychotherapy. *Archives of General Psychiatry, 37*, 471–481.

Luborsky, L., Singer, B., & Luborsky, L. (1975). Comparative studies of psychotherapies. *Archives of General Psychiatry, 32*, 995–1008.

Lyon, J. S., & Howard, K. I. (1991). Main effects analysis in clinical research: Statistical guidelines for disaggregating treatment groups. *Journal of Consulting and Clinical Psychology, 59*, 745–748.

Lyons, L., & Woods, P. (1991). The efficacy of rational-emotive therapy: A quantitative review of the outcome research, *Clinical Psychology Review, 11*, 357–369.

Matarazzo, R., & Patterson, D. (1986). Methods of teaching therapeutic skill. In S. L. Garfield & A. E. Bergin (Eds.), *Handbook of psychotherapy and behavior change* (pp. 821–843). New York: Wiley.

McCarthy, P. (1982). Differential effects of self-disclosing versus self-involving counselor statements across counselor-client gender pairings. *Journal of Counseling Psychology, 26*, 538–541.

McClure, F. H., & Teyber, E. (1996). The multicultural-relational approach. In F. H. McClure & E. Teyber, *Child and adolescent therapy: A multicultural-relational approach* (pp. 1–32). Fort Worth, TX: Harcourt Brace.

McClure, F. H., & Teyber, E. (in press). *Multicultural case studies with children and adolescents.* Pacific Grove, CA: Wadsworth.

Morgan, R., Luborsky, L., Crits-Christoph, P., Curtis, H., & Solomon, J. (1982). Predicting the outcomes of psychotherapy by the Penn Helping Alliance Rating Method. *Archives of General Psychiatry, 39*, 397–402.

Najavits, L., & Strupp, H. H. (1994). Differences in the effectiveness of psychodynamic therapists: A process outcome study. *Psychotherapy, 31,* 114–123.

Nelson, M. L. (1993). A current perspective on gender differences: Implications for research in counseling. *Journal of Counseling Psychology, 46,* 200–209.

Orange, D. (1995). *Emotional understanding: Studies in psychoanalytic epistemology.* New York: Guilford.

Orange, D., Atwood, G., & Stolorow, R. (1998). *Working intersubjectively: Contextualism in psychoanalytic practice.* Hillsdale, NJ: Analytic Press.

Orlinsky, D. E., Grawe, K., & Parks, B. K. (1994). Process and outcome in psychotherapy. In A. E. Bergin & S. L. Garfield (Eds.), *Handbook of psychotherapy and behavior change* (4th ed., pp. 170–377). New York: Wiley.

Orlinsky, D. E., & Howard, K. (1986). Process and outcome in psychotherapy. In S. L. Garfield & A. E. Bergin (Eds.), *Handbook of psychotherapy and behavior change* (pp. 311–381). New York: Wiley & Sons.

Parloff, M., Waskow, I. I., & Wolfe, B. (1978). Research on therapist variables in relation to process and outcome. In S. L. Garfield & A. E. Bergin (Eds.), *Handbook of psychotherapy and behavior change* (2nd ed., pp. 233–282). New York: Wiley.

Patterson, C. H. (1984). Empathy, warmth and genuineness in psychotherapy: A review of reviews. *Psychotherapy, 21,* 431–438.

Piper, W. E., Azim, H. F., Joyce, A. S., McCallum, M., Nixon, G. W., & Segal, P. S. (1991). Quality of object relations versus interpersonal functioning as predictors of therapeutic alliance and psychotherapy outcome. *Journal of Nervous and Mental Disease, 179,* 432–438.

Piper, W. E., Joyce, A. P., McCallum, M., & Azim, H. F. (1993). Concentration and correspondence of transference interpretation in short-term dynamic psychotherapy. *Journal of Consulting and Clinical Psychology, 61,* 586–696.

Quintana, S. M., & Holahan, W. (1992). Termination in short-term counseling: Comparison of successful and unsuccessful cases. *Journal of Counseling Psychology, 39,* 299–305.

Rave, P. J., & Goldfried, M. R. (1994). The therapeutic alliance in cognitive-behavior therapy. In A. D. Hovarth & L. S. Greenberg (Eds.), *The working alliance: Theory, research, and practice* (pp. 131–152). New York: Wiley.

Remer, P., Roffery, B. H., & Buckholtz, A. (1983). Differential effects of positive versus negative self-involving counseling responses. *Journal of Counseling Psychology, 30,* 121–125.

Rennie, D. L. (1985, June). *The inner experience of psychotherapy.* Paper presented at the annual meeting of the Society for Psychotherapy Research, Chicago.

Rennie, D. L. (1992). Qualitative analysis of the client's experience of psychotherapy: The unfolding of reflexivity. In S. G. Toukmanian & D. L. Rennie (Eds.), *Psychotherapy process research: Paradigmatic and narrative approaches* (pp. 211–233). Newbury Park, CA: Sage.

Reynolds, C. L., & Fischer, C. H. (1983). Personal versus professional evaluations of self-disclosing and self-involving counselors. *Journal of Counseling Psychology, 30,* 451–454.

Rhodes, R. H., Hill, C. E., Thompson, B. J., & Elliott, R. (1994). Client retrospective recall of resolved and unresolved misunderstanding events. *Journal of Counseling Psychology, 41,* 473–483.

Ricks, D. F. (1974). Supershrink: Methods of a therapist judged successful on the basis of adult outcomes of adolescent patients. In D. F. Ricks, M. Roff, & A. Thomas (Eds.), *Life history research in psychopathology* (pp. 288–308). Minneapolis: University of Minnesota Press.

Robbins, S. B., & Jolkovski, M. P. (1987). Managing countertransference feelings: An interactional model using awareness of feeling and theoretical framework. *Journal of Counseling Psychology, 34,* 276–282.

Robinson, L., Berman, J., & Neimeyer, R. (1990). Psychotherapy for the treatment of depression: A comprehensive review of controlled outcome research. *Psychological Bulletin, 108,* 30–49.

Rogers, C. R. (1961). The characteristics of a helping relationship. In C. R. Rogers (Ed.), *On becoming a person* (pp. 39–58). Boston: Houghton Mifflin.

Russell, R. L. (Ed.). (1994). *Reassessing psychotherapy research.* New York: Guilford.

Safran, J. D., Crocker, P., McMain, S., & Murray, P. (1990). The therapeutic alliance rupture as a therapy event for empirical investigations. *Psychotherapy: Research and Practice, 27,* 154–165.

Safran, J. D., & Muran, J. C. (1995). Resolving therapeutic alliance ruptures: Diversity and integration. *Psychotherapy in Practice, 1,* 81–92.

Safran, J., Muran, J. C., & Samstang, L. W. (1994). Resolving therapeutic alliance ruptures: A task analytic investigation. In A. Horvath & L. S. Greenberg (Eds.), *The working alliance: Theory, research, and practice* (pp. 225–255). New York: Wiley.

Safran, J. D., & Segal, Z. V. (1990). *Interpersonal process in cognitive therapy.* New York: Basic Books.

Sanchez-Craig, M., Spivak, K., & Davila, R. (1991). Superior outcome of females over males after brief treatment for the reduction of heavy drinking: Replication and report of therapist effects. *British Journal of Addiction, 86,* 867–876.

Sanderson, W. C., & Woods, S. (1995). Manual for empirically validated treatments. *The Clinical Psychologist, 48*(4), 7–11.

Schon, D. A. (1987). *Educating the reflective practitioner.* San Francisco: Jossey-Bass.

Seligman, M. P. (1995). The effectiveness of psychotherapy: The *Consumer Reports* study. *American Psychologist, 50,* 965–974.

Sexton, T., & Whiston, S. (1991). A review of the empirical basis for counseling: Implications for practice and training. *Counselor Education and Supervision, 30,* 330–354.

Sexton, T., & Whiston, S. (1994). The status of the counseling relationship: An empirical review, theoretical implications, and research directions. *The Counseling Psychologist, 22*(1), 6–78.

Shafter, R. (1988). When the therapist is female: Transference, countertransference and reality. *Issues in Ego and Psychology, 11,* 32–42.

Shapiro, D. A., Barkham, M., & Irving, D. L. (1984). The reliability of a modified Helper Behavior Rating System. *British Journal of Medical Psychology, 57,* 45–48.

Shapiro, D. A., & Firth, J. A. (1987). Prescriptive vs. exploratory psychotherapy: Outcomes of the Sheffield Psychotherapy Project. *British Journal of Psychiatry, 151,* 790–799.

Shapiro, D. A., Firth-Cozens, J., & Stiles, W. B. (1989). Therapists' differential effectiveness: A Sheffield Psychotherapy Project addendum. *British Journal of Psychiatry, 154,* 383–385.

Shapiro, D., & Shapiro, D. (1982). Meta-analysis of comparative therapy outcome studies: A replication and refinement. *Psychological Bulletin, 92,* 581–604.

Smith, M., & Glass, G. (1977). Meta-analysis of psychotherapy outcome studies. *American Psychologist, 32,* 752–760.

Smith, M. L., Glass, G. V., & Miller, T. I. (1980). *The benefits of psychotherapy.* Baltimore: Johns Hopkins University Press.

Stein, D., & Lambert, M. J. (1995). Graduate training in psychotherapy: Are therapy outcomes enhanced? *Journal of Consulting and Clinical Psychology, 63,* 182–196.

Stern, D. (1985). *The interpersonal world of the infant.* New York: Basic Books.

Stiles, W. B., & Shapiro, D. A. (1989). Abuse of the drug metaphor in psychotherapy process-outcome research. *Clinical Psychology Review, 9,* 521–543.

Stolk, V., & Perlesz, A. J. (1990). Do better trainees make worse family therapists? A follow-up study of client families. *Family Process, 29,* 45–58.

Stolorow, R. D., & Atwood, G. E. (1992). *Contexts of being: The intersubjective foundations of psychological life.* Hillsdale, NJ: Analytic Press.

Stolorow, R. D., Brandchaft, B., & Atwood, G. E. (1987). *Psychoanalytic treatment: An intersubjective approach.* Hillsdale, NJ: Analytic Press.

Stolorow, R. D., Brandchaft, B., & Atwood, G. E. (1994). *The intersubjective perspective.* Northvale, NJ: Jason Aronson.

Strupp, H. H. (1962). Patient-doctor relationships: Psychotherapists in the therapeutic process. In A. J. Bachrach (Ed.), *Experimental foundations of clinical psychology* (pp. 576–615). New York: Basic Books.

Strupp, H. H. (1980a). Success and failure in time-limited psychotherapy: A systematic comparison of two cases (Comparison 1). *Archives of General Psychiatry, 37,* 595–603.

Strupp, H. H. (1980b). Success and failure in time-limited psychotherapy. Further evidence (Comparison 4). *Archives of General Psychiatry, 37,* 947–954.

Strupp, H. H., & Binder, J. L. (1984). *Psychotherapy in a new key: A guide to time-limited dynamic psychotherapy.* New York: Basic Books.

Strupp, H. H., & Hadley, S. (1979). Specific versus nonspecific factors in psychotherapy: A controlled study of outcome. *Archives of General Psychiatry, 36,* 1125–1136.

Sue, S. (1990). Culture-specific strategies in counseling: A conceptual framework. *Professional Psychology: Research and Practice, 21,* 424–433.

Sue, S., Fujino, D., Hu, L., Takeuchi, D., & Zane, N. (1991). Community mental health services for minority groups: A test of the cultural responsiveness hypothesis. *Journal of Counseling Psychology, 59,* 533–540.

Sue, S., & Zane, N. (1987). The role of culture and cultural techniques in psychotherapy: A critique and reformulation. *American Psychologist, 42,* 37–45.

Svartberg, M., & Stiles, T. (1992). Predicting patient change from therapist competence and patient-therapist complementarity in short-term anxiety-provoking psychotherapy. *Journal of Consulting and Clinical Psychology, 60,* 304–307.

Talley, P. F., Strupp, H. H., & Butler, S. F. (1994). *Psychotherapy research and practice: Bridging the gap.* New York: Basic Books.

Tasca, G. A., & McMullen, L. M. (1992). Interpersonal complementarity and antitheses within a stage model of psychotherapy. *Psychotherapy, 29,* 515–523.

Terrell, F., & Terrell, S. (1984). Race of counselor, client sex, cultural mistrust level, and premature termination from counseling among black clients. *Journal of Counseling Psychology, 31,* 371–375.

Teyber, E. C. (2000). *Interpersonal process in psychotherapy: A relational approach.* (4th ed.). Pacific Grove, CA: Brooks/Cole.

Teyber, E., McClure, F., & Robertson, M. (2000). Scale to measure "Sensitivity to countertransference issues." In E. Teyber (Ed.), *Student workbook to accompany interpersonal process in psychotherapy: A relational approach.* Pacific Grove, CA: Brooks/Cole.

Thompson, L., Gallagher, D., & Breckenridge, J. (1987). Comparative effectiveness of psychotherapies for depressed elders. *Journal of Consulting and Clinical Psychology, 55,* 385–390.

Wade, P., & Bernstein, B. (1991). Culture sensitivity training and counselor's race: Effects on black female clients' perceptions and attrition. *Journal of Counseling Psychology, 38,* 9–15.

Weinberger, J. (1995). Common factors aren't so common: The common factors dilemma. *Clinical Psychology: Science and Practice, 2,* 45–69.

Weiss, J. R., Weiss, B., Han, S. S., & Bringer, D. A. (1995). Effects of psychotherapy with and adolescents revisited: A meta-analysis of treatment outcome studies. *Psychological Bulletin, 117,* 450–468.

Weisz, J., Weiss, B., Alicke, M., & Klotz, M. (1987). Effectiveness of psychotherapy in children and adolescents: A meta-analysis for clinicians. *Journal of Counsulting and Clinical Psychology, 55,* 542–549.

Wierbicki, M., & Pekarik, G. (1993). A meta-analysis of psychotherapy dropout. *Professional Psychology: Research and Practice, 24,* 190–195.

Wiggins, J., & Giles, T. (1984). The relationship between counselors' and students' self-esteem as related to counseling outcomes. *The School Counselor, 32,* 18–22.

Wiley, D. B. (1984). Kohut, Kernberg, and accusatory interpretations. *Psychotherapy, 21,* 672–675.

Wiseman, H., Shefler, G., Caneti, L., & Ronen, Y. (1993). A systematic comparison of two cases in Mann's time-limited psychotherapy: An events approach. *Psychotherapy Research, 3,* 227–244.

Yeh, M., Eastman, K., & Cheung, M. (1994). Children and adolescents in community health centers: Does the ethnicity or the language of the therapist matter? *Journal of Community Psychology, 22,* 153–163.

Yeh, M., Takeuchi, D., & Sue, S. (1994). Asian-American children treated in the mental health system: A comparison of parallel and mainstream outpatient service centers. *Journal of Clinical Child Psychology, 23,* 5–12.

CHAPTER 5

STALKING THE ELUSIVE CLIENT VARIABLE IN PSYCHOTHERAPY RESEARCH

NANCY M. PETRY, HOWARD TENNEN, AND GLENN AFFLECK
University of Connecticut Health Center

For decades, researchers and clinicians have attempted to *identify client characteristics that are associated with responses to psychotherapy.* Early work focused primarily on the main effects of basic demographic and personality variables and their roles in psychotherapy retention and outcomes. More recent research has expanded to client-therapist or client-therapy interactions. This work has led to even more ambitious projects in which clients, depending on their pretreatment characteristics, are "matched" to a particular therapist or type of therapy.

Despite thousands of empirical articles and hundreds of reviews examining the roles of these main and interaction effects, we are left with only a rudimentary understanding of pretreatment client characteristics that seem to affect the response to psychotherapy. Our goal in this chapter is not to provide a definitive answer regarding client variables or to review the many other chapters that have so thoroughly explored this issue. Rather, our objectives are to: (1) provide a general overview of clients' characteristics thought to be associated with retention and outcomes, with a particular emphasis on personality; (2) critically evaluate the methods and findings from many of these reports; and (3) suggest areas for future investigation.

SOCIODEMOGRAPHIC CHARACTERISTICS

We begin by examining literature on the role of sociodemographic characteristics in predicting response to treatment. We first provide an overview of studies that examine each variable for retention or continuation in treatment. Next, the relationship of that characteristic with outcome, or benefit from treatment, is described. Finally, when applicable, we provide a summary of the effects of interactions between client-therapist or client-therapy.

Socioeconomic Status

Demographic characteristics in general, and socioeconomic status (SES) in particular, have received considerable attention as variables that may be associated with the response to psychotherapy. Generally, investigators have found a positive relationship between higher social class and retention in psychotherapy. For example, early research by Dodd (1970) and Fiester and Rudestam (1975) found a relationship between higher social status and length of stay in treatment. Berrigan and Garfield (1981) also reported a clear linear relation between higher SES and continuation in treatment, and more recent work by Armbruster and Fallon (1994) reveals that lower SES is associated with premature treatment termination among general psychotherapy clients.

Education is highly correlated with social class, and many studies report positive relations between the years of education and the length of stay in treatment (Garfield, 1986). Among outpatients at a general mental health clinic, for example, Rabinowitz and Renert (1997) found that the duration of treatment was significantly shorter for patients with less than a high school education than for patients with a high school degree. In the treatment of specific disorders like substance use, studies generally indicate that shorter length of stay is associated with lower educational attainment (Agosti, Nunes, & Ocepeck-Welikson,

1996; Epstein, McGrady, Miller, & Steinberg, 1994; McCusker, 1995).

Although some investigators have found no differences between psychotherapy completers and terminators in education and social status (e.g., Beck et al., 1987; MacDonald, 1994; Sledge, Moras, Hartley, & Levine, 1990), the general consensus is that higher SES (or education) and psychotherapy retention are positively related. This relationship probably reflects, in part, the fact that lower socioeconomic patients are more likely to be mandated to treatment rather than self-referred. Shorter retention among patients from lower socioeconomic backgrounds also may be related to their relative lack of understanding of the nature of psychotherapy or their role in it. Moreover, psychotherapists are more likely to be from the upper socioeconomic strata and, therefore, may be more similar to their middle- and upper-class patients, thereby increasing the likelihood that these patients remain longer in treatment.

When one examines "outcomes," such as reductions in symptoms or improvements in psychosocial functioning, as opposed to mere continuation in therapy, the protective effects of higher SES status appear to diminish. In an early review by Luborsky, Chandler, Auerbech, Cohen, and Bachrach (1971), for example, SES yielded no relationship to outcome. Similarly, Garfield (1978, 1986, 1994), Lorion (1973), and Schmidt and Hancey (1979) conclude that although higher socioeconomic status appears to be related to greater acceptance and longer duration in psychotherapy, it bears scant relationships to outcomes. These findings may reflect the fact that once one has made a commitment to therapy, SES and its associated characteristics are less likely to have an influence on responses to treatments.

Race

Race is another variable that has been investigated in relation to treatment retention and outcome. Several early studies, including one of 17 community mental health clinics (Sue, McKinney, Allen, & Hall, 1974), found that ethnic minority clients attended significantly fewer sessions than white clients (e.g., Greenspan & Kulish, 1985; Salzman, Shader, Scott, & Binstock, 1970). Other studies, however, have found no relation between race and premature termination (e.g., Sledge et al., 1990).

Some data suggest that race may be associated with poorer response to treatment. Rosen-heck, Fontana, and Cottrol (1995) found that African-American veterans with posttraumatic stress disorder were more likely to drop out of therapy earlier and were less likely to benefit from treatment than their white counterparts. Costello, Baillargeon, Biever, and Bennett (1979), however, found that Mexican-American patients fared as well or better than their Anglo counterparts in a two-year follow-up study.

Recent research is less concerned with race as a main effect and is more concerned with the role of the ethnic similarity between the client and therapist. Some of these studies report that when the client and therapist are from the same ethnic background, longer stays in treatment are more likely (Fujino, Okazaki, & Young, 1994; Rosenheck et al., 1995; Sue, Fujino, Hu, Takeuchi, & Zane 1991; Yeh, Eastman, & Cheung, 1994). Other studies, in contrast, have reported that the client's and therapist's racial similarity was not important in predicting retention (Ewing, 1974; Zane, Hatanaka, Park, & Akutsu, 1994) or outcomes (e.g., Flaskerud & Liu, 1991; Jones, 1978). In summary, the evidence is mixed concerning the role of race and client-therapist racial similarities in psychotherapy retention and outcome.

Gender

Clients' gender is assessed in virtually every study that evaluates treatment retention and outcome. Although women may be more likely to seek treatment than men, most studies show no gender difference in premature termination once therapy begins (Berrigan & Garfield, 1981; DuBrin & Zastowny, 1988; Garfield, 1994; Greenspan & Kulsih, 1985; Sledge et al., 1990). Likewise, studies generally have not shown gender effects in psychotherapy outcomes (Luborsky, Mintz, & Christoph, 1979; Siegel, Rootes, & Taub, 1977; Sloane, Staples, Cristol, Yorkston, & Whipple, 1975).

Despite the general lack of association between gender and response to treatment, numerous studies have investigated the role of patient-therapist gender pairings. Some studies have reported greater patient satisfaction with same-gender pairing (Liljestrand, Gerling, & Saliba, 1978), whereas others show preferences for opposite-gender matches (Willer & Miller, 1978). Fujino et al (1994) found that gender similarity was associated with increased retention in treatment and higher levels of posttreatment functioning; they also found that client-therapist gender similarity was most important in treating Asian-American women. Jones and Zoppel (1982) described two studies investigating the influence of the client's and therapist's gender on process and outcomes. Women therapists rated themselves as more successful, especially with women clients, but overall, gender and gender matches did affect outcomes. Flaskerud and Liu (1991) also found that client-therapist gender similarity had little effect on outcomes in a study of close to two thousand clients. In summary, gender and gender matches seem to bear little, or weak, relation to psychotherapy retention and outcome.

Age

A few reports suggest a negative relationship between an older age and treatment continuation (Greenspan & Kulish, 1985; Sue, McKinney & Allen, 1976), but most suggest that age is not important in psychotherapy retention (Berrigan & Garfield, 1981; DuBrin & Zastowny, 1988; Gunderson, Frank, Ronningstam, Wachter, Lynch, & Wolf, 1989; Sledge et al., 1990). In terms of treatment outcome, an early literature review by Luborsky et al. (1971) found four studies that indicated a negative relationship between age and outcome, two with a positive relationship, and five showing no effect. In a large-scale meta-analysis of outcome in psychotherapy, Smith, Glass, and Miller (1980) found a zero correlation between age and outcome. More recent studies of brief therapy indicate that benefits are unrelated to clients' ages (MacDonald, 1994). In summary, little evidence suggests that a patient's age is related to his or her propensity to remain in, or benefit from, therapy.

One exception to this summary is in the treatment of substance use disorders, in which a younger age has repeatedly been associated with shorter retention rates and poorer outcomes (e.g., Agosti et al., 1996). One explanation for this finding is that individuals tend to "outgrow" substance use, and hence reductions in substance use may parallel improved outcomes, with or without treatment, as clients age (e.g., Stephens, 1991).

Marital Status

Marital status has been widely evaluated in terms of its relation to psychotherapy retention and outcome. Several early studies seemed to indicate that marital status was not an important factor in treatment attrition in general outpatient psychotherapy (Frank, Gliedman, Imber, Nash, & Stone, 1957; Yalom, 1966), nor was it correlated with psychotherapy outcome measures (e.g., Garfield, 1994). Recent work by Schrader (1994) similarly found that marital status did not predict outcomes for depressed patients.

In contrast, being married generally is associated with longer treatment retention among persons with substance use disorders (e.g., Fortney, Booth, Blow, & Bunn, 1995). In a review of studies published between 1975 and 1992, Pfeiffer, O'Malley, and Shott (1996) also found that being married was a strong predictor for positive outcomes of hospitalized psychiatric patients. Durham, Allan, and Hackett (1997) found that being married was one of the most robust predictors of positive outcomes among individuals treated for anxiety disorders. In the treatment of refractory depression, Thase and Howland (1994) reported that nonresponses to both pharmacotherapy and psychotherapy are associated with inadequate social support and with being single.

Others have examined not only marital status but also relationship satisfaction. Milton and Hafner (1979) found that patients whose marriages were rated unsatisfactory before treatment fared much worse during and following treatment than did those with better marital relationships. Burns, Sayers, and Moras (1994) found that once pretreatment depression severity and relationship satisfaction levels were controlled, married patients were substantially less depressed following 12 weeks of treatment.

Turning to studies of interaction effects, we see that Luborsky, Mintz, and Christoph (1979) found that patients treated by therapists with similar marital status (e.g., both or neither married) had better outcomes. A study examining the interactions between marital status and the type of therapy found that married patients did better after receiving cognitive therapy, whereas single and noncohabitating patients improved more following interpersonal therapy (Barber & Muenz, 1996). In summary, married patients generally fare better in response to psychotherapy than nonmarried patients, although some contrary evidence has been reported. Studies examining interactions between patients' marital status and therapists' marital status or type of therapy have yielded intriguing results. These findings need to be replicated before drawing conclusions about their generalizability.

Intelligence

Although few studies have examined intelligence and treatment retention, certain types of therapy are perceived as requiring more intelligent clients. For example, psychoanalysis candidates are typically screened before acceptance into treatment, and the vast majority are college graduates, who presumably are above average in intelligence (Reder & Tyson, 1980; Weber, Solomon, & Bachrach, 1985). In contrast, behavioral therapists are usually unconcerned with clients' intelligence, accepting even mentally retarded patients.

Barron (1953b) found a moderate correlation between higher intelligence and more positive outcomes. In a review of the literature, Luborsky, Singer, and Luborsky (1975) reported that 10 of 13 studies showed a positive relationship between higher intelligence and superior outcomes. Rosenberg (1954) reported that higher intelligence was associated with more positive outcomes and that other, related characteristics (e.g., the ability to produce associations easily, lack of rigidity, wide-ranging interests, sensitivity to the environment, ability to feel deeply, and a high energy level) also predicted positive therapeutic outcomes. Meltzoff and Kornreich (1970) found that seven studies secured a positive relationship, but eight found no relationship between higher intelligence and positive treatment outcomes. In a study of 106 outpatients diagnosed with depression, dysthymia, or generalized anxiety disorder and treated with cognitive therapy, a weak negative relationship emerged between intelligence and outcome (Haaga, DeRubeis, Steward, & Beck, 1991). In his review chapter, Garfield (1994) concluded that even if intelligence were associated with psychotherapy outcomes, its influence appears to be modest.

Our review indicates little reason to expect these six basic demographic characteristics to play a major role in predicting clients' continuation in or response to psychotherapy. Perhaps because of this relatively meager association between demographics and treatment responses, researchers sought other individual differences that may be associated with the latter. We now review the role of psychological disturbance and motivation to change.

NATURE, DURATION, AND SEVERITY OF DISTURBANCE AND MOTIVATION TO CHANGE

Diagnosis, Duration, and Severity

Psychiatric diagnosis has been widely investigated in relation to the length of stay in outpatient psy-

chotherapy, but most reports concur that diagnosis is not a significant correlate of premature termination (e.g., Garfield, 1986). On the other hand, outcomes do seem to differ by diagnosis. Certain conditions have vacillating and reoccurring or chronic courses, whereas others are acute. In a review encompassing 25 years of research, Frank (1974) found that anxiety and depression symptoms improved most and somatic complaints exhibited the poorest outcomes. Others have reported that the presence of anxiety at the initiation of therapy is a positive prognostic sign (Kernberg, Burstein, Coyne, Applebaum, Horwitz, & Voth, 1972; Luborsky et al., 1975).

The duration of disturbance has also been examined in relation to treatment outcome. In the treatment of phobias, an older age of onset is associated with a poorer response to behavioral treatment (Cameron, Thyer, Feckner, & Nesse, 1986). In an review of treatments for major depression, longer duration of the illness was associated with poorer outcomes (Gasperini, Scherillo, Manfredonia, & Franchini, 1993). In contrast, the age of onset and symptom duration did not affect the treatment response for panic and avoidance disorders (Buller, Maier, Goldenberg, & Lavori, 1991).

In terms of severity of psychological symptoms, investigators have noted repeatedly that the severity of psychiatric disturbance seems to be related to poorer treatment response. Indeed, the Sloane et al. (1975) observation that less disturbance at intake is related to greater benefits from psychotherapy has been replicated over several decades. In psychoeducational treatments for depressive disorders, the degree of depression at the start of therapy correlates with depression at termination; moreover, lower pretreatment depression is the best predictor of positive outcomes (e.g., Steinmetz, Lewinsohn, & Antonuccio, 1983). Likewise, the best predictor of interpersonal therapy outcomes for depressed patients is their positive emotional health at initiation of treatment (Rounsaville, Weissman, & Prusoff, 1981). Hoberman, Lewinshon, and Tilson (1988) and Beckham (1989) also found that less intense pretreatment depression precedes positive therapeutic responses. Similarly, in the treatment of addictive disorders, patients with less severe psychiatric symptoms demonstrate the best treatment response (McLellan, Luborsky, Woody, Druley, & O'Brien, 1983).

The severity and type of psychopathology may also interact with the type of therapy.

Whereas psychoanalytic therapy was especially efficacious for individuals low in initial rates of psychiatric disturbances, behavior therapy was equally efficacious for those low or high in such initial psychopathology (Sloane et al., 1975). In large-scale studies on opioid-dependency, Woody et al. (1984; Woody, McLellan, Luborsky, & O'Brien, 1995) found that patients with high levels of psychopathology were more likely to improve in response to supportive-expressive or cognitive-behavioral therapy rather than to standard case management. In summary, lower initial levels of psychopathology, regardless of its nature or duration, have been associated with better responses to psychotherapy.

Motivation to Change

Motivation for treatment has intuitive appeal as a predictor of treatment responsiveness, with well-motivated patients seemingly having a much better chance of remaining in therapy and improving because of it (e.g., Luborsky et al., 1971). Early research by Cartwright and Lerner (1963) found that patients who were high on their "need to change" indicator improved more than those who were low. Strupp, Wallach, Wogan, and Jenkins (1963) found that pretherapy motivation predicted therapists' ratings of success in therapy. Kiethy, Samples, and Strupp (1980) obtained a positive association between ratings of motivation and therapists' ratings of outcomes but not patients' ratings of change. Luborsky et al. (1971) reviewed five studies and concluded that motivation was positively correlated with outcome. In contrast to these findings, however, Horowitz Marmar, Weiss, DeWitt, and Roseonbaum, (1984) found no significant relation between motivation and outcome when outcome was evaluated by independent clinical judges. Siegel and Fink (1962) placed patients in high- or low-motivation groups, based on observers' ratings, and they, too, found patients' motivation to be unrelated to outcome.

These conflicting findings probably result from inherent difficulties in studying motivation, which has been difficult to define and operationalize. Across studies, no standard instrument has been used, and raters of motivation vary from clients, therapists, and independent judges (cf. Butcher & Koss, 1978; Keithy et al., 1980; Malan, 1963; Sifneos, 1972). More recent research on the role of motivation has burgeoned from the substance abuse field. In studying cigarette smokers, Prochaska and DiClemente (1982, 1983) identi-

fied five distinct stages of the change process: (1) *precontemplation* (no perception of the problem or no desire to change, (2) *contemplation* (awareness of a problem; solicitation of information regarding the problem, but unreadiness to make a commitment to change); (3) *preparation* (decided and committed to change but not yet working on the problem); (4) *action* (actively initiating changes in themselves or their environment); and (5) *maintenance* (changes have been made, although difficulty in maintaining them may occur).

Numerous studies have concluded that the Stages of Change Scale (Prochaska & DiClemente, 1983) is highly reliable and can be used to predict treatment outcomes among drug-dependent individuals (e.g., DiClemente et al., 1991; McConnaughy, DiClemente, Prochaska, & Velicer, 1983; McConnaughy, Prochaska, & Velicer, 1989). This measure has also been adapted to predict continuation in and outcome of clients treated for panic disorder (Beitman, Beck, Deuser, Carter, Davidson, & Maddock, 1994) and generalized anxiety disorder (Wilson, Bell-Dolan, & Beitman, 1997). The general conclusion is that individuals scoring high on precontemplation typically change the least, and individuals scoring high on action improve the most. These studies have promoted the use of treatment strategies designed to increase a client's motivation for change, such as motivational enhancement therapy (Miller, Zweben, DiClemente, & Rychtarik, 1992). Although research evaluating the efficacy of such techniques in reducing substance use is promising (Miller et al., 1995), the therapy does not appear to have the specific effect of moving clients along the motivation continuum. From this pattern of findings, Albert Bandura (1997) has concluded, "The stage scheme reminds us that some people have no interest in changing their health habits. Others are riper for change. But this common knowledge hardly requires the encumbrance of stage theorizing" (p. 9).

PERSONALITY CHARACTERISTICS

Personality is another individual difference putatively related to psychotherapy outcomes. The remainder of this chapter reviews the role of personality characteristics in predicting retention and outcomes in psychotherapy. Early research on personality variables focused on the Minnesota Multiphasic Personality Inventory (MMPI) and the Rorschach. Sullivan, Miller, and

Smeizer (1958) found that several MMPI scales predicted retention in relatively large samples of patients, but different scales predicted retention in different groups of patients, and none of the scales held up for more than one group of patients. In other studies (e.g., Rosenzweig & Folmen, 1974; Walters, Solomon, & Walden, 1982; Wolff, 1967), MMPI personality profiles generally failed to demonstrate consistent predictive value for treatment continuation.

For treatment outcome, MMPI personality measures were correlated positively with a global measure of improvement in some studies (e.g., Baron, 1953a; Kernberg et al., 1972) but unrelated to outcome in others (Fiske, Cartwright, & Kirtner, 1964; Getter & Sunderland, 1962; Weber et al., 1985). For the prognostic significance of the Rorschach, Roberts (1954) found that none of 11 Rorschach indexes were related to outcome, and Rogers and Hammond (1953) found that 95 Rorschach signs and three types of clinical judgments of personality failed to differentiate improved from nonimproved patients. Interest in Rorschach predictions of treatment outcomes has diminished in recent years, and one of the more recent studies (Luborsky, Crits-Christophe, Mintz, & Auerbach, 1988) reported mixed findings at best.

These earlier findings of weak and relatively inconsistent findings concerning the predictive power of traditional measures of personality foreshadowed the discrepant views noted in today's literature about the value of studying personality as a moderator of psychotherapeutic change. Reflecting the more pessimistic perspective, Lambert and Supplee (1997) decided that their chapter on psychotherapy outcomes in the *Handbook of Personality* should not focus on the client personality because

> personality variables have not been used successfully to ideally match therapists and patients, to select patients for treatments, or to predict therapy outcome. It has proved difficult to identify salient personality characteristics and to effectively measure those that have been hypothesized to be important to the therapeutic process. (p. 948)

In striking contrast to this discouraging verdict, Harkness and Lilienfeld (1997), who take as their starting point not the history of psychotherapy but the history of scientific inquiry into individual differences, conclude, "The last 40 years of

individual differences research *require* the inclusion of personality trait assessment for the construction and implementation of any treatment plan that would lay claim to scientific status" (p. 349; our emphasis). Harkness and Lilienfeld argue that personality trait assessment, combined with a better understanding among clinicians of the science of individual differences, would enhance psychotherapeutic outcomes in four ways. First, by distinguishing more circumscribed problems from those closely linked to a client's broad personality dispositions, it would help clinicians to focus on aspects of their clients' lives where change is most possible, while helping the clinician to foster trait-consonant adaptations in these clients. Second, it would encourage realistic expectations by providing a better appreciation of the extent to which genetically influenced traits may be modified by environmental manipulations. Third, trait assessment and a working knowledge of the literature on individual differences could help match clients to the most effective treatment. Finally, personality trait assessment could offer a basis for empirically grounded increases in clients' self-knowledge.

Lambert and Supplee's (1997) bleak outlook for the role of individual differences in treatment planning and effectiveness is based on the disappointing track record of studies examining personality as a treatment moderator. Harkness and Lilienfeld's (1997) mandate to base psychotherapy on the science of individual differences turns on their opinion that personality has not been sufficiently or adequately studied (cf. Beutler, 1991) and in part on Costa and McCrae's (1994) distinction between *basic tendencies* (which are extremely resistant to change) and *characteristic adaptations*, which they believe make a more effective target of therapeutic influence. We now consider the possibility that this distinction between basic tendencies and characteristic adaptations can be further refined to offer new opportunities and methods to examine the role of personality in psychotherapeutic outcomes and a better understanding of aspects of personality more amenable to change. We acknowledge from the outset, however, that if history is any indicator of future efforts on this topic, the best we can muster is cautious optimism.

Levels of Personality and Possibilities for Therapeutic Change

McAdams (1994) draws from the work of Cantor (1990), Hogan (1987), and McClelland (1951) to distinguish three levels of personality: *dispositional traits, personal concerns,* and *life narratives.* He argues that the answer to the question of whether people can change during adulthood, through psychotherapy or through life experiences, depends on which level of personality we consider. McAdams describes traits, which have been the mainstay of the literature in examining personality's role in psychotherapy outcomes, as "relatively nonconditional, relatively decontextualized, generally linear, and explicitly comparative dimensions of personality" (p. 300). There is converging and abundant evidence that traits remain stable, particularly in adulthood (McCrae & Costa, 1990). The consistency of traits, as Harkness and Lilienfeld (1997) document, appears to derive in part from their genetic base and from the tendency of individuals to select social environments that support their dispositions. Among the many critiques of trait conceptions of personality, those most relevant to implications for psychotherapeutic change have been offered by Thorne and Mischel and Shoda. They argue convincingly that personality defined as traits leaves no room for "conditional patterns" (Thorne, 1989) or "if . . . then . . . situation-behavior relations as signatures of personality" (Mischel & Shoda, 1995). These conditional relations between the person and his or her world are captured in these statements, which are familiar to clinicians: "I lose my sense of control when I'm threatened" and "Life seems to lose its meaning when someone important leaves me." The notion of conditional patterns opens new opportunities not available in trait conceptions for the study of personality's role in psychotherapeutic change.

Personal concerns is McAdams's (1994) second level of personality. This level includes a person's current life tasks (Cantor, 1990), strivings (Emmons, 1986), personal projects (Palys & Little, 1983), and current concerns (Klinger, 1977). Personal concerns correspond to characteristic adaptations and refer to what a person wants at a particular point in life and how the person plans to get it. These are not traits, nor are they epiphenomena of a more "fundamental" aspect of personality. People are quite aware of this second level of their personalities because personal concerns guide everyday activities. Unlike Level 1, Level 2 is contextual and motivated. Although there is scant evidence about stability and change in Level 2, McAdams makes a strong case for the ebb and flow of personal concerns throughout life.

Positive changes at Level 2 have been documented in studies of adaptation to threatening events. For example, in response to life-threatening events and major personal loss, some individuals report significant changes in their personal concerns. When a women who received a life-threatening diagnosis remarks that personal relationships have become a focus of her everyday life in a way that is new and rewarding, she is describing a change in personality at Level 2. Or consider a young man who notes how, since his son's death, he has shifted his priorities from his work to the community. He now organizes a community program for chronically ill children, volunteers at a local hospital, and freely shares his time and expertise with the town's Little League. These generative efforts have given his life renewed purpose and reflect a change in personality at Level 2. Although such spontaneous changes are well documented, we know little about the effectiveness of intentional efforts directed toward them and even less about whether and how they might occur in a psychotherapeutic context. Nonetheless, the positive effects on well-being and physical health of positive changes in personal concerns (e.g., Affleck, Tennen, Croog, & Levine, 1987) should encourage clinicians to systematically investigate this potential avenue of therapeutic influence.

Personality at Level 3 concerns the individual's attempt to shape an identity by finding unity and purpose in life. This level of inquiry into personality processes has gained momentum among those who are interested in personal crisis and trauma (e.g., Herman, 1992) and has begun to capture the attention of clinicians who are studying psychotherapeutic change (Hermans & Hermans-Jansen, 1995). McAdams (1994) and others who draw on the narrative tradition to understand personality consider identity to be an "evolving story that integrates a reconstructed past, perceived present, and anticipated future into a coherent and vitalizing life myth" (p. 306). Personal myth, which Costa and McCrae (1994) view as part of the self-concept, cannot be reduced to traits or personal concerns. It is an internalized, unfolding narrative that is revised to give life a sense of direction, meaning, and continuity.

McAdams (1993) speculates that whereas traits remain stable throughout adulthood and personal concerns change in response to circumstances and life stage, identity is continuously being shaped—both consciously and without awareness—to provide narrative coherence and a sense of meaning and purpose to life and to fit personal experiences into this coherent account. The personal crises (called "nuclear episodes" or "nadirs" in McAdams's scheme) that propel people into psychotherapy may also provide the therapist with an opportunity to help clients' fit the crisis into their life narrative (see Neimeyer & Stewart, Chapter 16 in this volume). At this point, however, there is only scant evidence that deliberate attempts by therapists to shape or influence their clients' personal narratives will be helpful. Moreover, research participants have told us spontaneously and repeatedly that such efforts can easily be interpreted as insensitive, inept, or unwelcome attempts to minimize unique burdens and challenges.

We need to learn more about this third level of personality before we apply it to therapeutic endeavors. Nevertheless, intuitively, it seems as though life narratives may be closely tied to the therapeutic relationship. For example, some clients more readily incorporate therapists' suggestions into their personal narratives. Furthermore, aspects of the therapeutic interaction that at first appear to be therapist-induced hindrances may later modify a client's life narrative, although the empirical literature has yet to address these possibilities. There is, however, one personality characteristic—psychological reactance—that has been studied rather extensively as a predictor of therapeutic outcome. It is to this "client variable" that we now turn.

Psychological Reactance

From among more than 175 categories of clients' characteristics that have been examined as predictors of psychotherapy outcomes (Beutler, 1991), we have selected psychological reactance for special attention because: (1) it is a theoretically derived individual difference and one that is particularly relevant to the therapeutic interaction; (2) a priori hypotheses concerning its interaction with treatment are readily derived; and (3) it is one of the few individual differences for which a theory-driven statistical interaction between a client's attribute and the treatment method has been replicated (Shoham, Bootzin, Rohrbaugh, & Urry, 1996; Shoham-Salomon, Avner, & Neeman, 1989).

Reactance theory (J. W. Brehm, 1966; S. S. Brehm, 1976) is based on two central premises: (1) that people experience certain behaviors, thoughts, and attitudes as "free," meaning that they could engage in that thought, behavior, or attitude at any given time; and, (2) that a person will experience an aversive motivational state, *psychological reactance*, whenever a free behavior is threatened. In response to this threat, an individual will attempt to restore the free behavior, thought, or attitude. Sharon Brehm (1976) suggested that instances of noncompliance or resistance in psychotherapy might be understood as reactance phenomena in which clients are attempting to avoid being subject to the therapist's directives. She viewed reactance as a primarily negative, complicating factor in therapy, and she offered recommendations about ways in which therapists might avoid inducing this aversive client state. From another perspective, it can be argued that reactance phenomena can be *used*, even *mobilized* in the service of therapeutic change (Tennen & Affleck, 1991; Tennen, Eron, & Rohrbaugh, 1985; Tennen, Rohrbaugh, Press, & White, 1981), and that although reactance can be therapist-induced, it also can be measured as an individual difference variable (Dowd, 1996; Dowd, Milne & Wise, 1991). Before pursuing these clinical issues in greater detail, we briefly outline the basic tenets of reactance theory.

According to reactance theory, freedoms can be restored either directly or indirectly. If a therapist tries to tell a client what to do, the client could restore freedom directly by disobeying or doing other than that which the therapist requests. An indirect restoration of freedom might involve complying now but disregarding the therapist's next request. In the context of psychotherapy, reactance arousal as originally defined by S. S. Brehm (1976) is a psychological *state* construct, which is manifested behaviorally through noncompliance or entrenchment in already established and often maladaptive behavior patterns. J. W. Brehm (1966) proposed that the magnitude of reactance arousal is determined by three factors: (1) the importance of the threatened freedom; (2) the proportion of freedoms threatened with elimination; and (3) the magnitude of the threat. S. S. Brehm's most general recommendation to therapists is to avoid threatening a client's behavioral freedoms. One should be careful not to come on too strong, not to be too eager to persuade, not to oversell suggestions or directives, and not to put pressure on the client to comply.

Drawing on reactance theory's basic premises, Tennen et al. (1981, 1985) differentiated two types of clinical interventions: those in which therapeutic change derives from complying with the therapist's directive and those in which change results from defying the directive. *Compliance-based* interventions are effective because complying with the directive interrupts the process that maintains the client's symptoms. Symptom prescription, for example, seems to be most effective with anxiety and insomnia because these problems are maintained by attempts to stave them off. When clients comply with a symptom prescription and attempt to create the symptom, they interrupt the usual tactic of trying to prevent it. *Defiance-based* interventions are effective because people change by defying the therapeutic directive.

Two factors, both derived from reactance theory, determine whether to use compliance- or defiance-based interventions. One factor is the probability that the client will experience psychological reactance in response to a planned intervention. The second factor concerns the behavior or attitude to be influenced: does the client believe that it is "free"? Defiance-based strategies are most effective when the target behavior is free and reactance potential is high. Compliance-based interventions are most effective with "unfree" behaviors like symptoms and when reactance potential is low or when it is low and the target behavior is free.

Unlike S. S. Brehm (1976), Tennen et al. (1981, 1985) asserted that threatening a client's behavioral freedoms, coming on strong, being eager to persuade, overselling suggestions or directives, and authoritatively pressuring the client to comply may be therapeutically effective in the context of a defiance-based intervention. Yet like Brehm and most others who have considered reactance phenomena and psychological change processes, their conceptualization of reactance retained its original status as a psychological *state* induced by others' interpersonal influence attempts. Potentially stable individual differences in reactance potential, though given some attention, is prominent in neither formulation.

More recently, investigators have begun to consider psychological reactance as a quality of the individual that can be assessed before treatment and independent of the therapist's efforts to influence the client. In one of the first controlled studies of the causal role of reactance in psychotherapeutic change, Shoham-Salomon, Avner, and Neeman (1989) measured reactance from clients' content-filtered tone of voice, which according to Zuckerman, DePaulo, and Rosenthal (1986), is the least controlled channel of communication. At the beginning of their first therapy session for procrastination, participants were asked by the therapist to describe their problem and to estimate the extent to which it could be controlled and overcome without therapeutic assistance. The first 20 seconds of each participant's uninterrupted speech was rated (with acceptable levels of interjudge reliability) on three bipolar scales to form a reactance indicator. Shoham-Salomon et al. found that in subsequent treatments based on paradoxical interventions, individuals demonstrating higher initial reactance benefited more from therapy than did those with lower reactance scores. In treatments based on self-control principles, reactance did not moderate outcomes (cf. Shoham-Salomon & Jancourt, 1985). These investigators concluded that reactance could be conceptualized either as an individual difference variable or as one that is situationally aroused.

Dowd and associates have examined carefully individual differences in reactance. Citing evidence first reported by Brehm and Brehm (1981) that links reactance to an internal locus of control, Type A personality characteristics, and private self-consciousness, Dowd and Seibel (1990) offered a model of the developmental origins of characterological reactance. Dowd, Milne, and Wise (1991) developed the Therapeutic Reactance Scale (TRS) as an individual difference indicator of psychological reactance and reported that scores were normally distributed and reasonably stable over time. Dowd and Wallbrown (1993) and Dowd, Wallbrown, Sanders, and Yesenosky (1994) found that reactance measured by the TRS was correlated positively with dominance, independence, autonomy, denial, self-sufficiency, lack of tolerance, and lack of conformity. The overall pattern of findings support Dowd's (1996) formulation of psychological reactance as a potentially important individual difference variable related to therapeutic outcome.

The reactance-based model of therapeutic intervention is explicit in its endorsement of selecting interventions to match the therapist's expectation of compliance or resistance. With compliance-based interventions, the therapist attempts to maximize compliance by avoiding threats to behavioral freedom and framing interventions in a manner consistent with the client's own construct system. With defiance-based strategies, the therapist tries to maximize psychological reactance. The recent conceptualization of reactance as an individual difference variable offers the opportunity to extend the idea of treatment matching to this individual difference factor. Although several studies have failed to produce a statistical interaction between reactance and treatment when reactance was measured by a questionnaire as a personality characteristic (e.g., Dowd, Hughs, Brockbank, Halpain, Seibel, & Seibel, 1988; Horvath & Goheen, 1990), the findings from a study by Shoham et al. (1996) that used speech pattern ratings hold promise for continued inquiry in this area of individual differences in psychotherapeutic change.

Shoham et al. (1996) hypothesized that individual differences in psychological reactance measured before and during therapy would moderate differential treatment effects for insomnia, with more highly reactant individuals benefiting more from paradoxical interventions (PI), which involve prescribing the very symptom the client sought to change, and those low in reactance showing more favorable outcomes from progressive muscle relaxation (PMR). Clients who met DSM-IIIR criteria for primary sleep onset insomnia were randomly assigned to one of two PI conditions, to PMR, or to an attention-measurement control group. Psychological reactance was measured in the first session by content-filtered speech segments, following the previously described procedures of Shoham-Salomon et al. (1989). Clients' reactance moderated treatment effects as hypothesized: paradoxical interventions were more effective for high- than for low-reactance clients, and PMR was more effective for clients with low reactance. Findings such as these should stimulate further research into how individual differences, including differences in trait reactance, might be used effectively to match treatments to clients' characteristics.

Client Attribute X Treatment Interactions

The success of Shoham et al. (1996) and Shoham-Salomon et al. (1989) in demonstrating how an individual difference variable moderates the effectiveness of treatment is, unfortunately, an anomaly in the literature that has examined how treatments interact with clients' characteristics. This field has been termed aptitude-treatment interaction (ATI) research (Cronbach & Snow, 1997; Dance and Neufield, 1988):

> In its simplest form, subjects are measured on some aptitude (X) and then randomly assigned to . . . treatments. [R]egression equations are calculated within each treatment group, using the individual difference measure as a predictor of the outcome. . . . An interaction of aptitude with treatment is present when the obtained regression slopes differ. (Dance & Neufield, 1988, pp. 192–193)

After comprehensively reviewing ATI studies of anxiety disorders, depression, pain, and weight reduction, Dance and Neufield concluded, "There are no well-documented client characteristics that can serve as the basis for treatment selection" (p. 209).

The most ambitious effort to test client X treatment interactions is Project MATCH (Project MATCH Research Group, 1997a). This multisite, randomized clinical trial of matching alcoholism treatments to clients' characteristics consisted of two parallel matching studies, one that recruited participants from five outpatient sites and another that recruited participants from five aftercare treatment centers following inpatient or outpatient hospital treatment. The 952 outpatients and 774 aftercare clients in this study were randomly assigned to one of three treatments: cognitive behavioral coping skills therapy (CBT; Kadden et al., 1992), motivational enhancement therapy (MET; Miller et al., 1992), and twelve-step facilitation therapy (TSF; Nowinski, Baker & Carroll, 1992). The Project Match Research Group was careful to select theoretically derived a priori matching hypotheses to 10 client characteristics including severity of alcohol involvement, gender, and a composite typology index. Despite its large sample, random assignment to well-defined treatments that were selected to differentially influence the selected client characteristics, use of multidimensional assessment, and inclusion of psychological and demographic client characteristics as matching variables, Project MATCH found extremely limited support for the hypothesis that individual differences among clients interact with treatment modality to differentially influence drinking outcomes. Only one of the 10 client characteristics examined, psychiatric severity, demonstrated a reliable matching effect: less severely impaired outpatients showed greater abstinence following treatment when treated with TSF than those treated with CBT. As psychiatric severity increased, TSF and CBT were comparable. Even client characteristics that had previously produced hypothesized matching results in smaller and less well-controlled studies at single treatment sites (e.g., sociopathy) yielded no evidence that these characteristics were differentially responsive to the three treatments. These (null) findings echo the lack of evidence for attribute X treatment interactions in the broader psychotherapy literature (Smith & Sechrest, 1991; Snow, 1991).

These investigators also examined hypotheses related to 11 secondary client attributes including psychopathology, religiosity, self-efficacy, readiness to change, social functioning, anger, and interpersonal dependence (Project MATCH Research Group, 1997b). Although two of these client attributes showed modest client X treatment interactions, the authors are appropriately conservative in their interpretation of both the primary and secondary findings in view of the numerous statistical contrasts performed. With more than thirty predicted contrasts performed to test matching hypotheses, the investigators were forced to conclude,

> [T]he number of hypotheses tested leaves open the possibility that these were attributable to chance. . . . Matching effects of this magnitude and specificity, as presently understood, will likely have limited practical clinical significance . . . the intuitively appealing notion that matching can appreciably enhance treatment effectiveness has been severely challenged. (p. 1690)

A CRITIQUE OF RETENTION AND OUTCOME STUDIES

Our review of the literature demonstrates that demographic characteristics, severity of psychological disturbance, and personality have been investigated extensively in relation to treatment response. These efforts have rarely converged on the importance of personal characteristics in influencing psychotherapy retention and outcome. We can draw one of two conclusions based on these null results: (1) client variables may have little influence on psychotherapy or (2) the studies that have addressed these issues have varied so markedly in subject populations, methodology, and outcome measurements that they render comparisons between studies difficult at best. Before considering the first conclusion, it is necessary to address the second.

The type and nature of client populations studied, as well as the clinical setting, varies immensely across the different studies cited, and these factors surely influence outcomes. People seek therapy for a multitude of reasons. Some initiate treatment voluntarily, some are referred for therapy, and still others are mandated to it. From each of these categories, a subset of individuals is offered and accepts treatment, others are not offered treatment or are referred elsewhere, and some are offered but refuse therapy. To further differentiate these subsets, individuals who seek treatment at community mental health centers are likely to differ from those who are seen at private clinics, in terms of the nature, duration and extent of disturbance, as well as demographic factors. Both of these groups of clients may differ substantially from patients seen as part of research studies who generally meet specific diagnostic characteristics and undergo an extensive battery of assessments before treatment is initiated. Thus, research participants may be substantially different from general treatment-seeking populations.

The distinction between treatment retention and outcome also deserves closer scrutiny. Retention simply refers to receiving psychotherapy, whereas outcome refers to obtaining some benefit. Some patients leave treatment after one or two sessions because they have already achieved the desired beneficial effect. Others may leave after the same interval because they are experiencing neither positive nor negative effects. Some may continue in therapy for long periods of time but not experience beneficial effects. Unfortunately, patients' characteristics alone are not the sole factor in the decision to discontinue treatment. Differences in reimbursement schedules, financial circumstances, and clinic policies also affect retention.

Even among studies addressing only retention, the definition of retention varies considerably. Some studies consider premature termination to mean not appearing for the first treatment session. Approximately 40% of patients who attend intake evaluations and are offered therapy do not keep their first appointment (e.g., Fordney-Settlage, 1975; Phillips & Fagan, 1982; Sue et al., 1976). Others evaluate only those who show up for the first therapy session, whereas still others include only patients who receive a certain number of sessions. Some studies focus on the actual number of sessions received, whereas other studies categorize patients into therapy completers vs. terminators. The definition of a completer varies dramatically across studies, with patients who attend at least 6 sessions, for example, considered to have successfully completed a course of therapy in some studies, and other studies classifying patients who received fewer than 26 sessions as premature terminators. Thus, one study's completer would be considered a premature terminator in another study. In most of these reports, moreover, the reason for therapy discontinuation is not reported. Because duration of treatment is rarely standardized in typical clinical settings, the definition of completers and noncompleters may be further obscured by therapists' interpretations or individual judgments (e.g., Pekarik, 1983).

Therapeutic outcomes also demonstrate wide variations in definition and measurement. Criteria for appraising outcome range from therapists' judgments, clients' judgments, independent judges' ratings, tests and questionnaires, and behavioral tasks. The variety of outcome indicators and the relatively few attempts to establish their concordance create significant challenges for those wishing to compare predictors of outcomes across studies.

Furthermore, psychotherapy outcome studies have been dominated by the use of "common" outcome measures for all study participants and have focused on changes in *levels* of these measures rather than changes in their temporal patterning or changes in their relation to other conceptually relevant variables. In regard to using common outcome measures, Shoham-Salomon and Hannah (1991) make a compelling argument that within the same therapy, different clients may experience different but equally worthwhile outcomes. They demonstrate this possibility by pointing to the Shoham-Salomon et al. (1989) study in which the investigators hypothesized and found that, when provided with paradoxical interventions, high-reactance clients became more effective in their daily activities, whereas low-reactance clients reported an enhanced sense of self-efficacy for dealing with the problem that brought them to treatment. Employing theoretically derived outcome measures that do not require all clients to change in the same way might not only strengthen the study of how individual differences contribute to treatment outcome but also shed light on individual differences in the *process* of change. Similarly, Dance and Neufield (1988) have recommended that treatment outcome measures assess multiple dimensions of improvement. This is necessary, they argue, because ATIs may not appear for self-report measures,

but they may emerge for behavioral outcome measures (recall the parallel argument about measuring reactance as a client's characteristic).

If we take seriously the possibility that personality at the level of personal concerns and life narratives might itself change as the result of psychotherapeutic intervention, we may need to reconsider the range of indicators we use to measure change even further than suggested by Shoham-Salomon and Hannah (1991) and Dance and Neufield (1988). Lambert, Shapiro, and Bergin's (1986) observation that change in personality (construed as dispositional tendencies) is considered irrelevant in most treatment studies is an accurate appraisal of the psychotherapy outcome literature, in large part because the most widely used indexes of change are those measuring depressive symptoms, anxiety, and global symptoms (Lambert & Supplee, 1997). Yet therapeutically generated changes in personal concerns or shifts in life narratives might leave some individuals "sadder but perhaps wiser." Those who confront and overcome challenges become more virtuous (McAdams, 1993) but not necessarily more hopeful or less distressed. For example, an individual whose personal narrative emphasizes tragic features may successfully come to grips with a major personal failure or loss without losing the tragic appreciation that such success is never unalloyed. Global symptom measures or counts of depressive symptoms, while informative, seem unable to fully capture the positive changes in personality that McAdams labels Levels 2 and 3.

Defining personality at Level 2 in terms of "conditional patterns" (Thorne, 1989) or "*if . . . then . . .* situation-behavior relations" (Mischel & Shoda, 1995) creates further challenges to the accurate assessment of therapeutic change. We believe that the best way to measure conditional patterns is not by questionnaire-based retrospective reports but rather through "real-time" data-collection strategies, using daily and within-day assessments (Stone & Shiffman, 1994; Tennen & Affleck, 1996). People are notoriously poor at reconstructing contingent probabilities (Jenkins & Ward, 1965), and we suspect that such reconstructions become increasingly inaccurate as the factors involved in these patterns become more personally relevant. Nearly all psychotherapy outcome measures reflect *levels* of the variable of interest rather than their *temporal patterning* or contingent *relation* to other clinically relevant variables.

Temporal patterns and temporally contingent relations need not be limited to the measurement of McAdams's (1994) Level 2 personal concerns. For example, among individuals facing more stressful events, prospectively measured, daily self-esteem instability predicts the greatest increase in depressive symptoms over time (Kernis et al., 1998; Roberts and Monroe, 1992). To adequately capture the temporal patterns inherent in the concept of esteem stability, psychotherapy outcome studies would need to turn to pre-post designs that include within-person measures of daily esteem over days or weeks.

Self-esteem stability is an indicator of temporal patterning. Contingent relations are another, as yet untapped category of outcome indicators. In a recent study, we measured pain and sleep quality every day for 30 days in a cohort of patients suffering from the widespread pain and disturbed sleep associated with fibromyalgia (Affleck & Tennen, 1998). Patients who met DSM-III-R criteria for major depression showed no relation between today's pain and tonight's sleep, whereas their nondepressed counterparts slept better after days of decreasing pain. Although *level* of sleep quality, *level* of pain, and *intensity* of depressive symptoms are important outcome indicators for any therapeutic intervention directed at these chronic pain sufferers, we believe that the within-person pain-sleep nexus is equally important and can be captured only through real-time within-person assessment of *contingent relations* over days or weeks.

The distinction in the personality literature between basic tendencies and characteristic adaptations reinforces our call for psychotherapy outcome indicators that capture temporally unfolding contingent relations. For example, individuals high on neuroticism (N) demonstrate a basic tendency to experience worry and depression, and it is unlikely that any therapeutic effort will change a high-N individual into someone who is carefree and happy. But high-N individuals also typically respond to threatening circumstances with heightened emotional reactivity (above their high baseline of negative affectivity). Therapeutic interventions that address the reactive component of N may be more successful than those attempting to change the basic tendency to experience negative affect, and a sensitive measure of that success would need to assess the emotional reactivity as it unfolded in an individual's everyday life. Daily process outcome indicators can be burdensome for clients, therapists, and investigators,

and at this point it is not clear if such complex measures might themselves become unintended interventions. Despite these challenges, we believe that the concepts of conditional patterns and characteristic adaptations require the development of new treatment outcome measures. Their development holds the promise of changing our focus from the study of *outcome variables* to the study of *outcome processes*.

Finally, we offer a word of caution about measuring individual differences and the implications of measurement for replicating individual difference main effects and treatment interactions. Beutler (1991) has urged investigators interested in individual differences to work toward reducing measurement redundancy across concepts and toward increasing the measurement consistency of comparable concepts. Although it may seem obvious that theoretically related individual difference concepts should employ related indicators, and even more obvious that any particular individual difference concept examined across studies should be measured with indicators that relate strongly to one another, this is often not the case. Beutler offered several examples of client variables that have been measured inconsistently across studies, resulting in only weak relations between indicators of the same individual difference. Perhaps the most striking example is in the measurement of reactance. Whereas studies using the TRS as a measure of reactance have generally failed to obtain reactance X treatment interactions, the two studies that have measured reactance by having raters code content-filtered speech segments (Shoham et al., 1996; Shoham-Salomon et al., 1989) have obtained interactions consistent with theory. Although differences in sample size, therapies, therapists, and a host of other factors may explain the inconsistent findings, we believe that one need not look further than the correlation between the TRS and content-filtered speech ratings, which is essentially zero (Shoham, personal communication, May 1998). Before investigators turn beyond the more than 175 client variables that have already been examined to explain therapeutic outcomes, they should be sure that those constructs that have not received replicable support have been investigated with comparable measures.

FUTURE DIRECTIONS

As our review thus far demonstrates, although there has been no shortage of background, personality and emotional characteristics of the client purported to predict therapeutic outcomes, few of these individual differences have withstood replication, and at best the findings can be described as inconsistent (Garfield, 1978, 1986, 1994). Shoham-Salomon and Hannah (1991) offered three significant challenges to investigators wishing to continue the pursuit of treatment-relevant client characteristics. First, they remind us that most of the background characteristics examined such as gender, age, and socioeconomic status are best thought of as proxies for psychologically meaningful factors. Second, many of these individual differences, such as treatment motivation, though typically considered stable qualities of the individual, tend to be themselves influenced by therapy in ways that make them either diminish or enhance their predictive power during treatment. Finally, because most of the client variables studied have been based on theoretically devoid post hoc expeditions (see Smith & Sechrest, 1991) or extracted out of context from other areas of research, "serendipitous (findings) remain exactly that, and there is little reason to expect them to be replicated" (Shoham-Salomon & Hannah, 1991, p. 220). The repeated failure of attempts to find meaningful client variables that predict outcomes has led to familiar post hoc (and to us unconvincing) explanations: methodological limitations of the studies, relatively small samples, and the ever elusive possibility that there may yet be a neglected client variable that reliably predicts or moderates treatment outcomes.

The idea that characteristics of the client influence psychotherapy outcomes, nevertheless, is as intuitively appealing now as it was over thirty years ago when Kiesler (1966) urged investigators to dispel the myth of "patient uniformity." Yet, our review, like previous reviews of client variables, suggests that those main effects that have been replicated are rather mundane. Less mundane effects, such as that individuals who need treatment least benefit most, are disheartening. Equally appealing in the absence of main effects is the prediction of client X treatment interactions. One needs to be exceptionally optimistic to interpret these findings as encouraging. Although the literature includes occasional support for theoretically derived client X treatment interactions (Beutler et al., 1991; Shoham-Salomon et al., 1989), such interactions often provide little improvement over separate linear effects (Dawes, 1988; Smith & Sechrest, 1991) and their clinical implications are often negligible.

We agree that efforts to match clients to treatments might be enhanced by (1) considering different outcomes as relevant for different clients (Shoham-Salomon & Hannah, 1991); (2) focusing on theory-driven interactions that include competing models in designs that attend to statistical power and other statistical requirements (Beutler, 1991; Cronbach & Snow, 1977; Smith & Sechrest, 1991); (3) using reliable instruments (Dance & Neufield, 1988) and, as we have suggested in this chapter, indicators of multiple levels of personality; (4) retaining the integrity of treatments regardless of the resources this may demand (Dance & Neufield, 1988); (5) applying the technique of manipulated assessment in which therapists are assigned randomly either to receive assessment information or to receive no assessment information to determine how such information contributes to treatment efficacy (Hayes, Nelson, & Jarrett, 1987; Harkness & Lilienfeld, 1997); (6) distinguishing treatment models from specific treatment interventions and focusing on the latter (Shoham & Rohrbaugh, 1995); and (7) considering how characteristics of clients' relationships with spouses or significant others may indicate different intervention strategies (Shoham, Rohrbaugh, Stickle, & Jacob, in press). Still, we find it difficult to be devoted to the proposition that client variables may influence treatment outcomes.

In the decades since Kiesler (1966) called for studies to dispel the patient uniformity myth, this area of inquiry has produced more heat than light. The evidence does not appear to support the notion that client variables relate to treatment outcomes (Dance & Neufield 1988; Project MATCH Group, 1997a, 1997b). To remain hopeful, one would need to selectively scan and weigh data, evaluate new pieces of evidence separately rather than collectively, and ignore negative results. These are the cognitive processes that define wishful thinking (Elster, 1983), not the scientific attitude that should guide our study of the psychotherapy process.

Smith and Sechrest (1991) suggested that after exerting so much effort to find individual differences relating to psychotherapy outcomes, we may now find it too painful to abandon the cause. It is hard to disagree that something other than the available evidence seems to drive the search for the ever elusive client variable in psychotherapy outcome and efficacy research. On the other hand, there was a time not too long ago when it was fashionable to claim that psychotherapy had no demonstrable superiority over a placebo ("Psychotherapy Caveat," 1974). Smith and Glass's (1977) meta-analysis of psychotherapy outcome studies proved otherwise, and more recent meta-analyses of specific therapies for specific conditions (e.g., Gloaguen, Cottraux, Cucherat, & Blackburn, 1998), along with support for a number of "empirically supported treatments" (Chambless, 1996), makes Eysenck's (1965) claim that clients improve comparably whether or not they receive treatment seem antiquated. A decade from now, as investigators more regularly turn to reliable, theoretically derived, multidimensional individual difference indicators applied in large multisite studies, we may wonder how we could have concluded that there was scant evidence that clients' attributes influence treatment outcome and even less evidence that matching treatment to clients' characteristics enhances the effectiveness of psychotherapeutic efforts. For now, without benefit of prescience, however, we cannot conclude otherwise.

REFERENCES

Affleck, G., & Tennen, H. (1998, May). *Selective evaluations and coping efforts as daily processes in adaptation to chronic pain*. Paper presented at the annual meeting of the American Psychological Society, Washington, DC.

Affleck, G., Tennen, H., Croog, S., & Levine, S. (1987). Causal attribution, perceived benefits, and morbidity following a heart attack: An eight-year study. *Journal of Consulting and Clinical Psychology, 55*, 29–35.

Agosti, V., Nunes, E., & Ocepeck-Welikson, K. (1996). Patient factors related to early attrition from an outpatient cocaine research clinic. *American Journal of Drug and Alcohol Abuse, 22*, 29–39.

Armbruster, P., & Fallon, T. (1994). Clinical, sociodemographic, and systems risk factors for attrition in a children's mental health clinic. *American Journal of Orthopsychiatry, 64*, 577–585.

Bandura, A. (1997). Health promotion from the perspective of social cognitive theory. *Psychology and Health, 12*, 1–27.

Barber, J. P., & Muenz, L. R. (1996). The role of avoidance and obsessiveness in matching patients to cognitive and interpersonal psychotherapy: Empirical findings from the Treatment for Depression Collaborative Research Program. *Journal of Consulting and Clinical Psychology, 64*, 951–958.

Barron, F. (1953a). An ego-strength scale which predicts response to psychotherapy. *Journal of Consulting Psychology, 17*, 327–333.

Barron, F. (1953b). Some test correlates of response to psychotherapy. *Journal of Consulting Psychology, 17*, 235–241.

Beck, N. C., Lamberti, J., Gamache, M., Lake, E. A., Fraps, C. L., McReynolds, W. T., Reaven, N., Heisler, G. H., & Dunn, J. (1987). Situational factors and behavioral self-predictions in the identification of clients at high risk to drop out of psychotherapy. *Journal of Clinical Psychology, 43*, 511–520.

Beckham, E. E. (1989). Improvement after evaluation in psychotherapy of depression: Evidence of a placebo effect? *Journal of Clinical Psychology, 45*, 945–950.

Beitman, B. D., Beck, N. C., Deuser, W. W., Carter, C. S., Davidson, J. R. T., & Maddock, R. J. (1994). Patient stage of change predicts outcome in a panic disorder medication trial. *Anxiety, 1*, 64–69.

Berrigan, L. P., & Garfield, S. L. (1981). Relationship of missed psychotherapy appointments to premature termination and social class. *The British Journal of Clinical Psychology, 20*, 239–242.

Beutler, L. E. (1991). Have all won and must all have prizes? Revisiting Luborsky et al.'s verdict. *Journal of Consulting and Clinical Psychology, 59*, 226–232.

Beutler, L. E., Engle, D., Mohr, D., Doldrup, R. J., Bergan, J., Meredith, K., & Merry, W. (1991). Predictors of differential response to cognitive, experiential, and self-directed psychotherapeutic procedures. *Journal of Consulting and Clinical Psychology, 59*, 333–340.

Brehm, J. W. (1966). *A theory of psychological reactance*. New York: Academic Press.

Brehm, S. S. (1976). *The application of social psychology to clinical practice*. Washington, DC: Hemisphere Press.

Brehm, S. S., & Brehm, J. W. (1981). *Psychological reactance: A theory of freedom and control*. New York: Academic Press.

Buller, R., Maier, W., Goldenberg, I. M., & Lavori, P. W. (1991). Chronology of panic and avoidance, age of onset in panic disorder, and prediction of treatment response: A report from the Cross-National Collaborative Panic Study. *European Archives of Psychiatry and Clinical Neuroscience, 240*, 163–168.

Burns, D. D., Sayers, S. L., & Moras, K. (1994). Intimate relationships and depression: Is there a causal connection? *Journal of Consulting and Clinical Psychology, 62*, 1033–1043.

Butcher, J. N., & Koss, M. P. (1978). Research on brief and crisis-oriented psychotherapies. In S. L. Garfield & A. E. Bergin (Eds.), *Handbook of psychotherapy and behavior change* (2nd ed., pp. 725–768). New York: Wiley.

Cameron, O. G., Thyer, B. A., Feckner, S., & Nesse, R. (1986). Behavior therapy of phobias:

Predictors of outcome. *Psychiatry Research, 19,* 245–246.

Cantor, N. (1990). From thought to behavior: "Having" and "doing" in the study of personality and cognition. *American Psychologist, 45,* 735–750.

Cartwright, R. D., & Lerner, B. (1963). Empathy, need to change, and improvement with psychotherapy. *Journal of Consulting Psychology, 27,* 138–144.

Chambless, D. L. (1996). In defense of dissemination of empirically supported psychological interventions. *Clinical Psychology: Science and Practice, 3,* 230–235.

Costa, P. T., Jr., & McCrae, R. R. (1994). Set like plaster? Evidence for the stability of adult personality. In T. F. Heatherton and J. L. Weinberger (Eds.), *Can personality change?* (pp. 21–40). Washington, DC: American Psychological Association.

Costello, R. M., Baillargeon, J. G., Biever, P., & Bennett, K. (1979). Second-year alcoholism treatment outcome evaluation with a focus on Mexican-American patients. *American Journal of Drug and Alcohol Abuse, 6,* 97–108.

Cronbach, L. J., & Snow, R. E. (1977). *Aptitudes and instructional methods.* New York: Irvington.

Dance, K. A., & Neufield, R. W. J. (1988). Aptitude-treatment interaction research in the clinical setting: A review of attempts to dispel the "patient uniformity" myth. *Psychological Bulletin, 104,* 192–213.

Dawes, R. M. (1988). *Rational choice in an uncertain world.* New York: Harcourt Brace Jovanovich.

DiClemente, C. C., Prochaska, J. O., Fairhurst, S., Velicer, W. F., Velasquez, M., & Rossi, J. S. (1991). The process of smoking cessation: An analysis of precontemplation, contemplation and preparation stages of change. *Journal of Consulting and Clinical Psychology, 59,* 295–304.

Dodd, J. A. (1970). A retrospective analysis of variables related to duration of treatment in a university psychiatric clinic. *Journal of Nervous and Mental Disease, 151,* 75–85.

Dowd, E. T. (1996). *Resistance and personality.* Paper presented at the annual meeting of the Association for the Advancement of Behavior Therapy, New York.

Dowd, E. T., Hughes, S. L., Brockbank, L., Halpain, D., Seibel, C., & Seibel, P. (1988). Compliance-based and defiance-based intervention strategies and psychological reactance in the treatment of free and unfree behavior. *Journal of Counseling Psychology, 35,* 370–376.

Dowd, E. T., Milne, C. R., & Wise, S. L. (1991). The Therapeutic Reactance Scale: A measure of psychological reactance. *Journal of Counseling and Development, 69,* 541–545.

Dowd, E. T., & Seibel, C. A. (1990). A cognitive theory of resistance and reactance: Implications for treatment. *Journal of Mental Health Counseling, 12,* 458–469.

Dowd, E. T., & Wallbrown, F. (1993). Motivational components of client reactance. *Journal of Counseling and Development, 71,* 533–538.

Dowd, E. T., Wallbrown, F., Sanders, D., & Yesenosky, J. M. (1994). Psychological reactance and its relationship to normal personality variables. *Cognitive Therapy and Research, 18,* 601–612.

DuBrin, J. R., & Zastowny, T. R. (1988). Predicting early attention from psychotherapy: An analysis of a large private practice cohort. *Psychotherapy, 25,* 393–408.

Durham, R. C., Allan, T., & Hackett, C. A. (1997). On predicting improvement and relapse in generalized anxiety disorder following psychotherapy. *British Journal of Clinical Psychology, 36,* 101–119.

Elster, J. (1983). *Sour grapes: Studies in the subversion of rationality.* New York: Cambridge University Press.

Emmons, R. (1986). Personal strivings: An approach to personality and subjective well-being. *Journal of Personality and Social Psychology, 51,* 1058–1068.

Epstein, E. E., McCrady, B. S., Miller, K. J., & Steinberg, M. (1994). Attrition from conjoint alcoholism treatment: Do dropouts differ from completers? *Journal of Substance Abuse, 6,* 249–265.

Ewing, T. N. (1974). Racial similarity of client and counselor and client satisfaction with counseling. *Journal of Consulting Psychology, 21,* 446–469.

Eysenck, H. J. (1965). The effects of psychotherapy. *Journal of Psychology, 1,* 97–118.

Fiester, A. R., & Rudestam, K. E. (1975). A multivariate analysis of the early dropout process. *Journal of Consulting and Clinical Psychology, 43,* 528–535.

Fiske, D. W., Cartwright, D. S., & Kirtner, W. L. (1964). Are psychotherapeutic changes predicable? *Journal of Abnormal and Social Psychology, 69,* 418–426.

Flaskerud, J. H., & Liu, P. Y. (1991). Effects of an Asian client-therapist language, ethnicity and gender match on utilization and outcome of therapy. *Community Mental Health Journal, 27,* 31–42.

Fordney-Settlage, D. S. (1975). Heterosexual dysfunction: Evaluation of treatment procedures. *Archives of Sexual Behavior, 4,* 367–387.

Fortney, J. C., Booth, B. M., Blow, F. C., & Bunn, J. Y. (1995). The effects of travel barriers and age on the utilization of alcoholism treatment aftercare. *American Journal of Drug and Alcohol Abuse, 21,* 391–406.

Frank, J. D. (1974). Therapeutic components of psychotherapy. A 25-year progress report of research. *The Journal of Nervous and Mental Disease, 159,* 325–342.

Frank, J. D., Gliedman, L. H., Imber, S. D., Nash, E. H., Jr., & Stone, A. R. (1957). Why patients leave psychotherapy. *Archives of Neurology and Psychiatry, 77,* 283–299.

Fujino, D. C., Okazaki, S., & Young, K. (1994). Asian-American women in the mental health system: An examination of ethnic and gender match between therapist and client. Special issue: Asian-American mental health. *Journal of Community Psychology, 22,* 164–176.

Garfield, S. L. (1978). Research on client variables in psychotherapy. In S. L. Garfield & A. E. Bergin (Eds.), *Handbook of psychotherapy and behavior change* (2nd ed., pp. 191–232). New York: Wiley.

Garfield, S. L. (1986). Research on client variables in psychotherapy. In S. L. Garfield & A. E. Bergin (Eds.), *Handbook of psychotherapy and behavior change* (3rd ed., pp. 213–256). New York: Wiley.

Garfield, S. L. (1994). Research on client variables in psychotherapy. In S. L. Garfield & A. E. Bergin (Eds.), *Handbook of psychotherapy and behavior change* (4th ed., pp. 72–113). New York: Wiley.

Gasperini, M., Scherillo, P., Manfredonia, M. G., & Franchini, L. (1993). A study of relapses in subjects with mood disorder on lithium treatment. *European Neuropsychopharmacology, 3,* 103–110.

Getter, H., & Sunderland, D. M. (1962). The Barron ego-strength scale and psychotherapy outcome. *Journal of Consulting Psychology, 26,* 195.

Gloaguen, V., Cottraux, J., Cucherat, M., & Blackburn, I. (1998). A meta-analysis of the effects of cognitive therapy in depressed patients. *Journal of Affective Disorders, 49,* 59–72.

Greenspan, M., & Kulish, N. M. (1985). Factors in premature termination in long term psychotherapy. *Psychotherapy, 22,* 75–82.

Gunderson, J. G., Frank, A. F., Ronningstam, E. F., Wachter, S., Lynch, V. J., & Wolf, P. J. (1989). Early discontinuance of borderline patients from psychotherapy. *Journal of Nervous and Mental Disease, 177,* 38–42.

Haaga, D. A., DeRubeis, R. J., Steward, B. L., & Beck, A. T. (1991). Relationship of intelligence with cognitive therapy outcome. *Behaviour Research and Therapy, 29,* 277–281.

Harkness, A. R., & Lilienfeld, S. O. (1997). Individual differences science for treatment planning: Personality traits. *Psychological Assessment, 9,* 349–360.

Hayes, S. C., Nelson, R. O., & Jarrett, R. B. (1987). The treatment utility of assessment: A functional approach to evaluating assessment quality. *American Psychologist, 42,* 963–974.

Herman, J. L. (1992). *Trauma and recovery: The aftermath of violence from domestic abuse to political terror.* New York: Basic Books.

Hermans, H., & Hermans-Jansen, E. (1995). *Self-narratives: The construction of meaning in psychotherapy.* New York: Guilford.

Hoberman, H. M., Lewinshon, P. M., & Tilson, M. (1988). Group treatment of depression: Individual predictors of outcome. *Journal of Consulting and Clinical Psychology, 56,* 393–398.

Hogan, R. (1987). Personality psychology: Back to basics. In J. Aronoff, A. I. Rabin, & R. A. Zucker (Eds.), *The emergence of personality* (pp. 79–104). New York: Springer.

Horowitz, M. J., Marmar, C., Weiss, D. S., DeWitt, K. N., & Roseonbaum, R. (1984). Brief psychotherapy of bereavement reactions: The relationship of process to outcome. *Archives of General Psychiatry, 41,* 438–448.

Horvath, A. O., & Goheen, M. D. (1990). Factors mediating the success of defiance- and compliance-based interventions. *Journal of Counseling Psychology, 37,* 363–371.

Jenkins, H. M., & Ward, W. C. (1965). Judgment of contingency between responses and outcomes. *Psychological Monographs: General and Applied, 79,* 1–17.

Jones, E. E. (1978). Effects of race on psychotherapy process and outcome: An exploratory investigation. *Psychotherapy: Theory, Research, and Practice, 15,* 226–236.

Jones, E. E., & Zoppel, C. L. (1982). Impact of client and therapist gender on psychotherapy process and outcome. *Journal of Consulting and Clinical Psychology, 50,* 259–272.

Kadden, R., Carroll, K. M., Donovan, D., Cooney, N., Monti, P., Abrams, D., Litt, M., & Hester, R. (1992). *Cognitive-behavioral coping skills manual: A clinical research guide for therapists treating individuals with alcohol abuse and dependence.* NIAAA Project MATCH Monograph, Vol. 3. DHHS Publication No. (ADM) 92-1895. Washington, DC: U.S. Government Printing Office.

Keithy, L. J., Samples, S. J., & Strupp, H. H. (1980). Patient motivation as a predictor of process and outcome in psychotherapy. *Psychotherapy and Psychosomatics, 33,* 87–97.

Kernberg, O. F., Burstein, E. D., Coyne, L., Applebaum, A., Horwitz, L., & Voth, H. (1972). Psychotherapy and psychoanalysis: Final report of the Menninger Foundation's Psychotherapy Research Project. *Bulletin of the Menninger Clinic, 36,* 1–276.

Kernis, M. H., Whisenhunt, C. R., Waschull, S. B., Greenier, K. D., Berry, A. J., Herlocker, C. E., & Anderson, C. A. (1998). Multiple facets of self-esteem and their relations to depressive symptoms. *Personality and Social Psychology Bulletin, 24,* 657–668.

Kiesler, D. J. (1966). Some myths of psychotherapy research and the search for a paradigm. *Psychological Bulletin, 65,* 110–136.

Klinger, E. (1977). *Meaning and void: Inner experience and the incentives in people's lives.* Minneapolis: University of Minnesota Press.

Lambert, M. J., Shapiro, D. A., & Bergin, A. E. (1986). The effectiveness of psychotherapy. In S. L. Garfield & A. E. Bergin (Eds.), *The handbook of psychotherapy and behavior change* (3rd ed., pp. 157–212). New York: Wiley.

Lambert, M. J., & Supplee, E. C. (1997). Trends and practices in psychotherapy outcome assessment and their implications for psychotherapy and applied personality. In S. Briggs (Ed.), *Handbook of personality psychology* (pp. 947–967). New York: Academic Press.

Liljestrand, P., Gerling, E., & Saliba, P. A. (1978). The effects of social sex-role stereotypes and sexual orientation on psychotherapeutical outcomes. *Journal of Homosexuality, 3,* 361–372.

Lorion, R. P. (1973). Socioeconomic status and traditional treatment approaches reconsidered. *Psychological Bulletin, 79,* 262–270.

Luborsky, L., Chandler, M., Auerbach, A. H., Cohen, J., & Bachrach, H. M. (1971). Factors influencing the outcome of psychotherapy: A review of quantitative research. *Psychological Bulletin, 75,* 145–185.

Luborsky, L., Crits-Christoph, P., Mintz, J., & Auerbach, A. (1988). Who will benefit from psychotherapy? *Predicting therapeutic outcomes.* New York: Basic Books.

Luborsky, L., Mintz, J., & Christoph, P. (1979). Are psychotherapeutic changes predictable? Comparison of a Chicago Counseling Center project with a Penn Psychotherapy Project. *Journal of Consulting and Clinical Psychology, 47,* 469–473.

Luborsky, L., Singer, B., & Luborsky, L. (1975). Comparative studies of psychotherapies. Is it true that "Everyone has won and all must have prizes"? *Archives of General Psychiatry, 32,* 995–1007.

MacDonald, A. J. (1994). Brief therapy in adult psychiatry. *Journal of Family Therapy, 16,* 415–426.

Malan, D. H. (1963). *A study of brief psychotherapy.* London: Tavistock.

McAdams, D. P. (1993). *The stories we live by: Personal myths and the making of the self.* New York: William Morrow.

McAdams, D. P. (1994). Can personality change? Levels of stability and growth in personality across the life span. In T. F. Heatherton & J. L. Weinberger (Eds.), *Can personality change?* (pp. 299–313). Washington, DC: American Psychological Association.

McClelland, D. (1951). *Personality.* New York: Holt, Rinehart & Winston.

McConnaughy, E. A., DiClemente, C. C., Prochaska, J. O., & Velicer, W. F. (1989). Stages of change in psychotherapy: A follow-up report. *Psychotherapy, 26,* 494–503.

McConnaughy, E. A., Prochaska, J. O., & Velicer, W. F. (1983). Stages of change in psychotherapy: Measurement and sample profiles. *Psychotherapy: Theory, Research and Practice, 20,* 368–375.

McCrae, R. R., & Costa, P. T., Jr. (1990). *Personality in adulthood.* New York: Guilford.

McCusker, J. (1995). Outcomes of a 21-day drug detoxification program. Retention, transfer to further treatment, and HIV risk reduction. *American Journal of Drug and Alcohol Abuse, 21,* 1–16.

McLellan, A. T., Luborsky, L., Woody, G. E., Druley, K. A., & O'Brien, C. P. (1983). Predicting response to alcohol and drug abuse treatments: Role of psychiatry severity. *Archives of General Psychiatry, 40,* 620–625.

Meltzoff, J., & Kornreich, M. (1970). *Research in psychotherapy.* New York: Atherton.

Miller, W. R., Brown, J. M., Simpson, T. L., Handmaker, N. S., Bien, T. H., Luckie, L. R., Montgomery, H. A., Hester, R. K., & Tonigan, J. S. (1995). What works? A methodological analysis of the alcohol treatment outcome literature. In R. K. Hester (Ed.), *Handbook of alcoholism treatment approaches: Effective alternatives* (2nd ed., pp. 12–44). Boston: Allyn & Bacon.

Miller, W. R., Zweben, A., DiClemente, C. C., & Rychtarik, R. G. (1992). *Motivational enhancement therapy manual. A clinical research guide for therapists treating individuals with alcohol abuse & dependence* (Vol. 2, pp. 1–121). Rockville: MD: National Institute on Alcohol Abuse and Alcoholism.

Milton, F., & Hafner, J. (1979). The outcome of behavior therapy for agoraphobia in relation to marital adjustment. *Archives of General Psychiatry, 36,* 806–811.

Mischel, W., & Shoda, Y. (1995). A cognitive-affective system theory of personality: Reconceptualizing situations, dispositions, dynamics, and invariance in personality structure. *Psychological Review, 102,* 246–268.

Nowinski, J., Baker, S., & Carroll, K. (1992). *Twelve step facilitation therapy manual: A clinical research guide for therapists treating individuals with alcohol abuse and dependence.* NIAAA Project MATCH Monograph (Vol. 1). DHHS Publication No. (ADM) 92-1893. Washington, DC: U.S. Government Printing Office.

Palys, T. S., & Little, B. R. (1983). Perceived life satisfaction and the organization of personal project systems. *Journal of Personality and Social Psychology, 44*, 1221–1230.

Pekarik, G. (1983). Follow-up adjustment of outpatient dropouts. *American Journal of Orthopsychiatry, 53*, 501–511.

Pfeiffer, S., O'Malley, D. S., & Shott, S. (1996). Factors associated with the outcome of adults treated in psychiatric hospitals: A synthesis of findings. *Psychiatric Services, 47*, 263–269.

Phillips, E., & Fagan, P. (1982, August). *Attrition: Focus on the intake and first therapy interviews.* Paper presented at the 90th annual convention of the American Psychological Association, Washington, DC.

Prochaska, J. O., & DiClemente, C. C. (1982). Transtheoretical therapy: Toward a more integrative model of change. *Psychotherapy: Theory, Research, and Practice, 19*, 276–288.

Prochaska, J. O., & DiClemente, C. C. (1983). Stages and process of self-change in smoking: Toward an integrative model of change. *Journal of Consulting and Clinical Psychology, 5*, 390–395.

Project MATCH Research Group (1997a). Matching alcoholism treatments to client heterogeneity: Project MATCH Posttreatment Drinking Outcomes. *Journal of Studies on Alcohol, 58*, 7–29.

Project MATCH Research Group (1997b). Project MATCH secondary a priori hypotheses. *Addiction, 92*, 1671–1698.

Psychotherapy caveat (1974, December). *APA Monitor*, p. 7.

Rabinowitz, J., & Renert, N. (1997). Clinicians' predictions of length of psychotherapy. *Psychiatric Services, 48*, 97–99.

Reder, P., & Tyson, R. L. (1980). Patient dropout from psychotherapy: A review and discussion. *Bulletin of the Menninger Clinic, 44*, 229–251.

Roberts, J. E., & Monroe, S. M. (1992). Vulnerable self-esteem and depressive symptoms: Prospective findings comparing three alternative conceptualizations. *Journal of Personality and Social Psychology, 62*, 804–812.

Roberts, L. K. (1954). The failures of some Rorschach indices to predict the outcome of psychotherapy. *Journal of Consulting Psychology, 18*, 96–98.

Rogers, L. S., & Hammond, K. R. (1953). Prediction of the results of therapy by means of the Rorschach test. *Journal of Consulting Psychology, 17*, 8–15.

Rosenberg, S. (1954). The relationship of certain personality factors to prognosis in psychotherapy. *Journal of Clinical Psychology, 10*, 341–345.

Rosenheck, R., Fontana, A., & Cottrol, C. (1995). Effect of clinician-veteran racial pairing in the treatment of posttraumatic stress disorder. *American Journal of Psychiatry, 152*, 555–563.

Rosenzweig, S. P., & Folman, R. (1974). Patient and therapist variables affecting premature termination in group psychotherapy.

Psychotherapy: Theory, Research, and Practice, 11, 76–79.

Rounsaville, B. J., Weissman, M. M., & Prusoff, B. A. (1981). Psychotherapy with depressed outpatients. Patient and process variables as predictors of outcome. *British Journal of Psychiatry, 138*, 67–74.

Salzman, C., Shader, R. I., Scott, D. A., & Binstock, W. (1970). Interviewer anger and patient dropout in walk-in clinic. *Comprehensive Psychiatry, 11*, 267–273.

Schmidt, J. P., & Hansey, R. (1979). Social class and psychiatric treatment: Application of a decision-making model to use patterns in a cost-free clinic. *Journal of Consulting and Clinical Psychology, 47*, 771–772.

Schrader, G. (1994). Natural history of chronic depression: Predictors of change in severity over time. *Journal of Affective Disorders, 32*, 219–222.

Shoham, V., Bootzin, R. R., Rohrbaugh, M., & Urry, H. (1996). Paradoxical versus relaxation treatment for insomnia: The moderating role of reactance. *Sleep Research, 24a*, 365.

Shoham, V., & Rohrbaugh, M. J. (1995). Aptitude X treatment interaction (ATI) research: Sharpening the focus, widening the lens. In M. Aveline & D. Shapiro (Eds.), *Research foundations for psychotherapy practice* (pp. 73–95). Sussex, Eng.: Wiley.

Shoham, V., Rohrbaugh, M. J., Stickle, T. R., & Jacob, T. (in press). Demand-withdraw couple interaction moderates retention in cognitive-behavioral vs. family-systems treatments for alcoholism. *Journal of Family Psychology*.

Shoham-Salomon, V., Avner, R., & Neeman, R. (1989). You're changed if you do and changed if you don't: Mechanisms underlying paradoxical interventions. *Journal of Consulting and Clinical Psychology, 57*, 590–598.

Shoham-Salomon, V., & Hannah, M. T. (1991). Client-treatment interaction in the study of differential change processes. *Journal of Consulting and Clinical Psychology, 59*, 217–225.

Shoham-Salomon, V., & Jancourt, A. (1985). Differential effectiveness of paradoxical interventions for more versus less stress-prone individuals. *Journal of Counseling Psychology, 32*, 443–447.

Siegel, N., & Fink, M. (1962). Motivation for psychotherapy. *Comprehensive Psychiatry, 3*, 170–173.

Siegel, S. M., Rootes, M. D., & Taub, A. (1977). Symptom change and prognosis in clinic psychotherapy. *Archives of General Psychiatry, 34*, 321–331.

Sifneos, P. E. (1972). *Short-term psychotherapy and emotional crisis.* Cambridge, MA: Harvard University Press.

Sledge, W. H., Moras, K., Hartley, D., & Levine, M. (1990). Effect of time-limited psychotherapy on patient dropout rates. *American Journal of Psychiatry, 147*, 1341–1347.

Sloane, R. B., Staples, F. R., Cristol, A. H., Yorkston, N. J., & Whipple, K. (1975). *Psychotherapy versus behavior therapy.* Cambridge, MA: Harvard University Press.

Smith, B., & Sechrest, L. (1991). Treatment of aptitude X treatment interactions. *Journal of Consulting and Clinical Psychology, 59*, 233–244.

Smith, M. L., & Glass, G. V. (1977). Meta-analysis of psychotherapy outcome studies. *American Psychologist, 32*, 752–760.

Smith, M. L., Glass, G. V., & Miller, T. I. (1980). *The benefits of psychotherapy.* Baltimore: Johns Hopkins University Press.

Snow, R. E. (1991). Aptitude-treatment interaction as a framework for research on individual differences in psychotherapy. *Journal of Consulting and Clinical Psychology, 59*, 205–216.

Steinmetz, J. L., Lewinsohn, P. M., & Antonuccio, D. O. (1983). Prediction of individual outcome in a group intervention for depression. *Journal of Consulting and Clinical Psychology, 51*, 331–337.

Stephens, R. C. (1991). Towards a role theoretic model of heroin use. In R. C. Stephens (Ed.), *The street addict role* (pp. 39–65). Albany: State University of New York Press.

Stone, A., & Shiffman, S. (1994). Ecological momentary assessment (EMA) in behavioral medicine. *Annals of Behavioral Medicine, 16*, 199–202.

Strupp, H. H., Wallach, M. S., Wogan, M., & Jenkins, J. W. (1963). Psychotherapists' assessment of former patients. *Journal of Nervous and Mental Disorders, 137*, 222–230.

Sue, S., Fujino, D. C., Hu, L., Takeuchi, D. T., & Zane, N. W. S. (1991). Community mental health services for ethnic minority groups: A test of the cultural responsiveness hypothesis. *Journal of Consulting and Clinical Psychology, 59*, 533–540.

Sue, S., McKinney, H., & Allen, D. B. (1976). Predictors of the duration of therapy for clients in the community mental health system. *Community Mental Health Journal, 12*, 365–375.

Sue, S., McKinney, H., Allen, D., & Hall, J. (1974). Delivery of community mental health services to black and white clients. *Journal of Consulting and Clinical Psychology, 42*, 794–801.

Sullivan, P. L., Miller, C., & Smeizer, W. (1958). Factors in length of stay and progress in psychotherapy. *Journal of Consulting Psychology, 1*, 1–9.

Tennen, H., & Affleck, G. (1991). Paradox-based treatments. In C. R. Snyder & D. R. Forsyth (Eds.), *Handbook of social and clinical psychology: The health perspective* (pp. 624–643). Elmsford, NY: Pergamon.

Tennen, H., & Affleck, G. (1996). Daily processes in coping with chronic pain: Methods and analytic strategies. In M. Zeidner and N. S. Endler (Eds.), *Handbook of coping* (pp. 151–180). New York: Wiley.

Tennen, H., Eron, J. B., & Rohrbaugh, M. (1985). Paradox in context. In G. Weeks (Ed.), *Promoting change through paradoxical interventions* (pp. 187–214). Homewood, IL: Dorsey Press.

Tennen, H., Rohrbaugh, M., Press, S., & White, L. (1981). Reactance theory and therapeutic paradox: A compliance-defiance model. *Psychotherapy: Theory, Research, and Practice, 18*, 14–22.

Thase, M. E., & Howland, R. H. (1994). Refractory depression: Relevance of psychosocial factors and therapies. *Psychiatric Annals, 24*, 232–240.

Thorne, A. (1989). Conditional patterns, transference, and the coherence of personality across time. In D. M. Buss & N. Cantor (Eds.), *Personality psychology: Recent trends and emerging directions* (pp. 149–159). New York: Springer-Verlag.

Walters, G. C., Solomon, G. S., & Walden, V. R. (1982). Use of the MMPI in predicting persistence in groups of male and female outpatients. *Journal of Clinical Psychology, 38*, 80–83.

Weber, J. J., Solomon, M., & Bachrach, H. M. (1985). Characteristics of psychoanalytic clinic patients: Report of the Columbia Psychoanalytic Center Research Project (I). *International Review of Psychoanalysis, 12*, 13–26.

Willer, B., & Miller, G. H. (1978). On the relationship of client satisfaction to client characteristics and outcome of treatment. *Journal of Clinical Psychology, 34*, 157–160.

Wilson, M., Bell-Dolan, D., & Beitman, B. (1997). Application of the Stages of Change Scale in a clinical drug trial. *Journal of Anxiety Disorders, 11*, 395–408.

Wolff, W. M. (1967). Psychotherapeutic persistence. *Journal of Consulting Psychology, 31*, 429.

Woody, G. E., McLellan, A. T., Luborsky, L., & O'Brien, C. P. (1995). Psychotherapy in community methadone programs: A validation study. *American Journal of Psychiatry, 152*, 1302–1308.

Woody, G. E., McLellan, A. T., Luborsky, L., O'Brien, C. P., Blaine, J., Fox, S., Herman, I., & Beck, A. T. (1984). Severity of psychiatric symptoms as a predictor of benefits from psychotherapy: The Veterans Administration–Penn study. *American Journal of Psychiatry, 141*, 1172–1177.

Yalom, I. D. (1966). A study of group therapy dropouts. *Archives of General Psychiatry, 14*, 393–414.

Yeh, M., Eastman, K., & Cheung, M. K. (1994). Children and adolescents in community health centers: Does the ethnicity or the language of the therapist matter? Special Issue: Asian-American mental health. *Journal of Community Psychology*, *22*(2), 153–163.

Zane, N., Hatanaka, H., Park, S. S., & Akutsu, P. (1994). Ethnic-specific mental health services: Evaluation of the parallel approach for Asian-American clients. Special Issue: Asian-American mental health. *Journal of Community Psychology*, *22*(2), 68–81.

Zuckerman, M., DePaulo, B. M., & Rosenthal, R. (1986). Humans as deceivers and lie detectors. In P. D. Blanck, R. Buck, & R. Rosenthal (Eds.), *Nonverbal communication in clinical context* (pp. 13–35). University Park: Pennsylvania State University Press.

CHAPTER 6

CHANGE AT
DIFFERING STAGES

JAMES O. PROCHASKA
University of Rhode Island

What causes people to take therapeutic action? The answer to this key question depends on what type of action is to be taken. What causes them to seek therapy? Why do the vast majority of people with mental health and behavioral health problems never seek therapy? What causes people to continue therapy? Why does half of the patient population discontinue psychotherapy and chemotherapy prematurely? What causes people to progress in therapy? Answers to these questions can provide better alternatives to one of the field's most pressing concerns: what types of treatment programs can have the greatest impact on entire populations with mental health and behavioral health problems?

What causes people to change? The answer to this question depends in part on where they start? What causes people to begin thinking about change can be different from what moves them to prepare to take action. Once they are prepared, different forces or influences can cause them to take the action or, once the action is taken, to maintain the change. We also need to be concerned about the forces or influences that move people backward, that cause them to regress or relapse back to their troubled behavior.

Fortunately, the answers to this complex set of questions may be simpler or at least more systematic than the questions themselves. To appreciate these answers, we need to begin by considering the transtheoretical model of change.

The transtheoretical model uses stages of change to integrate processes and principles of change from across major theories of intervention—hence the name transtheoretical. This model emerged from a comparative analysis of leading theories of psychotherapy and behavior change. The search was for a systematic integration of a field that had fragmented into more than three hundred theories of psychotherapy (Prochaska, 1979). The comparative analysis identified only 10 processes of change, such as consciousness raising from the Freudian tradition, contingency management from the Skinnerian tradition, and helping relationships from the Rogerian tradition.

In an empirical analysis of self-changers compared to smokers in professional treatments, we assessed how frequently each group used each of the 10 processes (DiClemente & Prochaska, 1982). Our research participants kept saying that they used different processes at different times in their struggles with smoking. These naive subjects were teaching us about a phenomenon that was not included in any of the multitude of therapy theories. They were revealing to us that behavior change unfolds through a series of stages (Prochaska & DiClemente, 1983).

THE STAGES OF CHANGE

Stages are fundamental in understanding change for a number of reasons. First, the concept of stages provides a temporal dimension, and change is a phenomenon that unfolds over time. Second, stages are at a middle level of abstraction between personality traits and psychological states. Stages have a stable quality like traits in that they tend to endure over relatively long periods of time. But traits are usually construed as not being particularly open to change. Stages are dynamic in nature and thus are open to change, but unlike states they do not change so easily and thus require special efforts or interventions. Stages, then, are both relatively stable, as well as dynamic in nature. The types of chronic problems that we see in therapy also have the dual nature of being both stable over time and yet open to change.

The concept of stages has also proven to be a remarkably fruitful dimension for integrating core constructs from across diverse systems of psychotherapy and competing theories of behavior change. Empirically, the stages of change have been useful in integrating processes of change from seven different systems of psychotherapy (Prochaska & DiClemente, 1983, 1984, 1985), as well as the self-efficacy construct from Bandura's (1977, 1982) social-cognitive theory and the decisional balance concept from Janis and Mann's (1977) theory of decision making, conflict, and commitment. To appreciate these integrative discoveries, we need to first describe in more detail each of the stages of change.

Precontemplation is the stage in which people are not intending to take action in the foreseeable future, usually measured as the next six months. People may be in this stage because they are uninformed or underinformed about the consequences of their behavior. Or they may have tried to change a number of times and become demoralized about their abilities to do so. Both groups tend to avoid reading, talking, or thinking about their high-risk behaviors. They are often characterized in other theories as resistant or unmotivated clients or as not ready for therapy or health-promotion programs. The fact is that traditional treatment programs were not ready for such individuals and were not motivated to match their needs.

People in precontemplation underestimate the benefits of changing and overestimate the costs. But they are typically not aware that they are making such mistakes. If they are not conscious of making such mistakes, it will be difficult for them to change. Thus, many remain stuck in the precontemplation stage for years, doing considerable damage to their bodies, themselves, and others. We have found no inherent motivation for people to progress from one stage to the next. These are not like stages of human development, in which children have an inherent motivation to progress from crawling to walking, even though crawling works very well and even though learning to walk can be painful and embarrassing.

We have identified two major forces that can move people toward progress. The first is devel-opmental events. In our research the *mean* age of smokers who finally quit and reach long-term maintenance is 39. Those of us who have gone through age 39 know that it is a "mean" age. It is an age to reevaluate how we have been living and whether we want to die because of the way we have been living or whether we want to enhance the quality and quantity of the second half of our lives.

The other naturally occurring force is environmental events. One of my favorite examples is a couple that we followed who were both heavy smokers. Their dog of many years died of lung cancer. This eventually caused the wife to quit smoking. The husband bought a new dog. So even the same events can be processed differently by different people.

There has been a common belief that people with addictions must hit bottom before they will be motivated to change. So family, friends, and physicians wait helplessly for a crisis to occur. But how often do people turn 39 or have a dog die? When people show the first signs of a serious physical illness, like cancer or cardiovascular disease, others around them can become mobilized to help them seek early intervention. We know that early interventions are often lifesaving, and we wouldn't wait for such patients to hit bottom. We shall see that we have created a third force to help troubled patients and populations in precontemplation to progress. It is called planned intervention.

Contemplation is the stage in which people are intending to take action in the next six months. They are more aware of the pros of changing, but are also acutely aware of the cons. When people begin to seriously contemplate giving up their long-term favorite substances, their awareness of the costs of changing can increase. There is no free change. This balance between the costs and benefits of changing can produce profound ambivalence. This profound ambivalence can reflect a type of love-hate relationship with an addictive substance, for example, and it can keep people stuck in this stage for long periods of time. We often characterize this phenomenon as chronic contemplation or behavioral procrastination. These people are not ready for traditional action-oriented programs.

Preparation is the stage in which people are intending to take action in the immediate future, usually measured as the next month. They have typically taken some significant action in the past year. These individuals have a plan of action, such as going to a recovery group, consulting a counselor, talking to their physician, buying a self-help book, or relying on a self-change approach. These are the people we should recruit for action-oriented treatment programs.

Action is the stage in which people have made specific, overt modifications in their lifestyles within the past six months. Because action is observable, behavior change has often been equated with action. But in the transtheoretical model, action is only one of six stages. Not all modifications of behavior count as action in this model. People must attain a criterion that scientists and professionals agree is sufficient to reduce risks for disease or other self-defeating or self-destructive consequences. In smoking, for example, only total abstinence counts. With alcoholism and alcohol abuse, there are many who believe that only total abstinence can be effective, whereas there are those who accept controlled drinking as effective action. With most mental health problems, we want people to be free from symptoms and to be able to live a normal life.

Maintenance is the stage in which people are working to prevent relapse but do not apply change processes as frequently as do people in action. They are less tempted to relapse and increasingly more confident that they can continue their changes. Based on temptation and self-efficacy data, we estimated that maintenance lasts from six months to about five years.

One of the common reasons that people relapse early in action is that they are not well prepared for the prolonged effort needed to progress to maintenance. Many think the worst will be over in a few weeks or a few months. If they ease up on their efforts too early, they are at great risk for relapse.

To prepare people for what is to come, we encourage them to think of overcoming a chronic problem as similar to running a marathon rather than a sprint. They may have wanted to enter the 100th running of the Boston Marathon. But if they had little or no preparation, they know they would not succeed and so would not enter the race. If they had done some preparation, they might make it for several miles before failing to finish the race. Only those well prepared could maintain their efforts, mile after mile.

In the Boston Marathon metaphor, people know they have to be well prepared if they are to survive Heartbreak Hill, which hits after 20 miles. What is the behavioral equivalent of Heartbreak Hill? The best evidence we have across chronic problems is that the majority of relapses occur at times of emotional distress. Times of depression, anxiety, anger, boredom, loneliness, stress, and distress are when we are at our emotional and psychological weakest (Prochaska, Norcross, & DiClemente, 1994).

How does the average American cope with such troubling times? The average American drinks more, eats more, smokes more, and takes more drugs (Mellinger, Balter, Uhlenhuth, Cisin, Manheimer, & Rickels, 1978). It is not surprising, therefore, that people struggling to overcome addictions will be at greatest risk of relapse when they face distress without their substance of choice. We cannot prevent emotional distress from occurring. But we can help prevent relapse if our patients have been prepared to cope with distress without falling back on addictive substances or other self-defeating behaviors.

If so many Americans rely on oral consumption as a way to manage their emotions, what is the healthiest oral behavior they could follow? Talking with others about one's distress is a means of seeking support that can help prevent relapse. Acute distress is the main reason people seek psychotherapy—to have someone to talk to who is supportive and helpful (Mellinger et al., 1978). Another healthy alternative that can be relied on by large numbers of people is exercise. Not only does such physical activity help manage moods, stress, and distress, but also for 60 minutes a week clients can receive over 50 health and mental health benefits (Reed, Velicer, & Prochaska, 1997). Exercise should be prescribed for all sedentary patients with addictions as the bargain basement of behaviors. A third healthy alternative is some form of deep relaxation, like meditation, yoga, prayer, massage, or deep muscle massage. Letting the stress and distress drift away from one's muscles and one's mind helps patients to keep progressing at the most distressing times.

As is now well known, most people taking action to modify chronic conditions like addictions do not successfully maintain their gains on their first attempt. With smoking, for example, successful self-changers make an average of five to six action attempts before they become long-term maintainers (Schachter, 1982). Many New Year's resolvers report five or more years of consecutive pledges before maintaining the behavioral goal for at least six months (Norcross & Vangarelli, 1989). Relapse and recycling through the stages occur quite frequently as individuals attempt to modify or cease addictive behaviors. Variations of the stage model are being used increasingly by behavior change specialists to investigate the dynamics of relapse (e.g., Brownell, Marlatt, Lichtenstein, & Wilson, 1986; Donovan & Marlatt, 1988).

Because relapse is the rule rather than the exception with problems like addictions, we found that we needed to modify our original stage model. Initially we conceptualized change as a linear progression through the stages; people were supposed to progress simply and discretely through each step. Linear progression is a possible but relatively rare phenomenon with many chronic conditions like addictions.

Figure 6.1 presents a spiral pattern that illustrates how many people actually move through the stages of change. In this pattern, people can progress from contemplation to preparation to action to maintenance, but many individuals will relapse. During relapse, individuals regress to an earlier stage. Some relapsers feel like failures—embarrassed, ashamed, and guilty. These individuals become demoralized and resist thinking about behavior change. As a result, they return to the precontemplation stage and can remain there for various periods of time. Approximately 15% of smokers who relapsed in our self-change research regressed back to the precontemplation stage (Prochaska & DiClemente, 1984).

Fortunately, this research indicates that the vast majority of relapsers—85% of smokers, for example—go back to the contemplation or preparation stages (Prochaska & DiClemente, 1984). They begin to consider plans for their next action attempt while trying to learn from their recent efforts. To take another example, fully 60% of unsuccessful New Year's resolvers make the same pledge the next year (Norcross, Ratzin, & Payne, 1989; Norcross & Vangarelli, 1989). The spiral model suggests that most relapsers do not revolve

endlessly in circles and that they do not regress all the way back to where they began. Instead, each time relapsers recycle through the stages, they potentially learn from their mistakes and try something different the next time around (DiClemente et al., 1991).

On any one trial, successful behavior change is limited in the absolute numbers of individuals who are able to achieve maintenance (Cohen et al., 1989; Schacter, 1982). Nevertheless, looking at a cohort of individuals, we see that the number of successes continues to increase gradually over time. However, a large number of individuals remains in the contemplation and precontemplation stages. Ordinarily, the more action taken, the better the prognosis. We need much more research to better distinguish between those who benefit from recycling and those who do not.

Termination is the stage in which individuals have zero temptation and 100% self-efficacy. No matter whether they are depressed, anxious, bored, lonely, angry, or stressed, they are sure they will not return to their old unhealthy habits as a way of coping. It is as if they never acquired the habits in the first place. In a study of former smokers and alcoholics, we found that less than 20% of each group had reached the criteria of no temptation and total self-efficacy (Snow, Prochaska, & Rossi, 1992). Whereas our ideal goal is to be cured or totally recovered, we recognize that for many people the best we can do is a lifetime of maintenance.

ENTERING INTO THERAPY

Too few studies have paid attention to one of the problems of professional treatment programs, that is, that such programs recruit or reach too few people with mental health and behavioral health problems. For example, across all DSM-IV diagnoses, in their lifetimes less than 25% of populations with these disorders ever enter professional therapy programs (Veroff, Douvon & Kulka, 1981a, 1981b). Among populations plagued by the major killers of our times, health behavior problems like smoking, sedentary lifestyles, obesity, unhealthy diets, and stress, fewer than 10% ever participate in therapy programs (e.g., U.S. Department of Health and Human Services, 1990).

Mental health and behavioral health problems are among the most costly of contemporary

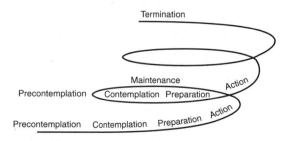

FIGURE 6.1 A spiral pattern for progressing through the stages of change.

conditions—to the individuals, their families and friends, their employers, their communities, and their health-care systems. Consider, for example, that of the $1 trillion a year in health-care costs in the United States, 7% to 8% are accounted for by pharmaceuticals. Behavior accounts for 50% to 60% of total costs. But the way behavior therapy and psychotherapy are currently practiced, less than 5% of these total costs are currently used effectively.

Depression is the second most costly disease in the United States. Yet most depressions go undiagnosed or misdiagnosed, untreated or mistreated. Addictions are among the most costly conditions, but they, too, go untreated or mistreated. This situation cannot and will not continue into the 21st century, if we are to bring health-care costs under control while at the same time providing quality care that enhances the health of clients and communities.

One of the world's largest health-care products and services corporation considered these conditions and concluded that there were huge unmet needs in behavior health. This means that there are great opportunities for this growth company. Their leaders decided that over the next 10 to 15 years, their company will transform itself into the world's leading behavior health company, with behavior change science rather than biological science as its major driver. Therapists will be able to participate in such growth opportunities, but only if they change the way they think and the way they practice.

No longer can we be prepared to treat problems like depression and addiction on just a case-by-case basis. Instead, we must develop therapeutic programs that can reach troubled individuals on a population basis. The early results of such efforts, however, are not encouraging.

There are governments and health-care systems that are seeking to treat such costly conditions on a population basis. But when they turn to the biggest and best clinical trials that are treating addictions and other problems on a population basis, what do they discover? Trial after trial is reporting disappointing outcomes (e.g., COMMIT, 1995; Ennett, Tabler, Ringwolt, & Fliwelling, 1994; Glasgow, Terborg, Hollis, Severson, & Boles, 1995; Luepher et al., 1994). Whether the trials were done at work sites, schools, or entire communities, the results are remarkably similar— no significant effects compared to the control conditions.

If we examine more closely one of these trials, the Minnesota Heart Health Study, we can find hints of what went wrong (Lando et al., 1995). With smoking as one of their targeted behaviors, nearly 90% of the smokers in treated communities reported seeing media stories about smoking. But the same was true with smokers in the control communities. Only about 12% of smokers in the treatment and control conditions said their physicians talked to them about smoking in the past year. If we look at what percentage participated in the most powerful behavior change programs—clinics, classes, and counselors—we find that only 4% of the smokers participated. If managed care offers free state-of-the-science cessation clinics, only 1% of smokers are recruited (Lichtenstein & Hollis, 1992). We simply cannot have much impact on the health of our nation if our best treatment programs reach so few people with the deadliest of addictions.

How do we motivate many more people with chronic problems to seek the appropriate help? By changing our paradigms and our practices. There are two paradigms that we need to contemplate changing. The first is an action-oriented paradigm that construes behavior change as an event that can occur quickly, immediately, discretely, and dramatically. Treatment programs that are designed to have people immediately stop abusing substances are implicitly or explicitly designed for the portion of the population who is in the preparation stage.

The problem here is that across 15 unhealthy behaviors (e.g., smoking, high-fat diets, and sun exposure) in 20,000 health maintenance organization (HMO) members, we find that typically less than 20% are prepared to take action (Rossi, 1992). The general rule of thumb is 40, 40, 20: 40% in precontemplation, 40% in contemplation, and 20% in preparation. When we offer action-oriented interventions, we are implicitly recruiting from less than 20% of the at-risk population. If we are to meet the needs of entire populations with problems, then we must design interventions for the 40% in precontemplation and the 40% in contemplation.

Offering stage-matched interventions and applying proactive or outreach recruitment methods in three large-scale clinical trials, we have been able to motivate 80% to 90% of smokers to enter our treatment programs (Prochaska, Velicer, Fava, Rossi, & Tsoh, 1999; Prochaska, Velicer, Fava, Ruggiero, Laforge, & Rossi, 1999).

This is a quantum increase in our ability to motivate many more people to start therapy.

The second paradigm change that this approach requires is movement from a passive-reactive approach to practice to a proactive approach. Most professionals have been trained to be passive-reactive: to passively wait for patients to seek services and then to react. The biggest problem with this approach is that the majority of people with problems never seek such services.

The passive-reactive paradigm is designed to serve populations with acute conditions. The pain, distress, or discomfort of such conditions can motivate people to seek the services of health professionals. But the major killers of our time are chronic conditions caused in large part by chronic lifestyle disorders.

If we are to treat the chronic conditions seriously, we simply must learn to recruit entire populations and offer them stage-matched therapies. Regions of the National Health Service in Great Britain are training health professionals in these new paradigms. Over 6000 physicians, nurses, counselors, and health educators have been trained to proactively interact at each stage of change with their entire patient populations who smoke, or abuse alcohol, drugs, and food.

What happens if professionals change only one paradigm and proactively recruit entire populations to action-oriented interventions. This experiment has been tried in one of the United State's largest managed care organizations (Lichtenstein & Hollis, 1992). Physicians spent time with smokers to get them to sign up for a state-of-the-art, action-oriented clinic. If that didn't work, nurses spent up to 10 minutes to get them to sign up, followed by 12 minutes by health educators and a counselor's call to home. The base rate was 1% participation. This most intensive recruitment protocol motivated 35% of smokers in precontemplation to sign up. But only 3% showed up, 2% finished, and none ended up better off. From a combined contemplation and preparation group, 65% signed up, 15% showed up, 11% finished, and a few percent ended up better off.

Given the growing evidence to date, we believe that we can provide an innovative and probably definitive answer to this question: what can move a majority of people to start a professional therapy program? One answer is professionals who are motivated and prepared to proactively reach entire populations and offer them interventions that match whatever stage of change they are in.

Retention

What motivates people to continue in therapy? Or conversely, what moves clients to terminate counseling quickly and prematurely, as judged by their counselors? A meta-analysis of 125 studies found that nearly 50% of clients drop out of treatment (Wierzbicki & Pekarik, 1993). Across studies there were few consistent predictors of premature termination, except that substance abuse, minority status, and lower education predicted more dropouts. Although important, these variables did not account for much of the variance in dropouts.

The dropout rates from drug treatments are remarkably similar. For antidepressants, about 50% of the patients stop taking their medication in the first month. With antibiotic medication that can cure ulcers, about 50% don't complete treatment. With lifesaving cholesterol medication, about 50% discontinue treatment in the first few months. It could be coincidence that 50% of patients drop out of psychotherapy and chemotherapy. Or it could be that understanding the causes of such negative changes could help enhance the health of huge numbers of people.

There are now at least seven studies on dropouts from a stage model perspective on a broad spectrum of psychiatric disorders, substance abuse, smoking, obesity, and drug treatment for hypertension and HIV/AIDS (e.g., Medeiros, Prochaska, & Prochaska, in press; Prochaska, Norcross, Fowler, Follick, & Abrams, 1992). These studies found that stage related variables outpredicted demographics, type of problem, severity of problem, and other patient- and problem-related variables. Figure 6.2 presents the stage profiles of the three groups of patients with a broad spectrum of psychiatric disorders (Medeiros et al., in press). In this study we were able to predict 93% of the three groups: premature terminators, early but appropriate terminators, and continuers in therapy.

Figure 6.2 shows that the pretherapy profile of the entire group who dropped out quickly and prematurely (40%) was a profile of people in the precontemplation stage. The 20% who finished quickly but appropriately had a profile of patients who were in the action stage when entering therapy. Those who continued in longer-term treatment were a mixed group, with the majority in the contemplation stage.

We cannot treat people in the precontemplation stage as if they are starting in the same place

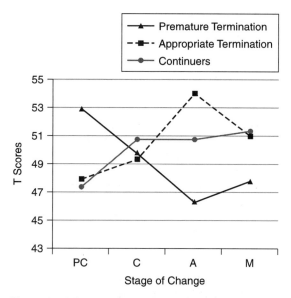

FIGURE 6.2 **Pretherapy stage profiles for premature terminators, appropriate terminators, and continuers (in standardized T scores with *M* = 50, *SD* = 10).**

as those in the action stage and expect them to continue in therapy. If we try to pressure them to take action when they are not prepared, should we expect to retain them in therapy? Or do we drive them away and then blame them for not being motivated enough or not being ready enough for our action-oriented interventions?

With patients entering therapy in the action stage for an addiction, what would be an appropriate approach? One alternative would be to provide relapse prevention strategies according to Marlatt and Gordon (1985). But would relapse prevention strategies make any sense with the 40% of patients who enter in the precontemplation stage? What might be a good match here? We would recommend a dropout prevention approach because we know that these patients are likely to leave early if we don't help them to continue.

With clients starting therapy in precontemplation, I typically tell them my key concerns: "I'm concerned that therapy may not have a chance to make a significant difference in your life because you may be tempted to leave early." I may then explore whether they have been pressured to enter therapy. How do they react when someone tries to pressure or coerce them into changing when they are not ready? Can they let me know if they feel that I am trying to pressure or coerce them? I do want to help them but will

only encourage them to take steps when they are most ready to succeed.

Fortunately, we now have four studies with stage-matched interventions in which we can examine retention rates of people entering interventions in the precontemplation stage. What is clear is that when treatment is matched to stage, people in precontemplation continue at the same high rates as those who started in the preparation stage. This result held for clinical trials when people were recruited proactively (we offered help), as well as in participants recruited reactively (they called us for help). Unfortunately, these studies have been done only with smokers. But if they hold up across problems, we will be able to offer a practical answer to this question: what motivates people to continue in therapy? The answer is receiving treatments that match their stage.

Progress

What moves people to progress in therapy and to continue to progress after therapy? Figure 6.3 presents an example of what is called the *stage effect*. The stage effect predicts that the amount of successful action taken during treatment and after treatment is directly related to the stage people are in at the start of treatment (Prochaska, DiClemente, & Norcross, 1992). In this example interventions with smokers ends at six months. The group of smokers who started in the precontemplation stage show the least amount of effective action as measured by abstinence at each assessment point. Those who started in the

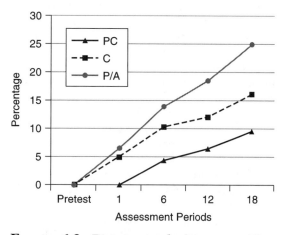

FIGURE 6.3 **Percentage abstinent over 18 months for smokers in precontemplation (PC), contemplation (C), and preparation (P/A) stages before treatment (*n* = 570).**

contemplation stage made significantly more progress. And those who entered treatment already prepared to take action were quite successful at every assessment.

The stage effect has been found across a variety of problems and populations, including rehabilitative success for brain injury and recovery from anxiety and panic disorders following random assignment to placebo or effective medication (Beitman, Beck, Deuser, Carter, Davidson, & Maddock, 1994; Lam et al., 1988). In the latter clinical trial, the psychiatrist concluded that patients would need to be assessed for their stage of readiness to benefit from such medication and would need to be helped through the stages so that they were well prepared before being placed on the medication.

Here is one strategy for applying the stage effect clinically. We have already seen that if we try to move all people with chronic conditions to immediate action, it is likely that the majority will not show up for therapy or not finish. An alternative is to set realistic goals for brief encounters with clients at each stage of change. A realistic goal is to help clients progress through one stage in brief therapy. If the client moves relatively quickly, then we can help them progress through two stages. The results to date indicate that if clients progress through one stage in one month, they double the chances that they are taking effective action by six months. If they progress through two stages, they increase their chances of taking effective action by three to four times (Prochaska, Velicer, Fava, Laforge, & Rossi, 1999). Setting such realistic goals can enable many more people to enter therapy, continue in therapy, progress in therapy, and continue to progress after therapy.

The first results reported back from England, where the 6000 health professionals have been trained in the stage approach, is a dramatic increase in their morale. They can now see progress with the majority of their patients, whereas they once saw failure when immediate action was the only criterion for success. They are much more confident that they have treatments that can match the stage of all of their patients, rather than just the 20% or so who are prepared to take immediate action. These reactions indicate that the stage model is helpful for the professionals, as well as their patients.

As I teach my students, the models of therapy that we choose should be good for our mental health, as well as the mental health of our clients. After all, we are involved in therapy for a lifetime, whereas most of our clients are involved for only a brief time.

As managed care organizations move to briefer and briefer therapies for mental health and behavior health disorders, there is a danger that most health professionals will feel pressured into having to produce immediate action. If this pressure is then transferred to patients who are not prepared for such action, we will repeat the past—not reaching most patients and not retaining most patients. We can help move a majority of patients to progress in relatively brief encounters, but only if we set realistic goals for them and for us. Otherwise we risk demoralizing and demotivating both our clients and ourselves.

Process

If we are to help motivate patients to progress from one stage to the next, we will need to know principles and processes of change that can produce such progress. Following are six principles and nine processes of change that can be applied in therapy to help people progress through the stages of change.

Principle 1. *The Advantages of Changing Must Increase for People to Progress from Precontemplation.* We found that in 12 out of 12 studies the advantages were higher in contemplation than in precontemplation (Prochaska et al., 1994). This pattern held true across 12 areas: use of cocaine, smoking, delinquency, obesity, sedentary lifestyles, high-fat diets, and sun exposure; and encouragement for consistent condom use, safer sex, radon testing, mammography screening, and physicians practicing behavioral medicine. It has also been found to hold true for the pros and cons of being in therapy (Medeiros et al., in press).

Here's a technique we use in our population-based programs. Ask a patient in precontemplation to tell you all the benefits of a particular action, such as quitting cocaine or completing therapy. Patients typically can list four or five. Let them know there are 8 to 10 times that amount. Challenge them to double or triple their list for your next meeting. If their list of pros for therapy starts to indicate many more motives, like better moods, less stress, more energy, healthier immune system, better sex life, enhanced self-esteem, fewer problems, and increased incomes, they will be more motivated to seriously contemplate continuing therapy.

Principle 2. The disadvantages of changing must decrease for people to progress from contemplation to action. In 12 out of 12 studies we found that the disadvantages were lower in action than in contemplation (Prochaska et al., 1994).

Principle 3. The pros and cons must cross over for people to be prepared to take action. In 12 out of 12 studies the cons of changing were higher than the pros in precontemplation, but in 11 out of 12 the pros were higher than the cons in the action stage. The one exception was quitting cocaine, which was the only population with a large percentage of inpatients. We interpret this exception to mean that with these addicts, their action may have been more under the social controls of residential care than under self-control. At a minimum, their pattern would not bode well for immediate discharge.

It should be noted that if we used raw scores to assess these patterns, we would often find that the pros of changing are higher than the cons even for people in precontemplation. It is only when we use standardized scores that we find clear patterns, with the cons of changing always higher than the pros. Thus, compared to their peers in other stages, people in precontemplation underestimate the pros and overestimate the cons. We interpret this to mean that they are not particularly conscious of making these mistakes because they don't know how they compare to their peers.

Principle 4. The *strong principle* of progress holds that to progress from precontemplation to effective action, the pros of changing must increase 1 standard deviation (Prochaska, 1994). Across 12 different problem behaviors, the pros of changing were found to increase 1 standard deviation from precontemplation to action.

Principle 5. The *weak principle* of progress holds that to progress from contemplation to effective action, the cons of changing must decrease 1/2 standard deviation. Across the same 12 problem behaviors, the cons of changing were found to decrease only 1/2 standard deviation from contemplation to action.

Because the pros of changing must increase twice as much as the cons decrease, we place twice as much emphasis on the benefits of changing than on the costs. What is striking here is that we believe we have discovered mathematical principles for how much positive motivations must increase and how much negative motivations must decrease. Such principles can produce much more sensitive assessments for guiding our interventions, giving us and our patients feedback for when therapeutic efforts are producing progress and when they are failing. Together we can modify our methods if we are not seeing as much movement as is needed for becoming adequately prepared for action.

Principle 6. We need to match particular processes of change to specific stages of change. Table 6.1 presents the empirical integration that we have found between processes and stages of change. Guided by this integration, we would apply the following processes with patients in precontemplation.

1. *Consciousness raising* involves increased awareness about the causes, consequences, and cures for a particular problem. Interventions that can increase awareness include observations, confrontations, interpretations, feedback, and education like bibliotherapy. Some techniques, like confrontation, are high risk in terms of retention and are not recommended as much as motivational enhancement methods such as personal feedback about the current and long-term consequences of continuing with the addiction (Miller, Benefield, & Tonigan, 1993). Increasing the cons

TABLE 6.1. **Processes of Change Emphasized at Particular Stages of Change**

Precontemplation	Contemplation	Preparation	Action	Maintenance
Consciousness raising Dramatic relief Environmental reevaluation		Self-reevaluation Self-liberation	Contingency management Helping relationship Counterconditioning Stimulus control	

of not changing is the corollary of raising the pros of changing. So clearly part of applying consciousness raising is designed to increase the pros of changing.

2. *Dramatic relief* involves emotional arousal about one's current behavior and relief that can come from changing. Fear, inspiration, guilt, and hope are some of the emotions that can move people to contemplate changing. Psychodrama, role playing, grieving, and personal testimonies are examples of techniques that can move people emotionally.

We should note that earlier behavior change literature concluded that interventions like education and fear arousal did not motivate behavioral change. Unfortunately, many interventions were evaluated by their ability to move people to immediate action. Processes like consciousness raising and dramatic relief are intended to move people to contemplation, not immediate action. Therefore, we should assess their effectiveness by whether they produce the progress they are expected to produce. Fortunately, the field never stopped believing that education and emotion can move people, in spite of what some studies said.

3. *Environmental reevaluation* combines both affective and cognitive assessments of how an addiction affects one's social environment and how changing would impact that environment. Empathy training, value clarification, and family or network interventions can facilitate such reevaluation.

Here is a brief media intervention aimed at smokers in precontemplation. A man clearly in grief says, "I always feared that my smoking would lead to an early death. I always worried that my smoking would cause lung cancer. But I never imagined it would happen to my wife." Beneath his grieving face appears this statistic: "50,000 deaths per year are caused by passive smoking, the California Department of Health." In 30 seconds we have consciousness raising, dramatic relief, and environmental reevaluation. No wonder such media interventions have been evaluated as an important part of California's successful reduction of smoking.

4. *Self-reevaluation* combines both cognitive and affective assessments of one's self-image when free from a chronic condition. Imagery, healthier role models, and value clarification are techniques that can move people evaluatively. Clinically, we find people first looking back and reevaluating themselves as troubled individuals. As they progress into preparation, they begin to develop more of a future focus as they imagine more

how their life will be free from their chronic conditions.

5. *Self-liberation* is both the belief that one can change and the commitment and recommitment to act on that belief. Techniques that can enhance such willpower include public rather than private commitments. Motivational research also suggests that if people have only one choice, they are not as motivated as if they have two choices (Miller, 1985). Three is even better, but four does not seem to enhance motivation. Whenever possible we try to provide people with three of the best choices for applying each process. With smoking cessation, for example, we used to believe that only one commitment really counted and that was quitting cold turkey. We now know there are at least three good choices: (1) cold turkey, (2) nicotine replacement, and (3) nicotine fading. Asking clients to choose which alternative they believe would be most effective for them, and which they would be most committed to use, can enhance their motivation and their self-liberation.

6. *Counterconditioning* requires the learning of healthier behaviors that can substitute for troubled behaviors. We just discussed three healthier alternatives to smoking. Earlier we discussed three healthier alternatives for coping with emotional distress rather than relapsing. Counterconditioning techniques tend to be quite specific to a particular behavior and include desensitization, medication, assertion, and cognitive counters to irrational self-statements that can elicit distress.

7. *Contingency management* involves the systematic use of reinforcements and punishments for taking steps in a particular direction. Because we find that successful self-changers rely much more on reinforcement than punishment, we emphasize reinforcements for progressing rather than punishments for regressing. Contingency contracts, overt and covert reinforcements, and group recognition are procedures for increasing reinforcement and incentives that increase the probability that healthier responses will be repeated.

To prepare people for the longer term, we teach them to rely more on self-reinforcements than social reinforcements. We find clinically that many clients expect much more reinforcement and recognition from others than that which others actively provide. Too many relatives and friends can take action for granted too quickly. Average acquaintances typically generate only a couple of positive consequences early in action.

Self-reinforcements are obviously much more under self-control and can be given more quickly and consistently when temptations to lapse or relapse are resisted.

8. *Stimulus control* involves modifying the environment to increase cues that prompt healthier responses and decrease cues that are tempting. Avoidance, environmental reengineering such as removing addictive substances and paraphernalia, and attending self-help groups can provide stimuli that elicit healthier responses and reduce risks for relapse.

9. *Helping relationships* combine caring, openness, trust, and acceptance, as well as support for changing. Rapport building, a therapeutic alliance, counselor calls, buddy systems, sponsors, and self-help groups can be excellent resources for social support. If people become dependent on such support for maintaining change, we need to take care in fading out this support so that termination of therapy does not become a condition for relapsing.

Competing theories of therapy have implicitly or explicitly advocated alternative processes of enhancing motivation for change. Do cognitions move people or emotions? Is it values, decisions, or dedication? Are contingencies what motivate us, or are we controlled by environmental conditions or conditioned habits? Or is it the therapeutic relationship that is the common healer across all therapeutic modalities?

Our eclectic answer to each of these questions is yes. Our integrative answer is that therapeutic processes originating from competing theories can be compatible when they are combined in a stage-matched paradigm (Table 6.1). With patients in earlier stages of change, we can facilitate change through more experiential processes that produce healthier cognitions, emotions, evaluations, decisions, and commitments. In later stages, we seek to build on such solid preparation and motivation by emphasizing more behavioral processes that can help condition healthier behaviors, reinforce these behaviors, and provide physical and social environments that support healthier lifestyles free from chronic conditions.

MATCHING THERAPY TO STAGE

Matching therapy to the client's stage and level of change is one of the most important strategies for creating a therapeutic alliance. A client and therapist each working at different stages is one of the most common sources of resistance. If the therapist is an action-oriented therapist and the client is in the precontemplation stage, then the client will experience the therapist as insensitive and coercive, such as a parent pressuring change when the child is not convinced that change is needed. Cocaine and heroin addicts in the precontemplation stage, for example, perceived that they were in therapy more out of coercion than choice (Medeiros et al., in press). Conversely, if the client is prepared to take action and the therapist relies almost exclusively on consciousness raising and self-reevaluation processes, the client will experience therapy as moving much too slowly and the therapist might believe that the client is at risk for acting out.

Similarly, clients who believe that immediate situational changes will improve their symptoms are likely to be resistant to spending much time in becoming more conscious of their childhood. Conversely, therapists who rely heavily on situationally focused techniques like desensitization can experience resistance from clients who are convinced that their phobias are rooted in much deeper levels, which they want to understand. A client who was being treated with systematic desensitization for a social phobia by one of our graduate students complained, "It seems to me that the therapy you are using is like treating a cancer with aspirin."

The most resistant clients are those in the precontemplation stage, particularly those who have been pressured into therapy by spouses who are threatening to leave them, employers who are threatening to fire them, schools that are threatening to expel them, or judges who are threatening to imprison them. To help such clients accept therapy, we need to be able to empathize with their situation—to let them know we have a sense of how it must feel to be in therapy when they are not convinced that they need to change or when they are convinced that other people are the problem. At times, we engage such resistant clients by helping them to learn how they can change someone else. In the process, they will have to change their ways as well, but at least they are less defensive about learning how people change.

One of the most serious technical errors is to fail to match treatment to the client's stage of change. Clients are likely to have enough sources of resistance to change and do not need therapeutically produced resistance. Traditionally, too many clients have dropped out of therapy, only to be blamed for not being motivated rather than being provided with processes appropriate to the stage at which they are motivated to work.

Therapists who are well matched to the client's stage of change are likely to experience the therapeutic process as progressing more smoothly. Of course, clients can become stuck in a stage, but at least the therapist is aware of not contributing to that problem. Clients who have been stuck in the contemplation stage tend to substitute thinking and reflecting for acting. At times, we refer to these individuals as chronic contemplators. They can be very comfortable with therapists who prefer to rely on more contemplation-oriented processes such as consciousness raising and self-reevaluation. But encouraging such clients to go deeper and deeper into more levels of their problems can be iatrogenic; that is, the therapy can produce difficulties by feeding into clients' problems. At some point, action must be taken. But if the therapists have not been trained to use action-oriented processes effectively, they might prefer to avoid action in the same way that chronic contemplators can avoid action. After years and years of archeological expeditions into the deepest levels of their problems, such clients may yell out (as the character on the cover of *New York* magazine): "Help, I'm being held captive in psychotherapy!"

At some point, therapy must terminate. These days, therapy usually terminates before the clients' problems are eradicated. This is one of the reasons why there can be a fair amount of anxiety around the termination process. Intuitively, all parties know that the client is not yet free. Even with our most effective techniques for agoraphobia, for example, by the end of treatment, fewer than 30% of clients have recovered or reached normal levels of functioning (Jacobson, Wilson, & Tupper, 1988). Many more have improved, but they are not symptom-free. Similarly, with addictive problems, fewer than 30% of clients will be free from their addictions a year after they have terminated the best therapies available (Hunt, Barnett, & Branch, 1971). Most clients are not willing or able to cover the costs of continuing therapy until they have reached the termination stage.

Three criteria are usually used to decide on when termination should occur: (1) clients are feeling good; (2) they ask for less frequent sessions; and (3) they are solving problems on their own. Perhaps the most common is the client's criterion of feeling good enough to go back to coping on his or her own. Clients may communicate this directly or they may use indirect methods such as missing some weekly sessions or asking to have sessions less frequently. The worst case is when clients terminate therapy unilaterally, without even discussing it with the therapist. I find that clients are often ready to terminate therapy before the therapist is ready, especially the student therapist.

One of the themes of transtheoretical therapy is to work in harmony with how people change naturally. One of the natural termination processes is to gradually fade out therapy once effective action is being taken. Thus, once the action criterion is reached, termination begins with biweekly sessions in place of weekly ones; then we progress to monthly meetings. Most clients experience such changes in scheduling as rewarding, both as signs of the excellent progress they have been making and as saving time, money, and effort.

A particularly good sign that clients are ready to terminate is when they are functioning so effectively as self-changers that they solve some problems that have not been the focus of therapy. We know that our clients are not going to be problem-free, but we also know that we have truly helped clients when they are free to overcome their most pressing problems on their own.

THE THERAPEUTIC RELATIONSHIP AT EACH STAGE

The stance of the therapist varies with the stage clients are in. With clients in the precontemplation stage, therapists need to be more active in keeping them from dropping out of therapy and to help them to begin to explore problems in the face of considerable resistance and defensiveness. Therapists may need to be more active in asking questions to help precontemplators to participate; they may need to inform clients about the many advantages of therapy, for example, that the salaries of clients increase faster than control comparisons, because these clients seriously underestimate the benefits of therapy; and they need to teach clients about how people change and where the clients' current experiences fall within the cycle of change. Therapists need to be able to identify with the precontemplators' defensiveness rather than react to it, and in this sense to join with clients and their uncomfortable place in therapy. Reflecting clients' resentments or reservations about being in therapy can help resistant clients to feel that this therapist can be on their side rather than joining with the forces who were pressuring them to enter therapy in the first place.

With clients in the contemplation stage, the therapist's work is easier. The therapist can be more passive and leave much of the contemplative work to those clients who are eager to explore and to understand but slow to act. Therapists may need to be more active at times in helping clients remain more focused on the levels of change that are most appropriate to their problems. As actors, clients can often shift to *situational* attributions, whereas therapists, as observers, tend to be biased toward dispositional attributions like those at the intrapersonal level (Jones & Nisbett, 1972). According to attribution research, actors tend to attribute negative behaviors, like excessive drinking, to situational determinants ("I was unemployed"). Observers tend to attribute the same behaviors to the actor's disposition or personality ("The client has an addictive or dependent personality"). As more objective observers, therapists can help shift the focus of sessions to the levels that have been assessed to be most crucial in causing or controlling clients' particular problems.

Therapists will also have to be prepared to become more active with chronic contemplators. If in previous therapy clients have spent many months and even years analyzing their issues, therapists will need to become more directive and help clients to start to take at least some small steps toward action.

With clients who are prepared to take action, therapists have a number of useful alternatives. The first is to review the client's plan of action to see if it has a high probability of success. If so, then the therapist can sit back and let the client go forward. If therapists know that there are particularly effective action plans available for particular problems, such as sensate focusing for sexual dysfunctions (Masters & Johnson, 1970) or in vivo desensitization for phobias (Wolpe, 1973), then these should be shared and encouraged. Typically, we try to provide clients with choices for action, including their own creative plans, so that they can maximize their commitments to plans rather than feel that their only choices are to follow their therapist's directions or resist.

If clients are not adequately prepared to take action, then they are encouraged to engage in further contemplation or preparation processes. Clients, for example, who are tempted to use situational-level actions (e.g., moving to a warm climate) to solve interpersonal-level problems (e.g., marital conflicts) are likely to discover that such travel therapy is ineffective. Such ineffective action would be analogous to what psychodynamic therapists view as acting out.

The amount of responsibility that therapists assume varies with the stage clients are in. The greatest burden is with precontemplators because they are least able to change themselves and most likely to resist therapy. But the therapist's responsibility is to help clients become less defensive and more open to exploration and understanding, to help them progress to the contemplation stage and not to pressure for premature changes such as taking action. With clients who are prepared to take action, much more of the burden will fall on the client for carrying out an action plan because most of this activity will occur between therapy sessions. The therapists' responsibilities include adequately reviewing an action plan to make sure it is realistic and potentially effective and to revise the plan in aspects that are not working well.

The therapist's stance at different stages can be characterized as follows. With precontemplators, often the role is that of a *nurturing parent*, who can join with the resistant and defensive youngster who is both drawn to and repelled by the prospects of becoming more independent. With contemplators, the role is more that of a *Socratic teacher*, who encourages clients to achieve their own insights into their condition. With clients who are in the preparation stage, the stance is more that of *an experienced coach*, who has been through many important matches and can provide a fine game plan or can review the person's own plan. With clients who are progressing into action and maintenance, the therapist becomes more of *a consultant*, who is available to provide expert advise and support when action is not progressing as smoothly as expected. As termination approaches in long-term therapy, the therapist is consulted less and less often as the client experiences greater autonomy and the ability to live a life freer from past patterns and problems that were disabling. In some ways, this sequence of stances parallels the changing roles that effective parents play as their children grow through stages of personal development. In this sense, the therapeutic relationship changes and evolves as clients progress through stages of intentional change. In long-term therapy, the therapist can be seen by the client first as a nurturing parent, then as a favorite teacher, next as a caring coach, and finally as a concerned consultant relating to a more self-directed client. Like parents, therapists should not strive to be perfect role models but "good enough" guides who can help clients through the complexities of changing.

Outcomes and Impacts

What happens when we combine all of these principles and processes of change to help patients and entire populations to progress toward action? What are the outcomes that can be produced with groups of patients and the impacts on entire populations when stage-matched interventions are proactively delivered to entire populations? We examine a series of clinical trials that apply stage-matched interventions to see what lessons we might learn about the future of behavioral health and mental health care.

In the first large-scale clinical trial we compared four treatments: (1) one of the best home-based, action-oriented cessation programs (standardized); (2) stage-matched manuals (individualized); (3) expert system computer reports plus manuals (interactive); and (4) counselors plus computers and manuals (personalized). We randomly assigned by stage 739 smokers to one of the four treatments (Prochaska, DiClemente, Velicer, & Rossi, 1993).

In the computer condition, participants completed by mail or telephone 40 questions that were entered into our central computers and generated feedback reports. These reports informed participants about their stage of change, their pros and cons of changing, and their use of change processes appropriate to their stages. At baseline, participants were given positive feedback on what they were doing correctly and guidance on which principles and processes they needed to apply more to progress. In two progress reports delivered over the next six months, participants also received positive feedback on any improvement they made on any of the variables relevant to progressing. Thus, demoralized and defensive smokers could begin progressing without having to quit and without having to work too hard. Smokers in the contemplation stage could begin taking small steps, such as delaying their first cigarette in the morning for an extra 30 minutes. They could choose small steps that would increase their self-efficacy and help them become better prepared for quitting.

In the personalized condition, smokers received four proactive counselor calls over the six-month intervention period. Three of the calls were based on the computer reports. Counselors

reported much more difficulty in interacting with participants without any progress data. Without scientific assessments, it was much harder for both clients and counselors to tell whether any significant progress had occurred since their last interaction.

Figure 6.4 presents point prevalence abstinence rates for each of the four treatment groups over 18 months, with treatment ending at 6 months. The two self-help manual conditions paralleled each other for 12 months. At 18 months, the stage-matched manuals moved ahead. This is an example of a *delayed action effect*, which we often observe with stage-matched programs specifically and with self-help programs generally. It takes time for participants in early stages to progress all the way to action. Therefore, some treatment effects as measured by action will be observed only after considerable delay. But it is encouraging to find treatments producing therapeutic effects months and even years after treatment ended.

The computer alone and computer plus counselor conditions paralleled each other for 12 months. Then, the effects of the counselor condition flattened out while the computer condition effects continued to increase. We can only speculate about the delayed differences between these two conditions. Participants in the personalized condition may have become somewhat dependent

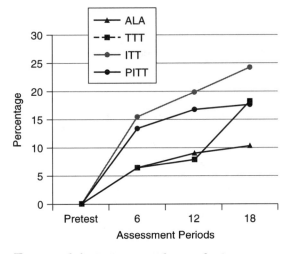

FIGURE 6.4 Point prevalence abstinence (%) for four treatment groups at pretest and at 6, 12, and 18 months. (ALA = standardized manuals; TTT = individualized stage-matched manuals; ITT = interactive computer reports; PITT = personalized counselor calls).

on the social support and social control of the calls. The last call was after the 6-months assessment, and benefits would be observed at 12 months. Termination of the counselors could result in no further progress because of the loss of social support and control. The classic pattern in smoking cessation clinics is rapid relapse as soon as the treatment is terminated. Some of this rapid relapse could well be due to the sudden loss of social support or social control provided by the counselors and other participants in the clinic.

The next test was to demonstrate the efficacy of the expert system when applied to an entire population recruited proactively. With over 80% of 5170 smokers participating and fewer than 20% in the preparation stage, we demonstrated the significant benefits of the expert system at each six-month follow-up (Prochaska, Velicer, Fava, Rossi, & Tsoh, 1999). Furthermore, the advantages over proactive assessment alone increased at each follow-up for the full two years assessed. The implications here are that expert system interventions in a population can continue to demonstrate benefits long after the intervention has ended.

We then showed remarkable replication of the expert system's efficacy in an HMO population of 4000 smokers with 85% participation (Prochaska, Velicer, Fava, Ruggiero, Laforge, & Rossi, 1999). In the first population-based study, the expert system was 34% more effective than assessment alone; in the second, it was 31% more effective. These replicated differences were clinically significant as well. While working on a population basis, we were able to produce the level of success normally found only in intense clinic-based programs with low participation rates of much more selected samples of smokers. The implication is that once expert systems are developed and show effectiveness with one population, they can be transferred at much lower cost and produce replicable changes in new populations.

Enhancing Interactive Interventions

In recent benchmarking research, we have been trying to create enhancements to our expert system to produce better outcomes. In the first enhancement in our HMO population, we added a personal hand-held computer designed to bring the behavior under stimulus control. This commercially successful innovation was an action-oriented intervention that did not enhance our expert system program on a population basis. In fact our expert system alone was twice as effective

as the system plus the enhancement. There are two major implications here: (1) more is not necessarily better and (2) providing interventions that are mismatched to the stage can make outcomes markedly worse.

Counselor Enhancements

In our HMO population, counselors plus expert system computers were outperforming expert systems alone at 12 months. But at 18 months the counselor enhancement had declined and the computers alone had increased. Both interventions were producing identical outcomes of 23.2% abstinence, which are excellent for an entire population. Why did the effect of the counselor condition drop after the intervention? Our leading hypothesis is that people can become dependent on counselors for the social support and social monitoring that they provide. Once these social influences are withdrawn, people may do worse. The expert system computers, on the other hand, may maximize self-reliance. In a current clinical trial, we are fading out counselors over time as a method for dealing with dependency on the counselor. If fading is effective, it will have implications for how counseling should be terminated: gradually over time rather than suddenly.

We believe that the most powerful change programs will combine the personalized benefits of counselors and consultants with the individualized, interactive, and data-based benefits of expert system computers. But to date we have not been able to demonstrate that the more costly counselors, who had been our most powerful change agents, can actually add value over computers alone. These findings have clear implications for the cost effectiveness of expert systems for entire populations needing behavior health programs.

Interactive vs. Noninteractive Interventions

Another important aim of the HMO project was to assess whether interactive interventions (computer-generated expert systems) are more effective than noninteractive communications (self-help manuals) when controlling for the number of intervention contacts (Velicer, Prochaska, Fava, Laforge, & Rossi, 1999). At 6, 12, and 18 months for groups of smokers receiving a series of one, two, three, or six interactive vs. noninteractive contacts, the interactive interventions (expert system) outperformed the noninteractive manuals in all four comparisons. In three of the comparisons (one, two, and three), the difference at 18 months was at least five percentage points, a difference between treatment conditions assumed to be clinically significant. These results clearly support the hypothesis that interactive interventions will outperform the same number of noninteractive interventions.

These results support our assumption that the most powerful health-promotion programs for entire populations will be interactive. In the reactive clinical literature it is clear that interactive interventions like behavioral counseling produce greater long-term abstinence rates (20% to 30%) than do noninteractive interventions such as self-help manuals (10% to 20%). It should be kept in mind that these traditional action-oriented programs were implicitly or explicitly recruiting for populations in the preparation stage. Our results indicate that even with proactively recruited smokers with less than 20% in the preparation stage, the long-term abstinence rates are in the 20% to 30% range for the interactive interventions and in the 10% to 20% range for the noninteractive interventions. The implications are clear. Providing interactive interventions through computers is likely to produce better outcomes than relying on noninteractive communications, such as newsletters, media, or self-help manuals.

Proactive vs. Reactive Results

We believe that the future of behavior health programs lies with stage-matched, proactive, and interactive interventions. Much greater impacts can be generated by proactive programs because of much higher participation rates, even if efficacy rates are lower. But we also believe that proactive programs can produce comparable outcomes to traditional reactive programs. It is counterintuitive to believe that comparable outcomes can be produced with people whom we recruit as with people who call us for help. But that is what informal comparisons strongly suggest. In a comparison of 18-month follow-ups for all subjects who received our three expert system reports in our previous reactive study and in our current proactive study, the abstinence curves were remarkably similar (Prochaska et al., 1993; Prochaska, Velicer, Fava, Ruggiero, Laforge, & Rossi, 1999).

The results with our counseling plus computer conditions were even more impressive. Proactively recruited smokers working with counselors and computers had higher abstinence

rates at each follow-up than did the smokers who had called for help. One of the differences is that our proactive counseling protocol had been revised and, it is hoped, improved, based on previous data and experience. But the point is this: if we offer people improved behavioral change programs that are appropriate for their stage, we probably can produce efficacy or abstinence rates at least equal to those we produce with people who come to us for help. Unfortunately, there is no experimental design that could permit us to randomly assign people to proactive vs. reactive recruitment programs. We are left with informal but provocative comparisons.

If these results continue to be replicated, therapeutic programs will be able to produce unprecedented effects on entire populations, which we believe will require scientific and professional shifts:

1. From an action paradigm to a stage paradigm
2. From reactive to proactive recruitment
3. From expecting participants to match the needs of our programs to having our programs match their needs
4. From clinic-based to population-based programs that still apply the field's most powerful individualized and interactive intervention strategies

VISION FOR THE FUTURE

If our field makes these paradigm shifts, then we can envision a future in which behavior health intervention programs will receive the emphasis they require. No longer will only a small minority of people with major mental health and behavior health problems be reached. A health-care delivery system will be developed to reach 80% or more of people with major behavioral killers and disablers.

Hospitals were designed for births, deaths, and surgery. Outpatient practices were designed to deliver diagnoses and drugs. Both of these systems were designed to deliver acute care to acute conditions like infectious diseases. But the major killers of our time are chronic diseases, caused in large part by chronic behavioral problems. The problem is that acute conditions stopped being the dominant killers of our society in the 20th century. The acute-care delivery systems are not designed to treat the chronic behavior conditions that are the major causes of chronic disease and premature death.

Historically, when goods needed to be delivered across the sea, shipping was developed as a major transportation system. When the goods reached land, a new delivery system needed to be developed, such as railroads. When the goods reached the end of the line, another delivery system was needed, namely, highways on which cars and trucks could deliver goods. In behavior health care we are faced with the equivalent of trying to drive a car on railroad tracks. No wonder it is such a bumpy ride. No wonder we worry about whether our vehicle will survive.

Where will be the primary site for behavior health-care delivery? Clearly not hospitals and not outpatient clinics, which are fine for acute care. However, they do not reach many people with the chronic behavior conditions that are the major killers and that drive up the most health-care costs. Home-based behavior health care will be the primary site, with telecommunication the primary delivery system.

Who will pay for building such a system? Who paid for the new highways? The government, through gasoline taxes. Here is one vision of how the new behavior health-care system could be built. Utilizing proactive telephone and mail recruitment, interactive computers, and 40,000 stage-matched counselors paid $50,000 per year, we could reach 80% of the smokers in the United States and reduce smoking by 20% to 25% in 18 to 24 months. This would have huge public health benefits and health-care savings. The system would also be in place to treat many other major behavioral health problems, like depression and addictions, on a population basis. All of this could be built for less than 5% of the recent settlement with the tobacco industry.

We can envision a day when stage-matched interactive technologies will be to behavior health and mental health therapies what medications are to biological medicine: the most cost-effective method for bringing the maximum amount of science to bear on important problems in entire populations in a user-friendly manner. Some therapists may be threatened by such a vision. But imagine physicians who could only rely on talking to patients and giving them printed pamphlets. What if they had no scientific assessments like magnetic resonance imaging and blood analyses? What if they had no new techniques for treating diseases, like medications or laser surgery? Who would go to such physicians? Did the status and salaries of physicians go down with new scientific assessments and interventions? Or did they go up?

Behavior change specialists working with be-havior change technologies will have the means to help entire patient populations progress at each stage of change. With new models of therapy and behavior change, with new technologies and delivery systems, we will be able to reach and help many more people than we ever thought possible.

REFERENCES

Bandura, A. (1977). Self-efficacy: Toward a unifying theory of behavior change. *Psychological Review, 84*, 191–215.

Bandura, A. (1982). Self-efficacy mechanism in human agency. *American Psychologist, 37*, 122–147.

Beitman, B. D., Beck, N. C., Deuser, W., Carter, C., Davidson, J., & Maddock, R. (1994). Patient stages of change predict outcome in a panic disorder medication trial. *Anxiety, 1*, 64–69.

Brownell, K. D., Marlatt, G. A., Lichtenstein, E., & Wilson, G. T. (1986). Understanding and preventing relapse. *American Psychologist, 41*, 765–782.

Cohen, S., Lichtenstein, E., Prochaska, J. O., Rossi, J. S., Gritz, E. R., Carr, C. R., Orleans, C. T., Schoenbach, V. J., Biener, L., Abrams, D., DiClemente, C. C., Curry, S., Marlatt, G. A., Cummings, K. M., Emont, S. L., Giovino, G., & Ossip-Klein, D. (1989). Debunking myths about self-quitting: Evidence from ten prospective studis of persons quitting smoking by themselves. *American Psychologist, 44*, 1355–1365.

COMMIT. (1995). The Community Intervention Trial of Smoking Cessation (COMMIT). Summary of cohort results. *American Journal of Public Health, 85*, 183–192.

DiClemente, C. C., & Prochaska, J. O. (1982). Self-change and therapy change of smoking behavior: A comparison of processes of change of cessation and maintenance. *Addictive Behaviors, 7*, 133–142.

DiClemente, C. C., Prochaska, J. O., Fairhurst, S. K., Velicer, W. F., Valesquez, M. M., & Rossi, J. S. (1991). The processes of smoking cessation: An analysis of precontemplation, contemplation, and preparation stages of change. *Journal of Consulting and Clinical Psycology, 59*, 295–304.

Donovan, D. M., & Marlatt, G. A. (Eds.). (1988). *Assessment of addictive behaviors: Behavioral, cognitive, and physiological procedures.* New York: Guilford.

Ennett, S. T., Tabler, N. S., Ringwolt, C. L., & Fliwelling, R. L. (1994). How effective is drug abuse resistance education? A meta-analysis of Project DARE outcome evaluations. *American Journal of Public Health, 84*, 1394–1401.

Glasgow, R. E., Terborg, J. R., Hollis, J. F., Severson, H. H., & Boles, S. M. (1995). Take heart: Results from the initial phase of a work-site wellness program. *American Journal of Public Health, 85,* 209–216.

Hunt, W., Barnett, L., & Branch, L. (1971). Relapse rates in addiction programs. *Journal of Clinical Psychology, 27,* 455–456.

Jacobson, N. S., Wilson, L., & Tupper, C. (1988). The clinical significance of treatment gains resulting from exposure-based interventions for agoraphobia: A reanalysis of outcome data. *Behavior Therapy, 19,* 539–559.

Janis, I. L., & Mann, L. (1977). *Decision making: A psychological analysis of conflict, choice and commitment.* New York: The Free Press.

Jones, E. E., & Nisbett, R. E. (1972). The actor and observer: Divergent perceptions of the causes of behavior. In E. E. Jones, D. Kanouse, H. H. Kelley, R. E. Nisbett, S. Valins, & B. Weiner (Eds.), *Attribution: Perceiving the causes of behavior* (pp. 79–94). Morristown, NJ: General Learning Press.

Lam, C. S., McMahon, B. T., Priddy, D. A., & Gehred-Schultz, A. (1988). Deficit awareness and treatment performance among traumatic head injury adults. *Brain Injury, 2,* 235–242.

Lando, H. A., Pechacek, T. F., Pirie, P. L., Murray, D. M., Mittelmark, M. B., Lichtenstein, E., Nothwehyr, F., & Gray, C. (1995). Changes in adult cigarette smoking in the Minnesota Heart Health Program. *American Journal of Public Health, 85,* 201–208.

Lichtenstein, E., & Hollis, J. (1992). Patient referral to smoking cessation programs: Who follows through? *The Journal of Family Practice, 34,* 739–744.

Luepker, R. V., Murray, D. M., Jacobs, D. R., Mittelmark, M. B., Bracht, N., Carlaw, R., Crow, R., Elmer, P., Finnegan, J., Folsom, A. R., Grimm, R., Hannan, P. J., Jeffrey, R. Lando, H., McGoern, P., Mullis, R., Perry, C. L., Pechacek, T., Pirie, P., Sprafka, J. M., Weisbrod, R., & Blackburn, H. (1994). Community education for cardiovascular disease prevention: Risk factor changes in the Minnesota Heart Health Program. *American Journal of Public Health, 84,* 1383–1393.

Marlatt, G. A., & Gordon, J. R. (Eds.). (1985). *Relapse prevention: Maintenance strategies in addictive behavior change.* New York: Guilford.

Masters, W., & Johnson, V. (1970). *Human sexual inadequacy.* Boston: Little, Brown.

Medeiros, M. E., Prochaska, J. O., & Prochaska, J. M. (in press). Predicting termination and continuation status in psychotherapy using the transtheoretical model. *Psychotherapy: Theory, research, practice, training.*

Mellinger, G. D., Balter, M. B., Uhlenhuth, E. H., Cisin, I. H., Manheimer, D. I., & Rickels, K. (1983). Evaluating a household survey measure of psychic distress. *Psychological Medicine, 13,* 607–621.

Miller, W. R. (1985). Motivation for treatment: A

review with special emphasis on alcoholism. *Psychological Bulletin, 98,* 84–107.

Miller, W. R., Benefield, R. G., & Tonigan, J. S. (1993). Enhancing motivation for change in problem drinking: A controlled comparison of two therapist styles. *Journal of Consulting and Clinical Psychology, 61,* 455–461.

Norcross, J. C., Ratzin, A. C., & Payne, D. (1989). Ringing in the New Year: The change processes and reported outcomes of resolutions. *Addictive Behaviors, 14,* 205–212.

Norcross, J. C., & Vangarelli, D. J. (1989). The resolution solution: Longitudinal examination of New Year's change attempts. *Journal of Substance Abuse, 1,* 127–134.

Prochaska, J. O. (1979). *Systems of psychotherapy: A transtheoretical analysis.* Chicago: Dorsey.

Prochaska, J. O. (1994). Strong and weak principles for progressing from precontemplation to action based on twelve problem behaviors. *Health Psychology, 13,* 47–51.

Prochaska, J. O., & DiClemente, C. C. (1983). Stages and processes of self–change of smoking: Toward an integrative model of change. *Journal of Consulting and Clinical Psychology, 51,* 390–395.

Prochaska, J. O., & DiClemente, C. C. (1984). *The transtheoretical approach: Crossing traditional boundaries of change.* Homewood, IL: Dow Jones/Irwin.

Prochaska, J. O., & DiClemente, C. C. (1985). Common processes of change in smoking, weight control, and psychological distress. In S. Shiffman & T. Wills (Eds.), *Coping and substance abuse.* New York: Academic Press.

Prochaska, J. O., DiClemente, C. C., & Norcross, J. C. (1992). In search of how people change: Applications to the addictive behaviors. *American Psychologist, 47,* 1102–1114.

Prochaska, J. O., DiClemente, C. C., Velicer, W. F., & Rossi, J. S. (1993). Standardized, individualized, interactive and personalized self-help programs for smoking cessation. *Health Psychology, 12,* 399–405.

Prochaska, J. O., Norcross, J. C., Fowler, J., Follick, M., & Abrams, D. B. (1992). Attendance and outcome in a work-site weight control program: Processes and stages of change as process and predictor variables. *Addictive Behavior, 17,* 35–45.

Prochaska, J. O., Norcross, J. C., & DiClemente, C. C. (1994). *Changing for good.* New York: William Morrow.

Prochaska, J. O., Velicer, W. F., Fava, J. L., Laforge, R. G., & Rossi, J. S. (1999). *Stage, interactive, dose response, counseling and stimulus control effects in a managed care population of smokers.* Manuscript in preparation.

Prochaska, J. O., Velicer, W. F., Fava, J., Rossi, J., & Tsoh. (1999). *A stage matched expert system intervention with a total population of smokers.* Manuscript under review.

Prochaska, J. O., Velicer, W. F., Rossi, J. S., Goldstein, M. G., Marcus, B. H., Rakowski, W., Fiore, C., Harlow, L., Redding, C. A., Rosenbloom, D., & Rossi, S. R. (1994). Stages of change and decisional balance for twelve problem behaviors. *Health Psychology, 13*, 39–46.

Reed, G. R., Velicer, W. F., & Prochaska, J. O. (1997). What makes a good staging algorithm: Examples from regular exercise. *American Journal of Health Promotion, 12*, 57–66.

Rossi, J. S. (1992). *Stages of change for 15 health risk behaviors in an HMO population.* Paper presented at the 13th meeting of the Society for Behavioral Medicine, New York.

Schacter, S. (1982). Recidivism and self-cure of smoking and obesity. *American Psychologist, 37*, 436–444.

Snow, M. G., Prochaska, J. O., & Rossi, J. S. (1992). Stages of change for smoking cessation among former problem drinkers: A cross-sectional analysis. *Journal of Substance Abuse, 4*, 107–116.

U.S. Department of Health and Human Services. (1990). *The health benefits of smoking cessation: A report of the Surgeon General.* DHHS Publication No. CDC 90–8416. Washington, DC: U.S. Government Printing Office.

Velicer, W. F., Prochaska, J. O., Fava, J. L., Laforge, R. G., & Rossi, J. S. (1999). Interactive versus and non-interactive interventions and dose-response relationships for stage matched smoking cessation programs in a managed care setting. *Health Psychology, 18*, 21–28.

Veroff, J., Douvan, E., & Kulka, R. A. (1981a). *The inner America.* New York: Basic Books.

Veroff, J., Douvan, E., & Kulka, R. A. (1981b). *Mental health in America.* New York: Basic Books.

Wierzbicki, M., & Pekarik, G. (1993). A meta-analysis of psychotherapy dropout. *Professional Psychology: Research and Practice, 29*, 190–195.

Wolpe, J. (1973). *The practice of behavior therapy.* Elmsford, NY: Pergamon.

CHAPTER 7

HOPE THEORY:

UPDATING A COMMON

PROCESS FOR

PSYCHOLOGICAL CHANGE

C. R. SNYDER, STEPHEN ILARDI, SCOTT T. MICHAEL, AND JEN CHEAVENS
University of Kansas, Lawrence

SO MANY PSYCHOTHERAPIES, SO FEW COMMON PROCESSES

By one count (Karasu, 1986), there are at least four hundred distinct approaches to psychotherapy. By the turn of the millennium, this number will swell to over five hundred (Snyder, Michael, & Cheavens, 1999). Amidst all of these purportedly differing approaches, what can be discerned about possible *shared* frameworks that can bridge this multitude of psychotherapy techniques? This is the core question that we seek to answer in the present chapter.

Despite this proliferation of individual psychotherapies, four decades of outcome research have yielded a startling result, namely, *clinical improvement in psychotherapy is produced by a large number of different psychotherapy protocols with very few differences in efficacy among them* (Elkin et al., 1989; Garfield, 1981; Luborsky, Singer, & Luborsky, 1975; Miller, Duncan, & Hubble, 1997; Smith & Glass, 1977; Smith, Glass, & Miller, 1980). This uniformity in treatment outcome appears to be even more marked when the differing approaches have similar psychotherapeutic foci (Frank & Frank, 1991). In referring to the ubiquitous phenomenon of outcome equivalency, Luborsky, Singer, and Luborsky (1975) subtitled their influential article "Everyone Has Won and All Must Have Prizes," an allusion to the Dodo Bird's verdict in *Alice in Wonderland;* the researchers concluded that all psychotherapy approaches are worthy of prizes because they all appear to "work" to an equal degree.

Findings of equal efficacy among varying psychotherapies has catalyzed the further study of common processes across psychotherapies. In the past, these processes have been called nonspecific or common factors (Lambert, 1992). Uncomfortable with these terms, Kazdin (1980) decries the fact that they imply "nebulous influences in treatment that mysteriously alter client behavior" (p. 325). Although we concur with this critique, we believe there is one such common factor that is not vague inasmuch as it reflects a *specific* concept (and an accompanying framework) that is worthy of consideration. That bridging concept is hope. Accordingly, this chapter explores the explanatory role of hope as a core process in facilitating positive psychotherapeutic change.

CARRYING THE TORCH OF HOPE LIT BY JEROME FRANK

We are by no means the first to advance hope as a useful mechanism for understanding the common processes in psychological change. The seminal thinker on this point was Jerome Frank, who through the 1960s and 1970s (see Frank, 1961, 1968, 1971, 1973), published several compelling papers and books suggesting that the generation of hope was a core mediational mechanism across differing psychotherapies. Although Frank continued to advocate the importance of hope in subsequent writings (see Frank, 1989), including the two revisions of his classic *Persuasion and Healing* (Frank, 1973; Frank & Frank, 1991), his retirement understandably has left a rather large vacuum in the championing of this perspective.[1]

We agree with Frank's view that hope constitutes an important mediational mechanism in successful therapy, and our goal in this chapter is to continue the discussion of the psychotherapeutic power of hope that he so eloquently advanced over the last several decades. Accordingly, we present a new and expanded theory of hope and, thereafter, briefly summarize the correlates of higher hope. Finally, in the major portion of this chapter, we explore how this new hope theory helps to explicate the shared, beneficial processes of psychotherapy.

A NEW THEORY OF HOPE

From the late 1950s to the 1960s, theorists' definitions of hope centered on persons' positive expectations for goal attainment (Cantril, 1964; Farber, 1968; Frank, 1975; Frankl, 1992; Melges & Bowlby, 1969; Menninger, 1959; Schactel, 1959; Stotland, 1969). This view portrayed hope simply as the perception that one's goals can be attained (Snyder, Cheavens, & Michael, 1999; Snyder, Sympson, Michael, & Cheavens, in press). Subsequent, in-depth examinations by our research team into such hopeful perceptions, however, have led to a somewhat more complex model than this unidimensional, goal-expectancy conceptualization. Expanding on previous unidimensional models of hope as goal-directed thought, we suggest that hope also includes both an agentic and a planning component. Accordingly, our new model of hope has three interrelated cognitive components, referred to as *goals*, *agency*, and *pathways*. In this section, we describe these components and discuss the manner in which they interact to form our model of hope.

Goals

We begin with the assumption that purposive human actions are goal-directed. As such, goals are the targets of mental action sequences. Thus,

goals reflect the cognitive component that anchors hope theory (Snyder, 1994a, 1994b). According to this theory, such goals must be sufficiently important to motivate people. Goals that motivate should be attainable and yet contain some inherent uncertainty. Furthermore, goals can vary in their temporal nature, ranging from short to long term.

Pathways Thoughts

To attain imagined goals, people must perceive that they are capable of producing viable routes to them. This component of hope, called pathways thought, entails an appraisal of capabilities for finding one or more effective routes to the desired goal. The capacity to envision at least one pathway is shown in Figure 7.1.

Although pathways thought typically involves the perceived ability to imagine one principal avenue to the desired end point, we have found that high-hope persons often believe that they can come up with many ways to reach their goals (Irving, Snyder, & Crowson, 1998; Snyder et al., 1991). This latter capacity for pathways thinking becomes especially marked when the person encounters a blockage to a desired goal. On this point, our research reveals that high-hopers perceive that they can generate alternate routes when confronted with such impediments; equally important, high-hopers actually produce more alternative routes when blocked (Irving et al., 1998; Snyder, 1994a, 1994b; Snyder et al., 1991).

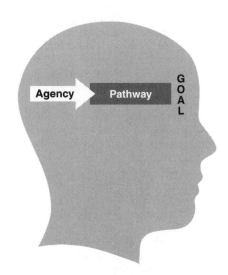

FIGURE 7.1 Schematic of agentic and pathways goal-related thoughts in hope theory.

---

[1] In suggesting that hope is a shared process in successful psychotherapy, we also would hasten to acknowledge that other writers have promulgated this perspective (e.g., Erickson, Post, & Paige, 1975; Menninger, 1959; Stotland, 1969).

Agency Thoughts

The third component of this new theory of hope is called agency thought, or the perceived capacity to begin *and* sustain movement along the envisioned pathways to a desired goal. This goal-directed initiative often appears in such self-affirming statements as "I know I can do this" and "I will get this done." Indeed, in our laboratories, we have found that such agentic self-talk is embraced by high- as compared to low-hope people (Snyder, LaPointe, Crowson, & Early, 1998). As can be seen in the hypothetical protagonist of Figure 7.1, her agentic thought is being applied to the particular imagined pathway to a desired goal. An additional characteristic of such agentic thought is that it allows people to channel their positive mental energies to alternate pathways *when impediments are encountered* (Irving et al., 1998; Snyder, 1994b; Snyder et al., 1991).

Necessity of Both Agency and Pathways Thoughts

Elsewhere, we have offered a specific definition of hope as "a positive motivational state that is based on an interactively derived sense of successful (a) agency (goal-directed energy), and (b) pathways (planning to meet goals)" (Snyder, Irving, & Anderson, 1991, p. 287).[2] Some amplification of

this definition may help the reader to gain a fuller sense of the fact that both agency and pathways goal-directed thoughts are necessary for the hope process. That is, effective goal-directed thinking requires both the perceived capacity to envision workable routes *and* goal-directed energy. Those who practice psychotherapy, for example, may readily think of a client who is filled with pathways thoughts but simply cannot get moving because of deficiencies in agentic thoughts. Conversely, another client may be brimming with agentic thought but lack the pathways thinking to

---

[2]One may rightfully ask about the relationship of hope theory to previous theoretical perspectives. Self-efficacy theory evolved from the influential work of Albert Bandura (1977, 1982, 1986, 1989a, 1989b, 1995, 1997; Maddux, 1995), and it should be noted that hope theory bears similarities and differences relative to this earlier theory. Briefly, Bandura argues that goal-directed behavior results through the assessment of (1) outcome expectancies, which tap the degree to which a person believes that a particular behavior will produce a given outcome, and (2) efficacy expectancies, which tap the degree to which the person perceives that he or she can engage in those requisite behaviors. The outcome and efficacy expectancies, respectively, are similar to pathways and agency thinking in hope theory. Such expectancies, according to Bandura, are situation-specific and therefore vary from the premise of hope theory that goal-directed cognitions appear across a variety of goal arenas. Bandura also suggests that the efficacy expectancies are the most critical determinants of actual goal-directed activity, whereas hope theory holds that agentic and pathways thoughts are equally and iteratively involved throughout goal pursuit activities. There are other differences in the

---

components that are worthy of mention. For example, the agency component of hope theory differs from efficacy expectancies in that agency goes beyond the perception of effectively carrying out a goal-directed sequence of activities; more specifically, agency also entails a willingness to direct one's mental energy to initiating and sustaining movement toward the goal. Again, because of the across-goal nature of hope theory, agency taps a general propensity to perceive oneself as using pathways in general. Likewise, pathways thinking not only taps the propensity to understand the contingent route for a given situation but also reflects a more general propensity to foresee multiple pathways. Finally, recent research reveals that hope factors differently than self-efficacy, and hope provides unique predictive variance of well-being beyond self-efficacy (Magaletta & Oliver, 1999).

Scheier and Carver (1985, 1987) define optimism as a generalized expectancy that good things will happen. Although optimism and hope theory share views about the importance of expectancies across situations and both are cast within the context of goal-directed behavior, the two theories differ in how expectancies operate. Scheier and Carver hold that expectancies are the most important predictor of outcomes. Although the agency component is similar to their expectancies notion, the pathways component is not explicitly part of the optimism model. Also, unlike the optimism model, wherein generalized outcome expectancies are theorized to be the most important predictor of outcomes, hope theory equally emphasizes the iterative roles of agentic and pathways thoughts. In the work in our laboratory, the agency component of various hope scales correlates with the Life Orientation Test (LOT), whereas the pathway component does not show very strong relations (see Snyder et al., in press, for a detailed comparison of optimism and hope).

For a discussion of hope theory in relation to other theories such as helplessness, resourcefulness, the Type A behavior pattern, achievement motivation, self-esteem, and so on, see Snyder (1994b) and Snyder, Irving, and Anderson (1991).

guide this energy to the desired goals. Neither one of these persons (i.e., the low-agency/high-pathway pattern or the high-agency/low-pathway pattern) can be said to have high hope. (For more detailed descriptions of the low-agency/high-pathway or the high-agency/low-pathway patterns of thought, including case histories, see Snyder, 1994b, pp. 34–40.)

As posited by the theory, our research shows that agency and pathways thoughts are additive and iterative in nature (Snyder et al., 1991). They are additive in that neither agency nor pathways thoughts alone will yield successful goal attainment. They are iterative in that increases in one component typically should lead to increases in the other. For example, increasing pathways thoughts should ignite the associated agentic thoughts. The inverse also follows, however, in that a rush of agentic thoughts should be yoked to particular pathways thoughts. Typically, both components work together to enhance goal-directed thinking.

Hope Cognitions and Emotions

Hope theory posits that the unimpeded pursuit of goals should result in positive emotions, whereas blockages should produce negative affect. Research in our laboratory, utilizing both correlational and longitudinal causal designs, shows that goal blockages yield negative emotional responses (Snyder et al., 1996). This premise of hope theory is also supported in the findings from other laboratories. That is, difficulties in the pursuit of important goals have been shown to undermine perceived well-being (Diener, 1984; Emmons, 1986; Little, 1983; Omodei & Wearing, 1990; Palys & Little, 1983; Ruehlman & Wolchik, 1988), and perceived blockages or lack of progress toward major goals have caused decreases in perceived well-being rather than the other way around (Brunstein, 1993; Little, 1989). Stated succinctly, goal pursuit thoughts drive emotional experiences.

Although blockages do produce negative emotional reactions, it should be emphasized that high- as compared to low-hope people do not experience the same degree of negative affect when blocked. A major reason for this is that higher hope people can generate additional, alternative paths when the original path is impeded. Also, higher hope people are likely to perceive that they can and will use their alternate routes when confronted with blockages (Irving et al., 1998; Snyder, 1994a, 1994 b; Snyder et al., 1991).

WHAT DOES HIGHER HOPE IN THIS MODEL TELL US ABOUT PEOPLE?

In this section, we provide a brief overview of the instruments we have developed and the correlations that we have obtained with scores on these hope scales in relations with other instruments. This latter review serves as a bridge from the benefits of hope for people in general to the subsequent major discussion in this chapter of the underlying benefits of hope for persons in psychotherapy.

Hope Scales

We believe that it would be useful for practitioners and researchers to have self-report hope measures based on our new model. Accordingly, we have developed three instruments for measuring hope. We describe these briefly in this section.

Trait Hope Scale

The Trait Hope Scale (Snyder et al., 1991) consists of four agency items, four pathways items, and four filler items. It asks respondents to imagine themselves across time and situational contexts. This instrument demonstrates both internal and temporal reliability, with two separate and yet related factors, as well as an overarching hope factor (Babyak, Snyder, & Yoshinobu, 1993). Several convergent and discriminant validity studies have supported its posited relationships with many other related measures. (See Appendix A for the Trait Hope Scale.)

State Hope Scale

The State Hope Scale (Snyder et al., 1996) has three agency and three pathways items. It asks respondents to describe how they perceive themselves "right now." Numerous studies support the internal reliability and factor structure, as well as the construct validity of the State Hope Scale. (See Appendix B for the State Hope Scale.)

Children's Hope Scale

The Children's Hope Scale (Snyder et al., 1997), for children ages 8 to 16, is made up of three agency and three pathways items. It asks children to give their usual thoughts in responding to the items. The scale's internal and test-retest reliabilities have been documented, as has its two-factor structure. Relevant studies also support the convergent and discriminant validities of the Children's Hope Scale. (See Appendix C for the Children's Hope Scale.)

Summary of Hope Measures

Together, these three indexes offer brief and valid means of tapping hopeful thinking in children and adults. We turn next to a discussion of what we have learned from administering these scales to various clinical and nonclinical populations.

Correlates of Hope

Our research shows that the active, cognitive approach to accomplishing goals, which characterizes hopeful persons, is associated with several benefits (see Snyder, 1994b; Snyder, Cheavens, & Michael, 1999; Snyder et al., in press) for children and adults. Because progress in psychotherapy may covary with a client's psychological adjustment, physical health, and life achievements, we have partitioned the relevant hope data into these three categories for review.

Psychological Adjustment

High-hope persons have more positive and fewer negative thoughts than individuals low in hope (Snyder et al., 1991, 1996); they have higher self-esteem, and report being more energized, confident, and challenged by their goals (Snyder et al., 1991). Furthermore, they generally see themselves in a favorably biased light and engage in positive self-presentations (Curry, Snyder, Cook, Ruby, & Rehm, 1997; Snyder et al., 1991, 1996, 1997). In this latter regard, Taylor and her colleagues (Taylor & Armor, 1996; Taylor & Brown, 1988, 1994) have described such positive self-illusions as adaptive coping strategies. Thus, high-hope individuals may benefit from their somewhat elevated sense of control over stressful events and an overly roseate view of the future (see Snyder, 1989).

Low-hope people think negatively about their goal pursuits and are overwhelmed by them. Their futures are filled with perceived uncertainties and serious concerns about their ability to cope. They tend to present themselves in an understated and self-effacing manner. Similarly, low-hope persons not only prefer negative self-referential statements but also are especially prone to remember personal weaknesses (see Snyder, LaPointe, Crowson, & Early, 1998). That is, low-hope persons tend to ruminate on the negative aspects of their goal pursuits. This set of characteristics, as well as this latter tendency to gravitate to negative self-referential information,

should make it more difficult for low-hope persons to change in the therapy process.

Health

We expected to find that high hope confers some benefits in health-related problems, both through increased pathway thinking about strategies for coping with illnesses and through increased agency to use these potentially adaptive strategies. One of the earliest findings was that high-hope persons are more likely to engage in physical exercise (Harney, 1990) and that aerobic exercise increases agency-related thinking (McCann & Holmes, 1984; Roth & Holmes, 1987). Also, aerobic exercise has been shown to play a role in preserving such agentic thought during major life stressors (Holmes, 1993; Seraganian, 1993). Research on this latter point shows that higher hope is associated with more adaptive coping and lower risk of depression after spinal cord injury (Elliott, Witty, Herrick, & Hoffman, 1991). Also, high-hope burn survivors engaged in fewer activities that were counterproductive to recovery, and they interacted more positively with caregivers (Barnum, Snyder, Rapoff, Mani, & Thompson, 1998).

Studies on pain tolerance (in response to a cold pressor task) reveal that high-hope persons not only report less pain but also tolerate it for twice as long as low-hope persons (Snyder & Brown, 1997; Snyder & Hackman, 1998). Also, high-hope women are more knowledgeable about breast cancer and reported that they would use more effective coping methods in response to cancer (Irving et al., 1998). Finally, Affleck and Tennen (1996; see also Tennen & Affleck, 1999) report that higher hope among fibromyalgia patients is associated with the ability to find more benefits from the disease condition, as well as the ability to remind oneself of these benefits (this finding also holds when controlling statistically for optimism/pessimism). Together, these studies suggest that hope is associated with more adaptive coping responses, a more positive outlook, and an ability to find meaning in illness-related situations.

Achievement

Although higher hope is *not* related significantly to intelligence, it is related to superior performance on standardized achievement measures (Snyder et al., 1991, 1997; Snyder, Wiklund, & Cheavens, 1999). For example, higher hope predicts better semester grades (Curry et al., 1997;

Snyder et al., 1991), as well as higher cumulative grades and eventual graduation rates (these latter relationships remained even while the influence of ACT scores was statistically controlled) (Snyder, Wiklund, & Cheavens, 1999).

Higher hope is also associated with superior athletic performances. In this regard, Curry et al. (1997) report that trait and state hope together accounted for 56% of the variance related to a college track meet performance and that this relationship remained significant when statistically controlling for the shared variances related to rated natural ability (by coaches), amount of training, self-esteem, confidence, and locus of control. In sum, the findings that more hopeful thought relates to superior academic and athletic achievements may have implications for facilitating related outcomes in the psychotherapy process.

Overview: Beneficial Correlates of Higher Hope

When it comes to adjustment, coping with illness, and achievement, it appears that higher hope is related to benefits across a broad spectrum of outcome markers. Noteworthy here is the fact that these relationships often have held when the shared variances related to other psychological and aptitude measures have been removed statistically. These findings suggest that the underlying hopeful, goal-directed thoughts are useful in predicting outcomes in several important life arenas. We submit that psychotherapy is one such important arena. In the remainder of this chapter, we see how well hope theory accounts for the experience of the typical person undergoing successful psychotherapy.

AGENCY THOUGHTS AND PSYCHOLOGICAL CHANGE

According to hope theory, agentic thought provides the motivational spark enabling clients to initiate and sustain movement toward their therapeutic goals. As such, agency is the engine propelling persons to desired outcomes. In this section, we explore what can be learned by applying the agency concept to various psychotherapy processes. Our approach is eclectic, in that we do not focus on any particular therapeutic approach (for specific application of hope theory to cognitive behavioral theory, see Snyder, Ilardi, Cheavens, Michael, Yamhure, & Sympson, in press; for general application across approaches, see Snyder, Michael, & Cheavens, 1999). We explore

agentic thought before and during early sessions, as well as throughout the course of therapy and subsequent follow-ups; moreover, the implications of agency for understanding placebo response is described.

Agency in Early Psychotherapy Improvement

During the first four weeks of treatment, many clients improve considerably (Fennell & Teasdale, 1987; Howard, Kopta, Krause, & Orlinsky, 1986; Howard, Lueger, Maling, & Martinovich, 1993; Ilardi & Craighead, 1994; Rush, Kovacs, Beck, Weissenburger, & Hollon, 1981; Uhlenhuth & Duncan, 1968). Sometimes, the mere promise of therapy can ignite the positive change process. On this point, 40% to 66% of clients have reported getting better before attending their first session (Howard et al., 1986; Lawson, 1994; Weiner-Davis, de Shazer, & Gingerich, 1987). Likewise, the beginning diagnostic intake interview also produces substantial improvements for many clients (Frank, Nash, Stone, & Imber, 1963; Kellner & Sheffield, 1971; Piper & Wogan, 1970). Furthermore, 56% to 71% of the total change variance in psychotherapy has been observed in the very early stages of treatment (Fennell & Teasdale, 1987; Howard et al., 1993).

This consistent surge of improvement before and shortly after initiating psychotherapy cannot reflect any of the psychotherapy techniques specific to a given psychotherapy protocol because these interventions have not had time to be implemented (e.g., the supposed "active" components of the change mechanisms have not been introduced and implemented in cognitive behavior therapy within this early time period) (Ilardi & Craighead, 1994). So what underlies this positive change? We suggest that *it is the increase in agentic thinking that drives this phenomenon of rapid early psychotherapeutic improvement* (for other discussions of early session beneficial increases in hope-related processes, see Goldstein, 1962; Ilardi & Craighead, 1994; Peake & Archer, 1984; Peake & Ball, 1987; Wickramasekera, 1985; and Wilkins, 1979, 1985).

By deciding to seek psychotherapy, the potential client has made a choice to seek help that goes beyond the sources from which it is usually obtained. That is, research suggests that informal sources of help such as family and friends are the first line of help (Cowen, 1982; Norcross & Prochaska, 1986; Veroff, Douvan, & Kukla, 1981). Whatever the malaise and indecision may have been before making the appointment with the mental health professional, this act serves as a manifestation of the client's determination and commitment (to self and others) to "get better." All of the perceived benefit that the potential client has attributed to psychotherapy—which is considerable, based on the results of recent surveys (Seligman, 1995)—increases the client's motivation to change. Indeed, the social influence perspective in psychotherapy argues that the therapists' power and influence engender a strong belief by clients that they can make positive changes (see Strong, 1987, 1991; Strong & Claiborn, 1982; Strong, Wambach, Lopez, & Cooper, 1979).

The sense of willpower that therapists convey for their approaches is infectious and frequently "caught" by their clients. For example, smoking cessation and weight-loss programs that persuade clients that they have the necessary agentic motivation have been found to be more successful in sustaining positive psychotherapy changes over time than no-persuasion comparison conditions (Nicki, Remington, & MacDonald, 1984; Weinberg, Hughes, Critelli, England, & Jackson, 1984). There is also evidence that higher agency in therapists is positively correlated with higher agency (as measured by the Hope Scale) in clients (Crouch, 1989). Furthermore, it is the client's positive expectancy regarding his or her ability to effectively utilize coping strategies (i.e., agency) that most strongly predicts superior psychotherapy outcome (Kirsch, Mearns, & Catanzaro, 1990; see also Kirsch, 1990)

Another agency-enhancing process is the establishment during early psychotherapy sessions of a therapeutic alliance (see Horvath & Greenberg, 1986, 1989, for a discussion of measurement of this construct). A sense of trust is crucial for the therapeutic relationship, and such trust enhances clients' sense of agency to change (see Strong, 1991). Clients have reported that one of the most notable parts of the psychotherapy process is whether they feel liked and respected by their therapists (Strupp, Fox, & Lessler, 1969). Indeed, in the 1970s, it was common for psychotherapy researchers to place the establishment of a warm and supportive therapeutic relationship at the core of the clinical change process (Gurman, 1977; Truax & Mitchell, 1971). We believe, however, that the establishment of a warm, support alliance is important primarily because it implies that clients are motivated (i.e., have increased agency) to work on their problems.

Feeling cared for may help to induce agency thoughts that things can change for the better, and research to test this posited relationship would be useful.

Agency in Later Psychotherapy Improvement

To this point, we have reviewed several ways in which a sense of goal-directed agency is critical in the early stages of psychotherapy. It would be unwise to suppose, however, that such mental energy is not equally important in the latter stages of the therapy process. In this section, we explore briefly the role of agentic thought throughout the course of psychotherapy.

Several writers have posited that agency-like thoughts are crucial for sustaining positive changes in psychotherapy. For example, Howard (1986; Howard & Conway, 1986) has posited that self-determination is a key for sustaining psychological change. Luborsky, Crits-Christoph, Mintz, and Auerbach (1988) found that clients' motivation predicts subsequent successful psychotherapy outcomes. Similarly, other recent writers have advanced notions of willfulness and effortful thought as crucial to the successful change process (Axsom, 1989; Cross & Markus, 1990; Kolb, Beutler, Davis, Crago, & Shanfield, 1985; Yalom, 1989).[3] In a review of 50 published articles, Grencavage and Norcross (1990) examined what appeared to be the core factors that contributed to the course of psychotherapeutic change. They found that one of the key factors was the client's expectancies that he or she was capable of producing targeted life changes.

In a test of the importance of such agency-like factors for positive psychological change, Hanna and Ritchie (1995) conducted an in-depth analysis of what people report as critical contributors to this improvement. On a five-point scale of perceived potency (1 = not at all, 2 = somewhat, 3 = definite, 4 = necessary, and 5 = sufficient), effort/willfulness had a mean rating of 3.6 (one of the highest average scores in a list of 24 variables). From the perspective of the persons

---

[3]For earlier writings on the topic of will, we would recommend (in chronological order), Wundt (1894), McDougall (1908), Lewin (1951), Adler (in Ansbacher & Ansbacher, 1956), White (1959), deCharms (1968), Deci (1975), Rank (1929/1978), and Ajzen and Fishbein (1980).

actually undergoing positive changes, therefore, a sense of agency appears to play a vital role.

In examining the clinical course of clients following psychotherapy completion, it is instructive to explore those factors that tend to be associated with the maintenance of treatment gains. Not surprisingly, clients' perceived mastery in dealing with their problems is crucial not only for short-term improvement but also for the *maintenance* of such improvement (see Liberman, 1978). Such mastery thoughts reflect, in large part, a continued willingness to grapple with whatever difficulties the person may encounter. In a related line of investigation, Eisenberger and colleagues (Eisenberger & Masterson, 1983; Eisenberger, Mitchell, & Masterson, 1985; Eisenberger & Shank, 1985) suggest that adaptive learning should be rewarded expressly by therapists to foster agency-like persistence. Thus, clients learn to believe that their effortful thoughts and actions are critical *for maintaining gains.*

In an extensive program of research aimed at helping children, Carol Dweck and her colleagues have found it very useful to teach *effortful,* rather than *trait,* attributions (Diener & Dweck, 1978; Dweck, 1986). That is, motivation is more consistently maintained over time when children are taught that their outcomes in life are linked more to their efforts than to their seemingly unchangeable natural abilities (reviewed in Murdock & Altmaier, 1991, pp. 568–570). A similar pattern is discerned among adults—specifically, clients' clinical gains are maintained more fully and longer when clients attribute successes to their internal effortful and agentic thoughts rather than to the therapists' expertise (Colletti & Kopel, 1979; Colletti & Stern, 1980; Jeffrey, 1974; Sonne & Janoff, 1979).

Additional support for the importance of agency enhancement in psychotherapy is found in the meta-analysis of Barker, Funk, and Houston (1988). These investigators examined only those studies in which the positive expectancies of the nonspecific, control-group conditions (e.g., simple discussion without treatment, active listening, and systematic ventilation) were equal to those in an active treatment group. These nonspecific, or common factor, conditions may be considered analogous to agency enhancement alone (without specific intervention techniques). The agency-enhancement groups (i.e., nonspecific control) were significantly superior to the no-treatment control groups in posttreatment outcome analyses, with a difference in effect size of .47 standard deviations. Furthermore, at follow-up (after the termination of treatments) the agency-enhancement groups were still significantly superior to the no-treatment groups, but the effect size had increased to .73 standard deviations. The results of Barker et al. (1988), while controlling more carefully for expectancies than previous studies, nevertheless replicate earlier meta-analytic studies showing that agency-alone (common factors) groups are reliably superior (roughly .5 standard deviations) to no-treatment control groups (Landman & Dawes, 1982; Prioleau, Murdock, & Brody, 1983; Shapiro & Shapiro, 1982; Smith et al., 1980).

Enhanced perceptions of personal agency vis-à-vis desired goals have been shown to influence a variety of therapy-related outcomes. In a longitudinal study of heavy smokers who were attempting to stop, those with higher agency at the beginning of treatment were more likely to do so (Carey & Carey, 1993). Part of this effectiveness of perceived agency is evidently related to the ability to handle especially problematic circumstances (Strecher, Becker, Kirscht, Eraker, & Graham-Tomasi, 1985). That is, motivation is crucial for tough problems. Furthermore, it appears that agency increases from the time of deciding to enter treatment through the initial and maintenance phases (DiClemente, Prochaska, Fairhurst, Velicer, Velasquez, & Rossi, 1991).

One of the more difficult to treat health-related problems is diabetes, and increased agentic thinking is related to better self-management (McCaul, Glasgow, & Shafer, 1987; Padgett, 1991). Another thorny treatment goal is weight loss. Perceived agency at the beginning of treatment successfully predicts maintenance of weight loss over time (Leon, Sternberg, & Rosenthal, 1984); likewise, the more that agentic thoughts about weight loss are fostered over the course of treatment, the more likely people are to lose the weight and keep it off (Bernier & Avard, 1986).[4]

Agency as a Proxy for Placebo

The term *placebo* (Latin for "I shall please") was adopted by psychological research from the field

---

[4]The power of such agentic expectancies is revealed both before and during treatment. These expectancies correlate with improvement before treatment (Friedman, 1963; Goldstein, 1960), and they determine whether or not specific treatment strategies (pathways thinking in the present context) are used (Kirsch et al., 1990).

of medicine, where it meant the ingestion of a pharmacologically inert substance (Critelli & Neumann, 1984; White, Tursky, & Schwartz, 1985a, 1985b). Indeed, the history of medicine before the 17th century has been described as the history of placebo effects (Shapiro, 1971). By using the placebo pill in double-blind studies, in which neither the client nor the researcher purportedly is aware of the inert or "real" content of the pill, the researcher intends to ascertain the incremental amount of change related to the active ingredients of the particular drug over the comparison placebo (Rosenthal & Frank, 1956; Thorne, 1952; Wilkins, 1984). Likewise, placebos supposedly enable researchers to differentiate between the active physiological effects of a "real" psychiatric drug and the psychological effects of the placebo.

Before proceeding further, however, it is appropriate to call into question two important implicit assumptions of researchers in this area. First, double-blind studies on psychoactive drugs do *not* guarantee that patients or researchers are not aware of whether the placebo or actual drug is being ingested (Fisher & Greenberg, 1997a, 1997b, 1997c). Relevant research shows that because of the marked side effects associated with the "real" drugs and the muted sensory effects of the placebo, both researchers and patients can break the supposed double-blind and correctly identify the "sensorially brighter" active drugs (Fisher & Greenberg, 1993). Second, it is also inaccurate to conclude that "real" drugs act exclusively through biology or physiology, whereas placebos act through nonbiological variables (Evans, 1985; Fisher & Greenberg, 1997a). Rather than pose a scientifically untenable mind/body dualism, we suggest that placebos ultimately influence behavior through brain changes in a similar manner as do, for example, antipsychotic drugs; moreover, the field has no clearer understanding of the underlying physiological mediating effects of "real" drugs than it does of those mediating placebos (for a review, see Fisher & Greenberg, 1997b).

The emerging view of placebo comparison groups in psychotherapy research is that they serve as a means of controlling for the effective *common* ingredients in all psychotherapies. Increasingly, especially among cognitive psychotherapists, the view of placebos as therapeutically inert variables has been replaced with a newer perspective that emphasizes their active role for successful psychotherapeutic change

(Kirsch, 1978). As such, placebos serve as a proxy for agentic thinking about one's ability to change; placebos thus reflect motivational expectancies for improvement (Frank & Frank, 1991).

One indication of the power of pill placebos is that a great number of studies (especially regarding the treatment of depression) have found very little difference in efficacy between placebos and drugs for adults (Fisher & Greenberg, 1989, 1997a, 1997b, 1997c; Greenberg & Fisher, 1997; White et al., 1985a, 1985b) and children (Fisher & Fisher, 1997). These findings are even more marked in light of the previous point that drug studies do not successfully produce a true double-blind condition. Thus, for persons who are receiving placebos and know it (this evidently being most participants), their expectancies probably are not as strong as for those receiving the "real" drug; nevertheless, the placebo condition subjects often perform as well as the drug condition subjects (see Roberts, 1994, 1995). Psychiatrist Walter Brown (1994a, 1994b), who is an expert in placebo research, has gone so far as to suggest that a placebo per se may be recommended as a recognized therapy, especially for depression.

It is important to note that the efficacy of placebos (along with the efficacy of "real" drugs) appears to be moderated by the attitude communicated by those administering the pills. For example, Wheatley (1967) found that optimistic psychotherapists engendered better therapy outcomes than did their pessimistic counterparts when dispensing antianxiety drugs. Another relevant study (Uhlenhuth, Cantro, Neustadt, & Payson, 1957) compared a psychiatrist having a favorable attitude toward antianxiety drugs with one who held a far less favorable attitude. Patients of the former psychiatrist had significantly better outcomes. Likewise, in a study of physicians who were trained to be either enthusiastic or skeptical about an antianxiety drug, the enthusiastic training generated more favorable outcomes (Fisher, Cole, Rickels, & Uhlenhuth, 1964). Similar findings were reported in an expanded replication study (Uhlenhuth, Rickes, Fisher, Park, Lipman, & Mock, 1966).

Summary of Agency-related Literature

We have reviewed data pertinent to the role of the client's agentic thought before entering psychotherapy, during early and later treatment sessions, and in posttreatment. Although previous writers and researchers have not expressly used the term *agency*, their focal concepts clearly fit our present definition of agentic thought. What we see, across differing methodologies and samples, is that agentic thought provides a crucial spark for igniting *and* sustaining psychotherapeutic change. Furthermore, an examination of the placebo literature makes it clear that placebo conditions facilitate agentic thought in a manner similar to that observed in psychotherapy; moreover, enhanced agentic thinking catalyzes clinical improvement, whether it occurs in psychotherapy or in a placebo control condition. For any therapist who has worked with a client mired in an unmotivated state, or for anyone who has had the subjective experience of lacking such agentic mental energy, these findings about the importance of agentic thought will come as no surprise.

Having described agency as the motivational driver of psychotherapeutic change, we turn next to the important topic of pathways thinking, which is the perceived "roadmap" for achieving movement toward psychotherapeutic goals.

PATHWAYS THOUGHTS AND PSYCHOLOGICAL CHANGE

In this section, we review the role of pathways thinking as a common process that undergirds all psychotherapeutic approaches. That is, whatever the specifics of a particular psychotherapeutic approach may be, it invariably will teach clients to *believe in their capacities to find the successful means of reaching the desired therapy and life goals*. Variations on this theme are presented in this section.

Admitting Need for Professional Help and Setting the Initial Appointment

We noted in the previous section that the act of seeking professional help leads to increased agency. Similarly, this decision serves as a bellwether in terms of the client's search for a route toward the goal of positive life changes. To initiate psychotherapy reflects a momentous decision, in which the client typically taps into the rich societal lore about psychotherapy as a vehicle for making improvements. This thought—that therapy actually may help—is perhaps the first pathways-enhancing thought in the sequence of psychotherapy. Despite the oftentimes humorous and misleading portrayals of psychotherapists on television (e.g., "Bob Newhart Show" and "Frasier") and in the movies (e.g., *One Flew over*

the Cuckoo's Nest), psychotherapy and its practitioners are afforded considerable respect in our society. Thus public opinion toward psychotherapy in general is quite positive (see Seligman, 1995). Such respect for psychotherapy undoubtedly contributes to elevated pathways thinking as people embrace the psychotherapeutic path and decide to begin professional treatment.

Prefatory Programs Enhancing Clients' Belief in Psychotherapy

One intervention that probably enhances clients' pathways thinking is the provision of a prefatory session (or sessions) before therapy so that clients will be more prepared once they actually begin treatment (Heitler, 1973; Lambert & Lambert, 1984; Mayerson, 1984; Strupp & Bloxom, 1973; Zwick & Attkisson, 1985). As Jerome Frank (1978) wrote, "A patient will probably not remain in therapy or profit from it unless his expectations are in accord with what actually transpires" (p. 19). After examining this literature, our speculation is that such pretreatments increase clients' expectancies about the hopeful pathways thinking that will be "taught" in their subsequent treatment.

Irving, Snyder, Gravel, Hanke, Hilberg, and Nelson (1997) sought to test this idea in a community mental health center. Clients were randomly assigned to either a five-week orientation group or a five-week waiting list prior to 12 weeks of individual therapy. The orientation group had 5 weekly 1.5-hour meetings. The orientation meetings were designed to prepare clients for individual therapy, and they emphasized notions, congenial to hope theory, of establishing goals to address problems and coming up with strategies to achieve these goals (i.e., pathways thinking). Clients assigned to the wait-list were required to wait 5 weeks from completion of intake to the beginning of individual therapy. Independent variables included pretreatment assignment (yes or no) and level of hope (high or low) as measured by the Hope Scale at intake. Dependent measures of well-being (four items developed expressly for this study, with an alpha of .79), level of functioning (Howard et al., 1993), and the State Hope Scale were administered at intake and four times during individual therapy. The final sample ($n = 98$) was largely female, white, unmarried, and high school educated. The design was a 2 [Trait Hope: High, Low (based on a median split of Hope Scale scores)] × 2 (Pretreatment Pathways Hope: Yes, No/Waiting List) factorial. Compared with high-hope people, those low in hope reported greater responsiveness to the pretherapy hope pathways orientation on the dependent measures of well-being, level of functioning, and state hope. Thus, the clients who initially were lowest in overall hope profited the most by the pathways thinking that was taught in the pretreatment. This empirical finding lends further support to the importance of the *early* role of pathways thinking for subsequent successful psychotherapy.

Whatever therapists can do to demonstrate their perceived expertise should help to solidify the new clients' pathways thinking. It is interesting that one of the core results of pretreatment training is that it also increases the clients' perception of the efficacious power of the therapists' techniques (see, for discussion, Beutler, Clarkin, Crago, & Bergan, 1991). This perceived technical expertise also appears to be dependent on the therapist's inherent belief in his or her therapeutic approach, as well as a willingness to "sell" this approach in a simple, convincing, and articulate manner. This perspective is similar to that presented by Beck, Rush, Shaw, and Emery (1979) in their classic manual, *Cognitive Therapy of Depression*, in which therapists are encouraged in early sessions to present convincing and credible rationales to enhance their clients' beliefs in subsequent pathways-related activities.

Teaching Alternate Pathways

The principle of providing individuals with alternate pathways when their intended paths become blocked is an inherent part of most cognitive therapies. For example, Beck et al. (1979) suggest that cognitive therapy for depression works by "providing the patient with symptom relief by translating his major complaints into solvable problems" (p. 167). Thus, one of the cognitive therapist's primary goals is to help clients perceive themselves as capable of producing new routes to their desired goals.

Problem-solving therapies also focus on teaching clients to produce alternative pathways to their goals (D'Zurilla & Nezu, 1980; Nezu & D'Zurilla, 1981a); moreover, they teach people to select the most adaptive among several alternatives (Nezu & D'Zurilla, 1979, 1981b). Related research suggests that it is advantageous to produce multiple pathways (Claerhout, Elder, & Janes, 1982; Getter & Nowinski, 1981), inasmuch as it increases the likelihood of discovering a few high-quality paths (D'Zurilla & Nezu, 1980). It is

important to emphasize that it is clients' enhanced *perception* that they can find successful routes to their goals that actually appears to drive the attainment of their therapeutic goals (Heppner & Hillerbrand, 1991; Heppner & Petersen, 1982).

Teaching Mental Rehearsals

Another pathways-producing strategy that cuts across differing psychotherapeutic approaches is that of teaching clients to engage in mental rehearsals of important upcoming events (Snyder, 1994b). Although mental rehearsals were first examined in the context of athletics (see Mahoney & Avener, 1977), this approach to enhancing pathways thinking has been shown to result in beneficial outcomes in a variety of domains (Markus & Ruvolo, 1989). Some of the most compelling empirical evidence in support of the effectiveness of imaginal techniques in helping persons to achieve their desired performance goals comes from the work of Shelley Taylor and her colleagues (see Taylor & Pham, 1996; Taylor & Schneider, 1989). These rehearsals involve helping the client to anticipate any potential blockages and to visualize what can be done to surmount those problems (Bruce & Newman, 1978; Carbonell, 1981; Wilensky, 1983). Such rehearsals are especially effective for what Honeycutt, Zagacki, and Edwards (1989) have called "imagined interactions," or those anticipated important interchanges with significant others. Because many of the problems that people bring to psychotherapy involve such interactions with important others, this rehearsal approach has widespread applicability.

Stepping

One of the adaptive characteristics of high-hope people is that they tend to break down complex long-term goals into several smaller substeps (Snyder, 1994b). Indeed, this approach is common to several psychotherapies (Greeno, 1978), as clients learn to plan their activities in incremental steps that lead to a long-term therapy goal. By concentrating on the salient steps toward goals that are temporally close to the client, the client is freed from maladaptive preoccupation with unattained long-term goals (Vallacher & Wegner, 1987; Vallacher, Wegner, & Somoza, 1989). Another advantage of short-term steps is that the client can more readily perceive when gains are made, and several therapeutic approaches use the attainment of such subgoals as opportunities for clients to reward themselves for progress. Finally, substeps are typically more concrete than vague, long-term goals and thus are more easily visualized by clients.

Pathways Effects Beyond Agentic Placebo Effects

Psychotherapy research has often used a three-group design to test the effects of specific treatments. First, there typically is a control group of patients who are asked to wait while the persons in the other two conditions receive their interventions. The intent of this no-treatment control group is to provide a baseline for any changes that may naturally occur over time in the patient population. Second, there may be a so-called psychotherapy placebo group, in which clients receive some form of motivational feedback and the therapist's attention but no specific techniques associated with a particular protocol. Note that the "placebo" group, in this sense, is not the same as the placebo pill approach described earlier. The intent of the psychotherapy placebo condition is analogous to the administration of the pill placebo, however, in that the researcher is attempting to control for positive expectancies (agency, in the present context) and to find out to what degree the *specific* intervention strategies (pathways, in the present context) augment desired therapeutic changes. Third, a group of clients is assigned to treatment with a specific intervention. If clients' outcomes in this treatment group are found to be superior to those in the no-treatment control, then it can be inferred that a particular psychotherapeutic technique is efficacious. If the treatment group is superior to the placebo control, then one can deduce the specific efficacy of a particular psychotherapeutic technique *beyond that attributable to basic expectancies* (i.e., agency).

Instead of describing particular studies that have employed this methodology to test the effectiveness of each given psychotherapy approach, we begin by describing the results of meta-analytic studies that incorporate many such studies. One of the most illuminative was conducted by Barker et al. (1988). Discussed earlier in this chapter, this study used the three basic groups described above but selected for inclusion only those psychotherapy placebo studies in which the client's expectancies for the placebo actually matched those for the active treatment. By assuring these equal expectancies, Barker et al., helped ensure that any superior effects of the spe-

cific treatments would be attributable to the procedures specific to those techniques. As noted previously, clients in the placebo groups improved an average of .47 standard deviations more on treatment outcome measures than did no-treatment controls. Additionally, the specific treatment groups improved an average of .55 standard deviations more on clinical measures than did the placebo control groups. Thus, the specific treatments appeared to augment the amount of nonspecific clinical improvement by about .50 standard deviations.[5] As such, it may be inferred that specific pathways training (across varying psychotherapy approaches) does produce effects beyond the basic agency thinking of the psychotherapy placebo groups.

Although the analysis of Barker et al. (1998) was superior to previous studies by virtue of equating treatment and therapy placebo groups for agency-like positive expectancies, it should be noted that other studies have also found significant increments in psychotherapeutic improvement for treatment as compared to therapy placebo control groups (Landman & Dawes, 1982; Prioleau et al., 1983; Shapiro & Shapiro, 1982; Smith et al, 1980).

Group Study of Pathways vs. Agency Training

Ellen Klausner, at the Clinical Research Center for Geriatric Depression of the New York Hospital/Cornell Medical Center, has tested a set of agency plus pathways interventions against interventions that target only agency for psychotherapeutic efficacy change (Klausner, Clarkin, Spielman, Pupo, Abrams, & Alexopoulas, in press; Klausner, Snyder, & Cheavens, in press). Older outpatients (age $m = 67$) who met DSM-IV diagnostic criteria for major depressive disorder were randomly assigned in this study to either an agency plus pathways group ($n = 13$) or an agency-alone group ($n = 13$). For the former, explicit interventions were drawn from *The Psychology of Hope* (Snyder, 1994b) to develop an 11-session program to help the participants set goals

---

[5]Although the Barker et al. (1988) study did find significant differences in the treatment and placebo groups at the end of psychotherapy, it is curious that in follow-up sessions the treatment groups were only .17 standard deviations superior to the placebo groups. Evidently, either the robustness of the specific interventions decayed over time or the power of the placebo groups remained especially strong.

(e.g., plant a rose bush or go to the shopping center) and think about their goals in order to produce pathways and related agency motivation. Therapy included weekly homework assignments and discussions about how this new type of thinking was working, as well as behavioral practice assignments. The agency-alone group was based on Butler's (1974) life review model, and it involved reminiscences about various stages in the participants' lives. Such reminiscences elicited self-perceptions of vigor that were felt during earlier times in participants' lives, and therefore it mostly activated agency-like thoughts and feelings. This reminiscence approach serves as a very stringent agency comparison group because previous research shows that it significantly reduces depressive symptoms in older persons (Arean, Perri, Nezu, Schein, Christopher, & Joseph, 1993).

Participants were evaluated at the beginning and end of the group-based interventions. Assessments included self-report and observational indexes. Both groups experienced significantly reduced depression over the course of treatments. However, only the agency plus pathways intervention group experienced significant reductions in hopelessness and anxiety, as well as increases in the State Hope Scale scores; furthermore, the number of interactions with family members increased for the agency plus pathways intervention but not for the agency-alone group. The former intervention produced a 15-point decline in the Hamilton (1960) Depression Rating Scale (HDRS), moving the mean from a level indicative of major depression to a level consistent with no depression at all. In contrast, the agency-alone group experienced a mean drop of only 4.6 points on the HDRS, leaving the mean level of symptomology in the major depression range. Not only was this effect statistically significant ($p < .001$), but also the effect size (gamma 1.58) was very strong (Cohen, 1988).

Individuals in the agency plus pathways intervention group became very proactive over the course of the sessions; they routinely furnished refreshments, and group members thanked everyone involved and even gave small gifts at the wrap-up session. The agency-alone group, on the other hand, became quite passive; they generally were unengaged, with one member exclaiming spontaneously, "I'm not baking anything!" In summary, this agency plus pathways intervention group provides a vivid sense of the manner in which pathways-related intervention strategies

can produce a lively and effective psychotherapeutic milieu for generating hope, even among a difficult-to-treat sample of depressed older adults.

Summary of Pathways-related Literature

In this section, we have seen that people generally hold the practice of psychotherapy in high regard. Indeed, a wide range of psychotherapies evidently provides viable pathways-enhancing interventions. Furthermore, prefatory psychotherapy programs not only prepare clients for the particular pathways strategies that they will be taught in psychotherapy but also result in improved outcomes. Finally, meta-analytic studies generally indicate that the pathways thinking engendered by specific psychotherapy techniques increases clinical improvement beyond that which is due merely to placebo-like agentic thinking. The addition of pathways thinking through *specific* techniques roughly doubles the effect of psychotherapy beyond that obtained by agentic thinking alone (i.e., expectancy controls).[6] On this latter point, a group study with depressed older adults also yielded a similar result—the addition of pathways to agency training alone helped to significantly augment clients' improvement. Therefore, we conclude that pathways thinking is necessary for clients' attainment of the full beneficial effects of psychotherapy.

AGENCY AND PATHWAYS RIPPLES

Although we have distinguished between the roles of agency and pathways as they contribute to successful psychotherapy outcomes, this distinction is less clear in the actual thinking patterns of clients (Snyder, 1994b). That is, in fact, agency and pathways thinking are intertwined, so that it is difficult to think of one component without also thinking of the other. In this section, we describe how agency and pathways are intimately and reciprocally related.

The Agency to Pathways Push

As noted in the previous section, psychotherapy gains appear to be more pronounced when path-

---

[6]It is our view, similar to others (Brown, 1994a, 1994b; Horvath, 1988), that placebos are alternative treatments that can be compared to other forms of partial or full psychotherapy.

ways strategies are added to agency-driven improvements. For the full beneficial effect of psychotherapy to be derived, both agency and pathways thinking are necessary. For example, Fennell and Teasdale (1987) found that within two weeks of beginning treatment in either cognitive-behavioral therapy (CBT) or treatment-as-usual (TAU) for depressed patients, they were able to distinguish between depressed participants who were rapid responders (the "steeps") and slow or non-responders (the "slights"). What is noteworthy about their findings, however, is that only the rapid responders who received CBT maintained and enhanced their gains over the course of treatment. On the other hand, the steeps in the TAU condition neither maintained nor enhanced their early treatment changes. Thus, the changes of the CBT steeps reflected their early determination to meet goals (agency thinking), along with the ability to generate pathways to continue and maintain their improvements (pathways thinking).

This point is further illuminated, we believe, by the following case history (a client of the senior author) that shows how agentic thinking increases first, with subsequent pathways thinking then kicking in to complement the enhanced agency thought. The client came to psychotherapy because of "depressed feelings." As he described his life, it was apparent that he was expending as little physical energy as possible to get through each day. Therefore, as an initial therapeutic intervention, he was asked to begin an exercise program. After hearing a description of several possible types of exercise, including swimming, aerobic weight lifting, and so on, he opted for a program of walking. At first, this involved a walking regimen in his apartment, with later increases in length and speed as he went outside. In light of considerable research showing how exercise is related to increases in agentic thought, it was expected that this man would increase his sense of willfulness, which he did. As he began to attain an increase in such agentic thinking, however, he immediately also began to think of ways in which he could attain his desired therapeutic goals. That is, his pathways thinking appeared to rise in conjunction with his agency thinking. In his own words, "With all of this energy I am feeling, I need to find some ways to channel it." One of the pathways that he initiated was a walking group at his work site, where he and other interested employees would take walks during breaks. This helped him to achieve one of his therapeutic goals, which was to connect better with other

people. The point in this case is to suggest that the therapist can attend to agency, and chances will be good that the other component, pathways thinking, will provide the conduit for this increased sense of willfulness.

The Pathways to Agency Push

Sometimes in working with clients, it makes the most sense to begin working first on improving their pathways thinking. This decision may be made when the therapist perceives that the client is most lacking in such pathways thought. Again, an example from the practice of the senior author may help to elucidate this process. Clients sometimes come into treatment, reporting that they "do not know what to do." What this often means is that they cannot come up with ways to achieve their goals. Perhaps even more fundamentally, they cannot even think of themselves as capable of finding such routes to desired goals. In one prototypical case, a college professor reported that he no longer could write his books because of the arthritis pain in his hands. Over the years, he had written several books by drafting them in long hand on yellow pads, after which secretaries transcribed his writings into typed form. In an effort to find other means of achieving his goal of publication, we discussed other routes that he might take. An initial strategy involved transcribing his ideas into a dictaphone, but he found that this did not allow him to engage in a give-and-take revision process as he developed his ideas. Thus, this approach was rejected, but not without an accompanying lesson—namely, he was encouraged to think about this first trial not as a failure per se but rather as a useful piece of feedback that might help him find some better approach. This technique is taken from research documenting what high-hope persons do after one strategy does not work (Snyder, 1994b). That is, a failure is not seen as catastrophic feedback about the person but rather as informative situational feedback about what does not work.

The next pathways-related approach with this client was to learn to type, using a computer word-processing program. Somehow, over the years, the professor had avoided learning how to type. This new plan worked well in that it did not elicit the full-scale arthritic pain in his hands, and it enabled the professor to engage in the important manuscript revision process. In this case, therefore, the client learned a skill (typing) that served as a pathway to his cherished book-writing activities. Once this pathway was discovered, the professor was filled with agency to use it. Furthermore, in the process of finding appropriate pathways to his desired goals, the professor learned the more general process of remaining flexible in finding workable routes to desired goals. In this regard, it should be noted that flexibility characterizes the adaptive pathway thinking of high-hope people (Snyder, 1994b).

Agency and Pathways: Two-way Interaction for Goal-directed Thought

Consider the instance in which the client begins to think about desired goals. This person also immediately begins to think about the requisite level of effort and persistence (i.e., agentic thoughts) associated with them (Latham & Locke, 1975; Locke, 1966). Likewise, thinking about desired goals has been shown to elicit thoughts about how to attain them, that is, pathways thinking (Latham & Baldes, 1975). Further research suggests that upon thinking about goals, people immediately imagine their capacities to work toward them (agency) and ways to reach them (pathways) (Gagne, 1984). Thus, by helping clients clearly articulate their goals, we may be helping them to start *both* their agentic and their pathways thinking.

Because of the inherent relationship between agency and pathways thinking [these two components typically correlate approximately .40 to .50 (Snyder et al., 1991, 1996, 1997)], it should not be surprising that the two continually iterate back and forth throughout the sequence of moving toward one's desired therapeutic goals. In the degree to which any of the hope components—goal setting, agency, and pathways thinking—can be strengthened, the chances of improving overall hope are also increased (Snyder, 1994b).

PSYCHOTHERAPIES INTO THE 21ST CENTURY: A HOPEFUL AGENDA

Psychotherapy researchers have frequently assumed that psychotherapy approaches, to be considered efficacious, must yield client outcomes that are statistically superior to placebo, nonspecific factors or high-expectancy control comparison groups (Eysenck, 1961; Kazdin, 1978; Paul, 1966; Shapiro, 1971). Likewise, psychotherapy outcome research has adopted a horse race mentality in which treatment approaches are judged in terms of how well they compare to other approaches. The hope theory that forms the basis of this chapter, however, suggests that an equally compelling perspective involves how various therapeutic approaches all achieve their effectiveness by teaching effective pathways for reaching desired goals, as well as by promoting the agency to use them (Snyder, Michael, & Cheavens, 1999). It should be emphasized, however, that the typical approach to psychotherapy outcome research rarely, if ever, has focused on the shared treatment elements that appear to underlie much of the positive therapeutic changes. Instead, in an unfortunate manifestation of the American desire to be unique (see Snyder & Fromkin, 1980; Wallach & Wallach, 1983), the proponents of specific psychotherapy approaches appear to have concentrated on tests designed to document the superior (i.e., "special") viabilities of their preferred theoretical approaches.

Although the present zeitgeist of psychotherapy research emphasizes "empirically supported" treatments (Chambliss, 1996; Crits-Christoph, 1996; Wilson, 1996), we still have a relatively meager understanding of the underlying mechanisms by which psychotherapy derives its beneficial effects (Garfield, 1996). In this regard, we would like to suggest that more of our future energies be placed on investigating the similarities in psychotherapy change processes that produce favorable outcomes. The central question of what works would not thereby be abandoned, but theorists and researchers might recast it in more cooperative, integrative terms.

In this chapter, we have presented just one construct—hope—for exploring the common factors that underlie the beneficial psychotherapy change process. As we move into the 21st century, we believe that the search for other common factors will continue to advance our collective understanding of beneficial psychotherapy processes. To the extent that we discover the common processes that facilitate psychological change, we will be able to construct a truly solid foundation for psychotherapy. In turn, we then may dispel the perception among some critics who describe the psychotherapy enterprise as a baseless "house of cards" (see Dawes, 1995).

REFERENCES

Affleck, G., & Tennen, H. (1996). Construing benefits from adversity: Adaptational significance and dispositional underpinnings. *Journal of Personality*, *64*, 899–922.

Ajzen, I., & Fishbein, M. (1980). *Understanding attitudes and predicting social behavior*. Upper Saddle River, NJ: Prentice Hall.

Ansbacher, H. L., & Ansbacher, R. R. (1956). *The individual psychology of Alfred Adler*. New York: Basic Books.

Arean, P. A., Perri, M. G., Nezu, A. M., Schein, R., Christopher, F., & Joseph, T. (1993). Comparative effectiveness of social problem-solving therapy and reminiscence therapy as treatments for depression in older adults. *Journal of Consulting and Clinical Psychology*, *61*, 1003–1010.

Axsom, D. (1989). Cognitive dissonance and behavior change in psychotherapy. *Journal of Experimental Social Psychology*, *25*, 234–252.

Babyak, M. A., Snyder, C. R., & Yoshinobu, L. (1993). Psychometric properties of the Hope Scale: A confirmatory factor analysis. *Journal of Research in Personality*, *27*, 154–169.

Bandura, A. (1977). Self-efficacy: Toward a unifying theory of behavior change. *Psychological Review*, *84*, 191–215.

Bandura, A. (1982). Self-efficacy mechanism in human agency. *American Psychologist*, *37*, 122–147.

Bandura, A. (1986). *Social foundations of thought and action: A social cognitive theory*. Upper Saddle River, NJ: Prentice Hall.

Bandura, A. (1989a). Human agency in social cognitive theory. *American Psychologist*, *44*, 1175–1184.

Bandura, A. (1989b). Self-regulation of motivation and action through internal standards and goal systems. In L. A. Pervin (Ed.), *Goal concepts in personality and social psychology* (pp. 19–85). Hillsdale, NJ: Erlbaum.

Bandura, A. (Ed.). (1995). *Self-efficacy in changing societies*. New York: Cambridge University Press.

Bandura, A. (1997). *Self-efficacy: The exercise of control*. New York: Freeman.

Barker, S. L., Funk, S. C., & Houston, B. K. (1988). Psychological treatment versus nonspecific factors: A meta-analysis of conditions that engender comparable expectations for improvement. *Clinical Psychology Review*, *8*, 579–594.

Barnum, D. D., Snyder, C. R., Rapoff, M. A., Mani, M. M., & Thompson, R. (1998). Hope and social support in the psychological adjustment of children who have survived burn injuries and matched controls. *Children's Health Care*, *27*, 15–30.

Beck, A. T., Rush, A. J., Shaw, B. F., & Emery, G. (1979). *Cognitive therapy of depression*. New York: Guilford.

Bernier, M., & Avard, J. (1986). Self-efficacy, outcome and attrition in a weight reduction program. *Cognitive Therapy and Research*, *10*, 319–338.

Beutler, L. E., Clarkin, J., Crago, M., & Bergan, J. (1991). Client-therapist matching. In C. R. Snyder & D. R. Forsyth (Eds.), *Handbook of social and clinical psychology: The health perspective* (pp. 699–716). New York: Pergamon.

Brown, W. A. (1994a). Placebo as a treatment for depression. *Neuropsychopharmacology*, *10*, 265–269.

Brown, W. A. (1994b). Reply to commentaries. *Neuropsychopharmacology*, *10*, 287–288.

Bruce, B., & Newman, D. (1978). Interacting plans. *Cognitive Science*, *2*, 195–233.

Brunstein, J. C. (1993). Personal goals and subjective well-being: A longitudinal study. *Journal of Personality and Social Psychology*, *65*, 1061–1070.

Butler, R. (1974). Successful aging and the role of life review. *Journal of the American Geriatric Society*, *22*, 529–535.

Cantril, H. (1964). The human design. *Journal of Individual Psychology*, *20*, 129–136.

Carbonell, J. (1981). Counterplanning: A strategy-based model of adversary planning in real-world situations. *Artificial Intelligence*, *16*, 295–329.

Carey, K. B., & Carey, M. P. (1993). Changes in self-efficacy resulting from unaided attempts to quit smoking. *Psychology of Addictive Behaviors*, *7*, 219–224.

Chambliss, D. L. (1996). In defense of dissemination of empirically supported psychological interventions. *Clinical Psychology: Science and Practice*, *3*, 230–235.

Claerhout, S. J., Elder, J., & Janes, C. (1982). Problem-solving skills of rural battered women. *American Journal of Community Psychology*, *10*, 605–612.

Cohen, J. (1988). *Statistical power analysis for the behavioral sciences* (2nd ed.). Hillsdale, NJ: Erlbaum.

Colletti, G., & Kopel, S. A. (1979). Maintaining behavior change: An investigation of three maintenance strategies and the relationship of self-attribution to the long-term reduction of cigarette smoking. *Journal of Consulting and Clinical Psychology*, *47*, 614–617.

Colletti, G., & Stern, L. (1980). Two-year follow-up of a nonaversive treatment for cigarette smoking. *Journal of Consulting and Clinical Psychology*, *48*, 292–293.

Cowen, E. L. (1982). Help is where you find it: Four informal helping groups. *American Psychologist*, *37*, 385–395.

Critelli, J. W., & Neumann, K. F. (1984). The placebo: Conceptual analysis of a construct in transition. *American Psychologist*, *39*, 32–39.

Crits-Christoph, P. (1996). The dissemination of efficacious psychological treatments. *Clinical Psychology: Science and Practice*, *3*, 260–263.

Cross, S. E., & Markus, H. R. (1990). The willful self. *Personality and Social Psychology Bulletin*, *16*, 726–742.

Crouch, J. A. (1989). *The Hope Scale and head injury rehabilitation: Staff ratings as a function of client characteristics.* Unpublished doctoral dissertation, University of Kansas, Lawrence.

Curry, L. A., Snyder, C. R., Cook, D. L., Ruby, B. C., & Rehm, M. (1997). The role of hope in student-athlete academic and sport achievement. *Journal of Personality and Social Psychology, 73,* 1257–1267.

Dawes, R. (1995). *House of cards: Psychology and psychotherapy built on myth.* New York: Free Press.

deCharms, R. (1968). *Personal causation.* New York: Academic Press.

Deci, E. L. (1975). *Intrinsic motivation.* New York: Plenum.

DiClemente, C. C., Prochaska, J. O., Fairhurst, S. K., Velicer, W. F., Velasquez, M. M., & Rossi, J. S. (1991). The process of smoking cessation: An analysis of precontemplation, contemplation, and preparation stages of change. *Journal of Consulting and Clinical Psychology, 59,* 295–304.

Diener, C. I., & Dweck, C. S. (1978). An analysis of learned helplessness: Continuous changes in performance, strategy, and achievement cognitions following failure. *Journal of Personality and Social Psychology, 36,* 451–462.

Diener, E. (1984). Subjective well-being. *Psychological Bulletin, 95,* 542–575.

Dweck, C. S. (1986). Motivational processes affecting learning. *American Psychologist, 41,* 1040–1048.

D'Zurilla, T. J., & Nezu, A. (1980). A study of the generation-of-alternatives process in social problem solving. *Cognitive Therapy and Research, 4,* 67–72.

Eisenberger, R., & Masterson, F. A. (1983). Required high effort increases subsequent persistence and reduces cheating. *Journal of Personality and Social Psychology, 44,* 593–599.

Eisenberger, R., Mitchell, M., & Masterson, F. A. (1985). Effort training increases generalized self-control. *Journal of Personality and Social Psychology, 49,* 1294–1301.

Eisenberger, R., & Shank, D. M. (1985). Personal work ethic and effort training affect reduces cheating. *Journal of Personality and Social Psychology, 49,* 520–528.

Elkin, I., Shea, T., Watkins, J. T., Imber, S. D., Sotsky, S. M., Collins, J. F., Glass, D. R., Pilkonis, P. A., Leber, W. R., Docherty, J. P., Fiester, S. J., & Parloff, M. B. (1989). National Institute of Mental Health treatment of depression collaborative research program: General effectiveness of treatments. *Archives of General Psychiatry, 46,* 971–983.

Elliott, T. R., Witty, S., Herrick, S., & Hoffman, J. T. (1991). Negotiating reality after physical loss: Hope, depression, and disability. *Journal of Personality and Social Psychology, 61,* 608–613.

Emmons, R. A. (1986). Personal strivings: An approach to personality and subjective well-being. *Journal of Personality and Social Psychology, 51,* 1058–1068.

Erickson, R. C., Post, R., & Paige, A. (1975). Hope as a psychiatric variable. *Journal of Clinical Psychology, 31,* 324–329.

Evans, F. J. (1985). Expectancy, therapeutic instructions, and the placebo response. In L. White, B. Tursky, & G. E. Schwartz (Eds.), *Placebo: Theory, research, and mechanisms* (pp. 215–234). New York: Guilford.

Eysenck, H. J. (1961). The effects of psychotherapy. In H. J. Eysenck (Ed.), *Handbook of abnormal psychology: An experimental approach* (pp. 697–725). New York: Basic Books.

Farber, M. L. (1968). *Theory of suicide.* New York: Funk & Wagnalls.

Fennell, M. J., & Teasdale, J. D. (1987). Cognitive therapy for depression: Individual differences and the process of change. *Cognitive Therapy and Research, 11,* 253–271.

Fisher, R. L., & Fisher, S. (1997). Are we justified in treating children with psychotropic drugs? In S. Fisher & R. P Greenberg (Eds.), *From placebo to panacea: Putting psychiatric drugs to the test* (pp. 307–322). New York: Wiley.

Fisher, S., Cole, J. O., Rickels, K., & Uhlenhuth, E. H. (1964). Drug-set interaction: The effect of expectations on drug response in outpatients. *Neuropsychopharmacology, 3,* 149–156.

Fisher, S., & Greenberg, R. P. (Eds.) (1989). *The limits of biological treatments for psychological distress: Comparisons with psychotherapy and placebo.* Hillsdale, NJ: Erlbaum.

Fisher, S., & Greenberg, R. P. (1993). How sound is the double-blind design for evaluating psychotropic drugs? *Journal of Nervous and Mental Disease, 181,* 345–350.

Fisher, S., & Greenberg, R. P. (1997a). The curse of the placebo: Fanciful pursuit of a pure biological therapy. In S. Fisher & R. P. Greenberg (Eds.), *From placebo to panacea: Putting psychiatric drugs to the test* (pp. 3–56). New York: Wiley.

Fisher, S., & Greenberg, R. P. (Eds.). (1997b). *From placebo to panacea: Putting psychiatric drugs to the test.* New York: Wiley.

Fisher, S., & Greenberg, R. P. (1997c). What are we to conclude about psychoactive drugs? Scanning the major findings. In S. Fisher & R. P. Greenberg (Eds.), *From placebo to panacea: Putting psychiatric drugs to the test* (pp. 359–384). New York: Wiley.

Frank, J. D. (1961). *Persuasion and healing.* Baltimore: Johns Hopkins University Press.

Frank, J. D. (1968). The role of hope in psychotherapy. *International Journal of Psychiatry, 5,* 383–395.

Frank, J. D. (1971). Therapeutic factors in psychotherapy. *American Journal of Psychotherapy, 25,* 350–361.

Frank, J. D. (1973). *Persuasion and healing: A comparative study of psychotherapy* (rev. ed.). Baltimore: Johns Hopkins University Press.

Frank, J. D. (1975). The faith that heals. *The Johns Hopkins Medical Journal, 137,* 127–131.

Frank, J. D. (1978). Expectation and therapeutic outcome—The placebo effect and the role induction interview. In J. D. Frank, R. Hoehn-Saric, S. D. Imber, B. L. Liberman, & A. R. Stone (Eds.), *Effective ingredients of successful psychotherapy* (pp. 1–34). New York: Brunner/Mazel.

Frank, J. D. (1989). Non-specific aspects of treatment: The view of a psychotherapist. In M. Sheppherd and N. Sartorius (Eds.), *Non-specific aspects of treatment* (pp. 95–114). Toronto: Hans Huber.

Frank, J. D., & Frank, J. B. (1991). *Persuasion and healing* (3rd ed.). Baltimore: Johns Hopkins University Press.

Frank, J. D., Nash, E. H., Stone, A. R., & Imber, S. D. (1963). Immediate and long-term symptomatic course of psychiatric outpatients. *American Journal of Psychiatry, 120,* 429–439.

Frankl, V. E. (1992). *Man's search for meaning: An introduction to logotherapy* (4th ed.). Boston: Beacon Press.

Friedman, H. J. (1963). Patient expectancy and symptom reduction. *Archives of General Psychiatry, 8,* 61–67.

Gagne, R. M. (1984). Learning outcomes and their effects: Useful categories of human performance. *American Psychologist, 39,* 377–386.

Garfield, S. C. (1981). Psychotherapy: A 40-year appraisal. *American Psychologist, 35,* 174–183.

Garfield, S. C. (1996). Some problems associated with "validated" forms of psychotherapy. *Clinical Psychology: Science and Practice, 3,* 218–229.

Getter, H., & Nowinski, J. K. (1981). A free response test of interpersonal effectiveness. *Journal of Personality Assessment, 45,* 301–308.

Goldstein, A. P. (1960). Patients' expectancies and non-specific therapy as a basis for (un)spontaneous remission. *Journal of Clinical Psychology, 16,* 399–403.

Goldstein, A. P. (1962). *Therapist-patient expectancies in psychotherapy.* Elmsford, NY: Pergamon.

Greenberg, R. P., & Fisher, S. (1997). Mood-mending medicines: Probing drug, psychotherapy, and placebo solutions. In S. Fisher & R. P Greenberg (Eds.), *From placebo to panacea: Putting psychiatric drugs to the test* (pp. 115–172). New York: Wiley.

Greeno, J. G. (1978). Nature of problem-solving abilities. In W. K. Estes (Ed.), *Handbook of learning and cognitive processes: Vol. 5. Human information processing.* Hillsdale, NJ: Erlbaum.

Grencavage, L. M., & Norcross, J. C. (1990). Where are the commonalities among the therapeutic common factors? *Journal of Mental Health Counseling, 13,* 372–378.

Gurman, A. S. (1977). The patient's perception of the therapeutic relationship. In A. S. Gurman & A. M. Razin (Eds.), *Effective psychotherapy: A handbook of research* (pp. 503–543). New York: Pergamon.

Hamilton, M. (1960). A rating scale for depression. *Journal of Neurology, Neurosurgery, and Psychiatry, 23,* 56–62.

Hanna, F. J., & Ritchie, M. H. (1995). Seeking the active ingredients of psychotherapeutic change: Within and outside the context of therapy. *Professional Psychology: Research and Practice, 26,* 176–183.

Harney, P. (1990). *The Hope Scale: Exploration of construct validity and its influence on health.* Unpublished master's thesis, University of Kansas, Lawrence.

Heitler, J. B. (1973). Preparation of lower-class patients for expressive group psychotherapy. *Journal of Consulting and Clinical Psychology, 41,* 251–260.

Heppner, P. P., & Hillerbrand, E. T. (1991). Problem-solving training implications for remedial and preventive training. In C. R. Snyder & D. R. Forsyth (Eds.), *Handbook of social and clinical psychology: The health perspective* (pp. 681–698). Elmsford, NY: Pergamon.

Heppner, P. P., & Petersen, C. H. (1982). The development and implications of a personal problem-solving inventory. *Journal of Counseling Psychology, 29,* 66–75.

Holmes, D. S. (1993). Aerobic fitness and the response to psychological stress. In P. Seraganian (Ed.), *Exercise psychology: The influence of physical exercise on psychological processes* (pp. 39–63). New York: Wiley.

Honeycutt, J. M., Zagacki, K. S., & Edwards, R. (1989). Interpersonal communication and imagined interactions. In C. Roberts & K. Watson (Eds.), *Intrapersonal communication processes: Original essays* (pp. 167–184). Scottsdale, AZ: Gorsuch Scarisbrick.

Horvath, A. O., & Greenberg, L. S. (1986). The development of the Working Alliance Inventory. In L. S. Greenberg & W. M. Pinsof (Eds.), *The psychotherapeutic process: A research handbook* (pp. 367–390). New York: Guilford.

Horvath, A. O., & Greenberg, L. S. (1989). The development of the Working Alliance Inventory. *Journal of Counseling Psychology, 36,* 223–253.

Horvath, P. (1988). Placebos and common factors in two decades of psychotherapy research. *Psychological Bulletin, 104,* 214–215.

Howard, G. S. (1986). *Dare we develop a human science?* Notre Dame, IN: Academic Publications.

Howard, G. S., & Conway, C. G. (1986). Can there be an empirical science of volitional action? *American Psychologist, 41,* 1241–1251.

Howard, K. I., Kopta, S. M., Krause, M. S., & Orlinsky, D. E. (1986). The dose-effect relationship in psychotherapy. *American Psychologist, 41,* 159–164.

Howard, K. I., Lueger, R. J., Maling, M. S., & Martinovich, Z. (1993). A phase model of psychotherapy outcome: Causal mediation of change. *Journal of Consulting and Clinical Psychology, 61,* 678–685.

Ilardi, S. S., & Craighead, W. E. (1994). The role of nonspecific factors in cognitive-behavior therapy for depression. *Clinical Psychology: Science and Practice, 1,* 138–156.

Irving, L. M., Snyder, C. R., & Crowson, J. J., Jr. (1998). Hope and the negotiation of cancer facts by college students. *Journal of Personality, 66,* 198–214.

Irving, L., Snyder, C. R., Gravel, L., Hanke, J., Hilberg, P., & Nelson, N. (1997, April). *Hope and effectiveness of a pre-therapy orientation group for community mental health center clients.* Paper presented at the Western Psychological Association Convention, Seattle.

Jeffrey, D. B. (1974). A comparison of the effects of external-control and self-control on the modification and maintenance of weight. *Journal of Abnormal Psychology, 83,* 404–410.

Karasu, T. B. (1986). The specificity versus nonspecificity dilemma: Toward identifying therapeutic change agents. *American Journal of Psychiatry, 143,* 687–695.

Kazdin, A. E. (1978). Nonspecific treatment factors in psychotherapy outcome research. *Journal of Consulting and Clinical Psychology, 47,* 846–851.

Kazdin, A. E. (1980). *Research design in clinical psychology.* New York: Harper & Row.

Kellner, R., & Sheffield, B. F. (1971). The relief of distress following attendance at a clinic. *British Journal of Psychiatry, 118,* 195–198.

Kirsch, I. (1978). The placebo effect and the cognitive-behavioral revolution. *Cognitive Therapy and Research, 2,* 255–264.

Kirsch, I. (1990). *Changing expectations: A key to effective psychotherapy.* Pacific Grove, CA: Brooks/Cole.

Kirsch, I., Mearns, J., & Catanzaro, S. J. (1990). Mood regulation expectancies as determinants of dysphoria in college students. *Journal of Counseling Psychology, 37,* 306–312.

Klausner, E. J., Clarkin, J. F., Spielman, L., Pupo, C., Abrams, R., & Alexopoulas, G. S. (in press). Late-life depression and functional disability: The role of goal-focused group psychotherapy. *International Journal of Geriatric Psychiatry.*

Klausner, E. J., Snyder, C. R., & Cheavers, J. (in press). A hope-based group treatment for depressed older adult outpatients. In G. M. Williamson, P. A. Parmelee, & D. R. Shaffer (Eds.), *Physical illness and depression in older adults: A handbook of theory, research, and practice.* New York: Plenum.

Kolb, D. L., Beutler, L. E., Davis, C. S., Crago, M., & Shanfield, S. B. (1985). Patient and therapy process variables relating to dropout and change in psychotherapy. *Psychotherapy, 22,* 702–710.

Lambert, M. J. (1992). Implications of outcome research for psychotherapy integration. In J. C. Norcross & M. R. Goldfried (Eds.), *Handbook of psychotherapy integration* (pp. 94–129). New York: Basic Books.

Lambert, R. G., & Lambert, M. J. (1984). The effects of role preparation for psychotherapy on immigrant clients seeking mental health services in Hawaii. *Journal of Community Psychology, 12,* 263–275.

Landman, J. T., & Dawes, R. M. (1982). Psychotherapy outcome: Smith and Glass' conclusions stand up under scrutiny. *American Psychologist, 37,* 504–516.

Latham, G. P., & Baldes, J. J. (1975). The practical significance of Locke's theory of goal setting. *Journal of Applied Psychology, 60,* 122–124.

Latham, G. P., & Locke, E. A. (1975). Increasing productivity with decreasing time limits: A field replication of Parkinson's law. *Journal of Applied Psychology, 60,* 524–526.

Lawson, D. (1994). Identifying pretreatment change. *Journal of Counseling and Development, 72,* 244–248.

Leon, G. R., Sternberg, B., & Rosenthal, B. S. (1984). Prognostic indicators of success or relapse in weight reduction. *International Journal of Eating Disorders, 3,* 15–24.

Lewin, K. (1951). Intention, will, and need. In D. Rappaport (Ed.), *Organization and pathology of thought* (pp. 95–153). New York: Columbia University Press.

Liberman, B. L. (1978). The role of mastery in psychotherapy: Maintenance of improvement and prescriptive change. In J. D. Frank, R. Hoehn-Saric, S. D. Imber, B. L. Liberman, & A. R. Stone (Eds.), *Effective ingredients of successful psychotherapy* (pp. 35–72). New York: Brunner/Mazel.

Little, B. R. (1983). Personal projects: A rationale and method for investigation. *Environment and Behavior, 15,* 273–309.

Little, B. R. (1989). Personal projects analysis: Trivial pursuits, magnificent obsessions, and the search for coherence. In D. M. Buss and N. Cantor (Eds.), *Personality psychology: Recent trends and emerging directions* (pp. 15–31). New York: Springer-Verlag.

Locke, E. A. (1966). The relationship of intentions to level of performance. *Journal of Applied Psychology, 50,* 60–66.

Luborsky, L., Crits-Christoph, P., Mintz, J., & Auerbach, A. (1988). *Who will benefit from psychotherapy? Predicting therapeutic outcomes.* New York: Basic Books.

Luborsky, L., Singer, B., & Luborsky, L. (1975). Comparative studies of psychotherapies. Is it true that "everyone has won and all must have prizes"? *Archives of General Psychiatry, 32,* 995–1008.

Maddux, J. E. (Ed.). (1995). *Self-efficacy, adaptation, and adjustment: Theory, research, and application.* New York: Plenum.

Magaletta, P. R., & Oliver, J. M. (1999). The hope construct, will and ways: Their relative relations with self-efficacy, optimism, and general well-being. *Journal of Clinical Psychology, 55,* 539–551.

Mahoney, M. J., & Avener, M. (1977). Psychology of the elite athlete: An exploratory study. *Cognitive Therapy and Research, 1,* 135–141.

Markus, H., & Ruvolo, A. (1989). Possible selves: Personalized representations of goals. In L. A. Pervin (Ed.), *Goal concepts in personality and social psychology* (pp. 211–241). Hillsdale, NJ: Erlbaum.

Mayerson, N. H. (1984). Preparing clients for group therapy: A critical review and theoretical formulation. *Clinical Psychology Review, 4,* 191–213.

McCann, L., & Holmes, D. S. (1984). Influence of aerobic exercise on depression. *Journal of Personality and Social Psychology, 46,* 1142–1147.

McCaul, K. D., Glasgow, R. E., & Shafer, L. C. (1987). Diabetes regimen behaviors: Predicting adherence. *Medical Care, 25,* 868–881.

McDougall, W. (1908). *An introduction to social psychology.* London: Methuen.

Melges, R., & Bowlby, J. (1969). Types of hopelessness on psychopathological processes. *Archives of General Psychiatry, 20,* 690–699.

Menninger, K. (1959). The academic lecture on hope. *The American Journal of Psychiatry, 116,* 481–491.

Miller, S. D., Duncan, B. L., & Hubble, M. A. (1997). *Escape from Babel: Toward a unifying language for psychotherapy practice.* New York: Norton.

Murdock, N. L., & Altmaier, E. M. (1991). Attribution-based treatments. In C. R. Snyder and D. R. Forsyth (Eds.), *Handbook of social and clinical psychology: The health perspective* (pp. 563–578). Elmsford, NY: Pergamon.

Nezu, A., & D'Zurilla, T. J. (1979). An experimental evaluation of the decision-making process in social problem solving. *Cognitive Therapy and Research, 3,* 269–277.

Nezu, A., & D'Zurilla, T. J. (1981a). Effects of problem definition and formulation on decision making in the social problem-solving process. *Behavior Therapy, 12,* 100–106.

Nezu, A., & D'Zurilla, T. J. (1981b). Effects of problem definition and formulation on generation of alternatives in the social problem-solving process. *Cognitive Therapy and Research, 5,* 265–271.

Nicki, R. M., Remington, R. E., & MacDonald, G. A. (1984). Self-efficacy, nicotine-fading/self-monitoring and cigarette-smoking behavior. *Behavior Research Therapy, 22,* 477–485.

Norcross, J. C., & Prochaska, J. O. (1986). The psychological distress and self-change of psychologists, counselors, and laypersons. *Psychotherapy, 23,* 102–114.

Omodei, M. M., & Wearing, A. J. (1990). Need satisfaction and involvement in personal projects: Toward an integrative model of subjective well-being. *Journal of Personality and Social Psychology, 59,* 762–769.

Padgett, D. K. (1991). Correlates of self-efficacy beliefs among patients with non-insulin dependent diabetes mellitis in Zagreb, Yugoslavia. *Patient Education and Counseling, 18,* 139–147.

Palys, T. S., & Little, B. R. (1983). Perceived life satisfaction and organization of personal projects systems. *Journal of Personality and Social Psychology, 44,* 1221–1230.

Paul, G. L. (1966). *Insight vs. desensitization in psychotherapy.* Stanford, CA: Stanford University Press.

Peake, T. H., & Archer, R. P. (1984). *Clinical training in psychotherapy.* New York: Haworth.

Peake, T. H., & Ball, J. D. (1987). Brief psychotherapy: Planned therapeutic change for changing times. *Psychotherapy in Private Practice, 5,* 53–63.

Piper, W. E., & Wogan, M. (1970). Placebo effect in psychotherapy: An extension of earlier findings. *Journal of Consulting and Clinical Psychology, 34,* 447.

Prioleau, L., Murdock, M., & Brody, N. (1983). An analysis of psychotherapy versus placebo studies. *The Behavioral and Brain Sciences, 6,* 275–310.

Rank, O. (1978). *Will therapy.* New York: Norton. (Original work published 1929).

Roberts, A. H. (1994). "The powerful placebo" revisited: Implications for headache treatment and management. *Headache Quarterly, Current Treatment and Research, 5,* 208–213.

Roberts, A. H. (1995). The powerful placebo revisited: Magnitude of nonspecific effects. *Mind Body Medicine, 1,* 35–43.

Rosenthal, D., & Frank, J. D. (1956). Psychotherapy and the placebo effect. *Psychological Bulletin, 53,* 294–302.

Roth, D. L., & Holmes, D. S. (1987). Influence of aerobic exercise training and relaxation training on physical and psychological health following stressful life events. *Psychosomatic Medicine, 49,* 355–365.

Ruehlman, L. S., & Wolchik, S. A. (1988). Personal goals and interpersonal support and hindrance as factors in psychological distress and well-being. *Journal of Personality and Social Psychology, 55,* 293–301.

Rush, A. J., Kovacs, M., Beck, A. T., Weissenburger, J., & Hollon, S. D. (1981). Differential effects of cognitive therapy and pharmacotherapy on depressive symptoms. *Journal of Affective Disorders, 3,* 221–229.

Schactel, E. (1959). *Metamorphosis.* New York: Basic Books.

Scheier, M. F., & Carver, C. S. (1985). Optimism, coping, and health: Assessment and implications of generalized outcome expectancies. *Health Psychology, 4,* 219–247.

Scheier, M. F., & Carver, C. S. (1987). Dispositional optimism and physical well-being: The influence of generalized outcome expectancies. *Journal of Personality, 55,* 169–210.

Seligman, M. E. P. (1995). Effectiveness of psychotherapy: The *Consumer Reports* study. *American Psychologist, 50,* 965–974.

Seraganian, P. (Ed.). (1993). *Exercise psychology: The influence of physical exercise on psychological processes.* New York: Wiley.

Shapiro, A. K. (1971). Placebo effects in medicine, psychotherapy, and psychoanalysis. In A. E. Bergin & S. C. Garfield (Eds.), *Handbook of psychotherapy and behavior change: Empirical analysis* (pp. 439–473). New York: Wiley.

Shapiro, D. A., & Shapiro, D. (1982). Meta-analysis of comparative therapy outcome studies: A replication and refinement. *Psychological Bulletin, 92,* 581–604.

Smith, M. L., & Glass, G. V. (1977). Meta-analysis of psychotherapy outcome studies. *American Psychologist, 32,* 752–760.

Smith, M. L., Glass, G. V., & Miller, T. I. (1980). *The benefits of psychotherapy.* Baltimore: Johns Hopkins University Press.

Snyder, C. R. (1989). Reality negotiation: From excuses to hope and beyond. *Journal of Social and Clinical Psychology, 8,* 130–157.

Snyder, C. R. (1994a). Hope and optimism. In V. S. Ramachandren (Ed.), *Encyclopedia of human behavior* (Vol. 2, pp. 535–542). San Diego, CA: Academic Press.

Snyder, C. R. (1994b). *The psychology of hope: You can get there from here.* New York: Free Press.

Snyder, C. R., & Brown, J. (1997). *Hope and pain tolerance.* Unpublished manuscript, University of Kansas, Lawrence.

Snyder, C. R., Cheavens, J., & Michael, S. T. (1999). Hoping. In C. R. Snyder (Ed.), *Coping: The psychology of what works* (pp. 205–231). New York: Oxford University Press.

Snyder, C. R., & Fromkin, H. L. (1980). *Uniqueness: The human pursuit of difference.* New York: Plenum.

Snyder, C. R., & Hackman, A. (1998). *Hope and pain tolerance: A replication.* Unpublished manuscript, University of Kansas, Lawrence.

Snyder, C. R., Harris, C., Anderson, J. R., Holleran, S. A., Irving, L. M., Sigmon, S. T., Yoshinobu, L., Gibb, J., Langelle, C., & Harney, P. (1991). The will and the ways: Development and validation of an individual differences measure of hope. *Journal of Personality and Social Psychology, 60,* 570–585.

Snyder, C. R., Hoza, B., Pelham, W. E., Rapoff, M., Ware, L., Danovsky, M., Highberger, L., Rubinstein, H., & Stahl, K. (1997). The development and validation of the Children's Hope Scale. *Journal of Pediatric Psychology, 22,* 399–421.

Snyder, C. R., Ilardi, S. S., Cheavens, J., Michael, S. T., Yamhure, L., & Sympson, S. (in press). *The role of hope in cognitive behavior therapies. Cognitive Therapy and Research.* University of Kansas, Lawrence.

Snyder, C. R., Irving, L. M., & Anderson, J. R. (1991). Hope and health. In C. R. Snyder and D. R. Forsyth (Eds.), *Handbook of social and clinical psychology: The health perspective* (pp. 285–305). Elmsford, NY: Pergamon.

Snyder, C. R., LaPointe, A. B., Crowson, J. J., Jr., & Early, S. (1998). Preferences of high- and low-hope people for self-referential feedback. *Cognition and Emotion, 12,* 807–823.

Snyder, C. R., Michael, S. T., & Cheavens, J. (1999). Hope as a psychotherapeutic foundation of common factors, placebos, and expectancies. In M. A. Huble, B. Duncan, & S. Miller (Eds.), *Heart and soul of change* (pp. 179–200). Washington, DC: American Psychological Association.

Snyder, C. R., Sympson, S., Michael, S. T., & Cheavens, J. (in press). The optimism and hope constructs: Variants on a positive expectancy theme. In E. C. Chang (Ed.), *Optimism and pessimism.* Washington, DC: American Psychological Association.

Snyder, C. R., Sympson, S. C., Ybasco, F. C., Borders, T. F., Babyak, M. A., & Higgins, R. L. (1996). Development and validation of the State Hope Scale. *Journal of Personality and Social Psychology, 70,* 321–335.

Snyder, C. R., Wiklund, C., & Cheavens, J. (1999, August). *Hope and academic performance in college.* Paper presented at the American Psychological Association, Boston. University of Kansas, Lawrence.

Sonne, J., & Janoff, D. (1979). The effect of treatment attributions on the maintenance of weight reduction: A replication and extension. *Cognitive Therapy and Research, 3,* 389–397.

Stotland, E. (1969). *The psychology of hope.* San Francisco: Jossey-Bass.

Strecher, V. J., Becker, M. H., Kirscht, J. P., Eraker, S. A., & Graham-Tomasi, R. P. (1985).

Psychological aspects of changes in cigarette-smoking behavior. *Patient Education and Counseling, 7,* 249–262.

Strong, S. R. (1987). Interpersonal influence theory as a common language for psychotherapy. *International Journal of Integrative and Eclectic Psychotherapy, 6,* 173–184.

Strong, S. R. (1991). Social influence and change in therapeutic relationships. In C. R. Snyder & D. R. Forsyth (Eds.), *Handbook of social and clinical psychology: The health perspective* (pp. 540–562). New York: Pergamon.

Strong, S. R., & Claiborn, C. D. (1982). *Change through interaction: Social psychological processes of counseling and psychotherapy.* New York: Wiley-Interscience.

Strong, S. R., Wambach, C. A., Lopez, F. B., & Cooper, R. K. (1979). Motivational and equipping functions of interpretation in counseling and psychotherapy. *Journal of Counseling Psychology, 26,* 98–107.

Strupp, H. H., & Bloxom, A. L. (1973). Preparing lower class patients for group psychotherapy: Development and evaluation of a role-induction film. *Journal of Consulting and Clinical Psychology, 41,* 373–384.

Strupp, H. H., Fox, R. E., & Lessler, K. (1969). *Patients view their psychotherapy.* Baltimore: John Hopkins University Press.

Taylor, S. E., & Armor, D. A. (1996). Positive illusions and coping with adversity. *Journal of Personality, 64,* 873–898.

Taylor, S. E., & Brown, J. D. (1988). Illusion and well-being: A social psychological perspective on mental health. *Psychological Bulletin, 103,* 193–210.

Taylor, S. E., & Brown, J. D. (1994). Positive illusions and well-being: Separating fact from fiction. *Psychological Bulletin, 116,* 21–26.

Taylor, S. E., & Pham, L. B. (1996). Mental simulation, motivation, and action. In P. E. Gollwitzer & J. A. Bargh (Eds.), *The psychology of action: Linking cognition and motivation to behavior* (pp. 219–235). New York: Guilford.

Taylor, S. E., & Schneider, S. K. (1989). Coping and the simulation of events. *Social Cognition, 7,* 174–194.

Tennen, H., & Affleck, G. (1999). Finding benefits in adversity. In C. R. Snyder (Ed.), *Coping: The psychology of what works* (pp. 279–304). New York: Oxford University Press.

Thorne, F. C. (1952). Rules of evidence in the evaluation of the effect of psychotherapy. *Journal of Clinical Psychology, 8,* 38–41.

Truax, C. B., & Mitchell, K. M. (1971). Research on certain therapist interpersonal skills in relation to process and outcome. In A. E. Bergin & S. L. Garfield (Eds), *Handbook of psychotherapy and behavior change: An empirical analysis* (pp. 299–344). New York: Wiley.

Uhlenhuth, E. H., Cantro, A., Neustadt, J. D., & Payson, H. E. (1957). The symptomatic relief with meprobamate, phenobarbital, and placebo. *American Journal of Psychiatry, 115,* 905–910.

Uhlenhuth, E. H., & Duncan, D. B. (1968). Subjective change with medical student therapists: Some determinants of change in psychoneurotic outpatients. *Archives of General Psychiatry, 18,* 532–540.

Uhlenhuth, E. H., Rickels, K., Fisher, S., Park, L. C., Lipman, R. S., & Mock, J. (1966). Drug, doctor's verbal attitude and clinic setting in the symptomatic response to pharmacotherapy. *Psychopharmacologia, 9,* 392–418.

Vallacher, R. R., & Wegner, D. M. (1987). What do people think they're doing? Action identification and human behavior. *Psychological Review, 94,* 3–15.

Vallacher, R. R., Wegner, D. M., & Somoza, M. (1989). That's easy for you to say. Action identification and speech fluency. *Journal of Personality and Social Psychology, 56,* 199–208.

Veroff, J. B., Douvan, E., & Kukla, R. A. (1981). *The inner American: A self-portrait from 1957 to 1976.* New York: Basic Books.

Wallach, M. A., & Wallach, L. (1983). *Psychology's sanction for selfishness: The error of egoism in theory and therapy.* San Francisco: Freeman.

Weinberg, R. S., Hughes, H. H., Critelli, J. W., England, R., & Jackson, A. (1984). Effects of preexisting and manipulated self-efficacy on weight loss in a self-control program. *Journal of Research in Personality, 18,* 352–358.

Weiner-Davis, M., de Shazer, S., & Gingerich, W. (1987). Building on pretreatment change to construct the therapeutic solution: An exploratory study. *Journal of Marital and Family Therapy, 13*(4), 359–364.

Wheatley, D. (1967). Influence of doctors' and patients' attitudes in the treatment of neurotic illness. *Lancet, 2,* 1133–1135.

White, L., Tursky, B., & Schwartz, G. E. (1985a). Placebo in perspective. In L. White, B. Tursky, & G. E. Schwartz (Eds.), *Placebo: Theory, research, and mechanisms* (pp. 3–8). New York: Guilford.

White, L., Tursky, B., & Schwartz, G. E. (Eds.). (1985b). *Placebo: Theory, research, and mechanisms.* New York: Guilford.

White, R. W. (1959). Motivation reconsidered: The concept of competence. *Psychological Review, 66,* 297–333.

Wickramasekera, I. (1985). A conditioned response model of placebo effect: Predictors form the model. In L. White, B. Tursky, & G. Schwartz (Eds.), *Placebos: Theory, research and mechanisms* (pp. 255–287). New York: Guilford.

Wilensky, R. (1983). *Planning and understanding: A computational approach to human reasoning.* Reading, MA: Addison-Wesley.

Wilkins, W. (1979). Expectancies in therapy research: Discriminating among heterogeneous nonspecifics. *Journal of Consulting and Clinical Psychology, 47,* 837–845.

Wilkins, W. (1984). Psychotherapy: The powerful placebo. *Journal of Consulting and Clinical Psychology, 52,* 570–573.

Wilkins, W. (1985). Placebo controls and concepts in chemotherapy and psychotherapy research. In L. White, B. Tursky, & G. Schwartz (Eds.), *Placebos: Theory, research and mechanisms* (pp. 83–109). New York: Guilford.

Wilson, G. T. (1996). Empirically validated treatments: Reality and resistance. *Clinical Psychology: Science and Practice, 3,* 241–244.

Wundt, W. M. (1894). *Lectures on human and animal psychology.* (J. E. Creighton & E. B. Titchener, Trans.). New York: Macmillan.

Yalom, I. D. (1989). *Loves' executioner and other tales of psychotherapy.* New York: HarperCollins.

Zwick, R., & Attkisson, C. C. (1985). Effectiveness of a client pretherapy orientation program. *Journal of Counseling Psychology, 32,* 514–524

THE TRAIT
HOPE SCALE

Directions: Read each item carefully. Using the scale shown below, please select the number that best describes YOU and put that number in the blank provided.

1 = Definitely False
2 = Mostly False
3 = Somewhat False
4 = Slightly False
5 = Slightly True
6 = Somewhat True
7 = Mostly True
8 = Definitely True

_____ **1.** I can think of many ways to get out of a jam.

_____ **2.** I energetically pursue my goals.

_____ **3.** I feel tired most of the time.

_____ **4.** There are lots of ways around any problem.

_____ **5.** I am easily downed in an argument.

_____ **6.** I can think of many ways to get the things in life that are important to me.

_____ **7.** I worry about my health.

_____ **8.** Even when others get discouraged, I know I can find a way to solve the problem.

_____ **9.** My past experiences have prepared me well for my future.

_____ **10.** I've been pretty successful in life.

_____ **11.** I usually find myself worrying about something.

_____ **12.** I meet the goals that I set for myself.

When administering the scale, it is called The Future Scale. The Agency subscale score is derived by summing items 2, 9, 10, and 12; the Pathway subscale score is derived by adding items 1, 4, 6, and 8. The total Hope Scale score is derived by summing the four Agency and the four Pathway items.

From C. R. Snyder et al., The will and the ways: Development and validation of an individual differences measure of hope, *Journal of Personality and Social Psychology*, © 1991, vol. 60, p. 585. Reprinted with the permission of the American Psychological Association and the senior author.

B

THE STATE HOPE SCALE

Directions: Read each item carefully. Using the scale shown below, please select the number that best describes *how you think about yourself right now* and put that number in the blank before each sentence. Please take a few moments to focus on yourself and what is going on in *your life at this moment*. Once you have this "here and now" set, go ahead and answer each item according to the following scale:

1 = Definitely False
2 = Mostly False
3 = Somewhat False
4 = Slightly False
5 = Slightly True
6 = Somewhat True
7 = Mostly True
8 = Definitely True

_____ 1. If I should find myself in a jam, I could think of many ways to get out of it.

_____ 2. At the present time, I am energetically pursuing my goals.

_____ 3. There are lots of ways around any problem that I am facing now.

_____ 4. Right now, I see myself as being pretty successful.

_____ 5. I can think of many ways to reach my current goals.

_____ 6. At this time, I am meeting the goals that I have set for myself.

The Agency subscale score is derived by summing the three even-numbered items; the Pathways subscale score is derived by adding the three odd-numbered items. The total State Hope Scale score is derived by summing the three Agency and the three Pathways items. Scores can range from a low of 6 to a high of 48. When administering the State Hope Scale, it is labeled as the Goals Scale for the Present.

From C. R. Snyder et al., Development and validation of the State Hope Scale, *Journal of Personality and Social Psychology*, © 1996, vol. 70, p. 335. Reprinted with the permission of the American Psychological Association and the senior author.

THE CHILDREN'S HOPE SCALE

Directions: The six sentences below describe how children think about themselves and how they do things in general. Read each sentence carefully. For each sentence, please think about how you are in most situations. Place a check inside the circle that describes YOU the best. For example, place a check (√) in the circle (O) above "None of the time" if this describes you. Or if you are this way "All of the time," check this circle. Please answer every question by putting a check in one of the circles. There are no right or wrong answers.

1. I think I am doing pretty well.

O	O	O	O	O	O
None of the time	A little of the time	Some of the time	A lot of the time	Most of the time	All of the time

2. I can think of many ways to get the things in life that are most important to me.

O	O	O	O	O	O
None of the time	A little of the time	Some of the time	A lot of the time	Most of the time	All of the time

3. I am doing just as well as other kids my age.

O	O	O	O	O	O
None of the time	A little of the time	Some of the time	A lot of the time	Most of the time	All of the time

4. When I have a problem, I can come up with lots of ways to solve it.

O	O	O	O	O	O
None of the time	A little of the time	Some of the time	A lot of the time	Most of the time	All of the time

5. I think the things I have done in the past will help me in the future.

O	O	O	O	O	O
None of the time	A little of the time	Some of the time	A lot of the time	Most of the time	All of the time

6. Even when others want to quit, I know that I can find ways to solve the problem.

O	O	O	O	O	O
None of the time	A little of the time	Some of the time	A lot of the time	Most of the time	All of the time

When administered to children, this scale is not labeled The Children's Hope Scale, but is called "Questions About Your Goals." To calculate the total Children's Hope Scale score, add the responses to all six items, with "None of the time" = 1; "A little of the time" = 2; "Some of the time" = 3; "A lot of the time" = 4; "Most of the time" = 5; "All of the time" = 6. The three odd-numbered items tap agency, and the three even-numbered items tap pathways.

From C. R. Snyder et al., The development and validation of the Children's Hope Scale, *Journal of Pediatric Psychology* © 1997, vol. 22(3), p. 421. Reprinted with the permission of the Journal and the senior author.

Chapter 8

The Long and Short of Psychological Change: Toward a Goal-centered Understanding of Treatment Durability and Adaptive Success

Paul Karoly and Cindy Wheeler Anderson
Arizona State University

Living well requires passion, resilience to challenges, and a reasoned, morally tenable maintenance of commitments.

Mardi Horowitz (1998)

Over the last 100 years, conceptual and data-based articles, chapters, and books numbering in the hundreds of thousands have been written to explain the nature of "mental illness" and to suggest potential modes of social, psychological, and biochemical remediation. Yet, as we enter the next millennium, a sense of cumulative wisdom is difficult to detect. With respect to appraising psychopathology, at least a dozen conceptual models, often with non-overlapping foci and assumptions, are currently available.[1] In addition, novel forms of treatment for psychological disorders regularly appear, often encased in only the thinnest veneer of empirical support. Apparently undaunted by a lack of consensus about such foundational issues as the delineation of normal vs. abnormal adjust-

ment, the interplay of biogenetic and environmental factors in psychopathology, or the causal nature of "personality" and its "disorders" (cf. Bergner, 1997; Depue & Zald, 1993; Pervin, 1994; Wakefield, 1992), the fields of clinical psychology, psychiatry, social work, counseling, criminal justice, and allied human services disciplines appear to be operating from a relatively optimistic stance. The optimism stems in part from the growing belief that, on the one hand, many of the over four hundred varieties of psychological intervention are effective (i.e., superior to no treatment or to "nonspecific" elements) and, on the other hand, that no single brand of treatment has emerged as significantly better than the others (with a few disorder-specific exceptions) (cf. Landman & Dawes, 1982; Lipsey & Wilson, 1993; Smith & Glass, 1977; Smith, Glass, & Miller, 1980). Despite the fact that if one examines the empirical literature closely, many qualifications of these two beliefs can be found, the practicing clinician and clinical researcher nonetheless have taken them to heart.

As a counterbalance to the generally upbeat appraisal of psychotherapy in the clinical sciences, we ask in this chapter some different and decidedly more difficult questions about human change processes and their relation to adjustive "outcomes." One fulcrum on which we balance our arguments is the dimension of *time*, or more pointedly, the temporal trajectory of psychological change as it is played out in formal helping sit-

---

[1]The available models of psychopathology include the moderated stress illness (differential vulnerability), the biomedical, the interpersonal and self-presentational, the psychodynamic (classical and contemporary), the functional-behavioral, the information processing, the cognitive social-learning, the sociocultural, the developmental, the adaptive systems, the evolutionary and sociobiological, the common personality factors (e.g., the five factor), and the self-regulatory approaches.

uations. A consideration of the lastingness or durability of therapeutic ministrations will be presented here to explore the divergent meanings behind the idea of "therapeutic movement."

In this chapter, the term *psychotherapy* denotes a formal process in which a patient or patient system (dyad, family, etc.), manifesting a pattern of personal or social dysfunction [typically reflected in the descriptions of Axis I and Axis II disorders in the Diagnostic and Statistical Manual (DSM) of the American Psychiatric Association, D], undergoes systematic assessment and (re)education to alleviate or modulate the most pressing complaints; establish a self-enhancing lifestyle; and/or achieve acceptable levels of personal control, comfort, self-confidence, self-awareness, and/or decisional flexibility (cf. Kanfer & Goldstein, 1991). Pharmacotherapy per se is omitted from consideration as a psychological intervention (although its use in combination with psychological treatments would be included). The present definition is somewhat restrictive, given the enormous variety of help-giving/help-seeking activities currently in vogue. Nonetheless, the majority of empirical studies of clinical intervention has centered on DSM-listed problems among persons identified (by themselves or others) as requiring professional assistance.

This chapter pursues two main objectives: (1) to critique the therapy outcome literature on the basis of its conceptual narrowness and its failures to demonstrate convincingly short-term, treatment-specific gains, as well as robustness, or durability of treatment influence, and (2) to offer a goal-based motivational alternative to the symptom-centered, state-change models of human adjustment that have dominated clinical science. These dual objectives are independent, in that readers need not accept the premises of an emerging goal systems framework to appreciate the questionable nature of the current evidence concerning psychotherapy potency. However, in skeptically appraising the short- and long-term change literature, a search for some new organizing principles seems a logical necessity. Although we acknowledge that the interpretive problems we raise here eventually may yield to procedural refinements and better data-analytic methods, and that the apparent willingness of practitioners and researchers to adapt to a managed care vision of personal change may well be a healthy development, we nonetheless offer an alternative meta–theory from which to appraise the effectiveness of modern psychotherapeutics.

AN ALTERNATIVE FRAMEWORK

Almost a half-century ago, Eysenck (1952) challenged psychotherapists of all persuasions to demonstrate that their formal, clinical interventions could produce significant adaptive change over and above that brought about by the mere passage of time (so-called "spontaneous remission"). He thus moved clinical science ahead by galvanizing researchers and clinicians to conduct credible, bottom-line effectiveness studies. Unfortunately, in our view, he also locked clinical science into a mechanistic, efficient-cause style of thinking that has seriously constrained its potential for growth and development (cf. Rychlak, 1998). Unintentionally, Eysenck's challenge set a comparatively low standard of proof that we believe has led to an arguably unhealthy level of cross-disciplinary complacency. As Sechrest, McKnight, and McKnight (1996) have noted, the general belief that psychotherapy helps people with problems may be akin to the assertion that "food reduces hunger," with the more substantive but neglected questions being how much help does it provide (clinically rather than statistically) and under what circumstances? We agree with Sechrest and his colleagues but contend that the question of "whether" therapy works remains open and that yet another vital question—for how long?—is either not being pursued widely or is being investigated in a conceptually restrictive fashion. Furthermore, we would argue that the psychotherapy outcome literature more accurately reduces to the assertion that "something is better than nothing" (clearly an even *less* empirically useful statement than "food reduces hunger").[2]

Our skepticism about contemporary approaches to psychological change stems not only from a critical interpretation of the formal logic of outcome research, some of which we discuss in this chapter, but also from an allegiance to an alternative organizing framework about the nature of human adaptation and its problems and about the proper role of would-be clinical interventionists. Thus, we contend that even if one were to accept the positive interpretations of the available outcome research, there is reason to question the premises on which these findings are built. Although a complete statement of an alternative

---

[2]When outcome research involves a comparison of a treatment to a placebo condition, then the assertion becomes "something is better than nothing special."

framework is well beyond the scope of the present chapter, a brief articulation here will help ground our critique of traditional concepts of therapeutic outcome.

First, the reader is reminded that the dominant approach to remediating human problems, although not easy to succinctly summarize, should be quite familiar to almost anyone living in a modern industrial society. Psychological change agents (whatever their professional identification) are viewed, by themselves, as well as their clients and the general public, as performing their duties in a manner akin to physicians (or other technical experts). That is, they are trained to distinguish among an array of "mental" (rather than physical) problems and then to offer skillful repairs that, like coronary bypass surgery, are designed to remove dangerous or functionally unacceptable ways of being in an expeditious fashion, thereby returning the individual to pre-illness levels of adaptation for the foreseeable future. Clinical science clearly has been influenced by a biomedical worldview in the formulation of its key concepts, theories, and methods of empirical validation. Practitioners likewise have been socialized into thinking about "illnesses," "diseases," "patients," "symptoms," "syndromes," "illness episodes," "comorbidity," "cures," "dose-response relations," "relapses," "placebos," "follow-ups," and "clinical trials," among other things.

Within the received, biomedically inspired view, adjustment problems of all sorts, including phobias, obsessive rituals, prolonged depressive affect, drug addiction, hyperactivity, high-risk sexual behavior, and repeated criminal activity, are considered to be aberrant states of functioning (or of functional disability) that although unfolding in naturalistic settings, can be "transported to" and treated in the context of a consulting room, clinic, school, or prison. Within an "aberrant states of functioning" perspective, problems are mostly discrete and episodic, and "change" or "therapeutic movement" is usually a matter of engineering the appropriate modification in some malfunctioning component(s) of a relatively stable supporting structure. That some types of human adjustive problems fit quite well within such a mechanistic worldview is *not* at issue. However, to the extent that a great many psychological problems diverge in form and function from an acute illness metaphor, we contend that an appreciation of the full scope of human maladaptation can be (and has been) seriously obscured.

Within the aberrant states tradition, practitioners also seem to be convinced, despite divergences in their theories about what causes aberrant functioning, that interventions can be instantiated in accordance with a *treatment equifinality principle*, that is, the view that there are many operationally divergent yet equally efficacious pathways to psychological change (including the biochemical, intrapsychic, behavioral, and interpersonal). The treatment equifinality principle has been strengthened in recent years by the results of scores of meta-analytic reviews (revealing few differences in efficacy between diverse types of treatment), by the psychotherapy integration movement, and by the broad-ranging discussion of "common factors" purportedly underlying therapeutic success (cf. Frank, 1973; Gold, 1996; Goldfried, 1995; Weinberger, 1995).[3] In addition, when change factors fail to take hold (or take hold in a less than ideal fashion), therapists working in the aberrant states tradition can employ especially sensitive statistical techniques (such as survival or multistate analysis) to better track the time course to relapse or premature dropout (cf. Hartmann, Schulgen, Olschewski, & Herzog, 1997) and/or seek to enhance or strengthen treatment potency through the use of technical solutions such as treatment fading, booster sessions, relapse prevention or problem-solving training, and preinterventive efforts at matching patients' needs and motives with congruent therapeutic modalities (Eyberg, Edwards, Boggs, & Foote, 1998; Goldstein & Kanfer, 1989; Karoly, 1980, 1991b).

The present position is that especially in the short run—immediately after therapy termination and extending sometimes to several years posttreatment—positive changes in a state provide minimal information about the redirective power of formal therapy. Meaningful "therapeutic movement" should reflect much more than ei-

---

[3]Note that we are not suggesting that the treatment equifinality principle is *inherently* flawed, but rather that it tends to be invoked on a post hoc basis to explain the apparent equivalence of effects across therapeutic modalities. An equifinality effect may be expected on the basis of a higher order mechanism of human adaptive functioning that is capable of being triggered by alternative routes—such as situational priming, specific self-generated thoughts, autonomic arousal, and so on. If such a mechanism is postulated, it should be theoretically possible to study its operation on an a priori basis (e.g., experimentally) rather than merely inferring its existence after the fact.

ther a short- or long-term reduction of symptoms. Rather, it should indicate a *continuing process of self-regulated, rule-based, flexibly negotiated, optimally paced, integrated, and balanced goal directedness.*

To elaborate on the meaning of this six-process conception, it is first necessary to point out that modern Western societies require individuals to achieve (at varying levels of specificity) a number of "normative tasks," including the acquisition of world knowledge and self-knowledge, the establishment of social ties, and the attainment of self-sufficiency (vocational independence and problem-solving skills). People's day-to-day goals or personal strivings emerge from their interpretation of these broad, culturally molded "life task" domains (cf. Cantor, 1990, 1994; Cantor & Zirkel, 1990; Ford, 1992; Ryan, Sheldon, Kasser, & Deci, 1996).

Adjustive difficulty (psychopathology) can occur in response to prolonged task failure or to personally or situationally mediated threats to task engagement and/or as a consequence of dysfunctions in goal selection, the setting of goal achievement levels, goal justification, goal representation (i.e., cognitions concerning the unfolding process of goal striving), goal framing (i.e., goal-centered information-processing styles), goal structuring (i.e., relations among representational features), and/or strategies of goal pursuit (cf. Bandura, 1986; Baumeister, Heatherton, & Tice, 1994; Carver & Baird, 1998; Carver & Scheier, 1990; Karoly, 1991a, 1993a, 1993b, 1998; Karoly & Ruehlman, 1995; Kuhl, 1992; Lecci, Karoly, Ruehlman, & Lanyon, 1996; McGregor & Little, 1998; Strauman, 1989; Van Hook & Higgins, 1988). A DSM-IV disorder or psychopathology is taken to be the result of ineffective life-task management under the influence of inadequate or dysfunctional self-regulation and/or dysfunctional environmental affordances. Within this emerging framework, stressful or transitional events do not necessarily have a direct causal connection to psychological or physical symptoms. Rather, stressful events affect adjustment by potentially threatening or challenging the cognitive construal and/or pursuit of valued goals and beliefs (and the personal theories that contain them) or by pressing for the enactment of new (unfamiliar or risky) personal strivings (cf. also Martin & Sugerman, 1997; Park & Folkman, 1997). Symptoms may represent temporary system accommodations or long-term system reorganization under the guidance of self-defeating

goals. But whatever their origin, symptoms are "secondary" phenomena.

Rather than adopting a unitary prior cause orientation, the guiding meta–theory behind this emerging framework is *teleological* (final cause-oriented), as well as traditionally deterministic. In other words, we are willing to inquire not only about probabilistic antecedent-consequent linkages but also about the ends or anticipated futures for the sake of which people act. With goals as the pivotal feature of this conception, the basic unit of analysis is self-regulated locomotion toward goals, and the idea of effective or therapeutic movement translates to *getting and staying on track toward distant yet meaningful goals in the face of obstacles; unavailable, reduced, or unpredictable external supports; and/or difficult life transitions.* A trajectory-based conception of therapeutic movement stands in sharp contrast to a strict efficient cause model whose focus is on eliminating or weakening the deleterious effects of a presumably pathogenic personal history (cf. also H. Goldstein, 1984). Nonetheless, the trajectory conception does not reject the efficient cause model but rather includes it as a special case of dysfunctional self-regulation.

Changes in aberrant states (often, but not always, identified as symptoms) are certainly meaningful to the individual and/or to society, especially when the reduction of unwanted (or the increase in desirable) attributes contributes to personal and social well-being and to a sense of control. However, a motivational model conceives of aberrant states as *resulting from* dysfunctions in strategic goal selection, representation, and/or guidance, with the last involving deficits in the activation, organization, modification, emotive modulation, maintenance, social support mobilization, and/or inhibition of purposeful action patterns (Karoly, 1996). Consequently, symptoms can be *motivationally informative* only when shown to be related functionally to ineffective goal pursuit or self-defeating goal cognition. Insofar as providing a benchmark for differentiating "normal" from "pathological" adjustment, the regulatory view of psychopathology is more causally specific and temporally grounded than either the *harmful dysfunction* (Wakefield, 1992) or the *restrictions on deliberate action* (Bergner, 1997) perspectives that have gained currency of late (cf. Lilienfeld & Marino, 1995).

From a self-regulatory vantage, then, people can be diagnosed (i.e., understood) more usefully in terms of *deviations from what they want or need to be doing right than in terms of what or how they are unintentionally doing wrong.* Although unintentional or unskilled "wrongdoing" is clinically and socially important and experientially salient, it need not be viewed as the most basic or defining aspect of psychological maladaptation.[4] Moreover, the locus of change and directional guidance in the long run must be the client (the person whose life is dysregulated) rather than a powerful external source such as a therapist or a mood-altering drug. The justification for emphasizing client-centeredness of change derives not only from a commitment to a self-regulatory meta–theory but also from the empirically supported belief that self-directed change promises to be among the most *practical, generalizable, and cost-effective* methods of intervention, provided one takes the long view when assessing the benefits of treatment (Kanfer & Schefft, 1988; Karoly, 1980; Karoly & Kanfer, 1982; Klar, Fisher, Chinsky, & Nadler, 1992; Linden & Wen, 1990).

The self-regulatory meta–theory that is being proposed here is hardly revolutionary. Most practitioners of psychotherapy probably would agree that the overall purpose of treatment is to help equip patients with the self-knowledge and instrumental skills necessary to allow them to take charge of their goal-directed movement through life—their *psychological wayfaring*—in such a manner that dysfunctional thoughts, feelings, or actions are eliminated or kept to a manageable (or at least an acceptable) level and personal meaning is achieved. That the reduction in DSM-described symptoms, for convenience's sake, has been used as a proxy indicator of successful psychological wayfaring is understandable. However, the deliberate reification of the proxy may be a serious miscalculation. Moreover, the reluctance to erect a life-span developmental model of psychological wayfaring (self-regulation) in favor of minimodels that focus on the tangible expressions and products of human misguidance (failures to stay on track) has yielded a plethora of short-term, decontextualized corrective maneuvers currently being marketed as empirically validated treatments.

As noted previously, at least six critical features are associated with effectively and self-

consciously staying on track toward one's aspirations and commitments. These features require some elaboration.

First, it was suggested that goal directedness should be self-regulated. This means that most forms of treatment should instill the skills and motives that will permit adults to serve as *active self-therapists*, responsibly (some might say, "wisely") guiding their lives, not only with respect to modulating aberrant states of functioning, but also with regard to regulating such ongoing tasks as finding meaning; managing behavior, thought, and affective expression in response to inevitable life transitions; and generally moving in a prosocial fashion toward self-defining commitments (cf. Patterson & Hidore, 1997; Sternberg, 1998). The fact that goals or standards originate in a social world (i.e., evolve out of social exchange) simply implies that the content of what is meaningful or self-defining or prosocial is socially and culturally driven; it does not diminish the importance of internalized, self-reflective, and autonomous goal pursuit as the key criterion of adaptive mastery. Although the automatized regulation of certain biological goals is part of the architecture of the evolved human brain (Bogdan, 1994), a person's path through life in an open society nonetheless remains largely a matter of relatively unconstrained action and personal decision making. At base, an effective self-regulator is considered to be one who is reliably guided by *standards* (goals) and by *feedback* (accurately gathered information about the discrepancies between activated goals or standards and current performance accomplishments). Consequently, a great many common psychological symptoms can be traced to failures or dysfunctions in feedback-centered guidance to goal (Karoly, 1991a, 1993a, 1993b, 1996; Power & Dalgleish, 1997; Teasdale & Barnard, 1993; Wells & Matthews, 1994).

Second, it was asserted that rule-based movement toward distant goals is a desirable feature of an adaptive motivational system. If goal-directed movement is equated with a journey, it should be possible to locomote from point A to a distant point B in a haphazard fashion, switching direction in response to immediate cues and contingencies but eventually arriving at one's stated destination. Alternatively and preferably, one could travel with a palpable degree of deliberateness, driven in part by the use of forethought, if-then reasoning, and rule-based cognition (cf. Bandura, 1986) that ostensibly facilitates the avoidance of costly and time-consuming side trips and detours.

---

[4]We use the terms *right* and *wrong* to denote functional rather than moral or didactic processes. Within the realm of "wrongdoing," we would also include "wrongthinking" and "wrongfeeling."

On the other hand, being *rigidly* rule-oriented is a decided disadvantage in an ever-changing world. Thus, a third criterion of adaptive goal pursuit is that the traveler must seek to negotiate multiple objectives and changing states of value in a flexible or open-minded manner. The ability to make finely tuned discriminations about when and where to employ a psychological rule-of-the-road and when it is appropriate to compromise are related to what Cantor and Kihlstrom (1987) have called "social intelligence." It is important to note that although the rigid use of problem-solving strategies may not produce noticeable adjustment problems during the early phases of a psychological change program (a time when overlearned strategies are most likely to fit the situations being encountered), such a style can nonetheless hinder treatment generalization and transfer.

A fourth dimension of potentially effective goal pursuit is optimal pacing. Optimally paced goal pursuit refers to movement that is based on a desire to achieve in accord with reasonably high yet realistic standards; such goal pursuit is *not* characterized by premature termination (giving up), slowing down of efforts, or lowering of performance standards under conditions of task failure. Optimal pacing reflects what Ford (1992) has called the *optimal challenge principle* and is consistent with what Locke and Latham (1990) have shown to be the myriad practical advantages of adherence to specific and relatively difficult goals (in contrast to vague and overly easy ones). A central causal component underlying optimal pacing is the possession of a strong sense of *self-efficacy*, the conviction that one has the power to produce given levels of task attainment (Bandura, 1997). Included among the consequences of optimal pacing should be a sense of coherence, control, and optimism.

The fifth suggested criterion of adaptive goal directedness is the requirement that goal systems be relatively unconflicted (or *integrated*). Whether an individual has a great many or just a few personal goals, to the extent that the active goals in the system are incompatible, operating at cross purposes from the standpoint of instrumental performance or their typical effects on the environment, then the likelihood of goal achievement is reduced. Research has shown, for example, that goal conflict or ambivalence is predictive of physical and psychological symptoms, whereas integrated goals are associated with greater life satisfaction (Emmons, 1996; McGregor & Little, 1998).

Finally, goal systems function best when there is balance. For example, there should not be an overrepresentation of goals in just one or two major categories of life-task pursuit because of the restriction in sources of satisfaction that such an arrangement almost invariably entails. Even when a variety of goal types are being actively pursued, individuals may yet tend to overvalue one or two categories, thereby creating an artificial hedonic restriction. The threat of a loss of an overvalued goal may precipitate depression (Champion & Power, 1995) in some and violence in others (Baumeister, 1997). And, distinct from the question of how many and what sorts of eggs one has in the goal system basket lies the balance between aspirations that carry implications for self-definition and self-worth (and that are typically more complex and difficult to achieve) and those aspirations that are associated with more routine but nonetheless enjoyable and readily attained outcomes. Little (e.g., 1993) refers to the last desideratum as the need to balance *meaning* and *manageability*.

PLAN OF THE CHAPTER

Even by dint of this relatively brief presentation of a goal-based, motivational conception of adjustment, it should be clear that the short-term change-in-state emphasis that characterizes the modern clinical literature falls far short of demonstrating that psychotherapy can be an effective vehicle for assisting individuals to skillfully regulate their psychological wayfaring through time to "live well"—as aptly defined by Horowitz (1998) in the quotation that opened this chapter. The plan for the remainder of this chapter is, therefore, to offer a minority viewpoint about therapeutic movement, one that is orchestrated in five parts. First, we assert that the meta-analytic literature on treatment effects cannot be unambiguously interpreted to mean that "therapy works!" Nonspecific elements may play a dominant role in the short-term change equation. Yet, even if all the meta-analytic findings on short-term outcome were accepted at face value, the question of posttermination durability remains. Although many formal psychotherapeutic systems appear to recognize the importance of the long-term or extended effects of treatment, we contend that robustness of treatment remains a significantly understudied issue. To illustrate this point, we briefly review the change missions of several prominent psychotherapy perspectives, noting the extent to which recently published research emanating from these frameworks has tended to downplay the extended effects question. Following this, we review the available meta-analytic findings on the extended outcomes of treatment. We further contend that even if the meta-analytic findings on long-term change were much stronger than those surveyed, a fourth concern would be the absence of data supporting the self-regulated, or internalized, nature of therapeutic change.

A Skeptical Perspective on Short-term Treatment Success

Why shouldn't clinical scientists be overly impressed with the evidence (see, e.g., Nathan & Gorman, 1998) that favors empirically validated therapies and the attendant practice guidelines that have emerged in their wake? At one level, of course, we *should* be impressed. We should be confident that the Eysenck null hypothesis can be safely rejected as it pertains to a variety of interventions and many (though certainly not all) types of patients.[5] However, a skeptical reading is still possible, given our construal of clinical change.

The present incredulous interpretation stems in part from the view that (1) certain identifiable mechanisms (often called nonspecific effects) capable of producing immediate improvements in patterns of adjustment tend to be a part of almost any serious, professionally enacted effort to change people; (2) these mechanisms are not as likely to operate in the typical attention placebo or minimal treatments employed as control or comparison methods as they are in thera-

pies to which investigators are conceptually committed; and (3) these mechanisms may have a brief or time-limited impact on adjustment.

It is also important to note that complex organisms are expected to evidence *rhythms, cycles, periodicities, fluctuations,* or *oscillations* in their adaptive activities (cf. Mahoney, 1991; Weiner, 1989). In other words, change and volatility are natural for both adaptive and aberrant patterns. If what goes down eventually comes up again, then time-limited, pre-post, group measurement cannot be trusted to unerringly capture the developmental dynamics of either adaptive growth or symptomatic recurrences (Hayes, Barlow, & Nelson-Gray, 1999; Haynes, 1992; Hollon & Cobb, 1993).[6] Taking a long-range, iterative view of adjustment means identifying and, if necessary, modifying and bringing under volitional control those psychological pacemaker processes that tune or align patterned (nonrandom) oscillations of action, thought, and affect to fluctuating yet salient environmental or social events (Karoly, 1996). This dynamic, transactional view stands in contrast to the conventional wisdom that seeks proof of treatment effectiveness mainly through short-term changes in mean levels of functioning.

What sorts of evaluative analyses of psychotherapeutic effectiveness would we therefore like to see employed? First, the supposed active and unique ingredients in formal therapies currently considered empirically proven need to be tested against other potentially psychoactive in-

---

[5]Prioleau, Murdock, and Brody (1983) have countered the traditional wisdom by arguing that the effect size of .42, which Smith, Glass, and Miller (1980) interpreted as evidence of psychotherapy's general effectiveness, is not supportive of such an interpretation. They contend that the benefits of therapy over placebo treatment is "vanishingly small." By contrast, we are accepting the superiority of psychotherapy over placebo controls but are arguing that the difference stems from nonspecific effects that are more abundant in formal therapy than typical placebo conditions.

[6]At this point, some readers may object to the idea that pathological conditions show oscillations, by pointing to the "obvious" stability or persistence of deviant patterns such as schizophrenia, alcoholism, criminal behavior, cigarette smoking, social phobia, and a host of other clinical conditions. Cures, they would argue, may be fleeting, but psychopathology tends to remain in effect unless acted on by powerful forces. Such reasoning is tantamount to the assertion that *bad habits are strong* whereas *good habits are weak*. Clearly, there are no principle(s) of learning that would support such a view. Moreover, the day-to-day actions, thoughts, and emotional expressions of most patient groups are, in fact, quite variable. Alcoholics are not always drunk, schizophrenics are not always delusional, and psychopaths are not always taking advantage of others; rather their overall patterns of symptom display tend over time to fluctuate around either short-lived or extended equilibrium states of maladaptation. This is precisely why short-term measurement of symptom levels is not recommended as a method of indexing treatment efficacy.

terventions that are easier and cheaper to instantiate, for example, meditation, physical exercise, self-help books, group treatments conducted by paraprofessionals, or simply informal helping contacts with others (cf. Cooper, Coker, & Fleming, 1995; Frank, 1982; Gould & Clum, 1993). Moreover, approaches vying for the label "empirically proven" need to be tested against those nonspecific change mechanisms that are most apt to be activated in systematic, relationship-centered, and professionally orchestrated treatment programs, but not in particularly large or uniform doses in the usual control-group conditions employed in outcome research.[7]

The incredulous or skeptical view, therefore, differs from the received view in its assumption that whereas random assignment of patients to conditions might be capable of controlling for such potent patient factors as readiness or expectancy to change, trust in caregivers, level of distress, initial level of self-efficacy and the like, it cannot equalize experimental and ostensibly credible control groups in terms of the so-called nonspecific factors because these factors are loaded into most experimental-group conditions but are lacking or minimal in amount amid no-treatment, attention-placebo, and many treatment-as-usual conditions. Neither can the randomized trials approach per se eliminate the problem of insensitive or inappropriate outcome measurement (cf. Frank, 1982; Parloff, 1986; Prioleau, Murdock, & Brody, 1983; Sechrest, McKnight, & McKnight, 1996). We further contend, unlike those who advocate considering powerful and pervasive nonspecific factors to be the building blocks of treatment, that many of these change mechanisms (to be discussed mo-

mentarily) can be relatively short-lived and nonuniform in their action (i.e., subject to individual variation); and, therefore, they cannot yet be touted as the singular or homogeneous cornerstones of the therapeutic edifice. Nonetheless, the idea that nonspecific factors might interact with potent facilitators of self-directedness (i.e., the skills, knowledge, and content-sensitive attributions necessary to direct behavior under conditions of uncertainty) to enhance the possibility of lasting therapeutic change is a hypothesis that we would like to see tested.

Mechanisms of Short-term Change

The first explicit, time-limited mechanism of change to be considered is actually a perceptual-attributional process that ostensibly allows almost any new, organized, and professionally presented "treatment" program to appear effective: *confirmation (or confirmatory) bias* (Lewicka, 1998; Myers, 1999). Specifically, when a novel treatment program is in effect, both the patient and the therapist (provided the therapist has a genuine allegiance to the methods being used) will display a tendency to interpret evidence of *change* as evidence of *improvement*. This tendency reflects the biased process of searching for data that fit one's existing beliefs or expectancies (and also is known as *selective hypothesis testing*). If, as many observers claim, people enter therapy at times of extreme distress, demoralization, or desperation (cf. Frank, 1982), then the normal process of return to a baseline state of tolerable (although not ideal) socioemotional functioning will feed some genuine, naturalistic improvement into the mix, thereby enhancing confirmatory thinking. Moreover, regardless of the staying power of selective hypothesis testing, shortly after therapy ends and patients (and therapists) are reviewing their experiences, confirmatory bias may alter their recall of events, prompting them to remember the initial symptoms as worse than they actually were and, therefore, to rate the posttherapy level of improvement as greater than it actually is (Barone, Maddox, & Snyder, 1997; Lord, Ross, & Lepper, 1979).

Certainly, treatment as usual (i.e., no intervention or promise thereof) for demoralized patients, by definition, has failed to yield perceived improvements; so it neither will serve as a source of confirmation bias nor act as a control for its effects. Similarly, no-treatment control conditions lack the power to induce positive expectancy effects, as do many earnestly but unsystematically

---

[7]Barker, Funk, and Houston (1988) conducted a meta-analysis in which they sought to evaluate the effects of treatment vs. nonspecific factors specifically in studies that reported no significant difference between participants' expectations for improvement between the treatment and nonspecific control conditions. They were able to find only 17 studies (out of many hundreds) that met their inclusion criteria. This fact should only dampen the enthusiasm of those who claim that psychotherapy's superiority over mere expectancy has been widely studied. Moreover, the finding that the studied treatments were relatively more effective than nonspecific factor control by .55 *SD* units (the "good news") should be tempered by the fact that this difference was only .17 *SD* units at follow-up ("the bad news").

invoked placebo interventions. When reviewers (e.g., Lipsey & Wilson, 1993) point to the meta-analytic finding that "positive treatment effect sizes cannot be accounted for entirely by generalized placebo effects" (p. 1197) and that, in fact, placebo effects are typically "modest" in scope, we do not disagree. However, novel and superficially convincing treatments of any sort (whether medical or psychological), evaluated in a pre-post design, have much more going for them than do most placebo comparison conditions used in contemporary research. Therefore, the information value of typical placebo conditions as comparative anchors in meta-analytic syntheses are dubious.

But most important for the present argument, it is questionable whether the effects of confirmatory bias, optimism, or similar positive expectancy mechanisms endure for a significant period of time in the absence of genuine growth in the patient's capacity for cognitive-emotional regulation—instrumental goal directedness or what Bandura, (1986, 1997) calls "self-enablement." When positive expectancies do, in fact, endure, their lastingness is likely the result of skill-based performance accomplishments in addition to goal-directed thinking. Moreover, we do not believe that positive expectancies will continue unabated after formal treatment terminates, *if the treatment did not seek to actively build or restructure patients' cognitive and behavioral regulatory systems* (cf. also Chapter 7 in this volume). Consistent with this interpretation, Higginbotham, West, and Forsyth (1988) concluded their extensive review of expectancy effects in psychotherapy with the following assertions: that outcome expectancies tend to fluctuate over the course of treatment, that they tend not to endure past the early stages of treatment, and that they have little impact on complex psychological problems (aberrant states of functioning) that require extensive training.

A second mechanism, *cognitive dissonance* (Festinger, 1957), remains a significant potential ally of novel, complex, and effortful interventions—at least in the short run. Having invested time, energy, and money in a "change" program, even one that hasn't produced tangible results, patients will be motivated to perceive their work as worthwhile and themselves as having "improved," often in direct proportion to how much they have invested. Such cognitive restructuring allows patients to then achieve the affectively acceptable state of "consonance" (cf. Brehm & McAllister, 1980; A. P. Goldstein, 1962). Even individuals

with a negative view of themselves (a view that they are supposedly motivated to maintain) may, when investing in a program of psychotherapy, simply disavow any personal responsibility for the perceived improvement, attributing it instead to the skill and dedication of the therapist (cf. Barone, Maddox, & Snyder, 1997, chap. 7). If, in fact, so-called placebo treatments are typically not as elaborate or as emotionally involving as the to-be-validated treatments, then cognitive dissonance and reality negotiation effects would be more likely to occur in the latter than in the former.

Individuals taking part in formal therapies are typically motivated to view themselves as engaging in a discernible change process because patients, like all self-aware people, tend to reflect on what they are doing; and they will invariably define for themselves what Vallacher and Wegner (1985) have dubbed *act identities*. That is, when observing the stream of their own behavior over time, individuals usually come to symbolically represent what is occurring in terms of higher order identities, convictions, or self-conceptions. For example, a physician on her way to work in the morning, if asked, "What are you doing?" will respond by saying something like "I am going to start my shift in the emergency room" or "I am going to train a new crop of interns" rather than "I am putting one foot in front of the other" or "I am moving in the direction of the county hospital." Likewise, individuals involved in a formal therapeutic program (say, marital therapy) are likely to represent their actions in terms of "trying to learn how to be a better husband." By contrast, persons assigned to an attention-placebo treatment may, by virtue of the unscripted or minimally scripted nature of the encounter, see themselves as "sitting in a room and talking" or "letting off steam." Thus, the more organized and believable the intervention, the greater the press for a higher order "patient" identity.

But will this identity persist in the absence of specific and potent treatment? According to Vallacher and Wegner (1985), the more complex and time-consuming a set of actions, the more action flexibility (interchangeability of means) is required. If few or no problem-solving and/or self-regulatory skills are being learned or if rigid attitudes are not being actively challenged in therapy, the requisite enactive flexibility is unlikely to emerge—and the would-be "patient" is apt to move to a lower level of identification and ultimately abandon the therapeutic goal.

Although we could describe other short-acting change mechanisms that accompany formal interventions more than placebo treatments, the point is sufficiently made. Short-term improvement, especially when judged in relation to nothing (or nothing special), isn't very clinically convincing.

Disciplinary Interest in Treatment Durability

Some readers may now be asking, "Why are you railing against short-term, placebo-driven improvements and an obviously imperfect outcome research literature (in which credible control conditions are difficult to enact because of constraints like time and money) when most psychotherapeutic systems place a premium on the achievement of long-lasting cures?"

We acknowledge that what most therapists do in their treatment sessions may not be adequately represented by the typical psychotherapy outcome study. However, *because most practicing therapists do not routinely conduct systematic follow-up evaluations of their own patients, and therefore can accrue no direct evidence of their personal effectiveness,* they must rely on the admittedly constrained and artificial research to lend credence to their expectations that treatment works and that its effects endure. Assuming that the question of psychotherapy's effectiveness relative to a control group is open to skeptics, we can at least credit clinical professionals with caring about and documenting the durability or temporal robustness of their interventions. As we show next, concern with treatment lastingness certainly exists—but it varies across therapeutic schools and is hardly overwhelming in any absolute sense.

To determine the extent of interest in extended outcomes among contemporary psychotherapy researchers, we went not to scholarly pronouncements from the major schools but to the published literature of the last 7 to 10 years as indexed in three computerized databases: PsycINFO (from 1989 to June 1998), Medline Express (1991 to June 1998) and Dissertation Abstracts (1992 to June 1998). Although it is clear that methodological strides have been made since the time of Eysenck's (1952) critique, at this point we sought not to appraise the quality of the research but merely to count it.

Consequently, a search was conducted of the various databases, using the keywords *treatment* and *disorder* and then the convergence of these two words. The next step was the inclusion into the word search of the following terms defining seven active interventive modalities: *psychoanalytic, cognitive, behavioral, cognitive-behavioral, family therapy, interpersonal,* and *narrative-constructivist.* The final step was to identify the number of studies associated with each modality of treatment that focused on the question of durability. We accomplished this by searching for the words *maintenance, follow-up, generalization,* or *relapse prevention* appearing in concert with each of the seven treatment types.

As shown in Table 8.1, genuine concern for the durability of treatment is reflected in the publication of 7,618 studies out of a total of 67,314 (see the row marked TX + D, and sum the number of studies under Maintenance, Follow-up, Generalization, and Relapse Prevention). However, when indexed by the seven schools of treatment, the relative focus on long-term outcomes did not fare as well. Although we cannot accurately characterize the types of treatment modalities used in the almost 50,000 studies that could *not* be matched to any of the seven selected schools (at least by virtue of key words appearing in their titles and abstracts), we nonetheless discover that for the seven identified brands of formal therapy, interest in maintenance, follow-up, generalization, and relapse prevention was generally in the 0% to 10% range during the period covered in our search. (Readers should also consult the modality-specific chapters in this volume to learn how advocates from a wider assortment of treatment systems conceptualize the durability question.)

Clearly, the relative neglect of durability issues appears to be at variance with the clinical rhetoric associated with each of the schools of therapy sampled, all of which claim that successful treatment should involve not simply the removal of symptoms but also a systematic and robust restructuring of clients' styles or habits of personal and social functioning.

Illustratively, classical and contemporary psychoanalytic viewpoints are well known for their concern with the alteration of complex intrapsychic structures (emphasizing not only the "self" system but the structure of symbolized interpersonal relationships as well). Dealing with misdirected defensiveness; conflict and compromise; and misguided efforts at thought, feeling, and behavior control loom larger as therapeutic objectives within contemporary refinements of Freudian theory than do efforts at taming the id or relieving intrapsychic tension. Similarly, cog-

TABLE 8.1 Word Search of the PsycINFO Database for the Time Period 1989–May 1998, Medline Express 1991–June 1998, and Dissertation Abstracts 1992–May 1998

Keyword	Total	Maintenance	Follow-up	Generalization	Relapse Prevention
Treatment (TX)	511,663				
Disorder* (D)	259,802				
TX + D	67,314	2,036	4,943	236	403
		(.03)	(.07)	(.00)	(.01)
Psychoanalytic	1,109	17	53	2	6
+ TX + D		(.02)	(.05)	(.00)	(.01)
Cognitive	6,332	242	642	60	134
+ TX + D		(.04)	(.10)	(.01)	(.02)
Behavioral	6,575	302	639	80	131
+ TX + D		(.05)	(.10)	(.01)	(.02)
Cognitive-Behavioral	1,111	80	180	24	61
+ TX + D		(.07)	(.16)	(.02)	(.05)
Family Therapy	988	48	5	15	24
+ TX + D		(.05)	(.01)	(.02)	(.03)
Interpersonal	1,380	79	111	10	20
		(.06)	(.08)	(.01)	(.01)
Narrative/Constructivist	106	13	21	2	0
+ TX + D		(.12)	(.19)	(.02)	(.00)

Values enclosed in parentheses represent the percentage of concern for treatment durability. Disorder* refers to any of the following range of disorders: adjustment, adolescent, affective, anxiety, attention-deficit, behavior, bipolar, cognitive, conduct; depressive, dissociative, eating, emotional, mental, mood, obsessive-compulsive, panic, personality, posttraumatic, phobic, psychiatric, psychotic, schizophrenic, sexual, somatic, sleeping, substance, or traumatic stress.

nitive therapies seek to alter long-standing attitudes, beliefs, schemas, and/or expectancies thought to underlie maladaptive action and emotion and to train specific skills (e.g., social, problem-solving, and emotion management skills) that contribute to the development and maintenance of DSM symptoms. Behavioral interventionists, although focused on the alteration of specific symptoms, are strongly committed, as a result of their learning-theory background, to demonstrating that pathologic patterns have been permanently extinguished and that newly acquired, adaptive responses are resistant to extinction. Among the indicators of robustness are response maintenance over time and settings and transfer of training. Because behaviorists have sought to teach (or "program") extended skills acquisition, they clearly are invested in the evaluation of long-term effects.

Cognitive-behaviorists, for their part, share the concern for durability of treatment influences expressed by their cognitive and behavioral forebears, and moreover they have pioneered the use

of *relapse prevention* technologies especially designed to anticipate and forestall expectable setbacks in therapeutic progress (e.g., Daley, 1989; Eldridge, 1998; Marlatt & Gordon, 1985; Wanigaratne, Wallace, Pullin, Keaney, & Farmer, 1990; Wilson, 1992). Although family therapy can be undertaken from within psychoanalytic, behavioral, experiential, and other guiding philosophies, it generally has been associated with a general systems worldview, within which family dynamics and complex patterns of communication assume central importance. Solving a particular problem within a family may be the immediate task, but restructuring the working relations among family members is the ultimate goal. In such a framework, long-range change and stabilization is as important as any short-term strategic accommodations family members might make. Interpersonal therapies as applied to individual patients (in contrast to families as patients) likewise focus on "problems in living" brought about by dysfunctional communication patterns and the need to remediate the patient's self-defeating "styles" of relating to others. If what occurs in the therapy room fails to generalize to real-world interaction patterns, nothing meaningful has happened. An ecological (social-environmental) framework by definition concerns itself with time-sensitive, as well as with place-sensitive, changes. Finally, narrative-constructive approaches to treatment reflect a philosophy of change that is inimical to the linear, reactive, product-focused, circumscribed, and "objectivist" nature of the "aberrant states of functioning" tradition. In tune with the goal systems model discussed in this chapter, narrative-constructivist therapists are relatively unconcerned with eliminating defects or symptoms, focusing instead on facilitating long-term personal development (i.e., supporting a meaningful trajectory toward the future) by helping people to rewrite their life stories (Neimeyer, 1993; see also Chapter 16 in this volume). Clearly, one critical test of the adequacy of narrative repair, or "rebiographing," is whether it facilitates the emergence of a coherent and durable (albeit not necessarily permanent or fixed) script revision.

In short, we feel confident that given the central role of durability of change in their theories, researchers working within each of the seven major therapeutic schools should have displayed strong(er) commitments to examining treatment lastingness. That psychoanalytic researchers showed no interest in generalization or relapse prevention is not surprising, as these constructs are most compatible with behavioral and cognitive-behavioral theorizing. That narrative-constructivists (the newest formal school) have published the least amount of research also was not surprising; but their proportional interest in follow-up (19%) was heartening. Nonetheless, the overall trends seem to reveal comparatively little effort on the part of contemporary clinical scientists to systematically appraise the durability of their interventive methods.

It is possible, however, that the general lack of concern over durability of therapeutic effects among those psychotherapy proponents who should be concerned stems from the nature of the clinical problems being treated within the major schools. If a significant proportion of effort is being focused on rather self-limiting but cyclical problems (e.g., acute depression, situational anxiety, identity issues, and marital strain), then clinicians and researchers might well expect both short-term success and inevitable recurrence of similar difficulties (rather than a return of former

symptoms). Such a pattern might justify a relatively immediate focus of research attention. But what about chronic problems that are known to be difficult to treat, as well as relapse-prone? Surely, a stricter temporal standard of evaluation would be applied to these problems. To assess whether problems known to be habitual and resistant to change, such as addiction or substance abuse, were more apt to be examined for maintenance, follow-up, generalization, and relapse prevention, we conducted PsychINFO and Medline searches, using the key words *addiction, substance abuse,* and *treatment* and the names of six major therapeutic schools. As can be seen in Table 8.2, the 0% to 10% empirical interest figures are maintained, with the exception of the relatively high interest in relapse prevention among cognitive-behaviorists (24%).

Finally, an exclusive focus on psychology and psychiatry as the core disciplines charged with implementing therapeutic change may well underestimate the efforts of allied disciplines whose focus is also on severe, relapse-prone human problems. To partially investigate this possibility, a word search was conducted of the Criminal Justice Abstracts Database, keyed to the concepts of *criminal behavior, violence, aggression,* and *abuse.* When the key word *treatment* was added to the mix, followed by *maintenance, follow-up,* and the like, the results tended to mirror those previously reported (see Table 8.3).

Meta-analyses of Long-term Treatment Effects: A Brief Review

Although controlled appraisals of long-term therapy outcomes may represent only a small portion of contemporary research efforts, the research syntheses that are available nonetheless may be clear and encouraging. Indeed, if there is widespread empirical support for the persistence of treatment-specific (in contrast to nonspecific) effects across a variety of disorders and clinical modalities, this might explain the relatively scant interest among contemporary researchers in the costly enterprise of further delineating robustness (cf. Landman & Dawes, 1982; Nicholson & Berman, 1983). Accordingly, a number of meta-analytic studies were reviewed to help put the question of treatment durability into perspective. The reader should note that in evaluating the robustness question, at least two types of analyses are possible: (1) an examination of comparative or controlled effect sizes, in which a treatment is appraised from termination to follow-up relative to

TABLE 8.2 Word Search of the PsycINFO Database for the Time Period of 1989–June 1998 and Medline Express 1991–June 1998

Keyword	Total	Maintenance	Follow-up	Generalization	Relapse Prevention
Addiction or Substance	50,281				
Addiction or Substance + TX	14,191	1,010 (.07)	896 (.06)	19 (.00)	305 (.02)
Addiction or Substance + TX + Psychoanalytic	107	7 (.06)	2 (.02)	1 (.01)	5 (.05)
Addiction or Substance + TX + Cognitive	748	50 (.07)	64 (.09)	5 (.01)	90 (.12)
Addiction or-Substance + TX + Behavioral	1,285	106 (.08)	85 (.07)	7 (.01)	83 (.06)
Addiction or Substance + TX + Cognitive-Behavioral	157	6 (.04)	17 (.11)	3 (.02)	39 (.24)
Addiction or Substance + TX Family Therapy	291	20 (.07)	23 (.08)	0 (.00)	20 (.07)
Addiction or Substance + TX + Interpersonal	260	17 (.06)	13 (.05)	0 (.00)	11 (.04)
Addiction or Substance + TX + Narrative/ Constructivist	19	0 (.00)	0 (.00)	0 (.00)	0 (.00)

Values enclosed in parentheses represent the percentage of concern for treatment durability.

TABLE 8.3 Word Search of the Criminal Justice Database for the Time Period 1968–March 1998

Keyword	Total	Maintenance	Follow-up	Generalization	Relapse Prevention
Criminal Behavior	1,774				
Violent	4,137				
Aggressive or Aggression	1,684				
Abuse	5,725				
CB + V + Ag + Ab	11,814				
CB + V + Ag + Ab + TX	2,684	87 (.03)	172 (.06)	9 (.00)	240 (.09)
CB + V + Ag + Ab + Rehab	582	20 (.03)	24 (.04)	3 (.01)	76 (.13)

Values enclosed in parentheses represent the percentage of concern for treatment durability.

a comparison condition that is similarly appraised, and (2) an examination of raw within-group effect sizes for a given treatment (from termination to follow-up). No warrant is offered for the completeness of the following review, as meta-analytic studies are increasingly available (and any comprehensive review would be dated by the time it went to press). We did attempt a thorough search; and, we believe the research syntheses to be discussed are representative of those being published. In light of the thoroughness of Lambert and Bergin's (1994) review in the Bergin and Garfield (1994) handbook, we begin by briefly summarizing the work reported by these authors. Next, we discuss meta-analyses published since the appearance of that review.

First, to the broad question "Are patients who improve in therapy able to maintain their gains?" Lambert and Bergin's (1994) answer was generally affirmative, taking as their point of embarkation the carefully conducted and oft-cited meta-analysis of Nicholson and Berman (1983). Nicholson and Berman concluded that psychotherapeutic gains are indeed so durable that costly follow-up procedures should be employed very selectively. A closer examination of the pattern of findings, however, reveals treatment robustness occurring most prominently for so-called neurotic disorders (somatic disorders, depression, anxiety, phobias, lack of assertiveness, etc.), treated largely by behavioral or cognitive-behavioral methods and *indexed by follow-up periods averaging less than one year*. Other investigators examining the maintenance question in disorders known to be relapse-prone (such as obesity, substance abuse, high-risk sexual behavior, marital discord, and the like) have found the maintenance data unavailable, largely impressionistic, or disappointing (relative to the notable effect sizes and lack of differences from posttreatment to follow-up as reported by Nicholson and Berman).

When dealing with chronic, recurring psychological problems such as addiction and criminality, even normally potent behavioral and cognitive-behavioral methods have proven insufficient for the job; and this fact prompted the development of relapse prevention and maintenance enhancement techniques, all built on the recognition that principles of change initiation or response acquisition may be distinct from principles of generalization, transfer, and maintenance (Goldstein & Kanfer, 1979; Horner, Dunlap, & Koegel, 1988; Karoly, 1991b, 1995; Karoly & Kanfer, 1982; Marlatt & Gordon, 1985).

Through the use of such diverse *robustness-promoting* procedures as coping-skills training, planning, values clarification, self-monitoring, stimulus control, rational emotive therapy, self-statement modification, self-reward, schedule thinning, booster sessions, goals clarification, decisional balance sheets, conflict resolution, attributional retraining, relaxation and affect management procedures, assertiveness training, social skills enhancement, planned (programmed) relapses, self-efficacy training, social support recruitment, and a variety of other cognitive-behavioral mechanisms, the clinician can presumably work to ensure that newly acquired adaptive responding, particularly among treatment-resistant clients, persists into the foreseeable future. In contrast to the view that "many patients who undergo therapy achieve healthy adjustment for long periods of time," Lambert and Bergin (1994, p. 152) eventually report on a number of studies with disappointingly high rates of recidivism and then appear to endorse the view that for patients who enter various high-risk situations after treatment termination, some type of maintenance-enhancement/relapse-prevention training is required. One therefore leaves the Lambert and Bergin chapter with a sense that the question of long-term treatment effects has not yet been definitively addressed but that cautious optimism is warranted.

Among the important post–Lambert and Bergin analyses of the literature is Carroll's (1996) narrative (non-meta-analytic) review of relapse prevention efforts for addiction. Controlled trials of various relapse prevention programs for substance use disorders (the sort of persistent problems for which relapse prevention methods are ideally suited) were evaluated. For cigarette smoking, alcohol use, and drug-taking problems, relapse prevention procedures proved most clearly effective only when compared to nothing (no treatment). When compared to attention-placebo conditions, relapse prevention was superior in only 50% of the studies. And when compared to alternative treatments, relapse prevention appeared to be equivalent but not clearly superior. Although questions of statistical power and experimental-design adequacy limit the conclusions one can draw safely, Carroll's narrative review does little to bolster one's faith in relapse prevention as the technological solution to psychotherapy's durability problem. Similarly, a review by Laws (1995) of the theory and practice of relapse prevention suggests that although it may well be the treatment of choice for certain intractable problems (addictions and sexual misconduct), "its present evidentiary status vis-a-vis its main rivals (i.e., any kind of cognitive-behavioral therapy) is not particularly good" (p. 469). Finally, Dimeff and Marlatt (1998) have concluded that although relapse prevention does not literally inoculate those with addictive problems against the possibility of relapse, it may assist in reducing the harmful consequences of drug use reinitiation.

Meta-analytic reviews of comparative long-term treatment effects for modalities other than relapse prevention were gathered from published sources dating from the beginning of 1995 to the middle of 1998. Searching the PsycINFO database, Psychological Abstracts, and relevant articles and books yielded a small collection of research syntheses characterized by diversity in sample sizes, disorders, treatment methods, types of control or comparison conditions, and length of follow-up (ranging from 2 weeks to 20 years). What follows is a brief summary, in chronological order, of the meta-analytic literature reviews.

Anderson and Lambert (1995) subjected 26 studies to several meta-analyses in an attempt to resolve conflicting data on the effectiveness of short-term psychodynamic psychotherapies. Although no evidence could be found to demonstrate the superiority of short-term psychodynamic therapies over other treatments, the follow-up effects suggested that short-term treatments marginally outperformed alternative modalities when the follow-up occurred at a point six months or more after termination (but not before). However, before we can judge the meaning of the marginal durability advantage, or sleeper effect, for short-term dynamic treatments, three other meta-analytic findings reported by Anderson and Lambert warrant our attention. These analyses are particularly critical in light of the arguments presented earlier in this chapter. Recall our assertion that comparing a particular brand of treatment to wait-list controls (i.e., nothing) or to attention-placebo controls (nothing special) could be misleading and that comparisons to active, alternative treatments would afford a fairer test of both the specific potency (effectiveness) and the relative value (cost effectiveness) of a to-be validated form of psychotherapy. When Anderson and Lambert meta-analyzed the data from all three types of comparisons, the pattern was startling—but completely in accord with our skeptical predictions; namely, short-term psycho-

dynamic therapies achieved a moderate effect size (ES) of $d = .71$ relative to no treatment, a small ES of $d = .34$ relative to minimal treatments, and an insignificant ES of $d = -.02$ relative to alternative treatments. Thus, there is little reason to view short-term dynamic therapy as a *uniquely effective* clinical modality. The fact that it yields a slight advantage in the durability of effects may be its most notable accomplishment (although this could simply reflect the durability of its placebic elements).

Feske and Chambless (1995) conducted a meta-analytic comparison of 21 studies testing the effectiveness of cognitive-behavioral therapy (CBT; $n = 12$) and exposure-only treatments ($n = 9$) for social phobia, finding both modalities to be equally effective. Addressing follow-up, the reviewers also found no advantage for CBT over exposure in pretest-to-follow-up improvement. The authors did comment, however, on the variability in potency of cognitive-behavioral therapies across studies, a fact that weakens our ability to evaluate the short- and long-term comparative effectiveness of cognitive-behavioral treatments for social phobia.

Panic disorder was the focus of a meta-analytic investigation by Gould, Otto, and Pollack (1995) of 43 controlled studies. These investigators compared cognitive-behavioral therapy to pharmacotherapy and to a combination of both for the treatment of panic disorder. Cognitive treatments produced the highest effect sizes (ES = .68) relative to drug treatments (ES = .47) and to combination treatments and yielded fewer treatment dropouts. More important for our present purposes, using a minimum follow-up period of six months, Gould, Otto, and Pollack calculated the overall within-group (raw) effect size for 12 studies that had determinable follow-up periods. They explained their willingness to forego an examination of controlled effect sizes as follows:

> Conclusions about the long-term efficacy of panic interventions are limited by the difficulties in maintaining patients in control conditions over time. In many studies, subjects in control conditions are given a treatment intervention at posttreatment, thus making it impossible to derive a "controlled" effect size at follow-up. (p. 836)

They opted for raw effect sizes to allow more studies to be included in their meta-analysis. They therefore calculated effect sizes by subtracting the mean of a treatment group at posttreatment from the mean of the group at follow-up, divided by the posttreatment standard deviation. With such a formula, a negative effect size would indicate that subjects failed to maintain their posttreatment gains. The results were informative, albeit disappointing. The average ES for all studies was $-.17$. For drug treatments, the mean ES was $-.46$. Combined treatments yielded an ES of $-.07$. The most promising finding was that cognitive-behavioral groups yielded an ES of .06. Because of the small sample sizes, comparisons of these within-group effects yielded differences that were not statistically significant.

The final meta-analysis for 1995 is that of Hall (1995), who examined sexual offender recidivism through a meta-analysis of 12 treatment studies. A small overall effect was found for treatment relative to control conditions ($r = .12$). However, again the author of the meta-analysis found it necessary to comment on the variability in the data. Hall reported larger effect sizes in studies with higher base rates of recidivism and with follow-ups of longer than five years. One interpretation of these findings is that treatment works best for the most serious offenders and when longer posttreatment time periods are used. Yet Hall pointed out that sexual offenders continue to be at risk for recidivism for over 20 years and that less effective treatments may produce changes that wear off within 5 years. Although the number of studies included and the average effect size were both small, Hall noted with cautious optimism that the findings were "robust." That is, using the so-called file drawer method, Hall was able to calculate how many null studies would have to be discovered in researchers' file drawers to render nonsignificant the obtained p value for the overall effect. That fail-safe number was 88.

The immediate and extended effects of cognitive behavioral therapy were compared against pharmacological treatments for generalized anxiety disorder (GAD) in the first 1997 meta-analytic investigation (Gould, Otto, Pollack, & Yap, 1997). When inquiring, "Do treatments for GAD maintain their salutary effects over time?" the authors set a minimum criterion of six months for follow-up and discovered that only 6 of their original 35 studies could be examined. The raw (uncontrolled) effect size across 16 treatments was $-.10$. Interpreting this negative figure as not different from zero, the authors concluded that "reductions in anxiety were largely maintained at

follow-up" (p. 299). The durability findings for CBT were also good (ES = .05), but pharmacotherapy was not readily evaluated because of a paucity of follow-up data.

A second meta-analysis at this time examined the effects of cognitive-behavioral treatments for bulimia (Lewandowski, Gebing, Anthony, & O'Brien, 1997). In general, although the authors reported strong treatment effects (r's in the .60s) when both behavioral and attitudinal outcome measures were used, the follow-up effect sizes appeared to be less impressive. The overall follow-up effect size was $r = .27$, and both the measures used and the follow-up periods were quite variable.

Reinecke, Ryan, and DuBois (1998) examined cognitive-behavioral therapy for depression in adolescents. Using a modified effect size formula to correct for small sample bias, which is calculated so that negative scores indicate *superiority* of the treatment group over the controls, these authors reported, based on six studies, that the overall follow-up control comparison was $-.61$. Although this finding is impressive and robust (the fail-safe n to invalidate the follow-up finding is 62 null studies in the file drawer), the authors are nonetheless cautious in their claims. The average number of subjects per group was 20, and the majority of studies used dysphoric rather than clinically depressed adolescents. Furthermore, the effectiveness of cognitive-behavior therapy was usually contrasted to a wait-list or relaxation control condition "rather than with pharmacotherapy or another accepted form of psychotherapy" (p. 31).

The year 1998 also saw the publication of at least two reviews of recidivism in sexual offenders. Hanson and Bussiere (1998) examined evidence from 61 studies (far more than Hall's 1995 meta-analysis reported above) and discovered that although the overall rate of relapse was low (13.4% in an n of 23,393), subgroups of offenders recidivated at higher rates. In their analyses, the average follow-up period was four to five years. In contrast to Hall, Hanson and Bussiere were interested in identifying predictors of recidivism and differences among sexual and nonsexual violent offenders rather than evaluating the long-term effects of treatment per se. However, they addressed issues that relate to the overall theme of this chapter. First, they found that measures of subjective distress were unrelated to any type of recidivism. Echoing our view that symptoms are starting points (rather than end points or outcome indexes), the authors noted, "Subjective distress is a transient state, and no measure of highly changeable states would be expected to predict sexual offense recidivism years later" (p. 357). Second, the authors suggested that despite the fact that treatment effectiveness was not addressed directly, there was evidence to suggest that offenders who at least attend and cooperate with some formal program are less likely to relapse than those who drop out of treatment. Thus, treatment may serve a *monitoring function* if not a rehabilitative one.

VanLankveld (1998) conducted a meta-analysis of a dozen controlled studies of bibliotherapy for sexual dysfunction. Recall that we suggested earlier that bibliotherapy represents a reasonable standard of comparison to appraise not only the clinical effectiveness but also the cost effectiveness of various formal therapies. The present review revealed that at posttreatment the effect size was a respectable .68, although it eroded at follow-up. The possibility of combining bibliotherapy with short-term CBT has not yet been investigated, but it may offer a way of enhancing treatment durability while seeking to minimize costs.

Finally, Kibby, Tyc, and Mulhern (1998) conducted a meta-analysis of 42 studies involving psychological interventions for children and adolescents with varying medical conditions. They found that not only were psychological interventions effective at posttreatment (mean overall ES = 1.12), but also no significant decline in effect size was noted between termination and 6- and 12-month follow-up periods. Despite the existence of methodological problems, such as small sample sizes, a lack of random assignment to treatment groups, and high attrition rates, the findings are encouraging.

In sum, the relatively positive appraisals of the extended effects of psychotherapy that prompted Lambert and Bergin (1994) and Nicholson and Berman (1983) to recommend foregoing *short-term* (6-month) *follow-ups* seems reasonable in the case of certain disorders (like depression) and certain modalities (such as cognitive-behavioral treatments). However, the longer-term (1-, 2-, 5-, or 10-year) effectiveness for relapse-prone disorders as treated by therapies other than cognitive-behavioral is far from being unambiguously established. Our current review suggests that enduring outcomes that transcend the verbal or behavioral measurement of symptom frequency are by no means assured,

even when maintenance (relapse prevention) is specifically programmed. The glass is half empty.

Are Long-term Effects "Self"-regulated?

Again, the point can be made that even if the meta-analytic findings were more strongly indicative of impressive, widespread, and unambiguous treatment durability, an additional interpretive issue would remain: do treatment effects persist as a result of patients' empowerment or are they attributable to patients' dependence on the continued availability of powerful social contingencies or the temporary removal of external threats or challenges?

It is instructive to note that before the advent of today's cross-disciplinary optimism, a leading psychotherapy researcher (Strupp, 1982) asserted that of the many problems associated with evaluating therapy outcome, one of the most critical was the general neglect of the need to strengthen patients' goal-directedness:

> . . . to feel better about themselves, their relationships with others, and their behavior in general, patients must learn to make changes within themselves and in their environment . . . therapy is designed *not to impose change on the patient* but to create the conditions that allow change to occur within the patient. (p. 46; our emphasis)

In fact, more than a decade before Strupp's plea, cognitive-behavioral investigators, most notably Fred Kanfer and his colleagues (e.g., Kanfer & Karoly, 1972; Kanfer & Phillips, 1970), were affirming the decidedly nonbehavioristic view that *self-determined* and *self-initiated change* were the hallmarks of a meaningful therapeutic encounter. Moreover, the process of regulating or redirecting one's actions, thoughts, and emotions over time (changing one's lifestyle) was taken to be as important as instigating focal changes, usually reductions, in problematic behaviors, thoughts, or feelings per se (cf. Kanfer & Schefft, 1988; Karoly, 1995).

Nonetheless, several decades after Strupp's admonition and Kanfer's pioneering work, the field of psychotherapy not only seems to be preoccupied with techniques of change imposition but also has succumbed to the rather pernicious mind sets of immediacy, passivity, and conceptual precision. That is, current ways of thinking have directed the efforts of professionals toward rapid results, decontextualized problem formulations, and the technical correctness or recipe-driven nature of planned interventions. The notion of the patient as a dysfunctional or would-be self-regulator in errant pursuit of personal autonomy and valued goals and in need of new or better strategies for the promotion of extended self-directedness has found little room to thrive in a "health technology" environment. Most unfortunately, the null hypothesis that most forms of psychotherapy have no lasting impact on patients' self-regulatory capacity has been difficult to reject on the basis of contemporary outcome research.

For example, attempts to appraise self-regulation-centered therapies have been piece-meal (usually focusing on such subcomponents of the overall regulatory process as self-monitoring or self-administered rewards), cross-sectional, and time-limited insofar as the number and adequacy of follow-up periods are concerned (Karoly, 1995). Although the meta-analytic evaluative strategy may provide the best estimate of the clinical yield for the self-regulation domain, not many meta-analyses are currently available.

One of the earliest attempts to appraise a component of self-regulatory intervention was Dush, Hirt, and Schroeder's (1983) meta-analysis of self-statement modification. Sixty-nine studies yielding 221 comparisons were examined, with 54 of the comparisons of self-statement modification referring to placebo groups, 62 to wait-list controls, and 31 to assessment-only controls. The average ES was .74 when comparing self-statement modification to wait-list or assessment-only controls. Effect sizes were generally lower when self-statement modification was compared to placebo groups.

In light of our earlier discussion of the value of such "minimalist" comparisons as reported by Dush et al. (1983), it isn't clear that self-statement modification truly outperforms nonspecific factors. Moreover, Dush et al. noted wide variations in the potency of this approach across different disorders (with complex phobias yielding the best and psychotic symptoms yielding the poorest ESs). Therapist differences and differences in the format of treatment also affected effect sizes. As in meta-analyses being conducted in the late 1990s, however, this 1983-vintage report indicated that neither therapist experience nor duration of therapy bore any relation to overall therapeutic gain. Oddly, male therapists seemed to outperform females in the conduct of self-statement modification. Most problematic, from the standpoint of this chapter, is the lack of data

on the degree to which patients independently initiated self-statement modification outside the therapeutic context and the absence of information on its long-term use.

A more recent meta-analysis by Febbraro and Clum (1998) sought to examine the effectiveness of several hypothesized components of self-regulation, that is, self-monitoring, self-evaluation, and self-reinforcement (cf. Kanfer & Karoly, 1972), in the treatment of habit disturbances, anxiety, depression, and health-related problems in adults. In view of the fact that these components could be employed as supportive or adjunctive elements in almost any form of clinical intervention, the results of this meta-analysis could bear on the key question of whether therapies have the potential to build clients' self-directedness. Unfortunately, the Febbraro and Clum meta-analysis, despite its attempt to relate effectiveness to self-regulation theory, suffered as a result of methodological weaknesses in the extant literature, including: (1) the prevalence of minimally informative control conditions (wait-list, no treatment, and minimal contact); (2) the limited follow-up periods used in the available research (ranging from one to eight *weeks*); (3) variability within the self-regulatory interventions used; and (4) the small number of studies available to evaluate persistence (stability) of effects for self-regulatory interventions. The overall effect size for combinations of self-regulatory components compared to no intervention was a modest $d = .25$. Furthermore, the authors concluded that "it is unclear at this time whether subjects using self-regulatory interventions can maintain their treatment gains" (p. 158).

In short, 15 years after Dush, Hirt, and Schroeder (1983) failed to clearly establish that self-regulation training of a specific sort could produce self-initiated and lasting change, Febbraro and Clum (1998) generally failed to support (or even adequately test) the hypothesis that training in key elements of self-regulation could produce self-regulated behavioral change in adults.

It appears that humans, when characterized as complex systems embedded in complex systems and evolving in a nonlinear fashion over time, simply cannot be assumed to be amenable to "regularized," semipermanent solutions such as the context-specific emission of a learned "coping strategy," the strategic self-reinforcement of a desired behavior, or the neuromodulating action of a prescribed psychoactive drug taken in response to a particular emotionally arousing event. In an organizing model that does not assume perfect rationality or centralized control and that gives equal weight to change and stability, even failure-prone movement toward multiple and distant peaks of adaptive success (generalized goal directedness) may be a more useful criterion of "adjustment" than any single, all-or-none strategic (behavioral) accommodation or any structural (attitudinal) transformation. And if the attainment of a steady state of adjustment (i.e., a "normal" state of functioning) is an unnatural and misguided objective, it may well be time to abandon the metaphors of the past and adopt a more dynamical approach to life-span conceptions of person-environment transactions (Barton, 1994; Eidelson, 1997; Mahoney, 1991).

Summary

This chapter has presented a series of self-correcting assertions about the effectiveness of psychotherapy. First, the meta-analytic findings that have been so widely used as a basis for proclaiming that many forms of psychotherapy have yielded measurable effects when compared against the passage of time, professional attention, and/or other credible "control" interventions were reinterpreted in light of the contention that nonspecific change elements are the main success-inducing ingredients. However, even if this assertion were proven wrong (and therapy-specific factors were credited with producing statistically and clinically significant effect sizes), an added problem is that the effects are usually short term. We therefore asserted that long-range outcomes have not been sufficiently addressed and that the extant literature on such effects remains inconclusive. Consequently, treatment gains for complex and chronic problems generally cannot be expected to persist. In view of this interpretation, the field's apparent unwillingness to invest in empirical assessments of long-range outcomes can be characterized as both short-sighted and self-serving. However, once again, if these assertions were proven incorrect (and long-term maintenance were shown to be the rule rather than the exception), there is yet another interpretive obstacle: the robust effects have not been shown to be self-regulated. And finally, even if durable treatment effects could be unequivocally attributed to the skills, motives, and efforts of patients, the majority of the findings reflect only symptomatic change—and the premises underlying

most of the extant models of human psychopathology and psychotherapy do not support the persistence of a symptom-free state as a truly meaningful criterion of mental health.

We conclude that if a genuine science of therapeutic movement is ever to become a reality, the 21st century must see greater attention to the therapy-assisted instantiation of what psychodynamicists have labeled *character development*, of what Adlerians call *lifestyle modification*, of what behaviorists refer to as *an adaptive social repertoire*, of what cognitivists call *flexible schemas*, of what humanists mean when they specify a *fully functioning person*, of what narrative constructionists term *life story repair*, and of what has in this chapter been referred to as *goal-guided self-regulation*.

References

Anderson, E. M., & Lambert, M. J. (1995). Short-term dynamically oriented psychotherapy: A review and meta-analysis. *Clinical Psychology Review, 15*, 503–514.

Bandura, A. (1986). *Social foundations of thought and action: A social-cognitive theory*. Upper Saddle River, NJ: Prentice Hall.

Bandura, A. (1997). *Self-efficacy: The exercise of control*. New York: Freeman.

Barker, S. L., Funk, S. C., & Houston, B. K. (1988). Psychological treatment versus nonspecific factors: A meta-analysis of conditions that engender comparable expectations for improvement. *Clinical Psychology Review, 8*, 579–594.

Barone, D. F., Maddox, J. E., & Snyder, C. R. (1997). *Social cognitive psychology: History and current domains*. New York: Plenum.

Barton, S. (1994). Chaos, self-organization, and psychology. *American Psychologist, 49*, 5–14.

Baumeister, R. F. (1997). Esteem threat, self-regulatory breakdown, and emotional distress as factors in self-defeating behavior. *Review of General Psychology, 1*, 145–174.

Baumeister, R. F., Heatherton, T. F., & Tice, D. M. (1994). *Losing control*. San Diego, CA: Academic Press.

Bergin, A. E., & Garfield, S. L. (Eds.). (1994). *Handbook of psychotherapy and behavior change* (4th ed.). New York: Wiley.

Bergner, R. M. (1997). What is psychopathology? And so what? *Clinical Psychology: Science and Practice, 4*, 235–248.

Bogdan, R. J. (1994). *Grounds for cognition: How goal-guided behavior shapes the mind*. Hillsdale, NJ: Erlbaum.

Brehm, S. S., & McAllister, D. A. (1980). A social psychological perspective on the maintenance of therapeutic change. In P. Karoly & J. J. Steffen (Eds.), *Improving the long-term effects of psychotherapy* (pp. 381–406). New York: Gardner.

Cantor, N. (1990). From thought to behavior: "Having" and "doing" in the study of personality and cognition. *American Psychologist, 45*, 735–750.

Cantor, N. (1994). Life task problem solving: Situational affordances and personal needs. *Personality and Social Psychology Bulletin, 20*, 235–243.

Cantor, N., & Kihlstrom, J. F. (1987). *Personality and social intelligence.* Upper Saddle River, NJ: Prentice Hall.

Cantor, N., & Zirkel, S. (1990). Personality, cognition, and purposive behavior. In L. A. Pervin (Ed.), *Handbook of personality theory and research* (pp. 135–164). New York: Guilford.

Carroll, K. M. (1996). Relapse prevention as a psychosocial treatment: A review of controlled clinical trials. *Experimental and Clinical Psychopharmacology, 4*, 46–54.

Carver, C. S., & Baird, E. (1998). The American dream revisited: Is it *what* you want or *why* you want it that matters? *Psychological Science, 9*, 289–292.

Carver, C. S., & Scheier, M. F. (1990). Principles of self-regulation: Action and emotion. In E. T. Higgins & R. M. Sorrentino (Eds.), *Handbook of motivation and cognition* (Vol. 2, pp. 3–52). New York: Guilford.

Champion, L. A., & Power, M. J. (1995). Social and cognitive approaches to depression: Towards a new synthesis. *British Journal of Clinical Psychology, 34*, 485–503.

Cooper, P. J., Coker, S., & Fleming, C. (1995). An evaluation of the efficacy of cognitive-behavioral self-help for bulimia nervosa. *Journal of Psycho-somatic Research, 40*, 281–287.

Daley, D. C. (1989). *Relapse prevention: Treatment alternatives and counseling aids.* Blue Ridge Summit, PA: TAB Books.

Depue, R. A., & Zald, D. H. (1993). Biological and environmental processes in nonpsychotic psychopathology: A neurobehavioral perspective. In C. G. Costello (Ed.), *Basic issues in psychopathology* (pp. 127–237). New York: Guilford.

Dimeff, L. A., & Marlatt, G. A. (1998). Preventing relapse and maintaining change in addictive behaviors. *Clinical Psychology: Science and Practice, 5*, 513–525.

Dush, D. M., Hirt, M. L., & Schroeder, H. (1983). Self-statement modification with adults: A meta-analysis. *Psychological Bulletin, 94*, 408–422.

Eidelson, R. J. (1997). Complex adaptive systems in the behavioral and social sciences. *Review of General Psychology, 1*, 42–71.

Eldridge, H. (1998). *Therapist guide for maintaining change: Relapse prevention for adult male perpetrators of child sexual abuse.* Thousand Oaks, CA: Sage.

Emmons, R. A. (1996). Striving and feeling: Personal goals and subjective well-being. In P. M. Gollwitzer & J. A. Bargh (Eds.), *The psychology of action: Linking cognition and motivation to behavior* (pp. 313–337). New York: Guilford.

Eyberg, S. M., Edwards, D., Boggs, S. R., & Foote, R. (1998). Maintaining the treatment effects of parent training: The role of booster sessions and other maintenance strategies. *Clinical Psychology: Science and Practice, 5*, 544–554.

Eysenck, H. J. (1952). The effects of psychotherapy: An evaluation. *Journal of Consulting Psychology, 16*, 319–324.

Febbraro, G. A. R., & Clum, G. A. (1998). Meta-analytic investigation of the effectiveness of self-regulatory components in the treatment of adult problem behaviors. *Clinical Psychology Review, 18*, 143–161.

Feske, U., & Chambless, D. L. (1995). Cognitive behavioral versus exposure only treatment for social phobia: A meta-analysis. *Behavior Therapy, 26*, 695–720.

Festinger, L. (1957). *A theory of cognitive dissonance.* Stanford, CA: Stanford University Press.

Ford, M. E. (1992). *Motivating humans: Goals, emotions, and agency beliefs.* Newbury Park, CA: Sage.

Frank, J. D. (1973). *Persuasion and healing.* Baltimore: Johns Hopkins University Press.

Frank, J. D. (1982). Therapeutic components shared by all psychotherapies. In J. H. Harvey & M. M. Parks (Eds.), *Psychotherapy research and behavior change: The master lecture series* (Vol. 1, pp. 9–37). Washington, DC: American Psychological Association.

Gold, J. R. (1996). *Key concepts in psychotherapy integration.* New York: Plenum.

Goldfried, M. R. (1995). *From cognitive-behavior therapy to psychotherapy integration.* New York: Springer.

Goldstein, A. P. (1962). *Therapist-patient expectancies in psychotherapy.* New York: Macmillan.

Goldstein, A. P., & Kanfer, F. H. (Eds.). (1979). *Maximizing treatment gains: Transfer enhancement in psychotherapy.* New York: Academic Press.

Goldstein, H. (1984). *Social learning and change: A cognitive approach to human services.* New York: Tavistock/Methuen.

Gould, R., & Clum, G. (1993). A meta-analysis of self-help treatment approaches. *Clinical Psychology Review, 13*, 169–186.

Gould, R., Otto, M. W., & Pollack, M. (1995). A meta-analysis of treatment outcome for panic disorder. *Clinical Psychology Review, 15*, 819–844.

Gould, R., Otto, M. W., Pollack, M., & Yap, L. (1997). Cognitive behavioral and pharmacological treatment of generalized anxiety disorder: A preliminary meta-analysis. *Behavior Therapy, 28*, 285–305.

Hall, G. C. N. (1995). Sexual offender recidivism revisited: A meta-analysis of recent treatment studies. *Journal of Consulting and Clinical Psychology, 66,* 702–708.

Hanson, R. K., & Bussiere, M. T. (1998). Predicting relapse: A meta-analysis of sexual offender recidivism studies. *Journal of Consulting and Clinical Psychology, 66,* 348–362.

Hartmann, A., Schulgen, G., Olschewski, M., & Herzog, T. (1997). Modeling psychotherapy outcome as event in time: An application of multistate analysis. *Journal of Consulting and Clinical Psychology, 65,* 262–268.

Hayes, S. C., Barlow, D. H., & Nelson-Gray, R. O. (1999). *The scientist-practitioner: Research and accountability in the age of managed care.* Boston: Allyn & Bacon.

Haynes, S. N. (1992). *Models of causality in psychopathology.* New York: Macmillan.

Higginbotham, H. N., West, S. G., & Forsyth, D. R. (1988). *Psychotherapy and behavior change: Social, cultural, and methodological perspectives.* New York: Pergamon.

Hollon, S. D., & Cobb, R. (1993). Relapse and recurrence in psychopathological disorders. In C. G. Costello (Ed.), *Basic issues in psychopathology* (pp. 377–402). New York: Guilford.

Horner, R. H., Dunlap, G., & Koegel, R. L. (Eds.). (1988). *Generalization and maintenance: Lifestyle changes in applied settings.* Baltimore: Paul H. Brookes.

Horowitz, M. J. (1998). *Cognitive psychodynamics: From conflict to character.* New York: Wiley.

Kanfer, F. H., & Goldstein, A. P. (1991). Introduction. In F. H. Kanfer & A. P. Goldstein (Eds.), *Helping people change* (4th ed.). New York: Pergamon.

Kanfer, F. H., & Karoly, P. (1972). Self-control: A behavioristic excursion into the lion's den. *Behavior Therapy, 3,* 398–416.

Kanfer, F. H., & Phillips, J. S. (1970). *Learning foundations of behavior therapy.* New York: Wiley.

Kanfer, F. H., & Schefft, B. K. (1988). *Guiding the process of therapeutic change.* Champaign, IL: Research Press.

Karoly, P. (1980). Person variables in therapeutic change and development. In P. Karoly & J. J. Steffen (Eds.), *Improving the long-term effects of psychotherapy* (pp. 195–261). New York: Gardner.

Karoly, P. (1991a). Goal systems and health outcomes across the life span: A proposal. In H. Schroeder (Ed.), *New directions in health psychology: Assessment* (pp. 65–93). Bristol, PA: Hemisphere.

Karoly, P. (1991b). On the robustness and flexibility of clinical interventions. In C. R. Snyder & D. R. Forsyth (Eds.), *Handbook of social and clinical psychology* (pp. 717–736). New York: Pergamon.

Karoly, P. (1993a). Goal systems: An organizing framework for clinical assessment and treatment planning. *Psychological Assessment, 5,* 273–280.

Karoly, P. (1993b). Mechanisms of self-regulation: A systems view. *Annual Review of Psychology, 44,* 23–52.

Karoly, P. (1995). Self-control theory. In W. O'Donohue & L. Krasner (Eds.), *Theories of behavior therapy: Exploring behavior change* (pp. 259–285). Washington, DC: American Psychological Association.

Karoly, P. (1996). *A self-regulatory/goal systems perspective on directional change and resistance to change in psychotherapy: Strengthening the motivational face of clinical science.* Unpublished manuscript, Arizona State University, Tempe.

Karoly, P. (1998, May). *Intentional mindsets: Goal framing in seven dimensions.* Address presented at the 10th Annual Convention of the American Psychological Society, Washington, DC.

Karoly, P., & Kanfer, F. H. (Eds.). (1982). *Self-management and behavior change: From theory to practice.* New York: Pergamon.

Karoly, P., & Ruehlman, L. S. (1995). Goal cognition and its clinical implications: Development and preliminary validation of four motivational assessment instruments. *Assessment, 2,* 113–129.

Kibby, M. Y., Tyc, V. L., & Mulhern, R. K. (1998). Effectiveness of psychological intervention for children and adolescents with chronic medical illness: A meta-analysis. *Clinical Psychology Review, 18,* 103–117.

Klar, Y., Fisher, J. D., Chinsky, J. M., & Nadler, A. (Eds.). (1992). *Self change: Social psychological and clinical perspectives.* New York: Springer-Verlag.

Kuhl, J. (1992). A theory of self-regulation: Action versus state orientation, self-discrimination, and some applications. *Applied Psychology: An International Review, 41,* 95–173.

Lambert, M. J., & Bergin, A. E. (1994). The effectiveness of psychotherapy. In A. E. Bergin & S. L. Garfield (Eds.), *Handbook of psychotherapy and behavior change* (pp. 143–189). New York: Wiley.

Landman, J. T., & Dawes, R. M. (1982). Psychotherapy outcome: Smith and Glass's conclusions stand up under scrutiny. *American Psychologist, 37,* 504–516.

Laws, D. R. (1995). A theory of relapse prevention. In W. O'Donohue & L. Krasner (Eds.), *Theories of behavior therapy* (pp. 445–473). Washington, DC: American Psychological Association.

Lecci, L., Karoly, P., Ruehlman, L. S., & Lanyon, R. I. (1996). Goal-relevant dimensions of hypochondriacal tendencies and their relation to symptom manifestation and psychological distress. *Journal of Abnormal Psychology, 105,* 42–52.

Lewandowski, L. M., Gebing, T. A., Anthony, J. L., & O'Brien, W. H. (1997). Meta-analysis of cognitive-behavioral treatment studies for bulimia. *Clinical Psychology Review, 17,* 703–718.

Lewicka, M. (1998). Confirmation bias: Cognitive error or adaptive strategy of action control? In M. Kofta, G. Weary, & G. Sedek (Eds.), *Personal* control in action: Cognitive and motivational mechanisms* (pp. 233–258). New York: Plenum.

Lilienfeld, S. O., & Marino, L. (1995). Mental disorder as a Roschian concept: A critique of Wakefield's "harmful dysfunction" analysis. *Journal of Abnormal Psychology, 104,* 411–420.

Linden, W., & Wen, F. K. (1990). Therapy outcome research, health care policy, and the continuing lack of accumulated knowledge. *Professional Psychology, 21,* 482–488.

Lipsey, M. W., & Wilson, D. B. (1993). The efficacy of psychological, educational, and behavioral treatment: Confirmation from meta-analysis. *American Psychologist, 48,* 1181–1209.

Little, B. R. (1993). Personal projects and the distributed self: Aspects of a conative psychology. In J. Suls (Ed.), *Psychological perspectives on the self: The self in social perspective* (pp. 157–185). Hillsdale, NJ: Erlbaum.

Locke, E. A., & Latham, G. P. (1990). *A theory of goal-setting and task performance.* Upper Saddle River, NJ: Prentice Hall.

Lord, C. G., Ross, L., & Lepper, M. R. (1979). Biased assimilation and attitude polarization: The effects of prior theories on subsequently considered evidence. *Journal of Personality and Social Psychology, 37,* 2098–2109.

Mahoney, M. J. (1991). *Human change processes.* New York: Basic Books.

Marlatt, G. A., & Gordon, J. R. (1985). *Relapse prevention: Maintenance strategies in the treatment of addictive behaviors.* New York: Guilford.

Martin, J., & Sugerman, J. (1997). The social-cognitive construction of psychotherapeutic change: Bridging social constructionism and cognitive constructionism. *Review of General Psychology, 1,* 375–388.

McGregor, I., & Little, B. R. (1998). Personal projects, happiness, and meaning: On doing well and being yourself. *Journal of Personality and Social Psychology, 74,* 494–512.

Myers, D. G. (1999). *Social psychology* (6th ed.). New York: McGraw-Hill.

Nathan, P. E., & Gorman, J. M. (Eds.). (1998). *A guide to treatments that work.* New York: Oxford University Press.

Neimeyer, R. A. (1993). An appraisal of constructivist psychotherapies. *Journal of Consulting and Clinical Psychology, 61,* 221–234.

Nicholson, R. A., & Berman, J. S. (1983). Is follow-up necessary in evaluating psychotherapy? *Psychological Bulletin, 93,* 261–278.

Park, C. L., & Folkman, S. (1997). Meaning in the context of stress and coping. *Review of General Psychology, 1,* 115–144.

Parloff, M. B. (1986). Placebo controls in psychotherapy research: A sine qua non or a placebo for research problems? *Journal of Consulting and Clinical Psychology, 54,* 79–87.

Patterson, C. H., & Hidore, S. C. (1997). *Successful psychotherapy: A caring loving relationship.* Northvale, NJ: Jason Aronson.

Pervin, L. A. (1994). A critical analysis of current trait theory. *Psychological Inquiry, 5,* 103–113.

Power, M., & Dalgleish, T. (1997). *Cognition and emotion: From order to disorder.* Hove, Eng.: Psychology Press.

Prioleau, L., Murdock, M., & Brody, N. (1983). An analysis of psychotherapy versus placebo studies. *Behavioral and Brain Sciences, 6,* 275–285.

Reinecke, M. A., Ryan, N. E., & DuBois, D. L. (1998). Cognitive-behavioral therapy of depression and depressive symptom during adolescence: A review and meta-analysis. *Journal of the American Academy of Child and Adolescent Psychiatry, 37,* 26–34.

Ryan, R. M., Sheldon, K. M., Kasser, T., & Deci, E. L. (1996). All goals are not created equal: An organismic perspective on the nature of goals and their regulation. In P. M. Gollwitzer & J. A. Bargh (Eds.), *The psychology of action: Linking cognition and motivation to behavior* (pp. 7–26). New York: Guilford.

Rychlak, J. F. (1998). How Boulder biases have limited possible theoretical contributions of psychotherapy. *Clinical Psychology: Science and Practice, 5,* 233–241.

Sechrest, L., McKnight, P., & McKnight, K. (1996). Calibration of measures for psychotherapy outcome studies. *American Psychologist, 51,* 1065–1071.

Smith, M. L., & Glass, G. V. (1977). Meta-analysis of psychotherapy outcome studies. *American Psychologist, 32,* 752–760.

Smith, M. L., Glass, G. V., & Miller, T. I. (1980). *The benefits of psychotherapy.* Baltimore: Johns Hopkins University Press.

Sternberg, R. J. (1998). A balance theory of wisdom. *Review of General Psychology, 2,* 347–365.

Strauman, T. J. (1989). Self-discrepancies in clinical depression and social phobia: Cognitive structures that underlie emotional disorders? *Journal of Abnormal Psychology, 98,* 14–22.

Strupp, H. H. (1982). The outcome problem in psychotherapy: Contemporary perspectives. In J. H. Harvey & M. M. Parks (Eds.), *Psychotherapy research and behavior change: The master lecture series* (Vol. 1, pp. 43–71). Washington, DC: American Psychological Association.

Teasdale, J. D., & Barnard, P. J. (1993). *Affect, cognition, and change: Re-modeling depressive thought.* Hove, Eng.: Erlbaum.

Vallacher, R. R., & Wegner, D. M. (1985). *A theory of action identification.* Hillsdale, NJ: Erlbaum.

Van Hook, E., & Higgins, E. T. (1988). Self-related problems beyond the self-concept: Motivational consequences of discrepant self-guides. *Journal of Personality and Social Psychology, 55,* 625–633.

vanLankveld, J. J. D. M. (1998). Bibliotherapy in the treatment of sexual dysfunctions: A meta-analysis. *Journal of Consulting and Clinical Psychology, 66,* 702–708.

Wakefield, J. C. (1992). Disorder as harmful dysfunction: A conceptual critique of DSM-III-R's definition of mental disorder. *Psychological Review, 99,* 232–247.

Wanigaratne, S., Wallace, W., Pullin, J., Keaney, F., & Farmer, R. (1990). *Relapse prevention for addictive disorders.* Oxford: Blackwell.

Weinberger, J. (1995). Common factors aren't so common: The common factors dilemma. *Clinical Psychology: Science and Practice, 2,* 45–69.

Weiner, H. (1989). The dynamics of the organism: Implications of recent biological thought for psychosomatic theory and research. *Psychosomatic Medicine, 51,* 608–635.

Wells, A., & Matthews, G. (1994). *Attention and emotion: A clinical perspective.* Hove, Eng.: Erlbaum.

Wilson, P. H. (1992). *Principles and practice of relapse prevention.* New York: Guilford.

CHAPTER 9

ENHANCING PERCEIVED CONTROL IN PSYCHOTHERAPY

SUZANNE C. THOMPSON AND MICHELLE WIERSON
Pomona College

Those who have a strong sense of personal control judge that they can obtain desired outcomes and avoid misfortunes through their own actions. In contrast, those with low perceptions of control believe that their fortunes cannot be influenced through personal action; chance, fate, or powerful others determine their life's course. These judgments are pervasive throughout our lives—both the day-to-day routine and the more momentous drama—as we take stock of our future prospects, assess our self-worth, decide which goals to pursue and which to abandon, and contemplate whether it will be worthwhile to put our energies into trying to change ourselves or our lives.

Beliefs about controllability are some of the most widely used and influential concepts in psychology. Several major theories, including learned helplessness (Seligman, 1972), social cognitive theory (Bandura, 1997), cognitive adaptation (Taylor, 1983), social learning theory (Rotter, 1966), and personal causation theory (deCharms, 1968), assign a central role to perceptions of control in emotional well-being and adaptive performance. Numerous research studies have confirmed the benefits of perceived control in a variety of areas. Perceptions of control are associated with better coping in stressful life circumstances (Glass, McKnight, & Valdimarsdottir, 1993; Litt, 1988; Shnek et al., 1997; Thompson, Nanni, & Levine, 1994; Thompson, Sobolew-Shubin, Galbraith, Schwankovsky, & Cruzen, 1993) and with protection against the deleterious effects of stress on physiological and immune functioning (Dantzer, 1989; Sieber et al., 1992; Visintainer, Volpicelli, & Seligman, 1982; Wiedenfled, O'Leary, Bandura, Brown, Levine, & Raska, 1991). In addition, those with a stronger sense of perceived control are more likely to take needed action to improve or protect their physical health (Peterson & Stunkard, 1989; Rodin, 1986), and they generally have better physical health (Peterson & Stunkard, 1989; England & Evans, 1992). A sense of personal control can also affect how one interacts with others. For example, parents who believe that they cannot control their child's behavior have a higher potential for child abuse (Bugental, Blue, & Cruzcosa, 1989; Stringer & LaGreca, 1985) and are more likely to have a coercive and abusive parenting style (Bugental et al., 1989). Elder caregivers with a sense of control are more satisfied and less depressed than those who judge their control to be low (Wallhagen, 1993). In almost every area of life, personal control has implications for emotional well-being, for the likelihood that action is taken, for physical health, and for general adaptive functioning.

Given the pervasive importance of personal judgments of control, it is not surprising that they can play a central role in the process and outcomes of psychotherapy. Clients' perceived control may affect how much effort they put into therapy, the extent to which progress is made in therapy, and the likelihood that gains generalize to new settings. Our purpose in this chapter is to review the implications of perceived control for psychotherapy and to suggest ways in which perceived control can be enhanced in the therapeutic process. The role of perceived control in the etiology of psychological disorders, the decision to obtain treatment, assessment, and the treatment process are all discussed. We also address problematic areas that are relevant to the goal of enhancing personal control. These include group and cultural differences in the desire for and adaptiveness of perceived control and the tradeoff between blame and helplessness. Because a confusing array of control-related terms has been used throughout the general control literature, we start with a section that identifies and distinguishes various concepts.

DEFINING CONCEPTS REGARDING CONTROL

Numerous distinctions among control-related concepts have been made. Six of them are particularly relevant in understanding the ideas discussed in this chapter: perceived control, actual control, locus of control, self-efficacy, primary control, and secondary control.

Perceived vs. Actual Control

In this chapter we mainly focus on perceived control, defined as indicated in the opening paragraph of this chapter: the belief that one can obtain desired outcomes and avoid bad ones through one's own actions. Having a sense of control does not mean that one has tested that belief, that one is necessarily going to act on it, or that the belief is veridical. Perceived control is usually assessed through self-report scales such as the Mastery Scale (Pearlin & Schooler, 1978) and more rarely through the observation of behavior. An example is Langer's (1975) research on illusions of control that uses decisions made in gambling situations to measure beliefs that one can control the outcome.

In contrast, actual control refers to the objective circumstances. Actors with actual control are in situations that can be influenced through personal action available to the actors, although they may not recognize or believe that they possess this control. For example, a therapist may judge that a client is capable of acting to get desired outcomes (i.e., has actual control), but the client may not believe that he or she has the control (i.e., low perceived control).

The distinction between actual and perceived control is important because actual control may only benefit individuals who feel confident that they can take effective action (Litt, 1988). Those who feel unsure about their relevant skills may feel less anxiety and cope better without actual control.

The Components of Perceived Control: Locus of Control and Self-Efficacy

Several theoretical approaches propose that personal control is made up of two judgments. The first type of judgment, termed *locus of control* (Rotter, 1966), *control ideology* (Gurin, Gurin, & Morrison, 1978), or *contingency beliefs* (Weisz & Stipek, 1982), refers to beliefs about the sources of reinforcement: is what happens to individuals due to their own action or to forces outside of their control? Locus of control is not necessarily a personal judgment about one's own control but rather a set of beliefs about the source of causality for people in general: within (internal) or outside (external) the individual. The second component in personal control is called *self-efficacy* (Bandura, 1977), *competence* (Weisz & Stipek, 1982), or *agency beliefs* (Chapman, Skinner, & Baltes, 1990) and refers to perceptions of one's own ability to enact the necessary action to obtain the outcome.

Perceived control is a combination of both locus of control (or contingency) and self-efficacy (or competence) (Weisz, 1986). For example, people have perceived control of satisfying relationships if they believe that good relationships are based on actions individuals perform (internal locus of control) and that they possess the skills that are needed to perform those actions (self-efficacy). However, individuals who judge that the quality of relationships is strongly influenced by chance or the actions of powerful others (external locus of control) or believe that they are not personally capable of performing the actions that cause satisfying relationships (low self-efficacy) will have low perceptions of control. In other words, low perceived control could be due to perceptions of noncontingency between individual actions and the outcome or to low beliefs in one's own competence to enact the needed actions.

Some of the most common confusions about control concepts are related to locus of control, self-efficacy, and perceived control. Often these terms are used interchangeably, mudding the conceptual waters. Some scales make it more confusing by purporting to measure locus of control yet containing items that measure perceived control and vice versa. The distinction, however, is an important one because locus of control, self-efficacy, and perceived control will not always have the same effects. Those with an internal control ideology do not necessarily judge that they personally have control. In fact, an internal locus of control combined with low self-efficacy may be particularly problematic. For example, Seligman and Miller (1979) refer to a situation of external locus of control and low self-efficacy that they call universal helplessness—the individual cannot exert control and neither can others. This is not as devastating as personal helplessness, which involves judgments of internal locus of control and low self-efficacy—effective control is possible, but the individual does not have the skills necessary to exercise it. For the therapeutic process, it is important to know whether a client has low perceived control because of perceived noncontingency or because of low competence (or both). The different situations suggest different remedies.

Primary and Secondary Control

Almost all of the research on perceived control has focused on the benefits associated with it—the belief that you can influence existing realities. However, another approach to undesirable outcomes is to use acceptance—gaining control by accepting things as they are, either yourself or the circumstances. Rothbaum, Weisz, and Snyder (1982) term the first approach "primary control" and contrast it with "secondary control," or acceptance that involves adjusting to the situation as it is. Unlike earlier perspectives, such as learned helplessness theory, the two-process model of control proposed by Rothbaum et al. recognizes that positive emotional outcomes and a greater overall sense of perceived control can be realized by accepting, rather than trying to change, some less-than-desirable situations. Secondary control may involve relying on chance or fate, adjusting expectations to be in line with likely outcomes, turning control over to others, and finding positive interpretations of an undesirable situation. Secondary control is distinguished from helplessness by more positive emotional reactions and an acceptance of the situation as it is.

The important point that Rothbaum et al.'s (1982) theory adds to views on control is that good outcomes and an overall sense of perceived control can be achieved by using acceptance in some areas. A number of studies support this view. Secondary control has been associated with better psychological outcomes for men with HIV (Thompson, Nanni, & Levine, 1994), persons with disabilities (Krantz, 1995), and children undergoing treatment for leukemia (Weisz, McCabe, & Dennig, 1994). In addition, positive effects of secondary control have been found for older adults coping with aging-related appearance changes (Thompson et al., 1998).

THE ROLE OF CONTROL IN PSYCHOPATHOLOGY AND THERAPY

The therapy process is complex and multifaceted, with a myriad of factors contributing to its success; of these, perceived control is only one component that needs to be considered. It is not our purpose here to suggest that control is the *primary* factor in clinical treatment. However, when addressing control as a *central* factor, it is possible to conceptualize therapy entirely within the context of control. First, lack of perceived control itself may be viewed as creating psychological vulnerability for the development of psychopathology, both in the general sense and through its role in specific disorders and psychological issues. In this way, perceived control sets the stage for the therapeutic process. Second, and more important, the therapy process itself can be conceptualized in relationship to perceived control. Specifically, at the onset of therapy, clients are in a state of low perceived control; they may even feel out of control and helpless. The therapist's goal during therapy, then, is to help clients claim or reclaim personal control by providing support, empowerment, and skills. And in the end, treatment is thought to be successful if clients leave feeling less helpless and in a state of higher perceived control. By viewing therapy from this perspective, it is possible to use a construct like perceived control in all phases of the counseling process. In fact, Frank (1982) argues that perceived control is a construct that cuts across theoretical orientations and schools of psychotherapy. Thus, perceived control becomes a useful conceptual tool to the therapist and lends itself well to the application of specific strategies in the clinical setting, regardless of the therapist's training background.

General Issues in Perceived Control in Psychopathology

To some extent, all psychopathology is related to low perceived control, whether it plays an etiological role in the disorder or an exacerbating role as it interferes in the process of coping with the disorder. Many theoretical models of psychopathology incorporate control-related constructs. For example, Frank (1982) describes a state of distress that all clients share—he refers to this state as *demoralization*—characterized by feelings of personal incompetence, hopelessness, low self-esteem, and helplessness (all of which may be viewed as dimensions of low perceived control). Demoralization is related to the development of psychological symptoms and may lead to problems in daily functioning or, for those already exhibiting a psychological disorder, may contribute to the increased manifestation of symptoms. Arnkoff and Mahoney (1979) see disorders concerned with control as central to psychopathology. They note the Western cultural consensus that life is controllable; as a result, any individual's lack of belief in personal control is viewed as pathological in and of itself. Therefore, within Western culture, low perceived control is equal to psychopathology. Arnkoff and Mahoney describe the role of control in multiple categories of psychopathology, including "neurosis," mood disorders, and personality disorders. Similarly, Mineka and Kihlstrom (1978) propose that personal perceptions of the environment as uncontrollable and unpredictable serve to create neurosis, and Barlow (1988) argues that anxiety disorders are characterized by illusions of uncontrollability. Indeed, he claims that changing perceptions of helplessness is central in managing any psychological disorder.

Control in the Etiology of Specific Psychopathologies

Whereas low perceived control might increase an individual's general vulnerability to any psychological distress, it is especially implicated in the development of depressive and anxiety disorders. Perhaps the best-known application is Seligman's (1972) theory of learned helplessness and depression, which postulates that people become depressed when they see no causal connection between their own behavior and environmental consequences—that is, when they have low perceived control. Two decades of research have provided a record of empirical support for the theory that low control can lead to depression (Peterson, Maier, & Seligman, 1993). In turn, increasing perceptions of control reduces depression in clients (Hollon & DeRubeis, 1992), generates a

higher frequency of problem-solving attempts (Ross & Mirowsky, 1989), reduces self-criticism and hopelessness, and elicits coping behaviors (Beck, Rush, Shaw, & Emery, 1979).

Perceived control is also considered important in the etiology of many anxiety disorders, including obsessive-compulsive disorder, panic disorder, social phobia, posttraumatic stress disorder, and generalized anxiety disorders. For example, the very nature of obsessive-compulsive disorder (OCD) is related to control. On the one hand, most clients with OCD view their obsessive and intrusive thoughts as uncontrollable and unmanageable (Purdon & Clark, 1994); on the other hand, those who view themselves as more responsible for the obsessions (i.e., have higher perceived control) may actually have a poorer prognosis because of the shame and guilt that accompany the intrusive thoughts. In response, compulsive behaviors are often illusory attempts at controlling either the obsessions or the environmental consequences victims believe will occur without the behavior. Like many depressed individuals, those with OCD feel at the mercy of their disorder, with little belief in their own ability to combat the symptoms. This state of helplessness can become so pathological that the compulsive behaviors themselves control the individual's life.

Cloitre, Heimberg, Liebowitz, and Gitow (1992) argue that perceptions of diminished control are an undercurrent of all anxiety disorders, but they specifically focus on panic disorder and social phobia. Using Levenson's (1981) locus of control scale, they demonstrated that individuals with panic disorder score lower on the internality scale than do normal controls and that they score higher on the chance subscale—that is, they perceive events as random in nature and out of their own control. This perception, in turn, probably exacerbates symptoms when they do occur, as there is no sense that symptoms can be deescalated or abated by personal control or even by the utilization of others. These data are supported by a recent review of studies on panic disorder (Rapee, 1995), showing consistently that panic-disordered individuals experience a higher frequency and intensity of panic symptoms (affective, cognitive, and physiological) if they have low perceptions of control over those symptoms. Additional information is offered by Shear (1995), who argues that panic attacks occur when individuals believe that there is a threat to their safety and well-being that is unpredictable and uncontrollable.

In contrast to panic disorder, social phobics show a different pattern in control-related issues. Cloitre et al. (1992) showed that whereas individuals with social phobia do have lower perceptions of personal control (internality) than do community controls, they also view events as controlled by powerful others in their environment. That is, events are not considered random in nature but rather outcomes controlled by people other than themselves, often people who are sources of potential scrutiny and criticism. It is this fear of negative evaluation, coupled with the belief that their own behavior cannot influence or control that evaluation, that exacerbates the symptoms of social phobia (Leung & Heimberg, 1996).

A common link in the discussion of anxiety disorders is clients' low perceptions of personal or internal control over events in their lives and over their own response to such events. For example, Eifert, Coburn, and Seville (1992) argue that the interpretation of the physiological component of anxiety is as important as the response itself. Specifically, if physiological cues are interpreted by anxious individuals as out of their control and inevitably leading to catastrophe (e.g., cardiac arrest), then the symptoms may escalate or become more pervasive. One goal of treatment, then, is to help individuals identify a link between their behavior and a resulting reduction or escalation of physiological responding. Hibbert (1984) makes a similar argument about the cognitive aspect of anxiety, in that symptoms escalate because the individual believes there is an imminent loss of self-control.

Judgments of control can also play a role in reactions to traumatic events. The likelihood that an individual will develop symptomatic posttraumatic stress disorder (PTSD) is mediated by the interpretation of the controllability of the event. But here perceptions of control may actually work in the opposite way than in the development of other anxiety disorders. Foa, Steketee, and Rothbaum (1989) suggest that victims who have a high sense of perceived control are more likely to blame themselves for the traumatic event and to experience more guilt and suffering than individuals with a more externalized sense of control (i.e., "events are caused by something/someone other than myself"). Moreover, based on a summary of literature on reactions to trauma, symptoms of PTSD are more likely in individuals who

experience a loss of predictability over the environment when they previously believed they possessed it. In this way, the trauma disrupts their worldview and their sense of perceived control. Thus, treatment goals may focus more on the reestablishment of control, rather than the introduction of it, or on the acceptance of some events as uncontrollable and unpredictable.

Although it is clear that perceived control is an important construct in the etiology of major diagnosable disorders, it is also important to note that control is a factor in other psychological contexts. For example, parents who have a low sense of perceived control over their children's behavior are more likely to exhibit poor parenting skills and to engage in a coercive behavioral cycle with their children (Patterson, 1988). One of the major goals of parent-training programs is to help parents feel more competent (i.e., higher self-efficacy) and more in control of their homes (Forehand & McMahon, 1981). Spousal abuse provides another example of how perceived control might be important in family interactions. Two patterns of men at high risk for physically or verbally abusing their spouses or partners have been identified (Prince & Arias, 1994). Both types have a low sense of personal control. In one pattern this is combined with low self-esteem and low desired control, and in the other pattern it occurs along with high self-esteem and high desire for control. In this case, intervention may require a balance between increasing perceived control in some circumstances and increasing acceptance of and coping with uncontrollability in others.

In conclusion, then, perceived control is a central factor in the development of specific psychopathology and psychological symptoms. In some cases, low perceived control serves to contribute to the development of the disorder. In other cases, low perceived control contributes to escalation in the frequency and severity of symptoms. In still other cases, low perceived control may actually serve as a buffer in the development of the disorder. And, certainly, perceived control becomes a prognostic factor for the remediation of these disorders.

Initiation of Treatment: Entering Therapy

Control appears to be an issue in etiology of psychopathology—or *need for treatment*—and one may reasonably argue that perceived control is central in the therapeutic process itself, although very little attention has been given to the role that control may play in the initiation of treatment. Entering therapy involves some insight and awareness of the need for the intervention, but what is it that drives individuals to seek help for their distress? We propose that it is an individual's perceived loss of control (e.g., "I used to have control but not any longer" or "I feel out of control) that is essential to the initiation of treatment.

The role of loss of control is borne out by the few studies on the issue. Frank (1982) argues that clients seek treatment because they recognize the presence of symptoms and believe that they cannot control or change them on their own. Shapiro, Bates, Greenzang, and Carrere (1994) examined a psychiatric outpatient sample and found that at the beginning of treatment, when asked, "What brings you here today?" over half of the statements made by clients reflected a loss of control or a fear of losing control. Only 15% of the total statements indicated having control or the belief that control could be regained; this demonstrates a significant theme of loss of control when entering therapy. Shapiro, Schwartz, and Astin (1996) argue that this loss of control is significantly different than that found in non-clinic samples, who tend to make a higher proportion of self-control statements. Similarly, Simoni, Adelman, and Nelson (1991) showed that a majority of a college student sample seeking therapy had lower perceived control than their counterparts who were not seeking therapy. Those who wished to enter therapy endorsed the desire to increase personal control as a goal in the therapeutic process. Even when problems have been chronic and continuing over a long period of time (e.g., alcohol abuse), it is when individuals reach the point at which they feel out of control that they tend to seek therapy. In fact, it is arguable that a loss of perceived control is *necessary* for an individual to initiate the therapeutic process.

Assessment Phase

Even though perceived control can be seen as central to therapy, it is not sufficient to merely presume that it is an issue and to proceed from there. For example, in some cases high perceived control is useful and should be encouraged, whereas in other cases a high need for control is a barrier to stable functioning (e.g., as in the face of an uncontrollable or low-control situation). And although increasing perceived control is generally viewed as beneficial, there is some evidence that it

can actually result in greater distress for some individuals. Thus, simply working to increase control in all therapeutic situations is ineffective and, at times, even damaging. Shapiro et al. (1996) argue that comprehensive assessment is the critical variable in developing appropriate and effective treatment strategies.

Though it is hardly revelational that assessment is an essential part of therapy, Shapiro et al. (1996) propose a specific assessment of control that is particularly useful for our purposes. Four areas of control need to be assessed during this phase: (1) environmental affordances (i.e., how controllable are the circumstances?); (2) behavioral skills and abilities for enacting control; (3) self-efficacy and responsibility for control (including locus of control); and (4) desire for control. If, for example, the environment is controllable but there is low desire for control, increasing skills and promoting self-responsibility are not good short-term intervention strategies. Similarly, if environmental affordances are low, then increasing active control strategies may actually result in increased helplessness. In either case, interventions that focus on "positive yielding" modes of control (i.e., acceptance and secondary or palliative coping) or "emotion-focused" coping are more likely to be effective. In contrast, if environmental affordances and desire for control are high, traditional techniques for enhancing behavioral skills and self-efficacy are appropriate. Clearly, then, it is the assessment of these dimensions that is key.

Individual Differences in Reactions to Control

Another assessment issue concerns individual differences in the effects of perceived control. Most research in this area has assumed that perceived control is universally beneficial. However, a number of studies have called this assumption into question. Liberman (1978) found that internal locus of control patients showed more improvement in a condition in which they were encouraged to attribute improvement to their own efforts, whereas external patients did better when improvement was attributed to a placebo pill. Similarly, a self-control intervention was more effective for hyperactive children with perceptions of high personal causality. The children with low beliefs in their personal causality did better with a social reinforcement program (Bugental, Whalen, & Henker, 1977). Reich and Zautra

(1991) investigated the effects of a control enhancement intervention that involved assessing one's control in daily life and attempting to increase it in controllable areas and to accomodate in uncontrollable situations. Participants were randomly assigned to the intervention, a no-contact control group, or a placebo control group that just involved social contact. Participants with a high internal locus of control benefited most from the intervention, but those with a low internal perspective improved the most with the placebo, or social contact, group. The researchers concluded that low internal participants may have found that relying on external social resources was more helpful than relying on personal action. These studies suggest that not everyone may benefit from programs intended to increase personal control.

What are the implications of these findings of individual differences in reactions to control-enhancing conditions? One conclusion might be that some people do not want control over their outcomes. Although there are undoubtedly some situations in which that is the case (see Burger, 1989; Rodin, Rennert, & Solomon, 1980; Thompson, Cheek, & Graham, 1988, for discussions of when control is not desired), it is more likely that these individual differences reflect preferences for different ways of achieving control. Some people may prefer to believe that they can get desired outcomes through their own direct action, and some may prefer using more indirect means such as getting comfort or guidance from others, being in a more structured environment, or using aids (e.g., medication) rather than personal action. Rothbaum et al. (1982) describe two types of primary control: relying on one's own action and relying on a more indirect type, one that uses secondary control processes but with the aim of getting what one wants, not to accomodate to reality. For example, some people may use vicarious control—identifying with and depending on powerful others—as a way of adjusting to a situation (secondary control). Others may rely on vicarious control to get what they want by aligning themselves with powerful others who will act on their behalf. In the latter case, they are still invested in getting what they want but are using an indirect method of primary control. It may be that those with an external locus of control are more likely to get a sense of mastery from the indirect strategies. For example, rather than relying on direct action, they may associate with supportive others whose actions can help them get desired outcomes.

These interaction effects in control enhancement interventions suggest that programs to increase personal control need to be sensitive to different ways of achieving it. For example, an assessment of people's preferred ways of getting what they want would help determine preferences for direct or indirect influence.

Assessment Tools

An assessment of control areas can be conducted in several ways, none of which is entirely adequate. Some control-related questionnaires and instruments are available (e.g., Levenson's, 1981, locus of control scale or Pearlin and Schooler's, 1978, mastery scale). There are also a variety of specialized control scales to measure beliefs about control in particular domains such as health, academic achievement, and relationships. For example, Nelson (1993) developed a scale to measure perceived control in social, health, and cognitive domains. To assess control beliefs related to living with a chronic illness, Shnek et al. (1997) used a helplessness measure developed by Stein, Wallston, Nicassio, and Castner (1988) for arthritis patients and a self-efficacy scale developed by Schiaffino, Revenson, and Gibofsky (1991).

One problem is that most control scales have been designed for research rather than clinical purposes. In contrast, the Shapiro Control Content Analysis Scale is a multidimensional measure of control that does assess many domains and lends itself nicely to developing "control profiles" that point to particular interventions (Shapiro et al., 1994). However, it does not provide a comprehensive measure of an individual's skills and abilities. In the end, augmenting paper-and-pencil measures with comprehensive clinical interviews is much more likely to yield the depth of information that will be most useful clinically. For example, asking clients about past controllable and uncontrollable events, as well as their responses to them, will help provide a picture of perceived control, skills, and behavioral competencies. It also helps to pinpoint whether clients are flexible in their response to events, for example, whether they are able to use acceptance as a reasonable coping strategy in the face of uncontrollable events or rather rigidly attempt to use active control strategies even when they are ineffective. Once previous and present strategies have been identified, treatment goals for enhancing or modifying control strategies become clearer.

ENHANCING CONTROL IN TREATMENT

Personal control can be enhanced in a variety of ways. We discuss general strategies for creating a situation in therapy that encourages a client's sense of control. Then we cover strategies for enhancing control for particular control-related problems: low self-efficacy, low-control circumstances, and general personal helplessness.

Setting the Context for Enhancing Control

In any therapeutic setting, regardless of whether the clients' low personal control is an issue in the etiology or maintenance of the problem, increasing a sense of control is a desirable goal. According to Frank (1982), one key characteristic of successful therapies is not so much that they reduce clients' symptoms as that they instill a sense of control that counteracts the demoralization that brings many people into therapy.

Clients who have a stronger sense of perceived control are more likely to persist in the face of setbacks, to put more effort into their therapy, and to internalize their successes. As examples, outpatient children and adolescents with a stronger sense of personal control have better therapy outcomes, presumably because they are more likely to work at problem solving (Weisz, 1986). In addition, Wilson (1979) suggests that giving clients control in the form of having choices can be effective in reducing their resistance to treatment.

Four components can help provide a control-enhancing context for therapy: a sense of contingency, involvement in therapeutic tasks, a setting that encourages personal responsibility for change, and a balance between the client's and therapist's control.

To have a sense of control, people need to know that they are operating in a context where there is a contingency between personal action and outcomes. In other words, clients need to have positive expectations about the effectiveness of the program that will be followed—that their efforts in therapy will, in fact, pay off. Several control enhancement studies have raised perceptions of control just by reminding the participants that they can and should expect to have control. In one study, physiotherapy patients in the control-enhancing condition were told that they were being offered an effective program to control their symptoms and that the more effort they

exerted, the more they would improve. The other group of patients was not given this information. The control-enhanced group had higher perceptions of control and made more progress in therapy (Johnston, Gilbert, Partridge, & Collins, 1992). Similarly, Langer and Rodin's (1976) research on increasing control among nursing-home residents found that a simple message from the director that residents could effect change in the setting (along with the receipt of a plant to take care of) led to positive emotional and physical outcomes. It appears that strengthening the perception that personal action can lead to desired outcomes strengthens personal control and thereby increases motivation and persistence.

One way for therapists to set clients' expectations of contingency between personal action and outcome is to directly address this issue at the beginning of therapy. Consider the following message from a therapist: "I can see that you are in a difficult, painful situation. It won't be easy, but I really believe that we can make a difference and improve your situation. I will do my part and you will have to do your part as well." This message acknowledges the seriousness of a clients' problems but also communicates the therapist's expectation that the clients' efforts in therapy will be rewarded.

Becoming involved in the work of therapy also contributes to a sense of control. Research on perceived control has found that people who act for themselves, who get more involved in a behavior, and who expend more effort have a stronger sense that their action caused a successful outcome (Langer, 1975). If we apply this to the context of therapy, getting the client involved in the process through homework assignments, journal keeping, role playing, reality-testing experiments, and other exercises can help strengthen a sense of control over the treatment outcome.

As therapy proceeds and positive changes are made, it is important that clients see themselves as responsible for the changes. Progress that is attributed to the therapist or to chance is unlikely to persist when therapy is completed, nor it is likely to generalize to other areas of life. It may be especially difficult for individuals with a pessimistic attribution style, which externalizes credit for positive outcomes, to adopt internal attributions for positive changes. Phares (1993), for example, tells the story of a client in psychotherapy who refused to take credit for any progress during the course of the treatment. If his application for a vocational school was successful, it must be because there was no competition. If a woman responded to his attentions, she must not have many friends. His successful efforts to make positive changes were never attributed to his own skills. Cognitive-restructuring techniques that challenge externalizing credit for progress in therapy may help to overcome this tendency. One way to accomplish this is by directly addressing attributions for positive changes that occur. First, the client is asked to identify positive changes that have occurred since the beginning of therapy. Then, the therapist and client discuss what the client is doing differently that has produced the positive effects. Eventually, the therapist introduces the idea that it was mainly the client's skills and efforts that produced the changes, for example, by suggesting that the client's creativity and skill in applying the ideas generated in therapy is a major reason that they were successful.

A final general strategy for enhancing control concerns the balance of responsibility between the therapist and the client. It would be tempting to conclude that a situation with maximum actual control is the best way to nurture perceptions of control. However, when the client is given too much actual control too early, it could have the unfortunate effect of undermining expectations of an effective treatment and reducing a sense of control. Optimum personal control develops when individuals are given choices within a structured environment (Skinner, 1995).

A three-step model in which control is transferred from the therapist to the client over the course of therapy provides both the structure and the freedom that are necessary for nurturing strong perceptions of control. The therapist acts as a guide in the initial stages of therapy by making suggestions for the client to implement. The role of knowledgeable guide helps to foster trust in the therapist and to enhance the belief of an effective and powerful treatment. As treatment progresses, the therapist adopts the role of a collaborator, who works with the client to decide how to implement changes. Gradually, more decisions are transferred to the client. By the end of treatment, the therapist's role becomes that of a consultant—someone who can be sought for additional consultation as problems arise when therapy has ended.

Therefore, to increase clients' personal control, therapists should make clear their beliefs in the effectiveness of the program, involve the clients in the process, take opportunities to point out the clients' personal responsibilities for successes, challenge and correct statements that externalize credits, and provide a context with enough structure to impart security and enough freedom to allow effective personal choices. We now turn to specific control-related problems.

Interventions for Common Control-related Problems

Enhancing Self-efficacy

One type of control-related problem that clients may present is a low sense of self-efficacy. Phobias and some anxiety disorders are often related to underlying low self-efficacy concerning a set of behaviors. Individuals with snake phobia or social anxiety, for example, may have an adequate sense of personal control in many areas of their lives but little or no confidence that they can perform in the phobia-related area. According to social cognitive theory, treatments for phobia are effective when they increase self-efficacy for performance related to the phobia (Bandura, 1997). Research in this tradition has extensively studied how to increase self-efficacy for specific phobia disorders, using the techniques of guided mastery experiences, modeling, and verbal persuasion (Bandura, 1997).

Enactive mastery experiences that involve the successful performance of a behavior related to the phobia have been found to be the most effective routes to strengthening self-efficacy (Bandura, 1997; Bandura, Adams, & Beyer, 1977). A key component to guided mastery is the use of mastery aids that create environmental conditions that optimize the chance of a successful experience. For example, breaking down a more complex behavior into more easily accomplished substeps, performing the behavior jointly with the therapist, being exposed to a model who demonstrates how to cope with the feared situation, and using graduated time when the initial exposure to the anxiety-provoking stimulus is brief are mastery aids that can be used to prompt initial behavior and increase the likelihood that it will be successful.

Also included in Bandura's (1997) program of self-efficacy establishment is verbal persuasion by the therapist to encourage the translation of successful performance into a higher sense of efficacy. Schunk and Rice (1987) found that just giving children practice in using effective strategies to improve academic performance was not sufficient to increase self-efficacy. The children needed to be reminded that their use of strategies was effective. In addition, protective aids can be used in situations in which a phobic reaction has been encountered to protect against the feared negative effects of the experience. For example, someone with a dog phobia might be asked to approach a dog that is muzzled, so the fear of being attacked is reduced. Intervention programs with these elements have been found to successfully reduce phobic reactions and avoidance (e.g., Bandura, Jeffery, & Wright, 1974).

Increasing Personal Control in Low-control Circumstances

Another type of control-related dysfunction occurs when a traumatic incident has undermined general feelings of control and safety. According to cognitive adaptation theories (Janoff-Bulman & Freize, 1983; Taylor, 1983; Thompson & Janigian, 1988), a stressful negative life event such as the loss of a loved one or the diagnosis of a life-threatening disease can undermine adaptive beliefs of personal control and relative invulnerability. Survivors may feel vulnerable to disaster and unable to protect themselves in a wide range of situations, even those not connected to the traumatic event. Numerous studies find that low feelings of control during or in the aftermath of a traumatic experience are associated with poor emotional outcomes such as depression and anxiety (Lowery, Jacobsen, & McCauley, 1987; Shnek et al., 1997; Thompson, et al., 1994) and less successful coping strategies (Wallhagen, 1993). One goal in therapy is to reestablish a sense of security and personal control despite the low-control circumstances and, in some cases, the continual erosion of control that may characterize individuals' lives. Techniques that can help reestablish a general sense of safety and control include the use of acceptance (secondary control), goal reassessment, and cultivation of control.

Emphasizing and Increasing Acceptance

Throughout our lives we face situations in which the potential for control is low or nonexistent. In addition, there may be aspects of ourselves that we find undesirable yet difficult to change. A basic idea in Rothbaum et al.'s (1982) two-process model of control (primary and secondary) is that an adaptive way of dealing with these low-control situations is to recognize the lack of contingency and accept the situation as it is. Secondary control—the acceptance of these situations—allows individuals to avoid the sense of helplessness and

deterioration in perceived control that would ensue if they continually experienced ineffectual action. Thus, acceptance can help maintain a high overall sense of control.

Several researchers on the therapeutic process have commented on the role of acceptance in good therapeutic outcomes. Frank (1982) states, "Psychotherapy also often includes helping the patients to accept and endure suffering as an inevitable aspect of life that can be used as an opportunity for personal growth" (p. 10). Similarly, in her discussion of the long-term treatment of anxiety disorder patients, Shear (1995) acknowledges that not all symptoms can be successfully treated and that one goal in psychotherapy might be to encourage the acceptance of a certain level of continuing symptomatology as a natural part of life.

The question of when one should try to make changes or to adjust to things as they are is not an easy one. The most obvious answer is expressed in folk sayings such as "Change what can be changed; accept what cannot be changed; and have the wisdom to know the difference." One difficulty with this approach is that there is no easy, direct, or often even *any* way to tell what is changeable. Certainly, at times the control of a situation is not in doubt. The death of a loved one, irreversible paralysis, or a miscarriage cannot be undone. But often the extent of individuals' control in a situation is not known. We have all heard tales of individuals who persisted in the face of seemingly hopeless odds and who eventually achieved their goals.

A more useful approach than assuming that clients or therapists can tell what is controllable has been suggested by a control enhancement model that focuses on identifying ways in which the outcome may be achieved, doing an assessment of self-relevant skills, and determining whether the costs of exercising the control are worth the benefits (Thompson, 1991a). This approach does not assume that controllability can be accurately assessed but instead concentrates on assessing the costs and benefits of continuing to pursue a goal. Clients can be helped to identify potential ways to achieve a goal and to assess their skills along those lines, but it is up to the individual to decide whether the potential outcome is worth the costs of exercising control and the possibility of eventual failure. If it is not, then the issue becomes how to accept and adjust to the less desirable circumstances.

There has not been much research on how to

foster acceptance of undesirable situations. Rothbaum et al. (1982) discuss four types of secondary control processes: illusory, predictive, interpretive, and vicarious. Of these, interpretive secondary control (finding positive meaning in the event) seems most amenable to intervention and, in fact, is consistent with several models of how people cope with stressful life events (e.g., Janoff-Bulman & Freize, 1983; Taylor, 1983; Thompson & Janigian, 1988). Finding positive meaning can be achieved by focusing on side benefits associated with the event and by making downward comparisons. To the extent that individuals see some positive aspects to their experience, judge that the situation could be worse, or compare themselves with others who are worse off, they should find it easier to accept their current circumstances. As an example of how this is done, Krantz (1995) discusses common mechanisms used by persons with disabilities to find benefits from their situation, for example, choosing language that puts the present situation in a positive light, choosing not to interpret the situation as a loss, and recognizing the special knowledge they have gained from their experience.

Many studies have found benefits associated with the ability to adopt a positive interpretation of a stressful, undesirable event. Stroke patients and their family caregivers who stated that the stroke helped them appreciate life and their spouses more and that they had grown from the experience were more likely to have found meaning in their experiences with the stroke (Thompson, 1991b). In addition, downward comparison has been associated with better coping for breast cancer patients (Taylor, Wood, & Lichtman, 1983), for mothers of infants in newborn intensive-care units (Affleck, Tennen, Pfeiffer, Fifield, & Rowe, 1987), and for adults undergoing bone marrow transplantation (Ersek, 1992). Thus, there is evidence that making a more positive interpretion of the event or comparing oneself to those who are worse off are ways to increase acceptance of a traumatic experience.

The process of finding meaning in a negative experience can be promoted in therapy through discussion of how the client generally finds meaning in life situations. Many individuals may use traditional religious beliefs or spirituality to provide a meaningful context for their experience. Just asking about these types of beliefs may encourage people to use them to find meaning. A second way to promote the search for meaning is to provide ways for the client to connect to others who have dealt with a similar loss. For example, parents of a child with leukemia might be encouraged to join a support group for parents of cancer patients, find a chat room on the Web with a similar focus, or read a book written by a parent in those circumstances. However the topic of finding meaning is broached, it is important to remember that the search for meaning has to be initiated by the individual. Most people will not find it beneficial to be told to focus on what is positive about their loss or to have others identify positive aspects that might give a sense of meaning. Discussions of spiritual beliefs and hearing about others' experiences will be useful if they help begin the process whereby people identify a positive meaning for themselves.

Negative emotions about a loss may be overwhelming for some individuals and make it difficult for them to acknowledge and deal with their situation. Thus a useful approach in fostering acceptance of circumstances that cannot be changed is to help clients directly address and handle their feelings about the loss and begin the process of finding control in other areas. This could be accomplished by helping them to identify their unexpressed feelings about the loss. For children, this might involve reading stories about a child in similar circumstances and discussing how that child feels and what works for coping with those feelings. For example, good books are available for both younger and older children that describe a divorce from a child's point of view. Hearing about the reactions and feelings of other individuals in similar circumstances helps normalize the client's feelings and makes it easier to accept the loss. A sense of self-blame may make it difficult to accept the loss and keeps people focused on achieving the idealized outcome, rather than adjusting to and coping with the situation as it is. Here, too, providing opportunities for clients to discover that they are not unique or isolated in their experience helps pave the way to acceptance.

It is important to be clear that accepting a difficult situation is not equivalent to repression, in which the implications of a trauma are not acknowledged or dealt with. Nor is acceptance associated with helplessness, which continues a focus on the idealized outcome but without any sense that it can be achieved. Instead, the acceptance of a difficult loss is based on first recognizing and dealing with the pain associated with the loss and then with finding a sense of control in other areas so that one is not left feeling helpless.

The focus of control shifts from getting the idealized outcome to other important outcomes, such as feeling a sense of efficacy in dealing with the situation. Thus, acceptance is closely tied to the next component in increasing personal control in low-control circumstances: changing to goals that can be reached despite the loss.

Changing to Reachable Goals

Goals are an important facet of a sense of control in life. The perception that one is making progress toward reaching one's goals contributes to a sense of mastery and a general sense of personal control. One reason that control is eroded by a traumatic life event is that goals that had formerly given structure and meaning to life are no longer reachable. In addition, people may have tenuous control over more mundane situations. For instance, patients in treatment for cancer may not be able to set their own daily schedule and, therefore, find it hard to work toward goals in everyday life.

Individuals who are able to invest in goals that are more compatible with their current life circumstances will see less threat to their sense of control and also will find it easier to accept the loss. Brandstadter and Rothermund (1994) found that many adults successfully buffered losses by rescaling goals. They did so by shifting their preferences and downplaying the personal importance of domains in which losses occurred. Persons with disabilities may find other areas for gratification, for example, using the disability as an impetus to switch to a more satisfying career and one that is more attainable, given the current situation (Krantz, 1995). Cancer patients who reported changing to goals that were more internal and less materialistic after their diagnosis had a stronger sense of meaning than those who did not (Thompson & Pitts, 1992).

Disengaging from previous goals and investing in new ones can be a difficult process. Clients need first to acknowledge and grieve the loss of former personal goals before they are able to redirect attention and energy in new directions. A therapist might use here the techniques discussed in the section on acceptance. Then the therapy can focus on evaluating potential new goals that are worth pursuing and are reachable. This could be done by discussing options and suggesting that the client make some initial efforts in the area of the new goal to see if that will be a satisfying field

of endeavor. For example, a woman whose career as a dancer has been cut short by a disability might want to pursue a different goal in the field of dance, such as opening a dance studio, or might consider goals in very different areas, such as writing, training in the legal profession, or volunteering. She might begin by teaching a dance class or taking a course in law to see if that new area is a promising goal to pursue.

Finding and Creating Personal Control

There may be a variety of ways of cultivating personal control even in low-control circumstances. One involves the relationship between predictability and perceived control. In general, individuals feel greater control when they have a sense of what is going to happen, even if the possibilities for exerting influence to get what one wants are low (Thompson, 1981). Getting information about one's situation either through experts or individuals who have gone through similar circumstances can contribute to a sense of personal control, although it may not increase actual control. Individuals with a chronic physical illness or a diagnosis of a psychological disorder might gather information about treatment and prognosis from medical journals, friends, and the Internet. Perhaps even more valuable would be information about the course of their illness from a support group of other people with a similar diagnosis. Knowing what is likely to happen and the options for treatment imparts a sense that the situation is not totally out of one's control, perhaps because predictability allows one to prepare strategies in advance.

Another way to cultivate personal control in low-control circumstances is by finding or creating areas that are amenable to personal control. In their study of cancer patients, Thompson et al. (1993) made a distinction between central control (perceived control over the course of the cancer) and consequence control (control over the effects of the cancer on one's life). Although it may seem that curing oneself of cancer would be the most important outcome for this group, consequence control over the effects of cancer on emotions and day-to-day life had a much stronger association with psychosocial outcomes. This indicates that benefits can be realized by a sense of control over the more manageable aspects of life with a chronic illness: individuals can use what seem like less central (but more controllable) areas to increase their sense of control. Because consequence control is more amenable to intervention than is central control, the message that consequence control is more important for psychosocial outcomes is a hopeful one.

Work on finding and creating control in therapy can include several components. One is helping clients to recognize actual control that they already possess. Because people often operate in an automatic, "mindless" state, they are not cognizant of the control that they do exercise (Langer, 1989). Activities that call attention to ways in which control is being exercised in everyday life can help increase a sense of control. A therapist can review with clients ways in which they are successfully enacting control despite their low-control situation.

A second way to build a sense of control in therapy is to actively create areas where it is salient, for example, engaging in activities that highlight the relationship between action and outcome. Even simple activities like cleaning off one's desk; running; or playing a sport like racquetball, where the effect of one's physical action can be felt, highlight a connection between one's action and an outcome. One woman with breast cancer joined a rowing team of breast cancer survivors and found that the physical act of rowing was a strong reminder of the effectiveness of her actions (Mitchell, 1997). A therapist can help clients identify activities that will give them a sense of accomplishment and areas where the results of one's actions are obvious as a start at recapturing a sense of control. Changing to reachable goals, as discussed in the previous section, will also create more opportunities to have actual control.

In summary, perceptions of control in low-control circumstances can be increased by knowing how to accept some aspects of the situation, by finding goals that can be reached in the situation, by reducing uncertainty, by recognizing one's current control, and by cultivating control in other areas.

General Feelings of Helplessness

General feelings of helplessness may occur in individuals who do not appear to be in low-control circumstances. Even though they have experienced no major traumatic loss and appear to have adequate resources and abilities, these individuals have a low sense of mastery that has generalized to many areas of life, resulting in a negative self-image, feelings of failure, and a sense of hopelessness. There are a variety of ways to help reestablish a sense of effective functioning. Some of these come from research on how individuals estimate their control.

According to a recent review of the literature, people use a control heuristic to judge the extent of their personal influence over outcomes (Thompson, Armstrong, & Thomas, 1998). We judge that we have controlled outcomes when we believe we intended the outcome and see a connection between our action and the outcome. Both ideas of intentionality and connection can explain the circumstances in which individuals will overestimate, underestimate, and accurately estimate their control. In the case of people who feel generally helpless, there may be an underestimation of personal control.

Several factors have been found to influence the control heuristic process (Thompson, Armstrong, & Thomas, 1998). One consideration is whether the individual is focused on success or failure. When people are focused on success, they are inclined to believe that they intend success, to remember more of their current successes than failures, and to have available information about their past successes. All of this leads to higher estimates of personal control. In contrast to an emphasis on success, individuals with low feelings of general control most likely focus on failure. This leads them to expect failure, to be biased in their memory of past behavior (overremembering failures relative to successes), to be surprised by successes, and thus to have lower perceptions that the success came about because of their intentional actions. Successes do not contribute to enhanced personal control when the focus is on failure because the low sense of intentionality and low perception of connection between one's actions and the success are not conducive to an estimate of control.

A focus on success is increased by enhancing the expectation of good outcomes, by situations or tasks that remind one of past effective actions, by tasks with a high reinforcement rate, by comparing oneself to less competent others, and by a patterning of successes so that it appears earlier rather than later in the responding (Thompson, Armstrong, & Thomas, 1998).

How could this information about how people judge their control be used to help individuals with a low sense of general mastery? It suggests that activities that focus attention on success, such as diary or journal writing, in which individuals keep accounts of daily successes as they occur, and homework assignments to recall success in a particular area would be of value to help enhance a sense of control. Also useful would be cognitive-restructuring work to counteract the tendency to externalize the cause of positive outcomes so that clients see the connection between their behavior and the success. One technique for accomplishing this is automatic thought recording, in which clients describe an event and their automatic thoughts in response to it and are then required to counter that thought (Beck, 1976; Beck et al., 1979). For example, a client may recount a success ("My suggestions in a work meeting were well received"), the automatic thought it evoked ("It was just luck. I'll never be able to repeat it"), and a more adaptive answer to that thought ("I had good ideas in the last meeting, too, so maybe I am good at identifying solutions").

Another approach to increasing a general personal control in treatment is focused on future behaviors. Goals and plans for reaching them give a sense of personal control because they highlight both intentionality and the connection between one's action and desired outcomes. That is, just clarifying and specifying one's goals and developing a plan for reaching them can increase feelings of control. Problem-solving techniques that involve identifying goals, making plans, and starting with small changes that have a high probability of success can be useful here. Like individuals in low-control circumstances, those with a general sense of helplessness may also benefit from treatment that helps them recognize their current control and foster new areas for effective action. A depressed mother, for example, may actually be accomplishing a great deal in her parenting and work roles but not recognize her effective actions. The techniques of reviewing current effective action, setting reachable goals, and breaking plans into small reachable steps with a high probability of success could be useful.

Another type of low-mastery individual has to be acknowledged. For some individuals, a low sense of control may be an accurate assessment of their chances of good outcomes because they lack the necessary skills to be effective. For example, Dunning and Story (1991) found that depressed students were more pessimistic than the nondepressed about their prospects for the upcoming term, but at the same time the depressed group overestimated their chances for good outcomes. In other words, in actuality, the depressed individuals had fewer positive experiences and more negative experiences over the course of the term. This may have occurred because the depressed group had fewer skills to bring about the outcomes they desired. In these cases, the identification and amelioration of skill deficits may be needed through programs such as anger management or training in parenting, social skills, or assertiveness.

Overcontrolling

Throughout this chapter, we have focused on the benefits of perceived control and on techniques to help clients with low self-efficacy, a loss of control due to traumatic circumstances, or general helplessness. A different type of control-related problem occurs in individuals who are excessively focused on personal control. These are individuals who are compelled to assert personal control even in areas that could be better or more appropriately managed by others or areas that are not amenable to control. Having a sense of control is generally adaptive, but feeling that you need to use your control to influence all situations, including attempting to control other people, can increase personal and interpersonal stress.

Several steps are necessary to reduce the tendency to be overly focused on exerting control. First, clients have to be aware of their propensity to overcontrol. Next, they need to be cognizant of the deleterious effects of exaggerated control on their interpersonal relationships and personal stress levels. Finally, individuals with this tendency need to learn skills and strategies for changing their style of control.

Because one aspect of the Type A syndrome involves a strong need to exert control in most situations (Carver & Humphries, 1982), interventions that have been found to reduce Type A behavior may be an effective way to help clients who are overcontrolling. One study found that group counseling sessions for cardiac patients significantly reduced Type A behavior and resulted in a lower recurrence rate of myocardial infarctions (Friedman et al., 1986). The group sessions had four components: (1) exercises that established awareness of one's Type A behavior, such as watching tapes of Type A individuals and talking with spouses who described their partner's Type A behaviors; (2) drills that helped participants establish non–Type A behaviors, such as deliberately driving in the slow lane and making a point of telling someone, "Maybe I'm wrong"; (3) stress reduction training; and (4) keeping a dream diary as a source of information about frustrations. Several aspects of this intervention seem particularly well suited to reducing overcontrolling tendencies. For example, clients could be helped to identify areas in which they are overcontrolling and given drills that help them practice letting go of control. This might involve allowing one's spouse to make the final decision on how to handle a domestic issue or trusting a fellow worker to complete a task. An important part of this process is not just letting go of some control but also reducing the tendency to second-guess, closely supervise, or harshly criticize the decisions made by others. After the completion of some drills, the benefits of less involvement can be identified and discussed.

CASE STUDY

I (MW) first met Annie, age 11, when she came into my office with her mother. I had been working with her parents toward managing the mental illness of Annie's older sister, Renee. Renee was a 22-year-old with moderate mental retardation, a history of sexual abuse, and a pattern of severe anxiety symptoms. The family was referred to me after Renee had a psychotic break that resulted in hospitalization. At the time that Annie presented with her own problems, Renee was stable on antipsychotic medication, antianxiety medication, relaxation training, individual support, and family therapy.

Ms. Hart, Annie's mother, brought Annie in because of recent episodes of crying and withdrawal. Ms. Hart remarked that Annie was "totally out of control" and "not coping well" in the family environment. During intake, Annie acknowledged this, saying that she "lost it" frequently. It quickly became evident that issues of perceived control were primary in this case.

Assessment focused primarily on interviews with Annie; however, this was quite a task. According to her mother, Annie vowed never to talk in therapy. Thus, although Annie was polite and cooperative, she was unwilling to disclose much of anything about her family and her feelings about Renee, instead shrugging and saying, "I don't know" or claiming that things were fine at home. This resistance was not surprising—it was perhaps the only tool of control and power that Annie had. However, it made me question whether I was the right person to help Annie;

perhaps I should refer her to someone who did not already know her family. Yet Annie's mother preferred to work with me and reported that Annie was willing as well. Skeptical, I agreed to try.

Part of being able to gain control in therapy is, ironically, the need to relinquish control to the therapist. Understanding how difficult this would be for Annie, I incorporated two strategies for helping her give up some initial control to me. The first, which may seem counterintuitive, was to give her complete control over talking to me. I used three exercises. One, I developed a written contract, explicitly stating that nothing Annie said (if she talked at all) would be disclosed to her parents. She, her mother, and I signed this document. Second, I gave Annie a tape recorder to use in the therapy sessions. She could tape them, and at the end of the time, erase the tape so that the words "no longer existed." Third, I told her I would wait indefinitely for her to talk, and that is what I did—I waited. All of these techniques were designed to put Annie in charge, toward the goal of increasing her sense of control over the therapy process. It was hoped that if she felt more power, she would feel more comfortable in giving some of it away in the therapeutic process.

In the meantime (and several sessions passed with nothing but polite conversation with this 11-year-old), I tried to apply the concept of the "shadow side" (borrowing from David Greenwald). Clearly, Annie was expressing her sadness and anxiety, but her anger and fear were not being expressed, living instead in the shadows. Toward this end, I employed many typical techniques (following Robert Shapiro) for working with children, including storytelling; The Talking, Feeling, and Doing Game drawing; and role playing. Annie was on to this ploy immediately—in fact, she once said to me, slyly, "It is obvious these cards are rigged for me" and promptly quit playing the game.

Daunted, I was ready to refer but decided to try one more thing. I asked Ms. Hart to schedule Annie's appointment when no one else would be in the office and then to leave us alone there. I got a phone book and placed it in front of Annie, challenging her to rip it up in a timed race with me. My goal was to use it as an anger expression technique, but this did not happen. As Annie started to rip up those pages, she began to laugh, then to rip faster, then to laugh more. Following her lead, I cheered her on, I ran around the room, and I screamed and emoted and exclaimed (very foolishly, very "out of control" myself); soon her laughing led to hysterical laughing, until she fell on the floor and held her side. Finally, Annie had relinquished control of her emotions. Anger expression—the goal—did not occur, but Annie *had* become carried away. That was the turning point in therapy, about five appointments into treatment.

In the meetings afterward, Annie began to talk more about her family, though still in a guarded way; and, so, leaving her in control of the disclosure process, I did not push her. When she talked, Annie described her sister's mental illness and how much time her parents spent dealing with her. Annie admitted that she was angry, but she also said that it was "hopeless" and that nothing could be done to change the situation. After all, that was just the way Renee was. "I have to accept it," she said.

In a way, Annie was right—acceptance, a secondary control strategy, certainly applied here to an unpredictable course for her sister. Renee's illness was lifelong; in many ways, Renee would always demand more time and energy from their parents than was fair. However, Annie was depressed and feeling helpless in response to this situation, so I decided to focus on primary control strategies at first and return to acceptance later.

The control and coping strategies introduced were emotion-focused coping, problem-solving strategies, and the use of the spiritual and religious. First, it became clear that Annie was angry with Renee and with her mother but that she truly felt uncomfortable talking about it. Though Ms. Hart attempted to normalize these feelings for Annie, they weren't being expressed. Instead, I employed the help of Annie's father. Mr. Hart (Renee's stepfather) shared many of Annie's feelings—anger, frustration, hurt, deprivation, and guilt—and he was willing to talk to Annie about them. After one session together, they agreed to have regular "gripe fests" about their frustrations. Providing Annie with an acceptable outlet for expressing her anger seemed to be helpful, and both daughter and father valued this special time together.

Once Annie was expressing anger more at home, she also was more willing to talk to me about it in therapy. She described "losing it" (i.e., her crying and subsequent withdrawal) as something that happened unexpectedly and that she did not know how to handle. We worked for two sessions on this issue; first, we identified environmental cues (e.g., Renee's escalation in anxiety symptoms and her mother's increased attention to Renee) and internal cues (e.g., stomach tightening and a lump in the throat) that tended to precede the episodes. Next, we developed a list of things Annie could do when she observed the cues, such as riding her bike, talking to her dad, listening to music, climbing the wall in her backyard, and singing aloud in her room. Certainly none of these techniques was magical; and, in fact, Annie rarely used them at all. But the list was in her room and it provided a reminder to her that she *could, in fact, choose* to control her reaction to the situation.

A third control strategy was to use the religious life of this family, who were very devout Christians. Annie's parents had drawn on family prayer in the past to help deal with her distress, but the impact had been small, even though prayer was a large part of Annie's world. Once Annie had a better strategy for dealing with things at home, however, it was time to reintroduce prayer and the concept of "God's plan" (a paramount value in this family). We talked in sessions about God's plan for Annie, for Renee, and for her family, and Annie was able to verbalize family messages such as "Renee is God's special child" and "God has a plan for me; that's why I don't have Renee's problems." These messages were more acceptable to Annie once she felt more control. Tapping into spiritual coping, then, served to further increase the perception of control for Annie and for her family.

Finally, it was time to return to acceptance. In the last session before termination, Annie and I discussed the way things were at home—that, in fact, they weren't always fair; that, in fact, Renee would always have this problem in some form or another and Annie would just have to deal with it. In this session, Annie said to me, "Yep, I can't change Renee but I can change me." In this way, acceptance became a positive thing for Annie rather than further feeding into hopelessness, as it had at the initiation of therapy.

In our terminating session, Annie said that she thought things were better and that she could "take a break" from therapy. I still see Annie's family and expect that some of these themes will recur as Annie grows and has to face the pressures of adolescence. Perhaps she will return, feeling out of control again. But, for now, she has regained control for herself; as she put it when we ended our work together (with a shrug and a smile), "Things aren't perfect, but I haven't lost it in a very long time."

ADDITIONAL COMPLEXITIES IN ENHANCING CONTROL IN THERAPY

Distinguishing Control and Responsibility

When individuals are dealing with being victimized, the belief that one has control in that area can have many benefits, including enhanced self-esteem and feelings of being protected from future harm. However, there can be a downside to a sense of control because it is closely linked to feeling responsible for the outcome. Rape victims, for example, may feel protected from further harm if they feel that they had some control over the victimization because that helps them to identify ways to avoid further victimization. One concern, however, is that this sense of control could lead to a feeling of blame and responsibility for the rape.

Because control and blame can be closely linked, it is important that efforts to enhance control be done in a way that does not hold the victims responsible for their plight. One way to make this important distinction is through an explicit discussion of the difference between responsibility for a situation and gaining control over the situation. A batterer is entirely responsible for spousal abuse, for example, because no one deserves this sort of treatment. At the same time, it can be useful for battered spouses to identify ways in which they could have protected themselves and can protect themselves in the future. Language that distinguishes between responsibility for the violence and responsibility for personal safety can help increase control without reinforcing self-blame (Dutton, 1992): "It is important to help the battered woman examine her goals . . . and take responsibility for acting to meet them. She is not always in absolute control over her safety, but she can take control of her actions in attempting to insure it" (p. 123).

Another way to distinguish control from blame involves models of helping by Brickman, Rabinowitz, Karuza, Cortes, Cohn, and Kidder (1982). This perspective distinguishes between the cause of an problem and the solution. One helping model, termed "enlightenment," involves not holding victims responsible for the cause of their plight but seeing them as having some responsibility for the solution. Depressed clients, for example, can be encouraged to see that they are not responsible for being depressed but that they can assume responsibility for finding a solution. Responsibility might involve getting information, working in therapy, or taking medication—whatever strategy seems to be a way to reach the desired outcome.

Cultural Differences in the Effects of Perceived Control

Although perceived control is generally adaptive, therapists should be sensitive to cultural differences in control styles. Differences in mean levels of control have been associated with demographic factors, such as class, age, and ethnic group. In general, those who have lower socioeconomic status (SES), either lower income (Lachman & Weaver, 1998; Mirowsky, 1995) or less education (Gurin et al., 1978; Mirowsky, 1995), have lower perceptions of control. Ethnic group differences in control have also been found in some studies. Whites have been found to score higher on primary control measures than do Chinese Americans (Peng & Lachman, 1993), and they generally have a higher sense of personal mastery than do African Americans (Gurin et al., 1978). However, in contrast, Graham's (1994) review of control issues found that beliefs about personal control were high among African Americans. The lower perceived control of ethnic group members may be an accurate reflection of their relatively lower power over their circumstances because of restricted access to resources. The lower control ratings could also be due to an ethic that places value on group power (collectivism) rather than individual power (individualism).

Studies of age differences in personal control have generally found stable judgments of control throughout the adult years (Gatz & Karel, 1993), with decrements coming only in the later years (Mirowsky, 1995; Nelson, 1993) or not at all (Lachman, 1991; Peng & Lachman, 1993).

It is not clear if the lower levels of personal control that are sometimes found with lower SES, ethnic groups, and older persons are a reflection of the lack of control in life circumstances characterized by reduced resources or if instead they mean that direct personal control is not a preferred style in those groups. Although it seems most likely that the former explanation is correct, it would seem wise to be sensitive to possible differences associated with control preferences in lower SES, older, and ethnic group clients and to assess control strategy preferences.

CONCLUSION

Guiding clients through treatment in a way that maximizes positive outcomes is a complex process. We suspect that enhancing a sense of control in treatment is already a desired treatment outcome for most therapists, although they may not state it in exactly those terms. Furthermore, there may be a number of other goals that therapists wish to accomplish in this journey, in addition to bolstering clients' perceptions of control. Nonetheless, making control enhancement an explicit focus throughout the therapeutic process has a number of advantages. First, when increasing control is a central goal, decisions about treatment can be evaluated in light of their potential effects on clients' perceived control, thereby improving the chances of successfully enhancing control. Second, progress in improving control can be assessed as therapy proceeds, and adjustments can be made if necessary. Third, because people often enter therapy because of a sense that important parts of their lives are out of control, treatment that is explicitly focused on helping them regain a sense of control is a motivating and easily understood rationale for work in therapy.

In this chapter, we have identified a variety of routes for enhancing clients' sense of control and have pointed out complexities that arise when attempting to increase personal control. Our goal is to integrate the research and clinical literature about perceived control in a way that gives an overview of this intersection and also to present practical applications of how the theory and research can be used to help individuals find more control in their lives. Our hope is that this integration will prove useful to therapists as they engage in the treatment process and that it will spur further research that investigates the nature and applications of perceived control.

REFERENCES

Affleck, G., Tennen, H., Pfeiffer, C., Fifield, C., & Rowe, J. (1987). Downward comparison and coping with serious medical problems. *American Journal of Orthopsychiatry, 57*, 570–578.

Arnkoff, D. B., & Mahoney, M. J. (1979). The role of perceived control in psychopathology. In L. C. Perlmuter & R. A. Monty (Eds.), *Choice and perceived control* (pp. 155–174). Hillsdale, NJ: Erlbaum.

Bandura, A. (1997). *Self-efficacy.* New York: Freeman.

Bandura, A., Adams, N. E., & Beyer, J. (1977). Cognitive processes mediating behavioral change. *Journal of Personality and Social Psychology, 35*, 125–139.

Bandura, A., Jeffery, R. W., & Wright, C. L. (1974). Efficacy of participant modeling as a function of response induction aids. *Journal of Abnormal Psychology, 83*, 56–64.

Barlow, D. H. (1988). *Anxiety and its disorders: The nature and treatment of anxiety and panic.* New York: Guilford.

Beck, A. T. (1976). *Cognitive therapy and the emotional disorders.* New York: International Universities Press.

Beck, A. T., Rush, A. J., Shaw, B. F., & Emery, G. (1979). *Cognitive therapy for depression.* New York: Guilford.

Brandstadter, J., & Rothermund, K. (1994). Self-percepts of control in middle and later adulthood: Buffering losses by rescaling goals. *Psychology and Aging, 9*, 265–273.

Brickman, P., Rabinowitz, V. C., Karuza, J., Jr., Coates, D., Cohn, E., & Kidder, L. (1982). Models of helping and coping. *American Psychologist, 37*, 368–384.

Bugental, D. B., Blue, J., & Cruzcosa, M. (1989). Perceived control over caregiving outcomes: Implications for child abuse. *Developmental Psychology, 25*, 532–539.

Bugental, D. B., Whalen, C. K., & Henker, B. (1977). Causal attributions of hyperactive children and motivational assumptions of two behavior-change approaches: Evidence for an interactionist position. *Child Development, 48*, 874–884.

Burger, J. M. (1989). Negative reactions to increases in perceived personal control. *Journal of Personality and Social Psychology, 56*, 246–256.

Carver, C. S., & Humphries, C. (1982). Social psychology of the type A coronary-prone behavior pattern. In G. S. Saunders & J. Suls (Eds.), *Social psychology of health and illness* (pp. 33–64). Hillsdale, NJ: Erlbaum.

Chapman, M., Skinner, E. A., & Baltes, P. B. (1990). Interpreting correlations between children's perceived control and cognitive performance: Control, agency, or means-ends beliefs? *Developmental Psychology, 26*, 246–253.

Cloitre, M., Heimberg, R. G., Liebowitz, M. R., & Gitow, A. (1992). Perceptions of control in panic disorder and social phobia. *Cognitive Therapy and Research, 16*, 569–577.

Dantzer, R. (1989). Neuroendocrine correlates of control and coping. In A. Steptoe & A. Appels (Eds.), *Stress, personal control and health* (pp. 277–294). New York: Wiley.

deCharms, R. (1968). *Personal causation.* New York: Academic Press.

Dunning, D., & Story, A. L. (1991). Depression, realism, and the overconfidence effect: Are the sadder wiser when predicting future actions and events? *Journal of Personality and Social Psychology, 61*, 521–532.

Dutton, M. A. (1992). *Empowering and healing the battered woman*. New York: Springer.

Eifert, G. H., Coburn, K. E., & Seville, J. L. (1992). Putting the client in control: The perception of control in the behavioral treatment of anxiety. *Anxiety, Stress, and Coping, 5*, 165–176.

England, S. L., & Evans, J. (1992). Patients' choices and perceptions after an invitation to participate in treatment decisions. *Social Science and Medicine, 34*, 1217–1225.

Ersek, M. (1992). The process of maintaining hope in adults undergoing bone marrow transplantation for leukemia. *Oncology Nursing Forum, 19*, 883–889.

Foa, E. B., Steketee, G., & Rothbaum, B.O. (1989). Behavioral/cognitive conceptualizations of post-traumatic stress disorder. *Behavior Therapy, 20*, 155–176.

Forehand, R., & McMahon, R. (1981). *Helping the noncompliant child*. New York: Guilford.

Frank, J. D. (1982). Therapeutic components shared by all psychotherapies. In J. H. Harvey & M. M. Parks (Eds.), *Psychotherapy research and behavior change* (Master lecture series, Vol. 1, pp. 9–37). Washington DC: American Psychological Association.

Friedman, M., Thoresen, C., Gill, J., Ulmer, D., Powell, L., Price, V., Brown, B., Thompson, L., Rabin, D., Breall, W., Bourg, E., Levy, R., & Dixon, T. (1986). Alteration of type A behavior and its effects on cardiac recurrences in post myocardial infarction patients: Summary results of the recurrent coronary prevention project. *American Heart Journal, 112*, 653–675.

Gatz, M., & Karel, M. J. (1993). Individual change in perceived control over 20 years. *International Journal of Behavioral Development, 16*, 305–322.

Glass, D. C., McKnight, J. D., & Valdimarsdottir, H. (1993). Depression, burnout, and perceptions of control in hospital nurses. *Journal of Consulting and Clinical Psychology, 61*, 147–155.

Graham, S. (1994). Motivation in African Americans. *Review of Educational Research, 64*, 55–117.

Gurin, P., Gurin, G., & Morrison, B. M. (1978). Personal and ideological aspects of internal and external control. *Social Psychology, 41*, 275–296.

Hibbert, G. A. (1984). Ideational components of anxiety: Their origin and content. *British Journal of Psychiatry, 144*, 618–624.

Hollon, S. D., & DeRubeis, R. J. (1992). Cognitive therapy and the prevention of depression. *Applied and Preventive Psychology, 1*, 89–95.

Janoff-Bulman, R., & Frieze, I. H. (1983). A theoretical perspective for understanding reactions to victimization. *Journal of Social Issues, 39*(2), 1–17.

Johnston, M., Gilbert, P., Partridge, C., & Collins, J. (1992). Changing perceived control in patients with physical disabilities: An intervention study with patients receiving rehabilitation. *British Journal of Clinical Psychology, 31*, 89–94.

Krantz, S. E. (1995). Chronic physical disability and secondary control: Appraisals of an undesirable situation. *Journal of Cognitive Psychotherapy: An International Quarterly, 9*, 229–248.

Lachman, M. E. (1991). Perceived control over memory aging: Developmental and intervention perspectives. *Journal of Social Issues, 47*(4), 159–175.

Lachman, M. E., & Weaver, S. L. (1998). The sense of control as a moderator of social class differences in health and well-being. *Journal of Personality and Social Psychology, 74*, 763–773.

Langer, E. J. (1975). The illusion of control. *Journal of Personality and Social Psychology, 32*, 311–328.

Langer, E. J. (1989). *Mindfulness*. Reading, MA: Addison-Wesley.

Langer, E. J., & Rodin, J. (1976). The effects of choice and enhanced personal responsibility: A field experiment in an institutional setting. *Journal of Personality and Social Psychology, 34*, 191–198.

Leung, A. W., & Heimberg, R. G. (1996). Homework compliance, perceptions of control, and outcome of cognitive-behavioral treatment of social phobia. *Behaviour, Research, and Therapy, 34*, 423–432.

Levenson, H. (1981). Differentiating among internality, powerful others, and chance. In H. M. Lefcourt (Ed.), *Research with the locus of control construct* (Vol. 1, pp. 15–63). New York: Academic Press.

Liberman, B. L. (1978). The role of mastery in psychotherapy: Maintenance of improvement and prescriptive change. In J. D. Frank, R. Hoehn-Saric, S. E. Imber, B. L. Liberman, & A. R. Stone, *Effective ingredients of successful psychotherapy*. New York: Brunner/Mazel.

Litt, M. D. (1988). Self-efficacy and perceived control: Cognitive mediators of pain tolerance. *Journal of Personality and Social Psychology, 4*, 149–160.

Lowery, B. J., Jacobsen, B. S., & McCauley, K. (1987). On the prevalence of causal search in illness situations. *Nursing Research, 36*, 88–93.

Mineka, S., & Kihlstrom, J. F. (1978). Unpredictable and uncontrollable events: A new perspective on experimental neurosis. *Journal of Abnormal Psychology, 87*, 256–271.

Mirowsky, J. (1995). Age and the sense of control. *Social Psychology Quarterly, 58*, 31–43.

Mitchell, J. (1997, May 28). Paddling toward life. *The Oregonian*, D, 1, 3.

Nelson, E. A. (1993). Control beliefs of adults in three domains: A new assessment of perceived control. *Psychological Reports, 72*, 155–165.

Patterson, G. R. (1988). Family process: Loops, levels, and linkages. In N. Bolger, A. Caspi, G. Downey, & M. Moorehouse (Eds.), *Persons in context: Developmental processes* (pp. 114–151). New York: Cambridge University Press.

Pearlin, L. I., & Schooler, C. (1978). The structure of coping. *Journal of Health and Social Behavior, 19,* 2–21.

Peng, Y., & Lachman, M. E. (1993). *Primary and secondary control: Age and cultural differences.* Paper presented at the 101st Annual Convention of the American Psychological Association, Toronto.

Peterson, C., Maier, S. F., & Seligman, M. E. P. (1993). *Learned helplessness: A theory for the age of perceived control.* New York: Oxford University Press.

Peterson, C., & Stunkard, A. J. (1989). Personal control and health promotion. *Social Science and Medicine, 28,* 819–828.

Phares, E. J. (1993). From therapy to research: A patient's legacy. In G. G. Brannigan & M. R. Merrens (Eds.), *The undaunted psychologist* (pp. 157–171). New York: McGraw-Hill.

Prince, J. E., & Arias, I. (1994). The role of perceived control and the desirability of control among abusive and nonabusive husbands. *The American Journal of Family Therapy, 22,* 126–134.

Purdon, C., & Clark, D. A. (1994). Perceived control and appraisal of obsessional intrusive thoughts: A replication and extension. *Behavioural and Cognitive Psychotherapy, 22,* 269–285.

Rapee, R. M. (1995). Psychological factors influencing the affective response to biological challenge procedures in panic disorder. *Journal of Anxiety Disorders, 9,* 59–74.

Reich, J. W., & Zautra, A. J. (1991). Experimental and measurement approaches to internal control in at-risk older adults. *Journal of Social Issues, 47*(4), 143–158.

Rodin, J. (1986). Aging and health: Effects of the sense of control. *Science, 233,* 1271–1276.

Rodin, J., Rennert, K., & Solomon, S. K. (1980). Intrinsic motivation for control: Fact or fiction. In A. Baum & J. E. Singer (Eds.), *Advances in environmental psychology: Applications of personal control* (pp. 131–148). Hillsdale, NJ: Erlbaum.

Ross, C. E., & Mirowsky, J. (1989). Explaining the social patterns of depression: Control and problem solving—or support and talking? *Journal of Health and Social Behavior, 30,* 206–219.

Rothbaum, F., Weisz, J. R., & Snyder, S. S. (1982). Changing the world and changing the self: A two-process model of perceived control. *Journal of Personality and Social Psychology, 42,* 5–27.

Rotter, J. B. (1966). Generalized expectancies for internal versus external control of reinforcement. *Psychological Monographs, 80*(1, Whole No. 609).

Schiaffino, K. M., Revenson, T. A., & Gibofsky, A. (1991). Assessing the impact of self-efficacy beliefs on adaptation to rheumatoid arthritis. *Arthritis Care and Research, 4,* 150–157.

Schunk, D. H., & Rice, J. M. (1987). Enhancing comprehension skill and self-efficacy with strategy value information. *Journal of Reading Behavior, 19,* 285–302.

Seligman, M. E. P. (1972). Learned helplessness. *Annual Review of Medicine, 23,* 407–412.

Seligman, M. E. P., & Miller, S. M. (1979). The psychology of power: Concluding comments. In L. S. Perlmuter and R. A. Monty (Eds.), *Choice and perceived control* (pp. 345–370). Hillsdale, NJ: Erlbaum.

Shapiro, D. H., Bates, D. E., Greenzang, T. R., & Carrere, S. (1994). A control content analysis scale applied to verbal samples of psychiatric outpatients: Correlation with anxiety and hostility scales. *Psychologia, 34,* 86–97.

Shapiro, D. H., Schwartz, C. E., & Astin, J. A. (1996). Controlling ourselves, controlling our world. *American Psychologist, 51,* 1213–1230.

Shear, M. K. (1995). Psychotherapeutic issues in long-term treatment of anxiety disorder patients. *The Psychiatric Clinics of North America, 18,* 885–894.

Shnek, Z. M., Foley, F. W., LaRocca, N. G., Gordon, W. A., DeLuca, J., Schwartzmann, H. G., Halper, J., Lennox, S., & Irvine, J. (1997). Helplessness, self-efficacy, cognitive distortions, and depression in multiple sclerosis and spinal cord injury. *Annals of Behavioral Medicine, 19,* 279–286.

Sieber, W. J., Rodin, R., Larson, L., Ortega, S., Cummings, N., Levy, S., Whiteside, T., & Herberman, R. (1992). *Brain, Behavior, and Immunity, 6,* 141–156.

Simoni, J. M., Adelman, H. S., & Nelson, P. (1991). Perceived control, causality, expectations, and help-seeking behaviour. *Counselling Psychology Quarterly, 4,* 37–44.

Skinner, E. A. (1995). *Perceived control, motivation, and coping.* Thousand Oaks CA: Sage.

Stein, M. J., Wallston, K. A., Nicassio, P. M., & Castner, N. M. (1988). Correlates of a clinical classification schema for the arthritis helplessness subscale. *Arthritis and Rheumatism, 31,* 876–881.

Stringer, S. A., & LaGreca, A. M. (1985). Correlates of child abuse potential. *Journal of Abnormal Child Psychology, 13,* 217–226.

Taylor, S. E. (1983). Adjustment to threatening events: A theory of cognitive adaptation. *American Psychologist, 38,* 1161–1173.

Taylor, S. E., Wood, J. V., & Lichtman, R. R. (1983). It could be worse: Selective evaluation as a response to victimization. *Journal of Social Issues, 39*(2), 19–40.

Thompson, S. C. (1981). Will it hurt less if I can control it? A complex answer to a simple question. *Psychological Bulletin, 90,* 89–101.

Thompson, S. C. (1991a). Intervening to enhance perceptions of control. In C. R. Snyder & D.

Forsyth (Eds.), *Handbook of social and clinical psychology* (pp. 607–623). New York: Pergamon.

Thompson, S. C. (1991b). The search for meaning following a stroke. *Basic and Applied Social Psychology, 12,* 81–96.

Thompson, S. C., Armstrong, W., & Thomas, C. (1998). Illusions of control, underestimations, and accuracy: A control heuristic explanation. *Psychological Bulletin, 123,* 143–161.

Thompson, S. C., Cheek, P. R., & Graham, M. A. (1988). The other side of perceived control: Disadvantages and negative effects. In S. Spacapan & S. Oskamp (Eds.), *The social psychology of health* (pp. 69–93). Beverly Hills, CA: Sage.

Thompson, S. C., & Janigian, A. (1988). Life schemes: A framework for understanding the search for meaning. *Journal of Social and Clinical Psychology, 7,* 260–280.

Thompson, S. C., Nanni, C., & Levine, A. (1994). Primary versus secondary and disease versus consequence-related control in HIV-positive men. *Journal of Personality and Social Psychology, 67,* 540–547.

Thompson, S. C., & Pitts, J. (1992). In sickness and in health: Chronic illness, marriage, and spousal caregiving. In S. Spacapan & S. Oskamp (Eds.), *Helping and being helped* (pp. 115–151). Newbury Park, CA: Sage.

Thompson, S. C., Sobolew-Shubin, A., Galbraith, M. E., Schwankovsky, L., & Cruzen, D. (1993). Maintaining perceptions of control: Finding perceived control in low-control circumstances. *Journal of Personality and Social Psychology, 64,* 293–304.

Thompson, S. C., Thomas, C., Rickabaugh, C. A., Tantamjarik, P., Otsuki, T., Pan, D., Garcia, B., & Sinar, E. (1998). Primary and secondary control over age-related changes in physical appearance. *Journal of Personality, 66,* 583–605.

Visintainer, M. A., Volpicelli, J. R., & Seligman, M. E. P. (1982). Tumor rejection in rats after inescapable or escapable shock. *Science, 216,* 437–439.

Wallhagen, M. I. (1993). Perceived control and adaptation in elder caregivers: Development of an explanatory model. *International Journal of Aging and Human Development, 36,* 219–237.

Weisz, J. R. (1986). Contingency and control beliefs as predictors of psychotherapy outcomes among children and adolescents. *Journal of Consulting and Clinical Psychology, 54,* 789–795.

Weisz, J. R., McCabe, M. A., & Dennig, M. D. (1994). Primary and secondary control among children undergoing medical procedures: Adjustment as a function of coping style. *Journal of Consulting and Clinical Psychology, 62,* 324–332.

Weisz, J. R., & Stipek, D. J. (1982). Competence, contingency, and the development of perceived control. *Human Development, 25,* 250–281.

Wiedenfeld, S. A., O'Leary, A., Bandura, A., Brown, S., Levine, S., & Raska, K. (1991). Impact of perceived self-efficacy in coping with stressors on components of the immune system. *Journal of Personality and Social Psychology, 59,* 1082–1094.

Wilson, G. T. (1979). Perceived control and the theory and practice of behavior therapy. In L. C. Perlmuter & R. A. Monty (Eds.), *Choice and perceived control* (pp. 175–189). Hillsdale, NJ: Erlbaum.

PART IV

PSYCHOTHERAPEUTIC
APPROACHES

●

PSYCHODYNAMIC APPROACHES TO PSYCHOTHERAPY: PHILOSOPHICAL AND THEORETICAL FOUNDATIONS OF EFFECTIVE PRACTICE

DOUGLAS A. VAKOCH AND HANS H. STRUPP
Vanderbilt University

MODELS OF PSYCHODYNAMIC PSYCHOTHERAPY

In this chapter, we address several aspects of psychodynamic psychotherapy—its theoretical foundations, from several perspectives; its analysis of the relationship between patient and therapist; and the underlying ways of viewing the world that are characteristic of psychodynamic approaches. Although our emphasis is on examining psychodynamic psychotherapy, at times we do so by contrasting this orientation with other orientations. We begin by examining some of the basic theories laid out by Freud and elaborated and modified by subsequent generations of dynamic thinkers.

Freud's Drive Model

To understand the foundations of Freud's model of psychodynamic functioning, it is essential to understand the scientific context in which it arose. As a medical doctor in the late 19th century, Freud was trained as a neurologist. This training helped inculcate the habit of dealing with disturbances of the human psyche in physicalistic terms. In contradistinction to philosophical and religious examinations of the mind and soul, Freud attempted to use a rigorously scientific approach to understanding human psychological distress.

One of the core scientific models that influenced Freud's thinking was Charles Darwin's (1859) evolutionary theory. A central assumption of this theory is that life is a struggle for scarce resources, in which only the strong, "red in tooth and claw," survive to reproduce. And much to the dismay of Victorian sensibilities, Darwin claimed that evolutionary principles hold sway over all living beings. Human beings were not to be seen as somewhere between angels and beasts, but as continuous in their deepest needs with other animals.

Drawing on this Darwinian framework, Freud emphasized the primacy of the innate drives of sexuality and aggression. In Freud's view, these biological drives become manifest during the child's development, taking on different forms during the psychosexual stages that he termed oral, anal, phallic, latency, and genital. For example, both drives are evident in the oedipal conflict, in which the young child in the phallic stage seeks a sexual relationship with the opposite-sex parent and fears retaliation from the same-sex parent for this wish.

But in Freudian drive theory, these impulses are not always acted on. The individual may express these desires as fantasies—either conscious or unconscious—rather than acting them out. But whether the wishes are acted out or fantasized, the individual often encounters obstacles to their expression. Constraints are imposed by parental figures or the broader society that bring the desiring individual into a state of conflict. This conflict can be manifested in many ways. For example, the individual may want to act in sexual or aggressive ways and yet feel guilty for these desires.

Ego Psychology

In his later writings, Freud discussed how one aspect of the conflicted person, the ego (Latin for "I"), attempts to deal with impulses of the id

(Latin for "it"). As Freud (1923/1960) contrasted the two, "The ego represents what may be called reason and common sense, in contrast to the id, which contains the passions" (p. 15). The id is ruled by the pleasure principle, through which individuals attempt to gratify all of their desires immediately. By contrast, the ego attempts to govern the psyche through the reality principle, in which drives are not satisfied directly or immediately but through compromises with societal restrictions.

The ego-psychological approach to psychoanalysis is a direct outgrowth and development of Freud's writings on the ego. Psychoanalysts such as Anna Freud (1966) attempted to explain ways in which the ego acts to defend against threats to the self, for example, by repressing or sublimating instinctual drives. However, another perspective has viewed the ego as operating more broadly, in response to the individual's larger environment, not merely to conflicts (Hartmann, 1958; Pine, 1990). From this perspective, the individual is seen as having a built-in tendency to make sense of the world. Consistent with the drive model, ego psychology sees the ego functioning through biologically determined, evolutionarily adaptive processes. The hard-wired perceptual and cognitive apparatus of the infant, as it develops through interaction with its environment, provides the foundation for the reality principle.

From an ego-psychological perspective, development is seen not primarily in terms of successive manifestations of innate urges, but as a process of learning to construct a meaningful model of the world from a complex array of experiences. The infant attempts to incorporate as much relevant information as possible into this model of how the world works, all the while being restricted by cognitive limitations. If the infant is fortunate and has a sufficiently stable and predictable environment, an adequate model of the world can be constructed, thereby allowing the infant to comprehend subsequent experiences.

Problems arise when the infant's maturing ego is unable to construct a sufficiently coherent model of the world. In an attempt to reduce anxiety over living in a world where some experiences do not "fit in" in a meaningful way, the infant may block out certain information. Historically, this has been described as the work of various defense mechanisms. The particular defenses used by any given individual are determined by interrelated factors including the person's innate temperament, the type of stresses en-

countered during childhood, and how well various defenses were rewarded in childhood (McWilliams, 1994).

For example, the schizoid individual characteristically responds through the defense of *withdrawal*. In part, this may reflect a temperamental sensitivity to stimulation. The acutely sensitive person is more prone to withdraw from the world, a tendency that is particularly rewarded if it allows the child to escape from caretakers who are too emotionally demanding. Whereas withdrawal may be an adaptive response in childhood, as the person's life situation changes the patient may begin seeing this habitual response as overly truncated. In short, the defense of withdrawal might come to be seen as *ego dystonic*, or alien to the person's central sense of self.

Defenses that are too pervasive or too rigidly applied give rise to a split in the patient's ego (Sterba, 1934). One part, the *experiencing ego*, corresponds to the patient's direct emotional experience. The other part, the *observing ego*, has some awareness of and distance from the experiencing ego. From this perspective, those patients who experience their problems as ego-dystonic (i.e., in conflict with the observing ego) have the best prognosis. Unless the problem is something subjectively felt as needing to be changed, the patient will not have the motivation to seek more flexible means of responding.

Object Relations Theory

Both drive theory and ego psychology recognize that the child interacts with other people during the maturational process. Neither of these theoretical approaches, however, places the other person in a central role, as does an *object relations* perspective. In Freud's drive theory, sexual and aggressive impulses can be directed toward other persons, but they can be directed equally well toward nonhuman targets. For ego psychologists, the developing child attends to other people, providing the child's nascent ego with important information. But the ego is not specifically defined in terms of other individuals. In the object relations perspective, however, relationships with other people (called objects) are at the core of the individual's development. Different theorists have proposed specific ways that individual development unfolds in response to interactions with others. In the following paragraphs, we summarize the views of an influential object relations theorist, Melanie Klein, and then contrast her approach with that of other object relations theorists.

Although developmental issues were a central concern to Freud, he did not base his theory of psychosexual stages on direct observations of children. Rather, he derived his theory primarily from clinical work with adults. By contrast, Klein attempted to conduct psychoanalysis directly with children. Although she was not able to apply standard psychoanalytic approaches to children because of their limited verbal and cognitive abilities, she came to understand their central preoccupations through play therapy. Contrary to Freud's theories, the children whom Klein observed did not devote much time to restraining their libidinal drives. Instead, they primarily focused on elaborating their interpersonal worlds, particularly through their relationships with their mothers, their primary caregivers.

Unlike other major object relations theorists, Klein emphasized Freud's early notions about the *death instinct* to help explain infant development. Klein viewed the death instinct as a powerful inner force that would result in self-destruction if not checked. The infant dealt with this force by *projecting* the struggle between life and death onto the external world in a way that affects the perception of other human beings. This projection results in an external world that—in the mind of the infant—is populated with "bad objects." But the child also projects some libidinal energy to create "good objects" in the external world. The child then *introjects*, or internalizes, these objects as hateful and loving feelings.

Klein describes the child's development in terms of the conflict between these loving and hateful feelings. In the first stage, the child meets the first object, the breast. The infant recognizes the goodness of the breast through the nurturance it provides. But equally important, the child responds to the breast as if it were malicious. The infant "bites and tears up the breast, devours it, annihilates it; and he feels that the breast will attack him in the same way" (Klein, 1952/1975, p. 63; cited in Cashdan, 1988, p. 7). The infant deals with these contrary feelings by separating them into distinct categories corresponding to good and bad objects.

As children mature, they begin to treat their mothers as entities, whole objects that are both good and bad. As a consequence, the child reacts to the mother with both love and hate. One consequence of the child's expression of negative feelings is a sense of guilt over hurting the mother through expressed anger. This guilt then leads to a sense of sorrow for inflicting pain on the mother. This concern for the other provides the foundation for the later development of empathy in the child.

Other major object relations theorists deemphasize or ignore the role of the death instinct. For example, Fairbairn (1954) contended that the bad object arises from the infant's experiences of the mother's insufficiency. That is, children are not merely fantasizing that mothers are aggressive, but are also responding to true instances of dealing with frustrations and deprivations when not getting what they want.

A recurrent theme of object relations theorists is the infant's tendency to split experiences into good and bad objects. If the child matures in a healthy way, the same person can be seen as having both good and bad aspects. When this does not occur, the person typically has extreme and chaotic relationships with others as an adult, as occurs for individuals with borderline features (Kernberg, 1975).

Many object relations theorists discuss development toward healthy integration, although they may conceptualize the stages in different ways. For example, Mahler, Pine, and Bergman (1975) described the steps by which a child becomes separate and individuated from the mother, whereas Fairbairn (1954) spoke of the child's move from dependence to mutuality and interdependence. For Kohut (1971, 1977), maturation involves the move from feelings of narcissistic omnipotence to a more realistic sense of self in which one's limitations are acknowledged.

Interpersonal Theory

In many respects, Harry Stack Sullivan's interpersonal approach is very similar to object relations approaches and, in fact, some consider Sullivan's approach to be an American version of British objects relations theory. As with the object relations theorists, Sullivan stressed the development of the individual.

At times, the language that Sullivan (1953) uses to describe development makes his view sound like a drive theory. For example, he wrote, "*The observed activity of the infant arising from the tension of needs induces tension in the mothering one, which tension is experienced as tenderness and as an impulse to activities toward the relief of the infant's needs*" (p. 39; emphasis in original). His use of words like *tension* and *impulse*, however, should not obscure Sullivan's emphasis on the individual's most central needs being directed toward significant others. In fact, in Sullivan's view, the development of personality and a sense of self requires contact with others. For Sullivan, the self is formed out of internalizations of one's interactions with others. Without these interactions, no fully formed self would exist.

Although Sullivan (1953) placed considerable emphasis on early childhood, his developmental concerns did not end there. Rather, he proposed stages of development that went through late adolescence. One implication of this extension of interpersonal development beyond childhood is that it provides a framework for understanding the remediation of interpersonal deficits that sometimes occur in adolescence. Sullivan maintained that if the preadolescent is able to form a close relationship with a same-sexed friend, or "chum," this friendship can help compensate for inadequacies experienced in childhood. Furthermore, by carefully following the development of the individual through early adulthood, the stage is set for the therapist and researcher to focus carefully on the interactions between the patient and therapist that occur within the session. The theoretical focus on interpersonal interactions directs the attention of the therapist and researcher to social *transactions* and interpersonal communication. These phenomena, that is, social transactions, are intrinsically observable and, therefore, are easily accessible to empirical investigation. Likewise, social transactions can be shown to follow general "laws" governing the oscillating sequences of each participant's contributions to the ongoing interaction (Anchin & Kiesler, 1982).

THERAPEUTIC DIMENSIONS OF PSYCHODYNAMIC PSYCHOTHERAPY

Transference

For Freud, psychopathology was the result of an unconscious conflict between the socialized ego and the threatened expression of unsocialized, libidinal (sexual and aggressive) impulses. The neurotic conflict can be abolished by teaching the ego to accept, tolerate, and modify the subjectively threatening impulse. In the Freudian view, the patient's entire psychological system resists conscious awareness of the libidinal impulses, as well as awareness or memory of the original conflict. Repression of the conflict has two results: one is maintenance of the status quo; the other is a tendency to act out, or repeat attitudes and emotions relevant to the conflict, rather than

consciously remembering it. This repetition brings relief to the individual because it restores the person to an earlier psychic state. In Sigmond Freud's (1920/1966) framework, this repetition is driven by a "regressive instinct."[1]

The conflicts between id and ego are thus reenacted continually in the patient's life. When they occur within the consulting room and in interaction with the therapist, these repetitions are referred to as *transference*. That is, patients transfer the conflict from their own psyches into the interpersonal interactions with therapists. The existence of transference is very fortunate from a therapeutic perspective because it provides an arena in which the therapist can help the patient to uncover the underlying conflict. By becoming an ally of the patient's observing ego, the therapist fosters the patient's awareness and, ultimately, the acceptance of id impulses. In short, the unconscious is made conscious, which allows for change.

Differing schools of psychodynamic psychotherapy provide alternative explanations for the therapeutic efficacy of dealing with the transference. For the classical drive theorist, addressing the transference is effective because it focuses on an intrapsychic conflict between ego and id and thus frees the patient from the regressive instinct. That is, with the conflict resolved, or at least made tolerable, the patient no longer needs to retreat to an earlier psychic state.

For object relations theorists, on the other hand, transference is not driven by the patient's purely intrapsychic conflict. Rather, transference is based on the patient's internalized representations of past interactions with significant others—either actual or fantasied. As we learned previously, individuals incorporate good and bad objects into their psychic worlds with varying degrees of integration. From an object relations perspective, these representations are *projected* onto the therapist (Guntrip, 1973). That is, regardless of the true nature of the interaction between the patient and therapist, the patient comes to see the therapist in terms of internalized objects. Through the process of *projective identification*, therapists come to act in manners consistent with the objects that patients have projected onto them.

The nature of projective identification is specified clearly by interpersonal theorists, al-

---

[1] We are indebted to the contributions of Dr. Stephen F. Butler in our formulation of the following material.

though they use different language to do so. A central concept in an interpersonal account of transference is *complementarity*. That is, the actions of one partner in any interaction tend to "pull" for a certain reaction from others that will complement the original action. One common approach in characterizing such complementarity has been to look for a few underlying dimensions along which the complex array of interactions can be classified.

Two of the most frequently identified dimensions, which go by different names, are the dimensions of *control* (dominance vs. submission) and *affiliation* (love vs. hate) (Benjamin, 1982; Leary, 1957). From these dimensions, two types of complementarity can be recognized. On the control dimension, interactions are driven by the principle of *reciprocity*. Thus, if one person acts in a controlling, dominating fashion, this has a tendency to pull for reciprocal submissiveness in the other person. And, likewise, an initially submissive act by one person extends an invitation to the other to take charge. Complementarity along the control dimension, by contrast, involves *corresponding* actions. That is, a kind, loving action from one person will elicit a similarly caring response from the other; likewise, a hateful action by one person will naturally pull for a similar negative reaction from the other.

The explanatory framework offered by interpersonal theorists provides a means for understanding and predicting interactions. Although the researcher and therapist may have an explicit understanding of the rules guiding these interactions, patients may not be aware of the impact that their actions have on others. Whereas many people generally can judge the context of a situation and respond appropriately to others, less fortunate individuals are more rigid in their responses. As a consequence, the latter may misread others' intentions and react in a self-defeating manner. For instance, a patient who grew up in a very hostile family may misread the friendly actions of others as being manipulative attempts to gain an advantage. Whereas this might have been an accurate reading of the patient's parents, it may be a distortion of the actions of other significant persons whom the patient meets as an adult.

The hallmark of an interpersonal approach to psychodynamic psychotherapy is to increase the patient's flexibility in interacting with others. First and foremost, through in-session interactions and analyses of transference, patients understand their habitual interactional styles and become more effective in responding to others.

Countertransference

In classical Freudian psychoanalysis, the phenomenon of transference is not limited to the patient. Because of analysts' unresolved conflicts, they can undergo the same processes of projection. This process of analysts' projections onto patients, called *countertransference*, is seen as a breach of analytic neutrality. The ideal stance is analytic objectivity, and the distortions introduced by countertransference are seen as a hindrance to effective therapy. Freud considered countertransference such a large obstacle that he required a personal analysis of all would-be analysts, in part to gain insights into their transferences.

With the development of psychodynamic thinking, however, countertransference no longer is seen as completely negative. Instead, it is recognized as a potential tool for assessing patients and providing feedback to them. For example, distinctions can be drawn between nonproductive countertransference and "objective countertransference," the latter referring to those strong feelings of the therapist toward the patient that are based on the patient's real actions and personality. To misunderstand the true nature of objective countertransference reactions would deprive the therapist of potentially useful information about the patient. Analysts stress the importance of therapists' tolerance of strong negative feelings toward patients, without acting on these feelings. Also, objective countertransference provides the therapist with information to be given to patients about their impacts on others. The value of objective countertransference has become accepted widely in psychodynamic circles (e.g., Epstein, 1979; Menninger & Holzman, 1973).

One recent elaboration of the psychotherapeutic value of objective countertransference is seen in Cashdan's (1988) approach to object relations. Cashdan maintains that patients use four major projective identifications: power, dependency, ingratiation, and sexuality. In this model, the therapist is often not aware of countertransferential reactions in early therapy. As the therapeutic relationship develops, however, the therapist responds to the patient's projective identifications similarly to others' reactions. As the countertransference increases, the therapist feels strong emotional reactions to the patient. Treatment consists of helping patients understand how they elicit these feelings from most others, therapists included.

In this approach, objective transference is inevitable. Throughout treatment, the therapist remains alert to emotional pulls to respond in a certain way. As Kiesler (1982) notes, "The therapist cannot *not* be hooked by the client" (p. 18; our emphasis). However, the therapist *does* have the power to stop responding in the expected complementary manner, and this is an essential component of interpersonal therapy. In addition, the therapist meta-communicates with the patient about the patient's "evoking style" (Kiesler, 1982; Strupp & Binder, 1984). The goal is to help the patient to become aware of alternative and more beneficial interactional styles.

Negative Complementarity: A Research Perspective

Although the phenomena of countertransference are discussed somewhat differently by divergent psychodynamic schools, the core processes are the same. One of the challenges to investigators of psychodynamic approaches is to operationalize the psychotherapeutic process. Interpersonal theory provides a useful framework for this purpose through its emphasis on complementarity. In this section, we review research studies that highlight the dangers of negative responses by therapists to patients' hostility, that is, *negative complementarity*.

Although some psychodynamic theorists continued to emphasize the importance of countertransference in the 1960s and 1970s, psychotherapy researchers interested in the nature of the therapist's influence focused on the more general question of the differential influence of *specific* (technique) vs. *nonspecific* (common or relational) factors. Vanderbilt I was one such study. Its major purpose was to determine the relative contribution of these two factors on treatment outcomes (see Chapter 7 in this volume). In this study, treatments conducted by professional therapists (representing technique plus common factors) were contrasted with treatments conducted by college professors who had been judged very helpful to students (representing only common factors). If the specific techniques used by therapists were important above and beyond common factors, then patients working with trained therapists should have better outcomes than those patients paired with college professors ("alternate therapists"). Contrary to expectation, there were no statistically significant differences in group comparisons of therapy outcomes, despite adequate power (Strupp & Hadley, 1979).

Marked differences in the interpersonal process across therapies were apparent, however, in a subsequent series of systematic qualitative

case studies. "Research-informed case studies" (Soldz, 1990) were conducted by first identifying and characterizing patient-therapist dyads, using quantitative measures. Thereafter, fine-grained qualitative analyses were conducted on the selected cases (Strupp, 1980a, 1980b, 1980c, 1980d). Specifically, for each selected therapist, a case with a good outcome was contrasted with one with a poor outcome. In the last comparison in this series, Strupp (1980d) summarized the impact of negative complementarity, as follows:

> . . . as therapists we have not adequately faced up to the negative reactions engendered in us by patients. . . . The plain fact is that any therapist—indeed any human being—cannot remain immune from negative reactions to the suppressed and repressed rage regularly encountered in patients with moderate to severe disturbances. (p. 953)

Strupp concluded by noting the pervasiveness of the problem: "In our study we failed to encounter a single instance in which a difficult patient's hostility and negativism were successfully confronted or resolved . . . therapists' negative responses to difficult patients are far more common and far more intractable than has been generally recognized" (Strupp, 1980d, p. 954).

These qualitative analyses in the series of case studies by Strupp were confirmed by an independent reanalysis of the same cases, using quantitative measures based on interpersonal theory. Specifically, Benjamin's (1974) structural analysis of social behavior (SASB), which allows coding of the interpersonal process, using the dimensions of control and affiliation, showed that significantly fewer negative interactions occurred in cases with good outcomes (Henry, Schacht, & Strupp, 1986). Consistent with the cyclical nature of communication posited by interpersonal theorists, both patients' and therapists' communications were significantly more problematic in poor outcome cases. These problems took two forms. First, poor outcome cases showed more instances of a hostile utterance being followed by a hostile response, that is, direct evidence of negative complementarity. Second, poor outcome cases included more verbalizations with "mixed" interpersonal implications. An example of such a communication is a comment that is simultaneously both blaming and supportive. Because these analyses were conducted on early sessions, it appears that a negative process occurring at a very early stage may cause problems of lasting significance.

To examine the impact of negative complementarity at different stages of psychotherapy, Tasca and McMullen (1992) completed new SASB ratings of Vanderbilt I patient-therapist dyads. Unlike the earlier study cited above, however, they coded segments of sessions from three stages of therapy, each of which emphasized different tasks. In their model, toward the beginning of therapy, a vital therapeutic task is to establish a strong alliance with the patient. By the middle of treatment, the therapist focuses on work that is more confrontational. The final stage of therapy is characterized by a consolidation of the alliance and confrontational work. The investigators demonstrated that the negative complementarity associated with poor outcome cases was not restricted to the early stage of treatment: "The hostility that emerged from the very beginning of unsuccessful cases was pervasive across sessions" (p. 519). Consistent with their stage theory, they found that the negative process was most pronounced during the early and late stages of treatment, during which times alliance formation and alliance consolidation, respectively, are most important.

To better understand the process by which negative complementarity is maintained over the course of treatment, Tasca and McMullen (1992) also examined the sequences of negative exchanges. Their results point to the role played by patients in drawing their therapists into hostile interactions. Specifically, the patients in poor outcome cases made significantly more attempts to elicit hostile responses than did patients with good outcomes. This suggests that poor outcome patients easily engage in cyclical maladaptive patterns (Strupp & Binder, 1984) in their interpersonal transactions. This conclusion is supported by Kiesler and Watkins's (1989) observation, using a different assessment of complementarity: at least in the early phase of therapy, hostile displays by the patient have a profound impact on therapeutic interaction, with patients contributing more than therapists to the deterioration of the alliance.

Klee, Abeles, and Muller (1990) used different measures of both the process and the outcome, but their results also indicated that patients could draw their therapists into negative interactions. They showed that when patients contributed negatively to the therapeutic alliance from the start of therapy, therapists also tended to intervene in a hostile manner. This negativity on the part of the therapist, however, was unrelated to the therapist's positive contributions to the alliance. Thus, therapists may try assiduously to interact positively even with very difficult patients, but they remain prone to negative reactions.

Vanderbilt II: A Manual-guided Approach

In the 1980s and 1990s, American psychotherapy outcome research has focused on developing and assessing "manualized" treatments. The goal of this manualization is to systematize the conceptualization and delivery of psychotherapies so that research studies can validly and precisely evaluate the relative efficacy of psychotherapies, contrasted either with one another or with pharmacotherapies. Therapists using manualized treatments in controlled outcome studies are expected to restrict themselves to interventions covered by the particular manual being used, and the use of other interventions is strongly discouraged (Goldfried, Greenberg, & Marmar, 1990).

Given the problems that therapists had dealing with negative complementarity in the Vanderbilt I study and other research projects described previously, would therapists do better if their practices were guided by a manual focusing on transference issues? The Vanderbilt II project (Strupp, 1993) was conducted to answer this question for one type of manual-guided brief therapy: time-limited dynamic psychotherapy, or TLDP (Strupp & Binder, 1984). This model of therapy emphasizes the identification and amelioration of maladaptive interpersonal patterns, especially as manifested in the patient-therapist relationship. The study's design may be unique insofar as it compares the performance of therapists before and after a year of TLDP training rather than contrasting TLDP with another treatment. This design was chosen to more closely examine the effects of training on treatment efficacy.

Thus TLDP was created to address the sort of deficits therapists showed in the Vanderbilt I study. As noted previously, that study was designed to test the relative contributions of specific (technique) vs. nonspecific (common or relational) factors. One finding was that even experienced psychodynamic therapists displayed significant hostile reactions to difficult patients. The pervasiveness of this negative complementarity was surprising given the theoretical centrality of countertransference in psychodynamic therapies.

Nevertheless, it appeared that the therapists were lacking in specific techniques central to a psychodynamic treatment of these patients' problems. Thus, in the Vanderbilt II study, TLDP training emphasized a more systematic and earlier focus on transference and countertransference phenomena.

On the one hand, TLDP training succeeded in the Vanderbilt II study. After training, therapists' *adherence* to manual-guided techniques increased, and during supervision sessions therapists became more sensitive to observing the interpersonal process of both their own videotaped therapy sessions and the taped sessions of their fellow therapists. In more important ways, however, many of the therapists failed to improve significantly in their ability to deal effectively with essential transference and countertransference issues within actual sessions. That is, although the therapists increased their awareness of the specific techniques that constitute psychodynamic therapy and they could reflect with some insight on the interpersonal process *after* the sessions were completed, they continued to show deficits in effectively conducting TLDP in the here-and-now of their sessions. In fact, only about one-fourth of the posttraining cases were judged to have been completed with at least a minimum level of skill (Bein et al., 1997). Moreover, after training, therapists displayed *more* hostile and complex responses to patients, apparently because they were more active in sessions (Henry, Schacht, Strupp, Butler, & Binder, 1993).

After TLDP training, the therapists more often executed techniques prescribed by the manual, but frequently in an unnatural or ineffective manner. For instance, therapists often probed for patients' feelings about the therapist, but they did so when no evidence of transference was being manifested. At other times, therapists made transference interpretations that had no basis in material previously discussed in therapy. Even when therapists were on target with their transference interpretations, they seemed to lack the skills to facilitate the patient's greater self-understanding and emotional expression. In sum, the changes in technique that occurred as a result of training were relatively superficial. Although the therapists may have adhered more completely to manual-prescribed interventions, few clinically meaningful improvements in conducting therapy resulted.

For example, in the third session of one of the posttraining therapies (Butler & Strupp, 1989), a female patient disclosed concerns about her ability to remain sexually faithful in significant heterosexual relationships. Rather than exploring the patient's fears further, the male therapist immediately began probing to determine whether there was a "pattern" in her selection of men. In the midst of the patient's anxious confusion about this question, the therapist abruptly raised the issue of her feelings for him. Though she denied any feelings for the therapist, he continued to force the issue. After awhile the patient said, "I don't feel I've really opened up much yet," and she switched the conversation away from her sexual concerns toward her panic symptoms. Although the therapist was attempting to adhere to TLDP by detecting an interpersonal pattern and then relating it to the therapeutic relationship, his effort was concrete and mechanical and too vague, insensitive, and ill timed to foster any security in self-exploration on the part of the patient.

A somewhat more skillful attempt was also made in a third session. The patient and therapist discussed the patient's fantasy that people watching the videotape of their session would laugh at her. This was followed by the report of a previous therapist who had laughed at her. The therapist empathized with her humiliation and connected this with what she said earlier about repeated experiences of humiliation and devaluation from her father. He then asked, "Do you imagine that I might be feeling something like that too, in my reaction to you?" After an initial denial, the patient admitted to wondering whether the therapist might see her problems as "not that serious" and feel that she should be able to straighten things out for herself. Further exploration revealed fresh data about her masochistic inclination to aggressive self-attack in failing to meet perfectionistic standards, followed by more intimate vignettes of seeing herself as being a disappointment to her harsh and critical father.[2]

We have focused on the acquisition of TLDP skills by therapists as a whole, but there were considerable individual differences in the therapists' learning of the skills and in their implications. Notably, the most adherent therapists were themselves self-blaming and self-controlling. These therapists had worse outcomes than other therapists in the study (Henry et al., 1993). Similarly, more self-indicting therapists showed less

---

[2]We are indebted to Dr. Stephen F. Butler for assistance in formulating these cases.

warmth and friendliness toward their patients in sessions. In short, therapists cannot be treated as interchangeable units. There was no attempt in the Vanderbilt II study to individualize the way therapists would execute TLDP techniques with different types of patients, but such training might have been useful. Some tailoring of the training program to each therapist's personal characteristics might have helped to overcome the countertransferential responses that were most problematic for each therapist.

Should it be thought that the negative process is only problematic for therapists new to a psychodynamic approach, consider the course of a therapy conducted by the principal investigator of the Vanderbilt II study. Strupp (1990) published the case of a woman he treated during the course of a therapy that ran aground. The treatment ended prematurely after 13 sessions when, in anger, the patient precipitously terminated. Early in the treatment of this professional woman, she and the therapist identified a prepotent interpersonal theme of feeling exploited by and disappointed in men, as well as a conviction that men could not understand her experience. Both patient and therapist struggled with the manifestations of this theme within the therapeutic relationship but eventually succumbed to it. As Strupp observed after the patient quit, "One might argue that these feelings complemented precisely the patient's unconscious intent, in other words, they pointed to a central transference problem. I tried to avoid a power struggle but, in the end, failed" (p. 655).

The Limitations of Manualized Therapy

In a recent article on the role of the university in the information age, Noam (1995), a professor of finance and economics at Columbia University, made a point that is of considerable significance for psychotherapy: "True teaching and learning," the author asserted, "are more than information and its transmission. Education is based on mentoring, internalization, identification, role modeling, guidance, socialization, interaction, and group activity" (p. 249). With equal validity, we might say that psychotherapeutic treatment is considerably more than the application of techniques set forth in a treatment manual. As a large psychodynamic literature has long attested, therapeutic change is also a function of mentoring, internalization, identification, role modeling, guidance, socialization, and interaction.

Early in the history of psychoanalysis, Freud characterized psychotherapy as a form of "after-education" (*Nacherziehung*)—in other words, a teaching and learning process (Alexander & French, 1946). He understood that psychotherapy is not a treatment, except in a metaphorical sense, and that it can never be a product or a commodity delivered by a technician to a passive individual. Rather, the therapist serves as a model of adult living whose attitudes and values patients can internalize and with whom they can identify. Furthermore, the therapist provides guidance, as well as a benign and nurturing social milieu in which the patient can "grow" and mature. The therapist is also in a position to demonstrate beliefs and patterns of behavior to the patient that have been self-defeating, painful, and troublesome. In other words, the therapist effectively mediates *unlearning*, which typically is a prerequisite to new learning. Clearly, such a *corrective emotional experience* cannot be prescribed, easily packaged and dispensed, nor can it be readily mediated through manuals.

Indeed, one of Freud's most original and impressive contributions was to have created a vehicle—psychodynamic psychotherapy—that emphasizes the counterproductive childhood "lessons" that can interfere with happiness as an adult. In short, the therapist helps the patient to discover what works and what does not work in interpersonal living. As Sullivan (1954) advised in a memorable phrase, "Work toward uncovering those factors which are concerned in the person's recurrent mistakes, and which lead to his taking ineffective and inappropriate action. There is no necessity to do more" (p. 239).

Whereas the general principles of what constitutes therapeutic unlearning and learning are well understood, their application *in a specific case* often calls for consummate empathic understanding, sensitivity, tact, and *skill* on the therapist's part. At its best, each therapeutic hour is highly personalized and specially designed to meet the needs of a particular patient. The therapist must pinpoint the patient's current difficulty and frame communications to be helpful to the patient at this juncture. Often this means "not getting in the way," staying out of power struggles, and avoiding interpretations that might be complementary to the patient's provocations. In each instance, there are probably several ways to accomplish these goals, and there is no single absolute formula for success. On the other hand, there undoubtedly are many ways in which the therapist can undercut, sabotage, or otherwise derail the therapeutic process.

How does the therapist acquire the requisite skills to help another person? As in any complex and intricate process, it takes time, effort, instruction, and practice. A treatment manual can be a useful *beginning* or reference. Perhaps this is the most that can be expected. Similarly, an adherence measure can provide only a gross index of what the therapist does, and it can only rarely capture the essence of the therapist's communications. The trap for unwary researchers and managed-care companies alike is that of reifying a living process.

Where does this leave us in regard to the use of manuals in the training of psychodynamic therapists? Shall we return to the traditional supervisory model of training therapists? Indeed, the current preoccupation with manuals may have exceeded their usefulness, and further emphasis on the standardization of "techniques" may impede, rather than further, the advancement of productive models for therapists' training.

Currently, instruction in psychotherapy based on manuals tends to be brief, and it provides little opportunity for practicing and exploring the wide range of psychotherapeutic issues. Some therapists, especially those with self-blaming and self-controlling introjects (Henry, Schacht, & Strupp, 1990), may be excellent in adhering to a manualized model, but they may have difficulty in communicating with patients what they have learned without sounding mechanical or artificial. These therapists (like other novices) may rely rigidly on technical rules that, in practice, may interfere with full attention to the patient's communications. Often, as shown in the Vanderbilt II study, acquiring new psychotherapy skills may involve an extended period of disorganization and awkwardness. Furthermore, enhancing the skills of therapists is a complex and demanding process that calls for a new—and perhaps radical—reconceptualization of psychotherapy training procedures.

PSYCHODYNAMIC WAYS OF SEEING

Thus far we have approached psychodynamic psychotherapy through an examination of its theories and practices, that is, at levels usually discussed by both researchers and clinicians. As we have seen, however, an exclusive focus on these levels may leave the practitioner unable to ad-

dress some of the greatest challenges of psychotherapy, such as the problem of negative complementarity.

In this section, we argue that a more complete understanding of psychodynamic approaches can be gained by looking at *therapists' and patients' tacit ways of seeing the world.* Our point is that certain styles of thinking and visions of reality are particularly characteristic of, and consistent with, a psychodynamic approach. The degree to which any given patient's style matches or fails to match a therapist's style can affect such clinically important issues as the development of the therapeutic alliance and the therapist's prognosis for a patient. Thus, both therapists' and patients' styles will be considered, as well as the implications of the match between them (Berzins, 1977). The rationale for this focus on matching is that increased compatibility of the patient and therapist should allow for maximal interpersonal attraction and communication, which facilitate psychotherapy (see reviews in Byrne, 1969, 1971).[3]

Metaphor and Psychodynamic Reasoning

Some of the most obvious differences among therapeutic approaches are their underlying fundamental theoretical constructs, such as ideas about transference or projective identification. For example, Houts (1984) manipulated a simulated patient's implicit view of the nature of that person's problem so that it would be either compatible or incompatible with the theoretical orientation of the therapists who judged the prognosis. Houts found that psychodynamic therapists were more optimistic about the prognosis of patients whose explanatory biases were consistent with a psychodynamic conceptualization.

Less obvious differences, however, may be as important for understanding patient-therapist compatibility. In addition to the theoretical framework of each orientation, there are also implicit views about appropriate methods of gaining an understanding about the world, others, and the self that characterize different orientations. The distinction between a theoretical perspective and an epistemological style can be understood in terms of how broadly theories and epistemologies can be applied. Theories tend to focus on one particular realm, for example, psychological func-

---

[3]We gratefully acknowledge the contributions of Dr. Marvin R. Goldfried to this section.

tioning. Epistemologies are more pervasive and influence how one evaluates many seemingly disparate aspects of reality. For example, one individual may have a tendency to reason by using analogies, whereas another emphasizes concrete observations of the external world, and still another may try to evaluate the logical consistency of arguments. These different epistemological styles can influence such widely different activities as assessing the prognosis of a patient, deciding who was at fault in an automobile accident, or choosing a career. Using the categories developed by Royce (1964), we discuss three different styles of understanding, or epistemological styles: metaphorism, empiricism, and rationalism. Given the relative emphasis on metaphorism in psychodynamic psychotherapy, this is our primary focus.

Metaphorism

The metaphorical epistemological style has been described as a reliance on symbolizing as a means of expression (Diamond & Royce, 1980). Traditionally, the importance of interpreting the symbolic significance of a patient's speech has been associated with psychoanalysis. For example, one of Sigmund Freud's (1961) central therapeutic techniques involved uncovering the latent meaning behind the manifest symbols of dreams.

The use of metaphor in psychotherapy has been conceptualized in at least three major ways. Some psychoanalytic theorists have stressed the patient's defensive use of metaphor (Evans, 1988). By avoiding a literal expression of underlying conflict, patients can begin to explore the basis of their problems while simultaneously protecting themselves from greater self-awareness than they are ready for at that time (Aleksandrowicz, 1962; Ekstein, 1966; Reider, 1972; Yeomans, Clarkin, Altschul, & Hull, 1992). Alternatively, metaphor can be understood as a direct means of expressing that which is not explicable in literal terms (Evans, 1988). Finally, metaphors may have their impact by the heightened affective arousal that frequently accompanies their symbolic and imaginal forms.

Consistent with the historical emphasis on metaphor in psychoanalysis, psychoanalytic therapists show greater preference than do behavior therapists for an epistemological style that emphasizes metaphorism (Schacht & Black, 1985; Vakoch, 1996). Similarly, a group of behavioral scientists who initiated the behavior modification movement relied less on metaphorism than did a nonbehavioral comparison group (Krasner & Houts, 1984).

Although these differences have historical origins, they may also reflect psychodynamic therapists' greater emphasis on complex thought. Such complexity can be understood in terms of the high value placed on ambiguity by psychodynamic therapists (Messer & Winokur, 1986). This is consistent with empirical evidence that psychodynamic therapists see themselves as quite complex and serious (Walton, 1978). As might be expected, more cognitively complex individuals prefer insight therapy over behavior therapy (Neufeldt, 1978).

Alternatively, the psychoanalytic emphasis on metaphor may reflect the importance of interpretation and the exploration of emotion as interventions. This is consistent with the high prevalence of figurative language in psychodynamic interpretations (Yeomans et al., 1992). Such language and symbolism may contribute to the heightened emotional experiencing that psychodynamic therapists facilitate during those portions of sessions judged to be particularly good (Wiser & Goldfried, 1993).

Empiricism and Rationalism

The second epistemological style, empiricism, "says we know to the extent that we perceive correctly" (Royce, 1976, p. 21). Pure empiricism emphasizes an inductive process of gaining knowledge about the external world. In his attempt to gather information without being biased by preexisting theories, Sir Francis Bacon (1620/1960) exemplifies an empiricist approach. Writing about the third style, rationalism, Diamond and Royce (1980, p. 34) noted, "The person whose view of reality is largely determined by his commitment to rationality would test the validity of his view of reality by its logical consistency." Writing only a decade after Bacon, René Descartes (1630/1971) formalized the rationalist epistemology in his third rule for the proper use of the mind: "As regards any subject we propose to investigate, we must inquire not what other people have thought, or what we ourselves conjecture, but what we can clearly and manifestly perceive by intuition or deduce with certainty. For there is no other way of acquiring knowledge" (p. 153). Thus, the rationalist begins with clear and evident truths and, following the structure of syllogistic reasoning, arrives at a logically deduced proof.

Virtually all therapists use each of the three epistemological styles to some extent, but the metaphorical style is particularly evident in many psychodynamic therapists. By contrast, behavioral therapists and cognitive-behavioral therapists show greater preferences for both empirical and rational styles than do psychodynamic therapists (Schacht & Black, 1985; Vakoch, 1996).

Although so far we have emphasized the epistemologies that are most often associated with different theoretical orientations, it is important to remember that it is the individual person who has an epistemological style. Although we can characterize each orientation by prevalent epistemological styles, not all therapists within an orientation share the dominant style (Vasco, Garcia-Marques, & Dryden, 1993). Nor does the degree of dissonance remain constant throughout a therapist's career. Most often, dissonance between therapists' personal epistemologies and the dominant epistemology of their orientation increases with therapists' experience (Vasco et al., 1993). Although it is tempting to assume that this reflects increasingly eclectic practice with more experience (Smith, 1982), this is not always the case. In fact, therapists of different orientations tend to do different things when their personal epistemologies are discordant with the dominant epistemology of their chosen orientation. Cognitive therapists and behavioral therapists whose own personal epistemologies are dissonant with their orientation (i.e., therapists with a predominantly metaphorical style) tend not to let the theories in which they were trained dictate their clinical practice. In comparison, cognitive and behavioral therapists whose personal epistemologies are consistent with their orientations are more likely to use the theories of their orientations to guide their practice. The pattern seems to be just the opposite for psychodynamic therapists. When personal epistemology and dominant epistemology of their orientation are in conflict (i.e., when the therapist is primarily empirical or rational), they tend to rely on psychodynamic theory even more, reminiscent of Bartley's (1962) "retreat to commitment" (Vasco et al., 1993).

Worldviews

The same sort of dissonance that occurs between a therapist's personal epistemology and the dominant epistemology of a given theoretical orientation can also occur between the epistemologies of the patient and therapist. The implications of such dissonance are highlighted in studies on worldviews, that is, constructs that include epistemological styles as well as notions about the nature of reality (Harris, Fontana, & Dowds, 1977). In other words, worldviews describe both people's epistemologies (ways of knowing) and their assumptions about the world (e.g., whether or not things can be described mechanistically). In one study relevant to this issue, pairs of friends were more likely to predict that they would remain friends if they had compatible worldviews (Harris et al., 1977). Though this study did not involve a clinical population, it may have implications for the development of the bond aspect of the therapeutic alliance, which refers to the mutual trust, liking, and attachment between the therapist and patient (Bordin, 1979; Horvath & Greenberg, 1986, 1989). Similarly, friends were more likely to predict that they would harmoniously work together on an academic project if they had compatible worldviews (Harris et al., 1977). This may have implications for the development of both (1) the task aspect of the therapeutic alliance, which refers to the degree of agreement between the patient and therapist about the specific activities of therapy, and (2) the goal aspect of the alliance, that is, the extent to which the patient and therapist agree about the aims and end points of therapy (Bordin, 1979; Horvath & Greenberg, 1986, 1989).

Compatibility of worldviews also can affect therapists' perceptions and patients' responses to therapy. Therapists viewed their first sessions with their patients as being more positive and less negative when patients and therapists had compatible worldviews; similarly, patients attended more sessions with their therapists when the two had compatible worldviews (Harris et al., 1977). In this study, compatibility of worldviews seemed more important than the specific character of the worldviews. When Harris et al. examined whether or not a preference for any of four worldviews, either by the patient or the therapist, accounted for ratings of positivity or negativity of their interactions, no such preferences were found.

Visions of Reality

Several studies show that psychodynamic therapists are less optimistic about their patients' prognoses than cognitive-behavior therapists. For example, in a study of peer reviewers for the American Psychological Association and Civilian

Health and Medical Program of the Uniformed Services, psychodynamic reviewers rated patients as more disturbed than did behavior therapists (Cohen & Oyster-Nelson, 1981). Similar results were found when therapists with a wider range of clinical experience were examined. In a study of clinical judgments by graduate students, postdoctoral students, residents, and faculty members, Langer and Abelson (1974) found that psychodynamic therapists rated an interviewee who was labeled a patient as being more disturbed than behavior therapists rated the same interviewee. When subjects were restricted to clinical trainees, again psychodynamic as compared to either cognitive or behavioral therapists were more pessimistic about the patient's responsiveness to treatment (Houts, 1984). These observations are consistent with self-report-based findings that psychodynamic therapists have a more pessimistic view of the world than cognitive-behavioral therapists (Vakoch, 1996).

One way to understand this psychodynamic pessimism is in terms of the views of human nature that characterize different theoretical orientations of psychotherapy (Messer & Winokur, 1980). Each of the "visions of reality" discussed by Messer and Winokur is based on literary forms, for example, comedies and tragedies. Consistent with the literary use of these terms, comedies end in a resolution of conflict by the elimination of a situational obstacle, whereas in tragedies the protagonists are responsible for their own demise because of personal characteristics. One way in which different theoretical orientations may differ is in the extent to which they emphasize such important views of human nature. This has been suggested by Messer and Winokur (1986) in their account of how orientations differ in emphasizing the tragic view and thus how they may differ in their degree of pessimism: "Behavior therapy has a far less somber outlook than psychoanalysis, and the kind of hope for cure it holds out is greater. Its emphasis on learning through modeling and reinforcement, direct and vicarious, allows for greater optimism regarding people's ability to change" (pp. 118–119).

In a study of conceptualizations of interpersonal issues by psychodynamic and cognitive-behavior therapists, Vakoch and Goldfried (in press) found support for these differences in tragic and comic views across orientations: psychodynamic therapists more frequently referred to concepts related to masochism, inadequacy, and guilt, whereas cognitive-behavior therapists emphasized assertiveness and control.

The more frequent use of concepts related to both masochism and inadequacy by psychodynamic therapists suggests an emphasis on patients' deficiencies, which is compatible with a tragic vision. In addition, psychodynamic therapists tended to use the tragic notion of guilt more often than did cognitive-behavior therapists. This also is consistent with Jones and Pulos's (1993) observation that psychodynamic therapists focus on patients' feelings of guilt to a greater extent than cognitive-behavior therapists.

In contrast, psychodynamic therapists conceptualized patients' problems in terms of assertiveness less frequently than did cognitive-behavior therapists. This suggests less emphasis among psychodynamic therapists on a comic vision, in which conflict "can be eliminated by effective manipulative action" (Messer & Winokur, 1980, p. 823). Similarly, the psychodynamic therapists' less frequent use of terms related to control also indicates their downplaying of a comic vision, which "emphasizes the familiar, controllable, and predictable aspects of situations and people" (p. 823).

Another difference between orientations was the greater emphasis on attachment in psychodynamic conceptualizations, which is also consistent with differences in visions of reality. As we have already noted, psychodynamic therapists often focus on conflicts of childhood origin that have not been adequately resolved. In contrast, cognitive-behavior therapists do not focus on the past to as great an extent but are instead more oriented toward the present and future.

Therapeutic Flexibility

One of the greatest challenges for the psychodynamic therapist is to gain a perspective on the obstacles to conducting this type of therapy. The research literature reviewed earlier highlights the difficulty of dealing with negative complementarity, even when this is an explicit focus of training. In a similar manner, certain characteristics of the therapist may make it more difficult to work with patients who differ on fundamental ways of viewing the world.

Just as therapists must be aware of countertransference to deal effectively with negative complementarity, they may benefit by a greater understanding of their habitual ways of thinking and envisioning the human condition. Certain styles may come more naturally for each therapist, but conscious awareness of alternatives and an intention to remain flexible can make therapists more open to other ways of viewing reality. Although our understanding of implicit judgment processes of psychotherapists and patients is still in its infancy, greater attentiveness to these differences between individuals could have a significant impact on day-to-day practice.

FUTURE DIRECTIONS

Freud's and Breuer's discoveries led to the realization that talking could help people who suffer from serious, debilitating symptoms. Despite early reliance on quasi-biological and mechanistic formulations, these ideas laid the groundwork for an appreciation of the power of communication in human affairs, for good or ill. As the theory and practice of psychodynamic psychotherapy developed and matured, the role of interpersonal communication has taken center stage. This development has led to efforts by interpersonal theorists to describe the laws that govern communications between people. Furthermore, the emphasis on communication has reflected an increased recognition of the importance of viewing causal relationships in circular rather than linear terms. Circular causality and the principles of feedback, mutual influence, and complementarity have proven to be extremely powerful ideas, both in the clinical and research domains.

However, recent dissatisfactions with the traditional experimental designs and clinical trial methodologies used to study psychotherapy have led to calls for the development of new and creative methodologies for investigating psychotherapy (Greenberg, 1986; Strupp, 1986). In particular, we believe that the place to begin is to study the interactions and communications occurring between two people when one of them is in distress and seeks help from the other. Greenberg has stressed the necessity for basic descriptive work along these lines, with the goal of creating a "shared descriptive framework" or descriptive language for therapeutic phenomena. This may require, for instance, observations of the same archival therapy sessions by researchers in different settings. Without such a shared language, based on direct observations of the same therapies, psychotherapy researchers will have difficulty in communicating with one another, let alone arriving at a consensus on the nature of communications between patients and therapists.

The problems inherent in such an undertaking are legion. Consider, for example, the fact that our perception of language is intrinsically context-dependent (e.g., Bransford & Franks, 1971; Neisser, 1976). This means that the same words have different meanings, depending on the unique characteristics of a given situation. How to account for such contextual differences from therapy to therapy, even from session to session, is the foremost scientific hurdle for psychotherapy research; it may also represent *the* scientific and methodological frontier for the foreseeable future (Butler & Strupp, 1986; Rice & Greenberg, 1984; Stiles, 1988).

Although we have emphasized concepts central to psychodynamic psychotherapies in this chapter, the same ideas are relevant to a range of psychotherapy orientations. Such training issues as definitions of competent performance, the relationship between adherence and skill, problems with difficult patients, establishing a workable interpersonal climate, and awareness of preferred epistemologies and visions of reality, should all be concerns for therapists and researchers from differing theoretical persuasions. By focusing the meager fiscal resources available for psychotherapy research on the resolution of these fundamental issues, we might profit from a greater understanding of the science and art of psychotherapy.

REFERENCES

Aleksandrowicz, D. B. (1962). The meaning of metaphor. *Bulletin of the Menninger Clinic, 26,* 92–101.

Alexander, F., & French, T. M. (1946). *Psychoanalytic therapy: Principles and applications.* New York: Ronald Press.

Anchin, J. C., & Kiesler, D. J. (1982). *Handbook of interpersonal psychotherapy.* New York: Pergamon.

Bacon, F. (1960). *The new organon.* Indianapolis: Bobbs-Merrill. (Original work published 1620)

Bartley, W. W. (1962). *The retreat to commitment.* New York: Knopf.

Bein, E., Anderson, T., Strupp, H. H., Henry, W. P., Schacht, T. E., Binder, J. L., & Butler, S. F. (1997). *The effects of training in time-limited dynamic psychotherapy: changes in therapeutic outcome.* Manuscript submitted for publication.

Benjamin, L. S. (1974). Structural analysis of social behavior. *Psychological Review, 81,* 392–425.

Benjamin, L. S. (1982). Use of structural analysis of social behavior (SASB) to guide intervention in psychotherapy. In J. C. Anchin & D. J. Kiesler (Eds.), *Handbook of interpersonal psychotherapy* (pp. 190–212). New York: Pergamon.

Berzins, J. I. (1977). Therapist-patient matching. In A. S. Gurman & A. M. Razin (Eds.), *Effective psychotherapy: A handbook of research* (pp. 190–212). New York: Pergamon.

Bordin, E. S. (1979). The generalizability of the psychoanalytic concept of the working alliance. *Psychotherapy: Theory, Research, and Practice, 16,* 252–260.

Bransford, J. D., & Franks, J. J. (1971). The abstraction of linguistic ideas. *Cognitive Psychology, 2,* 331–350.

Butler, S. F., & Strupp, H. H. (1986). "Specific" and "nonspecific" factors in psychotherapy: A problematic paradigm for psychotherapy research. *Psychotherapy, 23,* 30–40.

Butler, S. F., & Strupp, H. H. (1989, June). *Issues in training therapists to competency: The Vanderbilt experience.* Paper presented at the meeting of the Society for Psychotherapy Research, Toronto.

Byrne, D. (1969). Attitudes and attraction. In L. Berkowitz (Ed.), *Advances in experimental social psychology* (Vol. 4, pp. 36–89). New York: Academic Press.

Byrne, D. (1971). *The attraction paradigm.* New York: Academic Press.

Cashdan, S. (1988). *Object relations therapy.* New York: Norton.

Cohen, L. H., & Oyster-Nelson, C. K. (1981). Clinicians' evaluations of psychodynamic psychotherapy: Experimental data on psychological peer review. *Journal of Consulting and Clinical Psychology, 49,* 583–589.

Darwin, C. R. (1859). *On the origin of species by means of natural selection, or, The preservation of favoured races in the struggle for life.* London: Murray.

Descartes, R. (1971). Rules for the direction of the mind. In E. Anscombe & P. T. Geach (Eds. & Trans.), *Descartes: Philosophical writings* (pp. 151–180). Indianapolis: Bobbs-Merrill. (Original work published 1630)

Diamond, S. R., & Royce, J. R. (1980). Cognitive abilities as expressions of three "ways of knowing." *Multivariate Behavioral Research, 15,* 31–56.

Ekstein, R. (1966). *Children of time and space, of action and impulse.* New York: Appleton-Century-Crofts.

Epstein, L. (1979). The therapeutic function of hate in the countertransference. In L. Epstein & A. H. Feiner (Eds.), *Countertransference: The therapist's contribution to the therapeutic situation* (pp. 213–234). New York: Jason Aronson.

Evans, M. B. (1988). The role of metaphor in psychotherapy and personality change: A theoretical reformulation. *Psychotherapy, 25,* 543–551.

Fairbairn, W. R. D. (1954). *An object relations theory of the personality.* New York: Basic Books.

Freud, A. (1966). *The ego and the mechanisms of defense.* New York: International Universities Press. (Original work published 1936)

Freud, S. (1960). *The ego and the id.* New York: Norton. (Original work published 1923)

Freud, S. (1961). The interpretation of dreams. In J. Strachey (Ed. & Trans.), *The standard edition of the complete psychological works of Sigmund Freud* (Vols. 4 & 5, pp. 339–627). London: Hogarth. (Original work published 1900)

Freud, S. (1966). Resistance and repression. In *Introductory lectures on psychoanalysis* (pp. 286–302). New York: Norton. (Original work published 1920)

Goldfried, M., Greenberg, L., & Marmar, C. (1990). Individual psychotherapy: Process and outcome. *Annual Review of Psychology, 41,* 659–688.

Greenberg, L. S. (1986). Research strategies. In L. S. Greenberg & W. M. Pinsof (Eds.), *The psychotherapeutic process: A research handbook* (pp. 707–734). New York: Guilford.

Guntrip, H. (1973). *Psychoanalytic theory, therapy, and the self.* New York: Basic Books.

Harris, M., Fontana, A. F., & Dowds, B. N. (1977). *Journal of Personality Assessment, 41,* 537–547.

Hartmann, H. (1958). *Ego psychology and the problem of adaptation.* New York: International Universities Press. (Original work published 1939)

Henry, W. P., Schacht, T. E., & Strupp, H. H. (1986). Structural analysis of social behavior: Application to a study of interpersonal process in differential psychotherapeutic outcome. *Journal of Consulting and Clinical Psychology, 54,* 27–31.

Henry, W. P., Schacht, T. E., & Strupp, H. H. (1990). Patient and therapist introject, interpersonal process, and differential psychotherapy outcome. *Journal of Consulting and Clinical Psychology, 58,* 768–774.

Henry, W. P., Schacht, T. E., Strupp, H. H., Butler, S. F., & Binder, J. L. (1993). The effects of training in time-limited dynamic psychotherapy: Mediators of therapists' response to training. *Journal of Consulting and Clinical Psychology, 61,* 441–447.

Horvath, A. O., & Greenberg, L. S. (1986). The development of the Working Alliance Inventory. In L. S. Greenberg & W. M. Pinsof (Eds.), *The psychotherapeutic process: A research handbook* (pp. 529–556). New York: Guilford.

Horvath, A. O., & Greenberg, L. S. (1989). The development and validation of the Working Alliance Inventory. *Journal of Counseling Psychology, 36,* 223–233.

Houts, A. C. (1984). Effects of clinician theoretical orientation and patient explanatory bias on initial clinical judgments. *Professional Psychology: Research and Practice, 15,* 284–293.

Jones, E. E., & Pulos, S. M. (1993). Comparing the process of psychodynamic and cognitive-behavioral therapies. *Journal of Consulting and Clinical Psychology, 61,* 306–316.

Kernberg, O. F. (1975). *Borderline conditions and pathological narcissism.* New York: Jason Aronson.

Kiesler, D. J. (1982). Interpersonal theory for personality and psychotherapy. In J. C. Anchin & D. J. Kiesler (Eds.), *Handbook of interpersonal psychotherapy* (pp. 3–24). New York: Pergamon.

Kiesler, D. J., & Watkins, L. M. (1989). Interpersonal complementarity and the therapeutic alliance: A study of relationship in psychotherapy. *Psychotherapy, 26,* 183–196.

Klee, M. R., Abeles, N., & Muller, R. T. (1990). Therapeutic alliance: Early indicators, course, and outcome. *Psychotherapy, 27,* 166–174.

Klein, M. (1975). Some theoretical conclusions regarding the emotional life of the infant. In M. Klein (Ed.), *Envy and gratitude and other works, 1946–1963* (pp. 61–93). New York: Delacorte. (Original work published 1952)

Kohut, H. (1971). *The analysis of the self.* New York: International Universities Press.

Kohut, H. (1977). *The restoration of the self.* New York: International Universities Press.

Krasner, L., & Houts, A. C. (1984). A study of the "value" systems of behavioral scientists. *American Psychologist, 39,* 840–850.

Langer, E. J., & Abelson, R. P. (1974). A patient by any other name . . . : Clinician group difference in labeling bias. *Journal of Consulting and Clinical Psychology, 42,* 4–9.

Leary, T. (1957). *Interpersonal diagnosis of personality.* New York: Ronald Press.

Mahler, M., Pine, F., & Bergman, A. (1975). *The psychological birth of the human infant.* New York: Basic Books.

McWilliams, N. (1994). *Psychoanalytic diagnosis: Understanding personality structure in the clinical process.* New York: Guilford.

Menninger, K. A., & Holzman, P. S. (1973). *Theory of psychoanalytic technique* (Vol. 2). New York: Basic Books.

Messer, S. B., & Winokur, M. (1980). Some limits to the integration of psychoanalytic and behavior therapy. *American Psychologist, 35,* 818–827.

Messer, S. B., & Winokur, M. (1986). Eclecticism and the shifting visions of reality in three systems of psychotherapy. *International Journal of Eclectic Psychotherapy, 5,* 115–124.

Neisser, U. (1976). *Cognition and reality.* San Francisco: Freeman.

Neufeldt, S. A. (1978). Client cognitive characteristics and preference for counseling approaches. *Journal of counseling psychology, 25,* 184–187.

Noam, E. M. (1995). Electronics and the dim future of the university. *Science, 210,* 247–249.

Pine, F. (1990). *Drive, ego, object, and self: A synthesis for clinical work.* New York: Basic Books.

Reider, N. (1972). Metaphor as interpretation. *International Journal of Psycho-Analysis, 53,* 463–469.

Rice, L. N., & Greenberg, L. S. (1984). *Patterns of change.* New York: Guilford.

Royce, J. R. (1964). *The encapsulated man.* Princeton, NJ: Van Nostrand.

Royce, J. R. (1976). Psychology is multi: Methodological, variate, epistemic, world-view, systemic, paradigmatic, theoretic, and disciplinary. In J. Coles & W. J. Arnold (Eds.), *Nebraska Symposium on the Conceptual Foundations of Theory & Method in Psychology* (pp. 1–63). Lincoln: University of Nebraska Press.

Schacht, T. E., & Black, D. A. (1985). Epistemological commitments of behavioral and psychoanalytic therapists. *Professional Psychology: Research and Practice, 16,* 316–323.

Smith, D. (1982). Trends in counseling and psychotherapy. *American Psychologist, 37,* 802–809.

Soldz, S. (1990). The therapeutic interaction: Research perspectives. In R. A. Wells & V. J. Gianetti (Eds.), *Handbook of the brief psychotherapies* (pp. 27–54). New York: Plenum.

Sterba, R. F. (1934). The fate of the ego in analytic therapy. *International Journal of Psycho-Analysis, 15,* 117–126.

Stiles, W. B. (1988). Psychotherapy process—outcome correlations may be misleading. *Psychotherapy, 25,* 27–35.

Strupp, H. H. (1980a). Success and failure in time-limited psychotherapy: A systematic comparison of two cases. (Comparison 1.) *Archives of General Psychiatry, 37,* 595–603.

Strupp, H. H. (1980b). Success and failure in time-limited psychotherapy: A systematic comparison of two cases. (Comparison 2.) *Archives of General Psychiatry, 37,* 708–716.

Strupp, H. H. (1980c). Success and failure in time-limited psychotherapy: With special reference to the performance of a lay counselor. (Comparison 3.) *Archives of General Psychiatry, 37,* 831–841.

Strupp, H. H. (1980d). Success and failure in time-limited psychotherapy: Further evidence. (Comparison 4.) *Archives of General Psychiatry, 37,* 947–954.

Strupp, H. H. (1986). Psychotherapy: Research, practice and public policy (how to avoid dead ends). *American Psychologist, 41,* 120–130.

Strupp, H. H. (1990). The case of Helen R.: A therapeutic failure? *Psychotherapy, 27,* 644–656.

Strupp, H. H. (1993). The Vanderbilt psychotherapy studies: Synopsis. *Journal of Consulting and Clinical Psychology, 61,* 431–433.

Strupp, H. H., & Binder, J. L. (1984). *Psychotherapy in a new key: A guide to time-limited dynamic psychotherapy.* New York: Basic Books.

Strupp, H. H., & Hadley, S. W. (1979). Specific versus nonspecific factors in psychotherapy: A controlled study of outcome. *Archives of General Psychiatry, 36,* 1125–1136.

Sullivan, H. S. (1953). *The interpersonal theory of psychiatry*. New York: Norton.

Sullivan, H. S. (1954). *The psychiatric interview*. New York: Norton.

Tasca, G. A., & McMullen, L. M. (1992). Interpersonal complementarity and antitheses within a stage model of psychotherapy. *Psychotherapy, 29*, 515–523.

Vakoch, D. A. (1996). *Predictors of prognosis for patients with interpersonal problems: The role of therapists' epistemology, experience, optimism, and theoretical orientation*. Unpublished doctoral dissertation, State University of New York, Stony Brook.

Vakoch, D. A., & Goldfried, M. R. (in press). Psychodynamic and cognitive-behavioral perceptions of interpersonal therapeutic issues. *Psychotherapy Research*.

Vasco, A. B., Garcia-Marques, L., & Dryden, W. (1993). "Psychotherapist know thyself!": Dissonance between metatheoretical and personal values in psychotherapists of different theoretical orientations. *Psychotherapy Research, 3*, 181–196.

Wiser, S. L., & Goldfried, M. R. (1993). A comparative study of emotional experiencing in psychodynamic-interpersonal and cognitive-behavioral therapies. *Journal of Consulting and Clinical Psychology, 61*, 892–895.

Yeomans, F. E., Clarkin, J. F., Altschul, E., & Hull, J. W. (1992). The role of figurative language in the inductive phase of expressive psychotherapy. *Journal of Psychotherapy Practice and Research, 1*, 270–279.

CHAPTER 11

INTEGRATIVE PSYCHOTHERAPY: INTEGRATING PSYCHODYNAMIC AND COGNITIVE-BEHAVIORAL THEORY AND TECHNIQUE

DREW WESTEN

Harvard Medical School and The Cambridge Hospital/Cambridge Health Alliance

One of the most important reasons for considering integrating various therapeutic modalities is that those of us who practice clinically all fail to some extent at some percentage of our cases. Although the literature concerning therapy outcome clearly has documented that patients in any form of psychotherapy do substantially better than those who receive no treatment, claims of specific advantages of one approach over another often have evaporated under further investigation (particularly when investigator allegiance is held constant) (Luborsky et al., 1999; Smith, Glass, & Miller, 1980; Stiles, Shapiro, & Elliot, 1986); moreover, even some of the best findings do not look so impressive on closer examination (see the Karoly chapter in this volume).

Consider, for example, the data for cognitive therapy of depression, the prototype of empirically validated treatments for depression (Task Force on Promotion and Dissemination of Psychological Procedures, 1995). Careful inspection of the data suggest that, like virtually every other short-term manualized treatment ever studied, data at follow-up intervals of two years or more are virtually nonexistent and, where they do exist, are not supportive (Morrison & Westen, 1999). For example, when the NIMH multisite collaborative depression project compared cognitive

therapy to both imipramine and interpersonal therapy in one of the first truly objective studies ever conducted (that is, a study not conducted by partisans of the treatment under investigation), it proved no better than the other two treatments and slightly worse for severely depressed patients (Elkin et al., 1995). Perhaps more importantly, the relapse rate at the two-year follow-up was extremely high, as it was for the other two treatments (Shea et al., 1992). Across treatments, only 24 percent of patients recovered and remained recovered at follow-up. Were this cancer research, we would not likely refer to such treatments as empirically validated or even "empirically supported."

Furthermore, when subject selection criteria are considered, the picture painted of the utility of cognitive therapy (and virtually every psychotherapy ever studied using randomized control trials) for general practice grows considerably dimmer. Consider an outcome study reported by Thase et al. (1992), which is representative of well-conducted research in this area. The investigators screened over 130 depressed patients, of whom 76 were deemed suitable for the treatment protocol (slightly more than half, which is actually high for this literature). Of those included, 23 were described as fully recovered and 27 partially recovered at the end of treatment, for a full recovery rate of roughly 33 percent and a reasonable outcome for roughly two-thirds of patients treated. Within a year, however, 16 of these 50

Author's note The author thanks Hal Arkowitz, Stan Messer, Rick Snyder, and Laura Arkowitz Westen for their comments on a draft of this paper.

successful to moderately successful cases had fully relapsed, leaving 34 fully or partially successful treatments at follow-up. This is slightly above 40% of patients *treated* in the study, and only *20%* of depressed patients who walked into the clinic. When one considers the implications for clinicians who cannot turn away half the patients who present for treatment, and the fact that the only studies that have provided outcome data at two years show that *half of the patients who are recovered at one year are sick again a year later*, skepticism about the comprehensiveness of such treatments seems appropriate.

I choose cognitive therapy for depression as the case in point because it is one of the *best* validated psychotherapies for any disorder. The situation is certainly no better for psychodynamic forms of treatment, for which we do not have data that would allow us to examine similar success rates when all factors are taken into account, despite some impressive scattered studies of treatment efficacy (e.g., Blatt, Ford, Berman, et al., 1994; Fonagy & Moran, 1990). If the empirical data do support one conclusion, however, it is probably that we currently have solid empirical grounds for humility. Clearly we have not yet amassed the data that would allow us to choose between alternative therapeutic approaches, except for a handful (or perhaps a fingerful) of disorders, such as simple phobia.

In clinical psychology, adherents of the two major contemporary approaches—psychodynamic and cognitive-behavioral therapy[1]—rarely read each other's journals or attend each other's conferences. As a result, practitioners from each camp are easily caught in a self-reinforcing system that reaffirms the truth of their position. Although many, if not most, clinicians today describe themselves as integrative or eclectic (Norcross & Prochaska, 1988), the assumptions of psychodynamic and cognitive-behavioral theory and therapy are so different and often contradictory that even those practitioners who recognize a need for integration have difficulty finding a theoretical position from which to practice (see Messer, 1986).

This chapter has three aims. The first is to show why integrating psychodynamic and cognitive-behavioral therapy can at times be useful, by examining the complementary strengths and weaknesses inherent in the two approaches. The second is to describe briefly the history of efforts at psychotherapy integration. The third is to explore three theoretical domains, each derived from both research and clinical observation, that may have important implications for integrative clinical practice. Throughout, I focus on integrations of psychoanalytic and cognitive-behavioral approaches, although these are by no means the only integrations possible (e.g., Greenberg, Rice, & Elliott, 1993; Greenberg & Safran, 1987).

Before beginning, a caveat is in order. Integrative therapies are relatively new, tremendously varied, typically not highly prescriptive, and generally tailored to individual patients. By their nature they tend to defy manualization and are not easily studied using the methods that have formed the basis of the efficacy literature (Kazdin, 1996). Thus, I will not describe a body of outcome research bearing on their efficacy. In theory, integrative treatments may be testable through the standard dismantling strategy used in randomized controlled trials (e.g., comparing cognitive-behavioral therapy for depression with psycho-dynamic therapy and a combination of cognitive-behavioral therapy and psychodynamic therapy). However, we will probably learn more about the relative utility of both pure and hybrid treatment strategies through naturalistic studies of treatment effectiveness. These strategies carefully assess the psychotherapy process (through recording of sessions) and correlate process with outcome variables, to see what works, for which kinds of patient, and at what points in treatments. Despite the lack of controlled outcome studies of treatments that involve integrative elements, I nevertheless intend to argue for the potential value of such treatments *empirically*, by drawing substantially on basic science research that bears on integrative treatment approaches, particularly research in cognitive neuroscience.

WHY INTEGRATE? FOUR HORROR STORIES, AND THREE REASONS FOR THEM

To make the case for the potential utility of therapy integration, I first briefly present four therapeutic horror stories—cases that demonstrate what happens when one does *not* think and practice integratively. I then describe, theoretically,

---

[1] Research over the past 20 years has consistently shown these to be the two most common orientations of clinicians (Pope, Tabachnick, & Keith-Spiegel, 1987).

why each approach alone can be *expected* to be less than optimally effective in a substantial number of cases.

Tales from the Analytic Crypt

I begin with two psychoanalytic horror stories, which should humble any but the most self-assured psychoanalyst. I do not exclude myself from such humblings; indeed, my own therapeutic failures have been the primary impetus to my interest in modes of treatment to which I did not gravitate by temperament or training.

The first case is a patient who was seen for five years in psychoanalysis by a prominent analyst. The patient presented with a wide range of complaints, including depression and a general sense of interpersonal isolation. After five years on the couch, little had changed, and he terminated treatment. He subsequently entered treatment with a psychodynamically trained psychotherapist who discovered, upon inquiry in the first session, that the patient had a serious problem with alcohol and had in fact been intoxicated throughout much of his analysis. The analyst had never known because he did not believe in asking direct questions in the initial interviews of a psychoanalysis; rather, he preferred for material to emerge "in the transference" and at the patient's own pace.

Now an apologist for psychoanalysis could clearly argue that this is simply an example of bad treatment: The analyst *should* have conducted a thorough initial intake evaluation, and at the very least should at some point have recognized that all those allusions to screwdrivers and wall-bangers were not just phallic derivatives. But two arguments militate against this rejoinder. First, the analyst was no mere novice; he was a training analyst, specially selected by his peers as a master clinician designated to play a major role in training the next generation of analysts in his community. At the very least, this demonstrates that analytic institutes have some serious problems with quality control. Second, suppose the analyst had discovered the drinking problem on initial intake, as any competent clinician should have, and thus elected to see the man in face-to-face therapy, at least until the alcoholism was under control. How, then, would he proceed? How many psychoanalytic clinicians would know where to turn to find an analytically informed approach to the treatment of addictions (particularly approaches with any scientific evidence supporting their effectiveness)?

The second case cannot be as readily explained away. The therapist was a well-trained, highly talented clinician, to whom I would refer my mother (and I *like* my mother, at least most of the time). The patient presented with problems including interpersonal difficulties and panic attacks. The therapist addressed both problems psychodynamically and discovered what appeared to be some important links between the two, such as the relation between the panic attacks and the patient's intense difficulties with being alone. The panics would typically occur when she was by herself at night. Not surprisingly, bedtime difficulties had been a salient aspect of her developmental history. With treatment, the panics decreased in frequency and intensity, but they did not completely abate.

The therapist noted that the patient seemed preoccupied with her *fear* of panicking and interpreted this as a resistance against dealing with the underlying issues. Although this would not, on the face of it, be an unreasonable hypothesis to consider, it does not take into consideration a body of cognitive-behavioral research on the way panic patients develop classically conditioned fear responses to their own interoceptive cues (Barlow, 1988). Patients become hypervigilant to their own internal responses (shortness of breath, racing heart, and so forth), and their fear of their own fear actually contributes to triggering the attacks. The most efficacious treatment for such a fear is one based on classical conditioning, and involves desensitizing the person to these interoceptive cues.

This second case is not one of an incompetent therapist. One could perhaps fault her for not knowing of the relevant behavioral literature (although this particular treatment occurred in the late 1980s, before the work of Barlow, Clark, and others was as widely known as it is today), but the problem is deeper: Talking someone out of a conditioned emotional response is not easy. It *can* sometimes be done psychodynamically. As Freud was the first to note, a crucial aspect of the treatment of phobias is repeated exposure to the phobic stimulus without retraumatization, so that the person no longer finds it so frightening. Fenichel (1945) echoed that sentiment in a classic psychoanalytic work. However, few psychoanalytic practitioners would recognize the fear of fear as a conditioned emotional response in panic patients, and no psychoanalyst would consider having a patient run up and down stairs to expose her to the feeling of being short of breath. Conditioned emotional responses can be triggered subcortically, via thalamo-amygdala pathways that involve no direct cortical input (LeDoux, 1995). A verbal intervention is a very blunt instrument with which to try to break problematic subcortical connections, although it can be helpful in convincing the person to expose herself to the stimulus enough times to extinguish an emotional response.

A Nightmare on Ellis Street

Cognitive-behavioral readers may be deriving considerable satisfaction from these analytic horror stories, reinforced in their view that their psychodynamic colleagues practice in the Twilight Zone. So let me present two brief cognitive-behavioral horror stories. The first was a patient with borderline personality disorder and a history of quite lethal suicide attempts, who lived her life from one crisis to the next. Her affects were intense and poorly regulated, and her suicidality reflected this affective intensity, as well as a tendency toward impulsivity and a vulnerability to rejection. During one of her crises, the patient began seeing a cognitive-behavioral therapist, who informed her that she had trouble relaxing and needed to learn relaxation techniques. After several sessions of relaxation training, the patient took a serious overdose.

Treating a borderline patient with relaxation training is arguably analogous to treating a patient with rabies for a sore throat. An apologist could note that this event, like the second analytic horror story described above, also occurred during the late 1980s, before Marsha Linehan's (1993) cognitive-behavioral approach to borderline personality disorder was widely known. That response, however, is as problematic as the response of the analytic apologist. It is no accident that the cognitive-behavioral literature contained virtually no references to personality disorders until the early 1990s, and that few cognitive-behavioral therapists were trained or competent to diagnose them until recently. To have a concept of personality disorder, one must first have a concept of personality *structure* or *organization*—at the very least a coherent, comprehensive theory that allows a formulation of a patient's enduring, interacting patterns of thought, feeling, motivation, and behavior. The best the apologist could do is to say that since the rise of behavior therapy in the 1950s, behaviorally oriented clinicians were misdiagnosing and failing to treat the broader pathology of an entire class of patients for 40 years, but they are not doing this anymore. As we will see, the assumptions behind each approach made it inevitable that psychoanalysts would have begun noticing and classifying personality pathology in the 1930s, 60 years before these disorders entered the language of cognitive-behavioral theory and therapy.

A second case should leave even the most stalwart cognitive-behavioral hairs standing on end (or at least in need of conditioning). The patient was a man who presented with a driving phobia and "trouble getting along with people." During the course of the first session, as he was describing his relationship with his wife, I noticed a peculiar smirk on his face as he described an incident in which he seemed to enjoy watching her squirm. As we moved into other areas of his life and I observed the same smirk at other times, such as when he made a passing comment about his sexual relationship with his wife and with previous girlfriends, I asked an unusual question, and one that a cognitive-behavioral therapist treating a phobic would certainly never ask: "What kind of pornography do you read?" The smirk turned into a broad grin, and he told me that it is not the kind one can buy over the counter.

In fact, the patient was attracted to extremely violent sadomasochistic pornography, and as the evaluation proceeded, several facts became clear. Although he had never apparently acted on his aggressive impulses in any dangerous ways, he had a seething anger and an enjoyment of watching people squirm. When we traced the origins of his driving phobia, we discovered its association to a fantasy of hitting pedestrians who did not "show him respect," a pervasive theme in his interpersonal encounters. Indeed, as we traced some of his associations to driving, he recalled, with a mixture of surprise and anxiety, an event in which he had frightened himself by driving too quickly toward a pedestrian who angered him by crossing the street against the light and denying him his "right of way."

The patient had been treated for a year by a cognitive therapist, from whom I received an account of their work together, which she considered highly successful. She focused on his "workaholism" and "poor social skills," using homework assignments (e.g., to spend more time with his wife), role playing, and social skills training. She did not focus, however, on something I learned in my second session with him that seemed highly relevant to his interpersonal problems: He had harbored fantasies of raping and mutilating her throughout the treatment, fantasies on which he had no intention of acting but which he found quite pleasurable. When I asked how he and his therapist had understood these fantasies, he replied, with the same grin to which I was becoming accustomed, that she did not know about them. Why not, I naïvely inquired? "She never asked." And why *would* she ask? What, in the models that guide cognitive-behavioral practice, would lead a therapist to ask a person with poor social skills and workaholism about his feelings toward her, or in particular about his fantasies about her?

Now suppose instead that the patient had presented to her with his driving phobia. She would surely not have explored his associations and discovered the connection between the aggressive impulses that were, empirically, associatively connected to this phobia, and that appeared to be connected to his problems behind the wheel, in the office, and under the sheets. (I say *empirically* because, in fact, we only discovered the connection by following his associations, much as contemporary cognitive neuroscientists learn about associative connections through time-honored techniques such as word-association tests). Instead, the therapist would likely have used standard exposure techniques to treat the phobia, and might even have done so successfully. So would one call that a successful treatment outcome? In behavioral research on phobias, one certainly would. I doubt, however, that his wife, co-workers, or many pedestrians would concur.

Complementary Strengths and Weaknesses

At this point I have, no doubt, convinced many readers that I am being unfair to their approach and presenting it in caricature. (I suppose I can take heart in having succeeded in influencing psychoanalytic and cognitive-behavioral readers to share at least *one* belief.) But as I hope to show, these examples demonstrate some of the complementary strengths and weaknesses of the two approaches to treatment. Three are of particular importance: the relative attention to macro versus micro processes, the focus on motivation versus cognition, and the understanding of consciousness. Each of these areas demonstrates both what each approach has to offer and where it can fall short.

Attention to Macro Versus Micro Processes

One of the biggest differences between psychodynamic and cognitive-behavioral theory and technique is their relative attention to macro versus micro processes. This difference has existed since the beginning of each approach. Freud tended to think in terms of broad constructs—the id, the unconscious, and so forth. In contrast, Skinner and other behaviorists focused on the determinants of discrete behaviors.

One of the major pitfalls of psychoanalytic theory, and of the language of psychoanalysis more generally, is the tendency to rely too heavily on diffuse and often unoperationalized or unoperationalizable constructs, as in contemporary constructs such as "self pathology," "projective identification," and "narcissistic vulnerability." These terms may have empirical referents, but they often carry too many disparate meanings to be theoretically or empirically useful. For example, a very competent psychoanalytical therapist described both members of a couple she was treating as having "severe narcissistic vulnerabilities." I could see how that term could apply to the husband, who had been diagnosed by his therapist with a narcissistic personality disorder and had shown ample evidence of it. However, the wife, who was my patient, had in many respects the opposite problem—deep-seated feelings of inadequacy and low self-esteem, which led her, among other things, to tolerate barrages of devaluing comments from her husband. Now at some level, both spouses had profound concerns about their own worth and loveability, and in this sense I could understand what my colleague meant. But clearly this is an imprecise way of speaking, when the same term can be applied to someone who is grandiose and self-centered and also someone who is self-deprecating and other-centered, and who as a couple have interpersonal styles that are complementary rather than similar.

One of the virtues of contemporary cognitive-behavioral therapy, in contrast, is its focus on specific processes. Thus, Barlow (1988) distinguishes conditioned responses to interoceptive cues (such as heart racing) from catastrophic cognitions ("I'm going crazy") in the maintenance of panic attacks, and has developed different strategies for addressing each. In general, cognitive-behavioral therapists are more effective in *targeting* processes and behaviors for change, rather than assuming that all symptoms will dissipate with an often vaguely specified combination of "emotional insight" and something-or-other that could go on in the therapeutic relationship. (I am being somewhat unfair here to the psychoanalytic theory of change, although in clinical case discussions I rarely hear a level of sophistication much above this, and never, for example, hear discussion of the role of crucial variables such as exposure in treating thoughts or impulses associated with anxiety; see Weinberger, 1995.) Particularly when a patient has a symptom such as panic or alcoholism, it is difficult to see how "the relationship"—including even the most accurate transference interpretations—will cure it, except insofar as, for this particular patient, the relationship is a powerful enough source of soothing to help regulate the affects that may underlie the symptom (and the patient and therapist are able to work together in such a way as to foster internalization of this soothing capacity over time). Clearly the relationship is part of the process, but *which* part of the relationship, for which patient, at which particular times in the treatment, and with which more focused interventions, is an important frontier for theoretical and empirical investigation for both psychoanalysis and cognitive-behavioral therapy.

On the other hand, one of the greatest strengths of psychoanalytic theory in understanding complex phenomena, particularly related to personality, is its attention to the myriad ways in which cognitive, affective, and motivational processes interact. A psychodynamic approach assumes the interdependence of symptoms, but more importantly, it assumes that personality *has organization*. According to Kernberg (1975, 1984), an individual's personality can be organized at any point along a continuum of pathology. In psychotic forms of personality organization, reality-testing is severely impaired and interpersonal relationships are seriously compromised. At a less disturbed but still severely personality-disordered level (which he calls *borderline personality organization*), the person has poorly regulated affects, a tendency toward impulsivity, a tendency toward idiosyncratic thoughts and attributions, and poorly integrated representations of the self and others. Individuals whose personality is organized at a neurotic to healthy level may have symptoms such as depression and anxiety but are fundamentally able to form relationships, function in the workplace, find meaning in life, and tolerate the normal stresses of life. From this point of view, the fact that virtually all studies of

Axis I disorders find extraordinarily high rates of comorbidity with other Axis I and Axis II conditions suggests that symptoms may not be so readily understood as independent phenomena that can be treated one at a time using specific techniques outlined in a manual. One of the key assumptions underlying randomized controlled trials of manualized treatments for specific Axis I disorders—that symptoms are discrete and can be treated as such—may be neither theory-neutral nor empirically validated.

In contrast to psychodynamic theories, cognitive-behavioral theories are less able to explain, except in a very ad hoc way, why certain personality symptoms empirically tend to co-occur, such as wrist-cutting, identity confusion, and rejection sensitivity in borderline personality disorder. Not all wrist-cutting occurs after a rejection, and identity confusion does not logically seem related to either of these other symptoms, yet empirically, all three tend to occur in borderline patients. Without a theory that specifies how personality is organized—that is, how cognitive, affective, behavioral, and motivational processes interact and develop—one cannot explain constellations of symptoms that are not intuitively obvious in their patterns of covariation.

The importance of focusing on organization has become clear over the past 20 years in research on attachment (see Sroufe & Waters, 1977) and longitudinal studies of personality (Block, Gjerde, & Block, 1991; Shedler & Block, 1990). Both domains of research have found that a specific behavior may be too simple a unit for sophisticated analysis over time. Attachment researchers, for example, have discovered that two very discrete behaviors—providing affectively barren or defensively sparse descriptions of relationships with significant others, and having difficulty feeling comfortable with physical intimacy with one's baby—are derived from similar experiences in one's own attachment relationship from childhood. It can ultimately derive from the same internal working models that cause the perception of attachment relationships as threatening (Main et al., 1985). Similarly, depression in childhood may to some degree predict depression in adulthood, but an even more important predictor of adult depression may be under- versus overcontrol of impulses in childhood: For boys, undercontrol predicts later depression, whereas for girls, overcontrol predicts later depressive tendencies (Block et al., 1991). Only a concept of personality structure can explain such predictions.

The Roles of Motivation and Cognition

A second area in which the two approaches have complementary strengths and weaknesses is in their relative focus on motivational versus cognitive processes. Psychodynamic therapists typically begin with the question, "What could motivate this person to have this symptom?" Thus, when presented with a depressed, self-critical patient who cannot tolerate compliments and deflects them at every turn, the question the therapist asks herself is "How can this person be motivated to attack himself and avoid hearing compliments?" Pursuing this question, the therapist might find that the person had a very critical parent, a common experience in self-critical people with depressive tendencies (see Blatt & Homann, 1992), and that the individual has essentially taken the parent into his head and continued where the parent left off. Alternatively, the therapist might learn, as was the case with a high-functioning patient who nonetheless suffered with anxiety, depression, and residual symptoms of an eating disorder, that self-criticism was more bearable than feelings related to loss, rejection, or separation: It gave her a paradoxical sense of control over her pain, which she could attribute to herself and hence have the hope of changing by changing herself.

A psychodynamic therapist would assume that negative thoughts about oneself are so painful to maintain that people would give them up as soon as possible if they could, so that something must motivate them to maintain negative self-representations (Westen, 1985). In this sense, psychoanalysts are the true behaviorists, assuming that through a process akin to operant conditioning, self-representations that are punishing should be extinguished unless they are somehow reinforced. Thus, a patient whose parent or parents were critical and who seems bound on maintaining a negative view of self might (1) respect the parent and hence be motivated to maintain a "shared" belief in his worthlessness, (2) fear that the parent is right and hence feel like a fraud if he allows himself to think good things about himself, (3) obtain a sense of virtue by attacking himself and hence identifying with his parent, (4) fight off a sense of pride that has previously been associated with criticism and hence has taken on an aversive affective coloring, or (5) use self-punishment as a way of assuaging guilt, etc. These are very important possibilities to consider, and dovetail with motives for self-consistency—that is, desires to confirm our preexisting self-

images (Swann, 1992)—which may arise in part because of the motivated nature of many self-representations.

Indeed, although Freud's drive theory was problematic in numerous respects, Freud emphasized three things about human motivation that have turned out empirically to be right (see Westen, 1998a; Westen & Gabbard, in press). First, motivation has its origin in our bodies, so that below an elegant cortex is a relentless hypothalamus that differs little from that of other primates. Second, motives need not develop in harmony with one another and can often come into conflict. Third, motives may be either conscious or unconscious, as recently documented experimentally (Bargh, 1997; McClelland, Koestner, & Weinberger, 1989).

On the other hand, the correlative weakness of the psychodynamic approach is precisely its *assumption* of the primacy of motivation. Sometimes a learned behavior is just a learned behavior, or a skills deficit is just a skills deficit. For example, for years psychoanalysts explained the malevolent worldview of patients with borderline personality disorder as a projection of their own impulses outward (Kernberg, 1975). Sometimes that explanation is valid, as in the example of a patient who often ended relationships by flying into a rage. In treatment, her fear was that her therapist would do the same to her. She thus made a suicide gesture after expressing anger toward her therapist as a way of trying to keep the therapist from abandoning her, which of course the therapist had no intention of doing. Yet this projected aggression hypothesis led analysts for years to ignore a simpler social learning hypothesis, that borderline patients may sometimes expect abuse at the hands of others because that is what they have experienced. Research over the last decade, in fact, has shown a particular association between borderline personality disorder and a history of childhood abuse (Herman, Perry, & Van der Kolk, 1989; Ogata et al., 1990; Zanarini, 1997).

Matters are more complicated, however, than either a psychodynamic or a cognitive-behavioral account alone can explain: *Sexual* abuse seems more specifically related to the malevolent worldview of borderline patients than *physical* abuse (Westen, Ludolph, Misle, Ruffins, & Block, 1990); the latter ought, according to a social learning explanation, to be equally, if not more consistently, related to malevolent expectancies. Further, abuse experiences affect both expectations and motivations in ways that lead some borderline patients to *precipitate* later abuse experiences, which then confirm their schemas (on cyclical processes of this sort, see Wachtel, 1997).

Similarly, regardless of the way a skills deficit emerges, once it is in place, a therapist cannot simply assume that it will go away without specifically targeting it. Psychodynamic therapists do skills training all the time—such as addressing transference patterns related to passivity and fear of confrontation in patients with these issues— but they do not do so systematically, and they often fail to make enough effort to help their patients generalize the gains they make in treatment outside the consulting room. Consider the case of a patient with a mixed personality disorder, who had a host of problems that appeared to stem in part from her relationship with her very erratic, self-preoccupied mother. Aside from these intrapsychic conflicts and concerns, the patient was also quite off-putting to people because of idiosyncrasies in her interpersonal style, such as standing too close in face-to-face interactions and making silly, inappropriate puns and facial expressions that seemed to reflect anxiety and interpersonal unease but were covered by a veneer of false confidence. Now perhaps generic psychotherapeutic interventions that would ultimately alter her ability to empathize with others and maintain appropriate boundaries would "trickle down" to such subtle aspects of procedural knowledge. Or perhaps not. But in either case, failure to address social skills deficits of this sort could leave her continuing to alienate people for years, reinforcing many of her defenses against feeling rejected, maintaining her need for defensive withdrawal from other people, and so forth, and hence would *impede the psychodynamic work*. Simply because a conflict is resolved does not mean that the constellation of subtle behaviors associated with it, which may have taken on functional autonomy as they became woven into the fabric of the individual's behavioral repertoire, will all change. In more cognitive terms, because several aspects of procedural knowledge (such as the distance one stands from another person or the way one defensively uses humor) may have arisen during the same period and possibly as a response to the same situation does not mean that the conditions that elicit these responses, or the circumstances that might alter them, will later always co-occur.

Cognitive-behavioral theories, in contrast, assume the primacy of cognition (see, e.g., Beck, 1976, 1993). They generally lack any explicit theory of motivation, assuming that feelings primarily follow from thoughts (or in a more behavioral rendition, that actions are controlled by environmental events). This is a highly problematic stance, because the way people behave is likely to depend as much on the motives they pursue as on the expectations they have of what will happen if they pursue one course of action or another. Consider the literature on the intergenerational transmission of attachment patterns (e.g., Main, 1996; Main et al., 1985; van IJzendoorn, 1995). Results of numerous studies demonstrate that experiences with attachment figures shape not only children's internal working models of relationships but also their *motives*. As noted above, children whose primary attachment figures are uncomfortable with intimacy and physical touch gradually learn to shut off their wishes for closeness, and as adults, they deny such wishes and report positive feelings about their parents even as their electrophysiological reactions suggest otherwise (Dozier & Kobak, 1992). The idea that experiences shape cognition but not motives is untenable, yet it is implicit in cognitive theories of psychopathology. These latter cognitive approaches have no in-depth theorization about underlying general or dysfunctional motives, except insofar as these motives reflect dysfunctional thoughts (such as "it's important that everyone like me") that are relatively clear to the naked eye.

Consider the therapeutic approach taken by Aaron Beck in a videotaped interview with a man with prominent sociopathic and narcissistic features, who had a terribly disrupted attachment history in which he had been sent to live with multiple caretakers. This experience had clearly shaped both his *expectations* of intimate relationships and what dynamic psychotherapists would refer to as his *capacity to invest emotionally in other people* (for empirical research on this variable and its relation to developmental experiences such as disrupted attachments, see Westen, 1991b; Westen, Ludolph, Block, Wixom, & Wiss, 1990). The man complained of being unloved and said that if he dropped off the face of the earth, no one would really feel the difference. Beck tried to work with him on the cognitive distortions underlying this belief, but in fact, I suspect the patient was right: He *was* unlovable because he could not himself love anyone else and was, in reality, both interpersonally exploitative and easily enraged. The problem lay not with his negative self-concept but with his difficulty trusting and caring for others, which led to unsatisfactory relationships; these in turn reinforced a negative view of himself, the world, and his future *that was in many respects accurate.*

The Role of Consciousness

A third area of complementary strengths and weaknesses pertains to the role of consciousness. In psychoanalysis, the assumption is that the deeper the better: The more the clinician gets to the "real" conflict underneath, the more likely the cure (Wachtel, 1997). Paradoxically, despite Freud's early formulation of the aim of psychoanalytic treatment as making the unconscious conscious, psychoanalytic theory tends to devalue the role of conscious thoughts and feelings by treating them as surface manifestations of underlying unconscious dynamics. To the extent that the patient's problems reflect unconscious conflicts or defenses against unpleasant thoughts, feelings, or memories, standard psychoanalytic assumptions about manifest versus latent content are sensible. A primary aim of the treatment should be to help the patient rethink decisions from the past (such as being wary of, or oppositional toward authority figures) that may have once even been adaptive (such as when dealing with an authoritarian father in childhood) but that now play themselves out relatively automatically without conscious intent.

To the extent, however, that other factors also are involved, one cannot simply relegate consciousness to the role of providing clues to unconscious material. Consciousness evolved for a reason; it monitors and controls the internal and external environments, and helps us make choices in the short-run that may override our habitual tendencies. Altering conscious beliefs, strategies, and consciously chosen behaviors can have an enormous impact, if often time-limited, on the emotions people experience, the memories and expectancies they retrieve that can in turn influence their behaviors, and the choices they make (see Dalgleish & Power, 1997) that can alter or reinforce enduring, often unconscious beliefs and associations.

With respect to consciousness, cognitive therapists tend, again, to be the mirror image of their psychodynamic counterparts. Cognitive therapists address depression by focusing on the conscious or almost conscious beliefs patients have and the things they say to themselves that contribute to the maintenance of their depression. When people are depressed, they do, in fact, tend to make conscious attributions and retrieve information in a negatively biased way that exacerbates their depression (see Mathews &

Macleod, 1994). Calling attention to these processes can be very useful (and is, I suspect, an intervention made by all good therapists, regardless of theoretical orientation). Other patients have deficits in affect regulation that require treatment aimed at teaching them new conscious patterns to replace old dysfunctional patterns, or to build responses in the absence of effective affect-regulatory procedures. Thus, it is no wonder that Linehan's (1993) treatment is successful, at least in the short-term, in treating certain aspects of borderline psychopathology using cognitive-behavioral techniques that are aimed at helping these patients regulate their intense, labile emotions—because the inability to do so is a central feature of the disorder (see also Westen, 1991b).

Once again, however, the strengths and weaknesses of an approach tend to spring from the same wells. Along with the emphasis of cognitive-behavioral therapy on cognitive processes is an inattention to unconscious processes, which flies in the face of a decade of research on implicit thought and memory in cognitive science (e.g., Holyoak & Spellman, 1993; Reber, 1992; Schacter & Buckner, 1998). Indeed, as discussed later, one could argue that cognitive science and psychodynamic treatment have much more in common than cognitive science and cognitive therapy. To the extent that cognitive-behavioral clinicians consider motives, they tend to assume a serial processing model of motivation (i.e., that all active motives are conscious or semi-conscious and guide behavior one at a time), despite the amassing evidence that many mental processes (including motivational processes) occur in parallel and influence behavior whether or not they attain consciousness.

In fact, a plethora of studies across cognitive, social, personality, and developmental psychology have now documented the existence and importance of unconscious cognitive, affective, motivational, and defensive processes (for reviews, see Westen, 1998a, in press), and any therapeutic system that ignores these processes does so at its peril. For example, McClelland, Koestner, and Weinberger (1989) have shown that self-report and projective (TAT) measures of motivation do not correlate with each other, but each has predictable external correlates: Self-reported motives predict behavior when consciousness is focused on conscious goals, whereas projective motives predict behavior over the long run (such as entrepreneurial success over 20 years) as people's implicit motives guide their behavior. Bargh (1997) has shown that surreptitiously activating motives (such as having people unscramble words related to achievement or affiliation) influences motivated behavior in subsequent tasks even though experimental participants have no idea what motives have been activated. Shedler, Mayman, and Manis (1993) have documented that people who defend against negative views of themselves—who believe they are psychologically healthy despite evidence to the contrary—show autonomic hyperreactivity related to heart disease. Several research teams have demonstrated substantial correlations between reliably coded unconscious defensive processes and various measures of psychiatric outcome (Perry & Cooper, 1989; Roston, Lee, & Vaillant, 1992; Westen, Muderrisoglu, Fowler, Shedler, & Koren, 1997).

The distinction between implicit and explicit processes may help explain the paradoxical finding that cognitive therapy for depression (at least in the laboratory) tends to be very effective in the short run but ineffective in the long run. Cognitive therapies largely target explicit thought and memory, focusing on the way people consciously think and talk to themselves. Particularly when the treatment is relatively brief, as in the cognitive therapies conducted in randomized controlled trials to date, cognitive therapy is unlikely to lead to either (1) changes in implicit associational networks that contribute to the recurrence of depressive or anxiety states over time or (2) automatization of the conscious processes that *are* learned in treatment. This would allow either of these two latter processes to be activated implicitly alongside the long-standing implicit associations and procedures that increase vulnerability to these states. Similarly, behaviorally oriented interventions that focus on generalized coping strategies such as relaxation can be expected to produce primarily short-term effects in treating anxiety because of their reliance on conscious activation (and the presence of the therapist to assure their activation). In contrast, behavioral interventions directed at *specific* cognitive-affective associations—such as associations between anxiety states and particular stimuli, thoughts, or interoceptive cues—should be much more effective in the long run. Altering these associations *in vivo* not only alters conscious cognitions but also alters the implicit associational networks that register regularities in the world over time (including in the person's own reactions, e.g., to feeling a tightening in chest

muscles). This could explain the relatively greater success of treatments such as Barlow's panic control treatment over longer periods of time. Not only do such techniques change the person's "gut" reactions, but they also increase feelings of self-efficacy in the face of anxious feelings that re-emerge and allow the person time and enough of a sense of control to activate explicit coping strategies that may help prevent relapse.

To summarize, psychodynamic approaches tend to focus on large and complex phenomena, motivational explanations, and interactive, unconscious processes. Cognitive-behavioral approaches tend to focus on discrete processes, cognitive explanations, and processes that are conscious or can readily be made conscious. Unfortunately, we cannot assume that the patients who walk into our offices have problems that fall on the appropriate side of each of these antinomies to suit our theoretical and therapeutic (and probably temperamental) predilections. Sometimes one or the other is appropriate. More often, however, neither side of the antinomy alone is accurate or sufficient: We need an integrative theory that can point us toward the interaction of discrete processes, of motivation and cognition, and of conscious and unconscious processes.

APPROACHES TO PSYCHOTHERAPY INTEGRATION

Arkowitz (1997) has provided a comprehensive summary of the history of psychotherapy integration, which I will not duplicate here. (For handbooks that describe the major approaches, see Norcross & Goldfried, 1992; Stricker & Gold, 1993; and the *Journal of Psychotherapy Integration*, published by the Society for the Exploration of Psychotherapy Integration.) Arkowitz distinguishes three avenues of integration, which cover much of the landscape: technical eclecticism, common factors, and theoretical integration.

Technical Eclecticism

Technical eclecticism is probably the most common form of integration (see Norcross, 1986). Many clinicians who consider themselves technically eclectic pick and choose interventions from different approaches, usually with one approach dominating the way they practice. A more sophisticated form of technical eclecticism is empirically guided eclecticism, in which the therapist attempts to select interventions with particular patients or at particular points in the treatment based on controlled outcome trials (Beutler & Clarkin, 1990; Prochaska & Norcross, 1994). Thus, a therapist might treat a depressed patient with cognitive or interpersonal therapy but integrate empirically supported experiential techniques into the treatment (see Greenberg, Rice, & Elliott, 1993) if the patient's depression appears to reflect, in part, "unfinished business" with a parent who has recently died and with whom the patient had a very conflicted relationship. The term "technical eclecticism" originated with Arnold Lazarus, whose "multimodal therapy" is largely a blend of cognitive and behavioral strategies (Lazarus, 1976, 1981).

Although many clinicians probably do successfully integrate techniques from multiple perspective at different times, technical eclecticism has many pitfalls. One is the dearth of data on the *long-term* impact of virtually any intervention. What works in controlled trials in producing an initial response to treatment may, in fact, not be what works in the long run; it may even be counterproductive. For example, research on emotional disclosure of painful experiences finds that initially it may lead to increased distress and autonomic reactivity but ultimately produces substantial emotional and physical benefits (Pennebaker, 1997). Further, as Arkowitz (1997) points out, there are so many patient and therapist variables, which could influence which intervention to employ at which time, that we are a long way off from a true science of differential therapeutics (see the Petry, Tennen, & Affleck chapter in this volume). For example, as noted earlier, virtually all controlled therapy trials have excluded between 10% and 90% of potential patients because of comorbid conditions that are the norm in clinical practice. In addition, as Messer has argued (e.g., Messer & Warren, 1995), the importation of a technical strategy from one form of treatment to another may change its meaning to the patient; doing so also may require validation in its new context, because it may function differently in a different therapeutic milieu. For example, a behavioral intervention during dynamic treatment could engender a very different kind of reaction from the patient who has come to expect a less structured therapeutic stance, which may in turn affect its efficacy.

Common Factors

A second approach to psychotherapy integration is a common factors approach, which seeks common ingredients across therapies that account for their success (see the chapter by Snyder, Ilardi, Michael, & Cheavens in this volume). One of the most important common factors approaches actually arose before the advent of behavior therapy, namely, Alexander and French's (1946) concept of *corrective emotional experience*. According to Alexander and French, whose position led to their "excommunication" from psychodynamic circles at the time (but has returned in many guises since then), the basic therapeutic principle underlying many forms of treatment is the same: "To reexpose the patient, under more favorable circumstances, to emotional situations which he could not handle in the past" (p. 66). In psychoanalysis, an emphasis on exposure has never been as explicit, either before or after this classic work. As I will suggest, this remains one of the major reasons psychodynamic therapists could profit from integrating theory and technique from their cognitive-behavioral colleagues (Weinberger, 1995).

From a theoretical perspective, Jerome Frank set the agenda for the common factors approach in a series of publications beginning with his classic book, *Persuasion and Healing* (1961, 1973). Drawing on a range of evidence, including anthropological studies, Frank argued that the common factors that explain much of therapeutic success involve restoring hope and morale, eliciting emotional arousal, providing corrective emotional experiences, encouraging behavioral change outside sessions, and helping the patient develop new perspectives of the self and others. From a broader perspective, he suggested that psychotherapy provides an emotionally charged relationship with a person perceived as a healer, who provides a sensible way of understanding the symptom and avenues for change (a schema or myth), and a ritualized procedure for healing.

In general, many theorists and researchers have concluded that not only the therapeutic relationship but also presenting the patient with new experiences (conceived as learning in behavioral treatment and insight in psychodynamic therapy) are crucial components of therapeutic success. Weinberger (1995) offers a relatively succinct summary of the state of the art, pointing to five common factors that appear empirically related to therapeutic change: the therapeutic relationship, expectations of therapeutic success, confronting the problem, providing an experience of mastery or cognitive control, and attribution of success to internal factors (e.g., new skills, personality change) rather than external ones (e.g., the presence of the therapist). One of the main phenomena that has bolstered the common factors approach is the repeated finding that most therapies tend to produce equivalent results, despite radically different methods and frequent claims for the superiority of one treatment over another, which typically evaporate when investigator allegiance is controlled.

A useful analogy in thinking about the common factors approach comes from the field of intelligence, where many researchers since Spearman have argued that intelligence reflects both general intelligence (the "common factor") and specific intelligences (the particular techniques used by adherents of different approaches, which likely lead to different kinds of change, or perhaps to different kinds of change in different kinds of patients). Indeed, studies that have examined psychotherapy *process* in rich detail have typically found the presence of both common and specific factors that correlate with treatment outcome (Ablon & Jones, 1998; Goldfried, 1991).

Although the common factors approach has much to commend it, it, too, is not without its critics (see Messer & Warren, 1995). For example, similar mean change scores may emerge across different treatment conditions for many reasons, including the presence in any sample of individuals who respond to different forms of treatment; common factors that lead to improvement in the short run (such as hope, or nonspecific aspects of the relationship) but wear off over time and are never discovered because of the pervasive inadequacy of follow-up intervals in psychotherapy research; and the lack of clinically sophisticated change measures that address subtle aspects of personality change that may predict long-term outcome. Further, with the exception of research by Goldfried (1991) and a few others, the level of generality of descriptions of common factors may conceal as much as it reveals. "The relationship" in cognitive-behavioral therapy and psychoanalysis are very different, both in style of relating and in attention to the relationship itself as a laboratory for exploring wishes, fears, fantasies, and relationship paradigms. As Schacht (1984) has noted, salt in one's soup is very different from salt in one's gas tank. At times, a more passive analytic stance could be a help or a hindrance; the same is true of a more active cognitive-behavioral stance. In both cases, aspects of "the relationship" can have very different effects at different points in the treatment. Finally, as Weinberger (1995) has pointed out, "common

factors aren't so common;" that is, most approaches to therapy capitalize on common factors accidentally rather than systematically, because their theories emphasize the "uncommon factors" that distinguish their therapeutic approach.

Theoretical Integration

The most thorough form of psychotherapy integration is integration at the level of theory. In this approach, technical integrations evolve from theoretical integrations. The most important early effort at psychotherapy integration was Dollard and Miller's (1950) pathbreaking effort to integrate psychoanalytic ideas with the Hullian behavioral theory of the time and with an understanding of culture, something missing in most accounts of psychotherapy until the emphasis on diversity emerged in the political arena over 30 years later. Although this book is filled with insights that are likely to be rediscovered, two are probably the most important. First, Dollard and Miller argued for a relation between anxiety reduction and reinforcement, suggesting that behaviors (or thought processes) that reduce anxiety are reinforcing. Indeed, Miller (1992) has documented empirically the way a thought can become associated with anxiety through classical conditioning procedures. From there it takes little imagination to use a two-factor learning model to suggest that classically conditioned emotional responses to thoughts can, like conditioned emotional responses to other stimuli, lead to avoidance—in this case avoidance of the thought. This was the second major insight, the conceptualization of repression as a form of avoidance learning, in which the person learns to avoid thoughts to minimize anxiety.

There can be no doubt that the watershed event in the history of psychotherapy integration, which catalyzed the formation of The Society for the Exploration of Psychotherapy Integration (SEPI) in 1983, was the publication of Paul Wachtel's (1977) *Psychoanalysis and Behavior Therapy*, which remains the most important and sophisticated attempt at theoretical integration in the field. In many respects Wachtel's book took off from three starting points: (a) Dollard and Miller's (1950) insights on anxiety and anxiety reduction; (b) Perry London's (1964) conclusion that insight and action are the primary change agents in psychoanalysis and behavior therapy, respectively, and that a treatment that incorporated both might well be more effective than either alone; and (c) more interpersonally oriented psychodynamic traditions, such as the work of Harry Stack Sullivan (1953) and Karen Horney (1950).

Wachtel was trained psychoanalytically but through observation of skilled behavior therapists came to believe that many of his anti-behavioral biases were not well grounded. On the one hand, he remained committed to psychoanalytic concepts of conflict, unconscious processes, and the importance of childhood experiences for subsequent interpersonal functioning—three theoretical assumptions that have now amassed substantial empirical support (Westen, 1998a). Thus, he rejected the radical behaviorist assumption of the time that thoughts and feelings were nonexistent, epiphenomenal, unimportant, or in any case not worthy of scientific (or therapeutic) attention. On the other hand, he equally rejected the psychoanalytic view that getting to the bottom of things psychodynamically means getting to the most deeply repressed or "primitive" layers of the personality. Indeed, in his pithy summary of his critique of the dominant approach to psychoanalysis at the time, "Personality is a process, not an onion" (p. xvi). His point was that psychotherapy should not be a process of peeling the psychic onion down until the therapist reaches the center, in search of repressed pockets of functioning preserved intact despite years of development like a "wooly mammoth" encased in ice for millenia. Rather, he argued, many of the patterns that give people trouble in their lives reflect their *current* ways of thinking, feeling, and behaving interpersonally, which perpetuate the problem.

This central point is easily misunderstood. What Wachtel proposed is that, based on their childhood experiences, people bring ways of thinking, feeling, and behaving into their current relationships. In so doing, however, they often perpetuate and exacerbate the problem through a process of "cyclical psychodynamics," in which their actions produce precisely what they fear. Hence a self-reinforcing spiral of disappointment and avoidance is created, in which they feel certain that the dangers they are trying to avoid are justified because they keep re-creating them. Thus, a patient who as a child experienced his mother as distant and uncomfortable with closeness is likely to push people away, leading them to become more distant with him, and confirming his view that intimacy is to be avoided. Subsequent research has corroborated many aspects of this theory, such as research on avoidant attachment styles (Dozier & Kobak, 1992) and Swann's (Swann, Stein-Seroussi, & Giesler, 1992) work on

self-verification processes, which finds that people who are depressed, for example, tend to prefer people who give them negative rather than positive feedback.

Wachtel did not propose a new form of therapy based on his theory (to his credit, I believe, given the 400 plus schools that exist today). Instead, he described what behavior therapists could learn from dynamic therapists and vice versa, providing concrete suggestions of ways dynamic therapists, for example, could incorporate more active interventions into their treatments. His own therapeutic approach is a modified psychodynamic one; indeed, he has written what is probably the best book ever published on how actually to talk to patients (Wachtel, 1993), which can be used by therapists of any orientation but is most appropriate for more open-ended, exploratory psychotherapies.

Technically, Wachtel's work has been most influential in fostering what is probably the most important form of contemporary psychotherapy integration, which Messer (1992) has called *assimilative integration*. In assimilative integration, a therapist primarily grounded in one theoretical orientation incorporates perspectives or practices from another perspective in a considered fashion, after examining its meaning and implications within his or her own therapeutic system. (For useful case examples, see Stricker & Gold, 1996; Wachtel, 1991.)

Although Wachtel is the most comprehensive and influential integrative theorist, others have offered important advances in this respect as well. Horowitz (1987) has proposed an assimilative psychodynamic approach that integrates psychoanalysis and cognitive science at the theoretical level. Ryle (1990) has been developing a cognitive-analytic short-term therapy that resembles Horowitz's approach in certain respects but is more explicit in terms of the implications for technique. Greenberg and his colleagues (e.g., Greenberg & Safran, 1987) have been evolving an approach that integrates Gestalt, Rogerian, and more recently cognitive elements at the level of both theory and technique. Kohlenberg has offered an approach based on contemporary behavioral theory that integrates aspects of psychoanalytic therapy such as a focus on the therapeutic relationship (Kohlenberg & Tsai, 1991).

Similar to the other forms of integration described by Arkowitz, theoretical integration has its critics (Messer, 1986). Perhaps the two major criticisms are the selective nature of integration and the problem of incompatible worldviews. First, any integrative effort is selective. The concept of discriminative stimuli in behavioral theory (stimuli that signal certain contingencies are operative) is highly compatible with the psychoanalytic notion that certain dynamics become activated under certain conditions but not in others, such as hostility in the face of the demands of an authority figure. On the other hand, a radical behavioral stance that denies causal status to mental events or eschews the concept of motivation is incompatible with any psychodynamic construct. Second, cognitive-behavioral therapists tend to be optimists and to be less interested in the interpretation of meaning than psychoanalytic therapists. They believe that through changing circumstances or confronting irrationalities in thinking, people can become happy, and that the important data in psychotherapy are relatively observable and do not require substantial inference to find. As Messer (1986) has pointed out, in contrast, psychoanalytic psychotherapists tend to have a more "tragic" view of the nature of human life as filled with inevitable conflicts and frustrations. Their interest is in affect and meaning, and their intellectual bent is more toward literary criticism (interpretation of narratives) than engineering (see the Vakoch and Strupp chapter in this volume).

Whether the two approaches can be bridged at the theoretical level is probably an empirical question, in two respects. First, we will probably not know whether such an integration is possible until we see one. In the study of perception, competing positions (e.g., top-down versus bottom-up approaches, or trichromatic versus opponent-process theories of color vision) have frequently appeared incompatible, only to be resolved by later recognition of their applicability at different levels of the nervous system or at different points in the sensory-perceptual process. Personally, I suspect such a possibility would be much more likely in the field of psychotherapy if researchers and clinicians did not devalue each other and if adherents of the major approaches would consider undue certainty about their own position and their own preferred form of data (and lack of knowledge or derision of competing points of view) as a countertransference problem. I am not, however, at all sanguine that this will happen anytime soon. Second, if psychotherapy researchers decide at some point to (a) pursue ecologically valid strategies for testing therapeutic effectiveness (e.g., with samples of patients

who resemble patients seen in clinical practice, who have multiple concerns and symptoms, rather than with artificially homogeneous samples that are representative of no known human population); (b) study outcome at clinically and scientifically defensible follow-up intervals, given known patterns of relapse (e.g., two to ten years, rather than zero to one year); (c) include outcome measures that capture the range of outcomes, which clinicians from differing theoretical orientations find compelling, rather than assessing only one symptom in people who are typically polysymptomatic; and (d) include sophisticated process measures that can be correlated with outcome in naturalistic samples, in order to learn about what interventions and interactional styles actually predict positive outcome—then clinicians may pay attention to the findings and adjust their practices accordingly.

ASSOCIATIVE NETWORKS, AFFECT REGULATION, AND SOCIAL COGNITION: NEW AVENUES FOR THEORETICAL INTEGRATION

Wachtel's pioneering efforts focused on integrating aspects of psychoanalysis with behavioral theory and technique in the mid-1970s. Both approaches have developed substantially since then, as reflected in the new edition of his classic work published in 1997, which links his approach to developments in relational psychoanalysis in the intervening years. In many respects these relational approaches have rediscovered the assimilative psychodynamic stance Wachtel had been advocating for 20 years, in which the patient is seen as a collaborator; enactments in the treatment are treated as opportunities to learn about and change enduring maladaptive ways of interacting in relationships; and interpersonal dynamics in the here-and-now are viewed as important and legitimate objects of inquiry in their own right instead of just as clues to primitive unconscious fantasies unmodified by years of experience.

In the two decades since Wachtel published *Psychoanalysis and Behavior Therapy*, another major change has occurred in the psychology of considerable relevance to the field of psychotherapy integration: The emergence of cognitive science as a major approach to the mind (and cognitive neuroscience as an approach to mind-brain relationships). In what follows, I briefly explore three theoretical domains informed by this new development: networks of association, affect regulation, and social cognition and object relations. Each has considerable relevance for integrative clinical practice and may lead to a "second generation" of integrative theory.

Associational Networks

One area of potential integration between psychodynamic and cognitive-behavioral theory and technique lies in the concept of associational networks. Indeed, associationism is a common ancestor of psychoanalysis, behaviorism, *and* cognitive science. Behaviorist theory always has viewed associations—between stimuli and responses, between two stimuli, between a primary and secondary reinforcer, etc.—as the key to learning. Psychoanalysis and cognitive science both propose that a large proportion of knowledge is stored along networks of association, which operate unconsciously (in psychoanalytic language) or implicitly (in cognitive language). Information becomes organized along associational networks through experience, although as research from the behaviorist tradition has demonstrated, some associations are more readily learned than others (Garcia & Koelling, 1966). Associative links between units of information are strengthened by their repeated conjunction, either in thought or in reality.

The parallels between psychodynamic and cognitive views of associational networks have increased since the advent of connectionist models in cognitive science, notably parallel distributed processing (PDP) models (Rumelhart, McClelland, and the PDP Group, 1986; Smith, 1998). From a connectionist perspective, the meaning of an object or concept is not found in a particular location in the brain (an "engram"). Rather, a representation is distributed across a network of processing units that, through experience, have become activated in tandem. Each of these units attends to some small aspect of the representation, and none alone represents the entire concept. The presence of some units implies the likely presence of others, whereas the presence of others implies the likely absence of others. In connectionist models, the connection between two units (*nodes* in the network) can thus have a positive or negative weight (or a zero weight if the presence of one does not predict the presence of the other), indicating whether the connectionist is excitatory or inhibitory.

In other words, the brain represents knowledge through the interaction of thousands or millions of neurons, which can either excite or inhibit each other, spreading activation to or away from a particular way of interpreting, categorizing, or responding. The more extensive the match between current experience and previously activated networks of association representing a concept, memory, behavior, and so forth, the more likely the person is to categorize an object as a member of that class, remember the incident, or produce the previously performed behavior. Complicating matters is that at any given time multiple networks (or parts of networks) are activated simultaneously because many stimuli have overlapping features. Settling on a "solution" to the problem (whether the problem is one of categorization, remembering, choosing among various options, etc.) involves a process of *parallel constraint satisfaction*, in which the brain essentially tries out multiple possible solutions and finds the best fit to the data. Once the system has arrived at a solution that appears most consistent with the data, alternative solutions are inhibited.

To provide a simple example, when two initially unconnected processes repeatedly co-occur (such as the detection of two crossed lines by a child who is first learning the letter x), a network begins to be formed and is strengthened each time the child encounters an x. This network comes to take on a particular meaning (in this case, a letter), and a stimulus that resembles the stored concept to a substantial enough degree (e.g., a hand-scrawled x that is not a perfect exemplar of the letter) will activate enough of the connected units to activate the whole representation. Upon seeing an imperfect instance of an x, such as a handwritten version, networks representing both x and a t may be simultaneously activated. In this case, the broader context of the letter, such as its place in the word in which it is embedded (e.g., either *e tra* or *ex ra*) provides an additional set of constraints that would favor one interpretation of the letter and inhibit another.

To give a more complex clinical example, if enough features of an interaction with a therapist match prior experiences with a parent, the representation of the parent (or self-in-relation-to-parent) will be activated, leading to assimilation of the therapist to a representation from the past (in psychoanalytic terms, a transference reaction). For example, during a period in which I was traveling extensively, I repeatedly had to shift therapy appointments around to avoid missing too many sessions. This had a particular impact on one patient, whose father, a successful businessman, had traveled extensively—and in the process had met another woman for whom he had left the patient's mother. The patient at first seemed to respond to my absences with tremendous flexibility. However, over time he seemed to become cold and distant. In one session, as I was just becoming aware of the pattern, I wondered with him about a look I was beginning to see in his eyes, which seemed steely. My comment led to associations and, thus, to memories of how abandoned he had felt by his father, particularly when his father left the family, and how at first he had tried to impress his father and press for extra time with him but eventually had just "given up" and distanced himself. In this case, my own actions inadvertently activated a prototype from the past, along with the attendant feelings and responses to those feelings.

As this example suggests, one way psychodynamic and behaviorist theory can augment connectionist views in cognitive science is in the recognition that many of the same principles apply to affective and motivational processes as to strictly cognitive ones. Feelings, wishes, and fears are associated with representations of people and situations and are activated unconsciously along with other forms of information when part of the network is primed by an environmental or mental event. As in the example of the transference reaction already mentioned, nothing about the mind's architecture requires that people be conscious of the triggers of their affective reactions or of the activation of many of the processing units that may ultimately lead to a conscious feeling. As described earlier, a considerable body of experimental literature documents the existence of implicit or unconscious affective and motivational processes, much like the implicit cognitive processes studied by cognitive scientists. For example, if an experimenter repeatedly pairs a word (e.g., "poodle") with mild electric shock and then presents the word subliminally, participants will show an electrophysiological response, such as increased skin conductance or an evoked-related brain potential (ERP), even though they have no conscious awareness of having seen or heard the word that elicited the affective response (see, e.g., Wong, Shevrin, & Williams 1994). Neurological evidence suggests that affective associative memory involves different neural pathways than conscious, explicit memory, and that affective associations may linger long after a conscious, declarative memory has dissipated. For example, Johnson, Kim, and Risse (1985) found that Korsakoff's patients, who cannot remember any of the information taught them about two fictional characters, nevertheless subsequently prefer the character who had been described more positively.

These phenomena have substantial clinical implications because they suggest the importance of techniques that allow the therapist and patient access to unconscious or implicit associational networks that may influence thought, feeling, and behavior yet be inaccessible to consciousness. For example, one patient, who had a pattern of rejecting men once she started to become close to them, inexplicably became "disgusted" with a man with whom she had spent an exciting romantic evening three days earlier. When asked why, she shrugged and said, "I don't know, I just thought, when he was about to come over Friday night, 'Yuck, I don't like this guy.'" After trying unsuccessfully to find out what thought processes had intervened during the week, I used what might be called *directed free association*, suggesting that because neither she nor I knew why her feelings had changed, it might be useful for her simply to place herself mentally back in the moments before the man arrived at her house Friday night and let her mind wander to whatever thoughts or feelings came up. Her associations led to several other encounters with men and to a revelation to both of us, that she had never had comfortable sex except under the influence of alcohol. Eventually she associated to a time in her late adolescence when she was beginning to receive considerable attention from boys and starting to experiment with sex. Shortly after that time she developed somatic symptoms that led her to withdraw from her social group and halt sexual activity, which she found conflictual.

Advances in the understanding of associative networks in cognitive neuroscience provide a theoretical rationale for precisely this kind of free-associative technique, because it is now clear that people do not have conscious access to such networks, which nonetheless regulate their thoughts, feelings, and behavior. The best way to begin to "map" the networks related to a patient's symptoms is to follow the associative links between nodes on the network when the patient tries to suspend the normal conscious regulation of thought and memory and say whatever comes to mind.

These considerations also suggest ways that more structured cognitive-behavioral therapy techniques can be extended in a way that may be useful to both psychodynamic and cognitive-behavioral therapists. For example, one patient, an assistant professor on a tenure track line, was completely stymied in his efforts to write. The relation between this symptom and a history of humiliations at the hands of a parent who had apparently responded more with envy than pride at the patient's achievements, was readily apparent, but the dynamic work was slow, and unfortunately the tenure clock was fast. Concerned that we might be fiddling while Rome burned, I supplemented our dynamic work with a behavioral plan, which met, as well, with only a modicum of success. As we explored what happened as he tried to work, what became clear is that neither his associations in the session nor his reports of what he thought and felt as he tried to write were providing us with enough insight into the networks of association or the conscious thought processes that were stopping him. All he could report was that his mind would drift to everything but the paper. So I suggested that the next time he sit down to write, he essentially free associate in the margins, to try to give us more access to the networks activated in real life rather than in my office, which I suspected was priming different associations for both dynamic reasons (resistance) and cognitive ones (it was not the setting in which his resistances to writing were active). What we learned, in fact, was a surprise to both of us: That he was essentially keeping a running commentary in the margins of self-critical comments that were virtually in the syntax of his critical parent. I suspect we might have gotten to that material eventually, but real-life considerations contraindicated a more standard analytic stance. (I must again point out here that these interventions were not undertaken without constant consideration of the transference-countertransference dynamics implicit in my making a "homework" assignment, even though I explained to him why I thought it might be useful and collaborated with him on how to implement it.)

Affect Regulation

A second fertile area for theoretical integration, drawing heavily on the work of Dollard and Miller (1950), Wachtel (1997), and Bowlby (1969), involves affect regulation (Schore, 1994; Westen 1985, 1994b, 1997a, 1997b). Feelings (including both emotions and sensory pleasure–pain states) can be conceived as evolved mechanisms for the selective retention of behavioral and mental processes. That is, humans have evolved a set of affective proclivities that regulate both thought

and action, e.g., fear and anxiety, which, under normal conditions, become attached to representations of stimuli that threaten bodily integrity, survival, reproduction, survival of related others, and so forth. The feelings associated with a mental or behavioral event influence the tendency to reproduce or avoid it in the future under similar conditions. Thus, people avoid committing actions that make them feel anxious, ashamed, or guilty, just as they avoid eating foods that taste bitter. They can regulate their affects through behaviors, conscious coping strategies, or unconscious defenses.

This approach is consistent with a large body of research on operant conditioning, because it suggests that the consequences of an action determine whether or not it is reproduced. Although it is not consistent with the antimentalist philosophy of science associated with Skinnerian behaviorism, affect regulation is, I believe, consistent with the assumptions of most behavior therapists, who have long known the importance of helping people deal with unwanted affective reactions and their influence on subsequent behavior. This approach to affect regulation also is consistent with many theories and research paradigms in the behavioral tradition, such as two-factor learning theory (Mowrer, 1947), which proposes that the consequences that influence behavior are largely affective, and Gray's (1990) hypothesis of neurologically distinct motivational systems for appetitive and avoidant behavior associated with positive and negative affect, respectively. The cognitive-social theories of Mischel (1979) and Bandura (1977, 1986) add that people also act on the basis of their *expectancies* about evaluatively significant events.

From a cognitive perspective, affect regulation mechanisms are a form of procedural knowledge—that is, skills activated, often without conscious involvement, when current circumstances match prior conditions in which the procedure was associated with reducing unpleasant feelings or enhancing pleasant ones. Thus, if distraction proves useful in handling an anxiety-provoking situation, the person is likely to use it again. Clinically, what now appears to be maladaptive affect-regulatory processes (such as dissociation that disrupts functioning or leads to further abuse in trauma survivors, or the use of intellectualizing defenses that interfere with intimacy in more obsessional patients) may have been useful or even may have been adaptive efforts to regulate affects at a prior time in which more adaptive strategies were not available. Unfortunately, once such strategies become associated with affect regulation, they are likely to be automatically activated under similar conditions in the future, and efforts to tinker with them may lead to resistance.

Talking about affect-regulatory strategies in this way with patients can often allow them to hear about and acknowledge highly maladaptive aspects of their personality that would otherwise evoke shame or denial (see Linehan, 1993; Wachtel, 1993). For example, one patient was able to begin addressing his tendency to behave in very passive–aggressive ways when presented with an interpretation like the following: "Given how controlled you felt by your father, and how sternly he punished disobedience, I can see why you would have developed some very subtle ways to express your anger and autonomy—by passively resisting. But it seems now as if that strategy is getting you in more trouble than it's worth because you're not in your father's house any more, and quietly refusing to do things just makes people angry."

As this example suggests, from a psychodynamic perspective, mental processes, like behaviors, can be selectively retained, that is, reinforced, based on their affect-regulatory properties, a point recognized by Dollard and Miller (1950), who viewed repression as an internal flight mechanism (see also Wachtel, 1997). Defenses, in this conceptualization, are unconscious procedures for regulating affect. A further contribution of psychodynamic thinking to the understanding of affect regulation is the insight that people typically regulate multiple affects simultaneously, leading to compromise solutions called *compromise formations* (see Brenner, 1982). For example, a patient who had deeply conflictual feelings toward women and commitment found himself repeatedly committing too soon, then feeling trapped and angry, and then feeling compelled to have constant "us" conversations with the women. The outcome of these conversations was always the same: He would say that perhaps they should see other people, she would cry, he would comfort her and reassert his commitment, and then he would again feel trapped and ultimately enraged. We gradually came to understand the multiple motives involved, including a fear of being tied to a woman (related to his experience of his father as tethered to his mildly disabled mother as a child), his wish to be honest about his feelings and desires, his aggressive impulses toward women (again forged in his rela-

tionship with his mother, who he experienced as using her disability to control him through guilt), and his need to atone for hurting the woman's feelings. He thus fashioned a compromise formation that was inherently unsatisfying in a general sense but momentarily seemed to maximize multiple affective constraints. He essentially tortured the woman with his constant "us" conversations but then did penance by swearing fidelity and committing himself in ways that felt deeply unpleasant but punished him for his aggression and his sexual desires, which he considered at some level illegitimate.

Operating from an integrative conceptualization of affect regulation vastly expands the range of clinical interventions open to the practitioner and allows clinicians to address phenomena they otherwise may have left unaddressed, such as defensive processes in cognitive-behavioral therapy or conscious coping mechanisms in psychodynamic therapy. Thus, working integratively, a therapist can conceptualize a case psychodynamically while still using behavioral techniques to help a patient regulate uncomfortable affective states. For instance, consider the patient described earlier (under "therapeutic horror stories") who was treated psychodynamically for panic attacks. To help the patient reduce her vulnerability to anxiety and improve her life over the long term, the therapist appropriately explored issues around separation, for example, by examining the patient's thoughts and feelings in current relationships in which she feared loss or abandonment, including the relationship with the therapist (e.g., her reactions to the therapist's vacations, which tended to engender separation distress). At the same time, nothing would stop a clinician in this circumstance from offering the patient a "double-barreled" treatment, aimed at addressing both the characterological conditions that render the person vulnerable to anxiety and the classically conditioned responses that maintain the panic symptoms. Thus, particularly until the panic symptoms are under control, the clinician could either sequentially or simultaneously help the patient learn to regulate her affect directly by teaching her relaxation techniques such as diaphragmatic breathing and guided imagery and desensitizing her to feelings of shortness of breath that predict impending panics by having her practice running in place until she masters the feeling of breathlessness.

Any response the patient has to the more structured aspects of such a treatment—such as feeling distant from or controlled by the therapist when the therapist is more actively teaching relaxation techniques or prescribing running exercises—could then be explored in terms of its transferential meanings (Wachtel, 1987). My own limited experience integrating such straightforwardly behavioral techniques into dynamic therapies has been that patients almost uniformly develop transferential reactions to behavior plans (particularly feeling controlled), regardless of how collaboratively these plans are developed, and that their reactions can provide useful avenues for exploration of issues of control and authority. Whether the better strategy is to integrate behavioral strategies into dynamic treatments in this way or to refer the patient for adjunctive cognitive-behavioral therapy (and whether this differs for different patients) is unclear and worthy of empirical attention.

A theoretical synthesis that integrates behavioral conceptions of conditioned emotional responses and incorporates the importance of exposure with psychodynamic conceptions of defense and associative networks can prove technically useful in less obvious ways. For example, one patient, who was extremely successful in his line of work, tended to be "invisible" in his social life. I realized after some time in working with him that I had never heard him discuss any of his successes for more than a few seconds at a time, after which he would move on to something troubling to him. What became clear in exploring this was that he tended to overregulate his positive affect, particularly feelings of pride, because of his childhood experience of receiving minimal praise when he would try to elicit a gleam in his parents' eyes for his successes. Discussing this, however, did not lead him to do anything different because pride for him was strongly associated with aversive feelings (thwarted wishes for admiration), and simply knowing about the origins of this connection did not break those associations.

Thus, with an exposure model in mind, I shared with him my understanding of why he was afraid to feel proud, and suggested that we spend the next couple of sessions working our way through his history of accomplishments, beginning with his childhood. I used the analogy of someone who has a phobia of dogs, who avoids dogs by walking across the street and hence never sheds the fear, and suggested that he was a "pride phobic," and that he needed to pet the dog. Over the course of the next couple of sessions, he ambivalently shared some of his accomplishments

with me, and we analyzed his resistance when he would, frequently, try to get off topic. He clearly got pleasure from having someone significant in his life take an interest in his achievements, but, as is the case with anyone who has a phobia, found the experience at times uncomfortable. From a psychoanalytic self-psychology perspective, of course, I could have conceptualized this as providing mirroring that he never received as a child, and that was clearly part of what the intervention was about. On the other hand, the self-psychological view underplays his *conflict* in receiving mirroring at this point (a classical psychoanalytic point of view) and the importance of actively structuring the situation so that he would be exposed to a feared experience (a behavioral intervention).

Social Cognition and Object Relations

A third area of convergence of psychodynamic and cognitive-behavioral theory is their mutual interest in patients' representations of self, others, and relationships (see Blatt, Auerbach, & Levy, 1997; Horowitz, 1987; Westen, 1991b). A common link between psychoanalytic theories of object relations (see Greenberg & Mitchell, 1983), experimental work in social cognition (see Fiske, 1993), and cognitive approaches to therapy (Beck, 1976; Safran & Segal, 1991; Segal, 1988) is the concept of schema, which was actually first introduced into the psychotherapy literature by psychoanalytic ego psychologists (Hartmann, 1950) and object relations theorists (Sandler & Rosenblatt, 1962). A schema is an organized pattern of mental activity that influences perception, thought, and memory (Neisser, 1976) and includes both conscious and unconscious elements. Although psychodynamic and cognitive-behavioral theories differ considerably in their views of the role of representations in psychopathology—such as their relative emphases on emotion and motivation versus thought, unconscious versus conscious processes, etc.—considerable areas of convergence also have appeared in the two literatures, such as the distinction between two kinds of depression, one involving self-criticism and feelings of inadequacy relative to internal standards and the other involving concerns about loss, separation, loneliness, and abandonment (Clark, Steer, Beck, & Ross, 1995; Blatt & Zuroff, 1992). Considerable work needs to be done in both cognitive therapy and psychoanalysis as the competing assumptions and implications of various models of representation (such as prototypes, schemas, and associational networks) become clarified (see Smith, 1998).

Several dimensions of social cognition and object relations are important targets of clinical evaluation and intervention (Westen, 1991a, 1998b). Among the most important are (a) the cognitive structure of representations (complexity and integration); (b) the affects associated with various specific and generalized representations (such as whether the person tends to associate anxiety, sadness, guilt, shame, and so forth with people, females, maternal figures, maternal figures who resemble mother in some specific way, etc.); (c) the capacity to invest emotionally in relationships (as opposed to the tendency to treat others as means to one's ends, the most extreme example of which occurs in patients with antisocial personality disorder); (d) the nature of the individual's investment in values and moral standards; (e) the ability to understand social and psychological causality (which is disrupted in many patients with personality disorders, who have difficulty understanding in realistic ways why people do what they do); (f) the capacity to manage aggressive impulses; (g) the dominant interpersonal concerns (wishes, fears, and what Higgins [1990] calls chronically accessible schemas) that emerge in people's narratives in psychotherapy;[2] (h) the behavioral and social patterns and skills the person characteristically produces; and (i) the patient's prominent identifications with important others (who may be psychologically "sitting on the person's shoulder") as well as attempted disidentifications with people the patient feels or fears she is like (McWilliams, 1998).

Another set of variables of considerable relevance to psychoanalysis and cognitive-behavioral therapy includes aspects of self. Although the concept of "self" is prominent in both approaches today, distinctions among various aspects of self have rarely been clearly conceptualized from either perspective (see Segal, 1988; Westen, 1992). The *sense of self*, or Jamesian (1890) "I," refers to individuals' experience of themselves as the thinker of their thoughts, feeler of their feelings,

and agent of their actions. This dimension is sometimes disrupted in patients who have experienced childhood sexual trauma (see Westen, 1994a). Other self-related dimensions include (a) conscious and unconscious representations of self and their patterns of activation; (b) self-with-other schemas (the self-representations embedded in particular relationship schemas, such as *self feeling guilty for having sexual impulses*, which is common in many kinds of patients, such as anorexics); (c) conscious and unconscious self-esteem; (d) feared, wished-for, and valued self-representations that serve as standards or guides for behavior (see Higgins, 1990; Strauman, Lemieux, & Coe, 1993); (e) desires to produce particular representations of the self in others, which elicit efforts at strategic self-presentation (e.g., Jones & Pittman, 1982); and (f) identity (Erikson, 1963; Marcia, 1994), a complex construct that involves the integration or coherence of multiple self-representations, the experience of self as recognized by significant others and the broader social milieu, and the emotional weighting of elements of self (such as roles and characteristics) the person experiences as self-defining.

I have presented these three domains of potential theoretical integration—associational networks, affect regulation, and social cognition/object relations—as distinct, but in reality they are typically intertwined. Connectionist models to date have focused on only one form of constraint satisfaction that influences thought and memory, namely *cognitive* constraint satisfaction (that is, equilibrating to a solution that best fits the data). However, much of the time our cognitions, particularly about ourselves and significant others, reflect *affect-regulatory* constraints as well (Westen, 1998a, in press). For example, one patient, whose emotionally ill father had terrorized his family with violent tirades, had a largely loving relationship with his significant other of many years but would occasionally erupt in vicious verbal outbursts, which he insisted were completely understandable because he was provoked. Remarkably, the patient never consciously associated his outbursts with his father's, and stressed in multiple areas of life how he differed from his father and would never be like him.

Now one could, of course, offer a strictly cognitive interpretation of this patient's failure to make the connection between himself and his father, or an attributional explanation of how he came to view his behavior as justified. From a psychoanalytically informed connectionist per-

---

[2] Researchers from various perspectives have studied these under different rubrics, such as core conflictual relationship themes (Luborsky & Crits-Christoph, 1990), relationship schemas (Baldwin, 1993; Horowitz, 1987), and internal working models of relationships (Bowlby, 1969; Main, Kaplan & Cassidy, 1985).

spective, however, the conscious association between father and self was blocked by its affective consequences. Affect—in this case, anxiety and guilt—placed an additional set of constraints on what he could think by inhibiting conscious recognition of an obvious similarity. To put it another way, the affects that are attached to nodes in a network (and to links between them) can inhibit their conscious activation. Thus, even though the patient's behavior (procedural knowledge) reflected his history with his father, his conscious, declarative representations of father and self were completely divorced.

Similarly, the fact that the patient repeatedly came to the conclusion that his anger was justified reflects a combination of cognitive constraints (being provoked is indeed an appropriate explanation to *consider* when one becomes furious) and affective constraints (imagining that he could be like his father would have been extremely painful). These affective constraints shifted the equilibrated solution away from the one that best fit the data from a strictly cognitive point of view to an alternative, less threatening explanation (at least consciously). A major goal of the treatment was to help this patient work through his identifications with his father. In technical terms, this required exposing him to a set of previously warded-off self-representations (see Horowitz, 1987) in a supportive atmosphere that allowed him to recognize the links between himself and his father without bolstering his defenses against them or rupturing the therapeutic relationship. My own experience is that confronting patients with painful information about themselves such as this often is much more successful if interpretive comments are both classically dynamic, in the sense of linking current behavior to past, and somewhat psychoeducational and matter-of-fact, such as helping the person see how his behavior is both understandable and natural in light of that past. Thus, the patient was able to hear and acknowledge an aspect of himself he had dreaded for years with a simple statement like the following: "You know, much of who we are is modeled after the important people in our lives when we're young. One of the hardest things to deal with is when the people we naturally most love and admire, like your father, are also the people we hate the most for the things they did. I can see why you'd hate many things about your father and why you vowed never to be like him, but it's hard to imagine that you didn't also pick up some things from him, both good and bad. Our task, I think, is to figure out which parts you want to keep and which parts you want to try to get rid of."

CONCLUSION

Integrating psychodynamic and cognitive-behavioral theory and practice may at times be essential for optimal treatment because the two perspectives have complementary strengths and weaknesses. Psychodynamic approaches offer a complex understanding of cognitive-affective interactions, motivation, and unconscious processes. However, they too often rely on broad, vaguely specified terms such as "narcissistic injury" that do not facilitate the targeting of specific processes; assume that symptoms reflect motivational processes, thus discounting the role of learning and cognition; and fail to address adequately patients' problems regulating conscious processes (such as ruminative thoughts) and behaviors that may require direct intervention. Cognitive-behavioral approaches, in contrast, focus on highly specific processes that can be targeted for intervention, cognitive processes involved in psychopathology, and conscious processes and behaviors. However, they lack a concept of personality structure and hence fail to address complex interactions of cognition, emotion, and motivation involved in many symptoms and in personality disorders; assume that problematic affective processes reflect dysfunctional thoughts and so discount the role of problematic and conflicting motives; and fail to attend to unconscious cognitive, affective, and motivational processes that have now been demonstrated in experimental research, particularly in cognitive neuroscience. Psychotherapy integration can occur at the level of technical eclecticism, common factors, and theoretical integration. Theoretical integration is the most thoroughgoing form of integration. Integrative theoretical approaches to associational networks, affect regulation, and the psychological processes that mediate the capacity to develop and maintain intimate relationships may provide important avenues for integration.

Although I have argued in this chapter for the potential importance of therapy integration, the barriers to therapeutic integration at both the conceptual and the practical level are substantial. Therapists choose their orientation for a reason, and they tend to find an approach whose theoretical postulates match their own personal attitudes and dynamics. As Jung once said, every psychological theory is the personal confession of the psychologist. Therapists typically are drawn to an approach by virtue of either personal characteristics or more accidental events and allegiances (such as where they did their graduate training or who their mentor happened to be). Thus, even *considering* integrative theories or techniques can engender various sources of resistance, such as fears of being disloyal to people and paradigms, fears of making mistakes, fears of not knowing, and so forth. Practicing within a paradigm is certainly more comfortable.

Practicing within a paradigm is, I think, far preferable to a willy-nilly eclecticism of the "I'll try some of this and some of that" variety. The latter is likely to lead to treatments that lack coherence, to confusion for patients, and to the potential for considerable therapeutic acting-in, because therapists without a strong theoretical compass are likely to find themselves either completely at sea or swayed by the currents of their countertransference, that is, by feelings that pull them in one direction or another. Indeed, one of my constant cautions to supervisees who want to try interjecting a cognitive-behavioral intervention into a psychodynamic treatment is to *know whose affect you're regulating.* Cognitive-behavioral work is more active, structured, and predictable and hence tends to have fewer affective tugs on the therapist. Thus, integrative therapists working from a psychodynamic home base are as likely to become more active and integrative when their own anxiety is aroused as when their patients' anxiety needs regulating.

On the other hand, a business as usual psychodynamic stance, traditionally described as *neutral,* is no more free of countertransference than is an integrative stance. The decision to be less active is, like every psychological act, a compromise formation. A less active stance can reflect varying degrees of good therapeutic technique, passive aggression, passive withholding, fear of saying something wrong, identification with mentors who stressed therapeutic abstinence, fear of intimacy, desire for dominance, and so forth. *Every* technical stance needs to be understood as a compromise formation, which is partly idiosyncratic, partly culturally constructed within a particular therapeutic community, and partly based on clinical wisdom. We should look for that wisdom wherever we can find it—in our own clinical experience, in scientific studies, and even sometimes in the writing of clinicians, theorists, and researchers who think very differently from ourselves.

REFERENCES

Ablon, J. S., & Jones, E. E. (1998). How expert clinicians' prototypes of an ideal treatment correlate with outcome in psychodynamic and cognitive-behavioral therapy. *Psychotherapy Research, 8*(1), 71–83.

Alexander, F., & French, T. M. (1946). *Psychoanalytic therapy: Principles and application.* New York: Ronald Press.

Andersen, S., & Cole, S. (1991). Do I know you? The role of significant others in general social perception. *Journal of Personality and Social Psychology, 59,* 384–399.

Arkowitz, H. (1997). Integrative theories of therapy. In P. Wachtel & S. Messer (Eds.), *Theories of psychotherapy: Origins and evolution* (pp. 227–288). Washington, D.C.: American Psychological Association Press.

Baldwin, M. (1992). Relational schemas and the processing of social information. *Psychological Bulletin, 112,* 461–484.

Bandura, A. (1977). *Social learning theory.* Englewood Cliffs, New Jersey: Prentice-Hall.

Bandura, A. (1986). *Social foundations of thought and action.* Englewood Cliffs, New Jersey: Prentice-Hall.

Bargh, J. (in press). The automaticity of everyday life. In J. S. Wyer, Jr. (Ed.), *Advances in social cognition* (Vol. 10). Hillsdale, N.J.: Lawrence Erlbaum.

Bargh, J., & Barndollar, K. (1996). Automaticity in action: The unconscious as repository of chronic goals and motives. In P. M. Gollwitzer & J. Bargh (Eds.), *The psychology of action* (pp. 457–481). New York: Guilford.

Bargh, J. A. (1997). The automaticity of everyday life. In R. S. Wyer, Jr. (Ed.), *The automaticity of everyday life: Advances in social cognition* (Vol. 10, pp. 1–61). Mahwah, N.J.: Erlbaum.

Barlow, D. H. (1988). *Anxiety and its disorders.* New York: Guilford Press.

Beck, A. T. (1976). *Cognitive therapy and the emotional disorders.* New York: International Universities Press.

Beck, A. T. (1993). Cognitive therapy: Past, present, and future. *Journal of Consulting and Clinical Psychology, 61,* 194–198.

Beitman, B. D., Goldfried, M. R., & Norcross, J. C. (1989). The movement toward integrating the psychotherapies: An overview. *American Journal of Psychiatry, 146,* 138–147.

Bergin, A. E., & Garfield, S. L. (1994). *Handbook of psychotherapy and behavior change* (4th ed.). New York: Wiley.

Beutler, L., & Clarkin, J. (1990). *Differential treatment selection: Toward targeted therapeutic interventions.* New York: Brunner/Mazel.

Blatt, S., Auerbach, J., & Levy, K. (1997). Mental representations in personality development, psychopathology, and the therapeutic process. *Review of General Psychology, 1,* 351–374.

Blatt, S., Ford, R., Berman, W., Cook, B., Cramer, P., & Robins, C. E. (1994). *Therapeutic change: An object relations perspective.* New York: Plenum.

Blatt, S. J., & Homann, E. (1992). Parent-child interaction in the etiology of dependent and self-critical depression. *Clinical Psychology Review, 12,* 47–91.

Blatt, S. J., & Zuroff, D. (1992). Interpersonal relatedness and self-definition: Two prototypes for depression. *Clinical Psychology Review, 12,* 527–562.

Block, J. H., Gjerde, P., & Block, J. H. (1991). Personality antecedents of depressive tendencies in 18-year-olds: A prospective study. *Journal of Personality and Social Psychology, 60,* 726–738.

Bowlby, J. (1969). *Attachment and loss.* (Vol. I). *Attachment.* New York: Basic Books.

Brenner, C. (1982). *The mind in conflict.* New York: International Universities Press.

Clark, D., Steer, R. A., Beck, A. T., & Ross, L. (1995). Psychometric characteristics of revised sociotropy and autonomy scales in college students. *Behaviour Research & Therapy, 33,* 325–334.

Dalgleish, T., & Power, M. Eds. (in press). *Handbook of cognition and emotion.* New York: Wiley.

Dalgleish, T., & Power, M., Eds. (1999). *Handbook of cognition and emotion.* New York: Wiley.

Dollard, J., & Miller, N. (1950). *Personality and psychotherapy: An analysis in terms of learning, thinking, and culture.* New York: McGraw-Hill.

Dozier, M., & Kobak, R. (1992). Psychophysiology in attachment interviews: Converging evidence for deactivating strategies. *Child Development, 63,* 1473–1480.

Elkin, I., Shea, M. T., Watkins, J. T., Gibbons, R. D., Sotsky, S., & Pilkonis, P. (1995). Initial severity and differential treatment outcome in the National Institute of Mental Health Treatment of Depression Collaborative Research Program. *Journal of Consulting and Clinical Psychology, 63,* 841–847.

Erikson, E. (1963). *Childhood and society.* New York: Norton.

Fenichel, O. (1945). *The psychoanalytic theory of neurosis.* New York: Basic Books.

Fiske, S. (1993). Social cognition and social perception. *Annual Review of Psychology, 44,* 155–194.

Fonagy, P., & Moran, G. S. (1990). Studies on the efficacy of child psychoanalysis. *Journal of Consulting and Clinical Psychology, 58,* 684–695.

Frank, J. D. (1961). *Persuasion and healing.* Baltimore: Johns Hopkins Press.

Frank, J. D. (1973). *Persuasion and healing* (2nd ed.). Baltimore: Johns Hopkins Press.

Garcia, J., & Koelling, R. (1966). Relation of cue to consequence in avoidance learning. *Psychonomic Science, 4,* 123–124.

Goldfried, M. (1991). Research issues in psychotherapy integration. *Journal of Psychotherapy Integration, 1,* 5–25.

Gray, J. A. (1990). Brain systems that mediate both emotion and cognition. *Cognition and Emotion, 4,* 269–288.

Greenberg, J. R., & Mitchell, S. (1983). *Object relations in psychoanalytic theory.* Cambridge: Harvard University Press.

Greenberg, L., Rice, L., & Elliott, R. (1993). *Facilitating emotional change: The moment-by-moment process.* New York: Guilford.

Greenberg, L., & Safran, J. (1987). *Emotion in psychotherapy: Affect, cognition, and the process of change.* New York: Guilford.

Hartmann, H. (1950). *Ego psychology and the problem of adaptation.* Madison, CT: International Universities Press. (Original work published 1939).

Herman, J., Perry, J. C., & Van der Kolk, B. A. (1989). Childhood trauma in borderline personality disorder. *American Journal of Psychiatry, 146,* 490–495.

Higgins, E. T. (1990). Personality, social psychology, and person-situation relations: Standards and knowledge activation as a common language. In L. Pervin (Ed.), *Handbook of personality: Theory and research* (pp. 301–338). New York: Guilford Press.

Holyoak, K., & Spellman, B. (1993). Thinking. *Annual Review of Psychology, 44,* 265–315.

Horney, K. (1950). *Neurosis and human growth: The struggle toward self-realization.* New York: W. W. Norton.

Horowitz, M. (1988). *Introduction to psychodynamics.* New York: Basic Books.

Horowitz, M. J. (1987). *States of mind: Configurational analysis of individual psychology,* 2nd ed. New York: Plenum.

James, W. (1890). *Principles of psychology.* New York: Henry Holt.

Johnson, M. K., Kim, J. K., & Risse, G. (1985). Do alcoholic Korsakoff's syndrome patients acquire affective reactions? *Journal of Experimental Psychology: Learning, Memory, & Cognition, 11,* 22–36.

Jones, E. E., & Pittman, T. S. (1982). Toward a general theory of strategic self-presentation. In J. Suls (Ed.), *Psychological perspectives on the self.* Hillsdale, N.J.: Lawrence Erlbaum.

Kazdin, A. (1996). Combined and multimodal treatments in child and adolescent psychotherapy: Issues, challenges, and research directions. *Clinical Psychology: Science and Practice, 3,* 69–100.

Kernberg, O. (1975). *Borderline conditions and pathological narcissism.* New York: Jason Aronson.

Kernberg, O. (1984). *Severe personality disorders.* New Haven: Yale University Press.

Kohlenberg, R. J., & Tsai, M. (1991). *Functional analytic psychotherapy: Creating intense and curative therapeutic relationships.* New York: Plenum.

Landman, J. T., & Dawes, R. M. (1982). Psychotherapy outcome: Smith and Glass' conclusions stand up under scrutiny. *American Psychologist, 37,* 504–516.

Lazarus, A. (1976). *Multimodal behavior therapy.* New York: Springer.

Lazarus, A. (1981). *The practice of multimodal therapy.* New York: McGraw-Hill.

LeDoux, J. (1995). Emotion: Clues from the brain. *Annual Review of Psychology, 46,* 209–235.

Linehan, M. (1993). *Cognitive-behavioral treatment of borderline personality disorder.* New York: Guilford.

London, P. (1964). *The modes and morals of psychotherapy* (2nd ed.). New York: Holt, Rinehart, & Winston.

Luborsky, L., & Crits-Christoph, P. (1990). *Understanding transference: The core conflictual relationship theme method.* New York: Basic Books.

Luborsky, L., Digurer, L., Seligman, D. A., Rosenthal, R., Krause, E. D., Johnson, S., Halperin, G., Bishop, M., Berman, J. S., Schweizer, E. (1999). The researcher's own therapy allegiances: A "wild card" in comparisons of treatment efficacy. *Clinical Psychology: Science and Practice, 6,* 95–106.

Main, M. (1996). Introduction to the special section on attachment and psychopathology: 2. Overview of the field of attachment. *Journal of Consulting and Clinical Psychology, 64,* 237–243.

Main, M., Kaplan, N., & Cassidy, J. (1985). Security in infancy, childhood, and adulthood: A move to the level of representation. In I. Bretherton & E. Waters (Eds.), *Growing points of attachment theory and research. Monographs of the Society for Research in Child Development, 50.* (No. 1–2, 67–104).

Marcia, J. E. (1994). The empirical study of ego identity. In H. A. Bosma, T. L. G. Graafsma, H. D. Grotevant, & D. J. de Levita (Eds.), *Identity and identity development: Interdisciplinary approaches* (pp. 67–80). Thousand Oaks, CA: Sage Publications, Inc.

Mathews, A., & Macleod, C. (1994). Cognitive approaches to emotion. *Annual Review of Psychology, 45,* 25–50.

McClelland, D. C., Koestner, R., & Weinberger, J. (1989). How do self-attributed and implicit motives differ? *Psychological Review, 96,* 690–702.

McWilliams, N. (1998). Relationship, subjectivity, and inference in diagnosis. In J. Barron & D. Wolitzky (Eds.), *Making diagnosis meaningful: Enhancing evaluation and treatment of psychological disorders* (pp. 197–226). Washington, D.C.: American Psychological Association Press.

Messer, S. (1986). Behavioral and psychoanalytic perspectives at therapeutic choice points. *American Psychologist, 41,* 1261–1272.

Messer, S. (1992). A critical examination of belief structures in integrative and eclectic psychotherapy. In J. Norcross & M. Goldfried (Eds.), *Handbook of psychotherapy integration* (pp. 130–168). New York: Basic Books.

Messer, S., & Warren, C. S. (1995). *Models of brief psychodynamic therapy: A comparative approach.* New York: Guilford.

Miller, N. E. (1992). Some examples of psychophysiology and the unconscious. *Biofeedback and Self-Regulation, 17,* 3–16.

Mischel, W. (1979). On the interface of cognition and personality: Beyond the person-situation debate. *American Psychologist, 34,* 740–754.

Morrison, K., & Westen, D. (1999). The empirical validity of empirically validated therapies. (Unpublished data, Harvard Medical School).

Mowrer, O. H. (1947). On the dual nature of learning: A reinterpretation of "conditioning" and "problem-solving." *Harvard Educational Review, 17,* 102–148.

Neisser, U. (1976). *Cognition and reality.* San Francisco: Freeman.

Norcross, J., (Ed.) (1986). *Handbook of eclectic psychotherapy.* New York: Brunner/Mazel.

Norcross, J., & Goldfried, M. (1992). *Handbook of psychotherapy integration.* New York: Basic Books.

Norcross, J., & Prochaska, J. (1988). A study of eclectic (and integrative) views revisited. *Professional Psychology: Research and Practice, 19,* 170–174.

Ogata, S., Silk, K. R., Goodrich, S., Lohr, N. E., Westen, D., & Hill, E. (1990). Childhood abuse and clinical symptoms in borderline personality disorder. *American Journal of Psychiatry, 147,* 1008–1013.

Pennebaker, J. (1997). *Opening up: The healing power of expressing emotions* (Rev. ed.). New York: Guilford Press.

Perry, J. C., & Cooper, S. (1989). An empirical study of defense mechanisms. I. Clinical interview and life vignette ratings. *Archives of General Psychiatry, 46,* 444–460.

Pope, K., Tabachnick, B., & Keith-Spiegel, P. (1987). Ethics of practice: The beliefs and behaviors of psychologists as therapists. *American Psychologist, 42,* 993–1006.

Power, M., & Dalgleish, T. (1997). *Cognition and emotion: From order to disorder.* East Sussex, England: Psychology Press.

Prochaska, J., & Norcross, J. (1994). *Systems of psychotherapy: A transtheoretical analysis* (3rd ed.). Pacific Grove, CA: Brooks/Cole.

Reber, A. (1992). The cognitive unconscious: An evolutionary perspective. *Consciousness and Cognition, 1,* 93–133.

Roston, D., Lee, K., & Vaillant, G. (1992). A Q-sort approach to identifying defenses. In G. Vaillant (Ed.), *Ego mechanisms of defense: A guide for clinicians and researchers* (pp. 217–233). Washington, D.C.: American Psychiatric Association Press.

Rumelhart, D. E., McClelland, J. L, & The PDP Research Group (1986). *Parallel distributed processing: Explorations in the microstructure of cognition, Vol. 1: Foundations.* Cambridge, Massachusetts: MIT Press.

Ryle, A. (1990). *Cognitive-analytic therapy: Active participation in change.* New York: Wiley.

Safran, J., & Segal, Z. (1991). *Interpersonal process in cognitive therapy.* New York: Basic Books.

Sandler, J., & Rosenblatt, B. (1962). The concept of the representational world. *Psychoanalytic Study of the Child, 17,* 128–145.

Schacht, T. (1984). The varieties of integrative experience. In H. Arkowitz & S. Messer (Eds.), *Psychoanalytic therapy and behavior therapy: Is integration possible?* (pp. 107–132). New York: Plenum.

Schacter, D. L. (1992). Understanding implicit memory: A cognitive neuroscience approach. *American Psychologist, 47,* 559–569.

Schacter, D. L., & Buckner, R. L. (1998). Priming and the brain. *Neuron, 20,* 185–195.

Segal, Z. (1988). Appraisal of the self-schema construct in cognitive models of depression. *Psychological Bulletin, 103,* 147–162.

Shea, M. T., Elkins, I., Imber, S., Sotsky, S., Watkins, J. T., Colins, J. F., Pilkonis, P., Beckham, E., Glass, D. R., Dolan, R. G., & Parloff, M. B. (1992). Course of depressive symptoms over follow-up: Findings from the National Institute of Mental Health Treatment of Depression Collaborative Research Program. *Archives of General Psychiatry, 49,* 782–787.

Shedler, J., & Block, J. (1990). Adolescent drug use and psychological health: A longitudinal inquiry. *American Psychologist, 45,* 612–630.

Shedler, J., Mayman, M., & Manis, M. (1993). The illusion of mental health. *American Psychologist, 48,* 1117–1131.

Smith, E. R. (1998). Mental representation and memory. In D. T. Gilbert, S. T. Fiske, et al. (Eds.), *The handbook of social psychology* (Vol. 2, 4th ed., pp. 391–445). Boston: McGraw-Hill.

Smith, M. L., Glass, G. V., & Miller, F. I. (1980). *The benefits of psychotherapy.* Cambridge, Massachusetts: Harvard University Press.

Sroufe, L. A., & Waters, E. (1977). Attachment as an organizational construct. *Child Development, 48,* 1184–1199.

Stiles, W. B., Shapiro, D. A., & Elliott, R. (1986). Are all psychotherapies equivalent? *American Psychologist, 41,* 165–180.

Strauman, T., Lemieux, A., & Coe, C. (1993). Self-discrepancy and natural killer cell activity: Immunological consequences of negative self-evaluation. *Journal of Personality and Social Psychology, 64,* 1042–1052.

Stricker, G., & Gold, J. R. (1993). *Comprehensive handbook of psychotherapy integration.* New York: Plenum.

Stricker, G., & Gold, J. R. (1996). Psychotherapy integration: An assimilative psychodynamic approach. *Clinical Psychology: Science and Practice, 3,* 47–58.

Sullivan, H. S. (1953). *The interpersonal theory of psychiatry.* New York: W. W. Norton.

Swann, W., Stein-Seroussi, A., & Giesler, R. B. (1992). Why people self-verify. *Journal of Personality and Social Psychology, 62,* 392–401.

Task Force on Promotion and Dissemination of Psychological Procedures (1995). Training in and dissemination of empirically-validated psychological treatments: Report and recommendations. *The Clinical Psychologist, 48,* 3–23.

Thase, M. E., Simons, A. D., McGeary, J., Cahalane, J., Hughes, C., Harden, T., & Friedman, E. (1992). Relapse after cognitive behavior therapy of depression: Potential implications for longer courses of treatment. *American Journal of Psychiatry, 149,* 1046–1052.

van IJzendoorn, M. (1995). Adult attachment representations, parental responsiveness, and infant attachment: A meta-analysis on the predictive validity of the Adult Attachment Interview. *Psychological Bulletin, 117,* 387–403.

Wachtel, P. (1977). *Psychoanalysis and behavior therapy: Toward an integration.* New York: Basic Books.

Wachtel, P. L. (1987). *Action and insight.* New York: Guilford.

Wachtel, P. L. (1991). From eclecticism to synthesis: Toward a more seamless psychotherapeutic integration. *Journal of Psychotherapy Integration, 1,* 43–54.

Wachtel, P. L. (1993). *Therapeutic communication: Principles for effective practice.* New York: Guilford.

Wachtel, P. L. (1997). *Psychoanalysis, behavior therapy, and the relational world.* Washington, D.C.: American Psychological Association Press.

Weinberger, J. (1995). Common factors aren't so common: The common factors dilemma. *Clinical Psychology: Science and Practice, 2,* 45–69.

Westen, D. (1985). *Self and society: Narcissism, collectivism, and the development of morals.* New York: Cambridge University Press.

Westen, D. (1991a). Social cognition and object relations. *Psychological Bulletin, 109,* 429–455.

Westen, D. (1991b). Cognitive-behavioral interventions in the psychodynamic psychotherapy of borderline personality disorders. *Clinical Psychology Review, 11,* 211–230.

Westen, D. (1992). The cognitive self and the psychoanalytic self: Can we put ourselves together? *Psychological Inquiry, 3,* 1–13.

Westen, D. (1994a). The impact of sexual abuse on aspects of self. In D. Cicchetti & S. Toth (Eds.), *Rochester Symposium on Developmental Psychopathology,* (Vol. 5, pp. 641–667). Rochester: University of Rochester Press.

Westen, D. (1994b). Toward an integrative model of affect regulation: Applications to social-psychological research. *Journal of Personality, 62,* 641–647.

Westen, D. (1995). A clinical-empirical model of personality: Life after the Mischelian ice age and the NEO-lithic era. *Journal of Personality, 63,* 495–524.

Westen, D. (1997a). Divergences between clinical and research methods for assessing personality disorders: Implications for research and the evolution of Axis II. *American Journal of Psychiatry, 154,* 895–903.

Westen, D. (1997b). Toward an empirically and clinically sound theory of motivation. *International Journal of Psycho-Analysis, 78,* 521–548.

Westen, D. (1998a). The scientific legacy of Sigmund Freud. Toward a psychodynamically informed psychological science. *Psychological Bulletin, 124,* 333–371.

Westen, D. (1998b). Case formulation and personality diagnosis: Two processes or one? In James Barron (Ed.), *Making diagnosis meaningful* (pp. 111–138). Washington, D.C.: American Psychological Association Press.

Westen, D. (in press). Psychodynamic theory and technique in relation to research on cognition and emotion: Mutual implications. In T. Dalgleish & M. Power (Eds.), *Handbook of cognition and emotion.* New York: Wiley.

Westen, D., & Gabbard, G. (in press). Psychoanalytic approaches to personality. In L. Pervin & O. John (Eds.), *Handbook of personality: Theory and research* (2nd ed.). New York: Guilford.

Westen, D., Lohr, N., Silk, K., Gold, L., & Kerber, K. (1990). Object relations and social cognition in borderlines, major depressives, and normals: A TAT analysis. *Psychological Assessment: A Journal of Consulting and Clinical Psychology, 2,* 355–364.

Westen, D., Ludolph, P., Block, J., Wixom, J., & Wiss, F. C. (1990). Developmental history and object relations in psychiatrically disturbed adolescent girls. *American Journal of Psychiatry, 147,* 1061–1068.

Westen, D., Ludolph, P., Misle, B., Ruffins, S., & Block, M. J. (1990). Physical and sexual abuse in adolescent girls with borderline personality disorder. *American Journal of Orthopsychiatry, 60,* 55–66.

Westen, D., Muderrisoglu, S., Fowler, C., Shedler, J., & Koren, D. (1997). Affect regulation and affective experience: Individual differences, group differences, and measurement using a Q-sort procedure. *Journal of Consulting and Clinical Psychology, 65,* 429–439.

Wong, P., Shevrin, H., & Williams, W. J. (1994). Conscious and nonconscious processes: An ERP index of an anticipatory response in a conditioning paradigm using visually masked stimuli. *Psychophysiology, 31,* 87–101.

Zanarini, M. (Ed.). (1997). *The role of sexual abuse in the etiology of borderline personality disorder.* Washington, D.C.: American Psychiatric Association Press.

CHAPTER 12

EXISTENTIAL APPROACHES TO PSYCHOTHERAPY

CONSTANCE T. FISCHER, BRIAN MCELWAIN, AND J. TODD DUBOISE
Duquesne University

INTRODUCTORY COMMENTS

In this chapter, we review characterizations of existential psychotherapy by founding and contemporary practitioner-authors. The first sections, Existentialism and From Existential-Phenomenological Philosophy to Existential Psychology, present historical philosophical background along with corrections to common misunderstandings. We outline the following philosophical themes that ground existential psychotherapy: humans are always in relation with the self, others, and the world; intersubjectivity is our access to one another; lived bodily experience and reflection are our access to our own construals of meaning; and we are responsible for meaning and choice even though these occur within the context of our being decidedly limited by contingencies, including the prospect of death. The next section, Existential Psychotherapy: Case Example, brings this psychotherapy approach to life with an example of therapy. In the subsequent and largest section, The Practice of Existential Psychotherapy, we discuss a *framework* for practice, drawn from writings of contemporary authors, under three headings: relationship, understanding, and flexibility. These themes present existential psychotherapy as an *approach* to clients and their situations; this therapy is not a system of techniques. Finally, the Concluding Comments present further clarifications and review major points.

An existential approach fosters clients coming to terms with personal meanings of various life circumstances, as well as taking responsibility for their present options. Within an existential *philosophical* framework, the psychotherapist also considers *theories* and known patterns of personality development and disorder in order to be sensitive to clients' situations. The therapist, however, resists translating clients' lives into constructs and is slow to pathologize. Instead, the therapist respects the normality and necessity of clients both making and coming to terms with their life circumstances and their choices.

For example, a client, Sharon, and her psychotherapist readily agreed that in the aftermath of her mother's death six month ago, she had met DSM criteria for dysthymia. But treating the depression was not the therapist's goal, although she did provide suggestions for getting on with work and life, suggestions that also helped Sharon to take initiatives that countered her sense of being helpless. Rather, the goal was for Sharon to discover the meanings of her mother's death, not only for her future but also for her sense of history with her mother. In this instance, Sharon developed an understanding that throughout her life she had felt that her brothers were favored by both parents. She had become a devoted daughter, determined to win love through service to her parents, even to the point of bringing her mother to live with her after her father died. In brief, her mother's death announced that Sharon could no longer hope that her lifelong project of winning love through service would finally be fruitful; indeed, her mother's death announced to Sharon that her efforts apparently had been doomed from the beginning. Following this acknowledgment, Sharon successfully struggled to own her earlier choices and to find ways to continue her life, while still valuing service and appreciating whatever love came her way; however, she no longer bargained service for love. After many months, she found herself "amazingly free and peaceful," even as she continued to deal seriously with life, as we all must. This account lends itself to several theoretical understandings with which many existentially oriented psychotherapists would agree. The point here is that an existential dilemma was dealt with as such.

In practice, existentially oriented psychotherapists utilize techniques found in many forms of talk therapy (see the subsequent case example of Jim). Many existential psychotherapists suggest assignments; invite clients to try cognitive, imaginative, and/or behavioral exercises; and so on. Whatever the means, the goals in existential psychotherapy are to help clients to (1) become aware at some level of their previously implicit values and ways of shaping their lives and (2) explore altered courses that are still consistent with their histories and hopes. Each effort implicates the other. Out of such new awareness and exploration, clients find their own ways of revising and reorganizing their lives. The reader may consult Fischer (1991, 1998) for exercises and approaches developed by existential-phenomenological psychotherapists.

Existential psychotherapists try not to impose either their own values or psychology's notions of psychopathology. But they may share their reactions with clients as part of the joint project to better understand the clients' shaping of their worlds. In this process, it becomes apparent to clients that the therapist, too, struggles with existential responsibility for dealing with the dilemmas of daily life.

EXISTENTIALISM

Existentialism comes from the Latin *ex-istere*, meaning to "stand out toward, to emerge into possibilities, to become." But to become, we must deal with our situation and context, and indeed with the unalterable aspects of our lives. Hence, a central dialectic of living is a continual play between limitation and possibility. When our lives are focused on either pole of the dialectic, we find ourselves stuck, suffering and often presenting difficulties for other persons. In more flexible living, the polarity is not dualistic or binary but complementary. Existentialism is a philosophy that addresses this human condition of being responsible for our lives, despite remarkable limitations and the absence of guarantees about life's meanings and meaningfulness.

Critics of existentialism have claimed that this philosophy itself emphasizes limitation, at the expense of possibility, and hence leads inevitably to despair, nihilism, and intractable depression. This misunderstanding ignores the fact that the acknowledged father of existentialism—Søren Kierkegaard (1813–1855)—passionately explored the dialectics of faith (1843/1941). Similarly, this misunderstanding overlooks Max Scheler's (1928/1962) discussion of sympathy, Friedrich Nietzsche's (1887/1967) life-affirming will to power, Martin Buber's (1923/1958) relationship with the Thou, Eric Fromm's (1941) freedom, Gabriel Marcel's (1951/1978) spiritual relationships, Martin Heidegger's (1959/1966) releasement, and so forth.

A second misunderstanding is that existentialism gives priority to freedom. Humanistic traditions that emphasize potential, possibility, and transcendence resemble Gnostic more than existential traditions. From an existential perspective, the call to choice and freedom is conditional. Possibilities of engagement are bound by both general finitude and by the givens of our particular situations. Indeed, Jean Paul Sartre (1943/1975) reminded us that we have no choice but to choose: we are "condemned to choice," and we inevitably choose in terms of our personal projects. Many individuals have taken Sartre's comment to mean that our lives are purely the construction of our choices and actions. This misunderstanding, however, ignores the formative and limiting events that existentialists have addressed, including traumatic loss, war and other disasters, interpersonal abuse, and cultural responses to race, along with the "accidents" of one's genetic makeup, historical era, country of birth, physical limitations, age, and gender.

From an existential perspective, our choices occur in what the humanistic psychologists have named "the here and now." The understanding of temporality of which the here and now is one moment, however, is quite different from that of the natural sciences in which most of psychology has been based. Where much of natural scientific psychology focuses on the linear influence of the past on the present, existential psychology recognizes that one's past is alive in the present and is influenced by the call or anticipation of the future. Moreover, revised goals and shifts in our ongoing ways of relating to the world lead to a similarly revised reading of the past, as well as of future possibilities. Hence both psychoanalytic and behavioral therapists' criticism of existential and humanistic psychotherapists for dwelling too much in the present are unfounded. Besides, most existentially oriented therapists do support clients' explorations of their pasts as a means for discovering both old and revised ways of coauthoring their lives.

Professionals who have read only theoretical work on existentialism sometimes assume that existentially oriented therapy involves only heady, conceptual discussions. To the contrary, existential therapists respect the meanings evident in the body's language. Moreover, behavior as action is core material both for reflection and as alternatives with which to experiment. Philosophically, our comportment and "bodying forth," as Erwin Straus (1952) and Maurice Merleau-Ponty (1942/1962) have noted, orient us in an upright and facing-forward posture as we move from past to what may be ahead. Applied existentialism, therefore, *elucidates situated freedom in terms of a person's embodied-being-in-the-world*. Our freedom is expanded to the extent that we take our limitations into account. As we do so, we find that our actions modify the world even as circumstances shape our actions. World and person coconstitute each other; each participates in forming the other.

Of course, the world with which we are always in relation includes other people. Heidegger (1927/1962) delineated *mitsein*, being with others, as a dimension of human being in the world (*Dasein*). Among existential philosophers who addressed the negative side of this inescapable being with others, Jean-Paul Sartre (1943/1975) emphasized that of the other person's gaze toward us. We too often allow ourselves to be objectified or fixed by that gaze. Sartre is also well known for his statement that Hell is other people. Heidegger alerted us to the pull of anonymous society (the "they"), and Nietzsche (1967) condemned our willingness to go with "the herd." Likewise, van den Berg (1971) described relational alienation as a route to psychopathology.

In contrast, Martin Buber (1923/1958) described positive human relations as "encounters" in which we genuinely meet the other as being similar to but also as different from ourselves. We respectfully find ourselves interested in those dif-

ferences. Buber differentiated the objectifying and exploitative quality of I-It relationships from those of I-Thou encounters, which occur in an atmosphere of respect, freedom, and collaboration.

FROM EXISTENTIAL-PHENOMENOLOGICAL PHILOSOPHY TO EXISTENTIAL PSYCHOLOGY

The following section is oversimplified in its review of major themes. Readers who are unfamiliar with the area at least can develop a feel for the issues, and interested readers can look into selected concepts through the references provided.

There is no single system of existential thought, nor are there competing schools of existential psychology. Rather, existential psychology is an approach of like-minded persons looking for correctives to determinism, materialism, and realism—correctives that allow for fuller humanness while also addressing the difficulties and opportunities of dealing with the human condition in our daily lives. Psychologists who identify themselves as existential have looked to existential-phenomenological philosophy to address those features of human existence for which our natural science tradition is not suited. Stances developed within existential psychology have evoked critiques and challenges from traditional psychology, moving existentially oriented therapists to further clarify their foundational notions of human existence. Research methodologies and clinical practices have been developed and refined both from within this human science orientation and from dialogue and argument with psychology's natural science tradition. As with any challenging conversation, though, misunderstandings, misrepresentations, and confusions are inevitable. As we proceed in this chapter from existential-phenomenological philosophy to existential psychology and later into psychotherapy, we highlight and correct some of these misconceptions.

Many clinical scientists are skeptical of the move from philosophy to psychology. Unfortunately, the central figures in existential-phenomenological philosophy, namely, Martin Heidegger (1889–1976), Jean Paul Sartre (1905–1980), and Maurice Merleau-Ponty (1908–1961), often wrote so abstractly that they seem to belie their call to remain rigorously close to experience. However, this close description is necessary for developing life-based understandings independent of prior theory. Traditional psychology supposedly is based on firmer data that are subject to the formulation of hypotheses, which can then be tested to determine reality. Hence, the skeptics wonder whether an existential approach, based on such different premises, can have much in common with traditional psychology.

In turn, existential psychologists wonder how psychology can claim to be rigorous in the absence of explicit understandings about the meaning of being human. Martin Heidegger's (1927/1962) wisdom in asking questions such as "What is the nature of Being?" was to awaken thinkers from the slumber of unthought, although lived, experience. Likewise, existential psychology asks, "How can we care therapeutically for individuals and communities unless we have a clearer understanding of what we assume to be human existence?" In fact, existential psychology arose largely in response to Wilhelm Wundt's (1832–1920) and Wilhelm Dilthey's (1833–1911) differing efforts to characterize human nature.

Wilhelm Dilthey's 1894 article, "Ideas About a Descriptive and Structural Psychology," marks the beginning of existential-phenomenological psychology (Dilthey, 1924 & 1927/1977). Dilthey was dissatisfied with Wundt's approach to human beings, which was derived from physical science methodology. Dilthey made the important distinction between *Naturalwissenschaften*, or natural science, and *Geistewissenschaften*, or human science (literally, "spiritual science," or science of the mind). In brief, natural science *explains* phenomena by the analysis of interacting but isolated elements, whereas human science *understands* phenomena by way of holistic description. This very distinction, though, has drawn further criticism.

Is not the division of science into "natural" and "human" a return to Cartesian dualism, the very split that existential psychology intends to undo? Are we suggesting that humans are not biological and physical creatures like the rest of the animal kingdom? Are we guilty of anthropocentric elitism, inviting unnecessary oppression of "lower" forms of existence?

Existential psychology has addressed these important questions. Dilthey's distinction between natural and human sciences need not be a binary or antagonistic one. We are situated inescapably in our worlds like any other animal. Existential psychology, however, suggests that what natural science offers is not the whole story. For example, knowing the neurophysiology of traumatic stress response does not tell us the complete story about the lived experience of the child who is a victim of sexual abuse. We do not see fear of spiders by looking solely at levels of adrenaline in a person's system. Many existential psychologists applaud the fact that psychotropics alter neurochemical imbalances, as long as we remember that medication changes more than chemicals in the brain; it changes lived and experienced worlds, just as the latter can change our chemistry.

Merleau-Ponty (1942/1962, 1942/1963), known as the philosopher of embodiment—of the incarnate character of being human—remained faithful to the physical basis for all knowledge but resisted the reduction of the body to a mere biological and mechanical apparatus. In short, the human and natural sciences *complement* each other; they do not *replace* each other. Each approach offers a *qualitatively* different point of access to phenomena. Qualitative clarification offers much to quantitative analysis. Neither picture of human existence is complete without the other. Given this clarification, we can turn to other contributions to the foundations of existential psychology.

Edmund Husserl (1859–1938) and his student Martin Heidegger drew from Dilthey's project and developed what came to be known as phenomenology, the study of how things appear to humans. This study of how humans participate in what can be known provides a salient epistemology (philosophy of knowledge) for all of psychology. Husserl's (1913/1962) transcendental phenomenology and Heidegger's existential phenomenology have both influenced the evolution of existential psychology. Briefly, transcendental phenomenology made the transition into existential phenomenology by way of Heidegger's, Sartre's, and Merleau-Ponty's works, which in turn grounded the development of existential-phenomenological psychology through the work of Karl Jaspers (1883–1969), Ludwig Binswanger (1881–1966), and Medard Boss (1903–1990).

Karl Jaspers incorporated Dilthey's and Husserl's work into the areas of psychopathology and therapeutic intervention. This transition did not impose a theoretical structure "from above." Quite the contrary, Jaspers emphasized rigorous, detailed, descriptive analysis of phenomena. In his major work, *General Psychopathology*, Jaspers (1913/1963) resisted the traditional move to reduce human experience to isolated, scientific datum such as a person's physiological chemistry, internal thought processes, or reactions to surrounding stimuli. Jaspers held that patients' existences are accessible through disciplined attention to communication amid inescapable "boundary situations" in *Existenz:* suffering, chance, death, conflict, and guilt.

Ludwig Binswanger (1923/1947) wrote "About phenomenology," in which he addressed the coconstitution of human beings and their worlds. Binswanger firmly held that a full description of individuals' participation in the world requires attention to their lived, prereflective, and daily experiences. He elaborated existential psychology's position that so-called internal mental processes occur *in the world*—the lived world, known through action, affect, anticipation, and so on, and always through particular situations. Elucidating lived worlds became the project of existential phenomenology, to which Binswanger (1963) contributed many case examples.

Medard Boss (1957/1963, 1979/1994), following Heidegger, also believed that the starting point for psychological understanding was with our "primal being together in a shared world" (1979/1994, p. xxxi). Boss's psychology and clinical practice, known as *Daseinanalysis* (analysis of a person's being-in-the-world), emphasized its "openness." Boss was convinced that meaningfulness is discovered by remaining open to experience. Temporality, spatiality, bodyhood, coexistence in a shared world, attunement, memory based in historicity, and mortality provide the framework, or existential givens, from which people consider and choose.

Each of these existential dimensions, whose combinations are endless, implies the others. Boss noted that these possibilities are to be understood existentially rather than in physical, geometric, or mathematical terms. Physical proximity to another may not have much to do with existential "closeness" with that person. Lived time cannot be measured or plotted graphically. We experience our pasts through our situated presents, leaning into anticipated futures. Anticipation opens our capacities for awareness of recollection. Boredom occurs in slowed time, anxiety in accelerated time, and unresolved grief in frozen time. Boredom, anxiety, and grief are bodily experiences, located in our comportment and attunement to our worlds. Our "bodyhood" (or bodiliness) discloses our shared world. Without a shared world, time, space, and body would be

nonsensical. Presence, choice, and understanding presuppose the *mutual interplay* of these existential possibilities.

One's openness to the interplay of these existential possibilities is not passive, but rather it necessitates choice, decision, and engagement. Boss suggested existential alternatives to many of traditional psychology's notions: from psyche to human being-in-the-world; from consciousness in the person to openness in the world; from psychic unconscious to hiddenness; from drives to existential relatedness; from causality to meaning. Boss foreshadowed many existential clinicians' understanding of the unconscious as being our prereflective, lived experience. Upon reflection, we can see both developmental and motivational aspects of our perceptions and actions, but all of this occurs in our relations, not in "psyches."

Many "family resemblances," to use Wittgenstein's phrase, to existential psychology have been developed since Jaspers's, Binswanger's, and Boss's work. Among the more prominent are Sartre's (1953) existential analysis, R. D. Laing's (1960) existential-phenomenological psychology, Eric Fromm's (1941) and Rollo May's (1958) different brands of existential-humanistic psychology, and Victor Frankl's (1967) logotherapy. These developments led to both positive and negative consequences. On the positive side, the potential and power of the existential position became evident in psychological research and in clinical assessment and psychotherapy. On the negative side, existentialism was everywhere, and thus, ironically, its implications for psychology were not widely addressed.

Existential psychology has continued its diverse dialogues with psychoanalysis (e.g., Foucault, 1954/1985; Fromm, 1970). Transpersonal psychology has been incorporated into a textbook on existential-phenomenological psychology (Valle, 1998). National and international sources include the works of Eugene Minkowski in Paris; Erwin Straus, V. E. von Gebsattel, and Victor von Weizsacker in Germany; G. Bally and Ronald Kuhn in Switzerland; J. H. van den Berg and F. J. Buytendijk in Holland; Hans Kohn and Ernesto Spinelli in England; and Rollo May, E. Angel, and H. Ellenberger (1958), James Bugental (1987), Irvin Yalom (1980), and many faculty members of the psychology departments of Duquesne University, the University of Dallas, Saybrook University, Seattle University, and the State University of West Georgia in the United States.

EXISTENTIAL PSYCHOTHERAPY: CASE EXAMPLE

Introduction

The following simple instance of existential psychotherapy serves to ground the sometimes abstract discussion in this chapter. It also reflects existential psychotherapy's similarities to many other approaches. This example illustrates its mutual respect between participants, the nonimposition of psychopathology schemes, the therapist's disciplined use of self and of openness to the client's experience, an invitation to the client to reflect on continuing choices, and the power of revised meanings to allow the client to reorganize his or her world.

The Case Example

Jim was a forty-year-old minister who was racked with guilt over his obsession with women's breasts. He entered therapy to eliminate this "evil" from his life, an evil that was causing tremendous marital strife. The more he resisted his roaming eye and the accompanying fantasies, the more they persisted.

In therapy meetings, Jim would begin to lament over his sinfulness. Each attempt of the therapist to join Jim was met with continued obsessions about his inadequacies. Jim had read some self-help books on addiction and felt that maybe this was an addiction, originating from never having had enough breast milk from his mother. The therapist asked how Jim felt about this loss and about other missed opportunities for fulfillment. Jim rejected the question as suggesting hopelessness of repairing his damaged soul. The therapist attempted to join Jim by revealing his own sadness both at Jim's predicament and in regard to his own losses. Jim ignored the attempt, drowning the possibility of connection with self-flagellation. The therapist then tried to explore Jim's flagellation, which seemed to be based on his assumptions that as a minister he should be "above the limitations of his flock." Jim grew angry at the therapist for "suggesting that lust was allowed."

The therapist then told Jim how he was beginning to feel about him. The therapist pointed out that Jim blocked all kinds of nurturing attempts by the therapist to connect with him. The therapist also invited Jim to notice that Jim's private ruminations were isolating him from positive acknowledgment and benefits in his relational world; he was starving himself. Jim's wife and children had said similar things to him. The therapist then told Jim how sad he felt watching Jim block relational nurturance and mentioned his own pull to stop trying to connect—something he did not want to do.

Jim began to soften and to take in the feedback from the therapist. As he did, he noticed that he relaxed the tightness in his body, and he felt the subsequent warmth of his interchange with the therapist. He remarked that he had not felt this way since he was converted and "accepted Jesus into his heart." Jim and the therapist reflected together on how their openness to life and relationships may invite gifts. In fact, they reflected on how just the very activity of being open is itself a gift. As Jim was leaving, he snickered. When the therapist inquired about this, Jim said, "You know, here toward the end, I forgot about the breasts. Now they don't even call my attention."

THE PRACTICE OF EXISTENTIAL PSYCHOTHERAPY

In the following overview of the practice of existential psychotherapy, two related organizing principles are drawn from earlier sections, Existentialism and From Existential-Phenomenological Philosophy to Existential Psychology. The first is "situated freedom", our human condition of being radically limited by circumstances and yet always engaged in shaping our futures—always becoming. "Becoming" points to the dynamic, in-process nature of human existence that is central to all psychotherapeutic change (Cohn, 1984). A second organizing principle is the importance of maintaining profound respect for subjective or lived experience. Honoring clients' perceptions, thoughts, values, anticipations, and so on allows both clients and psychotherapists to better grasp how clients experience and shape their worlds.

There is no single or even major school of existential psychotherapy, a fact that perhaps reflects a philosophical disinclination of existentialists to impose order. Several existential clinicians have written that the practice of psychotherapy is much more akin to improvised artistic performance than to a technical application of scientific findings or procedures (e.g., Abroms, 1993; Bergantino, 1981; Bugental, 1976, 1987). Nevertheless, we readily identify three motifs that convey the spirit of existential psychotherapy evident in contemporary writing: relationship, understanding, and flexibility.

Relationship

Many approaches to psychotherapy emphasize the therapeutic relationship. Indeed, agreement about its importance is probably more widespread than views about any other aspect of psychotherapy. Research findings across theoretical orientations link the quality of the "working alliance" to various positive outcomes (e.g., Horvath & Symonds, 1991; Marziali & Alexander, 1991). However, views about the role of the relationship vary greatly. For example, the therapeutic relationship is viewed variously as a mediating variable, a tool to manage social influence, the object of interpretations, or the means of therapeutic change itself. The last of these is closest to the position of existential therapists.

A common misunderstanding of existential approaches to psychotherapy is that they are extremely individualistic. Specifically, the misunderstanding is that existential therapists are said to see an individual's experience as independent and valid in itself. On the contrary, existential psychotherapists conceive of persons and reality in relational terms. This misconception is probably related to an inadequate appreciation of the existential emphasis on the importance of respecting a person's subjective experience. This emphasis was in part a response to the dismissive attitude toward consciousness of both traditional behaviorism and many schools of psychoanalysis. Moreover, contrary to the Western emphasis on separable psyches, existential philosophy regards human phenomena as better understood in terms of interpersonal relationships.

Indeed, existential psychotherapists speak of all human awareness and reflection as being interpersonally derived. In consciousness, "objects" in the world are inseparably interdependent (Spinelli, 1994). We are contingent beings who, despite our proud efforts, can never stand apart from the contexts that are our "life supports." Van Deurzen-Smith (1997) writes that our interpersonal relationships are primary and formative of all our experience, including our self-conceptions. Similarly, Spinelli contends that selves are only definable as "focal points" in relationships; hence selves are in no way separate, fixed, or complete and stand-alone entities.

Having addressed the common misunderstanding of existential psychotherapy as being individualistic, we now turn to the practical implications of our philosophical reflections. First, we acknowledge the irony, given the relational emphasis of existential theory, that most accounts of existential psychotherapy describe working with individual clients. Among the few exceptions are Goldberg and Goldberg (1973) about group therapy, Lantz (1993) about family therapy, and Charny (1992) and Spinelli (1997) about couples therapy.

Most existential psychotherapists, at opportune moments, divulge to the client some impressions of their encounters. Together they can better appreciate the clients' intentions, styles of carrying them out, and outcomes for both clients and others. Similarly, in these discussions, therapists often learn of their misperceptions, styles, and impact on the self and clients. Often, clients find that these interchanges have altered the meaning of their earlier patterns and that without necessarily resolving to change, change has occurred.

Existential therapists frequently invoke notions such as "authenticity," "encounter," "genuine presence," and "mutuality" to distinguish their relations to clients from those of therapists of some other orientations. Perhaps it would be helpful to introduce Sullivan's (1953) notion of the therapist as a "participant-observer" as a point of reference. In his "interpersonal theory of psychiatry," Sullivan pointed out that observing scientists participate in the very events and processes that they study; thus a psychiatrist cannot attain a distant, "above the fray" position from which to make observations. Sullivan's view can be contrasted sharply with the classical Freudian analytic effort to obtain uncontaminated "objective" knowledge of intrapsychic processes by adopting the cool, dispassionate stance of a surgeon (Freud, 1912/1963). For Freud, it was essential that the analyst minimize his or her personal presence in the consulting room so that both parties could focus their attention on the analysand's "internal" world; he hoped that this kind of personal neutrality would allow him to claim objectivity for his observations, as well as to legitimize psychoanalysis as a (natural) science.

There are many contemporary instances of Freud's legacy of attempted objectivity in the therapeutic relationship. Across schools of psychotherapy, practitioners have their own personal and/or theoretical reasons for attempting to maintain such a posture. However, from the existential premise about the inescapable relationality of human existence, attempting to attain objective observer status seems counterproductive to the therapeutic relationship. Hence many existential psychotherapists have embraced Sullivan's participant-observer perspective as a much needed corrective to the classical analytic stance (e.g., van Kaam, 1966; Yalom, 1989).

Existential therapists are active participants in the therapeutic relationship. They take advantage of their intersubjective participation in clients' experiences to comprehend what it must be like to live in the clients' worlds. Interpretations, questions, challenges, suggestions, and affirmations are useful to the extent that the therapist is attuned to the client's experience, meanings, and present situation. A warm, caring, respectful relationship fosters open, honest, and direct communication for both the client and the therapist (Edwards, 1982; Potash, 1994). Although rarely mentioned in writings, it is our experience that this relationship in the support of the serious enterprise of psychotherapy is accompanied by occasional joint laughter. In short, the quality of the relationship may shape the manner and the degree to which the client's experience is expressed (van Kaam, 1966). The achievement of an "authentic encounter" depends substantially on the therapist's ability and willingness to be genuinely present with the client as another human being.

If their meetings go well, the client and therapist encounter each other's similarities and differences. The "feel" of such a relationship is distinctly less hierarchical than is the case in some other theoretical stances (Owen, 1994). For example, Cannon (1991) has noted that Sartre objected to the essentially authoritarian stance of the psychoanalyst who assumes the role of expert. In such relationships, clients are treated as "objects" of study; "things" to be fixed; or dark, "unconscious" spaces to be illuminated. In contrast, existential psychotherapists seek more symmetrical, collaborative therapeutic relationships; clients are not passive objects but active, purposive, and unpredictable beings. Nevertheless, despite emphasis on shared humanness, psychotherapists are responsible for maintaining a disciplined psychotherapeutic frame, for giving priority to clients' well-being, and for revising their approach in light of continued exposure to relevant literatures.

Colm (1966) pointed out that genuine participation in a relationship necessarily involves tensions, anger, irritation, affection, and so on, on both sides. She further noted that without the possibility of criticism and disagreement, acceptance loses meaningful depth. In short, courage, honesty, and tolerance of differences are funda-

mental to the establishment and ongoing maintenance of the kind of collaborative relationship that is fundamental to existential psychotherapy.

If the psychotherapist does allow mutuality to develop through recognition of shared humanity, the shift from the initial acknowledgment of unequal social roles to a less dependent relationship is palpable (van den Berg, 1971; Willis, 1994). Such a relationship between the therapist and client necessarily involves both in an intimately affective manner that exposes them to the risk of personal change (Bugental, 1976; Cannon, 1991). Indeed, May (1983) asserts that not only does effective psychotherapy inevitably change both of its participants but also clients' openness to changing is facilitated by therapists' openness to being changed. Spinelli (1997) agrees that therapists who adopt personally or professionally defensive postures implicitly encourage their clients to do the same, and thus stifle their willingness to take risks. Willis (1994) holds that therapists' self-disclosure about the ongoing therapeutic relationship, and possibly other subjects, is characteristic of existential therapy. The relevant questions then become when, how much, and to what specific ends do therapists' self-disclosure relate. Our own position is that therapists' self-disclosure should always be for the sake of the therapy and not for the therapists' other interests.

In summary, from an existential perspective, all understandings are derived from and maintained by relationships; therefore, dynamic, process-inclusive understandings will always be preferable to static, individualistic ones. The importance of attending to relational process, as well as to reported content, is axiomatic for many existential psychotherapists (e.g., Bugental, 1978; Spinelli, 1994; Yalom, 1989). Attending to the process dimensions of the therapeutic relationship enhances accessibility to clients' interpersonal strengths and struggles. With this in mind, we now turn to the place of understanding in existential psychotherapy.

Understanding

Although usually taken for granted, a psychotherapist's understanding of the client's particular experience of the world is fundamental. Too often therapists are preoccupied with diagnostics, techniques, and office management. When such preoccupations interfere with the therapist's attention to the client's personal world, they may find themselves working at cross purposes.

When the client's world is adequately understood, both the client and the psychotherapist are positively affected. In this process, however, psychotherapists typically are not overwhelmed by emotion. Contrary to concerns raised by critics, existential therapists continue to act effectively as facilitators even while experiencing affect in sessions. Existential therapists warn that intellectual understandings and explanations are inadequate by themselves and that it is affectively toned understandings and experiences in relationship to others that can be deeply transformative (Boss, 1957/1963; May, 1958; Yalom, 1989). Indeed, compassion characterizes the affective dimension of a therapist's experience in relation to a client. This compassion is integral to the hoped for "corrective emotional experience" of psychotherapy.

Compassionate understanding involves empathizing with the particular clients' lives as they experience them. Instead of seeing the client primarily from the outside in a search for symptoms of psychopathology or for behaviors or cognitions to work on, existential psychotherapists value "experience-near" understandings of their clients. That is, they try to stay close to the client's experience and to speak in descriptive terms rather than moving to abstract levels of explanations, hypothetical constructs, and theories (Owen, 1994; Potash, 1994). As King and Citrenbaum (1993) have put it, psychotherapists ought to work within a client's worldview—within his or her "existential reality."

Although it certainly is true that theory always is derived from someone's personal experience, formalized theories can become quite depersonalized. Existential psychotherapists are keenly aware that the more they become caught up in theoretical speculations, the less they will be able to attend to the particularities of clients' lives.

Although theory can effectively serve psychotherapeutic work, it is important to remain cognizant of its concrete basis in personal experience. The notions of *transference* and *countertransference* are good examples. These psychoanalytic terms refer to the inevitably selective, biased aspects of our adult perceptions and reactions, which are based on significant childhood experiences with our parents. Psychotherapists, of course, should be sensitive to transference and countertransference processes in the therapeutic relationship (van Deurzen-Smith, 1997). However, many therapists become so focused on the

transference and on reconstructing the distant past by means of its appearance in therapy that they abandon the adult who is consulting them in the present. Without dismissing the phenomena to which transference and countertransference refer, existential therapists emphasize the importance of attending to the ongoing client and therapist relationship (Willis, 1994).

Unfortunately, transference and countertransference can be (and often are) invoked as a means to disown one's current experience vis-à-vis another (Spinelli, 1997). If a therapist is unable or unwilling to engage the client authentically, then that client may be stuck in a kind of "countertransference relationship" that closes off future possibilities (Prochaska, 1979). But the major point in this context is that theoretically encumbered explorations of transference and countertransference are not "experience-near." A substantially more experience-near kind of interpretation favored by existential therapists highlights ways in which a client attempts to avoid authentic engagement with the therapist (Bugental, 1986; May, 1983; Prochaska, 1979).

In addition to efforts to become attuned to and close to the client's experience, an existential therapist brackets—puts aside—his or her own desires to effect *specific* client change, cure, and/or growth (Spinelli, 1994, 1997; Strasser, 1996; van Deurzen-Smith, 1988, 1997). Clients find their own meaningful ways of integrating revised views and associated action into their ongoing lives. The aim of an existential therapist, then, is to jointly develop understandings of the client's life world, not to directly change it. This is an important and seemingly counterintuitive point. The process of this approach primarily involves reflecting on the client's experience and activities, without necessarily setting behavioral goals to be accomplished. Some existential psychotherapists suggest trying out different behaviors as a way for the client to discover and develop personally viable alternatives. But the goal is not to prescribe particular behavior. Not surprisingly, then, existential psychotherapists are often oriented toward long-term work, but even Strasser's (1996) time-limited approach involves letting go of expectations that something specific must be accomplished within given time constraints.

Existential psychotherapists may bend this general frame if they believe that circumstances render a client unable to reflect and choose over time. For example, they may urge a client to call a family member right on the spot to explain his or her plan to commit suicide. In addition, some existentially oriented psychotherapists might agree, for example, to assist a client who wants to stop smoking. Here, too, therapist and client would clarify the meaning to the client of smoking, and they might imagine the client's world without cigarettes. They also might use Bugental's "but what's stopping you" technique of successively affirming what the client sees as obstacles until they reach what the client now recognizes that he or she has not wanted to risk or to give up. The client may then stop smoking or opt to continue.

Among the clarifications that existential psychotherapists pursue with clients are their ways of dealing with the "givens of existence" (Spinelli, 1997; Strasser, 1996). Yalom (1980) has provided the most widely cited account of these basic human limitations, or "existential givens"—death, freedom, existential isolation, and meaninglessness. Although it is possible and often quite useful to speak in terms of one's characteristic responses to the limitations and uncertainties of being human, it is important to remember that one is constantly choosing those responses; thus, one's "characteristics" are, in an important sense, one's habitual choices. Van Deurzen-Smith (1988, 1997) has noted that an existential psychotherapist's task is *not* to help clients become more responsible for their choices and the course they take as a result, but rather to help them to recognize that they are always already responsible and *to invite them to reassess their ongoing choices.* According to van Deurzen-Smith, the optimal therapeutic posture is one of radical questioning of all that the client, and the therapist for that matter, takes for granted, but without assuming that the client necessarily needs to change as a result.

This absence of emphasis by existential psychotherapists on a particular change is important for creating a meeting place where clients can more freely and fully disclose and explore their most private anxieties, hopes, beliefs, values, and so on. In contrast, emphasizing change subtly implies criticism of a client's current position. An accepting and respectful stance on the therapist's part encourages clients to adopt a similar posture in respect to themselves, and it increases the likelihood that they will be able to openly and nondefensively disclose and explore their experiences (Spinelli, 1997). As they do so, it becomes increasingly likely that they, together with their therapists, will come to elucidate anxieties, hopes,

beliefs, values, and so on that they had previously lived without awareness. In more radical Sartrean terms, such encounters would allow for the illumination both of one's "fundamental project of being" and of choices about becoming who one is and who one shall be (Cannon, 1991; Sartre, 1953).

The existential psychotherapist initiates a respectful questioning of what clients have taken for granted; this questioning becomes a mutual endeavor. The therapist forsakes dependence on any particular program or therapeutic technique, and instead allows his or her interventions to flow from continuously evolving understandings of the client's experience (Heuscher, 1964; May, 1958; Misiak & Sexton, 1973; Prochaska, 1979). Furthermore, the existential psychotherapist humbly maintains a stance of "un-knowing," attempting to remain as open as possible to whatever is presented (Spinelli, 1997).

Because the therapist cannot know a client in a complete or final sense, remaining open to and encouraging further exploration is ongoing. This openness includes being receptive to challenges to one's own limiting assumptions. When the therapist remains grounded within the client's worldview and works alongside the client, his or her comments are not received as assaults from an outsider. An existential psychotherapist is drawn into the client's world and yet respects the differences between their experiences (van Deurzen-Smith, 1997). In the absence of this stance, there can be no genuine encounter between the partcipants. As the client begins to participate in this relationship more fully, new understandings, perspectives, and possibilities become accessible. New possibilities open as the therapist and client jointly and nonjudgmentally explore and elucidate the client's self-construct (Spinelli, 1997). Although expansion of awareness of possibilities does not necessarily lead to the resolution of particular problems, it contributes to the client's general well-being and sense of empowerment (Bugental, 1978).

Flexibility

As we address flexibility, our third theme in the practice of existential psychotherapy, it may be helpful to make another general distinction between this approach and humanistic psychotherapies. In contrast to some humanistic psychotherapies that tend to be lopsidedly optimistic about "human potential," suggesting that persons can soar to ever greater heights as they perfect their consciousness, existential psychotherapists incline toward what they see as a more even-handed and grounded attitude. Because both humanistic and existential therapists respond to deterministic personality theories by emphasizing human freedom, however, they commonly are lumped together as an "existential-humanistic" (or vice versa) or "third-force" approach. Although these two approaches both stress human possibilities, identifying the two approaches too closely on that basis elides important differences between them.

Existential psychotherapists recognize and respect the substantial limitations on freedom (e.g., Allers, 1961; Cannon, 1991; Sartre, 1953; van Deurzen-Smith, 1988; van Kaam, 1966). We humans have been "thrown" into the world and repeatedly find ourselves in situations that we have not chosen; but we do have some choice in our responses to the "givens" that confront us (Cohn, 1995; du Plock, 1997). Indeed, the specific pattern of our chosen responses to the givens of our particular existence contributes to its shape, as well as to determining the kinds of future situations that we will inhabit. Yet we are inescapably embodied and situated. We owe our birth and continuing existence to physical, chemical, biological, social, cultural, and ethical laws and customs that preceded us and, though they may change to some degree during our limited time here on earth, will outlast us. Any proud attempt of ours to live outside these unyielding dictates may lead instead to reduced options or even to death. Boss (1979/1994) wrote of the "freedom-finiteness" dialectic that characterizes human existence. This dialectic provides an important point of contrast between some humanistic and existential psychotherapies.

On a conceptual level, the goal of an existential psychotherapist is to help increase flexible "response-ability" on the part of the client, that is, his or her facility in flexibly responding to the particular givens of life circumstances (van Kaam, 1966). Although existential psychotherapists typically do not speak in terms of psychopathology, rigidity, meaninglessness, and alienation are central to their notions of problematic human behavior. For Boss (1979/1994), "illness" and "pathology" of any sort, including "medical" problems such as broken bones, are fundamentally about the impairment of human freedom; hence "healing" involves recovery and/or enhancement of one's accessible possibilities. This perspective is based on a dynamic process-understanding of being human. Existentialists like to remind us that *being* is a verb—so integrally connected with *becoming* that a constant process of change is a basic characteristic of human beings. Excessive constancy is indicative of problems (Potash, 1994). A "healthy" sense of self must remain plastic in order to stay in harmony with one's dynamic living in the world. The more static one's sense of self, the more limited one's capacity will be to embrace the varied experiences that inevitably will be encountered (Spinelli, 1997). We might say that if one has only a single lens through which to see oneself, then one will be able to see things only in that specific light and, consequently, will miss much of what is there to be seen and will be locked into unbalanced, repetitive patterns of behavior. Even so, Spinelli (1994) points out that "sedimented" beliefs are the fundamental building blocks of one's sense of self—of one's image of who one is.

In that such beliefs are unavoidable, the important question is whether particular aspects of one's "self-construct" or "existential project" have become too restrictive and now conflict with one's current experience. If so, then self-deception is necessary to maintain the familiar but confining self-construct or project. From the perspective of many existential psychotherapists, efforts to discover who one "really" is, to establish an unchanging sense of self, or to shore up ego structures are misguided attempts to somehow hold still the dynamic processes of being human. These therapists see letting go of a static, object-like self-concept, and of thereby increasing flexible living, as more valuable (e.g., Cannon, 1991; King & Citrenbaum, 1993). Because being human means being in an ever-changing process, therapists and clients need not try to make change happen. Instead, we can let go of our efforts to remain the same and can become aware of and embrace the processes of change in which we are always participating (van Deurzen-Smith, 1997). Increasing awareness of the ways in which we have constrictedly defined ourselves and our world enables us to envision and to enact new alternatives, as well as, as if for the first time, choosing to do what we had previously done mechanically (Bugental & Bracke, 1992; van Kaam, 1966). Having choices where one had previously felt compelled and experiencing an increased range and flexibility of awareness are empowering and enlivening (Bugental, 1976, 1987). The successful outcome of therapy is a client's empowerment, a growing sense of being able (King & Citrenbaum, 1993), even while being circumspect about limitations and choices. Specific behavioral changes accompany these processes rather than being primary objectives.

Insofar as an existential psychotherapist's goal for the client is empowerment through flexibility, the theory and practice of therapy must manifest similar flexibility. Several existential therapists have pointed out that a client will not be encouraged to find more flexibility than is shown by the therapist in the session room (e.g., Bergantino, 1981; Edwards, 1982; Spinelli, 1994). For a client to experience expanding personal flexibility, the therapist must be willing to risk venturing out of his or her comfort zone to provide up-close examples of flexibility. Insofar as therapists are commited to personal and professional securites and conventions, they are of limited help to clients who are similarly stuck (King & Citrenbaum, 1993).

Being circumspect is an aspect of therapists' flexibility. Thus existential therapists are mindful that sessions are a small segment of clients' worlds. Although the client-therapist relationship is one means through which clients revise their understandings and options, circumspect therapists know that clients' ongoing worlds are powerful maintainers of the status quo. So despite our emphasis in this chapter on the therapeutic relationship, within that relationship therapists flexibly respond to and evoke clients' daily situations of being engaged with family, friends, supervisors, medical conditions, finances, and so forth.

We turn now to the therapist's role in facilitating and maintaining a flexible course of psychotherapy. We have already mentioned that an existential psychotherapist does not become overly attached to any particular theoretical perspective. The issue is that if we have only one lens, we make do with it, and most likely we will not even recognize our perspective as such because we cannot imagine observing in any other way. Many existential therapists are concerned about the development of subtle, and not so subtle, dogmatism among the theorists and practitioners of various schools of therapy, including existential psychotherapy. Frankl (1979) asserts that logotherapy has no fixed dogma and that it is open to the evolutionary influences of divergent views both among its practitioners and from other schools of therapy. This represents an ideal of existential psychotherapists generally, but maintaining this kind of openness is much easier said than done. Hence Spinelli (1994) and van Deurzen-Smith (1997) call for disciplined self-

reflection on the part of therapists, toward continual illumination, clarification, and criticism of their own implicit, sedimented personal and theoretical assumptions. This discipline of "unknowing" is central for achieving and maintaining a "beginner's mind," which is as free as possible of preconceptions and thus open, indeed eager, to hear and learn from each client's unique experience (King & Citrenbaum, 1993). Without the humility and flexibility of such an approach, the kind of authentic encounter that is crucial in existential psychotherapy would be limited.

The flexibility in theory that opens a therapist to the understandings of others must be coupled with flexibility in practice. In the same way that philosophical and theoretical questions about, for example, what is "healthy" and "unhealthy," or "good" and "bad," cannot be answered absolutely or outside of a particular context, so too "technical" questions about therapy must be addressed contextually; each instance must be considered in light of its own particular and changing contingencies (Charny, 1992). A consistent finding in the written accounts of existential psychotherapy that we have reviewed for this chapter was the variability across therapists, clients, and situations that characterizes the practice of existential therapy (e.g., Bugental, 1978; du Plock, 1997; May, 1958; Norcross, 1987; Potash, 1994; Prochaska, 1979). Any of a wide variety of modalities and specific interventions can and should be employed as long as they are not used in a merely technical manner but rather in a way that is consistent with a genuinely caring and understanding human encounter (May & Yalom, 1995; Moss, 1989).

The practice of existential psychotherapy cannot be codified or prescribed because it depends on developing an evolving understanding of the particular client's dynamic, momentary experiences and on responding in ways that one hopes will be helpful in light of that inevitably incomplete understanding (Potash, 1994). Furthermore, because the process of psychotherapy is infinitely fluid; complex; and variable across therapists, clients, contexts, and moments; the impact of one's responses will always be unpredictable—even unknowable in a complete sense. A therapist's strict adherence to an agenda or treatment plan based on previously useful patterns of understanding and intervention may interfere with the therapist's openness and ability to helpfully respond to a particular client. Thus, Frankl (1967) wrote that the therapeutic process involves constant improvisation in relation to each individual. Furthermore, several existential therapists have contended that effective psychotherapy is much more an intuitive, artistic practice than the application of a technical-scientific procedure (Abroms, 1993; Bergantino, 1981; Bugental, 1976, 1987). The practice of an existential psychotherapy is perhaps best characterized by a "methodological eclecticism and theoretical pluralism" within a "disciplined openness" (Fischer, 1991).

CONCLUDING COMMENTS

The editors of this volume asked if we could estimate the proportion of psychotherapists who practice with an existential approach. We have no way of doing that, in large part because many clinicians utilize much of its framework without regarding themselves as exclusively existential. One can adopt the techniques and interests of many approaches within an existential frame, including psychodyanic approaches. When we respond to those infernal checklists, asking for "theoretical orientation," we are inclined to check most of the items, all the while protesting that the list mixes philosophy, theory, and methods. For example, during psychotherapy, through familiarity with object relations theory we might become attuned to certain dynamics, and we might ask if the client would be interested in trying a cognitive-behavioral exercise to explore his or her habitual responses. Within the existential frame, however, our goal would be for clients to discover their participation in their routine ways of being, and thereby to invite them to find their own modifications.

When prospective clients ask about our approach to psychotherapy, it doesn't occur to us to say that we are existential psychotherapists, even though we are affiliated with a major institutional home of human-science psychology, one with an historical emphasis on existential phenomenology. Instead, we answer more to the point, that is, along the lines that we talk with clients to help them reflect on their lives, explore ways of thinking of their history, and find some revised ways of continuing their journey. We may mention that we sometimes incorporate imaginative exercises, readings, looking at family dynamics, journaling, behavioral exercises, and so on.

We looked for empirical research on outcomes of existential psychotherapy but found none. Upon reflection, this is not surprising.

Most psychotherapists who agree that they practice within an existential framework would object to artificially restricting their practice to meet research criteria and to participating in manualized psychotherapy research. However, there is considerable research on topics salient to existential psychotherapy, such as personal meaning, purpose, spirituality, values, and personal projects (e.g., Wong & Fry, 1998). There is also considerable research on experiential psychotherapy and on the relation of emotion and change in psychotherapy (e.g., Greenberg, 1993; Greenberg & Safran, 1987).

In this chapter, we have often mentioned the overlap of existential and other psychotherapy approaches. What ultimately differentiates it is *consistency* in honoring the significance and power of clients' meaning, making efforts to deal with our human condition, similarly refusing to explain through mechanisms, and refusing to reduce problems in living to psychopathology and in respecting the interpersonal and intersubjective character of psychotherapeutic encounters. Both personal construct and narrative psychotherapy (see Chapter 16 in this volume), although coming from different histories, share most of these features.

In conclusion, we have outlined three interconnected themes—relationship, understanding, and flexibility—through which we have characterized the practice of contemporary existential psychotherapists. We hope that many readers find that these themes are consonant with their own theoretical orientation and practice of psychotherapy. To the extent that psychotherapists subordinate theory and technique to an openness to clients' worlds, support their attempts to deal authentically with limits and possibility, and encourage them to attain flexibility and empowerment through their participation in changing meanings, they work with individuals' existential conditions.

REFERENCES

Abroms, E. M. (1993). *The freedom of the self: The bio-existential treatment of character problems.* New York: Plenum.

Allers, R. (1961). *Existentialism and psychiatry.* Springfield, IL: Thomas.

Bergantino, L. (1981). *Psychotherapy, insight, and style: The existential moment.* Boston: Allyn & Bacon.

Binswanger, L. (1947). Uber phanomenologie. In *Ausgewahlte vortrage und afstatze, Band 11.* Bern: Franke. (Original work published 1923)

Binswanger, L. (1963). *Being-in-the-world*. (J. Needleman, Ed.). New York: Basic Books.

Boss, M. (1963). *Psychoanalysis and Daseinsanalysis*. (L. Lefebre, Trans.). New York: Basic Books. (Original work published 1957)

Boss, M. (1994). *Existential foundations of medicine and psychology*. (S. Conway & A. Cleaves, Trans.). Northvale, NJ: Aronson. (Original work published 1979)

Buber, M. (1958). *I and thou*. New York: Scribner. (Original work published 1923)

Bugental, J. F. T. (1976). *The search for existential identity: Patient-therapist dialogues in humanistic psychotherapy*. San Francisco: Jossey-Bass.

Bugental, J. F. T. (1978). *Psychotherapy and process: The fundamentals of an existential-humanistic approach*. New York: Random House.

Bugental, J. F. T. (1986). Existential-humanistic psychotherapy. In I. L. Kutash & A. Wolf (Eds.), *Psychotherapists' casebook* (pp. 222–236). San Francisco: Jossey-Bass.

Bugental, J. F. T. (1987). *The art of the psychotherapist*. New York: Norton.

Bugental, J. F. T., & Bracke, P. E. (1992). The future of existential-humanistic psychotherapy. *Psychotherapy, 29*(1), 28–33.

Cannon, B. (1991). *Sartre and psychoanalysis: An existentialist challenge to clinical metatheory*. Lawrence: University of Kansas Press.

Charny, I. W. (1992). *Existential/dialectical marital therapy: Breaking the secret code of marriage*. New York: Brunner/Mazel.

Cohn, H. W. (1984). An existential approach to psychotherapy. *British Journal of Medical Psychology, 57*, 311–318.

Cohn, H. W. (1995). Misconceptions in existential psychotherapy. *Journal of the Society of Existential Analysis, 6*(1), 20–27.

Colm, H. (1966). *The existentialist approach to psychotherapy with adults and children*. New York: Grune & Stratton.

Dilthey, W. (1977). *Descriptive psychology and historical understanding*. (R. M. Zaner & K. L. Heiges, Trans.). The Hague: Martinus Nijhoff. (Original work published 1924 and 1927)

du Plock, S. (1997). Introduction. In S. du Plock (Ed.), *Case studies in existential psychotherapy and counselling* (pp. 1–11). New York: Wiley.

Edwards, D. G. (1982). *Existential psychotherapy: The process of caring*. New York: Gardner.

Fischer, C. T. (1991). Phenomenological-existential psychotherapy. In M. Hersen, A. E. Kazdin, & A. S. Bellack (Eds.), *The clinical psychology handbook* (2nd ed., pp. 534–550). New York: Pergamon.

Fischer, C. T. (1998). Phenomenological, existential, and humanistic foundations for psychology as a human science. In A. S. Bellack & M. Hersen (Eds.), *Comprehensive clinical psychology. Vol. 1: Foundations*. (pp. 449–472). Oxford: Pergamon.

Foucault, M. (1985). Dream, imagination, and existence. *Review of Existential Psychology and Psychiatry, 19*, 31–78. (Original work published 1954)

Frankl, V. E. (1967). *Psychotherapy and existentialism: Selected papers on logotherapy*. New York: Simon & Schuster.

Frankl, V. E. (1979). Introduction. In J. B. Fabry, R. P. Bulka, & W. S. Sahakian (Eds.), *Logotherapy in action* (pp. ix–xii). New York: Jason Aronson.

Freud, S. (1963). Recommendations for physicians on the psychoanalytic method of treatment. In *Therapy and technique*. New York: Collier. (Original work published 1912)

Fromm, E. (1941). *Escape from freedom*. New York: Holt, Rinehart and Winston.

Fromm, E. (1970). *The crisis of psychoanalysis: Essays on Freud, Marx, and social psychology*. Greenwich, CT: Faucett.

Goldberg, C., & Goldberg, M. C. (1973). *The human circle: An existential approach to the new group therapies*. Chicago: Nelson-Hall.

Greenberg, L. S. (1993). Emotion and the change process in psychotherapy. In M. Lewis & J. M. Haviland (Eds.), *Handbook of emotions* (pp. 499–510). New York: Guilford.

Greenberg, L. S., & Safran, J. D. (1987). *Emotion in psychotherapy: Affect, cognition, and the process of change*. New York: Guilford.

Heidegger, M. (1962). *Being and time* (J. Macquarrie & E. Robinson, Trans.). San Francisco. (Original work published 1927)

Heidegger, M. (1966). *Discourse on thinking*. (John M. Anderson & E. Hans Freud, Trans.). New York: Harper & Row. (Original work published 1959)

Heuscher, J. E. (1964). What is existential psychotherapy? *Review of Existential Psychology and Psychiatry, 4*(2), 158–167.

Horvath, A. O., & Symonds, B. D. (1991). Relation between working alliance and outcome in psychotherapy: A meta-analysis. *Journal of Counseling Psychology, 38*(2), 139–149.

Husserl, E. (1962). *Ideas: General introduction to pure phenomenology*. New York: Collier. (Original work published 1913)

Jaspers, K. (1963). *General psychopathology*. (J. Hoenig & M. W. Hamilton, Trans.). Chicago: Regeny Press. (Original work published 1913)

Kierkegaard, S. (1983). *Kierkegaard Anthology*. Princeton: Princeton University Press.

King, M. E., & Citrenbaum, C. M. (1993). *Existential hypnotherapy*. New York: Guilford.

Laing, R. D. (1960). *The divided self: An existential study in sanity and madness*. London: Tavistock.

Lantz, J. (1993). *Existential family therapy: Using the concepts of Viktor Frankl*. Northvale, NJ: Jason Aronson.

Marcel, G. (l978). *Homo viator: Introduction to a metaphisic of hope*. Glouster, MA: Peter Smith. (Original work published 1951)

Marziali, E., & Alexander, L. (1991). The power of the therapeutic relationship. *American Journal of Orthopsychiatry*, *61*(3), 383–391.

May, R. (1958). Contributions of existential psychotherapy. In R. May, E. Angel, & H. F. Ellenberger (Eds.), *Existence: A new dimension in psychiatry and psychology* (pp. 37–91). New York: Basic Books.

May, R. (1983). *The discovery of being: Writings in existential psychology*. New York: Norton.

May, R., Angel, E., & Ellenberger, H. F. (Eds.). (1958). *Existence: A new dimension in psychiatry and psychology*. New York: Basic Books.

May, R., & Yalom, I. D. (1995). Existential psychotherapy. In R. J. Corsini & D. Wedding (Eds.), *Current psychotherapies* (5th ed., pp. 262–292). Itasca, IL: Peacock.

Merleau-Ponty, M. (1962). *Phenomenology of perception*. New York: Humanities Press. (Original work published 1942)

Merleau-Ponty, M. (1963). *The structure of behavior*. Boston: Beacon Press. (Original work published 1942)

Misiak, H., & Sexton, V. S. (1973). *Phenomenological, existential, and humanistic psychologies: A historical survey*. New York: Grune & Stratton.

Moss, D. (1989). Psychotherapy and human experience. In R. S. Valle & S. Halling (Eds.), *Existential-phenomenological perspectives in psychology: Exploring the breadth of human experience* (pp. 193–213). New York: Plenum.

Nietzsche, F. (1967). *On the geneology of morals*. (W. Kaufman, Trans.). New York: Vintage Books. (Original work published 1887)

Norcross, J. C. (1987). A rational and empirical analysis of existential psychotherapy. *Journal of Humanistic Psychology*, *27*(1), 41–68.

Owen, I. R. (1994). Introducing an existential-phenomenological approach: Part 2—Theory for practice. *Counselling Psychology Quarterly*, *7*(4), 347–358.

Potash, H. M. (1994). *Pragmatic-existential psychotherapy with personality disorders*. Madison, NJ: Gordon Handwerk.

Prochaska, J. O. (1979). *Systems of psychotherapy: A transtheoretical analysis*. Homewood, IL: Dorsey.

Sartre, J.-P. (1953). *Existential psychoanalysis*. (H. E. Barnes, Trans.). New York: Philosophical Library.

Sartre, J.-P. (1975). *Being and nothingness: A phenomenological essay on ontology*. (H. E. Barnes, Trans.). New York: Washington Square Press. (Original work published 1943)

Scheler, M. (1962). *Man's place in nature*. New York: Farrar, Straus, & Cudahy. (Original work published 1928)

Spinelli, E. (1994). *Demystifying therapy*. London: Constable.

Spinelli, E. (1997). *Tales of Un-knowing: Eight stories of existential therapy*. New York: New York University Press.

Strasser, F. (1996). Time-limited existential therapy: A structural view. *Journal of the Society for Existential Analysis*, *8*(1), 46–56.

Straus, E. (1952). The upright posture. *Psychiatric Quarterly*, *26*, 529–561.

Sullivan, H. S. (1953). *The interpersonal theory of psychiatry*. New York: Norton.

Valle, R. (1998). *Phenomenlogical inquiry in psychology: Existential and transpersonal dimensions*. New York: Plenum.

van den Berg, J. (1971). What is psychotherapy? *Humanitas*, *7*, 321–370.

van Deurzen-Smith, E. (1988). *Existential counseling in practice*. Newbury Park, CA: Sage.

van Deurzen-Smith, E. (1997). *Everyday mysteries: Existential dimensions of psychotherapy*. New York: Routledge.

van Kaam, A. (1966). *The art of existential counseling*. Wilkes-Barre, PA: Dimension.

Willis, R. J. (1994). *Transcendence in relationship: Existentialism and psychotherapy*. Norwood, NJ: Ablex.

Wong, P. T. P., & Fry, P. S. (Eds.). (1998). *The human quest for meaning: A handbook of psychological research and clinical applications*. Mahwah, NJ: Erlbaum.

Yalom, I. D. (1980). *Existential psychotherapy*. New York: Basic Books.

Yalom, I. D. (1989). *Love's executioner and other tales of psychotherapy*. New York: Basic Books.

CHAPTER 13

INTERPERSONAL PSYCHOTHERAPY

IAN H. GOTLIB AND PAMELA K. SCHRAEDLEY
Stanford University

Whereas it is almost certainly the case that there are core elements common to many of the major approaches in psychotherapy, it is equally true that each approach has a different emphasis or focus in attempting to bring about therapeutic change. Most traditional approaches to psychotherapy focus primarily on intrapersonal processes in the patient as both key targets of treatment and critical mechanisms of change. It is important to realize, however, that most psychological disorders have a significant interpersonal, as well as intrapersonal, component and that evaluating the interpersonal context of the patient is almost certain to expand and elucidate the clinical picture. For example, a woman seeking treatment for depression following a divorce may experience symptom relief from pharmacotherapy; similarly, cognitive therapy may help her to believe that she is still a worthwhile person despite a failed marriage. However, without directly addressing the divorce and her interpersonal difficulties that might have contributed to it and that may also make her transition from married to single life more difficult, the clinical picture would be incomplete and the possibility of recurrence high.

There is a reasonably long history of theoretical approaches in understanding the etiology and maintenance of psychopathology that focus on interpersonal functioning. The interpersonal school of psychiatry, developed by Harry Stack Sullivan (1953), was among the first to systematically specify connections between interpersonal context and psychiatric disorders. Sullivan was strongly influenced by Adolph Meyer (1957), whose approach to psychopathology at that time was unique in its focus on the patient's adaptations to his or her environment. Meyer believed that patients' responses to stress in adulthood were determined in large part both by their early experiences, including family interactions, and by associations with particular social groups in adulthood. Sullivan developed and elaborated on Meyer's perspective, postulating that psychiatric difficulties were a result of disordered communication and problematic interpersonal relations. Although he believed that the roots of interpersonal dysfunction lay in early childhood experiences, Sullivan felt that the most important manifestations of these experiences, and ultimately their resolution, were in the individual's current social relationships and interactions. Therefore, according to Sullivan, the emphasis of treatment needed to shift from the individual and the resolution of past relationships (which was at that time the modal focus of psychoanalysis) to the successful development of current, satisfying interpersonal interactions.

This notion of the importance of disturbed interpersonal relationships in the genesis of psychiatric disorders was first applied systematically to the study of families of schizophrenic patients by Gregory Bateson and his colleagues at the Mental Research Institute in Palo Alto, California. These investigators formulated a "double-bind theory" to explain the development of schizophrenia in the context of dysfunctional family communications. Double-bind communications are those in which individuals are "damned if they do and damned if they don't," in which it is impossible for them to give a "correct" response. Double-bind situations are clearly stressful, and Bateson and his colleagues proposed that exposure to these stressful communication patterns over time increases individuals' risk for developing symptoms of schizophrenia. Although this theory has not received unequivocal empirical support, it did provide a framework for examining the communication patterns of families as an etiologic factor in psychological disorder and ultimately led to the development of family-focused therapies for this disorder (see Goldstein & Miklowitz, 1995, for a review of this area of research).

At the same time, general systems theory, developed by von Bertalanffy (1950) in the physical sciences, was beginning to receive attention in the social sciences as well, particularly for the study of family dynamics. General system theory maintains that complex systems of interrelated elements can only be fully understood by examining the nature of the relationships among the elements. More important, this theory proposes that the behavior of an element of a system can be better understood with increasing knowledge of the system of which it is a member. The extension of this theory to the field of psychology and to the study of psychiatric disorders highlighted the importance of considering the individual's interpersonal environment in attempting to understand the etiology and maintenance of that person's psychological difficulties and, more important, in efforts to treat the psychological disorder.

Spurred in part by these theoretical perspectives, investigators began to document empirically the presence of interpersonal problems and adverse interpersonal environments that were associated with a number of discrete psychiatric disorders. For example, as we describe in more detail later, compared with nonpsychiatric controls, depressed persons, individuals with eating disorders, patients with panic disorder, and persons experiencing difficulties with substance abuse have all been found to have smaller and less supportive social networks (e.g., Billings & Moos, 1985; Markowitz et al., 1989; Tiller et al., 1997). Individuals experiencing high levels of depression, anxiety, or alcoholism have also been found to report significant marital difficulties (e.g., Gotlib & Hooley, 1988; Hand, Lamontagne, & Marks, 1974; Moos, Finney, & Gamble, 1982). In fact, recent research now suggests that living with spouses or parents who are highly critical or negative in their comments and behavior places both depressed and schizophrenic patients at increased risk for relapse or recurrence of the disorder (e.g., Hooley & Teasdale, 1989; Kavanagh, 1992).

Findings such as these offer empirical support for aspects of interpersonal theories of psychopathology and provided the impetus for Klerman, Weissman, Rounsaville, and Chevron

(1984) and his colleagues to develop interpersonal psychotherapy (IPT) for depression. Perhaps not surprisingly, given the results of studies that have demonstrated the widespread existence of interpersonal difficulties across a variety of psychiatric diagnoses, IPT is now also being modified for use in the treatment of a number of other disorders and problems. In this chapter we focus primarily on IPT for depression, but we also describe a number of these extensions of IPT to other difficulties. We begin by briefly describing the results of empirical research that led to the development and use of IPT, and then discuss in detail IPT for depression. We describe the objectives of IPT, the three stages of this therapy, and the four major problems on which it focuses. We then describe the results of studies conducted to examine the efficacy of IPT for depression. Following this discussion, we examine extensions of IPT to forms of depression other than major depressive disorder in adults, including depressed adolescents and older adults, adults with dysthymia or recurrent depression, and depression seen in primary-care settings. We also examine recent extensions of IPT to problems and disorders other than depression, including general dysphoria, bulimia, and substance abuse. Finally, we conclude this chapter by discussing a number of questions raised by the literature we have reviewed and by offering suggestions for future research. We turn now to a discussion of the literature that forms the empirical foundation for the practice of IPT.

RATIONALE FOR AN INTERPERSONAL APPROACH TO PSYCHOTHERAPY

As noted, there is considerable empirical evidence that a number of psychological disorders are characterized by difficulties in interpersonal functioning. For example, depressed individuals have consistently been shown to have smaller and less supportive social networks than do community controls (e.g., Billings, Cronkite, & Moos, 1983; Billings & Moos, 1985; Brim, Witcoff, & Wetzel, 1982). Similar findings have been reported among individuals diagnosed with eating disorders (Tiller, Sloane, Schmidt, Troop, Power, & Treasure, 1997), panic disorder (Markowitz et al., 1989), and substance abuse (Hawkins & Fraser, 1985). The results of a number of investigations suggest that it may be important to distinguish between general social contact and close relationships. For example, although individuals who have recovered from depression do not show deficits in the number of their network contacts, they do report having fewer friends and close relationships than do never-depressed controls, a pattern of interpersonal difficulties that seems to mirror that found when these individuals were symptomatic. These results suggest, therefore, that the interpersonal functioning of depressed patients in more intimate relationships remains impaired after their symptoms have abated (cf. Billings & Moos, 1985).

Much of the research on functioning in close relationships has focused on marriage. Marital difficulties have been linked to several psychological disorders, including depression (see Gotlib & Hooley, 1988; Gotlib & McCabe, 1990, for reviews), anxiety disorders (Hand, Lamontagne, & Marks, 1974), and alcoholism (Moos et al., 1982). It is interesting that although investigators have linked depression and marital difficulties quite consistently, marital dysfunction has not always been found to be characteristic of other disorders. In fact, it is possible that marital difficulties are associated with some psychiatric disorders, such as anxiety, because of their comorbidity or co-occurrence with depression. Thus, individuals with pure agoraphobia, who do not exhibit comorbid clinical depression, have been found to demonstrate levels of marital functioning comparable to those that characterize nonpsychiatric controls (e.g., Arrindell & Emmelkamp, 1986; Burglass, Clarke, Henderson, Kreitman, Kreitman, & Presley, 1977). Investigators have also uncovered distinctive associations between marital functioning and depression that do not appear to hold for other disorders. For example, although marital difficulties have been found to persist after recovery from depression (e.g., Rounsaville, Prusoff, & Weissman, 1980; Weissman & Paykel, 1974), recovery from other disorders, such as alcoholism, has been associated with improvement in marital functioning (Moos et al., 1982). It appears, therefore, that depression, perhaps to a greater extent than is the case with other emotional disorders, is strongly associated with marital dysfunction and, furthermore, that marital functioning may not improve with recovery from depression without being targeted explicitly for intervention.

It is important that marital relationships and social support have been shown not only to be associated with psychopathology but also to influence the course of the disorder, including onset (e.g., Huba, Wingard, & Bentler, 1980; Paykel et al., 1969), treatment outcome (e.g., Booth, Russell, Soucek, & Laughlin, 1992; Tucker, 1982; Wills, 1990), and relapse (e.g., Rounsaville, Weissman, Prusoff, & Herceg-Baron, 1979). In fact, one of the strongest predictors of relapse is a construct referred to as expressed emotion (EE). Expressed emotion encompasses emotional over-involvement and criticism of the distressed individual by a family member or spouse. Living in a high-EE household has been found to predict rates of relapse for patients diagnosed with schizophrenia and with affective disorders (e.g., Hooley & Teasdale, 1989; Kavanagh, 1992; Miklowitz et al., 1988; Simoneau, Miklowitz, & Saleem, 1998).

It is also important to realize that the interpersonal context of individuals experiencing psychiatric disorders is often stressful. In addition to marital conflict and divorce, other important life transitions may create upheaval in the interpersonal realm. It has been estimated, for example, that 75% of individuals diagnosed with anorexia or bulimia experience a severe life stressor in the year leading up to the onset of the disorder (Schmidt, Tiller, Andrews, Blanchard, & Treasure, 1997). Similarly, Brown and Harris (1989) found that more than two-thirds of depressive episodes are preceded by a severe stressor, with most occurring within a few weeks of onset. Compounding these difficulties, individuals who are experiencing emotional disturbance are characterized by poor coping skills. For example, compared to controls, bulimic women have been found to use more avoidance and wishful thinking, to seek less social support, and to exhibit more helplessness and less mastery in response to stressful events (e.g., Troop, Holbrey, Trowler, & Treasure, 1994; Troop & Treasure, 1997). Similarly, depressed individuals have been found to exhibit dysfunctional coping, including self-blaming, venting anger on others, denial, and pessimism (e.g., Bifulco & Brown, 1996; Haenninen & Aro, 1996).

In sum, therefore, individuals experiencing diverse forms of psychopathology have been found to exhibit a range of difficulties in their interpersonal functioning. It is not clear, however, whether these difficulties represent a cause or a consequence of the disorder or both. Diathesis-stress models of psychopathology propose that an underlying vulnerability puts one at risk for disorder in the face of life stress (cf. Monroe & Simons, 1991). One version of this type of model posits that low levels of social support from family and friends leave individuals vulnerable to disorder when they experience stressful life events (e.g., Brown & Harris, 1978). Consistent with this position, several researchers have demonstrated that low levels of social support, combined with high levels of life stress, predict depressive symptoms better than do levels of social support or stress alone (e.g., Monroe, Imhoff, Wise, & Harris, 1983; Phifer & Murrell, 1986).

Another possibility is that disordered individuals play an active role in *creating* the stressful life events that they experience, essentially creating difficulties with the people around them. For example, although depressed individuals have been found repeatedly to report greater stress in their lives than do nondepressed controls (e.g., Billings & Moos, 1982; Lloyd, 1980a, 1980b), the results of recent research suggest that they may actually help to create some of this stress. Hammen (1991) makes an important distinction between *independent* stressful life events (i.e., events over which the individual has no control) and *dependent* stressful events (i.e., events that the individual may have had a role in creating). For example, whereas the death of a loved one is an independent event (assuming that the individual did not have a hand in the loved one's death), a fight with a family member may be a dependent event. Hammen (1991) has demonstrated that whereas depressed individuals experience the same number of independent events as do their nondepressed counterparts, they experience a greater number of dependent events. More important for the purposes of this chapter, these dependent events tend to be interpersonal in nature. Consistent with this perspective, there is a growing literature demonstrating that depressed individuals have an adverse interpersonal impact on others with whom they interact, eliciting negative behaviors and reactions from those around them (e.g., Gotlib & Robinson, 1982; Gurtman, 1986; Howes & Hokanson, 1979).

It is clear, therefore, that a strong interpersonal component is associated with depression, as well as with other forms of psychopathology. Because interpersonal dysfunction has been found not only to serve as a risk factor for depression but also to be a consequence of emotional disturbance, it is important that treatment approaches address both of these processes. We turn now to a more detailed discussion of IPT for depression.

INTERPERSONAL PSYCHOTHERAPY FOR DEPRESSION

Drawing on empirical findings like those described above, demonstrating consistent interpersonal difficulties in depression, Klerman et al. (1984) developed IPT as a short-term therapy for this disorder and published a treatment manual. This therapy is based on a conceptualization in which depression is assumed to be maintained and/or exacerbated by interpersonal problems and in which improvement in interpersonal functioning is assumed to decrease the number and intensity of depressive symptoms. Klerman et al. state explicitly that this improvement in depression is expected to occur regardless of whether the interpersonal problems are primary in causing the depression or are a concomitant of the disorder.

The primary objective of IPT, like any therapy, is the relief of depressive symptoms. Unlike other forms of therapy, however, IPT focuses on interpersonal functioning as the key mechanism of therapeutic change. More specifically, IPT focuses on interpersonal problems as they relate to the onset, maintenance, and exacerbation of depressive symptoms. One of four major interpersonal problems is selected as the explicit focus for treatment: grief, role disputes, role transitions, or interpersonal deficits. (We discuss specific strategies for targeting each problem later in this chapter.) It is important that IPT focuses on current interpersonal relationships rather than on the past. Whereas early significant relationships may be useful in demonstrating consistent patterns of interpersonal functioning, the main target of change in IPT is the patient's functioning in current relationships. The focus of IPT, therefore, is on the here and now. Because IPT is a time-limited therapy, usually lasting only 12 to 16 weeks, it is necessary to maintain a tight focus on the specific problem that is targeted and to keep the discussion centered on the patient's current functioning and on ways in which it can be improved.

Interpersonal psychotherapy is conducted in three stages. In the initial sessions, the depressive symptoms are assessed, the syndrome of depression is named and described for the patient, and the patient is given the "sick role." In addition, the patient describes his or her interpersonal relationships in detail, and the depressive disorder is examined in the context of these interpersonal relationships. From this examination, the major interpersonal problem that will become the focus of treatment in the intermediate sessions—grief, role disputes, role transitions, or interpersonal deficits—is identified. Finally, the therapist's understanding of the problem is described to the patient and a treatment plan is developed. In the intermediate sessions, the interpersonal problem is further developed as the patient and therapist work through the problem together, outlining more precisely its nature, plans for change, and strategies for achieving a positive outcome. Finally, in the sessions prior to termination, the therapist helps the patient to accept the termination of the therapeutic relationship and to develop independent competencies that will aid in maintaining the gains achieved in therapy. We turn now to a more detailed discussion of these three stages of treatment.

Initial Sessions

In the first two or three sessions, the patient describes the problems for which he[1] is seeking therapy. Depressive (and other) symptoms are assessed, and a brief overview of the patient's depressive history is obtained. Once the therapist feels confident of the diagnosis of depression, it is discussed with the patient. Naming the disorder for the patient helps him to realize that the various symptoms are part of a common syndrome and that these symptoms and the syndrome of depression are treatable. It is important for the therapist to emphasize that depression is a disorder that often responds to psychotherapy, thereby giving the patient hope for improvement. Naming the syndrome and discussing the efficacy of treatment help the patient adopt the "sick role." The sick role is one in which the patient is exempt from normal social obligations and other responsibilities and focuses on the job of getting well. This conceptualization emphasizes the active role the patient must take in his treatment. In addition, the sick role is presented as an undesirable but time-limited state. The patient may have a history of problems relating to depression and may see it as a part of his personality. Placing the depression in the context of an illness of limited duration helps the patient to believe both that the problems are treatable and that they are not fundamental, unchangeable features of his personality.

Once the patient understands that the symptoms he has been experiencing are attributable to the depression, the therapist and patient begin to explore the interpersonal context of the depression. The patient is asked to complete an interpersonal inventory, which explores current and past relationships, especially as they relate to the patient's current episode of depression. The patient is asked to describe the nature of his current relationships, the expectations that he believes are held by both parties in each significant relationship, and whether or not those expectations are being fulfilled. In addition, the patient is asked to describe changes that he believes would improve the relationships that are problematic. The goal of the interpersonal inventory is to frame the depression in terms of its interpersonal context and to identify key interpersonal issues that may eventually become targets of change in the subsequent intermediate sessions. Finally, the discussion of interpersonal problems that may be related to the depression encourages the patient to begin looking at potential solutions to his problems, rather than simply focusing on the unpleasant nature of the depressive symptoms.

Once the patient's interpersonal context is fairly well developed and understood, the therapist shares her understanding of the patient's problems and how they relate to the depression. The specific goals, assumptions, and features of IPT are explained to the patient, including the interpersonal focus, the time-limited duration of therapy, and its emphasis on the here and now. Together, the therapist and the patient outline the specific problem area (or areas) that will become the focus of treatment, and they form a plan for the remainder of the therapy sessions.

Intermediate Sessions

Once the target problem is defined, the intermediate sessions (sessions 4–12) are used to help the patient work through the issues and problems related to that target. The patient is encouraged to direct the flow of the discussions, although the therapist does guide the patient back to the target problem if he persists in discussing irrelevant material. In the initial sessions the therapist and patient together selected one, or possibly two, of the four major problems as the target(s) for change. We outline below the goals and strategies for therapeutic work in each of these areas, as well as the mechanisms through which IPT is hypothesized to bring about change in each area.

---

[1]In describing the process of therapy in the remainder of this chapter, we try to alternate the gender of the patient and therapist, solely for ease of presentation.

Grief

When a loved one dies, it is normal for people to react with grief. Whereas normal grief shares some features with depression, such as a sad mood and social withdrawal, it does not generally require psychiatric treatment. Indeed, most people who experience grief do not seek treatment, and the symptoms of grief begin to decrease in a matter of a few months as the bereaved individual comes to terms with the loss. Several abnormal grief reactions, however, may complicate this pattern and lead to depression. For example, in delayed reactions, individuals who experienced a prior loss but who did not complete a normal grieving process may subsequently exhibit a profound grief reaction when faced with a less significant loss or with a reminder of the original loss. This delayed reaction may not be accurately diagnosed because of the different time frame of the response.

The goals of IPT are to help the patient deal more effectively with a loss by facilitating healthy mourning for the loved one and developing other relationships or interests. The patient's mourning of the loss and development of new relationships are hypothesized to lead to an abatement of the depressive symptoms through a sharper sense of acceptance of the loss and the increase in the support now available to deal both with the grief and with other stressors that might emerge.

Role Disputes

When the patient and at least one significant other have incompatible expectations in their relationship, the therapist and patient may select interpersonal role disputes as the target for treatment. Klerman et al. (1984) have observed that role disputes that are unresolved and repetitious tend to be related to the onset, maintenance, or exacerbation of depressive symptoms. The patient may feel that he does not have control of his relationships, or he may be afraid of losing the relationship with the other person.

The goals of IPT are, first, to identify the dispute; second, to formulate a plan of action to resolve the dispute; and finally, to modify communication patterns or change expectations to bring about a satisfactory resolution. Role disputes generally fall into one of three stages: *renegotiation*, in which both parties are aware of the dispute and are trying to bring about a solution; *impasse*, in which negotiation has stopped between the two parties, leaving only an unspoken hostility; and *dissolution*, in which the relationship is damaged beyond recovery. In renegotiation, the therapist's task is to help the patient utilize more adaptive communication patterns in the relationship. In the case of an impasse, the therapist may attempt to reopen negotiations in hopes for a successful resolution of the dispute. And with dissolution, the therapist tries to help the patient see that the relationship is in fact over and encourages her to seek other interests and relationships that will help to fill the void left by the lost relationship.

In exploring a role dispute, it is important to determine whether the dispute is indicative of a more general pattern of functioning that was also present in past disputes of a similar nature. If this is the case, the therapist can explore this pattern with the patient and can examine possible explanations for the repetitive dispute, including an examination of what the patient may gain from such a pattern.

Improvement in depressive symptoms as a result of focusing on the patient's role disputes may come about through an acceptance of the loss of a relationship and the formation of new relationships, as is the case with grief. Alternatively, if the relationship is preserved, the renewed strength of that relationship should increase the patient's perceived social support, and the successful resolution of the dispute will reduce or eliminate a chronic stressor that was associated with the maintenance of the patient's depression. Finally, analysis of repetitive patterns of disputes and communication patterns would be expected to help the patient behave more adaptively in future encounters with significant others.

Role Transitions

A large literature has linked depression with stressful life changes. Many of these changes are associated with a transition in the social role in which the individual finds himself. Although role transitions that are negative (e.g., losing a job) may understandably be associated with depression, it is critical to recognize that even role transitions that are on the surface positive may also lead to depression. For example, receiving a promotion at work may be accompanied by the stresses of the new job, fear of failing at the new position, or fear of not being worthy of the promotion. The most common role transitions are those that are associated with changes in the life cycle, including biological changes such as menopause, and those that involve changes in a social role, such as marriage or retirement. In general, role transitions that are associated with depression are characterized by feelings of helplessness in coping with the transition, by the loss of members in the social support network, and/or by the need to develop new social skills. Klerman et al. (1984) report that in most cases, the patient is aware of the transition and of the stress it is causing.

In treating depression by focusing on a role transition, IPT aims to help the patient shed the old role, mourning it if necessary, and then to acquire new skills, coping strategies, or social supports to deal more successfully with the transition. Treatment may also help the patient to see his new role in a more positive light, if this has been a problem. As the patient learns to develop and use new coping skills, including seeking social support, he will not only become better equipped to handle the stressors that are contributing to the current depression but also will learn skills that should help him to negotiate future transitions more successfully.

Interpersonal Deficits

Some depressed individuals may not have a specific interpersonal problem—a death, role transition, or dispute—on which to focus therapeutic treatment. They may, instead, demonstrate a pattern of isolation that suggests that interpersonal deficits should be the focus of treatment. Patients with interpersonal deficits have generally had trouble throughout their lives in forming and maintaining relationships. An individual with adaptive interpersonal functioning maintains close relationships with family and intimate others, comfortable relationships with friends, and appropriate relationships with work acquaintances. A depressed patient who displays interpersonal deficits may show problems in one or more of these domains as a function of maladaptive social skills, or she may exhibit a more general pattern of social isolation, with few if any meaningful relationships (cf. Gotlib & Whiffen, 1991).

Because there may be no significant current relationships on which to focus treatment, a therapist who is attempting to target interpersonal deficits may focus on past relationships, or even on the patient's relationship with the therapist, as a starting point for change. Treatment from this perspective may involve the use of communication analysis for examining relationship skills, as well as practicing role plays and techniques learned from the relationship with the therapist as strategies for fostering new relationships. The

utilization of such strategies for reducing isolation should help the patient to develop a new social network that will both reduce her current loneliness and serve as a buffer for her against future stressors.

Final Sessions

In the final three or four sessions, the therapist should address the termination of treatment. The patient may worry that he will not be able to deal with future problems without the help of the therapist. In particular, more socially impoverished patients may become anxious at the thought of losing the relationship they have developed with the therapist. Certainly, it is important to acknowledge these feelings and allow the patient to express these concerns. At the same time, however, the therapist should encourage the patient to try out and practice his newly learned strategies and techniques on his own. Independent successes achieved throughout treatment should be reinforced and highlighted to bolster the patient's confidence and self-esteem, and techniques for how the patient will handle future problems should also be discussed.

Some patients may, in fact, require further treatment after the IPT protocol has been completed. In particular, patients with more chronic personality disturbances, recurrent depressives who need maintenance treatment, and patients who do not respond successfully to treatment with IPT are most likely to need either to continue treatment in IPT or to participate in another form of therapy. For these patients, a new, longer-term therapeutic contract may be negotiated. It is important to realize, however, that most patients will experience some apprehension at the termination of treatment, and this should not be interpreted as an indication that further treatment is warranted. In fact, Klerman et al. (1984) recommend that patients wait from four to eight weeks to determine whether further treatment is necessary and appropriate.

Efficacy of IPT for Depression

The efficacy of IPT for depression has been examined in a number of clinical trials. In the first systematic study of IPT, Weissman, Prusoff, DiMascio, Neu, Goklaney, & Klerman (1979) compared acute (i.e., 16-week) IPT with or without amitriptyline with a nonscheduled control treatment, in which patients were assigned a psychiatrist they could contact but in which no treatment sessions were scheduled. The results of this study indicated that both IPT and amitriptyline alone were more effective than was the control treatment in reducing levels of depressive symptoms. Although these two treatments were equally effective in symptom reduction, they appeared to target different symptoms. Whereas IPT led to improved mood and work performance and reduced suicidal ideation and guilt, amitriptyline appeared to improve sleep, appetite disturbance, and somatic symptoms (the more "vegetative" symptoms of depression). Perhaps because of this differential symptom impact, the combination of IPT and amitriptyline was more effective than either treatment alone and more effective than the control condition (DiMascio, Weissman, Prusoff, Neu, Zwilling, & Klerman, 1979; Weissman et al., 1979). In a one-year follow-up, Weissman, Klerman, Prusoff, Sholomskas, and Padian (1981) reported that patients who had received IPT, either alone or in combination with amitriptyline, were functioning better in social activities and with their families than were patients who had received drugs alone or who were in the control treatment.

In addition, IPT was tested in the National Institute of Mental Health (NIMH) Treatment of Depression Collaborative Research Program (Elkin et al., 1989). This large-scale, multisite study tested the efficacy of IPT, cognitive-behavioral therapy (CBT), and imipramine, compared to a placebo-clinical management control condition, over a 16-week period with 250 randomly assigned depressed outpatients. Elkin et al. reported that IPT was as effective as imipramine and CBT in reducing overall symptoms of depression from pre- to posttreatment. In a secondary analysis of these data, Elkin et al. (1995) examined the role of the initial severity of the depression in the outcome of the four treatments. They found that whereas there were no significant differences among the treatment conditions for initially less severely depressed patients, imipramine and in some cases IPT were both superior to CBT for more severely depressed patients. Despite its focus on interpersonal functioning, IPT was no more effective in increasing general social functioning immediately following treatment than were the other conditions (Imber et al., 1990). There is now some evidence, however, that IPT is more effective in improving social functioning of patients with relatively better pretreatment social functioning; moreover, IPT had the worst outcome for patients with the lowest initial levels of social functioning (Sotsky et al., 1991). It appears, therefore, that for depressed patients to benefit from IPT, they must have a minimally adequate level of adaptive social functioning at the time they enter treatment.

INTERPERSONAL PSYCHOTHERAPY FOR DIFFERENT POPULATIONS OF DEPRESSED PERSONS

Although IPT was developed by Klerman et al. (1984) as a treatment for adults diagnosed with major depressive disorder, it has since been extended and adapted for other depressed populations, including adolescents, older adults, adults with recurrent depression, adults diagnosed with dysthymia, depressed adults with marital disputes, and depressed adults in primary-care settings. In this section we briefly describe these extensions of IPT.

For Depression in Adolescents (IPT-A)

It is becoming increasingly clear that the prevalence of depression among adolescents is similar to, if not greater than, that found in adults (e.g., Kessler, McGonagle, Nelson, Hughes, Swartz, & Blazer, 1994; Lewinsohn, Hops, Roberts, Seeley, & Andrews, 1993). Surprisingly, however, there has been little research on the efficacy of therapies for depression in this population (cf. Petersen, Compas, Brooks-Gunn, Stemmler, Ey, & Grant, 1993). As is the case in adulthood, there is considerable evidence that depression in adolescence is associated with interpersonal difficulties (Gotlib, Lewinsohn, & Seeley, 1995). Based on this literature, Mufson, Moreau, Weissman, and Klerman (1991, 1993) developed a manualized version of IPT for depressed adolescents.

Like the original adult version of IPT, IPT-A targets a specific problem. However, IPT-A adds a fifth problem to the four contained in IPT: the single-parent family. Mufson et al. (1991) reasoned that in addition to grief, role disputes, role transitions, and interpersonal deficits, many depressed adolescents are dealing with the separation from or loss of a parent and with authority issues that accompany the single-parent situation. Another change from the original version of IPT is the increased use of phone contact to provide additional support and establish trust between the adolescent and the therapist; the adolescent is encouraged to call the therapist as needed. The therapist is also encouraged to maintain contact with the adolescent's school system, so that progress and/or problems at school can be monitored and discussed. Finally, IPT-A also focuses on the role of the parent(s) in the adolescent's depression. Not only are therapists trained to be sensitive to concerns of the parent(s), but in addition they may be directly involved in the therapy sessions if the nature of the problems being addressed closely involves one or both parents.

Despite these differences, the goals and proposed mechanisms of IPT-A in alleviating depression are very similar to those of IPT. Data on the efficacy of IPT-A have not yet been reported; nevertheless, its manual-based format and its reliance on principles of IPT suggest that it should be a promising treatment for depression in adolescents.

For Depression in Older Adults

Although older adults have lower rates of depression than do their younger counterparts, the fact remains that between 10 and 15 percent of community-residing older adults suffer from depression at any time (Blazer & Williams, 1980; Butler & Lewis, 1982). Because older adults are more likely than younger adults to be on medications that interact adversely with antidepressants, it is critical that psychotherapeutic interventions be developed that are tailored specifically for this population. In this context, IPT may be a particularly appropriate form of psychotherapy for older adults, in large part because the foci of IPT, grief, role transitions, and social isolation (all of which have been found to be related to depression), are more common among older than younger adults.

Rothblum, Sholomskas, Berry, and Prusoff (1982) have reported the results of studies that suggest that IPT may be an effective treatment for depression in later life. Whereas IPT-LL (late life) follows the basic format we described for IPT, it has been modified from the original therapy to include concerns specific to older adults (Frank et al., 1993; Sholomskas, Chevron, Prusoff, & Berry, 1983). For example, older people who are lonely may be more likely to become dependent on the therapist, and they may seek help with practical matters such as financial problems or health-care needs. Consequently, the therapist is trained to give practical support to the patient when appropriate but also to encourage independent problem-solving skills in this population.

A second consideration for older adults is that in general they have smaller social networks than do their younger counterparts. Thus, it may not be appropriate to suggest that they discontinue or disengage from upsetting relationships. Rather, therapists working from an IPT-LL framework are trained to encourage older adults to alter their responses to these significant others and to help them to manage more adaptively any negative effect caused by contact with them. Third, Rothblum et al. (1982) note that the typical 50-minute session may be too rigid for older adults, who may not be used to talking for that long about themselves. Moreover, silences during the session that might have the effect of drawing out younger patients may be interpreted by older adults as rejection. Consequently, conducted sessions from an IPT-LL perspective may be shorter than is typical, and the therapist may make a concerted effort to be more active in the sessions. Finally, because older adults may quickly become hopeless if they do not see immediate gains in social functioning, the IPT-LL therapist is trained to select the target problem with a rapid change in mind.

For Dysthymia

Dysthymia, or chronic subthreshold depression, affects approximately 3% of adults (Weissman, Leaf, Bruce, & Florio, 1988). It is very common, however, among psychiatric outpatients, affecting up to 36% of individuals seeking psychiatric treatment (Markowitz, Moran, Koscis, & Frances, 1992). As do individuals suffering from major depression, dysthymic individuals show impairment in marital and family, leisure, and work functioning (Koscis et al., 1988a). Dysthymia has also been found to be associated not only with a high rate of comorbidity with other Axis I and Axis II disorders but also with a reduced quality of life and elevated rates of morbidity (Wells et al., 1989). Although medications can be effective in the treatment of dysthymia, up to 40% of patients either refuse medications or do not respond to them successfully (Koscis et al., 1988b).

For the treatment of dysthymia, IPT is difficult for several reasons. First, because dysthymia is a chronic state, there is quite often no acute stressor or situation that is related to the onset of the disorder. Nevertheless, a stressor may have exacerbated dysthymic symptoms, in which case that stressor should be addressed in IPT. Second, dysthymics are highly likely to show comorbid personality pathology. Indeed, investigators have estimated that the prevalence rate of Axis II disorders among individuals diagnosed with dysthymia is between 34% and 47% (e.g., Koscis et al., 1986; Koenigsberg, Kaplan, Gilmore, & Cooper, 1985). In large part because patients with characterological psychopathology may resist the idea that they have a disorder, dysthymia with Axis II comorbidity is difficult to treat with a short-term therapy such as IPT. Finally, broad interpersonal deficits are more clearly characteristic of dysthymia than they are of major depression. Although it is tempting to focus IPT for dysthymia on these broad interpersonal deficits, it is important that another, more narrow target area be chosen as well.

Mason, Markowitz, and Klerman (1993) reported pilot data from a trial of IPT for dysthymia. In this study, patients diagnosed with dysthymia who had refused medications or who had failed to respond to pharmacotherapy after 10 weeks were seen for an average of 12 weekly sessions of IPT. These patients were compared to a randomly selected subset of patients who completed at least 3 weeks of pharmacotherapy. The results of this study suggest that IPT is as effective as antidepressant medication in reducing the symptoms of dysthymia, with five of the nine patients recovering in each group. In fact, Mason et al. report that 78% of the patients who received IPT were characterized as partial or full responders to treatment, indicating that IPT may be effective in alleviating symptoms associated with dysthymia.

As Long-term Maintenance Treatment for Recurrent Depression (IPT-M)

Depression has consistently been found to be a recurrent disorder. Over 80% of depressed patients experience more than one episode over the course of their lives (Belsher & Costello, 1988; Keller, 1985). More specifically, investigators have reported that over 50% of depressed patients relapse within two years of recovery (cf. Keller & Shapiro, 1981), and data from the NIMH Collaborative Study indicate that individuals with three or more previous episodes of depression may have a relapse rate as high as 40% within only 12 to 15 weeks after recovery (Mueller et al., 1996). From the perspective of IPT, it is important to note that patients with a history of recurrent depression continue to show occupational and social impairment even after their symptoms have remitted (Billings & Moos, 1985; Frank et al., 1993). Therefore, IPT-M does not focus on the interpersonal context of an onset of a depressive episode but rather on the ongoing interpersonal context of the remitted state. The goal of IPT-M is to help the patient develop more effective strategies for coping with interpersonal stresses and to reduce or prevent recurrence of the depression.

Although IPT-M is similar to IPT in its focus on interpersonal problems, because of the longer-term nature of IPT-M more than one problem may become the focus of therapeutic change. Individuals who experience recurrent depression, especially those with comorbid personality disturbance, may be quite used to being in the sick role. Often, these patients require assistance in making the transition from the role of sick person to well person. In addition, patterns may emerge in the area of interpersonal disputes, with one or two key relationships being chronic sources of distress. In these cases the therapist helps the patient identify and modify maladaptive communication patterns that are repeatedly associated with these difficulties.

It is important to remember that IPT-M was developed in part to address interpersonal deficits that do not improve with remission of the depressive episode. Thus, the therapist using IPT-M works in a long-term fashion to encourage social contact and improve existing relationships or to help the patient form new relationships. Grief is generally addressed in short-term therapy and is not a common focus in IPT-M. If, however, a death occurs during the course of IPT-M, it is handled in much the same way as it is in acute IPT. Finally, in IPT-M, patients are instructed to monitor depressive symptoms that may indicate the early stages of a recurrence. If the therapist feels that the patient is moving toward recurrence, the therapist and patient can develop strategies to prevent it.

Klerman, DiMascio, Weissman, Prusoff, and Paykel (1974) compared an early version of IPT-M with a low-contact control treatment in a sample of women who were recovering from an acute depressive episode. Patients were assigned either to eight months of weekly IPT or to brief monthly visits (low contact) and, in addition, received amitriptyline, a placebo, or no pill. Patients who received IPT-M exhibited better occupational and family functioning than did patients who received low-contact treatment (Weissman, Klerman, Paykel, Prusoff, & Hanson, 1974); however, patients who received IPT also demonstrated greater rates of symptom relapse than did patients who were given amitriptyline (Paykel, DiMascio, Haskell, & Prusoff, 1975). Finally, patients who received a combination of IPT and amitriptyline had lower rates of relapse and better social functioning than did patients in the other treatment groups. Differences in social functioning among the groups were not apparent immediately following treatment but began to emerge six to eight months later.

More recently, Frank et al. (1990) examined the efficacy of IPT-M with a sample of patients who were experiencing their third or later episode of depression. Patients were treated with a combination of acute IPT and imipramine. Patients who responded well to treatment entered a 20-week continuation phase, in which they were seen biweekly for 8 weeks, then monthly, and were maintained on imipramine. At the end of the 20-week continuation phase, patients were randomly assigned to one of five conditions: IPT-M, IPT-M with imipramine, IPT-M with placebo, clinic visits with imipramine, or clinic visits with placebo. Patients were seen monthly for 3 years or until they had a recurrence. Results indicated that imipramine (alone or in combination with IPT-M) was highly successful in delaying the recurrence of depression. Whereas IPT-M alone or with a placebo was more effective in delaying a recurrence than were clinic visits with a placebo, IPT-M was not significantly better than maintenance imipramine in delaying recurrence. Frank et al. suggest that IPT-M may be especially useful in preventing a recurrence in patients for whom antidepressant medications are not a viable form of maintenance therapy.

For Depressed Patients with Marital Disputes (IPT-CM)

Major depression is frequently associated with marital discord (Gotlib & Beach, 1995; Gotlib & Whiffen, 1989; Weissman, 1987). Consequently, the interpersonal disputes that are examined in IPT often involve problems with a spouse. Conjoint IPT (IPT-CM) was developed by Rounsaville and colleagues (unpublished manual, cited in Weissman & Klerman, 1993) as an adaptation of IPT that included the spouse in the treatment sessions. The identified depressed patient attends sessions with his or her spouse, and although the focus of the therapy remains on alleviating depressive symptoms, the target problem is most typically the dysfunctional interpersonal relationship of the couple. Thus, IPT-CM focuses on identifying maladaptive communication patterns between the spouses and on encouraging role renegotiation in the couple's relationship.

Foley, Rounsaville, Weissman, Sholomskas, and Chevron (1989) conducted a pilot study of the efficacy of IPT-CM. This study included 18 couples in which one partner had sought treatment for depression and had identified marital disputes as the major problem associated with the onset or maintenance of the depressive episode. Patients were randomly assigned to receive 16 weeks of IPT or IPT-CM. Patients in both groups showed an improvement in both depressive symptoms and social functioning from intake to termination, and there were no significant differences between the two groups with respect to these variables. However, marital adjustment improved significantly more for patients who received IPT-CM than for those who received IPT. Given the apparent dissociation between improvement in depression and improvement in marital functioning, it will be important for investigators to examine more explicitly and systematically the nature of the association between these two variables.

In Primary-care Settings

Rates of depressive disorders have been found to be consistently higher among patients being treated by a primary-care physician than in the general population. For example, Katon and Schulberg (1992) estimated the prevalence of diagnosable depressive disorder among primary-care patients to be between 15% and 22%; moreover, individuals with affective disorders visit their doctors more frequently than do individuals without psychiatric difficulties (Katon et al., 1990). Although pharmacotherapy is an established form of treatment for depressive disorders in primary-care settings (cf. Beardsley, Gardocki, Larson, & Hidalgo, 1988), psychotherapy would clearly be valuable for those patients who refuse or do not respond successfully to medications.

In a randomized clinical trial of IPT in a primary-care setting, Schulberg and his colleagues (e.g., Brown, Schulberg, Madonia, Shear, & Houck, 1996; Schulberg et al., 1995) compared IPT with pharmacotherapy and usual care in the treatment of depression and of comorbid depression and anxiety. Both treatments lasted eight months and included an acute phase and a continuation phase. Schulberg et al. found that IPT and pharmacotherapy were equally effective in reducing depressive symptoms over the course of treatment, although IPT had a lower attrition rate than did pharmacotherapy. Nearly two-thirds of the depressed patients treated by either IPT or pharmacotherapy recovered from their depression by the completion of the study. Although patients with comorbid depression and generalized anxiety disorder also responded equally well to both treatments, only one-third of depressed patients with comorbid panic disorder had recovered by the end of treatment (about half of the recovery rate obtained for pure depression). These findings suggest that depression that is comorbid with panic disorder may represent a particularly intractable form of the disorder.

EXTENSIONS OF IPT TO OTHER DISORDERS AND PROBLEMS

For Subclinical Disorders and Emotional Distress

Whereas a considerable proportion of primary-care patients are suffering from a diagnosable affective disorder, a far greater number are likely to be experiencing lower levels of dysphoria due to life stresses. Patients who enter the primary-care system with physical complaints that may be due in large part to psychological distress may be better treated with psychotherapy than with pharmacotherapy. Unfortunately, it is not feasible to expect trained therapists to be on hand to offer psychotherapy in such cases. With this in mind, Weissman and Klerman (1988) developed interpersonal counseling (IPC) for treating stress and distress in a primary-care setting. This is a brief intervention of up to six 30-minute sessions that can be administered by nurse practitioners or other medical staff after 8 to 12 hours of training. Modeled after IPT, IPC is a condensed therapy that addresses one of the four problems outlined in IPT, with the exception that loneliness and social isolation is substituted for the area of interpersonal deficits. The goals of IPC are to reduce stress, enhance social functioning, and ultimately to reduce inappropriate or excessive use of the physical health-care system. Weissman and Klerman suggest that patients be referred to IPC if they exhibit signs of stress or distress, either observed by the intake worker or derived through a questionnaire such as the General Health Questionnaire (GHQ; Goldberg, 1979).

During the first two sessions of IPC, the therapist and patient review the patient's psychological symptoms, and the patient completes a life events checklist and interpersonal inventory. The therapist offers a formulation of the patient's stress and distress in one of the four problems. In the intermediate three sessions, the therapist and patient discuss strategies for coping with the problem. Finally, in the sixth session, they deal with issues of termination, including encouragement of the patient's independent use of the coping strategies he has learned and discussion of how he will deal with further stresses, either on his own or with the help of his support network.

Unlike IPT, if a patient feels better at any point during the intervention she is not encouraged to continue with IPC. Another difference between IPC and IPT is that homework is assigned explicitly in IPC in an attempt to alleviate distress in the shorter time frame. For example, the life events checklist may be assigned to the patient to complete for homework after the first session; or patients may be instructed to try a new strategy for dealing with the problem between sessions, and the results of the homework are then discussed in the next session.

Klerman et al. (1987) examined the effectiveness of IPC in a pilot study with 128 patients in a primary-care clinic who scored a 6 or higher on the GHQ; half of these patients participated in IPC, and the 64 gender-matched control patients were followed with care as usual. Patients referred for IPC were screened for psychiatric diagnoses, and although many were experiencing depression, dysthymia, phobias, or other disorders, only two were referred for psychiatric care because of severe psychopathology. Patients receiving IPC completed the GHQ again after the last session; whereas the control patients completed the GHQ six weeks after inclusion in the study. By the end of treatment, 83% of the IPC group scored 4 or lower on the GHQ (the normal range), whereas only 63% of the control patients attained this "recovered" status. Only 22% of the subjects completed all six sessions, and symptom reduction was found to be unrelated to the number of sessions completed. The two groups did not differ significantly in subsequent health-care utilization; in fact, there was a trend for patients in the IPC group to use the health-care system *more* than those in the control group in the year following the intervention.

Similar results were reported by Mossey, Knott, Higgins, and Telerico (1996), who examined the efficacy of IPC for older adults suffering from "sub-dysthymic depressive symptoms." Mossey et al. found that compared to usual care, older adults who received IPC showed improved depressive symptoms, general health, and physical and social functioning three months after treatment. The gains for depressive symptoms remained significant six months after the intervention. Clearly, therefore, although IPC appears to be a promising treatment, further research is required both to examine the mechanism through which it may work and to attempt to refine the treatment to reduce subsequent health-care utilization of IPC participants.

For Bulimia

Although the primary difficulties in bulimia involve body image and eating dysfunction, patients are also typically characterized by elevated levels of depressive and anxious symptoms, as well as by impaired social functioning. For many bulimic individuals, their self-worth is derived from their weight or appearance. Because of the anxiety and low self-esteem that stems from this judgment, many bulimic individuals experience considerable social isolation.

A reasonably large body of empirical research has supported the use of CBT in the treatment of bulimia (cf. Fairburn, Agras, & Wilson, 1992). It has been found to be as effective as antidepressant medication for reducing the binging and purging of individuals with eating disorders, and it appears to have a powerful effect on the level of dietary restraint. Fairburn and colleagues (Fairburn et al., 1991; Fairburn, Jones, Peveler, Hope, & O'Connor, 1993) included IPT in a treatment outcome study of CBT as a comparison form of therapy that did not address self-monitoring or education about eating and weight issues. Whereas the symptoms of patients who received CBT improved more rapidly during therapy than did symptoms of patients who received IPT, the latter continued to improve over the one-year follow-up period, demonstrating a reduction of symptoms over that period that was equivalent to that exhibited by CBT patients. This is an intriguing finding because weight and body concerns were addressed only in the initial phase in which patients identified interpersonal problems that they believed brought on or exacerbated their eating problems. Patients in both treatment groups demonstrated improved social functioning following therapy, with no significant differences between patients who received CBT and those who were treated with IPT. Thus, IPT appears to be a promising treatment for bulimia. In fact, IPT is currently being compared to CBT in both efficacy and mechanisms of action in a

multisite study of 200 bulimic women (cf. Fairburn, 1993).

For Substance Abuse

Individuals who abuse drugs have been found to experience widespread psychological impairment. Compared with their nonabusing counterparts, they are more likely to be depressed (Rounsaville, Weissman, & Kleber, 1983; Rounsaville, Weissman, Kleber, & Wilbur, 1982) and to demonstrate impairments in their social and interpersonal functioning (McLellan et al. 1981; Ramer, Zaslove, & Langan, 1971). Based on these findings, Rounsaville and his colleagues (e.g., Carroll, Rounsaville, & Gawin, 1991; Rounsaville & Carroll, 1993; Rounsaville, Glazer, Wilber, Weissman, & Kleber, 1983) adapted IPT for substance-abusing patients.

Traditionally, opioid-addicted patients do not respond well to psychotherapeutic interventions. They either fail to become engaged in treatment or they discontinue treatment early, have a high relapse rate, and engage in impulsive behaviors that can sabotage the benefits of therapy (e.g., Brill, 1977). However, there is recent evidence that psychotherapy can be effective for opioid-addicted patients who are receiving maintenance methadone treatment (Woody et al., 1983). Thus, Rounsaville, Glazer, Wilber, Weissman, and Kleber (1983) conducted a clinical trial in which IPT was compared with a low-contact control condition in the treatment of methadone-maintained opioid addicts. As expected, attrition was high in both groups, with only 38% of the patients in the IPT group and 54% of the patients in the control group completing the 24 weeks of treatment. Nevertheless, patients in both groups improved as a result of treatment. Patients who received IPT did not exhibit greater improvement than did patients in the low-contact control condition, who received only one 20-minute session each month, in which a clinician reviewed the patient's situation but avoided giving feedback. Similar results were reported by Carroll et al. (1991), who compared the efficacy of IPT with that of relapse prevention (RP) in the treatment of cocaine-abusing patients. Again, attrition was high, with only 38% of the patients assigned to IPT and 66% of the patients assigned to RP completing the 12 weeks of treatment. Consistent with Rounsaville et al.'s results, Carroll found no overall outcome differences between the two treatment groups, although RP was more effective than IPT in helping the most severe abusers achieve abstinence. It appears, therefore, that IPT is not effective in the treatment of substance abuse, either as the primary treatment or as an adjunct to pharmacotherapy.

CONCLUDING COMMENTS

In this chapter we described the theoretical and empirical foundations for the use of interpersonal therapy for depression and other psychiatric or emotional disorders. Overall, and consistent with the theoretical underpinnings of IPT, the empirical evidence indicates that compared to low-contact or usual-care control conditions, IPT is effective in reducing symptoms of depression, dysthymia, subclinical distress, and bulimia (e.g., Elkin et al., 1989; Fairburn et al., 1991, 1993; Klerman et al., 1987; Mason et al., 1993; Mossey et al., 1996; Weissman et al., 1979); it is interesting that IPT was found to be no more effective than low-contact care in the treatment of substance abuse (Carroll et al., 1991; Rounsaville, Glazer, Wilber, Weissman, & Kleber, 1983). In reviewing this body of research, it is clear that a major unresolved issue involves the mechanisms through which IPT reduces depressive symptoms. In this final section, therefore, we discuss this issue, as well as a number of related concerns, and we offer suggestions for future research in this area.

Klerman et al. (1984) posit that IPT reduces symptoms of depression or dysphoria by improving interpersonal functioning. Data on the posttreatment social functioning of patients who have received IPT suggest that this may not be the mechanism by which IPT works. Indeed, there has not been a single study in which patients treated with IPT exhibited a greater improvement in social functioning following treatment than those who received other forms of therapy. In fact, advantages in social functioning for patients treated with IPT do not seem to occur until at least 6 to 12 months after therapy, which is often several months after they have exhibited symptomatic improvement (Imber et al., 1990; Paykel et al., 1975; Weissman et al., 1981). The fact that depressive symptoms are reduced in many patients over the course of treatment with IPT suggests that this therapy does not improve depression by changing the patients' quality of interpersonal functioning, or at least does not reduce levels of depression by improving interper-

sonal functioning to a greater degree than is the case with antidepressant medication or other forms of psychotherapy.

In the case of bulimia, symptom reduction takes a slower course and actually resembles more closely the time course represented by changes in interpersonal functioning (Fairburn et al., 1991, 1993). Part of the reason for the different time course for depression and bulimia treated with IPT may involve the presence in therapy of an explicit focus on problematic symptoms. Whereas IPT for depression targets depressive symptoms explicitly in treatment sessions, IPT for bulimia does not deal directly with dieting and weight issues. Thus, the slower course of symptom reduction in bulimia may be due to the indirect focus on symptomatic improvement. It is possible, of course, that the gradual interpersonal gains exhibited by bulimic patients in IPT over the follow-up year led to the reduction of symptoms over that same time frame. The comparable treatment results of IPT and CBT in these studies, of course, render this possibility less parsimonious than one would like. Nevertheless, there are no studies explicitly testing this possibility, and this is clearly a critical direction for future research. Indeed, studies that include repeated assessments of interpersonal functioning over a long follow-up period will undoubtedly be instructive in helping to understand the mechanisms by which symptoms of bulimia remit in response to treatment with IPT and CBT.

However, IPT does appear to effect long-term changes in interpersonal functioning that are observed in patients up to a year following treatment (Weissman et al., 1981), and it is reasonable from Klerman et al.'s (1984) model of therapy to expect that these changes would prevent or delay relapse. In fact, this does not appear to be the case. Instead, IPT has been associated with a *higher* rate of relapse than pharmacotherapy (Paykel et al., 1975). Moreover, IPT does not seem to delay the recurrence of depression beyond the effects accounted for by antidepressant medications (Frank et al., 1990). The fact that improvement in interpersonal functioning emerges gradually in the year following treatment, rather than during the treatment phase, suggests that these are stable changes in behavior. The ineffectiveness of this interpersonal improvement in preventing future depressive episodes, however, calls into question the strategy of targeting interpersonal functioning as a vehicle for effecting lasting therapeutic change.

Finally, the literature that we have reviewed in this chapter suggests that there are several patient groups for whom IPT is more or less effective. For example, there is some evidence that it is more effective for those individuals who are characterized by higher levels of pretreatment social functioning (Sotsky et al., 1991). In addition, although combining IPT-M with maintenance pharmacotherapy seems broadly to increase the prevention of depression relapse (Paykel et al., 1975), this does not appear to be the case for individuals who experience recurrent episodes of depression (Frank et al., 1990). Consistent with the current emphasis in psychotherapy research on matching treatments and patients, it is important that future studies examine more explicitly the effectiveness of IPT for different subgroups of individuals, perhaps stratified by initial levels of interpersonal functioning or by subtype of depression.

To conclude, there is little question that IPT is an effective treatment for several disorders, including depressive disorders, subclinical distress, and bulimia. The mechanisms by which IPT achieves its effects, however, are less clear and do not appear to be those formulated by Klerman et al. (1984). Moreover, the broad types of disorders and subtypes of patients for whom IPT is most effective have yet to be determined. It is imperative that future research focus both on an examination of the "active ingredients" of IPT, that is, the mechanisms through which IPT effects changes in symptoms, and on the conditions under which IPT is most successful in bringing about therapeutic change. Such foci should serve to refine IPT and improve its efficacy, as well as to help us gain a better understanding of the nature of the relation between interpersonal functioning and symptoms of psychopathology.

CASE EXAMPLE

Bob S., a 25-year-old Hispanic male, sought treatment for depression. He reported that he first began to experience symptoms of depression in college after he moved away from his family in Mexico. Throughout the past several years, he has experienced a persistent sad mood, as well as sleep disturbance, fatigue, and feelings of worthlessness. He has also been plagued by recurrent thoughts of suicide and reports having constructed elaborate plans to kill himself. During these bouts of suicidality, he reports calling friends, contact with whom would boost his mood. Until now he has avoided seeking treatment, believing that he should be able to work through his problems on his own; his friends have now convinced him, however, to seek help from a mental health professional.

Mr. S.'s primary difficulty is with loneliness. He feels that the people he has met since moving to the United States do not exhibit the same level of love and concern for others as the people with whom he grew up. He does not believe that he needs psychological treatment, and he states repeatedly that if people were kinder to him, he would not be depressed. He has not made any close friends in the seven years since he moved, but he does remain in contact with two close friends from Mexico, as well as with his mother and sister.

Initial Phase (Sessions 1–2)

Upon being probed about the interpersonal context of his depression, Mr. S. reports that his depression is primarily due to a failure to find a loving romantic partner. He does occasionally date, but these brief contacts do not lead to intimacy or love. Several years earlier, he dated a woman for several months, during which time his depression lessened. She broke off contact with him, however, without explanation. He spends considerable time and effort in seeking love and intimacy, both from romantic partners and from friends, but has not been successful. In reporting a recent failed date, Mr. S. becomes quite emotional. During this emotional reporting, he states that his father died in a car accident when he was 13 years old. He does not believe that his father's death is relevant to his current depression, and he resists talking about any feelings of grief. The association of his father's death with rejection by a woman, compounded by Mr. S.'s avoidance of the topic, suggests to the therapist that the grief has not been adequately resolved.

Because of the severity of Mr. S.'s depression and the level of his suicidal ideation, the therapist decides that he would benefit from immediate pharmacotherapy. In addition, the therapist selects two problem areas in dealing with the interpersonal context of Mr. S.'s depression. First, the therapist determines that grief for the death of Mr. S.'s father must be resolved before any strides can be taken in current relationships. The general strategy in dealing with Mr. S.'s grief is to explore in detail his reaction to his father's death, facilitating a normal mourning process if appropriate.

Second, Mr. S. exhibits problems with interpersonal deficits. He clings strongly to the relationships he has, and his inappropriate level of emotional dependence on new acquaintances appears to frighten away potential friends and partners. Mr. S. self-discloses excessively to new acquaintances, telling them about his depression and suicidality very soon after meeting them, which serves to thwart his efforts to make new social contacts.

By the second session, Mr. S. is still quite depressed but is no longer suicidal. He agrees to discuss his father's death, so long as that is not the sole focus of therapy. It soon becomes evident that Mr. S. stepped into the role of "man of the house" shortly after his father's death. He reports crying at his father's funeral and then "putting away his tears and taking care of his family." Mr. S. is extremely loyal, and his family is the most important thing in his life. When asked who took care of him during this emotional period, Mr. S. laughs and said that he took care of himself. His mother and sister reportedly depend heavily on him. His mother constantly states that she would be lost without her son. When he did show sadness or weakness, his mother would "fall apart," saying that she had nothing left to live for. Mr. S. soon learned to keep his feelings to himself.

Intermediate Phase (Sessions 3–8)

In session 3, Mr. S. further discusses the period following his father's death. He acknowledges that he had never really mourned his father and that he resents his mother in some ways for forcing him to grow up too quickly. He also discusses his fear of entering a relationship with a woman in which he could not show his feelings. Mr. S. realizes that his excessive displays of emotion early in relationships frighten most people away; he feels, however, that only people who "stick with him through it" are worth having in his life. When asked if he would be lonely if he could not find such a person, Mr. S. becomes visibly upset. Toward the end of the session, the therapist asks Mr. S. how his mother is doing now and how she might respond if he were to voice his buried feelings of grief to her. He says that she is doing much better and that he will give it a try. They agree that he will talk to his mother about his grief that week and discuss it in the following session.

In session 4, Mr. S. reports that he did indeed see his mother during the past week and that he told her that he needed to talk about his father.

His mother acknowledged that she had leaned on him heavily after his father died and that he had helped her to get through it. He then asked her who had helped him to get through it. His mother held him as they both cried and talked about Mr. S.'s father and the things they missed about him. Although he acknowledges that the talk with his mother went well, he is angry at the therapist for raising old feelings. Mr. S. feels that he has gotten over his father's death and that the therapist is disturbing his peace. The session is spent discussing the difference between ignoring feelings and true acceptance of the death. By the end of the session, Mr. S. acknowledges that talking to his mother was helpful in resolving the anger he has felt since his father's death. Together, the therapist and Mr. S. decide to move on to Mr. S.'s problem with loneliness.

Mr. S. begins session 5 by apologizing to the therapist for his behavior the previous week. He states that he thought about his father all week and that he can now begin to think about that time in his life without feeling angry or hostile. Although thoughts of his father still elicit sadness, Mr. S. says that it is a "good sadness" of missing his father rather than feeling abandoned by his father and used by his family. For the remainder of the session, the therapist asks Mr. S. to talk about his expectations in relationships, both friendships and romances. Mr. S. indicates that he is looking for genuine and caring people, but he places much less emphasis on their ability to deal with his depression than he did in session 3. In fact, he now seems much less depressed than he had in the previous sessions. Mr. S. still reports experiencing a sad mood but, at the same time, notes that he is sleeping better and seems to have more energy.

The therapist suggests that Mr. S.'s early disclosures may be scaring people off before they get a chance to really know him. Mr. S. and the therapist discuss strategies for starting to develop friendships without high levels of emotional disclosure. Together they identify other interests that Mr. S. could talk about with new social partners. Mr. S. agrees to seek new friendships and to refrain from disclosing highly personal information and emotions until the other person has indicated an interest in deepening the friendship.

In session 6, Mr. S. discusses his frustration at trying to meet new people. He reports approaching several coworkers and asking them to go to lunch or for drinks after work, but he did not yet have any luck in this regard. The therapist suggests that Mr. S. try to think of ways to get people together based on common interests, and they discuss strategies to meet this goal. Mr. S., an avid rock climber, decides to organize a rock-climbing excursion for some coworkers who had expressed an interest in this activity. He also decides to join a wine-tasting group organized by his sister. The therapist and Mr. S. discuss his expectations for these group activities, making sure that they are realistic. They discuss Mr. S.'s hopes for instant friendship and outline a more reasonable time frame for the development of close relationships. Mr. S. again expresses his dislike of "American coldness" but concedes that his expectations in prior relationships have not led to success.

By session 7, Mr. S. had gone to his first wine-tasting group and had met several new people. He states that he had a very good time but expresses disappointment that he had not felt an immediate bond with anyone there. He also organized a rock-climbing trip with three of his male coworkers to take place in the coming week. Mr. S. is disappointed that none of the women at work expressed an interest in the trip. These feelings are consistent with a pattern on Mr. S.'s part to enter social interactions with unrealistically high expectations, which are seldom met. The therapist and Mr. S. spend the remainder of the session discussing these expectations. Although Mr. S. is not as depressed as he was in earlier sessions, he nevertheless continues to be dissatisfied with his life. Mr. S. agrees with the therapist that because he receives all of his enjoyment from close relationships, he places very high expectations on every social encounter, hoping it will lead to deep friendship or love. Consequently, the therapist and Mr. S. spend the remainder of the session examining domains from which Mr. S. may get satisfaction other than close social ties.

Session 8 finds Mr. S. in a significantly better mood. The rock-climbing excursion was a success, and he has already planned a second trip. Because Mr. S. was the only one with climbing experience, he took on the role of instructor for the group, teaching them about safety practices and climbing technique. He feels good that his coworkers have seen him as competent, and he is proud of his mastery of this sport. In addition, Mr. S. was also able to satisfy, at least to some extent, his need for intimacy because his coworkers trusted him to set up the rope anchors and backup systems to ensure that no one got hurt. Mr. S. reports that he is looking forward to the next trip, and a larger number of coworkers are interested in going. He has decided to continue the rock-climbing trips but stop attending the wine tastings because he hasn't felt any connection with the people there.

Termination Phase (Sessions 9–12)

In session 9, Mr. S. reports that he went to lunch with his mother and had a wonderful time. He has developed a much closer relationship with her since they talked intimately several weeks earlier. Mr. S. also went for drinks after work with one of the men from the rock-climbing trip. The therapist raises the issue of termination, and Mr. S. becomes rather quiet. When the therapist probes Mr. S. about his feelings, Mr. S states that he hasn't yet built any close relationships and does not feel ready to leave the therapeutic relationship. The therapist encourages Mr. S to consider the progress he has made since the start of therapy and reminds him that they have three sessions remaining.

In session 10 the therapist and Mr. S. discuss Mr. S.'s progress in therapy and talk about strategies for maintaining this improvement after termination. The therapist assures Mr. S. that he is on the right track. His relationship with his mother has improved, and he is starting to form closer friendships with his coworkers. Mr. S. also has a framework set up for meeting new people. Finally, the therapist and Mr. S. discuss how he can continue to maintain reasonable expectations as his relationships with coworkers and other acquaintances become closer.

In session 11, Mr. S. expresses some dissatisfaction with the distance he is maintaining in his new relationships. He reports feeling that he is being "phony" by holding back his emotions, and he expresses doubts that he will ever get close to these new friends if he does not share his feelings. The therapist discusses appropriate disclosure with Mr. S. They role-play, and Mr. S. practices reading social signals from partners that would indicate whether they are ready for more intimate disclosure. The therapist raises the issue of termination again, and in this session Mr. S. seems more accepting of it. He asks the therapist if he can call if he has a crisis, and they agree that that would be appropriate. The therapist and Mr. S. also decide that he should continue on maintenance medication until he feels more stable in his nondepressed state.

In session 12, the final session, the therapist reviews Mr. S.'s progress with him. They discuss the success of his new style of dealing with acquaintances and how that style would transfer to potential romantic partners. The therapist congratulates Mr. S. on the strides he has taken and encourages him to continue to pursue outside interests even after his social network becomes stronger. Mr. S. expresses his satisfaction with the therapy and thanks the therapist for helping him through a difficult time.

Summary

Mr. S. experienced nearly a complete remission over the course of therapy. His grief was adequately resolved, which also led to a strengthened relationship with his mother. His interpersonal deficits were also somewhat improved, and he was able to start up several social relationships. His social network was still quite delicate at the end of therapy, but Mr. S. learned skills that could help him to build a more stable social network. Given his interpersonal deficits and because his symptoms responded to IPT, Mr. S. is a likely candidate for IPT-M.

References

Arrindell, W. A., & Emmelkamp, P. M. G. (1986). Marital adjustment, intimacy, and needs in female agoraphobics and their partners: A controlled study. *British Journal of Psychiatry, 149,* 592–602.

Beardsley, R., Gardocki, G., Larson, D., & Hidalgo, J. (1988). Prescribing of psychotropic medication by primary care physicians and psychiatrists. *Archives of General Psychiatry, 45,* 1117–1119.

Belsher, G., & Costello, C. G. (1988). Relapse after recovery from unipolar depression: A critical review. *Psychological Bulletin, 104,* 84–96.

Bifulco, A., & Brown, G. W. (1996). Cognitive coping response to crises and onset of depression. *Social Psychiatry and Psychiatric Epidemiology, 31,* 163–172.

Billings, A. G., Cronkite, R. C., & Moos, R. H. (1983). Social-environmental factors in unipolar depression: Comparisons of depressed patients and nondepressed controls. *Journal of Abnormal Psychology, 92,* 119–133.

Billings, A. G., & Moos, R. H. (1982). Psychosocial theory and research on depression: An integrative framework and review. *Clinical Psychology Review, 2,* 213–237.

Billings, A. G., & Moos, R. H. (1985). Psychosocial processes of remission in unipolar depression: Comparing depressed patients with matched community controls. *Journal of Consulting and Clinical Psychology, 53,* 314–325.

Blazer, D. G., & Williams, C. D. (1980). Epidemiology of dysphoria and depression in an elderly population. *American Journal of Psychiatry, 137,* 439–444.

Booth, B. M., Russell, D. W., Soucek, S., & Laughlin, P. R. (1992). Social support and alcoholism treatment: An exploratory analysis. *American Journal of Drug and Alcohol Abuse, 18,* 87–101.

Brill, L. (1977). The treatment of drug abuse: Evolution of a perspective. *American Journal of Psychiatry, 134,* 157–160.

Brim, J., Witcoff, C., & Wetzel, R. D. (1982). Social network characteristics of hospitalized depressed patients. *Psychological Reports, 50,* 423–433.

Brown, C., Schulberg, H. C., Madonia, M. J., Shear, M. K., & Houck, P. R. (1996). Treatment outcomes for primary care patients with major depression and lifetime anxiety disorders. *American Journal of Psychiatry, 153,* 1293–1300.

Brown, G. W., & Harris, T. O. (1978). *Social origins of depression.* London: Free Press.

Brown, G. W., & Harris, T. O. (1989). Depression. In G. W. Brown & T. O. Harris (Eds.), *Life events and illness* (pp. 49–93). New York: Guilford.

Burglass, D., Clarke, A. J., Henderson, A. S., Kreitman, A., Kreitman, N., & Presley, A. S. (1977). A study of agoraphobic housewives. *Psychological Medicine, 7,* 73–86.

Butler, R. N., & Lewis, M. (1982). *Aging and mental health* (3rd ed.). St. Louis, MO: Mosby.

Carroll, K. M., Rounsaville, B. J., & Gawin, F. H. (1991). A comparative trial of psychotherapies for ambuatory cocaine abusers: Relapse prevention and interpersonal psychotherapy. *American Journal of Drug and Alcohol Abuse, 17,* 229–247.

DiMascio, A., Weissman, M. M., Prusoff, B. A., Neu, C., Zwilling, M., & Klerman, G. L. (1979). Differential symptom reduction by drugs and psychotherapy in acute depression. *Archives of General Psychiatry, 36,* 1450–1456.

Elkin, I., Gibbons, R. D., Shea, M. T., Sotsky, S. M., Watkins, J. T., Pilkonis, P. A., & Hedeker, D. (1995). Initial severity and differential treatment outcome in the National Institute of Mental Health Treatment of Depression Collaborative Research Program. *Journal of Consulting and Clinical Psychology, 63,* 841–847.

Elkin, I., Shea, M. T., Watkins, J. T., Imber, S. D., Sotsky, S. M., Collins, J. F., Glass, D. R., Pilkonis, P. A., Leber, W. R., Docherty, J. P., Fiester, S. J., & Parloff, M. B. (1989). National Institute of Mental Health Treatment of Depression Collaborative Research Program. *Archives of General Psychiatry, 46,* 971–982.

Fairburn, C. G. (1993). Interpersonal psychotherapy for bulimia nervosa. In G. L. Klerman & M. M. Weissman (Eds.), *New applications of interpersonal psychotherapy* (pp. 353–378). Washington, DC: American Psychiatric Press.

Fairburn, C. G., Agras, W. S., & Wilson, G. T. (1992). The research on the treatment of bulimia nervosa: Practical and theoretical implications. In G. H. Anderson & S. H. Kennedy (Eds.), *The biology of feast and famine: Relevance to eating disorders* (pp. 318–340). New York: Academic Press.

Fairburn, C. G., Jones, R., Peveler, R. C., Carr, S. J., Solomon, R. A., O'Connor, M. E., Burton, J., & Hope, R. A. (1991). Three psychological treatments for bulimia nervosa: A comparative trial. *Archives of General Psychiatry, 48*, 463–469.

Fairburn, C. G., Jones, R., Peveler, R. C., Hope, R. A., & O'Connor, M. E. (1993). Psychotherapy and bulimia nervosa: Longer term effects of interpersonal psychotherapy, behavior therapy, and cognitive behavior therapy. *Archives of General Psychiatry, 50*, 419–428.

Foley, S. H., Rounsaville, B. J., Weissman, M. M., Sholomskas, D., & Chevron, E. (1989). Individual versus conjoint interpersonal psychotherapy for depressed patients with marital disputes. *International Journal of Family Psychiatry, 10*, 29–42.

Frank, E., Frank, N., Cornes, C., Imber, S. D., Miller, M. D., Morris, S. M., & Reynolds, C. F. (1993). Interpersonal psychotherapy in the treatment of late-life depression. In G. L. Klerman & M. M. Weissman (Eds.), *New applications of interpersonal psychotherapy* (pp. 167–198). Washington, DC: American Psychiatric Press.

Frank, E., Kupfer, D. J., Perel, J. M., Cornes, C., Jarrett, D. B., Mallinger, A. G., Thase, M. E., McEachran, A. B., & Grochocinski, V. J. (1990). Three-year outcomes for maintenance therapies in recurrent depression. *Archives of General Psychiatry, 47*, 1093–1099.

Goldberg, D. P. (1979). Detection of and assessment of emotional disorders in primary care. *International Journal of Mental Health, 8*, 30–48.

Goldstein, M. J., & Miklowitz, D. J. (1995). The effectiveness of psychoeducational family therapy in the treatment of schizophrenic disorders. *Journal of Marital and Family Therapy, 21*, 361–376.

Gotlib, I. H., & Beach, S. R. H. (1995). A marital/family discord model of depression: Implications for therapeutic intervention. In N. S. Jacobson & A. S. Gurman (Eds.), *Clinical handbook of couple therapy* (pp. 411–436). New York: Guilford.

Gotlib, I. H., & Hooley, J. M. (1988). Depression and marital distress: Current status and future directions. In S. Duck (Ed.), *Handbook of personal relationships* (pp. 543–570). Chichester, Eng.: Wiley.

Gotlib, I. H., Lewinsohn, P. M., & Seeley, J. R. (1995). Symptoms versus a diagnosis of depression: Differences in psychosocial functioning. *Journal of Consulting and Clinical Psychology, 63*, 90–100.

Gotlib, I. H., & McCabe, S. B. (1990). Marriage and psychopathology: A critical examination. In F. Fincham & T. Bradbury (Eds.), *The psychology of marriage: Conceptual, empirical, and applied perspectives* (pp. 226–257). New York: Guilford.

Gotlib, I. H., & Robinson, L. A. (1982). Responses to depressed individuals: Discrepancies between self-report and observer-rated behavior. *Journal of Abnormal Psychology, 91*, 231–240.

Gotlib, I. H., & Whiffen, V. E. (1989). Depression and marital functioning: An examination of specificity and gender differences. *Journal of Abnormal Psychology, 98*, 23–30.

Gotlib, I. H., & Whiffen, V. E. (1991). The interpersonal context of depression: Implications for theory and research. In W. H. Jones & D. Perlman (Eds.), *Advances in personal relationships* (Vol. 3, pp. 177–206). London: Jessica Kingsley.

Gurtman, M. B. (1986). Depression and the response of others: Reevaluating the reevaluation. *Journal of Abnormal Psychology, 95*, 99–101.

Haenninen, V., & Aro, H. (1996). Sex differences in coping and depression among adults. *Social Science and Medicine, 43*, 1453–1460.

Hammen, C. (1991). The generation of stress in the course of unipolar depression. *Journal of Abnormal Psychology, 100*, 555–561.

Hand, I., Lamontagne, Y., & Marks, I. M. (1974). Group exposure (flooding) in vivo for agoraphobics. *British Journal of Psychiatry, 124*, 588–602.

Hawkins, J. D., & Fraser, M. W. (1985). Social networks of street drug users: A comparison of two theories. *Social Work Research and Abstracts, 21*, 3–12.

Hooley, J. M., & Teasdale, J. D. (1989). Predictors of relapse in unipolar depressives: Expressed emotion, marital distress, and perceived criticism. *Journal of Abnormal Psychology, 98*, 229–235.

Howes, M. J., & Hokanson, J. E. (1979). Conversational and social responses to depressive interpersonal behavior. *Journal of Abnormal Psychology, 88*, 625–634.

Huba, G. J., Wingard, J. A., & Bentler, P. M. (1980). Applications of a theory of drug use to prevention programs. *Journal of Drug Education, 10*, 25–38.

Imber, S. D., Pilkonis, P. A., Sotsky, S. M., Elkin, I., Watkins, J. T., Collins, J. F., Shea, M. T., Leber, W. R., & Glass, D. R. (1990). Mode-specific effects among three treatments for depression. *Journal of Consulting and Clinical Psychology, 58*, 352–359.

Katon, W., & Schulberg, H. (1992). Epidemiology of depression in primary care. *General Hospital Psychiatry, 14*, 237–247.

Katon, W., Von Korff, M., Lin, E., Lipscomb, P., Russo, J., Wagner, E., & Polk, E. (1990). Distressed high utilizers of medical care:

DSM-III-R diagnoses and treatment needs. *General Hospital Psychiatry, 12*, 355–362.

Kavanagh, D. J. (1992). Recent developments in expressed emotion and schizophrenia. *British Journal of Psychiatry, 47*, 665–671.

Keller, M. B. (1985). Chronic and recurrent affective disorders: Incidence, course, and influencing factors. In D. Kemali & G. Recagni (Eds.), *Chronic treatments in neuropsychiatry* (pp. 111–120). New York: Raven Press.

Keller, M. B., & Shapiro, R. W. (1981). Major depressive disorder: Initial results from a one-year prospective naturalistic follow-up study. *Journal of Nervous and Mental Disorders, 169*, 761–768.

Kessler, R. C., McGonagle, K. A., Nelson, C. B., Hughes, M., Swartz, M., & Blazer, D. G. (1994). Sex and depression in the National Comorbidity Survey: II. Cohort effects. *Journal of Affective Disorders, 30*, 15–26.

Klerman, G. L., Budman, S,. Berwick, D., Weissman, M. M., Damico-White, J., Demby, A., & Feldstein, M. (1987). Efficacy of a brief psychosocial intervention for symptoms of stress and distress among patients in primary care. *Medical Care, 25*, 1078–1088.

Klerman, G. L., DiMascio, A., Weissman, M. M., Prusoff, B. A., & Paykel, E. S. (1974). Treatment of depression by drugs and psychotherapy. *American Journal of Psychiatry, 131*, 186–191.

Klerman, G. L., Weissman, M. M., Rounsaville, B. J., & Chevron, E. S. (1984). *Interpersonal psychotherapy of depression.* New York: Basic Books.

Koenigsberg, H. W., Kaplan, R. D., Gilmore, M. M., & Cooper, A. M. (1985). The relationship between syndrome and personality disorder in DSM-III experience with 2,462 patients. *American Journal of Psychiatry, 142*, 207–212.

Koscis, J. H., Frances, A. J., Voss, C., Mason, B. J., et al. (1988a). Imipramine and social-vocational adjustment in chronic depression. *American Journal of Psychiatry, 145*, 997–999.

Koscis, J. H., Frances, A. J., Voss, C., Mann, J. J., et al. (1988b). Imipramine treatment for chronic depression. *Archives of General Psychiatry, 45*, 253–257.

Koscis, J. H., Voss, C., Mann, J. J., et al. (1986). Chronic depression: Demographic and clinical characteristics. *Psychopharmacology Bulletin, 22*, 192–195.

Lewinsohn, P. M., Hops, H., Roberts, R. E., Seeley, J. R., & Andrews, J. A. (1993). Adolescent psychopathology: I. Prevalence and incidence of depression and other DSM-III-R disorders in high school students. *Journal of Abnormal Psychology, 102*, 133–144.

Lloyd, C. (1980a). Life events and depressive disorder reviewed. I. Events as predisposing factors. *Archives of General Psychiatry, 37*, 529–535.

Lloyd, C. (1980b). Life events and depressive disorder reviewed. II. Events as precipitating factors. *Archives of General Psychiatry, 37*, 541–548.

Markowitz, J. C., Moran, M. E., Koscis, J. H., & Frances, A. J. (1992). Prevalence and comorbidity of dysthymic disorder. *Journal of Affective Disorders, 24*, 63–71.

Markowitz, J. S., Weissman, M. M., Ouellette, R., Lish, J. D., & Klerman, G. L. (1989). Quality of life in panic disorder. *Archives of General Psychiatry, 46*, 984–992.

Mason, B. J., Markowitz, J. C., & Klerman, G. L. (1993). Interpersonal psychotherapy for dysthymic disorders. In G. L. Klerman & M. M. Weissman (Eds.), *New applications of interpersonal psychotherapy* (pp. 225–264). Washington, DC: American Psychiatric Press.

McLellan, A. T., Luborsky, L., Woody, G. E., & O' Brien, C. P. (1981). Are the "addiction related" problems of substance abusers really related? *Journal of Nervous and Mental Disease, 168*, 26–33.

Meyer, A. (1957). *Psychobiology: A science of man.* Springfield, IL: Charles Thomas.

Miklowitz, D. J., Goldstein, M. J., Nuechterlein, K. H., Snyder, K. S., & Mintz, J. (1988). Family factors in the course of bipolar disorder. *Archives of General Psychiatry, 45*, 225–231.

Monroe, S. M., Imhoff, D. F., Wise, B. D., & Harris, J. E. (1983). Prediction of psychological symptoms under high-risk psychosocial circumstances: Life events, social support, and symptom specificity. *Journal of Abnormal Psychology, 92*, 338–350.

Monroe, S. M. , & Simons, A. D. (1991). Diathesis-stress theories in the context of life stress research: Implications for the depressive disorders. *Psychological Bulletin, 110*, 406–425.

Moos, R. H., Finney, J. W., & Gamble, W. (1982). The process of recovery from alcoholism: II. Comparing spouses of alcoholic patients and spouses of matched community controls. *Journal of Studies on Alcohol, 43*, 888–909.

Mossey, J. M., Knott, K. A., Higgins, M., & Talerico, K. (1996). Effectiveness of a psychosocial intervention, interpersonal counseling, for subdysthymic depression in medically ill elderly. *Journal of Gerontology, 51*, 172–178.

Mueller, T. I., Keller, M. B., Leon, A. C., Solomon, D. A., Shea, M. T., Coryell, W., & Endicott, J. (1996). Recovery after 5 years of unremitting major depressive disorder. *Archives of General Psychiatry, 53*, 794–799.

Mufson, L. H., Moreau, D., Weissman, M. M., & Klerman, G. L. (1991). Interpersonal psychotherapy for adolescent depression: Description of modification and preliminary application. *Journal of the American Academy of Child and Adolescent Psychiatry, 30,* 642–651.

Mufson, L. H., Moreau, D., Weissman, M. M., & Klerman, G. L. (1993). Interpersonal psychotherapy for adolescent depression. In G. L. Klerman & M. M. Weissman (Eds.), *New applications of interpersonal psychotherapy* (pp. 129–166). Washington, DC: American Psychiatric Press.

Paykel, E. S., DiMascio, A., Haskell, D., & Prusoff, B. A. (1975). Effects of maintenance amitriptyline and psychotherapy on symptoms of depression. *Psychological Medicine, 5,* 67–77.

Paykel, E. S., Myers, J. K., Dienelt, M. N., Klerman, G. L., Lindenthal, J. J., & Pepper, M. P. (1969). Life events and depression: A controlled study. *Archives of General Psychiatry, 21,* 753–760.

Petersen, A. C., Compas, B. E., Brooks-Gunn, J., Stemmler, M., Ey, S., & Grant, K. E. (1993). Depression in adolescence. *American Psychologist, 48,* 155–168.

Phifer, J. F., & Murrell, S. A. (1986). Etiologic factors in the onset of depressive symptoms in older adults. *Journal of Abnormal Psychology, 95,* 282–291.

Ramer, B. S., Zaslove, M. O., & Langan, J. (1971). Is methadone enough? The use of ancillary treatment during methadone maintenance. *American Journal of Psychiatry, 127,* 1040–1044.

Rothblum, E. D., Sholomskas, A. J., Berry, C., & Prusoff, B. A. (1982). Issues in clinical trials with the depressed elderly. *Journal of the American Geriatrics Society, 30,* 694–699.

Rounsaville, B. J., & Carroll, K. M. (1993). Interpersonal psychotherapy for patients who abuse drugs. In G. L. Klerman & M. M. Weissman (Eds.), *New applications of interpersonal psychotherapy* (pp. 319–352). Washington, DC: American Psychiatric Press.

Rounsaville, B. J., Glazer, W., Wilber, C. H., Weissman, M. M., & Kleber, H. D. (1983). Short-term interpersonal psychotherapy in methadone-maintained opiate addicts. *Archives of General Psychiatry, 40,* 629–636.

Rounsaville, B. J., Prusoff, B. A., & Weissman, M. M. (1980). The course of marital disputes in depressed women: A 48 month follow-up study. *Comprehensive Psychiatry, 21,* 111–118.

Rounsaville, B. J., Weissman, M. M., & Kleber, H. D. (1983). An evaluation of depression in opiate addicts. *Research in Community & Mental Health, 3,* 257–289.

Rounsaville, B. J., Weissman, M. M., Kleber, H. D., & Wilber, C. H. (1982). Heterogeneity of psychiatric diagnosis in treated opiate addicts. *Archives of General Psychiatry, 39,* 161–166.

Rounsaville, B. J., Weissman, M. M., Prusoff, B. A., & Herceg-Baron, R. L. (1979). Marital disputes and treatment outcome in depressed women. *Comprehensive Psychiatry, 20,* 483–490.

Schmidt, U. H., Tiller, J. M., Andrews, B., Blanchard, M., & Treasure, J. (1997). Is there a specific trauma precipitating the onset of an eating disorder? *Psychological Medicine, 27,* 523–530.

Schulberg, H. C., Madonia, M. J., Block, M. R., Coulehan, J. L., Scott, C. P., Rodriguez, E., & Black, A. (1995). Major depression in primary care practice: Clinical characteristics and treatment implications. *Psychosomatics, 36,* 129–137.

Sholomskas, A. J., Chevron, E. S., Prusoff, B. A., & Berry, C. (1983). Short-term interpersonal therapy (IPT) with the depressed elderly: Case reports and discussion. *American Journal of Psychotherapy, 37,* 552–566.

Simoneau, T. L., Miklowitz, D. J., & Saleem, R. (1998). Expressed emotion and interactional patterns in the families of bipolar patients. *Journal of Abnormal Psychology, 107,* 497–507.

Sotsky, S. M., Glass, D. R., Shea, M. T., & Pilkonis, P. A. (1991). Patient predictors of response to psychotherapy and pharmacotherapy: Findings in the NIMH Treatment of Depression Collaborative Research Program. *American Journal of Psychiatry, 148,* 997–1008.

Sullivan, H. S. (1953). *The interpersonal theory of psychiatry.* New York: Norton.

Tiller, J. M., Sloane, G., Schmidt, U., Troop, N., Power, M., & Treasure, J. L. (1997). Social support in patients with anorexia nervosa and bulimia nervosa. *International Journal of Eating Disorders, 21,* 31–38.

Troop, N. A., Holbrey, A., Trowler, R., & Treasure, J. L. (1994). Ways of coping in women with eating disorders. *Journal of Nervous and Mental Disease, 182,* 535–540.

Troop, N. A., & Treasure, J. L. (1997). Psychosocial factors in the onset of eating disorders: Responses to life events and difficulties. *British Journal of Medical Psychology, 70,* 373–385.

Tucker, M. B. (1982). Social support and coping: Applications for the study of female drug abuse. *Journal of Social Issues, 38,* 117–137.

von Bertalanffy, L. (1950). An outline of general systems theory. *British Journal of the Philosophy of Science, 1,* 134–165.

Weissman, M. M. (1987). Advances in psychiatric epidemiology: Rates and risks for major depression. *American Journal of Public Health, 77,* 445–451.

Weissman, M. M., & Klerman, G. L. (1988). *Interpersonal counseling (IPC) for stress and distress in primary care settings.* New York: New York State Psychiatric Institute.

Weissman, M. M., & Klerman, G. L. (1993). Conjoint interpersonal psychotherapy for depressed patients with marital disputes. In G. L. Klerman

& M. M. Weissman (Eds.), *New applications of interpersonal psychotherapy* (pp. 103–128). Washington, DC: American Psychiatric Press.

Weissman, M. M., Klerman, G. L., Paykel, E. S., Prusoff, B. A., & Hanson, B. (1974). Treatment effects on the social adjustment of depressed patients. *Archives of General Psychiatry, 30,* 771–778.

Weissman, M. M., Klerman, G. L., Prusoff, B. A., Sholomskas, D., & Padian, N. (1981). Depressed outpatients: Results one year after treatment with drugs and or interpersonal psychotherapy. *Archives of General Psychiatry, 38,* 51–55.

Weissman, M. M., Leaf, P. J., Bruce, M. L., & Florio, L. (1988). The epidemiology of dysthymia in five communities: Rates, risks, comorbidity, and treatment. *American Journal of Psychiatry, 145,* 815–819.

Weissman, M. M., & Paykel, E. S. (1974). *The depressed woman: A study in social relationships.* Chicago: University of Chicago Press.

Weissman, M. M., Prusoff, B. A., DiMascio, A., Neu, C., Goklaney, M., & Klerman, G. L. (1979). The efficacy of drugs and psychotherapy in the treatment of acute depressive episodes. *American Journal of Psychiatry, 136,* 555–558.

Wells, K. B., Stewart, A., Hays, R. D., Burnam, A., Rogers, W., Daniels, M., Berry, S., Greenfield, S., & Ware, J. (1989). The functioning and well-being of depressed patients: Results from the Medical Outcomes Study. *Journal of the American Medical Association, 262,* 914–919.

Wills, T. A. (1990). Multiple networks and substance use. Special issue: Social support in social and clinical psychology. *Journal of Social and Clinical Psychology, 9,* 78–90.

Woody, G. E., Luborsky, L., McLellan, T., O'Brien, C. P., Beck, A. T., Blaine, J., Herman, I., & Hole, A. (1983). Psychotherapy for opiate addicts: Does it help? *Archives of General Psychiatry, 40,* 639–645.

CHAPTER 14

MARITAL THERAPY: THEORY, PRACTICE, AND EMPIRICAL STATUS

DONALD H. BAUCOM
University of North Carolina

NORMAN EPSTEIN
University of Maryland

KRISTINA COOP GORDON
University of North Carolina

MARITAL THERAPY: THEORY, PRACTICE, AND EMPIRICAL STATUS

As Halford, Markman, and Fraenkel (in press) point out in their review of marital distress, most adults marry and look to their marriage to meet many of their important psychological and physical needs. Unfortunately, many of these same couples experience extreme disappointment in their relationship over time. In Western countries, adulthood implies a married lifestyle, with more than 90% of the population becoming married by age 50 (DeGuilbert-Lantione & Monnier, 1992; McDonald, 1995). Married individuals generally expect a great deal from their marriage (Millward, 1990) and, in general, turn to their partners as primary sources of support (Levinger & Huston, 1990). Unfortunately, in many instances, these high expectations for support, affection, and intimacy are not met satisfactorily, or they erode over time. As a result, divorce rates are high in Western countries, with the United States reporting the highest rate of approximately 55% (McDonald, 1995).

Given the alarming rate of both marital distress and dissolution, it is fortunate that clinicians and researchers have devoted considerable effort to developing and evaluating interventions for treating marital problems. In the current chapter, we will provide a representative overview of the major models of marital therapy[1], along with a discussion of the empirical status of these various theoretical models. Given that such a review must be selective, we will discuss only those approaches to marital distress that have at least some empirical support for their efficacies. This decision is not intended to imply that other approaches are not useful for couples; hopefully, investigators interested in these other marital therapy approaches will conduct well-controlled treatment outcome investigations to evaluate their efficacies.

Whereas couple-based interventions are used in a variety of contexts, this chapter will focus solely on the treatment of marital discord. Couple interventions also have been developed for prevention and enhancement purposes; for a review of the status of these interventions, the reader is referred to Baucom, Burnett, Van Widenfelt, et al. (in press) and Sayers, Kohn, and

---

[1]Although the term *couples therapy* appears to be gaining in prominence and is more general than the term *marital therapy*, acknowledging that many couples in intimate relationships might not be married, the interventions described have been evaluated almost exclusively with married couples. Therefore, the term *marital therapy* will be employed, and the utility of these interventions with individuals in intimate relationships but who are not married is largely unknown.

Heavey (in press). Similarly, couple and family-based interventions have been evaluated for the treatment of individual adult psychological problems; the efficacies of these couple-based intervention strategies are discussed in Baucom, Shoham, Mueser, Daiuto, and Stickle (1998). Finally, a number of couple-based interventions have been developed for assisting individuals experiencing medical difficulties; the efficacies of these interventions are discussed in Schmaling and Sher (1997).

In evaluating the efficacy of various approaches to marital therapy, we have adopted the criteria developed by Chambless and Hollon (1998) for empirically supported interventions. Briefly, for a treatment to be evaluated as efficacious, these authors hold that it must be superior to a wait-list condition or equivalent to another efficacious treatment; moreover, there must be sufficient statistical power to detect treatment effects. It also is important for the treatment to be employed readily by persons other than those who developed the intervention. Accordingly, Chambless and Hollon require that the efficacy of a treatment must be corroborated by at least two independent teams of investigators, and that the preponderance of the evidence must support its efficacy. If the intervention has been successful in only one study or in multiple studies by the same investigator, then the intervention is viewed as "possibly efficacious" (see Chambless & Hollon, 1998, and the special issue of the *Journal of Consulting and Clinical Psychology* in which their article appears for an in-depth discussion of the strengths and weaknesses of this approach to evaluating psychotherapy research).

Given the emphasis we are placing upon the demonstrated efficacies of these intervention strategies, we will describe the various theoretical models in terms of how they have been operationalized in treatment outcome investigations. For example, behavioral marital therapy (BMT) is the most thoroughly evaluated form of marital therapy. Since the time when the first controlled empirical investigations were conducted in the United States in the mid-1970s, a great deal of theoretical development and clinical innovation has occurred in BMT during the intervening years. Although several derivative approaches have appeared, the treatment outcome investigations have been based on the original BMT treatment model described later in this chapter. We will note where there have been recent promising developments in a given theoretical perspective, although no empirical data presently are available to evaluate their efficacy.

The differing approaches to marital therapy vary greatly around two foci. First, some approaches focus strongly on overt behavioral patterns, whereas other approaches place greater emphasis on internal experience, such as cognitions and affect. Second, some theoretical approaches emphasize the role of each individual in contributing to the development of the marriage; other approaches emphasize the couple's interaction patterns or relationship. Therefore, in describing these various approaches, we will attempt to describe the degree to which each approach emphasizes (a) overt behavior versus internal experiences, including both cognition and affect, and (b) a focus on the individual versus the couple. No approach focuses exclusively on one pole of these various dimensions, but there are notable differences in their relative emphases.

BEHAVIORAL MODELS

As suggested by the title of the model, behavioral marital therapists take a systematic approach to the assessment and modification of couples' behaviors (e.g., Jacobson & Margolin, 1979; Liberman, 1970; O'Leary & Turkewitz, 1978; Stuart, 1980; Weiss, Hops, & Patterson, 1973). Behavioral marital therapy was developed from the theoretical models of social exchange theory (Thibaut & Kelley, 1959) and social learning theory (Bandura, 1977; Rotter, 1954). Social exchange theory proposes that levels of relationship satisfaction depend on the person's ratio of positive to negative experiences in that relationship. Similarly, social learning theory suggests that members of a couple shape each other's behavior by providing positive or negative consequences for each other's actions.

Basic Concepts
Behavior

Empirical investigations have supported the social exchange conceptualization of intimate relationships, such that self-reported relationship satisfactions are correlated (a) positively with the frequencies of their partners' positive actions, and (b) negatively to an even stronger degree with the frequencies of the partners' negative actions (Weiss & Heyman, 1990). Thus, distressed couples are more likely to demonstrate a high rate of negative behaviors and a low rate of positive behaviors; conversely, nondistressed spouses are more likely to engage in more positive behaviors toward their partners than negative ones (Gottman, 1994).

In addition, other findings indicate that distressed married couples are prone to aversive, destructive patterns of communication, such as a demand-withdraw pattern in which one partner pursues an issue while the other withdraws (Christensen & Heavey, 1990; Christensen & Shenk, 1991). Furthermore, distressed couples are more likely to engage in negatively linked social exchanges in which one person's bitter, barbed comment is reciprocated with even greater intensity by the receiving partner. As noted previously, communication behaviors expressing contempt, hostility, defensiveness, and stubbornness also contribute significantly to marital distress (Gottman, 1994; Gottman & Krokoff, 1989).

Cognition

As will be discussed subsequently, behavioral marital therapy has evolved into cognitive-behavioral marital therapy, a therapeutic modality that places significant emphasis on partners' cognitions. Even from a more behavioral perspective, however, cognitions are important because of their relationship to behavior. In general, behavior therapists see cognition as relating to behaviors in at least two ways. First, a person's evaluation or impact of a partner's behaviors as positive or negative depends, in part, on the recipient's subjective experience of these behaviors (Baucom & Epstein, 1990.). For example, a husband may present an expensive day at a beauty spa as a gift to his wife. The wife may either interpret this behavior as an attempt to enhance her well-being by giving her an opportunity to relax and be pampered, or she may interpret his gesture as his dissatisfaction with her appearance and an attempt to improve her looks. These different interpretations of the same behavior likely would have differing impacts on the wife's feelings toward her husband; in the former case, she is likely to feel positively toward him, and in the latter case, negatively. Second, behavioral marital therapists believe that whether an individual decides to engage in a particular behavior will be influenced by his or her subjective expectancies or predictions regarding the consequences of that behavior (e.g., reinforcement or punishment from a partner for behaving in that manner). For example, over time a wife might stop demonstrating physical affec-

tion toward her spouse if she believes that he will not respond positively to her efforts. Thus, behaviorists include a focus on cognitions because cognitive processes will influence the impact of a partner's behavior, as well as whether an individual chooses to engage in a given behavior.

Affect

In addition to cognition, behavioral marital therapists have noted that affect has a great influence on couples' behaviors and relationship satisfaction. Studies of couples' behavioral interactions have shown that distressed partners are more likely to respond negatively to each other's expressions of negative affect than are members of nondistressed couples (negative reciprocity); furthermore, these expressions of negative affect are not as likely to be offset by high levels of positive affect as they are in nondistressed relationships (Gottman, 1994). This emotional linkage also is echoed in couples' physiological responses; distressed as compared to nondistressed partners, particularly males, are likely to have higher heart rates and greater skin conductance levels (reflecting emotional arousal) during conflict. Gottman's (1994) findings indicated that when in conflict, distressed couples are flooded by high levels of negative affect and, thus, are less likely to think clearly or to engage in skillful behaviors that would dampen the counterproductive affect. Gottman and Levenson (1988) suggested that this high negative arousal is so aversive that it leads distressed partners, especially males, to withdraw from conflict, thus preventing distressed couples from reaching successful resolutions of the problems under discussion. These reactions have strong implications for the future of the relationship; both strong emotional and physiological responses of spouses predicted increased marital distress three years later (Levenson & Gottman, 1985).

Despite the aforementioned potential difficulties associated with negative affect, behavioral marital therapists do *not* view all negative affect as destructive. Instead, findings suggest that the expression of negative affect can be healthy in a relationship, depending on how these feelings are addressed. For example, Gottman and Krokoff (1989) reported results from two three-year longitudinal studies in which couples' anger and disagreements during discussions of high-conflict relationship topics were associated with their *current* relationship distress; however, for husbands, the initial expression of negative affect significantly predicted *improvement* in satisfaction over the three years (with a nonsignificant effect in the same direction for wives). On the other hand, other research suggests that expressions of negative affect that involve stubbornness, defensiveness, withdrawal, and contempt are likely to contribute to marital distress (Gottman, 1994; Gottman & Krokoff, 1989). Based on the present inconsistent findings, it is not possible to conclude when a couple's expression of negative emotions is destructive or beneficial.

Although couples' communication behaviors are linked with their affect, Weiss and Heyman (1997) note that correlations between couples' behavioral exchanges and their levels of relationship satisfaction tend to be modest, and that satisfaction appears to be influenced significantly by each partner's overall subjective sentiment toward the other, a phenomenon that they term *sentiment override*. These observations point to the central importance of affect in marriage and to the inherent difficulties of a model that is overly dependent upon changing behaviors without adequate attention to the partners' global feelings toward each other.

Contributions of the Couple Versus the Individual in Marital Distress

Not surprisingly, with a major focus on interactive processes as a primary source of marital distress, behavioral marital therapists place a strong emphasis on the contribution of the couple as a dyad rather than the individual's unique characteristics. The basic principles of social learning theory emphasize that spouses' behaviors are both learned and impacted by their partners' behavior. The behavioral approach also is based on social exchange theory principles that link the couple's satisfaction to higher ratios of pleasing versus displeasing exchanged behaviors. Thus, the behavioral model suggests that a couple's ability to maintain a satisfying relationship is based on their skills for providing each other with reinforcing and effective behavioral exchanges. As a result, the interventions described subsequently are focused primarily on altering behavioral exchanges between the couple and developing more effective communication skills. Little attention is given to understanding the unique characteristics of each partner, and how individual factors, including both strengths and vulnerabilities, contribute to marital adjustment.

Approaches to Treatment
Behavior

Because a central tenet of the behavioral model is that distress is caused by a low ratio of positive to negative exchanges, behavioral couple therapists have used behavior-exchange procedures such as *love days* (Weiss et al., 1973) or *caring days* (Stuart, 1980). These procedures involve each partner agreeing to enact certain positive behaviors requested by his or her partner in order to increase the percentage of positive exchanges. Similarly, couples have been taught to develop behavioral contracts in which each person agrees to behave in specific ways desired by the partner, and contingencies are placed upon the enactment of these behaviors. Although behavioral contracting appears to be less emphasized in current behavioral approaches to assisting distressed couples, it served as a major intervention strategy in many of the treatment outcome investigations that have been conducted. In addition, in order to increase the likelihood that couples will experience more reinforcing interactions, behavior therapists teach couples specific communication skills and guidelines for (a) expressing thoughts and feelings, (b) engaging in empathic listening, and (c) problem-solving. By developing these skills, it is believed that couples will enhance their abilities to negotiate more satisfying solutions to conflicts, as well as their abilities to experience more intimacy through skillful expression of feelings. Typically, these behavioral interventions use a collaborative approach with the clients in which the therapist describes the goals and procedures, models the specific behaviors, and coaches the partners as they practice the skills before attempting them at home.

Cognition

In their text on behavioral marital therapy, Jacobson and Margolin (1979) recommended that therapists instruct couples to monitor and record their cognitions at home; moreover, these researchers indicated that behavior therapy would have little impact on distressed couples unless it altered distorted cognitions. In addition, Stuart (1980) promoted the concept of relabeling, which essentially involves challenging the couples to alter their negative interpretations of ambiguous situations. Both types of cognitive restructuring procedures involve the therapist offering more benign interpretations as substitutes for the partners' negative attributions concerning the causes of each other's displeasing behaviors. Furthermore, cognitive restructuring provides a challenge to the partners' unrealistic beliefs about their relationships, such as the expectation that loving partners should be able to mind-read each other's needs. Unfortunately, descriptions of cognitive restructuring in early behavioral texts are quite brief, and they typically do not give therapists a great deal of guidance in how to accomplish this goal. It also should be noted that cognitive interventions were not systematically employed in the treatment outcome studies discussed subsequently.

Affect

Behavioral approaches to couple relationships have viewed emotions (e.g., anger, sadness) as reactions to specific behavioral interactions. They see distress as resulting from particular behavioral patterns that are repetitive, ingrained, and reciprocal. Consequently, behaviorists' approaches to modifying affect typically have depended on the behavioral interventions described previously. However, this approach of altering affect through changing behavior may be problematic for some distressed couples. Weiss and Heyman (1990) noted that unless treatments directly address the partners' sentiments toward each other, long-term improvement is less likely. Related research findings on limited associations between partner behaviors and satisfaction indicate that it is not safe to assume that planned behavioral changes will overcome existing negative feelings toward the partner (e.g., Halford, Sanders, & Behrens, 1993; Iverson & Baucom, 1990).

Empirical Support

Behavioral marital therapy is the most widely evaluated marital treatment, having been a focus of approximately two dozen well controlled treatment outcome studies. Behavioral marital therapy has been reviewed in detail in several previous publications, including findings from specific investigations (e.g., Alexander, Holtzworth-Munroe, & Jameson, 1994; Baucom & Epstein, 1990; Baucom & Hoffman, 1986; Baucom et al., 1998; Bray & Jouriles, 1995; Jacobson & Addis, 1993; Lebow & Gurman, 1995), as well as meta-analyses (Dunn & Schwebel, 1995; Hahlweg & Markman, 1988; Shadish, Montomery, Wilson, Wilson, Bright, & Okwumaba, 1993). All of these reviews reach the same conclusion: Behavioral marital therapy is an efficacious intervention for

maritally distressed couples. (See Table 14.1 for a description of the controlled marital therapy outcome investigations that have been conducted.)

A large number of investigations have compared behavioral marital therapy to wait-list control conditions, consistently finding that behavioral marital therapy is more efficacious than the absence of systematic treatment. Several early investigations of behavioral marital therapy also have compared it to nonspecific or placebo treatment conditions, with behavioral marital therapy generally being more efficacious than nonspecific treatment conditions (Azrin, Besalel, Bechtel, et al., 1980; Crowe, 1978; Jacobson, 1978); meta-analyses have confirmed these findings (Dunn & Schwebel, 1995; Hahlweg & Markman, 1988; Shadish et al., 1993).

The overall findings suggest that, after receiving behavioral marital therapy, between one to two-thirds of couples will be in the nondistressed range of marital satisfaction. Most couples appear to maintain these gains for short time periods (6 to 12 months); however, long-range follow-up results are not as encouraging. In a two-year follow-up of BMT, for example, Jacobson, Schmaling, and Holtzworth-Munroe (1987) found that approximately 30% of couples who had recovered during therapy had relapsed subsequently. In addition, Snyder, Wills, and Grady-Fletcher (1991) reported that 38% of couples receiving BMT had divorced during a four-year follow-up period. Thus, brief behavioral marital therapy improvements are not maintained for many couples over a number of years, although some couples maintain and even improve upon their gains.

COGNITIVE-BEHAVIORAL MODELS

Cognitive-behavioral marital therapy (CBMT) evolved from behavioral marital therapy and is consistent with behavior therapy trends during the 1980s and 1990s to incorporate cognitive factors into behavioral conceptualizations of maladaptive responses. Consequently, most of the BMT theoretical perspectives and interventions described previously have been incorporated into CBMT. The much greater emphasis of cognitions in cognitive-behavioral marital therapy is its primary difference relative to BMT in its original formulations. Whereas BMT noted the importance of cognitions to behavior change, the CBMT model additionally proposes that cogni-

**TABLE 14.1 Empirical Status of Marital Therapy for the Treatment
of Marital Distress**

	Efficacious and Specific Treatments		
Treatment	**Reference**	**Treatment Conditions**	**Major Results**[a]
Behavioral (BMT)	Azrin, Besalel, Betchel Michalicek, Mancera, Carroll, Shuford, & Cox (1980)	1. BMT ($n = 28$) 2. Attention/Placebo ($n = 27$)	$1 > 2$
	Baucom (1982)	1. BMT ($n = 18$) 2. Communication/Problem Solving ($n = 18$) 3. Behavioral Contracting ($n = 18$) 4. Wait List ($n = 18$)	$1 = 2 = 3 > 4$
	Baucom & Lester (1986)	1. BMT ($n = 8$) 2. BMT + Cognitive Restructuring ($n = 8$) 3. Wait List ($n = 8$)	$1 = 2 > 3$
	Baucom, Sayers, & Sher (1990)	1. BMT + Cognitive Restructuring for Couples + Emotional Expressiveness Training ($n = 12$) 2. BMT ($n = 12$) 3. BMT + Cognitive Restructuring for Couples ($n = 12$) 4. BMT + Emotional Expressiveness Training ($n = 12$) 5. Wait List ($n = 12$)	$1 = 2 = 3 = 4 > 5$
	Bennun (1985)	1. Conjoint BMT ($n = 19$) 2. Group BMT ($n = 19$) 3. Individual BMT ($n = 19$)	$1 = 2 = 3$
	Boelens, Emmelkamp, MacGillavry, & Markvoot (1980)	1 Behavioral Contracting ($n = 8$) 2. Systematic Therapy ($n = 8$) 3. Wait List ($n = 5$)	$1 = 2 > 3$
	Crowe (1978)	1. BMT ($n = 14$) 2. Group Analytic Therapy ($n = 14$) 3. Attention/Placebo ($n = 14$)	$1 = 2 = 3$

TABLE 14.1 *(Continued)*

Efficacious and Specific Treatments

Treatment	Reference	Treatment Conditions	Major Results[a]
	Emmelkamp, van der Helm, MacGillavry, & van Zanten (1984)	1. Communication/Problem Solving + Behavioral Contracting (*n* =) 2. Behavioral Contracting + Communication/ Problem Solving (*n* = 17)	1 = 2
	Emmelkamp, van Linden van den Hewell, Ruphan, Sandlerman, Scholing, & Stroink (1988)	1. BMT (*n* = 16) 2. Cognitive Restructuring for Couples (*n* = 16)	1 = 2
	Ewart (1978)	1. BMT (*n* = 18) 2. Wait List (*n* = 6)	women: 1 > 2 men: 1 = 2
	Girodo, Stein, & Dotzenroth (1980)	1. BMT (*n* = 6) 2. Minnesota Couples' Communication Program (*n* = 12) 3. Wait List (*n* = 6)	1 = 2 = 3
	Hahlweg, Revenstorf, & Schindler (1982)	1. BMT (*n* = 17) 2. Group BMT (*n* = 16) 3. Emotional Expressiveness Training (*n* = 16) 4. Group Emotional Expressiveness Training (*n* = 19) 5. Wait List (*n* = 17)	1 = 2 = 3 > 4 = 5
	Halford, Sanders, & Behrens (1993)	1. BMT (*n* = 13) 2. BMT + Cognitive Restructuring + Affect Exploration + Generalization Training (*n* = 13)	1 = 2
	Jacobson (1977)	1. BMT (*n* = 5) 2. Wait List (*n* = 5)	1 > 2
	Jacobson (1978)	1. BMT + Good Faith Behavioral Contracting (*n* = 8) 2. BMT + Quid Pro Quo Behavioral Contracting (*n* = 9) 3. Attention/Placebo (*n* = 7) 4. Wait List (*n* = 6)	1 = 2 > 3, 4

286

TABLE 14.1 (*Continued*)

Efficacious and Specific Treatments

Treatment	Reference	Treatment Conditions	Major Results[a]
	Jacobson (1984)	1. BMT ($n = 9$) 2. Communication/Problem Solving ($n = 9$) 3. Behavior Exchange ($n = 9$) 4. Wait List ($n = 9$)	$1 = 2 = 3 > 4$
	Johnson & Greenberg (1985)	1. Emotion Focused Therapy ($n = 15$) 2. Communication/Problem Solving ($n = 15$) 3. Wait List ($n = 15$)	$1 > 2 > 3$
	Liberman, Levine, Wheeler, Sanders, & Wallace (1976)	1. BMT ($n =$) 2. AP ($n =$)	$1 > 2$
	Snyder& Wills (1989)	1. BMT ($n = 29$) 2. Insight-Oriented Marital Therapy ($n = 30$) 3. Wait List ($n = 20$)	$1 = 2 > 3$
	Tsoi-Hoshmund (1976)	1. BMT ($n = 10$) 2. Attention/Placebo ($n = 6$) 3. Wait List ($n = 4$)	$2 = 3$ $1 > 2, 3$
	Turkewitz & O'Leary (1981)	1. Emotional Expressiveness Training ($n = 10$) 2. BMT ($n = 10$) 3. Wait List ($n = 10$)	$1 = 2 = 3$
	Wilson, Bornstein, & Wilson (1988)	1. Group BMT ($n = 5$) 2. Conjoint BMT ($n = 5$) 3. Wait List ($n = 5$)	$1 = 2 > 3$

Efficacious and Possibly Specific Treatments

Treatment	Reference	Treatment Conditions	Major Results[a]
Emotion-Focused (EFT)	Dandeneau & Johnson (1994)	1. EFT ($n = 12$) 2. Waring Cognitive Therapy ($n = 12$) 3. Wait List ($n = 12$)	$1 = 2 = 3$
	Goldman & Greenberg (1992)	1. EFT ($n = 14$) 2. Systematic Therapy ($n = 14$) 3. Wait List ($n = 14$)	$1 = 2 > 3$

TABLE 14.1 *(Continued)*

Efficacious and Possibly Specific Treatments

Treatment	Reference	Treatment Conditions	Major Results[a]
	James (1991)	1. EFT + Emotional Expressiveness Training ($n = 14$) 2. EFT ($n = 14$) 3. Wait List ($n = 14$)	$1 = 2 > 3$
	Johnson & Greenberg (1985)	See above entry under BMT.	
	Walker, Johnson, Manion, & Cloutier (1996)	1. EFT ($n = 16$) 2. Wait List ($n = 16$)	$1 > 2$

Possibly Efficacious Treatments

Treatment	Reference	Treatment Conditions	Major Results[a]
Cognitive (CT)	Emmelkamp et al. (1988)	See above entry under BMT.	
	Huber & Milstein (1985)	1. Cognitive Restructuring for Couples ($n = 9$) 2. Wait List ($n = 8$)	$1 > 2$
Cognitive-Behavioral (CBT)	Baucom & Lester (1986)	See above entry under (BMT).	
	Baucom, Sayers, & Sher (1990)	See above entry under BMT.	
	Halford, Sanders, & Behrens (1993)	See above entry under BMT.	
Insight-Oriented (IOMT)	Snyder & Wills (1989)	See above entry under BMT.	
Systemic Therapy (ST)	Goldman & Greenberg (1992)	See above entry under EFT.	

[a] Major results include statistically significant differences among treatment conditions at posttest; see text for follow-up results. Treatments are designated by number from the previous column. $1 > 2$ indicates that treatment 1 is statistically superior to treatment 2 in improving marital adjustment at posttest.

tive change is important in its own right. That is, in many instances, a couple might *not* need to change their behavior in order to increase their relationship satisfaction. For example, a husband might change his attribution for his wife's coming home late as avoidance of him to her attempt to work extra hours to help the family's financial well-being; accordingly, he may become less distressed without any behavioral change on her part. Similarly, a wife with an extreme standard for her husband's behavior (e.g., that he should want to spend all of his free time with her) is dissatisfied when he does not meet her standard. Helping her to reevaluate and change the stringency of her standard might be the intervention of choice, rather than a behavior change on either person's part. Thus, CBMT builds upon the behavioral model by suggesting that increasing relationship satisfaction involves a balance of behavioral and cognitive changes, both of which hold the potential for important emotional change.

Basic Concepts

Cognition

Systematic attention to cognition has been developed within CBMT (Baucom & Epstein, 1990; Baucom, Epstein & Rankin, 1995; Dattilio & Padesky, 1990; Epstein & Baucom, 1989; Epstein, Baucom, & Daiuto, 1997). The CBMT researchers have identified five major types of cognitions involved in couple relationship functioning (Baucom, Epstein, Sayers, & Sher, 1989). Empirical studies suggest that these cognitions are associated with, or even lead to, partners' negative affective and behavioral responses to each other (Epstein & Baucom, 1993; Fincham, Bradbury, & Scott, 1990; Noller, Beach, & Osgarby, 1997).

The first cognitive variable is selective attention, which involves how each member of a couple idiosyncratically notices, or fails to notice, particular aspects of relationship events. Selective attention contributes to distressed couples' low rates of agreement about the occurrence and quality of specific events, as well as negative biases in perceptions of each other's messages (Noller et al., 1997).

The second major category of cognition is attributions, or inferences made about the determinants of partners' positive and negative behaviors. The tendency of distressed partners to attribute each other's negative actions to global, stable traits has been referred to as *distress-maintaining attributions* because they leave little room for future optimism that one's partner will behave in a more pleasing manner in other situations (Holtzworth-Munroe & Jacobson, 1985). Epstein (1984) described how the attributions of distressed spouses are similar to those of depressed individuals' hopelessness about positive change. Bradbury and Fincham (1990) have thoroughly reviewed the empirical support for the importance of partners' attributions in relationship functioning.

The third major category is expectancies, or predictions that each member of the couple makes about particular relationship events in the immediate or more distant future. Negative relationship expectancies have been associated with lower satisfaction, stemming from pessimism about improving the relationship (Fincham & Bradbury, 1989; Pretzer, Epstein, & Fleming, 1991).

The fourth and fifth categories of cognition are forms of what cognitive therapists have referred to as basic or core beliefs shaping experience of the world. These include (a) the assumptions, or beliefs, that each individual holds about the characteristics of individuals and intimate relationships, and (b) the standards, or each individual's personal beliefs, about the characteristics that an intimate relationship and its members *should* have (Baucom & Epstein, 1990; Baucom et al., 1989). Couples' assumptions and standards are associated with current relationship distress, either when these beliefs are unrealistic or when the partners are not satisfied with how their personal standards are being met in their relationship (Baucom, Epstein, Rankin, & Burnett, 1996; Halford, Kelly & Markman, 1997).

Affect

The cognitive-behavioral model of marital therapy also addresses four aspects of affect that influence marital distress. One important affective factor is the degree to which each person experiences positive and negative emotions toward the partner and the relationship. Clients who possess strong negative emotions toward each other are almost certain to be distressed within their relationship. Also, their positive emotions buffer their distress (Gottman, 1994), as well as affect their treatment motivation and the eventual success of the treatment. A second factor addressed by CBMT is partners' abilities to understand their emotions and their causes. Often clients lack the ability to differentiate between categories of emotion such as anger and anxiety, or the degrees of emotion, such as irritation and anger. This lack of knowledge may result in confusing messages sent to their partners about their emotional experiences and hamper the effective expression of emotion.

Third, how effectively individuals can express their emotions to their partners is important. A failure to express emotions may not reflect skill deficits. As such, beliefs about the appropriateness of expressiveness (e.g., it is a sign of weakness to express vulnerable feelings) may prevent clients from appropriately expressing their emotions. Finally, maladaptive emotions and related symptoms (e.g., clinical depression or anxiety) can interfere significantly with the couple's relationship adjustment. For example, several studies have documented a close relationship between marital distress and depression; however, the causal direction between these constructs is complex (Beach & O'Leary, 1992; O'Leary, Riso, & Beach, 1990).

Behavior

Cognitive-behavioral marital therapists hold views of behavior in marriage that are similar to those in traditional behavioral marital therapy. The behavioral factors that are most likely to impact a couples' adjustment are (a) the ratio of exchanges of positive versus negative actions, (b) the partners' skills for expressing and active listening to each other's thoughts and feelings, (c) the partners' problem-solving skills, and (d) the partners' abilities to provide effective reinforcement for each other within their relationship. The cognitive-behavioral approach assumes that behavior, cognition, and affect mutually influence each other, so that a well-timed appropriate behavioral intervention that challenges a client's previously held cognition also may produce a shift in the client's affect (Baucom & Epstein, 1990). For example, a wife may feel that her husband does not really care about her because he no longer demonstrates romantic behaviors. If she is asked to monitor and observe the positive things he does daily for her or the family, she may notice more positive aspects of her husband's behavior, thus altering her feelings toward him.

Contributions of the Couple Versus the Individual in Marital Distress

Cognitive-behavioral couple therapists see relationship problems as developing not only from behavioral excesses and deficits within the couple but also from each individual's cognitions that either elicit distress or impede the resolution of conflicts (Epstein, Baucom, & Rankin, 1993). Thus, some of the problematic cognitions that the therapist identifies may have developed from each individual's history, including the current marriage, previous romantic relationships, the family of origin, and society at large. For example, depending on how a husband experienced his mother's seemingly sudden and unexpected divorce from his father, he might overgeneralize,

believe that women cannot be trusted, and predict that his wife will abandon him some day (even without obvious signs of her departure). Thus, many of the problematic behavioral interactions between spouses may evolve from the partners' relatively stable cognitions about the relationship. Unless these cognitions are taken into account, successful intervention is likely to be compromised. Therefore, cognitive-behavioral marital therapists attend to how each person thinks about and experiences the relationship. On many occasions, the treatment explores one partner's cognitions, while the other partner listens and contributes to the process. In this way, the unique characteristics, learning histories, and current thoughts and cognitions of each partner are integrated into the couple's ongoing interactions.

Similarly, although CBMT focuses on dyadic behavioral interaction patterns, such as the common demand–withdraw cycle, the model also considers each partner's behavioral learning history. Consistent with the BMT model, the cognitive-behavioral approach assumes that each partner's learning history includes the development of particular behavioral responses and skills that he or she is likely to exhibit in the current relationship. For example, individuals from families in which parents modeled minimal communication about feelings and punished their children for expressing negative emotions may be predisposed to similar avoidant communications with their partners. Thus, individuals' current behavior toward their partners can be influenced both by their pre-existing behavioral patterns and by the consequences (reinforcement and punishment) provided for each other's responses.

Approaches to Treatment
Cognition

This approach has integrated assessment and intervention procedures from cognitive therapies (Beck et al., 1979; Meichenbaum, 1977) with traditional skills-oriented behavioral strategies. CBMT teaches partners to monitor and test the appropriateness of their cognitions. It incorporates some standard cognitive restructuring strategies, such as (a) considering alternative attributions for a partner's negative behavior, (b) asking for behavioral data to test a negative perception concerning a partner (e.g., that the partner never complies with requests), and

(c) evaluating an extreme standard by generating lists of the advantages and disadvantages of expectations to live up to this standard. In general, a hallmark of the cognitive-behavioral approach is a collaboration between the therapist and couple, the goal of which is to facilitate clients conducting their own cognitive assessments and modifications.

In addition, several of Jacobson and Christensen's (1996) integrative marital therapy interventions to promote partners' acceptance of their differences and problems also appear to involve cognitive restructuring. For example, one strategy focuses on *empathic joining*, or the shifting away from attributing displeasing partner behaviors to negative or dysfunctional traits to understandable responses and common differences that exist between the partners. Another strategy used by Jacobson and Christensen involves asking a couple to role-play negative behaviors during therapy, after which each partner discusses ongoing thoughts and emotions so as to clarify the understanding of the underlying motivations behind the behaviors. Such interventions help individuals to shift their attributions for their partners' negative behaviors from negative to more benign intentions.

Affect

The traditional cognitive therapy approach to emotions is based on the premise that when a behavioral event occurs, the individual cognitively interprets it and, based upon that interpretation, responds emotionally. Consequently, behavior, cognition, and emotion are viewed as integrally related. Therefore, cognitive-behavioral marital therapists commonly monitor partners' emotional reactions to each other during therapy sessions and guide the couple in uncovering their own cognitions about each other's actions that contribute to their emotional responses. As the therapist works to improve both members' understanding of the determinants of their own and each other's emotions, the goal is to increase the couple's skills in assessing their moment-to-moment affective shifts. A common procedure for increasing the identification of factors eliciting emotional responses is to focus the person's attention on the thoughts and visual images that spontaneously occur just before or during particular emotional responses. For example, a husband may think, "She doesn't care about me or our relationship" when he becomes angry while talking

with his wife. Furthermore, cognitive-behavioral therapists employ communication skills training to aid spouses in effectively expressing their emotions to one another.

In cases where an individual's emotional responses are less associated with the couple's interactions than with a broader set of individual difficulties (e.g., clinical depression that pre-dated the relationship), the therapist might suggest individual treatment for that partner.

Behavior

Given that cognitive-behavioral marital therapy evolved from earlier behavioral models of couple functioning, the therapist uses the same behavioral interventions we have described for behavioral marital therapy. There are differences, however, in how behavior is considered within this broader cognitive-behavioral model. As noted earlier, behavior change is not the ultimate goal of all cognitive-behavioral marital therapists. At times, internal changes involving both cognitions and affects are the foci of such interventions. Therefore, the therapist might focus on behavior changes to (a) alter the current behaviors of the couple if they are maladaptive or (b) provide evidence for modifying their cognitions. For example, to change a wife's expectancy that her husband will not respond to her attempts to talk with him about his work difficulties, the therapist might ask the couple to set aside time at home expressly for this purpose. The wife might be asked to monitor carefully how her husband responds to her concern for his plight. In such an instance, the conversation itself may be beneficial, but the wife also is gathering information relevant to her beliefs about their relationship. Along with such daily behavioral experiments, the therapist monitors the partners' behavioral and emotional responses to each other during sessions. The partners' in-session behavioral and emotional responses are used as cues to elicit thoughts about their relationship, and the therapist can intervene immediately to alter counterproductive cognitions.

Empirical Support

The efficacy of cognitive interventions has been explored in two ways—as the sole intervention or as part of a broader set of therapeutic strategies to assist distressed couples (see Table 14.1).

Huber and Milstein (1985) compared cognitive marital therapy with a waiting-list control condition. Their cognitive marital therapy focused primarily on irrational relationship standards and assumptions that were highlighted by Epstein and Eidelson (1981), along with specific irrational marital beliefs noted by Ellis (1977). Six weeks of cognitive marital therapy was more effective than the waiting-list condition. Applying the Chambless and Hollon criteria (1998), cognitive therapy would be classified as a possibly efficacious treatment for marital distress.

In current practice, cognitive interventions are typically used with a variety of behavioral interventions, as well as interventions focusing on couples' emotions. Based on the description of cognitive-behavioral marital therapy already provided, Baucom and colleagues (Baucom & Lester, 1986; Baucom, Sayers, & Sher, 1990) supplemented traditional behavioral marital therapy with cognitive restructuring interventions targeted at couples' marital attributions and their marital standards. In these two studies, both traditional behavioral marital therapy and cognitive-behavioral therapy were more effective than a waiting-list condition in improving the couples' marital adjustment and communication. However, there were no significant differences between the two treatment conditions. These results were replicated in a similar investigation by Halford, Sanders, and Behrens (1993). Furthermore, the magnitude of change produced for various dependent measures appears to be consistent with what has been found in a number of behavioral marital therapy investigations. Thus, the findings to date suggest that CBMT is as efficacious as BMT alone, but it does not produce enhanced treatment outcomes. In interpreting these findings, it is important to note that couples were randomly assigned to treatment conditions. Some couples might benefit more from a central focus on cognitive change, whereas others may need extensive alterations in how they behave toward each other. At present, no reported investigations have addressed this later matching issue.

SYSTEMS MODELS

Since the 1960s, the predominant conceptual model used by family therapists to understand relationship functioning is general systems theory, developed by the biologist Von Bertalanffy (1968). Family therapists who have drawn from systems concepts have used the fields of biology, physiology, cybernetics, and anthropology. The basic idea underlying systems theory is that members of families form complex patterns of mutual interdependence and influence (Nichols & Schwartz, 1998). As Nichols and Schwartz note, systems theory is not a well-defined model but rather a general set of principles that guides thinking about mutual influence patterns. A premise of the systems approach to family functioning is that in order to understand an individual's behavioral, cognitive, and affective responses, those responses should be viewed in the context of significant interpersonal relationships. Systems theorists emphasize circular causality in interpersonal relationships, in which each family member's behavior is both a cause and an effect of other family members' behaviors. An example of circular causality is the demand–withdraw cycle, in which one individual's demands increases the probability that the other person will withdraw, and, in turn, the latter person's withdrawal increases the former's demands.

Furthermore, systems theory proposes that the interpersonal system is influenced by the larger systems in which it is embedded. Thus, a couple is influenced by and, in turn, influences the rest of the nuclear family; moreover, the nuclear family has patterns of mutual influence with their extended family and the community systems (e.g., schools).

Adopted from the field of physiology, another key concept in systems theory is *homeostasis*, or the organism's tendency to use regulatory mechanisms to maintain relative stability in the face of forces pushing for change. Thus, a couple's ability to maintain stability in meeting their interpersonal needs depends on their strategies for dealing with normative and unexpected events that threaten the status quo. For example, any couple must achieve a balance between togetherness and autonomy. After attaining a mutually satisfactory balance in this area, the birth of a first child forces changes in their pattern (e.g., how much individual activity each partner will give up to care for the child; how they will maintain cohesion as a couple when they have less time alone together). There are two opposing system-regulating mechanisms that allow it to maintain its viability. On the one hand, there are *morphostasis* mechanisms that restrain change. Thus, when each member of the couple attempts to cope with the demands of the newborn child by pursuing individual activities, the other person gets upset, and individualistic behavior decreases. On the other hand, *morphogenesis* mechanisms allow or seek change in the system's structure in order to meet changing needs. For example, the new parents may begin to share their thoughts and feelings with each other more, increasing the depth of their intimacy even though their amount of time together has decreased. Systems theorists focus on such dynamic processes in couples' interaction patterns. In working with a distressed couple, they examine ways in which the couple's strategies for dealing with life events and problems have either exacerbated or created new problems.

Basic Concepts

Cognition

Although family systems models focus primarily on the interactions among family members and the ways in which these interactions create, maintain, or exacerbate existing problems, they also allow for the influence of each member's cognitions upon these interactions. More specifically, two major categories of cognition and behavior that systems therapists tend to evaluate are power and connectedness (Fraenkel, 1997).

Family systems therapists of differing theoretical orientations have observed that couples commonly differ in their ideas about how power should be shared between them. For example, spouses may disagree about the extent to which there is a relationship hierarchy and who should have more power in that hierarchy. In addition, distressed couples are likely to disagree about the ways and degree to which they wish to be connected; i.e., they are likely to argue about boundaries, both between each other and between themselves and other people.

Structural family therapists (e.g., Minuchin, 1974; Todd, 1986) hold that a certain degree of power differential is necessary in order for any social system to function effectively in meeting the members' needs. A system without any clear hierarchy (i.e., lacking leadership) is vulnerable to chaos and dysfunction when encountering stressors and problems. Structural family therapists not only pay attention to behavioral patterns that reflect degrees of hierarchy in couple and family relationships but also address the individuals' beliefs about the distribution of power. For example, when a young couple initially formed their relationship, perhaps the husband assumed a leadership role, and the wife was comfortable with that hierarchy because she had grown up in a family with traditional gender roles. As the wife matured further and gained self-confidence, however, she developed a belief that their relationship

should be egalitarian. The husband may resist the wife's attempts to change the hierarchy, because he experiences the potential change as threatening to his power. Structural family therapists' use of *reframing* interventions to alter family members' perceptions of each other is a form of cognitive restructuring. Thus, the therapist may label the wife's efforts to change the hierarchy as evidence of her deep caring for her husband and her desire to reduce stress that he has experienced from taking on so much responsibility. On the other hand, systems-oriented therapists implicitly acknowledge the importance of family members' cognitions, using such reframing as a technique for modifying behavioral patterns. Family members' cognitions about desirable and appropriate boundaries between individual members and subsystems (e.g., setting areas of privacy for a couple, vis-à-vis their children) also are implicitly important to systems-oriented family therapists.

Furthermore, family systems theorists propose that these beliefs about power and connectedness derive, in part, from a particular subculture and family of origin. For example, Giordano and Carini-Giordano (1995) describe how cultural differences in values and preferences concerning expressiveness and boundaries can contribute to marital and family distress. In addition to socializing individuals into a particular subcultural set of values and beliefs, the family of origin also may add its unique contribution to marital difficulties through unresolved hurts and transgressions. Boszormenyi-Nagy and colleagues (1986; Boszormenyi-Nagy, Grunebaum, & Ulrich, 1991) term this process the *revolving slate*. One partner has been injured in the family of origin, and this injury is unresolved; consequently, he or she carries the injury-related cognitions and emotions into the present family. This is termed *destructive entitlement* and reflects the injured partner's belief that because of such injury, she or he is owed something in return, is allowed to inflict punishment on others to make up for the original injury. Not surprisingly, Boszormenyi-Nagy indicates that these cognitions can create great marital conflict.

Strategic and solution-focused systems theorists, less so than structural family therapists (and much less than those applying intergenerational models such as those of Bowen and Boszormenyi-Nagy), are concerned with the origin of a couple's problematic beliefs or values. To the extent that these latter therapists pay attention to internal processes at all, they are most concerned with the couple's current cognitions about their problem. Strategic and solution-focused therapists assume that thinking about life problems in narrow and rigid ways leads to limited and rigid problem solving. In this regard, a common, fundamental error is to assume that, when their behavioral problem-solving strategy has not worked, the only alternative is to try more of the same behavior (Nichols & Schwartz, 1998; O'Hanlon & Weiner-Davis, 1989). For example, when spouses interpret each other's behavior as attempts to dominate, they try to solve this problem by exercising power in return. If such coercions are misguided attempts to increase togetherness and intimacy, the strategy will backfire, creating greater distance. The self-defeating pattern will continue if the individuals conclude that they must try harder to coerce each other to behave intimately. Strategic and solution-focused therapists change partners' interpretations of each other's behavior and the rules governing relationship patterns. Thus, by reframing their mutual coercion as attempts to get closer because they value each other, the therapist attempts to foster collaborative rather than coercive behavior.

Furthermore, strategic and solution-focused therapists do not believe that a particular kind of structure (such as a certain degree of hierarchy or boundaries) is necessary for positive relationship functioning. Instead, they focus primarily on what is "working" or "not working" for a couple. The facilitating cognitions are the partners' beliefs about the possibility of change and each partner's current definition and understanding of the couple's problem. They believe that a couple's definition of the problem as global and stable (and therefore hopeless) contributes to distress and to maladaptive coping strategies. As in structural family therapy, these cognitions are targeted for change through therapist-initiated reframing, thereby providing the partners with more benign explanations for each other's distressing behavior.

Increasingly, the narrative approach has gained prominence among systems-oriented family therapists. Narrative therapy is based on the assumption that individuals' responses to their life experiences depend on the personal meanings that they attach to those experiences (Freedman & Combs, 1996; White & Epston, 1990; see also the chapter in this volume by Niemeyer and colleagues). Nichols and Schwartz (1998) note that narrative therapists have recognized that reframes used by strategic therapists will have lasting impact only if they are consistent with the life stories that individuals have constructed about themselves and their close relationships. For example, reframing spouses' coercive behavior toward each other as attempts to achieve closeness may have limited impact if one or both partners have developed general views of themselves as being unlovable. Nichols and Schwartz (1998) note that narrative therapists have moved away from traditional systems thinking, focusing much less on family behavioral patterns than on the members' idiosyncratic cognitions about themselves and their relationships, which contribute to their rigid approaches to their problems. Individuals' family histories are considered very important in shaping their life stories; a central therapeutic goal is to help persons broaden their conceptualizations of their alternatives in life. Finally, it should be noted that the narrative theoretical model clearly has considerable overlap with the cognitive-behavioral model.

Affect

The role of affect varies widely among the different family systems models. According to the Bowenian model of therapy (Bowen, 1978; Papero, 1995), which focuses more on family members' internal experiences than most systems approaches, family dysfunction arises when the members respond with diffuse and intense anxiety to problems such as conflicts concerning intimacy. In this model, these affective responses dominate cognition and result in dysfunctional behaviors. For example, members of a couple who are experiencing conflict commonly *triangle* a third party, drawing in the individual as an ally. Another response used to cope with anxiety in family relationships is an *emotional cutoff*, in which an individual distances from a family member physically and/or psychologically. In the Bowen model, these responses fail to resolve family problems, and children raised by parents whose coping is dominated by negative affect develop similar deficits in their functioning. Consequently, the focus of therapy involves identifying and developing more constructive ways to cope with anxiety.

Systems therapists propose that an individual's emotional responses are influenced by the ways that interactional processes influence family members' connections with each other (Minuchin, 1974). For example, disengaged couples are less likely to be aware of and responsive to each other's emotions, leading to lessened feelings of closeness, support, and intimacy; conversely, enmeshed couples are likely to overreact to one another's affect, leading to greater feelings of anger or anxiety.

Systems theorists who take an intergenerational perspective also attend to how a partner's family of origin may influence his or her current expression of affect. Emotional responses that may have been adaptive in the family of origin may be problematic in the current relationship (Miller, 1994). For example, a child who grew up with a volatile alcoholic parent may have developed a pattern of withdrawing in fear when the parent was became emotionally upset. If the individual continues this pattern of withdrawal later in adulthood when his or her partner becomes emotional, however, this withdrawal is likely to increase relationship conflict. Thus, an intergenerational systems perspective can be helpful in understanding a partner's experiences of, and responses to, emotions.

On the other hand, strategic and solution-focused systems therapists are less likely to take an intergenerational systems approach, or to look for influences of affect on dysfunctional behavioral patterns. Instead, they view displays of negative affect as reflections of rigid, chronic, and ineffective strategies used to solve relationship problems. Thus, couples who try to resolve unfulfilled intimacy desires by attempting to coerce each other to behave more intimately are likely to become angry when this strategy fails. Changes in affect are assumed to follow from interventions that shift the couple or family toward more constructive interactions.

Family therapists who use the narrative approach (e.g., White & Epston, 1990) view emotions as arising from the ways in which the members of a couple or family have labeled and understood their relationship experiences. For example, both members of a couple may label the husband's blue moods and irresponsible behavior as depression. Consequently, the partners may continue to support these responses by interpreting them with a depression label that suggests the husband is helpless to behave differently. The wife, thus, might assume responsibility for unpleasant tasks and reduce her relationship expectancies because her husband "has" clinical depression. Her responses further confirm the husband's own life narrative as being an ineffective, depressed person, and they allow him to withdraw further from intimacy and responsibility in the relationship, which in turn offers more evidence of his "disability."

Behavior

A systems theory view of behavior in couple and family relationships examines the functional payoffs of particular behaviors within the system. Each person is viewed as playing a role in the family or marital system, and the partners are rewarded, punished, and noticed based upon their performances within the system. In addition, behavior patterns that comprise a relationship generally are either symmetrical or complementary (Fraenkel, 1997). Any system will only work when patterned interactions between the partners meet each person's needs and expectations (Colapinto, 1991; Minuchin, 1974; Todd, 1986). If these needs are not met, the behavioral patterns will result in the partners becoming more polarized (Shoham, Rohrbaugh, & Patterson, 1995). For example, if both partners respond to each other's expression of negative affect with more negative affect, this negative symmetrical pattern increases conflict and decreases problem resolution. Within a complementary marital system, one partner might have the role of being the responsible partner, and the other is allowed to be more spontaneous and irresponsible. This complementary pattern will function effectively only when both partners are comfortable in their roles and the system has the flexibility to adapt to other life stresses that may require assuming different roles.

As noted previously, therapists who apply general systems theory to family relationships commonly focus on the organizational parameters of boundaries and hierarchy in the family system. The flexibility and adaptability of the system along these dimensions often determine whether the system can adapt well to any developmental or outside stresses. In our earlier example, one spouse may have taken on the "weak" spouse role and, thus, be lower in the marital hierarchy. Through his or her own individual growth, however, this spouse may become less comfortable in the one-down position. In this case, if the hierarchy and balance of power between the partners are too rigid, the couple encounters considerable conflict and distress when the nondominant spouse seeks more relationship autonomy and control. A problem with boundaries might occur when a young couple marries and attempts to establish autonomy from their families of origin. If the boundaries between themselves as a couple and other family members are too permeable, then the families of origin may become too intrusive and prevent the young couple from making decisions and establishing an identity of their own.

As noted previously, strategic and solution-focused systems therapists (e.g., Haley, 1976; Madanes, 1981, 1991; O'Hanlon & Weiner-Davis, 1989) also propose that the problematic behaviors bringing clients to therapy (e.g., escalating arguments) often are maladaptive solutions to relationship problems. For example, a wife's "nagging" may be aimed at getting her husband to take more responsibility, whereas the husband's refusal reflects an avoidance of her "nagging." Thus, each partner's attempts to reduce or change the other's displeasing behavior unwittingly increase the likelihood of the negative behavior.

Contributions of the Couple and the Individual in Marital Distress

Systems theorists conceptualized relationship dysfunction and distress as resulting from the couple's ineffective solutions to relationship issues. As a result, these models approach marital distress with an emphasis on how the couple as a unit creates, maintains, and exacerbates relationship conflict. Due to limitations or inflexibility in the relationship-interaction patterns (e.g., structural characteristics such as boundaries and hierarchy) or the use of maladaptive solutions that escalate rather than resolve marital conflicts, systems theorists see the partners as engaged in repetitive, self-defeating patterns of mutual influence that must be disrupted through therapeutic interventions. Whereas structural and strategic-systems theorists' interventions generally address how the couple is currently functioning as a unit, some other systems theorists examine the contributions of the individual's family of origin to the marital distress. In Bowen's model (Bowen, 1978; Papero, 1995), the individual's application of cognitive skills for problem solving is shaped in the family of origin. Narrative therapists (e.g., White & Epston, 1990) also focus on the internal processes through their identification of each person's construction of his or her life story.

Approaches to Treatment
Cognition

The systems approaches that emphasize the impact of a couple's current interaction pattern on their level of discord and distress (e.g., structural, strategic, solution-focused) have the goal of modifying dysfunctional patterns. One common ther-apeutic strategy is to use reframing techniques to shift the partners' perspectives of each other and their relationship problems. The therapist's goal is to create a plausible framework for helping partners to understand the necessity of changing their behaviors and trying new solutions to relationship problems. For example, if a wife can understand how her nagging sets up a defensive reaction from her husband, and how the nagging permits him to justify his withdrawal from responsibility, she may be more amenable to trying a different method to bring about behavior change. Similarly, if the husband understands how his withdrawal increases the likelihood of his wife's nagging, he may be encouraged to find another solution to avoid her nagging, such as performing agreed-upon behaviors on time. In addition, as described earlier, providing spouses with more benign interpretations of each other's distressing behaviors can encourage more empathic and supportive behavior.

In addition, intergenerational systems therapies use information about family of origin and intergenerational transmission of patterns to help couples understand and reframe problematic relationship behaviors. For example, an adult who learned to withdraw from an alcoholic parent might similarly withdraw in his or her current relationships. The therapist would help each partner to understand how the husband's adaptive behavior in the course of growing up with an unpredictable parent is no longer adaptive or needed within the current environment. Thus, this intervention helps the couple to depathologize the behavior, allows the wife to empathize with her husband's difficulty, and yet acknowledges its current problematic effect and the need for change.

Recent developments in narrative therapy have altered the focus from couple and family interaction patterns as the major cause of relationship problems to the identification of the individuals' internalized conceptualizations of themselves, particularly in relation to significant others (e.g., Freedman & Combs, 1996; White & Epston, 1990). This focus on cognition is a significant paradigm shift away from traditional systems theory thinking (Nichols & Schwartz, 1998), and the compatibility of narrative therapy with the cognitive-behavioral model (particularly the role of schemata) is notable. Narrative therapists assume, however, that a change in an individual's life story is a prerequisite for behavior change; in comparison, the cognitive-behavioral model assumes that behavior changes can produce cognitive shifts.

Affect

As noted previously, therapists who follow Bowen's model assume that family members' dysfunctional responses to life problems result when anxiety and other strong affective responses interfere with rational, cognitive problem solving. Thus, a major goal for this type of systems therapy is to assist family members in solving problems with rational thought processes rather than automatic responses based on emotions. Because the origin of such emotions is assumed to be past conflicts and unresolved issues in the family of origin, the goal of therapy involves fostering the individuals' *differentiation*, which involves three therapeutic processes. First, the therapist helps individuals to function effectively and autonomously from their families of origin, balancing autonomy with healthy degrees of connection and mutual support with their other family members. This process fosters the individual's ability to remain relatively unenmeshed when other family members' behaviors are being driven by anxiety. Second, the therapist may aid individuals in developing the capacity to separate cognitive and emotional functioning by helping them understand that what people feel is not always what is realistically occurring. Finally, the therapist may help individuals to see how their current significant relationships are different from those in their families of origin.

Other systems theorists view negative affect as stemming from problems in the structure of the couple's system. As a result, a primary goal of therapy is to shift the couple's structural characteristics to a more adaptive system. It is assumed that the emotional responses will change as the structure is modified in ways that better meet the couple's needs. For example, if a therapist construes a wife's depression as loneliness stemming from the couple's emotional disengagement, then the therapist would target the wife's depression by interventions designed to increase the couple's connectedness.

Behavior

In the beginning of therapy, systems therapists closely assess the circular processes and sequences of behaviors that occur between members in a relationship in order to determine the couple's structure. The structure of the relationship is composed of repetitive behavioral patterns, such

as those defining the clarity of the partners' boundaries. Thus, the continuum ranging from disengagement to enmeshment that has been described by structural family therapists (e.g., Minuchin, 1974) is assessed in terms of behaviors such as the amount of open, direct communication between the two people and the degree to which the couple shares time and activities. A couple is viewed as having a clear but permeable boundary if they exhibit a balance between sharing and autonomy. An example of a communication pattern that reflects conflict over boundaries is one in which one partner pursues discussion of topics while the other partner increasingly distances him- or herself from such discussions. Because these conflict-producing behavioral patterns are viewed as maladaptive solutions to relationship problems, the structural or strategic therapist's goal is to help the couple shift to a more constructive behavioral solution.

The methods that systems therapists employ to help the clients discover new interaction patterns can be direct or indirect. Some systems therapists are likely to assign new behaviors to the couple based upon their theoretical considerations of what is healthy in a marriage, as well as what the couple believes needs to change in their relationship (Boszormenyi-Nagy, 1986; Boszormenyi-Nagy et al., 1991; Fraenkel, 1997; Madanes, 1991). The focus of these behavioral directives typically would be on changing the couple's boundaries or their hierarchy as needed; for example, the therapist might attempt to make the couple's boundaries more or less permeable or help them to clarify their hierarchical structure. In contrast to behavioral marital therapy, systems-oriented therapists commonly design these interventions without collaboration with the couple, based on the assumption that constructive change only requires that the therapist induce behavioral changes, whether or not the clients understand the rationale.

Strategic therapists who ascribe to variations of the problem-focused family systems model, such as the Mental Research Institute (MRI) approach (e.g., Watzlawick, Weakland, & Fisch, 1974) and the approaches of Haley (e.g., 1976) and Madanes (e.g., 1981), focus primarily on the dysfunctional behavioral patterns demonstrated by the couple and then help the partners to decrease these destructive behaviors. In contrast, therapists who follow the solution-focused model of family systems therapy (e.g., O'Hanlon & Weiner-Davis, 1989; Weiner-Davis, 1992) focus on uncovering what has worked successfully for the couple in the past and encouraging them to increase these behaviors.

When strategic therapists anticipate or experience a couple resisting change, they are likely to use indirect and *paradoxical directives*, such as "prescribing the symptom" (Shoham et al., 1995). The purposes of these interventions often are hidden deliberately from the couple; the ultimate goal usually is to induce behaviors that are opposite to the actions prescribed by the therapist. For example, to help a resistant couple stop arguing, the therapist may ask them to argue more, giving them the rationale that they are not arguing enough and, thus, never able to reach a resolution. The assumption behind such an intervention is that when the therapist prescribes the arguments, the couple responds as any system that has mechanisms maintaining stability by resisting forces acting to induce change. Paradoxical directives are intended to activate the couple's tendency to resist input from an outsider and to use that motivation to produce constructive change. Therefore, it is assumed that the couple may resist the therapist's attempts to control the couple's behavior and actually argue less. As can be seen from this example, strategic therapists at times do not focus on helping clients gain insight into the causes of their problems or the factors involved in solving their difficulties. For strategic therapists, the goal is for clients to change the problematic behaviors for which they sought help, regardless of whether the clients understand the mechanisms underlying such change.

Empirical Support

At present, there is very little research exploring the efficacy of family systems approaches to treating marital distress. There has been one published, well-controlled treatment study in which systems therapy was compared to emotion-focused therapy (see subsequent description), as well as to a waiting-list condition (Goldman & Greenberg, 1992). The systemic marital therapy relied upon the following intervention strategies to change couple interactions: (a) reframing or positively connoting the couples' symptoms or the functioning of the system and (b) interrupting vicious behavioral cycles by prescribing the symptom or the pattern of interaction that is targeted for change. The findings indicated that both active treatment conditions were superior to the wait-list condition. In addition, both were equally

efficacious in altering marital adjustment. The findings from this single investigation place systemic marital therapy into the category of possibly efficacious treatments (Baucom et al., 1998). Given the variety of different perspectives represented within a broad systems approach to understanding couple functioning, much more treatment outcome research is needed to clarify the utility of these approaches to assisting married couples. Systems approaches are perhaps the most widely employed approaches used by couple therapists in applied settings, yet there is a dearth of research exploring their efficacy.

PSYCHODYNAMIC MODELS

Just as there is no singular behavioral theory of marital distress and marital therapy, there is a variety of psychodynamic viewpoints and approaches to understanding marital distress. However, what these psychodynamic approaches have in common is their emphasis on early relationship experiences in understanding current, adult intimate relationships such as marriage. Most contemporary psychodynamic approaches are consistent with aspects of Snyder's (in press) insight-oriented marital therapy (IOMT), which emphasizes "interpersonal schemas and relationship dispositions rather than instinctual impulses or drive derivatives" (p. 10).

Psychodynamic therapists assist clients in reconstructing information about their significant early relationships, including their affective quality and strategies the individual developed for gratification of emotional needs, as well as for anxiety containment. A central goal of such therapy is to increase each partner's insight into consistencies between the interpersonal conflicts and coping styles in their current and past significant relationships. Furthermore, individuals are helped to see how the coping strategies that were adaptive in prior relationships are inappropriate for achieving emotional intimacy and other personal needs in their current relationships.

Basic Concepts
Cognition

Psychodynamic approaches view clients' cognitions as a system of internalized representations that function as models of how relationships should and do work. These internalized representations (e.g., introjects in the object relations framework and working models in attachment theory) are comprised of characteristics that the client either observed or experienced in early relationships with parents or similar caregiving figures. These representations comprise schemas about the world and one's relationship to the world that may be beyond awareness but are influential in how one interacts with one's partner and how one interprets situations in the relationship. For example, attachment theorists (e.g., Johnson & Greenberg, 1994; Kobak, Ruckdeschel, & Hazan, 1994) suggest that a person's working relationship model is made up primarily of tacit assumptions about his or her partner's degree of physical and emotional availability. If individuals believe that people are unlikely to be available to meet their needs, then they may feel a great deal of anxiety in interpersonal relationships and require either excessive reassurance or emotional distance to feel comfortable in a relationship. Additionally, if persons internalize hostile, abusive relationships, then they may quickly attribute threat or hostility to ambiguous situations in later relationships.

Affect

Psychodynamically oriented couple therapists propose that emotions experienced within the context of interacting with a partner have a major impact on the overall relationship. Many of these emotional responses to one's mate are believed to be influenced by the individual's developmental history. As mentioned previously, an insecure working model or an internalized representation (introject) of a hostile, rejecting other that stems from earlier caregiving relationships may cause a person to feel extreme anxiety or anger in later adult relationships. In response to these emotions, the individual may use defensive responses (e.g., withdrawal, denial, projection) that lead to distortions in the individual's interactions with a partner (Scharff, 1995).

In addition, attachment theorists consider some strong emotions to be primary, whereas other emotions (often anger) are secondary and are used as a defense to avoid experiencing more threatening primary emotions (Johnson, 1996). Primary attachment emotions such as sadness and anxiety communicate the individual's needs to the caregiver, which in turn should elicit comforting responses from the caregiver. For example, anxiety may be a primary emotion because it indicates that a person's attachment to an important other is threatened (Kobak et al., 1994). Consequently,

fear of losing the other can motivate the individual to send a partner messages about an increased need for reassurance and comfort. Kobak et al. note that when individuals' working models are secure, they expect that caregivers will attend to their attachment needs; therefore, the individuals are more likely to express their emotions so as to facilitate attachment (e.g., expressing anger as a reflection of concern about distance in the relationship rather than as a personal attack on the caregiver). In contrast, individuals with insecure attachment working models may expect that direct expressions of attachment needs and emotions will lead to negative responses from caregivers, which result in high levels of anxiety about their ability to maintain attachments. As a result, individuals may develop strategies for coping with this anxiety, such as detachment or hypervigilance and exaggerated expressions of emotion intended to gain the attention of the caregivers. Unfortunately, these coping mechanisms are unlikely to elicit the desired nurturing responses, and the caregiver is unlikely to decipher the vulnerable attachment needs underlying such behavior. Consequently, the individual's insecure working model is reconfirmed when the caregiver does not respond in a comforting, nurturing manner.

Behavior

As has been mentioned, psychodynamically oriented marital therapists believe that adults' behavioral responses in their relationships are influenced by previous relationship experiences that complicate an individual's ability to respond adaptively to the present relationship. The internalized working models, introjects, or schemas concerning intimate relationships with attachment figures create a tendency to behave in particular ways to cope with perceived relationship dynamics (Kobak et al., 1994; Scharff, 1995). For example, individuals who have secure working models of attachment usually have confidence that the significant others will respond positively to their expressions of need. Therefore, they are more likely to express thoughts and emotions directly, giving the other persons information that allows an appropriate response to individual needs. These experiences further reinforce the working models of the nurturing significant other (Kobak et al., 1994). However, individuals with insecure working models usually do not anticipate reassuring responses from attachment figures (Kobak et al., 1994). Consequently, these individuals are more likely to communicate their needs in unclear, indirect ways. This behavior decreases the likelihood that the significant other will be able to respond effectively to the person's underlying attachment needs, thus reinforcing the insecure attachment model. Attachment theorists suggest, and empirical findings demonstrate, that such working models and individuals' typical behavioral responses to attachment concerns are relatively stable over time and throughout the lifespan (Berman, Marcus, & Berman, 1994; Bowlby, 1989; Davila & Bradbury, 1996; Davila, Burge, & Hammen, 1997; Rothbard & Shaver, 1994).

In addition, as previously mentioned, the object relations conceptualization of couple relationships suggests that individuals' perceptions of partners are commonly distorted by their projecting onto the partners their own denied, unacceptable, and/or threatening characteristics (Scharff, 1995). If the partner provides corrective information about aspects of the projections that are inaccurate, the individual's own introjected views of the self are modified, and he or she can distinguish better between self and other. However, if the partners are struggling with their own internal conflicts, they are not likely to tolerate the others' projections and may behave in aversive ways that confirm distorted projections. Thus, as described by Scharff (1995), marital distress occurs when these unconscious processes do not result in correction of distortions and reduction of anxiety.

Contributions of the Couple and the Individual in Marital Distress

Of all the models presented in this chapter, the psychodynamic models perhaps tend to place the most emphasis on the individual's contribution to the relationship. Although these theorists do attend to the couple's interactions, their focus on these interactions is primarily based upon how the partners reinforce or change each other's working models or internalized representations. Thus, a great deal of attention is given to what characteristics and histories the individual partners bring to the relationship. However, the extent to which psychodynamic therapists focus on early childhood and unconscious processes varies. For example, within insight-oriented marital therapy (IOMT), which was developed and evaluated by Snyder and his colleagues (Snyder & Wills, 1989; Snyder et al., 1991), a major goal of therapy is to make these unconscious, individual processes clearer to both members of the couple and to develop the individuals' empathy with each other as each struggles to correct distorted schemas. On the other hand, although Greenberg and Johnson's emotion-focused therapy (Greenberg & Johnson, 1988; Johnson & Greenberg, 1995) emphasizes the importance of early attachment relationships in the etiology of marital distress, their interventions focus on the current marriage as the context for best addressing attachment issues.

Approaches to Treatment
Cognition

Psychodynamically oriented therapists believe that much of a couple's distress results from underlying processes and schemas that are either unconscious or generally accessible but beyond awareness. Therefore, the therapy first focuses on identifying the content of these internalized representations and then interprets them to clients in order to create insight into the effects their past relationship histories have on their current reactions to their partners. It is assumed that once the partners develop insight into these processes, this insight then allows them to modify their schemas in light of current data (Kobak et al., 1994). That is, a major goal is to separate the past from the present and to assist both individuals in responding to the present, rather than basing their responses on earlier relationships.

Furthermore, in emotion-focused marital therapy—an approach based on attachment theory (e.g., Johnson & Greenberg, 1995)—the therapist encourages persons to express vulnerable feelings related to their insecure attachments. Emotion-focused theorists believe that these expressions of vulnerability in turn should foster empathy from the other partner. It is hypothesized that the empathic shift toward viewing the partner's negative behavior as arising from attempts to cope with vulnerable feelings rather than from malicious motives results in a significant cognitive change in the individual's attributions about the partner.

In addition to creating empathy through exploring the partners' vulnerability regarding their insecure attachment models, the therapist also attempts to change the partners' cognitions about current negative interactions through a process of reframing, which is an intervention common to many theoretical approaches. These reframes typically redefine the couple's problems as dyadic and as consisting of circular processes, a perspective intended to counteract the distressed partners' tendencies to blame each other. The therapist also reframes each person's behavior in a more benign manner than it has been viewed by the other person; for example, framing an individual's aggressive criticism as desperate attempts to cope with fear of being abandoned by the partner, whose love he or she values and desires. These reframes generally arise from the therapist's assessment of the attachment issues involved in each person's contribution to the couple's negative interaction pattern. Therefore, they serve two purposes in the therapy: (a) they increase the individuals' insight into their own issues, promoting further exploration and expression of vulnerable feelings, and (b) they help the partners gain more insight into each other's sources of anxiety, thus fostering empathy for the vulnerabilities that underlie negative behavior.

Additionally, for therapists who adopt an object relations perspective, the role of the therapist is to identify and interpret for the clients their largely unconscious intrapsychic needs, conflicts, and defenses against anxiety. In addition, the object relations therapist uses the interpersonal dynamics suggested by the partners' transference responses toward the therapist (Scharff, 1995). For example, the client may act as if the therapist is a hostile, controlling authority figure when, in fact, the therapist has maintained a neutral stance. In this case, the client's reaction can be seen as a clue to the nature of his or her internalized representations of relationships.

Affect

Psychodynamic therapists consider clients' emotional responses to be a key source of information about partners' internal dynamics. Moments in which an individual experiences emotion during therapy sessions (e.g., toward the partner, self, or therapist) are viewed as potential windows into unconscious material from childhood that is assumed to have contributed to the current emotion. When appropriate, the therapist attempts to identify and interpret the intrapsychic, developmental meaning of these emotional responses. By helping the couple understand the significance of these emotions and their origins, the therapist helps the partners tolerate anxiety. Furthermore, each partner becomes better able to provide for the other's personal needs because of their increased understanding of, and empathy for, each

other. Therefore, a central goal of marital therapy is to access the partners' negative working models through identifying the emotions elicited by them, and then help the individuals scrutinize and modify them in light of disconfirming information from the current relationship (Kobak et al., 1994).

In addition, object relations therapists employ their own emotional reactions to the couple as an indication of what the partners may experience in their interactions with each other. For example, the therapist may feel frustrated with the passivity of one of the partners and, thus, gain insight into the reactions of the other partner. This reaction can then be interpreted to the couple to help partners obtain clearer understandings of the kinds of reactions that their behaviors are likely to elicit, even from a supposedly objective source.

Behavior

Both object relations theorists and attachment theorists suggest that when adults perceive that their attachment relationships with significant others are currently threatened, natural negative behavioral responses to such threats to their security are elicited. Changing such problematic responses necessitates first identifying the relevant working models or introjects, bringing them to the couple's attention, and reevaluating them in light of more current material. In addition, the therapist assists individuals in developing more constructive interactions with their partners, such as direct, nonhostile communication, that increase the probability of receiving reassuring responses and greater intimacy (Johnson & Greenberg, 1995; Scharff, 1995). Although the therapist and couple may set general goals of improving communication and relationship functioning, specific behavioral targets typically are not identified. It is assumed that as each individual understands himself/herself more clearly and develops greater empathy for the partner, this provides the context for adaptive behavior change.

Empirical Support

Snyder and Wills (1989) compared the relative effectiveness of IOMT and traditional behavioral marital therapy and found both treatments to be efficacious relative to a waiting-list condition. There were no differences between insight-oriented marital therapy and traditional behavioral marital therapy; however, in altering posttest marital adjustment. Furthermore, at posttest, the two therapies had similar rates of couples who moved from the distressed range of relationship functioning to the nondistressed range. Whereas IOMT and traditional behavioral marital therapy were comparable on marital adjustment at a six-month follow-up, the findings changed significantly when long-term follow-up was considered. In the longest follow-up to date on the efficacy of marital therapy, Snyder et al. (1991) recontacted 96% of the treated couples four years after the completion of therapy. At four-year follow-up, significantly more of the traditional behavioral marital therapy couples had experienced divorce relative to insight-oriented marital therapy couples. Similar patterns were found when levels of marital adjustment were considered: at four-year follow-up, insight-oriented marital therapy couples demonstrated significantly higher levels of marital adjustment than behavioral marital therapy couples. Furthermore, at four-year follow-up, traditional behavioral marital therapy demonstrated significantly higher rates of deterioration relative to insight-oriented marital therapy (see Table 14.1). Finding meaningful differences between active treatment conditions is rare in the field of marital therapy, and in psychotherapy research in general; thus, Snyder's findings call for replication to determine whether the long-term impact of IOMT is consistently superior to skills-based behavioral interventions. Based on the results from this one investigation, IOMT would be classified as possibly efficacious.

There have been several investigations of emotion-focused therapy (EFT) addressing various issues about its efficacy, and the findings to date indicate that EFT is of significant benefit to distressed couples (Baucom et al., 1998; Johnson, Hunsley, Greenberg, & Schindler, in press). Emotion-focused therapy has been shown to be superior to behavioral marital therapy and a wait-list condition at posttest, although it should be noted that the authors specify that this is with moderately distressed couples only (Johnson & Greenberg, 1985). In another study, emotion-focused therapy was equally effective as a family systems approach at posttest, and both were superior to a wait-list control group (Goldman & Greenberg, 1992). Finally, James (1991) compared traditional emotion-focused therapy to an enhanced version of emotion-focused therapy that also included communication training. Both treatments were superior to the wait-list condition in terms of marital functioning; however, the

two treatment groups did not significantly differ. In addition, James (1991) reported that approximately 90% of couples receiving the two versions of emotion-focused therapy improved with treatment, and 75% were no longer distressed at the end of treatment.

Furthermore, when emotion-focused therapy is restricted to moderately distressed couples, the posttest findings appear to be relatively unchanged at follow-up (James, 1991; Johnson & Greenberg, 1985). The pattern of findings is different, however, in the one investigation that employed more distressed couples. Goldman and Greenberg (1992) found that EFT and systemic marital therapy were not different from each other at posttest, but at four-month follow-up, the systemic therapy was superior to EFT. This difference between treatments resulted from the couples in the EFT treatment experiencing significant relapse during the follow-up period. The investigators caution that, with severely distressed couples, time-limited EFT might not be powerful enough to create sufficient intimacy to maintain posttest gains. Considering the overall results from these empirical investigations, EFT is classified as an efficacious treatment in assisting moderately distressed couples.

CONCLUSIONS

Although more information is needed about the relative overall efficacy of cognitive-behavioral, systems-oriented, and psychodynamic marital therapies, findings to date suggest that all of these theoretical approaches can be of assistance to at least some maritally distressed couples. In addition, no single theoretical approach has established itself as superior to other theoretical perspectives in terms of treatment efficacy. If this pattern of empirical findings continues into the future, then investigators and clinicians might well devote effort to studies that examine optimal matches between types of interventions and couples' needs and problems. At least two major factors evident in the marital interaction and therapy literature underscore the need for couple-to-treatment matching: (a) variation in couples' characteristics and needs, and (b) variations in the degrees to which the existing theoretical approaches to marital therapy address internal versus interpersonal factors and current versus long-standing issues in the partners' lives.

First, couples vary in the degree to which their relationship problems are associated with individual versus dyadic dysfunction, current versus long-standing processes, and behavioral, cognitive, or affective responses. Research findings have provided evidence of bi-directional causal links between individual psychopathology and relationship functioning, indicating that clinicians need to assess the degree to which individual and conjoint therapy are appropriate. Similarly, findings concerning the effects on marital functioning of partners' dispositional characteristics, such as attachment styles, point to the need for treatment planning that takes into account individual difference variables as well as current couple interaction patterns. Furthermore, results of therapy outcome studies indicate that for some couples, training in behavioral skills such as expressiveness, empathic listening, and problem-solving is sufficient to resolve marital problems. For others, however, there likely is a need to identify and modify broader relationship patterns such as power inequities, boundary issues, and deficits in emotional intimacy. Thus, marital treatment must take into account the fact that couples enter therapy with varying characteristics and needs, and depending on those individual differences, they are likely to respond differentially to alternative interventions.

Second, our review illustrates how psychodynamic, systems-oriented, behavioral, and cognitive-behavioral marital therapies involve different assumptions about the essential phenomena that affect relationship dysfunction. Some approaches focus considerably more than others on the personal characteristics that the two partners bring to their relationship, as well as on a historical, developmental perspective on the individuals' functioning. Other approaches focus more on how the current organization of the couple's interaction pattern impacts marital discord and distress. Furthermore, the theoretical approaches vary in their attention to the behavioral, cognitive, and affective domains of partners' functioning in their relationships. These differences in conceptualization of relationship problems can lead to marked differences in therapeutic procedures. For example, because Bowen family systems therapists emphasize disruptive effects of anxiety on individuals' functioning, they structure therapy sessions in ways that maximize cognitive processing (e.g., using genograms to foster insight into intergenerational family patterns) and minimize clients' emotional responses (e.g., holding sessions with individual members of a couple, so they will not trigger each other's

emotions). In contrast, emotion-focused marital therapists elicit partners' emotional responses to each other during sessions as a path to understanding and modifying problematic insecure working models.

Our review suggests that currently all of the major theoretical approaches to marital therapy address some potentially important facets of intimate relationships, but none provide an adequate balance of attention to both the couple and individual factors that therapists must be prepared to assess and treat. In addition, the alternative approaches attend differentially to what can be labeled *micro behaviors* (specific communication skills and other discrete acts) versus *macro behaviors* (broad interaction patterns, such as the distribution of power or interpersonal influence in the dyad). Although macro patterns are ultimately comprised of sets of micro behaviors, the alternative theoretical approaches tend to vary in the degree to which they increase couples' awareness of the broader thematic issues that affect their level of marital satisfaction. For example, behavioral marital therapy has a strong record of identifying and modifying specific behaviors that partners experience as distressing in each other, but considerably less attention has been paid to understanding the broader classes of such behaviors that make them distressing. Thus, a partner's behaviors may be experienced, overall, as emotional disengagement, although such a pattern is not clear from a specific interaction. In contrast, psychodynamic marital therapies tend to focus on macro themes in couples' relationships, but commonly such approaches pay less attention to specific behavioral patterns that can be modified to better meet the partners' needs.

It is beyond the scope of this chapter to conduct a thorough comparative analysis of the prominent approaches to marital therapy. Rather, we believe that an essential lesson from our consideration of these approaches is that much is to be gained from finding means for integrating their strengths. The existing empirical results do not support a loose eclecticism but rather the development of multilevel assessment and intervention, taking into account both individual and couple characteristics, historical (developmental) and current functioning, micro- and macro-level patterns, and the three domains of behavior, cognition, and affect. The achievement of a truly integrative treatment approach for distressed couples requires both additional research on client-treatment matching and the flexibility of therapists in stepping beyond boundaries of traditional theoretical schools.

REFERENCES

Alexander, J. F., Holtzworth-Munroe, A., & Jameson, P. B. (1994). The process and outcome of marital and family therapy: Research review and evaluation. In S. L. Garfield & A. E. Bergin (Eds.), *Handbook of psychotherapy and behavior change* (4th ed., pp. 595–630). New York: John Wiley and Sons.

Azrin, N. H., Besalel, V. A., Betchel, R., Michalicek, A., Mancera, M., Carroll, D., Shuford, D., & Cox, J. (1980). Comparison of reciprocity and discussion-type counseling for marital problems. *American Journal of Family Therapy, 8*, 21–28.

Bandura, A. (1977). *Social learning theory*. Englewood Cliffs, NJ: Prentice-Hall.

Baucom, D. H. (1982). A comparison of behavioral contracting and problem-solving/communications training in behavioral marital therapy. *Behavior Therapy, 13*, 162–174.

Baucom, D. H., Burnett, C. K., VanWidenfelt, B., Schilling, E., Sandin, E., & Ragland, L. (in press). The prevention of marital discord and divorce: An international perspective. In K. Hahlweg, D. H. Baucom, R. Bastine, & H. J. Markman, (Eds.), *Preddiktion und prevention von beziehungsstvungen und scheidung [Prediction and prevention of marital distress and divorce]*. Bonn: BMFS.

Baucom, D. H., & Epstein, N. (1990). *Cognitive-behavioral marital therapy*. New York: Brunner/Mazel.

Baucom, D. H., Epstein, N., & Rankin, L. A. (1995). Cognitive aspects of cognitive-behavioral marital therapy. In N. S. Jacobson & A. S. Gurman (Eds.), *Clinical handbook of couple therapy* (pp. 65–90). New York: Guilford Press.

Baucom, D. H., Epstein, N., Rankin, L. A., & Burnett, C. K. (1996). Assessing relationship standards: The Inventory of Specific Relationship Standards. *Journal of Family Psychology 10*(1), 72–88.

Baucom, D. H., Epstein, N., Sayers, S. L., & Sher, T. G. (1989). The role of cognitions in marital relationships: Definitional, methodological, and conceptual issues. *Journal of Consulting and Clinical Psychology, 57*, 31–38.

Baucom, D. H., & Hoffman, J. A. (1986). The effectiveness of marital therapy: Current status and application to the clinical setting. In N. S. Jacobson & A. S. Gurman (Eds.), *Clinical handbook of marital therapy* (pp. 597–620). New York: Guilford Press.

Baucom, D. H., & Lester, G. W. (1986). The usefulness of cognitive restructuring as an adjunct to behavioral marital therapy. *Behavior Therapy, 17*, 385–403.

Baucom, D. H., Sayers, S. L., & Sher, T. G. (1990). Supplementing behavioral marital therapy with cognitive restructuring and emotional *expressiveness* training: An outcome investigation. *Journal of Consulting and Clinical Psychology, 58*, 636–645.

Baucom, D. H., Shoham, V., Mueser, K. T., Daiuto, A. D., & Stickle, T. R. (1998). Empirically supported couple and family interventions for marital distress and adult mental health problems. *Journal of Consulting and Clinical Psychology, 66*, 53–88.

Beach, S. R., & O'Leary, K. D. (1992). Treating depression in the context of marital discord: Outcome and predictors of response of marital therapy versus cognitive therapy. *Behavior Therapy, 23*, 507–528.

Beck, A. T., Rush, A. J., Shaw, B. F., & Emery, G. (1979). *Cognitive therapy of depression*. New York: Guilford Press.

Bennun, I. (1985). Behavioral marital therapy: An outcome evaluation of conjoint, group and one spouse treatment. *Scandinavian Journal of Behaviour Therapy, 14*, 157–168.

Berman, W. H., Marcus, L., & Berman, E. R. (1994). Attachment in marital relations. In M. B. Sperling & W. H. Berman (Eds.), *Attachment in adults: Clinical and developmental perspectives* (pp. 204–231). New York: Guilford Press.

Bertalanffy, L. Von (1968). *General systems theory*. New York: George Braziller.

Boelens, W., Emmelkamp, P., MacGillavry, D., & Markvoort, M. (1980). A clinical evaluation of marital treatment: Reciprocity counseling vs. system-theoretic counseling. *Behavior Analysis and Modification, 4*, 85–96.

Boszormenyi-Nagy, I. (1986). Contextual therapy and the unity of therapies. In J. C. Hansen (Ed.), *The interface of individual and family therapy* (pp. 65–72). Rockville, MD: Aspen Publications.

Boszormenyi-Nagy, I., Grunebaum, J., & Ulrich, D. (1991). Contextual therapy. In A. S. Gurman & D. P. Kniskern (Eds.), *Handbook of family therapy* (Vol. II, pp. 200–238). New York: Brunner/Mazel.

Bowen, M. (1978). *Family therapy in clinical practice*. New York: Aronson.

Bowlby, J. (1989). The role of attachment in personality development and psychopathology. In S. Greenspan & G. Pollock (Eds.), *The course of life: Vol. 1. Infancy* (pp. 229–270). Madison, CT: International Universities Press.

Bradbury, T. N., & Fincham, F. D. (1990). Attributions in marriage: Review and critique. *Psychological Bulletin, 107*, 3–33.

Bray, J. H., & Jouriles, E. N. (1995). Treatment of marital conflict and prevention of divorce.

Journal of Marital and Family Therapy, 21, 461–473.

Chambless, D. L., & Hollon, S. D. (1998). Defining empirically supported therapies. *Journal of Consulting and Clinical Psychology, 66,* 7–18.

Christensen, A., & Heavey, C. L. (1990). Gender and social structure in the demand/withdraw pattern of marital conflict. *Journal of Personality and Social Psychology, 59,* 73–81.

Christensen, A., & Shenk, J. L. (1991). Communication, conflict, and psychological distance in nondistressed, clinic, and divorcing couples. *Journal of Consulting and Clinical Psychology, 59,* 458–463.

Colapinto, J. (1991). Structural family therapy. In A. S. Gurman & D. P. Kniskern (Eds.), *Handbook of family therapy* (Vol. II, pp. 417–443). New York: Brunner/Mazel.

Crowe, M. J. (1978). Conjoint marital therapy: A controlled outcome study. *Psychological Medicine, 8,* 623–636.

Dandeneau, M. L., & Johnson, S. M. (1994). Facilitating intimacy: Interventions and effects. *Journal of Marital and Family Therapy, 20,* 17–33.

Dattilio, F. M., & Padesky, C. A. (1990). *Cognitive therapy with couples.* Sarasota, FL: Professional Resource Exchange.

Davila, J., & Bradbury, T. N. (1996, November). *Attachment stability in the early years of marriage.* Paper presented at the annual meeting of the Association for Advancement of Behavior Therapy, New York.

Davila, J., Burge, D., & Hammen, C. (1997). Why does attachment style change? *Journal of Personality and Social Psychology, 73,* 826–838.

Dunn, R. L., & Schwebel, A. I. (1995). Meta-analytic review of marital therapy outcome research. *Journal of Family Psychology, 9,* 58–68.

Ellis, A. (1977). The nature of disturbed marital interactions. In A. Ellis & R. Grieger (Eds.), *Handbook of rational-emotive therapy* (pp. 170–176). New York: Springer.

Emmelkamp, P., van der Helm, M., MacGillavry, D., & van Zanten, B. (1984). Marital therapy with clinically distressed couples: A comparative evaluation of system-theoretic, contingency contracting, and communication skills approaches. In K. Hahlweg & N. S. Jacobson (Eds.), *Marital interaction: Analysis and modification* (pp. 36–52). New York: Guilford Press.

Emmelkamp, P. M. G., van Linden van den Heuvell, C., Ruphan, M., Sanderman, R., Scholing, A., & Stroink, F. (1988). Cognitive and behavioral interventions: A comparative evaluation with clinically distressed couples. *Journal of Family Psychology, 1,* 365–377.

Epstein, N. (1984). Depression and marital dysfunction: Cognitive and behavioral linkages. *International Journal of Mental Health, 13*(3–4), 86–104.

Epstein, N., & Baucom, D. H. (1989). Cognitive-behavioral marital therapy. In A. Freeman, K. M. Simon, L. E. Beutler, & H. Arkowitz (Eds.), *Comprehensive handbook of cognitive therapy* (pp. 491–513). New York: Plenum.

Epstein, N., & Baucom, D. H. (1993). Cognitive factors in marital disturbance. In K. S. Dobson & P. C. Kendall (Eds.), *Psychopathology and cognition* (pp. 351–385). San Diego: Academic Press.

Epstein, N., Baucom, D. H., & Daiuto, A. (1997). Cognitive-behavioral couples therapy. In W. K. Halford & H. J. Markman (Eds.), *Clinical handbook of marriage and couples intervention* (pp. 415–449). Chichester, England: John Wiley and Sons.

Epstein, N., & Eidelson, R. J. (1981). Unrealistic beliefs of clinical couples: Their relationship to expectations, goals and satisfaction. *American Journal of Family Therapy, 9*(4), 13–22.

Ewart, C. K. (1978, August). *Behavior contracts in couple therapy: An experimental evaluation of quid pro quo and good faith models.* Paper presented at the annual meeting of the Association for Advancement of Behavior Therapy, Toronto.

Fincham, F. D., & Bradbury, T. N. (1989). The impact of attributions in marriage: An experimental analysis. *Journal of Social and Personal Relationships, 6,* 69–86.

Fincham, F. D., Bradbury, T. N., & Scott, C. K. (1990). Cognition in marriage. In F. D. Fincham & T. N. Bradbury (Eds.), *The psychology of marriage: Basic issues and applications* (pp. 118–149). New York: Guilford Press.

Fraenkel, P. (1997). Systems approaches to marital therapy. In W. K. Halford & H. J. Markman (Eds.), *Clinical handbook of marriage and couples interventions* (pp. 379–414). Chichester, England: John Wiley & Sons.

Freedman, J., & Combs, G. (1996). *Narrative therapy: The social construction of preferred realities.* New York: Norton.

Giordano, J., & Carini-Giordano, M. A. (1995). Ethnic dimensions in family treatment. In R. H. Mikesell, D. D. Lusterman, & S. H. McDaniel (Eds.), *Integrating family therapy: Handbook of family psychology and systems theory* (pp. 347–356). Washington, D.C.: American Psychological Association.

Girodo, M., Stein, S. J., & Dotzenroth, S. E. (1980). The effects of communication skills training and contracting on marital relations. *Behavioral Engineering, 6,* 61–76.

Goldman, A., & Greenberg, L. (1992). Comparison of integrated systemic and emotionally focused approaches to couples therapy. *Journal of Consulting and Clinical Psychology, 60,* 962–969.

Gottman, J. M. (1994). *What predicts divorce?* Hillsdale, NJ: Lawrence Erlbaum.

Gottman, J. M., & Krokoff, L. J. (1989). Marital

interaction and satisfaction: A longitudinal view. *Journal of Consulting and Clinical Psychology, 57,* 47–52.

Gottman, J. M., & Levenson, R. W. (1988). The social psychophysiology of marriage. In P. Noller & M. A. Fitzpatrick (Eds.), *Perspectives on marital interaction* (pp. 182–200). Clevedon, England: Multilingual Matters, Ltd.

Greenberg, L. S., & Johnson, S. M. (1988). *Emotionally focused therapy for couples.* New York: Guilford Press.

Hahlweg, K., & Markman, H. J. (1988). Effectiveness of behavioral marital therapy: Empirical status of behavioral techniques in preventing and alleviating marital distress. *Journal of Consulting and Clinical Psychology, 56,* 440–447.

Hahlweg, K., Revenstorf, D., & Schindler, L. (1982). Treatment of marital distress: Comparing formats and modalities. *Advances in Behavior Research and Therapy, 4,* 57–74.

Haley, J. (1976). *Problem-solving therapy.* San Francisco: Jossey-Bass.

Halford, W. K., Kelly, A., & Markman, H. J. (1997). The concept of a healthy marriage. In W. K. Halford & H. J. Markman (Eds.), *Clinical handbook of marriage and couples intervention* (pp. 3–12). Chichester, England: Wiley.

Halford, W. K., Markman, H. J., & Fraenkel, P. (in press). Relationship problems. In M. Hersen & A. Bellack (Eds.), *Comprehensive clinical psychology: Vol. 6. Adult disorders: Clinical formulation and treatment.* New York: Elsevier.

Halford, W. K., Sanders, M. R. & Behrens, B. C. (1993). A comparison of the generalization of behavioral marital therapy and enhanced behavioral marital therapy. *Journal of Consulting and Clinical Psychology, 61,* 51–60.

Holtzworth-Munroe, A., & Jacobson, N. S. (1985). Causal attributions of married couples: When do they search for causes? What do they conclude when they do? *Journal of Personality and Social Psychology, 48,* 1398–1412.

Huber, C. H., & Milstein, B. (1985). Cognitive restructuring and a collaborative set in couples' work. *American Journal of Family Therapy, 13*(2), 17–27.

Iverson, A., & Baucom, D. H. (1990). Behavioral marital therapy outcomes: Alternate interpretations of the data. *Behavior Therapy, 21,* 129–138.

Jacobson, N. S. (1977). Problem-solving and contingency contracting in the treatment of marital discord. *Journal of Consulting and Clinical Psychology, 45,* 92–100.

Jacobson, N. S. (1978). Specific and nonspecific factors in the effectiveness of a behavioral approach to the treatment of marital discord. *Journal of Consulting and Clinical Psychology, 46,* 442–452.

Jacobson, N. S. (1984). A component analysis of behavioral marital therapy: The relative effectiveness of behavioral exchange and communication/problem-solving training. *Journal of Consulting and Clinical Psychology, 52,* 295–305.

Jacobson, N. S., & Addis, M. E. (1993). Research on couples and couple therapy: What do we know? Where are we going? Special Section: Couples and couple therapy. *Journal of Consulting and Clinical Psychology, 61,* 85–93.

Jacobson, N. S., & Christensen, A. (1996). *Integrative couple therapy: Promoting acceptance and change.* New York: Norton.

Jacobson, N. S., & Margolin, G. (1979). *Marital therapy: Strategies based on social learning and behavior exchange principles.* New York: Brunner/Mazel.

Jacobson, N. S., Schmaling, K. B., & Holtzworth-Munroe, A. (1987). Component analysis of behavioral marital therapy: 2-year follow-up and prediction of relapse. *Journal of Marital and Family Therapy, 13,* 187–195.

James, P. S. (1991). Effects of a communication training component added to an emotionally focused couples therapy. *Journal of Marital and Family Therapy, 17,* 263–275.

Johnson, S. M. (1996). *The practice of emotionally focused marital therapy: Creating connection.* New York: Brunner/Mazel.

Johnson, S. M., & Greenberg, L. S. (1985). Differential effects of experiential and problem-solving interventions in resolving marital conflict. *Journal of Consulting and Clinical Psychology, 53,* 175–184.

Johnson, S. M., & Greenberg, L. S. (1994). Emotion in intimate relationships: Theory and implications for therapy. In S. M. Johnson & L. S. Greenberg (Eds.), *The heart of the matter: Perspectives on emotion in marital therapy* (pp. 3–22). New York: Brunner/Mazel.

Johnson, S. M., & Greenberg, L. S. (1995). The emotionally focused approach to problems in adult attachment. In N. S. Jacobson & A. S. Gurman (Eds.), *Clinical handbook of couple therapy* (pp. 121–141). New York: Guilford Press.

Johnson, S. M., Hunsley, J., Greenberg, L., & Schindler, D. (in press). Emotionally focused couples therapy: Status and challenges. *Clinical Psychology.*

Kobak, R., Ruckdeschel, K., & Hazan, C. (1994). From symptom to signal: An attachment view of emotion in marital therapy. In S. M. Johnson & L. S. Greenberg (Eds.), *The heart of the matter: Perspectives on emotion in marital therapy* (pp. 46–71). New York: Brunner/Mazel.

Lebow, J. L., & Gurman, A. S. (1995). Research assessing couple and family therapy. *Annual Review of Psychology, 46,* 27–57.

Levenson, R. W., & Gottman, J. M. (1985).

Physiological and affective predictors of change in relationship satisfaction. *Journal of Personality and Social Psychology, 49,* 85–94.

Levinger, G., & Huston, T. L. (1990). The social psychology of marriage. In F. D. Fincham, & T. N. Bradbury (Eds.), *The psychology of marriage* (pp. 19–58). New York: Guilford.

Liberman, R., Levine, J., Wheeler, E., Sanders, N., & Wallace, C. J. (1976). Marital therapy in groups: A comparative evaluation of behavioral and interaction formats. *Acta Psychiatrica Scandinavica, 266,* 1–34.

Liberman, R. P. (1970). Behavioral approaches to family and couple therapy. *American Journal of Orthopsychiatry, 40,* 106–118.

Madanes, C. (1981). *Strategic family therapy.* San Francisco: Jossey-Bass.

Madanes, C. (1991). Strategic family therapy. In A. S. Gurman & D. P. Kniskern (Eds.), *Handbook of family therapy* (Vol. II, pp. 396–416). New York: Brunner/Mazel.

McDonald, P. (1995). *Families in Australia.* Melbourne: Australian Institute of Family Studies.

Meichenbaum, D. (1977). *Cognitive-behavior modification.* New York: Plenum.

Miller, S. G. (1994). Emotion in the context of systemic marital therapy. In S. M. Johnson & L. S. Greenberg (Eds.), *The heart of the matter: Perspectives on emotion in marital therapy* (pp. 151–171). New York: Brunner/Mazel.

Millwood, C. (1990). What marriage means to young adults. *Family Matters, 29,* 26–28.

Minuchin, S. (1974). *Families and family therapy.* Cambridge, MA: Harvard University Press.

Nichols, M. P., & Schwartz, R. C. (1998). *Family therapy: Concepts and methods* (4th ed.). Boston: Allyn & Bacon.

Noller, P., Beach, S., & Osgarby, S. (1997). Cognitive and affective processes in marriage. In W. K. Halford & H. J. Markman (Eds.), *Clinical handbook of marriage and couples therapy* (pp. 43–71). Chichester, England: Wiley.

O'Hanlon, W. H., & Weiner-Davis, M. (1989). *In search of solutions: A new direction in psychotherapy.* New York: Norton.

O'Leary, K. D., Riso, L. P., & Beach, S. R. (1990). Attributions about the marital discord/depression link and therapy outcome. *Behavior Therapy, 21,* 413–422.

O'Leary, K. D., & Turkewitz, H. (1978). Marital therapy from a behavioral perspective. In T. J. Paolino & B. S. McCrady (Eds.), *Marriage and marital therapy: Psychoanalytic, behavioral and systems theory perspectives* (pp. 240–297). New York: Brunner/Mazel.

Papero, D. V. (1995). Bowen family systems and marriage. In N. S. Jacobson & A. S. Gurman (Eds.), *Clinical handbook of couple therapy* (pp. 11–30). New York: Guilford Press.

Pretzer, J., Epstein, N., & Fleming, B. (1991). Marital Attitude Survey: A measure of dysfunctional attributions and expectancies. *Journal of Cognitive Psychotherapy: An International Quarterly, 5,* 131–148.

Rothbard, J. C., & Shaver, P. R. (1994). Continuity of attachment across the life span. In M. B. Sperling & W. H. Berman (Eds.), *Attachment in adults: Clinical and developmental perspectives* (pp. 31–71). New York: Guilford Press.

Rotter, J. B. (1954). *Social learning and clinical psychology.* Englewood Cliffs, NJ: Prentice-Hall.

Sayers, S. L., Kohn, C. S., & Heavey, C. (in press). Prevention of marital dysfunction: Behavioral approaches and beyond. *Clinical Psychology Review.*

Scharff, J. S. (1995). Psychoanalytic marital therapy. In N. S. Jacobson & A. S. Gurman (Eds.), *Clinical handbook of couple therapy* (pp. 164–193). New York: Guilford Press.

Schmaling, K. B., & Sher, T. G. (1997). Physical health and relationships. In W. K. Halford & H. J. Markman (Eds.), *Clinical handbook of marriage and couples interventions* (pp. 323–345). Chichester, England: Wiley.

Shadish, W. R., Montomery, L. M., Wilson, P., Wilson, M. R., Bright, I., & Okwumabua, T. (1993). Effects of family and marital psychotherapies: A meta-analysis. *Journal of Consulting and Clinical Psychology, 61,* 992–1002.

Shoham, V., Rohrbaugh, M., & Patterson, J. (1995). Problem- and solution-focused couple therapies: The MRI and Milwaukee models. In N. S. Jacobson & A. S. Gurman (Eds.), *Clinical handbook of marital therapy* (pp. 142–163). New York: Guilford Press.

Snyder, D. K. (in press). Affective reconstruction in the context of a pluralistic approach to couple therapy. *Clinical Psychology: Science and Practice.*

Snyder, D. K., & Wills, R. M. (1989). Behavioral versus insight-oriented marital therapy: Effects on individual and interspousal functioning. *Journal of Consulting and Clinical Psychology, 57,* 39–46.

Snyder, D. K., Wills, R. M., & Grady-Fletcher, A. (1991). Long-term effectiveness of behavioral versus insight-oriented marital therapy: A 4-year follow-up study. *Journal of Consulting and Clinical Psychology, 59,* 138–141.

Stuart, R. B. (1980). *Helping couples change: A social learning approach to marital therapy.* New York: Guilford Press.

Thibaut, J. W., & Kelley, H. H. (1959). *The social psychology of groups.* New York: Wiley.

Todd, T. C. (1986). Structural-strategic marital therapy. In N. S. Jacobson & A. S. Gurman (Eds.), *Clinical handbook of marital therapy* (pp. 71–105). New York: Guilford Press.

Tsoi-Hoshmand, L. (1976). Marital therapy: An integrated behavioral-learning approach. *Journal of Marriage and Family Counseling, 2,* 179–191.

Turkewitz, H., & O'Leary, K. D. (1981). A comparative outcome study of behavioral marital therapy and communication therapy. *Journal of Marital and Family Therapy, 7,* 159–169.

Walker, J. G., Johnson, S., Manion, I., & Cloutier, P. (1996). Emotionally focused marital intervention for couples with chronically ill children. *Journal of Consulting and Clinical Psychology, 64,* 1029–1036.

Watzlawick, P., Weakland, J., & Fisch, R. (1974). *Change: Principles of problem formation and problem resolution.* New York: Norton.

Weiner-Davis, M. (1992). *Divorce-busting.* New York: Summit Books.

Weiss, R. L., & Heyman, R. E. (1990). Observation of marital interaction. In F. D. Fincham & T. N. Bradbury (Eds.), *The psychology of marriage: Basic issues and applications* (pp. 87–117). New York: Guilford Press.

Weiss, R. L., & Heyman, R. E. (1997). A clinical-research overview of couples interactions. In W. K. Halford & H. J. Markman (Eds.), *Clinical handbook of marriage and couples intervention* (pp. 13–41). Chichester, England: Wiley.

Weiss, R. L., Hops, H., & Patterson, G. R. (1973). A framework for conceptualizing marital conflict, a technology for altering it, some data for evaluating it. In L. A. Hamerlynck, L. C. Handy, & E. J. Mash (Eds.), *Behavior change: Methodology, concepts, and practice* (pp. 309–342). Champaign, IL: Research Press.

White, M., & Epston, D. (1990). *Narrative means to a therapeutic end.* New York: Norton.

Wilson, G. L., Bornstein, P. H., & Wilson, L. J. (1988). Treatment of relationship dysfunction: An empirical evaluation of group and conjoint behavioral marital therapy. *Journal of Consulting and Clinical Psychology, 56,* 929–931.

CHAPTER 15

GROUPS AS CHANGE AGENTS

DONELSON R. FORSYTH AND JOHN G. CORAZZINI
Virginia Commonwealth University

This chapter is dedicated to the memory of John Corrazinni, who died unexpectedly in October of 1999. With his passing, we have lost not only a wonderful person but a precious resource—a superb combination of psychotherapist and academician. His legacy is the cadre of students who are better therapists because of their time with Jack.

The Center Therapy Group had been meeting in a counseling center, which was located in an urban university, for the past three years. Membership had changed during that period as new members joined and mature members departed, but at the present time eleven individuals were attending regularly. They reported a range of psychological problems, including difficulties in establishing intimate relationships, confusion about their sexual identities, mood and thought disturbances, and problems relating to members of their families. Ann, for example, had been sexually abused by her father and would emotionally abuse her husband. When she told her mother about the abuse, her mother abandoned her in favor of her father. John came to therapy seeking the skills he needed to establish an intimate relationship with a woman. He had dropped out of college and spent some time in the military, but now he was back to finish his degree requirements. Gene had a very close, protective relationship with his mother. He held women, in general, in very high regard, and was reluctant to achieve independence from his mother. Bob had been sexually abused by both his mother and her girlfriend. He had a great deal of difficulty calling it to mind. Linda suffered from esteem problems, resulting in part from conflict with her mother who criticized her constantly. Linda often dressed in black with fishnet stockings, depicting the hated role of the "slut" that had been given her by her mother. Barry came from an abusive family. He protected himself by deflecting onto his brother the abuse his father might give to him.

He and Ann identified with each other in the group. Carl was gay and immature. In addition to several developmental issues, he dealt with the deaths of many friends from AIDS. Jerome lacked self-confidence and talked about settling for romantic partners who were less than what he wanted but would not reject him.

These eleven members of the Center Therapy Group were guided in their therapeutic journey by three mental health professionals. One therapist, a male, had worked as the group's leader during its entire three-year history. A woman cotherapist had been with the group for two years and an intern had been working in the group for several months. These therapists actively orchestrated the content and direction of the hour-long weekly sessions, shifting the group's attention to various concerns shared by the members.

The Center Therapy Group helped most of its members with their problems. Some individuals dropped out of the group before achieving the change they sought, but many more underwent substantial growth and experienced improved psychological adjustment during their tenure in the group. Why? What powerful interpersonal dynamics does the group therapist harness to promote adjustment and beneficial change in members? This chapter examines these questions by scrutinizing both professionally guided groups used to sustain well-being and mental health (e.g., psychotherapy groups, training groups) as well as spontaneous, grassroots groups that also provide members with psychological sustenance (e.g., self-help groups, support groups). We consider the history of group approaches and the forms they currently take before appraising their overall utility.

VARIETIES OF CHANGE-PROMOTING GROUPS

That a group can be used as a change-promoting agent is not a new idea. Throughout history, personal change often has been achieved through social mechanisms rather than individualistic, asocial processes. Ettin (1992), for example, argues persuasively that the groups used by Socrates and described in the Dialogues—where he examined important philosophical and value issues through guided discussion and questioning—differ little from educational and training groups used today. Marsh (1935, p. 382) similarly suggests that most religious movements that developed around charismatic leaders were therapeutic in nature, for devotees were "partly seekers for knowledge, but they were also seekers for emotional help." Such groups were "a form of group therapy as well as a form of education."

The types of groups that are most numerous today—the therapy group, the interpersonal learning group, and the self-help group—emerged in their contemporary forms between 1910 and 1950. During this period, psychotherapy itself emerged as a means of helping people deal with mental and emotional problems. In some cases, physicians, psychiatrists, psychologists, and other mental health practitioners applied these basic change principles in group settings. These applications often began as local, setting-specific methods but evolved into more general, widely dispersed treatment procedures.

Early Group Therapists

Although the precise point of origin, that first group formed by a mental health professional and that focused on therapeutic goals, is much debated, most sources trace the systematic use of groups as agents of therapeutic change back to 1905 and Joseph Hersey Pratt's group approach to treating patients suffering from tuberculosis. Pratt, a physician with a background in psychology and theology, arranged for patients to gather in groups so that he could give them instruction in personal hygiene. He turned to the group format because it was so efficient: "I originally brought the patients together as a group simply with the idea that it would save my time" (Pratt,

1922, p. 403). But he soon recognized that group-level processes were contributing to the success of his treatments; accordingly, he gradually put less stress on the informational aspects of the groups and increased their interpersonal dynamics. Many of the groups developed tendencies seen in modern-day self-help groups, including sharing of information among members, encouraging testimonial sessions by veteran members, and robust cohesiveness. Pratt refined his methods to focus more on psychological gains, and expanded his groups to include people who suffered from other physical illnesses (e.g., diabetes) and psychological disturbances. By the 1930s he was leading "Thought Control Classes" with individuals who were suffering from nervous disorders (Pratt, 1922).

Pratt was not the only practitioner experimenting with groups during this period. Psychiatrist Edward Lazell, for example, felt that progress in individual therapy sessions would be faster if he delivered information to patients about common psychosexual developmental issues in a group format. So, he gathered his patients together—many of whom were suffering from substantial thought disorders—for lectures on such topics as fear of death, inferiority feelings, narcissism, and overcompensation (Lazell, 1921). At about this same time, Cody Marsh, who most sources describe as a "minister turned psychiatrist" (e.g., Ettin, 1992; Scheidlinger, 1993), was stressing the interpersonal dynamics of groups over the informational content he provided to the group members. He believed that psychological problems weren't rooted in psychosexual problems or biochemical imbalances, but in difficulties in one's interpersonal relations. He summed up his approach with the slogan "By the crowd they have been broken, by the crowd they shall be healed" (Marsh, 1933, p. 407). Marsh also anticipated milieu therapies by opening up his sessions to all members of the community.

A number of early psychoanalytically oriented therapists also turned to group techniques, either in part or exclusively. Kanzer (1983) even goes so far as to suggest that Freud's famous Viennese Circle, which met from 1901 to 1907, was, in some respects, a therapy group. The explicit purpose of the group was to explore and refine Freud's ideas regarding therapy and the nature of personality, but many of the members experienced deep personal change as a result of their participation in the group. The group was an extremely turbulent one, however, and Roth

(1993) suggests that Freud's leadership style and close control over the group process undermined the group's therapeutic value. Indeed, the group ended with the rebellion of Adler, who went on to establish group-centered treatment methods with families and with unrelated patients. He and his colleagues (most notably, Dreikurs, 1959) called this method "Collective Therapy," which stressed self-insight by observing one's interactions with other people.

Trigant Burrow (1927), though trained as a psychoanalyst and a founding member of the American Psychoanalytic Association, also rejected individual analysis in favor of a group approach. He argued that most psychological disorders could be traced back to social relationships rather than intrapsychic turmoil. As such, individual psychoanalysis was artificial because it cut the patient off from contact with other people. He guided his groups in an exploration of the meaning behind any interpersonal processes that occurred in the groups, and has been credited with such concepts as group analysis, group-as-a-whole, and the development of the here-and-now approach with colleague Hans Syz (Rosenbaum, 1963).

Slavson, Moreno, and Legitimization of Group Approaches

Group approaches to change in various mental health facilities were used more and more routinely in the years before and after World War II. Publications describing group methods, with such titles as "Group psychotherapy: A study of its application" (Wender, 1940), "The psychoanalysis of groups" (Wolf, 1949), "Results and problems of group psychotherapy in severe neurosis" (Schilder, 1939), and "Group activities in a children's ward as methods of psychotherapy" (Bender, 1937) signaled the growing acceptance of the method by professionals and the lay public. (Ettin [1992], Kibel [1992], and Rosenbaum [1965] provide extensive histories of the development of group therapy.)

Samuel Slavson and Jacob Moreno were two of the most vocal advocates of group therapy during this period of growth and legitimization. Slavson initially used a group approach with adolescents who were isolated from their peers or suffered from poor relations with their parents. His small, eight- to ten-person *activity groups* met for two hours under the watchful eye of a permissive, nondirective therapist. The activities included art projects, crafts, cooking, and interac-

tive games, but the children were permitted to set their own agendas, even to the point of withdrawing from the group's activities altogether. Slavson noted that such groups could be very boisterous and even violent initially, but that over time group structures developed and interactions became routinized. Slavson, who drew on psychoanalytic theory, believed that submersion in such a group increased self-worth, impulse control, and insight: "The new feeling of security they have found in the special group is applied to other life situations, and their egos are further strengthened and their feelings about themselves become more positive and wholesome" (Slavson, 1950, p. 43).

With adults, Slavson practiced what he called *analytic group therapy*, which emphasized interviews of the patients by the therapist and group discussion. These sessions were conducted much like individual psychoanalytic therapy, stressing transference, catharsis, ego-strengthening, insight, and reality testing, but with these advantages: the presence of people with similar problems helped members speak more freely about their difficulties; supportive friendships developed; and the group helped members deal with the transference problems causing tension between the patient and therapist.

Slavson is responsible for many advances in the use of therapeutic groups, including the founding of the American Group Psychotherapy Association in 1942 and the *International Journal of Group Psychotherapy* in 1951. He has also been credited with coining the phrase *group dynamics*, although he explicitly discounted the relevance of group-level processes in his analytic therapy groups. Unlike his predecessors, Slavson stressed individual functioning and considered the group to be a catalyst only. When in groups, an individual's hidden concerns often surface, allowing the therapist to recognize them quickly and then confront them. The group's dynamics, however, were largely irrelevant to Slavson.

The latter view contrasts sharply with Jacob Moreno's. Moreno conducted therapeutic groups perhaps as early as 1910, and he used the term *group therapy* in print in 1932. Moreno believed that the interpersonal relations that developed in groups provided the therapist with unique insights into each member's personality and proclivities, and that by taking on roles the members become more flexible in their behavioral orientations. He made his sessions experientially powerful by developing psychodrama techniques. During psychodrama sessions, the group members reenacted specific turbulent episodes from group members' lives or events that happened within the group. Moreno believed that psychodrama's emphasis on physical action was more involving than passive discussion, and that the drama itself helped members overcome their reluctance to discuss critical issues (Kipper, 1978; Sacks, 1993). Moreno also developed sociometry to aid him in the analysis of the interpersonal relations linking group members and founded a journal with that name in 1938 (now titled *Social Psychology Quarterly*).

Contemporary Practices

Years ago, practitioners questioned the relative value of group approaches and relied on them only when circumstances made individual approaches impossible. But this view eventually gave way as group approaches emerged as appropriate treatments for a variety of problems, including addiction, thought disorders, depression, eating disorders, and personality disorders (Kaplan & Sadock, 1993; Long, 1998; Spira, 1997). Therapists who traditionally used only dyadic, one-on-one methods added group sessions, either supplementing or completely replacing their individual sessions. Not only did these therapists draw on the earlier work of such pioneers as Marsh, Burrow, Moreno, and Slavson, but they also integrated these approaches with their personal, and often eclectic, approach to treatment. Extensive reviews of the field by Brabender and Fallon (1993), Dies (1992), Ettin (1992), Kaplan and Sadock (1993), Spira (1997), and Yalom (1995) identify an array of approaches, including psychoanalytic, systems, object relations, problem-solving, educative, interpersonal, developmental, transactional, existential, Gestalt, humanistic, and cognitive-behavioral methods. We consider some of these contemporary methods next, after noting that this review is far from exhaustive. Indeed, the variety of contemporary group approaches is enormous.

Psychoanalytic Groups

Psychoanalysis, by tradition, is an individual treatment modality. The analyst, through directives, free association, interpretation, and transference, creates a powerful relationship with the client, who then gains insight into unresolved conflicts. But in *Group Psychology and the Analysis of Ego*, Freud (1922) explained a person's willingness to submit to the authority of a leader in terms of transference processes: Individuals accept their group leaders as authority figures, and other group members come to take the place of siblings. Group membership becomes an unconscious means of regaining the security of the family, and the emotional ties that bind members to their groups are like the ties that bind children to their family (Kohut, 1984).

Psychoanalysis in groups exploits these transference mechanisms to promote change in members. The therapist becomes the central authority in such groups, and usually relies on the traditional tools of the analyst as he or she directs the session and summarizes the group's efforts. By shifting attention from one patient to the next during the course of a single group session, members change their roles during the session—sometimes acting as the patient seeking help, at other times the observer of another's problems, and on occasion the helper who gives counsel to a fellow group member. This rotation gives patients an opportunity to observe others' responses to situations that are similar to their own, and also to observe the dynamic interplay between the authority and their "sibling." Although individual therapy usually stimulates parental transference, during group psychoanalysis sibling transference also occurs. Members may find themselves reacting to one another inappropriately, but their actions, when examined more closely, may parallel the way they treated a brother or a sister when they were young (Day, 1981; Kutash & Wolf, 1993; Rutan & Stone, 1993).

Freudian principles permeate most group approaches. Rare is the therapist who does not deal with transference processes, the interpretation of fantasies or dreams, familial tensions, and other latent conflicts. Treatments generally divaricate, however, in their emphasis on individual versus group processes. Many analysts agree with Slavson by stressing the importance of the individual in the group, rather than the group itself. Wolf (1949), for example, called his approach "psychoanalysis *in* groups" rather than "psychoanalysis *of* groups," and argued against spending too much time considering dynamic relationships within the group. Those who adopt this view suggest that the term *group psychotherapy* is a "misnomer for a technique that, although conducted in a group, is designed to aid an individual patient; it is a treatment of ailing individual patients in a group setting, not a treatment of ailing groups, because only individual patients have intrapsychic dynamics" (Kutash & Wolf, 1993,

p. 126; see, too, Kibel & Stein, 1981; Slavson, 1957; Wolf & Schwartz, 1962).

The group-as-a-whole approach reaches a very different conclusion. Although these approaches embrace psychoanalytic assumptions of unconscious motivations, personality conflicts, and transference, they strive to integrate the treatment of the individual with the analysis of the group-as-a-whole. Rather than ignoring the tension between individuality and group membership, the group-as-a-whole approaches capitalize on these tensions to promote growth and development. This approach is rooted in the work of Foulkes (1964) and Bion (1961), who argued that psychological problems are always interpersonal ones. Bion maintained that just as individuals rely on defense mechanisms to cope with ego threats, groups use strategies to cope with uncertainties and anxieties. Many of these strategies are rooted in dependence, for the group members engage in collective projective identification in an attempt to transfer responsibility for their problems from themselves to the leader. Groups also engage in fight-or-flight reactions and often concentrate their attention on pairs of members within the group, in a process Bion called *basic assumption pairing*. Bion felt that group members gain tremendous insights into both individual and collective defensive processes by examining these ubiquitous, but essentially maladaptive, processes. His work provided the basis for the Tavistock Institute of Human Relations (Ettin, Cohen, & Fidler, 1997; Horwitz, 1993).

Cognitive-Behavioral and Behavioral Therapy Groups

Cognitive-behavioral and behavioral approaches, which have emerged as influential and effective treatment methods in recent decades (e.g., Ingram, Kendall, & Chen, 1991), provide the theoretical and technical basis for some group therapies. These approaches do not focus on unconscious conflicts, interpersonal transactions, or group-as-a-whole dynamics, but instead assume that symptomatic thoughts and behaviors can be controlled through careful application of learning principles (Skinner, 1953, 1971). Behavior therapies tend to focus more on explicit, observable behaviors, such as social or relationship skills. Cognitive-behavioral approaches, such as Ellis's (1973) rational-emotive therapy, Meichenbaum's (1977) cognitive-behavior modification, and Beck's (1976) cognitive therapy, focus on changing cognitive processes. Beck,

for example, helps individuals overcome mood disorders by training them to recognize and eliminate such errors in thinking as overgeneralizing, catastrophizing, blaming oneself, and black–white thinking.

These approaches often are used in one-on-one settings, but they also can be applied in group settings (Flowers, 1979; Hollander & Kazaoka, 1988; Rose, 1993). Behavioral therapists tend to be more active within their groups, and the groups themselves are usually more structured. The goals and methods of the group are clearly described to participants, who may go through a period of pregroup training. During this period a staunch behaviorist—one who stresses objective measurement of symptoms before, during, and after treatment—would identify the specific behaviors and cognitions that will be modified and devise the means of assessing them. Clients also may watch videotaped examples of group therapy sessions, with the deliberate intention of creating change-enhancing expectancies and the identification of specific therapeutic goals (Higginbotham, West, & Forsyth, 1988). At this point the therapist also might ask the patients to sign a behavioral contract that describes in objective terms the goals the group members are trying to achieve.

During treatment, therapists rely on a number of behavioral methods, including modeling, rehearsal, and feedback. The group leaders may engage in a one-minute conversation with each other, videotape the interaction, and then play it back to the group while identifying the nonverbal and verbal behaviors that made the conversation flow smoothly. During rehearsal, group members practice particular skills themselves, either with one another or through role-playing exercises. These practice sessions can be videotaped and played back to the group so the participants can see precisely what they are doing correctly and what aspects of their behavior need improvement. This feedback phase involves not only reassurance and praise from the leaders but also support from the other group members (Bellack & Hersen, 1979; Curran, 1977; Galassi & Galassi, 1979).

Interpersonal Group Psychotherapy

Irvin D. Yalom, in his well-received *The Theory and Practice of Group Psychotherapy* (1995), describes his interpersonal approach to treatment. This approach assumes that because most problems, such as depression, anxiety, and personality disorders, can be traced back to social sources, then social sources can be used to provide relief (Kiesler, 1991). Yalom's (1995) interpersonal group psychotherapy (also called interactive group psychotherapy) uses the group as a *social microcosm* where members respond to one another in ways that are characteristic of their interpersonal tendencies outside of the group. Therapy groups, as groups, display a full array of group dynamics, including social influence, structure, conflict, and development. The therapist takes advantage of the group's dynamics to help members learn about how they influence others, and how others influence them. Members do not discuss problems they are facing at home or work, but instead focus on interpersonal experiences within the group: the *here-and-now* rather than the *then-and-there*. When, for example, two members begin criticizing each other, a client uses powerful influence tactics, or another refuses to get involved in the group's meetings, therapists prompt group members to examine and explain the members' interaction (Yalom, 1995).

Yalom's interpersonal model is unique in its emphasis on identifying, and exploiting, curative factors in groups. In examining group methods, Yalom distinguishes the *front* from the *core*. A therapeutic method's front includes its procedures, techniques, and nuances: a Gestalt therapist uses different techniques than a psychoanalyst, who in turns acts very differently from a cognitive-behavior therapist. But beneath these various fronts, Yalom finds a shared core of mechanisms that promote change and sustain well-being. He terms these shared core qualities *curative factors*, and his list includes the installation of hope, universality, the imparting of information, altruism, the corrective recapitulation of the primary family group, the development of socializing techniques, imitative behavior, interpersonal learning, group cohesiveness, catharsis, and existential factors. Some of the factors on Yalom's list are mechanisms that are responsible for facilitating change, whereas others describe the general group conditions that should be present within effective groups.

Interpersonal Learning Groups

Lakin (1972), in his insightful review of types of change-promoting groups, draws a distinction between therapeutic groups and learning groups. Therapeutic groups, as described earlier, are typically led by a mental health professional, and patients are suffering from diagnosed clinical conditions. Participants in learning groups, in contrast, seek to become more aware of, and skilled at, interpersonal relationships. Learning groups are often considered "therapy for normals." Lakin also discusses expressive groups, in which participants strive to express their emotions more completely. Expressive groups are relatively rare.

Analyses of the roots of interpersonal learning groups generally began with Kurt Lewin (1936). Indeed, it was Lewin who stated the basic law of change in groups: "It is easier to change individuals formed into a group than to change any of them separately" (1951, p. 228). Lewin believed that, in many cases, groups and organizations fail because their members aren't trained in human relations. He therefore recommended close examination of group experiences to give people a deeper understanding of themselves and their group's dynamics. Other theorists expanded on this basic idea, and by 1965 the human potential movement was in high gear (Back, 1973; Gazda & Brooks, 1985; Lakin, 1972). Varieties included T groups, encounter groups, and structured training groups.

Training Groups (T Groups)

Although groups have long been used to help members explore their relationships with others and their interpersonal skills, contemporary use of learning groups can be traced to a workshop held on the campus of the State Teachers College in Connecticut in 1946 (Benne, 1964). The procedures used in the workshops were designed by Kenneth Benne, Leland Bradford, and Ronald Lippitt. Kurt Lewin and his students were on hand to document their effectiveness. The trainers had planned to rely on relatively unstructured group discussions in their teaching, but during an evening review session, the organizers realized that much more could be gained if members could review the processes that were occurring within their discussion groups. This discovery is generally credited to Kurt Lewin, who permitted the trainees to sit in on the review sessions even though the researchers were discussing the trainees' behaviors. Lippitt (interviewed by Back, 1973, pp. 8–9) describes this unique event as follows:

> And on this particular night, three of the trainees, three school teachers who hadn't gone home that evening, stuck their heads in the door and asked if they could come in, sit, and observe and listen, and Kurt (Lewin)

was rather embarrassed, and we all were expecting him to say no, but he didn't, he said, "Yes, sure, come in and sit down." And we went right ahead as though they weren't there, and pretty soon one of them was mentioned and her behavior was described and discussed, and the trainee and the researcher had somewhat different observations, perceptions of what had happened, and she became very agitated and said that wasn't the way it happened at all, and she gave her perception. And Lewin got quite excited about this additional data and put it on the board to theorize it, and later on in the evening the same thing happened in relation to one of the other two. . . . And the next night the whole fifty were there and were every night, and so it became the most significant training event of the day as this feedback and review of process of events that had gone on during the work sessions of the day.

This serendipitous discovery prompted Lewin's students and the trainers to stress the importance of group process analysis when they created a curriculum for use in a time-limited residential community located in Bethel, Maine (Bradford, Gibb, & Benne, 1964). The training setting was termed a laboratory because the experiences were stimulating, experimental, but drawn from theoretical analyses relevant to behavior change. The laboratory, which was initially sponsored by the National Education Association, the Research Center for Group Dynamics, and the Office of Naval Research (ONR), assumed skills are most easily acquired by actually experiencing human relations. Hence, they were termed training groups, or T groups. As one advocate of group training explained, "The training laboratory is a special environment in which they learn new things about themselves. . . . It is a kind of emotional re-education" (Marrow, 1964, p. 25). After Lewin's death in 1947, his colleagues organized the National Training Laboratory (NTL), and during the last 50 years, thousands of educators, executives, and leaders have participated in its programs (Bednar & Kaul, 1979; Burke & Day, 1986; R. E. Kaplan, 1979).

Structured Training Groups

In NTL groups, the activities of trainees are carefully planned, but much of the time is spent in open-ended group meetings. These groups include a facilitator or trainer who acts primarily as a catalyst for discussion rather than as director of the group. In most cases, the group members experience considerable conflict during the first few days of a session as members grapple with situational ambiguity and they pressure the trainer for leadership support. This ambiguity is built into the curriculum, however, for it shifts responsibility for structuring, understanding, and controlling the group's activities to the participants. During this period, the members reveal their preferred interaction styles to others, and they learn to disclose their feelings honestly, gain conflict-reduction skills, and find enjoyment from working in collaborative relationships.

Structured learning groups, in contrast, are planned interventions that focus on a specific interpersonal problem or skill. Integrating behavioral therapies with interpersonal learning, the group leaders identify specific learning outcomes before the sessions. They then develop behaviorally focused exercises that will help members practice these targeted skills. If the session deals with problems with communication, members may be split into pairs, and the pairs then practice sending messages using only nonverbal channels. During assertiveness training, group members might practice saying no to one another's requests. In a leadership training seminar, group members may be asked to role-play various leadership styles in a small group. These exercises are similar in that they actively involve the group members in the learning process.

Thousands of local and national institutes use structured learning groups in their seminars and workshops. Although the formats for these structured experiences differ substantially, most include (a) an orientation session in which the leader, usually in a lecture format, reviews the critical issues and focuses members on the exercise's goals; (b) an experiential phase during which the group members complete a highly structured exercise; (c) a debriefing phase when the group discusses the experience, with the leader providing interpretations and guidance; and (d) an application phase when the group members use their newfound knowledge to enhance their relationships at work and home (Forsyth, 1999).

Growth Groups

During the 1950s and 1960s, a version of the T group emerged that focused explicitly on enhancing positive emotions and the quality of one's relations. As the purpose of the training shifted from learning about various group processes to enhancing spontaneity, personal growth, and sensitivity to others, a new label developed for such groups: sensitivity training, or encounters (Johnson, 1988; Lieberman, 1994).

Moreno first discussed the concept of an encounter in his 1914 *Invitation to an Encounter* (Moreno, 1953, p. 7), but the technique did not gain momentum until political and social changes increased the value placed on empathy, emotional understanding, and close interpersonal relations. Carl Rogers's client-centered methods, although often used in both individual and group therapies, initially provided the foundation for growth groups. Drawing on Rogers's self-psychology, these methods assumed that members too often experience self-rejection because their needs for approval and love are rarely satisfied. To minimize expected rejection from others, people tend to keep their interpersonal relations relatively superficial. Encounter groups help members restore their trust in their own feelings, their acceptance of their personal qualities, and promote openness in interactions with others. During sessions members are encouraged to open up to one another by displaying their inner emotions, thoughts, and worries, and the group coordinator stresses mutual understanding by modeling empathy and unconditional positive regard. In most groups, leaders make use of experiential exercises that help members express intense feelings of anger, caring, loneliness, and helplessness. Stripped of defensiveness and facades, Rogers believed, group members would encounter each other *authentically*.

Large Group Awareness Training (LGAT)

Back (1973) calls the rise of growth groups in the 1960s and 1970s a social movement: a deliberate, relatively organized attempt to achieve a change in a social system. But the movement has matured in recent years, and in doing so has changed from a social movement into a social movement *organization*. Social movement organizations still strive to achieve change, but they have lost their local, parochial flavor. Like any organization they have clearly defined goals, rational planning, and bureaucratic leadership structures (Snow & Oliver, 1995).

These organizations, which Lieberman (1994) calls LGATs (Large Group Awareness Training), include EST, FORUM, and Lifespring. Their members seek to improve their overall level of satisfaction and interpersonal relations, but instead of joining a local encounter group, they become members of these large organizations. Lieberman notes that these organizations use methods that combine aspects of structured training groups and encounter groups. Lifespring, for example, uses music, role-play exercises, lectures, and guided group interaction in an attempt to increase self-awareness, self-confidence, positive thinking, and skilled interaction with others. Lieberman suggests that at least 1.3 million Americans have taken part in LGAT sessions.

Self-Help Groups

Self-help groups (SHGs) existed long before practitioners began to make use of groups for therapeutic purposes. Because SHGs are voluntary associations that form spontaneously when individuals who share a common problem meet to exchange information and social support, they are rarely formally documented in the literature on groups. SHGs, which are also known as mutual support groups, likely have primordial origins.

The variety of self-help groups is enormous. SHGs exist for nearly every major medical, psychological, or stress-related problem, including groups for sufferers of heart disease, cancer, liver disease, and AIDs; groups for people who provide care for those suffering from chronic disease, illness, and disability; groups to help people overcome addictions to alcohol and other substances; groups for children of parents overcome by addictions to alcohol and other substances; and groups for a variety of problems in living, such as groups for helping people with money or time management problems. These groups differ from each other in many ways, but most are self-governing, with members rather than experts or mental health professionals determining activities. They also tend to stress the importance of treating all members fairly and giving everyone an opportunity to express their viewpoints. The members face a common predicament, problem, or concern, so they are "psychologically bonded by the compelling similarity of member concerns" (Jacobs & Goodman, 1989, p. 537). These groups all stress the importance of reciprocal helping, for members are supposed to both give help to others as well as receive it from others. SHGs usually charge little in the way of fees, and they form because the members' needs are not being met by existing educational, social, or health agencies.

Self-help groups are growing in terms of numbers and members, with perhaps as many as 8 million people in the United States alone belonging to such groups (Christensen & Jacobson, 1994; Goodman & Jacobs, 1994; Jacobs & Goodman, 1989). Jacobs and Goodman explain the rise of SHGs in terms of the erosion of the family, increase in the number of people still living with significant diseases, erosion of confidence in care providers, lack of mental health services, increased faith in the value of social support as a buffer against stress, and increased media attention provided by TV docudramas. Jacobs and Goodman feel that self-help groups will continue to increase, and that they will eventually take a large portion of the mental health dollar away from more traditional approaches.

The best-known self-help group, Alcoholics Anonymous, can be traced back to a specific individual and date of origin: Bill Wilson and 1935. Wilson, a confirmed alcoholic, relapsed many times before, he claims, he had a profound, mystical experience forcing a recognition of his powerlessness over his alcoholism but also his oneness with the universe. To explain the experience, he examined the writings of psychologists William James and Carl Jung, and eventually concluded that such experiences could be triggered by periods of negativity, depression, and helplessness. Wilson built AA around this spiritual experience, and required that members submit to a larger force and abandon their sense of individuality by remaining anonymous. Wilson then connected with a small group-based primitive spiritual group, the Oxford Group Movement, and his friend, physician, and fellow alcoholic William D. Silkworth. The result was a system of behavioral change that stressed self-examination, admitting past wrongs, rebuilding relationships and making amends, and reliance on and helping others.

Wilson's program formed the basis of Alcoholics Anonymous (AA), which became an international organization with millions of members. Despite AA's size, change is still achieved through local chapters of alcoholics who meet regularly to review their success in maintaining sobriety. AA assumes that alcoholism is a disease and that it has no cure. Individuals must remain abstinent, and social drinking is not considered an option. Many of the rituals and structures of AA are designed to prevent drinking, often through mutual support and providing positive examples. AA also makes the goal of sobriety attainable by requiring members to concentrate on not drinking each day,

rather than consider long-range methods for controlling their drinking.

AA groups are ubiquitous yet rarely scrutinized by researchers. They have been spared this scrutiny, in part, because their anonymity makes study complex for investigators. Moreover, AA tends to be value-laden in its approach to treating alcoholism, and hardnosed researchers often avoid studying such groups. But, as Miller (1995) notes, AA is one of the most widely used methods for treating addictions.

SOURCES OF CHANGE IN GROUPS

The members of the Center Therapy Group all experienced benefits from their membership. Before treatment they were troubled by feelings of low self-esteem, depression, misgivings about their ability to relate effectively to others, and a variety of specific behavioral and psychological problems. These problems had, however, abated as the group reached its scheduled dissolution. Why? What processes were at work within the group that helped the members improve their psychological functioning?

We preface our analysis of these issues by looking more closely at the processes that operated within a typical session of the Center Therapy Group. The transcript excerpts a longer session, and is a concrete illustration of the psychological and interpersonal processes that lie at the foundation of group approaches to treatment. In this particular session eight members were present, and the discussion focused on family and interpersonal relations.

Bob: I saw my girl friend the other day. She was waiting to talk to me. To reach closure about our relationship.

Gene: Do you feel bad about the breakup? Do you feel responsible?

Bob: I think it is over. I don't feel complete but I don't think there is any chance we can work it out.

Male therapist: One of the themes of this group has been no hope; passivity.

Bob: It affects everything. You want to be in the middle, but you stand on the outside.

Male therapist: Like in here, too?

Bob: Yah! You know what's going on in here but I feel so stupid. My mind is so cluttered. This applies to everything. Like I'm hiding behind a wall.

Male therapist: There is this "reluctance" or

"passivity" in the group. It's more than one person's issue.

John: I feel like this all the time. Like there is a governor in me. I'd like to be full throttle. I'm not alive because of that. I need to apologize for not being here for several weeks and to you, Jill [female leader], especially.

John then explained why he could not attend group. John had not attended the Center Therapy Group since the group's co-leader, Jill, had confronted him.

John: I feel bad about this.

Male therapist: Any chance if you were free, there would still be some reluctance about coming to therapy?

John: Yes, some fear.

Male therapist: Fear of what?

John: The woman in red. [Jill wore a red dress that day.]

Male therapist: But what is so intimidating about her?

John: I don't know.

Male therapist: Maybe someone in the group can help. Is anyone else afraid of Jill?

John: I just feel overwhelmed.

Male therapist: Are there any other women in the group that have the same effect on you?

John: I feel like all women have some affect on me, but it is not as intense.

After some probing as to what it was about Jill, John admitted he was romantically attracted to her.

Male therapist: Can you tell the group how you are feeling right now?

John: I'm really feeling very anxious.

Gene: I'm the opposite. I have a harder time dealing with guys. My friends in high school were women. I'm not afraid of her.

Male therapist: You'd rather sit next to her.

Ann: I'm totally intimidated by her. It's like she is the totally complete package. She's pretty, smart, and carries herself well.

Male therapist: You relate better with men than you do with other women.

Ann: Yes, but I also relate better to Linda [another female group member]. Thank God that she is here. Jill is just too together. I'd like to be like her. To carry myself like that.

John: I've been clobbered in my relationships with women. What would a slob like me do in a relationship with a woman like Jill?

Male therapist: So you have feelings for her. Yet you wonder what chance a slob like you would have with a woman like her.

Co-therapist: I [Jill] have noticed you. I said you are attractive and I feel you haven't heard me.

John: I have trouble with trust. I've been clobbered so often.

Male therapist: Let's get some other reactions.

Jerome: I see her as the ideal mother. She listens and is insightful. My mom doesn't listen.

Barry: She's not perfect. She doesn't talk enough. She doesn't have enough milk for me.

Linda: I had to defend myself from my mother. She called me a slut. I'm intimidated by this whole thing. I don't feel close to my mother.

Intern: I wonder if you're afraid if Jill or I will judge you?

Linda: Yes, I am.

Male therapist: What would it take you to see Jill or other women as women who are different from those that you have known?

Ann: Women's relationships are different. They are very powerful. You tell other women your soul. I don't know what men talk about. Probably cars or something. Women want deep connections. If another woman knows your stuff, they could really hurt you.

Linda: My mother betrayed me.

Male therapist: You used quiet to take care of yourself. Your passivity has been positive. Where are some of the others in the group with these issues?

Gene: I'm comfortable with my mother. I want to hear more from my dad [pointing to the male group leader sitting in the circle opposite to him]. My mother is always right. Women know everything. I just want to hear more from my dad. Women have played a very powerful role in my life; you need to take what they say. For example, when I told my mother I was in group therapy, she asked if the group was talking about her yet. I told her no. But one month later we were talking about her. See, they know.

Male therapist: And when your girlfriend said she was going to commit suicide if you left her . . .

Gene: She tried to. Women are magnificent. They have all the right answers and everything you need.

Male therapist: You can't be who you are without their support; you're beholden to them. Isn't that right, Bob?

Bob: I don't know. I sort of blanked out. I'm feeling confused [*Bob begins to cry*]. My thoughts are all jumbled; I can't make them out.

Jerome: I want to see women as equal instead of up here [*points to a place over his head*].

Barry: But it's weird. I feel like this woman thing is going to fix me. This is my salvation. Women just don't have enough milk for me.

Gene: I didn't date in high school. They kept me at their control. They let me be their friend, but not their boyfriend. No one gave me a chance.

Male therapist: You felt used.

Linda: Guys only wanted me for sex.

Intern: How did that make you feel?

Linda: Shitty!

Carl: They are the ones that are sluts. I like you and I don't want to have sex with you.

Male therapist: We've been talking about how moms have often been inadequate in our lives. That they haven't been enough in some cases. Bob, if Jill could help you right now, what would you want from her?

Bob: She reminds me of my mom's best friend.

Male therapist: Is she a nice person?

Bob: Yes, but she likes to sleep around. I do see her as a mother figure, too.

Male therapist: That has to be very confusing.

Bob: Yes.

Male therapist: I wouldn't know how to relate to her. What do you do with all of this, Jill? Bob says you're not enough and others are afraid of you. I wonder what they are going to do?

The group ended with a number of members stating what they wanted to do in future sessions.

Linda: I'd like to hear more about your feelings, Jill.

Ann: I'd like to hear about how not to be so judgmental.

This session of the Center Therapy Group is consistent with prior analysis of the therapeutic mechanisms that operate in groups. It hints at the processes identified by Lakin (1972), who argued that the successful group must facilitate emotional expression and feelings of belongingness, but it also must stimulate interpersonal comparisons and provide members with an interaction forum. The session also underscores Bednar and Kaul's (1978) concept of a "developing social microcosm," "interpersonal feedback and consensual validation," and "reciprocal opportunities to be both helpers and helpees in group settings" (p. 781). Yalom's (1995) curative factors, which were noted earlier, can also be detected in the session (e.g., Butler & Fuhriman, 1983a, 1983b; Crouch, Bloch, & Wanlass, 1994; Markovitz & Smith, 1983; Maxmen, 1973, 1978; Rohrbaugh & Bartels, 1975; Rugel & Myer, 1984; Sherry & Hurley, 1976; Yalom, 1995; Yalom & Vinogradov, 1993). Yalom gleaned these factors from his clinical experience and empirical research, but the list is generally consistent with theoretical analyses of groups in general (Forsyth, 1996). Table 15.1 summarizes some of these change-promoting factors, and we discuss them next.

Universality and Hope

One of the first, and most fundamental, sources of psychological sustenance in groups is a sense of shared calamity and misfortune. Even Pratt (1922), although originally only interested in using groups to reach a larger number of patients, was struck by they way his discouraged, pessimistic patients became hopeful and optimistic in their groups. When group members first join their groups they often feel that their problems are unique ones, but by comparing themselves to others in the group they come to recognize the *universality* of the problems they face. This idea is consistent with such phrases as "strength in numbers," "we are all in the same boat," and "we are not alone."

The sense of universality is a consequence of social comparison processes that naturally occur in groups. When individuals feel threatened or confused, they often affiliate with others. Schachter's (1959) classic study of women waiting to receive electric shocks, for example, confirmed the tendency people have to seek group membership in times of stress. Through affiliation, people secure social support, but they also can acquire information about their condition from other group members. Indeed, when people are with others who face similar problems or troubling events, they feel better in terms of self-esteem and mood than when they are with dissimilar people (Frable, Platt, & Hoey, 1998). Many groups—and self-help groups in particular—encourage social comparisons through rituals and traditions. Everyone at an AA meeting, for example, publicly states, "I am an alcoholic," and this ritual reassures each participant that his or her problems are shared by others.

Groups also provide members with targets for both downward social comparison and up-

TABLE 15.1 **Factors that Promote Change in Groups**

Factor	Definition	Meaning to Member
Universality	Recognition of shared problems, reduced sense of uniqueness	We all have problems.
Hope	Increased sense of optimism from seeing others improve	If other members can change, so can I.
Vicarious Learning	Developing social skills by watching others	Seeing others talk about their problems inspired me to talk, too.
Interpersonal Learning	Developing social skills by interacting with others	I'm learning to get along better with other people.
Guidance	Accepting advice and suggestions from the group members	People in the group give me good suggestions.
Cohesion	Feeling accepted by others	The group accepts me and understands me.
Self-disclosure	Revealing personal information to others	I feel better for sharing things I've kept secret for too long.
Catharsis	Releasing pent-up emotions	It feels good to get things off my chest.
Altruism	Increase sense of efficacy from helping others	Helping other people has given me more self-respect.
Insight	Gaining a deeper understanding of oneself	I've learned a lot about myself.

Source: D. R. Forsyth, *Group dynamics* (3rd ed.). Pacific Grove, Ca: Brooks/Cole, (1999).

ward social comparison. Most individuals, when given a choice, make comparisons that will provide them with reassuring as well as accurate information. By comparing themselves with someone who is experiencing even more severe hardships than themselves or someone who is not coping with problems effectively (downward social comparison), members' sense of victimization decreases and their overall sense of self-esteem increases (Gibbons & Gerrard, 1989; Wood, Taylor, & Lichtman, 1985). And when they compare themselves to people who are coping effectively with their problems, the upward social comparison helps members identify ways to improve their own situation (Buunk, 1995; Taylor & Lobel, 1989). Although such *supercopers* may threaten members by drawing their attention to their own limitations, they also reassure members that their problems can be overcome. In general, although contact with such people is reassuring, direct comparison with them is not (Taylor & Lobel, 1989).

Snyder and his colleagues believe that people's sense of hope is one of the best predictors of their mental health and adjustment. Individuals who are hopeful can identify many ways to reach their goals (pathways) and are also relatively confident that they can carry out the actions that are

necessary to reach their goals (agency). Hope, in Snyder's model, is more then just a sense of confidence or task persistence. Rather it is an enhanced motivational state that is sustained by clearly identified goals, pathway thoughts, and a sense of agency (Klausner, Snyder, & Cheavens, in press; Snyder, 1994; Snyder, Cheavens, & Sympson, 1997; see also Snyder, Ilardi, Michael, & Cheavens, this volume).

Klausner, Snyder, and Cheavens (in press) confirmed the value of a hope-based group intervention in a study of outpatients receiving antidepressant treatment at a geriatric center. These patients met for 11 weeks in groups that stressed individualized goal formulation and training in both pathway and agency thinking. By the end of treatment the subjects' levels of depression had dropped significantly, and the change was greater than that shown by a second set of patients who participated in a control group. Worthington, Hight, Ripley, Perrone, Kurusu, and Jones (1997) also verified the value of raising group members' sense of hope in a study of marital enrichment programs. These researchers, to offset the pessimism felt by many married people about their chances of avoiding divorce, developed a hope-enrichment therapy that stressed the components of Snyder's hope model. Clients were encouraged to take the initiative in improving their relationship and they were taught specific behaviors they could use to accomplish this goal. Trained couples had higher relationship satisfaction and better interaction skills than couples in a control condition.

Social Learning

Most theorists, when comparing group approaches to individuals ones, underscore the value of groups as arenas for interpersonal learning (Lieberman, 1980; Yalom, 1975, 1995). In groups, individuals gain information about themselves, their problems, and social relationships with others. They "become aware of the significant aspects of their interpersonal behavior: their strengths, their limitations, their parataxic distortions, and their maladaptive behavior that elicits unwanted responses from others" (Yalom, 1975, p. 40).

Of the 10 curative factors in Table 15.1, vicarious learning, interpersonal learning, and guidance (direct instruction) are most closely related to social learning processes. Unlike strict behavioral approaches that assume only actions followed by positive reinforcers are learned, social learning theory maintains that people can acquire new attitudes and behaviors by observing others' actions (Bandura, 1977). When a therapist carefully coaxes a member into expressing her pent-up hostility, observing group members learn how they can express emotions that they have been suppressing. Group leaders also can model desirable behaviors by treating the group members in positive ways and avoiding behaviors that are undesirable (Dies, 1994). Coleaders can model social interactions that the group members considered difficult or anxiety provoking. The leaders can then help the group members perform these same behaviors through the use of role-play procedures. Groups that use explicit modeling methods show greater improvement than groups that only discuss the problematic behaviors (Falloon, Lindley, McDonald, & Marks, 1977).

Groups also promote change by providing members with feedback about their personal and interpersonal qualities. When interacting with others in a supportive group setting, members receive direct feedback from the other group members about their qualities. The individual who is lonely because he alienates everyone by acting rudely may be told, "You should try to be more sensitive" or "You are always so judgmental, it makes me sick." Some groups exchange so much evaluative information that members withdraw from the group rather than face the barrage of negative feedback (Scheuble, Dixon, Levy, & Kagan-Moore, 1987). Most group leaders, however, are careful to monitor the exchange of information between members so that individuals learn the information they need to change in positive ways.

Interpersonal learning also occurs indirectly, as group members implicitly monitor their impact on the other people within their group, and draw conclusions about their own qualities from others' reactions to them—other group members become, metaphorically, a mirror for self-understanding (Cooley, 1902). A group member may begin to think she has good social skills if the group always responds positively each time she contributes to the group discussion. Another member may decide he is irritating if, each time he interacts in the group, the rest of the members respond with anger and hostility. This indirect feedback helps members perceive themselves more accurately. Individuals who are socially withdrawn, for example, tend to evaluate their social skills negatively even though their fellow group members view them positively (Christensen & Kashy, 1998). Individuals also tend to rate themselves as more anxious than others do (Marcus & Wilson, 1996). Extended contact with others in a group setting may repair these negative perceptions.

Interpersonal learning also occurs as members become recipients, willing or not, of the advice and guidance of both the leader and the other group members. When researchers analyzed recordings of therapy sessions, they discovered that therapists respond to clients at several levels. They provide information and guidance, ask a variety of questions, repeat and paraphrase the client's statements, confront the client's interpretations of problems, offer their own interpretation of the causes of client's problems, and express their approval of and support for the client (Hill, Helms, Tichenor, Spiegel, O'Grady, & Perry, 1988).

Although most would agree that the therapist should guide the group, experts disagree when discussing *how much* guidance a leader should provide. On the one hand, many clinicians advocate the leader-centered approaches typical of psychoanalytic, Gestalt, and behavioral groups. In such groups, the leader is the central figure. He or she guides the course of the interaction, assigns various tasks to the group members, and occupies the center of the centralized communication network. In some instances, the group members may not even communicate with one another but only with the group leader. In contrast, other therapists advocate a nondirective style of leadership in which all group members communicate with one another. These group-oriented approaches, which are typified by encounters or T groups, encourage the analysis of the group's processes, sometimes with the therapist/leader facilitating the process, but other times providing no direction whatsoever.

Studies of groups indicate that both directive and nondirective leaders are effective agents of change so long as they are caring, help members interpret the cause of their problems, keep the group on course, and meet the members' socio-emotional needs (Lieberman, Yalom, & Miles, 1973). Moreover, just as effective leaders in organizational settings sometimes vary their interventions to fit the situation, so do effective leaders in therapeutic settings shift their methods as the group matures. During the early stages of treatment, members may respond better to a task-oriented leader, whereas in the later stages, a socioemotional leader may be more helpful (Kivlighan, 1997).

Several studies suggest that groups with two leaders are more effective than groups with only one leader. Co-leadership eases the burdens put on the group's leader. The two leaders can lend support to each other and also can offer the group members their combined knowledge, insight, and experience. Also, male/female teams may be particularly beneficial because they offer a fuller perspective on gender issues, and serve as models of positive but nonromantic heterosexual relationships. The advantages of co-leadership, however, are lost if the leaders are unequal in status or engage in power struggles during group sessions (Thune, Manderscheid, & Silbergeld, 1981).

Cohesion and Development

Cohesion may not be a sufficient condition for effective groups, but it may be a necessary one (Yalom, 1985). Without cohesion, feedback would not be accepted, norms would never develop, and groups could not retain their members. In emphasizing the value of highly cohesive groups, Yalom and his colleagues join a long line of researchers who have reached similar conclusions. As early as 1951, Dorwin Cartwright suggested that if groups were to be used as change

agents, the members should have a strong sense of group identity and belonging or otherwise the group would not exert sufficient influence over them. Others, too, have noted that the "cotherapeutic influence of peers" in the therapy group requires group cohesion (Bach, 1954, p. 348; Frank, 1957; Goldstein, Heller, & Sechrest, 1966).

Cohesive groups, in general, tend to provide healthier environments than noncohesive groups, at least at the psychological level. Because people in cohesive groups respond to one another in a more positive fashion than members of noncohesive groups, people experience less anxiety and tension in such groups (Myers, 1962; Shaw & Shaw, 1962). Studies conducted in industrial work groups, for example, indicate that employees reported less anxiety and nervousness when they worked in cohesive groups (Seashore, 1954). Investigations of therapeutic groups routinely find that the members improve their overall level of adjustment when their group is a cohesive one (Marziali, Munroe-Blum, & McCleary, 1997), perhaps because they are stronger sources of social support (Posluszny, Hyman, & Baum, 1998). People also cope more effectively with stress when they are in cohesive groups (Bowers, Weaver, & Morgan, 1996; Zaccaro, Gualtieri, & Minionis, 1995). Membership in a cohesive group can prove problematic for some members, however, if they become too dependent (Forsyth & Elliott, 1999).

Cohesion likely influences the curative impact of a group by increasing the psychological intensity of the therapeutic experience. People in cohesive groups more readily accept the group's goals, decisions, and norms. Furthermore, pressures to conform are greater in cohesive groups, and an individual's resistance to these pressures is weaker (Back, 1951). When the group norms emphasize the value of cooperation and agreement among members, members of highly cohesive groups avoid disagreement more than members of noncohesive groups (Courtwright, 1978). Members of cohesive groups also sometimes react very negatively when a group member goes against the group consensus, and they take harsh measures to bring dissenters into line (Schachter, 1951).

A group's cohesiveness fluctuates over time, depending on its longevity, membership stability, and stage of development. Even when the group's task is a therapeutic one, time is needed to achieve cohesiveness. In one study, investigators observed and coded the behaviors displayed by adolescents in a program of behavioral change. These groups did not immediately start to work on self-development issues, nor did the group members try to help one another. Rather, the groups first moved through orientation, conflict, and cohesion-building stages before they began to make therapeutic progress (Hill & Gruner, 1973).

Other studies also suggest that the success of the group depends to a large extent on its movement through stages of development. Although the stages receive various labels from various theorists, many accept the five emphasized by Tuckman (1965): forming, storming, norming, performing, and adjourning. During the forming stage, individual members are seeking to understand their relationship to the newly formed group and strive to establish clear intermember relations. During the storming stage, group members often find themselves in conflict over status and group goals and, in consequence, hostility, disruption, and uncertainty dominate group discussions. During the next phase, norming, the group strives to develop a group structure that increases cohesiveness and harmony. The performing stage is typified by a focus on group productivity and decision making. Last, when the group fulfills its goals, it reaches its final stage of development, adjourning. If a group does not move through these stages, its members will not be able to benefit from the experience (MacKenzie, 1994, 1996; Yalom, 1995).

Dennis Kivlighan and his colleagues studied the impact of group development on therapeutic outcomes by matching interventions to the developmental maturity of the group. Group members were given structured help in expressing either anger or intimacy before either the fourth or ninth group session of their therapy. The information dealing with anger clarified the value of anger as a natural part of group participation and provided suggestions for communicating it. In contrast, the information dealing with intimacy clarified the value of intimacy in groups and provided suggestions for its appropriate expression toward others. As anticipated, when the interventions were matched to the most appropriate developmental stage—for example, group members received the information on anger during the storming phase (session four) or the information on intimacy during the norming phase (session nine)—the subjects displayed more comfort in dealing with intimacy, more appropriate expres-

sions of intimacy and anger, fewer inappropriate expressions of intimacy, and more congruence between self-ratings and other ratings of interpersonal style (Kivlighan, McGovern, & Corazzini, 1984).

Disclosure and Catharsis

Groups become more unified the more the members engage in self-disclosure: the sharing of personal, intimate information with others (Corey & Corey, 1992; Leichtentritt & Shechtman, 1998). When groups first convene, members usually focus on superficial topics and avoid saying anything too personal or provocative. In this orientation stage, members try to form a general impression of each other and make a good impression themselves. In the exploratory affective stage, members discuss their personal attitudes and opinions, but avoid intimate topics. This stage is often followed by the affective stage, when a few topics remain taboo. When the group reaches the final stage, stable exchange, all personal feelings are shared (Altman & Taylor, 1973).

Self-disclosure can be a challenge for some individuals. Individuals experiencing personality and psychological disturbances, for example, often disclose the wrong sorts of information at the wrong time (McGuire & Leak, 1980). Men and boys, too, generally are more reserved in their rate of self-disclosure (Brooks, 1996; Kilmartin, 1994; Shechtman, 1994). In consequence, therapists sometimes must take special steps to induce the male members of therapy groups to share personal information about themselves, including modeling disclosure and the incorporation of disclosure rituals in groups (Horne, Jolliff, & Roth, 1996).

Self-disclosure and cohesion are reciprocally related. Each new self-disclosure deepens the group's relationship intimacy, and this increased closeness then makes further self-disclosures possible (Kaul & Bednar, 1986; Roark & Sharah, 1989; Tschuschke & Dies, 1994). By sharing information about themselves, members are expressing their trust in the group and signaling their commitment to the therapeutic process (Rempel, Holmes, & Zanna, 1985). Self-disclosure of troubling, worrisome thoughts also reduces the discloser's level of tension and stress. Individuals who keep their problems secret, but continually ruminate about them, display signs of physiological and psychological distress. On the other hand, individuals who have the opportunity to disclose these troubling thoughts are healthier and happier (Pennebaker, 1990).

Members also can vent strong emotions in groups. The group offers members the opportunity to express strong emotions that they cannot express in any other circumstances; this catharsis might ease their level of anxiety. Emotional release has been identified by some as a great benefit of groups, but others suggest that "blowing off steam" may actually heighten members' psychological distress and upset (see Ormont, 1984).

Altruism

The group's leader is not the only source of help available to group members. In some instances, fellow group members can draw on their own experience to offer insights and advice to one another. This mutual assistance provides benefits for both parties. Even though the group's leader, and not the group members, is the official expert in the group, people often are more willing to accept help from people who are similar to them (Wills & DePaulo, 1991). The helper, too, "feels a sense of being needed and helpful; can forget self in favor of another group member; and recognizes the desire to do something for another group member" (Crouch et al., 1994, p. 285). Mutual assistance teaches group members the social skills that are essential to psychological well-being (Ferencik, 1992).

Mutual assistance is particularly important in self-help groups. Mended Hearts, a support group that deals with psychological consequences of open-heart surgery, tells members that "you are not completely mended until you help mend others" (Lieberman, 1993, p. 297). AA groups formalize and structure helping in the twelve-step procedures. Newcomers to the group are paired with sponsors, who meet regularly with the new member outside of the regular group meetings.

Insight

Individuals' perceptions of their personal qualities are generally accurate. Individuals who think of themselves as assertive tend to be viewed that way by others, just as warm, outgoing individuals are viewed as friendly and approachable (Kenny, Kieffer, Smith, Ceplenski, & Kulo, 1996; Levesque, 1997). In some cases, however, individuals' self-perceptions are inaccurate (Andersen, 1984). Individuals may believe that they are unattractive, socially unskilled, or friendly, when in fact they are attractive, interpersonally competent, or hostile.

Groups promote self-understanding by exposing members to unknown areas of the self. Although people are not particularly open to feedback about their attributes—especially their negative ones—when several individuals provide the same feedback, they are more likely to internalize this information (Jacobs, 1974; Kivlighan, 1985). Also, when the feedback is given in the context of a long-term, reciprocal relation, it cannot be dismissed so easily as being biased or subjective. Group leaders, too, often reward members for accepting rather than rejecting feedback, thus making the setting itself work to intensify self-awareness. In a supportive, accepting group, members can reveal hidden aspects of themselves, and therefore feel more open and honest in their relationships. Finally, Luft (1984) maintains that even qualities that are unknown both to the individual and to others can emerge and be recognized during group interactions.

Studies of group members' evaluations of the therapeutic experience also attest to the importance of self-insight. When participants in therapeutic groups were asked to identify events that took place in their groups that helped them the most, they stressed universality, interpersonal learning, cohesion (belonging), and insight. During later sessions they stressed interpersonal learning even more, but universality became less important (Kivlighan & Mullison, 1988; Kivlighan, Multon, & Brossart, 1996). Other studies that asked group members to rank or rate the importance of these curative factors generally found that group members emphasize self-understanding, interpersonal learning, and catharsis (Butler & Fuhriman, 1983a; Markovitz & Smith, 1983; Maxmen, 1973, 1978; Rohrbaugh & Bartels, 1975; Rugel & Meyer, 1984). In general, individuals who stress the value of self-understanding tend to benefit the most from participation in a therapeutic group (Butler & Fuhriman, 1983b).

THE EFFECTIVENESS OF GROUPS

Groups are used in a wide variety of settings to help individuals achieve personal change. This increasing reliance on groups is due, in part, to an increased concern for both cost and efficiency in an era of managed care that favors methods that can deliver effective services to more individuals at less cost (Hellman, Budd, Borysenko, McClelland, & Benson, 1990; MacKenzie, 1997).

But how effective are groups as treatment vehicles?

As with studies of individual therapies, calibrating the positive benefits of treatment has been difficult and controversial. Reviewers, after sifting through hundreds of studies evaluating the effectiveness of group interventions, rejected many as so methodologically flawed that they yielded no information (Bednar & Kaul, 1978, 1979, 1994; Burlingame, Kircher, & Taylor, 1994; Fuhriman & Burlingame, 1994; Kaul & Bednar, 1986). Groups are even more difficult to study than individuals, and so studies of their effectiveness often suffer from fatal flaws in design and execution. The use of varied and undocumented therapeutic methods, with different types of clients, by therapists who differ in skills and experience, in studies that too frequently lack valid measures and inadequate controls, make it difficult to draw firm conclusions. But those studies that do use valid methods, although far from unanimous in their support of group approaches, are for the most part positive.

Reviews of Group Outcomes

Most narrative reviews of the outcome literature are favorable, although they usually bemoan the methodological flaws that undermine the scientific adequacy of the database (Back, 1974; Meltzoff & Kornreich, 1970). Meltzoff and Kornreich, for example, were guardedly optimistic about the utility of group therapies because 80% of the methodologically sound studies reported either major or minor benefits for clients, whereas nearly all of the studies that reported no benefit were methodologically flawed. Bednar and Kaul's comprehensive and long-term monitoring of group methods are guardedly positive, although they continue to lament the lack of rigor in research (Bednar & Kaul, 1978, 1979, 1994; Kaul & Bednar, 1986). In like fashion Kanas (1986) examined 33 inpatient and 10 outpatient studies dating back to 1950 and concluded that group therapy was effective in 67% of the inpatient studies and 80% of the outpatient studies. He also reported that long-term therapy (more than three months) was especially useful, as were approaches that focused on interpersonal processes. Toseland and Siporin (1986) reviewed over 30 studies that compared individual and group therapies, and concluded that in 25% of these studies, the group therapy was significantly more effective than individual. Spitz (1984) presented a generally favorable review of the use of groups with a variety of client populations, including borderline and narcissistic personality disorders, physically ill patients, and chronic psychiatric patients.

Reviews of experiential groups also are generally positive (Bates & Goodman, 1986; Knapp & Shostrom, 1976; Smith, 1975, 1980). Knapp and Shostrom found that in those studies that used the Personality Orientation Inventory (POI) to assess outcome, most participants showed a consistent pattern of increased self-actualizing scores. Berman and Zimpfer (1980), in a systematic review of 26 controlled studies of personal growth groups, restricted their analysis to studies that (a) used both pretest and posttest measures, (b) met for at least 10 hours, and (c) had a long-term follow-up (at least one month after termination). Summarizing these methodologically superior studies, Berman and Zimpfer concluded that group treatments result in enduring positive changes, particularly at the self-report level.

Studies of the use of group therapies with particular populations also have yielded generally positive results. Kilmann and his colleagues (Sotile & Kilmann, 1977), although initially frustrated by the low quality of the research procedures in studies of group treatments for sexual dysfunctions, concluded that group therapy is an effective means of treating female orgasmic dysfunction and behavioral secondary erectile dysfunction (Mills & Kilmann, 1982). Zimpfer (1987), in his review of 19 studies of group therapy for the elderly, found that group treatments were differentially effective depending on the problems experienced by the client. He concluded that treatments that provide social support and sustain health-promoting actions and attitudes were most effective. Brandsma and Pattison (1985) and Flores (1997), after reviewing the empirical literature pertaining to group therapy with alcoholics, concluded that group interventions are an effective means of treating alcoholics who require therapeutic treatment.

The effectiveness of groups also can be gleaned from a methodologically questionable but empirically intriguing study of 4,000 individuals who responded to a *Consumer Reports* (1995) questionnaire concerning mental health services (see also Ingram, Hayes & Scott, this volume). This survey's conclusions are obviously limited by sampling biases and the reliance on client's self-reports (Seligman, 1995, 1996). The results, however, provide a strong confirmation of clients' satisfaction with psychological treatments, in general, and group methods, in particular. Nearly one-third of the sample reported membership in a treatment group, often in combination with individual or medical treatments. These individuals rated the experience positively, and felt that groups "seemed to help" (*Consumer Reports*, 1995, p. 738). AA received particularly positive evaluations in this study, described as "overwhelming approval." The analysis suggests that the benefits of AA may result from a dosage effect, because members are required to attend a meeting every day for the first 90 days of treatment, and then three meetings a week after that. This level of treatment far surpasses the treatment frequencies of most other therapies.

Meta-Analytic Reviews

Researchers have conducted enough studies of group and individual approaches to permit reviewers to carry out meta-analytic reviews of prior work (Davis, Olmsted, Rockert, Marques, & Dolhanty, 1997; Fuhriman & Burlingame, 1994; Hoag & Burlingame, 1997; Robinson, Berman, & Neimeyer, 1990; Shapiro & Shapiro, 1982; Smith, Glass, & Miller, 1980; Tillitski, 1990). These quantitative reviews, like the qualitative narrative reviews, generally suggest that group approaches are equivalent in effectiveness to individual approaches. For example, Smith, Glass, and Miller (1980), in their precedent-setting review of therapeutic treatments, found that individual and group treatments were roughly equivalent in terms of effectiveness. Miller and Berman (1983) discovered that cognitive-behavioral treatments were more effective than other methods, irrespective of whether they were carried out in an individual or a group format. Similarly, Addie Fuhriman and Gary M. Burlingame (1994), after reviewing 700 group therapy studies and seven meta-analytic reviews of prior research, concluded that group methods are effective treatments for a wide variety of psychological problems.

McRoberts, Burlingame, and Hoag (1998) also discovered that both individual and group approaches are effective in their meta-analytic review of 23 studies that directly compared individual and group treatment methods. These investigators examined a large number of other treatment and procedural variables that past researchers identified as key determinants of outcome, including theoretical orientation of the therapy use, treatment stardardization, dosage,

number of sessions, diagnosis of client, therapist gender and experience, and the presence of a cotherapist. The only factors that covaried significantly with outcome were client diagnosis, number of treatment sessions, and the year in which the study was conducted. Individual therapies tended to be more effective than group therapies when clients were classified using a formal diagnostic system, but group approaches were more effective when clients had "circumscribed symptomology" such as chemical dependencies and job-related stress. Group approaches also were more effective when clients were seen only briefly. When respondents attended only 10 or fewer sessions, group treatments were superior to individual ones. As for the year in which the study was conducted, studies conducted prior to 1980 favored groups, those conducted between 1981 and 1987 favored neither type, and those conducted after 1987 favored individual approaches. Other variables, such as the theoretical orientation of the therapist or type of group intervention, were unrelated to outcome.

Faith, Wong, and Carpenter (1995), in a meta-analytic review of sensitivity-training studies, also confirm the value of such groups. They searched for studies that utilized one of the following methods: T group, encounter group, marathon group, experiential training group, sensitivity training, enhancement training, empathy training, microcounseling, or human relations training. They did not include studies that were conducted in organizational or industrial settings, or ones that were specifically forms of group psychotherapy or cognitive-behavioral therapy. After examining the 63 studies that met their criteria, they concluded that these groups generally led to increases in self-actualization and self-esteem, and improved interpersonal relations. They noted that these effects increased in larger groups, when the groups met for longer periods of time, and when the measures focused on behavioral outcomes rather than self-reported ones. Burke and Day's (1986) analysis of the long-term effectiveness of T groups in organization-development interventions reached similar conclusions.

Comparisons of Group Therapies

McRoberts, Burlingame, and Hoag (1998) are not the only researchers who failed to distinguish between effective and ineffective types of group therapies. Group approaches conform to no single set of procedures, for some groups are leader-centered (psychoanalytic or Gestalt groups), whereas others are group-focused (encounter and T groups), and the group's activities can range from the highly structured (social skill training groups, such as assertiveness-training groups) to the unstructured (encounter groups). Group practitioners also vary greatly in their orientations and techniques; some focus on emotions with Gestalt exercises, others concentrate on the here-and-now of the group's interpersonal process, and others train members to perform certain behaviors through videotaped feedback, behavioral rehearsal, and systematic reinforcement.

In spite of this diversity, most studies attest to the relative equality of the different types of group therapy. Lieberman, Yalom, and Miles, for example, investigated the overall impact of a twelve-week experiential group on members' adjustment (Yalom, 1985; Lieberman, Yalom, & Miles, 1973). Using a pool of 206 Stanford University students who were enrolled for course credit, Lieberman, Yalom, and Miles randomly assigned each person to one of 18 different therapy groups representing 10 theoretical orientations: Gestalt, transactional analysis, T groups, Synanon, Esalen, psychoanalytic, marathon, psychodrama, encounter tape, and encounter. Trained observers coded the group's interactions, with particular attention to the leader's style. Before, during, immediately after, and six months following the participation they administered a battery of items assessing group members' self-esteem, attitudes, self-satisfactions, values, satisfaction with friendships, and so on. Measures also were completed by the co-members, the leaders, and by group members' acquaintances.

Somewhat unexpectedly, the project discovered that no one theoretical approach had a monopoly on effectiveness. For example, two separate Gestalt groups with different leaders were included in the design, but the members of these two groups evidenced widely discrepant gains. One of the Gestalt groups ranked among the most successful in stimulating participant growth, but the other group yielded fewer benefits than all of the groups. These findings may have resulted from the lack of experience of the group leaders, as Russell (1978) suggests, but more recent studies provide general confirmation for the equivalency among treatments reported by Lieberman, Yalom, and Miles (Berah, 1981; Coche, Cooper, & Petermann, 1984; Falloon, 1981; Gonzalez-Menendez, 1985; Hajek, Belcher,

& Stapleton, 1985; Knauss, Jeffrey, Knauss, & Harowski, 1983; Markham, 1985; Rosenberg & Brian, 1986; Sanchez, Lewinsohn, & Larson, 1980; Weinstein & Rossini, 1998; cf. Graff, Whitehead, & LeCompte, 1986; Kaplan, 1982).

Forsyth (1991) draws on Stiles, Shapiro, and Elliott's (1986) analysis of the apparent equivalence of individual therapies to account for this "no difference" result. First, the various group therapies may be differentially effective, but researchers' measures may not be sensitive enough to detect these variations. Second, as Kiesler's (1966) dismissal of the *uniformity myth* suggests, it may be that effectiveness is a complex product of the interaction of groups, therapists, clients, and circumstances. As Paul (1967) stated, the question isn't "Is Therapy A more effective than Therapy B?" but "What type of group run by which therapist is effective for this individual with this type of problem?" When researchers ignore the fit between treatment, therapist, client, and problem, the result is global, but undifferentiated, effectiveness. Third, although extant group interventions are based on widely divergent theoretical assumptions, these assumptions may not lead to differences in practice. A leader of a Gestalt group and the leader of a psychodynamic group, for example, may each explain their goals and methods in very different theoretical terms, but they may nonetheless rely on identical methods when in their groups. Last, as Yalom's (1995) concept of curative factors suggests, all groups—as groups—may promote change no matter what their specific qualities because they often generate curative processes.

Qualifications and Uncertainties

The available evidence pertaining to therapeutic outcomes of groups supports Bednar and Kaul's conclusion: the "accumulated evidence indicates that group treatments have been more effective than no treatment, than placebo or nonspecific treatments, or than other recognized psychological treatments, at least under some circumstances" (Bednar & Kaul, 1994, p. 632).

This positive conclusion, however, requires some qualification. First, and most important, the empirical evidence is not definitive. Whereas a number of reviews are positive, others conclude that group therapy is not as potent as individual therapy (e.g., Abramowitz, 1977; Dush, Hirt, & Schroeder, 1983; Engels & Vermey, 1997; Kilman & Stotile, 1976; Nietzel, Russel, Hemmings, & Gretter, 1987; Parloff & Dies, 1977; Solomon,

1982; Stanton & Shadish, 1997). Solomon, for example, found that outcome studies that compare individual and group therapy for alcoholism treatment do not recommend one treatment over the other. Parloff and Dies, after reviewing the results of studies of group therapies with a range of client types (schizophrenics, psychoneurotics, juveniles and adult offenders), concluded that the results are disappointing. Abramowitz reaches a similar conclusion in her review of outcome research on children's activity, behavior modification, play, and verbal therapy groups. Also, evidence pertaining to marathon groups is relatively negative (Kilmann & Stotile, 1976).

Second, the changes brought about by group experiences *may* be more perceptual than behavioral. Bednar and Kaul (1979), after culling the studies of change in groups that were methodologically flawed, concluded that most studies had reported changes only on self-report data, rather than behavioral data. Reviews of experiential groups also generally find stronger evidence of perceptual changes than of behavioral changes (Bates & Goodman, 1986; Berman & Zimpfer, 1980; Budman, Demby, Feldstein, & Gold, 1984; Ware, Barr, & Boone, 1982). Faith, Wong, and Carpenter (1995), however, did not confirm this tendency in their recent review.

Third, in some cases, groups can do more harm than good for participants. As Bednar and Kaul (1979) note, a participant may decide to leave the group before he or she has benefited in any way; such an individual is usually labeled a premature termination, or dropout (Holmes, 1983). A casualty, in contrast, is significantly harmed by the group experience. A casualty might, for example, commit suicide as a result of the group experience, require individual therapy to correct harm caused by the group, or report continued deteriorations in adjustment over the course of the group. The number of casualties reported in studies has ranged from none among 94 participants in a human-relations training lab followed up after five months (Smith, 1975, 1980) to a high of 8% of the participants in a study of 17 encounter groups (Lieberman, Yalom, & Miles, 1973). A relatively high casualty rate (18%) was obtained in one study of 50 married couples who participated in marathon encounter groups, but this rate was inflated by the problems the couples were experiencing before entering the group (Doherty, Lester, & Leigh, 1986). No evidence is available concerning the rate of casualties in self-help groups, but

statistics maintained by the NTL indicate that 25 individuals who participated in the program prior to 1974 experienced a severe psychological reaction (Back, 1974). This number is less than 0.2% of the participants. Casualties can be minimized by limiting conflict during sessions and making certain that the group atmosphere is supportive, nonevaluative, and nonthreatening (Mitchell & Mitchell, 1984; Scheuble et al., 1987).

THE FUTURE OF GROUP APPROACHES TO CHANGE

Groups are not all benefit without cost. Groups can demand great investment of time and energy from their members. While groups provide social support, they also are the source of considerable stress for their members. Groups, too, can socialize members in ways that are not healthy and set social identity processes in motion that increase conflict between groups (Forsyth & Elliott, 1999).

Their checkered impact in no way, however, detracts from their significance in shaping mental health. Groups are essential to human life. Groups help their members define and confirm their values, beliefs, and identities. When an individual is beset by problems and uncertainties, groups offer reassurance, security, support, and assistance. Groups are places where people can learn new social skills, and discover things about themselves and others. Groups, too, can produce changes in members when other approaches have failed. Both researchers and mental health professionals who understand groups agree with Lewin's law: "It is easier to change individuals formed into a group than individuals who are alone" (1951, p. 228).

Practitioners have not yet fully exploited the power of groups, however, and researchers have only begun to explain the dynamic interrelationship between a group and its members. Even though therapeutic applications that utilize a group setting (group therapy) and the scientific field devoted to the analysis of groups in general (group dynamics) always have been intertwined, this shared ancestry has yet to inform fully the scientific analysis or the therapeutic application of change methods in group contexts (Forsyth, 1997; Forsyth & Strong, 1986).

This research–practice gap should be closed if the science and practice of groups is to evolve and grow stronger, and this integration should focus on several levels of integration (Forsyth & Leary, 1991, 1997). Curriculum and training procedures should nurture the scholar's interest in groups in general and therapy groups in particular. Changes in graduate school training that could reduce this insularity include (a) a requirement for studying "real groups" (including families and therapy groups) in social psychology, (b) revision of curriculum to focus on more group topics (e.g., leadership, group structure), (c) updating of textbooks to include clinical topics, and (d) the revision of group-practice texts to include a more defensible foundation in theory and also research in group dynamics (Steenbarger & Budman, 1996).

The gap also should be closed at the professional and practice level. Curiously, when psychology emerged as a mental health field after World War II, many of its central practitioners were academicians who specialized in the study of group processes: Lewin was the prime example of an individual who prospered in the science and in the practice of groups. Over time, however, the professional identity of researchers and therapists diverged until now their shared roots are nearly unrecognizable. Even though group researchers and group therapists likely share many foundational assumptions—both recognize the causal power of a group and have seen the change that it can produce—they likely adopt differing views about the nature of science, and how our understanding of groups can be furthered best. The founding of new organizations, such as Division 49 of the American Psychological Association (Group Psychology and Group Psychotherapy), and the publication of texts and journals that integrate research and practice strive to restore this lost link.

Our understanding of groups as change agents has expanded considerably in the years since Pratt convened his first fledgling groups, but much work remains to be done. Those who study groups and make use of them to promote change agree that groups are essential to human life. Through membership in groups, we define and confirm our values and beliefs and take on or refine a social identity. When we face uncertain situations, in groups we gain reassuring information about our problems and security in companionship. In groups we learn about relations with others, the type of impressions we make on others, and the way we can relate with others more effectively. Given their central importance, we must accept the charge of developing more elaborate conceptualizations of groups that take into account both their change-producing properties and their properties as groups *per se*.

REFERENCES

Abramowitz, C. V. (1977). The effectiveness of group psychotherapy with children. *Annual Progress in Child Psychiatry and Child Development*, pp. 393–408.

Altman, I., & Taylor, D. A. (1973). *Social penetration: The development of interpersonal relationships.* New York: Holt, Rinehart & Winston.

Andersen, S. M. (1984). Self-knowledge and social inference: II. The diagnosticity of cognitive/affective and behavioral data. *Journal of Personality and Social Psychology, 46,* 294–307.

Bach, G. R. (1954). *Intensive group psychotherapy.* New York: Ronald Press.

Back, K. W. (1973). *Beyond words: The story of sensitivity training and the encounter movement.* Baltimore: Penguin Books.

Back, K. W. (1974). Intervention techniques: Small groups. *Annual Review of Psychology, 25,* 367–387.

Back, K. W. (1951). Influence through social communication. *Journal of Abnormal and Social Psychology, 46,* 9–23.

Bandura, A. (1977). *Social-learning theory.* Englewood Cliffs, NJ: Prentice Hall.

Bates, B., & Goodman, A. (1986). The effectiveness of encounter groups: Implications of research for counselling practice. *British Journal of Guidance and Counselling, 14,* 240–251.

Beck, A. T. (1976). *Cognitive theory and the emotional disorder.* Madison, CT: International Universities Press.

Bednar, R. L., & Kaul, T. (1978). Experiential group research: Current perspectives. In S. L. Garfield and A. E. Bergin (Eds.), *Handbook of psychotherapy and behavior change* (2nd ed., pp. 769–815). New York: John Wiley and Sons.

Bednar, R. L., & Kaul, T. (1979). Experiential group research: What never happened. *Journal of Applied Behavioral Science, 15,* 311–319.

Bednar, R. L., & Kaul, T. (1994). Experiential group research: Can the canon fire? In S. L. Garfield and A. E. Bergin (Eds.), *Handbook of psychotherapy and behavior change* (4th ed., pp. 631–663). New York: Wiley.

Bellack, A., & Hersen, M. (1979). *Research and practice in social skills training.* New York: Plenum.

Bender, L. (1937). Group activities in a children's ward as methods of psychotherapy. *American Journal of Psychiatry, 93,* 1151–1173.

Benne, K. D. (1964). History of the T-group in the laboratory setting. In L. P. Bradford, J. R. Gibb,

& K. D. Benne (Eds.), *T-group theory and laboratory method: Innovation in re-education* (pp. 80–135). New York: Wiley.

Berah, E. F. (1981). Influence of scheduling variations on the effectiveness of a group assertion-training program for women. *Journal of Counseling Psychology, 28*, 265–268.

Berman, J. J., & Zimpfer, D. G. (1980). Growth groups: Do the outcomes really last? *Review of Educational Research, 50*, 505–524.

Bion, W. (1961). *Experiences in groups.* New York: Basic Books.

Bowers, C. A., Weaver, J. L., & Morgan, B. B., Jr. (1996). Moderating the performance effects of stressors. In J. E. Driskell & E. Salas (Eds.), *Stress and human performance* (pp. 163–192). Mahwah, NJ: Erlbaum.

Brabender, V., & Fallon, A. (1993). *Models of inpatient group psychotherapy.* Washington, D.C.: American Psychological Association.

Bradford, L. P., Gibb, J. R., & Benne, K. D. (1964). Two educational innovations. In L. P. Bradford, J. R. Gibb, & K. D. Benne (Eds.), *T-group theory and laboratory method: Innovation in re-education* (pp. 1–14). New York: John Wiley & Sons.

Brandsma, J. M., & Pattison, E. M. (1985). The outcome of group psychotherapy alcoholics: An empirical review. *American Journal of Drug and Alcohol Abuse, 11*, 151–162.

Brooks, G. R. (1996). Treatment for therapy-resistant men. In M. P. Andronico (Ed.), *Men in groups: Insights, interventions, and psychoeducational work* (pp. 7-19). Washington, D.C.: American Psychological Association.

Budman, S. H., Demby, A., Feldstein, M., & Gold, M. (1984). The effects of time-limited group psychotherapy: A controlled study. *International Journal of Group Psychotherapy, 34*, 587–603.

Burke, M. J., & Day, R. R. (1986). A cumulative study of the effectiveness of managerial training. *Journal of Applied Psychology, 71*, 232–245.

Burlingame, G. M., Kircher, J. C., & Taylor, S. (1994). Methodological considerations in group psychotherapy research: Past, present, and future practices. In A. Fuhriman & G. M. Burlingame (Eds.), *Handbook of group psychotherapy: An empirical and clinical synthesis* (pp. 41–82). New York: John Wiley & Sons.

Burrow, T. (1927). The group method of analysis. *Psychoanalytic Review, 10*, 268–280.

Butler, T., & Fuhriman, A. (1983a). Curative factors in group therapy: A review of the recent literature. *Small Group Behavior, 14*, 131–142.

Butler, T., & Fuhriman, A. (1983b). Level of functioning and length of time in treatment variables influencing patients' therapeutic experience in group psychotherapy. *International Journal of Group Psychotherapy, 33*, 489–505.

Buunk, B. P. (1995). Comparison direction and comparison dimension among disabled individuals: Toward a refined conceptualization of social comparison under stress. *Personality and Social Psychology Bulletin, 21*, 316–330.

Cartwright, D. (1951). Achieving change in people: Some applications of group dynamics theory. *Human Relations, 4*, 381–392.

Christensen, A., & Jacobson, N. S. (1994). Who (or what) can do psychotherapy: The status and challenge of nonprofessional therapies. *Psychological Science, 5*, 8–12.

Christensen, P. N., & Kashy, D. A. (1998). Perceptions of and by lonely people in initial social interaction. *Personality and Social Psychology Bulletin, 24*, 322–329.

Clark, R. D., III, & Sechrest, L. B. (1976). The mandate phenomenon. *Journal of Personality and Social Psychology, 34*, 1057–1061.

Coche, E., Cooper, J. B., & Petermann, K. J. (1984). Differential outcomes of cognitive and interactional group therapies. *Small Group Behavior, 15*, 497–509.

Consumer Reports (1995, November). Mental Health: Does therapy help? pp. 734–739.

Cooley, C. H. (1902). *Human nature and the social order.* New York: Scribners.

Corey, M., & Corey, G. (1992). *Groups: Process and practice* (4th ed.). Pacific Grove, CA: Brooks/Cole.

Courtright, J. A. (1978). A laboratory investigation of groupthink. *Communication Monographs, 43*, 229–246.

Crouch, E. C., Bloch, S., & Wanlass, J. (1994). Therapeutic factors: Interpersonal and intrapersonal mechanisms. In A. Fuhriman & G. M. Burlingame (Eds.), *Handbook of group psychotherapy: An empirical and clinical synthesis* (pp. 269–315). New York: John Wiley & Sons.

Curran, J. P. (1977). Skills training as an approach to the treatment of heterosexual-social anxiety: A review. *Psychological Bulletin, 84*, 140–157.

Davis, R., Olmsted, M., Rockert, W., Marques, T., & Dolhanty, J. (1997). Group psychoeducation for bulimia nervosa with and without additional psychotherapy process sessions. *International Journal of Eating Disorders, 22*, 25–34.

Day, M. (1981). Psychoanalytic group therapy in clinic and private practice. *American Journal of Psychiatry, 138*, 64–69.

Dies, R. (1992). The future of group therapy. *Psychotherapy, 29*, 58–61.

Dies, R. (1994). Therapist variables in group psychotherapy research. In A. Fuhriman & G. M. Burlingame (Eds.), *Handbook of group psychotherapy: An empirical and clinical synthesis* (pp. 114–154). New York: John Wiley & Sons.

Doherty, W. J., Lester, M. E., & Leigh, G. K. (1986). Marriage encounter weekends: Couples who win and couples who lose. *Journal of Marital and Family Therapy, 12*, 49–61.

Dreikurs, R. (1959). The contribution of group psychotherapy to psychiatry. *Group Psychotherapy, 9*, 115–125.

Dush, D. M., Hirt, M. L., & Schroeder, H. (1983). Self-statement modification with adults: A meta-analysis. *Psychological Bulletin, 94*, 408–422.

Ellis, A. (1973). *Humanistic psychotherapy: The rational-emotive approach.* New York: Julian Press.

Engels, G. I., & Vermey, M. (1997). Efficacy of nonmedical treatments of depression in elders: A quantitative analysis. *Journal of Clinical Geropsychology, 3*, 17–35.

Ettin, M. F. (1992). *Group psychotherapy: A sphere of influence.* Boston: Allyn & Bacon.

Ettin, M. F., Cohen, B. D., & Fidler, J. W. (1997). Group-as-a-whole theory viewed in its 20th-century context. *Group Dynamics: Theory, Research, and Practice, 1*, 329–340.

Faith, M. S., Wong, F. Y., and Carpenter, K. M. (1995). Group sensitivity training: Update, meta-analysis, and recommendations. *Journal of Counseling Psychology, 42*, 390–399.

Falloon, I. R. (1981). Interpersonal variables in behavioural group therapy. *British Journal of Medical Psychology, 54*, 133–141.

Falloon, I. R., Lindley, P., McDonald, R., & Marks, I. M. (1977). Social skills training of outpatient groups: A controlled study of rehearsal and homework. *British Journal of Psychiatry, 131*, 599–609.

Ferencik, B. M. (1992). The helping process in group therapy: A review and discussion. *Group, 16*, 113–124.

Flores, P. J. (1997). *Group psychotherapy with addicted populations: An integration of twelve-step and psychodynamic theory* (2nd ed.). New York: Haworth Press.

Flowers, J. (1979). Behavioral analysis of group therapy and a model for behavioral group therapy. In D. Upper & S. Ross (Eds.), *Behavioral group therapy, 1979: An annual review.* Champaign, IL: Research Press.

Forsyth, D. R. (1991). Change in therapeutic groups. In C. R. Snyder & D. R. Forsyth (Eds.), *Handbook of social and clinical psychology: The health perspective* (pp. 664–680). New York: Pergamon.

Forsyth, D. R. (1996). *The functions of groups.* Paper presented at the annual meetings of the American Psychological Association. Toronto, Canada.

Forsyth, D. R. (1997, August). The scientific study of groups. *Group Dynamics: Theory, Research, and Practice, 1*, 3–6.

Forsyth, D. R. (1999). *Group dynamics* (3rd ed.). Pacific Grove, Ca: Brooks/Cole.

Forsyth, D. R., & Elliott, T. R. (1999). Group dynamics and psychological well-being: The impact of groups on adjustment and dysfunction. In R. Kowalski & M. R. Leary (Eds.), *The social psychology of emotional and behavioral problems: Interfaces of social and clinical psychology* (pp. 339–361). Washington, D.C.: American Psychological Association.

Forsyth, D. R., & Leary, M. R. (1991). Metatheoretical and epistemological issues. In C. R. Snyder & D. R. Forsyth (Eds.), *Handbook of social and clinical psychology: The health perspective* (pp. 757–773). New York: Pergamon.

Forsyth, D. R., & Leary, M. R. (1997). Achieving the goals of the scientist-practitioner model: The seven interfaces of social and counseling psychology. *The Counseling Psychologist, 25*, 180–200.

Forsyth, D. R., & Strong, S. R. (1986). The scientific study of counseling and psychotherapy: A unificationist view. *American Psychologist, 41*, 113–119.

Foulkes, S. (1964). *Therapeutic group analysis.* New York: International Universities Press.

Frable, D. E. S., Platt, L., & Hoey, S. (1998). Concealable stigmas and positive self-perceptions: Feeling better around similar others. *Journal of Personality and Social Psychology, 74*, 909–922.

Frank, J. D. (1957). Some determinants, manifestations, and effects of cohesiveness in therapy groups. *International Journal of Group Psychotherapy, 7*, 53–63.

Freud, S. (1922). *Group psychology and the analysis of the ego.* London: Hogarth.

Fuhriman, A., & Burlingame, G. M. (1994). Group psychotherapy: Research and practice. In A. Fuhriman & G. M. Burlingame (Eds.), *Handbook of group psychotherapy: An empirical and clinical synthesis* (pp. 3–40). New York: John Wiley & Sons.

Galassi, J. P., & Galassi, M. D. (1979). Modification of heterosocial skills deficits. In A. S. Bellack & M. Hersen (Eds.), *Research and practice in social skills training.* New York: Plenum.

Gazda, G. M., & Brooks, D. K. (1985). The development of the social/life skills training movement. *Journal of Group Psychotherapy, Psychodrama and Sociometry, 38*, 1–10.

Gibbons, F. X., & Gerrard, M. (1989). Effects of upward and downward social comparison on mood states. *Journal of Social and Clinical Psychology, 8*, 14–31.

Goldstein, A. P., Heller, K., & Sechrest, L. B. (1966). *Psychotherapy and the psychology of behavior change.* New York: John Wiley & Sons.

Gonzalez-Menendez, R. (1985). La psicoterapia de grupo didactica en psicoticos hospitalizados: Estudio comparativo de tres variantes. (Didactic group psychotherapy in hospitalized psychotic patients: Comparative study of three variations.) *Revista del Hospital Psiquiatrico de La Habana, 26*(4, Suppl.), 212–228.

Goodman, G., & Jacobs, M. K. (1994). The self-help,

mutual-support group. In A. Fuhriman & G. M. Burlingame (Eds.), *Handbook of group psychotherapy: An empirical and clinical synthesis* (pp. 489–526). New York: John Wiley & Sons.

Graff, R. W., Whitehead, G. I., & LeCompte, M. (1986). Group treatment with divorced women using cognitive-behavioral and supportive-insight methods. *Journal of Counseling Psychology, 33,* 276–281.

Hajek, P., Belcher, M., & Stapleton, J. (1985). Enhancing the impact of groups: An evaluation of two group formats for smokers. *British Journal of Clinical Psychology, 24,* 289–294.

Hellman, C. J., Budd, M., Borysenko, J., McClelland, D., & Benson, H. (1990). A study of the effectiveness of two group behavioral medicine interventions for patients with psychsomatic complaints. *Behavioral Medicine, 16,* 165–173.

Higginbotham, H. N., West, S. G., & Forsyth, D. R. (1988). *Psychotherapy and behavior change: Social, cultural, and methodological perspectives.* New York: Pergamon.

Hill, C. E., Helms, J. E., Tichenor, V., Spiegel, S. B., O'Grady, K. E., & Perry, E. S. (1988). Effects of therapist response modes in brief psychotherapy. *Journal of Counseling Psychology, 35,* 222–233.

Hill, W. F., & Gruner, L. (1973). A study of development in open and closed groups. *Small Group Behavior, 4,* 355–381.

Hoag, M. J., & Burlingame, G. M. (1997). Evaluating the effectiveness of child and adolescent group treatment: A meta-analytic review. *Journal of Clinical Child Psychology, 26,* 234–246.

Hollander, M., & Kazaoka, K. (1988). Behavior therapy groups. In S. Long (Ed.), *Six group therapies* (pp. 257–326). New York: Plenum.

Holmes, P. (1983). "Dropping out" from an adolescent therapeutic group: A study of factors in the patients and their parents which may influence this process. *Journal of Adolescence, 6,* 333–346.

Horne, A. M., Jolliff, D. L., & Roth, E. W. (1996). Men mentoring men in groups. In M. P. Andronico (Ed.), *Men in groups: Insights, interventions, and psychoeducational work* (pp. 97–112). Washington, D.C.: American Psychological Association.

Horwitz, L. (1993). Group-centered models of group psychotherapy. In H. I. Kaplan & B. J. Sadock (Eds.), *Comprehensive group psychotherapy* (3rd ed., pp. 156–165). Baltimore: Williams & Wilkins.

Ingram, R. E., Kendall, P. C., & Chen, A. H. (1991). Cognitive-behavioral interventions. In C. R. Snyder & D. R. Forsyth (Eds.), *Handbook of social and clinical psychology: The health perspective* (pp. 509–522). New York: Pergamon.

Jacobs, A. (1974). The use of feedback in groups. In A. Jacobs & W. W. Spradlin (Eds.), *The group as an agent of change.* New York: Behavioral Publications.

Jacobs, M. K., & Goodman, G. (1989). Psychology and self-help groups: Predictions on a partnership. *American Psychologist, 44,* 536–545.

Johnson, F. (1988). Encounter group therapy. In S. Long (Ed.), *Six group therapies* (pp. 115–158). New York: Plenum.

Kanas, N. (1986). Group therapy with schizophrenics: A review of controlled studies. *International Journal of Group Psychotherapy, 36,* 339–351.

Kanzer, M. (1983). Freud: The first psychoanalytic group leader. In H. I. Kaplan & B. J. Sadock (Eds.), *Comprehensive group psychotherapy* (2nd ed., pp. 8–14). Baltimore: Williams & Wilkins.

Kaplan, D. A. (1982). Behavioral, cognitive, and behavioral-cognitive approaches to group assertion training therapy. *Cognitive Therapy and Research, 6,* 301–314.

Kaplan, H. I., & Sadock, B. J. (Eds.). (1993). *Comprehensive group psychotherapy* (3rd ed.). Baltimore: Williams & Wilkins.

Kaplan, R. E. (1979). The conspicuous absence of evidence that process consultation enhances task performance. *Journal of Applied Behavioral Science, 15,* 346–360.

Kaul, T. J., & Bednar, R. L. (1986). Experiential group research: Results, questions, and suggestions. In S. L. Garfield & A. E. Bergin (Eds.), *Handbook of psychotherapy and behavior change* (3rd ed., pp. 671–714). New York: Wiley.

Kenny, D. A., Kieffer, S. C., Smith, J. A., Ceplenski, P., & Kulo, J. (1996). Circumscribed accuracy among well-acquainted individuals. *Journal of Experimental Social Psychology, 32,* 1–12.

Kibel, H. D. (1992). Inpatient group psychotherapy. In A. Alonso & H. Swiller (Eds.), *Group therapy in clinical practice* (pp. 93–112). Washington, D.C.: American Psychiatric Press.

Kibel, H., & Stein, A. (1981). The group-as-a-whole approach: An appraisal. *International Journal of Group Psychotherapy, 31,* 409–427.

Kiesler, D. J. (1991). Interpersonal methods of assessment and diagnosis. In C. R. Snyder & D. R. Forsyth (Eds.), *Handbook of social and clinical psychology: The health perspective* (pp. 438–468). New York: Pergamon.

Kiesler, D. J. (1966). Some myths of psychotherapy research and the search for a paradigm. *Psychological Bulletin, 65,* 110–136.

Kilmann, P. R., & Sotile, W. M. (1976). The marathon encounter group: A review of the outcome literature. *Psychological Bulletin, 83,* 827–850.

Kilmartin, C. T. (1994). *The masculine self.* New York: Macmillan.

Kipper, D. A. (1978). Trends in the research on the effectiveness of psychodrama: Retrospect and prospect. *Group Psychotherapy, 31,* 5–18.

Kivlighan, D. M., Jr. (1985). Feedback in group psychotherapy: Review and implications. *Small Group Behavior, 16,* 373–386.

Kivlighan, D. M., Jr. (1997). Leader behavior and therapeutic gain: An application of situational leadership theory. *Group Dynamics: Theory, Research, and Practice, 1,* 32–38.

Kivlighan, D. M., Jr., McGovern, T. V., & Corazzini, J. G. (1984). Effects of content and timing of structuring interventions on group therapy process and outcome. *Journal of Counseling Psychology, 31,* 363–370.

Kivlighan, D. M., Jr., & Mullison, D. (1988). Participants' perception of therapeutic factors in group counseling: The role of interpersonal style and stage of group development. *Small Group Behavior, 19,* 452–468.

Kivlighan, D. M., Jr., Multon, K. D., & Brossart, D. F. (1996). Helpful impacts in group counseling: Development of a multidimensional rating system. *Journal of Counseling Psychology, 43,* 347–355.

Klausner, E. J., Snyder, C. R., & Cheavens, J. (in press). A hope-based group treatment for depressed older adult outpatients. In G. M. Williamson, P. A. Parmelee, & D. R. Shaffer (Eds.), *Physical illness and depression in older adults: A handbook of theory, research, and practice.* New York: Plenum.

Knapp, R. P., & Shostrom, E. L. (1976). POI outcomes in studies of growth groups: A selected review. *Group and Organization Studies, 1,* 187–202.

Knauss, M. R., Jeffrey, D. B., Knauss, C. S., & Harowski, K. (1983). Therapeutic contact and individual differences in a comprehensive weight loss program. *Behavior Therapist, 6,* 124–128.

Kohut, H. (1984). *How does analysis cure? Contributions to the psychology of the self.* (A. Goldberg, Ed., with the collaboration of P. Stepansky). Chicago: University of Chicago Press.

Kutash, I. L., & Wolf, A. (1993). Psychoanalysis in groups. In H. I. Kaplan & M. J. Sadock (Eds.), *Comprehensive group psychotherapy* (3rd ed., pp. 126–138). Baltimore: Williams & Wilkins.

Lakin, M. (1972). *Experiential groups: The uses of interpersonal encounter, psychotherapy groups, and sensitivity training.* Morristown, N.J.: General Learning Press.

Lazell, E. W. (1921). The group treatment of dementia praecox. *Psychoanalytic Review, 8,* 168–179.

Leichtentritt, J., & Shechtman, Z. (1998). Therapist, trainee, and child verbal response modes in child group therapy. *Group Dynamics: Theory, Research, and Practice, 2,* 36–47.

Levesque, M. J. (1997). Meta-accuracy among acquainted individuals: A social relations analysis of interpersonal perception and metaperception. *Journal of Personality and Social Psychology, 72,* 66–74.

Lewin, K. (1936). *Principles of topological psychology.* New York: McGraw-Hill.

Lewin, K. (1951). *Field theory in social science.* New York: Harper.

Lieberman, M. A., Yalom, I., & Miles, M. (1973). *Encounter groups: First facts.* New York: Basic Books.

Lieberman, M. A. (1980). Group methods. In F. H. Kanfer & A. P. Goldstein (Eds.), *Helping people change.* New York: Pergamon.

Lieberman, M. A. (1993). Self-help groups. In H. I. Kaplan & M. J. Sadock (Eds.), *Comprehensive group psychotherapy* (3rd ed., pp. 292–304). Baltimore: Williams & Wilkins.

Lieberman, M. A. (1994). Growth groups in the 1980s: Mental Health Implications. In A. Fuhriman & G. M. Burlingame (Eds.), *Handbook of group psychotherapy: An empirical and clinical synthesis* (pp. 527–558). New York: John Wiley & Sons.

Long, S. (Ed.). (1988). *Six group therapies.* New York: Plenum.

Luft, J. (1984). *Groups process: An introduction to group dynamics* (3rd ed.). Palo Alto, CA: Mayfield.

MacKenzie, K. R. (1994). Group development. In A. Fuhriman & G. M. Burlingame (Eds.), *Handbook of group psychotherapy: An empirical and clinical synthesis* (pp. 223–268). New York: Wiley.

MacKenzie, K. R. (1996). Time-limited group psychotherapy: Has Cinderella found her prince? *Group, 20,* 95–111.

MacKenzie, K. R. (1997). Clinical application of group development ideas. *Group Dynamics: Theory, Research, and Practice, 1,* 275–287.

Malloy, T. E., Albright, L., Kenny, D. A., Agatstein, F., & Winquist, L. (1997). Interpersonal perception and metaperception in nonoverlapping social groups. *Journal of Personality and Social Psychology, 72,* 390–398.

Mann, L. (1988). Cultural influence on group processes. In M. H. Bond (Ed.), *The cross-cultural challenge to social psychology* (pp. 182–195). Thousand Oaks, CA: Sage.

Marcus, D. K., & Wilson, J. R. (1996). Interpersonal perception of social anxiety: A social relations analysis. *Journal of Social and Clinical Psychology, 15,* 471–487.

Markham, D. J. (1985). Behavioral rehearsals vs. group systematic desensitization in assertiveness training with women. Special Issue: Gender roles. *Academic Psychology Bulletin, 7,* 157–174.

Markovitz, R. J., & Smith, J. E. (1983). Patients' perceptions of curative factors in short term group psychotherapy. *International Journal of Group Psychotherapy, 33,* 21–39.

Marrow, A. J. (1964). *Behind the executive mask.* New York: American Management Association.

Marsh, L. C. (1933). An experiment in group treatment of patients at Worchester State Hospital. *Mental Hygiene, 17,* 396–416.

Marsh, L. C. (1935). Group therapy and the psychiatric clinic. *Journal of Nervous and Mental Disorders, 82,* 381–393.

Marziali, E., Munroe-Blum, H., & McCleary, L. (1997). The contribution of group cohesion and group alliance to the outcome of group psychotherapy. *International Journal of Group Psychotherapy, 47,* 475–497.

Maxmen, J. (1973). Group therapy as viewed by hospitalized patients. *Archives of General Psychiatry, 28,* 404–408.

Maxmen, J. (1978). An educative model for in-patient group therapy. *International Journal of Group Psychotherapy, 28,* 321–338.

McGuire, J. P., & Leak, G. K. (1980). Prediction of self-disclosure from objective personality assessment techniques. *Journal of Clinical Psychology, 36,* 201–204.

McRoberts, C., Burlingame, G. M., & Hoag, M. J. (1998). Comparative efficacy of individual and group psychotherapy: A meta-analytic perspective. *Group Dynamics: Theory, Research, and Practice, 2,* 101–117.

Meichenbaum, D. (1977). *Cognitive behavior modification: An integrated approach.* New York: Plenum.

Meltzoff, J., & Kornreich, M. (1970). *Research in psychotherapy.* New York: Atherton Press.

Milgram, S. (1963). Behavioral study of obedience. *Journal of Abnormal and Social Psychology, 67,* 371–378.

Miller, N. S. (1995). *Treatment of addictions: Applications of outcome research for clinical management.* New York: The Haworth Press.

Miller, R. C. & Berman, J. S. (1983). The efficacy of cognitive behavior therapies: A quantitative review of the research evidence. *Psychological Bulletin, 94,* 39–53.

Mills, K. H., & Kilmann, P. R. (1982). Group treatment of sexual dysfunctions: A methodological review of the outcome literature. *Journal of Sex and Marital Therapy, 8,* 259–296.

Mitchell, R. C., & Mitchell, R. R. (1984). Constructive management of conflict in groups. *Journal for Specialists in Group Work, 9,* 137–144.

Moreno, J. L. (1953). *Who shall survive? Foundations of sociometry, group psychotherapy and sociodrama.* Beacon, NY: Beacon House.

Myers, A. E. (1962). Team competition, success, and the adjustment of group members. *Journal of Abnormal and Social Psychology, 65,* 325–332.

Nietzel, M. T., Russell, R. L., Hemmings, K. A., & Gretter, M. L. (1987). Clinical significance of psychotherapy for unipolar depression: A meta-analytic approach to social comparison. *Journal of Consulting and Clinical Psychology, 55,* 156–161.

Ormont, L. R. (1984). The leader's role in dealing with aggression in groups. *International Journal of Group Psychotherapy, 34,* 553–572.

Parloff, M. B., & Dies, R. R. (1977). Group psychotherapy outcome research 1966–1975. *International Journal of Group Psychotherapy, 27,* 281–319.

Paul, G. L. (1967). Strategy of outcome research in psychotherapy. *Journal of Consulting Psychology, 31,* 109–118.

Pennebaker, J. W. (1990). *Opening up: The healing power of confiding in others.* New York: Morrow.

Posluszny, D. M., Hyman, K. B., & Baum, A. (1998). Group interventions in cancer: The benefits of social support and education on patient adjustment. In R. S. Tindale, L. Heath, J. Edwards, E. J. Posavac, F. B. Bryant, Y. Suarez-Balcazar, E. Henderson-King, & J. Myers (Eds.), *Theory and research on small groups* (pp. 87–105). New York: Plenum.

Pratt, J. H. (1922). The principles of class treatment and their application to various chronic diseases. *Hospital Social Services, 6,* 401–417.

Rempel, J. K., Holmes, J. G., & Zanna, M. P. (1985). Trust in close relationships. *Journal of Personality and Social Psychology, 49,* 95–112.

Roark, A. E., & Sharah, H. S. (1989). Factors related to group cohesiveness. *Small Group Behavior, 20,* 62–69.

Robinson, L. A., Berman, J. S., & Neimeyer, R. A. (1990). Psychotherapy for the treatment of depression: A comprehensive review of controlled outcome research. *Psychological Bulletin, 108,* 30–49.

Rohrbaugh, M., & Bartels, B. D. (1975). Participants' perceptions of curative factors in therapy and growth groups. *Small Group Behavior, 6,* 430–456.

Rose, S. D. (1993). Cognitive-behavioral group psychotherapy. In H. I. Kaplan & M. J. Sadock (Eds.), *Comprehensive group psychotherapy* (3rd ed., pp. 205–214). Baltimore: Williams & Wilkins.

Rosenbaum, M. (1963). Resistance to group psychotherapy in a community mental health clinic. *International Journal of Social Psychiatry, 9,* 1–4.

Rosenbaum, M. (1965). Group psychotherapy and psychodrama. In B. B. Wolman (Ed.), *Handbook of clinical psychology* (pp. 1254–1274). New York: McGraw-Hill.

Rosenberg, H., & Brian, T. (1986). Group therapy with alcoholic clients: A review. *Alcoholism Treatment Quarterly, 3,* 47–65.

Roth, B. E. (1993). Freud: The group psychologist and group leader. In H. I. Kaplan & M. J. Sadock (Eds.), *Comprehensive group psychotherapy* (3rd ed., pp. 10–21). Baltimore: Williams & Wilkins.

Rugel, R. P., & Meyer, D. J. (1984). The Tavistock group: Empirical findings and implications for group therapy. *Small Group Behavior, 15,* 361–374.

Russell, E. W. (1978). The facts about encounter groups: First facts. *Journal of Clinical Psychology, 34,* 130–137.

Rutan, J. S., & Stone, W. (1993). *Psychodynamic group psychotherapy* (2nd ed.). New York: Guilford Press.

Sacks, J. M. (1993). Psychodrama. In H. I. Kaplan & M. J. Sadock (Eds.), *Comprehensive group psychotherapy* (3rd ed., pp. 214–228). Baltimore: Williams & Wilkins.

Sanchez, V. C., Lewinsohn, P. M., & Larson, D. W. (1980). Assertion training: Effectiveness in the treatment of depression. *Journal of Clinical Psychology, 36,* 526–529.

Schachter, S. (1951). Deviation, rejection, and communication. *Journal of Abnormal and Social Psychology, 46,* 190–207.

Schachter, S. (1959). *The psychology of affiliation.* Stanford, CA: Stanford University Press.

Scheidlinger, S. (1993). History of group psychotherapy. In H. I. Kaplan & B. J. Sadock (Eds.), *Comprehensive group psychotherapy* (3rd ed., pp. 3–10). Baltimore: Williams & Wilkins.

Scheuble, K. J., Dixon, K. N., Levy, A. B., & Kagan-Moore, L. (1987). Premature termination: A risk in eating disorder groups. *Group, 11,* 85–93.

Schilder, P. (1939). Results and problems of group psychotherapy in severe neurosis. *Mental Hygiene, 23,* 87–98.

Seashore, S. E. (1954). *Group cohesiveness in the industrial work group.* Ann Arbor, MI: Institute for Social Research.

Seligman, M. E. P. (1995). The effectiveness of psychotherapy: The *Consumer Reports* study. *American Psychologist, 50,* 965–974.

Seligman, M. E. P. (1996). Science as an ally of practice. *American Psychologist, 51,* 1072–1079.

Shapiro, D. A., & Shapiro, D. (1982). Meta-analysis of comparative therapy outcome studies: A replication and refinement. *Psychological Bulletin, 92,* 581–604.

Shaw, M. E., & Shaw, L. M. (1962). Some effects of sociometric grouping upon learning in a second grade classroom. *Journal of Social Psychology, 57,* 453–458.

Shechtman, Z. (1994). The effect of group psychotherapy on close same-gender friendships among boys and girls. *Sex Roles, 30,* 829–834.

Sherry, P., & Hurley, J. R. (1976). Curative factors in psychotherapeutic and growth groups. *Journal of Clinical Psychology, 32,* 835–837.

Skinner, B. F. (1953). *Science and human behavior.* New York: Macmillan.

Skinner, B. F. (1971). *Beyond freedom and dignity.* New York: Knopf.

Slavson, S. R. (1950). Group psychotherapy. *Scientific American, 183*(6), 42–45.

Slavson, S. R. (1957). Are there dynamics in therapy groups? *International Journal of Group Psychotherapy, 7,* 131–154.

Smith, M. L., Glass, G. V., & Miller, T. I. (1980). *The benefits of psychotherapy.* Baltimore: Johns Hopkins University Press.

Smith, P. B. (1975). Controlled studies of the outcome of sensitivity training. *Psychological Bulletin, 82,* 597–622.

Smith, P. B. (1980). The outcome of sensitivity training and encounter. In P. B. Smith (Ed.), *Small groups and personal change* (pp. 25–55). New York: Methuen.

Snow, D. A., & Oliver, P. E. (1995). Social movements and collective behavior: Social psychological dimensions and considerations. In K. S. Cook, G. A. Fine, & J. S. House (Eds.), *Sociological perspectives on social psychology* (pp. 571–599). Needham Heights, MA: Allyn & Bacon.

Snyder, C. R. (1994). *The psychology of hope: You can get there from here.* New York: Free Press.

Snyder, C. R., Cheavens, J., & Sympson, S. C. (1997). Hope: An individual motive for social commerce. *Group Dynamics: Theory, Research, and Practice, 1,* 107–118.

Solomon, S. D. (1982). Individual versus group therapy: Current status in the treatment of alcoholism. *Advances in Alcohol and Substance Abuse, 2,* 69–86.

Sotile, W. M., & Kilmann, P. R. (1977). Treatments of psychogenic female sexual dysfunctions. *Psychological Bulletin, 84,* 619–633.

Spira, J. L. (1997). Understanding and developing psychotherapy groups for medically ill patients. In J. L. Spira (Ed.), *Group therapy for medically ill patients* (pp. 3–52). New York: Guilford Press.

Spitz, H. I. (1984). Contemporary trends in group psychotherapy: A literature survey. *Hospital and Community Psychiatry, 35,* 132–142.

Stanton, M. D., & Shadish, W. R. (1997). Outcome, attrition, and family-couples treatment for drug abuse: A meta-analysis and review of the controlled, comparative studies. *Psychological Bulletin, 122,* 170–191.

Steenbarger, B. N., & Budman, S. H. (1996). Group psychotherapy and managed behavioral health care: Current trends and future challenges. *International Journal of Group Psychotherapy, 46,* 297–309.

Stiles, W. B., Shapiro, D. A., & Elliott, R. (1986). "Are all psychotherapies equivalent?" *American Psychologist, 41,* 165–180.

Storr, A. (1988). *Solitude: A return to the self.* New York: The Free Press.

Taylor, S. E., & Lobel, M. (1989). Social comparison activity under threat: Downward evaluation and upward contacts. *Psychological Review, 96,* 569–575.

Thune, E. S., Manderscheid, R. W., & Silbergeld, S. (1981). Sex, status, and cotherapy. *Small Group Behavior, 12,* 415–442.

Tillitski, L. (1990). A meta-analysis of estimated effect sizes for group versus individual versus control treatments. *International Journal of Group Psychotherapy, 40,* 215–224.

Toseland, R. W., & Siporin, M. (1986). When to recommend group treatment: A review of the clinical and the research literature. *International Journal of Group Psychotherapy, 36,* 171–201.

Tschuschke, V., & Dies, R. R. (1994). Intensive analysis of therapeutic factors and outcome in long-term inpatient groups. *International Journal of Group Psychotherapy, 44,* 185–208.

Tuckman, B. W. (1965). Developmental sequences in small groups. *Psychological Bulletin, 63,* 384–399.

Ware, R., Barr, J. E., & Boone, M. (1982). Subjective changes in small group processes: An experimental investigation. *Small Group Behavior, 13,* 395–401.

Weinstin, M., & Rossini, E. D. (1998). Academic training in group psychotherapy in clinical psychology doctoral programs. *Psychological Reports, 82,* 955–959.

Wender, L. (1940). Group psychotherapy: A study of its application. *Psychiatric Quarterly, 14,* 708–718.

Wills, T. A., & DePaulo, B. M. (1991). Interpersonal analysis of the help-seeking process. In C. R. Snyder & D. R. Forsyth (Eds.), *Handbook of social and clinical psychology: The health perspective* (pp. 350–375). New York: Pergamon.

Wolf, A. (1949). The psychoanalysis of groups. I. *American Journal of Psychotherapy, 3,* 525–558.

Wolf, A., & Schwartz, E. (1962). *Psychoanalysis in groups.* New York: Gruen and Stratton.

Wood, J. V., Taylor, S. E., & Lichtman, R. R. (1985). Social comparison in adjustment to breast cancer. *Journal of Personality and Social Psychology, 49,* 1169–1183.

Worthington, E. L., Jr., Hight, T. L., Ripley, J. S., Perrone, K. M., Kurusu, T. A., & Jones, D. R. (1997). Strategic hope-focused relationship-enrichment counseling with individual couples. *Journal of Counseling Psychology, 44,* 381–389.

Yalom, I. D. (1975). *The theory and practice of group psychotherapy* (2nd ed.). New York: Basic Books.

Yalom, I. D. (1985). *The theory and practice of group psychotherapy* (3rd ed.). New York: Basic Books.

Yalom, I. D. (1995). *The theory and practice of group psychotherapy* (4th ed.). New York: Basic Books.

Yalom, V. J., & Vinogradov, S. (1993). Interpersonal group psychotherapy. In H. I. Kaplan & M. J. Sadock (Eds.), *Comprehensive group psychotherapy* (3rd ed., pp. 185–195). Baltimore: Williams & Wilkins.

Zaccaro, S. J., Gualtieri, J., & Minionis, D. (1995). Task cohesion as a facilitator of team decision making under temporal urgency. *Military Psychology, 7,* 77–93.

Zimpfer, D. G. (1987). Groups for the aging: Do they work? *Journal for Specialists in Group Work, 12,* 85–92.

CHAPTER 16

CONSTRUCTIVIST AND NARRATIVE PSYCHOTHERAPIES

ROBERT A. NEIMEYER
University of Memphis
ALAN E. STEWART
University of Florida

We can no longer rest assured that human progress may proceed step by step in an orderly fashion from the known to the unknown. Neither our senses nor our doctrines provide us with the immediate knowledge required for such a philosophy of science. What we think we know is anchored only in our assumptions, not in the bedrock of truth itself, and that world we seek to understand remains always on the horizons of our thoughts.

George A. Kelly (1977)

Although we rarely consider it, systems of psychotherapy result from the confluence of many philosophical, scientific, practical, and cultural factors. So it is with constructivism. Like behavior therapy, constructivist psychotherapies represent the clinical implementation of a particular philosophy of science, although the two approaches differ sharply in their philosophical allegiances. As with cognitive therapy, constructivism draws from contemporary scientific research, although it is more aligned with broader ethological and linguistic field studies than with the highly controlled laboratory experimentation of cognitive science. Along with family systems approaches, constructivist therapies have gained impetus from a dissatisfaction with pathology-oriented forms of treatment, though each has generated different solution-oriented interventions for the self and system in which it is embed-

ded. And like psychoanalytic therapies, constructivist approaches express the cultural sensibilities of the era in which they emerged, although the two perspectives represent distillations of a modern focus on historical truth and a postmodern focus on narrative possibility, respectively. Our goal in this chapter is to reflect on the family of psychotherapies defined by their adherence to constructivist assumptions, including their shared histories and their contemporary expressions. We then focus on one integrative metaphor—lives as stories—which has proven fertile for many constructivist therapists, as a way of illustrating some of the practical implications of constructivism. Finally, we conclude with a few comments on psychotherapy research as viewed through a constructivist lens and some of the current and future challenges to be faced by theorists and practitioners working within this developing perspective.

A DEFINITIONAL BEGINNING

One of the features of constructivist thought that can make an encounter with it somewhat daunting is its abstractness. Certainly, the reader who opens a typical constructivist text and encounters terms like *modulation corollary, morphogenic nuclear structure, autopoiesis, landscape of intentionality*, and *the heterogeneously distributed self* can find the experience rather chilling, to say the least. To avoid having you read this chapter with the text in one hand and a dictionary in the other, we attempt to minimize our use of scholarly jargon and instead speak as clearly as possible about the central ideas that define a constructivist outlook. Because we hope that you will become sufficiently intrigued with this therapy approach to explore it further, however, we sometimes introduce key concepts in constructivist thought and accompany them with concise definitions. We begin with a definition of constructivism itself.

At its root, *constructivism* is an epistemological position, that is, a particular theory of knowledge. Rather than viewing human knowing as a straightforward matter of developing realistic "mental maps" of an external world, constructivists emphasize the personal and collective processes by which people organize their experience and coordinate their relationships with one another (R. A. Neimeyer, 1995a). In this view, persons are seen as actively constructing templates of meaning that help them interpret their past, negotiate their present, and anticipate their future. The degree to which their constructions are adequate in helping with this interpretive, anticipatory, and pragmatic task becomes the focus of psychotherapy.

Although some antecedents of constructivist thought can be found in the 19th century (and even earlier in Western history), this perspective has gained momentum in the postmodern era, corresponding roughly to the second half of the 20th century. *Postmodernism* is both a philosophy and a cultural movement, and it acknowledges the multiplicity of constructions that can be developed to account for and structure human social life (Anderson, 1990; Botella, 1995; Kvale, 1992). In contrast to a modern view of reality as stable, singular, and knowable, postmodernists view both the reality of the world and the self as subject to shifting, competing, and local constructions, none of which can claim ultimate authority as true or justified to the exclusion of others (Neimeyer & Stewart, 1998a). In view of the tensions that can arise among these competing constructions (alternative views of psychotherapy are only one example), it is not surprising that postmodernists are drawn toward the study of *discourse*. Discursive psychologists, therefore, study and critique the ways in which different individuals and groups use language about social life as a way to increase the plausibility of their own positions and marginalize or silence the voices of others (Burr, 1995).

Finally, *narrative approaches* to therapy adopt the metaphor of lives as texts and focus on attempts to construct meaningful—though not necessarily objectively "true"—accounts of experiences in storied form. Therapists working within this perspective attempt to help clients achieve a sense of authorship over their life stories and to develop a narrative form that is adequate in structuring past events, while also leading to a hopeful future (Parry & Doan, 1994; Snyder, McDermott, Cook, & Rapoff, 1997). The narrative trend in many contemporary psychotherapy traditions is coherent with a constructivist approach, insofar as both view the client as not only the chief protagonist of his or her life script but also the person who is most able to revise it in more satisfying directions.

To gain a fuller appreciation of constructivist and narrative approaches to therapy and to understand their alignments with other contemporary therapeutic traditions, it is helpful to trace their roots in philosophical and psychological thought. Doing so will help define the constructivist agenda and set the stage for a discussion of specific therapeutic approaches and strategies that translate these theoretical considerations into practical guidelines for psychotherapy researchers and practitioners.

CONSTRUCTIVISM RECONSTRUCTED

One tenet of constructivist thought is that the stories we tell serve both organizational and anticipatory functions, allowing us to account for the plot structure of our past while also orienting us toward a meaningful future. So it is with the history of constructivism. Although the earliest contributors to this system of thought certainly did so without awareness that they later would be considered as progenitors of a psychotherapeutic movement, they nonetheless have been claimed as conceptual forebearers by constructivist scholars (Mahoney, 1991; R. A. Neimeyer, 2000a). For our purposes, we touch briefly on the work of eight thinkers—ranging from 18th-century philosophers to 20th-century psychotherapists—who provided an assumptive foundation for the principles and practices of the constructivist psychotherapies that we explore later in this chapter.

Although most constructivist scholars and practitioners acknowledge that a real, ontologically substantive world exists, they are much more interested in understanding the nuances of the person's construction of the world than in evaluating the extent to which it accurately represents some external reality. Thus, constructivists emphasize the development of a viable or workable construction of people, things, and events over the attainment of a singularly veridical rendering of one's surrounds. This suggests that multiple meanings can be developed for the events in one's life and that each meaning may help the person to understand and respond creatively to experience.

Philosophical Foundations

The idea that people actively and continuously engage in meaning-making processes, that is, construction, dates at least to the ancient Greek philosopher Epictetus, who maintained that people were more perturbed by their views of reality than by reality itself. But it was the Italian rhetorician Vico (1668–1744) who systematized the rudiments of a truly constructivist philosophy, tracing the origins of human thought to the gradual acquisition of the power to transcend immediate experience. Vico argued that the origins of human thought lay in the attempt to understand the mysteries of the external world by projecting upon it the structures of human motives and actions in the form of myths and fables. This tendency to order experience through the application of such "imaginative universals" was displaced eventually, he thought, by the development of linguistic abstractions that permitted categorization of events and objects on the basis of single characteristics.

The work of the German philosopher Kant (1724–1804) also contributed significantly to a conception of the human mind as an active, form-giving structure. Specifically, Kant believed that experience and sensation were not passively written into the person but that the mind transforms and coordinates the multiplicity of sense data into integrated thought. Thus, we can come to "know" only those phenomena that conform to the human mind, with its penchant for organizing the world in three-dimensional terms and imputing causality to events. From Vico and Kant, constructivists borrowed a model of knowledge as an active structuring of experience, rather than a passive or receptive assimilation of a "noumenal" reality of "things in themselves," uncontaminated by human knowing.

At the threshold of the 20th century, the German analytic philosopher Vaihinger (1852–1933) embraced constructivist epistemology in asserting that people develop impressions of the real world and create *workable fictions* that help them to adjust and to meaningfully respond to people and events. Conceptual "artifices" (e.g., of mathematical infinity or of a "reasonable man"), although having no exemplars in "reality," perform a heuristic function in helping the person organize and integrate disparate pieces of knowledge or sensory data. Vaihinger (1925) categorized his *Philosophy of 'As If'* as a kind of "idealistic positivism," to acknowledge the dual reliance on hard data and impressions received by the sensory system along with an active, form-giving activity of the mind to create useful constructions.

Within this century, the work of Vaihinger influenced Korzybski's development of general semantics. Korzybski (1879–1950), a Polish intellectual working independently of established academic circles, essentially criticized the use of the verb *to be* and its conjugations because it tended to identify people or things with qualities or characteristics without acknowledging them as simply descriptions from the standpoint of a given observer. For example, rather than accepting the statement that "Bob is a depressive," Korzybski might note that Alan describes Bob as depressed and then only under certain conditions. Identifying things with states, Korzybski maintained, deemphasized the multiplicity of meanings and modes of existence that characterize most phenomena, living or inanimate, and it obscured the role of the speaker in attributing meaning to events. From Vaihinger and Korzybski, constructivists drew the implication that human beings operate on the basis of symbolic or linguistic constructs that help them navigate in the world without contacting it in any simple, direct way. Moreover, they suggested that such constructions are viable to the extent that they help us live our lives meaningfully and find validation in the shared understandings of others in our families, communities, and societies. Postmodern thinkers who follow in this constructivist vein further stress the extent to which we live in a world constituted by multiple social realities, no one of which can claim to be objectively true across persons, cultures, or historical epochs (Gergen, 1994). Instead, the constructions by which we live, and which could be constituted quite differently, are at best provisional ways of organizing ourselves and our activities.

Psychological Expressions

Constructivist epistemology provided a conceptual basis for several distinct psychologies in this century. First, the British researcher Bartlett (1886–1979) applied constructivist concepts in his investigations of human memory processes. In his classic work on remembering, Bartlett maintained that memories were reconstructed out of bits and pieces of recollected information. That is, memories did not consist of stored, complete representations of past events that were recalled in toto. Bartlett viewed memories as past information unified by *schemas*, the threads of constructive processes that exist at the time information is remembered.

The Swiss genetic epistemologist Piaget (1896–1980) was the second psychologist to establish a coherent theory founded on a constructivist basis. As a developmental psychologist with interests in children's forms of knowing, Piaget chronicled how children's schemas changed as a function of both physical growth and exposure to a succession of conceptually challenging experiences. Rather than representing a smooth learning curve over time, Piaget contended that cognitive development was punctuated at critical points by qualitative transformations in the very style and form of thinking, permitting the eventual emergence of abstract, formal thought with a level of plasticity that was unavailable earlier in childhood. Subsequent developmentalists in the Piagetian tradition have extended this model into adulthood, when subtle dialectical forms of thinking emerge to permit more adequate accommodation to the complexities of social life. Bartlett and Piaget are significant for the development of constructivist thought because they introduced the notion of schema, regarding it less as a cognitive "copy" of an objective reality than as a way of organizing a meaningful past and engaging the present in an adaptive fashion.

The Austrian physician Alfred Adler (1870–1937) was one of the first clinicians to incorporate constructivist epistemology into his theory of personality and psychotherapy, which is known as individual psychology (Adler, 1927; Ansbacher & Ansbacher, 1956). Vaihinger (1925) significantly influenced Adler in asserting that people developed fictional life goals that affected the ways in which they related supportively to others while seeking personal completion and fulfillment. Thus, Adler viewed individuals as actively reconstructing the past and anticipating their futures in terms of fictional goals in the present, giving rise to a unique "style of life." Adler believed that problems ensued either when the individual was blocked by oneself or others in

moving toward these aims or when the individual pursued them at the expense of other people. Adler's therapeutic approach, influenced by the insight-oriented strategies of his time, was designed to help persons become fully aware of their unique strivings and to seek their expression in a form compatible with the broader "social interest." To do this, Adler would perform early recollection exercises and analyses of birth order and family relationships, not so much for the historical information that they provided about early experiences, but as a way to help clients understand how their current goals affected the value they placed on life experiences. As a therapeutic school embracing early constructivist ideas, Adler's individual psychology continues to garner the interest of clinicians and researchers, as well as educators committed to fostering healthy child-care practices among nonprofessionals (A. E. Stewart, 2000).

Finally, the American clinical psychologist George Kelly (1905–1967) developed both a comprehensive personality theory and an approach to psychotherapy based on a constructivist epistemology (Fransella, 1996; R. A. Neimeyer, 2000b). Influenced by Korzybski's general semantics and Moreno's psychodrama (Stewart & Barry, 1991), Kelly viewed people as incipient scientists, striving to anticipate and control the events they experienced by developing a system of personal constructs that they tested and refined through experience. In his landmark work, *The Psychology of Personal Constructs*, Kelly (1955) elucidated the personal origins of constructs that people used to apprehend and anticipate the world and the way in which they functioned as complex meaning systems organized around core constructs that defined an individual's sense of self. Despite his focus on the uniqueness of personal meaning systems, Kelly also emphasized the commonality of construing in different cultural groups and the attempt to construe the construction processes of others in the development of role relationships. In keeping with this dual focus on the self and the social surround, Kelly viewed psychotherapy as a tool for helping people to understand both their own construing and that of others and then to actively experiment with novel outlooks and the related possible selves.

By making the reconstruction of personal belief systems the focus of psychotherapy, Adler and Kelly anticipated the work of later cognitive theorists and therapists. The emphasis of these two early constructivists on the centrality of the social dimension, however, distinguishes them from many later cognitive perspectives and aligns them more closely with contemporary systems therapies. More generally, Adler's and Kelly's deep respect for individuality and their bold experimentation with brief, practical interventions provided a sharp departure from the dominant psychotherapies of their day and set the stage for the focus on personal meanings and solution-oriented treatments exemplified by many current constructivist psychotherapists.

CONSTRUCTIVIST PSYCHOTHERAPIES

The last 10 to 20 years have witnessed a growing diversity of psychotherapeutic approaches that have embraced a constructivist epistemology. There is no single school of constructivist psychotherapy, no approved set of techniques that define constructivist interventions. Instead, constructivist views have percolated into most major traditions of therapy, from the psychoanalytic to the cognitive-behavioral, producing novel ways of conceptualizing therapeutic practice, as well as a broad variety of associated change strategies or techniques. Our goals in this section are to provide a succinct description of features shared by constructivist and narrative therapies generally and then to survey some of the specific expressions of the constructivist approach. This provides the backdrop for a deeper consideration of the concept of narrative, along with several interventions tailored to assist in therapeutic "reauthoring" of problematic life stories.

General Features

Seen through a constructivist lens, psychotherapy can be defined as the variegated and subtle interchange and negotiation of (inter)personal meanings in the service of articulating, elaborating, and revising those constructions that the client uses to organize her or his experience and action. Such a definition emphasizes several features of the psychotherapy process, including the delicacy with which the therapist must grasp the contours of the experiential world of the client, the dialogical and discursive basis of their interaction, and the contributions of both to their mutual inquiry. These emphases in psychotherapy in turn reflect a more basic human quest to seek relatedness, connection, and mutuality of meaning in spite of our uniqueness, using the common ground provided by our language and our embodiment to

form an intersubjective bridge between our phenomenal worlds. Although psychotherapy conceived along these lines can have many different concrete objectives, at an abstract level all of these involve joining with clients to develop a refined map of the often inarticulate constructions in which they are emotionally invested and that define what they regard as viable courses of action, and then extending or supplementing these constructions to enlarge the number of possible worlds clients might inhabit (R. A. Neimeyer, 1995b).

The emphasis on both the uniqueness of clients' meaning systems and the distinctive relationship between any given client and therapist lead constructivists to distrust highly standardized and manualized procedures for modifying human behavior. In addition, constructivist and narrative therapists reject methods that simply supply clients with supposedly more "functional" or "adaptive" ways of coping, thinking, or feeling as defined by the therapist. Thus, constructivism contrasts with forms of therapy that accord therapists the "expert" role in diagnosing and treating "disturbed" clients. Instead, constructivists are more likely to grant both participants in therapy their own expertise, regarding the client as an expert on his or her experience and the therapist as an expert in the facilitation of personal and social change (Feixas, 1992).

Consistent with this emphasis, constructivists eschew pathologizing diagnostic systems that focus on clients' deficits and deviations from supposedly normal patterns of behavior (Neimeyer & Raskin, 1999). Accordingly, they resist the common practice of applying universal categories of disorders that fail to capture the richness and subtlety of any given individual's way of interpreting the social world and constructing relationships with others. For instance, a diagnostic category such as major depression merely describes a presumably maladaptive mood disorder, without conveying any information about the way in which the person's meaning-making processes have ceased to be viable for engaging life.

In contrast, constructivists prefer assessment techniques and working conceptualizations that are idiographic or tailored to each case, which examine both the positive and negative implications (from the client's, family's, or society's standpoint) of clients' ways of construing their lives and problems (G. J. Neimeyer, 1993). The personalism of the therapeutic encounter requires that the therapist have a sensitive attunement to the unspoken nuances in the client's conversation and skill in using evocative and metaphorically rich language to help sculpt their mutual meaning making toward fresh possibilities (R. A. Neimeyer, 1996). To be successful, such structural coupling between client and therapist systems ultimately must move beyond bland generalizations about the nature of the working alliance and instead foster a unique "shared epistemology" (Glover, 1995) that is irreducible to the individual systems of either partner in the therapeutic relationship.

What outcomes might be valued in this constructivist approach to the counseling process? Although the specific aims of psychotherapy are necessarily defined by the participants, at an abstract level the goals of constructivist therapies include adopting a "language of hypothesis" (Kelly, 1969) by recognizing that one's constructions are at best working fictions rather than established facts. As such, they are amenable to therapeutic deconstruction (e.g., through subjecting the same events to alternative readings) and reconstruction (e.g., through acting on alternative interpretations to realize their effects). Although enhanced reflexivity or awareness of the self may be a legitimate aim of this work, it is ultimately less important than the aim of constructing a self with sufficient narrative coherence to be recognizable but with sufficient fluidity to permit continued tailoring to the varied social ecologies that the client inhabits.

The Constructivist Turn

Having outlined some of the general features of constructivist therapy, we now discuss how these emphases are expressed in several distinguishable therapeutic orientations, ranging from direct outgrowths of earlier constructivist thinkers to independent developments in traditions as distinct as psychodynamic, cognitive-behavioral, humanistic, and family systemic therapies. It is ineresting that each has found the concept of narrative to be a useful metaphor for therapeutic work, as we see in the next section.

Contemporary Personal Construct Therapy

As early as the 1940s, Kelly had begun to experiment with change strategies that foreshadowed postmodern trends in psychotherapy. For example, in *fixed role therapy*, Kelly (1955) combined narrative and dramaturgical procedures first to help clients identify and then to temporarily sus-

pend the assumptive frames they used to construct their relationships with others. This took the form of asking them to write an open-ended "character sketch" of themselves, as viewed from the standpoint of a sympathetic friend who knew them intimately, which then became the basis of a therapist-drafted "enactment sketch" of a hypothetical person contending with similar issues in different ways. To facilitate the client's experimenting with this initially foreign role, Kelly took pains to ensure that the new sketch did not violate the client's central identity constructs but instead offered a plausible but "orthogonal" construction of life that carried fresh implications for thought, feeling, and action. For example, a client who tended to construe relationships in terms of "controlling vs. being controlled" might be asked for a fixed period of time to become "Ed Venturous," who seeks out unusual aspects of others' outlooks, much as an anthropologist might seek to enter and explore an exotic culture. During this time, he would attempt to work at his job, negotiate with his parents, formulate his life goals, and even relate to his partner as Ed might, being guided by a daily rereading of the sketch and periodic role-playing sessions with the therapist (R. A. Neimeyer, 1993). At the end of this intensive period of engagement with an alternative construction of self, he would then be coached to "de-role," setting aside Ed and discussing any experiential learning that resulted. Unlike more prescriptive behavior therapies that use role-playing procedures, Kelly's form of role therapy made no assumption that the new ways of relating were preferred, or even would be retained, by the client. Instead, their primary function was to dislodge the client from his or her habitual assumptive world and convey the idea that even one's "normal" self is every bit as much a provisional, modifiable construction that could be "storied" differently.

One recent therapeutic procedure that extends the postmodern implications of Kelly's fixed role therapy is the multiple self-awareness (MSA) group format devised by Sewell, Baldwin, and Moes (1998). Adopting the position that the self consists not of a coherent, true personality but of a shifting coalition of often disparate identities, the MSA format allows for the exploration of the impact of these selves on one another and on one's interpersonal relationships over time. The group process consists of several sessions, which move from introducing the concept of multiple selves through various narrative exercises designed to elicit different identity characteristics (e.g., efficiency and people pleasing) and anthropomorphize these as different characters with descriptive names (e.g., the Robot and the Peacekeeper). Group members then are coached to write an autobiography of each of these characters, describing how and when they emerged and what role they have played in their subsequent lives. This sets the stage for psychodramatic techniques in which members select a particular self from their personal repertoires to enact in a group scenario. For example, members might be instructed to imagine that they have to decide on a sightseeing tour to embark on with the other members, each of whom is also enacting a dominant, marginalized, problematic, or resourceful self-role (e.g., the Whining Child and the General). Interactions among the partial identities of the various group members vividly portray relational patterns associated with each role, as well as the means by which each exerts its influence or adapts to the control attempts of other people. Later exercises invite group members to function as directors, casting one another as the multiple selves in the director's own cast of characters or comparing and contrasting their different fractional identities to discover the themes that distinguish them. Processing these and other narrative and dramaturgical exercises permits members to shed light on otherwise obscure personal dynamics, as well as to consider ways of renegotiating conflicts in their self by realigning existing characters or adding new ones.

Whereas other post-Kellian construct theorists have also devised modified role therapy procedures (e.g., Epting & Nazario, 1987), most therapists in this tradition work without the explicit use of therapeutic role playing in the majority of their cases. For example, Leitner (1988, 1995) has developed an approach for analyzing the ways in which clients protect themselves from the potential terror of intimate role relationships, based on a delicate reading of their moment-to-moment engagements with their therapists. Other present-day exponents of personal construct therapy (PCT) also adopt a process-relational stance in promoting the conversational coconstruction of meaning in family therapy (Loos, 1993) or developing tools for linguistically sculpting the therapeutic dialogue through the use of selective highlighting, contrasting, ambiguating, and structuring features of therapeutic discourse (R. A. Neimeyer, 1996). Thus, contemporary personal construct therapists have retained Kelly's focus on personal meanings and the construction of roles but have tended to adopt a more deeply relational emphasis in diagnosing clients' difficulties and treating them in therapy.

Cognitive Constructivism

A second tradition of constructivist therapy began to gain momentum in the late 1970s as an outgrowth of cognitive and cognitive-behavioral therapies emphasizing the role of the person's interpretations of events in a range of disorders. Michael Mahoney (1980), a pioneer of the cognitive trend, began to critique its reliance on rationalistic epistemologies that presumed that emotional adjustment was a straightforward matter of making one's cognitions realistic and in line with an observable world. Instead, Mahoney (1991) viewed "dis-orders" such as anxiety or depression as the necessary emotional preconditions to profound personal change, and he began to turn more attention to the nonconscious "core-ordering processes" by which persons construct and maintain a sense of self. By the early 1990s, this focus on the "deeper" self-schema had begun to augment traditional cognitive therapies (Freeman, 1993; Young, 1990), and even initially rationalistic approaches such as cognitive-behavioral modification began to adopt a narrative metaphor in place of the more mechanistic concepts on which they were once based (Meichenbaum, 1993).

A particularly systematic expression of cognitive constructivist therapy is the "postrationalist" approach developed by the Italian theorist Vittorio Guidano (1991, 1995a; Guidano & Liotti, 1983). Guidano grounds his analysis in ethological studies of primate behavior and developmental research on human bonding patterns, arguing that intense attachment relationships are fundamental to intersubjectivity and self-recognition. In the case of human infants, who learn to recognize and modulate their emotional lives in the context of attachment to parenting figures, this gives rise to prototypical emotional schemata, which are gradually elaborated into structured and integrated patterns of self-complexity. Thus, individuals construct explicit self-knowledge (the *me*), shaped in part by the way in which they are regarded by significant others, to account for their spontaneous emotional engagement in life (the *I*). This ongoing effort to construct a coherent sense of identity in the face of tacit experiences that are inevitably more complex can give rise to self-deception, on the one hand, and to the anxious confrontation with feelings that are incongruent with our existing model of self, on the other hand.

Guidano's approach to therapy focuses on this indispensable alternation between the experiencing *I* and explaining *me*. In the context of a secure therapeutic relationship, Guidano draws attention to troubling discrepancies between the client's working models of the self-and-world and his or her moment-to-moment experiencing. This sometimes takes the form of a Movieola technique (Guidano, 1995b), in which the therapist pans the "camera" of therapeutic attention over a problematic interpersonal scenario, occasionally asking the client to "zoom in" on significant observations that require "close-up" analysis. For example, a client who viewed herself as a poised and self-assured professional (the *me*) might report feeling inexplicably embarrassed and self-conscious (the *I*) following an apparently routine meeting with her male employer. The therapist might first coach the client to recount the scene in detail and then to focus intensively on subtle cues (e.g., the boss's facial expression and her own posture and emotions) that were discrepant with her usual understanding of herself as a career woman. Such a review might find, for instance, that the employer's raised eyebrow and sidelong glance at one point in their discussion triggered images of her father's characteristic dismissal of her in childhood, ushering in the feelings of inadequacy that she felt during this earlier time. Discussion of these observations might then permit a reordering of her self-knowledge (the *me*) to "own" her residual feelings of vulnerability to not being taken seriously by men, as well as to work out how to respond to this dynamic in her work relationships. Overall, the goal of postrationalist therapy is not to rationally dispute negative emotions, as in conventional cognitive therapy, but to use intensive exploration of such affect-laden experiences to extend the client's self-awareness in the direction of greater complexity and integration.

Psychoanalytic Constructivism

As the more relativistic philosophy of constructivism has become more widespread, it has begun to permeate even long-standing traditions of psychotherapy, such as psychoanalysis. One harbinger of this trend is Donald Spence (1982), who argued that analysis could not unearth the historical truth of the patient's life but only constitute a procedure for disclosing its narrative truth or

subjective meaning in the eyes of its author—the client. In keeping with the psychoanalytic tradition, however, constructivist analysts still tend to emphasize the usefulness of accessing and reviewing emotionally significant unconscious memories less as veridical insights than as inventions subject to the demand for narrative "smoothing," that is, reworking to accentuate its relevance as a story.

One interesting recent integration of constructivism and psychoanalytic treatment is the *depth-oriented brief therapy* developed by Bruce Ecker and Laurel Hulley. As constructivists, Ecker and Hulley (1996) regard symptoms and problems as the products of the constructs that individuals use for knowing and responding to the flux of experience. They regard most of these core-ordering processes as tacit or nonconscious, however, until brought into awareness in therapy. Thus, if problems are produced because the person holds at least one construction of reality that makes the symptom compellingly necessary to have, then therapists must help clients discover and integrate this unconscious *prosymptom* position. This contrasts sharply with the conscious *antisymptom* position that clients typically express at the outset of therapy, in which the symptom is seen as senseless and undesirable. Because they believe that cognitive insight into the deep structures responsible for symptom generation is rarely effective in changing such patterns, Ecker and Hulley lead their clients on an experiential search for the "emotional truth" of their prosymptom construction. This consists of prompting clients to discover these positions, integrate them into their conscious construction of self and life, and then transform them by experiencing their incompatibility with constructs brought into the same field of awareness.

Ecker and Hulley (2000) provide an example of this method in the case of a woman suffering from severe anxiety. The client reported paralyzing feelings of helplessness and dread in the face of an intense legal battle compounded by various health crises within her family, which threatened the well-being of her children, husband, and herself. Resisting the temptation to accept her anxiety as "normal" in the face of this stress, the therapist pursued the internal construction of self that necessitated her symptoms. This involved *radical questioning*, asking her to vividly conjure an image of the symptom as if it were happening now, and then asking, "Right now, let your imagination show you what attitude or behavior you could have that would make the anxiety diminish or stop happening." The woman quickly got in touch with how "fighting back" would reduce her feeling of helpless vulnerability. She was then invited to imagine really fighting back, which prompted her surprised recognition of her own strong resistance to doing so. This led to her identification of a previously unconscious image of herself as a "Good Girl," one who never made trouble, fought back, or was less than "nice," regardless of the provocation. Moreover, this position was coupled with a tacit purpose: Being a Good Girl would protect her from terrible things, an unspoken assumption that had shaped her way of responding to a lifetime of stressors. Discovering this position made sense of the overwhelming vulnerability that she was experiencing, which was necessitated by her not fighting back (like a Good Girl), even when under attack. The therapist assigned the homework of writing her prosymptom position on a card and reading it whenever her anxiety began to build, a strategy that promoted her conscious integration of it and her spontaneous reorganization of her self-image as she began to recognize its costs. Although this form of therapy typically requires four to eight sessions, in this case substantial and lasting improvement was achieved after a single session. This result clearly is in accord with Ecker and Hulley's claim that effective therapy can be both deep and brief.

Humanistic Constructivism

Another long-standing tradition to be influenced by a constructivist position is humanistic-existential psychotherapy, whose emphases on human choice, agency, and phenomenology (or the study of experience) converge with core themes in personal construct theory and related forms of constructivist thought. One outgrowth of this convergence is the *self-confrontation method* devised by the Dutch personality theorist Hubert Hermans (1995), which uses open-ended questions to elicit those "valuations," or important units of meaning, that a person uses to structure a sense of her or his past, present, and future. The client then rates these synoptic life experiences on a standard list of affect terms, which yields indexes expressing the degree of self-enhancement, union with others, negative emotions, and positivity associated with each, providing a basis for self-reflection or a method for mapping therapeutic changes in meanings over time.

A second example of the infusion of constructivist themes into humanistic therapy is the dialectical approach of the Canadian psychologists Leslie Greenberg and Juan Pascual-Leone (1995). In their view, new meanings are constructed in therapy by activating opposing emotional schemes in such a way that the client can spontaneously synthesize them into a new, emergent structure. Although the particular approach hinges on the nature of the therapeutic task as identified in a given therapeutic moment (Greenberg, 1992), it is significant that, as with Ecker and Hulley (1996), such tasks are more experiential than cognitive. For example, a depressed and self-critical client might be asked to become the critical voice of her conscience by using the Gestalt technique of sitting in another chair and angrily accusing herself as the client of her shortcomings. As this role playing progresses, the client might come to recognize the strong resemblance of these criticisms to those she received from her mother, at which point the therapist might encourage the client to return to her previous seat and express to her "mother" how such criticism felt to her and what she wants from her mother now. Through a series of these emotionally vivid dialectical exchanges, therapy might help the client synthesize two contradictory internal experiences (e.g., self-contempt and the need for comfort) into a new structure (e.g., self-acceptance). In keeping with the dialectical framework, the "selfhood processes" that are the focus of this approach are viewed as continually evolving toward greater internal complexity and more adequate symbolization.

Systemic Constructivism

Finally, family systems therapies have been revolutionized by a social constructionist perspective (R. A. Neimeyer, 1998b), adopting a nonauthoritarian view of therapy as a conversation whose goal is to alter what Anderson and Goolishian (1992) term the "problem determined system." In such approaches, the therapist functions less as an expert who is dispensing answers than as a conversation manager who promotes the sort of exchanges among family members that "dissolve" old problems by "languaging" about them in a new way (Efran, Lukens, & Lukens, 1990).

Other family therapists have adopted the constructivist metaphor of lives as stories and have devised novel means of helping clients free themselves from the dominant narratives that originate in particular families and cultures and that keep them from feeling like the authors of their own lives. For therapists such as Michael White in Australia and David Epston in New Zealand (White & Epston, 1990), *externalizing the problem* by reconstruing it as something separate from the client's self provides a useful first step toward recognizing its destructive impact on clients and the relationships in which they are engaged. Therapy can then turn toward recognizing and validating those exceptional occasions when a person begins to resist the dominant narrative and rewrite his or her life story along more hopeful lines (cf. Snyder, McDermont, Cook, & Rapoff, 1997).

For example, a client struggling with guilt over the breakup of his marriage might be asked to imagine guilt as an unwelcome invader of his life, who requires him to distance himself from his children, engage in endless acts of self-punishment, and condemn himself to a life of solitary confinement. The therapist then can help the client identify "sparkling moments," when he spontaneously resists these "real effects" (Monk, Winslade, Crocket, & Epston, 1996), for example, by arranging a family get-together that includes both his children and his new partner. Narrative therapists have devised numerous creative ways of *historicizing* such desirable changes (e.g., by searching for earlier signs of self-assertion that made them possible) and documenting progress (e.g., by conferring "certificates of achievement" for those who overcome a difficult problem). Moreover, in keeping with their systemic leanings, such therapists are concerned with *recruiting an audience* for the new and more hopeful story once it is consolidated, by sharing it with other persons within and beyond the family. For example, after escaping from the stark prison to which guilt had sentenced him, this client might be asked to write an "escape plan" for future clients who are contending with a similar problem.

Having introduced the philosophical underpinnings of the constructivist perspective and discussed their expression in several prominent traditions of psychotherapy, we now consider an integrative metaphor—that of *narrative*—that is adopted by many of these approaches. Doing so permits us to illustrate some of the novel implications of constructivist therapy for clinical problems before we close with a few reflections on the challenges currently facing this evolving clinical perspective.

NARRATIVE AS AN INTEGRATIVE THERAPEUTIC METAPHOR

Over the last 20 years, the metaphor of the self as narrative has exemplified the constructivist emphasis on meaning making both inside and outside of psychotherapy (MacIntyre, 1981; Mair, 1988; Terrell & Lyddon, 1995). This metaphor casts the person as both the author and principal character in the ongoing story of his or her life. In the role of author, the person actively creates a narrative by binding past experiences and ongoing life events into meaningful units across time, themes, and persons (Mancuso & Sarbin, 1983). Such stories both guide and are informed by the person's role as the main character in his or her story and in the stories of others.

Three discernible and related influences have contributed to the emergence of the narrative metaphor in recent years. First, Bruner (1986) argued that although some problems in psychology may be addressed optimally through logico-deductive, reductionistic paradigms, other problems and questions are best pursued through narrative means. The appeal of the narrative mode as a general scientific method stems from the observation that some phenomena, such as human agency, goals, and feelings, cannot be meaningfully reduced to constituent parts without substantial loss of meaning, especially for clinicians.

The second impetus for the emergence of narrative metaphors was provided by Sarbin (1986), who advocated the view that narrative was a primary "root metaphor" for many content areas within psychology. Sarbin believed that historical acts, which occurred within particular contexts (persons, relationships, and situations), made up the substantive content domain for all psychological inquiry. Sarbin maintained that narratives were the optimal explanatory vehicles for phenomena within this domain. Howard's (1991) application of the narrative metaphor to cross-cultural psychology and psychotherapy illustrates its relevance to diverse areas.

Finally, the use of narratives at both the individual and collective levels of psychological study has become much more widespread in recent years. At the individual level, the autobiographical "life sketch" has become an important method for helping the aged to understand the recurrent, meaningful, and integrated patterns in their life stories (Carlsen, 1989; Omer, 1993). In narrating a life history, the person may develop unique meanings and also discern parallels between his or her personal story and timeless themes and plots that appear in literature (Atkinson, 1995). Collective meaning making can also result in the development of cultural (Howard, 1991) and familial stories (Beiver & Franklin, 1998) that carry implications for the individuals living them (McNamee & Gergen, 1992).

Empirical Support for the Narrative Metaphor

Narrative conceptualizations of psychological processes provide more than apt analogies or intriguing clinical heuristics. Empirical research in domains that are central to self-definition (autobiographical memory and language use) have supported the utility and appropriateness of the narrative metaphor. In autobiographical memories, there is evidence of narrative structure in both memory patterns themselves and in the ways autobiographical episodes are recalled (Barclay, 1996; Howe & Courage, 1997; Rubin, 1998). Regarding the former, Linton (1986) and Barsalou (1988) have observed that as similar events are repeated over time, they become stored in large-scale structures in memory known as "event structures," or *extendures*. These fundamental units tend to integrate thematically related material over time and could underlie the narrative structure of the memories themselves (Robinson & Swanson, 1990).

The use of language also plays a critical role in the way meaning is attached to the self and to one's lived experiences (de Shazer, 1994; Shotter & Gergen, 1989). The person's particular "languaging" of a narrative can indicate the ways that she or he relates to it. For instance, the use of the first person *I* in narratives suggests both more vivid autobiographical memories and a greater level of agency or involvement (Rubin, 1998). Conversely, the predominant use of the second person *me* in the narrative might convey a more passive or observational involvement. The use of different verb tenses in a narrative can also reveal the person's temporal relationship to a particular experience or role (Pillener, Desrochers, & Erbanks, 1998).

Narrative Models of the Self

Building on the work in autobiographical memory and language use, we view narratives as being associated with situated identities that are enacted in different life roles and contexts. The person who assumes such a role in a situation typically constructs a narrative that relates to his or her preexisting sense of self. In adopting this role-theoretic view (McCall & Simmons, 1978), we believe that a *self*, consisting of the individual's sense of his or her identity, continuity, and self-images, emerges as the person repeatedly and progressively organizes roles and contexts through narratives. Although a person can assume many possible selves in this manner (Markus & Nurius, 1986), we believe a primary *dominant narrative* that corresponds to the *I* typically coalesces to coordinate the *me*'s, or selves-as-objects, in their respective roles and experiences (Neimeyer & Stewart, 1998b).

Narrative Conceptualizations of Problems in Living

Although there have been some attempts to characterize life problems as stemming from "broken," "decomposed," or "gapped" narratives (see Neimeyer & Stewart, 1998b, for a brief review), an adequate taxonomy of life problems from a storied perspective has yet to emerge. Although a more elaborate scheme for understanding narrative breakdown could take many forms, we believe that a clinically useful taxonomy should minimally focus on the following: (1) the person's *role* or self-characterization in the story; (2) the extent to which the person is able to make use of lived experiences adequately in terms of organizing life themes; (3) the *entry* and *exit* of significant characters, settings, or themes; and (4) the person's sense of *authorship* over the resulting narrative.

Numerous "narrative diagnoses" could be framed along these dimensions. For example, a client's immersion in a new geographic setting or the appearance of significant new characters in his or her emotional life may temporarily challenge the client's ability to incorporate them meaningfully into an existing narrative and force modification of a once familiar "story line" for life. Some clients may have little sense of authorship of their lives and instead feel compelled to live out a dominant (and sometimes oppressive) narrative "written" by others in their family or culture. Still other clients may grieve the loss of principal persons, places, projects, or even parts of the self, necessitating a profound revision of a once meaningful life script, which must now be reauthored along different thematic lines. We offer a few brief cases as illustrations of these forms of story disruption and suggest some corresponding strategies for narrative repair.

A person who habitually defers to the "casting needs" of others may benefit from interventions that help to restore a sense of authorship and control over his or her own life story (White & Epston, 1990). For instance, Kay was a housewife in her mid-60s, who prided herself in attending to the material and emotional needs of her children and husband. As her children left home and her husband retired, Kay found herself playing bit parts in their lives, without a significant story line of her own; over the years she simply had not created a life story that incorporated those things that were uniquely important to her. Therapy with Kay initially focused on helping her to discover how she fulfilled others' needs while almost always sacrificing her own. By completing a genogram, a procedure for systematically discussing the members of one's family of origin and their relationship patterns over successive generations (McGoldrick & Gerson, 1985), Kay was able to see how her caretaker role as the oldest child was carried over to her present family. In a joint session, Kay and her husband completed a bow-tie diagram with the therapist's help. This systemic technique allows family members to become aware of how their behaviors may reinforce their roles in others' stories and distinguish them from their own (R. A. Neimeyer, 1993). These techniques, along with other exercises in projecting and writing about possible alternative futures for her, helped Kay to catch herself when taking too much responsibility for others, and instead to begin enacting a role based more on her own preferences.

The loss of loved ones, work roles, life projects, or aspects of the self can challenge radically the assumptive underpinnings of existing narratives, thereby undercutting a structure that once made life meaningful and predictable. Persons who have experienced such losses can often benefit from interventions that help them draw on resources they used in meaningfully negotiating previous transitions. Such a strategy was used with Donnie, a 42-year-old masonry contractor who was paralyzed below the waist after a car accident. Donnie's portrayal of himself as a strong, physically skilled, and efficient worker before the accident left him grieving the loss of his former self during his recuperation. Donnie was administered a biographical grid (see Neimeyer & Stewart, 1998b) to assess how he responded to other periods of transition in his life and to help him mobilize unique responses to his injury. As an adaptation of Kelly's (1955) grid method, the biographical grid involved (1) listing significant life events or stages touching on prior losses (e.g., his

grade school receipt of an award for an art project and his readjustment following the death of his mother in his adolescence); (2) identifying life themes and meanings by comparing and contrasting these events (e.g., achievement vs. sense of failure); and (3) relating these themes to his important life events, including his present disability. Donnie and the therapist observed that one recurrent coping strategy involved "losing himself" in interesting books, identifying with the struggles of the hero as he attempted to overcome adversity. This suggested the value of selected readings about the historical figures who exemplified the valued themes in Donnie's biographical grid, despite the limitations imposed by a physical handicap or social prejudice (e.g., Franklin Roosevelt). Pursuing such literary means to therapeutic ends eventually triggered a spontaneous discussion of Donnie's long-held curiosity about beginning his college education and the possibility of pursuing another career after his graduation. The interpretation of profound loss as occasioning significant meaning reconstruction has prompted the development of dozens of specific narrative strategies for taking a perspective on unwanted transitions brought about by not only personal injury but also bereavement, job loss, and the breakdown of close relationships (R. A. Neimeyer, 1998a).

Finally, several constructivist clinicians have begun to work toward a narrative conceptualization of traumatizing life experiences (Neimeyer & Stewart, 1998b). Almost by definition, traumatic experiences fragment a client's narrative structure for organizing and anticipating life events, while presenting the survivor with urgent experiences that resist integration into his or her preestablished meaning system (Sewell, 1997). Perhaps even more dramatically, such events as being sexually assaulted, witnessing the murder of a loved one, surviving a combat fire fight, or watching one's home and family be washed away by a flash flood seem to disrupt even the sensory and autobiographical memory processes that make up narratives. That is, the sights, sounds, smells, and sensation experienced during the event, along with the person's felt experiences of fear, horror, or shock, are often bundled together and *become* the trauma memory. Because these memories were encoded in an intense, unelaborated, and primitive form, they resist assimilation into one's ordinary declarative memory, which is implicated in the construction of a narrative (van der Kolk & van der Hart, 1991). Such traumatic memories may be so poignant and isolated that they give rise to a traumatized self, unrelated to the survivor's previous sense of identity, but which can itself provide the person with an identity as a victim, refugee, widow, and so forth (Neimeyer & Stewart, 1998b). In severe cases of combat trauma, for example, this *role constriction* can take the form of nearly exclusive self-characterization as a Vietnam veteran, a role that carries fixed implications of being irreparably damaged and alienated from mainstream society (Klion & Pfenninger, 1996). Whereas preemptive identification with this constricted role may have had understandable survival value at an earlier point, subsequent inflexible identification with the traumatized self can set in motion a vicious circle of social validation for this reduced script, as others avoid or marginalize the survivor.

THE CASE OF GREG[1]

Greg was a 47-year-old Vietnam combat veteran who was admitted to a veterans administration (VA) hospital inpatient unit for acute heroin detoxification and containment of violence potential. Referral data described previous problems with suicidal depression, severe anger dyscontrol, and a host of serious medical problems. He had lived a violent, fringe lifestyle for years, using and trafficking in hard drugs while "enforcing" for a motorcycle gang and occasionally working stints as a concrete pourer. Relations with his ex-wife, adult sons, and siblings were very poor. He had greatly deteriorated psychologically and medically the past year, deeply grieved by his mother's recent death. Although he had begun to distance himself from the gang and was making genuine (but dangerous) attempts to quit alcohol and drugs cold turkey, he was nonetheless becoming overwhelmed by the unfamiliar experience of *guilt*, defined in personal construct theory as a sense that his behavior had dislodged him from once central identity commitments.

He was frequently awakened at night in a state of full-blown panic, triggered by horrifying nightmares of combat atrocities, and he also had random daytime panic attacks. The frequency and severity of panic had increased markedly

since his mother's death and his early efforts to quit heroin and cocaine. He had fled public places often and was increasingly homebound, trying alone to shake off decades of total drug dependence. This *alexithymic* man had virtually no system for labeling and processing emotions. In a very basic sense, his entire personality had been held together by the glue of heroin ever since his Marine combat tour. In the absence of the intoxicated state of mind, his personality had begun to *loosen* and *fragment*, lacking any coherent structure, and he was terrified. By the time of admission, he was agitated, paranoid, and dangerous to himself and others.

As he became detoxified and safety was established, Greg was enrolled in the multidisciplinary treatment program. Over the next 18 months, he moved from inpatient to outpatient status and accessed scheduled titration of his psychiatric medications, medical attention for his numerous health problems, active social work support, and group and individual psychotherapy based on Kelly's personal construct psychology and related constructivist therapy models.

Following Kelly's recommendation, a *transitive diagnosis* process was established with ongoing team input and the inclusion of Greg as an active partner in self-diagnosis. The *preemptive* diagnoses (immediate cognitive status; medical triage; the seven DSM-IV, Axis I and II, categories he "fit") served their descriptive and organizing functions for both Greg and the treatment team, and psychological testing, extended observation, and therapeutic interaction informed the more nuanced, transition-oriented personal construct diagnosis. Transitive diagnosis is evolving, functional, and interactive and is inseparable from the process of therapy. Its explicit goals are to illuminate meaning-making processes and problems and to guide the search for innovative, reconstructive solutions to problems in living.

Greg was experiencing a prolonged state of psychological *threat*, the awareness of impending transition in core identity. This was directly in response to his disorganized but potent emotions, memories, and conflictual values. In particular, he felt extremely *guilty*, an emotion he had not felt since he was in high school. He had eradicated the possibility of guilt in Vietnam as a means of survival. But now his mother had died, and although he had remained her closest son through the years, he knew that he'd let her down with his violent lifestyle. An adolescent wave of guilt was consuming him, and nothing made sense any-

---

[1]From David T. Pfenninger, praxis, Indianapolis, and Reid E. Klion, Indiana University School of Medicine, Indianapolis.

more. He was highly inconsistent in his actions and mood, flipping from brute rage to withdrawn terror over and over again, a dramatic instance of *contrast reconstruction* signaling the need to develop overarching core constructs of self, which are capable of modulating this unpredictability.

Like many Vietnam-era combat veterans, Greg had developed a severe *role constriction*, although he was not the sort to "advertise" his Vietnam history. In fact, he had avoided Vietnam altogether as a topic but was virulently antigovernment and rejecting of all authority. His military mementos were literally stuffed in a closet at home, not viewed for years. Still, he had transferred his jungle fighter *role construct system* to his next quarter-century of civilian life in toto, straight into the "jungle" of the urban drug wars. He wasn't a soldier, but he was an outlaw. The functional pattern of these roles was isomorphic. Other roles—son, father, husband, worker, citizen—had atrophied early on.

The gang enforcer role encouraged ongoing intoxication, which both fueled his violence and numbed him, blotting out awareness of any vulnerable emotions. Early in psychotherapy, as Greg struggled with his wariness toward the therapist and his own inarticulation, it was painfully obvious that he had never told his story to anyone. In fact, *he had no story*, only an unintegrated montage of memory fragments and images, unordered and with no discernible time line, plot flow, elaborated characters, or symbolic legacy. His subjective narrative, then, was bordering on *chaos*, and his lived role was intense and unpredictable, with wild affective and social oscillations. His physical status mirrored the chaos, with Greg's own summary of his health being "I'm a mess."

Greg was encouraged to slowly place *dependency* on the milieu, team, and therapist and was reassured that his unsettling experiences could be understood and helped. It took a long while for him to see the therapist as sympathetic and able to assist, especially given that he viewed the VA hospital as "the belly of the beast," that is, part of the military establishment that long ago had abandoned him. As *sociality* developed—the ability to see one another's viewpoint, allowing for a deepening of trust and dialogue—*communality* was created through discovery that certain values, ideas, and interests (e.g., basketball) were in fact shared.

Under these conditions of sustained support and acceptance, Greg was guided in the therapeutic dialogue to begin piecing together a life narrative that could enable him to make sense of his experiences and shed light on the current crisis and future options. He began a gradual process of *narrative anamnesis*, reconnecting with memories of a pleasant childhood and how he was still a "mama's boy" as a high school senior. He recalled, with sometimes startling intensity, his rapid transformation into a heroin-addicted combat marine half a world away at age 19. Without the benefit of psychological debriefing, he had lived out that same violent and stoned pattern, because *he could construe no other option*. His chemical dependency had in effect served to mute the emotional signals of *construct invalidation* over the years. His adult life was essentially *hostile*, in the personal construct theory sense of continuing to deploy a social role structure repeatedly and intensely, despite its consistent invalidation.

The emergent narrative helped him begin to pull himself together. Eventually, he developed a longitudinal, more historicized version of himself. With this came an increased ability for *time binding* and *event binding* of the traumatic combat memories, in essence acknowledging that his earlier actions were understandable responses to the experiences he confronted at that time, even if they were no longer appropriate to his current situation. He was successful in getting off hard drugs altogether, admittedly transferring some of his chemical dependency to prescribed medications, but this was nonetheless a considerable practical improvement. The developmental story line and connective fissures of the narrative were *elaborated* through conversational, behavioral-modeling, journaling, and other dialogical techniques. Indeed, the therapist incorporated an extensive technical array with Greg across the course of therapy, including relaxation and imagery procedures, panic-control cognitive treatment interventions, supportive and "camaraderie" reflections and disclosures, chemical-dependency relapse prevention sessions, and guided exposure for social phobic tendencies (e.g., lunching with other patients in the canteen). This multimodal approach was coordinated with the overall treatment team program as well.

Greg's newly constructed life story helped to significantly reduce his extreme state of polarized, fragmented conflict. He learned to delay habitual responses to situations and hence was better able to anticipate and guide new actions and roles. Forgiveness and the possibility of personal integrity and change were central themes of his story-in-progress. He would redeem himself to his mother by becoming a better man. Perhaps most important, "fighting against the world" was replaced by a future vision of living out his years in search of peace and spiritual fulfillment. For Greg, this eventually meant moving to his mother's old property in the country, fixing up the house, fishing the pond, and becoming involved with the local church and community.

Pfenninger and Klion's conceptualization of trauma is also apt for Barry, a 47-year-old man who sought therapy for himself and his stepson one month after a horrific murder-suicide in his home. Against a backdrop of recent marital turmoil, he returned home from work one afternoon to find that his wife had isolated herself in the back bedroom, as their teenage stepson, Mat, sat watching television in an adjacent room. Within minutes of his return, he heard his wife call their six-year-old daughter to her, after which two shots echoed through the house. As Barry came lunging through the bedroom door, he saw the crumpled body of his daughter lying in a pool of blood, just before he was slammed against the wall by a shot to his abdomen. At that point, the teenage boy rushed into the room and, with the help of his seriously injured but still standing stepfather, wrested the gun from his mother's grip. Both men then turned their attention to the dying girl, as the mother first sat unsteadily on the floor, then fell face forward and died from a previously unnoticed self-inflicted shot to her chest.

Although this (ongoing) case obviously involves many dimensions (e.g., attention to the marital discord that provided a context for the violence and family interventions with the two surviving family members), a focus on the traumatic event itself featured prominently in early treatment. Following Guidano's (1995b) Movieola technique, the therapist first moved both father and stepson through a slow-motion replay of the death scene, encouraging them to put into words experiences that had previously existed only as mute and terrifying images and feelings. This act of speaking aloud about the details of the event for the first time allowed each to begin to reconstruct a more coherent and shared, albeit tragic, story of the event, in a way that opened it to further interrogation. Eventually, this emotionally vivid recounting was supplemented by more muted, but still anguished, questioning by both the father (e.g., "Am I still a father?") and stepson (e.g., "What will my life be like without the one

person who really loved me?"). With the decimation of their previous life narratives, which assigned them and other family members clear roles, both groped ineffectually for some strands of meaning that would lead them toward a more coherent future. Therapeutic use of various narrative applications (e.g., unsent letters to the wife and mother and loss characterizations of their changed sense of self; cf. R. A. Neimeyer, 1998a) assisted with this process, although finding a workable account that gives meaning to the tragedy will be a long-term, perhaps lifelong, quest. Fortunately, creative clinicians have begun to devise procedures to support this reauthoring process in both individual and group therapy for trauma survivors (J. Stewart, 1995).

As these vignettes illustrate, the narrative metaphor invites novel conceptualization of significant life problems, as well as the creative use of therapeutic techniques. Although therapeutic metaphors of lives as texts only now are being elaborated in a systematic manner (Freedman & Combs, 1996; Parry & Doan, 1994), such perspectives provide a compelling and empirically supported heuristic that many clients will find engaging.

CHALLENGES TO CONSTRUCTIVIST PSYCHOTHERAPY

As philosophers of science have discovered, no emerging paradigm wins quick intellectual acceptance by those aligned with other perspectives (Kuhn, 1972). In the field of psychotherapy, moreover, the fate of novel approaches is determined by large-scale economic and cultural factors, as well as by the practitioners whose response facilitates or impedes the paradigm's acceptance. Our purpose in this final section is to comment briefly on a few of these challenges, supplementing coverage of related issues discussed elsewhere (R. A. Neimeyer, 1995c, 1997). We do so by considering three issues—research, relevance, and reflexivity—which pose both constraints and opportunities for the development and dissemination of constructivist and narrative therapies.

Research

At least in North American clinical and counseling psychology, the respect accorded to any given approach to psychotherapy rests largely with its scientific credentials. Therapies that can claim a substantial research base are more likely to attract adherents, to be presented as credible to successive generations of students, and to be included in influential handbooks like this one. Conversely, those that lack such a base, although they may flourish on the fringes of academic respectability, are at a disadvantage in recruiting the interest of serious students, therapists, and scholars who could help apply, refine, and extend their basic concepts and procedures.

Particularly as judged from a North American perspective, constructivism's response to this research challenge is an unusual and in some respects ambivalent one. Even setting aside the important issue of whether the demand for empirical validation of therapy serves powerful hidden interests, such as concentrating power in the hands of some therapy traditions at the expense of others (Bohart, O'Hara, & Leitner, 1998; Henry, 1998), it is striking that constructivists often position themselves as the loyal opposition to mainstream psychotherapy research. Thus, whereas some constructivists are enthusiastic participants in the field of outcome research, adopting its preferences for highly controlled designs and relevant variables, others are critical of its most basic epistemological and methodological assumptions. At times, this keen enthusiasm for and deep distrust of the formalization required by research even coexist within the same scientist-practitioner (R. A. Neimeyer, 1999). While not unique to constructivism, this sort of divided allegiance is remarkable and deserves at least brief consideration.

On the one hand, a number of constructivists have examined the treatment acceptability of their preferred approaches (Vincent & LeBow, 1995) or evaluated their efficacy by using conventional experimental and statistical designs. For example, Alexander and her colleagues conducted a careful comparison of the outcome of two alternative forms of group therapy for incest survivors, one of which was based on constructivist concepts and procedures (R. A. Neimeyer, 1988). They found both groups to be comparably effective in relieving symptoms of distress associated with abuse (Alexander, Neimeyer, Follette, Moore, & Harter, 1989), although the constructivist intervention seemed particularly beneficial to more sexually traumatized group members (Alexander, Neimeyer, & Follette, 1991). Comparably favorable outcomes have been reported for a range of constructivist therapies applied to a diverse set of presenting problems (Adams, Peircy, & Jurich, 1991; Fransella, 1972; James, 1991).

Although such results are useful in suggesting the efficacy of constructivist psychotherapies, most researchers working within this perspective have been critical of straightforward "horse race" comparisons. Instead, they have given more attention to the development of measures that permit rigorous assessment of processes of meaning reconstruction in psychotherapy, regardless of its particular brand or orientation. Personal construct theorists have been especially active in this quest for more idiographic instrumentation, creatively modifying such tools as repertory grid technique to trace changes in the content and structure of clients' and therapists' meaning systems across the course of treatment (Winter, 1992). Furthermore, methodological innovations are beginning to originate in a number of other constructivist approaches as well. For example, working from the standpoint of developmental therapy, Ivey (1991) and his colleagues have developed procedures for assessing the epistemic styles (from sensorimotor through dialectical) in which adult clients formulate their problems in therapy and the way in which these shift over the course of treatment. One of the more promising aspects of this research is the construction of highly reliable classificatory systems for coding the developmental level of a client's language, as well as appropriate forms of counselor inquiries tailored to each of the four basic epistemic processing styles (Rigazio-DiGilio & Ivey, 1990).

Although the possible substantive and psychometric contributions of constructivism to psychotherapy research deserve further extension, perhaps a more profound contribution would be at the level of the *fundamental approaches to explanation* that inform and constrain empirical inquiries. Rennie and Toukmanian (1992), for example, distinguish between a paradigmatic approach to the study of psychotherapy process, which tends to be deductive, demonstrative, and quantitative, and a narrative approach, which tends to be inductive, hermeneutic, and qualitative. Most of the existing body of psychotherapy research (even that generated by constructivist investigators) has been of the paradigmatic type, being concerned with the discovery of general "laws" or patterns through the study of clients' and therapists' behaviors and cognitive structures. Whereas a paradigmatic approach to explanation is valuable in its own right, Rennie and Toukmanian argue for the potential usefulness of a narrative perspective, which may be more adequate in rendering the meaning of the therapy experience from the standpoint of its participants. Although some hybrid research programs have been mounted in an attempt to draw on the strengths of both (Angus, 1992; Greenberg, 1992; Martin, 1994), the fundamentally different epistemologies that underpin these two perspectives may militate against their full integration. But the penchant of constructivists for posing and addressing difficult questions of this kind may eventually position them to play a distinctive role in the future development of psychotherapy research.

Relevance

At a time when psychotherapy itself seems to be under the assault of forces demanding greater accountability, efficiency, and cost effectiveness, there is good reason to raise questions about the relevance of any new orientation. Some observers have implied that constructivist approaches, with their emphasis on elaborating personal meanings, fostering self-exploration, and enhancing relationships, may face challenges from managed care's initiatives to limit psychotherapy sessions and to reimburse therapies with "proven effectiveness" (Snyder, 1996).

As with the relation between constructivism and psychotherapy research, the question of the real-world fit of the theories described in this chapter is a complex one. Certainly, the constructivist passion for theory has sometimes produced writings of greater interest to scholars than to practitioners, leading some opponents to dismiss it because it cannot be translated into applications with clients. Likewise, the nonpathologizing orientation of narrative work and the advocacy of therapy as a form of "intermittent long-term consultation" (Mahoney, 1991) may fly in the face of the "medical necessity" and time-limited goals that are the hallmark of managed-care systems. On the other hand, constructivists have long been at the leading edge of the quest for brief therapies, from Kelly's pioneering experimentation with fixed role therapy in the 1940s to the development of solution-oriented therapies (Berg & de Jong, 1998; de Shazer, 1994) in the 1990s and beyond (see Chapter 20 in this volume). Perhaps more importantly, constructivists would argue that developing effective time-limited interventions requires a more penetrating analysis and facilitation of human change processes, at both an individual and interpersonal level (Mahoney, 1991; R. A. Neimeyer, 1996), instead of simply trying to practice traditional therapy "harder" or for briefer periods of time.

Finally, the question of the relevance of any given orientation turns on more than its economics considered in isolation. A broader definition of relevance would entail goodness of fit with other cultural trends, such as growing globalization, increased attention to the needs of culturally diverse clients, and demonstrated sensitivity to issues of gender and class. In these respects, a postmodern constructivism would score high points for relevance, judging from the remarkable internationality of its adherents (R. A. Neimeyer, 1997), its explicit attention to cultural factors in the construction of self (Ivey, 1991), its convergence with feminist perspectives on therapy (Brown, 2000; see also Chapter 17 in this volume), and its extension into community practice with economically distressed groups (Saleebey, 1998). It is important to bear in mind, however, that relevance, like any attribution of meaning, is ultimately in the eyes of the beholder. As with any other orientation to therapy, constructivist and narrative approaches will be deemed uniquely relevant to the needs of some psychotherapists and apparently irrelevant to the concerns of others. This raises the question of the person of the therapist, the consideration of which brings the chapter to a close.

Reflexivity

Psychotherapists choose their preferred ways of working for other than merely intellectual reasons. Just as practical, goal-oriented therapists might be drawn to the apparent technical efficiency of cognitive-behavioral therapy, or those with a more tragic or ironic view of life might resonate to psychodynamic approaches (see Chapter 10 in this volume), it is reasonable to ask what sorts of therapists find constructivism particularly apt or attractive. In our experience, therapists who develop a fascination with meaning-making approaches have a high tolerance for, and even a positive evaluation of, the necessary ambiguity of life. They thus are drawn toward ways of working with clients that help articulate this complexity, even when it moves them and their clients into realms of subtle and tacit meanings that may only be captured in more poetic or metaphoric language. Their own epistemological humility—the acknowledgement that even as professional therapists they have no authoritative grasp on the realities of the client's life—also leads them to distrust highly prescriptive interventions, whether these take the form of psychoeducational exercises or expert interpretations. Instead, they are more apt to position themselves as intensely interested fellow travelers in the client's journey rather than as tour guides, having a fixed itinerary or preconceived destination.

Although assuming this position has its own obvious challenges, more demanding still may be the relational implications of functioning as a constructivist therapist. Certainly, listening to some of the most tragic narratives of the human heart—stories of abuse, neglect, and failure—denies the therapist the comfortable distance assumed by more objectivist orientations to the efficient classification and elimination of unwanted symptoms and behaviors. Yet as Mahoney (1995) observes, it is precisely this ability to stand close to the suffering of another, while respectfully trying to sift through its nuances and find a way forward, that may be the essence of effective psychotherapy. Sustaining this posture entails what Leitner (1995, p. 362) has referred to as *optimal therapeutic distance*, defined as "being close enough to the other to experience the other's feelings while being distant enough to recognize them as the other's feelings—not the therapist's own." This further implies a delicate understanding of some of the more unfinished business in the therapist's own life, a demand that is surpassed by only a few contemporary approaches to psychotherapy.

CONCLUSIONS

In this chapter we have tried to provide a gateway into constructivist and narrative approaches to clinical practice, a task that is made more daunting by their diversity of expression in virtually all living traditions of psychotherapy. Unlike models that originate in the vision of a single founder, constructivist perspectives represent the outgrowth of deep philosophic roots, which continue to bear fruit in the thinking of theorists associated with distinct orientations to therapy, even in orientations that historically were antagonistic. As a result, constructivist approaches are defined more by a "family resemblance," deriving from their shared epistemology, than by their loyal adherence to a set of precepts, principles, or practices associated with a defined school of thought (Neimeyer, 1995a).

Attempting to assess the status of this emerging field is a bit like trying to predict the form of

an unfinished Picasso painting—you might be able to describe the shapes and colors currently on the canvas, but you can be assured that the final work is likely to include a few surprises. This is especially the case in delineating the contribution of the narrative metaphor to psychotherapy, which may carry as yet unrealized implications for problem definition, therapeutic strategy, and even scientific research. We hope that you as a reader will glimpse something of personal relevance in this unfinished canvas and perhaps even collaborate in shaping its future.

REFERENCES

Adams, J., Peircy, F. P., & Jurich, J. A. (1991). Effects of solution focused therapy's "Formula First Session Task" on compliance and outcome in family therapy. *Journal of Marital and Family Therapy, 17,* 277–290.

Adler, A. (1927). *Understanding human nature.* (W. B. Wolfe, Trans.). New York: Greenberg. (Original work published 1927)

Alexander, P. C., Neimeyer, R. A., & Follette, V. M. (1991). Group therapy for women sexually abused as children: A controlled study and investigation of individual differences. *Journal of Interpersonal Violence, 6,* 219–231.

Alexander, P. C., Neimeyer, R. A., Follette, V. M., Moore, M. K., & Harter, S. L. (1989). A comparison of group treatments of women sexually abused as children. *Journal of Consulting and Clinical Psychology, 57,* 479–483.

Anderson, H., & Goolishian, H. (1992). The client is the expert: A not-knowing approach to therapy. In S. McNamee & K. J. Gergen (Eds.), *Therapy as social construction* (pp. 25–39). Newbury Park, CA: Sage.

Anderson, W. T. (1990). *Reality isn't what it used to be.* New York: Harper & Row.

Angus, L. E. (1992). Metaphor and the communication interaction in psychotherapy. In S. G. Toukmanian & D. L. Rennie (Eds.), *Psychotherapy process research* (pp. 187–210). Newbury Park, CA: Sage.

Ansbacher, H. L., & Ansbacher, R. R. (Eds.). (1956). *The individual psychology of Alfred Adler: A systematic presentation from his writings.* New York: Basic Books.

Atkinson, R. (1995). *The gift of stories.* Westport, CT: Bergin & Garvey.

Barclay, C. R. (1996). Autobiographical remembering: Narrative constraints on objectified selves. In D. C. Rubin (Ed.), *Remembering our past* (pp. 94–125). Cambridge: Cambridge University Press.

Barsalou, L. W. (1988). The content and organization

of autobiographical memories. In U. Neisser & E. Winograd (Eds.), *Remembering reconsidered* (pp. 193–243). Cambridge: Cambridge University Press.

Beiver, J. L., & Franklin, C. (1998). Social constructionism in action: Using reflecting teams in family practice. In C. Franklin & P. S. Nurius (Eds.), *Constructivism in practice* (pp. 259–276). Milwaukee, WI: Families International.

Berg, I. K., & de Jong, P. (1998). Co-constructing a sense of competence with clients. In C. Franklin & P. S. Nurius (Eds.), *Constructivism in practice* (pp. 235–258). Milwaukee, WI: Families International.

Bohart, A. C., O'Hara, M., & Leitner, L. M. (1998). Empirically violated treatments: Disenfranchisement of humanistic and other psychotherapies. *Psychotherapy Research, 8,* 141–157.

Botella, L. (1995). Personal construct theory, constructivism, and postmodern thought. In R. A. Neimeyer & G. J. Neimeyer (Eds.), *Advances in personal construct psychology* (Vol. 3, pp. 3–35). Greenwich, CT: JAI Press.

Brown, L. (2000). Discomforts of the powerless. In R. A. Neimeyer & J. Raskin (Eds.), *Constructions of disorder* (pp. 287–308). Washington, D.C.: American Psychological Association.

Bruner, J. (1986). *Actual minds, possible worlds.* Cambridge, MA: Harvard University Press.

Burr, V. (1995). *An introduction to social constructionism.* London: Routledge.

Carlsen, M. B. (1989). *Meaning making: Therapeutic processes in adult development.* New York: Norton.

de Shazer, S. (1994). *Words were originally magic.* New York: Norton.

Ecker, B., & Hulley, L. (1996). *Depth-oriented brief therapy.* San Francisco: Jossey-Bass.

Ecker, B., & Hulley, L. (2000). The order in clinical "disorder": Symptom coherence in depth-oriented brief therapy. In R. A. Neimeyer & J. Raskin (Eds.), *Constructions of disorder* (pp. 63–89). Washington, D.C.: American Psychological Association.

Efran, J. S., Lukens, M. D., & Lukens, R. J. (1990). *Language, structure, and change.* New York: Norton.

Epting, F. R., & Nazario, A. (1987). Designing a fixed role therapy: Issues, techniques, and modifications. In R. A. Neimeyer & G. J. Neimeyer (Eds.), *Personal construct therapy casebook* (pp. 277–289). New York: Springer.

Feixas, G. (1992). Personal construct approaches to family therapy. In R. A. Neimeyer & G. J. Neimeyer (Eds.), *Advances in personal construct psychology* (Vol. 2, pp. 217–255). Greenwich, CT: JAI Press.

Fransella, F. (1972). *Personal change and reconstruction.* London: Academic Press.

Fransella, F. (1996). *George Kelly.* London: Sage.

Freedman, J., & Combs, G. (1996). *Narrative therapy.* New York: Norton.

Freeman, A. (1993). A psychosocial approach for conceptualizing schematic development for cognitive therapy. In K. T. Kuehlwein & H. Rosen (Eds.), *Cognitive therapies in action* (pp. 54–87). San Francisco: Jossey-Bass.

Gergen, K. J. (1994). *Realities and relationships.* Cambridge, MA: Harvard University Press.

Glover, R. (1995). Personal theories in psychotherapy: Toward an epistemology of practice. In R. A. Neimeyer & G. J. Neimeyer (Eds.), *Advances in personal construct psychology* (Vol. 3). Greenwich, CT: JAI Press.

Greenberg, L. S. (1992). Task analysis. In S. G. Toukmanian & D. L. Rennie (Eds.), *Psychotherapy process research* (pp. 22–50). Newbury Park, CA: Sage.

Greenberg, L., & Pascual-Leone, J. (1995). A dialectical constructivist approach to experiential change. In R. A. Neimeyer & M. J. Mahoney (Eds.), *Constructivism in psychotherapy* (pp. 169–191). Washington, D.C.: American Psychological Association.

Guidano, V. F. (1991). *The self in process.* New York: Guilford.

Guidano, V. F. (1995a). Constructivist psychotherapy: A theoretical framework. In R. A. Neimeyer & M. J. Mahoney (Eds.), *Constructivism in psychotherapy* (pp. 93–108). Washington, D.C.: American Psychological Association.

Guidano, V. F. (1995b). Self-observation in constructivist psychotherapy. In R. A. Neimeyer & M. J. Mahoney (Eds.), *Constructivism in psychotherapy* (pp. 155–167). Washington, D.C.: American Psychological Association.

Guidano, V. F., & Liotti, G. (1983). *Cognitive processes and emotional disorders.* New York: Guilford.

Henry, W. P. (1998). Science, politics, and the politics of science: The use and misuse of empirically validated treatment research. *Psychotherapy Research, 8,* 126–140.

Hermans, H. (1995). *Self-narratives: The construction of meaning in psychotherapy.* New York: Guilford.

Howard, G. S. (1991). Culture tales: A narrative approach to thinking, cross-cultural psychology, and psychotherapy. *American Psychologist, 46,* 187–197.

Howe, M. L., & Courage, M. (1997). The emergence and early development of autobiographical memory. *Psychological Review, 104,* 499–523.

Ivey, A. E. (1991). *Developmental strategies.* Pacific Grove, CA: Brooks/Cole.

James, P. S. (1991). Effects of a communication training component added to an emotionally focused couples therapy. *Journal of Marital and Family Therapy, 17,* 263–275.

Kelly, G. A. (1955). *The psychology of personal constructs.* New York: Norton.

Kelly, G. A. (1969). The language of hypothesis. In B. Mahrer (Ed.), *Clinical psychology and personality* (pp. 147–162). New York: Wiley.

Kelly, G. A. (1977). The psychology of the unknown. In D. Bannister (Ed.), *New perspectives in personal construct theory* (pp. 1–19). San Diego, CA: Academic Press.

Klion, R. E., & Pfenninger, D. T. (1996). Role constriction in Vietnam combat veterans. *Journal of Constructivist Psychology, 9,* 127–138.

Kuhn, T. (1972). *The structure of scientific revolutions.* Chicago: University of Chicago Press.

Kvale, S. (1992). *Psychology and postmodernism.* Newbury Park, CA: Sage.

Leitner, L. M. (1988). Terror, risk, and reverence: Experiential personal construct therapy. *International Journal of Personal Construct Psychology, 1,* 251–261.

Leitner, L. M. (1995). Optimal therapeutic distance. In R. A. Neimeyer & M. J. Mahoney (Eds.), *Constructivism in psychotherapy* (pp. 357–370). Washington, D.C.: American Psychological Association.

Linton, M. (1986). Ways of searching and the contents of memory. In D. C. Rubin (Ed.), *Autobiographical memory* (pp. 50–67). Cambridge: Cambridge University Press.

Loos, V. (1993). Now that I know the techniques, what do I do with the family? In L. Leitner & G. Dunnett (Eds.), *Critical issues in personal construct psychotherapy* (pp. 239–263). Malabar, FL: Krieger.

MacIntyre, A. (1981). *After virtue: A study in moral theology.* South Bend, IN: University of Notre Dame Press.

Mahoney, M. J. (1980). Psychotherapy and the structure of personal revolutions. In M. J. Mahoney (Ed.), *Psychotherapy process* (pp. 157–180). New York: Plenum.

Mahoney, M. J. (1991). *Human change processes.* New York: Basic Books.

Mahoney, M. J. (1995). The psychological demands of being a constructive psychotherapist. In R. A. Neimeyer & M. J. Mahoney (Eds.), *Constructivism in psychotherapy* (pp. 385–399). Washington, D.C.: American Psychological Association.

Mair, M. (1988). Psychology as story telling. *International Journal of Personal Construct Psychology, 1,* 125–137.

Mancuso, J. C., & Sarbin, T. R. (1983). The self-narrative in the enactment of roles. In T. R. Sarbin & K. Scheibe (Eds.), *Studies in social identity* (pp. 233–253). New York: Praeger.

Markus, H., & Nurius, P. (1986). Possible selves. *American Psychologist, 41,* 954–969.

Martin, J. (1994). *The construction and understanding of psychotherapeutic change.* New York: Teachers College Press.

McCall, G. J., & Simmons, J. L. (1978). *Identities and interactions* (rev. ed.). New York: Free Press.

McGoldrick, M., & Gerson, R. (1985). *Genograms in family assessment.* New York: Norton.

McNamee, S., & Gergen, K. J. (1992). *Therapy as social construction.* Newbury Park, CA: Sage.

Meichenbaum, D. (1993). Changing conceptions of cognitive behavior modification: Retrospect and prospect. *Journal of Consulting and Clinical Psychology, 61,* 202–204.

Monk, G., Winslade, J., Crocket, K., & Epston, D. (1996). *Narrative therapy in practice.* San Francisco: Jossey-Bass.

Neimeyer, G. J., Ed. (1993). *Constructivist assessment: A casebook.* Newbury Park, CA: Sage.

Neimeyer, R. A. (1988). Clinical guidelines for conducting interpersonal transaction groups. *International Journal of Personal Construct Psychology, 1,* 181–190.

Neimeyer, R. A. (1993). Constructivist approaches to the measurement of meaning. In G. J. Neimeyer (Ed.), *Constructivist assessment: A casebook* (pp. 58–103). Newbury Park: CA: Sage.

Neimeyer, R. A. (1995a). Constructivist psychotherapies: Features, foundations, and future directions. In R. A. Neimeyer & M. J. Mahoney (Eds.), *Constructivism in psychotherapy* (pp. 11–38). Washington, D.C.: American Psychological Association.

Neimeyer, R. A. (1995b). An invitation to constructivist psychotherapies. In R. A. Neimeyer & M. J. Mahoney (Eds.), *Constructivism in psychotherapy* (pp. 1–8). Washington, D.C.: American Psychological Association.

Neimeyer, R. A. (1995c). Limits and lessons of constructivism: Some critical reflections. *Journal of Constructivist Psychology, 8,* 339–361.

Neimeyer, R. A. (1996). Process interventions for the constructivist psychotherapist. In H. Rosen & K. T. Kuehlwein (Eds.), *Constructing realities* (pp. 371–411). San Francisco: Jossey-Bass.

Neimeyer, R. A. (1997). Problems and prospects in constructivist psychotherapy. *Journal of Constructivist Psychology, 10,* 51–74.

Neimeyer, R. A. (1998a). *Lessons of loss: A guide to coping.* New York: McGraw-Hill.

Neimeyer, R. A. (1998b). Social constructionism in the counselling context. *Counselling Psychology Quarterly, 11,* 135–149.

Neimeyer, R. A. (1999). Research and practice as essential tensions: A constructivist confession. In L. M. Vaillant & S. Soldz (Eds.), *The sometime relationship.* Washington, D.C.: American Psychological Association.

Neimeyer, R. A. (2000a). Constructivist psychotherapies. *Encyclopedia of psychology.*

Washington, D.C.: American Psychological Association.

Neimeyer, R. A. (2000b). George Kelly. *Encyclopedia of psychology*. Washington, D.C.: American Psychological Association.

Neimeyer, R. A., & Raskin, J. (Eds.). (1999). *Constructions of disorder*. Washington, D.C.: American Psychological Association.

Neimeyer, R. A., & Stewart, A. E. (1998a). Constructivist psychotherapies. In H. S. Friedman (Ed.), *Encyclopedia of mental health* (pp. 547–559). San Diego, CA: Academic Press.

Neimeyer, R. A., & Stewart, A. E. (1998b). Trauma, healing, and the narrative emplotment of loss. In C. Franklin & P. S. Nurius (Eds.), *Constructivism in practice* (pp. 165–184). Milwaukee, WI: Families International.

Omer, H. (1993). Short term psychotherapy and the rise of the life sketch. *Psychotherapy, 30*, 668–673.

Parry, A., & Doan, R. (1994). *Story re-visions*. New York: Guilford.

Pillener, D., Desrochers, A., & Erbanks, C. (1998). Remembering the past in the present. In P. Thompson, D. Hermann, D. Bruce, J. Read, D. Payne, & M. Toglia (Eds.), *Autobiographical memory: Theoretical and applied perspectives* (pp. 145–162). Mahwah, NJ: Erlbaum.

Rennie, D. L., & Toukmanian, S. G. (1992). Explanation in psychotherapy process research. In S. G. Toukmanian & D. L. Rennie (Eds.), *Psychotherapy process research* (pp. 234–251). Newbury Park, CA: Sage.

Rigazio-DiGilio, S. A., & Ivey, A. E. (1990). Developmental therapy and depressive disorders: Measuring cognitive levels through patient natural language. *Professional Psychology, 21*, 470–475.

Robinson, J. A., & Swanson, K. L. (1990). Autobiographical memory: The next phase. *Applied Cognitive Psychology, 4*, 321–335.

Rubin, D. C. (1998). Beginnings of a theory of autobiographical remembering. In C. P. Thompson, D. J. Hermann, D. Bruce, J. Read, D. Payne, & M. Toglia (Eds.), *Autobiographical memory: Theoretical and applied perspectives* (pp. 47–67). Mahwah, NJ.: Erlbaum.

Saleebey, D. (1998). Constructing the community: Emergent uses of social constructionism in economically distressed communities. In C. Franklin & P. S. Nurius (Eds.), *Constructivism in practice* (pp. 291–310). Milwaukee, WI: Families International.

Sarbin, T. R. (1986). The narrative as a root metaphor for psychology. *Narrative psychology: The storied nature of human conduct*. New York: Praeger.

Sewell, K. W. (1997). Posttraumatic stress: Towards a constructivist model of psychotherapy. In G. J. Neimeyer & R. A. Neimeyer (Eds.), *Advances in personal construct psychology* (Vol. 4, pp. 207–235). Greenwich, CT: JAI Press.

Sewell, K. W., Baldwin, C. L., & Moes, A. J. (1998). The multiple self awareness group. *Journal of Constructivist Psychology, 11*, 59–78.

Shotter, J., & Gergen, K. J. (1989). *Texts of identity*. Newbury Park, CA: Sage.

Snyder, C. R. (1996). Construing more workable realities and revising our personal stories, or vice versa. *Contemporary Psychology, 41*, 658–659.

Snyder, C. R., McDermott, D., Cook, W., & Rapoff, M. A. (1997). *Hope for the journey*. Boulder, CO: Westview.

Spence, D. (1982). *Narrative truth and historical truth*. New York: Norton.

Stewart, A. E. (2000). Alfred Adler. *Encyclopedia of psychology*. Washington, D.C.: American Psychological Association.

Stewart, A. E., & Barry, J. R. (1991). Origins of George Kelly's constructivism in the work of Korzybski and Moreno. *International Journal of Personal Construct Psychology, 4*, 121–136.

Stewart, J. (1995). Reconstruction of the self: Life-span oriented group psychotherapy. *Journal of Constructivist Psychology, 8*, 129–148.

Terrell, C. J., & Lyddon, W. J. (1995). Narrative and psychotherapy. *Journal of Constructivist Psychology, 9*, 27–44.

Vaihinger, H. (1925). *The philosophy of 'as-if '*. (C. K. Ogden, Trans.). New York: Harcourt Brace.

van der Kolk, B. A., & van der Hart, O. (1991). The intrusive past: The flexibility of memory and the engraving of trauma. *American Imago, 48*, 425–454.

Vincent, N., & LeBow, M. (1995). Treatment preference and acceptability: Epistemology and locus of control. *Journal of Constructivist Psychotherapy, 8*, 81–96.

White, M., & Epston, D. (1990). *Narrative means to therapeutic ends*. New York: Norton.

Winter, D. A. (1992). *Personal construct psychology in clinical practice*. London: Routledge.

Young, J. E. (1990). *Cognitive therapy for personality disorders: A schema-focused approach*. Sarasota, FL: Professional Resource Exchange.

FEMINIST THERAPY

LAURA S. BROWN

Feminist therapy is the *practice of therapy informed by feminist political philosophy and analysis, grounded in the multicultural feminist scholarship on the psychology of women and gender. This approach leads both therapist and client toward strategies and solutions advancing feminist resistance, transformation, and social change in daily personal life and in relationships with the social, emotional, and political environment* (Brown, 1994). What makes practice feminist is not with whom the therapist works but how therapists *think* about what is being done in therapy. It is an orientation that gives attention to questions of the practitioner's epistemologies and underlying theoretical models rather than specific techniques in practice, the nature and sort of problems being treated, or the demographic makeup of the client population. Feminist therapy focuses awareness on the notion that this seemingly private and highly personal transaction occurs within a social and political framework that itself informs, transforms, or distorts the meanings given to individual experience. It is one among an emerging group of critical theory models in psychology (Fox & Prilleltensky, 1997) that challenge the moral, political, and scientific status of the behavioral sciences and mental health professions.

This definition of feminist practice is as true when the client is a child with a chronic illness (not the stereotypical image of the client of a feminist therapist) as when the client is an adult who is struggling with a minority sexual orientation (very much the stereotypical image of the feminist therapist's client). It holds fast when the practice is not therapy per se but rather supervision, expert legal testimony, training, research, or teaching (Worell & Johnson, 1997). Feminist

therapy aims to deprivatize the therapists' understanding of the lives of the people with whom they work by initiating inquiry into how each life and each pain are manifestations of processes extant in the layers of a larger social context. At the same time, feminist therapy requires therapists to treat each life experience as valuable, unique, and authoritative, an expert source of knowledge about both that person and the culture as a whole. Because of this privileging of individual meaning while still attending to public, political realities that inform such meaning, feminist therapy theoretically straddles the gap between positivist and postmodernist views of human behavior and change, owing allegiance to neither. It is most closely identified with social constructivist and critical psychology models, paradigms that challenge the scientific, moral, and political status of psychology (Fox & Prilleltensky, 1997).

Although the feminist practice of psychotherapy has been occurring for the last three decades, it is only in the past few years that it has yielded a clear theoretical model (Brabeck & Brown, 1997; Brown, 1994). This absence of theory for the bulk of the history of feminist practice largely reflects the heritage of its development. Unlike almost every other school of psychotherapy, feminist therapy has been a tradition without official leaders or gurus (Brown & Brodsky, 1992). There is no person in a position equivalent to Freud, Jung, Perls, Ellis, or Beck who can be identified as a founder or chief theorist, from whose work applications were developed. Although the field has had a plethora of "mothers" (e.g., women like Phyllis Chesler, 1972; Miriam Greenspan, 1983; and Hannah Lerman, 1987, who were among the first to ask the hard questions about sexism in psychotherapy), feminist practice has differed from other theories of therapy even in its developmental process.

The absence of founders reflects the feminist

Author's note: Portions of this chapter are adapted from the author's book, *Subversive Dialogues: Theory in Feminist Therapy.*

commitment to authorizing knowledge from the grass roots instead of according authority only or primarily to that delivered by a designated "expert" from above. Much of feminist therapy practice has developed as a convergence of the work of many practitioners (primarily women therapists) who are attempting to apply feminist political principles as we understand them to the practice of psychotherapy, coming together informally at meetings and formally through journals. Feminist therapy theory has followed on practice, emerging from a synthesis of the work shared over the past three decades.

Feminist therapy is also unique among schools of thought in therapy practice in that it derives its categories of analysis largely from political analysis rather than from the behavioral sciences. Behavioral science data and interventions designed by mental health professionals have then been adapted to work within those political constructs. Feminist therapists consciously situate their work within the larger social and political milieu; behavioral science becomes a source of data that informs practice, but the attention to larger social meaning is always primary. For feminist therapy, the root problem being addressed is not that of individual, couple, or family psychopathology; rather, it is that of cultural patriarchy, those social forms in which a hierarchy of value and power, based irrationally on gender, race, class, sexual orientation, ability, and age, pervades inner life and interpersonal relationships. Feminist practitioners see their work as one aspect of the overall feminist struggle to achieve social justice. Thus, therapy is not simply about personal change or the amelioration of distress achieved in a decontextualized manner. It is also about how to understand the roots of that distress, as well as its eventual healing, in the structures of culture in which a person, couple, or family has developed.

The linking of a social movement with an approach to psychotherapy is a very uncommon phenomenon. Although Wilhelm Reich in his earlier years attempted to draw connections between the social and economic oppression of the working class and its psychological difficulties, for the most part there have not been immediate and assumed links between progressive movements for social change and schools of psychotherapy. In the past, one paid homage to Marx or Freud but rarely to both. But because feminism as a social movement has interrogated those "personal" aspects of life, such as intimate relationships, sexuality, parenthood, and reproduction, and defined the personal as political, the linking of feminist therapy to the larger feminist movement has greater face validity.

Feminist therapy, as one aspect of the overall feminist movement for social change, has as a goal the subversion of patriarchal dominance as it is internalized and personified in the life of the therapist, the therapeutic relationship, and the lives of clients, colleagues, and communities. Unlike other expressions of feminism, which address themselves to external and overt manifestations of patriarchal oppression, such as discrimination in the workplace or the violence against women in its many forms that pervades media representations, feminist therapy largely concerns itself with the invisible and sometimes nonconscious ways in which patriarchy has become embedded in each person's daily life in identity development, manners of emotional expression, and experiences of personal power and powerlessness.

A goal of feminist practice is the development of feminist consciousness and movement toward feminist action (Brabeck & Brown, 1997). By feminist consciousness, feminist therapists mean "the awareness of women that they belong to a subordinate group; that they have suffered wrongs as a group; that their condition of subordination is not natural, but is societally determined; that they must join with other women to remedy these wrongs; and finally, that they must and can provide an alternate vision of societal organization in which women as well as men will enjoy autonomy and self-determination" (Lerner, 1993, p. 14). Current feminist therapy theory expands on this definition to include in feminist consciousness an awareness of racist, classist, heterosexist, and other forms of oppression and their respective and interactive effects on human functioning (Adleman & Enguidanos, 1995; Brabeck & Brown, 1997; Brown, 1994; Greene & Sanchez-Hucles, 1997).

Feminist therapy theory is a technically eclectic model in which the emphasis is placed on the therapist's epistemology and strategies for constructing the therapy relationship. As Luepnitz (1988) has elegantly phrased it, feminist therapy is "a sensibility, an aesthetic"; it is a philosophy and epistemology of human transformation that prescribes, not the tools for change per se, but the manner in which any tool shall be grasped and used and the skills with which to evaluate by feminist criteria the tools we choose. Much of what makes feminist practice "feminist" has to do with how the therapist conceptualizes the work of therapy and with the questions evoked by feminist analysis. This theory of therapy as a liberatory act that is a component of a larger social change project has led to some confusion about what constitutes feminist practice. Before the mid-1990s, when feminist therapy theory was first delineated, many therapists, both feminist and otherwise, assumed that it was isomorphic, with the phenomenon of women therapists treating women for a variety of "women's issues" such as incest, eating disorders, difficulties with assertion, and the like (cf. Brody, 1984, for an example of this trend). A practitioner was a feminist therapist because she called herself one, whatever the degree of thought and feminist analysis actually had gone into her work. Some feminists in psychology have debated whether there is a litmus test for feminist therapy (Caplan, 1992; Kitzinger & Perkins, 1993). As Perkins (1991) noted, "women's issues" therapy in the absence of feminist theory may in fact be counterfeminist by making women the focus of the problem rather than the social order that devalues women and other marginalized groups. Thus, feminist therapists are both women and men (although the majority of self-identified feminist practitioners continue to be female), and they work with women, men, and various relationship combinations.

DEFINING PATRIARCHY

To comprehend the feminist analysis at the core of feminist therapy theory, it is necessary to have a clear definition of what constitutes patriarchy. Patriarchy is *not* individual men; rather it is any social system in which the following assumptions hold sway:

1. That men and women are different in their essence, not only biologically, but also "in their needs, capacities and functions. Men and women also differ in the way they were created and in the social function assigned to them by God" (Lerner, 1993, pp. 3–4).
2. That men (and attributes associated with maleness) are "naturally superior, stronger, and more rational, thus designed to be dominant. . . . Women are naturally weaker, inferior in intellect and rational capacities, unstable emotionally" (p. 4).
3. That men, "by their rational minds, explain and order the world. Women by their nurturant function sustain daily life. . . . While

both functions are essential, that of men is superior to that of women" (p. 4).
4. That men have an "inherent right to control the sexuality and the reproductive functions of women" (p. 4), whereas women have no such reciprocal right.
5. That men speak to and for the Divine on behalf of women.

Lerner (1993), one of the most distinguished feminist historians, writes, "Patriarchal concepts are, therefore, built into all the mental constructs of (any patriarchal) civilization in such a way as to remain largely invisible" (p. 3). Framed in psychological terms, patriarchal assumptions are considered to be pervasive and nonconscious, what Bem and Bem (1970), early social psychological commentators on the matter, termed a "non-conscious ideology." More recent feminist thought expands Lerner's analysis of gender to affirm that such nonconscious assumptions also exist about other dominant groups (e.g., Caucasians, upper-class people, and able-bodied people) in relationship to the nondominant group.

Patriarchal constructs have both behavioral and intrapsychic representations. Sometimes patriarchy is manifested culturally as women's intentional and systemic exclusion from certain prestigious or well-paying activities or occupations. At other times and places, it can be seen in smaller and more subtle ways: the higher cost of women's clothes, the pressure on men to dissociate eros from emotion, and the association of humanness with maleness in the generic masculine language. Sometimes patriarchy takes the form of violence and the threat of violence targeted at girls and women and, often, gay men. Even in cultures outside the West, in which patriarchy takes a more collectivist form, the devaluation of women and that which is associated with women emerges, although its lineaments may be unfamiliar to white Western observers who mistake collectivist cultures for nonpatriarchal ones.

Feminist therapy theory posits that in whatever shape it takes, patriarchy leaves its psychological marks in the form of distortions to and limitations on each person's capacity for well-being and personal power. Patriarchal patterns of thought pervade all intellectual and philosophical systems operating in a patriarchy to the point where such notions appear to be "the truth" when they are not closely examined. Although the dangers of patriarchy to women's emotional, physical, and financial well-being tend to appear more obvious, there are meaningful and painful costs to most men as well for their participation in patriarchal systems, for instance, men's higher rates of violent behavior or the difficulties that many men experience in being vulnerable in intimate relationships (Stoltenberg, 1990). Whereas gender is an almost inescapable locus of oppression in patriarchy, almost every human difference is viewed through the patriarchal lens as a form of "less than."

DEFINING FEMINISM: A REVIEW OF UNDERLYING POLITICAL THEORIES

Feminism is the collection of political philosophies that aims to undermine and overthrow patriarchy by ending inequities based on gender categories through cultural transformation and radical social change. All forms of feminism define gender-based (and other status-based) inequities as problematic and inherently wrong. Feminist therapy approaches the task of ending inequities by addressing patriarchal oppression in the forms it takes as distress in people's lives. It attends as well to the ways in which people are too comfortable with prescribed "normal" patterns of being that are ultimately destructive to their integrity.

The philosophy in which feminist therapy is rooted is that of political feminism. Typically for many currently practicing feminist therapists, this has been one of several forms of political feminism promulgated by mostly white women in late twentieth-century North America. Such political feminism has been by no means unitary but rather has tended to express several central themes or trends with variations, both important and trivial, in how such themes are operationalized. There are limitations to the usefulness of each of these political models, to the degree that they derive their analysis from unicultural perspectives or fail to address how patriarchy might express itself in a diversity of patriarchal cultures. But what each of these perspectives on feminism shares with others has been a vision of women as treated wrongly by the culture in which they lived and a commitment to changing that state of affairs.

Three schools of feminist political thought have had an impact on feminist therapy theory and practice: reformist feminisms, radical feminisms, and postmodern feminisms. These schools of thought tend to have certain core feminist precepts: the concept that the personal is political, the use of gender and power as primary analytic categories, and the privileging of the experience of the social "other" and marginalized experiences as foundational to epistemology. There are also important differences among these three schools, which are now described.

Reformist Feminist Models

Reformist political feminism has tended to focus primarily on the problems from the denial of equal rights and equal access to women. A reformist perspective is not usually critical of the system and institutions of the dominant culture per se but rather attends solely or primarily to the ways in which women are discriminated against or excluded from them. For example, a reformist perspective may not question the value of marriage as an entity but rather the denial of equal rights to credit, property, or one's own name to women within marriage. The fight to get women the right to attend military schools is another well-known example of a reformist feminist strategy. The emphasis of reformist activism has been on getting women the equal opportunity to participate in the institutions of the culture in ways identical to those available to men, as well as increasing the number of women visible within those institutions. This version of feminism has focused on changing laws to guarantee equal rights to women and on identifying those aspects of existing law that could be utilized in favor of women's access; it is a perspective that places faith in, and makes a tool of, the jurisprudence and electoral systems. It is often the feminism described by popular culture.

Reformist feminism has also emphasized the placement of women in positions of power within the structure of the dominant culture, opening up to women career and work fields that traditionally had been male-dominated and identifying and modifying those barriers to women's advancement in the worlds of commerce and politics that denied economic and mainstream political power to women. There has been a parallel, although not as active, emphasis on encouraging men's participation in such careers as child care and nursing in which men traditionally have been underrepresented. Reformist feminism tended at first to see women and men as essentially similar to each other in all matters except those of reproductive biology and external genitalia. More recently, however, it has adopted a perspective on gender that sees women and men as uniquely different, although equal. Nonetheless, both views have been in the service of a norm that says, "Anything women want to do, they can learn to do" and "People should be treated the same regardless of gender."

For reformist feminisms, gender is the only important category of analysis. It tends to be explicitly or implicitly exclusionary of people for whom race, class, ability, sexual orientation, or culture is the more salient factor in their positioning on the matrix of power and dominance. Reformist feminist canons often seek to elevate women who stress their gender oppression over other forms of oppression (e.g., the widely shared quote by Shirley Chisholm, the first African-American woman presidential candidate, that she had been more oppressed for her gender than for her race).

As an enduring theoretical base for feminist therapy, reformist feminism has become problematic because of its subtle tendencies toward shaping women to fit the status quo, with a minimum of questioning of the values of its structures. Nonetheless, it has been a dominant political vision in the earliest work of feminist therapists. That literature has a heavy emphasis on teaching women the behaviors they will need to function successfully in the world of men: assertion training, overcoming the "fear of success," "fair fighting" in heterosexual relationships, and the like. Reformist feminist therapies have unconsciously taken on a view of women as deficient when compared to men and has aimed to help women correct those perceived deficiencies, thus subtly reflecting patriarchal attitudes that were so profoundly embedded that they were initially not visible to feminist therapists' analyses. Consequently, when many early feminist therapists first encountered the research showing that "mentally healthy male" and "mentally healthy human" were considered to be one and the same (Broverman, Broverman, Clarkson, Rosekrantz, & Vogel 1970), reformist feminist therapists of that earlier period often simply attempted to help women become more "human," that is, less womanly and more androgynous, ignoring at that moment the androcentrism of the concept of "human" as it was then understood by mental health professionals.

Similarly, the structures into which women were attempting to fit, such as the workplace, were not particularly subjected to criticism by early reformist-oriented feminist therapists; instead the focus was on helping women to do better in such institutions. Because all behavior was defined as a learned phenomenon, the principles of social learning theory and behavioral and cognitive-behavioral schools of psychotherapy were seen as admirably fitting the needs of feminist therapists in teaching women new ways of behaving. Humanistic theories also attracted feminist practitioners because of their emphasis on the right of people to self-actualize, which feminists interpreted as the right to not be the targets of discrimination (Lerman, 1992). Because these models of therapy were developing concurrently with second-wave feminism and offered alternatives to the misogyny and hegemony of psychoanalytic thought as practiced in North America during that era, they also appealed by seeming modern and untainted by sexist psychoanalytic assumptions.

This reformist vision in early feminist therapy strongly mirrors the times in which it arose, the late 1960s and early 1970s. This was a time in which individual behavioral change was seen by many as the answer to societal problems. This zeitgeist colored the understanding of most feminist therapists. It was quite radical, not to say dangerously revolutionary, in the early 1970s for women in the mental health disciplines to assert simply that women would benefit from having women rather than men as therapists or from learning to own their anger and assertion rather than see these feelings as evidence of "penis envy," "masculine protest," or other forms of pathology; many mental health professionals who made such assertions were met with hostility or worse. In the face of that sort of reception, the step of asking more dangerous questions about the very value of certain kinds of behavior that the dominant culture had placed at the top of the hierarchy of worth required more time and experience. By the end of the 1970s, however, this transition had taken place, and radical feminisms had become the predominant political theory underlying feminist therapy.

Radical Feminisms

Radical feminisms, which have included lesbian feminism, women-of-color feminism or womanism, and socialist feminism, have taken an entirely different perspective on the dilemma of women's inequality. These political models construe it as one of many forms of interlocking oppressions found in a patriarchal cultures. Women's difficulties are seen less as the result of the inequality of opportunity per se; rather, these problems are construed as the end products of the systematic devaluation of women and anything related to women's work and ways of being. This devaluation persists in the face of formally equal social structures. Patriarchy is seen as attempting to control and denigrate women through systematic violence against them, the silencing of women's voices, and the degradation of women's knowledge and ways of seeing and learning. Thus, radical feminisms posit that the oppression of women as a class will only be changed when there is change within the overall culture, a deconstruction of dominant hierarchies of discourse in which dominance/submission as a mode of relating is replaced by a cooperative, collaborative form of social discourse.

The placement of women into positions of power and authority in the mainstream has been interpreted by radical feminism as tokenism, more likely to coopt the individual women involved than to lead to change in patriarchal systems. Radical feminisms focus instead on changing those institutions of patriarchal cultures that promulgate the status quo, such as the family, educational institutions, and the justice system, and on developing an integrative analysis of oppression (Kanuha, 1990) that ties together racist, classist, heterosexist, and other forms of oppression with gender oppression.

Radical feminisms initially utilized a model of gender that constructed women and men as essentially quite different from each other at the level of primary psychological development and, for the most part, has continued to use this perspective, which can be described in general by the adjective *essentialist*. This term refers to a view of certain characteristics as being essential to membership in a certain class or group, for example, the notion that men are essentially more interested in genital sexuality than women or that women are essentially nurturing.

More recently, postmodern radical feminist critics, employing a social constructivist explanation of gender-based oppression, have analyzed the possible pitfalls inherent in such a position, arguing that to claim that there are essential differences between women and men reifies gender as defined in the dominant culture and opts into a dichotomous mode of categorizing, which may by and of itself be patriarchal in nature and reflective of a Eurocentric worldview. Social constructivism posits that all categories and divisions of human behavior, such as gender or race, are artificial

creations of a particular social discourse at a particular time and place, subject to change as the defining variables of the discourse itself are modified. Social constructivist radical feminists posit, rather, that differences between women and men, although meaningful within a particular social and interpersonal context, are simply artifacts of that context, built by the social discourse, as it were, rather than essential to and inherent in being female or male. Much of current feminist psychological research reflects this social constructivist perspective (Hare-Mustin & Marecek, 1990).

Radical feminist theories are most consistent with current practice, precepts, and meta-assumptions of feminist therapy. Radical feminisms generate models for therapy that *do* question why and whether women (or men) should aspire to forms of behavior and relating that have been associated with male dominance. These models view behavior in context and integrate a critical philosophy of science and sociology of knowledge that questions positivists' "truth" and "objectivity," thus also questioning the scientific canons on which practice is built.

This model of therapy, in which all patriarchal verities are questioned profoundly, affects how the success of therapy will be defined by feminist therapists and, ultimately, our clients. "Success" in these terms may be invisible as such to the eyes of dominant culture institutions, and it may even appear to be a form of failure to achieve, fit, or otherwise shape oneself and one's culture to the requirements of a narrow dominant norm. I have commented that a goal of feminist therapy is to maladjust people to patriarchy (Brown, 1994), consistent with the radical feminist notion that patriarchies are per se problematic. Because much feminist practice has occurred outside of academic settings, it is only recently that specific outcome research on feminist therapies has begun. Worell (1998) describes a current project studying outcomes and clients' satisfaction in feminist psychotherapy practice; at the time of this writing, however, the only available outcome data are anecdotal, in the form of clients' reports of satisfaction with feminist models for treatment.

Postmodern Feminisms

Finally, as stated earlier, feminist therapy theory rests on an informed and critical vision of gender and its construction and meanings. This basis in scholarship and in the enduring feminist discourse on gender and its meanings is of particular importance to feminist therapy theory because of the place of gender as a central category of analysis in feminist theory. Because gender and its meanings have been so controversial, so rife with stereotype and myth and so vulnerable to being framed in the terms of so-called conventional wisdom, an informed and critical view of gender is thus basic to feminist therapy theories. Postmodern feminisms have provided an important theoretical underpinning to the scholarly basis of feminist practice.

The postmodern radical feminist discourse has uncovered dominant cultural assumptions about gender and gendered phenomena. At its inception, this discourse tended toward an error rooted in dominant visions, that is, that gender and biological sex were initially defined as one and the same. This assumption quickly became problematic when feminist psychologists observed that this presumed isomorphism of sex and gender implied that behaviors observed at higher frequencies among one group were prima facie assumed by most nonfeminists to be biologically, instinctively mediated and thus immutable.

The postmodern radical feminist discourse on gender and its meanings draws on the dynamic tension between a biological explanation of gender and gendered behaviors perspective that defines all behaviors as only artificially linked by gender by a prevailing social discourse (Hare-Mustin & Marecek, 1990). This dialogue and dissension reflect different initial biases of scholars and practitioners toward how we understand and make sense of observed phenomena, as well as the reality that neither perspective is a complete source of explanation for gender-related behaviors. But the tension between these two perspectives is of particular importance to feminist therapy theory and to its connection to political feminisms as the latter evolve over time.

Most of feminist therapy scholarship in the 1980s reflected the essentialist bias of that era's radical feminism, best exemplified by the "different voice" paradigm for gender, which is best represented in the work of Gilligan and her colleagues (Gilligan, 1981; Gilligan, Rogers, & Tolman, 1992), Belenky and her colleagues (Belenky, Clinchy, Goldberger, & Tarule, 1986), and other feminist scholars who have attempted to comprehend women's experiences and realities as self-defined. The notion of apparent gender differences as biologically immutable (or even having necessary evolutionary advantages) provides a simple explication of many complex and often scary phenomena. The framing of these essentialist perspectives within the different voice paradigm is an attempt to place this long-standing patriarchal assertion about difference into a feminist lens by making "feminine" qualities explicitly valuable rather than devalued. What is problematic about such essentialist constructions of gender is that they can easily be given unwanted meanings by upholders of the status quo.

As social constructivists within feminist psychology such as Rachel Hare-Mustin and Jeanne Marecek (1990), Michelle Fine (1992), and Rhoda Unger (1989) have noted, gender as a stimulus variable and gender as an experience of identity are both fraught with excess meaning about power, status in certain kinds of hierarchy, and inter- and intrapersonal expectations, none of which can be explicated with ease by appeals to biological differences. Unger's research findings suggest that if the power positions in a hierarchy are scrambled out of their usual gender linkages in dominant culture (e.g., male = dominant; female = submissive), then the nondominant people in an exchange will exhibit behaviors similar to those found in the women in the work of Gilligan and other "woman's voice" scholars. Theories of feminist therapy reflect this dynamic tension; it is important to know and understand how members of nondominant groups have lived and to see those lived experiences as of value, not as the lesser lives imagined by the dominant culture. It is also necessary for feminist therapy theories not to assume the essentially gendered nature of *apparently* gender-linked phenomena.

KNOWLEDGE CLAIMS UNDERLYING FEMINIST THEORIES

A tension between feminist and other theories of therapy can frequently be found in the knowledge claims utilized by feminist therapy theorists. This reconfigured canon reflects both radical and postmodern feminist concerns about the sociology of knowledge and the problems inherent in overreliance on the positivist tradition that has guided much of behavioral science research, particularly in the field of psychology. Feminist therapy theories do not eschew the use of empirical data derived from positivist models. Such data are taken, however, not as "pure science" but rather are subjected, as are all sources of information, to critical questions about such factors as the identity of the researcher, the manner in which the research question was framed, the strategy for interpreting data emerging from the research, and the context in which the research is conducted. Also, feminist therapy theories draw on, and give somewhat equal weight to, data from other knowledge-gathering strategies; these include findings from qualitative research, data from the range of non–mental health social sciences, autobiographical materials by members of nondominant groups, and single-case studies. Data that derive from or offer information about diverse human groupings are particularly valued in feminist therapy theories.

Feminist therapy theorists have identified several reasons for the necessity of a feminist perspective on therapy in integrating multicultural knowledge claims and epistemologies. Kanuha's (1990) description of an "integrated analysis of oppression," which posits an interlocking matrix of experiences as core for understanding human behavior, provides a paradigm for this discussion. Her model posits that without such a complex and multidimensional scholarship basis, feminist therapies risk the loss of philosophical integrity, defaulting to the "women therapists with women" model, where perhaps the best that is done conceptually is to "add women of color and stir" (Espin & Gawelek, 1992). Also, feminist theorists have long decried the losses to paradigm development and data creation that are inherent in a monocultural theoretical perspective, noting the array of possible visions of normative human behavior that can only be gained by peering through multiple lenses (Brabeck & Brown, 1997; Brown, 1994; Comas-Diaz & Greene, 1994). Most salient in daily practice are the intangible effects on the therapist and the therapy process of committing to a multicultural perspective and knowledge base.

Another concern for feminist therapy theories is to avoid the use of dominant cultural norms as a comparison standard. Feminist therapy asks, instead, what is usual for a person from a particular background, within a particular context, and using a particular personal epistemology deriving from that experience and context. Feminist theories are interested in developing knowledge arising from nondominant paradigms of experience, not to grant privileges to those over mainstream perspectives but to place them side by side as equally valued sources of information.

Core Concepts in Feminist Therapy

Feminist therapy theorists have approached the task of defining the parameters of feminist ther-

apy from these underlying assumptions about political analysis and knowledge generation. Several different authors have proposed a set of core concepts assumed to demarcate those parameters. Each of these sets of criteria for feminist practice reflects these underlying assumptions; they are presented roughly in the chronological order of their appearance, so that the foundation of one set in another can be more easily visible.

Hannah Lerman (1987) was the first author to propose a theoretical framework for feminist therapy. She described eight "meta-assumptions" underlying feminist therapy theory building as criteria for a feminist theory of personality:

1. Clinically useful
2. Encompassing the diversity and complexity of women and their lives
3. Viewing women positively and centrally
4. Arising from women's experiences
5. Remaining close to the data of experience
6. Recognizing that the internal world is inextricably intertwined with the external world
7. Not confining concepts by particularistic terminology or in terms of other theories
8. Supporting feminist modes of psychotherapy

Whereas Lerman's criteria center on women (reflecting to a large degree the discourse in feminist practice at the time they were explicated, before conscious attention to larger issues of human diversity in feminist practice), they do not define feminist therapy theory as pertaining to women alone. Rather, Lerman's criteria suggest a lens through which the world can be viewed, in which knowledge claims coming from a nondominant perspective become central to the paradigm.

I offered the following as proposed core concepts in feminist therapy theory (Brown, 1994):

1. An understanding of the relationship of feminist political philosophies to therapeutic notions of change
2. An analysis and critique of the patriarchal notions of gender, power, and authority in mainstream approaches to psychotherapy
3. A feminist vision of the nature and meaning of psychotherapy as a phenomenon in the larger social context
4. Concepts of normal growth and development, distress, diagnosis, boundaries, and relationships in therapy that are grounded in feminist political analysis and feminist scholarship

5. An ethics of practice tied to feminist politics of social change and interpersonal relatedness

6. A multicultural and conceptually diverse base of scholarship and knowledge informing this theorizing

Brabeck and Brown (1997) described nine "tenets of feminist theory of psychological practice" developed during a consensus conference of feminist practitioners:

1. "Feminist theory of psychological practice is consciously a political enterprise and its goal is social transformation in the direction of feminist consciousness" (p. 32).

2. The notion that feminist consciousness should become as taken-for-granted a version of reality as patriarchal consciousness currently is in the work of psychological practice.

3. The "capacity to create theory comes from experience and human connections through any form or medium" (p. 32).

4. Gender is an important locus of oppression and interactive with other loci of oppression; a feminist practitioner is "self-reflective regarding her positions in these various hierarchies" (p. 32) of dominance and oppression.

5. "Feminist theory of practice embraces human diversity as a requirement and foundation for practice" (p. 32).

6. Authority must be given to the direct experiences of oppressed people, in their own voice and own modalities.

7. "Feminist practitioners expand the parameters of conceptions of identity or personhood . . . and seek models of human growth and development that describe a variety of ways that people have a sense of identities and multiple subjectivities" (p. 32).

8. Distress is conceptualized as complex and multidetermined in causation, with particular attention to sociopolitical causation. Dominant norms in which the dominant group is conceptualized as whole and center, and the nondominant as broken or marginal, are avoided in paradigms of good function and distress.

9. Feminist theories of practice cannot be static but must change to reflect new knowledge arising from feminist scholarship.

A review of these three sets of concepts indicates areas of overlap. Though not completely consistent with one another (or entirely internally consistent), there is a shared focus on the importance of diversity, the political and social-contextual nature of feminist practice, and the appreciation of knowledge and perspectives arising from the experiences of nondominant groups. These critical feminist analyses of both process and content tie the private and unique pain of the client, as well as the interventions most likely to empower that client, to the public and political realities that are the crucible of the problem's formation.

In addition, these concepts clarify that feminist therapy is not simply about women. The paradigms for understanding human experience proposed by these authors acknowledge that oppression occurs at many points in the social and political matrix; race, class, culture, sexual orientation, age, size, and disability, among others, are common variables along which patriarchal dichotomies of value operate to diminish the quality of life and well-being and from which experience and knowledge that are usually marginalized can be derived and utilized. In addition, these conceptual frameworks imply that the experiences of the dominant, the oppressor, are as transparent to and in need of feminist analysis in therapy as are those of the oppressed.

Feminist therapy theories posit that the processes that occur in feminist therapy will reflect these three conceptual frameworks. Feminist therapy authors have attended to several such processes that are considered to commonly emerge in the course of a feminist therapy. These include the capacity for resistance, subversion of patriarchal consciousness, and the development of one's own voice.

Resistance and Subversion

The models of personal change in feminist therapy promote resistance, which refers to the development of a resilient capacity to refuse to merge with dominant cultural norms and to attend in some manner to one's own voice and integrity (Gilligan, Rogers, & Tolman, 1992). A feminist theory of psychotherapy, rooted in the call for radical social change, seeks to highlight our understanding of and ability to identify and strengthen such personal resistance and to reframe it as a positive and healthy act within the feminist political context.

Feminist theory postulates that our very sense of self, much less our definitions of the self, have been domesticated and undermined by patriarchal consciousness. For example, in most current approaches to therapy (but not those informed by social constructivist models), people are assumed to have a "self." This construct, in turn, is defined by the dominant culture's mental health authorities as being a unitary, individuated phenomenon. In contrast, the referential, relational, and multiple selves that are experienced as normative by some cultures of color or non-Western cultures (or even the absence of a construct of self in certain cultures) consequently are implicitly defined as less socially desirable and less mentally healthy or are ignored and unrecognized by dominant culture models of human behavior (Landrine, 1992). Shame, the experience of self as bad, flawed, undeserving, and meant to be hidden, is a pervasive result of this constant oppressive corruption and domestication. Tacitly and implicitly, patriarchy and its institutions discourage a clear knowledge of self and encourage silence. Although feminist models affirm that everyone resists this false consciousness to some degree, even this resistance is frequently constrained, knowingly or inadvertently, by the dominant paradigms.

Each act of feminist therapy must have as a goal the uncovering of the presence of the patriarchy as a source of distress, in order to name, undermine, resist, and subvert such oppressive influences. Feminist therapy theorizes awareness and transformation in therapy as a teaching of skillful, self-protective, and self-respectful strategies for resistance. Such a learning process allows therapy participants to understand how the solutions and strategies that seem intuitively obvious, because they are made available under patriarchy, may instead be further, needless lessons in powerlessness. Accordingly, the point of therapy is to assist clients in honoring their attempts to develop effective strategies for resistance in the absence of support for this goal. Feminist therapy theorizes that these strategies are a form of truth telling about what actually happened, as well as truth telling about what is possible and available to each person as avenues for change.

People commonly enter therapy while experiencing themselves as "failures"; when explored by therapist and client, it is not unusual to discover that this means that they have not achieved the sort of power, status, or control over their distress that they would have "if only I tried hard enough." Feminist analysis can strip bare the assumptions informing this and similar perceptions. It replaces the illusions of level playing fields and

the denial of power differences that are embedded in patriarchal discourse with clear and more honest visions of oneself in the social context, where power is unevenly distributed and value parceled out according to arbitrary characteristics rather than effort or talent. Feminist therapy thus reframes the client's experience as success at engaging in "individual or collective acts of courage, strength, and integrity in response to violence, threat of harm, wrongdoing, or untruth" (Fredlund, 1992, p. 7), and it promotes clients' abilities to identify and credit themselves for participating in such acts of resistance. Feminist visions of psychotherapy must be capable of seeing beyond the options presented by the dominant culture and able to identify and support paths of resistance and subversion that are not authorized, valued, or easily visible in the patriarchy.

CASE STUDY: AN EXAMPLE OF SUBVERSIVE RESISTANCE

Angela had come to see me for therapy because, in her own words, "I have no idea who I am." She was in her early 30s, Caucasian, from a working- and middle-class background; she had graduated from college and spent the intervening decade in a series of unsatisfying jobs and unhappy relationships. She described herself as often depressed and uncertain. As we got to know one another, I learned that there was one place of certainty and passion in Angela's life—her gardening. She could spend hours in any weather digging in the dirt and was impressively knowledgeable about plants and their various needs, as well as the organic control of Seattle's ubiquitous slug population. Nonetheless, she actively discounted this locus of emotional energy in her life as "nothing special, just a little hobby of mine."

When I suggested that it might be interesting to explore how Angela had managed to make the most powerful place in her life invisible and unimportant to herself, we were both surprised by how terrified she was of this possibility. Her terror served as a signpost; this, in turn, led us to her growing awareness that in her family of origin, there was no official place or room for anyone's passion. What there were, instead, were hiding places. Her parents and grandparents (and as she eventually learned, her great-grandparents in at least one family line) had all had similar life experiences as Angela's. They had worked at difficult, emotionally deadening jobs while nurturing secret passions that were carefully discounted as meaningless hobbies. The family narrative was marked by the story of an uncle who had tried to make his passion for woodworking become a means of making a living, just as the Great Depression hit, and the devastation that this had wrought on him and his immediate family.

Placing the family narrative into class and historical contexts, we were able to see how Angela's family had resisted the destruction of its members' creative voices by finding a "safe" place in which to hide their creativity. The family had resisted the pull to banish creativity but had decided at one point that their class situation made personal investment in such creativity risky to basic physical well-being. So the message had been passed down that work would be of no meaning, and meaning and passion would be protected by diminution. This resistance strategy had worked quite well; Angela learned that many of her family members had "hobbies" like her own in which they were boldly and inventively creative. Her terror at the possibility of violating the family rule represented the survival necessities that lay at the core of this survival strategy. "People need first to eat," Angela remembered her maternal grandmother telling her.

By framing this family narrative as a means for survival and resistance, rather than as family pathology, Angela was able to avoid blaming her parents and grandparents for what they had taught her. We looked together at how social class and historical accident had made it difficult for her family to make a different sort of place for its members' creativity, and we marveled at the way in which pulls to kill or disown creativity were resisted. She became able to ask herself how she might best survive and resist in the present, with the skills, tools, and social context in which she herself existed.

She decided that her most effective resistance to a class structure that had taught her family that they could never make a living from their passions might be to learn how she could challenge that rule, given the changed economic circumstances between her uncle's time and her own. She took courses in setting up a small business and apprenticed herself to a specialty organic landscape artist whose work she had studied, noting to me that this woman made an excellent living, employed several people, even had her own radio call-in show, and complained about having to turn away work because of the lack of time and energy. Angela concluded that "there's business out there for me, too." She learned that not knowing who she was had been a protective device, taught to her in her family, for keeping her passions safe and that in that safety zone, she had become prepared to make her passion her living. And she learned that she could protect herself in other ways and still know her passion, and even make a very good living at it (even though, as she joked to me toward the end of therapy, she had to spend a lot of money on waterproof gear, a necessity for the Pacific Northwest gardener).

Finding Voice

Feminist therapy theorists frequently have used the notions of voice and silencing to describe the inner experience of people struggling to deal with the emotional aftermath of life exposure to patriarchy. Jack (1991), in her model of depression in women, speaks of the silenced self of women who learn to not listen to their own passions and desires and, in line with patriarchal imperatives, to instead subsume them to those of the culture and its institutions. Brabeck and Brown (1997) describe the process of feminist practice as a "de-silencing" of the oppressed (p. 26). I utilized (Brown, 1994) the metaphor of therapy as a process of learning the client's emotional "mother tongue," or "native language," in which an undistorted image of a person can be apparent, drawing on Grahn's (1984) concept of the "other mother tongue" of lesbian and gay cultures. Writers in feminist therapy utilize this concept of the development of voice and de-silencing as a strategy for discussing the essence of the person, without resorting to the positivist concept of self, which has been criticized by some authors as too embedded in a specific epistemology to be of use to the diverse feminist discourse (Hare-Mustin, 1994; Lykes, 1985).

The concept of voice or mother tongue has also been used as a framework for understanding the alienation experience of people in patriarchal consciousness. When certain feelings, relationships, and ways of being are either not present, or present only as devalued, in dominant usage, these experiences are silenced. The alienating language of patriarchal consciousness, although it appears to be the "natural" language of human relationships, is pathologizing of and distorting to realities and life experiences that have been marginalized. The metaphor of recovery of the mother tongue also pertains to how concretely the processes of oppression actually operate, for instance, how the destruction of language goes hand in hand with cultural genocide (as has been true for many indigenous cultures around the world whose mother tongues have been supplanted, frequently by English).

A goal of feminist therapy is to assist clients in identifying their own voices or mother tongues. An assumption is that until that mother tongue is found, the story that each person tells of oneself will be distorted to some degree by patriarchal structures and the silencing of one's own voice inherent in patriarchal consciousness. This image of listening for the voice within to comprehend the nature and sources of alienation and distress and to uncover the hidden paths toward the subversion of dominant introjects points to the fact that the conceptual process in feminist therapy is not one in which therapist and client are seeking the true *pathology* of the person; rather, it is a search for the client's sources of power.

These meta-goals of therapy proposed by feminist theories differ radically from the tasks of psychotherapy commonly proposed in the dominant culture. Psychotherapy in feminism is present not to soothe but to disrupt, not to adjust but to empower. Perkins (1991) has described how feminist models are especially challenged by those approaches to therapy that assume that emotional distress is prima facie evidence of pathology. When therapy is constituted to engender feminist consciousness (Brabeck & Brown, 1997), it cannot constitute a smoothing over of experience and will often lead to an enhanced awareness of painful social realities. Sometimes when feminist theory is working well in a therapy process, there may be temporary increases in subjective distress where formerly there were comfort and acceptance. The development of voice and of skills in resistance and subversion ultimately yield *more* awareness and, possibly, distress about certain destructive social realities than may have been present at the onset of therapy. Feminist therapy requires a theory that defines therapy as not simply a healing art, although healing is likely to take place. Therapy also must be constituted, consciously and intentionally, as an act of radical social change, with the goal of upsetting those social arrangements in which oppressive imbalances of power hold sway. To function in a frame of feminist revolution and social change, feminist therapy defines two kinds of distress. One, the distress engendered by the development of feminist consciousness and thus an awareness of what is wrong with patriarchy, is not a problem to be treated. It is a positive outcome of feminist therapy, the end point of the healing journey through the personal into an awareness of the political. The other, the distress engendered by oppression and silencing, becomes the target of alleviating interventions.

THE RELATIONSHIP IN FEMINIST THERAPY

Although all forms of psychotherapy focus on the therapist-client relationship to one degree or another, the models of relating that emerge from feminist calls for radical rearrangements of social relationships, together with the different meanings ascribed by feminist thought to the very processes of caring and relating, lead to a transformed discourse. Critical analysis of power arrangements in psychotherapy and attempts to develop a paradigm for an egalitarian, empowering therapy relationship are thematic to feminist discourse on this topic. Feminist theories have identified the importance of attending both to the symbolic relationship, that which is usually referred to in the psychotherapy literature as transference and countertransference, and the real, in-the-world-now encounter. Feminist therapy has been uniquely attuned among therapy theories to the manner in which the internal, symbolic components of the interaction are shaped and colored by the signifiers of gender, race, class, and culture that obtain and give our actions meaning in the social world. From the start, feminist therapists have struggled to make sense of a relationship whose parameters, as commonly defined, appear to have an inherent poor fit with the goals of feminist social change.

Psychotherapy, like other social institutions of patriarchy, models a dominance-submission hierarchy of unequal power. Even the client-centered model, which was intended by Rogers as a strategy to increase the importance of the client's position in the transaction, still gives the authority to assign meaning to the therapist, whose task it is to "accurately symbolize" the client's utterances. Psychotherapy as currently practiced in most parts of North America is a form of relating created by a series of white men, few of whom have questioned underlying assumptions about the role of the therapist as defined within patriarchal models of relating. This is true even in the face of the emerging demographics of psychotherapy practice, in which most of those practicing these white-male-created versions of reality are themselves women (also predominantly white). Consequently, most models of therapy invest expertise and authority in one person, in this case the therapist. The hierarchy of power and value is embedded in these models; much writing on therapy practice discusses the need for the therapist to manage and contain the client and the therapeutic process.

Power and its imbalances in therapy have proven to be especially thorny problems for feminist therapists, given the inherent imbalances in therapy itself. Because an analysis of power dynamics is so central to feminist theory, the solution to the puzzle of power relationships in therapy is a core theoretical challenge for feminist therapy. Strategies for addressing this have often run into the difficulties inherent in an attempt to merge two quite different epistemologies. One, political feminism, sees the individual as living within a social context of political meaning and is concerned with the rearrangement of social and political power. The other, psychotherapy, has been otherwise apolitical, seeing the transformation of individual lives as an end unto itself, with little concern or attention paid to social arrangements. This is, of course, a political statement, but one that represents a politics of upholding the status quo.

The Symbolic in the Feminist Therapy Relationship

A step toward bringing together these divergent epistemologies has been for feminist therapy theory to interrogate and make explicitly political the symbolic and nonconscious aspects of the therapy relationship. Initially, feminist therapists attempted to disclaim the notion of symbolic relationship in therapy; however, since the middle 1980s, with the work of Miller and her colleagues at the Stone Center (Jordan, Kaplan, Miller, Stiver, & Surrey, 1992), there have been explicit framings of the symbolic in the feminist political paradigm. Although it is perceived as existing within inner and intersubjective space, representing the interaction of immediate experience and resonances to the past, feminist theory construes this inner space as being in constant interaction with, and obtaining meaning from, the social and political milieu.

Feminist therapy theory describes the symbolic relationship as both more and different than transference as typically described. Therapists are never defined as neutral screens on whom inter-

nal reality is projected by a client, nor as objective observers. The client's end of the symbolic exchange will not be simply a projection or distortion of the therapist based on the client's prior experiences, although the potential for this to occur, as is true for all human relationships, is noted. Nor are such symbolic or affect-laden components of the relationship defined as necessarily derived from disrupted or disturbed elements in each person's past. Instead, the symbolic relationship in feminist therapy is lively and interactive in response to the changing meanings of the various factors, such as gender, race, class, and role, that carry symbolic significance to either participant in the therapeutic encounter. Whereas individuals' pasts lend significance and meaning to the relationship in feminist therapy, the present and its signifiers are given equal status in shaping and forming the symbolic layers of the interaction. The collective pasts of both the therapist's and client's cultures of origin are part of the symbolic relationship.

Feminist therapists are asked to consider how each of these factors has been socially constructed for themselves, their clients, and the particular therapeutic exchange in order to unpack the various strands of extant meaning (Fine, 1992). The interrogation of the symbolic layer of the therapy relationship makes it necessary for feminist therapists first to be skilled in decoding their own responses and then to assist clients in a similar demystification during therapy. Key to this process is the imagination of how these symbolic strands will affect the exchange and balance of power in the relationship. The therapist also continuously attends to the events of daily life in the social environment that shape these mutual meanings, rather than assuming the symbolic values to be relatively static.

Anna Julia Cooper, an early twentieth-century African-American suffragist, said, "When and where I enter, then and there the whole race enters with me" (in Giddings, 1984, p. 13). Her pithy statement contains the factors to which feminist therapists must attend in analyzing and comprehending the effects of gender, race, class, sexual orientation, and so on in therapeutic relationships. When and where the exchange is entered, both physically and temporally, as well as emotionally and spiritually, each client and therapy bring their heritage, the meaning that this heritage has to them, and the meaning carried by the life of the other. Feminist therapists must attempt to know who they are when they "enter" the lives of their clients to have an awareness of what symbolic markers they carry with them into the therapeutic encounter. And as feminists, they must acknowledge that the signifiers of race, class, and so on are more than simply symbolic representations of internal realities for their clients or distortions stemming from distress or difficulties in function. These signifiers reflect real-life encounters between clients and the groups to which therapists belong (or are perceived as belonging). Also, that relationship will be affected most intimately by the ongoing sociocultural reality of the world in which the therapeutic relationship is situated.

This vision of the symbolic relationship in therapy moves beyond that of transference and countertransference by placing it in a broader sociopolitical context. The client's response to the therapist concerns not only the therapist's symbolization as a parent or other caregiver but also the various social meanings developed by this client about the therapist's actual or assumed group memberships. Feminist therapy theory argues that to strip the symbolic relationship of these sociocultural factors is to decontextualize this nonconscious component of psychotherapy and thus deny its relevance to the world events outside the therapy office in which this therapeutic relationship is contained. Feminists who have now practiced through the trials of O. J. Simpson and the Clinton-Lewinsky affair, to identify only two cultural phenomena that are laden with symbolism about gender, race, and power, have seen how the events of the real world affect the content and process of what occurs in therapy and the meaning of the therapist and client to each other. Broadly construing the symbolic relationship is also an initial step toward situating the important aspects of human growth and development as occurring not simply in a familial context but also within the larger social world in which sexism, racism, classism, and heterosexism, among other oppressive dominant norms, inform and interact with any family system.

The Egalitarian Relationship in Feminist Therapy

Egalitarianism and asymmetry form two important competing tensions in the construction of a therapy relationship that is feminist. Feminist therapy interrogates and attempts to address the actual power arrangements in the relationship as it exists in the here and now. In attempting to accomplish this goal, authors in the field of feminist therapy have typically described it as being an "egalitarian relationship." "Egalitarian" has most often been construed by persons new to or unfamiliar with feminist therapy as suggesting that it denies the presence of a power imbalance in therapy. This simplistic equation of egalitarian with "equal" has never been correct, although the confusion of meanings has been persistent. However, feminist therapists recognized early on that pure equality was not possible. The simple fact of who decided when to meet for therapy and on whose turf and terms the transaction proceeded (always the therapist's decisions and settings) betrayed the asymmetries lying close to the surface of the exchange. The concept of the egalitarian relationship represents an attempt to acknowledge the absence of equality while striving toward it as an ultimate goal. Egalitarian relationships are those structured to move toward equality of power, in which artificial and unnecessary barriers are removed from the process. In this relationship, there is an equality of *value* between the participants and of respect for each person's worth. There continues to be some necessary asymmetry, however, to certain aspects of the exchange, asymmetries designed in part to empower the less powerful person but primarily to define and delineate the responsibilities of the more powerful one.

In an egalitarian psychotherapy relationship, a primary goal is for clients to come to know and value their own needs, voice, and knowledge as central and authoritative to their lives. Therapists are not to supplant this knowing with their own authority but rather to use their skills to reflect and engage the clients in their own process and to help them learn how such self-knowledge and self-value are obscured by patriarchal processes and institutions. This egalitarian image sees therapists, by virtue of the role itself, as temporarily possessing certain kinds of greater power. To satisfy the feminist analysis of power, it is necessary to theorize methodologies by which this power is shared and transmitted to the client in every aspect of the psychotherapeutic transaction. It is also important to plan ways to respect the client's power for the therapist so that empowerment of the client does not simply become a matter of the therapist's compliance or abdication of personal agency.

The temporary absence of absolute equality of power is punctuated and made conscious in feminist practice by the therapist's analysis of the complex and subtle power dynamics in the exchange. This requires close attention by the therapist in order to maintain the delicate balance and not to accidentally garner to the therapist those powers typically ascribed to that role in dominant modalities but eschewed in feminist methodologies (e.g., the power to define the other as pathological and the self as the norm). The methodologies for achieving this balance vary in their specifics across persons and situations. Each such solution will take into account the powers of both the therapist and client and will define power as an infinite rather than finite resource of multidimensional properties.

The Power of the Therapist

A necessary step for feminist therapists' understanding of how to create and maintain egalitarian relationships is to have a thorough, thoughtful, and complex understanding and acceptance of their power so that it is used to create egalitarianism, so that it is not abused or given away; the empowerment of the client is not, after all, the disempowerment of the therapist. Accomplishing this step is assisted by the broadest possible definitions of power, manifested in terms of impact, presence, and influence, in order to define those forms of powers that may exist and operate independent of power in the world as defined in dominant terms. The effects of the politics of the context on relational power to enhance or diminish effectiveness in relating and engaging with clients must be acknowledged, as well as the manner in which the therapists are powerful, both personally and politically, in the role of therapist and in relationship to any particular client. Early theories noted that one of the legitimate powers of a therapist in the feminist model is to remind people of the power that they already have but are unable or as yet unwilling to see, feel, hear, and name (Smith & Siegel, 1985).

Feminist theories have underscored the powers of presence and nurturance as sources of impact, of influence, and ultimately of authority for therapists. Such theories note that these skills have been devalued in patriarchal discourse. The power to skillfully create and sustain relationships, often felt to be present in the client's phenomenological reality, is of a sort derived from both the actual and the symbolic aspects of the role of therapist. It is the power found in the capacity to offer nurturance and care, the power to be present with and encompass emotions and experiences that are terrifying to others, that comes from simply sitting and listening unflinchingly to the client's story. The theorists of the Stone Center (Jordan et al., 1992) have focused in particular on the process of therapeutic mutuality as an aspect of therapist power that can be utilized to empower the client. For the clients who have been silenced or have had their truths distorted by individual experience or cultural oppression, the mutuality of the exchange, in which the therapist serves as an attentive witness to those truths, provides the most powerfully transformative experience imaginable. Mutuality does not, however, imply sameness of needs or feelings, a common misconception in the use of this concept; in some instances, the therapist's willingness to hold and acknowledge differences, to refuse to cover over disconnection but rather to name its presence in the relationship, can become the empowering act of mutuality.

The power invested in the role of the therapist per se is also subjected to analysis; the manner in which the cultural context will create variations in the degree of power available is of particular interest to feminist therapists in constructing egalitarian therapy relationships. For example, the therapists practicing in communities where therapists are highly valued have more role-related power than do many therapists in communities where therapy is ridiculed or seen as dangerous. The therapists working with some cultural groups may need to grasp the power of their role more firmly in order to respect the desire of these clients for an expert authority; this may be a case in which the most effective strategy for empowering clients is first to accept firmly the hierarchies they carry with them, rather than to disrespect them from the outset. Therapists working in institutional settings carry the power and authority of the organization with them, which may add to or detract from the unofficial powers available symbolically.

Feminist theories also acknowledge that there are certain aspects of therapists' power that are legitimate components of their rights, as workers, to define the terms and conditions of their working environment. These include the power to set fees; to decide the time, place, and circumstances in which therapy will be offered; to define the degree of appropriate self-disclosure; and to have the right to refuse to work with someone. These are asymmetries that often are felt acutely and painfully by clients as disliked forms of therapists' power; but a feminist model does not require the disempowerment of the therapist as a worker to facilitate the empowerment of clients. Because many feminist therapists are women, and thus have been the targets of socialization experiences that teach the silencing of the self and accenting the needs of the other, these asymmetries are often troubling to the feminist therapist who has the goal of empowering clients. If, however, therapists build disrespect for themselves into the meta-assumptions of a therapy relationship, it no longer will be egalitarian because it is predicated on the false consciousness that empowerment of one requires disempowerment of the other. In the egalitarian relationship, there will be conflicts and disagreements at times.

The Power of the Client

The feminist model of egalitarian relationship also constructs the client as powerful, although frequently in a manner different from that of the therapist. A feminist epistemology of power is one that connotes power at many different levels and in a diversity of forms. It remains important to note that acknowledgment of the client's power does not relieve the therapist of certain responsibilities to the client, the therapy relationship itself, the communities to which each belongs, or the community of therapists, nor does it negate or obscure the power of the therapist herself. Acknowledgment of the client's power is, however, an essential aspect of the creation of a genuinely feminist relational matrix in the therapeutic exchange.

The powers of the client reflect role, person, and context in a manner similar to that found for the therapist. Identifying these powers requires subtlety of analysis because the phenomenology of the client is most commonly the experience of powerlessness. Within the role of client, certain types of power otherwise available to the person are often ceded to the therapist or weakened by the nature of the symbolic dynamics in the therapy relationship. Clients in therapy, feminist or otherwise, usually feel subjectively younger ("regressed"), weaker, and in greater need in the context of this relationship than they do in other relationships with adults. All of these experiences may decrease the client's power interpersonally. Even clients who are powerful and knowledgeable, peers of or more important than the therapist in their roles outside of the therapy relationship, are likely to enter this space of greater need once in the therapeutic exchange.

One strategy for empowerment of the client is framing the willingness to enter into such a relationship of dependency as the expression of a type of power hidden in patriarchal realities. Some of the power of the client, which feminist therapists can identify and name, emerges from the very experiences that appear to enhance powerlessness. Green (1990) has argued that in the feminist lens, the ability to directly express dependency is itself a form of power, in that it subverts patriarchal requirements to hide or socially embed dependency needs. A feminist analysis of the client's power thus constructs the client's ability and willingness to become temporarily, yet voluntarily, dependent as a statement of resistance to these patriarchal norms, even when clients experience themselves as being in such pain as to have no choice but to be in this dependent relationship. Such ability to resist, to risk a dependent stance in a relationship even though it may be experienced initially by the client as a form of weakness or deficit, is one unique dimension of power inherent in the role of the client from the perspective of feminist therapy. What differentiates feminist therapy at this point from any mainstream theories of psychotherapy is the recognition of this dependency as a hidden form of power and resistance to patriarchal norms. In taking this stance of resistance, clients, often unknowingly, take their initial steps toward the challenge of dominant paradigms within their lives.

Feminist therapy theory empowers clients by defining them as the ultimate experts about the meaning of their lives and their pain, the goals of therapy, and the quality of treatment outcome. This perspective of clients as experts on matters that normally are in the purview of the therapist in dominant models is another radical departure from mainstream constructions of the client as knower. This construction purposely eschews the notion that the therapist has the unilateral ability to know these things. Clients are explicitly handed the power to define self, and the meaning of self, in the manner most individually and culturally consistent. The therapist in feminist therapy must see her wisdom in a new way. Wisdom becomes the ability and willingness to continuously empower knowledge and wisdom in another. Although clients frequently enter therapy with access to their knowledge, voice, and authority blocked or silenced, therapists' commitments to egalitarian relationships require the assumption that the knowledge, voice, and authority are present and must be carefully nurtured by the therapy process.

The Coexpert Model

The egalitarian relationship takes form as a cooperative partnership of differing forms of expertise. The therapist is defined in this model as having expertise in the processes of change and empowerment, specialized and yet generally available expertise that is neither mystical nor inaccessible. This paradigm for the healer's expertise is a departure from most other models because it defines the skills constituting this expertise as being open for acquisition by the client as well, rather than as mysteries to which only the initiated can be exposed. Also, feminist therapy theory defines the healer as limited in her ability to heal by whatever unwillingness she may have to engage the client as an equal partner. Constructing a feminist relationship in therapy in which the client can be an authoritative knower requires that we describe our expertise in language that is accessible to clients from a variety of life experiences and that we center knowledge and reason equally in the client as in the therapist. This decentering process, in turn, reaffirms the power of the client as knower and expert. In this model, as clients become more aware of and take more possession of their role as authors of their own life narratives, the role of the therapist as a copyeditor, not a coauthor, of that narrative becomes more visible (see Chapter 16 in this volume).

In uncovering this personal narrative and identifying it for the client as a strategy for intrapersonal power, a feminist therapist can empower the client to begin to change this story. Although all approaches to therapy will involve this process of rewriting personal stories to some degree or another, feminist analysis utilizes interpretations of experience that underscore a placement of the client's experiences within a social and political context, as well as how these experiences have been deformed by patriarchal imperatives. This placement acts as one of the powerful deprivatizing aspects of a feminist psychotherapy. Placing individual experience in context, the notion of the personal as political, is another strategy for empowerment of the client by reducing the burdens of shame, silence, and alienation that are the legacy of patriarchal consciousness. Assisting clients to discover that they can make up their own stories—realizing that *all* of the stories are manufactured by someone, with none more "true" than the next—and supporting them as they come to believe in that narrative more strongly than any other add to their sense of personal power. Clients begin to see themselves as important sources of good in their lives and those of the people around them as they rewrite their stories, and thus they start to understand how powerful they can be and have been in their own development and survival. This feminist strategy of making manifest the impact of culture and context thus allows clients to see that they already have powerfulness in their emotional and behavioral repertoires.

The Client as Actor in the Life of the Therapist

In theorizing the client's power in the egalitarian relationship model, it is also important that therapists acknowledge both to themselves and to clients the latter's power in their lives. The process of influence and impact is bidirectional, and the client is an important shaper of the therapist's life and narratives in ways that may be invisible to clients when they perceive themselves as only the recipients of what therapists do. It is not the case that therapists from the dominant perspective have ignored the impact of the client; rather, it commonly has been framed in such a manner as to infer only pathology to power, flowing from client to therapist. Typically, therapists have mainly noted the difficult and problematic aspects of this influence. Most such back-handed affirmations of clients' impacts portray therapists in the role of victim to the client, replete with complaints about "manipulation." Realistically, some of the people with whom therapists work can be difficult to be around and may employ interpersonal strategies that are disempowering to others. Individuals who have experienced abuse, oppression, or discrimination often respond to these experiences by being angry, rigid, or controlling. Sometimes the people we work with can be objectively dangerous to us. Clients can disrupt our weekend afternoons with calls for help; making suicide threats before, during, and after vacations; and being jealous of our partners, children, and sometimes even our pets.

So there is a dilemma for the feminist therapist, who wonders if she wants to affirm *this* particular example of the client's power or simply wishes that it would go away. Reframing some of these behaviors as examples of strategies learned by the client from patriarchal consciousness, recalling that egalitarian relationships do not require the disempowerment of the therapist either, is a necessary component of responding to problematic impacts of clients on therapists. Equally important, though, is that therapists note and acknowledge positive effects of clients on their lives. Clients need to know that they are important to us, powerful with us, in ways that transform their narratives of powerlessness and also challenge whatever images they may have of their power to only do ill.

The process of acknowledging the client's power lies at the core of the continuous unfolding of egalitarian relating in feminist therapy. Egalitarian relationships in therapy occur when therapists know and embrace the reality of their power to use responsibly, as an agent for justice and change, and when, simultaneously, the power of the client is made manifest and strengthened. Whether it is power within the self, power in the therapy relationship, or power to transform the broader social context, the client's power is a factor to which feminist therapists attend, celebrate, and punctuate. There are many and diverse ways to accomplish this goal, commensurate with the technical eclecticism of feminist therapy. Feminist analysis calls on the therapist to respect both where and how the clients are as yet uncomfortable with power, while continuously seeking strategies suited to the clients by which to convey that powerfulness, so that they see themselves in a mirror in which such power is visible.

The egalitarian relationship is thus one in which power as a factor and force in the process of psychotherapy is made explicit within the asymmetries of the relationship. The power of the client is emphasized, enhanced, and framed so as to become more tangible; the power of the therapist as a change agent is honored, but the client's ability to internalize that power and eventually leave in possession of those abilities is never allowed to slip entirely into the background. This generates a paradigm of relating that subverts patriarchal models of hierarchy, both of power and of value.

Understanding the relationship between the client and therapist in such a manner is, in consequence, an essential step toward a vision of how feminist therapy will unfold. The conscious attention to power and its various meanings, the continuing inquiry into the ways in which various social signifiers affect the interaction in both concrete and symbolic ways, and the emphasis on relationality, all in the service of a more egalitarian connection, are characteristics that must inform every aspect of feminist therapeutic practice. When the relationship is woven of such elements, then the fabric of the therapy is more likely to re-

main feminist because the central aspects of the interaction will be those most tied to feminist understandings and analysis. This aspect of the methodology of feminist therapy is crucial, in no small part because without it, the most basic form and substance of the therapeutic exchange will cease to be feminist, regardless of the content of what is examined in therapy or the therapist's own feminist politics in other contexts. This way of knowing about what makes a relationship feminist in psychotherapy helps to create more clearly the distinction between a feminist psychotherapy and other forms and approaches.

CONCEPTIONS OF DISORDER: DIAGNOSIS AND DISTRESS

Therapy of whatever sort exists to assist people in dealing with distressing emotions, cognitions, and behaviors, and most models of therapy include models of distress. Feminist therapy theories, however, have a long and ambivalent relationship with the construction of psychological distress as evidence of disorder or pathology. From its inception, feminist theories have argued that the oppressive forces of patriarchal cultures (sexism, racism, heterosexism, classism, ageism, to name but a few), as well as those cultures themselves, are the actual pathologies and disorders with which clinicians should concern themselves. Feminist theories have attempted to find a place in between the pathologizing of oppressive cultures and the recognition of clinical realities by constructing most psychological distress not as a form of disorder but rather as understandable, possibly inevitable, and therefore not per se disordered responses to a dangerous and painful social context.

Simultaneous with the critique and deconstruction of common diagnostic nosologies, some feminist authors have attempted intentionally to define as forms of disorder and pathology certain worldviews and patterns of behavior that are currently considered common and somewhat acceptable among the dominant classes of a culture (Caplan, 1995). This strategy of constructing as disorders those behaviors that are ignored or celebrated by the cultural mainstream, while building a theory that otherwise has avoided locating disorders in the person, has created an interesting dynamic tension in feminist thought.

A theme running through feminist frameworks (see the core concepts of feminist therapy, described earlier in this chapter) is that all behavior has meaning only as it is constructed within the politics of the culture in which it is viewed. To create a "norm," whether moral or statistical, and then construct the cultural vision of goodness as being equivalent to it is a political dynamic with which mental health diagnosis is saturated. The designation of behaviors as "abnormal" is highly culturally determined; psychological diagnosis represents, not a description of that which is clearly present, but a mutual decision by professionals to classify certain ways of being as outside the dominant norms. In the history of American psychiatry and psychology, behaviors as diverse as running away from slavery and student protests have been consigned to the category of mental illness (Lerman, 1996)

Consequently, to comprehend distress and its constructions and to eschew normative assumptions, feminist theories propose that the culture itself must be subjected to analysis and critique, along with the exposure of its underlying oppressive normative assumptions. To assign a behavior to a category of "disorder" involves a complex process of sorting distress (the phenomenological experience of pain and misery) from pathology (something wrong, disordered, or abnormal), even in those circumstances where the distress may lead to impairment in function. Feminist theories do not view distress as isomorphic with pathology. As noted earlier, distress may represent resistance and necessary noncompliance with social norms (Brown, 1994; Rivera, 1996); impairment in function may punctuate problems in assumptions about how humans "should" function in a particular setting, such as a family or marital relationship (Caplan, 1995; Luepnitz, 1988).

Thus, in North American cultures, characterized by dominance of Caucasian, middle-class, heterosexual, young, Christian, able-bodied men, both white women and people of color (as well as members of various other nondominant groups) are socially constructed as less rational, more physical or "closer to nature," weaker, and less mentally fit than the members of the dominant group (Hacker, 1976; Lerner, 1993). Differences between groups tend to be theorized in patriarchies by dominant naive theories of behavior as being inherent and biological, and thus inescapable or essential to the alleged nature of the individual. Biological explanations of behavior tend to be advanced over other, multifactored and psychosocial ones that would presume the mutability of human behavior rather than its inher-

ence. Such cultural assumptions pervade diagnostic models of disorder and abnormalcy.

In patriarchal cultures, the presumed inherent nature of human difference is frequently used as a rationale to support unequal, differential treatment of various nondominant groups. The notion that certain groups like being treated unequally is commonly found in this sort of reasoning. In psychology, the characteristics that are socially constructed into the identity of nondominant groups are frequently construed as problematic or pathological; not only in musical comedy do we find the insistent question of why a woman cannot be more like a man (e.g., "reasonable"). Diagnoses exist to describe the excesses of femininity but not those of masculinity. Conversely, whatever characteristics are currently associated with the dominant group tend to be those associated with mental health and also are more likely to be socially desirable (Broverman et al., 1970; Landrine, 1988).

The Power of Naming

Feminist theory has long identified the right to name as a form of power (Lakoff, 1975). If I can tell you who you are, I take over the authorship of your life narrative. Rivera (1996) quotes a person who grew up in a highly abusive environment on the issue of being called a "disorder": "Words are powerful symbols. . . . Our language does not enlighten my struggle; it increases it. I am aware that what was once adaptive is now rather messy, to put it mildly. But I am not crazy. I am not ill. I am not a disorder" (p. 4). One of the strategies of feminism has been to give names to the experiences of oppressed people (e.g., sexual harassment and marital rape) that were previously rendered invisible in society because there was no name for them. The power to name one's own distress thus becomes one of the elements of the egalitarian therapy relationship in feminist practice.

To reserve to the therapist the power to name the distress for the person is to hold the power to define another, to determine how that person may be treated both inside and outside of therapy. Standard models of diagnosis have come under extensive criticism by feminists, not only for taking the power to name distress away from those experiencing it and placing it into the hands of professionals, but also for the manner in which certain categories or classes of behavior have been assigned to or left out of the parameters of disorder (Caplan, 1995; Lerman, 1996). Why, asks feminist theory, are some common ways of being for selected people defined as abnormal or disordered, whereas other ways of being are defined as normal distress, and still others are sufficiently acceptable that they are not even worthy of diagnostic scrutiny?

Are There Useful Constructions of Disorder?

Even diagnoses that initially appear to be benign or helpful from a feminist perspective are potentially problematic when subjected to closer analysis because of their inherent assumptions. These are the assumptions that any form of distress must be evidence of the abnormality and disorderedness of the distress itself. The diagnostic manual is very explicit about this. For instance, the diagnosis of an adjustment disorder defines the problem as an "abnormal" response to nontraumatic psychosocial stressors, although the nature of a normal response to those same stressors is left undefined. Thus, the question is left in the hands of the professional to determine what constitutes abnormality, a judgment that can occur without awareness of context or culture.

Nowhere does this conflict between feminist theory and pathologizing constructions of distress appear more sharply than at the location of the diagnosis of posttraumatic stress disorder (PTSD). This diagnosis was welcomed by many feminist practitioners when it was included for the first time in DSM-III in 1980 because it explicitly referred to social context, particularly oppressive social contexts, as a factor in distress. But the initial version of this diagnosis was flawed by a false assumption of an invariant and detectable human norm for a response to events. A trauma could only be identified and diagnosed as causing PTSD if an experience was "outside the range of usual human experience" and "frightening or threatening to almost anyone" (American Psychiatric Association, 1980). This statement again assumed a generic, normative human and decontextualized the distress (Brown, 1991).

Thus, another question is raised for feminist analysis by the definition in DSM of the posttrauma response as a disorder and pathology. Empirical evidence does demonstrate that not all persons exposed to a traumatic stressor, no matter how that is defined, will develop the pattern of symptoms called PTSD. Some will experience other combinations of distress. Others will report an absence of distress or even exhilaration. But does this mean that the person who does experience PTSD after trauma exposure is manifesting a disordered response and a form of psychopathology? A common feminist frame for describing PTSD is that it represents a reasonable response to unreasonable events (Walker, 1989); this, however, begs the question of reasonable to whom because even that phraseology infers that there are unreasonable (and disordered?) responses to the events in question. Rivera (1996) has written that to define these responses as a disorder would be to "collude in the on-going process of . . . objectification" (p. 4); thus, even if one framed PTSD as a normal response, allowing the "disorder" term to stand continues to assign pathology to the behaviors and to invite denigration of those experiencing this response pattern. Root (1992) has suggested that for individuals subjected to lifelong oppression such as cultural racism, classism, sexism, and so on, there is an experience of "insidious traumatization" that over time can render certain apparently neutral stimuli life threatening, thus moving the location of "reasonable" to within the context of the person experiencing distress.

Feminist constructions thus question any nomothetic models. People's distress can only be evaluated and defined in relationship to their own baselines and their own cultural and social context. The feminist analysis raises other questions as well: is it possible that current discussions are locating the norm in the wrong place? That is, are those who do *not* develop a PTS response to trauma responding in an abnormal or disordered manner? It is possible to argue that a construction of the PTS responses of dissociation, numbing, hyperarousal, and intrusion in the aftermath of trauma as normal would relocate the abnormalcy in the events that traumatize people (Rivera, 1996; Root, 1992)?

Feminist Constructions of Distress

Feminist constructions of distress thus work to keep away from the notion of disorder in the individual. The model inquires into what would be usual for a given person/situation and person/culture encounter and then whether or not the forms taken by the individuals' distress are indeed disordered or within the usual continuum of responses to that encounter. In addition, distress is conceived of as a potential outcome of behaviors that are empowering and affirming to the person and/or the social network (the resistance strategies described above) rather than as evidence of the presence of disorder.

Feminist constructions of distress also attend to the functional values and practical usefulness of behavior to a person in their milieus, with even distressing or impaired behaviors framed as possible strategies for meeting certain valued interpersonal or intrapsychic goals. If, for instance, a person can achieve attachment and care only by self-abasement or dependent behaviors, then the agency and function of these behaviors and their goal-directedness would be highlighted, rather than any pathology. The immense diversity of possible interpersonal matrices leads to wide variability in the development of such strategies; no one strategy is defined as disordered per se because each might be highly functional under certain circumstances.

Ultimately, with the focus in feminist therapy on clients' empowerment and the development of effective strategies for resisting patriarchal consciousness, the diagnosis of distress becomes secondary to the "diagnosis" of strengths, skills, and resources. A biopsychosocial model of distress, in which the relative contributions of various factors (e.g., biological sensitivity, social context, individual coping strategies, and available resources) are all factored into the equation, is utilized when formal diagnosis is necessary (Brown, 1994). Psychopathology as a concept is replaced with distress; pathology is, wherever possible, located outside the person and in the patriarchal realities that shape and form distress and self-disempowering modes of function.

THERAPY IN THE FEMINIST LENS: SUMMARY AND NEW DIRECTIONS

Therapy, to rise to the challenges of feminism, is not an end in itself. A feminist theory creates a therapy that serves as a way station; it can be one place, although not the only place, in which a person learns to value connection, loses the shame of her or his wounds, and becomes accustomed to being the focus of high-quality attention. Therapy fails as an instrument of feminist transformation, however, if it does not become a tool for the client's development of a sense of entitlement to good, equal relationships in life outside of therapy. It fails if the client becomes satisfied with having only the somewhat unequal and asymmetrical associations available in a therapeutic context. This challenge inherent in the existence of therapy per se remains a continuous one to feminist practice and raises ongoing questions of whether it is possible to have a feminist ethic and also practice psychotherapy (see Kitzinger & Perkins, 1993, for an excellent exegesis of this argument by feminist psychologists). It requires careful feminist analysis by a therapist to attend to the ways in which everyday connections among and between members of oppressed groups are undermined by patriarchal oppression. Therapy as a manifestation of feminist goals must be careful not to become part of that devaluation by offering a contrasting sort of relationship that appears more valuable and satisfying than daily life.

Theorizing a therapy capable of responding to the critiques of psychotherapy by feminist analysis creates a vision of therapy as an instrument of feminist social change. Such a discourse on therapy is highly subversive to the assumptions about "mental health" and "helping professions," to which most therapists are socialized in the course of our professional education and training. For feminist therapists and their clients to have relationships that are liberatory and challenging to patriarchal consciousness, we therapists must engage in a continuous parallel subversion of patriarchal assumptions within ourselves. An aspect of the boundaries defining feminist therapy as a philosophy is this willingness always to question, to assume the possible danger of what is done as a therapist to the goals of feminism.

Feminist therapy is entering a new era—attempting to respond to the vicissitudes of corporate controls of therapy in the form of managed care (Reed, 1995) and to challenges to feminist practice arising from various backlash, antifeminist social movements (Brown, 1996). Feminism as a political movement also continues to develop, and feminist therapies doubtless will respond to these emerging models of social change. But the core of feminist therapy, with its emphasis on the vision of therapy as an act of political resistance, is likely to persist. In our training, most therapists are taught to pay very close and careful attention to the meaning of each word and gesture and to monitor our feelings, fantasies, and dreams for their possible relevance to our practice. When we enter feminist realities and position therapy within a feminist discourse, we commit ourselves to paying similar close attention to the questions raised by feminist politics and philosophies. This additional analysis is the defining characteristic of feminist therapy, differentiating it in meaning and application from whatever is done by a therapist without such a vision.

References

Adleman, J., & Enguidanos, G. (1995). *Racism in the lives of women: Testimony, theory and guides to anti-racist practice.* Binghamton, NY: Harrington Park Press.

American Psychiatric Association (1980). *Diagnostic and statistical manual of mental disorders, 3rd ed., rev.* Washington, D.C.: American Psychiatric Press.

Belenky, M. F., Clinchy, B. M., Goldberger, N. R., & Tarule, J. M. (1986). *Women's ways of knowing.* New York: Basic Books.

Bem, S. L., & Bem, D. J. (1970). Training the woman to "know her place": The power of a nonconscious ideology. In S. Cox. (Ed.) *Female psychology: The emerging self* (pp. 180–191). Chicago: SRA.

Brabeck, M., & Brown, L. S. (1997). Feminist theory and psychological practice. In J. Worell & N. Johnson (Eds.), *Shaping the future of feminist psychology: Education, research and practice* (pp. 15–36). Washington, D.C.: American Psychological Association.

Brody, C. M. (Ed.). (1984). *Women therapists working with women: New theory and process of feminist therapy.* New York: Springer.

Broverman, I. K., Broverman, D., Clarkson, F. E., Rosenkrantz, P., & Vogel, S. (1970). Sex-role stereotypes and clinical judgments of mental health. *Journal of Consulting and Clinical Psychology, 34,* 1–7.

Brown, L. S. (1991). Not outside the range: One feminist perspective on psychic trauma. *American Imago, 48,* 119–133.

Brown, L. S. (1994). *Subversive dialogues: Theory in feminist therapy.* New York: Basic Books.

Brown, L. S. (1996). The private practice of subversion: Psychology as Tikkun Olam. *American Psychologist, 52,* 449–462.

Brown, L. S., & Brodsky, A. M. (1992). The future of feminist therapy. *Psychotherapy: Theory, Research, Practice, Training, 29,* 51–57.

Caplan, P. (1992). Driving us crazy: How oppression damages women's mental health and what we can do about it. *Women and Therapy, 12,* 5–28.

Caplan, P. (1995). *They say you're crazy: How the world's most powerful psychiatrists decide who's normal.* Reading, MA: Addison-Wesley.

Chesler, P. (1972). *Women and madness.* Garden City, NY: Doubleday

Comas-Diaz, L., & Greene, B. (Eds.). (1994). *Women of color: Integrating ethnic and gender identities in psychotherapy.* New York: Guilford.

Espin, O. M., & Gawelek, M. A. (1992). Women's diversity: Ethnicity, race, class and gender in theories of feminist psychology. In L. S. Brown & M. Ballou (Eds.), *Personality and*

psychopathology: Feminist reappraisals (pp. 88–110). New York: Guilford.

Fine, M. (1992). *Disruptive voices: The possibilities of feminist research.* Ann Arbor: University of Michigan Press.

Fox, D., & Prilleltensky, I. (Eds.). (1997). *Critical psychology: An introduction.* London: Sage.

Fredlund, T. (1992). How we decide. *Sinister Wisdom, 17,* 6–12.

Giddings, P. (1984). *When and where I enter: The impact of black women on race and sex in America.* New York: Morrow.

Gilligan, C. (1981). *In a different voice.* Cambridge, MA: Harvard University Press.

Gilligan, C., Rogers, A., & Tolman, D. (1992). *Women, girls and psychotherapy.* New York: Haworth.

Grahn, J. (1984). *Another mother tongue: Gay words, gay worlds.* Boston: Beacon Press.

Green, G. D. (1990). Is separation really so great? In L. S. Brown & M. P. P. Root (Eds.), *Diversity and complexity in feminist therapy* (pp. 87–104). New York: Haworth.

Greene, B., & Sanchez-Hucles, J. (1997). Diversity: Advancing an inclusive feminist psychology. In J. Worell & N. Johnson (Eds.), *Shaping the future of feminist psychology: Education, research and practice* (pp. 173–202). Washington, D.C.: American Psychological Association.

Greenspan, M. (1983). *A new approach to women and therapy.* New York: McGraw-Hill.

Hacker, H. M. (1976). Women as a minority group. In S. Cox (Ed.), *Female psychology: The emerging self* (pp. 156–170.) Chicago: SRA.

Hare-Mustin, R. T. (1994). Discourses in the mirrored room: Postmodern analysis of therapy. *Family Process, 33,* 19–35.

Hare-Mustin, R. T., & Marecek, J. (1990). *Making a difference: Psychology and the construction of gender.* New Haven, CT: Yale University Press.

Jack, D. (1991) *Silencing the self: Depression and women.* Cambridge, MA: Harvard University Press.

Jordan, J. V., Kaplan, A. G., Miller, J. B., Stiver, I. P., & Surrey, J. L. (1992). *Women's growth in connection: Writings from the Stone Center.* New York: Guilford.

Kanuha, V. (1990). The need for an integrated analysis of oppression in feminist therapy ethics. In H. Lerman & N. Porter (Eds.), *Feminist ethics in psychotherapy* (pp. 24–36). New York: Springer.

Kitzinger, C., & Perkins, R. (1993). *Changing our minds: Lesbian feminism and psychology.* New York: New York University Press.

Lakoff, R. (1975). *Language and woman's place.* New York: HarperColophon.

Landrine, H. (1988). Revising the framework of abnormal psychology. In P. Bronstein & K. Quina (Eds.), *Teaching a psychology of people: Resources for gender and sociocultural awareness* (pp. 37–44). Washington, D.C.: American Psychological Association.

Lerman, H. (1987). *A mote in Freud's eye: From psychoanalysis to the psychology of women.* New York: Springer.

Lerman, H. (1992). The limits of phenomenology: A feminist critique of the humanistic personality theories. In L. S. Brown & M. Ballou (Eds.), *Personality and psychopathology: Feminist reappraisals* (pp. 8–19). New York: Guilford.

Lerman, H. (1996). *Pigeonholing women's misery: A history and critical analysis of the psychodiagnosis of women in the twentieth century.* New York: Basic Books.

Lerner, G. (1993). *The creation of feminist consciousness.* New York: Oxford University Press.

Luepnitz, D. A. (1988). *The family interpreted: Feminist theory in clinical practice.* New York: Basic Books.

Lykes, M. B. (1985). Gender and individualist versus collectivist notions about the self. *Journal of Personality, 53,* 356–383.

Perkins, R. (1991). Therapy for lesbians? The case against. *Feminism and Psychology, 1,* 325–338.

Reed, E. (1995, October). *Scheherezade or the 1001 sessions: Feminist therapy and the discourse of managed care.* Paper presented at the 12th Advanced Feminist Therapy Institute, Ithaca, NY.

Rivera, M. (1996). *More alike than different: Treating severely dissociative trauma survivors.* Toronto: University of Toronto Press.

Root, M. P . P. (1992). Reconstructing the impact of trauma on personality. In L. S. Brown & M. Ballou (Eds.), *Personality and psychopathology: Feminist reappraisals* (pp. 229–266). New York: Guilford.

Smith A. J., & Siegel, R. F. (1985). Feminist therapy: Redefining power for the powerless. In L. B. Rosewater & L. E. A. Walker (Eds.), *Handbook of feminist therapy: Women's issues in psychotherapy* (pp. 13–21). New York: Springer.

Stoltenberg, J. (1990). *Refusing to be a man.* New York: Meridian.

Unger, R. (Ed.). (1989). *Representations: Social constructions of gender.* Amityville, NY: Baywood Publishing.

Walker, L. E. A. (1980). Psychology and violence against women. *American Psychologist, 44,* 695–702.

Worell, J. (1998). Looking ahead: So what's new? *Psychology of Women, 25,* pp 1–2.

Worell, J., & Johnson, N. (Eds.). (1997). *Shaping the future of feminist psychology: Education, research and practice.* Washington, D.C.: American Psychological Association.

CHAPTER 18

CONTEMPORARY BEHAVIOR THERAPY

WILLIAM C. FOLLETTE AND STEVEN C. HAYES
University of Nevada, Reno

This chapter is intended to describe the part of contemporary behavior therapy that is strongly rooted in operant and respondent learning traditions. Contemporary behavior therapy of this kind is in the midst of a significant period of growth and reinvigoration, particularly over the last 10 years and particularly under the rubric of clinical behavior analysis (Dougher, in press). To some degree, this is surprising, given that cognitive-behavior therapy is widely believed to have eclipsed traditional forms of behavior therapy and behavior analysis in the 1970s and 1980s. In this chapter, we point to the several factors that have led to this reinvigoration.

HISTORICAL PERSPECTIVE

There is perhaps no greater historical burden for contemporary behavior therapy than that word *behavior*. It is a word that is often used in psychology as a term of distinction with thoughts, feelings, or other private experiences (as when someone might say, "thoughts, feelings, and behavior"). It is a term that is linked to behavior*ism*, and through that term, to the early behaviorists. Ironically, both of those connotations are misleading as they bear on the contemporary scene. To understand how this came to be, one must understand the agenda of the early behaviorists and how later behaviorists (particularly Skinner) revolted against it.

The Early Behaviorists

The father of behavioral thinking in psychology is usually said to be John B. Watson. Watson mixed ideas from American pragmatism, evolutionary biology, functionalism, and reflexology into a potent challenge on psychology as the study of mind and on introspection as its method of investigation (Watson, 1913, 1924, pp. 2–5). In its place, he advocated a science of behavior, defining that term to mean muscle movements and glandular secretions (Watson, 1924, p. 14). He was interested in and studied events such as thinking (Watson & Rayner, 1920), but even these events he thought could be resolved into subtle movements or secretions.

Thus, in the hands of the early behaviorists, behavior was indeed pitted against mental events, and it was indeed defined peripherally. This was not as incredible as it might first seem because there was a hope and belief that behavior, so defined, still did encompass thought and emotion. In addition to these substantive claims, which never became popular although they became extremely well known, Watson also claimed that psychology as a science could study only overt behavior in any case because only these psychological events could be directly and publicly viewed. The wide acceptance of this claim led to behavioristic methods being adopted in virtually every area of psychology, including the science of mind.

This earliest stage of behavioral thinking did not lead to a robust applied technology, but it is worth noting that several studies were conducted in this period that demonstrated the applicability of behavioral principles (e.g., Watson & Rayner, 1920). This foreshadowed a continuing alliance that would grow up between the basic and applied wings of the behavioral movement.

Behavior theory blossomed in the early and middle part of the twentieth century, establishing and working through a wide variety of behavioral principles. When traditional behavior therapy began in the late 1950s and early 1960s, there was a rich vein of behavioral principles (e.g., direct contingency principles and classical conditioning principles) to be mined.

The Two Traditions of the Behavior Therapy Movement

When behavior therapy began, it emerged both from the methodological and neobehaviorism of stimulus-response (S-R) learning theory (as represented by Joseph Wolpe, Arnold Lazarus, Stanley Rachman, Hans Eysenck, M. B. Shapiro, and others) and the behavior analytic thinking of B. F. Skinner (as represented by Donald Baer, Todd Risley, Teodore Ayllon, Nathan Azrin, and others). At first, the neobehavioristic tradition focused on relatively specific clinical problems such as phobias (Wolpe, 1958), whereas behavior analytic tradition focused on institutionalized or developmentally disabled populations in such areas as schizophrenia (Allyon & Azrin, 1968) and autism (Lovaas, 1977). With some notable exceptions, many of the most dramatic treatment successes took place when applied clinical behaviorists had a great deal of control over the environmental contingencies that affected behavior. Over time, the methodological, neobehaviorist wing expanded considerably into the entire range of traditional clinical problems. Behavior analysis did not, preferring instead to expand on its successes in more limited domains. In part because of their criticism of psychoanalytic approaches, early behavior therapists from both wings were generally cautious of the value of verbal psychotherapies more generally, whether behaviorally rationalized or not.

Despite their broad differences, both of these traditions were recognizably forms of behavior therapy in their embrace of "operationally defined learning theory and conformity to well established experimental paradigms" (Eysenck, 1972; Franks & Wilson, 1974, p. 7). Of the two, the more methodological and neobehavioristic wing was always much more dominant (Mahoney, Kazdin, & Lesswing, 1974, p. 15).

The Rise of Cognitive-Behavior Therapy

In the 1960s basic S-R learning theory crumbled, in part because it was simply unable to solve the challenge of cognition by using strictly associationistic principles (Jenkins & Palermo, 1964, is widely cited as the book that marked the end of the attempt). This wing of methodological behavioristic thinking transformed itself over a few short years into cognitive psychology by adopting much more flexible associationistic principles, based on the metaphor of the computer. Increasingly elaborate mediational models were developed of the hypothetical "internal machinery" that supposedly bridged the gaps between an external stimulus event and a response to it.

Within a decade, this change led to a similar liberalization inside behavior therapy. Led at first by social learning theory and related writings (e.g., Bandura, 1968, 1977; Staats, 1975), the cognitive-behavior therapy movement was born (e.g., Mahoney, 1974; Meichenbaum, 1977). This movement had several profound effects on behavior therapy. A broad range of verbal psychotherapies quickly entered into the technical armamentarium of behavior therapy, in part because of the obvious link between discourse and cognition. Researchers also began to look for mediating cognitive variables (e.g., self-efficacy) that could explain behavioral change. As treatment innovation occurred in the context of one-hour per week, office-based therapy, cognitive interventions such as rational-emotive therapy (Ellis, 1979; Ellis & Harper, 1961), and cognitive therapy for depression (Beck, Rush, Shaw, & Emery, 1979) became increasingly popular.

At first, however, most of the formal connections between cognitive-behavior therapy and cognitive psychology were loose or absent. Much of the new technology was based more on a folk psychology of cognition than on cognitive science. Over time, some of the leaders in cognitive therapy worked out such connections (e.g., Ingram, 1991; Ingram & Holle, 1992), but the applied and basic wings of cognitive thinking remain relatively orthogonal to this day.

Cognitive-behavior therapy is quite clearly the empirical clinical mainstream of behavior therapy today. The rapid rate of innovation seen in the 1970s and 1980s has clearly slowed, however. As cognitive therapy has begun to plateau, more notice has been given to innovations in clinical behavior analysis.

The Rise of Clinical Behavior Analysis

Just as the collapse of S-R learning theory set the stage for cognitive-behavior therapy, changes in basic behavior analysis have set the stage for the rise of clinical behavior analysis as the core of contemporary behavior therapy. We address these changes throughout the chapter, but three specific themes seem worth mentioning here.

Philosophical Refinement: Functional Contextualism vs. Mechanism

The first advance was a wider appreciation for the philosophical innovation represented by behavior analysis. Skinner was more of an intuitive philosopher of science than a self-conscious one, and there are numerous philosophical inconsistencies in his writings as a result. Behavior analysis also suffered under the burden of its terminological and historical connection to Watsonian thinking. For both of these reasons, behavior analysis is frequently interpreted as a mechanistic approach. In mechanistic positions, complex events can always be reduced to parts, relations, and forces, much as a machine can be similarly dissembled. Those who viewed behavior analysis as a mechanistic position tended to think of stimuli and responses as formal, ontological categories that are then pieced together by contingency and contiguity.

In contrast, much of what seemed original in Skinner's thinking is antithetical to mechanism, namely, his radical forms of functionalism and pragmatism. For example, Skinner (1974) denied ontological implications for his constructions, emphasizing instead that scientific knowledge "is a corpus of rules for effective action, and there is a special sense in which it could be 'true' if it yields the most effective action possible" (p. 235). Some behavior analysts, such as Willard Day (Leigland, 1992) had long emphasized this aspect of Skinner's thinking. In the late 1980s and early 1990s, behavior analysts began to cast the essence of behavior analysis in contextualistic, not mechanistic, terms (Hayes, Hayes, & Reese, 1988; Morris, 1988). Although not all behavior analysts agree, the modern work of clinical behavior analysis has followed this approach and views behavior analysis as a form of functional contextualism (Biglan & Hayes, 1996; Hayes, 1993).

The core analytic unit of contextualism or pragmatism is the ongoing act in context (Pepper, 1942). The core components of contextualism are (1) a focus on the whole event, (2) sensitivity to the role of context in understanding the nature and function of an event, and (3) a firm grasp on a pragmatic truth criterion. There are various forms of contextualism (Hayes, Hayes, Reese, &

Sarbin, 1993; Rosnow & Georgoudi, 1986). Like all forms of pragmatism, functional contextualism takes effective action to be the goal of science. It is distinguished, however, by its specific goals: behavior analysis studies whole organisms interacting in and with a historical and current situational context for the purposes of predicting and influencing these interactions and deriving principles adequate to that task that are both precise and broad in scope.

The empirical approach that comes from this philosophical stance emphasizes three features. First, behavior is understood in terms of its function, not its form or location. A whole event is organized by its function, and all else is secondary. For that reason, behavioral units can be of any size and content, depending only on the analytic purpose. Second, behavioral functions are products of historical and situational context, and thus all concepts, units, and principles are contextually situated. Finally, only those features that help achieve the unified goal of prediction and influence are emphasized. Thus, the environmentalism of behavior analysis is not foundational or dogmatic but is merely pragmatic, given its goals (Hayes & Brownstein, 1986). We later explore the profound liberalization that these features enable.

The Development of Principles of Derived Stimulus Relations

Behavior analysts were never interested in "the behavior of rats for its own sake" (Skinner, 1938, p. 441). Rather, the research strategy (see Hayes & Hayes, 1992) was that relatively simple nonhuman behaviors in relatively simple environments might provide useful tools for the analysis of complex human behavior. It was not assumed that this strategy had to work because, a priori, we "can neither assert nor deny continuity or discontinuity" (Skinner, 1938, p. 442). In fact it worked very well, at least until issues of language and cognition were encountered. From the beginning, Skinner worried that his approach might not be sufficient in this area (see the concluding section of 1938), but he later claimed that a straightforward operant analysis worked there as well (Skinner, 1957).

There is now broad agreement that the empirical findings in the area of derived stimulus relations fundamentally undermine Skinner's approach to language and cognition (Hayes & Wilson, 1993). To take only one example, one of the most important of Skinner's verbal units is the tact, which is a verbal operant produced by a history of generalized reinforcement for emitting a characteristic topography in the presence of a particular object or event. Put more simply, a tact is a label for something. As a verbal operant, it is maintained by people understanding what is being referenced. Yet we now know that it is easy to produce tactlike performances, even in human infants (Lipkens, Hayes, & Hayes, 1993), based on derived stimulus relations such as stimulus equivalence (Sidman, 1986). We can think of the basic phenomenon in terms of a triangle made up of three arbitrary events: train any two sides in one direction and normal humans will show all three sides in both directions. Four of the six relations will have been *derived*.

For example, suppose the child is trained, given the written word C-A-T, to say "cat" and not "dog," and to point to cats, not dogs. With these two trained relations (written word–oral name; written word–class of objects), four derived relations will probably emerge: being able to select the written word, given either the oral name or the object; finding the object, given the oral name; and saying the oral name, given the object. If the child now says "cat," given actual cats, this is not a tact because it is not based on a direct history of generalized reinforcement for saying "cat" in the presence of cats. Performances of this kind emerge well before a child is two years old (Devany, Hayes, & Nelson, 1986; Linehan, 1984). To date, such performances seem to be absent in nonhumans.

We analyze the importance of such findings later, in the analysis of clinical problems, but the broad implications can be stated here: basic behavior analysis now has an emerging science of language and cognition that breaks new ground conceptually and empirically. Contemporary behavior therapy is being profoundly influenced by these developments.

The Scientific Analysis of Private Events

The final basic change is the opening up of behavioral thinking to the analysis of thought and emotion. This analysis involves the coming together of the first two points we have already made. It is not widely known that Skinner's (1945) contextualism explicitly overthrew Watson's prohibition against introspection and the scientific analysis of thoughts and feelings. Skinner (1974) believed that behavior analysis "does not insist upon truth by agreement and can therefore consider events taking place in the

private world within the skin" (p. 16). The reason that this philosophically important step is not widely known is that Skinner (1953) also believed that private events such as thoughts and emotions are co-occurring products of the same contingencies that precipitate overt behaviors, which they are said to cause, and thus are of "no functional significance, either in a theoretical analysis or the practical control of behavior" (p. 181). Skinner, in other words, argued that analyzing private experience was both scientifically legitimate and practically unnecessary (Friman, Hayes, & Wilson, 1998).

The intellectual changes flowing from the study of derived stimulus relations have challenged this conclusion (Friman et al., 1998). Of prime importance is the finding that a broad variety of psychological functions can move through derived stimulus relations, including conditioned reinforcing functions (Hayes, Brownstein, Devany, Kohlenberg, & Shelby, 1987; Hayes, Kohlenberg, & Hayes, 1991), discriminative functions of public (Barnes & Keenan, 1993; de Rose, McIlvane, Dube, Galpin, & Stoddard, 1988; Gatch & Osborne, 1989; Hayes, Brownstein, Devany, Kohlenberg, & Shelby, 1987; Kohlenberg, Hayes, & Hayes, 1991; Wulfert & Hayes, 1988) and private (DeGrandpre, Bickel, & Higgins, 1992) stimuli, elicited conditioned emotional responses (Dougher, Auguston, Markham, Greenway, & Wulfert, 1994), extinction functions (Dougher et al., 1994), and sexual responses (Roche & Barnes, 1997). Furthermore, these functions can be actively transformed by the precise derived relation involved (Dymond & Barnes, 1995; Roche & Barnes, 1997). What this means is that it can matter a great deal whether a person calls a given psychological event "anxiety" or "excitement." One contingency may give rise to the bodily reaction (e.g., drinking a great deal of coffee), whereas another may give rise to its role in further behavior (e.g., labeling the arousal a panic attack that might lead to "losing my mind," which in turn may lead to social withdrawal and overt avoidance). Without an analysis of human verbal construction in this instance, there is no way to relate two important sets of contingencies, one direct and one derived. Thus, the bidirectionality of human language and cognition challenges Skinner's (1974) belief that "the change in feeling and the change in behavior have a common cause" (p. 62). In contrast to Skinner's view, modern behavioral thinking, in other words, seems to be leading to the conclusion that analyzing private experience is both scientifically legitimate and practically necessary.

That does not mean, however, that thoughts or feelings are usefully thought of as *causing* other forms of activity. In contextualistic systems, causality is not ontological but merely a practically useful way to speak in some circumstances. Given the goals of functional contextualism (particularly that of behavioral influence), it is not very useful to treat any psychological event as the cause of another because behavioral influence always requires the manipulation of the contextual features of a psychological interaction (Biglan & Hayes, 1996; Hayes & Brownstein, 1986). Two psychological events may indeed be related, but the "cause" of both and of their relationship is to be found in their context. That is why contemporary behavior therapy has pioneered the development of acceptance methods, mindfulness, cognitive deliteralization techniques, and other contextual procedures focused on the role of private events in the regulation of overt behavior.

These many changes in behavioral thinking cannot merely be an attempt to ape the cognitive therapy movement because they have been driven by changes within basic behavior analysis that largely preceded and were unrelated to that movement. Stimulus equivalence, for example, was first identified in 1971 (Sidman, 1971), although its significance took many years to become apparent. Furthermore, the analysis of private experience that is characteristic of contemporary behavior therapy is quite distinct from the cognitive-behavior therapy tradition, as we later show.

MISCONCEPTIONS ABOUT CONTEMPORARY BEHAVIOR THERAPY

Behavior therapy is often characterized in ways that discourage individuals from coming into the field or actually studying contemporary innovations. In the following section we will briefly outline six such myths. We have already outlined developments in the field that will make their mythical nature immediately apparent.

Myth 1. Behavior Therapy Is Mechanistic

This myth is both profoundly incorrect and ironic. Critics like to claim that behaviorists treat people like machines. There are indeed "push-pull, click-click" forms of behavior theory, but

they exist almost entirely in the pages of history. Contextualistic thinking is at the core of modern behavior therapy, and with it an interest in the whole psychological event—its history, context, and purpose. Scientific divisions among events are taken to be constructions, to be used for pragmatic analytic purposes, not ontological realities to be considered in isolation from other events. Thus, there are fluidity, humility, and tentativeness of contextual analysis that are entirely unlike mechanistic thinking.

The irony, of course, is that early versions of the information-processing wing of cognitive psychology used computer metaphors that made use of input/output models of cognition (see Ingram & Kendall, 1986, for a discussion of the heuristic value of the computer metaphor). More recently, research on neural networking is less clearly mechanistic and more dynamic in its approach to simulating cognitive processes (e.g., Tryon, 1995). The point is that old metaphors die hard. However, the contemporary behavior therapy we describe in this chapter is not the mechanistic model of the 1920s.

Myth 2. Behavior Therapy Is Reductionistic

This myth, too, is both incorrect and ironic. If, as we have stated, behavior can only be understood in the unique context in which it occurs, then any attempt to reduce behavior to isolated stimuli and responses is doomed because the essential quality of the whole event is lost. A person raising an arm is not engaging in "arm-raising behavior." Functionally speaking, we have no idea what the person is doing until we appreciate it in a historical and situational context. When we do, the functional unit of behavior might be "getting attention," "reaching for food," or "stretching." The event loses all meaning if it is reduced to an isolated component.

The irony is that reductionism is popular in all mechanistic approaches to behavior. It is common, for example, for mechanistic wings of cognitive psychology to claim that "mental processes are brain processes" (Ellis & Hunt, 1983, p. 11). This makes perfect sense because all machines can be reduced to their parts, and in that sense, all psychological events can be reduced to biological ones.

Myth 3. Behavior Therapy Ignores Thoughts and Feelings

One of the popular myths about behavior therapy is that private events are ignored because they take place inside the person. This characterization is not entirely unfair because it is made even by some prominent behavior researchers (Johnston & Pennypacker, 1980). As we have tried to show, however, for at least the last 50 years behavioral thinking has assumed that thoughts and feelings are legitimate objects of study. Traditional and contemporary behavior therapists alike have always dealt with thoughts and feelings because clients often present for therapy concerns about their private experiences. Behavior therapists, however, have always viewed thoughts and feelings as dependent variables, not independent variables. In the contemporary behaviorists' view, it is a goal of therapy to identify the functional relationship between environmental events and thoughts and feelings, as well as their relation to overt behavior. What is relatively new is that a variety of technical terms and analyses has arisen within behavior theory that makes it easier to analyze thoughts and feelings in technical terms.

Myth 4. Behavior Therapy Ignores the Whole Person

As we described, behavior therapists are not all concerned with individual, isolated behaviors. Rather, behaviors are understood only in the entire context in which psychological events occur. The context includes the person's repertoire, the person's history of similar actions and their effects, the time and place a psychological event occurs, the person's current motivational state (in technical terms, the presence of "establishing operations"), the reactions of other people to the action, the biological and genetic milieu of the person emitting the behavior, and a whole host of other features that may be relevant to how a psychological event comes about and why it is maintained.

In fairness, the misperception is not difficult to understand. Some of the pioneering behavior therapists were studying very dramatic behavior, and an intense focus on a specific behavioral event was warranted. When the behavior of study is something as dramatic as severe head banging and the person demonstrating that behavior is nonverbal, it can indeed appear as if the behavior therapist is focusing merely on isolated behavior. Whereas such an analysis may have been sufficient in those highly constrained cases, a more comprehensive analysis is required for most situations.

Myth 5. Behavior Therapy Assumes That People Are Just Like Animals

Many of the principles used to understand psychological events from a behavioral point of view have been derived from laboratory experimental work with nonhumans. There was never a belief that principles identified with nonhumans would necessarily apply in whole cloth to humans (Skinner, 1938, p. 442). The evolutionary assumption is that new contains old, not that old contains new, and cross-species consistency is between the tips of two temporal branches, not two rungs of a single temporal ladder. Thus, cross-species consistency involves a transition both from new to old (as we go back in time to a point before the two species diverged) and from old to new (as we come forward in time within the evolution of a given species). Nothing in evolutionary theory or behavior theory thus demands that principles identified in nonhumans will operate with humans. Rather there was a simple, strategic hope that animal learning would be a good place to begin to help find conceptual tools that would unlock the complexity of human behavior. It turned out that this hope was not in vain; but even when direct learning principles are involved, everyone realizes that humans are shockingly complex organisms. Just as a good physician realizes the limitations of studying a single cell in a petri dish and extrapolating that to a biological system as complex as an entire human being, behavior therapists understand the limits of generalizability from animal to human studies. Furthermore, it is now known that humans are the only organisms that readily derive arbitrary stimulus relations. Human language and cognition do indeed seem to involve some things that are new. We further address this topic later.

Myth 6. Behavior Therapy Ignores the Therapeutic Relationship

The considerable amount of pioneering research in behavior therapy was conducted on institutionalized individuals, developmentally disabled individuals, or individuals with fairly focused problems. The point of intervention for institutionalized or developmentally disabled clients was primarily effecting change in the environment. In the classic work by Allyon and Azrin (1968), significant improvement in institutionalized patients with severe mental disorders such as schizophrenia was achieved by implementing a behavioral intervention that focused on modifying staff and environmental contingencies. Similar dramatic improvements have been observed in efforts to teach language and other skills to developmentally disabled and autistic children (e.g., Bijou & Baer, 1961; Lovaas, 1977), who had little capacity to engage in social interaction. Later, behavior therapies in the outpatient setting were developed for highly focused problems. For example, treatments of phobias were based, in part, on the famous case report of Little Albert by Watson and Rayner (1920), with additional conceptual work by Mowrer (1939) on the acquisition and maintenance of anxiety classical and operant conditioning, and the pioneering clinical work of Joseph Wolpe (1958), who developed the method of reciprocal inhibition that gave rise to desensitization. Treatment was highly structured and in some cases involved the presentation of feared stimulus materials in homework or through automated presentation, with no therapist even present in the room. Thus, it is not difficult to see where the initial view that the therapeutic relationship was unimportant arose.

However, even in the early 1960s, behaviorists were writing about the role of the therapist in shaping clients' social and verbal behavior (e.g., Krasner, 1962, 1963). The more recent work in contemporary behavior therapy has tended to provide considerable emphasis on the therapeutic relationship. For example, dialectical behavior therapy (DBT; Linehan, 1993a), integrative couple's therapy (ICT; Jacobson & Christensen, 1996), and acceptance and commitment therapy (ACT; Hayes, Strosahl, & Wilson, 1999) all provide extensive guidance about how to develop and maintain a powerful therapeutic relationship with clients. Perhaps no contemporary behavior therapy is more explicit in this area, however, than functional analytic psychotherapy (FAP; Kohlenberg & Tsai, 1991). Follette, Naugle, and Callaghan (1996) describe how the FAP therapist establishes a therapeutic relationship that functions to facilitate the client's change. Recent empirical work provides support for the importance of these relationship development techniques in the clinical environment and for the value of using them in the context of analytically based behavior psychotherapy (Paul, Marx, & Orsillo, 1999). We describe this psychotherapy in more detail later in this chapter. A lack of attention to the therapeutic relationship is clearly not characteristic of contemporary behavior therapy.

BEHAVIORAL PRINCIPLES

Behavioral principles are ways of speaking about whole organisms interacting in a historical and situational context that allows these interactions to be predicted and influenced with precision (few alternative constructions for a given event), scope (the broad applicability of a limited set of constructions to many events), and depth (the coherence among constructions focused on different levels of analysis). Seen in this way, behavioral principles contain certain philosophical assumptions about the proper units of analysis of psychology, the nature of behavioral events, and so on. Before turning to a description of behavioral principles of importance to contemporary behavior therapy, we address these assumptions briefly.

Philosophical Assumptions Inherent in Behavior Principles
Units of Analysis
The unit of analysis suggested by the above definition of behavioral principles is inherently holistic. Behavior is never assessed as an isolated act, nor can it be separated from the whole. All aspects of a psychological interaction, including thoughts, feelings, bodily sensations, movements, and so on, are included. Furthermore, it is a whole organism that acts. Psychological events are not the responsibility of separate parts of the person such as brains or muscles. That is, one cannot understand behavior at the psychological level by examining separate parts of the person or separately from his or her history and the *entire* context that gives the act meaning.

There is a potential downside to this holistic quality, namely, that it becomes impossible to selectively focus on features of a total complex. What saves the analyst from endless consideration of the totality is the principle of pragmatic clinical utility. The clinical and analytic goal is to conduct an analysis that produces an understanding that has precision, scope, and depth and that allows us to effect change in a client's behavior.

Constructivism
The ontological and pragmatic nature of behavioral principles means that these concepts are treated as constructions. In other words, behavioral principles are there for the pragmatic purposes of the scientist and clinician. They do not literally "direct" behavior anymore than the law of gravity itself makes objects fall. This places contemporary behavior therapy clearly in the camp of philosophical constructivists.

The Primacy of Function

In the same way that scientific terms are evaluated on the basis of their utility, all behavioral events are evaluated in the way they produce a transition from one state of affairs to another. In other words, behavior is understood in terms of its function, not its form. Behaviors that have the same effect on the environment in a given situation (i.e., function in the same way) are treated as equivalent regardless of whether they resemble each other in form (topography). For example, a client may wish to avoid talking about how he or she feels about the therapist. Whenever the therapist starts to broach the subject of the client's feeling for the therapist, the client could change the subject, appear disinterested, become angry, start to cry, have to go to the bathroom, miss future sessions, or any number of other overt behaviors that all function to limit the discussion of feelings. Even though the topographies of all these behaviors differ, if they function equivalently they would be considered instances of the same class of behaviors.

Functional Response Classes

Behaviors that have different topographies but the same function are considered to be members of the same functional response class. A response class is a grouping of responses that shares the same effects in a given situation. Functions must be understood both historically and situationally. For behaviors with different topographies to be members of the same response class, we need to know the history of the person to understand them. For example, with the client described above, we would need to know why he or she was avoiding the expression of emotional matters. What were the circumstances that led to the expression of emotion being something to be avoided? What were the consequences in the past for expressing feelings and then for avoiding them? Furthermore, we would need to know what in the present circumstances in therapy caused the client to view this situation as similar enough to past situations to lead the client to avoid the expression of feelings in this situation as well. If the client were refusing to talk about emotions because when he or she had done so in other important relationships it was done poorly and the relationship suffered, the therapist might focus on improving the expression of feelings. If the difficulty with emotional expression had been inadvertently brought about because the therapist ignored direct expressions of feelings with this client, paying attention instead when the client seemed secretive or evasive, the difficulty in the expression of emotions would be a member of a very different response class, requiring quite different interventions.

Types of Behavioral Principles

Contemporary behavior therapy rests directly on the application of learning principles that were initially derived from basic laboratory sciences. Some of the principles are long-standing, well-established findings, as in the case of direct contingency principles (including operant and respondent learning), whereas others are newly emerging, as in the case of indirect contingency principles or principles of verbal control (Hayes & Hayes, 1992).

Two learning traditions contribute to the understanding of behavior and behavior change—respondent (classical) conditioning and operant (Skinnerian) conditioning. Although we cannot fully describe these principles, a brief overview will be helpful.

Respondent or Classical Conditioning

Figure 18.1 shows the general preparation in respondent or classical conditioning. In the former, the unconditioned stimulus (UCS) elicits an unconditioned response (UCR). No prior learning history is required. In Pavlov's famous experiment with dogs, the UCS was food powder, which elicited the UCR of salivation. This is shown as pathway 1 in Figure 18.1. Pavlov then presented a previously neutral stimulus (one that did not have an effect on salivation), a bell, before the presentation of the UCS. With repeated pairings of the bell with the UCS (shown as pathway 2), the bell ultimately comes to elicit the same response as the UCS. Once that happens, the bell is called a conditioned stimulus (CS). A response that is elicited by the presentation of the CS rather than the UCS is called a conditioned response (CR), shown as pathway 3.

Using a more clinical example, we now consider a person who experiences a spontaneous panic attack. Such spontaneous attacks are common and can elicit aversive feelings in their victims, including fear that they are having a heart attack or dying (American Psychiatric Association, 1994). In this scenario, the panic attack could be considered a UCS and the resulting fear a UCR. In some circumstances, if a person were driving (a previously neutral activity) and experienced multiple panic attacks, the act of driving it-

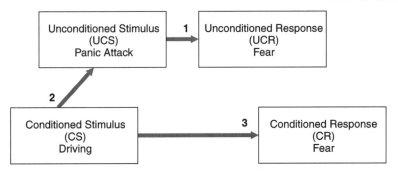

FIGURE 18.1. Representation of the Basic Respondent Conditioning Paradigm.

self (CS) could come to elicit fear (CR) even in the absence of an actual panic attack. In this example, there is a direct conditioning history of panic attacks and driving. The intervention of choice would be the presentation of the CS without the UCS. This is the application of the extinction principle for respondent conditioning. Wolpe's (1958) use of reciprocal inhibition is an application of extinction procedures for a variety of anxiety responses.

Operant Conditioning

The other type of direct conditioning that is often used as the basis of analysis of behavior in contemporary behavior therapy is operant conditioning (Skinner, 1938). For our purposes, we describe the familiar three-term contingency as follows:

$$S^D \bullet R \to S^R$$

In operant conditioning the S^D term indicates the discriminative stimulus, a stimulus in the presence of which the probability of a reinforcing consequence for a given behavior is greater than in its absence. Rather than being elicited, as in the respondent paradigm, the response R to the S^D is an emitted behavior that is under the control of the contingent stimulus S^R, frequently called the reinforcer. Thus, in the presence of a particular stimulus (or stimuli), a behavior is emitted. If it is followed by a reinforcing contingency, there is an increased probability that the response will be emitted again in the same or similar circumstances. If the behavior is emitted under particular stimulus conditions and then followed by a punishing contingency, there is a decreased likelihood that the same behavior will be emitted in the presence of the same or similar stimulus conditions.

Variations of this model add the notion of establishing operations to the three-term contingency. Establishing operations (EO) momentarily alter the reinforcing effectiveness of some event or stimulus (Michael, 1982, 1993a, 1993b). It is sometimes useful to think of establishing operations as motivational factors.

An operant is a behavior that operates on the environment (hence its name) in a characteristic manner. As an example of an operant, consider a situation in which a man wonders whether he should ask a woman out on a date. If the man looks at the woman's left ring finger and notices that there is no wedding or engagement ring, this could act as a discriminative stimulus for asking for a date. If he asks (the response in the presence of an apparently single woman) and the woman agrees (the reinforcing contingency), there is an increased likelihood that he will ask again under similar conditions. Notice that there are several ways in which this operant might fail to lead to a reinforcing consequence. First, the man may not recognize other stimulus features of the woman that might indicate that she was not likely to consent to an overture for a date. She may be avoiding eye contact or giving other social cues that she is not interested. Likewise, the man's behavioral repertoire may be deficient. He may appear to be pushy, overly confident, or otherwise undesirable. Finally, the woman's affirmative response may not act as a reinforcer if offered in a way that is unappealing ("Sure, I'd love to go out if the dinner is really expensive, but then I'll have to go right home because my boyfriend in California is calling me tonight").

Derived Stimulus Relations

Several modern behavior analytic approaches to human language take derived stimulus relations as their starting point. The experimental phenomenon originally emerged in the behavioral literature, using a matching-to-sample format (Sidman, Cresson, & Willson-Morris, 1974), and we describe the basic findings in those terms. In the standard experimental preparation, a sample stimulus (which could be anything, but here we suppose it is a graphical squiggle) is presented to a subject. The subject is then asked to select one of several comparison stimuli, none of which has any obvious formal similarity to the sample. Selection of one of the comparison stimuli is reinforced, and in the presence of other samples, selection of the other comparisons is reinforced. Of key importance is that even infants will show the bidirectional relation once a unidirectional relation is established (Lipkens et al., 1993). If A → B is trained, B → A will be derived. These bidirectionally derived stimulus relations can then combine into entire relational networks, and the psychological functions can move through that network, modified by the underlying relation.

There are many reasons to think that this process must be tracked separately from operant and classical conditioning (see Hayes & Hayes, 1992, for a review). Most important, organisms that come under the control of operant and classical contingencies do not necessarily show derived stimulus relations. To date, only humans do so. In addition, nothing in operant and classical conditioning would predict the outcomes achieved in the derived stimulus relations literature. Finally, even if deriving stimulus relations is a learned process, perhaps learned through operant contingencies (we would argue for that precise interpretation), it gives rise to forms of stimulus control that are otherwise unknown. Ironically, this means that there is a certain concordance between cognitive and contemporary behavioral perspectives: human language and cognition may indeed involve new behavioral processes. Equally ironically, it is the behavioral tradition that may be specifying precisely what those processes are.

Several lines of reasoning lead to the use of derived stimulus relations as a rough model of semantic meaning. First, derived stimulus relations are known to correlate with early indications of language performance (Barley et al., 1993; Devany et al., 1986; Dugdale & Lowe, 1990). Second, derived stimulus relation preparations are useful as language-training procedures (Sidman, 1971). Third, derived stimulus relations are arguably absent in nonverbal organisms (e.g.,

D'Amato, Salmon, Loukas, & Tomie, 1985; Dugdale & Lowe, 1990; Kendall, 1983; Lipkens, Kop, & Matthijs, 1988; Sidman, Rauzin, Lazar, Cunningham, Tailby, & Carrigan, 1982). Finally, derived stimulus relations produce behavior regulatory effects (reviewed earlier) that correspond with verbal regulatory effects.

Stimulus equivalence alone is not adequate as a model of semantic meaning, but if expanded it provides a good core of such a model. More recent research has shown that a wide variety of similarly derived stimulus relations occurs and that they combine into complex relational networks. This has been shown with relations of opposition (Steele & Hayes, 1991), difference (Steele & Hayes, 1991), and comparative relations such as greater than or less than (Dymond & Barnes, 1995). Thus, for example, those taught with sets of arbitrary stimuli to pick B given A, C given B, and D given C, in the presence of a cue that had earlier been established to control relations of opposition, will derive that A and D are opposite, but A and C are the same (i.e., the opposite of an opposite is the same; see Steele & Hayes, 1991). Relational frame theory (RFT) has provided a learning-based account of these multiply derived stimulus relations (Hayes, Gifford, & Wilson, 1996; Hayes & Hayes, 1992), but their exact nature and source are still being investigated. It is clear, however, that normal humans can bring a variety of stimulus relations to bear on arbitrary stimuli, given cues to do so.

The benefits of derived stimulus relations are considerable because they give humans the ability to acquire a great deal of what they know through indirect means. But it can also produce considerable problems. One of the most robust findings in the basic human operant literature is that verbal rules can produce rigid patterns of behavior that are frequently less sensitive to programmed contingencies than other forms of behavior (Hayes, Zettle, & Rosenfarb, 1989). This seems to be the result of at least two processes. First, verbal stimuli tend to excessively narrow the range of behavior available to contact contingencies (Hayes, Brownstein, Zettle, Rosenfarb, & Korn, 1986; Joyce & Chase, 1990). Second, verbal stimuli provide social standards against which behavior can be evaluated (e.g., Rosenfarb & Hayes, 1984; see Hayes et al., 1989, for a review).

An equally serious side effect is the tendency toward experiential avoidance. The bidirectionality of verbal knowledge means that self-awareness is painful when what is known is painful. For example, suppose a person recalls a trauma, say, an instance of sexual abuse. The original event was aversive, but now the verbal awareness and report of the event are aversive as well. This requires bidirectionality because classical conditioning and other unidirectional processes will not transfer the functions of the event that precedes the event that follows. That is, the functions of describing an aversive event, given only "event-description" training, will not be aversive by these direct learning processes, just as bell → food contingencies in classical conditioning do not alter the functions of the food but only those of the bell. Derived stimulus relations, however, are bidirectional. The tendency toward experiential avoidance is not a trivial matter because in a wide variety of clinical disorders experiential avoidance is known to play a part (Hayes, Wilson, Gifford, Follette, & Stroshahl, 1996).

METHODS IN CONTEMPORARY BEHAVIOR THERAPY: ASSESSMENT

The hallmark of contemporary behavior therapy is an individualized clinical assessment. This idiographic assessment is called functional analysis and has been described in several works (e.g., Hayes & Follette, 1992a, 1992b, 1993; Kanfer & Grimm, 1977; Kanfer & Saslow, 1969; Sturmey, 1996). We use the terms *functional analysis* and *functional assessment* interchangeably.

Functional assessment is the assessment and conceptualization of clinically relevant problem behaviors and their current and historical context to aid in selecting an appropriate intervention, to provide a means to monitor treatment progress, and to aid in the evaluation of the effectiveness of an intervention. In clinical practice, perhaps the primary standard of the quality of functional assessment is treatment utility: the demonstration that improved outcomes are achieved by the use of assessment as compared to its nonuse (Hayes, Nelson, & Jarret, 1987).

A schematic of the functional assessment process is shown in Figure 18.2. Step 1 in this process is familiar to most clinicians. At this point, the task is to identify the client's presenting problems and place them into some sort of hierarchy of clinical importance. In addition to a problem list, an evaluation of the client's assets and liabilities is made. Assets may include such features as functional social support, personal at-

tributes like financial resources and attractiveness, diversity in sources of social reinforcement, and robust health. Liabilities could entail such items as limited social opportunities, various disabilities, financial constraints, and legal problems.

The unique features of functional analysis become apparent in step 2. Here the functional analyst produces an analysis of the client's problems in terms of *behavioral principles.* Based on this application of behavioral principles, an intervention strategy is derived as shown in step 3. Once a principle-based intervention has been formulated, it is then implemented in step 4. The assessment of outcome begins in step 5 and then occurs continuously throughout treatment. The resultant outcome is repeatedly judged for adequacy in step 6. If the treatment is successful, as-

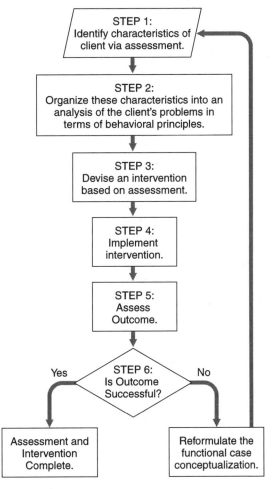

Classical Functional Analysis

FIGURE 18.2. Flow Diagram of a Functional Analysis.

sessment and intervention are complete. If not, the entire cycle is repeated. Successive iterations are usually more time-efficient because the assessment is based on much greater familiarity with the client, the situation, and assets.

Functional assessment is a well-established procedure, but there is still no precise direction about the kinds of things that should be attended to in this process. Haynes and O'Brien (1990) have suggested focusing on variables that are important, controllable, and causally related to the client's presenting problems. By important, Haynes and O'Brien mean that the variable in question could explain a significant portion of the variability in the presenting problem. For example, in increasing self-reported marital satisfaction for a couple, talking about emotional content in the relationship might be more important than reducing television watching. Controllability focuses the analysis on events that are current and manipulable. This does not preclude the examination of history, but it is not the dead history that would be important, only the history that is alive and in the present. For example, it is not sufficient to say that childhood sexual abuse explains a failure to sustain intimacy. Rather, one would have to specify how current events maintain the impact of this history in the present. Finally, causality means simply that a variable covaries with problem behavior and that upon manipulation of that variable, the target behavior changes. Of course, this is often not known in advance, but functional analyses can build on knowledge derived from previous analyses with others to make plausible guesses in that regard.

Functional Classification and Treatment Utility

The hallmark of functional assessment is an interest in treatment utility. For an assessment method to have treatment utility, there must be known and significant variation between treatments at the level of functional processes, assessment must detect at least some of the functional processes involved, and treatment must vary systematically and coherently with assessment. None of these characteristics pertains to the current DSM-IV nosology (e.g., Follette & Houts, 1996). First, treatment varies widely, but the differences in processes are unknown. Second, syndromal classification has no known relation to functional processes in almost every area of the current nosology. Finally, treatment varies more with the training of therapists than with assess-

ment. Cognitive-behavior therapy, for example, seems to work at least to a degree with almost every syndromal category of psychopathology. In this situation, there is little to be gained in terms of treatment outcome by syndromal classification.

This line of reasoning also suggests several instances when functional analysis should not be used (see Follette, Naugle, & Linnerooth, in press, for a discussion of limitations on demonstrating treatment utility). First, if standardized treatment packages are required in a given setting, based on symptom topography, then there is no reason to do functional analysis. Second, if a simple topographical analysis leads to effective treatment, there is likewise no reason to do functional analysis. For example, if most simple phobias are successfully treated by exposure, then the task is simply to deliver the treatment, not to understand the origin of the fear in a more detailed way. Third, if the problem has no known treatment, then functional analysis is useful only as an experimental tool, not a clinical tool per se. Fourth, if there are inexpensive packages that cover the range of treatment alternatives that might be applied, there is no reason to pursue a more detailed analysis. The empirical impact of this issue on treatment matching has been noted elsewhere (McKnight, Nelson, Hayes, & Jarrett, 1984).

Limitations of Functional Assessment

Given the long behavioral tradition behind functional analysis, it is worth considering why it has not become a staple of psychological assessment. There are several legitimate reasons. First, there is only a limited database showing that functional analysis can improve treatment outcome (for an example in this area, see Anderson, Freeman, & Scotti, 1999). Second, we know of no data that show that functional assessment is cost-effective. Third, functional analysis is still more of an art than a science because it is too poorly specified to be reliable and replicable (Hayes & Follette, 1992b) except in highly constrained circumstances, such as the identification of reinforcers with developmentally disabled populations (e.g., Iwata, 1994a, 1994b; Iwata et al., 1994). Thus, there is no clearly specified set of principles to be applied and no clear method of identifying a treatment plan.

Many possible solutions have been suggested (e.g., see Hayes & Follette, 1992b), but none have yet been tested. It seems likely that functional assessment will never come into its own until a functional classification system of known treatment utility has evolved. In the meantime, however, functional assessment seems to be more clinically useful to behavior therapists than alternative diagnostic systems.

METHODS IN CONTEMPORARY BEHAVIOR THERAPY: INTERVENTION

We have already described both operant and respondent conditioning. Clinical behavior analysts have often tried to understand clinical problems in terms of the difficulties that might arise from problems in the learning histories or environments of clients. Rather than attend to the typography of a client's presenting problem, the topography should be merely a starting point for identifying the relevant behavioral principles that need to be used to effect clinical change. Such an approach leads to a very different way of organiz-

ing problems than the syndromal approach used in DSM-IV.

Tables 18.1–18.3 provide a sample of problems and treatments as they might be conceptualized and organized from a behavior therapy perspective. The tables are arranged according to problems with different stimulus functions. Table 18.1 lists samples of difficulties with discriminative functions; Table 18.2 lists problems with response functions; and Table 18.3 lists problems with reinforcing or contingent functions. In the left most column of each table is an abstract behavioral concept that could be the source of clinical difficulties. This concept is rephrased more discursively in the next column. In the third column, an example or two is given of a clinical problem that might arise because of these behavioral processes. In the right most column, one or two behavioral treatments that might address these difficulties are listed. These tables are not meant to be comprehensive, either in principles,

TABLE 18.1 Behavioral Analysis of Clinical Problems and Interventions for Discriminative Stimulus Functions

Stimulus Domain Problem: *Discriminative Control*			
Functional Problem	**Description**	**Specific Problem Example**	**Possible Interventions**
Defective stimulus control	Response emitted under wrong conditions	Client gives too much interpersonal information for a given occasion	Social skills training
Discrimination deficits of private events	Person doesn't accurately tact (label) feelings	Client mislabels lust as love	Training in self-labeling
Inappropriate self-generated stimulus control; poor self-labeling	Self-generated cues for behavior lead to poor outcomes	Person inappropriately limits or emits behavior by under- or overestimating ability	Behavioral rehearsal
Overly rigid rule governance	Client is not under contingent control of environment or sensitive to environmental changes	Client does not see actual relationship between behavior and consequences	ACT (acceptance and commitment therapy)
Inffective arrangement of contingencies	Immediate environment not arranged to usefully control behavior	Inefficient dietary management; problems with schoolwork	Stimulus control and problem-solving training

TABLE 18.2 Behavioral Analysis of Clinical Problems and Interventions for Response Functions

Stimulus Domain Problem: *Response Problems*			
Functional Problem	Description	Specific Problem Example	Possible Interventions
Deficient or ineffective behavioral repertoire	Behaviors do not lead to reinforcement	Poor social skills, parental skills deficits, social isolation, and assertion deficits	FAP (functional analytic psychotherapy); parent effectiveness training
Aversive behavioral repertoire	Exhibits behavioral excesses or controlling behaviors that others find aversive	Aggressive or coercive behavior	Self-control training
Inappropriate conditioned emotional response	Has a classically conditioned response	Phobia and excessive fear	Exposure; modeling
Excessive self-monitoring of behavior	Is overly concerned with form of behavior rather than function	Perfectionism that impairs efficiency; obsessive-compulsive behavior	Thought stopping; response prevention
Behavioral excess	Exhibits excess behavior that interferes with access to reinforcers	Panic/anxiety; obsessive-compulsive behavior	Systematic desensitization; flooding; panic control therapy

problems, or treatments, but they give a small sample of some of the kinds of problems and procedures that are relevant to behavior therapy. Because of space limitations, it is not possible to describe in detail these procedures, but we do consider a few examples.

As one can see, once one identifies the applicable principle that establishes or maintains problematic behavior, the intervention is often self-evident, although sometimes difficult to actually implement. The basic principles themselves are straightforward. We briefly review some examples of broad classes of behavioral interventions before we describe recent innovations in contemporary behavior therapy.

Contingency Management

Contingency management procedures have long been the staple of applied clinical behavior analysis. The term describes a broad collection of procedures that include such reinforcement procedures as the shaping of successive approxi-

mations, token economies, time-out, and in some instances even the selective use of punishment to terminate self-destructive behavior.

Two classic examples of the application of contingency management procedures are the treatments for childhood autism (Bijou & Baer, 1961; Lovaas, 1977) and the management of the severely, chronically mentally ill inpatients by using a token economy (e.g., Allyon & Azrin, 1968). In both instances dramatic clinical improvements were observed following the application of contingency management procedures in previously intractable populations.

Childhood autism is characterized by profound disturbances in social relations and language with concurrent high rates of self-stimulatory and self-destructive behaviors. Prior to the application of behavioral principles, including contingency management, autistic children were often institutionalized. Because of the severity of their symptoms, many were functionally mute and others had to be physically restrained in their

TABLE 18.3 Behavioral Analysis of Clinical Problems and Interventions for Reinforcing Stimulus Functions

Stimulus Domain Problem: *Problems with Reinforcing Contingencies*			
Functional Problem	**Description**	**Specific Problem Example**	**Possible Interventions**
Behavior ineffectively controlled	Commonly controlling social/legal contingencies don't sufficiently reinforce or restrict behavior	Antisocial behavior	Establishment of conditioned reinforcers; environmental restriction
Inappropriate contingent control	Reinforcers socially unacceptable or lead to unacceptable outcomes for client or others	Pedophilia; substance abuse	Self-control training; social skills training; environmental restriction
Insufficient environmental reinforcement	Reinforcement of appropriate behaviors lacking	Living in social situation where some prosocial behavior isn't adequately supported	Pleasant activities planning and social skills training; environmental restructuring
Restricted range of reinforcement	Has limited set of reinforcing stimuli	Excessively dependent relationships; vulnerability to depression	Reinforcer sampling
Noncontingent reinforcement	Receives significant reinforcement for inadequate performance	Spoiled; school or work difficulties	Parent training; business management training
Overly punitive environment	Behavior is under aversive control rather than positive control	Mistrust; overcaution; misses opportunity for expanding behavioral repertoire	Social skills training; relationship-oriented approach
Excessively stringent self-reinforcement strategies	Standards set too high	Perfectionism; frequently disappointed in self or others	Self-instructional training; discrimination training
Excessive schedule dependence	Behavior is too dependent on high rates of reinforcement	Insecurity; easily frustrated and gives up too easily; doesn't attempt complex new skills	Self-control procedures; reinforcement schedule management

beds to minimize severe self-injurious behavior that frequently resulted in deafness, blindness, or brain damage in unrestrained autistic children. Children who were restrained experienced significant mortality from the consequences of being tied in bed for days at a time.

By applying operant principles, Lovaas (1977) was able to minimize or extinguish self-injurious behavior and subsequently establish language in a significant proportion of children. By reinforcing successive approximations of desired verbal behavior, Lovaas gradually moved from teaching the children to repeat words spoken to them (echolalia) to the establishment of a more complex vocabulary and finally to syntax and grammar. In subsequent studies, Lovaas (1987) was even able to establish normal or near normal social functioning by using intensive behavior therapy.

A similar dramatic success can be seen in the work of Allyon and Azrin (1968), who investigated the effects of altering the behavior of chronically psychotic patients who had been hospitalized for an average of approximately 13 years. Their intervention was to train the staff to ignore inappropriate behavior and reinforce appropriate behavior using tokens that were redeemable for items sold in a small store or for additional privileges. Dramatic improvements were noted in the use of these contingent management procedures. The benefits observed accrued to both patients and staff. These results have been replicated and refined by Gordon Paul (Paul & Lentz, 1977; Paul & Menditto, 1992).

Although these kinds of contingency management programs can produce dramatic beneficial effects, they require considerable control over the environment to produce large-magnitude changes. As a result, the major applications of contingency management programs have been in the treatment of institutionalized patients and the developmentally disabled and in effective parenting programs.

Exposure-based Interventions

Whereas contingency management programs follow an operant paradigm, exposure-based treatments are more closely tied to classical or respondent conditioning paradigms. Following the experimental work of Watson and Rayner (1920), which suggested that anxiety could be classically conditioned, and Mowrer's (1939) two-factor model, explaining why extinction did not readily occur, the development of treatments for anxiety has occupied behavior therapists for over thirty years.

The fundamental notion behind the behavioral treatment of fear and anxiety is that these are classically conditioned responses that should be extinguished when the client is exposed to the condition stimulus (the phobic object) without being exposed to the unconditioned stimulus. Mowrer (1939) argued that this extinction does not occur because the persons learn to avoid the phobic object; as they approach the conditioned stimulus, they become more fearful, and the subsequent escape and avoidance of the phobic object is negatively reinforced by the reduction of anxiety. Thus extinction does not occur because the persons do not experience the conditioned stimulus in the absence of the unconditioned stimulus, which would normally lead to the extinction of the conditioned fear response.

Forty years ago, Wolpe (1958) developed the exposure procedure called reciprocal inhibition, which has subsequently evolved into systematic desensitization. The treatment involves the graded exposure of fear-eliciting stimuli while the client engages in an alternative fear-incompatible response. Typically this incompatible response is relaxation.

Systematic desensitization involves three key steps: the construction of an anxiety hierarchy, training of an alternative response, and gradual exposure to the elements of the anxiety hierarchy either in vivo or by using imagery (see Goldfried & Davison, 1994, Chap. 6, for a complete description). Although the theoretical underpinnings of desensitization are not without weaknesses (e.g., see Blackledge & Hayes, in preparation), the general efficacy of the procedure is well established and the key feature of exposure seems to be the fear-eliciting stimuli in the absence of negative consequences, regardless of the order of presentation of items in the desensitization hierarchy (Emmelkamp, 1982; Emmelkamp & Kuipers, 1979).

Providing in vivo exposure to interoceptive cues has become increasingly important in the treatment of panic disorders (Barlow & Craske, 1989; Barlow, Craske, Cerny, & Klosko, 1989). Because persons with panic disorders frequently report feeling dizzy and they experience tachycardia, exposure exercises may include activities that induce these symptoms (e.g., running up stairs, CO_2 inhalation, or even twirling around until dizzy). Other interventions use even more dramatic procedures. For example, Stampl and Levis (1967) described implosion therapy, in which clients who manifest obsessive-compulsive discomfort about germs and the need to wash their hands may have their hands placed in a wastebasket full of coffee grounds, dirt, pencil shavings, and so on for long periods of time without an opportunity to escape or wash. Again, the key element in these kinds of interventions is exposure in the absence of a negative outcome.

Self-control Procedures

Contingency management strategies have been modified for use by individuals themselves in what are usually termed *self-control procedures*. These procedures are usually helpful when the short-term consequences of an action support a behavior that differs from that under long-term contingent control. For example, the short-term consequences of smoking may be immediately reinforcing through the reduction in nicotine craving and the reduction of anxiety, but the long-term consequences can include illness and death. These kinds of competing contingencies lead to what is termed a *behavioral trap* because the short-term consequences support behavior that is ultimately harmful. In contrast, a *behavioral fence* is a situation in which the short-term consequences of a behavior are aversive but the long-term consequences are positive. An example would be (for some people) exercise, for which tiredness and discomfort operate in the short term and increased health and cardiovascular fitness in the long term. To overcome such problems, clinicians might try to arrange for immediate discriminative cues that will strengthen the desired response. For the person having difficulty in jogging, scheduling the same time and place each day and arranging for a companion, while at the same time making sure that all other distracters are absent, can make the short-term contingencies support the long-term ones rather than compete with them.

What underlies the effectiveness of self-control procedures appears to be the proximal social contingencies. Thus, stating a goal publicly can have powerful social effects, whereas stating the same goal privately (i.e., no one else knows the goal exists) has minimal effects. Publicly stated goals alter the more immediate short-term contingencies because others respond differently to behaviors if they know whether or not a goal is being kept (Hayes, Rosenfarb, Wulfert, Munt, Zettle, & Korn, 1985).

Response Acquisition Procedures

In Table 18.2 we listed problems with ineffective behavioral repertoires. A common example of this problem is someone who exhibits ineffective social skills. By far the most commonly studied approach to teaching social skills to clinical populations involves a topographical analysis of social skills. This approach begins with the premise that is it both possible and desirable to identify the molecular behaviors that make up socially skillful behavior. Often the salient behaviors relevant to social skills are studied in both the clinical population (e.g., inpatients with schizophrenia) and skilled normal subjects. The behaviors are generally elicited from role-playing situations or conversations with confederates. Differences in repertoires are identified, with the intention of subsequently establishing those behaviors seen in the normal population that are absent in the clinical subjects. One might see that given our preference for valuing function over topography, contemporary behavior therapists have noted problems with this approach.

Rule Teaching and Following

Implicit in this approach is the assumption that the rules we might deduce from the study of skilled individuals are both correct and universally applicable to other individuals who are not skilled. On logical grounds, this is unlikely. The skilled individuals one studies are seen under limited circumstances so that there is no way to be certain that a sufficiently broad set of behaviors has been identified and taught. Beyond that, there is no compelling reason to believe that the skills that function well for one person are the ones that would work best for another. Are the skills used by a young, average-weight female the same ones that should be used by an older, obese male? Probably not.

There are other important problems with topographical skills training and rule following. For example, adherence to rules may make one insensitive to changing contingencies in the immediate environment. Behavioral research has shown that when people learn and follow rules in a changing environment, they are less able to recognize when their rules are no longer accurately representing the way contingencies operate (Hayes et al., 1986). Rule following becomes primary instead of tracking how the environment actually works.

But there is an even larger problem in teaching skills by the identify and training method. Though no one has claimed to have done so, let's assume that one could actually identify the 10 rules of successful social functioning. In real life, one does not follow a list of rules top down, but rather one has to select which subset of the 10 rules to follow and in which of the possible orders the behavior should be used. If one has to select all possible subsets and consider all possible orders, that results in 9,864,100 permutations of the combinations of the 10 original rules. It is obvious that teaching universally skillful behaviors is not possible, and years of research have provided empirical support for this conclusion.

Effectiveness as the Criterion Measure

One of the major difficulties in the social skills literature was the long-standing emphasis on teaching the proper topography or form of skillful behavior rather than effectiveness directly. The assumption has been that if less skilled people mimic the formal behavior of more skilled people, they will then be socially effective. In our opinion such an approach misses the point of social skills-training goals. It is social effectiveness that matters, not how one physically attempts to attain it. There are many ways in which one can make a good first impression, get a date, have a good job interview, and so on. To assume that another person can mimic behavior and have the same outcome is dubious at best. McFall (1982) recognized that merely attending to the formal properties of behavior missed the point because of the principle of equifinality, which he defines as "more than one good way to do something" (p. 17). He goes on to say, "In fact, the ultimate criterion for evaluating performance is its outcome or effect."

Learning Social Skills

In teaching social skills, it is useful to speculate about how skills, social or otherwise, are normally learned. From a behavior analytic perspective there is ample evidence to believe that skills are shaped and selected on the basis of the effect they have on the environment. The law of effect is one of the most well-researched principles in psychology. Operant conditioning principles are effective in shaping a variety of complex behaviors.

Watching young children on a playground suggests how social skills are learned. Johnny approaches Mary and says, "Gimme the ball." Mary says, "No; go away, Meanie." Johnny goes away for a moment and tries again. "Mary, let me have the ball, and you can chew this piece of gum I'm almost done with." Mary rebuffs him again, saying, "You are never nice to me. Go away." Finally Johnny says, "Mary, can I please play with you." And Mary agrees.

Without submitting these interactions to a technical analysis, it is sufficient to say that Johnny tries several approaches for achieving a goal. He tried and was clearly not reinforced for his initial efforts. A behavior is emitted and punished. The contingency is clear—Mary says no. It happens twice, and each time Johnny attempts a behavior, sees it doesn't work, and tries a new behavior after briefly licking his wounds. Ultimately

he finds an approach that allows him to accomplish the goal of playing with the ball. This is trial-and-error learning, and all that is theoretically necessary is that Johnny gets immediate feedback on whether his approach works.

In adulthood, regardless of the reason someone is not socially effective, the learning of a social repertoire still depends on people selecting from their behavioral repertoire, emitting a behavior, and keeping or refining the behavior according to its consequences.

Experimental work has suggested that teaching complex social skills might better be accomplished by teaching subjects to discriminate among the effects of their behavior on others and selecting and refining those that function successfully. Notice that the emphasis shifts from teaching specific behaviors to training subjects to discern the impact they are having, given their stated social goal. It is up to the subjects to select which topography they will emit from their entire repertoire of behaviors. The criterion against which clinical progress is measured is the improvement in effecting the desired social goal. There is experimental evidence that such contingency-shaped training procedures may be effective in teaching complex social behaviors. Initial work has produced some success in using a contingent-shaping approach in socially unskilled subjects (Azrin & Hayes, 1984), schizophrenics (Follette, 1992; Follette, Dougher, Dykstra, Compton, & Naugle, 1992; Follette, Dykstra, & Compton, 1992), and even psychotherapists (Follette & Callaghan, 1995). Thus, contemporary clinical behavior therapy, resting firmly on behavioral principles, seems to be producing progress where little has existed for several years.

The above overview of some of the long-standing behavioral principles and behavior-changing techniques is meant to give an overview of behavior therapy in general terms. In the next section, we briefly describe entirely new therapies that derive from long-standing and newly studied behavioral principles.

INNOVATIVE PSYCHOTHERAPIES IN CONTEMPORARY BEHAVIOR THERAPY

Several recent psychotherapeutic innovations are good examples of contemporary behavior therapy as defined here. We describe four, each of which was mentioned previously: functional analytic psychotherapy (FAP; Kohlenberg & Tsai, 1991), dialectical behavior therapy (DBT; Linehan, 1993a), integrative couple's therapy (ICT; Jacobson & Christensen, 1996), and acceptance and commitment therapy (ACT; Hayes et al., 1999). Each has its own distinct history. We briefly describe the nature of the approach and show that it fits the characteristics of contemporary behavior therapy as described here: treatments that attempt to apply behavioral principles to clinical problems and are also contextualistic; functionalistic; nonreductionistic; and concerned with private events and the therapeutic relationship, not just overt behavior.

Functional Analytic Psychotherapy (FAP)

Developed by Kohlenberg and Tsai (1991), FAP was originally designed to treat outpatients with a variety of interpersonal difficulties, including depression, anxiety, and personality disorders, that did not seem to respond to more traditional interventions, including cognitive therapy. The developers of this treatment recognized that the relationship themes that were the focus of psychodynamic therapy were clinically important but that psychodynamic accounts of therapy were based on an inadequate theoretical and scientific analysis. Thus, Kohlenberg and Tsai set out to use the principles of applied behavior analysis to modify complex interpersonal behavior, using the therapeutic relationship to identify clinically important behaviors and then to effect change. A functional analysis is used to understand what sorts of factors lead a client to behave in a particular way under a particular set of circumstances. Then, employing principles of reinforcement and generalization, the therapist begins to shape clinical improvements in client's behaviors by using an intense, curative therapeutic relationship as a means of shaping change. Clients appropriate for FAP are those who are likely to manifest a clinical problem during therapy and to be affected by the therapist's reactions.

There are three major components and several subcomponents in FAP. The first component is the establishment of a therapeutic relationship that is meaningful to the client. It follows that a relationship that is meaningful to the client is by necessity meaningful to the therapist. Because FAP focuses on interpersonal problems that are expected to appear during therapy, the key natural reinforcer to bring about and sustain clinical change is the positive reaction of the therapist to

therapeutic improvement. Kohlenberg and Tsai (1991) establish a genuine, honest, and caring relationship in which the therapist is committed to supporting the client's effort to change while at the same time honestly responding to the effect the client's behavior is having on him or her at any particular time. It is recognized that appropriate interpersonal responding is the natural reinforcer for successful relationships. Kohlenberg and Tsai correctly recognize that natural rather than arbitrary reinforcers (Ferster, 1967) will sustain generalized behavior change outside of therapy. Follette et al. (1996) have described their view of how the therapeutic relationship functions to initially support the general class of necessary therapy behaviors, such as just being in therapy and supporting the effort to change. As time goes on, more specific contingent reinforcement is provided that shapes closer approximations of targeted behaviors.

The second major component of FAP is the continuous functional analysis of clinically relevant behaviors (CRBs), which include both problem behaviors and desirable behaviors. The FAP therapists presume that their behavior will affect the clients through some direct contingent learning that is clearly grounded in operant and respondent conditioning. The therapists' in-session behavior is assumed to affect the clients by serving as a discriminative function, an eliciting function, or a reinforcing function. The therapist may function as a discriminative stimulus by asking a question such as "What's going on right now?" This sets the occasion for the client to respond in a socially useful manner. The therapist may serve an eliciting function when the client gets angry after the therapist asks, "Why were you late to this session?" Finally, if a useful therapeutic relationship has developed, the therapist can serve a reinforcer function for change. For example, a therapist may reinforce a client who has had difficulty expressing emotion when the client says, "It really makes me angry when therapy doesn't start on time" if the therapist acknowledges the problem and subsequently starts sessions more promptly.

Three types of CRBs are defined in FAP. A CRB1 is a client's problem that occurs in session. These are what would typically be thought of as the client's presenting problems, which should decrease in frequency as therapy progresses. For example, a client who has difficulty in forming close relationships and complains of feeling isolated may show a variety of behaviors that interfere with relationship formation. These can include being overly critical, interrupting others, or appearing to ignore what another person has just said. Each of these behaviors could be expected to occur during therapy and, with the appropriate contingent responding of the therapist, could be expected to decrease.

A CRB2 is an improvement in a client's behavior that occurs in session. In the previous example, the client may say to the therapist, "I've been waiting for you to say something, Doc, because you seem a little quiet today." The client's response shows attentiveness and patience, which are indicative of clinical improvement. The skilled FAP therapist would recognize this improvement and express genuine pleasure. The therapist may even naturally disclose why he or she is quieter than usual. As therapy progresses, one would expect to see an increase in CRB2s.

The CRB3s are instances of functional interpretations by clients of their own behaviors. That is, during the course of FAP, clients will come to understand the situations that give rise to both problematic and more useful behaviors in natural situations. When clients can describe the conditions under which behaviors will occur or fail to occur, they have shown a functional understanding of their environment. These are CRB3s and help the client understand and function effectively. The CRB3s are also shaped during therapy. Imagine the following hypothetical exchange.

Therapist: So, we've been talking about what it's like for you to go out looking for someone to get to know better. How's that been going?

Client: Like you'd really care.

Therapist: Whoa. Where did that come from?

In this exchange, the client is being prompted to recognize (discriminate) the conditions that gave rise to a rather off-putting response on his part. A discussion would ensue in which the therapist and client would try to functionally understand the exchange.

The therapist could respond contingently to the effect the client had on him. The above conversation could also proceed along the following therapeutic path:

Therapist: So, we've been talking about what it's like for you to go out looking for someone to get to know better. How's that been going?

Client: Like you'd really care.

Therapist: I'm confused. I was trying to under

stand what your experience of trying to date is like, and you responded in a way that could easily lead me to think you don't think I care, or perhaps you don't value the work we've been doing. I'm curious about whether that is what you intended to communicate.

Client: Sometimes I just get frustrated with you thinking all this is so easy.

Therapist: So you intended to express frustration with me?

Client: I guess so. Yes.

Therapist: Being able to tell me or anyone that you're frustrated with that person is useful. I'm all for doing that, but since what you said didn't communicate frustration to me as much as it did being dismissive, why don't you give it another try?

Client: Okay. Sometimes I just get frustrated with you.

Therapist: Much better. I didn't find myself getting annoyed with you. But it occurs to me that I still don't know why you're frustrated. Can you try it once more?

Client: When you describe a major problem in my life and then say, "So how's that going?" I feel like you think it's no big deal. It really *is* a big deal to me. Do you really know that?

Therapist: I do know that. I know it better now that you've told me in that way. It gives me a chance to tell you that I have some understanding of what you are going through, but I can't really walk in your shoes. I'm glad you told me what's really up. It gives me a chance to express my appreciation of your struggle better. Are there other times you wish I would do things differently?

Although we do not dissect each line in these two scenarios, it should be obvious that the therapeutic relationship provides opportunities for the therapist to be a discriminative stimulus, an eliciting stimulus, and a reinforcing stimulus almost simultaneously. At the same time, the client learns to recognize these functions for oneself and others.

Notice two things. First, unlike the traditional psychoanalytic conceptualization of the therapeutic relationship, which views the interpersonal processes between the client and therapist as a metaphor for some other unresolved relationship, FAP assumes that the client-therapist relationship itself is important. It is assumed that both problem behaviors and improvements are samples of clinically relevant behavior that has an important impact on the client's life outside of therapy. Second, unlike the notion of unconditional positive regard (Rogers, 1957), the FAP therapist unconditionally supports the client's effort to change but contingently responds to the function any change effort has on him or her. The therapist makes clear that the goal of therapy can only be attained if the client tries alternative behaviors and gets accurate feedback on their impact from the therapist.

It is apparent from the discussion of CRBs that the therapist is constantly conducting a functional analysis of the client's behavior. This analysis requires the therapist to postulate response classes, hypothesize about controlling variables, and discriminate among clinical improvements even when they are subtle. That is, FAP relies on direct conditioning principles and teaches the client to do the same.

To know what kinds of behaviors to augment or diminish, the therapist engages in a process of values clarification. Its purpose is to have the clients define those classes of behaviors that they find reinforcing and meaningful. Unless they can articulate those things to themselves, the clients cannot effectively let others in their environment know how they like to be treated and how they should learn to treat others.

Thus FAP has taken on a complex clinical subject matter, suboptimal interpersonal functioning, and applied behavioral principles to understanding how the therapeutic relationship can be understood and used to establish lasting change. It is an intensive, interpersonal therapy that requires a sophisticated assessment and behavior-shaping repertoire on the part of the therapist. As is typical of the other examples of contemporary behavior therapy, important clinical problems are being addressed by the use of the traditional values of the scientific study of behavior, and the effort seems to be paying dividends.

Dialectical Behavior Therapy (DBT)

A treatment designed for parasuicidal behavior (Linehan, 1984), DBT (Linehan, 1993a; Linehan, Armstrong, Suarez, Allmon, & Heard, 1991) has been applied effectively to borderline personality disorder (Linehan, 1993a), dissociative disorders (Barley et al., 1993), and drug abuse (Linehan, 1993b). Linehan describes clinical issues in terms of dialectics, in which an initial thesis is supplanted by its contradiction or antithesis, and finally by a synthesis, in which the apparent contradiction is resolved. In borderline personality disorder, for example, the primary dialectics identified in DBT are emotional vulnerability vs. self-invalidation, unrelenting crisis vs. inhibited grieving, and active passivity vs. apparent competence. It is the therapeutic task of DBT to work toward a synthesis of the two poles to undermine wide swings between them.

The intervention components designed to accomplish this are varied, distinct not so much in their form as in their purpose and overall coordinating logic. For example, DBT involves an extensive program of skills training, in which specific social and coping skills are targeted for acquisition or increases. Skills training is not unusual in behavior therapy, but DBT includes a number of unusual specific skills designed to help resolve dialectical processes. Mindfulness meditation skills are used, for instance, to help the client have a greater capacity to tolerate previously intolerable emotions, such as shame, guilt, or anger. Mindfulness is a focused, attentive, nonevaluative style of observation in the service of responding effectively to the situation. Difficult emotions are then deliberately sought out in therapy, so that the client can have the experience of contacting previously overwhelming emotions without running away or acting out and while practicing more adaptive coping skills. It is important that "maladaptive coping responses, including escape responses and other action tendencies, are blocked by the DBT therapist" (Linehan, 1993a, p. 344) to avoid automatic sources of reinforcement for maladaptive responding. The goal is often "tolerating emotions rather than changing them" (p. 347), although emotional change methods are also used in some circumstances. The therapeutic relationship established in DBT is deliberately intense but is used contingently. For example, clients may be given unusual access to therapists through phone contacts or beepers, but dramatically maladaptive behavior may result in *less* therapist contact rather than more.

Quite clearly DBT is a part of the innovative wave of contemporary behavior therapy. Behavioral principles are used deliberately throughout. Problems are defined and analyzed functionally, and a conscious attempt is made to orient toward the contextual features that define behavior as functional or nonfunctional. For example, emotions and thoughts are major targets of intervention, but the primary issue is not the form of these events but their function in a context. For that reason, emotional tolerance can be as important as emotional change: a clear example of concern for function over form. Finally, the therapeutic relationship is given significant attention.

Integrative Couple Therapy (ICT)

The development of ICT, which also combines elements of direct and indirect contingency learning (Jacobson & Christensen, 1996), followed the recognition that there was a substantial amount of marital distress that simply didn't succumb to traditional behavioral therapy (Jacobson & Margolin, 1979). Traditional behavioral marital therapy (BMT) used problem-solving and communications training and behavior exchange techniques in the assumption that marital dissatisfaction was a result of deficits in instrumental communication skills and inadequate mutual reinforcement. Whereas a significant number of couples did respond to this type of intervention, many cases did not (Jacobson, Follette, Revenstorf, Baucom, Hahlweg, & Margolin, 1984).

Jacobson and Christensen (1996) integrated several important notions of indirect verbal contingency learning into more traditional BMT. They describe a therapy in which couples change what is possible and then accept those aspects of the other and the relationship that cannot be changed. They are careful to draw a distinction between acceptance as resignation and acceptance as "letting go of the struggle to generate change in one's partner" (p. 14). They argue that acceptance can help couples by generating greater intimacy, using the conflict area to do so, generating tolerance, and generating change. Also, ICT makes considerable use of the distinction between rule-governed and contingency-shaped behavior (described earlier). The developers of the therapy recognize that the latter produces behaviors that are more flexible.

Once again we see in ICT some of the hallmarks of contemporary behavior therapy: the careful behavioral rationale and the emphasis on context and function over form. The use of acceptance procedures are a clear indication of this because it suggests that the form of an event is not inherently problematic. Emotions and thoughts are given equal emphasis with overt behavior, and the therapeutic relationship is given significant attention.

Acceptance and Commitment Therapy (ACT)

The psychotherapy approach of ACT (said as one word, not initials) is consciously based on functional contextualism and on clinical behavior analytic thinking as described in this chapter (Hayes, 1984, 1987; Hayes et al., 1999; Hayes & Wilson, 1993, 1994). Controlled research has shown that ACT produces positive clinical outcomes in a wide variety of adult disorders (e.g., Strosahl, Hayes, Bergan, & Romano, 1998; see Hayes et al., 1999, for a review). It pays particularly close attention to principles drawn from the study of derived stimulus relations. Like ICT and DBT, ACT takes a contextual approach to unwanted feelings and thoughts and often promotes acceptance in these areas rather than change. It pays perhaps even more attention to altering the contexts in which thoughts have literal meaning.

A core assumption in ACT is that verbal functions naturally lead to the avoidance of private events (Hayes & Gifford, 1997). For example, a person with a history of abuse will have difficulty when remembering the abuse because some of the psychological functions originally present will transfer to verbal awareness of the past through the bidirectional transfer of stimulus functions. It is a natural step, then, to avoid thinking about the abuse in order to "feel better."

This same process leads readily to the avoidance of a wide variety of unpleasant private events, a language-based tendency that is then greatly exacerbated by social processes. For example, it is not uncommon for even very young children to be told to "stop being afraid" or "stop crying or I'll give you something to cry about." Unfortunately, many of the means that are readily available to reduce or avoid private events cause other problems. A sexually abused person can avoid memory of the abuse by avoiding intimate relationships, for example, but at considerable cost. Thoughts or emotions can be avoided or suppressed but often at the cost of a paradoxical increase in these very thoughts or emotions in the long term. The usual course of ACT covers six stages.

The first stage, called *creative hopelessness*, essentially puts traditional, verbally guided problem-solving strategies on extinction to generate more innovative behavior. What the clients "think they need to do" is usually exactly what they *have* done; thus a real solution must lie outside that which initially seems reasonable. A direct change agenda, misapplied to the world inside the skin, needs to be put aside simply because it has not worked and will not work.

In the second stage, the misapplication of control is highlighted as a key problem. Here is a brief metaphor that captures some of the quality of this phase of ACT.

Therapist: Suppose I had you hooked up to the best polygraph machine that's ever been built. This is a perfect machine, the most sensitive ever made. When you are all wired up to it there is no way you can be aroused or anxious without my knowing it. So you have a very simple task here: all you have to do is stay relaxed. But I want to give you an incentive to do so, so I'm going to hold a pistol against your head. If you just stay relaxed, I won't blow your brains out, but if you get nervous I'm going to have to kill you. So just relax. . . . What do you think would happen?

This metaphor points to an extremely common clinical situation: a client is trying to follow a verbal rule that says that reduction in anxiety (for example) is necessary *or else*. Unfortunately, the natural response to imminent negative consequences is anxiety, not relaxation, and so the control effort is self-undermining.

In the third stage of ACT, the therapist uses experiential exercises and metaphors to help the client distinguish between the person who is aware of private events and the events known. This sense of "I" is important because it provides a basis from which acceptance of undesirable emotions or thoughts is possible without personal threat (see Hayes, 1984, for a behavioral analysis of this issue).

In the fourth stage of ACT, clients are taught emotional willingness and cognitive deliteralization skills. For example, ACT therapists ask clients at least temporally to adopt a particular verbal style in therapy, such as saying, "I am having the thought that I can't go to the mall" instead of simply stating, "I can't go to the mall." A variety of emotionally evocative exercises are used to help the clients open up to this previously avoided material.

In the fifth stage, the clients' values are explored in detail. In essence, after undermining an unworkable agenda, it becomes time to reconstruct a more workable one, and values provide the direction for that process.

In the final stage, overt behavioral commitments are pursued. In each case, situations are analyzed into values, goals, actions, and barriers. That is, clients resolve the clinical situation as follows: (1) What values do you intend to make manifest? (2) What concrete, achievable events are on that path? (3) What could you do now to produce those achievements? (4) What stands in the way of engaging in these actions? In essence, the first several steps of ACT are all about (4), whereas the last stages focus on (1)–(3). This final step is essentially indistinguishable from traditional behavior therapy and involves overt behavioral change. What defines ACT as part of the new wave of contemporary behavior therapy is its self-conscious use of behavioral principles and a functional approach and the radically contextual approach to private events. These steps in ACT flow directly from a contemporary behavioral account of language and how verbal functions can dominate other sources of behavioral regulation. The therapeutic relationship is also given great weight (Hayes et al., 1999).

Consistency Across These Examples

One of the things that may surprise readers most is that each of these four innovative examples of contemporary behavior therapy combines a serious concern with the application of behavioral principles with an equally serious interest in topics and procedures that are not always obviously "behavioral" in a traditional sense. This feature, it seems to us, marks a kind of maturing of the behavioral tradition. Behavioral psychology is an approach that had a strategic commitment to a study of the simple in order to understand the complex. In the 1960s, when the first wave of applications of behavioral principles began, only a certain level of complexity was addressed because behavior therapists only felt comfortable with a certain degree of extension. For example, issues of thoughts, emotions, and the therapeutic relationship were dealt with somewhat awkwardly or not at all. That has now changed, and clinical behavior analysts roam freely among some of the most complex topics in clinical psychology (e.g., self, purpose, meaning, and acceptance). A good part of the reason seems to be the rise of a new understanding of the contextualistic qualities of behavior theory and of the conceptual and empirical advances in the analysis of language and private events. Some of the originators of these procedures have spoken directly to these topics in ways that makes this interpretation more plausible. For example, Neil Jacobson, one of the developers of ICT, has shown considerable interest in contextualism as the philosophy underlying behavioral thinking (e.g., Jacobson, 1997), and Bob Kohlenberg, one of the developers of FAP, points to the basic behavior analytic work on rule governance as one of the findings that led him back into clinical behavior analysis.

CONCLUSION

In this chapter we have presented an overview of contemporary behavior therapy. Behavior therapy has come out of its doldrums, has begun to counter the mischaracterizations of its philosophical background, and is correcting the misconceptions that have impeded acceptance of what this scientifically based approach has to offer. New behavioral principles are emerging that address verbal behavior, long a stumbling block for a traditional analysis of complex human behavior. Of the recent therapeutic innovations in clinical psychology, contemporary behavior therapy, based on the application of behavior analytic principles, has produced some of the most exciting therapies of the last decade. There is ample opportunity for those who learn the basic behavioral principles to make important additional contributions well into the future.

REFERENCES

Allyon, T., & Azrin, N. H. (1968). *The token economy: A motivational system for therapy and rehabilitation.* New York: Appleton-Century-Crofts.

American Psychiatric Association. (1994). *Diagnostic and statistical manual of mental disorders* (4th ed.). Washington, DC: American Psychiatric Association.

Anderson, C. M., Freeman, K. A., & Scotti, J. R. (1999). Evaluation of the generalizability (reliability and validity) of analogue functional assessment methodology. *Behavior Therapy, 30,* 31–50.

Azrin, R. D., & Hayes, S. C. (1984). The discrimination of interest within a heterosexual interaction: Training, generalization, and effects on social skills. *Behavior Therapy, 15,* 173–184.

Bandura, A. (1968). A social learning interpretation of psychological dysfunctions. In P. London & D. Rosenhan (Eds.), *Foundations of abnormal psychology* (pp. 293–344). New York: Holt, Rinehart & Winston.

Bandura, A. (1977). *Social learning theory.* Upper Saddle River, NJ: Prentice Hall.

Barley, W. D., Buie, S. E., Peterson, E. W., Hollingsworth, A. S., Griva, M., Hickerson, S. C., Lawson, J. E., & Bailey, B. J. (1993). The development of an inpatient cognitive-behavioral treatment program for borderline personality disorder. *Journal of Personality Disorders, 7,* 232–240.

Barlow, D. H., & Craske, M. G. (1989). *Mastery of your anxiety and panic.* New York: Graywind.

Barlow, D. H., Craske, M. G., Cerny, J. A., & Klosko, J. S. (1989). Behavioral treatment of panic disorder. *Behavior Therapy, 20,* 261–282.

Barnes, D., & Keenan, M. (1993). The transfer of functions through derived arbitrary and non-arbitrary stimulus relations. *Journal of the Experimental Analysis of Behavior, 59,* 61–81.

Beck, A. T., Rush, A. J., Shaw, B. F., & Emery, G. (1979). *Cognitive therapy of depression.* New York: Guilford.

Biglan, A., & Hayes, S. C. (1996). Should the behavioral sciences become more pragmatic? The case for functional contextualism in research on human behavior. *Applied and Preventive Psychology: Current Scientific Perspectives, 5,* 47–57.

Bijou, S., & Baer, D. M. (1961). *Child development: A systematic and empirical theory.* New York: Appleton-Century-Crofts.

Blackledge, J. T., & Hayes, S. C. (in preparation). Contemporary behavioral therapies and their mechanisms: An analysis of mechanisms of action underlying traditional and contemporary exposure-based psychotherapies.

D'Amato, M. R., Salmon, D. P., Loukas, E., & Tomie, A. (1985). Symmetry and transitivity of conditional relations in monkeys (Cebus apella) and pigeons (Columba livia). *Journal of the Experimental Analysis of Behavior, 44,* 35–47.

DeGrandpre, R. J., Bickel, S., & Higgins, S. T. (1992). Emergent equivalence relations between interoceptive (drug) and exteroceptive (visual) stimuli. *Journal of the Experimental Analysis of Behavior, 58,* 9–18.

de Rose, J. T., McIlvane, W. J., Dube, W. V., Galpin, V. C., & Stoddard, L. T. (1988). Emergent simple discrimination established by indirect relation to differential consequences. *Journal of the Experimental Analysis of Behavior, 50,* 1–20.

Devany, J. M., Hayes, S. C., & Nelson, R. O. (1986). Equivalence class formation in language-able and language-disabled children. *Journal of the Experimental Analysis of Behavior, 46,* 243–257.

Dougher, M. J. (in press). *Clinical behavior analysis.* Reno, NV: Context Press.

Dougher, M. J., Auguston, E. M., Markham, M. R., Greenway, D. E., & Wulfert, E. (1994). The transfer of respondent eliciting and extinction functions through stimulus equivalence classes. *Journal of the Experimental Analysis of Behavior, 62,* 331–351.

Dugdale, N., & Lowe, C. F. (1990). Naming and

stimulus equivalence. In D. E. Blackman & H. Lejeune (Eds.), *Behavior analysis in theory and practice: Contributions and controversies* (pp. 115–138). Hillsdale, NJ: Erlbaum.

Dymond, S., & Barnes, D. (1995). A transformation of self-discrimination response functions through the arbitrarily applicable relations of sameness, more than, and less than. *Journal of the Experimental Analysis of Behavior, 64,* 163–184.

Ellis, A. (1979). The basic clinical theory of rational-emotive therapy. In A. Ellis & R. Grieger (Eds.), *Comprehensive handbook of rational-emotive therapy.* New York: Springer.

Ellis, A., & Harper, R. (1961). *New guide to rational living.* New York: Crown.

Ellis, H. C., & Hunt, R. R. (1983). *Fundamentals of human memory and cognition* (3rd ed.). Dubuque, IA: Brown.

Emmelkamp, P. M. (1982). *Phobic and obsessive-compulsive disorders: Theory, research and practice.* New York: Plenum.

Emmelkamp, P. M., & Kuipers, A. C. (1979). Agoraphobia: A follow-up study four years after treatment. *British Journal of Psychiatry, 128,* 86–89.

Eysenck, H. J. (1972). Behavior therapy is behavioristic. *Behavior Therapy, 3,* 609–613.

Ferster, C. B. (1967). Arbitrary and natural reinforcement. *The Psychological Record, 22,* 1–16.

Follette, W. C. (1992, May). *Contingency-shaped versus rule-governed learning of complex social behaviors.* Paper presented at the 18th annual convention of the Association for Behavior Analysis, San Francisco.

Follette, W. C., & Callaghan, G. M. (1995). Do as I do, not as I say: A behavior-analytic approach to supervision. *Professional Psychology: Research and Practice, 26,* 413–421.

Follette, W. C., Dougher, M. K., Dykstra, T. A., Compton, S. N., & Naugle, A. (1992, November). *Teaching complex social behaviors to subjects with schizophrenia using contingent feedback.* Paper presented at the 26th annual meeting of the Association for the Advancement of Behavior Therapy, Boston.

Follette, W. C., Dykstra, T. A., & Compton, S. N. (1992, November). *Contingent learning as an alternative to rule governance in teaching complex social behaviors to schizophrenics.* Paper presented at the 26th annual meeting of the Association for the Advancement of Behavior Therapy, Boston.

Follette, W. C., & Houts, A. C. (1996). Models of scientific progress and the role of theory in taxonomy development: A case study of the DSM. *Journal of Consulting and Clinical Psychology, 64,* 1120–1132.

Follette, W. C., Naugle, A. E., & Callaghan, G. M. (1996). A radical behavioral understanding of the therapeutic relationship. *Behavior Therapy, 27,* 623–641.

Follette, W. C., Naugle, A. E., & Linnerooth, P. J. N. (in press). Functional alternatives to traditional assessment and diagnosis. In M. J. Dougher (Ed.), *Clinical behavior analysis.* Reno, NV: Context Press.

Franks, C. M., & Wilson, G. T. (1974). *Annual review of behavior therapy: Theory and practice.* New York: Brunner/Mazel.

Friman, P. C., Hayes, S. C., & Wilson, K. G. (1998). Why behavior analysts should study emotion: The example of anxiety. *Journal of Applied Behavior Analysis, 31,* 137–156.

Gatch, M. B., & Osborne, J. G. (1989). Transfer of contextual stimulus function via equivalence class development. *Journal of the Experimental Analysis of Behavior, 51,* 369–378.

Goldfried, M. R., & Davison, G. C. (1994). *Clinical behavior therapy.* New York: Wiley.

Hayes, S. C. (1984). Making sense of spirituality. *Behaviorism, 12,* 99–110.

Hayes, S. C. (1987). A contextual approach to therapeutic change. In N. S. Jacobson (Ed.), *Psychotherapists in clinical practice: Cognitive and behavioral perspectives* (pp. 327–387). New York: Guilford.

Hayes, S. C. (1993). Analytic goals and the varieties of scientific contextualism. In S. C. Hayes, L. J. Hayes, H. W. Reese, & T. R. Sarbin (Eds.), *Varieties of scientific contextualism* (pp. 11–27). Reno, NV: Context Press.

Hayes, S. C., & Brownstein, A. J. (1986). Mentalism, behavior-behavior relations and a behavior analytic view of the purposes of science. *The Behavior Therapist, 9,* 175–190.

Hayes, S. C., Brownstein, A. J., Devany, J. M., Kohlenberg, B. S., & Shelby, J. (1987). Stimulus equivalence and the symbolic control of behavior. *Mexican Journal of Behavior Analysis, 13,* 361–374.

Hayes, S. C., Brownstein, A. J., Zettle, R. D., Rosenfarb, I., & Korn, Z. (1986). Rule-governed behavior and sensitivity to changing consequences of responding. *Journal of the Experimental Analysis of Behavior, 45,* 237–256.

Hayes, S. C., & Follette, W. C. (1992a). Behavioral assessment in the DSM era. *Behavioral Assessment, 14,* 293–295.

Hayes, S. C., & Follette, W. C. (1992b). Can functional analysis provide a substitute for syndromal classification? *Behavioral Assessment, 14,* 345–365.

Hayes, S. C., & Follette, W. C. (1993). The challenge faced by behavioral assessment. *European Journal of Psychological Assessment, 9*(3), 182–188.

Hayes, S. C., & Gifford, E. V. (1997). The trouble with language: Experiential avoidance, rules, and the nature of verbal events. *Psychological Science, 8,* 170–173.

Hayes, S. C., Gifford, E. V., & Wilson, K. G. (1996). Stimulus classes and stimulus relations:

Arbitrarily applicable relational responding as an operant. In T. R. Zental & P. M. Smeets (Eds.), *Stimulus class formation in humans and animals. Vol. 117, Advances in psychology* (pp. 279–299). New York: Elsevier.

Hayes, S. C., & Hayes, L. J. (1992). Verbal relations and the evolution of behavior analysis. *American Psychologist, 47*, 1383–1395.

Hayes, S. C., Hayes, L. J., & Reese, H. W. (1988). Finding the philosophical core: A review of Stephen C. Pepper's *World Hypotheses. Journal of the Experimental Analysis of Behavior, 50*, 97–111.

Hayes, S. C., Hayes, L. J., Reese, H. W., & Sarbin, T. R. (Eds.). (1993). *Varieties of scientific contextualism*. Reno, NV: Context Press.

Hayes, S. C., Kohlenberg, B. S., & Hayes, L. J. (1991). The transfer of specific and general consequential functions through simple and conditional equivalence classes. *Journal of the Experimental Analysis of Behavior, 56*, 119–137.

Hayes, S. C., Nelson, R. O., & Jarret, R. (1987). Treatment utility of assessment: A functional approach to evaluating quality of assessment. *American Psychologist, 42*, 963–974.

Hayes, S. C., Rosenfarb, I., Wulfert, E., Munt, E., Zettle, R. D., & Korn, Z. (1985). Self-reinforcement effects: An artifact of social standard setting? *Journal of Applied Behavior Analysis, 18*, 201–214.

Hayes, S. C., Strosahl, K., & Wilson, K. G. (1999). *Acceptance and commitment therapy: Emotion, cognition, and human suffering*. New York: Guilford.

Hayes, S. C., & Wilson, K. G. (1993). Some applied implications of contemporary behavior–analytic account of verbal events. *The Behavior Analyst, 17*, 289–303.

Hayes, S. C., & Wilson, K. G. (1994). Acceptance and commitment therapy: Altering the verbal support for experiential avoidance. *The Behavior Analyst, 17*, 289–303.

Hayes, S. C., Wilson, K. G., Gifford, E. V., Follette, V. M., & Stroshahl, K. (1996). Experiential avoidance and behavioral disorders: A functional dimensional approach to diagnosis and treatment. *Journal of Consulting and Clinical Psychology, 64*, 1152–1168.

Hayes, S. C., Zettle, R. D., & Rosenfarb, I. (1989). Rule following. In S. C. Hayes (Ed.), *Rule governed behavior: Cognition, contingencies, and instructional control* (pp. 191–220). New York: Plenum.

Haynes, S. N., & O'Brien, W. H. (1990). Functional analysis in behavior therapy. *Clinical Psychology Review, 10*, 649–668.

Ingram, R. E. (1991). Depressive cognition: Models, mechanisms, and methods. In R. E. Ingram (Ed.), *Contemporary psychological approaches to depression: Theory, research, and treatment* (pp. 169–195). New York: Plenum.

Ingram, R. E., & Holle, C. (1992). Cognitive science of depression. In D. J. Stein & J. E. Young (Eds.), *Cognitive science and clinical disorders* (pp. 187–209). San Diego, CA: Academic Press.

Ingram, R. E., & Kendall, P. C. (1986). Cognitive clinical psychology: Implications of an information processing perspective. In R. E. Ingram (Ed.), *Information processing approaches to clinical psychology* (pp. 3–21). Orlando, FL: Academic Press.

Iwata, B. A. (1994a). Functional analysis methodology: Some closing comments. *Journal of Applied Behavior Analysis, 27*, 413–418.

Iwata, B. A. (1994b). Toward a functional analysis of self-injury. *Journal of Applied Behavior Analysis, 27*, 197–209.

Iwata, B. A., Duncan, B. A., Zarcone, J. R., Lerman, D. C., Pace, B. A., & Gary, M. (1994). A sequential, test-control methodology for conducting functional analyses of self-injurious behavior. *Behavior Modification, 18*, 289–306.

Jacobson, N. S. (1997). Can contextualism help? *Behavior Therapy, 28*, 435–443.

Jacobson, N. S., & Christensen, A. (1996). *Integrative couple therapy: Promoting acceptance and change*. New York: Norton.

Jacobson, N. S., Follette, W. C., Revenstorf, D., Baucom, D. H., Hahlweg, K., & Margolin, G. (1984). Variability in outcome and clinical significance of behavioral marital therapy: A reanalysis of outcome data. *Journal of Consulting and Clinical Psychology, 52*, 497–504.

Jacobson, N. S., & Margolin, G. (1979). *Marital therapy: Strategies based on social learning and behavior exchange principles*. New York: Brunner/Mazel.

Jenkins, J. J., & Palermo, D. S. (1964). Mediation processes and the acquisition of linguistic structure. In U. Bellugi & R. Brown (Eds.), *The acquisition of language*. Monographs of the Society for Research in Child Development, 29 (Serial No. 92).

Johnston, J. M., & Pennypacker, H. S. (1980). *Strategies and tactics of human behavioral research*. Hillsdale, NJ: Erlbaum.

Joyce, J. H., & Chase, P. N. (1990). Effects of response variability on the sensitivity of rule-governed behavior. *Journal of the Experimental Analysis of Behavior, 54*, 251–262.

Kanfer, F. H., & Grimm, L. G. (1977). Behavioral analysis: Selecting target behaviors in the interview. *Behavior Modification, 1*, 7–28.

Kanfer, F. H., & Saslow, G. (1969). Behavioral diagnosis. In C. M. Franks (Ed.), *Behavior therapy: Appraisal and status* (pp. 417–444). New York: McGraw-Hill.

Kendall, S. B. (1983). Tests for mediated transfer in pigeons. *The Psychological Record, 33*, 245–256.

Kohlenberg, B. S., Hayes, S. C., & Hayes, L. J.

(1991). The transfer of contextual control over equivalence classes through equivalence classes: A possible model of social stereotyping. *Journal of the Experimental Analysis of Behavior, 56,* 505–518.

Kohlenberg, R. J., & Tsai, M. (1991). *Functional analytic psychotherapy.* New York: Plenum.

Krasner, L. (1962). The therapist as a social reinforcing machine. In H. H. Strupp & L. Luborsky (Eds.), *Research in Psychotherapy* (Vol. 2, pp. 61–94). Washington, DC: American Psychological Association.

Krasner, L. (1963). Reinforcement, verbal behavior, and psychotherapy. *American Journal of Orthopsychiatry, 33,* 601–613.

Leigland, S. (Ed.). (1992). *Radical behaviorism: Willard Day on psychology and philosophy.* Reno, NV: Context Press.

Linehan, M. M. (1984). *Dialectical behavior therapy: A treatment manual.* Seattle: University of Washington.

Linehan, M. M. (1993a). *Cognitive-behavioral treatment of borderline personality disorder.* New York: Guilford.

Linehan, M. M. (1993b). Dialectical behavior therapy for treatment of borderline personality disorder: Implications for the treatment of drug abuse. In L. Onken, J. Blaine, & J. Boren (Eds.), *Behavioral treatments for drug abuse and drug dependence* (pp. 201–215). NIDA research monograph series.

Linehan, M. M., Armstrong, H. E., Suarez, A., Allmon, D., & Heard, H. L. (1991). Cognitive-behavioral treatments of chronically parasuicidal borderline patients. *Archives of General Psychiatry, 48*(12), 1060–1064.

Lipkens, G., Hayes, S. C., & Hayes, L. J. (1993). Longitudinal study of derived stimulus relations in an infant. *Journal of Experimental Child Psychology, 56,* 201–239.

Lipkens, R., Kop, P. F. M., & Matthijs, W. (1988). A test of symmetry and transitivity in the conditional discrimination performances of pigeons. *Journal of the Experimental Analysis of Behavior, 49,* 395–409.

Lovaas, O. I. (1977). *The autistic child: Language development through behavior modification.* New York: Irvington.

Lovaas, O. I. (1987). Behavioral treatment and normal educational and intellectual functioning in young autistic child. *Journal of Consulting and Clinical Psychology, 55,* 3–9.

Mahoney, M. J. (1974). *Cognition and behavior modification.* Cambridge, MA: Ballinger.

Mahoney, M. J., Kazdin, A. E., & Lesswing, N. J. (1974). Behavior modification: Delusion of deliverance? In C. M. Franks & G. T. Wilson (Eds.), *Annual review of behavior therapy: Theory and practice* (pp. 11–40). New York: Brunner/Mazel.

McFall, R. M. (1982). A review and reformulation of the concept of social skills. *Behavioral Assessment, 4,* 1–33.

McKnight, D. L., Nelson, R. O., Hayes, S. C., & Jarrett, R. B. (1984). Importance of treating individually-assessed response classes in the amelioration of depression. *Behavior Therapy, 15,* 315–335.

Meichenbaum, D. H. (1977). *Cognitive-behavior modification: An integrative approach.* New York: Plenum.

Michael, J. (1982). Distinguishing between discriminative and motivational functions of stimuli. *Journal of the Experimental Analysis of Behavior, 37,* 149–155.

Michael, J. L. (1993a). *Concepts and principles of behavior analysis.* Kalamazoo, MI: Society for the Advancement of Behavior Analysis.

Michael, J. (1993b). Establishing operations. *Behavior Analyst, 16,* 191–206.

Morris, E. K. (1988). Contextualism: The world view of behavior analysis. *Journal of Experimental Child Psychology, 46,* 289–323.

Mowrer, O. H. (1939). A stimulus-response analysis of anxiety and its role as a reinforcing agent. *Psychological Review, 46,* 553–565.

Paul, G. L., & Lentz, R. (1977). *Psychosocial treatment of the chronic mental patient.* Cambridge, MA: Harvard University Press.

Paul, G. L., & Menditto, A. A. (1992). Effectiveness of inpatient treatment programs for mentally ill adults in public psychiatric facilities. *Applied & Preventive Psychology, 1,* 41–63.

Paul, R. H., Marx, B. P., & Orsillo, S. M. (1999). Acceptance-based psychotherapy in the treatment of an adjudicated exhibitionist: A case example. *Behavior Therapy, 30,* 149–162.

Pepper, S. C. (1942). *World hypotheses: A study in evidence.* Berkeley: University of California Press.

Roche, B., & Barnes, D. (1997). A transformation of respondently conditioned sexual arousal functions in accordance with arbitrarily applicable relations. *Journal of the Experimental Analysis of Behavior, 67,* 275–301.

Rogers, C. R. (1957). The necessary and sufficient conditions of therapeutic personality change. *Journal of Consulting Psychology, 21,* 95–103.

Rosenfarb, I., & Hayes, S. C. (1984). Social standard setting: The Achilles' heel of informational accounts of therapeutic change. *Behavior Therapy, 15,* 515–528.

Rosnow, R. L., & Georgoudi, M. (Eds.). (1986). *Contextualism and understanding in behavioral science.* New York: Praeger.

Sidman, M. (1971). Reading and auditory-visual equivalences. *Journal of Speech and Hearing Research, 14,* 5–13.

Sidman, M. (1986). Functional analysis of emergent verbal classes. In T. Thompson & M. D. Zeiler

(Eds.), *Analysis and integration of behavioral units* (pp. 213–245). Hillsdale, NJ: Erlbaum.

Sidman, M., Cresson, O., & Willson-Morris, M. (1974). Acquisition of matching-to-sample via mediated transfer. *Journal of the Experimental Analysis of Behavior, 22*, 261–273.

Sidman, M., Rauzin, R., Lazar, R., Cunningham, S., Tailby, W., & Carrigan, P. (1982). A search for symmetry in the conditional discriminations of rhesus monkeys, baboons, and children. *Journal of the Experimental Analysis of Behavior, 37*, 23–44.

Skinner, B. F. (1938). *The behavior of organisms*. New York: Appleton-Century-Crofts.

Skinner, B. F. (1945). The operational analysis of psychological terms. *Psychological Review, 52*, 270–277.

Skinner, B. F. (1953). *Science and human behavior*. New York: Free Press.

Skinner, B. F. (1957). *Verbal behavior*. New York: Appleton-Century-Crofts.

Skinner, B. F. (1974). *About behaviorism*. New York: Knopf.

Staats, A. W. (1975). *Social behaviorism*. Homewood, IL: Dorsey.

Stampfl, T. G., & Levis, D. J. (1967). Essentials of implosive therapy. A learning-theory based psychodynamic behavioral therapy. *Journal of Abnormal Psychology, 72*, 496–503.

Steele, D. L., & Hayes, S. C. (1991). Stimulus equivalence and arbitrarily applicable relational responding. *Journal of the Experimental Analysis of Behavior, 56*, 519–555.

Strosahl, K. D., Hayes, S. C., Bergan, J., & Romano, P. (1998). Assessing the field effectiveness of acceptance and commitment therapy: An example of the manipulated training research method. *Behavior Therapy, 29*, 35–64.

Sturmey, P. (1996). *Functional analysis in clinical psychology*. New York: Wiley.

Tryon, W. W. (1995). Neural networks for behavior therapists: What they are and why they are important. *Behavior Therapy, 26*, 295–318.

Watson, J. B. (1913). Psychology as a behaviorist views it. *Psychological Review, 20*, 158–177.

Watson, J. B. (1924). *Behaviorism*. New York: Norton.

Watson, J. B., & Rayner, R. (1920). Conditioned emotional reactions. *Journal of Experimental Psychology, 3*, 1–14.

Wolpe, J. (1958). *Psychotherapy by reciprocal inhibition*. Stanford, CA: Stanford University Press.

Wulfert, E., & Hayes, S. C. (1988). The transfer of conditional sequencing through conditional equivalence classes. *Journal of the Experimental Analysis of Behavior, 50*, 125–144.

CHAPTER 19

COGNITIVE AND
COGNITIVE-BEHAVIORAL THERAPIES

KEITH S. DOBSON
BARBARA J. BACKS-DERMOTT
University of Calgary
DAVID J. A. DOZOIS
University of Western Ontario

Until the 1970s it was clear that there were three primary forces in the field of psychotherapy: the psychoanalytic, behavioral, and humanistic models and methods. Only in the last three decades have the cognitive and cognitive-behavioral therapies grown to distinguish themselves from their forebears and to take the place of an identifiable "fourth force" in psychotherapy. Indeed, the cognitive-behavioral therapies have shown some of the strongest growth of any of the psychotherapy approaches to date (Robins, Gosling, & Craik, 1999) and have been applied to an increasing array of clinical disorders (Dobson, 1988; Freeman, Simon, Butler, & Arkowitz, 1989; Granvold, 1996; Hawton, Salkovskis, Kirk, & Clark, 1989; Salkovskis, 1996). In part because of the strong research evidence that they have been able to accrue (Chambless et al., 1996, 1998), they also figure prominently among the empirically supported treatments that are currently recognized in psychotherapy (Dobson & Craig, 1998).

In this chapter we provide a brief review of some of the major historical forces that led to the development of the cognitive-behavioral therapies (CBT). We then define the common characteristics among this increasingly diverse set of interventions, and in doing so also attempt to differentiate the cognitive-behavioral therapies from related approaches to psychotherapy. We then turn our primary focus to a description of the major models within the cognitive-behavioral paradigm and their current empirical status. The chapter concludes with a discussion of current issues related to the cognitive-behavioral therapies

and with predictions and suggestions for the future development of the approach.

HISTORICAL FORCES IN THE DEVELOPMENT OF THE COGNITIVE-BEHAVIORAL THERAPIES

As has been noted, the development of the cognitive-behavioral therapies can roughly be placed in the early 1970s (Mahoney, 1974; Meichenbaum, 1977). Although many descriptions of this development suggest that the cognitive-behavioral therapies grew out of the behavioral tradition (Dobson & Block, 1988; Mahoney, 1974), it may, in fact, be more accurate to suggest that there were two developmental pathways. The first was progressive and was derived from behaviorism; the second was more revolutionary and was derived from psychoanalysis. Each of these developmental parentages and their therapeutic offspring are described in turn.

The more traditional view of the cognitive-behavioral therapies is that they developed from a growing disaffection with the radical behavioral model and its exclusive attention to observable behavior as the object of study. Efforts to conceptualize thoughts as covert behaviors (e.g., Cautela, 1967; Homme, 1965) were not satisfactory, as the evidence required to document the lawful behavior of cognition could not be attained. Furthermore, increasing evidence began to emerge that even in the absence of behavioral experience, cognitive activities could predict behavioral change (e.g., the studies on observational learning by Bandura & Walters, 1963), or that in some instances cognitive predictors of behavior even outperformed behavioral predictors (Bandura, 1977).

From these research literatures it became increasingly clear that strict behavioral models could not adequately account for behavioral change. Increasingly, mediational models of change were introduced. For example, an early cognitive-behavioral intervention was covert sensitization (Cautela, 1967), in which the mental rehearsal of negative outcomes for behavior (e.g. imagining oneself vomiting all over one's clothing and being publicly embarrassed after drinking alcohol) was predicted to be a mediator for reducing actual alcohol consumption. A more elaborate model of cognitive-behavioral change was developed by Meichenbaum (1977; Meichenbaum & Goodman, 1971), in which individuals who were learning new, more adaptive behavior were taught to give themselves "self-instructional training," in which they mentally walked through the steps that would lead to adequate performance. Self-instructional training also included mental reinforcement for satisfactory outcomes.

The most complex of the early cognitive-behavioral therapies involved models that went beyond specific behavioral outcomes and tried to develop more generalizable models of behavioral change. Kanfer's emphasis on goal-directed behavioral change (Kanfer, 1996; Kanfer & Schefft, 1988) and the development of the problem-solving therapies (D'Zurilla & Goldfried, 1971) represent models of behavior change that incorporated ideas from the emerging cognitive mediational literature, but which kept a constant eye on measuring behavioral change as the key outcome variable.

In addition to the incremental approaches in developing the cognitive-behavioral therapies, a second developmental pathway must be recognized. Two of the major figures in the field, Aaron Beck and Albert Ellis, were trained in psychoanalysis and practiced this therapy approach early in their careers. Both theorists, however, came to reject some of the basic principles and practices of their early training, and they developed models of psychopathology and treatment that included internal (i.e., cognitive and emotional) processes but did not rest on assumptions of an unconscious process or the need for long-term, relationship-based treatment (Beck, 1970; Dryden & Ellis, in press). Both of these individuals developed perspectives that were "revolutionary," compared to their training, but that came to be incorporated into several later cognitive-behavioral models. Ellis's early work on irrationality as the basis of human suffering and his ABC model of cognitive mediation, for example, presage the development of many later ideas in the cognitive-behavioral tradition.

COMMON AND DISTINGUISHING FEATURES OF THE COGNITIVE-BEHAVIORAL THERAPIES

Partly because of the attention and growth of the approach, it is increasingly difficult to name the boundaries of the cognitive and cognitive-behavioral therapies. As early as 1988, it was suggested that there are at least 12 to 17 specific cognitive-behavioral models (Dobson & Block, 1988; Mahoney, 1988), and no doubt the number of therapies has grown since then (although we know of no recent taxonomy). Among the therapies that have been developed, there are conceptual and practical differences that can be used to classify them. For example, Dobson and Block (1988) argued that cognitive-behavioral therapies can be classified as one of the following types:

> *Coping skills therapies* focus on the learning or improvement of adaptive behavioral repertoires, often through cognitive mechanisms (e.g., self-instructional training).
> *Problem-solving therapies* teach a method of examining a problem from an adaptive perspective and determining how best to solve that problem.
> *Cognitive restructuring therapies* attempt to promote optimal functioning or healthy emotional responses by examining and changing dysfunctional thought processes (e.g., rational-emotive behavior therapy or cognitive therapy).

Our perspective is that the above conceptual framework continues to hold up well. At the same time, as the following review of specific therapies suggests, it is our sense that more recent developments in the cognitive-behavioral therapies have tended to focus less on the use of coping skills interventions and more on the formal process of problem solving or cognitive restructuring. We suggest that a strong factor in the relative development of various approaches to cognitive-behavioral therapy may lie in the explicit recognition of cognitive-restructuring therapies as effective treatments (Chambless et al., 1998).

THE REALISM ASSUMPTION AND THE PLACE OF CONSTRUCTIVISTIC THERAPIES

In his analysis of the cognitive-behavioral therapies, Mahoney (1988, 1991, 1995) has delineated a distinction between what he has termed the "rationalist" and the "constructivist" approaches to therapy. The distinction being drawn is much more than a focus on treatment or one based on particular therapeutic interventions. Indeed, the demarcation is based on a metaphysical perspective about the world and the nature of knowledge.

Rationalist therapies are predicated on the assumption of logical empiricism—that a real world exists and that it may be either perceived and understood accurately or misperceived. From this perspective, concepts such as cognitive distortions, cognitive errors, cognitive bias, and irrational beliefs make sense, as they reflect the extent to which the individual's perceptions are in line with reality. These therapies explicitly endorse the assumption of cognitive mediation—that emotional experience and behavioral choices follow from the cognitive appraisal of different situations. Rationalist cognitive therapies, therefore, focus on the accurate perception of events around the individual and on the adaptive response to those circumstances.

In contrast to the rationalist cognitive-behavioral therapies, the constructivistic therapies make no a priori assumption about the existence of an objective world, independent from experience. The value of cognition, from this perspective, is not in terms of its reality base but in terms of its coherence, order, and adaptiveness. Thus, the function of cognition is to order and make sense of experience, but cognition does not perforce define the nature of that experience, as the possibility of direct experiential and emotional "knowing" is also recognized. Direct cognitive mediation is rejected, therefore, because both "feedforward" and "feedbackward" mechanisms among emotional, physiological, behavioral, and cognitive systems are hypothesized (Mahoney, 1991, 1995).

One of the controversies between rationalist and constructivistic approaches to therapy deals with the role of emotion and its use in therapy. Rationalistic approaches view emotion as a conse-

quence of cognitive processing and, therefore, as an index of the negativity and the specific nature of that cognitive process. It has been argued that rationalist therapies view emotion as problems to be controlled by modifying dysfunctional thoughts (Mahoney, 1988, 1991; Neimeyer, 1995). For example, depression can be seen as a result of negative, distorted thoughts and should be treated by correcting these maladaptive cognitions. A constructivist paradigm, however, would view depression as a natural way of "knowing," and both the presence of depression, as opposed to some other emotional experience, and its intensity reflect aspects of that knowledge.

As has been articulated in *Back to Reality*, Held (1995) argues that constructivism itself comes in two forms. In the most extreme, what we label "metaphysical constructivism," the idea of an external reality is literally rejected. Within this perspective, humans are no more than the constructions we make of our experience, and no experience is inherently more accurate, honest, or justified than any other. Our lives are literally what we make of them, at a given place and time. Thus therapy involves a process of meaning-making and elaborative exploration. Choices are framed by the decision about what feels good to the individual and fits within his or her view of the world and self. No emotional, behavioral, or cognitive pattern is essentially "healthier" than any other. The point of contact between the therapist and client is language, which is the process by which meanings are elaborated.

In contrast, what we call "methodological constructivism" does not take the metaphysical position about the lack of external reality. Thus, this form of constructivism may include the idea that "the truth is out there," although the nature of that truth is potentially unknowable. From this perspective, what is key for optimal functioning is coherence and adaptation to the world *as we know it*. Methodological constructivism also uses language as the process for elaborating meaning in therapy; indeed, the techniques it encourages are largely those of metaphysical constructivism.

We have elaborated this distinction in part because of the growing interest in narrative forms of therapy (Gilligan & Price, 1993; White & Epston, 1990), the rise of postmodernism in psychology (Gergen, 1992, 1994), and the development of constructivist therapy (Guidano, 1991; Neimeyer, 1993, 1995). The *Handbook of Cognitive-Behavioral Therapies* (Dobson, 1988) included a chapter on this form of therapy. Increasingly, though, we are of the opinion that although methodological constructivism has some aspects of theory and methods of therapy in common with the cognitive-restructuring types of cognitive-behavioral therapies, both metaphysical and methodological constructivism belong to another approach to therapy. In particular, their rejection of the realism assumption places the manner in which problems are conceptualized, the way in which case conceptualizations are conveyed to the patient, the techniques that are chosen, and the ways in which outcomes are evaluated (indeed, the very idea of "outcomes") on a different plane from the other cognitive-behavioral therapies. Although this position can and no doubt will be contested, we have for this reason chosen not to address constructivist treatments further in this chapter.

SPECIFIC FORMS OF COGNITIVE-BEHAVIORAL THERAPY

In this section we address some of the major approaches of cognitive-behavioral therapy. Each form of therapy is given a definition and some historical reference. The treatment model is explained, as are some of the major treatment methods. Each section concludes with a discussion of the research findings for that approach.

Self-Instructional Therapies and Training

Self-instructional training (SIT) refers to a set of cognitive techniques designed to help individuals overcome cognitive deficits in such areas as problem solving, verbal mediation, and information seeking. Overt verbalizations of thought processes are modeled for the client and then are subsequently imitated and internalized by the client. Covert self-verbalizations follow, which result in the client's gaining verbal control over behavior. It is important to remember that SIT is an intervention strategy rather than a formalized theory (Kendall, Vitousek, & Kane, 1991).

Self-instructional training was originally developed by Meichenbaum and Goodman (1971; see also Meichenbaum, 1975) for use with impulsive or behavior-disordered children. This model was based on an understanding that impulsive children exercised less verbal control over their behavior than less impulsive children. Therefore,

a training procedure that promotes self-regulatory private speech was expected to be beneficial for such children. Meichenbaum (1977) later extended the use of self-instructional training to schizophrenic adults. Subsequent research has attempted to apply self-instructional training to individuals with mental retardation (e.g., Agran, Fodor-Davis, & Moore, 1986; Hughes, Hugo, & Blatt, 1996; Rusch, Morgan, Martin, Riva, & Agran, 1985; Whitman, Spence, & Maxwell, 1987).

Self-instructional training is a strategy for teaching self-instructional skills by using the following training sequences: (1) the trainer provides oral instructions while the subject observes; (2) the subject performs the task while the trainer instructs; (3) the subject performs the task while self-instructing aloud; (4) the subject performs the task while whispering; and (5) the subject performs the task while self-instructing covertly. Individuals are then taught to verbalize the following self-instructional statements: (1) stating the problem, (2) stating the response, (3) self-evaluating, and (4) self-reinforcing. Thus, individuals are taught to verbalize a sequence of statements when performing a task, and these vocalizations serve to direct the performance of appropriate responses (Meichenbaum, 1975; Meichenbaum & Goodman, 1971).

Initial results by the developers of self-instruction indicated that it was successfully used with impulsive children, as well as hospitalized schizophrenics (Meichenbaum, 1975, 1977; Meichenbaum & Goodman, 1971). Currently, although a considerable body of research suggests that self-instructional training is effective with children, there are few data about the effectiveness of self-instructional training with adults, including schizophrenic populations. Not surprisingly, there is also currently a dearth of research that meets the criteria for empirically supported treatment literature. To our knowledge, SIT has not been found to be an efficacious treatment for any adult disorder.

Problem-Solving Therapy

Problem-solving therapy (PST) was an early addition to the cognitive-behavioral field (D'Zurilla & Nezu, in press a; Kendall & Hollon, 1979). This approach flourished during the 1970s, with a number of PST programs being employed either alone or as part of a larger treatment package (D'Zurilla, 1988). As described below, it continues to be practiced both as a complete intervention and as an adjunct to other therapy approaches.

The underlying assumption of PST is that psychopathology can be conceptualized as an ineffective or maladaptive style of coping. According to this conceptualization, an individual's difficulties stem from ineffectual problem resolution and poor coping strategies. Ineffectual attempts to cope with or to resolve problems produce negative effects, such as physical symptoms, depression, anxiety, and the creation of new problems (D'Zurilla & Goldfried, 1971; D'Zurilla & Nezu, in press a). Thus PST utilizes a social problem-solving model in which effective problem solving as a general coping strategy increases general adaptiveness and prevents the adverse effects of stress from affecting one's well-being (D'Zurilla, 1990; D'Zurilla & Nezu, in press a, in press b; Nezu & D'Zurilla, 1989; Nezu, Nezu, & Houts, 1993).

Although there is a variety of social PST paradigms, this section focuses on the model developed by D'Zurilla and colleagues because it is representative of most problem-solving approaches. D'Zurilla and Goldfried (1971) originally presented a model of social problem solving, which was later refined by D'Zurilla and Nezu (1982, in press b). In this model, two processes are responsible for determining typical problem-solving outcomes. The first is *problem orientation*, which refers to the attentional and motivational aspects of the problem-solving process. Specifically, problem orientation concerns the ability to recognize problems as they occur. Related to this perceptual process is a set of relatively stable cognitive-emotional schemas or scripts that describe how a person typically thinks and feels about problems in living and one's own general problem-solving ability (D'Zurilla & Nezu, in press a). Individuals may have a positive or constructive problem orientation, which results in positive emotions and approach tendencies and maximizes the likelihood of effective problem-solving behavior. Alternatively, individuals may have a negative, dysfunctional problem orientation, which results in negative emotions and avoidance tendencies and reduces the likelihood of effective problem-solving behavior (D'Zurilla, 1988).

D'Zurilla and Nezu (in press a) proposed the following problem orientation variables: problem perception, problem attribution, problem appraisal, perceived control, and time-effort commitment. These are listed in sequential order, with each increasing or decreasing the likelihood of the next variable occurring. *Problem perception*

is defined as the general tendency to recognize problems when they occur. By doing so, problem perception activates the other problem orientation variables and thus sets the stage for problem solving proper. *Problem attribution* is defined as an individual's beliefs regarding problems. A positive problem attribution is the tendency to understand problems as normal and inevitable events for everyone. A negative problem attribution is the tendency to understand problems as a reflection of a personal and stable defect. *Problem appraisal* refers to an individual's assessment or analysis of the significance or relevance of a problem for one's own well-being. A positive problem appraisal is the tendency to view problems as challenges. A negative problem appraisal is the tendency to view problems as only harmful or threatening. *Perceived control* consists of both generalized problem-solving self-efficacy (the expectation or assumption that one is able to effectively solve problems) and generalized positive problem-solving outcome expectancy (the expectation or assumption that problems can be solved). Finally, *time-effort commitment* refers to the likelihood that the individual will accurately estimate and be able to commit to the amount of time and effort required for effective problem solving.

Problem solving refers to the process of attempting to arrive at an effective problem-solving solution by applying four primary problem-solving skills, which should maximize the likelihood of arriving at the most effective solution: problem definition and formulation, generation of alternative solutions, decision making, and solution implementation and verification (D'Zurilla & Nezu, in press a; Nezu et al., 1993). Although these skills are described sequentially, in reality individuals move back and forth between each of them in the attempt to arrive at the best solution for a particular problem (cf. Crick & Dodge, 1994).

The social problem-solving model presented provides a general framework for the use of PST. Assessment involves an analysis of negative life events, daily problems, emotional stress responses, and deficits in problem orientation and problem-solving skills. Then PST is utilized to reduce deficits and/or improve abilities in problem orientation and problem solving. This, in turn, is expected to increase coping skills and improve psychological well-being (D'Zurilla, 1988; D'Zurilla & Nezu, in press a).

An important objective of PST is identifying and resolving current life problems that are antecedents of an individual's maladaptive responses. A concomitant goal is teaching general skills that will enable an individual to deal more effectively and independently with future problems. In addition to solving these antecedent problems, PST can directly affect maladaptive responses, such as anxiety, depression, pain, overeating, or problem drinking, if they are viewed conceptually as "problems-to-be-solved" (D'Zurilla & Nezu, in press a). It is important to remember, however, that PST is not concerned solely with the amelioration of skills deficits but also with higher level functioning (D'Zurilla & Nezu, in press a).

Problem-solving therapy can be applied by using either a structured, time-limited format, focusing on psychotherapy and skills training, or a more traditional, open-ended framework (D'Zurilla & Nezu, in press a). The sequence or practice of PST involves moving through the major components of the social problem-solving model. At each stage, specific PST and general CBT techniques are used to facilitate a more adaptive or effective means of problem orientation and problem solving. However, it is important to remember that although the process of PST is described as sequential, in practice, it is much more fluid and flexible.

In the problem orientation phase, the goal is to help the client to adopt a more positive or adaptive problem orientation, to more accurately identify problems, and to recognize emotions as indications that a problem exists (D'Zurilla & Nezu, in press a). Specific techniques to facilitate this change include the reverse advocacy role-play technique, in which the therapist adopts a belief about problems that reflects a negative orientation. The client is asked to respond with reasons that a given assumption may be maladaptive or incorrect (D'Zurilla & Nezu, in press a). Other techniques include the use of problem checklists to help identify existing and possible problems, teaching clients how to use cues to help them stop and think before reacting impulsively in reaction to situations, and reframing emotional reactions as indications that a problem exists (D'Zurilla & Nezu, in press a).

In the problem definition and formulation phase, the intention is to help the client understand the nature of the problem and to generate realistic problem-solving goals (D'Zurilla & Nezu, in press a). Techniques used to facilitate this goal include teaching clients how to use the five "W" questions (who, what, when, where, and why) and the use of general cognitive restructur-

ing techniques to correct any faulty thinking. In the generation of alternative solutions phase, the goal is to produce as many solutions to the problem as possible. Clients are asked to suspend their judgment when generating these alternative solutions so that a variety of alternatives can be listed.

In the decision-making phase, the goal is to choose among the possible solutions and to develop a problem-solving plan. To do this, clients are taught to identify the possible consequences of each alternative in terms of their short- and long-term implications for themselves and others. Clients are also taught to evaluate whether a given solution will solve their problem and to achieve the most adaptive solution. Finally, in the solution implementation and verification phase of PST, the goal is to perform the chosen solution plan and to monitor and evaluate its outcomes. To do this, clients are taught self-monitoring techniques and are also encouraged to reward themselves for accurately predicting outcomes (D'Zurilla & Nezu, in press a).

In addition to the specific PST techniques described above, a variety of general CBT techniques are also used, including Socratic questioning, didactic instruction or psychoeducation, modeling, shaping, rehearsal, homework assignments, and reinforcement of positive changes (D'Zurilla & Nezu, in press a). Proponents of PST assert that general CBT techniques that are used in a given case should be integrated into the general PST framework (D'Zurilla, 1988; D'Zurilla & Nezu, in press a).

Treatment manuals have been developed for applying PST to a variety of populations and problems, including clinical depression (Nezu, 1986; Nezu, Nezu, & Perri, 1989; Nezu & Perri, 1989), cancer patients (Nezu et al., 1993), and substance abuse (Platt, Taube, Metzger, & Duome, 1988). In addition, D'Zurilla and Nezu (in press b) have recently completed a generic training manual. Moreover, PST has been utilized with a variety of populations, including adults and children, and clinical and nonclinical problems (e.g., depression, schizophrenia, anxiety disorders, suicidal behavior, substance abuse, marital and relationship problems, and mental retardation), health problems (e.g., cancer), and therapies (e.g., individual, group, marital, and family) (D'Zurilla & Nezu, in press a). Finally, PST has been used as a preventive approach (e.g., workshops and seminars).

Studies on a variety of populations have attested to the effectiveness of PST, including investigations of schizophrenia, depression, suicidal ideation and behavior, anxiety disorders, emotional and behavioral problems in individuals with mental retardation, marital problems, parenting problems, substance use, smoking, weight control, pain, cancer, and more generally community problems and issues (e.g., stress management training and competence enhancement) (D'Zurilla & Nezu, in press a). D'Zurilla and Nezu (in press b) have recently published a complete review of the outcome literature pertaining to PST. The developers of this approach acknowledge that there are limitations to this body of research that need to be addressed; however, their overall conclusion is that the bulk of the data support the efficacy of PST across different populations, problems, treatment settings, and ages (D'Zurilla & Nezu, in press a).

Beginning in the early 1980s, a number of studies have utilized the manualized treatment protocol to study the effectiveness of PST in treating depression. In general, results indicate that PST is as effective or more effective in reducing depressive symptoms as no treatment, control treatment (i.e., social reinforcement programs and problem-focused treatment without systematic training in problem-solving skills), or alternative treatments (i.e., PST without the problem orientation component, reminiscence therapy, and amitriptyline) (Arean, Perri, Nezu, Schein, Christopher, & Joseph, 1993, with depressed patients over 55; Hussian & Lawrence, 1981, with elderly individuals; Mynors-Wallis, Gath, Lloyd-Thomas, & Tomlinson, 1995, with depressed adults in primary care; Nezu, 1986, with clinically depressed adults; Nezu & Perri, 1989, with clinically depressed adults). Mynor-Wallis et al. documented that PST was as effective as amitriptyline in reducing depressive symptoms in a primary-care population. Additionally, a dismantling study (Nezu & Perri, 1989) found that improvements in depressive symptoms were significantly greater when the problem orientation component of PST was included than when it was not included.

However, there are problems with the available PST outcome literature. First, it is noteworthy that PST has not been systematically compared to other forms of CBT, which have been found to have empirical support according to the empirically supported treatment literature. Second, an adequate body of literature does not yet exist to support unequivocally the empirical status of PST. Thus, at present, the available research

suggests that PST for depression is a possibly efficacious treatment according to the empirically supported treatment literature (Chambless et al., 1998). Further evidence, using the generic PST treatment manual, as well as more focused trials, will help to establish the empirical status of PST.

Rational-Emotive Therapy and Rational-Emotive Behavior Therapy

Rational-emotive therapy (RET), developed by Albert Ellis in 1955 under the original title, rational psychotherapy, represented the first of what would later come to be known as the cognitive-behavioral therapies (Dryden & Ellis, in press; Ellis, 1997). Ellis subsequently changed the label again in 1993 to rational-emotive behavior therapy (REBT) in response to critics who argued that the previous label neglected behavior (Dryden & Ellis, in press; Ellis, 1993). Consistent with this recent development, we refer to this approach as REBT in this chapter.

Ellis purported that a number of factors affect the psychological well-being of individuals, including cognitive, emotional, behavioral, and environmental determinants (Dryden & Ellis, 1988). Toward this end, Ellis proposed the ABC model of human disturbance, in which A stands for the activating event; B refers to the person's rational or irrational beliefs, which influence the way that A is perceived; and C stands for the emotional, behavioral, and cognitive consequences that arise from B (Dryden & Ellis, in press; Ellis, 1995). The key assumption of this model is that our beliefs affect how we both feel and act, and the way we feel and act, in turn, affects our beliefs.

While acknowledging the interdependent and interactive nature of these variables in (mal)adaptive human functioning, REBT ascribes a central role to cognition, and in particular to evaluative beliefs, in accounting for psychological health and disturbance. In keeping with this emphasis on cognition, Ellis (1977) stressed that humans have two primary biological predispositions. The first is the tendency to think in a rigid and irrational manner. For example, individuals often interpret desires and preferences in absolutist terms (e.g., needs or demands). The extreme nature of these standards makes them very difficult to achieve and more likely to result in psychological distress when they are not met. Thus, the REBT model defines the term *irra-*

tional to mean that beliefs are rigid, inconsistent with reality, and illogical and that they usually (although not invariably) impede the pursuit of basic goals and desires (Dryden & Ellis, in press; Ellis, 1977). The second basic biological human tendency involves the capability for meta-cognition (i.e., to ponder over one's thinking) and therefore the potential for humans to modify irrational thinking.

The REBT model proposes that when individuals become psychologically disturbed because of the presence of absolutistic demands, they begin to make illogical assumptions or cognitive distortions or errors such as all-or-none thinking, fortune-telling, and jumping to conclusions (Dryden & Ellis, 1988, in press; Ellis, 1984). In this respect, REBT is similar to other CBT theories (e.g., Beck, Rush, Shaw, & Emery, 1979). Ellis's model differs from other conceptualizations, however, in that these cognitive distortions are believed to inevitably stem from the self-defeating demands or "musts" that the person has established. Absolutism (e.g., "must-urbation") is thought to be at the root of psychological disturbance, according to Ellis. Psychologically healthy individuals, in contrast, are purported to exhibit a philosophy of "relativism." These persons may have several wishes and preferences but do not convert their desires into absolutistic demands that must be met to attain happiness or self-satisfaction.

Ellis also proposed that low frustration tolerance works to perpetuate psychological disturbances. Individuals prefer familiarity and resist change, even though the temporary discomfort involved in change would result in the subsequent amelioration of subjective distress. Also, psychological disturbance is perpetuated because people have a tendency to act in ways consistent with their irrational beliefs (Dryden & Ellis, in press).

Given that irrational thoughts, absolutist demands, and unconditional shoulds or musts are at the crux of Ellis's theory, it follows that these are emphasized most in therapy. A major objective of REBT is to help individuals identify, challenge, and dispose of their irrationality and replace these beliefs with more rational and healthy thinking (Dryden & Ellis, 1988, in press; Ellis, 1995). Thus REBT strives for the elegant restructuring of an individual's core philosophy of demands and irrational beliefs. Although cognitive change is the primary focus of REBT, it is recognized that therapeutic change may also come from the alteration of activating events.

Therefore, REBT is an active, directive style of therapy in which therapists function as educators who teach clients to correct their irrational beliefs and to think more rationally. Clients learn how to use REBT methods to help themselves, which requires that they assume an active role in the therapy. Therapists in REBT consider a balanced therapeutic relationship to be an important but not necessary condition for effective therapy. Although an atmosphere of unconditional acceptance is promoted, undue warmth is considered to be counterproductive because it may reinforce clients' irrational beliefs about their need for approval or love.

Therapy progresses through a series of stages, beginning with assessment. During the assessment phase, therapists focus on understanding the client's current problem, and information is gathered regarding the ABCs of these difficulties (Dryden & Ellis, in press). Typically, extensive information about the client's history is neither collected nor deemed necessary. The assessment phase includes a therapeutic component, as it affords the opportunity for the clients to begin to understand the relationships among their activating events (A), their beliefs (B), and the consequences (C) of those beliefs (Ellis & Greiger, 1977).

The second stage of therapy is the disputing stage, in which clients are helped to gain some realization, on an intellectual level, that their musts and demands are not supported by reality (Dryden & Ellis, in press). The purpose of this stage is to help the clients understand that their irrational beliefs are responsible for their emotional disturbance and that more rational beliefs will lead to psychological health. This newly found intellectual insight is a necessary prerequisite for the next stage of therapy, the working-through phase. In this phase, a variety of techniques are used to help clients achieve greater emotional insight into their difficulties. According to REBT, attaining emotional insight helps to promote and reinforce new thoughts, feelings, and behaviors that are consistent with a rational belief system (Dryden & Ellis, in press).

Notwithstanding the theoretical distinctions that have been drawn between REBT and other modes of cognitive-behavioral therapy, in practice they may be indistinguishable (Dryden & Ellis, in press; Ellis, 1996). Thus REBT therapists are eclectic in the techniques they use. Specialized techniques derived from REBT theory, as well as general strategies adopted from CBT and from other schools of psychotherapy, are often employed. The therapeutic methods most preferred by REBT therapists are those most congruent with the overarching ABC model. For example, actively disputing irrational beliefs is generally favored over relaxation or other cognitive distraction techniques. The primary REBT techniques involve disputing irrational beliefs, examining the pros and cons of various situations, using imagery and bibliotherapy, and defining techniques (e.g., using language differently so that it is less self-defeating) (Dryden & Ellis, in press). A number of emotive techniques are also employed, including the use of humor, therapists' self-disclosure, stories and parables, humorous songs, shame-attacking exercises (e.g., clients are instructed to deliberately act shamefully in public to learn to tolerate discomfort and to accept themselves), and risk-taking exercises (e.g., clients force themselves to take a risk in an area in which they are trying to make a change).

A number of behavioral techniques are also essential to the practice of REBT, including in vivo desensitization and flooding. These more intense behavioral procedures are preferred to the gradual (e.g., systematic desensitization) procedures typically used in cognitive-behavioral therapy because a primary goal is to increase the client's frustration tolerance (Dryden & Ellis, in press; Ellis & Grieger, 1977).

According to Dryden and Ellis (in press), more than 1000 outcome studies have been conducted on RET and REBT, with the majority indicating that REBT is significantly more efficacious than no treatment. A number of reviews of available outcome studies have been conducted (Engels, Garnefski, & Diekstra, 1993; Haaga & Davison, 1993; Hollon & Beck, 1994). For example, Lyons and Woods, 1991, conducted a meta-analysis of 70 studies comparing RET to baseline, control groups, cognitive-behavioral modification, behavioral therapy, and other psychotherapies. The populations investigated included normal, phobic, neurotic, and emotional and somatic subjects. These reviewers found that RET was more effective than baseline and control groups but was no more effective than cognitive-behavioral modification and behavioral therapy.

Despite positive reviews, the outcome literature on RET and REBT has been criticized by several researchers. For example, Gossette and O'Brien (1992) reviewed the available research comparing the unique components of RET with wait-list, placebo, and other treatment conditions

and found that RET was effective in only 25% of the comparisons. These researchers cogently argued that many of the extant outcome studies that attest to the efficacy of RET are flawed because they have combined RET techniques with general CBT rather than addressing the unique features of RET. Dryden and Ellis (in press) also caution that the efficacy of REBT has not been systematically compared to other types of CBTs, including those developed by Beck, Bandura, Lazarus, and Meichenbaum. Kendall et al. (1995) recently noted that there is a paucity of well-controlled outcome studies that meet the criteria for establishing empirically supported treatments (e.g., APA Division 12 Task Force report on Promotion and Dissemination of Psychological Procedures). The empirically supported treatment literature does not presently include REBT as an efficacious treatment for any adult mental disorder (Chambless et al., 1998).

Cognitive Therapy

Cognitive therapy was originally developed by Beck et al. (1979) for the treatment of depression. Cognitive therapy is an active, direct, structured, short-term, psychoeducational psychotherapy that has now been adopted for the treatment of a variety of mental disorders, in addition to unipolar depression (e.g., Basco & Rush, 1996; Beck & Emery, 1985; Beck, Wright, Newman, & Liese, 1993; Dattilio & Freeman, 1994; Freeman et al., 1989). Cognitive therapy is based on the theoretical rationale that one's self-schema and related cognitive processes largely determine one's affect and behavior (Beck, 1976; Beck et al., 1979).

A core assumption of cognitive therapy is that the way in which an individual processes and interprets internal and external information must be modified to effect real change in psychological functioning and to prevent the recurrence of psychopathology. Thus, the principal emphasis in therapy entails the identification, evaluation, and modification of faulty information processing and underlying self-schemata. In cognitive therapy, clients are taught that the content and processes of their thinking style mediate emotional distress, that they can learn to systematically monitor and evaluate their beliefs and information-processing styles, and that the modification of these automatic thoughts and core beliefs will result in changes in affect and behavior. Cognitive therapy focuses on assisting clients to examine and understand the way in which they perceive themselves, their world, and the future and to experiment with more adaptive ways of responding in cognitive, emotional, and behavioral modes.

One of the primary tenets of cognitive-behavioral therapy is the use of collaborative empiricism, which refers to the fact that therapists and clients function together as a team, each contributing valuable information and expertise in an attempt to understand the clients' difficulties (via guided discovery), ameliorate their symptoms, and enhance their functioning (Beck et al., 1979). This collaboration extends to all aspects of the therapeutic encounter, from eliciting raw data to establishing homework assignments. A second important principle in cognitive therapy is its focus on the "here and now" (Beck et al., 1979). Although maladaptive thinking may have developed from early experiences, successful treatment does not require eliciting childhood memories or working through unconscious processes; rather, therapy focuses on how this thinking is currently activated and how one's maladaptive philosophies and beliefs might become more in line with objective evidence.

Assessment and diagnosis are essential components of cognitive-behavioral therapy. Also, it is imperative that the patient is provided with a rationale for cognitive therapy. Once the essential information has been gathered, and the clients have been educated about the cognitive model and what they can expect from the process of cognitive therapy, clients and therapists work together to formulate a cognitive understanding of the clients' problems (Persons, 1989; Persons & Davidson, in press). This formulation will ideally explain the cognitive distortions, behavioral issues, and emotional issues that contribute to an individual's psychological distress. This cognitive formulation forms the basis for the process and structure of therapy by establishing key objectives and action plans for change. Another key point in cognitive therapy is the establishment of an agenda at the beginning of each therapy session so that both the therapist and client collaboratively agree on the topics for each session. Throughout the course of therapy, the initial cognitive formulation or hypotheses about the client are tested and refined in accordance with available information.

Despite the title, cognitive therapy has from its inception used a variety of cognitive and behavioral techniques and strategies (Beck et al., 1979). In addition, cognitive-behavioral therapy does not ignore the importance of emotions, and in fact makes use of a number of emotional techniques as well (Beck et al., 1979). Primarily, though, cognitive techniques are aimed at eliciting understanding and altering the client's cognitive organization or construction of reality (e.g., beliefs and assumptions) (Beck et al., 1979). Cognitive techniques include cognitive restructuring, Socratic questioning, identifying illogical thinking, ascertaining the client's assumptions and previously unattested implicit rules, identifying automatic thoughts, examining and reality-testing automatic thoughts, reattributing responsibility, searching for alternative solutions, and recording dysfunctional thoughts.

As therapy proceeds and the client's symptoms abate, the focus of therapy changes from identifying cognitive errors to altering the maladaptive assumptions on which those errors are based (Beck et al., 1979). This focus is thought to have preventative effect in terms of increasing the clients' ability to cope with future problems and minimizing their risk of subsequent psychiatric distress. Maladaptive assumptions are believed to derive from self-schemata, which are the rules or internal working models with which the clients have learned to interpret themselves, the future, and the world. Different forms of psychopathology are believed to operate under this same basic system of cognitive biases, although they may be distinguished in terms of their content-specific cognitive profiles. For example, depression is often characterized by automatic thoughts and maladaptive beliefs that pertain to past loss, failure, and deprivation. The schemata involved in anxiety revolve around themes of future threat or danger. These schemata are maladaptive in that they are rigid, are excessive, and are thought to be activated when the individual experiences a situation that impinges on his or her specific vulnerability (e.g., acceptance-rejection) (Beck et al., 1979).

One important role of the therapist is to help clients question and assess the costs and benefits of their schemata, examine the evidence for these beliefs, generate alternative explanations, and develop more healthy beliefs. A technique that is often used to facilitate this stage is the downward arrow or vertical arrow technique (J. Beck, 1995), which asks a series of questions about the significance of an anticipated or past event in order to elicit the client's underlying beliefs (Belsher & Wilkes, 1994).

Socratic questioning involves asking a series of questions to help clients challenge the assumptions, beliefs, or behaviors that contribute to their presenting complaints (e.g., Rush & Nowels,

1994). An important distinction between CBT and REBT lies in this aspect of therapy. In REBT, active disputation of the clients' cognitions is undertaken to help the clients see the cognitive errors they are making. In CBT, Socratic questioning allows the clients to arrive at their own conclusions about their thinking and to identify their own cognitive errors rather than relying on the therapist to elicit and challenge them (Beck et al., 1979).

Behavioral techniques are also used in cognitive therapy. Their goals are to change behavior, elicit thoughts that are associated with specific behaviors, and test maladaptive cognitions or assumptions (Beck et al., 1979). In the early stages of therapy and with more severely depressed clients, for example, behavioral techniques (e.g., activity schedules, mastery and pleasure schedules, and graded task assignments) are utilized to fairly quickly provide the clients with some measure of symptom relief so that they are able to proceed with a course of therapy. These strategies often help to counteract patients' immobility, loss of motivation, and beliefs that they are ineffectual. Successful completion of behavioral techniques also provides the clients with information that is contrary to their beliefs that they are unable to accomplish any tasks. A key difference between the use of behavioral techniques by a cognitive therapist and that by a behavioral therapist is that the modification of behavior is the goal for the latter, whereas the modification of behavior is the means to an end, cognitive change, for the cognitive therapist (Beck et al., 1979). Homework is also an essential aspect of cognitive therapy, as it allows the clients to continue to work toward their goals between the therapy sessions and so encourages an active role for them in their own recovery (Beck et al., 1979).

Cognitive-behavioral therapy has also been adapted for use with a number of disorders other than unipolar depression, including anxiety disorders (e.g., Beck & Emery, 1985), personality disorders (e.g., Beck et al., 1990; Young, 1990, 1994), eating disorders (e.g., Fairburn, 1981, 1985; Garner & Bemis, 1982, 1985), substance abuse disorders (Beck et al., 1993), and bipolar disorder (Basco & Rush, 1996).

According to the empirically supported treatment literature, cognitive therapy for depression has been found to be an efficacious and specific treatment (Chambless et al., 1998). Thus, according to the available research, cognitive therapy is more efficacious for depression than no

treatment, control treatments, and other active treatments, such as nondirective therapy, traditional psychodynamic group therapy, interpersonal therapy, behavioral therapy, and problem-solving therapy (Chambless et al., 1998). Cognitive therapy has also been compared with pharmacotherapy in the treatment of depression, and in many instances has been found to be as effective or even more effective (Antonuccio, Danton, & DeNelsky, 1995; Bowers, 1990; De Rubeis & Feeley, 1990; Dobson, 1989; Evans et al., 1992; Hollon et al., 1992; Hollon, Shelton, & Loosen, 1991). Although more recent research indicates that the initial reports of the clear superiority of cognitive therapy may need to be adjusted, it remains to be seen whether cognitive therapy holds promise for preventing or delaying relapse and whether this is where its superiority lies (Antonuccio et al., 1995; Blackburn, Eunson, & Bishop, 1986; Dobson, Pusch, & Jackman-Cram, 1991; Fava, Rafanelli, Grandi, Conti, & Belluardo, 1998; Gortner, Gollan, Dobson, & Jacobson, 1998; Hollon et al., 1991; Segal, Gemar, & Williams, 1999; Simons, Murphy, Levine, & Wetzel, 1986). Even more encouraging has been the growing consensus that cognitive therapy is effective even for severely depressed individuals (Bowers, 1990; Evans et al., 1992; Hollon et al., 1992; Miller, Norman, Keitner, Bishop, & Dow, 1989; Thase, Bowler, & Harden, 1991).

Cognitive therapy has also been found to be an efficacious and specific treatment for generalized anxiety disorder (GAD) and panic disorder (Chambless et al., 1998). Thus, cognitive therapy is more effective than applied relaxation in the treatment of GAD, and more effective than exposure therapy or applied relaxation in the treatment of panic disorder. Also, in the treatment of social phobia, exposure on its own or in combination with cognitive restructuring were both found to be efficacious treatments. Cognitive therapy has also been found to be a possibly efficacious treatment for obsessive-compulsive disorder (OCD), although exposure and response prevention remain the most efficacious and specific treatment (Chambless et al., 1998).

The empirical status of cognitive therapy for other disorders is more tenuous than for depression and the anxiety disorders. Trials are under way to evaluate its efficacy in the area of substance abuse, bipolar disorder, posttraumatic stress disorder, and other domains. The field will no doubt pay considerable attention to these results.

Schema-focused Cognitive Therapy

Schema-focused therapy, or SFT (Young, 1990, 1994), is an adaptation of Beck's CBT that was developed for the treatment of personality disorders and chronic Axis I disorders (e.g., depression and anxiety). Schema-focused therapy differs from standard CBT in a number of ways. First, SFT places greater emphasis on the therapeutic relationship. Second, the role of affect is explicitly highlighted. Third, more discussion is focused on childhood origins of difficulties and developmental processes. Fourth, more attention is directed toward coping styles. Finally, there is more focus on identifying core themes or schemas. Thus, schema-focused therapy is an integrative approach that combines cognitive, behavioral, interpersonal, and experiential techniques.

Schema-focused therapy proposes four theoretical constructs to expand general CBT as proposed by Beck et al. (1979). The first of these is early maladaptive schemas, which are defined as "extremely stable and enduring themes that develop during childhood and are elaborated upon throughout an individual's lifetime . . . [and which] serve as templates for the processing of later experience" (Young, 1990, p. 9). Young also proposed three major processes, which explain how schemas function within an individual. Schema maintenance refers to processes, such as cognitive distortions and self-defeating behavioral patterns, that reinforce early maladaptive schemas. Schema avoidance refers to processes that act to avoid triggering the schema or experiencing the affect associated with it. Schema avoidance can include attempts at cognitive avoidance, affective avoidance, or behavioral avoidance. Finally, schema compensation refers to processes that overcompensate for early maladaptive schemas. Young (1990, 1994) has described a number of early maladaptive schemas that have been gleaned from clinical work, although he cautions that the list remains a work in progress.

Schema-focused therapy proceeds in two stages. In the first stage, the focus is on assessment and education. Specific steps to achieve these goals include identifying the clients' schemas and educating the clients about them, linking the schemas to the clients' current problems and to his/her life history, helping the patient become aware of the emotions associated with his/her schemas, and identifying the clients' dysfunctional coping styles. In the second stage of

therapy, the goal is change. Specific steps within this stage include cognitive work, such as restructuring the client's cognitions about his/her schemas; experiential work to help the clients grieve their early pain and regain some empowerment; a focus on the therapeutic relationship in order to "provide limited reparenting" as well as to work on confronting schemas and coping styles; and breaking of behavioral patterns by assigning and rehearsing behavioral change related to the client's current problems.

Schema-focused therapy is a rich approach that advances CBT in some clear directions. SFT also moves the field of the cognitive-behavioral therapies much closer to other schools of thought, such as both the constructivist therapies (see Chapter 16, this volume) and in particular the object-relations school of psychoanalysis schools. Unfortunately, at present there is a dearth of published research on the efficacy of schema-focused therapy. Even some of the basic assumptions of the approach (for example, the benefit of reprocessing early experience) require evaluation. The evolving place of SFT within the cognitive-behavioral therapies will no doubt be based in part on these evaluations.

A Case Example of Cognitive-Behavioral Therapy

"Dan" was a 43-year-old white-collar worker in a good-sized oil and gas firm, at least until the day he was told he was part of a "right-sizing" exercise the company he worked for was doing. As the only person laid off in his particular office, he began to question why he had been chosen. The company gave no answer; the settlement package they offered was a standard one, and the personnel officers offered no further clues.

Dan's wife of 14 years was anxious about the situation she and he were in. Mandy worried about mortgage payments and how they would afford to raise their two children. As Dan's initial attempts to obtain other work were unsuccessful, she became critical of him. His hope began to slip, and he found himself pulling away from both Mandy and other friends. By the time he recognized he was depressed and came for treatment, he had already entertained thoughts of running away and suicide as strategies to cope with his perceived incompetence.

The assessment of Dan revealed that he met the criteria for major depressive disorder. His Beck Depression Inventory score of 34 suggested moderately severe depression, and his manner reflected this assessment. He had become quite pessimistic about his work prospects, and he was not actively searching for new work. In fact, he spent a good deal of time watching television. Although he was helping out more around the house, both he and Mandy viewed this as a poor substitute for work. She was actively critical of him and had recently started to reject him in bed.

Dan's case is not terribly unusual, but it does raise important questions about how best to conceptualize and approach his problem. Simply by using the cognitive-behavioral therapies, potential approaches to this case include the following:

- Identifying the irrational beliefs he and his wife have about the need to work and its role in defining his value as a person. Thus REBT might have been used to educate Dan about his current beliefs and their consequences and then, using rational disputation, to broaden his view of his value.

- Treating his employment situation as a "problem" and using a problem-solving approach to his process of seeking reemployment. Techniques that could be used include generating various possible work situations, evaluating the advantages and disadvantages of each situation, defining optimal job strategies for the option that was chosen as the best from among those evaluated, and encouraging Dan to act on these plans.

- Using cognitive therapy strategies to assess situation-specific cognitive distortions in a variety of problematic areas, including job search and his relationship with Mandy, his children, and his friends. Using this approach, he could learn the process of how depression affects the view of what is possible, and new options for adaptive behavior and more effective thinking could arise.

- A more schema-focused cognitive therapy approach could have been employed to examine the origins of defining his worth by his work situation and how this schema defined his reaction to his layoff.

Which of the above conceptualizations was the "correct" one? Which one would lead to the best treatment plan and would be maximally effective in reducing Dan's depression, helping restore his relationship with Mandy, and get him to return to the work force (assuming these were his goals)? Which approach would he find the most acceptable? Should his wife be brought into the treatment office? Might a simple behavioral plan, without cognitive interventions, be just as effective? Are there any data to support one or the other of these plans for a depressed person with the profile of Dan?

It is an unfortunate reality that at present the research evidence does not support any one of these strategies over its competitors (or treatments from other supported approaches). The treatment of Dan was therefore based more on a clinical judgment about what he presented as his most salient problem (his work situation) and what he had tried previously that had not been successful (I always look for ineffective strategies and then use something else). In the end, a combination of problem solving and cognitive restructuring was used. We identified negative cognitions that were interfering with his job search, corrected these ideas (see the TIC-TOC strategy in Beck & Emery, 1985; J. Beck, 1995), and then used a more positive problem-solving approach to his employment situation. No doubt, his success in getting a new position was helpful in his recovery from depression, although the fact that it was at a lower income than his previous job left fertile ground for exploring the meanings he associated with position and economic value.

Indeed, it may not matter which approach was used with Dan. At this point in development we simply do not have a treatment algorithm to apply to individuals. (I [KD] predict we never will, and that clinical judgment will always play a role at the individual case level.) What this case does underscore for me, though, is the need for a case conceptualization (see also Persons, 1989; Persons & Davidson, in press) to plan the interventions that are applied.

CONCEPTUAL ISSUES AND FUTURE DIRECTIONS

As the previous sections attest, there is a wide range of cognitive-behavioral therapies, with a large number of interventions that can be applied to a broad range of clinical problems (Dobson & Craig, 1996; Granvold, 1996). Some of these therapies, such as REBT and cognitive therapy, represent systems, whereas other methods employ more focused intervention (e.g., SIT). Cognitive-behavioral therapies are generally garnering research evidence to support their development (Chambless, et al., 1998; Dobson & Craig, 1998), and it is likely that they will continue to be among the strongest developments in the years to come. Despite this generally rosy picture, it remains true that there are a number of conceptual and development challenges for the cognitive-behavioral therapies. In this section we review some of the most salient of these issues.

One Model or Several?

One of the conceptual issues that has been raised about the cognitive-behavioral therapies is whether they represent a single conceptual approach to psychotherapy, several related approaches, or a set of techniques (e.g., McMullin, 1986). Certainly, the cognitive-behavioral therapies we have discussed share the three essential elements first outlined by Dobson and Block (1988), in that they assume (1) cognitive activity affects behavior (the mediational hypothesis), (2) cognitive activity may be monitored and altered (the access hypothesis), and (3) desired behavioral change can be effected through cognitive change. They all share the idea that change in cognition, although a goal of therapy, is not sufficient to decide that therapy is concluded. Rather, behavioral change as an index of cognitive change is also a required element of successful therapy.

We have argued that the constructivist forms of therapy are not within the gambit of the cognitive-behavioral therapies because of their basic belief in the lack of a knowable, external reality. This perspective can be challenged (Held, 1995). We anticipate that considerable discussion about the "location" of the constructivist therapies within the taxonomy of psychotherapies in general will take place in the near future (see Chapter 16 in this volume).

Beyond the question of constructivist therapies, though, it would be to the field's advantage if a proper taxonomy of the cognitive-behavioral therapies could be evolved. Such a taxonomy could help to clarify whether some approaches "supercede" others and, conversely, if others are embedded with others. This taxonomy would be very helpful in the generation of comparative research studies. For example, it may be of value to contrast REBT, PST, and CBT in the treatment of depression. To do so, however, a more formalized taxonomy will be needed, with a clear exposition of which interventions "belong" to which therapies. Such research can help to clarify the effective ingredients of therapy or lead to the generation of new hybrid cognitive-behavioral models of intervention.

Efficacy and Efficiency

Although the cognitive-behavioral therapies are beginning to amass a solid database in terms of their efficacy (Chambless et al., 1998), it remains the case that the efficacy literature requires development. For example, although cognitive therapy is now considered to be effective in treating depression, its status with regard to other clinical issues is not as well developed. As discussed, there remain an insufficient number of well-controlled studies evaluating the efficacy of REBT. Some cognitive-behavioral therapies require further evidence to establish that they are more than "probably efficacious" (Chambless et al., 1996, 1998).

It is our perspective that as mental health treatments in general become more firmly established as having efficacy and as this evidence becomes more broadly known, several effects can be anticipated. First, as the public comes to learn about these data, people will seek these treatments. Third-party payers are acutely sensitive to funding what works, and so it can be expected that they will preferentially fund these treatments (indeed, this phenomenon is already occurring). Public policymakers and public agencies will always prefer to spend public funds on normative science and demonstrably evidence-based practice (Barlow, 1996). It is important to note that evidence-based practice and practice guidelines will favor all approaches that are given such support. Thus, although to date the cognitive-behavioral therapies distinguish themselves for their evidence, other therapy approaches may also garner such evidence.

A critical question is whether or not the methodology typically associated with clinical trials can provide convincing evidence about therapy effectiveness. Although the randomized clinical trial continues to be the optimal research design for evaluating therapy effectiveness, a number of conceptual issues remain, including the relative homogeneity of research participants, the manualization of treatment methods, the choice of outcome measures, the use of trained therapists, the nature of placebo or no-treatment controls, recruitment and sample sizes, the appropriate analysis of intent-to-treat and completer samples, the use of significance testing vs. other outcome assessments, and so on (see Chapter 2 in this volume; Jacobson & Christensen, 1996; Kazdin, 1994). In the design of any given study, the investigator will typically trade off one advantage for another methodological or statistical problem.

On top of the research issues that emerge in efficacy studies, that of efficiency has increasingly been raised. If a given therapy "works," how many sessions of it are required? Can it be organized in such a manner as to be more broadly applied or accepted by a higher proportion of patients? If two effective treatments exist for a given problem, is one more cost-effective, either in the short or long term (Hollon, 1996)? These questions require studies that take an existing effective treatment and then either modify it (e.g., compress it into fewer sessions) or compare it to some other approach in outcomes and other variables such as cost offset, patients' satisfaction, or some other measure of effectiveness (Howard, Moras, Brill, Martinovich, & Lutz, 1996). To date, such research is sparse. We therefore advocate greater attention to the issues of efficiency, as well as efficacy, in research on the cognitive-behavioral therapies (Hollon, 1996; Howard et al., 1996).

Mechanisms of Change

Although the techniques of the cognitive-behavioral therapies are fairly well explicated, it is the case that in large measure we do not well understand the mechanisms of change. Many of the therapies are complex, multifactorial approaches and involve several techniques appropriate to the patient's presenting problems and stage of therapy. Furthermore, many of the treatment manuals refer to the need for a particular form of therapeutic relationship and for certain structured elements of the therapy (e.g., session agendas and homework) regardless of the therapy content. Whether the effectiveness of the cognitive-behavioral therapies rests on the nature of the relationship, the structural elements, the techniques, or some combination of these (potentially also in interaction with other patient variables) is not well understood at present.

To investigate the effective ingredients of change, a number of research designs can be employed (Kazdin, 1994). Dismantling research paradigms has been used in examining the bases of the cognitive-behavioral therapies in such areas as depression (Gortner et al., 1998; Jacobson et al., 1996; Nezu & Perri, 1989), anxiety disorders (Emmelkamp, Mersch, Vissia, & van der Helm, 1985; Jerremalm, Jansson, & Ost, 1986), and marital therapy (Jacobson, 1984). Problem-solving therapies and panic control therapy, by virtue of their modular structure, recommend themselves for future research.

A variant of efficiency research that has been used in some studies but is still relatively underutilized in the cognitive-behavioral tradition is process research. For example, it is possible to assess the utilization of various techniques at various stages of treatment and to determine whether or not these techniques are associated with patient change. In a study of this type, DeRubeis and Feeley (1990) documented that cognitive therapy techniques early in the course of therapy were associated, more than general relationship factors, with a positive change in patients' depression scores. Similar research may provide clues about the mechanisms of change and has obvious implications for the optimal delivery of effective treatments.

The moderating role of various patient characteristics on cognitive-behavioral treatment outcomes is as yet a relatively understudied area. Beutler (Beutler & Baker, 1998; Beutler & Clarkin, 1990) has recommended the use of aptitude-by-treatment interactional research designs to examine these questions. Given that the cognitive-behavioral therapies are beginning to demonstrate a sufficient empirical base in general, it may be time to begin to study their relative effectiveness in specific populations or with specific patient characteristics (Beutler & Baker, 1998; Doyle, 1998). We recommend the strategies of aptitude-by-treatment research methods, although we are cognizant that such research requires larger sample sizes than those typically associated with work in the field.

Training, Adherence, and Competency Issues

One of the issues that has recently emerged in the research literature is that of therapists' training, adherence, and competency. The criteria for empirically supported therapies include the development of a treatment manual to help ensure that the treatment, if found effective, can be replicated. This requirement, though, begs the question of what type of training is necessary for outcome and efficiency research (Dobson & Shaw, 1988). Presumably, a treatment manual will help to control the content of any treatment that is being investigated; in other words, it will control the independent variable. Measures of therapists' adherence to a manual will constitute the operational definition of the manual's implementation. In addition to the issue of adherence, though, is that of competence. Competence rests on a level of skillful application of the techniques of the treatment that goes beyond simple adherence. The optimal test of a treatment model should be based on both an adherent and competent administration.

Unfortunately, the requirements of adherent and competent delivery of treatments are not often evaluated in treatment studies. Even in the research on cognitive therapy of depression, where this issue has been considered the most, standardized criteria for assessing adherence and competence are not yet available. It is not even clear who can be used as an evaluator of adherence and competence; for example, can trained undergraduates provide valid competency ratings, or must the raters be trained experts (Dobson & Shaw, 1988)? Unlike in drug protocols, where blood or urine assays can assess the dose being delivered to the patient, we have no similar evaluations in psychotherapy.

It is important to note that although adherence is a critical issue in randomized clinical trials, it is relatively unimportant in clinical settings. Indeed, one of the criticisms of the psychotherapy literature is that the treatments are too pure and that they do not relate well to clinical practice, where therapists typically operate by using an eclectic framework (Goldfried & Wolfe, 1996). What is critical for practitioners and service providers is how to be competent in delivery; adherence is relevant only if it can be demonstrated that a "pure" intervention is also the only competent way in which to deliver the treatment. Such questions require much more evaluation, both in general and with respect to the cognitive-behavioral therapies.

Dissemination

Predicated on the assumption that the cognitive-behavioral therapies are effective, as the database is beginning to show, an important issue emerges—how best to disseminate these treatments to interested and affected parties. Such parties include, but are not limited to, practitioners, patients, third-party payers, and policymakers. Organizations that promote the cognitive-behavioral therapies, such as the Association for the Advancement of Behavior Therapy or the International Association of Cognitive Psychotherapies, have a pivotal role to play in ensuring that dissemination takes place. Such methods as journals, books, conferences, workshops, press releases, political lobbying, and just plain old "boosterism" for psychotherapy all recommend themselves to us as sound strategies. The therapies that garner sound efficacy and effectiveness evidence, not limited to but certainly including the cognitive-behavioral therapies, deserve the opportunity to be used in clinical practice. Our patients deserve no less.

REFERENCES

Agran, M., Fodor-Davis, J., & Moore, S. (1986). The effects of self-instruction training on job-task sequencing: Suggesting a problem-solving strategy. *Education and Training of the Mentally Retarded, 21,* 273–281.

Antonuccio, D. O., Danton, W. G., & DeNelsky, G. Y. (1995). Psychotherapy versus medication for depression: Challenging the conventional wisdom with data. *Professional Psychology Research and Practice, 26,* 574–585.

Arean, P. A., Perri, M. G., Nezu, A. M., Schein, R. L., Christopher, F., & Joseph, T. X. (1993). Comparative effectiveness of social problem-solving therapy and reminiscence therapy as treatments for depression in older adults. *Journal of Consulting and Clinical Psychology, 61,* 1003–1010.

Bandura, A. (1977). Self-efficacy: Toward a unifying theory of behavior change. *Psychological Review, 84,* 191–215.

Bandura, A., & Walters, R. H. (1963). *Social learning and personality development.* New York: Holt, Rinehart and Winston.

Barlow, D. H. (1996). Health care policy, psychotherapy research, and the future of psychotherapy. *American Psychologist, 51,* 1050–1058.

Basco, M. R., & Rush, A. J. (1996). *Cognitive-behavioral therapy for bipolar disorder.* New York: Guilford Press.

Beck, A. T. (1970). Cognitive therapy: Nature and relation to behavior therapy. *Behavior Therapy, 1,* 184–200.

Beck, A. T. (1976). *Cognitive therapy and the emotional disorders.* New York: International Universities Press.

Beck, A. T., & Emery, G. (1985). *Anxiety disorders and phobias: A cognitive perspective.* New York: Basic Books.

Beck, A. T., Freeman, A., & Associates (1990). *Cognitive therapy of personality disorders.* New York: Guilford Press.

Beck, A. T., Rush, A. J., Shaw, B.F., & Emery, G. (1979). *Cognitive therapy of depression.* New York: Guilford Press.

Beck, A. T., Wright, F. D., Newman, C. F., & Liese, B. S. (1993). *Cognitive therapy of substance abuse.* New York: Guilford Press.

Beck, J. (1995). *Cognitive therapy: Basics and beyond.* New York: Guilford Press.

Belsher, G., & Wilkes, T. C. R. (1994). Middle phase of cognitive therapy: Intervention techniques for five steps in the therapeutic process. In T.C.R. Wilkes, G. Belsher, A. J. Rush, & E. Frank (Eds.), *Cognitive therapy for depressed adolescents* (pp. 132–243). New York: Guilford Press.

Beutler, L. E., & Baker, M. (1998). The movement

toward empirical validation: At what level should we analyze, and who are our consumers? In K. S. Dobson & K. D. Craig (Eds.) *Empirically supported therapies: Best practice in professional psychology.* (pp. 43–65). Thousand Oaks, California: Sage Publications.

Beutler, L. E., & Clarkin, J. (1990). *Systematic treatment selection: Toward targeted therapeutic interventions.* New York: Brunner/Mazel.

Blackburn, I., Eunson, K., & Bishop, S. (1986). A two-year naturalistic follow-up of depressed patients treated with cognitive therapy and pharmacotherapy and a combination of both. *Journal of Affective Disorders, 10,* 67–75.

Bowers, W. A. (1990). Treatment of depressed inpatients: Cognitive therapy plus medication, relaxation plus medication, and medication alone. *British Journal of Psychiatry, 156,* 73–78.

Cautela, J. (1967). Covert sensitization. *Psychological Reports, 20,* 459–468.

Chambless, D. L., Baker, M. J., Baucom, D. H., Beutler, L., Calhoun, K. S., Crits–Christoph, P., Daiuto, A., DeRebuis, R., Detweiler, J., Haaga, D.A.F., Bennett Johnson, S., McCurry, S. Mueser, K. T., Pope, K. S., Sanderson, W. C., Shoham, V., Stickle, T., Williams, D. A., & Woody, S. A. (1998). Update on empirically validated therapies, II. *The Clinical Psychologist, 51,* 3–16.

Chambless, D. L., Sanderson, W. C., Shoham, V., Bennett Johnson, S., Pope, K. S., Crits-Christoph, P., Baker, M., Johnson, B., Woody, S. R., Sue, S., Beutler, L., Williams, D. A., & McCurry, S. (1996). An update on empirically validated therapies. *The Clinical Psychologist, 49,* 30–33.

Crick, N. R., & Dodge, K. A. (1994). A review and reformulation of social information-processing mechanisms in children's social adjustment. *Psychological Bulletin, 115,* 73–101.

Dattilio, F. M., & Freeman, A. (1994). (Eds.). *Cognitive-behavioral strategies in crisis intervention.* New York: Guilford Press.

DeRubeis, R. J., & Feeley, M. (1990). Determinants of change in cognitive therapy for depression. *Cognitive Therapy and Research, 14,* 469–482.

Dobson, K. S. (Ed.). (1988). *Handbook of cognitive-behavioral therapies.* New York: Guilford Press.

Dobson, K. S. (1989). A meta-analysis of the efficacy of cognitive therapy for depression. *Journal of Consulting and Clinical Psychology, 57,* 414–419.

Dobson, K. S., & Block, L. (1988). Historical and philosophical bases of the cognitive-behavioral therapies. In K. S. Dobson (Ed.) *Handbook of cognitive-behavioral therapies* (pp. 3–38). New York: Guilford Press.

Dobson, K. S., & Craig, K. D. (Eds.). (1996). *Advances in cognitive-behavioral therapy.* Thousand Oaks, California: Sage Publications.

Dobson, K. S., & Craig, K. D. (Eds.). (1998). *Empirically supported therapies: Best practice in professional psychology.* Thousand Oaks, California: Sage Publications.

Dobson, K. S., Pusch, D., & Jackman-Cram, S. (1991). *Further evidence of the efficacy of cognitive therapy for depression: Multiple outcome measures and long-term effects.* Poster presented at the 25th Annual Association for Advancement of Behavior Therapy Convention, New York.

Dobson, K. S., & Shaw, B. F. (1988). Competency judgements in the training and evaluations of psychotherapists. *Journal of Consulting and Clinical Psychology, 56,* 666–672.

Doyle, A.-B. (1998). Are empirically validated treatments valid for culturally diverse populations? In K. S. Dobson & K. D. Craig (Eds.), *Empirically supported therapies: Best practice in professional psychology* (pp. 93–106). Thousand Oaks, California: Sage Publications.

Dryden, W., & Ellis, A. (1988). Rational-emotive therapy. In K. S. Dobson (Ed.), *Handbook of cognitive-behavioral therapies* (pp. 214–272). New York: Guilford Press.

Dryden, W., & Ellis, A. (in press). Rational-emotive behavior therapy. In K. S. Dobson (Ed.) *Handbook of cognitive-behavioral therapies (2nd edition).* New York: Guilford Press.

D'Zurilla, T. J. (1988). Problem-solving therapies. In K. S. Dobson (Ed.) *Handbook of cognitive-behavioral therapies* (pp. 85–135). New York: Guilford Press.

D'Zurilla, T. J. (1990). Problem-solving training for effective stress management and prevention. *Journal of Cognitive Psychotherapy: An International Quarterly, 4,* 327–355.

D'Zurilla, T. J., & Goldfried, M. R. (1971). Problem solving and behavior modification. *Journal of Abnormal Psychology, 78,* 107–126.

D'Zurilla, T. J., & Nezu, A. M. (1982). Social problem solving in adults. In P. C. Kendall (Ed.), *Advances in cognitive-behavioral research and therapy* (Vol. 1, pp. 202–274). New York: Academic Press.

D'Zurilla, T. J., & Nezu, A. M. (in press a). Problem-solving therapies. In K. S. Dobson (Ed.) *Handbook of cognitive-behavioral therapies (2nd edition).* New York: Guilford Press.

D'Zurilla, T. J., & Nezu, A. M. (in press b). *Problem-solving therapy: A social competence approach to clinical intervention* (2nd ed.). New York: Springer Press.

Ellis, A. (1977). The basic clinical theory of rational-emotive therapy. In A. Ellis & R. Grieger (Eds.), *Handbook of rational-emotive therapy* (pp. 3–34). New York: Springer.

Ellis, A. (1984). The essence of RET-1984. *Journal of Rational-Emotive Therapy, 2,* 19–25.

Ellis, A. (1993). Changing rational-emotive therapy (RET) to rational emotive behavior therapy (REBT). *Behavior Therapist, 16,* 257–258.

Ellis, A. (1995). Reflections of rational-emotive therapy. In M. J. Mahoney (Ed.), *Cognitive and constructive psychotherapies: Theory, research, and practice* (pp. 69–73). New York: Springer.

Ellis, A. (1996). Responses to criticism of rational emotive behavior therapy (REBT) by Ray DiGiuseppe, Frank Bond, Wendy Dryden, Steve Weinrach, and Richard Wessler. *Journal of Rational-Emotive & Cognitive-Behavior Therapy, 14*, 97–121.

Ellis, A. (1997). The evolution of Albert Ellis and rational emotive behavior therapy. In J. K. Zeig (Ed.), *The evolution of psychotherapy: The third conference* (pp. 69–82). New York: Brunner/Mazel.

Ellis, A., & Grieger, R. (Eds.). (1977). *Handbook of rational-emotive therapy.* New York: Springer.

Emmelkamp, P. M. G., Mersch, P. P., Vissia, E., & van der Helm, M. (1985). Social phobia: A comparative evaluation of cognitive and behavioral interventions. *Behaviour Research & Therapy, 23*, 365–369.

Engels, G. I., Garnefski, N., & Diekstra, R. F. W. (1993). Efficacy of rational-emotive therapy: A quantitative analysis. *Journal of Consulting and Clinical Psychology, 61*, 1083–1090.

Evans, M. D., Hollon, S. D., DeRubeis, R. J., Piasecki, J. M., Grove, W. M., Garvey, M. J., & Tucson, V. B. (1992). Differential relapse following cognitive therapy and pharmacotherapy for depression. *Archives of General Psychiatry, 49*, 802–808.

Fairburn, C. G. (1981). A cognitive behavioral approach to the management of bulimia. *Psychological Medicine, 11*, 707–711.

Fairburn, C. G. (1985). Cognitive-behavioral treatment for bulimia. In D. M. Garner & P. E. Garfinkel (Eds.), *Handbook of psychotherapy for anorexia nervosa and bulimia* (pp. 160–192). New York: Guilford.

Fava, G. A., Rafanelli, C., Grandi, S., Conti, S., & Belluardo, P. (1998). Prevention of recurrent depression with cognitive behavioral therapy. *Archives of General Psychiatry, 55*, 816–820.

Freeman, A., Simon, K., Butler, L., & Arkowitz, H. (Eds.). (1989). *Comprehensive handbook of cognitive therapy.* New York: Plenum.

Garner, D. M., & Bemis, K. M. (1982). A cognitive-behavioral approach to anorexia nervosa. *Cognitive Therapy and Research, 6*, 123–150.

Garner, D. M., & Bemis, K. M. (1985). Cognitive therapy for anorexia nervosa. In D. M. Garner & P. E. Garfinkel (Eds.), *Handbook of psychotherapy for anorexia nervosa and bulimia* (pp. 107–146). New York: Guilford.

Gergen, K. (1992). Towards a postmodern psychology. In S. Kvale (Ed.), *Psychology and postmodernism* (pp. 17–30). Newbury Park, CA: Sage.

Gergen, K. (1994). Exploring the postmodern: Perils or potentials? *American Psychologist, 49*, 412–416.

Gilligan, S., & Price, R. (Eds.). (1993). *Therapeutic conversations.* New York: Norton.

Goldfried, M. R., & Wolfe, B. E. (1996). Psychotherapy practice and research: Repairing a strained alliance. *American Psychologist, 51*, 1007–1016.

Gortner, E. T., Gollan, J. K., Dobson, K. S., & Jacobson, N. S. (1998). Cognitive-behavioral treatment for depression: Relapse prevention. *Journal of Consulting and Clinical Psychology, 66*, 377–384.

Gossette, R. L., & O'Brien, R. M. (1992). The efficacy of rational emotive therapy in adults: Clinical fact or psychometric artifact? *Journal of Behavior Therapy and Experimental Psychiatry, 23*, 9–24.

Granvold, D. K. (Ed.). (1996). *Cognitive and behavioral treatment: Methods and applications.* Belmont, CA: Brooks/Cole.

Guidano, V. F. (1991). *The self in process.* New York: Guilford.

Haaga, D. A. F., & Davison, G. C. (1993). An appraisal of rational-emotive therapy. *Journal of Consulting and Clinical Psychology, 61*, 215–220.

Hawton, K., Salkovskis, P. M., Kirk, J., & Clark, D. M. (Eds.). (1989). *Cognitive behaviour therapy for psychiatric patients: A practical guide.* Oxford: Oxford University Press.

Held, B. (1995). *Back to reality: A critique of postmodern theory in psychotherapy.* New York: Norton.

Hollon, S. D. (1996). The efficacy and effectiveness of psychotherapy relative to medications. *American Psychologist, 51*, 1025–1030.

Hollon, S. D. & Beck, A. T. (1994). Cognitive and cognitive-behavioral therapies. In A. E. Bergin & S. L. Garfield (Eds.), *Handbook of psychotherapy and behavior change* (pp. 428–466). New York: Wiley.

Hollon, S. D., DeRubeis, R. J., Evans, M. D., Wiemer, M. J., Garvey, M. J., Grove, W. M., & Tucson, V. B. (1992). Cognitive therapy and pharmacotherapy for depression: Singly and in combination. *Archives of General Psychiatry, 49*, 774–781.

Hollon, S., Shelton, R., & Loosen, P. T. (1991). Cognitive therapy and pharmacotherapy for depression. *Journal of Consulting and Clinical Psychology, 59*, 88–99.

Homme, L. (1965). Perspectives in psychology, XXIV: Control of coverants, the operants of the mind. *Psychological Reports, 15*, 501–511.

Howard, K., Moras, K., Brill, P., Martinovich, Z., & Lutz, W. (1996). Evaluation of psychotherapy: Efficacy, effectiveness, and patient progress. *American Psychologist, 51*, 1059–1064.

Hughes, C., Hugo, K., & Blatt, J. (1996). Self-instructional intervention for teaching generalized problem-solving within a functional task sequence. *American Journal on Mental Retardation, 100*, 565–579.

Hussian, R. A., & Lawrence, P. S. (1981). Social reinforcement of activity and problem-solving training in the treatment of depressed institutionalized elderly patients. *Cognitive Therapy and Research, 5*, 57–69.

Jacobson, N. S. (1984). A component analysis of behavioral marital therapy: The relative effectiveness of behavior exchange and communication/problem solving training. *Journal of Consulting and Clinical Psychology, 52*, 295–305.

Jacobson, N. S., & Christensen, A. (1996). Studying the effectiveness of psychotherapy: How well can clinical trials do the job? *American Psychologist, 51*, 1031–1039.

Jacobson, N. S., Dobson, K. S., Truax, P. A., Addis, M. E., Koerner, K., Gollan, J., Gortner, E., & Prince, S. E. (1996). A component analysis of cognitive-behavioral treatment for depression. *Journal of Consulting and Clinical Psychology, 64*, 295–304.

Jerremalm, A., Jansson, L., & Ost, L.-G. (1986). Cognitive and physiological reactivity and the effects of different behavioral methods in the treatment of social phobia. *Behaviour Research & Therapy, 24*, 171–180.

Kanfer, F. (1996). Motivation and emotion in behavior therapy. In K. S. Dobson and K. D. Craig (Eds.) *Advances in behavior therapy* (pp. 1–30). Thousand Oaks, California: Sage Publications.

Kanfer, F., & Schefft, B. K. (1988). *Guiding the process of therapeutic change*. Champaign, Ill: Research Press.

Kazdin, A. E. (1994). Methodology, design, and evaluation in psychotherapy research. In A. E. Bergin and S. Garfield (Eds.) *Handbook of psychotherapy and behavior change (4th edition)*. (pp. 19–71). New York: Wiley.

Kendall, P. C., Haaga, D. A. F., Ellis, A., Bernard, M., DiGiuseppe, R., & Kassinove, H. (1995). Rational-emotive therapy in the 1990s and beyond: Current status, recent revisions, and research questions. *Clinical Psychology Review, 15*, 169–185.

Kendall, P. C., & Hollon, S. D. (Eds.). (1979). *Cognitive-behavioral interventions: Theory, research, and procedures*. New York: Academic Press.

Kendall, P. C., Vitousek, K. B., & Kane, M. (1991). Thought and action in psychotherapy: Cognitive-behavioral approaches. In M. Hersen, A. E. Kazdin, & A. S. Bellack (Eds.), *The Clinical Psychology Handbook* (2nd ed., pp. 596–626). New York: Pergamon.

Lyons, L. C., & Woods, P. J. (1991). The efficacy of rational-emotive therapy: A quantitative review of the outcome research. *Clinical Psychology Review, 11*, 357–369.

Mahoney, M. J. (1974). *Cognition and behavior modification*. Cambridge, MA: Ballinger.

Mahoney, M. J. (1988). The cognitive sciences and psychotherapy: Patterns in a developing relationship. In K. S. Dobson (Ed.) *Handbook of cognitive-behavioral therapies* (pp. 357–386). New York: Guilford Press.

Mahoney, M. J. (1991). *Human change processes: The scientific foundations of psychotherapy*. New York: Basic Books.

Mahoney, M. J. (1995). Theoretical developments in the cognitive psychotherapies. In M. J. Mahoney (Ed.), *Cognitive and constructive psychotherapies: Theory, research, and practice* (pp. 3–19). New York: Springer.

McMullin, R. (1986). *Handbook of cognitive therapy techniques*. New York: Norton.

Meichenbaum, D. (1975). Self-instructional methods. In F. H. Kanfer & A. P. Goldstein (Eds.), *Helping people change* (pp. 357–391). New York: Pergamon.

Meichenbaum, D. (1977). *Cognitive-behavior modification: An integrative approach*. New York: Plenum.

Meichenbaum, D. H., & Goodman, J. (1971). Training impulsive children to talk to themselves: A means of developing self-control. *Journal of Abnormal Psychology, 77*, 115–126.

Miller, I. W., Norman, W. H., Keitner, G. I., Bishop, S. B., & Dow, M. G. (1989). Cognitive-behavioral treatment of depressed inpatients. *Behavior Therapy, 20*, 25–47.

Mynors-Wallis, L., Gath, D. H., Lloyd-Thomas, A. R., & Tomlinson, D. (1995). Randomised controlled trial comparing problem solving treatment with amitriptyline and placebo for major depression in primary care. *British Medical Journal, 310*, 441–445.

Neimeyer, R. A. (1993). Constructivist psychotherapy. In K. T. Kuehlwein & H. Rosen (Eds.), *Cognitive therapies in action* (pp. 268–300). San Francisco: Jossey-Bass.

Neimeyer, R. A. (1995). An appraisal of constructivist psychotherapies: Contexts and challenges. In M. J. Mahoney (Ed.), *Cognitive and constructive psychotherapies: Theory, research, and practice* (pp. 163–194). New York: Springer.

Nezu, A. M. (1986). Efficacy of a social problem-solving therapy approach for unipolar depression. *Journal of Consulting and Clinical Psychology, 54*, 196–202.

Nezu, A. M., & D'Zurilla, T. J. (1989). Social problem-solving and negative affective conditions. In P. C. Kendall & D. Watson (Eds.), *Anxiety and depression: Distinctive and overlapping features* (pp. 285–315). New York: Academic Press.

Nezu, C. M., Nezu, A. M., & Houts, P. S. (1993). Multiple applications of problem-solving principles in clinical practice. In K. T. Kuehlwein & H. Rosen (Eds.), *Cognitive therapies in action* (pp. 353–378). San Francisco: Jossey-Bass.

Nezu, A. M., Nezu, C. M., & Perri, M. G. (1989). *Problem-solving therapy for depression: Therapy, research, and clinical guidelines.* New York: Wiley.

Nezu, A. M., & Perri, M. G. (1989). Social problem solving therapy for unipolar depression: An initial dismantling investigation. *Journal of Consulting and Clinical Psychology, 57,* 408–413.

Persons, J. (1989). *Cognitive therapy in practice: A case formulation approach.* New York: Norton.

Persons, J., & Davidson, J. (in press). Cognitive-behavioral case formulation. In K. S. Dobson (Ed.), *Handbook of cognitive-behavioral therapies* (2nd ed.). New York: Guilford Press.

Platt, J. J., Taube, D. O., Metzger, D. S., & Duome, M. J. (1988). Training in interpersonal problem-solving (TIPS). *Journal of Cognitive Psychotherapy: An International Quarterly, 2,* 5–34.

Robins, R. W., Gosling, S. D., & Craik, K. H. (1999). An empirical analysis of trends in psychology. *American Psychologist, 54,* 117–128.

Rusch, F. R., Morgan, T. K., Martin, J. E., Riva, M., & Agran, M. (1985). Competitive employment: Teaching mentally retarded employees self-instructional strategies. *Applied Research in Mental Retardation, 6,* 389–407.

Rush, A. J., & Nowels, A. (1994). Adaptation of cognitive therapy for depressed adolescents. In T. C. R. Wilkes, G. Belsher, A. J. Rush, & E. Frank (Eds.), *Cognitive therapy for depressed adolescents* (pp. 3–21). New York: Guilford.

Salkovskis, P. M. (Ed.). (1996). *Frontiers of cognitive therapy.* New York: Guilford.

Segal, Z. V., Gemar, M., & Williams, S. (1999). Differential cognitive response to a mood induction following successful cognitive therapy or pharmacotherapy for unipolar depression. *Journal of Abnormal Psychology, 108,* 3–10.

Simons, A. D., Murphy, G. E., Levine, J. L., & Wetzel, R. D. (1986). Cognitive therapy and pharmacotherapy for depression: Sustained improvement over one year. *Archives of General Psychiatry, 43,* 43–48.

Thase, M., Bowler, K., & Harden, T. (1991). Cognitive behavior therapy of endogenous depression: Preliminary findings in 16 unmedicated patients. *Behavior Therapy, 22,* 469–477.

White, M., & Epston, D. (1990). *Narrative means to therapeutic ends.* New York: Norton.

Whitman, T. L., Spence, B. H., & Maxwell, S. (1987). A comparison of external and self-instructional teaching formats with mentally retarded adults in a vocational training setting. *Research in Developmental Disabilities, 8,* 371–388.

Young, J. E. (1990). *Cognitive therapy for personality disorders: A schema-focused approach.* Sarasota, FL: Professional Resource Exchange.

Young, J. E. (1994). *Cognitive therapy for personality disorders: A schema-focused approach* (rev. ed.). Sarasota, FL: Professional Resource Press.

CHAPTER 20

PLANNED SHORT-TERM PSYCHOTHERAPIES

BERNARD L. BLOOM
University of Colorado

Planned short-term psychotherapy, as a systematic field of inquiry and clinical practice, began as part of the community mental health movement that emerged in the early and mid-1960s. Initially, planned short-term psychotherapy was an uneasy compromise—promulgated as a strategy for coping with a greater proportion of the mental health needs of the community without undermining the principles or reputation of time-unlimited psychotherapy.

But what began as a fairly single-minded interest in making psychotherapy available to larger numbers of people slowly expanded as it became increasingly clear that brief psychotherapy (sometimes as brief as a single interview) could be remarkably effective. Indeed, were it not for the consistent evidence of the effectiveness of planned short-term psychotherapy, the writings in this field might have ended up simply as a footnote in the ongoing history of psychotherapy.

Developing an appreciation of the usefulness of planned short-term psychotherapy is not easy for therapists who have devoted years to the study, practice, and mastery of time-unlimited therapy. But initial critical attitudes toward planned short-term psychotherapy are undergoing an inexorable transformation as clinicians are coming to the conclusion that they may have underestimated how helpful they can be to people in brief periods of time. As the literature clearly shows, if we need confirmation of this state of affairs, we have only to ask our patients.

Starting in the early 1960s, coincident with the formal beginning of the community mental health movement, a series of major volumes appeared that described and evaluated some particular form of what was first called brief psychotherapy, but now somewhat more commonly, planned short-term psychotherapy. The word *planned* in the phrase *planned short-term psychotherapy* is important. These early writers, and all who followed them, describe short-term treatment that is intentionally designed to accomplish a set of therapeutic objectives within a sharply limited time frame. Planned short-term psychotherapy is thus short-term by design, not by default (Gurman, 1981; Weiss & Jacobson, 1981; Wells & Phelps, 1990), and should be distinguished from what might be called *unplanned short-term therapy*, that is, services that are brief typically because treatment is terminated unilaterally by the client.

While the current, rapidly increasing interest in planned short-term psychotherapy appears to be driven by changes in the organization, delivery, and payment mechanisms for health care services, it is important to remember that the beginnings of this interest long predated the beginning development of managed mental health care. Indeed, recent developments in the field of planned short-term psychotherapy should command the attention of mental health practitioners even if no changes were underway in the mental health service delivery system.

The growing interest in short-term therapy can be seen as part of the constantly developing history of psychotherapy. Early clinicians who wrote about brief psychotherapy came out of a psychoanalytic or psychodynamic orientation—an orientation that started out as relatively short-term but that now represents the longest of the psychotherapies. Marmor (1979) has noted that Freud's initial therapy cases were often very short in duration. Bruno Walter, the conductor, was successfully treated for a chronic cramp in his right arm in six sessions (Sterba, 1951). The composer Gustav Mahler was treated for an obsessional neurosis and severe marital difficulties in a single four-hour session that took place while strolling through the town of Leyden in Holland (Jones, 1955, Vol. 2, p. 80; see also Strupp, 1980, p. 379).

The current interest in short-term therapy thus can be seen, in part, as a response to growing dissatisfaction with the lengthening of traditional psychotherapy. Many writers in the field of time-limited psychotherapy are fully aware that psychotherapists ordinarily do not have the luxury of unlimited time with their patients. As a consequence, they have begun to search within their own experiences for wisdom they can share with those mental health professionals who have no alternative other than to try to be helpful to their patients in limited periods of time (Butcher & Koss, 1978, pp. 726-727).

THE ESSENTIAL CHARACTERISTICS OF PLANNED SHORT-TERM PSYCHOTHERAPIES

Short-term psychotherapy, as this term is currently defined, ranges in length from a minimum of one interview to a maximum of around 20 interviews, with an average duration of about six sessions. Few people now talk about therapies longer than 20 interviews as short-term, although the upper limit is not really agreed upon. Talley (1992) has suggested the term *very brief psychotherapy* for treatment episodes lasting less than eight sessions, reserving the term *brief psychotherapy* for episodes of between eight and 20 sessions.

At its simplest level, short-term psychotherapy can be defined as those therapies in which "the practitioner deliberately limits both the goals and the duration of treatment" (Wells, 1994, p. 2). To complicate this succinct definition somewhat, five fundamental components, other than actual duration, usually characterize planned short-term psychotherapy. These components

are (1) prompt intervention, (2) a relatively high level of therapist activity, (3) establishment of specific but limited goals, (4) the identification and maintenance of a clear focus, and (5) the setting of a time limit. There are, however, considerable differences in how writers use the term *focus*, what they mean by therapist activity, and how they go about setting a time limit.

Eckert (1993) has suggested that the components of planned short-term psychotherapy may be grouped into four categories—planning (rapid assessment, identification of focal issues, goal clarification, and treatment selection); collaboration (building a therapeutic alliance); timing (promptness of intervention, number, frequency, and duration of therapy sessions, inter-session tasks); and empowerment of the client (sharing control with the client, reducing the creation of dependency). Regarding empowerment, Trad (1991) has described the evolution from time-unlimited to planned short-term psychotherapy in terms of a fundamental change in the role of the therapist—from a passive one in which the gradual deconstruction of conflict is observed, to a more active one in which the therapist takes a more directive stance. Thus, both therapist and client appear to have been empowered in the move toward brief psychotherapy.

THERAPIST ATTITUDES TOWARD TIME-LIMITED PSYCHOTHERAPY

Advocacy for planned short-term therapy stands in contrast to a deeply ingrained mental health professional value system. In that value system, brief treatment is thought of as superficial, longer is equated with better, and the most influential and prestigious practitioners tend to be those who undertake intensive long-term therapy with a very limited number of clients.

Psychotherapists differ in the extent to which they are drawn to the basic ideas of planned short-term psychotherapy, in part because they have differences of opinion regarding the modification of human behavior, as well as the psychotherapeutic enterprise itself. According to Budman and Gurman (1983), while long-term therapists generally seek to change basic character, short-term therapists seek more parsimonious, limited, and conservative interventions. While long-term therapists believe that significant psychological change rarely occurs simply on the basis of experiences in day-to-day living, short-term therapists believe that significant psychological change in everyday life is not only common but is, in fact, inevitable.

In addition, long-term therapists tend to view presenting complaints as symptoms of deeper psychopathology, while short-term therapists tend to take these presenting complaints seriously and see their removal as a legitimate goal of therapy. Long-term therapists tend to view therapy as always benign and useful, and therefore they believe that there can hardly be too much therapy. In contrast, short-term therapists believe that therapy can under some circumstances be counterproductive, particularly if it goes on too long. Finally, long-term therapists tend to view being in therapy as the single most important aspect of a patient's life. In contrast, short-term therapists tend to view being in therapy as only one of many important activities in which patients are involved.

Hoyt (1985) has identified a number of related beliefs and tensions that may account for some of the continuing hesitancy of psychotherapists regarding short-term dynamic psychotherapy. The first of these beliefs is the conviction that more is better, that time-limited psychotherapy is necessarily inferior to time-unlimited therapy, simply because there can be less of it. A second belief is that some therapeutic techniques are simply impossible to carry out when faced with time constraints and that these specific techniques, such as uncovering or the provocation of affect, are essential to effective therapy.

Among the sources of tension generated by the prospect of planned short-term psychotherapy, Hoyt has noted a mismatch between some therapists' convictions of the clinical superiority of long-term therapy and many patients' interests in having their therapy be as brief as possible. A second source of tension is the fact that time-limited psychotherapy increasingly is recognized as more demanding and often more difficult for the therapist than time-unlimited therapy. A third difficulty identified by Hoyt is the fiscal complexity inherent in trying to derive an adequate income from one's professional activities while encouraging a high turnover in patients. Finally, Hoyt suggests that a short-term therapy practice inevitably results in repeated psychological losses to therapists, a phenomenon that often can result in considerable personal stress and discomfort (see also Carmona, 1988; Hoyt, 1987).

WHAT MAKES PLANNED SHORT-TERM PSYCHOTHERAPY COMPELLING?

In spite of these concerns, interest in planned short-term therapy is accelerating. This expanding attention has come about as a consequence of three interrelated factors: first, concern with efficiency and economy; second, changing concepts and theories of psychotherapy; and third, an accumulation of evidence that the effectiveness of planned short-term therapy appears to be indistinguishable from that of long-term treatment.

Efficiency and Economy

The efficiency and economy rationale for planned short-term therapy is stressed most notably by persons in the public sector. With limitations in both financial and staff resources, a community mental health facility, they argue, must derive the greatest possible effect from every available therapeutic hour. Treatment then would be more feasible for larger numbers of clients.

With the increasing demand for service, a planned short-term therapy orientation could result in the virtual elimination of waiting lists, which is a source of chronic tension for staff, clients, and the public (Kirkby & Smyrnios, 1992). Finally, for many clients, whether because of economic, cultural, or ideological considerations, planned short-term therapy is the only real alternative to no treatment at all (Avnet, 1965).

One setting that has attracted substantial interest in planned short-term psychotherapy is the university counseling center. Increased demand for psychotherapeutic services combined with reductions in budget allocations have drawn the attention of counseling center staff to the research literature that has served to document the potential benefits of a time-limited approach to student counseling and psychotherapy. As a consequence, there is growing interest in establishing short-term counseling programs. A number of reports recently have appeared that seem to suggest that such programs provide both effective as well as efficient care (Halligan, 1995; Pinkerton & Rockwell, 1994; Robbins & Zinni, 1988; Steenbarger, 1992, 1993).

The private sector also has become interested in the efficiency and economy of planned short-term therapy, but for a somewhat different set of reasons. First, third-party insurance reimbursement for outpatient psychotherapy is being reduced as part of the efforts to cope with the soaring cost of medical care and of medical insurance. Second, new organizational forms of health care are being developed. These various models offer the promise of reducing the cost of medical care by reducing overtreatment. Third, primary care physicians, who until recently, provided about two-thirds of all mental health services in the United States (Regier, Goldberg, & Taube, 1978), are continuing, if not expanding, their interest in providing mental health services. While surprisingly little is known about the nature of mental health services provided by primary care physicians, one thing is clear—those services are nearly always short-term in nature.

Changing Concepts in Psychotherapy

Among the relatively recent changes in psychotherapeutic theory pertinent to the growing interest in planned short-term therapy, the following should be mentioned: (1) acceptance of limited therapeutic goals; (2) emphasis in ego psychology on strengths as well as weaknesses of the client; (3) impact of behavior modification techniques; (4) increasing centrality of crisis theory and crisis intervention in service delivery system planning; and (5) greater attention being paid to current precipitating circumstances in contrast to past predisposing circumstances.

These changes have resulted in making treatment more promptly available; in the realization that when therapeutic time is limited, both client and therapist appear to work harder (Piper, Debbane, Bienvenu, & Garant, 1984). And in exploring the possibility that planned short-term therapy would be in many circumstances the treatment of choice even if it were not less expensive (Ewing, 1978, p. 19).

The treatment-of-choice argument comes in part from the growing realization that most treatment (planned or unplanned) is short-term (Hoffman & Remmel, 1975), and that there is some potential utility in making it advertently short-term. While it is true that most outpatient psychotherapy is short-term, however, it is important not to make too much of this fact. The 16% of clients who are in long-term psychotherapy account for nearly 63% of outpatient psychotherapy expenditures (Olfson & Pincus, 1994).

Mann (1973) states eloquently what a number of writers have noted:

There comes a point in the treatment of patients, whether in psychoanalysis or in psychotherapy, where time is no longer on the therapist's side insofar as the possibility of helping the patient to make further changes is involved, and where time serves far more the search by the patient for infantile gratification. (p. xi)

THE EVALUATION OF PLANNED SHORT-TERM PSYCHOTHERAPY

A large number of well-designed evaluation studies of planned short-term psychotherapy have appeared in the literature. Indeed, there are so many evaluation studies in the literature that even the number of reviews and critical analyses of these evaluations has become quite large (see Bloom, 1997). The empirical evaluation studies of short-term outpatient psychotherapy have found that planned short-term psychotherapies are, in general, as effective and long-lasting as time-unlimited psychotherapy, virtually regardless of client characteristics or treatment duration (Koss & Butcher, 1986; Smyrnios & Kirkby, 1993), and are essentially equally effective (see, for example, Laikin, Winston, & McCullough, 1991). Almost identical findings have been reported for short-term inpatient psychiatric care (see, for example, Bloom, 1984, pp. 98-101; Gelso & Johnson, 1983; Miller & Hester, 1986).

Indeed, perhaps no other finding has been reported with greater regularity in the mental health literature than the equivalence of effect of time-limited and time-unlimited psychotherapy. Schlesinger (1994) has noted the implications of this finding by commenting that "government and insurers fear that if left to their own devices, psychotherapists would tend to go on indefinitely. They are convinced that the prescription of 'long-term psychotherapy' guarantees only higher cost, not better results" (p. 2).

Representative of the most recent conclusions of the many reviews of the relationship of treatment duration to outcome is that of Koss and Shiang (1994) who concluded that brief therapies no longer are judged to be appropriate only for persons with lesser problems (as once was the view). The research related to this point reveals that brief therapy methods also are effective in lessening various health-related and psychological problems, including the chronic and severe ones. They noted that

. . . comparative studies of brief psychotherapy offer little empirical evidence of differences in overall effectiveness between time-limited and time-unlimited therapy or between alternate approaches to brief therapy. . . . Consequently, brief therapy results in a great saving of available clinical time and can reach more people in need of treatment. (p. 692)

Their conclusions are similar to those reported by Koss and Butcher in 1986 and by Butcher and Koss in 1978. In addition, Koss, Butcher, and Strupp (1986) have suggested that these findings may actually underestimate the effectiveness of planned short-term therapy because so few of the therapists participating in the evaluation studies had received formal training in brief therapy techniques.

It is important to underline the importance of Koss, Butcher, and Strupp's suggestion about the lack of training in the field of planned short-term psychotherapy by noting that in a recent study reported by Pekarik (1994), the role of training in improving clinicians' brief therapy skills clearly can be seen. Evaluating a ten-hour training program with a sample of 12 therapists who received the training program and a control sample of 10 therapists who did not, Pekarik found that in the case of 176 clients of these 22 therapists, in comparison with clients of the control group psychotherapists, clients of trained short-term psychotherapists received more brief therapy, reported greater treatment satisfaction, had lower dropout rates, and obtained better therapist ratings of outcome.

This general assessment of the evaluation literature is not meant to suggest that no further evaluations are needed, or that no persistent questions exist about the efficacy of brief episodes of psychotherapy. To the contrary, it may be as imprudent for mental health professionals to accept without question the implications of the research studies already conducted as to reject them out of hand. Gelso (1992), for example, who has written quite favorably about the effectiveness of brief episodes of care, still notes that more research is necessary before one should be entirely confident that planned short-term psychotherapy is as effective as longer episodes of care; that the changes noted in planned short-term psychotherapy are as long-lasting as those following longer episodes of care; or that since improvement is noted so quickly after psychotherapy has begun, only a few sessions of therapy are ever needed.

Dose-Response Studies

A number of studies of psychotherapy effectiveness have drawn on *dose-response methodology* from the field of pharmacology. That methodology examines the relationship between the amount of exposure to a treatment and the degree of improvement (see, for example, Howard, Kopta, Krause, & Orlinsky, 1986; Rush & Giles, 1982; Schlesinger, Mumford, Glass, Patrick, & Sharfstein, 1983). Whereas invoking dose-response methodology in the evaluation of psychotherapy effectiveness raises a number of complex issues (Stiles & Shapiro, 1989), the growing interest in dose-response relationships is understandable because if it can be shown that there is a significant relationship between the amount of exposure to a treatment and the degree of improvement, the likelihood that the relationship is a causal one is increased (MacMahon & Pugh, 1970).

Dose-response studies, which assume that drugs have some measurable effects on the body if they are administered in sufficient doses, seek to determine the characteristics of those effects. Efficacy is only one of those characteristics, however. In addition to efficacy, per se, dose-response studies examine treatment threshold, latency, potency, response variability and duration, treatment side effects, and margin of safety.

Most of these parameters have their parallels, at least theoretically, in the study of the effectiveness of psychotherapy. It thus seems clearly appropriate to examine psychotherapy effectiveness studies as if one were conducting dose-response investigations, assuming, of course, that the studies being examined meet minimal dose-response methodology requirements: (1) random assignment of clients into at least two treatments of differing levels of intensity, one of which could be an attention placebo group; (2) development of evaluation measures that have adequate psychometric robustness and employ appropriate levels of discrimination and numbers of data collection points; and (3) evaluation of therapeutic outcome by judges who are not aware of the experimental study group to which any given client is assigned.

Special considerations in the evaluation of psychotherapy outcome should be noted regarding outcome judgments made by the treating therapist. Reports in the literature suggest, first, that the likelihood of finding long-term therapeutic interventions superior to short-term interventions declines dramatically as one moves from outcome judgments made by therapists to judgments based on objectively measured psychological symptoms or characteristics (Bloch, Bond, Qualls, Yalom, & Zimmerman, 1977; Gelso & Johnson, 1983; Johnson & Gelso, 1980). Second, even though a substantial minority of patients are reported by their therapists as showing improvement after a relatively small number of sessions, it has frequently been suggested that therapists tend to be biased toward long-term therapy (Budman & Gurman, 1983; Burlingame & Behrman, 1987). Without adequate controls, that bias can fully account for the positive relationship often found in early studies of therapy duration and judged effectiveness.

Most early psychotherapy evaluation studies failed to meet dose-response methodological criteria. Untreated control or attention placebo groups were rarely created. Patients rarely were assigned randomly to treatment conditions of varying durations. Assessments of outcome were made nearly always either by the treating therapists, by judges (based upon data provided by the treating therapists), or by the treated patients themselves, and only at the time of discharge, that is, without adequate follow-up data collection. Finally, judgments of therapeutic outcome generally were made by using procedures and measures of undemonstrated reliability and validity.

As has been suggested, the study of the relationship of therapeutic dose and therapeutic outcome does not exhaust the potential contribution of the dose-response model to the understanding of psychotherapeutic effectiveness. The conclusions regarding the relationship of individual therapy outcome to treatment characteristics, based on scores of reasonably well-conducted evaluation studies (see Butcher & Koss, 1978; Koss & Butcher, 1986, for an extensive review of these studies), can now be reframed by returning to the variables that have been given special consideration in dose-response investigations.

Efficacy

Efficacy is defined as the maximum effect of a treatment employing its optimal dosage. Psychotherapy is unquestionably efficacious, but every psychotherapist would surely wish for its level of efficacy to be improved. While about two-thirds of treated patients are judged to have improved at the time of follow-up, one-third of untreated patients are also judged to have improved (Lambert, Shapiro, & Bergin, 1986). The treatment–no treatment dimension accounts for only 10% of the variability in outcome.

Threshold

Threshold is defined as the lowest dose capable of producing a discernible effect. Psychotherapy appears to have an extremely low threshold. As few as two or three sessions of psychotherapy repeatedly have been shown to have a significant effect in a large minority of cases, and there are numerous empirical as well as anecdotal reports of a single interview having a remarkable positive impact on some clients (Bloom, 1981; Cummings & Follette, 1976; Follette & Cummings, 1967; Talmon, 1990).

Latency

Latency is defined as the speed with which discernible effects are produced. Psychotherapy appears to have a remarkably low latency, and its initial positive effects are commonly reported during or immediately after the first interview. Indeed, positive effects have been reported between the time the initial appointment is made and actually takes place (see, for example, Howard et al., 1986, Table 3).

Potency

Potency is defined as the absolute amount of the treatment that is required to produce a specified effect. Psychotherapy has relatively high potency. Its maximum effects appear to be reached with small doses, and beyond that point, additional treatment appears to produce very little additional benefit (Bowers & Clum, 1988).

Duration of Effect

Duration of effect is defined as the amount of time that a given treatment outcome is sustained. Regardless of the duration of the treatment, psychotherapy has a relatively long-lasting effect, and there is evidence that improvement continues for at least one year after the conclusion of an episode of brief psychotherapy (Cross, Sheehan, & Khan, 1982; Gelso & Johnson, 1983; Husby, 1985).

Variability of Effect

The effectiveness of psychotherapy in general, and short-term psychotherapy in particular, appears to vary relatively little as a function of either therapist or therapy characteristics (Berman & Norton, 1985; Shiffman, 1987). This is not to suggest that therapists will have the same results regardless of whom they treat or what therapeutic approach they use. But determining the most appropriate treatment for a given patient in the hands of a given therapist is a task of considerable complexity, one that cannot be expected to yield significant results unless it is approached with care and dedication.

Side Effects and Margin of Safety

While there is a literature describing the harmful side effects of psychotherapy (see, for example, Gross, 1978; Hadley & Strupp, 1976; Rush & Giles, 1982; Sachs, 1983; Strupp, 1989; Tennov, 1975; Zilbergeld, 1983), these reports consist mainly of the description of negative consequences associated with scandalously unethical therapeutic practices. Psychotherapy in the hands of an ethical psychotherapist, however, appears to produce few, if any, untoward side effects.

APPROACHES TO PLANNED SHORT-TERM PSYCHOTHERAPY

The various approaches to planned short-term psychotherapy typically have been divided into three categories—psychodynamic, cognitive and behavioral, and strategic and systemic. It is useful to be aware of the various approaches to planned short-term psychotherapy for at least two reasons. First, a certain approach might prove to be superior for certain problems, or certain types of clients, for certain clinicians, or under certain circumstances. In this case, referrals or assignments to clinicians could be made on a more rational basis than is typically the case in most mental health agency settings, and one could anticipate general increases in therapeutic effectiveness. Second, exposure to different approaches to planned short-term therapy allows for the possibility that an individual clinician could develop a broader array of skills than might otherwise be the case. Under this circumstance, a specific clinician could be effective with a more varied array of clients or problems.

Psychodynamic Approaches

Marmor (1968) has described the psychodynamic therapeutic perspective very succinctly in terms of its five essential assumptions. First, behavior is motivated; second, motivation is largely concealed from awareness; third, personalities are shaped not only by biology but also by experiences; fourth, conflicting motivations can result in functional disturbances in cognition, affect, and behavior; and fifth, early developmental experiences are of significance in shaping adolescence and adulthood.

All psychodynamic approaches to planned short-term psychotherapy share a concern with the importance of transference phenomena and other aspects of the therapeutic relationship, and pay special attention to issues at termination and to the importance of the concept of the unconscious. But there is also a surprising amount of variability among the approaches.

In general, theorists vary in their aspirations, perhaps even their passions for short-term therapy, ranging from those who see it as equal to time-unlimited therapy in terms of its potential effectiveness to those who see it as useful but likely limited in its effect. Theorists vary in their relative emphasis on the patient's history versus emphasis on the present predicament as described by the patient. Theorists differ in terms of the transparency of their therapy, that is, in the sense of how aware the patient is likely to be of the hypotheses motivating the therapist's behavior. Theorists also differ in their activity level and in the nature of their interventions—confrontation versus support, challenge versus patient exploration.

In addition to attitudinal differences, psychodynamic psychotherapists vary in a number of aspects of their practice of planned short-term psychotherapy regarding duration of treatment, the usefulness of an initial diagnostic study and the establishment of a specific therapeutic contract, the use of the interpersonal approach to psychodynamic treatment, attention to transference phenomena, use of a mid-session intermission, planned follow-up interviews, and the judged importance of evaluation of outcome.

Principal proponents of the psychodynamic orientation to planned short-term psychotherapy include Lewis Wolberg (1968, 1980), Leopold Bellak (1984; see also Bellak & Small, 1978), Habib Davanloo (1978, 1980), Peter Sifneos (1979, 1987), Karl Lewin (1970), James Gustafson (1986, 1995), Mardi Horowitz (1976, 1991), and Gerald Klerman (1983; Klerman & Weissman, 1982, 1993; see also Bloom, 1997).

Cognitive and Behavioral Approaches

Cognitive and behavioral approaches to planned short-term psychotherapy have shown enough evidence of a productive union so that it seems appropriate to discuss them together. Cognitive theory has been significantly influenced by behavior therapy in the form of techniques such as social skills and relaxation training. At the same time, behavior therapy has become increasingly cognitive (Arkowitz & Hannah, 1989; Dobson, 1988). There is so much overlap between these two related forms of psychotherapy that many writers use the term *cognitive-behavioral* as a label for a single, general approach to psychological treatment.

Indeed, Koss and Shiang (1994) have suggested that it is sometimes difficult to separate the techniques of a behavioral approach from a cognitive approach. Both approaches try to identify the client's present predicament and the variables that maintain both the inappropriate behaviors as well as the inappropriate cognitions.

According to Dobson and Block (1988), cognitive and behavioral therapies share three fundamental beliefs: cognitive activity affects behavior, cognitive activity may be assessed and altered, and desired behavior change may be affected through cognitive change. The main attributes of both cognitive and behavior therapy are "a clear focus on the patient's complaints, devising specific treatment for specific problems, relatively brief periods of treatment, and systematic appraisals of outcome" (Bergin & Garfield, 1986, p. 6).

The radical behaviorist approach (see Wilson, 1978, 1981), which is identified with the work of Skinner, essentially holds that all behavior is under the control of environmental factors external to the person. More contemporary views of behavior therapy include the social learning perspective, with its emphasis on cognitive mediational processes and self-regulatory capacities. Thus, how external events determine behavior is mediated by internal cognitive processes and capacities that are, in turn, based on prior experience (for contemporary update, see Chapter 18).

Cognitive and behavioral therapies have grown rapidly in the past two decades, in part because of their successes with such a wide variety of clients, many of whom have presented problems that have been difficult to treat from a psychodynamic orientation (Phillips, 1985). If we begin with the assumption that thinking, feeling, and behaving are interdependent, then changes in one of these components have the potential to bring about changes in the others. If we change how we think about something or someone, we will likely change how we feel about, and how we behave toward, that something or someone. Cognitive and behavioral therapies focus on altering thought and behavior in the service of modifying emotional responses. To say it differently, emotional and behavioral responses are mediated by perceived meanings, or cognitions (Bedrosian & Bozicas, 1994, pp. 26 ff.).

Cognitive and behavioral theories share a set of values that dramatically distinguishes them from psychodynamic viewpoints (Jones & Pulos, 1993). While the psychodynamic approach views the origins of symptoms as unconscious and thus not easily accessible to clients, cognitive and behavioral theory suggests that the client is largely aware of these origins. According to cognitive and behavioral theory, dysfunctional feelings and behavior are largely due to ideas that produce biased judgments and cognitive errors, rather than to pathological motivation. Cognitive and behavioral theories and therapy also differ from psychodynamic theory and therapy in their central interest in the present, on the one hand, and their relative disinterest in the patient's past, in helping the patient achieve insight, in determining causes, or in exploring transference relationships, on the other hand.

Cognitive and behavioral theories have a number of important common elements including a careful and active assessment of current problems, the establishment of attainable and contracted therapeutic goals, the obtaining of prompt relief from the most pressing problems, and the use of a wide variety of empirically based interventions that increase the patient's sense of self-efficacy (Peake, Borduin, & Archer, 1988).

Cognitive and behavioral interventions can be thought of in three steps. First, clients are helped to find the thoughts and beliefs that are associated with their psychological problems and destructive behaviors. Second, clients are helped to analyze their thoughts and beliefs to determine their validity and functionality. Third, clients are helped to change their irrational thoughts, perceptions, and beliefs in the direction of greater rationality and usefulness so that the emotions associated with them will also change (McMullin, 1986; Schuyler, 1991).

Principal proponents of the cognitive and behavioral approach to planned short-term psychotherapy include Aaron Beck (1976; Beck, Rush, Shaw, & Emery, 1979; see also Bloom, 1997), Albert Ellis (1962, 1993), Frank Farrelly (Farrelly & Brandsma, 1974), and Lakin Phillips (1985; Phillips & Wiener, 1966).

Strategic and Systemic Approaches

Strategic therapy is a directive approach in which both individual and family problems are seen as being the expression of dysfunctional organizational patterns within the family. The therapist begins the therapy by negotiating the goals of therapy with the individual or the family and then "proceeds to develop a *strategy* for achieving these goals" (Simon, Stierlin, & Wynne, 1985, p. 335)—hence the term *strategic*.

Rosenbaum (1993) makes the same observation when he suggests that strategic therapy, rather than being a particular approach to psychotherapy or a particular theory of psychotherapy, can be defined as therapies of therapists directly taking responsibility for influencing clients, and using active planning strategies to affect change. Rosenbaum suggests that "Strategic therapists see clients' problems as being maintained by their attempted solutions. This being the case, strategic therapists usually work briefly, believing that frequently only a small change is necessary to resolve the presenting problem" (1993, p. 109; see also Rosenbaum, 1990).

Systemic psychotherapy concerns itself with the treatment of families and, more broadly, with the treatment of clients viewed as embedded in a social system (see, for example, Epstein, Bishop, Keitner, & Miller, 1990; Fraser, 1986). Rosenbaum (1990) links strategic and systemic psychotherapies by noting that "strategic therapists work with a systemic epistemology" (p. 356). But because strategic and systemic therapists believe that change can be brought about in a family system by changing a single element in the system, "family therapy" can be undertaken with individuals, and the theories and practices of strategic psychotherapists can be applied to individual as well as to family psychotherapy. The goals of strategic therapy are to change interpersonal interactions. Even when an individual is being treated, strategic and systemic therapists tend to think about that individual within a family context, that is, as part of a system of interacting individuals.

Strategic and systemic therapists have relatively little interest in the origin of problems (predisposing factors), in how the problems first manifested themselves (precipitating factors), or in even why they are so persistent (perpetuating factors). Rather, the principal interest is with how they are to be solved (Held, 1986; O'Hanlon & Weiner-Davis, 1989). Goldsmith (1986) characterizes this orientation in the following statement: "Strategic psychotherapeutic practice is concerned, after all, with getting patients to change rather than getting them to be more

aware of themselves" (p. 20). If the psychodynamic psychotherapist can be said to believe that "you are your past," and the cognitive or behavioral psychotherapist can be said to believe that "all that is really important is the present," the strategic or systemic psychotherapist can be said to believe that "we need to concentrate on the future—the present is important only in how it connects with the future."

De Shazer (1985), the founder of solution-focused psychotherapy, suggests that for an intervention to fit, it is not necessary to have detailed knowledge of the complaint. He goes on to observe that

> It is not necessary even to be able to construct with any rigor how the trouble is maintained in order to prompt solution. . . . Any really different behavior in a problematic situation can be enough to prompt solution and give the client the satisfaction he seeks from therapy. (p. 7)

O'Hanlon and Weiner-Davis (1989), among others, have written about the remarkable differences between the assumptions of past-oriented psychodynamic theories and present- and future-oriented cognitive or strategic theories. They have noted that traditional past-oriented theories tend to subscribe to the belief that (1) there are deep underlying causes for symptoms; (2) symptoms are functional; (3) insight into the causes of symptoms is necessary for symptom resolution; (4) symptom removal in the absence of insight is useless and may even be dangerous; (5) patients are resistant to psychotherapy and ambivalent about changing; (6) change takes time and brief interventions do not last; and (7) the fundamental task of psychotherapy is to identify and correct psychopathology.

In contrast, present- and future-oriented psychotherapeutic theories are based on a quite different set of beliefs: (1) patients bring with them into therapy the resources that are necessary to resolve their complaints; (2) personal change goes on continuously, with or without therapy; (3) the task of the psychotherapist is to identify and amplify change; (4) resolving symptoms does not require knowing the causes or the functions of the symptoms; (5) small changes are all that is necessary—these changes reverberate throughout the personality and can bring about changes in many areas of functioning; (6) patients define the goals for their own therapy; (7) rapid changes in behavior and problem resolution are possible; (8) there is no single right way to view symptoms; and (9) therapists should focus on what is possible and changeable rather than on what is impossible and intractable.

Principal proponents of the strategic and systemic approach to planned short-term psychotherapy include authors who elaborated on the work of Milton Erickson (Haley, 1973; O'Hanlon & Hexum, 1990), the Palo Alto Mental Research Institute group (Fisch, Weakland, & Segal, 1982; Haley, 1987; Weakland & Fisch, 1992), and Steve de Shazer (1982, 1994; see also Bloom, 1997).

GENERAL PRINCIPLES OF SHORT-TERM PSYCHOTHERAPY

A number of authors have identified the common characteristics of planned short-term psychotherapies. These characteristics—the limitation on time, the limitation on goals, the establishment of a focal issue, and a more active and flexible therapeutic approach—have been referred to already and little new can be added here.

Short-term psychotherapies may be equivalent in their effectiveness because everything inside the patient is connected to everything else. Whatever a caring, competent, and trustworthy therapist does, regardless of what specific techniques and theories are espoused, has the potential for being helpful. If the therapist simply asks patients to think more deeply about themselves, as virtually all psychotherapists do, such requests may have significant therapeutic potential. The request provides an opportunity for patients that is rarely present in normal social interactions. Exploration of the self can lead to discoveries that can clarify and demystify. A single discovery

about the self can lead the way to a significant change in how individuals think about themselves and others and in how they carry out their interpersonal interactions.

Freud made this point very clearly in his insistence that psychotherapy served the patient by helping make conscious the unconscious, that is, by increasing self-awareness. Describing his view of the difference between the conscious and the unconscious, Freud noted that everything conscious is subject to a process of wearing away, while what is unconscious is relatively unchangeable. Freud (1909/1953) once reconstructed his comments to a patient to whom he was pointing out the antiques standing about in his office as follows: "They were, in fact, I said, only objects found in a tomb, and their burial had been their preservation: the destruction of Pompeii was only beginning now that it had been dug up" (p. 313; see also Malcolm, 1987; Straker, 1986). Wearing away might not be good for the unburied treasures of Pompeii, but it is exactly what mental health professionals hope will happen in psychotherapy.

Shared Beliefs Among Short-Term Psychotherapists

A somewhat more empirical approach to the identification of general principles of planned short-term psychotherapy would be to look for specific shared beliefs among short-term psychotherapists, that is, principles or therapeutic techniques that many or most psychotherapists seem to subscribe to regardless of their particular approach to planned short-term psychotherapy. Our examination of the literature suggests that a number of shared beliefs likely do exist. A list of these shared beliefs, arranged from the more general to the more specific, is presented in the following table.

TABLE 20.1 Shared Beliefs Among Short-Term Psychotherapists

1. Where there is life there is change—with or without psychotherapy. The job of the therapist is to guide and accelerate that change.
2. Time-limited psychotherapy is hard work for the psychotherapist—intellectually and emotionally demanding, and requiring a high level of skill.
3. Available time should be filled wisely. When their schedules do not permit them to take on a new client, therapists cease being a resource to the community.
4. Virtually all clients can be helped and can be helped relatively quickly, regardless of diagnosis or problem severity.
5. Psychotherapy is better than no psychotherapy; planned short-term outpatient psychotherapy, except in relatively rare instances, is equal in effect to time-unlimited outpatient psychotherapy and to either time-limited or time-unlimited inpatient psychotherapy.
6. There is no evidence that any particular approach to planned short-term psychotherapy is significantly better than any other approach.

TABLE 20.1 (*Continued*)

7. Planned short-term psychotherapy requires a collaboration between client and therapist for establishing therapeutic goals, for the conduct of the therapeutic episode, and for bringing it to an agreed-upon conclusion.
8. Special training in planned short-term psychotherapy enhances clinical effectiveness.
9. The most critical question facing psychotherapists is how to know when enough psychotherapy has been done. Often that time tends to come sooner rather than later.
10. Psychotherapists significantly underestimate how helpful they can be to people in brief periods of time.
11. A successful episode of brief psychotherapy, however focused, can have a spreading effect throughout the personality of the client. Only small changes may be required to start a process that will lead to significant clinical improvement.
12. The effects of psychotherapy continue, and perhaps increase, long after the therapeutic episode has been concluded.
13. Clients have strengths as well as weaknesses, and have the capacity to make often quite major changes in their lives both during an episode of psychotherapy, as well as after an episode has been completed.
14. The leverage of the therapist, initially very high, decreases rapidly. Therapeutic efficiency and effectiveness can be maximized by keeping episodes as short as possible.
15. Psychotherapy should be thought of as a series of brief therapeutic episodes, each of which becomes an opportunity to accomplish some explicit set of objectives.
16. Psychotherapy should be considered as intermittent, that is, multiple individual brief treatment episodes within an ongoing therapeutic relationship. Clients always should feel that they are welcome to return for another therapeutic episode.
17. Therapists should maintain an optimal level of flexibility regarding the frequency and duration of appointments.
18. It is as important to avoid premature termination of the therapeutic episode as it is to avoid overtreatment.
19. Planned short-term therapists are not uneasy about being teachers at the same time that they are psychotherapists.
20. Short-term psychotherapists look to the time between sessions as a potentially valuable occasion for work to be done by the client. Homework can include keeping a log or a diary, establishing a schedule, having a conversation with a specific person on a specific topic, writing, reading, or rewarding oneself. They urge clients to keep track of, to think about, to try out, to follow up.
21. Once a focal issue is identified, detours should be avoided.
22. Empathic remarks, reassurance, and sympathetic listening facilitate therapeutic progress.
23. The psychological climax of every interview is a skillful intervention—a well-timed interpretation, a carefully considered activity plan designed to modify undesired behavior, or a proposal whose goal is to change interpersonal interaction.
24. Planned short-term psychotherapists believe that building a follow-up contact into the therapeutic episode not only creates the opportunity for them to evaluate the consequences of their work but also extends the life and the effectiveness of their interventions.

Illustrative Case History

While it is rare that a single case serves to illustrate the full spectrum of shared beliefs of planned short-term psychotherapists, many of the beliefs just described can be seen in the following illustrative case history.

A 27-year-old woman, referred by a former client, came in to discuss whether or not she should divorce her husband of four months who she "just allowed" herself to realize was an alcoholic. They had been living together for nine months before marrying, but in recent months he has been treating her like "dirt," drinking and leaving the house for a week or longer, and putting the blame on her for what he is going through. She feels that if she says the wrong thing it is going to bring on a drunken episode and has come to feel that she is not a good person. He is currently seeking help for his drinking and his anger and is now sometimes kind and loving. On those occasions she wants to continue the relationship.

At the conclusion of her long (7 minute) introductory statement, she says, "It makes sense that I am supposed to think well enough of myself to be able to, you know, stick this relationship out if I really want it, or walk out of it if I really don't want it. But I don't think I know. I don't think that I think that well of myself to be able to sit there and take it and stay there even though that's what I want. And maybe I don't think well enough of myself to be able to walk out if that's what I want. I just don't know." I asked her for how long she had not thought very well of herself, and she replied, "Oh, probably 27 years; that's how old I am." With that implicit permission to explore the antecedents of her low self-esteem, we spent the remainder of the single appointment discussing her past history and its pertinence to her current uncertainty about what to do regarding her marriage. At the tenth minute of the interview, the client says, "I don't think that it is a bad thing to be dependent on him but I think that it is a fault in my character in the ways sometimes that I am dependent on him. I think that all ties in together in why I don't know whether I am supposed to be walking out at certain times or not, or whether I am supposed to be just standing there and taking it." I replied, "And that is connected with feeling so badly about yourself as a person that you half-jokingly say has been true of you all your life."

We discussed her early as well as recent history with her parents and her two siblings during which time she was occasionally tearful, and found useful parallels between her dependence on her parents and her dependence on her husband. At the 38th minute of the interview, she said, "Before I could really start this marriage I had to put myself really low like I couldn't make it, you know, or something. Before I ever started anything in my life I went through crises of never thinking I could do it, and then I do it. But I always had to think that I could never make it, you know, and I don't know why I have to go through that. I want to find out why." But the origins of her early low self-esteem were a mystery to her.

My principal intervention following this and related lines of inquiry was to suggest that she contact her parents and sister, who was three years older than her, and try to learn more about events in her childhood that could have helped account for her low self-esteem. I said, "I guess I think you may have to make peace with your parents before you can be wise about what to do about your husband." We terminated the interview that lasted just about one hour with the agreement that we would keep in touch with each other by telephone. No additional appointments were scheduled.

I had three telephone conversations with her over the next five months. The road had not been altogether smooth but she and her husband were still together, he had entered and completed a 30-day treatment program for his alcoholism through his place of employment, and she had learned a great deal from her sister and mother about events in her childhood that helped her account for her low self-esteem. She seemed optimistic about the future, and did not feel that additional face-to-face appointments were needed.

THE CONCEPT OF THERAPEUTIC SUFFICIENCY

There is perhaps no question of greater current importance in the field of short-term psychotherapy than how to know when enough psychotherapy has been done. For, indeed, attention to this issue transforms the entire debate in short-term psychotherapy from one in which time is the central concept to one in which therapeutic sufficiency and the avoidance of both undertreatment and overtreatment are the central concepts.

Kane (1991) has observed that unlike surgery or the treatment of infectious disease, the end point in the treatment of mental illness is often not easy to determine. Sometimes, improvement can be viewed on a continuum. On other occasions judgments of improvement must be focused on a particular symptom or symptom pattern. He believes that

> It is the responsibility of the clinician to establish and continually reevaluate goals and objectives in treatment, and the patient should be informed of these assessments. Transference issues and unrealistic expectations of the therapist are important foci of treatment, and the good therapist knows how to manage them. (pp. 16-17)

In spite of the importance of the issue regarding the optimal duration of psychotherapy, suggestions about how to know when enough psychotherapy has been done are still uncommon. Most psychotherapists believe that clients cannot make significant clinical progress except in the presence of the therapist. Accumulating evidence suggests that therapists need to develop a greater appreciation of how and how much clinical improvement can take place as a consequence of a therapeutic process that is started but not necessarily witnessed by the therapist.

The greatest objection raised by traditional psychotherapists to the ideas promulgated by short-term therapists is usually what they see as an arbitrary, inflexible, and often capricious ceiling set by their agency or their clients' insurance coverage on the total number of psychotherapy sessions that will be permitted. If a mental health service delivery system functions on the basis of sufficiency instead of time, then it is possible to circumvent the issue of what constitutes the upper limit of short-term therapy, thus bypassing a profoundly refractory clinical objection to short-term psychotherapy. In place of an endless debate regarding how many interviews the agency should permit as its maximum, the issue becomes how to know when the therapy that already has been provided is sufficient to meet the patient's needs without running the risk of over-utilization. Schlesinger (1994), for example, has commented that if the therapist "would like to keep psychotherapy efficient by assuring that it takes no longer than it has to, the therapist must be able to determine when the patient has accomplished enough to permit him to continue on his own" (p. 15).

Issues regarding termination of treatment are particularly salient in the case of brief psychotherapy, where concerns about termination are, virtually by definition, always present. Indeed, Hoyt (1979, 1994) has suggested that in brief psychotherapy, termination may very well be *the* issue. In a sense, of course, therapeutic work is never completely finished, but our question asks when and for how long the therapist can step out of the picture to let clients continue the productive work of therapy on their own. There is relatively little in the published literature that can help in answering our question regarding when treatment can be terminated.

Termination criteria that derive from psychoanalytically based theories are, to say the least, difficult to operationalize and to evaluate. In their review of the literature regarding the process of termination in psychoanalysis and psychotherapy, Blanck and Blanck (1988) have reminded us of these somewhat imprecise traditional criteria: an optimal level of ego functioning;

relative independence of the ego from drives on the one hand and from the superego on the other hand; relative differentiation of self representations from object representations; genital primacy; when the unconscious has been made conscious; diminished need of the external object; resumption of phase-appropriate development; and so on. Each of these concepts poses daunting problems for the empirically oriented scholar-clinician (see also Budman, 1990).

In the psychoanalytic literature, termination is usually thought of as a sign of acting-out by the client, a narcissistic blow to the therapist, or a kind of mourning, a painful loss to therapist and client alike (de Bosset & Styrsky, 1986; Pekarik & Wierzbicki, 1986). The most common adjective that is used to modify the noun "termination" is "premature." That is, termination is often thought of in essentially negative terms.

Quintana (1993) has recently labeled this view the "termination-as-loss" model, and has suggested that this model, which has had a 40-year history, is in need of revision. One aspect of his proposed modernization is to understand the termination-as-loss model as consisting of two components—"termination-as-crisis" and "termination-as-development." According to Quintana, the crisis component of termination has been greatly overemphasized while the developmental opportunities inherent in termination of psychotherapy have been underappreciated. A more appropriate model of termination, particularly in the context of brief psychotherapy, would be to think of it as "termination-as-transformation"—transformation of how clients view themselves, their therapy, their therapists, and the client–therapist relationship.

Kupers (1988) seems to have this termination-as-transformation idea in mind when he summarizes his criteria for termination—"the amelioration of most of the symptoms, the resolution of the transference, the likelihood of continued psychological growth, and the therapist's confidence that longer therapy would not add anything to the client's potential in life." He adds, in the context of planned short-term psychotherapy, evidence that the client has become attuned to the psychological sphere, and that "the client has internalized the therapeutic message sufficiently well to be likely to return for another course of therapy when the need arises" (p. 120).

Traditional criteria for termination stand in opposition to the growing realization that we all face repeated challenges to our equilibrium and that a psychoanalysis followed by life-long psychic bliss is, sadly, the exception rather than the rule. With increasing frequency, we read that psychotherapy has to be seen as an ongoing process independent of treatment duration; that "conflicts, anxieties, losses, and changes are inevitably part of the human condition," which create the "potential for new conflicts to be activated . . . and . . . old ones reactivated" (Shectman, 1986, p. 521).

Studies have shown that patients anticipate that their treatment will be substantially shorter than their therapists think (Pekarik & Wierzbicki, 1986). While no significant correlation exists between therapy duration and outcome as judged by patients, there is a significant positive correlation between therapy duration and outcome as judged by therapists. In comparison with patients' evaluations of therapeutic outcome, therapists tend to underestimate the effectiveness of brief episodes of care and overestimate the effectiveness of long episodes of care (Bloom, 1992; O'Leary, 1995).

Termination can indicate not that all conflict has been fully and permanently resolved but that a significant piece of psychological work has been accomplished that permits clients to manage on their own. From this point of view, psychotherapy, particularly brief psychotherapy, can be seen as an encounter that starts a growth process that will continue long after the formal therapy has been concluded.

Thus, termination has begun to refer not to psychotherapy but *to this episode of psychotherapy*. This point of view leads to a distinction between the treatment episode and the treatment relationship. It is the relationship that endures over time. Productive treatment episodes of varying lengths may occur on occasion within this enduring treatment relationship (Edbril, 1994; Shectman, 1986). Thus, sufficiency of psychotherapy means sufficiency for now, not sufficiency forever. Walen, DiGiuseppe, and Dryden (1992) make a similar cognitively oriented point in the context of rational-emotive therapy when they note that "if therapy ends before behavior change is stabilized, the outcome may be less than desirable, although not terrible. Clients can always return to therapy for booster shots and further practice if needed" (p. 313).

Another aspect of the question of sufficiency of psychotherapy lies in the fact that both clinical and research studies suggest that the therapeutic gain associated with a single treatment session tends to diminish, and diminish rather sharply, as the number of sessions increases. While no precise computational formula exists for plotting session effect against number of previous sessions, data that have been reported (see, for example, Howard, et al. 1986; Seligman, 1995) suggests that after the first session, each additional session may only have about half of the therapeutic effect of the previous one. Thus, it does not take very long before additional treatment sessions have little discernible additive effectiveness. Accordingly, longer but fewer episodes of care would seem to have far greater potential for significant clinical improvement than shorter but multiple episodes of care.

Returning directly to the issue of therapeutic sufficiency, Fisch (1994) has suggested that

> How long or short therapy is also depends on whether the therapist knows when to stop. It may be trite to say, but if one has no idea of when something is done one runs the risk of going on interminably. Therapy, therefore, can be briefer if the therapist has some rather clear idea of what needs to occur to mark an endpoint of therapy. (p. 131)

What makes this comment particularly useful is its message that the therapist has an important role to play in deciding when psychotherapy can be ended. It isn't simply a matter of continuing psychotherapy because the client wants it to continue. Such a practice guarantees only that the cost of psychotherapy will be increased. Whether the result will be any better is clearly in doubt.

There are both positive and negative criteria for knowing when enough therapy has been done. On the positive side, enough therapy has been done when patients seem to have learned something important about themselves that they can chew on, and when they have a course of action or strategy that they can view within the context of an explicitly articulated, ongoing therapeutic relationship (see O'Hanlon, 1990).

On the negative side, not enough therapy has been done when the client has not finished his or her story, if for some reason the therapist is uneasy about terminating the therapy or has failed to define and communicate something the client needs to know, or if no coherent plan of action has been developed. Wise therapists will make sure that their psychotherapy is not terminated too soon just as they will make sure that they do not provide more psychotherapy than is needed.

PSYCHOTHERAPEUTIC FLEXIBILITY

The last two decades have witnessed a significant loosening of the rigid definitions of psychotherapeutic approaches. This increasing flexibility in attitudes regarding the conduct of psychotherapy may well be part of a generally growing diversity of attitudes toward human service delivery. In the case of psychotherapy in particular, this increasing flexibility can be seen in attitudes toward the therapeutic approach, toward the concept of cure, and toward the length and frequency of appointments.

Flexibility in Therapeutic Approach

Increasing liberalization of approaches toward how to conduct psychotherapy can be seen in a growing eclecticism that includes increasing recognition, even by therapists who are themselves very doctrinaire, of the important and necessary contributions of therapists with different theoretical persuasions. The common element among most psychotherapists is their interest in time and effectiveness. As a consequence they are drawn to intervention strategies that make creative use of their skills. The increasing eclecticism can be seen in the review of time-limited psychotherapy prepared by Budman and Stone (1983):

> It seems to us inevitable that brief therapy will increasingly become pragmatic eclectic therapy. As we have noted, the movement toward eclecticism is already affecting many therapists, regardless of whether they view themselves as doing brief treatment. (p. 944)

Eclecticism of theoretical approach can be seen in the shift from intrapsychic to interpersonal approaches (Horowitz & Vitkus, 1986) and in the growing integration of psychodynamic and strategic psychotherapy (Cummings & Sayama, 1995), strategic and cognitive psychotherapy (Feldman, 1994), and psychodynamic and cognitive behavioral psychotherapy (MacKenzie, 1988).

Just as a number of studies have examined how client characteristics may be related to therapeutic outcome in the case of planned short-term psychotherapy, the relationship of therapist characteristics (most of which transcend specific therapeutic approaches) to therapeutic outcome also has been studied. Sound research in this area is difficult to design. In a review of the literature examining the role of therapist characteristics to psychotherapy process and outcome, Lambert (1989) concluded that while some studies have found that some therapists (paraprofessionals as well as professionals) appear to be more effective than others, failure to randomize assignment of clients to therapists, small sample sizes, and a variety of other confounding variables make it impossible to come to any confident conclusions regarding how therapist characteristics impact therapy outcome. In spite of these methodological difficulties, some tentative assertions can be made regarding these relationships.

The most useful predictor of clinical outcome in brief psychotherapy appears to be interactional, namely, the nature of the alliance between client and therapist. The therapeutic alliance is generally defined as the ability of the client and therapist to work together collaboratively and with high levels of complementarity, and is usually assessed very early in the therapeutic episode. A strong therapeutic alliance provides the safety and security to clients that permits them to tolerate the anxiety often associated with clinical intervention. In general, good clinical outcomes seem to be more frequent when there is a productive alliance between client and therapist (Krupnick, Elkin, Collings, Simmens, Sotsky, Pilkonis, & Watkins, 1994; Mallinckrodt, 1993; Marmar, Weiss, & Gaston, 1989; Svartberg & Stiles, 1992). One therapist characteristic that is often a determinant of the therapeutic alliance is therapist empathy, and Free, Green, Grace, Chemus, and Whitman (1985) found that clients' ratings of therapist empathy were significantly and positively correlated with a number of outcome measures.

Other therapist variables offer intriguing clues to therapeutic effectiveness. Hill, Helms, Tichenor, Spiegel, O'Grady, and Perry (1988) examined verbatim transcripts of 127 sessions of eight cases of brief psychotherapy with anxious–depressed patients and found that experienced therapists had better immediate results when their behavior was characterized by relatively high levels of self-disclosure, interpretation, approval, paraphrasing, and asking open questions. Least helpful were confrontations, provision of information, and closed questions (see also Hill, 1992).

In an especially useful study, Jones, Cumming, and Horowitz (1988) found that with severely troubled patients, outcome was most positive when therapists gave explicit advice and guidance, when physical symptoms and body functions were discussed, when dialogue had a specific focus, and when the therapist was reassuring. In the case of patients whose difficulties were milder and less disabling, outcome was best when therapists explained the nature of psychotherapy and the rationale of their particular approach, when interpersonal relationships were a major theme of the sessions, when the patient's feelings and behavior in the present were linked to past situations, and when the therapist drew attention to the connections between the therapeutic relationship and other relationships. Thus, more traditional psychodynamic therapists appeared to be more effective for patients who were only mildly disturbed, whereas for patients who were more seriously disturbed, a more supportive and directive therapist seemed more likely to be helpful.

While empirical evidence is still sparse, the literature examining therapist characteristics that appear to be associated with positive therapeutic outcome has suggested a number of other variables that deserve further study. The first of these is therapist expertise. Clinical consensus is that planned short-term psychotherapy requires a greater level of experience and sophistication than does time-unlimited psychotherapy (see, for example, Bellak & Siegel, 1983). In particular, such experience brings with it the knowledge of what kinds of interventions have the potential to be helpful to the client.

Gelso and Johnson (1983) in their research studies in a university counseling center identified a number of other therapist characteristics that appear to be related to patient outcome. These characteristics include (1) the therapist's behavior reflects confidence that short-term therapy can be effective; (2) the therapist establishes challenging but limited therapeutic goals; (3) the therapist works toward insight but not to the exclusion of behavior change; (4) the therapist's goal is to start a therapeutic process that can continue after termination; and (5) the therapist follows up terminated patients to explore the consolidation of changes that has taken place.

As these studies indicate, certain therapist behaviors may be associated with unusually high levels of improvement. These studies need to be replicated and extended, but what seems clear is that under potentially specifiable conditions certain varieties of therapist behavior can result in significant increases in the likelihood of patient improvement, regardless of the theoretical approach to the therapy.

The fact that the list of specific therapist characteristics that are significantly associated with outcome measures is relatively short, however, may serve to underline the remarkable general effectiveness of planned short-term psychotherapy. To put it differently, the best explanation for the fact that empirical studies of the relationship between clinician characteristics and clinical outcome yield such equivocal results may be that planned short-term psychotherapy generally has a positive outcome almost regardless of how the therapist conducts the psychotherapy.

Flexibility Regarding the Concept of Cure

Mental health professionals in sharply increasing numbers are beginning to reconsider their earlier views of the goals of psychotherapy. That traditional perspective on the psychotherapeutic process, virtually unknown in the rest of the healing arts, is that, first, getting better will take a long time and, second, once you are better, you probably will never need to come back. Budman (1981, pp. 464–465) traces these beliefs to early Freudian thinking that Freud himself later repudiated, but not before the beliefs became firmly fixed as part of psychoanalytic folklore.

Cummings and VandenBos (1979) describe this belief system well:

> Any recontact with a former . . . patient is labeled . . . "relapse" and is . . . evidence that the earlier intervention was unsuccessful . . . We . . . act as if contact with a . . . psychologist is for a single, simple . . . problem, and that six sessions will solve everything forever. No other field of health care holds this conceptualization . . . (p. 433; see also Budman & Gurman, 1988, p. 248; Watzlawick, 1978, p. 159)

Most general human service providers—and mental health professionals in increasing numbers—hold an alternative point of view regarding cure, one that seems more persuasive in the context of planned short-term psychotherapy: First, let us try to help you as quickly as possible; and, second, something might very well go wrong in the future, in which case we will try to help you once again as quickly as possible. Kupers (1988) calls this kind of psychotherapy "therapy in pieces." He writes:

> More and more, clients enter therapy wishing to work through one or another

circumscribed issue, end the therapy when they feel satisfied with the immediate results, and then return to be in therapy again when another crisis arises. (p. 106)

As this discussion suggests, the medical concept of cure has largely been abandoned. The treatment relationship is interrupted when presenting problems are resolved, but is never terminated (Hoyt & Austad, 1992; Siddall, Haffey, & Feinman, 1988). With this orientation, commitment to the client can be seen from a new point of view. Rabkin (1977) described the short-term therapy orientation to that commitment well when he observed that under the best of conditions, relationships with professionals other than psychotherapists are not regarded as terminating at all. They are seen as intermittent. He continues,

For example, the accountant, lawyer, family doctor, or barber may have permanent relationships with clients and perhaps their families, although the actual face-to-face contacts occur only for specific tasks or problems. Particularly in relationships of confidence, as in the case of the accountant and the physician, the tie may last a lifetime. (p. 211)

Flexibility in Length and Frequency of Appointments

Two aspects of the growing flexibility—how one determines the length and frequency of clinical appointments and the duration of episodes of psychotherapy—deserve special note. First, there is increasing evidence that therapists are moving away from routinely scheduling 50-minute once-weekly interviews. And, second, attention is beginning to be directed to what may be the most profound question generated by the concept of short-term therapy, namely, how one is to know when enough psychotherapy has been provided (see following discussion).

Time-limited psychotherapy can be scheduled, as we have seen, in many different time frames: appointments generated one at a time; weekly one-hour sessions; half-hour sessions; meetings every two, three, or four weeks, or even twice a year; longer sessions of one and one-half or two hours' duration. Barkham (1989a, 1989b; Barkham & Shapiro, 1990; Day, 1993) has developed an interesting scheduling practice in which clients are regularly seen for two sessions one week apart followed by a third session three months later.

Budman and Stone (1983) have suggested, just as Barkham has, that it may be most effective to see patients initially on a weekly basis and then to move toward longer intervals between sessions. In addition, Budman proposes planned follow-up and periodic return visits. Such proposals "may be more in line with reality than the now-prevalent therapeutic cure model, where no provision is made for follow-up and maintenance of change by the patient often is not considered" (p. 943). Similarly, Goldsmith (1986) has noted that it is not unusual for intervals between sessions to be irregular, or to be every two to four weeks. The longer intervals provide more time for a consolidation of the therapeutic gains within the context of the patient's outside life. Longer intervals, suggests Goldsmith, can also indicate to a patient that the most important problem-solving efforts will be going on outside the therapeutic sessions. He goes on:

The irregularity of intervals between sessions, the variability in the length of the sessions, and the relatively lengthy time that can occur between sessions are all consistent with the belief that change is discontinuous. That is, the rate of therapeutic change that individuals manifest cannot be represented by a single sloping line on a graph. (p. 60)

PLANNED SHORT-TERM PSYCHOTHERAPY AND MANAGED CARE

The last several years have witnessed the beginnings of a profound change in the organization and financing of medical care in the United States. The traditional system of fee-for-service health care is being replaced by a variety of innovative organized health care systems. Well over 100 million Americans are now covered by some form of organized health care (Hoyt, 1995), and the number is increasing very rapidly. While the specific characteristics of the United States health care delivery system of the future are far from clear, there seems to be general agreement that fee-for-service health care is far too inefficient and expensive (Giles, 1993).

The cost of health care in the United States is growing at a rate three or four times that of the general inflation rate, and its unrestricted continuing growth cannot be sustained. In the last decade for which figures are available, expenditures for health care have more than doubled, exceeding one trillion dollars in 1996. This amount represents nearly 14% of the gross domestic product, an average of more than $3700 per person per year.

As the cost of health care increases, the cost of health insurance increases as well. As a consequence, access to health care is eroding. A growing number of Americans are not only unable to afford out-of-pocket medical expenses; they are also unable to afford to pay for health insurance. Ours is the most costly health care system in the world. More than 40 million people in the United States have no health insurance, and an additional million people a year lose the health insurance they have. In addition, insufficient attention is paid to the supply, quality, and distribution of health care services.

These problems are as true for mental health services as they are for general health services (Christianson & Osher, 1994; Feldman & Fitzpatrick, 1992; Shaffer, Cutler, & Wellstone, 1994). The organization and financing of mental health care has to be reformed, or to put this statement into more contemporary vocabulary, "managed." Planned short-term psychotherapy is playing a rapidly growing role in the thinking of health care policy analysts as they consider the implications of managed health care theory for the treatment of psychological disorders.

At the moment the move toward managed mental health care is far from a smooth one. Many health maintenance and mental health maintenance organizations are underfunded, poorly conceptualized, and excessively concerned about profitability. There are concerns about the possible loss of relationship confidentiality between health care provider and client. Managed care organizations appear and disappear. Their survival depends on the ongoing search for contracts with employer groups and on market forces, which often result in unpredictable changes in ownership.

The competitive environment among organized mental health care delivery systems has resulted in considerable instability so that the possibility of multiple brief episodes of psychotherapy within an ongoing therapeutic relationship is not always present. An ongoing therapeutic relationship is not possible when, for example, employers negotiate periodically with competing health care service delivery systems, thus moving their employees wholesale from one set of health care providers to another. Under these circumstances, therapeutic relationships are inevitably severed.

The most common and most serious objection that has been raised by mental health professionals to managed care is the possibility that patients will be undertreated, that is, that there will be too much attention to managed cost and too little attention to managed care (Hoyt, 1995). Managed mental health organizations are at financial risk. If the costs that are incurred in delivering mental health services exceed the income that is derived from fixed prepaid fees, the managed mental health organization cannot survive. Under these circumstances, there may be considerable pressure to reduce mental health treatment across the board or to disallow more costly interventions, which is a practice antithetical to responsible planned short-term psychotherapy that avoids overtreatment in order to conserve resources so that undertreatment also can be avoided. To put it differently, while a fee-for-service medical care system can run the risk of overtreating patients, there is a fear that a managed care system can run the risk of undertreating patients. A well-functioning health care delivery system should minimize both risks.

Reducing these risks depends precisely on a greater understanding of the concept of therapeutic sufficiency, that is, how to know when enough treatment has been delivered. It is the rare professional training program that provides even token attention to this issue. Many, perhaps a majority, of mental health professionals continue to believe, in spite of all the evidence to the contrary, that longer treatment episodes inevitably result in significantly greater clinical improvement.

Major Trends in Managed Care

The likely characteristics of managed care in the coming years can be extrapolated by examining recent trends in health care delivery. While such predictions must be presented with a good deal of caution, three major trends seem relatively clear.

First, managed care is here to stay. In the future there are likely to be fewer but larger managed care companies. This development will allow for far greater stability of mental health care in the future. One consequence of this emerging stability will be the increasing opportunity for both clients and staff to envision brief therapeutic episodes within an ongoing therapeutic relationship. Another consequence will be that managed care organizations will be able to devote more resources to those activities that have important but slow-to-appear consequences for improved physical and mental health. At the moment, with so much movement of clients in and out of health maintenance organizations, there is little incentive for the active development of, for example, stress management or social support enhancement programs. Such preventively oriented programs will more than likely benefit a different health maintenance organization than the one where the programs were developed.

Second, medical care, particularly mental health care, will continue to become increasingly empirically based—treatment plans will be developed as a function of an increased knowledge base. There will likely be a continued decrease in inpatient treatment. Greater attention will be paid to the cost of mental health personnel, with a better match between level of skill and training of mental health personnel, on the one hand, and treatment outcome, on the other. Mental health care should therefore become far more efficient and effective, while at the same time less costly. These developments should reduce the risk of undertreatment even more than might otherwise be the case.

Third, as mental health professionals become better trained in planned short-term psychotherapy and more secure about their abilities to be helpful to clients in brief periods of time, the need for an external utilization review will diminish. As a consequence, mental health professionals will be able to resume their primary responsibility for evaluating patient care and for making decisions about the resources that will be needed to complete a therapeutic episode successfully, without as great a need for onerous record keeping that is now usually required.

What is less easy to predict is the future relationship between mental health and physical health care. The difficulty in being sanguine about such a prediction can be seen in the current state of affairs. While the research literature makes a persuasive case that mental and physical health are remarkably interdependent, most managed mental health care seems to be developing on its own, but having little integration with physical health care.

These predictions are admittedly quite optimistic in character and suggest that managed care will become and then remain the primary mode for providing both physical and mental health services in the future. As time goes on, to continue this generally optimistic view, the risks of undertreatment and overtreatment should diminish, and mental health professionals should be-

come increasingly comfortable about making the most efficient use of time.

CONCLUDING COMMENTS

The field of planned short-term psychotherapy is quickly achieving all the hallmarks of an independent profession. About 150 English language books and edited collections of papers exclusively devoted to the topic have been published in the past 40 years, and nearly 2000 journal articles on the topic have appeared in print.

Courses on short-term therapy are increasingly available in graduate and continuing education programs. The field now has its own journals—the *Journal of Systemic Therapies*, founded in 1981; *International Journal of Short-Term Psychotherapy*, founded in 1986; and *Crisis Intervention and Time-Limited Treatment*, founded in 1993.

What is clear in the literature is that planned short-term psychotherapy is thought of as being applicable to a very wide variety of psychiatric disorders and to both acute and chronic stressful life circumstances in the case of both children and adults. In the case of specific psychiatric disorders, both clinical and research papers have discussed short-term psychotherapy in the treatment of alcoholism, anxiety disorders, chemical dependence, child sexual abuse, chronic pain, depression and other mood disorders, eating disorders, encopresis, panic disorders, personality disorders, phobic and obsessive-compulsive disorders, posttraumatic stress disorders, schizophrenia, and sexual dysfunctions.

Among acute as well as chronic stressful life circumstances, clinical studies have appeared discussing the role of planned short-term psychotherapy in helping clients cope with aging, bereavement, gay and lesbian issues, hostility, imprisonment, job-related stress, low self-esteem, military service, parent–infant issues, physical impairment, retirement, sexual abuse, single-parent families, and stress of university life. It is almost impossible to identify a disorder that has not been found to be responsive to one or another form of time-limited psychotherapy—again, an indication of its remarkable effectiveness (see Bloom, 1997).

Research provides overwhelming evidence that documents the effectiveness of short-term psychotherapy, the interest on the part of most consumers to be done with their therapy and get on with their lives, and the financial drain to society of long-term psychotherapy, which all have combined to raise serious questions about the continued application of time-unlimited approaches (Cochrane, 1972; MacKenzie, 1988). Most people who write about the future of psychotherapy believe that it will include vastly increased use of short-term interventions (see, for example, Luborsky, Docherty, Miller, & Barber, 1993; Magnavita, 1993; Norcross & Freedheim, 1992).

Goldin and Winston (1985) believe that short-term dynamic psychotherapy already has had a significant impact on traditional psychoanalytic psychotherapy, particularly regarding general therapeutic approach and the specific handling of resistance and transference reactions. Regarding their general approach, traditional psychoanalytic psychotherapists who observe the work of time-limited psychodynamic psychotherapists tend to "become more active, more courageous in pursuing feelings, appreciably more specific and concrete in delineating chief complaints, and generally more in control of the interview" (p. 69). In handling resistance, traditional psychodynamic psychotherapists appear to ask more detailed questions, and to be more assertive in thwarting regression on the part of the patient. Finally, in regard to dealing with transference reactions, traditional psychodynamic psychotherapists have tended to interpret the transference relationship earlier, and to decrease their encouragement of the regressive transference neurosis.

With remarkably few exceptions, short-term outpatient or inpatient psychotherapy appears to be equal in effectiveness to time-unlimited outpatient or inpatient care, and outpatient care appears to be equal in effectiveness to inpatient care. The implication of these conclusions for public policy is abundantly clear. In legal language, it is the policy of the *least restrictive alternative*, that is, the principle that psychotherapy should take place in that setting and in a manner that create the fewest personal restrictions on clients. Those restrictions are minimized by keeping the duration of treatment as short as possible.

The field of planned short-term psychotherapy has become an important specialty area and its clinical and research findings are having an increasing impact on the entire field of psychotherapy. Establishing standards by which clinicians can know when they have provided enough psychotherapy has been identified as one of the important empirical issues facing the field at this time. Avoiding overtreatment is the most com-

pelling strategy for assuring that additional treatment will be available when it is needed. Making sure that brief episodes of care are seen within the context of an ongoing therapeutic relationship can help assure that additional treatment will be requested.

The twin observations that planned short-term psychotherapy is indistinguishable from time-unlimited psychotherapy in its effects and that clients generally are quite satisfied with brief episodes of treatment are not only the most consistent findings in the psychotherapy literature; they are also the most affirmative. The repeatedly observed ability of mental health professionals to be helpful to their patients in remarkably short periods of time should bring an enormous sense of satisfaction to psychotherapists whose years of training have been designed to enhance their abilities to understand and be of help to troubled people.

Planned short-term psychotherapy started out life forty years ago as second best, offered to patients apologetically. Today, while there is continuing objection to across-the-board limitations on therapy duration, planned short-term psychotherapy has become one of the most exciting and professionally affirming developments in the field of clinical practice.

With the current concern about the high cost of medical care and with the growth of health maintenance organizations and other alternatives to fee-for-service health care, there is increasing interest in avoiding overtreatment, that is, in providing only those health-related services that are needed. The planned short-term therapy literature strongly suggests that long-term encounters may very likely provide more psychotherapy than is needed (Budman & Stone, 1983; Cummings, 1986; Klerman, 1983; McGuire & Frisman, 1983).

Closer examination of the evaluation literature suggests that the basic reason for the equivalence in outcome of brief and long-term psychotherapy lies not in the fact that long-term psychotherapy is of such limited effectiveness but rather that brief psychotherapy seems to yield such remarkably positive results. In a way, this finding should not be surprising. By petitioning for help, therapy clients signal their acceptance of a psychological component to their difficulties, their high motivation, as well as their willingness to change (see Chapter 7 in this volume on hope).

One set of clues that can help explain the effectiveness of planned short-term psychotherapy can be found in the work of Piper et al. (1984), who found that relatively short-term individual psychotherapy (average of 22 sessions within six-month maximum) was consistently superior to time-unlimited individual psychotherapy (average of 76 sessions within two-year maximum) on a variety of outcome measures collected from patients, therapists, and independent assessors blind to treatment assignment. They reported that short-term therapy patients and therapists "felt the need to work hard and relatively quickly. Attention was concentrated and focused. Affective involvement was high. . . . At completion most patients felt that they had received something valuable from the therapist" (p. 277). In contrast, long-term individual therapy patients and clinicians were less satisfied. "The length of time available coupled with the frequency of one session per week seemed to favor an increase in resistance and a decrease in working through. Thus, the patient tended to behave as if there was always plenty of time to work later" (p. 277).

It is important, however, not to promise more than can be delivered. Donovan (1987) has warned that when the proponents of time-limited psychotherapy suggest that their intervention is incontrovertibly the only reason for change in their patient's lives, they are engaging in clear speculation. People are in a constant state of change and they use a variety of situations and relationships to support that growth, including but certainly not limited to psychotherapy. In addition, Budman and Stone (1983) have reminded us that among the many development-promoting relationships are several courses of psychotherapy, not just one. Mental health professionals themselves seek an average of five therapies over their adult lives, even when one therapy has been a "full" psychoanalysis. These facts, according to Budman and Stone, throw into question the claims that one sequence of brief treatment should lead to definitive and permanent change (see also Budman, 1990). The question of how much psychotherapy is needed is not a trivial one, yet it has hardly been addressed in the theoretical or empirical literature.

In 1971, Parad concluded her review of the short-term treatment literature in the field of social welfare by noting that

> If the level of outcome effectiveness evidenced in the recent studies is further substantiated in future large-scale experimental research, it would be logical to infer that short-term treatment should

be the basic therapeutic approach for all but a relatively small selected group of applicants. . . . (p. 145)

Research that has been reported since that paper was published has repeatedly affirmed the remarkable efficacy of planned short-term psychotherapy. Happily, mental health professionals are beginning to accept with grace the affirmation of their effectiveness in brief periods of time and are proceeding to develop strategies for institutionalizing that effectiveness.

REFERENCES

Arkowitz, H., & Hannah, M. T. (1989). Cognitive, behavioral, and psychodynamic therapies: Converging or diverging pathways to change? In A. Freeman, K. M. Simon, L. E. Beutler, & H. Arkowitz (Eds.), *Comprehensive handbook of cognitive therapy* (pp. 143–167). New York: Plenum Press.

Avnet, H. H. (1965). How effective is short-term therapy? In L. R. Wolberg (Ed.), *Short-term psychotherapy* (pp. 7–22). New York: Grune & Stratton.

Barkham, M. (1989a). Brief prescriptive therapy in two-plus-one sessions: Initial cases from the clinic. *Behavioural Psychotherapy, 17,* 161–175.

Barkham, M. (1989b). Exploratory therapy in two-plus-one sessions: I—Rationale for a brief psychotherapy model. *British Journal of Psychotherapy, 6*(1), 81–88.

Barkham, M., & Shapiro, D. A. (1990). Brief psychotherapeutic interventions for job-related distress: A pilot study of prescriptive and exploratory therapy. *Counseling Psychology Quarterly, 3,* 133–147.

Beck, A. T. (1976). *Cognitive therapy and the emotional disorders.* New York: International Universities Press.

Beck, A. T., Rush, A. J., Shaw, B. F., & Emery, G. (1979). *Cognitive therapy of depression.* New York: Guilford Press.

Bedrosian, R. C., & Bozicas, G. D. (1994). *Treating family of origin problems: A cognitive approach.* New York: Guilford Press.

Bellak, L. (1984). Intensive brief and emergency psychotherapy. In L. Grinspoon (Ed.), *Psychiatry update: The American Psychiatric Association annual review* (Vol. 3, pp. 11–24). Washington, D.C.: American Psychiatric Press.

Bellak, L., & Siegel, H. (1983). *Handbook of intensive brief and emergency psychotherapy (B.E.P.).* Larchmont, NY: C.P.S. Inc.

Bellak, L., & Small, L. (1978). *Emergency psychotherapy and brief psychotherapy* (2nd ed.). New York: Grune & Stratton.

Bergin, A. E., & Garfield, S. L. (1986). Introduction and historical review. In S. L. Garfield & A. E. Bergin (Eds.), *Handbook of psychotherapy and behavior change: An empirical analysis* (3rd ed., pp. 3–22). New York: Wiley.

Berman, J. S., & Norton, N. C. (1985). Does professional training make a therapist more effective? *Psychological Bulletin, 98*, 401–407.

Blanck, G., & Blanck, R. (1988). The contribution of ego psychology to understanding the process of termination in psychoanalysis and psychotherapy. *Journal of the American Psychoanalytic Association, 36*, 961–984.

Bloch, S., Bond, G., Qualls, B., Yalom, I., & Zimmerman, E. (1977). Outcome in psychotherapy evaluated by independent judges. *British Journal of Psychiatry, 131*, 410–414.

Bloom, B. L. (1984). *Community mental health: A general introduction* (2nd ed.). Monterey, CA: Brooks/Cole.

Bloom, B. L. (1992). *Planned short-term psychotherapy: A clinical handbook* (1st ed.). Boston: Allyn & Bacon.

Bloom, B. L. (1997). *Planned short-term psychotherapy: A clinical handbook.* (2nd ed.). Boston, Allyn & Bacon.

Bowers, T. G., & Clum, G. A. (1988). Relative contribution of specific and nonspecific treatment effects: Meta-analysis of placebo-controlled behavior therapy research. *Psychological Bulletin, 103*, 315–323.

Budman, S. H. (1981). Looking toward the future. In S. H. Budman (Ed.), *Forms of brief therapy* (pp. 461–467). New York: Guilford Press.

Budman, S. (1990). The myth of termination in brief therapy: Or, it ain't over till it's over. In J. K. Zeig & S. G. Gilligan (Eds.), *Brief therapy: Myths, methods, and metaphors* (pp. 206–218). New York: Brunner/Mazel.

Budman, S. H., & Gurman, A. (1983). The practice of brief therapy. *Professional Psychology: Research and Practice, 14*, 277–292.

Budman, S. H., & Stone, J. (1983). Advances in brief psychotherapy: A review of recent literature. *Hospital and Community Psychiatry, 34*, 939–946.

Burlingame, G. M., & Behrman, J. A. (1987). Clinician attitudes toward time-limited and time-unlimited therapy. *Professional Psychology: Research and Practice, 18*, 61–65.

Butcher, J. N., & Koss, M. P. (1978). Research on brief and crisis-oriented therapies. In S. L. Garfield & A. E. Bergin (Eds.), *Handbook of psychotherapy and behavior change: An empirical analysis* (2nd ed., pp. 725–767). New York: Wiley.

Carmona, P. E. (1988). Changing traditions in psychotherapy: A study of therapists' attitudes. *Clinical Nurse Specialist, 2*, 185–190.

Christianson, J. B., & Osher, F. C. (1994). Health maintenance organizations, health care reform, and persons with serious mental illness. *Hospital and Community Psychiatry, 45*, 898–905.

Cochrane, A. L. (1972). *Effectiveness and efficiency: Random reflections on health services.* London: Nuffield Provincial Hospitals Trust.

Cross, D. G., Sheehan, P. W., & Khan, J. A. (1982). Short-and long-term follow-up of clients receiving insight-oriented therapy and behavior therapy. *Journal of Consulting and Clinical Psychology, 50*, 103–112.

Cummings, N. A. (1986). The dismantling of our health system: Strategies for the survival of psychological practice. *American Psychologist, 41*, 426–431.

Cummings, N. A., & Follette, W. T. (1976). Brief psychotherapy and medical utilization. In H. Dorken & Associates (Eds.), *The professional psychologist today: New developments in law, health insurance and health practice* (pp. 165–174). San Francisco: Jossey-Bass.

Cummings, N., & Sayama, M. (1995). *Focused psychotherapy: A casebook of brief, intermittent psychotherapy throughout the life cycle.* New York: Brunner/Mazel.

Cummings, N. A., & VandenBos, G. R. (1979). The general practice of psychology. *Professional Psychology: Research and Practice, 10*, 430–440.

Davanloo, H. (Ed.). (1980). *Short-term dynamic psychotherapy.* Northvale, NJ: Aronson.

Day, A. (1993). Brief prescriptive psychotherapy for depression with an incarcerated young offender: An application of Barkham's 2 + 1 model. *Journal of Offender Rehabilitation, 19*(1/2), 75–87.

de Bosset, F., & Styrsky, E. (1986). Termination in individual psychotherapy: A survey of residents' experience. *Canadian Journal of Psychiatry, 31*, 636–642.

de Shazer, S. (1982). *Patterns of brief family therapy: An ecosystemic approach.* New York: Guilford Press.

de Shazer, S. (1985). *Keys to solution in brief therapy.* New York: Norton.

de Shazer, S. (1994). *Words were originally magic.* New York: Norton.

Dobson, K. S. (Ed.). (1988). *Handbook of cognitive-behavioral therapies.* New York: Guilford Press.

Dobson, K. S., & Block, L. (1988). Historical and philosophical bases of the cognitive-behavioral therapies. In K. S. Dobson (Ed.), *Handbook of cognitive-behavioral therapies* (pp. 3–38). New York: Guilford Press.

Donovan, J. M. (1987). Brief dynamic psychotherapy: Toward a more comprehensive model. *Psychiatry, 50*, 167–183.

Eckert, P. A. (1993). Acceleration of change: Catalysts in brief therapy. *Clinical Psychology Review, 13*, 241–253.

Edbril, S. D. (1994). Gender bias in short-term therapy: Toward a new model for working with women patients in managed care settings. *Psychotherapy, 31*, 601–609.

Ellis, A. (1962). *Reason and emotion in psychotherapy.* New York: Stuart.

Ellis, A. (1993). Fundamentals of rational-emotive therapy for the 1990s. In W. Dryden & L. K. Hill (Eds.), *Innovations in rational-emotive therapy* (pp. 1–32). Thousand Oaks, CA: Sage.

Epstein, N. B., Bishop, D. S., Keitner, G. I., & Miller, I. W. (1990). A systems therapy: Problem-centered systems therapy of the family. In R. A. Wells & V. J. Giannetti (Eds.), *Handbook of the brief psychotherapies* (pp. 405–436). New York: Plenum.

Ewing, C. P. (1978). *Crisis intervention as psychotherapy.* New York: Oxford University Press.

Farrelly, F., & Brandsma, J. (1974). *Provocative therapy.* Cupertino, CA: Meta Publications.

Feldman, J. B. (1994). A multischema model for combining Ericksonian and cognitive therapy. In S. R. Lankton & K. K. Erickson (Eds.), *The essence of a single-session success* (pp. 54–74). New York: Brunner/Mazel.

Feldman, J. L., & Fitzpatrick, R. J. (Eds.). (1992). *Managed mental health care: Administrative and clinical issues.* Washington, D.C.: American Psychiatric Press.

Fisch, R., Weakland, J. H., & Segal, L. (1982). *The tactics of change.* San Francisco: Jossey-Bass.

Follette, W., & Cummings, N. A. (1967). Psychiatric services and medical utilization in a prepaid health plan setting. *Medical Care, 5,* 25–35.

Fraser, J. S. (1986). Integrating system-based therapies: Similarities, differences, and some critical questions. In D. E. Efron (Ed.), *Journeys: Expansion of the strategic-systemic therapies* (pp. 125–149). New York: Brunner/Mazel.

Free, N. K., Green, B. L., Grace, M. C., Chernus, L. A., & Whitman, R. M. (1985). Empathy and outcome in brief focal dynamic therapy. *American Journal of Psychiatry, 142,* 917–921.

Freud, S. (1909/1953). Notes upon a case of obsessional neurosis. In A. Strachey & J. Strachey (Eds.), *Sigmund Freud, M.D., LL.D. Collected papers* (Vol. 3, pp. 293–383). London: Hogarth Press.

Gelso, C. J. (1992). Realities and emerging myths about brief therapy. *Counseling Psychologist, 20,* 464–471.

Gelso, C. J., & Johnson, D. H. (1983). *Explorations in time-limited counseling and psychotherapy.* New York: Teachers College Press.

Giles, T. R. (1993). *Managed mental health care: A guide for practitioners, employers, and hospital administrators.* Boston: Allyn and Bacon.

Goldin, V., & Winston, A. (1985). The impact of short-term dynamic psychotherapy on psychoanalytic psychotherapy. In A. Winston (Ed.), *Clinical and research issues in short-term dynamic psychotherapy* (pp. 62–79). Washington, D.C.: American Psychiatric Press.

Goldsmith, S. (1986). *Psychotherapy of people with physical symptoms: Brief strategic approaches.* Lanham, MD: University Press of America.

Gross, M. L. (1978). *The psychological society.* New York: Random House.

Gurman, A. S. (1981). Integrative marital therapy: Toward the development of an interpersonal approach. In S. Budman (Ed.), *Forms of brief therapy* (pp. 415–457). New York: Guilford Press.

Gustafson, J. P. (1986). *The complex secret of brief psychotherapy.* New York: Norton.

Gustafson, J. P. (1995). *The dilemmas of brief psychotherapy.* New York: Plenum.

Hadley, S. W., & Strupp, H. H. (1976). Contemporary views on negative effects: An integrated account. *Archives of General Psychiatry, 33,* 1291–1302.

Haley, J. (1973). *Uncommon therapy: The psychiatric techniques of Milton H. Erickson, M. D.* New York: Norton.

Haley, J. (1987). *Problem-solving therapy* (2nd ed.). San Francisco: Jossey-Bass.

Halligan, F. R. (1995). The challenge: Short-term dynamic psychotherapy for college counseling centers. *Psychotherapy, 32,* 113–121.

Held, B. S. (1986). The relationship between individual psychologies and strategic/systemic therapies reconsidered. In D. E. Efron (Ed.), *Journeys: Expansion of the strategic-systemic therapies* (pp. 222–260). New York: Brunner/Mazel.

Hill, C. E. (1992). Research on therapist techniques in brief individual therapy: Implications for practitioners. *Counseling Psychologist, 20,* 689–711.

Hill, C. E., Helms, J. E., Tichenor, V., Spiegel, S. B., O'Grady, K. E., & Perry, E. S. (1988). Effects of therapist response modes in brief psychotherapy. *Journal of Counseling Psychology, 35,* 222–233.

Hoffman, D. L., & Remmel, M. L. (1975). Uncovering the precipitant in crisis intervention. *Social Casework, 56,* 259–267.

Horowitz, L. M., & Vitkus, J. (1986). The interpersonal basis of psychiatric symptoms. *Clinical Psychology Review, 6,* 443–469.

Horowitz, M. (1976). *Stress response syndromes.* Northvale, NJ: Aronson.

Horowitz, M. J. (1991). Short-term dynamic therapy of stress response syndromes. In P. Crits-Christoph & J. P. Barber (Eds.), *Handbook of short-term dynamic psychotherapy* (pp. 166–198). New York: Basic Books.

Howard, K. I., Kopta, S. M., Krause, M. S., & Orlinsky, D. E. (1986). The dose-effect relationship in psychotherapy. *American Psychologist, 41,* 159–164.

Hoyt, M. F. (1979). Aspects of termination in a time-limited brief psychotherapy. *Psychiatry, 42,* 208–219.

Hoyt, M. F. (1985). Therapist resistances to short-term dynamic psychotherapy. *Journal of the American Academy of Psychoanalysis, 13,* 93–112.

Hoyt, M. F. (1987). Resistance to brief therapy. *American Psychologist, 42,* 408–409.

Hoyt, M. F. (1994). Single-session solutions. In M. F. Hoyt (Ed.), *Constructive therapies* (pp. 140–159). New York: Guilford Press.

Hoyt, M. F. (1995). *Brief therapy and managed care: Readings for contemporary practice.* San Francisco: Jossey-Bass.

Hoyt, M. F., & Austad, C. S. (1992). Psychotherapy in a staff model health maintenance organization: Providing and assuring quality care in the future. *Psychotherapy, 29,* 119–129.

Husby, R. (1985). Short-term dynamic psychotherapy: IV. Comparison of recorded changes in 33 neurotic patients 2 and 5 years after end of treatment. *Psychotherapy and Psychosomatics, 43,* 23–27.

Johnson, D. H., & Gelso, C. J. (1980). The effectiveness of time limits in counseling and psychotherapy: A critical review. *Counseling Psychologist, 9,* 70–83.

Jones, E. (1955). *The life and work of Sigmund Freud.* New York: Basic Books.

Jones, E. E., Cumming, J. D., & Horowitz, M. J. (1988). Another look at the nonspecific hypothesis of therapeutic effectiveness. *Journal of Consulting and Clinical Psychology, 56,* 48–55.

Jones, E. E., & Pulos, S. M. (1993). Comparing the process in psychodynamic and cognitive-behavioral therapies. *Journal of Consulting and Clinical Psychology, 61,* 306–316.

Kane, J. M. (1991). Risk-benefit ratios in psychiatric treatment. In S. M. Mirin, J. T. Gossett, & M. C. Grob (Eds.), *Psychiatric treatment: Advances in outcome research* (pp. 15–20). Washington, DC: American Psychiatric Press.

Kirkby, R. J., & Smyrnios, K. X. (1992). The psychological health of children, cost-effectiveness, and brief therapy. *Australian Psychologist, 27,* 78–82.

Klerman, G. L. (1983). The efficacy of psychotherapy as the basis for public policy. *American Psychologist, 38,* 929–934.

Klerman, G. L., & Weissman, M. M. (1982). Interpersonal psychotherapy theory and research. In A. J. Rush (Ed.), *Short-term psychotherapies for depression* (pp. 88–106). New York: Guilford Press.

Klerman, G. L. & Weissman, M. M. (Eds.). (1993). *New applications of interpersonal psychotherapy.* Washington, D.C.: American Psychiatric Press.

Koss, M. P., & Butcher, J. N. (1986). Research on brief psychotherapy. In A. E. Bergin & S. L. Garfield (Eds.), *Handbook of psychotherapy and behavior change: An empirical analysis* (3rd ed., pp. 627–670). New York: John Wiley & Sons.

Koss, M. P., Butcher, J. N., & Strupp, H. H. (1986). Brief psychotherapy methods in clinical research. *Journal of Consulting and Clinical Psychology, 54,* 60–67.

Koss, M. P., & Shiang, J. (1994). Research on brief psychotherapy. In A. E. Bergin & S. L. Garfield (Eds.), *Handbook of psychotherapy and behavior change* (pp. 664–700). New York: John Wiley & Sons.

Krupnick, J. L., Elkin, I., Collings, J., Simmens, S., Sotsky, S. M., Pilkonis, P. A., & Watkins, J. T. (1994). Therapeutic alliance and clinical outcome in the NIMH treatment of depression collaborative research program: Preliminary findings. *Psychotherapy, 31,* 28–35.

Kupers, T. A. (1988). *Ending therapy: The meaning of termination.* New York: New York University Press.

Laikin, M., Winston, A., & McCullough, L. (1991). Intensive short-term dynamic psychotherapy. In P. Crits-Christoph & J. P. Barber (Eds.), *Handbook of short-term dynamic psychotherapy* (pp. 80–109). New York: Basic Books.

Lambert, M. J. (1989). The individual therapist's contribution to psychotherapy process and outcome. *Clinical Psychology Review, 9,* 469–485.

Lambert, M. J., Shapiro, D. A., & Bergin, A. E. (1986). The effectiveness of psychotherapy. In S. L. Garfield & A. E. Bergin (Eds.). *Handbook of psychotherapy and behavior change* (3rd ed., pp. 157–211). New York: John Wiley & Sons.

Lewin, K. K. (1970). *Brief encounters: Brief psychotherapy.* St. Louis, MO: Green.

Luborsky, L., Docherty, J. P., Miller, N. E., & Barber, J. P. (1993). What's here and what's ahead in dynamic therapy research and practice? In N. E. Miller, L. Luborsky, J. P. Barber, & J. P. Docherty (Eds.), *Psychodynamic treatment research: A handbook for clinical practice* (pp. 536–553). New York: Basic Books.

MacKenzie, K. R. (1988). Recent developments in brief psychotherapy. *Hospital and Community Psychiatry, 39,* 742–752.

MacMahon, B., & Pugh, T. F. (1970). *Epidemiology: Principles and methods.* Boston: Little, Brown.

Magnavita, J. J. (1993). The evolution of short-term dynamic psychotherapy: Treatment of the future? *Professional Psychology: Research and Practice, 24,* 360–365.

Malcolm, J. (1987). J'appelle un chat un chat. *The New Yorker, April 20,* 1987, 84–92, 95–102.

Mallinckrodt, B. (1993). Session impact, working alliance, and treatment outcome in brief counseling. *Journal of Counseling Psychology, 40,* 25–32.

Mann, J. (1973). *Time-limited psychotherapy.* Cambridge, MA: Harvard University Press.

Marmar, C. R., Weiss, D. S., & Gaston, L. (1989). Toward the validation of the California Therapeutic Alliance Rating System. *Psychological Assessment: A Journal of Consulting and Clinical Psychology, 1,* 46–52.

Marmor, J. (1968). New directions in psychoanalytic

theory and therapy. In J. Marmor (Ed.), *Modern psychoanalysis: New directions and perspectives* (pp. 3–15). New York: Basic Books.

Marmor, J. (1979). Short-term dynamic psychotherapy. *American Journal of Psychiatry, 136,* 149–155.

McGuire, T. G., & Frisman, L. K. (1983). Reimbursement policy and cost-effective mental health care. *American Psychologist, 38,* 935–940.

McMullin, R. E. (1986). *Handbook of cognitive therapy techniques.* New York: Norton.

Miller, W. R., & Hester, R. K. (1986). Inpatient alcoholism treatment: Who benefits? *American Psychologist, 41,* 794–805.

Norcross, J. C., & Freedheim, D. K. (1992). Into the future: Retrospect and prospect in psychotherapy. In D. K. Freedheim (Ed.), *History of psychotherapy: A century of change* (pp. 881–900). Washington, D.C.: American Psychological Association.

O'Hanlon, W. H. (1990). A grand unified theory for brief therapy: Putting problems in context. In J. K. Zeig & S. G. Gilligan (Eds.), *Brief therapy: Myths, methods, and metaphors* (pp. 78–89). New York: Brunner/Mazel.

O'Hanlon, W. H., & Hexum, A. L. (1990). *An uncommon casebook: The complete clinical work of Milton H. Erickson.* New York: Norton.

O'Hanlon, W. H., & Weiner-Davis, M. (1989). *In search of solutions: A new direction in psychotherapy.* New York: Norton.

O'Leary, M. G. (1995). Therapists' estimation of client satisfaction with services: Implications in an era of managed care. *Crisis Intervention and Time-Limited Treatment, 2,* 13–22.

Olfson, M., & Pincus, H. A. (1994). Outpatient psychotherapy in the United States: II. Patterns of utilization. *American Journal of Psychiatry, 151,* 1289–1294.

Parad, L. G. (1971). Short-term treatment: An overview of historical trends, issues, and potentials. *Smith College Studies in Social Work, 41,* 119–146.

Peake, T. H., Borduin, C. M., & Archer, R. P. (1988). *Brief psychotherapies: Changing frames of mind.* Thousand Oaks, CA: Sage.

Pekarik, G. (1994). Effects of brief therapy training on practicing psychotherapists and their clients. *Community Mental Health Journal, 30,* 135–144.

Pekarik, G., & Wierzbicki, M. (1986). The relationship between clients' expected and actual treatment duration. *Psychotherapy, 23,* 532–534.

Phillips, E. L. (1985). *A guide for therapists and patients to short-term psychotherapy.* Springfield, IL: Thomas.

Phillips, E. L., & Wiener, D. N. (1966). *Short-term psychotherapy and structured behavior change.* New York: McGraw-Hill.

Pinkerton, R. S., & Rockwell, W. J. K. (1994). Very brief psychological interventions with university students. *Journal of American College Health, 42,* 156–162.

Piper, W. E., Debbane, E. G., Bienvenu, J. P., & Garant, J. (1984). A comparative study of four forms of psychotherapy. *Journal of Consulting and Clinical Psychology, 52,* 268–279.

Quintana, S. M. (1993). Toward an expanded and updated conceptualization of termination: Implications for short-term, individual psychotherapy. *Professional Psychology: Research and Practice, 24,* 426–432.

Rabkin, R. (1977). *Strategic psychotherapy: Brief and symptomatic treatment.* New York: Basic Books.

Regier, D. A., Goldberg, I. D., & Taube, C. A. (1978). The de facto U.S. mental health services system. *Archives of General Psychiatry, 35,* 685–693.

Robbins, S. B., & Zinni, V. R. (1988). Implementing a time-limited treatment model: Issues and solutions. *Professional Psychology: Research and Practice, 19,* 53–57.

Rosenbaum, R. (1990). Strategic psychotherapy. In R. A. Wells & V. J. Giannetti (Eds.), *Handbook of the brief psychotherapies* (pp. 351–403). New York: Plenum.

Rush, A. J., & Giles, D. E. (1982). Cognitive therapy: Theory and research. In A. J. Giles (Ed.), *Short-term psychotherapies for depression* (pp. 143–181). New York: Guilford Press.

Sachs, J. S. (1983). Negative factors in brief psychotherapy: An empirical assessment. *Journal of Consulting and Clinical Psychology, 51,* 557–564.

Schlesinger, H. J. (1994). *Keeping psychotherapy efficient: How much is enough?* Unpublished manuscript.

Schlesinger, H. J., Mumford, E., Glass, G. V., Patrick, C., & Sharfstein, S. (1983). Mental health treatment and medical care utilization in a fee-for-service system: Outpatient mental health treatment following the onset of a chronic disease. *American Journal of Public Health, 73,* 422–429.

Schuyler, D. (1991). *A practical guide to cognitive therapy.* New York: Norton.

Seligman, M. E. P. (1995). The effectiveness of psychotherapy: The *Consumer Reports* study. *American Psychologist, 50,* 965–974.

Shaffer, E. R., Cutler, A. J., & Wellstone, P. D. (1994). Coverage of mental health and substance abuse services under a single-payer health care system. *Hospital and Community Psychiatry, 45,* 916–919.

Shectman, F. (1986). Time and the practice of psychotherapy. *Psychotherapy, 23,* 521–525.

Shiffman, S. (1987). Clinical psychology training and psychotherapy interview performance. *Psychotherapy, 24,* 71–84.

Siddall, L. B., Haffey, N. A., & Feinman, J. A. (1988). Intermittent brief psychotherapy in an HMO setting. *American Journal of Psychotherapy, 42,* 96–106.

Sifneos, P. E. (1979). *Short-term dynamic psychotherapy: Evaluation and technique.* New York: Plenum.

Simon, F. B., Stierlin, H., & Wynne, L. C. (1985). *The language of family therapy: A systemic vocabulary and sourcebook.* New York: Family Process Press.

Smyrnios, K. W., & Kirkby, R. J. (1993). Long-term comparison of brief versus unlimited psychodynamic treatments with children and their parents. *Journal of Consulting and Clinical Psychology, 61,* 1020–1027.

Steenbarger, B. N. (1992). Toward science-practice integration in brief counseling and therapy. *Counseling Psychologist, 20,* 403–450.

Steenbarger, B. N. (1993). Intentionalizing brief college student psychotherapy. *Journal of College Student Psychotherapy, 7*(2), 47–61.

Sterba, R. (1951). A case of brief psychotherapy by Sigmund Freud. *Psychoanalytic Review, 38,* 75–80.

Stiles, W. B., & Shapiro, D. A. (1989). Abuse of the drug metaphor in psychotherapy process-outcome research. *Clinical Psychology Review, 9,* 521–543.

Straker, G. (1986). Brief-term psychodynamic psychotherapy: A contradiction in terms? *South African Journal of Psychology, 16,* 57–61.

Strupp, H. H. (1980). Success and failure in time-limited psychotherapy with special reference to the performance of a lay counselor. *Archives of General Psychiatry, 37,* 831–841.

Strupp, H. H. (1989). Psychotherapy: Can the practitioner learn from the researcher? *American Psychologist, 44,* 717–724.

Talmon, M. (1990). *Single-session therapy: Maximizing the effect of the first (and often only) therapeutic encounter.* San Francisco: Jossey-Bass.

Tennov, D. (1975). *Psychotherapy: The hazardous cure.* New York: Abelard-Schuman.

Trad, P. V. (1991). The application of developmental strategies to short-term psychotherapy. *International Journal of Short-Term Psychotherapy, 6,* 219–235.

Walen, S. R., DiGiuseppe, R., & Dryden, W. (1992). *A practitioners guide to rational-emotive* therapy (2nd ed.). New York: Oxford University Press.

Watzlawick, P. (1978). *The language of change: Elements of therapeutic communication.* New York: Basic Books.

Weakland, J. H., & Fisch, R. (1992). Brief therapy— MRI style. In S. H. Budman, M. F. Hoyt, & S. Friedman (Eds.), *The first session in brief therapy* (pp. 306–323). New York: Guilford Press.

Weiss, R. L., & Jacobson, N. S. (1981). Behavioral marital therapy as brief therapy. In S. Budman (Ed.), *Forms of brief therapy* (pp. 387–414). New York: Guilford Press.

Wells, R. A., & Phelps, P. A. (1990). The brief psychotherapies: A selective overview. In R. A. Wells & V. J. Giannetti (Eds.), *Handbook of the brief psychotherapies* (pp. 3–26). New York: Plenum.

Wilson, G. T. (1978). On the much discussed nature of the term "behavior therapy." *Behavior Therapy, 9,* 89–98.

Wilson, G. T. (1981). Behavior therapy as a short-term therapeutic approach. In S. H. Budman (Ed.), *Forms of brief therapy* (pp. 131–166). New York: Guilford Press.

Wolberg, L. R. (1968). Short-term psychotherapy In J. Marmor (Ed.), *Modern psychoanalysis* (pp. 343–354). New York: Basic Books.

Wolberg, L. R. (1980). *Handbook of short-term psychotherapy.* New York: Thieme-Stratton.

Zilbergeld, B. (1983). *The shrinking of America: Myths of psychological change.* Boston: Little, Brown.

CHAPTER 21

LONG-TERM PSYCHOTHERAPY

PAUL CRITS-CHRISTOPH AND JACQUES P. BARBER
University of Pennsylvania

LONG-TERM PSYCHOTHERAPY

The emphasis on cost containment in health care, with the proliferation of health maintenance organizations and managed care, has created a sustained interest in the role of short-term psychotherapy. Research studies documenting the efficacy of short-term therapies of various types have furthered cemented the place of short-term therapy as a central treatment option for many clients seeking help. What then, is the possible role of *long-term psychotherapy* in the current environment? The intent of this chapter is to examine a variety of questions related to long-term therapy, including (1) How should long-term therapy be defined and differentiated from short-term therapy, and how often is long-term therapy delivered as a treatment in the community? (2) What are the major clinical approaches to long-term psychotherapy? (3) What does empirical research tell us about the efficacy of long-term therapy? (4) What are the types of patient problems for which long-term therapy might be indicated? and (5) What are the methodological issues involved in conducting research on long-term therapy?

Definition and Utilization of Long-Term Therapy

There are actually a variety of situations in which therapy might be described as *long term*. Long-term psychotherapy was traditionally associated with formal psychoanalysis or psychoanalytic psychotherapy, but there are other forms of long-term therapy as well.

Borrowing a strategy used in psychopharmacology studies, some psychotherapy has been referred to as maintenance therapy. In this form of treatment, an active phase treatment (e.g., once per week for 12 weeks) used to bring about symptom relief is followed by visits occurring less frequently (e.g., once per month for a year) that serve to protect against relapse. This approach has been used in the treatment of depression (Frank et al., 1990; Reynolds et al., 1997). Variations of this format are undoubtedly used in clinical practice, although there are no data available on how widespread this is.

Another form of long-term therapy involves recurrent brief therapies or recurrent crisis interventions. This format is also likely to be occurring somewhat in clinical practice. Patients are seen for brief periods of time mostly to deal with a crisis or to help resolve a more enduring problem in the framework of an intervention that might last up to 6 or 12 months. Once the patients have achieved a certain level of relief (mostly symptomatic), many of them leave therapy. Often when these patients experience either a recurrence or a new crisis, they will re-contact their therapists. Obviously, the chances they will get back into treatment increase the more their previous experience with therapy was positive. Such recurrent therapies have been described by McKenna and Todd (1997) in a recent analysis of nine patients who had multiple sequential experiences in psychotherapy.

A third kind of long-term therapy is a therapy that was intended to be short term but turns into a long-term event. Again, there are no data

Author note:

The preparation of this manuscript was funded in part by National Institute of Mental Health grants P50-MH-45178, K02-MH00756, and R01-MH40472.

on how often this occurs. However, our impression is that it is common for treatment centers that follow short term models (usually cognitive-behavioral) to have many patients that stay in treatment beyond brief therapy.

The fourth kind of long-term therapy is long-term by intent. This form of long-term therapy, like psychoanalysis, is the one that most people have in mind when thinking about long-term therapy. Formal psychoanalysis, with sessions held three to five times per week, is commonly carried out over a duration of five years or more. Long-term psychoanalytic psychotherapy, with sessions once or twice per week, is often recommended to be two to three years in duration. While these characterizations have some historical significance in the literature on long-term therapy, a modern definition of *long-term* therapy should be made with consideration of what is known about variations in the duration of psychotherapy as it is currently practiced.

Using data from clinics with a long-term psychodynamic therapy orientation, Howard, Davidson, O'Mahoney, Orlinsky, and Brown (1989) describe the durations of treatment for 405 patients. Only 16.3% of patients were in treatment for more than 52 sessions, and 4% received more than 104 sessions. Because patients rarely (in once-a-week therapy) attend 52 sessions in a year, these figures likely underestimate slightly the percentage of therapies that are greater than one or two years. The data presented by Pollak, Mordecai, and Gumpert (1992), who report on the attrition rates for 399 patients treated in a training setting that delivers long-term psychodynamic psychotherapy, confirm this: 28% of patients remained in treatment for one year or more.

It is quite possible that at the current time the average length of psychotherapy has decreased from the numbers reported by Howard et al. (1989) and Pollak et al. (1992) due to the increasing rationing of service by HMOs and managed care companies. In the Howard et al. sample, 9.5% of those patients with HMO plans remained in therapy for more than 52 sessions compared to 17.4% of those who did not have an HMO plan. Thus, increasing enrollment in HMO plans is likely to impact considerably on the utilization of long-term therapy. Alternatively, it is possible that many patients in long-term therapy seek treatment in private practice settings rather than a clinic setting, and therefore the Howard et al. and Pollak et al. studies do not provide accurate estimates of the proportion of psychotherapies that are long-term.

Regardless of whether there have been further changes in the utilization patterns for psychotherapy since the early 1990s, the existing data suggest that defining long-term therapy as two or more years in duration would lead to this type of therapy as largely being of theoretical interest but without much practical significance in the current service delivery system. However, considering that short-term therapy has often been defined as up to 25 sessions (weeks), long-term therapy must be of sufficient duration to be clearly beyond six months. Accordingly, we propose a definition of long-term therapy as one year or more in duration. Based upon this definition, data from Howard et al. (1989) and Pollak et al. (1992) suggest that between 16% and 28% of patients in treatment at clinics actually engage in long-term psychotherapy.

Many therapists, particularly those of a psychoanalytic orientation, might disagree with a definition of long-term therapy as one year or more. These therapists might consider one year of therapy as a relatively common, somewhat brief treatment, and long term as a more appropriate label for those treatments that last several years. However, their view of this is likely to be influenced by what Cohen and Cohen (1984) refer to as the *clinicians' illusion*. The clinicians' illusion has its source in the fact that, while the majority of patients attend relatively few sessions, the majority of therapists' time is spent with longer-term patients. In the Howard et al. (1989) sample, although only 16.3% of patients were in treatment for more than 52 sessions, these patients accounted for 56.1% of the treatment sessions provided. Because therapists spend a disproportionate percentage of their time with long-term patients, they tend to believe that long-term therapy is more common than it actually is.

Although the clinicians' illusion may bias providers in the direction of believing that long-term therapy is more common than it is, the extent to which long-term treatment is actually indicated as a treatment is a more complicated question. Many therapists, particularly psychodynamically oriented ones, generally prefer a long-term approach. In a survey of randomly selected clinical psychologists, Bolter, Levenson, and Alvarez (1990) found 65% of respondents adhering generally to a long-term model. Is attachment to a long-term model a self-serving belief, aimed at keeping practices full, or have managed care companies and HMOs ignored the need for long-term therapy and approved inadequate amounts of treatment for many patients? Within the limitations of the current scientific knowledge base, answers to these questions can be offered by examining the empirical literature on the efficacy of both short- and long-term psychotherapies, as well as examining investigations of the types of patients who benefit from short- versus long-term treatment. Before examining this literature, we turn first to a presentation of some of the major clinical approaches to long-term psychotherapy.

CLINICAL APPROACHES TO LONG-TERM PSYCHOTHERAPY

Psychoanalytic Approaches

There are actually many different models of the human mind and psychotherapy that are associated with the psychoanalytic tradition. Although psychoanalysis has its roots in Freud's work at the end of the 19th century, it has undergone many changes and split into different schools that have emphasized different aspects of psychological life (drive, ego, self or object relationships). Traditionally, the goal of psychoanalysis is to integrate into the present personality material that has not been previously integrated because it was repressed (forgotten). The origins of the repression are considered to be connected to the childhood neurosis that manifests itself in the transference neurosis during treatment. The analyst role is to provide a safe and neutral as possible environment where the core pathology of the patient can burgeon into a transference neurosis and be analyzed. This attempt to induce comprehensive change in the patient's personality by helping resolve the childhood neurosis as it is manifested in the transference neurosis is part of what, theoretically, sets apart traditional psychoanalysis from long-term dynamic therapy, which focuses on current conflicts and dynamic patterns.

Patients in psychoanalysis are instructed to say whatever is on their mind, even if the thoughts are unacceptable and unimportant. Following this rule creates all kinds of resistance that are interpreted in the analysis. Analysts who listen closely to the patients' associations learn about the associative network of their patients and more

generally about the organization of their thinking in terms of both process and content. Analysts look for disruptions and holes in the associative network to learn more about the use of defensive processes in the patients' psyches. Thus, analysts provide their patients with much teaching about their psychological functioning, what causes resistance, and which defenses are involved.

In long-term dynamic therapy, however, patients are not expected to say whatever is on their mind. Rather than uncovering the infantile neurosis as it manifests itself in the transference neurosis, dynamic therapists focus more on their patients' current conflicts as they manifest themselves in patients' relationships with themselves and others. In addition, therapists rarely use free association and therapy is more of a discussion between patients and therapists. The transference is addressed but not as much as in analysis. In contrast to psychoanalysis, where there is often an extensive reconstruction of the past, in long-term dynamically oriented therapy this reconstruction is very limited.

Another way in which long-term dynamic therapy can be distinguished from psychoanalysis is that long-term dynamic therapy is actually a family of therapies that can be described on a continuum ranging from expressive to supportive. In the more expressive or insight-oriented therapies, therapists use mostly interpretations, confrontations, and clarifications to increase patients' understanding of their feelings, behaviors, thoughts, and interpersonal relationships. In the relatively more supportive treatments, therapists attempt to support defenses and self-esteem and otherwise provide a supportive environment. The clinical lore is that patients with weaker egos and fewer resources such as poor frustration tolerance, impulse control, self-observation capacity, and psychological mindedness will benefit more from a supportive treatment than from an expressive therapy that requires both emotional and cognitive strengths.

Another model of long-term psychoanalytic therapy flows from the writings of Winnicott (1965), who was an English psychoanalyst and pediatrician. Winnicott saw the patient–therapist relationship as like the infant–mother relationship. He described the infant–mother relationship as a *holding environment*, meaning a state of dependence in which the infant's basic physical and psychological needs are always met. The caretaker encourages developmental growth while also making sure that the infant does not relinquish its dependency too early. Similarly, the therapist provides a non-judgmental environment of empathy, support, and acceptance, and is primarily concerned with the patient's needs rather than his or her own needs. This holding environment allows for healing and maturation, but a substantial amount of time is necessary for such a holding environment to have an important impact on the patient.

Cognitive-Behavioral Approaches

Although most behavioral and cognitive-behavioral treatment approaches are short-term, there are several examples of the development of longer-term cognitive-behavioral treatments. One of these is dialectical behavior therapy, or DBT (Linehan, 1993). Dialectical behavior therapy, although labeled by Linehan as a cognitive-behavioral treatment, is actually a complex treatment modality that is perhaps more accurately described as an eclectic rather than a traditional cognitive-behavior therapy per se. The treatment has two components: weekly group therapy and weekly individual sessions. Treatment duration is one year. The group therapy is psychoeducational and includes teaching interpersonal skills, distress tolerance/reality acceptance, and emotion regulation skills. Individual therapy sessions primarily involve directive, problem solving techniques, but also include supportive techniques such as empathy and acceptance. Behavioral goals are used to focus individual sessions. These goals are addressed in a sequential order, but goals previously addressed are readdressed if the problem returns. Examples of such goals include decreasing suicidal behaviors, decreasing therapy-interfering behaviors, decreasing behaviors that interfere with quality of life, increasing behavioral skills, and decreasing behaviors related to posttraumatic stress.

Linehan (1993) organizes the basic treatment strategies of dialectical behavior therapy into four categories: (1) dialectical strategies, (2) core strategies, (3) stylistic strategies, and (4) case management strategies. Dialectical strategies include techniques that allow the therapist to hold both sides of important polarities, with the hope that the patient will come to a new synthesis and increased flexibility arising out of the opposing positions. There are two major core strategies: acceptance (validation) and problem solving. Stylistic strategies refer to the form and style of therapeutic communications. Reciprocal communication strategies (responsiveness, self-disclo-

sure, warm engagement, and genuineness) are balanced with irreverent communication strategies that are intended to keep the patient off-balance. Case management strategies include interactions between the therapist and the community (e.g., consultants, family members, significant others).

Another example of longer-term cognitive-behavioral therapy is Beck and colleagues' cognitive therapy for personality disorders (Beck, Freeman, & Associates, 1990). Cognitive therapy for personality disorders rests on a concept that has some overlap with psychoanalytic theory, which is that *core* mental structures need to be identified and modified. While psychoanalytic theorists postulate that such core structures are unconscious and not easily available to the patient, cognitive theory holds that the products of such core cognitive structures are mostly within the realm of consciousness or can be brought into consciousness relatively easily. The core structures (schemas) produce biased judgments and cognitive errors that result in dysfunctional feelings and behavior. Patients with personality disorders have had such dysfunctional core schemas for much of their lives and therefore these schemas have become part of their "normal" cognitive organization. In addition, these patients generally avoid psychotherapy and are seemingly reluctant to change their patterns, seeing most problems they encounter in life as being external to them. These factors for such patients necessitate that cognitive therapy be long-term (Beck et al., 1990).

Group Therapy

Long-term group therapy has been proposed for a number of clinical problems and disorders, including sexual abuse survivors (Mennen & Meadow, 1992), eating disorders (Roth & Ross, 1988), and institutionalized patients with schizophrenia (Revere, Rodeffer, & Dawson, 1989). Although there are different theoretical models for long-term group therapy, the long-term format of these treatments leads to a number of advantages that these diverse treatments have in common compared to short-term group work. These advantages are reviewed by Mennen and Meadow and include increased group cohesiveness, increased personal and group-related discussion, and the greater likelihood of creating a social microcosm where maladaptive behavior patterns are re-created and therefore open to examination and change.

Informed Consent for Long-Term Therapy

Regardless of the specific treatment approach employed in a long-term format, one of the important clinical issues that needs to be addressed before long-term therapy begins is the issue of informed consent. Increasingly there are recommendations (e.g., Klerman, 1990) for implementation of informed consent procedures in mental health care in general. Wenning (1993) suggests that there are a variety of reasons why obtaining informed consent may be particularly important for long-term psychotherapy. One is that there is little empirical evidence justifying the use of long-term therapy, particularly in comparison to short-term therapy (see review in the next section). Long-term therapy is also generally more costly and certainly more time-consuming than brief therapy approaches. Therapists, because of their bias toward long-term therapy, and patients, because of lack of knowledge, may be vulnerable to engaging in long-term therapy without ever reviewing the issue of whether it is the most appropriate form of treatment, and whether, given a choice, the patient would elect to engage in long-term therapy.

A model for informed consent for long-term therapy is presented by Wenning (1993). Six issues are recommended for therapists to discuss with patients. The first is the diagnostic model used. Patients should know whether the therapist is applying a DSM diagnostic model, or some other model such as a psychoanalytic developmental model, in order to come to a recommendation for long-term therapy. Second, the risks and benefits of long-term therapy should be reviewed. The potential benefits for long-term therapy go beyond the symptomatic relief, which is typically the focus of short-term approaches, and include potential changes in personality, interpersonal functioning, and self-esteem. However, the risks that need to be considered include the possibility that no improvements are made despite the large investment of time and money. Occasionally, patients may actually be harmed by long-term therapy, sometimes because of the excessive dependency that can develop toward the therapist, which can undermine a sense of autonomy.

The third important issue of long-term therapy informed consent, according to Wenning (1993), is discussion of alternative treatment options. These include short-term therapy approaches, medication, self-help groups, pastoral counseling, reliance on friends or relatives, or no treatment at all. The benefits and risks connected to each of these alternatives should be discussed with the patient as well. Connected to the issue of alternatives is a fourth matter, the question of whether psychotherapy is essential or non-essential. When the person presenting for therapy has no overt symptoms and is functioning well, long-term psychotherapy needs to be described as an elective procedure (perhaps for the pursuit of personal growth) that is not a necessary treatment. A fifth issue is that patients need to be informed that insurance coverage for long-term therapy may be limited or even in some cases denied. The patient is then prepared to be financially responsible for treatment when insurance benefits are no longer available. A final aspect of Wenning's informed consent model is a quality assurance plan that includes methods for evaluating the patient's response to treatment. If no progress is made at specified time intervals, the therapist should stop treatment and consider other treatment options. In a discussion of the Wenning (1993) model, Gutheil (1993) adds that informed consent should be viewed as an ongoing process since unexpected symptoms and new information tend to emerge over the course of long-term psychotherapy.

The Efficacy of Long-Term Psychotherapy

The practical difficulties in designing and conducting an adequate scientific evaluation of the efficacy of long-term psychotherapy are many. It is therefore not surprising that the vast bulk of studies of psychotherapy have focused on short-term approaches. Moreover, the existing studies on long-term psychotherapy are extremely diverse in their methods and methodologies, thus rendering any attempt at a quantitative summary of results across studies (meta-analysis) meaningless. Instead, we present a description of selected research in order to give an overview of the state of knowledge about long-term psychotherapy.

Psychoanalysis and Psychodynamic Psychotherapy

There have been two extensive reviews of the efficacy of psychoanalysis and long-term psychoanalytic psychotherapy. Bachrach, Galatzer-Levy, Skolnikoff, and Waldron (1991) found six quantitative studies, two provisional quantitative studies, and a series of retrospective case reports that included interviews with patients who had been in psychoanalysis. However, of all of these studies, only one (Kernberg, Burstein, Coyne, Appelbaum, Horwitz, & Voth, 1972) was a prospective study with a comparison group, although random assignment was not used. This study will be briefly reviewed here.

The Menninger Foundation Psychotherapy Research Project (Kernberg et al., 1972; Wallerstein, 1986) is often described as the most systematic and extensive study of psychoanalysis yet performed. Detailed assessments at intake, termination, and two-year follow-up were made for 21 patients treated with psychoanalysis and 21 patients treated with psychotherapy. Patients in both psychotherapy and psychoanalysis were in treatment for over four years on average. The major focus of the project was on characterizing change and predicting treatment outcome, rather than comparing the two treatment conditions on outcome.

Average change from intake to follow-up on the Health–Sickness Rating Scale (Luborsky, 1975) was approximately 14 points for both treatment conditions, and in general no outcome differences were apparent. However, interpretation of a direct comparison of the two treatment modalities was hindered not only by the lack of random assignment but also by the fact that most of the psychoanalyses were conducted by student analysts while most of the psychotherapies were conducted by experienced clinicians. Moreover, Wallerstein's (1986) clinical analysis of the cases selected for psychoanalysis indicated that only 45% of the sample was judged to be suitable for this form of treatment. One-third of the patients in analysis had to be hospitalized at some point during their treatment and most of these more severely disturbed patients who were not suitable for psychoanalysis did not have favorable outcomes. Consistent with this clinical observation, the quantitative predictive analysis (Kernberg et al., 1972) found that initial, relatively higher ego-strength was associated with better outcome across the two treatment conditions. Another conclusion from the project was that there were supportive elements to all treatments, and that important changes can occur through such supportive elements alone (Wallerstein, 1986).

Bachrach et al.'s (1991) review of the Menninger study and other outcome studies concludes that patients suitable for psychoanalysis derive substantial therapeutic benefit. However, at best the literature reviewed by Bachrach et al. can be considered as consisting of promising, uncontrolled preliminary studies that point to the need for more rigorous studies. As discussed by Marshall, Vaughan, MacKinnon, Mellman, and Roose (1996), these studies have serious methodological weaknesses, such as lack of control for spontaneous remission (passage of time), selection bias, investigator bias, placebo response, and memory and recall biases (in the retrospective studies).

A number of additional studies on long-term psychoanalytic psychotherapy and psychoanalysis have been conducted or are ongoing. These studies have been recently reviewed by Fonagy, Käechele, Krause, Jones, and Perron (1999). All of these studies use heterogeneous patient samples, rather than focusing on a particular disorder or patient problem. As with the Bachrach et al. (1991) review, many of the studies located were retrospective, follow-up studies on patients previously treated with psychoanalysis or psychoanalytic psychotherapy (e.g., Teufel & Volk, 1988; Keller, Westhoff, Dilg, & Rohner, 1997; Leuzinger-Bohleber & Stuhr, 1997). Whereas these retrospective studies have limited value, several prospective naturalistic effectiveness studies have been reported (Monsen, Oldland, Faugli, Daae, & Eilersten, 1995; von Rad, Senf, & Braeutigam, 1998; Rudolf, 1991; Sandell, Bloomberg, & Lazar, 1997). A number of other studies, both naturalistic and randomized controlled trials, are ongoing, but results will not be available for several years.

Monsen et al. (1995) describe the results of a prospective study of the psychodynamic treatment of 25 patients with personality disorders. Treatment lasted an average of 25 months, and patients were assessed at intake, termination, and five years after termination. Significant change was found on measures of affect consciousness, defenses, and symptoms. At termination, 75% of patients who had an Axis I diagnosis at intake no longer met criteria for the disorder, and 72% of patients no longer had a personality disorder. These data illustrate the potential for long-term therapy to impact on Axis II conditions. The lack of comparison or control groups, however, makes it difficult to attribute the changes to treatment per se.

The Heidelberg Long-Term Psychotherapy Follow-Up Project (Kordy, von Rad, & Senf, 1989; von Rad, Senf, & Braeutigam, 1998) assessed the outcome of all types of long-term treatment provided at the Psychosomatic Clinic of the University of Heidelberg (Germany) for patients attending the clinic during a specified time period. Treatments included inpatient group therapy ($n = 63$), inpatient combined group and individual therapy ($n = 60$), inpatient individual therapy ($n = 16$), outpatient psychoanalysis (3 times/week; $n = 36$), and outpatient dynamic psychotherapy (once/week; $n = 33$). Patients were assessed at the beginning of treatment, termination of therapy, and follow-up 3.5 years later. The average duration of treatment was 2.6 years (146 sessions). Kordy et al. (1989) present a dose-response analysis of these data and conclude that the most effective dose was 2.5 years with 160 sessions. Von Rad et al. (1998) describe change in regard to individual therapy goals for patients in psychoanalysis versus those in dynamic psychotherapy. From pretreatment to follow-up, 18.8% of psychoanalysis patients, compared to 27.8% of dynamic psychotherapy patients, attained "moderate success" at achieving therapy goals, and 71.9% of psychoanalysis patients, compared to 50.0% of dynamic psychotherapy patients, attained "good success" at achieving their goals. Thus, both the dose-effect analysis and examination of attainment of therapy goals indicated that longer-term intensive treatment achieved better results than once-a-week dynamic psychotherapy.

Rudolf (1991) and Rudolf, Manz, and Õri (1994) report on a similar study in Germany that compared psychoanalysis ($n = 44$; average number of session = 265), dynamic psychotherapy ($n = 56$; average number of sessions = 60), and inpatient psychotherapy ($n = 164$; average length of stay = 2.6 months). Summarizing the results of the study as a whole, Fonagy et al. (1999) states that the patients treated with psychoanalysis improved considerably and to a greater extent than patients treated with either dynamic psychotherapy or inpatient treatment. However, Rudolf et al. indicate that very different types of patients were seen in the three treatment settings. Thus, direct comparisons between the outcomes of the three treatment settings are difficult.

In Sweden, long-term therapy is generally the treatment most often recommended. Long-term psychotherapy (primarily psychodynamic) or psychoanalysis is covered under Swedish national health insurance provided the therapist is an M.D. A study was begun in 1989 to evaluate the outcomes of these treatments, and preliminary information is now available (Sandell, Bloomberg, & Lazar, 1997; additional data reported by Fonagy et al., 1999). The study com-

pared psychoanalysis (three to five times per week; averaging 54 months in duration), psychodynamic psychotherapy (one to two times per week; averaging 43 months in duration), low-dose psychotherapy (e.g., low-frequency supportive therapy, brief therapy, couples therapy; averaging 21 months in duration), and no treatment. Although the study began as a randomized experiment, because of complaints by patients it was changed to a quasi-experimental design without random assignment. Fonagy et al. (1999) present effect size comparisons of the four groups at one- and two-year follow up assessments. The data indicated that although psychoanalysis and long-term psychotherapy were generally equivalent, both were superior to low-dose therapy (Cohen's d effect sizes ranging from .46 to .67) and to no treatment (effect sizes ranging from .18 to .46). A slight advantage of psychoanalysis over long-term psychotherapy was apparent at the second year follow-up (effect size = .23).

Two other outcome studies on long-term psychodynamic psychotherapy, not included in the reviews by Bachrach et al. (1991) or Fonagy et al. (1999), are worth mentioning. Stevenson and Meares (1992) evaluated psychodynamic therapy as a treatment of borderline personality disorder. The treatment was based upon the principles of self-psychology. In particular, therapy had a maturational goal that was accomplished through helping patients discover and elaborate their inner life. Empathy and attention to disruptions in empathy are central therapeutic techniques (Meares, 1987). The sample consisted of thirty patients with DSM-III borderline personality disorder treated with twice-per-week therapy for one year. Outcome was measured one year after termination of treatment. The results suggested that substantial and statistically significant ($p < .001$) reductions in violent behavior, drug use, medical visits, episodes of self-harm, time away from work, and symptoms were evident. Within-group effect sizes, calculated as the one-year post-therapy mean minus pre-therapy mean, divided by pre-therapy standard deviation, for these outcome measures were .47, .93, 1.10, .63, .76, and .94, respectively. Moreover, 30% of patients no longer met criteria for borderline personality disorder at the outcome assessment. However, no comparison or control group was used in this study. Nevertheless, the study does provide some preliminary, promising data on a self-psychological approach with difficult patients.

In another study involving patients with borderline personality disorder, Munroe-Blum and Marziali (1995) compared open-ended individual psychodynamic therapy with a manualized interpersonal group therapy for 110 patients. The group treatment lasted 30 sessions. No differences at one year (termination) or two years were found, although patients in general benefited from both treatments (pre–post effect size = .74 on a symptom checklist).

In evaluating the efficacy of long-term psychodynamic psychotherapy, an important question to ask is whether the treatment impacts upon nonsymptom-based outcomes, because the importance of such broader outcomes is one of the justifications for long-term treatment. Weiner and Exner (1991) report on such changes in long-term dynamic therapy compared to short-term therapy. In a naturalistic design, 88 patients engaged in long-term dynamic therapy were evaluated with the Rorschach test at the beginning of therapy and approximately one, two, and four years later, and compared to 88 short-term therapies evaluated at the same points in time. The average length of the short-term therapies was actually quite long by our standards, averaging 62.1 sessions. The long-term therapies, however, were significantly longer, with an average number of sessions of 452 at the four-year assessment (some patients were still in treatment at this assessment). Long-term therapy was usually twice or three time per week, while short-term therapy was once per week. Short-term therapy consisted of rational-emotive, gestalt, modeling, or assertiveness therapy. The Rorschach testing was performed by trained examiners who were not the treating therapist; these examiners had no information about the nature of the research study, the kind of therapy patients were receiving, or the stage of treatment (no examiner tested the same patient more than once).

The results indicated that although short- and long-term therapy patients looked similar by the one-year assessment, by the four-year outcome assessment the long-term therapy patients were significantly (p <.01) better than the short-term patients on 10 out of 27 measures scored from the Rorschach. These included Rorschach indices thought to measure (1) increasing ability to manage stress, (2) greater likelihood of dealing with experience attentively, openly, and consistently, (3) greater capability of modulating and enjoying emotional experience, (4) greater effectiveness of ideation, (5) less preoccupation and greater satisfaction with self, and (6) greater interest and comfort in interpersonal relationships.

Although this study has some notable strengths, including high external validity through the examination of therapies as practiced in the community, multiple assessment over an extended period of time (four years), and a relatively large sample size, the lack of random assignment and lack of control of the treatment variable render the study as preliminary, and the authors appropriately describe it as such. It may have been that the more difficult-to-treat patients ended up in short-term therapy and short-term therapists may have been less clinically competent than the long-term therapists. Moreover, intensity of treatment (once a week versus more than once a week) was confounded with duration of treatment. Finally, the validity of the indices derived from the Rorschach test has not been adequately demonstrated. Nevertheless, this study provides suggestive evidence indicating that long-term therapy may produce important benefits not attainable with short-term methods.

Long-Term Interpersonal Psychotherapy

Frank et al. (1990) describe one of the most rigorous scientific evaluations of a long-term psychotherapy. Interpersonal psychotherapy (Klerman, Weissman, Rounsaville, & Chevron, 1984) was examined as a maintenance treatment for recurrent depression. Interpersonal psychotherapy, while historically tied to psychodynamic therapy, has an emphasis on current life and interpersonal relationships. The treatment helps the patient develop more effective strategies of dealing with the interpersonal factors that are hypothesized to be involved in depression, including problems with grieving, role transitions, interpersonal role disputes, and interpersonal deficits. The design of the study was as follows: First, patients (n = 230) with recurrent major depression (three or more episodes) were treated to sustained remission (20 weeks of depressive symptoms in remission) of the current episode with a combination of antidepressant medication (imipramine) and interpersonal psychotherapy. At the end of this period, patients in remission were randomly assigned to one of five maintenance treatment conditions: (1) once-a-month sessions of interpersonal therapy, (2) monthly interpersonal therapy plus imipramine, (3) monthly interpersonal therapy plus placebo, (4) medication alone, or (5) pill placebo. Maintenance treatment lasted up to three years or until a recurrence of symptoms occurred. The results indicated that imipramine was highly successful and interpersonal therapy was modestly successful at preventing recurrences of depression. The average number of weeks until a recurrence of depression were 124 for imipramine, 131 for interpersonal therapy plus imipramine, 82 for interpersonal therapy, and 74 for interpersonal therapy plus placebo, and 45 for placebo. Although interpersonal therapy alone was not as successful as imipramine in preventing recurrences, it may have been that monthly sessions were not frequent enough. An ongoing study by the same group is comparing different frequencies of maintenance interpersonal therapy to directly examine this question.

Long-Term Cognitive-Behavioral Therapy

One randomized, controlled outcome study has been reported on dialectical behavior therapy lasting one year in duration. Linehan, Hubert, Suarez, Douglas, and Heard (1991) evaluated 44 women who evidenced para-suicidal behavior and were diagnosed as borderline personality disorder. Patients were randomized to either dialectical behavior therapy or treatment-as-usual in the community. The main results were that dialectical behavior therapy resulted in relatively fewer and less severe episodes of parasuicidal behavior and fewer days of hospitalization compared to treatment as usual. However, no differences between the two groups in depression, hopelessness, or suicidal ideation were found. The attrition rate for DBT (16.7%) was considerably lower than the attrition rate for treatment-as-usual (58.3%). Limitations of this study include the fact that the therapists in the treatment-as-usual condition did not have the same level of experience in treating patients with borderline personality disorder as the dialectical behavior therapists, and the fact that 27% of the control patients did not begin therapy although they were referred to a therapist. Thus, this study provides initial, promising data on the efficacy of dialectical behavior. However, the nature of the control condition prevents attribution of the relative differences between the conditions to the unique elements of dialectical behavior therapy versus alternative explanations.

Naturalistic Dose-Response Studies

Studies examining the relationship between length of psychotherapy and outcome have consistently found that more sessions lead to better outcome. Orlinsky and Howard's (1986) review indicated that 110 out of 114 studies reported just such a positive association between length of therapy and outcome. The large-scale *Consumer Reports* effectiveness study of psychotherapy (Seligman, 1995) also reported that longer-term treatment produced more benefits than shorter-term treatment, with more than two years of treatment showing the largest benefits. These studies, however, did not specify how much psychotherapy was sufficient to produce a certain rate of patient improvement.

An attempt to model a specific dose (number of sessions)-effect relationship for psychotherapy was made in the oft-cited study by Howard, Kopta, Krause, and Orlinsky (1986), who assembled data from 15 samples involving 2431 patients. Although Howard et al. found a positive relationship between dose and outcome (i.e., more sessions are better than fewer sessions), there was a negatively accelerating curve with diminishing returns at higher doses. Specifically, their data indicated that 30% of patients were improved by 2 sessions, 53% by 8 sessions, 74% by 26 sessions, 83% by 52 sessions, and 90% by 102 sessions. Certainly a managed care company is unlikely to invest in the difference in cost between 26 sessions and 52 sessions in order to gain an extra 9% of patients improved. Thus, the Howard et al. data appear to raise questions about the extent to which long-term therapy should typically be covered by health insurance.

Although the Howard et al. (1986) study was a valuable contribution to understanding the likely shape of the dose-effect relationship in psychotherapy, limitations render the data less useful as a guide to understanding the effect of specific doses of treatment. The major problem was with the definition of outcome: various global outcome ratings across the different samples were each dichotomized into a *improved* versus *not improved* scale. It is likely that included within the improved category were examples of relatively slight patient improvement, thereby biasing the results to indicate that relatively little psychotherapy is sufficient.

A later study (Kopta, Howard, Lowry, & Beutler, 1994) overcomes the limitations of the earlier Howard et al. (1986) report and arrives at completely different conclusions about the dose-effect relationship in psychotherapy. Kopta et al. examined the patterns of symptomatic recovery for 854 patients in psychotherapy. Items from a symptom checklist were separately analyzed for a dose-response relationship. Symptoms were found to fall into three clusters: acute distress symptoms that responded relatively quickly to therapy, chronic distress symptoms that responded more slowly, and characterological symptoms that responded even more slowly. Using established methodologies for calculating clinically significant change, Kopta et al. report that for chronic distress symptoms, it took up to 52 sessions until 60–86% (depending upon the specific symptom) of patients had clinically significant change. Selecting the acute distress and chronic distress symptoms that were most frequently present in the sample (i.e., at least 50% of the sample reported the symptom at intake), Kopta et al. estimate that it takes 58 sessions until 75% of patients achieve clinically significant change. The authors also note that these estimates apply to symptomatic recovery and that, based upon data reported by Howard, Lueger, Maling, and Martinovich (1993), we can expect that improvement in functioning will lag behind symptomatic recovery, thereby requiring even more sessions.

There are several strengths of the Kopta et al. (1994) study, including the large sample size and the fact that the data are naturalistic, drawn from actual clinical services in the real world. However, one limitation is that the treatments were primarily psychodynamic. It is possible that other forms of treatment less practiced in some settings, such as cognitive-behavioral therapy, would require fewer sessions to achieve clinically significant effects. Until such effectiveness studies are done that include large samples of patients treated with cognitive-behavioral therapy as delivered in the community, it is fair to conclude from the Kopta et al. study that long-term (i.e., one year or more) therapy should be considered a treatment option for many patients presenting with chronic distress and characterological symptoms.

Short- Versus Long-Term Therapy

Several authors have specifically reviewed the literature to evaluate the results of studies that directly compare short-term with long-term therapy. Luborsky, Singer, and Luborsky (1975) and Johnson and Gelso (1980) are perhaps the most comprehensive such reviews. These reviews, along with others, have uniformly concluded that there is no evidence that long-term therapy is superior to short-term therapy. Miller (1996), however, has recently re-evaluated these previous reviews. Of the 16 studies included in previous

reviews of short- versus long-term therapy, only one study compared brief therapy to long-term (one year or greater) in a prospective, randomized trial. Other studies actually compared two brief treatments (e.g, 4 versus 16 sessions), were retrospective, were duplicate reports of the same study, or did not contain a true time-limited treatment group. Thus, there is little basis for deciding whether short- or long-term treatment is better from controlled studies. However, Miller used relevant studies from the set of 16 to ask a related question: is there evidence that clinically determined treatment (patient and therapist decide how much treatment is appropriate) is better than time-limited therapy? Four comparative studies of individual therapy showed a superiority of clinically determined treatment over time-limited treatment, one showed no difference, and two studies of family therapy showed time-limited therapy to be superior to clinically determined treatment. Thus, at least for individual therapy, one common feature of long-term therapy as it is practiced (patient and therapist decide upon length as clinically appropriate) appears to be associated with greater benefits.

In regard to the treatment of children, one study has compared time-limited brief therapy to time-unlimited long-term therapy. Smyrnios and Kirkby (1993) compared time-limited (12 sessions) psychodynamic therapy to time-unlimited psychodynamic therapy (averaging 57 weeks) and also to a minimal contact control group for children and their parents seeking treatment at a child and family treatment program in Australia. Most of the children were diagnosed with anxiety or affective disorders, or conduct problems. At post-test, subjects in the minimal treatment group were significantly more improved than subjects in the time-unlimited condition, and at four-year follow-up, only the minimal treatment group reported significant changes (from pretreatment) in severity of target problems and measures of family functioning. This study, however, was small (10 children per treatment condition) and produced evidence against both time-limited and long-term therapy.

Efficacy of Short-Term Therapy

Studies on the efficacy of short-term psychotherapy are also relevant to understanding the potential clinical role of long-term therapy. In regard to the treatment of depression, the largest and most influential study has been the National Institute of Mental Health Collaborative Research Program (Elkin et al., 1989), which examined the efficacy of short-term manualized cognitive and interpersonal psychotherapies in comparison to medication and pill-placebo (plus clinical management) therapies. In describing the long-term effects of the treatments, Shea et al. (1992) conclude: "What is clear from our findings is that 16 weeks of these particular treatments is insufficient treatment to achieve full recovery and lasting remission" (p. 786). Only 24% of those patients that entered treatment and had complete follow-up data recovered from their depressive episode and continued to remain well (18 months after treatment). Such data strongly imply that long-term treatment, whether pharmacological or psychosocial, is likely to be indicated for many patients with major depressive disorder. In part, this may be because of the relatively high rate of recurrent or chronic major depression. In addition, relatively high numbers of patients with major depression have co-occurring Axis II diagnoses, which typically lead to failure of short-term treatment (see discussion of this issue later in this chapter).

For other Axis I disorders, brief treatment may be sufficient. Cognitive-behavioral treatments of panic disorders have demonstrated low relapse rates at follow-up assessments. For example, Beck, Sokol, Clark, Berchick, and Wright (1992) report that 83% of patients treated with 12 sessions of cognitive therapy were panic free at a one-year follow-up. In the treatment of generalized anxiety disorder, the picture is more mixed: Borkovec and Costello (1993) found that 59% of patients treated with 12 sessions of cognitive-behavior therapy had high end-state functioning at a one-year follow-up. This indicates fairly good success with brief treatment, but also some room for improvement.

Selection of Patients for Long-Term Psychotherapy
Clinical Lore

The overwhelming majority of the literature on who is a good candidate for long-term therapy is based on clinical experience and practice. However, if the question of who is to be recommended for long-term therapies would be asked to different clinicians, a wide range of answers would be given. One of the possible answers is that if the patient is interested in resolving his or her problems by increasing his or her self-understanding in long-term therapy, there are very few contraindications, if any, for long-term therapy. Most

likely, some clinicians will consider that regressed patients should not be seen in very intensive, exploratory, and reconstructive therapies such as psychoanalysis; although the same clinicians will not object to having these patients in more supportive long-term therapy. In other words, many clinicians would consider seeing patients with a wide range of psychological problems in long-term therapy. We do not believe that therapists would recommend long-term therapy only or mostly for pecuniary reasons, but rather they make this recommendation because the therapists believe that, everything else being equal, long-term therapy will be the treatment of choice for a variety of problems.

The literature on who is the best candidate for classical psychoanalysis (i.e., patient is lying on the couch three to five times a week for four to seven years using free associations) is voluminous. Fenichel (1945) refers to people who are not too old, intelligent, who suffer from severe neurosis, but without dangerous symptoms. In reviews of the concept of "analyzability," Bachrach (1980) and Bachrach and Reaf (1978) found that analysts considered high ego strength and good early relationships as good prognostic signs. In the early years of psychoanalysis in the United States, analysts tended to be selective and to take into analysis only those patients who fitted an almost ideal description. Thus, they tried to take into analysis only those kinds of patients who were sufficiently well put together that they could handle the frustration of the analytic situation. Over the years, psychoanalysts began seeing a wider range of patients, including schizophrenics and other psychotic patients, at a time when no other treatment was available for these patients. Thomä and Kächele (1987) term a suitable patient for psychoanalysis as "sick enough to need it and healthy enough to stand it" (p. 185). In the last 20 to 30 years, there has been clinical attention focused on two groups of difficult patients who might not have been treated previously with intensive analytic treatment: narcissistic and borderline personality disorders (Kohut, 1971; Kernberg, 1984). These are long-lasting and pervasive disorders.

Using more general terms, longer-term therapies are recommended for patients presenting with problems derived from a combination of environmental and constitutional factors. Among the environmental issues, we find an implicit assumption that the more severe, the earlier the onset of the disorder, and the earlier and longer the duration of trauma, the more likely a longer form of therapy is needed. Among the constitutional factors that will impact how the environment will be experienced, Beatson (1995) mentioned the degree of the childhood emotional resilience, the capacity to use whatever good experience is available, proneness to anxiety, and level of frustration tolerance. Thus, it is not surprising that long-term therapy is recommended for patients who suffer from some of the more severe personality disorders. A large part of the clinical literature on long-term therapy has focused specifically on individuals with narcissistic and borderline personality disorders (Gunderson, 1984; Kohut, 1971; Kernberg, 1984).

Research Evidence

Although there is extensive literature on factors predicting the outcome of psychotherapy (for reviews of this literature, see Garfield, 1994; Luborsky, Chandler, Auerbach, Cohen, & Bachrach, 1971; Luborsky, Crits-Christoph, Mintz, & Auerbach, 1988), few studies have directly addressed the question of what type of patients specifically benefit from long-term therapy. To answer this question fully, a study needs to examine predictors of both long- and short-term therapy. If only long-term therapy is examined, findings could not be used to suggest a basis for recommending long-term over short-term therapy, or vice versa. For example, if high ego-strength is associated with a relatively favorable outcome of long-term therapies (Kernberg et al. 1972), but is also associated with better outcome in short-term treatments, it would be a marker for treatment responsiveness in general, and not a basis for deciding which patients are appropriate for long-term therapy.

We are not aware of any studies that specifically compared predictors in long- versus short-term therapy. One of the intents of the large-scale Northwestern/Chicago research project (Howard, Orlinsky, & Lueger, 1995) is to characterize those patients who respond to long-term versus briefer therapy. No results on this topic have yet been published from the project. However, other data from the project on the rate of change over time of different types of outcome measures are relevant to the issue of understanding the possible role of long-term therapy. For example, Howard, Orlinsky, and Lueger (1995) present data demonstrating that self-esteem changes slowly over the course of psychotherapy. By session 16, less than 30% of patients showed reliable improvement in self-esteem, and only about 50% showed reliable improvement by session 48. More treatment, however, was consistently related to more patients benefiting in terms of self-esteem (particularly as the number of sessions increased between 28 and 48). Although it is an inference from these data, it is possible that increasing treatment to beyond one year would lead to more patients evidencing changes in self-esteem.

Another way to potentially shed light on the issue of who is appropriate for long-term therapy is through examination of studies that document who fails in short-term therapy. If a certain type of patient does poorly in a particular short-term therapy, an obvious recommendation is to try another form of short-term therapy. However, if there is evidence that certain patients consistently do poorly in a variety of short-term treatments, long-term therapy might be the only alternative to consider.

Consistent evidence does exist for the failure of short-term approaches to successfully treat patients with Axis II disorders. Studies of the impact of Axis II diagnoses on the outcomes of both psychosocial and psychopharmacological treatment for Axis I disorders have been reviewed by Reich and Vasile (1993) and earlier by Reich and Green (1991). The first review covered 21 studies and the second an additional 17. The major findings from these reviews are that patients with Axis I diagnoses and Axis II diagnoses have relatively worse outcomes with a wide range of both psychotherapy and medication treatments. In regard to findings relevant to specific treatment modalities, the following has been reported: (1) antisocial personality disorder (without a co-occurring diagnosis of depression) is associated with poor outcome in both cognitive and psychodynamic therapies for opiate addiction (Woody, McLellan, Luborsky, & O'Brien, 1985); (2) avoidant personality disorder predicts a relatively poorer outcome from exposure therapy for agoraphobia (Chambless, Renneberg, Goldstein, & Gracely, 1992); (3) presence of schizotypal personality disorder predicts a less favorable outcome of behavior therapy for obsessive-compulsive disorder (Minichiello, Baer, & Jenike, 1987); (4) presence of any personality disorder is associated with relatively poorer outcome of cognitive-behavioral group therapy for social anxiety (Turner, 1987); (5) patients with a personality disorder diagnosis demonstrate a slower response to imipramine plus interpersonal psychotherapy for recurrent unipolar depression (Frank, Kupfer, Jacob, & Jarrett, 1987); and (6) patients with a diagnosis in the anxious cluster of personality disorders display much poorer outcome with imipramine plus interpersonal therapy for recurrent unipolar depression (Pilkonis & Frank, 1988).

It is fair to conclude that the existing research evidence is consistent with the clinical lore regarding the treatment of personality disorders: that short-term treatment is insufficient. This conclusion takes on importance in the context of the prevalence of personality disorders. In community samples, about 10% of people have at least one personality disorder (Maier, Lichtermann, Klingler, Heun, & Hallmayer, 1992). Among individuals with an Axis I disorder, rates of Axis II disorders range from 48% of cocaine-dependent patients (Barber et al., 1996), to 36–75% (across studies) of those with anxiety disorders, and 36–65% of those with mood disorders (Ruegg & Frances, 1995).

Whether long-term therapy will successfully induce lasting change in patients with personality disorders is a question that has not been answered to date and is an important agenda for future research. However, there are some preliminary studies that are encouraging. In particular, Barber and Muenz (1996) have proposed a *theory of opposites* that hypothesizes that effective therapy for Axis II disorders requires the therapist to behave in a way that is antithetical to the interpersonal behavior, personality, and cognitive style of the patient. For example, effective interventions for the emotionally cold obsessive-compulsive personality disorder (OCPD) patient include responding in a warm and trusting manner, which in turn will assist moving the patient into the complementary realm of *histrionic*, where the patient becomes more emotional (Kiesler, 1986). According to the theory of opposites, OCPD patients who generally intellectualize and rationalize will be helped by psychodynamic/interpersonal interventions that neither rely on nor reinforce these defensive characterological patterns but rather introduce the discussion and expression of non-restricted affect. That is, the therapist attempts to work against the defenses instead of colluding with the OCPD's resistance and defenses. For avoidant personality disorder (AVPD) patients who tend to avoid feared social situations, the theory of opposites proposes that treatment that forces patients to confront anxiety-provoking social situations (e.g., by using homework or specific concrete instructions) is

more productive than treatment that explores the reasons for their avoidance. Partial support for this matching hypothesis comes from a study where one year of supportive-expressive psychodynamic psychotherapy was found to be more effective for OCPD patients than for AVPD patients (Barber et al., 1997). In order to more completely test the matching hypothesis, Barber and Muenz (1996), using a dimensional measure of personality disorder traits, re-analyzed data from the Treatment of Depression Collaborative Research Program (Elkin et al., 1989), which had shown no overall difference between cognitive therapy and interpersonal therapy. As predicted, results showed that as obsessiveness increased and avoidance decreased, patients did better in interpersonal therapy and worse in cognitive therapy; when avoidance increased and obsessiveness decreased, patients did worse in interpersonal therapy and better in cognitive therapy.

Integration of Clinical and Research Literature

There is a clear contradiction running through the clinical and research literature on the selection of patients for long-term therapy. On the one hand, patients with relatively high ego-strength and higher levels of functioning are considered candidates for long-term therapy, particularly psychoanalysis. On the other hand, patients with severe personality disorders, recurrent disorders, and failures from short-term therapy are also considered candidates for long-term therapy. Thus, it appears that both more severely disturbed and less severely disturbed patients are recommended for this kind of treatment. In part this confusion stems from the historical evolution of psychoanalysis mentioned earlier: psychoanalysis was originally conceived as a treatment for neuroses but then expanded into a treatment for personality disorders and other severe problems.

The resolution of this contradiction, however, resides in the recognition that long-term therapy can have at least two distinct functions. In regard to long-term formal psychoanalysis, treatment is best conceived of as an opportunity for relatively intact individuals to engage in a process of self-examination that may lead to greater enjoyment and satisfaction in life. Patients with high ego-strength can tolerate the slow pace of this treatment, the relative low frequency of therapist intervention, and the lack of explicit support by the therapist. This use of long-term treatment is less tied to a public health mission and more oriented toward personal self-actualization. With more severely disturbed patients, a public health justification of the use of long-term treatment is apparent. Such chronically lower functioning, highly symptomatic patients do not fare well in brief treatment, and therefore longer-term treatment appears to be the best recommendation. However, such patients are likely not to be appropriate for the intensive, exploratory climate of formal psychoanalysis.

In summary, we propose that, within the context of a public health service delivery system, long-term psychotherapy should be proposed for patients with recurrent and/or treatment-resistant Axis I disorders, such as recurrent major depression, as well as severe personality disorders. Long-term therapy could also be helpful to a large group of patients with dysfunctional, interpersonal self-defeating patterns that are recurrent and are not included or not often easy to diagnose based on the current DSM. For example, one of us has been treating patients who have difficulties developing and maintaining intimate and committed relationships (*commitophobia*). This issue is illustrated in the case example of a patient in long-term therapy presented in the next section. These patients tend to be in their late 30s when they come to treatment after having failed repeatedly to develop a satisfying relationship and have began to realize that something might be wrong with them rather than with their occasional partners. Many patients with problems associated with persistent low self-esteem may also benefit from long-term therapy. In the case of relationship problems and low self-esteem, however, it is likely that treatment of such problems will occur outside of the health care system (i.e., not covered by health insurance) unless a DSM-based diagnosis or other major symptom or problem (e.g., suicide risk) is apparent. Similarly, the use of long-term therapy for self-actualization and self-knowledge, while potentially having benefits to society through increased work productivity, will continue to be a use of long-term therapy that is not generally covered by health insurance.

Case Example

We present a case example of a patient in long-term therapy to illustrate some of the types of changes that are more likely to occur in longer-term treatment compared to brief therapy. Details of the case have been changed to protect confidentiality. Only a few aspects of the issues and changes observed in the treatment of the case are presented to keep this summary brief.

In his late thirties, Johnny began once a week therapy that eventually lasted more than two years. His initial complaint was that as soon as a woman fell in love with him, he would begin to lose interest in her. While remaining in the relationship, he would ruminate that he was going to hurt the woman when he was going to end the relationship. An associated fantasy was that any long-standing relationship he would have with a woman would end in a tragic manner. These thoughts were accompanied by very high levels of anxiety and depression. The bouts of anxiety and the obsessive-like thoughts recurred throughout the treatment. He had had five relationships of at least a two-year duration that had evolved in a similar manner. He had participated in different forms of psychotherapy and counseling, read many self-help books, and consulted several experts before this current treatment. It became clear that he had approached a therapist every time he reached a point where he could not bear remaining in a relationship with a woman and he had hoped that therapy would solve the problem for him.

Although he began to recognize that he had a problem, Johnny would vacillate between that recognition and the belief that if the women he was dating would be more beautiful, intelligent, exciting, and so on, he would have remained attracted to them. Outside of these intimate relationships, Johnny had few friends and few connections. He was successful in his career although he felt he should have been further along than he was.

To describe the intensity of his anxiety and depression related to his wishes to end a relationship, the following vignette is provided. During the therapist's summer vacation, Johnny had set a wedding date. After an initial period when he felt good about having finally taken the steps to commitment, he became increasingly distressed, anxious, and suicidal. He did not share any of his agony with his fiancée. At some point, the fiancée began to realize his distress and suggested that maybe he was not interested or ready for the commitment. This ended the relationship with this woman.

During the therapy, many topics were discussed including his getting anxious when an intimate relationship evolved. After months of therapy, his feelings that women would take power away from him were repeatedly addressed together with his tendency to be passive in the relationships. He learned that by passively consenting to do something he did not want to do, he developed resentment and angry feelings.

This issue played out in the relationship with the therapist as well. After a year of therapy, a number of incidents had been reviewed where the therapist had done something that had angered Johnny, but Johnny had responded passively and had not mentioned the incidents. These angry feelings were repeatedly explored in the transference relationship and increased his awareness of his negative feelings as well as some of his aggressive fantasies. Becoming aware of these feelings helped make them more acceptable and easier for him to handle. It is likely that his ability to experience increased levels of negative emotions also helped him increase his tolerance for positive feelings. While at the beginning of treatment he would say that his only emotional experience was anxiety, later on he slowly began to develop a range of feelings including some relatively warm, friendly feelings toward the therapist.

Concomitant to his increased awareness of multifaceted feelings, Johnny became more assertive. Initially his increased assertiveness was most apparent in the patient relationship with the therapist; then he became more assertive with his boss, which resulted in a very significant increase in his salary. Finally, he became assertive with the woman with whom he was currently living. By becoming more assertive with her, the relationship with her became tolerable and he could begin enjoying having a companion.

This case illustrates a number of aspects of long-term therapy. To the extent that a psychotherapy is focusing on problematic relationships, long-term therapy provides a forum in which a patient can examine multiple, current relationships occurring sequentially over a period of time, rather than relying upon retrospective analysis of past relationships or examination of one current relationship, as would necessarily be the case in a brief therapy. It is also likely that brief therapy is of too short a duration to actually document significant changes in being able to commit to a relationship. Moreover, the development of a wider range of emotional reactions, including greater comfort with positive emotions in the relationship with the therapist and outside relationships, is unlikely to be as evident within the context of brief therapy.

Methodological Issues in Conducting Outcome Research on Long-Term Therapy

There are a number of methodological issues that make accomplishing meaningful research on long-term therapy difficult. In particular, investigators interested in conducting a traditional "efficacy" trial, with the associated features of treatment standardization, fixed duration of therapy, and adequate control groups, encounter significant dilemmas when attempting to design a study of long-term therapy. Effectiveness studies, particularly those that rely upon naturalistic data, can circumvent some of these problems. However, such naturalistic studies are limited in their ability to produce strong evidence of causal connection between certain treatment techniques and improved outcome. We discuss several of the thornier methodological issues next.

Although there have been successful efforts (Barber et al., 1997; Linehan et al., 1991) at delivering a standardized psychotherapy for as long as one year, most therapists in the context of long-term therapy will tend to drift in a variety of directions rather than sticking to a specific treatment modality. Very general treatment manuals that specify principles of treatment rather than specific session-by-session instructions are likely to be better suited for investigations of long-term psychotherapy. Monitoring therapist adherence and competence at delivering a specific psychotherapy approach is a problem that can only be addressed by reviewing tapes of numerous sessions over the course of treatment—a practical problem for studies with relatively large numbers of patients and treatment sessions.

Duration of treatment is another problem. Several authors (e.g., Seligman, 1995) have argued that efficacy studies utilizing a fixed duration of therapy have limited generalizability to clinical practice where duration of treatment is not fixed. This argument is probably taken too far, given that the fact that duration of therapy is sometimes fixed in advance because of insurance limitations or because a clinic or practitioner adheres to a short-term model based upon a fixed number of sessions. However, in the context of investigating long-term therapy, a fixed duration of treatment appears even less justifiable. In part this is because the goals of long-term therapy—changing deeply rooted patterns, or schemas—are individualized to each patient, with wide variability in terms of the causes, duration, severity, and resistance to change of these patterns from patient to patient. Thus, some flexibility in tailoring duration of treatment to the patient's needs seems appropriate and consistent with most models of long-term treatment. Another factor to consider is that duration of long-term treatment will end up varying enormously even if an investigator attempted to fix duration in advance. This is because of the high likelihood that a significant number of patients will end treatment before the scheduled termination or, when more severely disturbed patients are involved, actually require ongoing additional treatment because of clinical concerns.

Perhaps the most difficult issue in attempting to study long-term therapy is the use and nature of control groups. For those that adhere to the importance of random assignment to treatment and control groups for documenting cause and effect relationships, such control groups are equally important for the study of treatment of any duration. Ethical questions arise, however, when considering a placebo-like control condition that would be scheduled to continue for a long duration. This concern can be alleviated to some degree by the careful monitoring of patients and breaking protocol when necessary to administer an active treatment. It is likely that, with more severely symptomatic and lower functioning patients, many patients would end up as "protocol violators" within a long-term placebo-like control condition. While deviation from protocol and dropout can be considered outcome measures in their own right, the occurrence of differential protocol violation and dropout in the control group, versus the experimental group, will bias outcome evaluation, thereby rendering interpretation of the data difficult if not impossible.

Given the above methodological conundrums, how should a study of long-term therapy be best designed? One answer to this question is that there is no single right answer. A variety of methodological approaches can be implemented, each with respective strengths and weaknesses and each more or less appropriate depending upon the specific scientific or practical question to be addressed. Fully naturalistic studies of long-term treatment are the best way to understand treatment as it is currently delivered in the community. These studies can provide information about dose of treatment (is one year enough, or are three years of therapy preferable for patients with borderline personality disorder?), pretreatment predictors of outcome, and correlational

analyses of process ingredients of therapy in relation to outcome.

If a randomized controlled experiment is to be attempted, several steps can be implemented to increase the interpretability of the data. Outcome should be assessed repeatedly through the course of treatment. If possible, outcome assessments should continue at fixed time intervals even for those patients who drop out of treatment or violate protocol. The data can then be analyzed via modern longitudinal methods, such as random regression analysis, using an intent-to-treat philosophy and including all data points. If one is successful in obtaining outcome data on a high proportion of patients, regardless of whether they are in treatment or not, then valid inferences about intention to treat can be made.

In terms of control conditions for a randomized clinical trial, consideration should be given to *treatment-as-usual* conditions. This was successfully implemented in Linehan et al.'s (1991) study of dialectical behavior therapy for borderline personality disorder. If a new, or newly standardized, long-term treatment is to be investigated, it seems meaningful to ask whether it is more effective than what is currently practiced in the community. Such a treatment-as-usual condition is likely to control for a variety of factors, such as expectations for change, the quality of the therapeutic relationship, and other common factors. Other factors, such as the training and quality of the psychotherapists, however, might be less well controlled in this design.

A second type of comparison condition that should be considered in terms of studies of long-term psychotherapy is maintenance medication. Frank et al. (1990) employed such a design in comparing long-term interpersonal psychotherapy to medication as treatments for recurrent depression. This type of comparison condition has great practical significance because long-term medication treatment is becoming increasingly common. In many cases, however, no medication has been developed for the types of patients who might be investigated in a study of long-term treatment (i.e., certain personality disorders).

CONCLUSIONS

Although much of the research and clinical writings of both authors of this chapter have focused on short-term treatment methods (e.g., Crits-Christoph & Barber, 1991), our primary conclusions from reviewing literature on long-term therapy is that the mental health field has probably turned its back on this modality too quickly. It appears that, for psychotherapy as it is currently practiced in the community, long-term treatment is indicated for sizable numbers of patients who present with recurrent disorders, chronic distress, and characterological problems. The current service delivery system may be providing inadequate treatment for these patients, leading to increased suffering and increased costs to society because of subsequent higher usage of other medical services (including hospitalization), reduced productivity at work, and other indirect costs. After several decades of research, we have accumulated some knowledge about the limitations of short-term therapy, particularly about the types of patients who do not achieve clinically meaningful benefits from brief treatment. What is exceptionally clear is that more research is needed on long-term therapy. Although there have been well over 1000 studies of psychotherapy, only a handful of meaningful studies have been performed on long-term therapy. We advocate a variety of approaches to the study of long-term therapy, depending upon the particular research question. Moreover, we remain optimistic that it is possible to conduct rigorous investigations of long-term therapy, including randomized clinical trials, provided steps are taken to deal with a host of methodological issues that are evident when attempting to conduct this type of research. In the meantime, until such research is performed, government, insurance companies, and health providers will need to continually attempt to arrive at a balance between the need to hold medical costs down and the need for more extensive mental health care for some individuals.

REFERENCES

Bachrach, H. M. (1980). Analyzability: A clinical-research perspective. *Psychoanalysis and contemporary thought, 3*, 86–116.

Bachrach, H. M., & Leaff, L. A. (1978). "Analyzability": A systematic review of the clinical and quantitative literature. *Journal of the American Psychoanalytic Association, 26*, 881–920.

Bachrach, H. M., Galatzer-Levy, R., Skolnikoff, A., & Waldron, S. (1991). On the efficacy of psychoanalysis. *Journal of the American Psychoanalytic Association, 39*, 871–915.

Barber, J. P., & Muenz, L. R. (1996). The role of avoidance and obsessiveness in matching patients to cognitive and interpersonal psychotherapy: Empirical findings from the Treatment for Depression Collaborative Research Program. *Journal of Consulting and Clinical Psychology, 64*, 951–958.

Barber, J. P., Frank, A., Weiss, R., Blaine, J., Siqueland, L., Moras, K., Calvo, N., Chittams, J., Mercer, D., Salloum, I. M. (1996). Prevalence and correlates of personality disorder diagnoses among cocaine dependent outpatients. *Journal of Personality Disorders, 10*, 297–311.

Barber, J. P., Morse, J. Q., Krakauer, I., Chittams, J., & Crits-Christoph, K. (1997). Change in obsessive-compulsive and avoidant personality disorders following time-limited supportive-expressive therapy. *Psychotherapy, 34*, 133–143.

Beatson, J. A. (1995). Long term psychotherapy in borderline and narcissistic disorders: When is it necessary? *Australian and New Zealand Journal of Psychiatry, 29*, 591–597.

Beck, A. T., Freeman, A., & Associates. (1990). *Cognitive therapy of personality disorders.* New York: Guilford Press.

Beck, A. T., Sokol, L., Clark, D. A., Berchick, R., & Wright, F. (1992). A crossover study of focused cognitive therapy for panic disorder. *American Journal of Psychiatry, 149*, 778–783.

Bolter, K., Levenson, H., & Alvarez, W. (1990). Differences in values between short-term and long–term therapists. *Professional Psychology: Research and Practice, 21*, 285–290.

Borkovec, T. D., & Costello, E. (1993). Efficacy of applied relaxation and cognitive-behavioral therapy in the treatment of generalized anxiety disorder. *Journal of Consulting and Clinical Psychology, 61*, 611–619.

Chambless, D. L., Renneberg, B., Goldstein, A., & Gracely, E. J. (1992). MCMI-diagnosed personality disorders among agoraphobic outpatients: Prevalence and relationship to severity and treatment outcome. *Journal of Anxiety Disorders, 6*, 193–211.

Cohen, P., & Cohen, J. (1984). The clinician's illusion. *Archives of General Psychiatry, 41*, 1178–1182.

Crits-Christoph, P., & Barber, J. P. (Eds.) (1991). *Handbook of short-term dynamic psychotherapy.* New York: Basic Books.

Elkin, I., Shea, M. T., Watkins, J. T., Imber, S. D., Sotsky, S. M., Collins, J. F., Glass, D. R., Pilkonis, P. A., Leber, W. R., Docherty, J. P., Fiester, S. J., & Parloff, M. B. (1989). NIMH Treatment of Depression Collaborative Research Program: General effectiveness of treatments. *Archives of General Psychiatry, 46*, 971–982.

Fenichel, O. (1945). *The psychoanalytic theory of the neuroses.* New York: Norton.

Fonagy, P., Käechele, H., Krause, R., Jones, E., & Perron, R. (1999). *An open door review of outcome studies in psychoanalysis.* London: International Psychoanalytical Association.

Frank, E., Kupfer, D. J., Jacob, M., & Jarrett, D.

(1987). Personality features and response to acute treatment in recurrent depression. *Journal of Personality Disorders, 1,* 14–26.

Frank, E., Kupfer, D. J., Perel, J. M., Cornes, C., Jarrett, D. B., Mallinger, A. G., Thase, M. E., McEachran, A. B., & Grochocinski, V. J. (1990). Three-year outcomes for maintenance therapies in recurrent depression. *Archives of General Psychiatry, 47,* 1093–1099.

Garfield, S. (1994). Research on client variables in psychotherapy. In A. E. Bergin & S. L. Garfield (Eds.). *Handbook of psychotherapy and behavior change* (4th ed. pp. 190–228). New York: John Wiley & Sons.

Gunderson, J. (1984). *Borderline personality disorders.* Washington, DC: American Psychiatric Press.

Gutheil, T. (1993). Informed consent in therapy. *Hospital and Community Psychiatry, 44,* 1005 (letter).

Howard, K. I., Davidson, C. V., O'Mahoney, M. T., Orlinsky, D. E., & Brown, K. P. (1989). Patterns of psychotherapy utilization. *American Journal of Psychiatry, 146,* 775–778.

Howard, K. I., Kopta, S. M., Krause, M. S., & Orlinsky, D. E. (1986). The dose-effect relationship in psychotherapy. *American Psychologist, 41,* 159–164.

Howard, K. I., Lueger, R. J., Maling, M. S., & Martinovich, Z. (1993). A phase model of psychotherapy outcome: Causal mediation of change. *Journal of Consulting and Clinical Psychology, 61,* 678–685.

Howard, K. I., Orlinsky, D. E., & Lueger, R. (1995). The design of clinically relevant outcome research: Some considerations and an example. In M. Aveline & D. A. Shapiro (Eds.), *Research foundations for psychotherapy practice.* New York: John Wiley & Sons.

Johnson, H. J., & Gelso, C. J. (1980). The effectiveness of time limits in counseling and psychotherapy: A critical review. *The Counseling Psychologist, 9,* 70–83.

Keller, W., Westhoff, R., Dilg, R., Rohner, H. H. (1997). *Studt and the study group on empirical psychotherapy research in analytical psychology.* Department of Psychosomatics and Psychotherapy, University Medical Center Benjamin Franklin, Free University of Berlin.

Kernberg, O. (1984). *Severe personality disorders.* New Haven: Yale University Press.

Kernberg, O. F., Burstein, E. D., Coyne, L., Appelbaum, A., Horwitz, L., & Voth, H. (1972). Psychotherapy and psychoanalysis: Final report of the Menninger Foundation Psychotherapy Research Project. *Bulletin of the Menninger Clinic, 36,* 3–275.

Klerman, G. (1990). The psychiatric patient's right to effective treatment: Implications of Osheroff v. Chestnut Lodge. *American Journal of Psychiatry, 147,* 409–418.

Klerman, G. L., Weissman, M. M., Rounsaville, B. J., & Chevron, E. S. (1984). *Interpersonal psychotherapy of depression.* New York: Basic Books.

Kohut, H. (1971). *The analysis of the self.* New York: International University Press,

Kopta, S. M., Howard, K. I., Lowry, J. L., & Beutler, L. E. (1994). Patterns of symptomatic recovery in psychotherapy. *Journal of Consulting and Clinical Psychology, 62,* 1009–1016.

Kordy, H., von Rad, M., & Senf, W. (1989). Empirical hypotheses on the psychotherapeutic treatment of psychosomatic patients in short and long-term time-unlimited psychotherapy. *Psychotherapy Psychosomatics 52,* 155–163.

Leuzinger-Bohleber, M., & Stuhr, U. (Hrsg). (1997). *Die Fähigkeit zu lieben, zu arbeiten und das Leben zu geniessen. Zu den vielen Facetten psychoanalytischer Katamneseforschung.* Psychosozial Verlag, Giessen.

Linehan, M. M. (1993). *Cognitive-behavioral treatment of borderline personality disorder.* New York: Guilford Press.

Linehan, M. M., Hubert, A. E., Suarez, A., Douglas, A., & Heard, H. L. (1991). Cognitive-behavioral treatment of chronically parasuicidal borderline patients. *Archives of General Psychiatry, 48,* 1060–1064.

Luborsky, L. (1975). Clinicians' judgments of mental health: Specimen case descriptions and forms for the Health-Sickness Rating Scale. *Bulletin of the Menninger Clinic, 35,* 448–480.

Luborsky, L., Chandler, M., Auerbach, A., Cohen, J., & Bachrach, H. (1971). Factors influencing the outcome of psychotherapy: A review of quantitative research. *Psychological Bulletin, 75,* 145–185.

Luborsky, L., Crits-Christoph, P., Mintz, J., & Auerbach, A. (1988). *Who will benefit from psychotherapy? Predicting therapeutic outcomes.* New York: Basic Books.

Luborsky, L., Singer, B., & Luborsky, L. (1975). Comparative studies of psychotherapies: Is it true that "everyone has won and all must have prizes"? *Archives of General Psychiatry, 32,* 995–1008.

Maier, W., Lichtermann, D., Klingler, T., Heun, R., & Hallmayer, J. (1992). Prevalences of personality disorders (DSM-III-R) in the community. *Journal of Personality Disorders, 6,* 187–196.

Marshall, R. D., Vaughan, S. C., MacKinnon, R. A., Mellman, L. A., & Roose, S. P. (1996). Assessing outcome in psychoanalysis and long-term dynamic psychotherapy. *Journal of the American Academy of Psychoanalysis, 24,* 575–604.

Meares, R. (1987). The secret and the self: On a new direction in psychotherapy. *Australian and New Zealand Journal of Psychiatry, 21,* 545–559.

Mennen, F. E., & Meadow, D. (1992). Process to recovery: In support of long-term groups for sexual abuse survivors. *International Journal of Group Psychotherapy, 42,* 29–44.

Miller, I. J. (1996). Time-limited brief therapy has gone too far: The result is invisible rationing. *Professional Psychology: Research and Practice, 27,* 567–576.

Minichiello, W. E., Baer, L., & Jenike, M.A. (1987). Schizotypal personality disorder: A poor prognostic indicator for behavior therapy in the treatment of obsessive-compulsive disorder. *Journal of Anxiety Disorders, 1,* 273–276.

Monsen, J. T., Oldland, T., Faugli, A., Daae, E., & Eilersten, D.E. (1995). Personality disorders: Changes and stability after intensive psychotherapy focusing on affect consciousness. *Psychotherapy Research, 5,* 33–48.

Munroe-Blum, H., & Marziali, E. (1995). A controlled trial of short-term group treatment for borderline personality disorder. *Journal of Personality Disorders, 9,* 190-198.

Orlinsky, D., & Howard, K. (1986). Process and outcome in psychotherapy. In S. L. Garfield & A. E. Bergin (Eds.), *Handbook of psychotherapy and behavior change* (pp. 311–381). New York: John Wiley & Sons.

Pilkonis, P. A., & Frank, E. L. (1988). Personality pathology in recurrent depression: Nature, prevalence, and relationship to treatment response. *American Journal of Psychiatry, 145,* 435–441.

Pollak, J., Mordecai, E., & Gumpert, P. (1992). Discontinuation from long-term individual psychodynamic psychotherapy. *Psychotherapy Research, 2,* 224–234.

Reich, J. H., & Green, A. I. (1991). Effect of personality disorders on outcome of treatment. *Journal of Nervous and Mental Disease, 179,* 74–82.

Reich, J. H., & Vasile, R. G. (1993). Effect of personality-disorders on the treatment outcome of Axis-I conditions—an update. *Journal of Nervous and Mental Disease, 181,* 475–484.

Revere, V., Rodeffer, C., & Dawson, S. (1989). Changes in long–term institutionalized schizophrenics with psychotherapy. *Journal of Contemporary Psychotherapy, 19,* 203–219.

Roth, D. M., & Ross, D. R. (1988). Long-term cognitive-interpersonal group therapy for eating disorders. *International Journal of Group Psychotherapy, 38,* 491–510.

Rudolf, G. (1991). Free University of Berlin: Berlin Psychotherapy Study. In L. Beutler & M. Crago (Eds.), *Psychotherapy research. An international review of programmatic studies.* (pp. 185-193). Washington, D.C.: American Psychological Association.

Rudolf, G., Manz, R., Öri, C. (1994). Ergebnisse der psychoanalytischen therapien. *Zsch psychosom Med, 40,* 25–40.

Ruegg, R., & Frances, A. (1995). New research on personality disorders. *Journal of Personality Disorders, 9,* 1–48.

Sandell, R., Bloomberg, J., & Lazar, A. (1997). When reality doesn't fit the blueprint: Doing research on psychoanalysis and long-term psychotherapy in a public health service program. *Psychotherapy Research, 7,* 333–344.

Seligman, M. E. P. (1995). The effectiveness of psychotherapy: *The Consumer Reports* study. *American Psychologist, 50,* 965–974.

Shea, M. T., Elkin, I., Imber, S. D., Sotsky, S. M., Watkins, J. T., Collins, J. F., Pilkonis, P. A., Beckham, E., Glass, D. R., Dolan, R. T., & Parloff, M. B. (1992). Course of depressive symptoms over follow-up: Findings from the National Institute of Mental Health Treatment of Depression Collaborative Research Program. *Archives of General Psychiatry, 49,* 782–787.

Smyrnios, K. X., & Kirkby, R. J. (1993). Long-term comparison of brief versus unlimited psychodynamic treatments with children and their parents. *Journal of Consulting and Clinical Psychology, 61,* 1020–1027.

Stevenson, J., & Meares, R. (1992). An outcome study of psychotherapy for patients with borderline personality disorder. *American Journal of Psychiatry, 149,* 358–362.

Teufel, R., & Volk, W. (1988). Erfolg und indikation stationärer psychotherapeutischer langzeit-therapie. In W. Ehlers, H. C. Traue, & D. Czogalik (Hrsg), *Bio-psycho-soziale medizin* (pp. 331–346). Berlin: Springer-PSZ-Drucke.

Thomä, H., & Käechele, H. (1987). *Psychoanalytic Practice: Vol. 1. Principles.* Berlin: Springer-Verlag.

Turner, R. M. (1987). The effects of personality disorder diagnosis on the outcome of social anxiety symptom reduction. *Journal of Personality Disorders, 1,* 136–144.

von Rad, M., Senf, W., Braeutigam, W. (1998). Psychotherapie und psychoanalyse in der Krankenversorgung: Ergebnisse des Heidelberger Katamnese-projektes. *Psychotherapie Psychosomatik Medizinische Psychologie, 48,* 88–100.

Wallerstein, R. (1986). *Forty-two lives in treatment: A study of psychoanalysis and psychotherapy.* New York: Guilford Press.

Weiner, I. B., & Exner, J. E. (1991). Rorschach changes in long-term and short-term psychotherapy. *Journal of Personality Assessment, 56,* 453–465.

Wenning, K. (1993). Long-term psychotherapy and informed consent. *Hospital and Community Psychiatry, 44,* 364–367.

Winnicott, D. W. (1965). *The maturational process and the facilitating environment.* New York: International Universities Press.

Woody, G. E., McLellan, A. T., Luborsky, L., & O'Brien, C. P. (1985). Sociopathy and psychotherapy outcome. *Archives of General Psychiatry, 42,* 1081–1086.

CHAPTER 22

PSYCHOPHARMACOLOGY IN CONJUNCTION WITH PSYCHOTHERAPY

MICHAEL E. THASE

University of Pittsburgh School of Medicine, Western Psychiatric Institute and Clinic

INTRODUCTION

In this chapter, I describe the conceptual basis for treatment plans that combine psychotropic medications and psychotherapy. I discuss pertinent tactical issues, and review evidence that such combinations have additive effects when compared to psychotherapy or pharmacotherapy alone for treatment of specific mental disorders. Psychotherapy–pharmacotherapy combinations, hereafter referred to as combined treatment, are important for a number of reasons. First, combined treatment strategies are widely employed to treat a broad range of DSM-IV mental disorders. Combined treatment approaches receive high marks from consumers (Seligman, 1995) and they are recommended frequently by expert consensus panels reviewing therapeutics for specific mental disorders (e.g., American Psychiatric Association, 1993, 1997, 1998; Ballenger, Davidson, Lecrubier, Nutt, International Consensus Group on Depression and Anxiety, Bobes, Beidel, Ono, & Westenberg, 1998; Depression Guideline Panel, 1993). It therefore is important for all mental health professionals to know the indications for, and limitations of, combined treatment strategies.

Second, combined treatment is generally more costly to deliver than the component monotherapies. Moreover, providing combined treatment routinely to all people seeking mental health care would tax existing treatment services to the breaking point. Therefore, there should be clear-cut evidence that combined treatment offers a definite additive effect. However, as will be reviewed in detail, research studies comparing combined treatments to the respective monotherapies do not uniformly document additive benefits. This points out the need to examine carefully the research methodologies used in randomized clinical trials to assess the possibility of "false negative" findings, as well as to consider potential biases that may lead professionals to overvalue combined treatment strategies.

Third, it is important to examine the evidence within groups of studies of specific mental disorders to identify particular subsets of patients who are more or less responsive to monotherapies. It is suggested that these patients represent particularly high risk/high yield candidates for more intensive combinations of psychotherapy and pharmacotherapy.

The Conceptual Basis for Psychotherapy–Pharmacotherapy Combinations

Combined treatment approaches have not always been viewed so positively by such a large proportion of mental health professionals. In the early years of the modern era of psychopharmacology, for example, there was widespread concern that medication treatment would interfere with the process of psychotherapy by relieving symptoms and hence reducing motivation for change (see, for example, the discussion by Klerman, Weissman, Markowitz, Glick, Wilner, Mason, & Shear, 1994). At a parallel level, psychodynamically oriented psychiatrists debated the potential impact of the act of prescription *per se* on the therapeutic relationship. Relevant concerns included that the prescribing therapist would be perceived by the patient as authoritarian or omnipotent. Conversely, there was concern that the therapist who chose not to prescribe might be seen as withholding or controlling. There was also an abiding ideological bias that pharmacotherapy was a superficial and often inadequate remedy (likened to a Band-Aid) for complex and multidetermined problems.

As evidence accumulated demonstrating the efficacy of selected pharmacotherapies for severe mental disorders (including schizophrenia, bipolar disorder, obsessive compulsive disorder, and psychotic depression), there was a change in professional attitudes. By the late 1960s and early 1970s, pharmacotherapy was viewed more commonly as an appropriate tool that could hasten relief from symptomatic suffering and help patients to make better use of psychotherapy (Klerman et al., 1994). In this spirit some of the earliest clinical trials on combined treatment were conducted (e.g., Klerman, DiMascio, Weissman, Prusoff, & Paykel, 1974; Hogarty, Ulrich, Mussare, & Aritigueta, 1976; May, 1968; Friedman, 1975). These studies yielded no evidence of negative interactions (see, for example, the review by Rounsaville et al., 1981). Moreover, the earlier studies on schizophrenia revealed that psychotherapy was not effective *unless* patients received concomitant antipsychotic medication (Hogarty et al., 1976; May, 1968).

The contemporary rationale for combining psychotherapy and pharmacotherapy is summarized by Table 22.1. Perhaps foremost is the fact that the best available single treatments or monotherapies for specific severe mental disorders are often incompletely effective. Moreover, no form of psychotherapy has been proven to be an effective monotherapy for schizophrenia, bipolar disorder, or major depressive disorders with psychotic features. For these disorders, if psychotherapies are used, they should be used in combination with pharmacotherapy. Thus, at the most pragmatic level, combining treatments may broaden the spectrum of efficacy as compared to the respective monotherapies. This type of treatment interaction is referred to as an additive effect (see Figure 22.1, Weissman, Prusoff, DiMascio, Neu, Goklaney, & Klerman, 1979). Nevertheless, the size of such an additive effect is smaller than would be expected from simple summation of the effects of the two monotherapies (i.e., $0.5 + 0.5 = 0.7$) (Klerman et al., 1994). I suspect that this is because both psychological and pharmacologic treatment effects capitalize on so-called nonspecific factors such as placebo-expectancy, therapeutic support, and spontaneous remission (Thase, in press). If such nonspecifics account for 50%–60% of an observed therapeutic effect (Depression Guideline Panel, 1993), the *maximum* possible additive effect for combined treatment could be estimated as about one-half of the magnitude of effect of the second treatment (i.e., $0.5 + 0.5/2 = 0.75$).

It is also possible that combining treatments could result in a so-called synergistic interaction (i.e., $0.5 + 0.5 = 1.5$). However, I am not aware of any examples of such synergy resulting from psychotherapy and pharmacotherapy combinations.

TABLE 22.1 Rationale for Combining Psychotherapy and Pharmacotherapy

- Combining treatments may increase the probability of response or improve the quality of remission.
- Combining treatments will broaden the therapeutic range of the intervention by capitalizing on dissimilar therapeutic mechanisms.
- Pharmacotherapy may control symptoms that disrupt psychotherapy (e.g., hallucinations or delusions) or reverse central nervous system abnormalities that impair learning or memory.
- Psychotherapy may add mode specific effects (e.g., social skills or interpersonal problem solving) that broaden the impact of pharmacotherapy.
- Psychotherapy may reduce the risk or frequency of noncompliance with pharmacotherapy.
- Combined treatment has broad support across mental health disciplines and consumer advocacy groups.

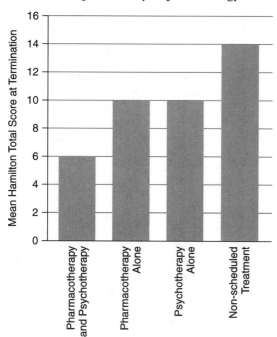

FIGURE 22.1 Additive effect of pharmacotherapy and psychotherapy on lowered depression. (Reprinted from DiMascio et al., 1979).

A second rationale is based on the assumption that pharmacotherapy and psychotherapy have dissimilar mechanisms of therapeutic action. Thus, the conceptual argument for combining treatments goes deeper than a simple "shotgun" approach to therapeutics, and the strategic use of dissimilar therapeutic actions has important implications for improving patient care. There is now some evidence of differential efficacy attributable to observable differences in patterns of brain activity. My colleagues and I have completed a study (Thase, Buysse, Frank, et al., 1997a) that examined the relationship between sleep neurophysiology and response to two of the better studied psychotherapies for depression, Beck's (1976) model of cognitive behavior therapy (CBT), and Klerman, Weissman, Rounsaville, and Chevron's (1984) interpersonal psychotherapy (IPT). In both studies a specific pattern of neurophysiologic disturbance was found to be associated with relatively poorer therapy outcomes. The EEG sleep disturbances associated with nonresponse to therapy included reduced eye movement (REM) sleep latency, poor sleep efficiency, and increased phasic REM sleep activity (Thase, Kupfer, Fasiczka, Buysse, Simons, & Frank,

1997b). Together, these disturbances are thought to reflect a state-dependent hyperarousal of limbic and brain stem circuits. Numerous studies have shown that, when effective, antidepressant medications dampen these circuits, as demonstrated by suppression of rapid eye movement in sleep (see, for example, Thase, 1998; Thase & Kupfer, 1987).

Our group and others have also found a parallel association between elevated plasma, or urinary-free cortisol levels (another indicator of hyperactive central nervous system responses), and poorer response to psychotherapy (Robbins, Alesi, & Colfer, 1989; Corbishley, Beutler, Quan, Bamford, Meredith, & Scogin, 1990; McKnight et al., 1992; Thase, Dubé, Bowler, Howland, Myers, Friedman, & Jarrett, 1996b; Thase & Friedman, 1999). Again, antidepressants appear to dampen such response at the systemic (DeBellis, Gold, Geracioti, Listwak, & Kling, 1993; Carroll, 1991; Thase, 1998) and perhaps cellular (Barden, Reul, & Holsboer, 1995; Duman, Heninger, & Nestler, 1997) levels. We predict that only those patients who manifest objective indicators of central nervous system dysfunction truly *require* pharmacotherapy (Thase et al., 1996; 1997) and that prospective assessment of these central nervous system mechanisms might actually facilitate a more judicious use of combined treatment.

A third rationale is the likelihood of mode-specific effects. These potential benefits are based on the use of targeted psychotherapeutic strategies, such as social skills training for people with schizophrenia or depression to improve relevant deficits and enhance quality of life over and above the effects expected with resolution of the illness state. Such effects would not necessarily convey greater improvements in the core symptoms of the patients' mental disorder but could be expected to lessen subsequent vulnerability.

A fourth rationale is that the addition of psychotherapy to a pharmacotherapy regimen may improve medication adherence and, for some patients with disorders, may permit reductions of daily medication dosages. Although routinely using lower doses of antidepressants may not always be such a good idea (Thase, 1983; 1992; Frank, Kupfer, Hamer, Grochocinski, & McEachran, 1992), the general principle of using the lowest dose that "works" does convey cost savings and lowers the incidence of some side effects. Improved compliance has obvious important implications because medication noncompliance is common across both nonpsychotic and psychotic mental disorders and is a major risk factor for both nonresponse and subsequent relapse.

The beneficial effect of psychotherapy on medication adherence is generally nonspecific, perhaps reflecting better acceptability of the more stigmatized treatment when paired with the more desired one. However, a specific psychotherapeutic focus on medication adherence also can have a substantial positive effect (Cochran, 1984). Conversely, concomitant pharmacotherapy may make participating in psychotherapy more acceptable to the smaller subgroup of patients who are uncomfortable with talking about thoughts and feelings. Such broadening of the acceptability of treatment may be particularly useful in conditions in which patient preference is more polarized (i.e., obsessive-compulsive disorder or major depressive disorder).

Tactical Issues

Psychotherapy-pharmacotherapy combinations are largely limited to three types of treatment teams: a psychiatrist working with a psychotherapist, a primary care physician working with a psychotherapist, and a psychiatrist providing both therapies. There is little evidence that one approach is inherently preferable to the others, and I am aware of only one prospective study that addressed this question. As reviewed later in more detail, the study of Blackburn, Bishop, Glen, Whalley, and Christie (1981) enrolled and treated depressed patients in two settings, a primary care clinic and a psychiatric clinic. They found that the combination of CBT and antidepressants was comparably effective regardless of whether the medication was prescribed by a psychiatrist or a primary care physician (see Figure 22.2). However, the study was rather small (cell n_s for the two combined treatment groups were 13 and 9) and patients were not randomized to provider teams (general practice patients were automatically treated by primary care physicians and speciality clinic patients were similarly always treated by psychiatrists).

There have been no studies comparing treatment by psychiatrists as the sole providers of combined therapy versus psychotherapist-physician treatment teams. The principal arguments for a single provider are parsimony, a more natural integration of treatments, and greater clarity of focus (Thase, 1997). For example, a psychiatrist has less chance of providing conflicting psychoeducation about the two modalities than a pair of clinicians and there is no chance of the pa-

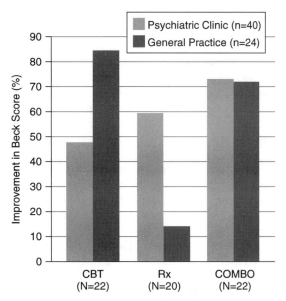

FIGURE 22.2 Cognitive-Behavior Therapy (CBT) and Pharmacotherapy (Rx) were differentially effective in psychiatric and general practice patients in Blackburn et al.'s (1981) study.

tient "splitting" between treatment providers (Thase, 1996). The main drawbacks of the single provider approach are limited availability (there are far too few psychiatrists to treat all the patients who receive combined therapy); expense (the hourly fee of a psychiatrist is generally higher than other providers); and psychotherapeutic experience (very few psychiatrists are trained to conduct the newer forms of psychotherapy that have received empirical verification). I have suggested elsewhere (Thase, 1997) that combined treatment provided by psychiatrists is most clearly indicated for patients with complex, comorbid disorders, such as a current episode of major depression superimposed on long-standing post-traumatic stress disorder or borderline personalty disorder. This suggestion has not, however, been tested prospectively by a "head-to-head" randomized clinical trial.

In the absence of data from prospective studies, some better understanding of practice patterns can be gleaned from studies of service utilization. In the United States, for example, it appears that psychiatrists provide no more than 10% of psychotherapy and 35% of the pharmacotherapy provided to patients with mental disorders (Regier, Hirschfeld, Goodwin, Burke, Lazar, & Judd, 1988; Wells, Burnam, Rogers, Hays, &

Camp, 1992). Thus, at least in the United States, primary care physicians provide a large majority of the pharmacotherapy and nonmedical psychotherapists conduct a large proportion of psychotherapy. Service utilization data also can be examined to determine the case complexity mixes and cost of various treatment teams. When compared to other providers, psychiatrists tend to treat more severely ill, complicated patients for longer periods of time (Wells et al., 1992). When such differences in case complexity are accounted for statistically, the presumed extra cost of care by psychiatrists dissipates (Goldman, McCulloch, Cuffel, Zarin, Suarez, & Burns, 1998).

Despite these data, the wider availability of combined treatment by physician–therapist teams and the millions of people who require such care necessitate the continued emphasis on the therapist–pharmacotherapist–patient triad. Given this reality, it is essential that we learn the characteristics and determinants of effective collaboration between primary care physicians and psychotherapists. For example, several studies of depressed patients suggest that indifferent, poorly executed pharmacotherapy offers little when added to a skillfully applied psychotherapy (e.g., Blackburn et al., 1981; Teasdale, Fennell, Hibbert, & Amies, 1984). It might similarly be inferred that a poorly executed psychotherapy has, at best, little additional value over and above competent supportive care (Frank et al., 1991).

The first critical element of an optimal combined approach is that the prescriber and therapist are collaborators and that their care is coordinated.

The Approval and Regulation of Pharmacotherapy

The medications used to treat specific mental disorders in the United States are subjected to three phases of research prior to approval by the Food and Drug Administration (FDA). The first phase primarily concerns dose-finding and documentation of safety. The second and third phases involve progressively larger clinical trials employing random assignment, appropriate control groups (i.e., an inert placebo and/or a standard, already approved medication), and double-blind evaluation. Despite strong opinions to the contrary (e.g., Rothman & Michaels, 1994), the FDA continues to require evidence that a novel medication is significantly more effective than a pill placebo before that medication can be considered for approval. In fact, it takes at least two positive placebo controlled trials before a novel psychotropic medication can be approved for treatment of a specific indication. The manufacturer of a novel drug will typically conduct as many as 8, 10, or even 12 Phase II and Phase III trials to ensure that adequate evidence of efficacy is obtained during the pre-submission evaluation process.

Approval by the FDA does not imply that a novel medication is dramatically effective. Further, FDA approval typically conveys no information about relative efficacy, i.e., as compared to other approved medications. Rather, no FDA-approved psychotropic medication even approaches the ideal of universal efficacy. FDA-approved medications have replicable, albeit limited therapeutic effects. For example, approximately 50% of all controlled trials of FDA approved antidepressants fail to demonstrate a statistically significant drug–placebo difference (Thase, 1999).

Approval does imply a certain degree of safety, typically on the basis of between 600 and 2,000 people treated with the novel compound. The clinical trials that lead to FDA approval thus generally overestimate the safety of novel medications because people with severe medical illnesses and those taking other, multiple medications largely have been excluded from research participation. A fourth, post-marketing phase of research is still necessary to observe rarer, but still important, toxicities and side effects (Thase, 1999). It is during this phase that the impressions of relative efficacy, tolerability, and ease of use also are formulated by practicing clinciians. Often, these impressions are based on the scantiest amount of data from controlled studies; they rest on clinical experience, expert opinion, and industry-sponsored marketing.

Although the FDA approves psychotropic medications for specific indications, the therapeutic effects of these medications almost always span diagnostic boundaries. For example, most sedative-hypnotic medications also have anxiolytic effects, and neuroleptic medications are useful for treatment of mania and psychotic depression, as well as schizophrenia. A large majority of antidepressant medications treat panic disorder effectively, and the more serotonergically active antidepressants have significant antiobsessional effects.

FDA approval of a new medication for one

indication, such as obsessive-compulsive disorder, thus should not strictly delimit the use of that treatment in clinical practice. The anticonvulsant medication carbamazepine, for example, is widely used as a second-line treatment of bipolar disorder even though it does not have formal FDA approval. Other common examples of *off-label* prescriptions include use of the antidepressant trazodone as a sleep aid and the antiobsessional medications clomipramine and fluvoxamine as antidepressants. Such off-label use may precede eventual FDA approval, as was the case with the anticonvulsant divalproex as a treatment of mania, or it may continue for years or even decades, as is the case for the use of tricyclic antidepressants for treatment of panic disorder. This is because the decision of a pharmaceutical company to seek FDA approval involves a commitment of millions of dollars of research and development costs. The manufacturer must consider these costs in relation to the patent life remaining for a medication and prospects for return on the investment. On occasion medications with promise for treatment of rarer conditions are given special status as *orphan drugs*, which permits additional research via an extension of patent life.

If the process that leads to approval of a novel psychotropic medication is compared to the development of a newer form of psychotherapy, a number of differences emerge. First, the procedures employed in Phase Two and Phase Three of treatment development yield much more evidence of efficacy from randomized clinical trials, in support of each newly approved medication, than there is for even the most extensively researched psychotherapy (Thase, 1995). Second, the efficacy of psychotropic medications has always been measured against a well-standardized attention–placebo condition. By contrast, the pursuit of a credible control condition is a methodologic challenge that has remained problematic for psychotherapy researchers. Third, FDA approval permits the manufacturer to market the new medication to physicians and, more recently, directly to consumers. A doctor can attend free seminars to learn how to prescribe a new medication, and receive conveniently packaged samples of that medication to give to patients at no cost. Although it is naïve to suggest that there is no commercialization of psychotherapy, it is also fair to state that there are several orders of magnitude difference in commercialization between these approaches to treatment.

The General Approach to Pharmacotherapy

With a few well-defined exceptions, physicians prescribe psychotropic medications to people who have explicitly assumed the social role of patients. Barring malfeasance or some other questionable practices, the physician prescribes a medication only after he or she has determined that the patient is suffering from a bona fide condition and that the chance of benefit outweighs the potential risks and cost of pharmacotherapy. If the physician is a psychiatrist, he or she is likely to have classified the condition as a mental disorder according to the DSM-IV, the official nomenclature of the American Psychiatric Association (1994). Physicians in primary care are less likely to employ this standardized approach to diagnosis, but they nonetheless prescribe treatment based on categorical assessments of disturbances such as insomnia, anxiety and depression, or chronic fatigue.

Treatment is intended to suppress or relieve symptoms and, when the scientific sophistication of the field permits, to counteract or correct more specific pathophysiological processes. The effectiveness of the treatment is monitored by observing changes in illness activity, which is typically gauged by the frequency or intensity of the patient's presenting signs and symptoms. Pharmacotherapy is conceptualized as consisting of three phases: acute, continuation, and maintenance phases of therapy (Kupfer, 1991; see Figure 22.3). Patients generally attend more frequent doctor visits (e.g., weekly or every other week) during the acute phase of treatment and less frequent visits after obtaining a response. If the initial medication is not effective, an alternate medication is selected and the acute phase is repeated until a satisfactory response is obtained. By convention, the four-to-six-month period of pharmacotherapy following stabilization is referred to as the continuation phase, with longer term preventative pharmacotherapy described as the maintenance phase (Depression Guideline Panel, 1993). Pharmacotherapy for most forms of mental disorder follows a medical or disease model, for chronic illnesses, analogous to the treatment of hypertension or peptic ulcer disease (Klerman et al., 1994).

Despite these parallels, the treatment of mental disorders differs from that of most other common medical conditions in several important respects. Patients with "mental problems" have much greater problems with stigma, for example,

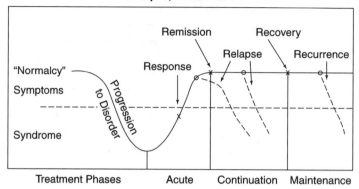

FIGURE 22.3 Response, remission, recovery, relapse, and recurrence of depression. (Reprinted from Kupfer, 1991.)

that may affect their acceptance of the diagnosis or adherence to the recommended subsequent treatment. The association of mental illness with images of moral or character weaknesses or between *psychiatric* medication and addiction or mind control are still quite prevalent in the popular culture. One only needs to look to contemporary cinema to see stereotypic characterization of the needy neurotic who uses medication as a crutch or the authoritarian psychiatrist who uses ECT (electroconvulsive therapy) to punish an unruly patient. Education for the patient and his or her family members is an important aspect of most approaches to disease management, and it may have a proportionally greater role in the treatment of mental disorders to help reduce stigma.

The ready availability of nonmedical approaches to treatment, specifically counseling and psychotherapy, also may be a more prominent consideration than in general medicine. In fact, several surveys have documented that the general public rates "seeing a counselor or therapist" ahead of "taking a medication" for management of depression (Roper, 1986). Here, patient choice represents an important yet often underexplored factor. It is not known if there are tangible differences between people who choose to see a physician or a therapist. If true, changes in health care delivery, particularly the use of a primary care physician as a "gatekeeper" for access to mental health delivery and the designation of a limited panel of providers, will alter a heretofore implicit process that has guided the way that people select their treatment. Finally, there is still not parity of insurance benefits between mental health treatment and general medical care. Thus, symptomatic people sometimes do not seek appropriate care because they believe that they can't afford it.

Combining Treatments: Conditions That Should Not Be Treated with Psychotherapy Alone

A person with a severe mental disorder should not be treated with psychotherapy alone if 1) there is little evidence that psychotherapy is an effective treatment; 2) there is ample evidence that some form of pharmacotherapy is effective; and 3) the patient has not already failed multiple treatment trials with all FDA-approved medications. Patients can make an informed choice to refuse pharmacotherapy, although most states have provisions for involuntary treatment of severe mental disorders when it is determined that the patients' ability to choose is impaired by the illness. Involuntary treatment is seldom used for conditions other than severe depression, bipolar disorder, or schizophrenia. Guardianship procedures are preferred when long-term treatment is indicated.

There are only a few mental disorders that should not be treated with psychotherapy alone: schizophrenia and psychotic disorders, manic and depressive states of bipolar affective disorder, psychotic major depressive episodes, and severe acute alcohol and sedative-hypnotic withdrawal states. Treatment of these conditions with psychotherapy alone, without appropriate concomitant pharmacotherapy, is tantamount to malpractice! Of course, mental disorders resulting from brain tumors, metabolic derangements, or central nervous system infections also should not be treated with psychotherapy alone. However, these conditions are also not properly managed with psychotropic medication unless appropriate neurological or medical care is provided.

Psychotherapy as an Adjunctive Therapy
Schizophrenia and Related Disorders

The value of adjunctive psychosocial intervention for people with schizophrenia has been evaluated during acute hospitalization following discharge (traditionally referred to as aftercare) and, for the chronically and persistently mentally ill, during long-term institutional care. The principal types of intervention have included milieu therapy, individual psychodynamic psychotherapy, and more recently, cognitive-behavioral therapies, behavior therapy targeting improved social skills, and various forms of family interventions.

Several conclusions are evident from the numerous studies of the value of inpatient psychosocial treatments for acute schizophrenia. First, a meta-analysis of 26 controlled studies demonstrated that there was no effect for inpatient psychosocial interventions during acute hospitalizations (Andrews, Brodaty, Hadzi-Pavlovic, et al., 1994). Indeed, studies conducted during the same era suggested that briefer hospitalizations yielded outcomes similar to longer admissions (e.g., Caffey, Galbrecht, & Klett, 1971; Herz, Endicott, & Spitzer, 1977), which indirectly supports the conclusion that extensive inpatient psychosocial treatment of acute schizophrenia has very limited value. Several large studies did demonstrate modest additive effects (Grinspoon, Ewalt, & Shader, 1972; May, 1968), and it is likely that the overall main effect of psychotherapy has been diluted by the contribution of studies that include therapy plus placebo conditions. However, the lengths of *acute* hospitalization in those studies are so long that the findings are virtually irrelevant to practitioners in 2000.

The de-emphasis of extensive inpatient treatment of schizophrenia naturally led to greater attention to the impact of psychosocial therapies in aftercare settings. Targets for intervention have included improved medication adherence, reduction of relapse and rehospitalization rates, improved social functioning, and better tolerance of psychosocial stressors. Of particular interest, a large body of research documented that overinvolvement of family, especially contact with significant others manifesting a high level of expressed emotion, greatly increased the risk of psychotic relapse (Brown, Birley, & Wing, 1972; Vaughn & Leff, 1976; Butzlaff & Hooley, 1998).

Results of controlled studies of aftercare, covering a wide range of psychosocial therapies, suggest some degree of psychotherapeutic specificity. For example, supportive individual interventions such as major role training (Schooler, Levine, Severe et al., 1980), occupational therapy (Liberman et al., 1998), and personal therapy have shown only modest additive benefit over pharmacotherapy alone. Of note, Hogarty, Greenwald, Ulrich et al. (1997b) found that whereas personal therapy had a modest positive effect for patients living with families, it had negative effects for those living alone, including increased risk of relapse. Because living arrangements are not randomly assigned, the mechanism underlying this interaction remains obscure. Perhaps schizophrenic people who live alone are adverse to too much interpersonal contact, along with the well-meaning attempts to provide therapeutic supports that actually are experienced as stressors. Conversely, those who are able to maintain significant social relations may be better able to engage in therapy.

Family-focused interventions have shown a consistent additive effect in terms of reduction of relapse risk and improved social functioning (Falloon, Boy, McGill et al., 1985; Hogarty, Anderson, Reiss et al., 1986; Randolph, Eth, Glynn et al., 1994). The magnitude of this effect can be substantial. For example, Randolph et al. (1994) found that the addition of a 25-session behavioral family management program reduced the relapse risk of schizophrenic patients from 55% (11/20) to 14% (3/21). Although psychoeducational family interventions are most commonly recommended for those from highly expressed emotion households, Randolph et al. (1994) found that the benefits were extended to patients across other living circumstances. One recent study further suggests that the benefit of family involvement may be conveyed by a relatively low-intensity, once-a-month group intervention (Schooler, Keith, Severe, et al., 1997).

A third area of research has focused on social skills training. Results of controlled studies demonstrate positive gains on measures of residual symptoms, social adjustment, and *in vivo* behavioral tests when social skills training is compared to supportive therapy control conditions

(Hogarty et al., 1986; Marder, Wirshing, Mintz et al., 1996; Liberman, Blackwell, Wallace, & Mintz, 1994). Hogarty et al. also found an additive effect between individual skills training and psycho-educational family therapy. In their most recent report, Liberman and colleagues (1998) found that the effects of social skills training were sustained across a two-year follow-up. The effects of skills training on relapse risk are less consistent across individual studies, but in aggregate there appears to be a significant reduction in the risk of rehospitalization (Benton & Schroeder, 1990).

The fourth area of research concerns the use of a modified form of Beck's (1976) CBT with schizophrenic patients already stabilized on antipsychotic medication. This approach is quite different from the more supportive and rehabilitative initiatives that have dominated this field for the past two decades. Specifically, the goal of CBT is to help patients learn to use the techniques of rational discourse to challenge and modify psychotic experiences (Perris, 1989). The results of two recent studies conducted in Great Britain indicate that this approach has considerable promise (Drury, Birchwood, Cochrane, & Macmillan, 1996; Kuipers, Garety, Fowler et al., 1997). In both trials the addition of weekly individual CBT sessions improved symptomatic outcomes when compared to pharmacotherapy alone. Moreover, in one study improvement following CBT was associated positively with the *strength* of delusions prior to treatment (Garety, Fowler, Kuipers et al., 1997). This is remarkable because the severity of psychotic symptoms typically predicts poorer outcomes in studies of a wide range of interventions for schizophrenia.

Research on the treatment of chronically ill institutionalized patients has yielded less consistently impressive results, but considering the alternative of providing only custodial care, there is evidence of clinical gains. In perhaps the most intensive study of chronically ill, institutionalized patients ever implemented, Paul and colleagues (1972, 1977) demonstrated that a systematic program based on contingency management principles resulted in improvements on a number of symptomatic and functional measures. Furthermore, many patients participating in this intensive program were able to decrease or even discontinue antipsychotic medication. Although it is likely that many, if not most, of these patients were actually not responsive to the phenothiazine antipsychotics that were withdrawn (Schooler, 1978), it is also true that these medications would not have been withdrawn without participation in the intensive psychosocial program. Moreover, prolonged exposure to high doses of antipsychotic medication is the leading risk factor for tardive dyskinesia, a potentially irreversible and disabling neurological syndrome. Intensive psychosocial treatment thus could have an important indirect benefit for patients who were not responsive to antipsychotic medications. Unfortunately, the program of Paul and colleagues was not widely disseminated and the feasibility of less costly alternatives has not been investigated systematically.

Another example of improved treatment of chronically ill schizophrenic patients was recently reported by Rosenheck, Tekell, Peters et al. (1998). This study of treatment-resistant, institutionalized veterans compared 122 patients treated for one year with the novel antipsychotic clozapine with 169 patients receiving conventional antipsychotic medications. Clozapine is a very expensive medication that has numerous annoying side effects and the risk of causing agranulocytosis, a potentially lethal form of bone marrow dysfunction. Nevertheless, clozapine has definite therapeutic effects for many patients who have not responded to standard antipsychotic medications. Rosenheck et al. found that the patients receiving clozapine treatment were significantly more likely to participate in supplemental psychosocial therapies. Furthermore, patients who participated in those therapies experienced improved outcomes on symptomatic and quality of life measures. Thus, pharmacotherapy with clozapine facilitated greater involvement in otherwise available psychosocial interventions, which in turn facilitated better outcomes.

In summary, there is compelling evidence that a range of individual and family-focused psychotherapies have definite beneficial effects when provided in combination with antipsychotic medications. There is recent evidence suggesting that CBT may offer yet another distinct psychosocial option for improving the course of schizophrenia.

Bipolar Affective Disorder

Although the prevalence of bipolar affective disorder is comparable to that of schizophrenia, research on additive psychosocial treatments has not received the same emphasis. Perhaps this is because the risk of chronicity is lower in bipolar disorder than schizophrenia, or perhaps it is because the standard pharmacotherapy for bipolar disorder, lithium salts, was perceived to be more effective than antipsychotics are for schizophrenia. In either event, there recently has been greater awareness that psychosocial therapies may play an important role in the treatment of a significant minority, if not a majority, of people with manic depression.

The rationale for adding psychotherapy to the treatment regimens for bipolar disorder has been discussed by Frank, Kupfer, Ehlers et al. (1994), Scott (1996), Miklowitz (1996), and Basco and Rush (1996), among others. Potential targets for adjunctive psychosocial treatment include improving management of psychosocial stressors, enhancing medication adherence, addressing stigma and losses related to the illness, and stabilizing chaotic interpersonal and functional routines. In addition, there is evidence that the expressed emotion of critical family members is as relevant to relapse risk in bipolar disorder as it is to schizophrenia (Butzlaff & Hooley, 1998; Vaughn & Leff, 1976).

Unfortunately, there are no definitive studies of combined treatment of bipolar disorder. There are, however, several promising preliminary reports and a number of uncontrolled studies demonstrating the potential value of adding psychosocial treatment to standard pharmacotherapy. In addition, large controlled studies are underway in the United States and in the United Kingdom.

Miklowitz (1996) has reviewed the early studies and concluded that family, group, and individual psychotherapies may indeed lead to improvements in functioning and adherence to pharmacotherapy. Scott (1996) notes, however, that these apparent effects could be attributable to relatively simple factors, such as improved psycho-education, better adherence, and nonspecific support. Although psycho-education and support are important aspects of all professional psychotherapies, they do not necessarily demand the expense and training of a formal treatment. Alternatively, psycho-education and focused attention to medication adherence could be accomplished efficiently with a highly focused, time-limited intervention. For example, Cochran (1984) found that a six-week course of CBT reduced medication noncompliance and lowered risk of re-hospitalization in a small but randomized study of 28 patients with bipolar disorder. Importantly, Cochran's adaptation of CBT *did not* focus on symptom management or use of cognitive techniques to address manic or depressive

distortions of thinking. The work reviewed earlier that is emerging from studies of schizophrenia suggests that cognitive interventions also might be applicable for symptom reduction in mania. Basco and Rush (1996) have published a treatment manual illustrating this approach.

Not all preliminary studies of psychosocial therapies of bipolar disorder are positive, and there is some evidence of possible iatrogenic psychotherapeutic effects. As part of a larger study of family treatment for hospitalized psychiatric patients, Clarkin, Glick, Haas et al. (1990) examined the outcomes of the subset of patients with affective disorders. Although the couples-oriented treatment had beneficial effects for the women, the men showed significant worsening on a measure of perceived family support and no additive benefit on symptomatic measures. It appears that couples treatment helped to shore-up the distressed marital relationships of women with affective disorders but aggravated the relationships of bipolar men. These findings raise the interesting, albeit complex, possibility of a three-way (i.e., gender × diagnosis × psychotherapy) interaction. Miklowitz and colleagues are conducting a randomized controlled trial of psycho-educational family therapy that may help to clarify these relationships.

Frank, Kupfer, Mallinger et al. (1999) recently reported preliminary results from a study of an individual therapy for bipolar disorder ongoing in Pittsburgh. Patients suffering from an acute episode of bipolar disorder (i.e., depressed, manic, or mixed) were randomly assigned to initial treatment that consisted of either a modified form of interpersonal psychotherapy (IPSRT; Frank et al., 1994) in combination with pharmacotherapy and clinical management or pharmacotherapy alone. The therapy builds upon conventional IPT by adding a component intended to help people with bipolar disorder achieve more regular social rhythms and greater day-to-day stability. After stabilization (a time course of at least 12 weeks), one-half of the patients in each randomization section are switched to the alternate strategy for an additional course of 24 months of maintenance therapy. Although the study is only about one-half finished, there is some evidence of an additive effect during the initial course of treatment. Specifically, IPSRT definitely improved social rhythm regularity and lifestyle (Frank, Hlastala, Ritenour et al., 1997). It also appears that the IPSRT group had lower levels of depressive symptoms across time. IPSRT has *not* yet been shown to have a preventative effect, however. The lack of a preventative effect may be because of an unexpected interaction between treatment assignment and phase of study. Specifically, during the maintenance phase both the patients withdrawn from IPSRT and those who had IPSRT added to their treatment regimen were at greater risk of relapse (Frank et al., in press). If these findings hold true in analyses of the completed sample, it would suggest that psychotherapy, once started, should not be abruptly discontinued after clinical stabilization. Moreover, it appears that there is some risk associated with adding psychotherapy to the treatment plan of a bipolar patient already stabilized with pharmacotherapy alone.

Major Depression with Psychotic Features

There are no studies concerning combined treatment of major depression with psychotic features. This is most unfortunate because psychotic depression is not uncommon and it is associated with higher rates of disability, recurrence, and suicide (Schatzberg & Rothschild, 1992). Beyond the characteristic delusions and hallucinations, psychotic depressions also are more neurobiologically disturbed, as reflected by all-night EEG sleep studies and various measures of hypercortisolism (Nelson & Davis, 1997; Thase, Kupfer, & Ulrich, 1986). Such abnormalities are not invariably corrected by pharmacotherapy, and sustained elevations of plasma cortisol levels may impair executive cognitive functioning and exacerbate reactivity to minor stressors (Thase & Howland, 1995). These difficulties could provide important targets for the forms of psychotherapy that have been developed for treatment of schizophrenia.

Disorders That May Respond Better to Combined Treatment Than to Psychotherapy Alone

There are a number of nonpsychotic DSM-IV mental disorders that can be treated effectively by psychotherapy alone. Based on the results of controlled clinical trials, these disorders include major (nonbipolar) depressive disorder (nonpsychotic, nonmelancholic subtype), dysthymia, panic disorder, obsessive compulsive disorder, social phobia, generalized anxiety disorder, bulimia, and primary insomnia. For each of these conditions, effective pharmacotherapies also exist. Thus, for the practicing psychotherapist, the rel-

evant question is "Should this patient also receive pharmacotherapy?" Conversely, physicians treating these nonpsychotic mental disorders need to be aware of the indications for adding a psychosocial therapy to pharmacotherapy. Although patient preference, availability, and cost are important practical considerations, an enlightened approach to differential therapeutics should also provide estimates about the likelihood of additive or differential benefit for combined treatment. The most useful way to obtain such empirical guidance is from controlled clinical trials, although relatively few studies have been completed and many studies have serious shortcomings.

Major Depressive Disorder

The principal psychotherapies studied in controlled clinical trials of combined treatment are various forms of behavior therapy, CBT, and IPT. I am not aware of a single published, controlled study of the combination of pharmacotherapy and psychodynamic therapy using factorial design and standard clinical trial methodology.

Meta-analyses of controlled studies of depressed outpatients have revealed relatively small additive effect sizes (Conte, Plutchik, Wild, & Karasu, 1986; Depression Guideline Panel, 1993). It would appear that the types of depression that typify the participants of these ambulatory trials, namely, mild to moderately severe, nonincapacitating disorders, do not justify the routine combination of modalities (Persons, Thase, & Crits-Christoph, 1996).

The results of a more recent meta-analysis of the original data of major depression patients are consistent with this conclusion (Thase, Greenhouse, Frank et al., 1997). Among the patients with milder depressions and those with midlife single (nonrecurrent) episodes, adding pharmacotherapy to IPT improved remission rates by about 20% when compared to IPT or CBT alone. However, remission rates were three times greater among the patients with more severe, recurrent depression receiving combined therapy when compared to those treated with IPT or CBT alone (see Figure 22.4).

Perhaps the most influential single study on combined therapy was the two-center trial of Klerman, DiMascio, Weissman, and colleagues (DiMascio, Weissman, Prusoff, Neu, Zwiling, & Klerman, 1979; Weissman, Prusoff, DiMascio, Neu, Goklaney, & Klerman 1979). These investigators studied IPT and amitriptyline, singly and

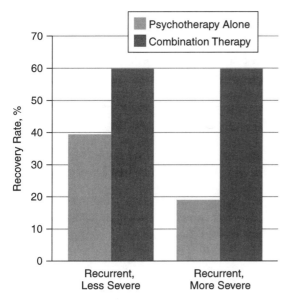

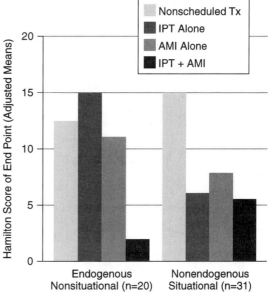

FIGURE 22.4   Recovery rates of patients in midlife (younger than 60 years) with recurrent major depression as a function of severity and treatment type. (Reprinted from Thase et al. 1997c).

FIGURE 22.5   Prusoff et al. (1980) found that only combined therapy was effective for treatment of endogenous, nonsituational depression, whereas all three active therapies were useful for nonendogenous, situational depression. (Adapted from Thase and Friedman, 1999.)

in combination, using a factorial design that included a low-contact, treatment-on-demand comparison group. The main findings indicated that the two component monotherapies were superior to the comparison group and that the combination condition was superior to the monotherapies on symptom measures and response rates (see Figure 22.1; DiMascio et al., 1979). Of note, a further analysis of various clinical subgroups indicated that the three active therapies were comparably effective for the subset of patients who met Research Diagnostic Criteria (Spitzer, Endicott, & Robins, 1978) for situational, nonendogenous major depressive disorder (Prusoff, Weissman, Klerman, & Rounsaville, 1980). By contrast, the additive benefit of the combination strategy was substantial among the subset of patients with nonsituational, endogenous depressive subtype (see Figure 22.5). These findings thus appear quite similar to the results of Thase et al. (1997c). Therefore, it would appear that clinicians could use either the severe/recurrent grouping or the endogenous depression construct to select depression cases likely to benefit from the combination of psychotherapy and antidepressant medication.

There are no other comparative studies of the combination of IPT and pharmacotherapy as

acute phase treatments. However, Frank and colleagues (1990) and Reynolds, Frank, Perel et al. (1999) evaluated this combination for prevention of recurrent depression. All of the patients who began these studies received combination therapy during the acute and continuation phases of treatment. During the 36-month, blinded preventive phase of the Frank et al. (1990) study, there was no evidence that continued monthly IPT sessions in combination with high-dose imipramine offered greater protection than pharmacotherapy alone (see Figure 22.6; Frank et al., 1990). This finding is similar to the results of an earlier, nine-month relapse prevention (continuation phase) study conducted by Klerman et al. (1974). Frank et al. did find that monthly IPT sessions alone had a significant preventative effect when compared to the group that was randomized to the placebo condition. Thus, a relatively minimal dose of IPT did offset the risk of recurrent depression after withdrawal of active pharmacotherapy. The protective effect also was significantly larger for patients who participated in dyads that achieved above-average therapeutic specificity (Frank, Kupfer, Wagner, McEachran, & Cornes, 1991). Frank and colleagues are now

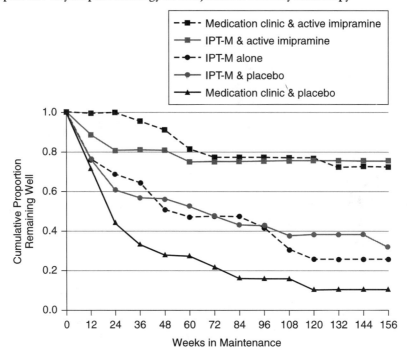

FIGURE 22.6 Outcome of the maintenance therapies in recurrent depression protocol. IPT-M = interpersonal psychotherapy maintenance. (Reprinted from Frank et al., 1990.)

conducting a study comparing three different doses of IPT (once monthly, every other week, and weekly) for women who responded to acute phase therapy with IPT alone.

The more recent study by Reynolds et al. (1999) enrolled 107 patients age 60 and above. All patients had stabilized after acute and continuation therapy with nortriptyline and IPT (total course: at least seven months of treatment). The findings from the double-blind, placebo-controlled maintenance phase were quite similar to those of Frank et al. (1990), with monthly maintenance IPT sessions having an intermediate effect between active nortriptyline and placebo. There was a trend suggesting that maintenance therapy with the combination approach was more effective than pharmacotherapy alone, particularly among patients over age 70.

There is little evidence from individual controlled studies that individual cognitive and behavioral therapies are more effective in combination with antidepressants than when provided alone to treat depressed outpatients (e.g., Beck, Hollon, Young, Bedrosian, & Budenz, 1985; Hersen, Bellak, Himmelhoch, & Thase, 1984; Hollon, DeRubeis, Evans, et al., 1992; Murphy,

Simons, Wetzel, & Lustman, 1984). These studies similarly yielded little evidence of an additive effect when combined therapy was compared to pharmacotherapy alone (Hersen et al., 1984; Hollon et al., 1992; Murphy et al., 1984).

It is possible that these studies have failed to show an advantage for combined treatment because of low statistical power, a ceiling effect, insensitive dependent measures, or some other methodological pitfall. Indeed, none of the trials reviewed previously had cell sizes large enough to give adequate statistical power to detect moderate effect sizes (e.g., a 15% to 20% difference in remission rates). It is also plausible that this generation of research was plagued by the necessity of using tricyclic antidepressants, which may have been less suitable for treatment of milder depressions, especially among women (Thase, Frank, Kornstein, & Yonkers, in press) and patients with reverse neurovegetative features (Stewart, Garfinkel, Nunes, Donovan, & Klein, 1998).

Nevertheless, Blackburn et al. (1981) did find a trend suggesting a small additive effect in their study, although this trend was evident only in one treatment setting. Among the more chronically and severely ill patients treated in a psychiatric clinic, combination treatment was somewhat more effective than both of the component monotherapies, which were comparable. By contrast, both combined treatment and CBT were substantially more effective than pharmacotherapy alone among general practice patients. Thus, the failure to detect an additive effect would appear to be the result of inadequate pharmacotherapy in the primary care setting. As illustrated in Figure 22.7, improvement in the CBT alone and in combination groups treated in the general practice clinic was almost identical. Moreover, response to combined therapy in the general practice setting also may have been dampened by significantly fewer sessions of CBT (five fewer therapy sessions than provided in the specialty clinic).

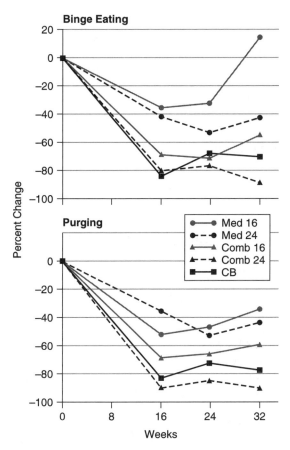

FIGURE 22.7 Changes in binge-eating and purging behavior of patients with bulimia nervosa treated with medication, Cognitive Behavioral Therapy (CBT), or a combination. (Reprinted from Agras et al., 1992.)

There is some preliminary evidence of a more meaningful additive effect in studies of CBT of hospitalized patients. There are two such studies that compared combined treatment with pharmacotherapy alone (Bowers, 1990; Miller, Norman, & Keitner, 1989); both reported trends favoring the combination strategy. A further analysis of Miller et al.'s study indicated that the combination strategy had an especially large effect for patients with high levels of dysfunctional attitudes; this subgroup responded quite poorly to pharmacotherapy alone (Miller, Norman, & Keitner, 1990). Using a dysfunctional attitudes index as a "screener" for the need of combined therapy has potentially meaningful implications because patients with such pessimistic and distorted patterns of thinking are at high risk of chronicity and relapse and are often overrepresented among treatment resistant populations (Thase, 1996). Further, this cognitive profile also has been associated with poor response to CBT alone (Whisman, 1993).

To date there are no published, controlled studies of combined treatment in chronically depressed outpatients. This is another significant gap in the literature because at least one-third of all depressions will run a chronic course at some point (Keller & Boland, 1998). Moreover, chronicity is associated with a relatively poorer response to both psychotherapy and pharmacotherapy as single modalities. A large multicenter trial (McCullough, Keller, Hirschfeld et al., 1996) comparing a modified form of CBT and pharmacotherapy with nefazodone, both singly and in combination, has recently been completed in a group of over 650 chronically depressed outpatients. Although the final results of the acute phase were not available at the time of writing this chapter, it appears that the group receiving combined treatment has substantially better response and remission rates than either of the monotherapy conditions.

One novel variation of the combined strategy is to add psychotherapy to ongoing pharmacotherapy, targeting residual symptoms. Fava and colleagues (1994; 1996; 1998a) studied this approach in a group of incompletely remitted antidepressant responders. A relatively brief, three-month course of a modified form of CBT was found to significantly reduce residual symptoms (Fava et al., 1994), improve chances for discontinuing medication without relapse (Fava et al., 1996), and convey a sustained decrease in recurrence risk (Fava et al., 1996, 1998a). A similar protective effect for sequential treatment was observed in a second study of patients with recurrent depression (Fava, Rafanelli, Cazzaro, Conti, & Grandi, 1998b).

Thase et al. (1997a) observed the converse effect among 38 patients who had not remitted fully with IPT. The addition of antidepressants (either imipramine or fluoxetine) after 8 to 16 weeks of individual IPT resulted in a 76% remission rate. This study was not controlled, and as a result, it is not possible to tease out the effects of active pharmacotherapy from those of spontaneous remission and placebo-expectancy. However, it is most unlikely that patients who could not benefit from up to four months of psychotherapy would have much of a placebo-expectancy response (Thase, in press; Stewart, McGrath, Quitkin, et al., 1993). The addition of pharmacotherapy should be considered as a treatment option if patients have not experienced symptomatic progress within two months of psychotherapy or if they seem to be "stuck" in an incomplete remission.

Bulimia Nervosa and Other Eating Disorders

Cognitive behavior therapy is considered by many to be the treatment of choice for bulimia nervosa, although there is evidence that interpersonal (Fairburn, Jones, Peveler et al., 1991) and supportive-dynamic (Freeman, Barry, Dunkeld-Turnbull, & Henderson, 1988) therapies may be helpful. Bulimia nervosa also is responsive to antidepressant medication (Walsh & Devlin, 1995). Results of several head-to-head comparisons have favored CBT over pharmacotherapy (Mitchell, Pyle, Eckert, Hatasukami, Pomeroy, & Zimmerman, 1990; Agras, Rossiter, Arnow et al., 1992), although there are notable individual differences in treatment responsiveness.

Three randomized clinical trials have studied combined treatment. Mitchell et al. (1990) found in their large ($n = 171$) factorial (2×2) study that the combination of imipramine (mean dose: 217 mg per day) and structured group CBT produced more pronounced improvements on measures of depression and anxiety than CBT plus pill placebo. Although the combined group did not experience greater improvements in frequency of binge eating or vomiting, this is likely to be the result of a ceiling effect because the improvements observed in the group CBT plus placebo group were substantial. Combined treatment also was significantly more effective than pharma-

cotherapy alone on a number of measures, even though the patients in the pharmacotherapy-alone group received 50 mg more medication daily (mean: 267 mg per day versus 217 mg per day).

Walsh, Wilson, Loeb et al. (1997) conducted a clinical trial employing two types of psychotherapy—CBT and supportive-psychodynamic therapy—in combination with either pill placebo or active pharmacotherapy. A fifth, unblinded condition received pharmacotherapy alone. The pharmacotherapy condition is noteworthy because patients in the active treatment condition received a two-stage intervention: the noradrenergically active tricyclic desipramine (up to 300 mg per day) followed, if necessary, by the selective serotonin reuptake inhibitor fluoxetine (up to 60 mg per day). By the end of the 16-week protocol, CBT was superior to supportive-dynamic therapy and active pharmacotherapy was superior to placebo. There was evidence of an additive effect for the combination of CBT and active pharmacotherapy but not for supportive-dynamic therapy when compared to the medication alone condition.

The third trial of combined treatment, by Agras et al. (1992), yielded less clear-cut evidence of a clinically meaningful additive effect across 24 weeks of protocol therapy: CBT plus desipramine was initially more effective than CBT alone, but there were no differences on most measures at week 16 (see Figure 22.7). The combined treatment group was significantly more effective than medication alone, and continued CBT sessions during medication discontinuation helped to reduce the risk of relapse. Pharmacotherapy in this study may have been compromised by a relatively low average dose (156.7 mg of desipramine per day; mean serum level 131 ng/ml). Moreover, with only 12 subjects in the combined cell, the study did not have the power to detect a moderate additive effect.

It would appear that bulimia nervosa responds best to either CBT or the combination of CBT and pharmacotherapy. The next generation of studies should focus on identifying indicators of additive benefit. A two-stage intervention (i.e., therapy alone, followed by the addition of pharmacotherapy) also warrants systematic study.

Panic Disorder

The best studied psychotherapies for panic disorder are CBT and, for patients with phobic avoidance, behavioral exposure (American Psychiatric Association, 1998). Effective pharmacotherapies include most antidepressants and potent benzodiazepines, such as alprazolam, clonazepam, and lorazepam. Comparisons across treatment modalities typically yield parity, although side effect complaints and relapse risk after medication discontinuation favor CBT (American Psychiatric Association, 1998). A further concern is that the potent benzodiazepines have a small but real liability for abuse and development of tolerance. Of note, CBT has been used to facilitate discontinuation of benzodiazepines after successful acute phase pharmacotherapy (Otto, Pollack, Sachs, Reiter, & Meltzer-Brody, 1993; Spiegel, Bruce, Gregg, & Nuzzarello, 1994).

A large number of studies have examined combined treatment of panic disorder, and many experts favor this approach (American Psychiatric Association, 1998). Although this literature is largely based on studies using tricyclic antidepressants, it is almost certain the results will generalize to pharmacotherapy with the SSRIs. A different story may emerge, however, from research using benzodiazepines as the antipanic medication (Spiegel & Bruce, 1997). Specifically, several early studies using moderate doses of lower-potency compounds such as diazepam failed to demonstrate additive effects (Hafner & Marks, 1976; Wardle, 1990). These findings heightened concerns regarding the amnestic effects of benzodiazepines (e.g., Curran, 1986), specifically, that medication effects might compromise learning during exposure therapy. Marks, Swinson, Basoglu et al. (1993) conducted a large, two-center, (London and Toronto) randomized trial comparing alprazolam (versus placebo) and exposure (versus relaxation) among 154 patients with panic disorder and agoraphobia. Results suggested that the addition of active alprazolam (up to five mg per day) to exposure had little beneficial therapeutic effects after the first four weeks of treatment. Further, combination therapy was more effective than alprazolam alone, reinforcing the conclusion that the behavior therapy had the stronger overall effect (Marks et al., 1993).

If one focuses on the small advantage for the combination early in treatment, this advantage must be weighed against longer-term outcomes. For example, relapse or symptomatic exacerbation after discontinuation of study medication occurred among slightly more than one-half of the patients who had received active alprazolam as compared to only 12% of the patients in the therapy plus placebo condition (Basoglu, Marks, Swinson, Noshirvani, O'Sullivan, & Kuch, 1994a). Closer examination of these data revealed a significant association between relapse risk and the patients' attribution of improvements to the benzodiazepine (Basoglu, Marks, Kilic, Brewin, & Swinson, 1994b).

It appears that the addition of benzodiazepines to behavior therapy does not actually disrupt learning *per se*, but may prevent the development of confidence in, and mastery of, the *in vivo* exposure strategies that are critical to successful treatment. In practice, when such a combination is used to hasten symptomatic responses, it would appear to be critical to help the patient recognize the value of the behavioral component and to de-emphasize the centrality of pharmacotherapy as the perceived mediator of change. The benzodiazepine should be subsequently tapered slowly, in concert with continued *in vivo* practice of behavioral strategies. These findings *do not* appear to apply to combination strategies employing antidepressants, probably because antidepressants do not rapidly suppress somatic cues of anxiety and, hence, do not undercut exposure. Nevertheless, there is a relapse risk associated with discontinuation of effective antidepressants that must be addressed. For this reason, sequential strategies may be preferred for many patients. CBT usually should be offered as a monotherapy, with the combination reserved for patients with more severe, chronic, or disabling disorders.

Obsessive Compulsive Disorder

The principal, empirically established treatments for obsessive compulsive disorder (OCD) include behavior therapy (emphasizing exposure and response prevention) and selected antidepressant medications with strong serotoninergic effects. Controlled studies consistently document that behavior therapy and pharmacotherapy with either selective serotonin reuptake inhibitors or the tricyclic clomipramine (Anafranil) benefit no more than 50% to 60% of people who begin treatment for OCD. Moreover, both forms of therapy have particular drawbacks. For example, relatively few practicing therapists provide the exposure-based behavioral intervention that is most useful for OCD and a significant minority of otherwise eligible patients declines to participate in exposure-based therapy (Mavissakalian, 1996). The serotoninergic antidepressants similarly are refused by a number of patients and these medications have intolerable side effects for 10% to

15% of those who agree to take pharmacotherapy (Griest, Jefferson, Kobak, Katzelnick, & Serlin, 1995).

Several studies have examined combined therapy for OCD (Marks, Stern, Mawson, Cobb, McDonald, 1980; Mawson, Marks, & Ramm, 1982; Van Balkom, De Haan, Van Oppen, Spinhoven, Hoogduin, & Van Dyck, 1998). Although not all studies are in agreement (Van Balkom et al., 1998), it appears that the effects of behavior therapy are enhanced or facilitated by concomitant antiobsessional pharmacotherapy. Conversely, it would appear that appropriate pharmacotherapy can be optimized by implementation of an exposure-based therapy. Several large studies on this topic have recently been completed and, hopefully, the results will permit a more definitive assessment of the magnitude of additive effects in the near future.

Other Anxiety Disorders

Social phobia, generalized anxiety disorder, and posttraumatic stress disorder are common and potentially disabling problems that can be treated effectively with psychotherapy or pharmacotherapy. The best documented psychotherapies are, yet again, behavioral and cognitive-behavioral therapies. Pharmacotherapies include antidepressants, the azapyrone compound buspirone (Buspar; GAD only), benzodiazepines (GAD only), and β-blockers (social phobia only).

Although the more chronic and severe forms of these disorders are logical indications for combined therapy, there are not yet any strong definitive studies in these areas that document additive effects (Beaudry, 1991; Mavissakalian, 1995). Until such data are available, clinicians would be well advised to consider sequential strategies instead of automatically recommending combinations. Researchers also would be wise to learn from the earlier studies of major depression and panic disorder to ensure that research on combined treatment effects is not compromised by low statistical power or design insensitivity.

Substance Abuse Disorders

The primary pharmacotherapies of substance abuse disorders are as follows: methadone maintenance (opiate dependence); naltrexone (opiate dependence and alcoholism); and disulfiram (relapse prevention of alcoholism). There are no effective pharmacotherapies approved for treatment of cocaine or marijuana abuse disorders. A number of other medications are used to manage acute drug and alcohol withdrawal states, which will not be considered further here.

The relative dearth of pharmacotherapies for substance dependence disorders is essentially matched by a limited number of "proven" psychotherapies. It does appear that the addition of CBT or supportive-dynamic psychotherapy improves the course of opiate dependent patients receiving methadone (Woody, McLellan, Luborsky et al., 1983), especially when patients have higher levels of anxiety or depressive symptoms (Woody et al., 1984). The combination of the tricyclic desipramine and CBT also was found to have additive effects for addicts with depressive symptoms in one study of cocaine dependence (Carroll, Rounsaville, Gordon et al., 1994). It appears that reduction of alcohol intake by a concomitant prescription of disulfiram similarly produced better improvements in a behavioral treatment program for polysubstance abusers. These types of studies should be seen as promising leads but in no way ensure that more is better. For example, Crits-Christoph and colleagues (in press) recently found in a large and well-controlled study of more than 400 cocaine addicts for whom the addition of CBT or supportive-dynamic therapy to a standard regimen of group drug counseling was no more effective than drug counseling alone. Moreover, adding professional psychotherapy to group drug counseling was significantly *less* effective than the treatment condition that received added sessions of individual drug counseling (Crits-Christoph et al., in press).

SUMMARY AND CONCLUSIONS

The combination of psychotherapy and pharmacotherapy offers substantial additive benefits for people suffering from a number of more severe mental disorders. There are numerous pragmatic and conceptual justifications for using psychotherapeutic and pharmacologic treatments in combination, but none is more compelling than reproducible evidence of higher response or remission rates or broader and more generalizable improvements in quality of life. Among the conditions that should not be treated with psychotherapy alone, schizophrenia and bipolar disorder are often treated with psychotherapy–pharmacotherapy combinations. When properly tailored as part of a psychosocial rehabilitation plan, social skills training, psycho-educational family therapy, and probably CBT have significant additive effects (when used in combination with appropriate antipsychotic medication) for those with schizophrenia. An emerging literature suggests that similar advantages for combined therapy may extend to treatment of bipolar disorder, although this research is still in the developmental stages.

Combined treatment does not have, as such, a reliable robust effect (when compared to competently administered monotherapies) that it should be championed as the treatment of choice for most patients with bulimia, OCD, panic disorder, or major depressive disorder, but it should not be reflexively championed (cf. Persons et al., 1996). It would appear that people with the symptomatically milder or less disabling forms of these common nonpsychotic disorders can be treated with a number of proven monotherapies at a lower cost than combined treatment, with case selection based on patient preference and availability. A more systematic approach to treatment sequencing could deliver even better outcomes when residual symptoms, medication discontinuation, or longer term prophylaxis are the targeted outcomes (e.g., Fava et al., 1994; Fava et al., 1998b; Spiegel et al., 1994).

For patients suffering from more severe or disabling episodes of depression, panic disorder, and bulimia, the extra cost of combined treatment is probably offset by evidence of better outcomes, both on symptomatic measures and selected mode-specific indicators (e.g., social functioning or assessments of cognitive distortions). The literature on major depressive disorder is the most fully developed and, for this indication, a combined treatment approach from the outset can be justified by high symptom severity and recurrent episodes, as well as inpatient status, psychiatric comorbidity, and chronicity. As very short average hospital stays mitigate against intensive inpatient treatment programs, the postdischarge phase of treatment should be the focus of psychosocial interventions.

The chances for additive effects can be enhanced by carefully integrating the two modalities. Such integration should include a clear rationale for both treatments, mutually supportive and coherent psycho-education, collaborative teamwork, and vigorous implementation of both strategies. These principles are particularly important when the treatments are provided by a team who conduct combined therapy, consisting of a nonmedical psychotherapist and a physician. Perhaps the most common team, consisting of a psychotherapist and a primary care physician, has received the least study, and it is worrisome that results from studies by specialists may not generalize automatically. Moreover, the indications for treatment by a single psychiatrist provider versus the standard, two-professional team still must be identified. A new generation of research must help to clarify if primary care physicians and psychotherapists can work effectively. Otherwise, practice guidelines based on empirical evidence should be revised to recommend that psychiatrists should conduct the majority of the pharmacotherapy.

REFERENCES

Agras, W. S., Rossiter, E. M., Arnow, B., Schneider, J. A., Telch, C. F., Raeburn, S. D., Bruce, B., Perl, M., & Koran, L. M. (1992). Pharmacologic and cognitive-behavioral treatment for bulimia nervosa: A controlled comparison. *American Journal of Psychiatry, 149*, 82–87.

American Psychiatric Association. (1993). Practice guideline for major depressive disorder in adults. *American Journal of Psychiatry, 150* (Suppl. 4), 1–26.

American Psychiatric Association. (1994). *Diagnostic and statistical manual of mental disorders.* Washington, D.C.: American Psychiatric Press.

American Psychiatric Association. (1997). Practice guideline for the treatment of patients with schizophrenia. *American Journal of Psychiatry, 154* (Suppl. 4), 1–63.

American Psychiatric Association. (1998). Practice guidelines for the treatment of patients with panic disorder. *American Journal of Psychiatry, 155* (Suppl. 5), 1–34.

Andrews, G., Brodaty, H., Hadzi-Pavlovic, D., Harvey, P. R., Holt, P., Tennant, C., & Vaughan, K. (1994). Treatment outlines for the management of schizophrenia: The Quality Assurance Project. *Australian and New Zealand Journal of Psychiatry, 28*, 14–22.

Ballenger, J. C., Davidson, J. R. T., Lecrubier, Y., Nutt, D. J., International Consensus Group on Depression and Anxiety, Bobes, J., Beidel, D. C., Ono, Y., & Westenberg, H. G. M. (1998). Consensus statement on social anxiety disorder from the International Consensus Group on Depression and Anxiety. *Journal of Clinical Psychiatry, 59* (Suppl. 17), 54–60.

Barden, N., Reul, J. M. H. M., & Holsboer, F. (1995). Do antidepressants stabilize mood through actions on the hypothalamic-pituitary-adrenocortical system? *Trends in Neuroscience, 18*, 6–11.

Basco, M. R., & Rush, A. J. (1996).

Cognitive-behavioral therapy for bipolar disorder. New York: Guilford Press.

Basoglu, M., Marks, I. M., Kilic, C., Brewin, C. R., & Swinson, R. P. (1994b). Alprazolam and exposure for panic disorder with agoraphobia attribution of improvement of medication predicts subsequent relapse. *British Journal of Psychiatry, 164,* 652–659.

Basoglu, M., Marks, I. M., Swinson, R. P., Noshirvani, H., O'Sullivan, G., & Kuch, K. (1994a). Pre-treatment predictors of treatment outcome in panic disorder and agoraphobia treated with alprazolam and exposure. *Journal of Affective Disorders, 30,* 123–132.

Beaudry, P. (1991). Generalized anxiety disorder. In B. D. Beitman, & Klerman, G. L. (Eds.), *Integrating pharmacotherapy and psychotherapy* (pp. 211–230). Washington, D.C.: American Psychiatric Press.

Beck, A. T. (1976). *Cognitive therapy and the emotional disorders.* New York: International Universities Press.

Beck, A. T., Hollon, S. D., Young, J. F., Bedrosian, R. C., & Budenz, D. (1985). Treatment of depression with cognitive therapy and amitriptyline. *Archives of General Psychiatry, 42,* 142–148.

Benton, M. K., & Schroeder, H. E. (1990). Social skills training with schizophrenics: A meta-analytic evaluation. *Journal of Consulting and Clinical Psychology, 58,* 741–747.

Blackburn, I. M., Bishop, S., Glen, A. I. M., Whalley, L. J., & Christie, J. E. (1981). The efficacy of cognitive therapy in depression: A treatment trial using cognitive therapy and pharmacotherapy, each alone and in combination. *British Journal of Psychiatry, 139,* 181–189.

Bowers, W. A. (1990). Treatment of depressed in-patients with cognitive therapy plus medication, relaxation plus medication, and medication alone. *British Journal of Psychiatry, 156,* 73–78.

Brown, G. W., Birley, J. L. T., & Wing, J. K. (1972). Influence of family life on the course of schizophrenic disorders: A replication. *British Journal of Psychiatry, 121,* 241–258.

Butzlaff, R. L., & Hooley, J. M. (1998). Expressed emotion and psychiatric relapse: A meta-analysis. *Archives of General Psychiatry, 55,* 547–552.

Caffey, E. M., Jr., Galbrecht, C. R., & Klett, C. J. (1971). Brief hospitlization and aftercare in the treatment of schizophrenia. *Archives of General Psychiatry, 24,* 81–86.

Carroll, B. J. (1991). Psychopathology and neurobiology of manic-depressive disorders. In B. J. Carroll & J. E. Barrett (Eds.), *Psychopathology and the brain* (pp. 265–285). New York: Raven Press.

Carroll, K. M., Rounsaville, B. J., Gordon, L. T., Nich, C., Jatlow, P., Bisighini, R. M., & Gawin, R. H. (1994). Psychotherapy and pharamcotherapy for ambulatory cocaine abusers. *Archives of General Psychiatry, 51,* 177–187.

Clarkin, J. F., Glick, I. D., Haas, G. L., Spencer, J. H., Lewis, A. B., Peyser, J., DeMane, N., Good-Ellis, M., Harris, E., & Lestelle, V. (1990). A randomized clinical trial of inpatient family intervention. V. Results for affective disorders. *Journal of Affective Disorders, 18,* 17–28.

Cochran, S. D. (1984). Preventing medical noncompliance in the outpatient treatment of bipolar affective disorders. *Journal of Consulting and Clinical Psychology, 52,* 873–878.

Conte, H. R., Plutchik, R., Wild, K. V., & Karasu, T. B. (1986). Combined psychotherapy and pharmacotherapy for depression: A systematic analysis of the evidence. *Archives of General Psychiatry, 43,* 471–479.

Corbishley, M., Beutler, L., Quan, S., Bamford, C., Meredith, K., & Scogin, F. (1990). Rapid eye movement density and latency and dexamethasone suppression as predictors of treatment response in depressed older adults. *Current Therapy Research, 47,* 846–859.

Crits-Christoph, P., Siqueland, L., Blaine, J., Frank, E. Luborsky, L., Onken, L., Muenz, L., Thase, M. E., Weiss, R. D., Gastfriend, D. R., Woody, G., Barber, J. P., Butler, S. F., Daley, D., Salloum, I., Bishop, S., Najavits, L. M., & Lis, J. (in press). Psychosocial treatment for cocaine dependence: Results of the National Institute on Drug Abuse collaborative cocaine treatment study. *Archives of General Psychiatry.*

Curran, H. V. (1986). Tranquillizing memories: A review of the effects of benzodiazepines on human memory. *Biological Psychology, 23,* 179–213.

DeBellis, M. D., Gold, P. W., Geracioti, T. D., Listwak, S. J., & Kling, M. A. (1993). Association of fluoxetine treatment with reductions in CSF concentrations of corticotropin-releasing hormone and arginine vasopressin in patients with major depression. *American Journal of Psychiatry, 150,* 656–657.

Depression Guideline Panel. (1993). Clinical practice guideline number 5. *Depression in primary care, Vol. 2. Treatment of major depression* (AHCPR Publication No. 93–0551). Rockville, MD: U.S. Department of Health and Human Services Agency for Health Care Policy and Research.

DiMascio, A., Weissman, M. M., Prusoff, B. A., Neu, C., Zwiling, M., & Klerman, G. L. (1979). Differential symptom reduction by drugs and psychotherapy in acute depression. *Archives of General Psychiatry, 36,* 1450–1456.

Drury, V., Birchwood, M., Cochrane, R., & Macmillan, F. (1996). Cognitive therapy and recovery from acute psychosis: A controlled trial. I. Impact on psychotic symptoms. *British Journal of Psychiatry, 169,* 593–601.

Duman, R. S., Heninger, G. R., & Nestler, E. J. (1997). A molecular and cellular theory of depression. *Archives of General Psychiatry, 54,* 597–606.

Fairburn, C. G., Jones, R., Peveler, R. C., Carr, S. J., Solomon, R. A., O'Connor, M. E., Burton, J., & Hope, R. A. (1991). Three psychological treatments for bulimia nervosa. A comparative trial. *Archives of General Psychiatry, 48,* 463–469.

Falloon, I. R., Boy, J. L., McGill, C. W., Williamson, M., Razani, J., Moss, H. B., Gilderman, A. M., & Simpson, G. M. (1985). Family management in the prevention of morbidity of schizophrenia: Clinical outcome of a two-year longitudinal study. *Archives of General Psychiatry, 42,* 887–896.

Fava, G. A., Grandi, S., Zielezny, M., Canestrari, R., & Morphy, M. A. (1994). Cognitive behavioral treatment of residual symptoms in primary major depressive disorder. *American Journal of Psychiatry, 151,* 1295–1299.

Fava, G. A., Grandi, S., Zielezny, M., Rafanelli, C., & Canestrari, R. (1996). Four-year outcome for cognitive behavioral treatment of residual symptoms in major depression. *American Journal of Psychiatry, 153,* 945–947.

Fava, G. A., Rafanelli, C., Cazzaro, M., Conti, S., & Grandi, S. (1998b). Well-being therapy. A novel psychotherapeutic approach for residual symptoms of affective disorders. *Psychological Medicine, 28,* 475–480.

Fava, G. A., Rafanelli, C., Grandi, S., Canestrari, R., & Morphy, M. A. (1998a). Six-year outcome for cognitive behavioral treatment of residual symptoms in major depression. *American Journal of Psychiatry, 155,* 1443–1445.

Frank, E., Hlastala, S., Ritenour, A., Houck, P., Tu, X. M., Monk, T. H., Mallinger, A. G., & Kupfer, D. J. (1997). Inducing lifestyle regularity in recovering bipolar disorder patients. Results from the maintenance therapies in bipolar disorder protocol. *Biological Psychiatry, 41,* 1165–1173.

Frank, E., Kupfer, D. J., Ehlers, C. L., Monk, T. H., Cornes, C., Carter, S., & Frankel, D. (1994). Interpersonal and social rhythm therapy for bipolar disorder: Integrating interpersonal and behavioral approaches. *The Behavior Therapist, 17,*143–149.

Frank, E., Kupfer, D. J., Hamer, T., Grochocinski, V. J., & McEachran, A. B. (1992). Maintenance treatment and psychobiological correlates of endogenous subtypes. *Journal of Affective Disorders, 25,* 181–190.

Frank, E., Kupfer, D. J., Mallinger, A., Thase, M. E., Swartz, H. A., Grochocinski, V. J., Houck, P. R. & Weaver, E. (1999). Early results from the Pittsburgh study of maintenance therapies in bipolar disorder I: Comparisons with prior controlled trials. (manuscript submitted for review).

Frank, E., Kupfer, D. J., Perel, J. M., Cornes, C., Jarrett, D. B., Mallinger, A. G., Thase, M. E., McEachran, A. B., & Grochocinski, V. J. (1990). Three-year outcomes for maintenance therapies in recurrent depression. *Archives of General Psychiatry, 47,* 1093–1099.

Frank, E., Kupfer, D. J., Wagner, E. F., McEachran, A. B., & Cornes, C. (1991). Efficacy of interpersonal psychotherapy as a maintenance treatment of recurrent depression. Contributing factors. *Archives of General Psychiatry, 48,* 1053–1059.

Freeman, C. P. L., Barry, F., Dunkeld-Turnbull, J., & Henderson, A. (1988). Controlled trial of psychotherapy for bulimia nervosa. *British Medical Journal, 296,* 521–525.

Friedman, A. S. (1975). Interaction of drug therapy with marital therapy in depressive states. *Archives of General Psychiatry, 32,* 619–637.

Garety, P., Fowler, D., Kuipers, E., Freeman, D., Dunn, G., Bebbington, P., Hadley, C., & Jones, S. (1997). London–East Anglia randomised controlled trial of cognitive-behavioural therapy for psychosis. II: Predictors of outcome. *British Journal of Psychiatry, 171,* 420–426.

Goldman, W., McCulloch, J., Cuffel, B., Zarin, D. A., Suarez, & Burns, B. J. (1998). Outpatient utilization patterns of integrated and split psychotherapy and pharmacotherapy for depression. *Psychiatric Services, 49,* 477–482.

Griest, J. H., Jefferson, J. W., Kobak, K. A., Katzelnick, D. J., & Serlin, R. C. (1995). Efficacy and tolerability of serotonin transport inhibitors in obsessive-compulsive disorder. *Archives of General Psychiatry, 52,* 53–60.

Grinspoon, L., Ewalt, J. R., & Shader, R. I. (1972). *Schizophrenia: Pharmacotherapy and psychotherapy.* Baltimore: Williams & Wilkins.

Hafner, J., & Marks, I. (1976). Exposure in vivo of agoraphobis: Contributions of diazepam, group exposure, and anxiety evocation. *Psychological Medicine, 6,* 71–88.

Hersen, M., Bellack, A. S., Himmelhoch, J. M., & Thase, M. E. (1984). Effects of social skill training, amitriptyline, and psychotherapy in unipolar depressed women. *The Behavior Therapist, 15,* 21–40.

Herz, M. I., Endicott, J., & Spitzer, R. L. (1977). Brief hospitalizations: A two-year follow-up. *American Journal of Psychiatry, 134,* 502–507.

Hogarty, G. E., Anderson, C. M., Reiss, D. J., Kornblith, S. J., Greenwald, D. P., Javna, C. D., Madonia, M. J., & Environmental Personal Indicators in the Course of Schizophrenia Research Group. (1986). Family psychoeducation, social skills training, and maintenance chemotherapy in the aftercare treatment of schizophrenia. *Archives of General Psychiatry, 43,* 633–642.

Hogarty, G. E., Greenwald, D., Ulrich, R. F., Kornblith, S. J., DiBarry, A. L., Cooley, S., Carter, M., & Flesher, S. (1997b). Three-year trials of personal therapy among schizophrenic patients living with or independent of family, II: Effects on adjustment of patients. *American Journal of Psychiatry, 154,* 1514–1524.

Hogarty, G. E., Ulrich, R. F., Mussare, F., & Aristigueta, N. (1976). Drug discontinuation among long term, successfully maintained schizophrenic outpatients. *Diseases of the Nervous System, 37,* 494–500.

Hollon, S. D., DeRubeis, R. J., Evans, M. D., Wiemer, M. J., Garvey, M. J., Grove, W. M., & Tuason, V. B. (1992). Cognitive therapy and pharmacotherapy for depression singly and in combination. *Archives of General Psychiatry, 49,* 774–781.

Keller, M. B., & Boland, R. J. (1998). Implications of failing to achieve successful long-term maintenance treatment of recurrent unipolar major depression. *Biological Psychiatry, 44,* 348–360.

Klerman, G. L., DiMascio, A., Weissman, M., Prusoff, B., & Paykel., E. (1974). Treatment of depression by drugs and psychotherapy. *American Journal of Psychiatry, 131,* 186–191.

Klerman, G. L., Weissman, M. M., Markowitz, J., Glick, I., Wilner, P. J., Mason, B., & Shear, M. K. (1994). Medication and psychotherapy. In A. E. Bergin & S. L. Garfield (Eds.), *Handbook of psychotherapy and behavior change* (pp. 734–782). New York: Raven Press.

Klerman, G. L., Weissman, M. M., Rounsaville, B. J., & Chevron, E. S. (1984). *Interpersonal psychotherapy of depression.* New York: Basic Books Inc.

Kuipers, E., Garety, P., Fowler, D., Dunn, G., Bebbington, P., Freeman, D., & Hadley, C. (1997). London–East Anglia randomised controlled trial of cognitive-behavioural therapy psychosis. *British Journal of Psychiatry, 171,* 319–327.

Kupfer, D. J. (1991). Long-term treatment of depression. *Journal of Clinical Psychiatry, 52* (Suppl. 5), 28–34.

Liberman, R. P., Blackwell, G., Wallace, C. J., & Mintz, J. (1994, May). *Reducing relapse and rehospitalization in schizophrenic patients treated in a day hospital: A controlled study of skills training vs psychosocial occupational therapy.* Presented at the 147th Annual Meeting of the American Psychiatric Association, Philadelpha, PA.

Liberman, R. P., Wallace, C. J., Blackwell, G., Kopelowicz, A., Vaccaro, J. V., & Mintz, J. (1998). Skills training versus psychosocial occupational therapy for persons with persistent schizophrenia. *American Journal of Psychiatry, 155,* 1087–1091.

Marder, S. R. Wirshing, W. C., Mintz, J., McKenzie, J., Johnston, K., Eckman, T. A., Lebell, M., Zimmerman, K., & Liberman, R. P. (1996). Two-year outcome of social skills training and group psychotherapy for outpatients with schizophrenia. *American Journal of Psychiatry, 153,* 1585–1595.

Marks, I. M., Swinson, R. P., Basoglu, M., Kuch, K., Noshirvani, H., O'Sullivan, G., Lelliott, P. T., Kirby, M., McNamee, G., Sengun, S., & Wickwire, K. (1993). Alprazolam and exposure alone and combined in panic disorder with agoraphobia: A controlled study in London and Toronto. *British Journal of Psychiatry, 162,* 776–787.

Marks, I. M., Stern, R. S., Mawson, D., Cobb, J., & McDonald, R. (1980). Clomipramine and exposure for obsessive-compulsive rituals: I. *British Journal of Psychiatry, 136,* 1–25.

Mavissakalian, M. R. (1995). Combined behavioral and pharmacological treatment of anxiety disorders. In L. J. Dickstein, M. B. Riba, & J. M. Oldham (Eds.), *Review of Psychiatry,* (Vol. 15, pp. 565–584). Washington, D.C.: American Psychiatric Press.

Mawson, D., Marks, I. M., & Ramm, L. (1982). Clomipramine and exposure for chronic obsessive-compulsive rituals: III. Two year follow-up and further findings. *British Journal of Psychiatry, 140,* 11–18.

May, P. R. A. (1968). *Treatment of schizophrenia.* New York: Science House.

McCullough, J. P., Keller, M. B., Hirschfeld, R. M. A., Russell, J. M., Dunner, D. L., Thase, M. E., & Kocsis, J. H. (1997). Collaborative study of nefazodone and CBT-CD in chronically depressed patients. *Biological Psychiatry, 42* (Suppl. 1), 254S.

McKnight, D. L., Nelson-Gray, R. O., & Barnhill, J. (1992). Dexamethasome suppression test and response to cognitive therpay and antidepressant medication. *Behavior Therapist, 23,* 99–111.

Miklowitz, D. J. (1996). Psychotherapy in combination with drug treatment for bipolar disorder. *Journal of Clinical Psychopharmacology, 16* (Suppl. 1), 56S–66S.

Miller, I. W., Norman, W. H., & Keitner, G. I. (1989). Cognitive-behavioral treatment of depressed inpatients: Six-and twelve-month follow-up. *American Journal of Psychiatry, 146,* 1274–1279.

Miller, I. W., Norman, W. H., & Keitner, G. I. (1990). Treatment response of high cognitive dysfunction depressed inpatients. *Comprehensive Psychiatry, 30,* 62–71.

Murphy, G. E., Simons, A. D., Wetzel, R. D., & Lustman, P. J. (1984). Cognitive therapy and pharmacotherapy. Singly and together in the treatment of depression. *Archives of General Psychiatry, 41,* 33–41.

Nelson, J. C., & Davis, J. M. (1997). DST studies in psychotic depression: A meta-analysis. *American Journal of Psychiatry, 154,* 1497–1503.

Otto, M. W., Pollack, M. H., Sachs, G. S., Reiter, S. R., Meltzer-Brody, S., & Rosenbaum, J. F. (1993). Discontinuation of benzodiazepine treatment: Efficacy of cognitive-behavioral therapy for patients with panic disorder. *American Journal of Psychiatry, 150,* 1485–1490.

Paul, G. L., & Lentz, R. J. (1977). *Psychosocial treatment of chronic mental patients.* Cambridge: Harvard University Press.

Paul, G. L., Tobias, L. L., & Holly, B. L. (1972). Maintenance psychotropic drugs in the presence of active treatment programs. *Archives of General Psychiatry, 27,* 106–115.

Perris, C. (1989). *Cognitive therapy of schizophrenia.* New York: Guilford Press.

Persons, J. B., Thase, M. E., & Crits-Christoph, P. (1996). The role of psychotherapy in the treatment of depression. Review of two practice guidelines. *Archives of General Psychiatry, 53,* 283–290.

Prusoff, B. A., Weissman, M. M., Klerman, G. L., & Rounsaville, B. J. (1980). Research diagnostic criteria subtypes of depression. Their role as predictors of differential response to psychotherapy and drug treatment. *Archives of General Psychiatry, 37,* 796–801.

Randolph, E. T., Eth, S., Glynn, S. M., Paz, G. G., Leong, G. B., Shaner, A. L., Strachan, A., Van Vort, W., Escobar, J. I., & Liberman, R. P. (1994). Behavioural family management in schizophrenia. Outcome of a clinic-based intervention. *British Journal of Psychiatry, 164,* 501–506.

Regier, D., Hirschfeld, R. M. A. Goodwin, F., Burke, J., Lazar, J., & Judd, L. (1988). The NIMH depression, awareness, recognition, and treatment program: Structure, aims and scientific basis. *American Journal of Psychiatry, 145,* 1351–1357.

Reynolds, C. F., III, Frank, E., Perel, J. M., Imber, S. D., Cornes, C., Miller, M. D., Mazumdar, S., Houck, P. R., Dew, M. A., Stack, J. A., Pollock, B. G., & Kupfer, D. J. (1999). Nortriptyline and interpersonal psychotherapy as maintenance therapies for recurrent major depression: A randomized controlled trial in patients older than 59 years. *Journal of the American Medical Association, 281,* 39–45.

Robbins, D. R., Alesi, N. E., & Colfer, M. V. (1989). Treatment of adolescents with major depression: Implications of the DST and the melancholic clinical subtype. *Journal of Affective Disorders, 17,* 99–104.

Roper. (1986). *Roper Report 86–8.* New York: Roper Organization.

Rosenheck, R., Tekell, J., Peters, J., Cramer, J.,

Fontana, A., Xu, W., Thomas, J., Henderson, W., Charney, D., for the Department of Veterans Affairs Cooperative Study Group on Clozapine in Refractory Schizophrenia. (1998). Does participation in psychosocial treatment augment the benefit of clozapine? *Archives of General Psychiatry, 55,* 618–625.

Rothman, K. J., & Michaels, K. B. (1994). The continuing unethical use of placebo controls. *The New England Journal of Medicine, 331,* 394–398.

Rounsaville, B. J., Klerman, G. L., & Weissman, M. M. (1981). Do psychotherapy and pharmacotherapy for depression conflict? Empirical evidence from a clinical trial. *Archives of General Psychiatry, 38,* 24–29.

Schatzberg, A. F., & Rothschild, A. J. (1992). Psychotic (delusional) major depression: Should it be included as a distinct syndrome in DSM-IV? *American Journal of Psychiatry, 149,* 733–745.

Schooler, N. R. (1978). Antipsychotic drugs and psychological treatment in schizophrenia. In M. A. Lipton, A. DiMascio, & K. F. Killam (Eds.), *Psychopharmacology: A generation of progress* (pp. 1155–1168). New York: Raven Press.

Schooler, N. R., Keith, S. J., Severe, J. B., Matthews, S. M., Bellack, A. S., Glick, I. D., Hargeaves, W. A., Kane, J. M., Ninan, P. T., Frances, A., Jacobs, M., Lieberman, J. A., Mance, R., Simpson, G. M., & Woerner, M. G. (1997). Relapse and rehospitalization during maintenance treatment of schizophrenia. The effects of dose reduction and family treatment. *Archives of General Psychiatry, 54,* 453–463.

Schooler, N. R., Levine, J., Severe, J. B., Brauzer, B., DiMascio, A., Klerman, G. L., & Tuason, V. B. (1980). Prevention of relapse in schizophrenia: An evaluation of fluphenazine decanoate. *Archives of General Psychiatry, 37,* 16–24.

Scott, J. (1996). Cognitive therapy of affective disorders: A review. *Journal of Affective Disorders, 37,* 1–11.

Seligman, M. E. P. (1995). The effectiveness of psychotherapy. The *Consumer Reports* study. *American Psychologist, 50,* 965–974.

Spiegel, D. A., & Bruce, T. J. (1997). Benzodiazepines and exposure-based cognitive behavior therapists for panic disorder: Conclusion from combined treatment trials. *American Journal of Psychiatry, 154,* 773–781.

Spiegel, D. A., Bruce, T. J., Gregg, S. F., & Nuzzarello, A. (1994). Does cognitive behavior therapy assist in slow-taper alprazolam discontinuation in panic disorder? *American Journal of Psychiatry, 151,* 876–881.

Spitzer, R. L., Endicott, J., & Robins, E. (1978). Research diagnostic criteria: Rationale and reliability. *Archives of General Psychiatry, 35,* 773–782.

Stewart, J. W., Garfinkel, R., Nunes, E. V., Donovan, S., & Klein, D. F. (1998). Atypical features and treatment response in the National Institute of Mental Health Treatment of Depression Collaborative Research Program. *Journal of Clinical Psychopharmacology, 18*, 429–434.

Stewart, J. W., McGrath, P. J., Quitkin, F. M., Rabkin, J. G., Harrison, W., Wager, S., Nunes, E., Ocepek-Welikson, K., & Tricamo, E. (1993). Chronic depression: Response to placebo, imipramine, and phenelzine. *Journal of Clinical Psychopharmacology, 13*, 391–396.

Teasdale, J. D., Fennell, M. J. V., Hibbert, G. A., & Amies, P. L. (1984). Cognitive therapy for major depressive disorder in primary care. *British Journal of Psychiatry, 144*, 400–406.

Thase, M. E. (1983). Cognitive and behavioral treatments for depression: A review of recent developments. In F. J. J. Ayd, I. J. Taylor, & B. T. Taylor, (Eds.), *Affective disorders reassessed: 1983* (pp. 234–243). Baltimore: Ayd Medical Communications.

Thase, M. E. (1992). Long-term treatments of recurrent depressive disorders. *Journal of Clinical Psychiatry, 53* (Suppl. 9), 32–44.

Thase, M. E. (1995). Re-educative psychotherapy. In G. O. Gabbard (Ed.), *Treatments of psychiatric disorders* (Vol. 1, pp. 1169–1204). Washington, D.C.: American Psychiatric Press.

Thase, M. E. (1996). The role of axis II comorbidity in the management of patients with treatment resistant depression. *Psychiatric Clinics of North America, 19*, 287–309.

Thase, M. E. (1997). Integrating psychotherapy and pharmacotherapy for treatment of major depressive disorder. Current status and future considerations. *The Journal of Psychotherapy Practice and Research, 6*, 300–306.

Thase, M. E. (1998). Depression, sleep, and antidepressants. *Journal of Clinical Psychiatry, 59* (Suppl. 4), 55–65.

Thase, M. E. (1999). How should efficacy be evaluated in randomized clinical trials of treatments for depression. *Journal of Clinical Psychiatry, 60* (Suppl. 4), 23–31.

Thase, M. E., Buysse, D. J., Frank, E., Cherry, C. R., Cornes, C. L., Mallinger, A. G., & Kupfer, D. J. (1997a). Which depressed patients will respond to interpersonal psychotherapy? The role of abnormal electroencephalographic sleep profiles. *American Journal of Psychiatry, 154*, 502–509.

Thase, M. E., Dubé, S., Bowler, K., Howland, R. H., Myers, J. E., Friedman, E., & Jarrett, D. B. (1996b). Hypothalamic-pituitary-adrenocortical activity and response to cognitive behavior therapy in unmedicated, hospitalized depressed patients. *American Journal of Psychiatry, 153*, 886–891.

Thase, M. E., Frank, E., Kornstein, S., & Yonkers, K. A. (in press). Sex-related differences in response to treatment of depression. In E. Frank (Ed.), *Sex, society, and madness: Gender and psychopathology*. Washington, D.C.: American Psychiatric Press.

Thase, M. E., & Friedman, E. S. (1999). Is psychotherapy, alone, an effective treatment for melancholia and other severe depressive states? *Journal of Affective Disorders, 54*, 1–19.

Thase, M. E., Greenhouse, J. B., Frank, E., Reynolds, C. F., III, Pilkonis, P. A., Hurley, K., Grochocinski, V., & Kupfer, D. J. (1997c). Treatment of major depression with psychotherapy or psychotherapy-pharmacotherapy combinations. *Archives of General Psychiatry, 54*, 1009–1015.

Thase, M. E., & Howland, R. H. (1995). Biological processes in depression: An updated review and integration. In E. E. Beckham & W. R. Leber (Eds.), *Handbook of depression* (pp. 213–279). New York: Guilford Press.

Thase, M. E., & Kupfer, D. J. (1987). Current status of EEG sleep in the assessment and treatment of depression. In G. D. Burrows & J. S. Werry (Eds.), *Advances in human psychopharmacology* (pp. 93–148). Greenwich, CT: JAI Press, Inc.

Thase, M. E., Kupfer, D. J., Fasiczka, A. L., Buysse, D. J., Simons, A. D., & Frank, E. (1997b). Identifying an abnormal electroencephalographic sleep profile to characterize major depressive disorder. *Biological Psychiatry, 41*, 964–973.

Thase, M. E., Kupfer, D. J., & Ulrich, R. F. (1986). Electroencephalographic sleep in psychotic depression: A valid subtype? *Archives of General Psychiatry, 43*, 886–893.

Van Balkom, A. J. L. M., De Haan, E., Van Oppen, P., Spinhoven, P., Hoogduin, K. A. L., & Van Dyck, R. (1998). Cognitive and behavioral therapies alone versus in combination with fluvoxamine in the treatment of obsessive-compulsive disorder. *The Journal of Nervous and Mental Disease, 186*, 492–499.

Vaughn, C. E., & Leff, J. P. (1976). The influence of family and social factors on the course of psychiatric illness. A comparison of schizophrenic and depressed neurotic patients. *British Journal of Psychiatry, 129*, 125–137.

Walsh, B. T., & Devlin, M. J. (1995). Psychopharmacology of anorexia nervosa, bulimia nervosa, and binge eating. In F. E. Bloom & D. J. Kupfer (Eds.), *Psychopoharmacology: The fourth generation of progress* (pp. 1581–1589). New York: Raven Press.

Walsh, B. T., Wilson, G. T., Loeb, K. L., Devlin, M. J., Pike, K. M., Roose, S. P., Fliess, J., & Waternaux, C. (1997). Medication and psychotherapy in the treatment of bulimia nervosa. *American Journal of Psychiatry, 154,* 523–531.

Wardle, J. (1990). Behavior therapy and benzodiazepines: Allies or antagonists? *British Journal of Psychiatry, 156,* 163–168.

Weissman, M. M., Prusoff, B. A., DiMascio, A., Neu, C., Goklaney, M., & Klerman, G. L. (1979). The efficacy of drugs and psychotherapy in the treatment of acute depressive episodes. *American Journal of Psychiatry, 136,* 555–558.

Wells, K. B., Burnam, M. A., Rogers, W., Hays, R., & Camp, R. (1992). The course of depression in adult outpatients. Results from the Medical Outcomes Study. *Archives of General Psychiatry, 49,* 788–794.

Whisman, M. A. (1993). Mediators and moderators of change in cognitive therapy of depression. *Psychological Bulletin, 114,* 248–265.

Woody, G. E., McLellan, A. T., & Luborsky, L. (1984). Psychiatric severity as a predictor of benefits from psychotherapy. *American Journal of Psychiatry, 141,* 1171–1177.

Woody, G. E., McLellan, A. T., Luborsky, L., O'Brien, C. P., Beck, A. T., Blaine, J., Herman, I., & Hole, A. (1983). Psychotherapy for opiate addicts: Does it help? *Archives of General Psychiatry, 40,* 639–645.

PART V

APPLICATIONS OF PSYCHOTHERAPY TO SPECIAL NEEDS

CHAPTER 23

PSYCHOTHERAPY WITH CHILDREN AND FAMILIES

MICHAEL C. ROBERTS, ERIC M. VERNBERG, AND YO JACKSON
The University of Kansas

PSYCHOTHERAPY WITH CHILDREN AND FAMILIES

Children, adolescents, and their families present a unique set of issues requiring specialized approaches from mental health professionals. Child applications of psychotherapy are perhaps more complex than adult-oriented psychotherapy given the multiple systems in which children interact (e.g., family, school, recreational and peer groups, juvenile justice, health care, social welfare). Today's psychotherapy, in contrast to that of 25 years ago and earlier, and in contrast to much adult therapy, requires the engagement of family members (nuclear and extended), peers, teachers, pediatricians and other health care professionals, police, social workers among others as needed. Interventions may range from an individual to a team approach to psychotherapy, often including families as active partners in the decision making.

The term *child psychotherapy* includes a full range of interventions for psychological and behavior change. As recommended in a model for training psychologists to provide services for children, adolescents, and families (Roberts, Carlson, Erickson et al., 1998), such strategies for change include:

1. Child–adolescent interventions (including individual psychotherapy, group psychotherapy, play therapy, behavioral and cognitive behavioral interventions, skills training, and psychopharmacology);

2. Parent interventions (including consultation and education/training);

3. Family interventions (including family therapy and systems, family empowerment/support); and

4. School and community interventions (including consultation with social services, the legal system, and medical settings). (p. 296)

In this chapter, we will provide an overview of these interventions.

Through interventions, professionals can target several aspects of the child's life including a) the child's behavior directly through intervention; b) the adult's behavior taken on behalf of the child (e.g., changing the child's immediate environment); c) the adult caregiver's behavior with the goal of changing the child's behavior (e.g., training parents or teachers in behavioral management techniques); d) the caregiver's own dysfunctional behavior (e.g., dealing with the adult's anger, anxiety, or depression); and, e) the institutions and the environment in general (e.g., changing juvenile justice laws or school behavior management policies).

There are several orientations or perspectives we hold as basic to understanding the process of psychological/behavior change in children, adolescents, and families. These include orientations to a) the developmental perspective; b) empirical foundations and competent services; c) family involvement; d) integrated comprehensive interventions; and e) prevention.

BASIC PERSPECTIVES FOR INTERVENTIONS WITH CHILDREN, ADOLESCENTS, AND FAMILIES

Developmental Perspective

The developmental perspective is a fundamental aspect of child and adolescent interventions. It recognizes that humans are in constant change;

for children and adolescents, this change process may be more accelerated and thus more evident. For children, the changes can be dramatic in the ability to think and reason, understand, and make decisions, in addition to the more obvious physical changes. Each domain of change may affect therapeutic interventions such as biological/physical, cognitive/intellectual, psychosocial, and moral development. In terms of psychotherapy, the developmental perspective includes determining when services might be most powerful in the developmental progression; when services are critically needed (i.e., when do problems most likely occur in the developmental pathways?); and what types of services are most effective (different interventions are likely more effective at different developmental levels). This perspective also includes improving the child's or adolescent's current situation, as well as preparing for later changes and possible interventions. Utilizing the developmental perspective, Vernberg, Routh, and Koocher (1992) coined the phrase *developmental psychotherapy* to connote the therapist's goal of returning the child to healthy developmental pathways.

Empirical Perspective

The reliance on empirically supported interventions is just as important for child and family therapy as it is for adult work. A downward extension of adult techniques and assumptions not only is inadequate, however, but it borders on unethical (see Roberts et al., 1998; Roberts, Erickson, & Tuma, 1985). Extending Gordon Paul's (1967) axiom, Saxe, Cross, and Silverman (1988) stated that psychotherapy with children should be based on research about treatment efficacy and effectiveness so that professionals can know "a) what therapy, b) under what conditions, c) for which children, d) at which developmental level, e) with which disorders, f) under what environmental conditions, and g) with which concomitant parental, familial, environmental, or systems intervention" (p. 803). Clinical research provides assistance in making these determinations. Unfortunately, however, Kazdin (1988) identified over 230 published forms of child therapy. We would suggest that the selection of a treatment strategy for different child problems should be based on its potential for effecting change, not on the clinician's loyalty to a modality (Shirk & Phillips, 1991). Thus, for particular cases, the selection should be from the modalities of empirically supported treatments. As we will show in later sections in this chapter, there is increasing

evidence for empirically supported interventions with children.

The American Psychological Association Division of Clinical Psychology has identified empirically supported interventions mostly for adult clients (Chambless, Baker, Baucom et al., 1998; Task Force on the Promotion and Dissemination of Psychological Procedures, 1995), whereas its Section on Clinical Child Psychology has evaluated the literature for psychosocial interventions for children and adolescents (Lonigan & Elbert, 1998). Additionally, there are other resources for evidence-based interventions with children (e.g., Frick, 1998; Hembree-Kigin & McNeil, 1995; Hibbs & Jensen, 1996; Hoagwood, Hibbs, Brent, & Jensen, 1995; Kazdin & Weisz, 1998; Silverman & Kurtines, 1996).

Family Orientation

Although many traditional child psychotherapy approaches have blamed the parent or family for the child's problems, newer approaches see the family in more complex interactions. This newer perspective implicates the family in the etiology and maintenance of problems; but, it also views parents as potent allies and confederates in implementing changes (Fauber & Long, 1991). From this perspective, the clinician also needs to know when not to involve the family (e.g., when a parent is not ready to make changes or help the therapy process). Instead of viewing family involvement as an either/or proposition, however, it should be viewed on a continuum. Fauber and Long suggest that by "working back from the problem," the clinician can identify and involve those specific interactive processes contributing to the child's dysfunction and necessitating family involvement.

Integrated/Comprehensive Interventions

Given the large number of settings in which children function, clinical child, pediatric, and school psychologists are recognizing that traditional individual psychotherapy often may not be appropriate. As a result, a new orientation has developed in which multiple strategies are implemented in an integrated, often multidisciplinary approach. These approaches are given different labels that reflect their origins, such as continuum of care, wraparound services, comprehensive and coordinated services, multisystemic therapy, and system of care. They generally share an integrative perspective involving recognition of the "complex, reciprocal interactions among social systems, including families, when problems are conceptualized and service systems are designed," and a collaboration of the various systems (formal and informal) involved with children and their families (Task Force on Comprehensive and Co-ordinated Psychological Services for Children, 1994, p. 18). Often conceptualized and implemented with particular target problems and theoretical orientations, the service integration model is not a psychotherapeutic intervention *per se* but a plan or vehicle for delivering psychological interventions. Several excellent implementations of these comprehensive interventions are available (e.g., Haapala, 1996; Hanley, 1996; Lutzker, 1996; Schoenwald, Henggeler, Pikrel, & Cunningham, 1996). Such an orientation to integrated, comprehensive care may be undertaken by a psychologist working in a large project or team, or by an independent practitioner who maintains ongoing contact and consultation with the various child or adolescent agencies and settings. Involving more than just a single person makes such interventions with children, adolescents, and their families quite complex.

Prevention

The concepts of prevention are, all too often, viewed as dichotomous from those of psychotherapy in that these prevention interventions are aimed at arresting the development of a problem in children so that subsequent psychotherapy is unnecessary. Thus, prevention typically is conceived as taking action before the problem occurs, or early enough to curtail development (Roberts & Peterson, 1984). Heller and colleagues (in this volume) offer an overview of prevention concepts. Only a few prevention programs, however, have received adequate empirical validation, including those for problems of "mental health, academics, physical health and sexuality, drug use, injuries, and physical abuse" (Durlak, 1997, p. 178).

Successful preventions involve the use of comprehensive, multilevel interventions, an emphasis on protective and positive factors (through the acquisition of coping and adaptive skills), the involvement of parents, the application of sound theoretical and empirical bases, and community or collaborative arrangements. A preventive orientation also involves clinical interventions to insure that current problems are not developed further, that potential problems are avoided, and that the child and family have learned adaptive behavior.

PSYCHOTHERAPY OUTCOMES AND EVALUATION

Whether psychotherapy works is a question that has been posed over several decades. In terms of psychotherapy outcomes with children, Hans Eysenck made the first narrative review of the extant literature in 1952. Based on a rather sparse literature, he concluded that children undergoing psychotherapy did not improve therapeutically more than children placed on a waiting list or in a baseline control condition. Other narrative reviews from this era reached similar conclusions (Levitt, 1957, 1963). That is, the then in-vogue forms of psychotherapy (traditional psychoanalysis and play therapy) were not better than spontaneous remission of symptoms. Later narrative and qualitative reviews have yielded more favorable conclusions as increasing numbers of studies have found that behavioral and cognitive-behavioral interventions result in positive outcomes relative to appropriate comparison groups.

Meta-Analytic Studies of Treatment Outcome

Relative to the earlier narrative reviews, meta-analytic procedures are more objective in their consolidation and integration of results from numerous treatment evaluation studies. In this meta-analytic approach, all reviewed studies are combined statistically to produce a mean effect size statistic. This statistic is based on calculating the posttreatment differences on psychological measures for those who receive treatment as compared to those who did not—the mean difference for the two-group comparison is then divided by the variability in the group (such as the standard deviation of the nontreated sample). Each individual study results in an effect size statistic. In meta-analysis, the effect sizes for all the studies are aggregated with a resulting mean effect size. Larger mean effect sizes reflect more effective treatments, using the following general interpretation ranges: small: 0.2–0.4; medium: 0.5–0.7; and large: 0.8–1.0.

The first meta-analysis of therapy with children (ages 12 years and younger) examined 64 studies and generated a moderately high mean effect size of 0.71; this meant that the children who received psychotherapy were better off in their posttreatment functioning than were 76% of the control group receiving no treatment (Casey & Berman, 1985). Comparing effect sizes according to broad categories, these researchers noted that behavioral treatments were more effective than nonbehavioral. Problems of design and methodological differences, however, led these researchers to conclude that there was no definitive evidence that one form of psychotherapy was more effective than any other. (Overall, their findings that support the efficacy of psychotherapy with children parallel those found in a meta-analysis of adult psychotherapy [Smith & Glass, 1977]).

A later meta-analysis by Weisz, Weiss, Alicke, and Klotz (1987) obtained a mean effect size of 0.79. Their analysis included 105 outcome studies in which interventions were made with children ages 4–18, with a range of presenting problems. They noted that there was a predominance of behaviorally based interventions in the later studies included in their analysis. Weisz et al. concluded that, across all therapy modalities and types of studies, children receiving psychological treatments were functioning better after treatment than were 79% of the children in the control groups. When only the best research designs were analyzed, the resulting effect sizes found that behavioral treatments received stronger support (0.93) than nonbehavioral interventions (0.45).

A third meta-analysis reviewed 223 studies of therapy outcomes with children and adolescents (Kazdin, Bass, Ayers, & Rodgers, 1990). This review obtained a mean effect of 0.88 for comparisons of treated children versus nontreated (i.e., on average, treated children had better outcomes than 81% of children without treatment). Other meta-analyses, with increasing degrees of sophistication in selecting the variables to include and control, have been conducted and similar results have been found (e.g., Weisz & Weiss, 1993; Weisz, Weiss, Han, Granger, & Morton, 1995). Some of the differences in effect size derive from methodological differences and inclusion of different studies. Over all the meta-analytic studies, two conclusions consistently can be drawn. First, psychotherapy with children results in large effects exceeding any change resulting from not receiving treatment. Second, these studies find that behaviorally based therapies produced better outcomes than more traditional approaches.

More focused studies using meta-analysis found medium to large mean effect sizes for cognitive behavioral interventions (Durlak, Fuhrman, & Lampman, 1991), prevention (Durlak & Wells, 1997), training social competence (Beelmann, Pfingsten, & Losel, 1994), family therapy

(Hazelrigg, Cooper, & Borduin, 1987), and child and adolescent behavior therapy (Allen, Tarnowski, Simonian, Elliott, & Drabman, 1991). On a broader scale, Lipsey and Wilson (1993) collected findings of 302 meta-analytic studies on a continuum of therapeutic modalities and outcomes with their associated mean effect sizes (many of them with child, adolescent, and family therapies). They analyzed the "overwhelmingly positive" effect sizes and concluded that "well-developed psychological, education, and behavior treatment is generally efficacious" (p. 1181). A grand mean effect size was calculated at 0.47 ($SD = 0.28$). These researchers suggest that effect sizes for psychological treatment are not trivial and generally demonstrate practical efficacy as well as statistical significance.

There are many criticisms and limitations raised about meta-analyses and the meaningfulness of the effect size statistic, as well as the selection criteria for the studies included (Weisz & Weiss, 1993). One particularly important limitation is that most studies included in meta-analyses were conducted in research or training clinics using analog situations rather than in the field, testing clinical practices. Thus, the generalizability of the findings is restricted in application to what clinicians actually may do in practice. Differentiation of the terms *efficacy* and *effectiveness* is being promoted to distinguish the proof of outcome in research clinics versus field utility.

Despite the research being conducted with a focus on both efficacy and effectiveness, the treatment clinicians report utilizing in their own practice, such as psychodynamic therapy, often is not what the leading edge researchers are examining, such as behavioral and cognitive-behavioral interventions (see Kazdin, 1993; Shirk & Russell, 1992). This discrepancy suggests two conclusions: a) clinical researchers should give greater attention to what the clinicians actually do in therapy; and b) practicing clinicians should give greater attention to what the research literature indicates are empirically supported therapeutic interventions (Roberts & Hurley, 1997).

Kazdin (1993) outlined seven research questions for research into psychotherapy outcome with children, adolescents, and families. Clinical researchers should examine

1. What is the outcome of treatment versus receiving no treatment?

2. What are the components of the intervention contributing to any changes?

3. What are the parameters of the intervention

that can be changed by the therapist in order to improve the outcome?

4. What is the relative effectiveness of the various interventions used for the problem?

5. What therapy approaches can be combined in order to improve treatment outcome?

6. What roles are played by different therapy processes in the treatment?

7. What is the impact of differing characteristics of client, family, or therapist singly or in combination with various treatment approaches?

Other Therapeutic Outcomes

The primary goal of psychotherapy with children, adolescents, and families is to improve the behavioral functioning of those exhibiting psychological problems. These are best measured by behavioral and psychological instruments such as are used in the treatment outcome studies included in the meta-analytic research. Several other measures are of interest in understanding the effects of psychotherapy. These will be noted briefly here.

Treatment Acceptability

Because a variety of therapeutic techniques is used by psychologists, clinical researchers have been interested in assessing their social validity. This is called *acceptability of treatment*, and includes the attitudes and judgments of clients, professionals, and the public about the psychological treatment procedures. That is, are the procedures considered reasonably useful and appropriate for the presenting problem and characteristics of the child or adolescent client? A fairly large literature has developed concerning acceptability of alternative treatments for children's presenting problems. These are summarized by Calvert and Johnston (1990). They found that acceptable interventions seemed to be those using positive reinforcement and practice, whereas unacceptable interventions included more negative techniques such as corporal punishment, shock, and paradoxical interventions. They found that quite a few common psychological interventions have not been evaluated sufficiently in terms of treatment acceptability, including play therapy, family therapy, and many cognitive behavioral techniques.

Client Satisfaction

A measure of the perception and attitudes during and after psychological treatment is known generally as consumer, or client, satisfaction with services. Additionally, the clinician may secure satisfaction ratings from the referral sources. These demonstrations of "quality of care" are useful ways of documenting practice patterns and of understanding the process of client change, if used appropriately. They are also subject to manipulation and bias (Roberts & Hurley, 1997). Related to child and family therapy, several excellent research examples are available regarding client and referral source satisfaction. For example, the evaluation of a pediatric psychology outpatient practice demonstrated the percentages of favorable perceptions of services and interventions (e.g., Schroeder, 1996; Schroeder, Gordon, Kanoy, & Routh, 1983). Satisfaction ratings for an HMO-based behavioral pediatrics clinic indicated parents liked the treatment recommendations (Charlop, Parrish, Fenton, & Cataldo, 1987; Finney, Riley, & Cataldo, 1991). Parental perceptions of services for children with special health needs provided feedback for improving psychological treatments and logistical issues of the agency (Krahn, Eisert, & Fifield, 1990). Referral source satisfaction for inpatient consultation and liaison services also have been generally favorable (e.g., Olson & Netherton, 1996; Rodrigue, Hoffman, Rayfield, et al., 1995). Most studies of the satisfaction with services have measured the parents' perceptions, and only a few have examined the perceptions of the child or adolescent client (e.g., Garland & Besinger, 1996).

Cost Offset

Some studies have examined the cost of mental health care, but one of the more intriguing comparisons relevant to issues of managed care is the question of whether providing psychological services reduces the client's use of other, more expensive medical services (Roberts & Hurley, 1997). This savings is called the *medical cost offset*. Early reports of health maintenance organizations (HMOs) found that medical costs are offset by psychological services (e.g., Cummings & Follette, 1968; Mumford, Schlesinger, Glass, Patrick, & Cuerdon, 1984). A few studies examined the offset effect for child psychological services. For example, Rosen and Wiens (1979) found that psychological evaluation and treatment of children reduced medical usage by 41%, reduced psychiatric inpatient hospitalizations by 35%, and also significantly reduced their number of prescriptions and number of presenting medical problems. Similar significant medical cost offsets have been found in studies of a neighborhood clinic for children and adolescents in a diverse cultural and ethnic population (Graves & Hastrup, 1981), of an HMO with long-term follow-up (Hankie, Starfield, Steinwachs, Benson, Livingston, & Katz, 1984); and of a behavioral pediatrics unit providing psychological consultation and services in a large medical plan (Finney et al., 1991; Finney, Lemanek, Cataldo, Katz, & Fuqua, 1989). In general, these clinical studies have found that multifaceted, brief interventions were effective and resulted in lower usage of medical services. Some have argued that offset gains are illusory (Fraser, 1996). Nonetheless, the cost benefit of psychotherapy with children requires additional examination.

BEHAVIORAL INTERVENTIONS

A large and growing literature supports the use of behaviorally based therapies with children (Powers & Rickard, 1992; Watson & Gresham, 1998). This theoretical approach covers a wide array of techniques, all related to the direct observation of the child in naturalistic settings and the careful changing of the contingencies controlling the child's behavior. Behavior therapy relies on the principles of learning applied through an experimental analysis of behavior (Bandura, 1969; Kanfer & Phillips, 1970). The underlying conceptualization is that all behaviors, adaptive and maladaptive, are governed by the same learning principles. Simply, behaviors that are learned can be unlearned. Furthermore, the important behaviors are observable and measurable in some way. The principal focus of behavior therapy is to modify the environmental contingencies producing the maladaptive behavior, while enhancing the conditions under which adaptive behavior is exhibited. There is little attention given to the past except in understanding the conditions of current behaviors. Traditional assessment techniques are not frequently employed by behavioral clinicians because they are not perceived to add useful information about the relationship of environmental events and the child's problematic behavior (Gresham & Lambros, 1998). Instead, behavior therapy relies on a careful assessment known as a functional analysis of behavior. This analysis is a systematic way of gathering information so that the behaviors can be described operationally and precisely, with an understanding of what conditions either produce or reduce the be-

haviors (generally known as contingencies). This procedure requires an examination of a problem behavior's antecedents, the behavior itself, and the environmental consequences following the behavior (frequently summarized as the A-B-C model). The behavioral approach assumes that effective interventions can be made by changing the contingency relationships of the behavior to its antecedents and consequences.

Given its bases in experimental methodology, behavior therapy utilizes detailed measurement and treatment procedures. Behavioral interventions can be implemented in a variety of settings such as the home and other living situations, school classrooms, and playgrounds. Frequently, the behavior therapist will observe and intervene with the child in his or her natural setting or in an analog situation. To implement the therapeutic changes, the behavioral intervention may include the child and the adults or peers in the child's environment. In order to assess and change the contingencies, the therapist may use others' observations such as a teacher's notes to parents about a child's misbehavior at school, the parents' records of a child's complaints about stomach pains, or the child's self-recording of bed wetting.

Behavioral interventions are most successful when discrete behaviors are identified for modification. Nonetheless, complex sequences of behaviors have been successfully addressed, such as changing parents' behavior specifically and generally toward their children (e.g., Hembree-Kigin & McNeil, 1995), altering child abusive behaviors (Lutzker, 1996), and replacing anxious and phobic responses to situations with adaptive behaviors (Silverman & Kurtines, 1996). The choice of which behavior to target in behavioral interventions typically is made by considering what is most troubling to caregivers or the child, and what problems seem most amenable to intervention. Behavioral interventions generally are categorized into operant techniques, respondent conditioning, and combinations of procedures. These will be defined briefly with examples.

Operant-Based Intervention

Skinner (1938, 1953) is credited with developing the principles of operant conditioning. Others have expanded substantially the literature demonstrating the experimental bases and empirically validated applications of the operant-based interventions.

Reinforcement

Positive reinforcement most frequently is used in interventions in which the presentation of a stimulus immediately after a targeted behavior occurs, thereby producing an increase in that behavior. In negative reinforcement, the removal of a stimulus contingent to a behavior increases the likelihood that the behavior will increase in frequency. Examples of positive reinforcement in treatment include systematic rewards or points redeemable for something valued. Rewards might include a toy or extra recess time for a child to stay in his seat or not talk in the classroom; stickers or access to special toys for a child with enuresis for having a dry bed in the morning; or access to the television, telephone, or computer for an adolescent who refrains from mouthing-off or who completes homework assignments.

Occasionally, teaching a child to perform specific behaviors or tasks requires breaking down the behaviors into smaller steps. In this situation, the therapist may have to shape small changes in the child's behavior by reinforcing approaches to the desired goal behaviors. Prompts may be given by the therapist, teacher, or parent to indicate to the child when a behavior should be exhibited. These prompts then are removed systematically or faded out so that the child does not need them to guide the performance of the desired behavior. The term *differential reinforcement of other behavior (DRO)* refers to the application of reinforcement to behaviors that are incompatible with or in place of the problem behavior. Thus, a child who is reinforced for studying may replace his disruptive behavior with this more positive behavior. When a child is reinforced for positive behaviors, these gradually replace the presenting problems. DiLorenzo (1988) and Powers and Rickard (1992) summarize the parameters of reinforcement to increase behaviors. Classrooms or housing units (e.g., group homes) often utilize a system of reinforcement wherein pupils or housemates are given reinforcements for desired behaviors. These systems are called token economies because they use tokens or points to stand in for the direct reinforcer. When a child earns a set number of points through adaptive behavior, he or she can trade them for backup reinforcers in the form of privileges of television watching or free time. The use of positive reinforcement has been favorably evaluated in treatment acceptability studies (Calvert & Johnston, 1990).

Extinction

When a reinforcement is withheld for a previously reinforced behavior, that behavior tends to decrease in frequency. When advised by a therapist to employ extinction or nonreinforcing behaviors, the parent or teacher is instructed to ignore the child's attention-getting behaviors, crying, or temper tantrums. Usually, this ignoring leads to an increase or burst of the maladaptive behavior, but if used consistently and with proper implementation, the child's behavior will not be reinforced and therefore no longer exhibited. Some behaviors are difficult to ignore over a period of time, so this procedure is used selectively (DiLorenzo, 1988).

Time-out from reinforcement sometimes is thought to be an extinction procedure in that, when an inappropriate behavior is exhibited, the child is removed from the environment so that no reinforcement is given for it and he or she also does not get to engage in other reinforcing activities. In practice, time-out may be placing a child in a chair or a room away from other activities (see Hembree-Kigin & McNeil, 1995). Time-out procedures vary with different clinical researchers and have been widely implemented, often inappropriately so that the technique loses its power to change behavior. Some conceptualizations include time-out as a punishment technique. Time-out is frequently recommended as part of parent training techniques such as Eyberg's Parent–Child Interaction Therapy (Hembree-Kigin & McNeil, 1995), and Barkley's interventions with defiant children and children with attention deficit hyperactivity disorder, known as ADHD (Barkley, 1997a).

Punishment

The application of a stimulus designed to reduce the probability of certain behaviors is designated in behavioral approaches as punishment. Several aspects of punishment have been researched in the behavioral literature. The application of noxious stimuli such as lemon juice, shock, water spray, bright lights, and noise have been used as contingent consequences for such behaviors as infantile gagging or rumination, biting, head banging and self-stimulatory behaviors (body rocking, teeth grinding). Spanking would be considered a punishment technique, but there is considerable controversy over its inclusion as a behavior control technique (e.g., Friedman & Schonberg, 1996). In a summary of the literature on treatment of ADHD, Pelham, Wheeler, and Chronis (1998) reported that negative consequences are "an effective and necessary component of classroom behavioral interventions" (p. 199). Overcorrection is a punishment technique used to reduce maladaptive behaviors by having a child correct his or her behavior not just to return to the previous situation but to improve or enhance the situation. For example, a disruptive boy might have to clean up not just a mess he created but the whole kitchen floor. Similarly, a girl who wet the bed at night might be required to clean the bed clothes in addition to making up the bed. In another punishment technique, response-cost refers to the withdrawal of a reinforcer or the application of a penalty or fine when a child exhibits a maladaptive behavior. Punishment techniques need to be clearly designed with immediate application and continually applied to be effective. Because punishment is effectively targeted at decreasing behavior excesses, most behavior therapists also design complementary reinforcement programs to increase more adaptive child behaviors. Programs of behavioral management frequently use systematic reinforcement and selective punishment through behavior contracts between the child and therapist or caregiver (e.g., Stokes, Boggs, & Osnes, 1986).

Respondent Conditioning

In contrast to operant techniques, respondent conditioning (or classical conditioning) has been used less in clinical applications. These techniques are based on Pavlovian principles in the pairing of behaviors and stimuli so that previously unrelated behaviors become automatically exhibited when a particular stimulus is produced. In behavioral interventions, respondent conditioning techniques are used in desensitization procedures to reduce a person's phobia or anxiety. The pairing of induced relaxation responses to anxious situations (*in vivo* desensitization) or anxiety arousing thoughts (systematic desensitization) diminishes the child's fears and phobias. For example, clinical research has demonstrated the efficacy of desensitization techniques with children's fears of animals, snakes, and school. Even when not employed in a desensitization procedure, the literature supports teaching children and adolescents relaxation skills so that they can self-induce a relaxed state that is incompatible with anxiety. An alternative to desensitization is flooding, in which the fearful child fully imagines

the worst end result of fears. Given the nature of referrals for clinical practice, however, desensitization and flooding techniques are infrequently employed.

Imitation and Modeling

Modeling employs the technique of having a model demonstrate a safe and successful interaction with a feared situation such that the child may imitate. Modeling has been used in the treatment of children's anxieties about hospitalization and surgery, fears of dogs and snakes, and social interactions (see review by Powers & Rickard, 1992). This technique has a supporting empirical research, but is infrequently used in clinical practice.

Behavioral Consultation

Child behavior therapists frequently assist others, particularly teachers and school personnel, in order to implement behavior management programs for whole classrooms as well as individual children. When the therapist does not do the actual intervention, behavioral consultation frequently is used to connote the process of assisting others to effectively use behavioral techniques of reinforcement (e.g., Bergan & Kratochwill, 1990; Erchul & Martens, 1997).

Parent Training

Over the last 25 years, one particularly well-developed form of behavioral interventions has been to train parents to manage their children's behavior in the home and in public. Parent training has taken several forms, but the most frequent is based on behavioral techniques for externalizing problems ranging from disobedience to conduct disorders (Brestan & Eyberg, 1998). Parent training and use of behavioral techniques by parents has been fairly well validated and treatment manuals exist to guide therapists (e.g., Barkley, 1997a; Forehand & McMahon, 1981; Hembree-Kigin & McNeil, 1995). Trade books directed at parents also have been published based on these techniques (e.g., Becker, 1971; Blechman, 1985; Forehand & Long, 1996; Patterson & Gullion, 1968). These can be effectively incorporated into a therapist's interventions through a bibliographic approach.

Issues About Behavioral Therapies

The numerous varieties of behavioral interventions have an extremely large literature only briefly touched on here. Objections are raised occasionally concerning interventions by therapists, parents, or others in the child's life being as being mechanistic and without acknowledgment of the child's emotional situation. Other objections include the assertion that giving rewards for good behavior by parents or teachers amounts to bribery, or that it undermines the child's intrinsic motivation. This latter argument ignores the rather obvious fact that most individuals are rewarded (at least financially, if not intrinsically) for doing what they ought to do (their jobs) and there is no reason to expect children to respond any differently to their environmental conditions. Furthermore, because the child typically is not intrinsically motivated to do the behavior before starting a reinforcement program, there is no motivation to undermine. Indeed, behavior therapists do not advise changing the contingencies of reinforcement for prosocial or the other positive behaviors that a child already exhibits. Another opposing argument is that the child or adolescent will develop new symptoms once the presenting problem is removed through effective behavioral interventions. There is little evidence that new or previously unrecognized maladaptive behaviors are created; moreover, behavior therapists would respond to this concern by noting that if such behaviors ever occurred, then behavioral techniques would work as well on those.

The generalizability of a child's behavior change also is noted as a problem in that behavioral changes in one situation are not necessarily exhibited in another situation. Behavior analysts have addressed this issue through the systematic programming of stimulus control (Stokes & Baer, 1977).

Social validity (Wolf, 1978) is a concept used by behavior interventionists to describe the "social significance of the goals of an intervention, the social acceptability of intervention procedures to attain those goals, and the social importance of the effects produced by the intervention" (Gresham & Lambros, 1998, p. 15). This concept basically requires the therapist to engage the environmental agents (e.g., teachers, parents) in bringing about behavior changes that the agents agree are desired. This concept also implies that behavioral therapists should utilize their powerful techniques only for those maladaptive behaviors truly judged to be clinically significant, not for those behaviors mildly troublesome to somebody but which are within the normal range of human behavior. Similarly, behavior therapists increasingly are endorsing the family-centered concepts of involving family members (including the af-

fected child) in decision making about what the interventions should target and entail.

The strength of behavioral interventions derives from its original and ongoing empirical-experimental approach. As noted in the meta-analyses described earlier, as well as in the recent reports of empirically supported interventions with children (Lonigan & Elbert, 1998), behavioral techniques provide stronger treatment effects than do other forms of intervention. Such findings probably reflect the fact that evaluative methodologies were part of behavioral interventions from the beginning, along with the sheer power of behavioral therapeutic interventions.

Another consideration in these interventions is that the process of child behavior therapy differs strongly from traditional child psychotherapy, which is based on a relationship between the therapist and the child. Some forms of behavior therapy do involve direct therapist contact, such as in systematic desensitization or other behavioral treatments for anxiety disorders (Ollendick & King, 1998; Silverman & Kurtines, 1996). In many behavioral interventions, however, parents, teachers, or houseparents are the most frequent intervenors because they are the resources actually in the child's or adolescent's environment.

COGNITIVE/BEHAVIORAL INTERVENTIONS

Along with accumulating research evidence over the last two decades, cognitive-behavioral interventions have become increasingly popular among child-oriented clinicians. These approaches incorporate many features of behavioral interventions (e.g., emphasis on learned nature of most behaviors), but with specific attention to the cognitions that underlie many actions and emotions. These cognitions are often a target for change, with the belief that such modifications will produce lasting behavioral or emotional changes. Behavior change continues to be a goal, and the full set of behavioral techniques, as described in the previous section, also may be used here. Unlike the behavioral approaches, cognitive-behavioral interventions emphasize a nonobservable aspect of human experience—cognition. The contents of such cognitions are thought to be acquired through experience, and to be governed by the laws of learning that have proved so powerful in explaining observable behavior.

Recently, important social-cognitive models of child psychopathology have appeared (e.g., Barkley, 1997b; Dodge, 1993; Slaby & Guerra, 1988). These models connect childhood experiences or biological states with the emergence of cognitive features (e.g., encoding or cue interpretation biases, attributional styles, impairments in executive functions) frequently found in children or adolescents with specific types of psychopathology, and they also identify targets for change. In the model proposed by Dodge (1993), early experiences set the stage for the development of knowledge structures, which in turn exert a pervasive influence on social information processing and behavior. Knowledge structures evolve over the course of a lifetime, and they are known by the more familiar terms of *schemas*, *scripts*, and *attitudes*. The content of knowledge structures is inferred from multiple sources of information, including overt behavior, verbalizations, and physiological responses. Some cognitive-behavioral interventions attempt to change these knowledge structures through directed activities; such activities aim to make the content more explicit and to increase conscious choices about their veracity. For example, one component of the cognitive mediation training (CMT) program offered to violent juvenile offenders by Guerra and Slaby (1990) focused on identifying the adolescents' attitudes and beliefs about violence, and then giving multiple challenges to the veracity or morality of beliefs that distinguish aggressive and nonaggressive adolescents. Changes in these attitudes and beliefs were accomplished via CMT, and they were accompanied by decreased aggressiveness. These changes in attitudes, beliefs, and aggressive behavior, however, did not endure at the two-year posttreatment follow-up. As such, the change of long-term adaptive knowledge structures may be questionable, especially if adolescents return to the same maladaptive circumstances.

Social information processing involves several steps: encoding information, assigning meaning, accessing responses, evaluating potential responses, and enacting responses (Dodge, 1993). Problem behavior may be linked to processing biases or deficits at any (or all) of these steps. Indeed a large body of research has found predictable biases or deficits for children with specific clinical disorders, including conduct disorder and depression (Dodge, 1993), attention deficit hyperactivity disorder (Barkley, 1997b), anxiety disorders (Costanzo, Miller-Johnson, &

Wencel, 1995), and autism (Ozonoff, Pennington, & Rogers, 1991). Examples of social information processing deficits include inability to encode nonverbal cues of emotion (autism or Pervasive Developmental Disorder [PDD]), impulsive responding (Attention Deficit Hyperactivity Disorder [ADHD]), or lack of access to a normal range of response options (depression, Conduct Disorder [CD]). Biases include such empirically-demonstrated phenomena as hostile attribution biases in highly aggressive children (labeled intention-cue detection deficit), inattention to positive cues (depression), or biases toward the selection of aggressive responses (CD). These social information deficits and biases are believed to arise from a combination of external events, such as patterns of interactions with caretakers and peers, and internal states, such as structural or biochemical characteristics of the central nervous system.

Core Procedures and Techniques
Problem-Solving Skills Training

Cognitive-behavioral interventions often attempt to influence social information processing and problem solving. A number of social problem-solving and social skills training programs are structured to address each component of an underlying social information-processing model (e.g., Guerra & Slaby, 1990; Kazdin, Siegel, & Bass, 1992; McGinnis & Goldstein, 1997; Pfiffner & McBurnett, 1997). Core elements across models typically include reading cues in self and others, sizing up the situation, generating and evaluating potential solutions, enacting the preferred solution, and evaluating outcomes. Early evaluations of general programs to improve social skills or social information processing in heterogeneous groups of children were not successful in demonstrating the efficacy of these programs (Ladd, 1985). Subsequent research has indicated that careful tailoring of general social information processing interventions to target an individual child's specific deficits or biases is more promising. Sustained effort and repeated practice in real-life situations also appear to be necessary (Kendall, Flannery-Schroeder, Panichelli-Mindel, Southam-Gerow, Henin, & Warman, 1997).

Verbal Self-Instruction

In this procedure, children are encouraged to invoke specific thoughts or self-statements when facing problematic situations. These may take the form of competence statements ("I am a brave boy; I can do this"), problem-solving statements ("I need to think about what I want to see happen"), coping statements ("Take a few deep breaths and relax my muscles"), or evaluative statements ("I did okay with that"). The use of self-instruction is generally encouraged through modeling, rewards, and practice (e.g., Graziano & Mooney, 1980; Snyder, McDermott, Cook, & Rapoff, 1997).

Self-Recording and Self-Monitoring

Increasing awareness of habits of thought and connections between experiences and emotions is often a goal in cognitive-behavioral treatments. Daily records of key thoughts or behaviors may provide cues about maladaptive thought patterns and also allow for reevaluation with the aid of a therapist. Such records of events and thoughts often are included in social problem-solving treatments (e.g., Kazdin, Siegel, & Bass, 1992). Preadolescents and early adolescents typically are limited in their ability to "think about thinking," and may need considerable help in generating useful records of their own thoughts and behaviors. If self-records are obtained by the therapist, they seem more likely to have value for early adolescents and younger children as a tool in generating alternative plans of action or reevaluating events than as a means to challenge automatic thoughts (Schrodt, 1992).

Relaxation Training

With proper presentation and environmental support, even relatively young children have been successfully taught to use relaxation techniques to cope with overarousal and fear (Graziano & Mooney, 1980; Kendall, 1994; Kendall et al., 1997). Imagery often is used with deep muscle relaxation.

Thought Stopping

This set of techniques is used by the therapist to help children cope with repetitive, intrusive thoughts that interfere with important functions such as sleep, academic performance, or social engagement. Typically, the child or adolescent is given an explanation as to why certain thoughts are irrational or maladaptive, along with how these can be ignored or blocked. For example, obsessive thoughts accompanying Obsessive Compulsive Disorder (OCD) have been framed as by-products of a biological disturbance that causes the mind to be oversensitive to fear cues

(March, Mulle, & Herbel, 1994), and the intrusive thoughts of Posttraumatic Stress Disorder (PTSD) are considered predictable sequelae to traumatic experiences (Yule & Williams, 1990). Techniques for stopping or ignoring such thoughts also are taught. Cognitive-behavioral therapists may tell youngsters with OCD to "boss back" the obsessive thoughts rather than letting the OCD boss them, and then be given practice and coaching in how to boss back in specific instances. In an example involving PTSD, adolescents were instructed to listen to soothing music when repetitive, intrusive thoughts interfered with their sleep (Yule & Williams, 1990). It is important to note that thought-stopping strategies should not be used in isolation. Rather, the intrusive thoughts are stopped or ignored when they interfere with important functions, and discussed and examined in therapy sessions.

In Vivo and Imaginal Exposure and Practice

Teaching children to use cognitive and behavioral strategies to cope with real-life problematic situations often requires practice and environmental support. For symptoms involving behavioral avoidance, exposure to the avoided situation may be accomplished through imagery, or in vivo, exposure. During exposure, it is important to help the child use the previously learned coping strategies and behavioral skills. The therapist often provides such help, but parents or other adults also may be enlisted to support exposure to previously problematic situations and to prompt the use of more adaptive behaviors and cognitions (Dadds, Heard, & Rapee, 1992; Graziano & Mooney, 1980; Kazdin et al., 1992).

Education and Information Giving

Explanations and information about the causes and consequences of problematic cognitions, feelings, and behavior are important components of many cognitive-behavioral treatments. Information giving often sets the stage for changing children's and family members' responses to troublesome circumstances (e.g., bossing back OCD symptoms, relaxing in the presence of irrationally feared stimuli). For example, in the manualized treatment for anxiety developed by Kendall, Kanda, Howard, and Siqueland (1990), the first eight treatment sessions focus on education and skills instruction, and the second eight on exposure and practice in real-life settings.

Issues About Cognitive Behavioral Therapies

Strengths

Cognitive-behavioral interventions have strong potential for treatment acceptability among children and parents. Most interventions clearly are focused on the concerns that brought the child to treatment and have a commonsense appeal and logic. Treatment duration is generally predictable, a characteristic that also appeals to managed care companies. Although many specific cognitive-behavioral interventions for children and adolescents have not yet received thorough treatment acceptability evaluation, those that have typically fared well.

A second strength is the availability of manualized cognitive-behavioral treatment programs. Treatment principles and techniques can be specified with a relatively high level of precision, facilitating outcome research and dissemination of treatments (Wilson, 1996). Some treatment manuals are organized around issues that cut across diagnostic groups, such as anger management (Lochman & Lenhart, 1993) and problem-solving and social skills (examples given earlier). Others address specific disorders or categories of disorders, including depression (Lewinsohn, Clarke, Hops, & Andrews, 1990; Temple, 1997), PTSD (Amaya-Jackson, March, Murray, & Schulte, 1998), anxiety disorders (Kendall et al., 1990), and OCD (March, Mulle, & Herbel, 1994).

A third positive attribute of cognitive behavioral psychotherapy is its firm foundation in empirically-supported conceptual models. The extensive research literature on cognitive psychology, social learning theory, and social information processing provides a strong rationale for many cognitive-behavioral treatments. Although the use of an empirically supported conceptual model does not guarantee clinical success, lacking such undermines the credibility of any form of child psychotherapy.

Developmental Focus

Adapting treatments to match the individual's developmental level requires careful attention to language, logic, and sequences of development (Shirk, 1998). For example, children's ability to use meta-cognitive strategies emerges gradually and follows a developmental sequence. Younger children (e.g., preschool and early elementary age) have difficulty recognizing the value of cognitive strategies or remembering to use them at the appropriate time. Mid-elementary-level children typically recognize the value of certain strategies, but fail to use them spontaneously. Clinically determined impaired children may function well below agemates in the acquisition of specific cognitive skills. Not only should the cognitive-behavioral skill represent the next step (rather than the final step) toward acquisition of mature skills, but also the rationale used with a specific child, the level of environmental support needed, and expectations for generalization and maintenance all depend on an accurate assessment of the child's current level of functioning.

Careful attention to the child's language skills also is paramount. Unfortunately, available evidence suggests that the use of language beyond the child's capacity for full comprehension occurs with some frequency in psychotherapy sessions (Russell, 1998).

State of Empirical Support

As a class, cognitive-behavioral interventions with children and adolescents have fared relatively well in treatment outcome research, reaching the "probably efficacious" level in many instances under current standards for establishing empirically supported treatments (Lonigan, Elbert, & Johnson, 1998). Open trial and single-subject studies provide substantial support, yet clinical trials with random assignment, using clinic-referred populations, remain to be conducted for most cognitive-behavioral treatments. Cognitive-behavioral treatments do not appear appropriate as a primary or sole therapy for certain disorders, including ADHD (Pelham et al., 1998), although they may play a useful role as auxiliary components or for addressing comorbid conditions.

Challenges

Uncertainty remains about the mechanisms by which cognitive-behavioral interventions work. Social-information processing itself seems difficult to modify, especially as patterns of perception and interpretation become more stable with increasing age (Crick & Dodge, 1994). Although improvements in symptoms often occur with CBT, supporting evidence for changes in basic social information processing is meager. Treatment generalization and maintenance of gains continue to be topics in need of further study. Evidence of durable effects for some treatments is emerging (e.g., Kendall & Southam-Gerow,

1996), and the conditions that promote long-term maintenance of treatment gains deserves increased attention. The combination of CBT for the child or adolescent, coupled with family or parent-focused treatments, appears particularly promising (Kazdin et al., 1992; Ollendick & King, 1998).

PSYCHODYNAMIC/ANALYTIC THERAPY

Next to physical medicine, psychoanalysis is the oldest form of treatment for child clinical disorders. Psychoanalytic therapy with children originated in classical Freudian psychoanalysis (Freud, 1974; Freud, 1955). This perspective suggests that maladaptive behavior is the product of mental forces and that psychological processes regulate behavior. Antecedents of behavior are assumed to be beyond the realm of conscious thought, and subsequent behavior is multiply determined and goal-directed.

Psychoanalytic treatment with children in its simplest form focuses on the use of the child's statements in therapy, often while playing, as a way of demonstrating hidden motives and anxieties. These statements then are used by the therapist or analyst to illustrate the causes of current conflicts and problems. When the child achieves insight and understanding of this connection, more adaptive responses can be taught. Similar to a medical approach, there is a long-held belief that the practice of psychoanalytic techniques (e.g., psychoanalysis) with children is restricted to only those who have been specifically trained. The psychoanalytically oriented therapist must have sufficient skill in empathy without overidentification so that he or she can efficiently observe and interpret the child's conduct. The therapist also must be comfortable with his or her own childhood conflicts so as to permit the child's free reenactment while in play therapy.

Core Concepts and Techniques
Rapport and Free Association

Typically, psychoanalytic treatment begins by building rapport so that the child will feel comfortable and unlikely to censor any ideas or thoughts that may come to mind. The goal of this therapeutic approach is to engage the child and reduce anxiety, which may have led the child to hold back information repressed from the past. When a sufficient degree of rapport is established, the child is usually in a comfortable enough position to free associate, that is, say anything that comes into mind. The therapist helps the child to reconnect each expression to prior ones, until the earliest memories are tapped. Thus, the child is to relive any unpleasant past experiences and eliminate any subsequent anxieties that underlie his/her present problems, such as ongoing parent–child relationships.

Dream Analysis

The analysis of dreams is aimed at uncovering hidden, influential material. Children are encouraged to describe their dreams, which are believed to provide another path to unpleasant experiences and thoughts. As such, even rather innocent objects are viewed as having a significance far beyond their basic appearance. The main task is to interpret the characters, objects, and their true significance in the dreams, which takes great skill on the analyst's part. During free association and dream analysis, the analyst closely attends to anything that the child seems reluctant to discuss. This behavior is regarded as a form of the child's resistance and it alerts the analyst to its possible significance.

Drawing and Storytelling

The analyst may also use drawing and storytelling techniques to elicit additional unconscious material and resolve conflicts. The therapist is to provide interpretations of the statements reported and to link these to the child's behavior. For example, a child might report a dream or a story where primary caretakers are stealing his or her arms and legs. To this, the analyst might say to the child that this dream is a reflection of the child's fear of forming deep attachments to parents because of fear damage (Lorand, 1964). An important rule in child psychoanalysis is that the child's symptoms must be assessed in the context of the interference they pose to normal development. That is, not all symptoms may be identified for intervention, but rather those behaviors that are likely to prevent healthy attachments and intra-psychic growth. The therapist relates the information to past and present experiences and behavior, and these interpretations are presented to the child so that they can be discussed and more adaptable responses can be developed.

Empirical Support for Psychoanalytic Therapy

A tremendous amount of literature demonstrates the use of the psychoanalytic technique for every type of childhood clinical disorder. The practice mainly is illustrated by examples and case histories (A. Freud, 1958). However, this vast literature should not be taken to indicate a substantial amount of empirical research support. There appears to be a significant absence of solid evidence regarding the validity of this approach or the benefits of its outcome. No study with satisfactory controls has demonstrated the efficacy of this approach for treating childhood disorders, or its superiority over other less expensive, readily available approaches. Clearly one of the problems in evaluating psychoanalysis for children is the fact that it rests more on clinical expertise than quantitative outcome (Feldman, 1968, Luborsky, 1971; Wallerstein, 1975). The course of psychoanalysis requires several sessions a week and can run for years. Therefore, it may be inappropriate for behavior problems that require more immediate remediation.

Psychodynamic Play Therapy

Aside from the more classical, Freudian psychoanalytic approach to childhood disorders, psychodynamic play therapy is another alternative. Although both approaches are predicated on the analysis of resistance and transference, the techniques are noticeably different. Dissimilar from other traditional modes of child therapy, the methods and outcomes of play intervention may not be observable immediately in the child's verbal behavior. That is, children may not orally describe what their issues are, how they are feeling about the treatment, or what they want from the therapist. Instead children are likely to play out these feelings and thoughts using the play medium (Landreth, 1982). In the beginning phase, the therapist is engaged in facilitating a therapeutic relationship with the child by meeting him or her at the child's developmental level.

In psychodynamic play therapy, toys are made readily available to the child. However, toys are seen as a stepping stone to the ultimate goal of treatment—enhancing the child's ability to verbalize conflicts and to aid the therapist in later interpretation. In some analytic approaches, observing the child's play is akin to noting an adult's free associations. A conservative view toward interpretation is that free play is inherently therapeutic by allowing the release of instinctual impulses and thereby reliving intrapsychic tension (Klein, 1932). For the Freudian therapist, however, play behavior is but one source of information for deriving inferences (Freud, 1946). Other sources, such as parent reports, later complete the picture, and the therapist waits for this additional information to clarify any possible interpretations; play alone is not believed to be sufficient for resolving hidden conflicts. A necessary next step is the interpretation wherein the therapist helps the child to make connections between present behaviors and past experiences.

Although the ultimate goals involve interpretation and insight, these tasks often are more difficult with children because their cognitive capabilities may be limited. Accordingly, the analytic play therapist often will use metaphors to illustrate an interpretation using characters or subjects in the child's play. Using the play metaphor is the first step in helping the child to learn to verbalize affect and conflict. Lewis (1974) has described several types of verbalizations that a psychoanalytic play therapist may use with play metaphors. These include focusing statements to bring the child's attention to the factual events in the play, reductive statements to identify unnoticed patterns of behavior by the child, situational statements to demonstrate the various situations that tend to produce consistent affective and behavioral responses from the child, transference interpretations to illustrate how the child's conflicts are related to the relationship with the therapist, and etiological statements to demonstrate the connection between the child's current behavior and past events.

The determination of specific psychoanalytic play objects differs from most other approaches to play therapy. The chief difference lies in having few available toys. The psychoanalytic play therapist holds that too many toys serve to confuse rather than to encourage engagement. Furthermore, the toys presented are consistent with the therapist's own sense of comfort. Therefore, for therapists who do not care to get dirty, paints and other potentially messy toys should not be used. The psychoanalytic approach encourages the therapist to have available materials for drawing, modeling clay, blocks of various sizes, small flexible family dolls, a few hand puppets, a toy nursing bottle, toys guns, a small rubber ball, and a few cars and trucks. It also is suggested that, for older children, a few board games be made available. Regardless of the types of toys, all of the materials should be geared toward encouraging the child's free play and verbalization of fantasy, affect, and conflict. For the older child and adolescent, free play is likely to be limited, and more classical psychoanalytic approaches may be used. However, even for older children, toys should be made available for particular times when the child may choose to play in regressive behavior as a way to resolve hidden conflicts. These requirements depart significantly from most other approaches to play therapy where what is needed for the child's treatment often is inconsistent with the therapist's comfort level. Furthermore, client-centered approaches to play therapy often encourage the selection of toys by providing a wide range of play activities (Landreth, 1992). Finally, psychoanalytic play therapists often encourage children to bring toys from home to the therapy session because these objects are likely to be chosen for their significance. This also represents a significant difference from other play therapy where this behavior would be seen as a lack of trust of the therapy and therapist.

Current Applications of Psychodynamic Therapy

At one time, psychoanalytic approaches were used for virtually all presenting problems. This uniform approach is much less likely today; the value of other interventions is recognized and the selective use of play therapy is more appropriate. Psychoanalytic approaches for children do not propose to ameliorate all of the presenting personality deficits and clinical difficulties. Instead, the focus is on negotiating the stringency of a punitive superego on a child's behavior and adjustment. Contrary to other forms of child psychotherapy, persistence of symptoms is not taken as a sign of failure as long as there is evidence of strengthened character formation. Symptom reduction is less significant to treatment outcome than the child's overall feeling of adjustment and need for further treatment. This often is measured as the child's willingness to manage daily life stressors and to engage in and maintain mutually satisfying relationships. The real test of child psychoanalysis may lie in the child's ability to withstand frustrations and difficulties later in life without regressing to prior maladaptive behaviors.

Surveys of clinical practice indicate a high utilization of psychoanalytic/dynamic concepts and approaches by practitioners (Kazdin et al., 1990; Koocher & Pedulla, 1977; Tuma & Pratt, 1982). Most of these surveys were taken prior to the burgeoning impact of managed care reimbursement systems, which tend not to pay for psychoanalytic therapy (Roberts & Hurley, 1997). Nonetheless, despite limited empirical support for these approaches, they are still endorsed by many therapists. Some commentators have called for greater research attention to psychoanalytic approaches, while others have argued that clinicians should use only those techniques demonstrated to be effective (and that psychoanalytic approaches have had ample time to demonstrate effectiveness). Fonagy and Target (1996) suggested that psychoanalytic concepts are useful in providing a broader conceptual view, even while other techniques, such as behavioral interventions, may address the immediate maladaptive behaviors. Additionally, some presenting problems are not readily amenable to behavioral or cognitive-behavioral interventions for which a psychoanalytic approach may be indicated (e.g., parent–child conflicts, family of origin problems).

ISSUES IN CHILD PSYCHOTHERAPY

Ethical and Legal Issues

Many ethical and legal issues surround psychotherapeutic interventions with children, adolescents, and their families (Koocher & Keith-Siegel, 1990; Rae, Worchel, & Brunnquell, 1995). Some of these issues have been mentioned already. We will emphasize a few points.

Training for Competence

The delivery of mental health services to children and families should be governed by the competent ability of the professional to provide specialty services (Shirk & Phillips, 1991). Achievement of competence is specifically linked to training. Many psychologists trained in a clinical psychology program, for example, are *de facto* specialists in *adult* assessment and intervention, but have minimal exposure to children in didactic coursework or clinical practicum. As noted at the beginning of this chapter, the downward extension of adult techniques is usually inadequate and often unethical. Comprehensive training models geared to provide services to children, adolescents, and their families are available to guide competence building (Roberts et al., 1985; Roberts et al., 1998; Roberts, 1998; Tuma, 1985). These models should be followed by students, trainers, and clinicians in preparation to conduct child psychotherapy.

Consent to Treatment

The legal and developmental consideration of whether children can consent to psychotherapy treatment is an important complicating factor in conducting psychotherapy with children and adolescents. The rights of children have been inadequately defined by federal and state laws. A Supreme Court ruling (Parham *v.* J. R., 1979) held that children could be committed to mental institutions by their parents. In contrast, some state laws have granted children the right to seek certain types of medical treatment without parental consent. A comprehensive policy does not exist for children and adolescents seeking or rejecting psychotherapy. The concept of *least restrictive alternative* generally guides mental health professionals in determining what therapeutic interventions should be considered. Additionally, the psychologist would want to involve the child or adolescent in the decision-making process about treatment and its goals to the degree that the child is capable (Gustafson & McNamara, 1987). Some commentators argue that children as young as seven years of age may be able to participate (Koocher & Keith-Siegel, 1990), while others have held that children below ages 11–13 do not have the developmental ability to give consent to treatment (Grisso & Vierling, 1978).

Confidentiality

Related to the consent issue is that of keeping confidential the information gained in a child psychotherapeutic relationship. The question arises as to whether a child has the same right to privacy granted to adult clients, or whether information may be shared with interested parties such as parents, the school, legal, and medical personnel. Although some professionals note the valid extension of adultlike rights to children, this is not always legally protected. Some commentators suggest that agreements made prior to beginning treatment can help define the degree of confidentiality accorded to a minor client (Gustafson & McNamara, 1987). A complexity of considerations may expand or preclude confidentiality for a child or adolescent (Koocher & Keith-Siegel, 1990). Legal limitations on confidentiality or privileged communication include the legal requirement to report suspected child abuse and expressed intent to harm self or others (Gustafson & McNamara, 1987; Koocher, 1989; Taylor & Adelman, 1989). Child-oriented psychotherapists, in addition to being competently trained in the techniques of assessment and intervention, need to be fully versed in the ethical and legal issues of children and adolescents involved in therapy.

Future Directions

We anticipate that the future of psychotherapy will be directed to a large degree by how psychologists and other mental health professionals respond to the challenges of managed care (Roberts & Hurley, 1997). The early development of psychotherapy was not related to the mechanisms for financing the care. Currently, and for the foreseeable future, the applications of known therapeutic interventions will be dictated by how much reimbursement is appropriate for certain problems, for what modes of interventions, and for how many sessions. The empirical validation of treatment techniques and the improved outcomes in functioning for children as a result of the use of empirically supported treatments will assist in insuring future contributions to the improved well-being of children, adolescents, and families through psychotherapy.

References

Allen, J. S., Tarnowski, K. J., Simonian, S. J., Elliott, D., & Drabman, R. S. (1991). The generalization map revisited: Assessment of generalized treatment effects in child and adolescent behavior therapy. *Behavior Therapy, 22,* 393–405.

Amaya-Jackson, L., March, J. S., Murray, M. C., & Schulte, A. (1998). Cognitive-behavioral psychotherapy for children and adolescents with posttraumatic stress disorder after a single-incident stressor. *Journal of the American Academy of Child and Adolescent Psychiatry, 37,* 585–594.

Bandura, A. (1969). *Principles of behavior modification.* New York: Holt, Rinehart, and Winston.

Barkley, R. A. (1997a). *Defiant children: A clinician's manual for assessment and parent training* (2nd ed.). New York: Guilford.

Barkley, R. A. (1997b). Behavioral inhibition, sustained attention, and executive functions: Constructing a unifying theory of ADHD. *Psychological Bulletin, 121,* 65–94.

Becker, W. C. (1971). *Parents are teachers: A child management program.* Champaign, IL: Research Press.

Beelmann, A., Pfingsten, U., & Losel, F. (1994). Effects of training social competence in children: A meta-analysis of recent evaluation studies. *Journal of Clinical Child Psychology, 23,* 260–271.

Bergan, J. R., & Kratochwill, T. R. (1990). *Behavioral consultation and therapy.* New York: Plenum.

Blechman, E. A. (1985). *Solving child behavior problems at home and at school.* Champaign, IL: Research Press.

Brestan, E. V., & Eyberg, S. M. (1998). Effective psychosocial treatments of conduct-disordered children and adolescents: 29 years, and 5272 kids. *Journal of Clinical Child Psychology, 27,* 180–189.

Calvert, S. C., & Johnston, C. (1990). Acceptability of treatments for child behavior problems: Issues and implications for future research. *Journal of Clinical Child Psychology, 19,* 61–74.

Casey, R. J., & Berman, J. S. (1985). The outcome of psychotherapy with children. *Psychological Bulletin, 98,* 388–400.

Chambless, D. L., Baker, M. J., Baucom, D. H., Beutler, L. E., Calhoun, K. S., Crits-Christoph, P., Daiuto, A., DeRubeis, R., Detweiler, J., Haaga, D. A. F., Johnson, S. B., McCurry, S., Mueser, K. T., Pope, K. S., Sanderson, W. C., Shoham, V., Stickle, T., Williams, D. A., & Woody, S. R. (1998). Update on empirically validated therapies II. *The Clinical Psychologist, 51,* 3–16.

Charlop, M. H., Parrish, J. M., Fenton, L. R., & Cataldo, M. F. (1987). Evaluation of hospital-based outpatient pediatric psychology services. *Journal of Pediatric Psychology, 12,* 485–503.

Costanzo, P., Miller-Johnson, S., & Wencel, H. (1995). Social development. In J. March (Ed.), *Anxiety disorders in children and adolescents* (pp. 82–108). New York: Guilford.

Crick, N. R., & Dodge, K. A. (1994). A review and reformulation of social information processing mechanisms in children's social adjustment. *Psychological Bulletin, 115,* 74–101.

Cummings, N. A., & Follette, W. T. (1968). Psychiatric services and medical utilization in a prepaid health plan setting: Part II. *Medical Care, 6,* 31–41.

Dadds, M., Heard, P., & Rapee, R. (1992). The role of family interventions in the treatment of child anxiety disorders: Some preliminary findings. *Behaviour Change, 9,* 171–177.

DiLorenzo, T. M. (1988). Operant and classical conditioning. In J. L. Matson (Ed.), *Handbook of treatment approaches in childhood psychopathology* (pp. 65–78). New York: Plenum.

Dodge, K. A. (1993) Social-cognitive mechanisms in the development of conduct disorder and depression. *Annual Review of Psychology, 44,* 559–584.

Durlak, J. A., Fuhrman, T., & Lampman, C. (1991). Effectiveness of cognitive-behavior therapy for maladapting children: A meta-analysis. *Psychological Bulletin, 110,* 204–214.

Erchul, W. P., & Martens, B. K. (1997). *School consultation: Conceptual and empirical bases of practice.* New York: Plenum.

Eysenck, H. J. (1952). The effects of psychotherapy: An evaluation. *Journal of Consulting Psychology, 16,* 319–324.

Fauber, R. L., & Long, N. (1991). Children in context: The role of the family in child psychotherapy. *Journal of Consulting and Clinical Psychology, 59,* 813–820.

Feldman, F. (1968). Results of psychoanalysis in clinic case assignments. *Journal of the American Psychoanalytic Association, 16,* 274–300.

Finney, J. W., Lemanek, K. L., Cataldo, M. F., Katz, H. P., & Fuqua, R. W. (1989). Pediatric psychology in primary health care: Brief targeted therapy for recurrent abdominal pain. *Behavior Therapy, 20,* 283–291.

Finney, J. W., Riley, A. W., & Cataldo, M. F. (1991). Psychology in primary health care: Effects of brief targeted therapy on children's medical care utilization. *Journal of Pediatric Psychology, 16,* 447–461.

Fonagy, P., & Target, M. (1996). A contemporary psychoanalytic perspective: Psychodynamic developmental theory. In E. D. Hibbs & P. S. Jensen (Eds.), *Psychosocial treatments for child and adolescent disorders: Empirically based strategies for clinical practice* (pp. 619–638). Washington, D.C.: American Psychological Association.

Forehand, R. L., & McMahon, R. J. (1981). *Helping the noncompliant child.* New York: Guilford Press.

Fraser, J. S. (1996). All that glitters is not always gold: Medical offset effects and managed behavioral health care. *Professional Psychology: Research and Practice, 27,* 335–344.

Freud, A. (1946). *The psychoanalytical treatment of children.* London: Imago Press.

Freud, A. (1958). Clinical studies in psychoanalysis. *Proceedings of the Royal Society of Medicine, 51,* 938–942.

Freud, A. (1974). The role of transference in the analysis of children. In *The writings of Anna Freud* (Vol. 1). New York: International Universities Press, Inc.

Freud, S. (1955). *The interpretation of dreams.* New York: Basic Books.

Frick, P. J. (1998). *Conduct disorders and severe antisocial behavior.* New York: Plenum.

Friedman, S. B., & Schonberg, S. K. (1996). The short- and long-term consequences of corporal punishment. *Pediatrics, 98,* 803–860.

Garland, A. F., & Besinger, B. A. (1996). Adolescents' perceptions of outpatient mental health services. *Journal of Child and Family Studies, 5,* 355–375.

Graziano, A. M., & Mooney, K. C. (1980). Family self-control instruction for children's nighttime fear reduction. *Journal of Consulting and Clinical Psychology, 48,* 206–213.

Gresham, F. M., & Lambros, K. M. (1998). Behavioral and functional assessment. In T. S. Watson & F. M. Gresham (Eds.), *Handbook of child behavior therapy* (pp. 3–22). New York: Plenum.

Grisso, T., & Vierling, L. (1978). Minor's consent to treatment: A developmental perspective. *Professional Psychology, 9,* 412–427.

Guerra, N. G., & Slaby, R. G. (1990). Cognitive mediators of aggression in adolescent offenders: 2. Intervention. *Developmental Psychology, 26,* 269–277.

Gustafson, K. E., & McNamara, J. R. (1987). Confidentiality with minor clients: Issues and guidelines for therapists. *Professional Psychology: Research and Practice, 18,* 503–508.

Haapala, D. A. (1996). The Homebuilders Model: An evolving service approach for families. In M. C. Roberts (Ed.), *Model programs in child and family mental health* (pp. 295–315). Mahwah, NJ: Lawrence Erlbaum Associates.

Hankie, J. R., Starfield, B. H., Steinwachs, D. M., Benson, P., Livingston, G., & Katz, H. P. (1984). The relationship between specialized mental health care and patterns of primary care use among children enrolled in a prepaid group practice. *Research in Community Mental Health, 4,* 203–230.

Hanley, J. H. (1996). Coordination of mental health services for children, adolescents, and their families. In M. C. Roberts (Ed.), *Model programs in child and family mental health* (pp. 285–293). Mahwah, NJ: Lawrence Erlbaum Associates.

Hazelrigg, M. D., Cooper, H. M., & Borduin, C. M. (1987). Evaluating the effectiveness of family therapies: An integrative review and analysis. *Psychological Bulletin, 101,* 428–442.

Hembree-Kigin, T., & McNeil, C. B. (1995). *Parent-child interaction therapy.* New York: Plenum.

Hibbs, E. D., & Jensen, P. S. (Eds.). (1996). *Psychosocial treatments for child and adolescent disorders: Empirically based strategies for clinical practice.* Washington, D.C.: American Psychological Association.

Hoagwood, K., Hibbs, E., Brent, D., & Jensen, P. (1995). Introduction to the special section: Efficacy and effectiveness in studies of child and adolescent psychotherapy. *Journal of Consulting and Clinical Psychology, 63,* 683–687.

Kanfer, F. H., & Phillips, J. S. (1970). *Learning foundations of behavior therapy.* New York: Wiley.

Kazdin, A. E. (1988). *Child psychotherapy: Developing and identifying effective treatments.* Elmsford, NY: Pergamon Press.

Kazdin, A. E. (1993). Psychotherapy for children and adolescents: Current progress and future research directions. *American Psychologist, 48,* 644–657.

Kazdin, A. E., Bass, D., Ayers, W. A., & Rodgers, A. (1990). Empirical and clinical focus of child and adolescent psychotherapy research. *Journal of Consulting and Clinical Psychology, 60,* 733–747.

Kazdin, A. E., Siegel, T. C., & Bass, D. (1990). Drawing on clinical practice to inform research on child and adolescent psychotherapy: Survey of practitioners. *Professional Psychology: Research and Practice, 21,* 189–198.

Kazdin, A. E., Siegel, T. C., & Bass, D. (1992). Cognitive problem-solving skills training and parent management training in the treatment of antisocial behavior in children. *Journal of Consulting and Clinical Psychology, 60,* 733–747.

Kazdin, A. E., & Weisz, J. R. (1998). Identifying and developing empirically supported child and adolescent treatments. *Journal of Consulting and Clinical Psychology, 66,* 19–36.

Kendall, P. C. (1994). Treating anxiety disorders in children: Results of a randomized clinical trial. *Journal of Consulting and Clinical Psychology, 62,* 100–110.

Kendall, P. C., Flannery-Schroeder, E., Panichelli-Mindel, S. M., Southam-Gerow, M., Henin, A., & Warman, M. (1997). Therapy for youths with anxiety disorders: A second randomized clinical trial. *Journal of Consulting and Clinical Psychology, 65,* 366–380.

Kendall, P. C., Kande, M., Howard, B., & Siqueland, L. (1990). *Cognitive-behavioral treatment of anxious children: Treatment manual.* (Available from authors, Department of Psychology, Temple University, Philadelphia, PA 19122.)

Kendall, P. C., & Southam-Gerow, M. A. (1996). Long-term follow-up of a cognitive-behavioral therapy for anxiety-disordered youth. *Journal of Consulting and Clinical Psychology, 64,* 724–730.

Klein, M. (1932). *The psychoanalysis of children.* London: Hogarth Press.

Koocher, G. P. (1989). Ethical issues in legally mandated child abuse reporting. *The Independent Practitioner, 9,* 43–44.

Koocher, G. P., & Keith-Siegel, P. C. (1990). *Children, ethics, and the law.* Lincoln, NE: University of Nebraska Press.

Krahn, G. L., Eisert, D., & Fifield, B. (1990). Obtaining parental perceptions of the quality of services for children with special health needs. *Journal of Pediatric Psychology, 15,* 761–774.

Ladd, G. (1985). Documenting the effects of social skills training with children: Process and outcome assessment. In B. H. Schneider, K. H. Rubin, & J. E. Ledingham (Eds.), *Children's peer relations: Issues in assessment and intervention* (pp. 243–269). New York: Springer-Verlag.

Landreth, G. (1992). *Play therapy, the art of the relationship.* Muncie, IN: Accelerated Development.

Levitt, E. E. (1957). The results of psychotherapy with children: An evaluation. *Journal of Consulting Psychology, 32,* 286–289.

Levitt, E. E. (1963). Psychotherapy with children: A further evaluation. *Behavior Research and Therapy, 60,* 326–329.

Lewinsohn, P. M., Clarke, G. N., Hops, H., & Andrews, J. (1990). Cognitive-behavioral treatment for depressed adolescents. *Behavior Therapy, 21,* 385–401.

Lewis, M. (1974). Interpretation in child analysis: Developmental considerations. *Journal of the American Academy of Child Psychiatry, 13,* 32–53.

Lipsey, M. W., & Wilson, D. B. (1993). The efficacy of psychological, educational, and behavioral treatment: Confirmation from meta-analysis. *American Psychologist, 48,* 1191–1209.

Lochman, J. E., & Lenhart, L. A. (1993). Anger coping intervention for aggressive children:

Conceptual models and outcome effects. *Clinical Psychology Review, 13*, 785–805.

Lonigan, C. J., & Elbert, J. C. (Eds.). (1998). Special issue on empirically supported psychosocial interventions for children. *Journal of Clinical Child Psychology, 27* (No. 2).

Lonigan, C. J., Elbert, J. C., & Johnson, S. B. (1998). Empirically supported psychosocial treatments for children: An overview. *Journal of Clinical Child Psychology, 27*, 138–145.

Lorand, S. (1964). Treatment of adolescents. In S. Lorand & H. Schneer (Eds.), *Adolescents: Psychoanalytic approach to problems and therapy* (pp. 238–250). Harper & Row.

Luborsky, L. (1971). Quantitative research on psychoanalytic therapy. In A. Bergin & S. Garfield (Eds.), *Handbook of psychotherapy and behavior change* (pp. 408–438). New York: Wiley.

Lutzker, J. R. (1996). An ecobehavioral model for serious family disorders: Child abuse and neglect; developmental disabilities. In M. C. Roberts (Ed.), *Model programs in child and family mental health* (pp. 33–46). Mahwah, NJ: Lawrence Erlbaum Associates.

March, J., Mulle, K., & Herbel, B. (1994). Behavioral psychotherapy for children and adolescents with obsessive-compulsive disorder: An open trial of a new protocol driven treatment package. *Journal of the American Academy of Child and Adolescent Psychiatry, 33*, 333–341.

McGinnis, E., & Goldstein, A. P. (1997). *Skillstreaming the elementary school child: New strategies and perspectives for teaching prosocial skills.* Champaign, IL: Research Press.

Mumford, E., Schlesinger, H. J., Glass, G. V., Patrick, C., & Cuerdon, T. (1984). A new look at evidence about reduced cost of medical utilization following mental health treatment. *American Journal of Psychiatry, 141*, 1145–1158.

Ollendick, T. H., & King, N. J. (1998). Empirically supported treatments for children with phobic and anxiety disorders: Current status. *Journal of Clinical Child Psychology, 27*, 156–167.

Olson, R., & Netherton, S. D. (1996). Consultation and liaison in a children's hospital. In M. C. Roberts (Ed.), *Model programs in child and family mental health* (pp. 249–264). Mahwah, NJ: Lawrence Erlbaum Associates.

Ozonoff, S., Pennington, B. F., & Rogers, S. J. (1991). Executive function deficits in high-functioning autistic individuals: Relationship to theory of mind. *Journal of Child Psychology and Psychiatry, 32*, 1081–1105.

Parham v. J. R. (1979). 442 U. S. 584.

Patterson, G. R., & Gullion, M. E. (1968). *Living with children: New methods for parents and teachers.* Champaign, IL: Research Press.

Paul, G. L. (1967). Outcome research in psychotherapy. *Journal of Consulting Psychology, 31*, 109–118.

Pelham, W. E., Wheeler, T., & Chronis, A. (1998). Empirically supported psychosocial treatments for attention deficit hyperactivity disorder. *Journal of Clinical Child Psychology, 27*, 190–205.

Pfiffner, L. J., & McBurnett, K. (1997). Social skills training with parent generalization: Treatment effects for children with attention deficit disorder. *Journal of Consulting and Clinical Psychology, 65*, 749–757.

Powers, S. W., & Rickard, H. C. (1992). Behavior therapy with children. In C. E. Walker & M. C. Roberts (Eds.), *Handbook of clinical child psychology* (2nd ed., pp. 749–763). New York: Wiley-Interscience.

Rae, W. A., Worchel, F. F., & Brunnquell, D. (1995). Ethical and legal issues in pediatric psychology. In M. C. Roberts (Ed.), *Handbook of pediatric psychology* (2nd ed., pp. 19–36). New York: Guilford.

Roberts, M. C. (1998). Innovations in specialty training: The Clinical Child Psychology Program at the University of Kansas. *Professional Psychology: Research and Practice, 29*, 394–397.

Roberts, M. C., Carlson, C. I., Erickson, M. T., Friedman, R. M., La Greca, A. M., Lemanek, K. L., Russ, S. W., Schroeder, C. S., Vargas, L. A., & Wohlford, P. F. (1998). A model for training psychologists to provide services for children and adolescents. *Professional Psychology, 29*, 293–299.

Roberts, M. C., Erickson, M. T., & Tuma, J. M. (1985). Addressing the needs: Guidelines for training psychologists to work with children, youth, and families. *Journal of Clinical Child Psychology, 14*, 70–79.

Roberts, M. C., & Hurley, L. K. (1997). *Managing managed care.* New York: Plenum.

Rodrigue, J. R., Hoffman, R. G., Rayfield, A., Lescano, C., Kubar, W., Streisand, R., & Banko, C. (1995). Evaluating pediatric psychology consultation services in a medical setting: An Example. *Journal of Clinical Psychology in Medical Settings, 2*, 89–107.

Rosen, J. C., & Wiens, A. N. (1979). Changes in medical problems and use of medical services following psychological intervention. *American Psychologist, 34*, 420–431.

Russell, R. L. (1998). Linguistic psychotherapy research: New directions and promising findings. *Journal of Clinical Child Psychology, 27*, 17–27.

Saxe, L., Cross, T., & Silverman, N. (1988). Children's mental health: The gap between what we know and what we do. *American Psychologist, 43*, 800–807.

Schoenwald, S. K., Henggeler, S. W., Pikrel, S. G., & Cunningham, P. B. (1996). Treating seriously troubled youths and families in their contexts: Multisystemic therapy. In M. C. Roberts (Ed.), *Model programs in child and family mental health* (pp. 317–332). Mahwah, NJ: Lawrence Erlbaum Associates.

Schrodt, G. R. (1992). Cognitive therapy of depression. In M. Shafii & S. L. Shafii (Eds.), *Clinical guide to depression in children and adolescents* (pp. 197–218). Washington, D.C.: American Psychiatric Press.

Schroeder, C. S. (1996). Mental health services in pediatric primary care. In M. C. Roberts (Ed.), *Model programs in child and family mental health* (pp. 265–284). Mahwah, NJ: Lawrence Erlbaum Associates.

Schroeder, C. S., Gordon, B. N., Kanoy, K., & Routh, D. K. (1983). Managing children's behavior problems in pediatric practice. In M. Wolraich & D. K. Routh (Eds.), *Advances in developmental and behavioral pediatrics* (Vol. 4, pp. 25–86). Greenwich, CT: JAI Press.

Shirk, S. R. (1998). Interpersonal schemata in child psychotherapy: A cognitive-interpersonal perspective. *Journal of Clinical Child Psychology, 27*, 4–16.

Shirk, S. R., & Phillips, J. S. (1991). Child therapy training: Closing gaps with research and practice. *Journal of Consulting and Clinical Psychology, 59*, 766–776.

Shirk, S. R., & Russell, R. L. (1992). A reevaluation of estimates of child therapy effectiveness. *Journal of the American Academy of Child and Adolescent Psychiatry, 31*, 703–709.

Silverman, W. K., & Kurtines, W. M. (1996). *Anxiety and phobic disorders: A pragmatic approach.* New York: Plenum.

Skinner, B. F. (1938). *The behavior of organisms.* New York: Appleton-Century-Crofts.

Skinner, B. F. (1953). *Science and human behavior.* New York: Macmillan.

Slaby, R. G., & Guerra, N. G. (1988). Cognitive mediators of aggression in adolescent offenders: 1. Assessment. *Developmental Psychology, 24*, 580–588.

Smith, M. L., & Glass, G. V. (1977). Meta-analysis of psychotherapy outcome studies. *American Psychologist, 32*, 752–760.

Snyder, C. R., McDermott, D., Cook, W., & Rapoff, M. A. (1997). *Hope for the journey: Helping children through good times and bad.* Boulder, CO: Westview Press.

Stokes, T. F., & Baer, D. M. (1977). An implicit technology of generalization. *Journal of Applied Behavior Analysis, 10*, 349–367.

Stokes, T. F., Boggs, S. R., & Osnes, P. G. (1986). Separation anxiety disorder and school phobia. In M. C. Roberts & C. E. Walker (Eds.), *Casebook in child and pediatric psychology* (pp. 71–93). New York: Guilford.

Task Force on Comprehensive and Coordinated Psychological Services for Children: Ages 0–10 of the American Psychological Association. (1994). *Comprehensive & coordinated services for children: A call for service integration.* Washington, D.C.: American Psychological Association.

Task Force on Promotion and Dissemination of Psychological Procedures, Division of Clinical Psychology, American Psychological Association. (1995). Training in and dissemination of empirically-validated psychological treatments: Report and recommendations. *The Clinical Psychologist, 48*(1), 3–23.

Taylor, L., & Adelman, H. S. (1989). Reframing the confidentiality dilemma to work in children's best interests. *Professional Psychology: Research and Practice, 20*, 79–83.

Tuma, J. M. (1985). *Proceedings: Conference on training clinical child psychologists.* Baton Rouge, LA: Section on Clinical Child Psychology.

Tuma, J. M., & Pratt, J. M. (1982). Clinical child psychology practice and training: A survey. *Journal of Clinical Child Psychology, 11*, 27–34.

Vernberg, E. M., Routh, D. K., & Koocher, G. P. (1992). The future of psychotherapy with developmental psychotherapy. *Psychotherapy, 29*, 72–80.

Wallerstein, R. (1975). *Psychotherapy and psychoanalysis.* New York: International University Press.

Watson, T. S., & Gresham, F. M. (Eds.). (1998). *Handbook of child behavior therapy.* New York: Plenum.

Weisz, J. R., & Weiss, B. (1993). *Effects of psychotherapy with children and adolescents.* Newbury Park, CA: Sage.

Weisz, J. R., Weiss, B., Alicke, M. D., & Klotz, M. L. (1987). Effectiveness of psychotherapy with children and adolescents: A meta-analysis for clinicians. *Journal of Consulting and Clinical Psychology, 55*, 542–549.

Weisz, J. R., Weiss, B., Han, S. S., Granger, D. A., & Morton, T. (1995). Effects of psychotherapy with children and adolescents revisited: A meta-analysis of treatment outcome studies. *Psychological Bulletin, 117*, 450–468.

Wilson, G. T. (1996). Manual-based treatments: The clinical application of research findings. *Behaviour Research and Therapy, 34*, 295–314.

Wolf, M. (1978). Social validity: The case for subjective measurement or how applied behavior analysis is finding its heart. *Journal of Applied Behavior Analysis, 11*, 203–214.

Yule, W., & Williams, R. (1990). Post traumatic stress reactions in children. *Journal of Traumatic Stress, 3*, 279–295.

CHAPTER 24

CHILDHOOD MALTREATMENT: TREATMENT OF ABUSE/INCEST SURVIVORS

ALAN J. LITROWNIK AND IDALIA CASTILLO-CAÑEZ
San Diego State University, and SDSU/UCSD Joint Doctoral Program in Clinical Psychology

In this chapter we focus on the problems of and methods for intervention with individuals who have been sexually abused during their childhood or adolescent years. This focus is unique in that survivors of child sexual abuse can come from diverse backgrounds (e.g., age, gender, culture, and class), as well as present with a variety of problems (e.g., sexual, substance use, interpersonal) and diagnoses (e.g., Posttraumatic Stress Disorder or PTSD, Multiple Personality Disorder, Borderline Personality Disorder). Our attempts to understand the role that this human-induced trauma has on victims and to develop interventions to alleviate resultant dysfunction have expanded rapidly in the last three decades of the 20th century. Prior to this period we experienced other epochs of interest (e.g., Tardieu in the mid-19th century France, Freud during the early 20th century in Austria) that were followed by disbelief, denunciation of the messengers, and in some cases recantation (see Goodwin, 1993; van der Kolk, Weisaeth, & van der Hart, 1996).

In a similar vein, our current concerns about the degree of suffering that results from child sexual abuse and how to develop and apply effective interventions have met with some criticism. While some of this criticism has the potential to be constructive (e.g., cautions about how to reconstruct memories, Loftus, 1993), much of it sounds quite familiar. That is, we hear emotional denials, people saying that they do not believe that adults could do such things to children, and selective attention to those inevitable cases of false positives while ignoring the many more cases of false negatives (Fish, 1998). An additional factor that has come into play more recently is the involvement of the legal, or judicial, system (criminal and civil) in adjudicating claims of abuse. Because there is a potential for the loss of individual liberty in the criminal justice system, the burden of proof used to determine if the crime occurred (i.e., beyond a reasonable doubt) protects against false positives, or those who are inappropriately accused. The cost of these protections (i.e., decreasing false positives) is an increase in false negatives.

What does this all portend for the 21st century? It is our belief that the current interest in the problem of child sexual abuse will not suffer from the same fate as prior periods did. Rather, our interest in child sexual abuse will continue as we become better able to understand its impact, and as a result develop more effective interventions. The general aims of this chapter are to first describe the state of our knowledge about the problem of child sexual abuse (and incest, more specifically), and then to suggest future directions for how we can continue to develop our approaches to treat its effects.

In an effort to accomplish these aims we present a discussion of child sexual abuse as it relates to Offord, Kraemer, Kazdin, Jensen, and Harrington's (1998) concept of *Burden of Suffering*, which provides one of the reasons why we believe that our interest in child sexual abuse, in general, and incest, more specifically, will not wane as we enter the 21st century. Following a discussion of some of the current thinking about how approaches to therapy should be developed and assessed, we review the approaches to understanding what child sexual abuse involves and the mechanisms (e.g., processes and mediating and moderating factors) that are responsible for the observed effects. This conceptual foundation is utilized to identify common themes or targets for treating adult survivors of child sexual abuse. Next, we review the empirical evidence for treatments applied to (1) child victims of sexual abuse, (2) adults who have experienced other kinds of trauma (e.g., rape) that result in similar symptom patterns (e.g., PTSD), and (3) adult survivors of child sexual abuse. Following this review we address some specific issues related to the treatment of incest or child sexual abuse survivors in clinical settings, and make suggestions about what needs to be accomplished as we enter the new millennium.

CHILD SEXUAL ABUSE

Definitions

It is important to note that child sexual abuse (CSA) is not a disorder or characteristic associated with a particular population as is the case with special populations that are the focus of other chapters in this section. Rather, it is something that is experienced by an individual during his or her childhood that increases the risk of subsequent problems. This risk factor is differentiated (Courtois, 1995) from other traumas (e.g., natural disasters, accidents) that individuals experience in a number of ways: (1) It is the result of another individual's premeditated action; (2) In most CSA cases it is committed by someone who is attached to the child (this is always the case with incest); (3) The sexual abuse usually occurs in the context of other abuse (e.g., threats not to tell, force); (4) The act is usually misrepresented to the child; (5) and it is usually chronic.

The core defining features of CSA include a sexual act that can vary in severity or intrusiveness (i.e., range from fondling to penetration). This act is initiated by an individual who is more mature than the victim, able to understand the action, and is receiving some sexual gratification from the encounter. In contrast, the victim is typically dependent, is developmentally immature, is not able to fully comprehend the act, and therefore does not have the knowledge or authority to give his or her consent (Crosson-Tower, 1999; Krugman & Jones, 1987).

CSA is further differentiated from other conditions based on the relationship of the perpetrator to the child victim. Specifically, intrafamilial sexual abuse (i.e., incest) involves a perpetrator who is part of the child's nuclear family or someone who assumes the role of surrogate parent. Thus, incest not only involves perpetrators who are biological fathers, but also stepfathers, older siblings, uncles, and boyfriends who may or may not be living in the victim's home (Crosson-Tower, 1999; Fischer & McDonald, 1998). We should note that the most common perpetrators are fathers and uncles, and that while we recognize that some cases of intrafamilial sexual abuse involve female perpetrators, the vast majority of cases do not (Crosson-Tower, 1999). In addition, there is empirical support for the claim that intrafamilial abuse more likely tends to involve female victims, have an earlier onset (i.e., the victims are younger), be of longer duration, involve more invasive acts, and result in greater physical injury than sexual abuse perpetrated by individuals outside the family or home (i.e., extrafamilial sexual abuse) (Fischer & McDonald, 1998; Gold, Ehai, Lucenko, Swingle, & Hughes, 1998).

While definitional issues (i.e., should acts that do not involve contact be considered sexual abuse?) continue to be debated, our interest is in providing readers with an understanding of what this risk factor (i.e., CSA) can involve. Of course, the specificity of definitions utilized in empirical studies that estimate the scope of the problem, as well as attempt to understand its impact, will be affected by these definitions and resultant inclusion criteria. When this might be the case in the following sections, we attempt to be more specific in identifying what we or other authors are referring to when we use the term *child sexual abuse* (CSA).

Burden of Suffering

As mentioned in the introduction, CSA has been identified in the past as a problem deserving of attention. Earlier interest in addressing this problem diminished when questions about how many children actually experienced CSA and, if they did, whether it impacted their health or functioning were raised. These questions were presented in an effort to challenge those who proposed explanations for psychological problems that ran counter to the prevailing cultural mores of the region and time (Courtois, 1995; Goodwin, 1993). Offord et al. (1998) recently introduced the concept *Burden of Suffering*. They propose that it is useful in ". . . estimating the importance of a condition or disorder, or a group of disorders, for a society" (Offord et al., 1998, p. 686). The assumption is that conditions or disorders with a greater burden deserve more attention. We believe that current challenges to our increased focus on CSA can be addressed by looking at the condition of CSA as it relates to this concept. Specifically, *Burden of Suffering* is described along three dimensions: (1) frequency of the disorder or condition, (2) short-term and long-term morbidity, and (3) costs, both fiscal and in human terms (Offord et. al., 1998).

Frequency: Incidence/Prevalence

The frequency or scope of a problem is typically estimated by using the epidemiological constructs of incidence and prevalence (National Research Council, 1993). Estimates of incidence, or the number of new cases over a period of time, for CSA come from the U.S. Department of Health and Human Services' National Child Abuse and Neglect Data System (NCANDS) annual report. The most recent report (USDHHS, 1998) provides summary descriptions of information from states about cases of abuse and neglect that came to their attention during 1996. While this is likely an underestimate of incidence because it only includes cases that were reported to state protective agencies, almost 1 million children (15 per 1000) of the over 2.5 million (40 per 1000) that were reported were identified as victims of abuse and neglect. Approximately 120,000, or 12%, of these victims were identified as having experienced CSA (1.8 per 1000). CSA victims were most often female (77%), while representing a diverse group of ethnicities (64.8% Caucasian, 19.2% African-American, 14.1% Hispanic, and 1.9% other).

Most of the empirical literature that has attempted to estimate the scope of CSA has examined lifetime prevalence, i.e., the percentage of individuals in the population who have experienced CSA. These estimates have varied widely (6% to over 60% for females, and 3% to over 30% for males), depending on sampling methods, definitions, and assessments. In an effort to address this variability Gorey and Leslie (1997) reviewed the empirical literature, selected 16 surveys of non-clinical samples in North America that excluded non-contact sexual abuse in their definition, and adjusted estimates for males and females according to reported response rates. Based on their analyses, Gorey and Leslie conclude that somewhere between 12%–17% of the female population and 5%–8% of the male popu-

lation have experienced CSA. Fish (1998) estimates that prevalence rates in clinical populations, in general, are at least twice those found in nonclinical populations, and much higher in some specific clinical populations such as those diagnosed with Posttraumatic Stress Disorder, Dissociative Identity Disorder, and Borderline Personality Disorder.

Few attempts have been made to distinguish between intrafamilial and extrafamilial prevalence rates in nonclinical populations. Nevertheless, Krugman and Jones (1987) estimate that between 3%–5% of adult women and 1%–2% of adult men are victims of intrafamilial sexual abuse. This is likely an underestimate because Fischer and McDonald (1998) found in their review of records that nearly half (i.e., 44%) of the substantiated CSA cases in two western Canadian cities involved intrafamilial abuse. Again, some of the discrepancies in prevalence estimates of intrafamilial abuse are probably due to the population that is examined. Specifically, Finkelhor (1986) comments that the majority of CSA cases do not involve incest (i.e., when nonclinical samples are examined), whereas the majority of CSA cases known to professionals (i.e., clinical samples) do involve incest.

Morbidity: Short- and Long-Term Effects

Long- and short-term effects of CSA have been summarized in a number of descriptive reviews (e.g., Beitchman, Zucker, Hood, DaCosta, Akman, & Cassavia, 1992; Beitchman, Zucker, Hood, DaCosta, & Akman, 1992; Kendall-Tackett, Williams, & Finkelhor, 1993) and a recent meta-analysis (Neumann, Jousekamp, Pollock, & Briere, 1996). The meta-analytic review selected 38 studies that examined the long-term impact of CSA in five broad areas (i.e., affective, behavioral, identity/relational, psychiatric sequelae, and general symptomatology) by assessing victims of CSA and a comparison group that was not victimized. Overall, the effect size, or differences in long-term impact between those who did and did not experience CSA, was in the small to moderate range, with larger effects found in clinical versus nonclinical samples. Specifically, CSA victims evidenced significant impairment in the following areas: anxiety, anger, depression, revictimization, self-mutilation, sexual problems, substance abuse, suicidality, self-concept, obsessions and compulsions, dissociation, posttraumatic stress, and somatization. After reviewing some of the same studies included in Neumann et al.'s (1996) meta-analytic review, Gorey and Leslie (1997) conclude that "Three decades of research on child abuse has clearly underscored its public health importance . . ." (p. 391).

In addition to the usual psychosocial or mental health sequelae of CSA that have been identified and empirically verified, recent reports suggest that numerous physical problems may also be related to a history of CSA (see Roy, 1998, for a review). While the relationship between CSA and some physical problems (e.g., chronic pelvic pain, gastrointestinal conditions, eating disorders) may be direct, we have suggested that some problems (e.g., HIV/AIDS) may not be directly related to CSA. Rather, the relationship between CSA and physical problems is mediated by behaviors that place individuals at increased risk for developing these problems (e.g., promiscuity, substance use) (Taussig & Litrownik, 1997). One example of how this might occur comes from some of the work of Jinich and his colleagues at the Center for AIDS Prevention Studies at the University of California, San Francisco (Jinich, Paul, Stall, Acree, Kegeles, Hoff, & Coates, 1998). Specifically, gay and bisexual men who were sexually abused prior to age 15 were more likely to engage in risky sexual behavior (i.e., unprotected anal intercourse with nonprimary partners) than those who had not been abused. And reported levels of HIV infection were significantly higher in those gay and bisexual men who had been sexually abused, especially those who experienced CSA accompanied by threats or coercion.

Costs

The costs, in human terms, are evident in the sequelae associated with the short- and long-term impact of CSA. These sequelae include direct as well as indirect mental and physical health problems of victims. In addition, problems associated with a CSA history (e.g., sexually reactive behavior, inappropriate parenting) can impact others (see Baynard, 1997; Morris, 1995). Specifically, males who have been sexually abused as children are at greater risk for becoming a perpetrator of sexual abuse. There are also numerous anecdotal reports of female victims of intrafamilial abuse placing their own children in situations where they are more likely to be victimized (e.g., leaving them in the care of the same family member who abused them).

The fiscal costs of CSA are associated with subsequent involvement in a variety of public as well as private systems of care (i.e., child welfare, criminal justice, and mental and physical health). Provision of services within these systems can cost the general public, private insurance companies, as well as the victims and their families. Though we are not aware of any specific attempts to estimate the costs of CSA, it is safe to assume that they would be quite high given the estimated prevalence of CSA in adult clinical populations (33%–57% of women, and 18%–48% of men) (see Fish, 1998).

Approaches to Intervention

Based on our review of the scope, morbidity, and costs of CSA, it is evident that the *Burden of Suffering* associated with this problem is quite high. Thus, it can be argued that CSA is a problem that is not only important to our society but also one that deserves our attention. While this attention and effort to reduce the *Burden of Suffering* that results from CSA should include prevention and early intervention approaches (e.g., universal and targeted interventions; see Offord et al., 1998), the focus of this chapter is on clinical interventions for adult survivors.

It is interesting to note that there have been many specific treatments suggested for CSA survivors, and more specifically for incest survivors, but currently there is little, if any, evidence that any of these recommended treatments work. This contrasts with an emerging empirical literature that has demonstrated the positive impact of (1) universal interventions (e.g., "Say no, run, and tell") that attempt to prevent CSA from occurring in the first place (Daro, 1996) and (2) targeted interventions for children who recently disclosed suspected CSA (see Jinich & Litrownik, 1999).

DEVELOPING AND EVALUATING TREATMENTS FOR CSA (INCEST) SURVIVORS

What is needed is a strategy that will move us from our current state of knowledge about treatments for CSA survivors to the desired point where we not only have evidence of the efficacy and effectiveness of specific treatment approaches but also begin to address the many practice issues that will be faced by professionals delivering these treatments. Models for how we can conceptualize this process (Burns, in press), as well as guidelines for identifying empirically supported treatments (Chambless & Hollon, 1998), have been proposed.

Specifically, Burns (in press) borrows from the National Institute of Drug Abuse Research Phase Model in identifying the necessary progression of research in the development of appropriate treatments. The first phase involves the formulation of a new treatment approach. This typically follows from specific conceptual or theoretical formulations and, in many cases, empirical studies that help us to understand the problem (i.e., what its origin is, processes involved in its development, etc.). It is during this first phase that small pilot studies are conducted. As a result of these the treatment is defined (e.g., manualized), measures of competence in delivering the treatment and adherence to the treatment are developed, feedback from clinicians and patients is received, and the treatment is refined. In the second phase, the treatment continues to be developed through a larger observational pilot test that assesses feasibility, acceptability, and the appropriate dosage. Randomized clinical trials (RCTs) should be utilized within the third and fourth phases when establishing the efficacy (phase 3) and then effectiveness (phase 4) of the treatment. The fifth and final phase addresses the effectiveness of the treatment in practice. This can include observational studies of usual patients, providers, and organizations compared with effect sizes from the efficacy studies. It is during this phase of further treatment refinement that issues of practice are likely to be encountered (e.g., variability in patient characteristics, severity and complexity of the problem or problems that brought the patient to the attention of the therapist, and therapist characteristics including competence in delivering the treatment).

There is a relative dearth of efficacy (phase 3) and effectiveness (phase 4) studies examining treatments for CSA, much less incest, survivors. Rather, specific treatments have been developed based on a particular conceptual or theoretical understanding of the problem, and in some cases pilot studies conducted (phases 1 and 2) or case studies reported (phase 5). Burns (in press) points out that the development of treatment approaches does not have to be unidirectional. That is, efficacy and effectiveness studies do not always have to follow the development of a specifically defined and pilot-tested treatment, but rather can be prompted by reports of promising new approaches to treatment that come from usual practice. Nevertheless, there is a need to establish the efficacy (Chambless & Hollon, 1998), as well as effectiveness (Hoagwood, Hibbs, Brent, & Jensen, 1995) of specific treatments. While much discussion of how this can be accomplished is currently taking place (i.e., proposed criteria for identifying empirically supported treatments), there has been little attention paid to the translation or dissemination of effective treatments to clinical settings in general.

The remainder of this chapter will be devoted to reviewing the current state of our attempts to develop, evaluate, and disseminate treatments for CSA survivors in general, and incest survivors more specifically. This review will begin with a consideration of what we know about the problem of intrafamilial and extrafamilial abuse, that is, its characteristics, effects, and processes/mechanisms that are responsible for the observed effects. Themes or specific targets for treatment approaches suggested by this conceptual understanding will be identified. Following the identification of suggested treatment targets, we review the empirical support for treatments that have actually been applied to (1) children who have experienced CSA, (2) adults who have experienced similar traumas (e.g., rape) and resultant PTSD, and (3) adult survivors of CSA. Again, we will attempt to identify common components of treatments that appear to hold some promise. Finally, a discussion of some of the most pressing practice issues will lead to suggestions for how we might effectively organize our future research and clinical work.

Understanding Intrafamilial Sexual Abuse

Descriptive Characteristics

If we hope to understand better how intrafamilial sexual abuse impacts an individual, we need to begin with a description of what is typically involved in the abuse. This not only includes the specific actions of the perpetrator and victim but also the context in which the abuse occurs. Important contextual factors that need to be considered include characteristics of the victim (e.g., developmental level, gender), perpetrator (e.g., age, gender, relationship to victim), and family (e.g., single parent, two-parent, stepparent, blended), as well as those that operate at the macro level (e.g., cultural norms and religious beliefs).

By definition, intrafamilial abuse involves an immature victim and a perpetrator who is in a position of authority, and oftentimes is directly responsible for the well-being of the child victim. This can occur in the context of a macrosystem that seemingly supports the actions of the perpetrator, which further limits the options of the victim. For example, Heggen (1996) identifies four religious beliefs that have been utilized to support abuse as well as negate or dismiss the negative responses of incest victims (God intends that men dominate and women submit; woman is morally inferior to man and cannot trust her own judgment; suffering is a virtue and women in particular have been designated to be "suffering servants"; and believers must quickly forgive and be reconciled with those who sin against them).

More specifically, the abuse involves some form of sexual behavior (from fondling to intercourse) that occurs once or over a period of time. The sexual behavior may stimulate the victim, is usually associated with negative emotions, can be confused with attention and love, and in some cases is followed by the perpetrator rewarding the victim (e.g., gifts, special privileges). Trust and vulnerability of the victim are manipulated to accomplish the perpetrator's sexual motives through force or trickery, reliance on misinterpreted beliefs (e.g., religious), threats (e.g., what will happen if it is not kept secret), and blaming the victim. Thus, the well-being of the victim is disregarded, expected care and protection from a caregiver is not forthcoming, and the victim cannot protect him/herself.

Intrafamilial sexual abuse typically involves female victims (more than 70%) and male perpetrators (more than 90%). In addition, it is likely to involve more invasive sexual activity (e.g., manipulation of genitalia and intercourse) and occur over a longer period of time than extrafamilial sexual abuse (Crosson-Tower, 1999; Fischer & McDonald, 1998). While there are naturally some differences in the specific characteristics of sexual abuse perpetrated on boys versus girls that are a function of anatomical differences (i.e., more anal intercourse), Gold et al. (1998) report that the characteristics of CSA in males and females are basically the same (e.g., age of onset, severity, duration, use of force).

These specific components or characteristics of intrafamilial abuse interact with contextual factors (e.g., victim, perpetrator, family, cultural, and religious characteristics) in determining specific processes (e.g., coping strategies) or changes (e.g., physiological and developmental lags or deviations) in victims. The observed result is a compendium of sequelae, disorders, or problem behaviors.

Effects

A number of reviews of the long-term effects of CSA identify the most common outcomes to be: emotional (fears, depression); cognitive (negative self-evaluation, helplessness, distrust of others); interpersonal (externalizing behavior problems); physical and sexual functioning (sexual difficulties, chronic pelvic pain); compulsive behaviors and behaviors of excess (substance abuse, eating disorders, self-destructive behaviors); and disorders (Posttraumatic Stress, Borderline Personality, and Dissociative Identity) (see Briere, 1996b; Browne & Finkelhor, 1986; Donaldson & Cordes-Green, 1994; Kendall-Tackett et al., 1993; Loewenstein, 1993; Lynskey & Fergusson, 1997; Neumann et al., 1996). Though these reviews identify some common sequelae of CSA, it has been pointed out that not all victims evidence symptoms, and that there does not appear to be a specific syndrome associated with a CSA history (Kendall-Tackett et al., 1993; Lynskey & Fergusson, 1997). Rather, the degree of symptomatology that results is a function of the characteristics (e.g., severity, duration) of and contexts (e.g., victim, perpetrator, family, and macrosystem characteristics) in which the abuse occurs.

Much of the research that has been reported in the literature has focused on detailing the outcomes of CSA (e.g., comparisons of CSA victims to the nonabused population), and relating differences in outcomes to characteristics of the abuse and/or individuals involved. While this body of work can serve as an initial step in our understanding of how CSA is related to specific outcomes, it is only the beginning of our understanding of how it is that CSA can lead to such problems. That is, when we can identify the processes or mechanisms that follow exposure to CSA, we will not only better understand (and predict) subsequent outcomes but also be able to develop conceptually based approaches to treatment (Feiring, Taska, & Lewis, 1996). As Kendall-Tacket et al. (1993) stated, "Researchers evince a great deal of concern about the effects of sexual abuse but disappointingly little concern about why the effects occur." Thus, there is a ". . . glaring inadequacy in the literature; a nearly universal absence of theoretical underpinnings in the studies being conducted on this subject to date" (p. 175).

Approaches to Understanding Mechanisms/Processes: Trauma

Though not all individuals who experience CSA evidence short-term, much less long-term, sequelae, it is the case that the most often reported long-term effect is PTSD. For example, Lipovsky, Swenson, Ralston, and Saunders (1998) estimate that more than 60% of those who are survivors of CSA will experience PTSD at sometime in their lives. It is understandable, then, that the majority of theorizing about how CSA impacts individuals would focus on trauma theory.

General Trauma Models

One approach has been to view CSA as any other trauma in attempting to understand how the experience leads to the observed outcome, i.e., PTSD. While recognizing that various forms of trauma (e.g., incest, rape, and combat) differ in important ways, the claim is that the effects, or observed symptoms of PTSD, are remarkably similar and that there are critical communalties in psychological experience (see Dye & Roth, 1991; Foa & Meadows, 1997; McCann, Sakheim, & Abrahamson, 1988). Foa and her colleagues (Foa & Jaycox, in press; Foa & Meadows, 1997; Jaycox, Zoellner, & Foa, 1997) and others (e.g., Roth & Newman, 1993) propose an Emotional Processing Theory of trauma that explains not only how some victims develop chronic disturbances but also how it is that recovery occurs. Foa proposes that the trauma places demands on the individual to process information that challenges core beliefs (e.g., the world is benign, the world is meaningful, self is worthy, and people are trustworthy), and that reconciling the traumatic experience with these beliefs, i.e., emotional processing, is necessary for recovery. Chronic psychological disturbances indicate that the information has not been effectively processed. Rather, the traumatic experience is represented in memory (e.g., the world is dangerous; I can't control what happens to me) in such a way that it increases stress, and this stress, along with the arousal associated with the trauma, further interferes with the processing of the traumatic event. The ability to complete this emotional processing is related to the pretrauma conceptions of the world and self, memory of the trauma, and the victim's interpretations

of the posttrauma experience (Jaycox et al., 1997).

The pervasive and sometimes debilitating arousal associated with the trauma is explained by basic learning theory. Specifically, the occurrence of the trauma in a context (i.e., contiguity) results in anxiety and fear, being inappropriately generalized to similar situations (e.g., males, going to bed at night). These classically conditioned responses then lead to responses that avoid feared situations, thus reinforcing the conditioned response as well as the avoidance behavior (Mowrer's Two-Factor Learning Model; Carlson, Furby, Armstrong, & Shlaes, 1997).

Hartman and Burgess (1993) propose a similar neuropsychological model of information processing of trauma. CSA is viewed as an extreme stressor (or trauma), which overwhelms the limbic system as it attempts to move information from active awareness and process it for memory storage. Resolution of the trauma occurs when sufficient processing allows for the storage of this information. When the traumatic event is not resolved it remains in active memory or becomes defended by cognitive mechanisms (i.e., denial, dissociation, or splitting) that result in PTSD (e.g., fragmented memory, re-experiencing the trauma). This limbic appraisal hypothesis assumes that stimuli are first processed by the limbic system before being transmitted to the neocortex where reactions are interpreted. If processing or routing of this information is compromised by dysregulation in the limbic system (e.g., it is overwhelmed), then meaning systems will also be affected.

While Carlson et al. (1997) recognize that PTSD is associated with CSA histories, especially incest, they question whether a general trauma model can be used to explain responses to CSA in all cases. Specifically, they argue that not all CSA is traumatic (i.e., involves threat that produces overwhelming fear responses and feelings of helplessness). As a result they claim that only those cases that conform to the criterion established for "trauma" in the DSM-IV for PTSD (American Psychiatric Association, 1994) can be explained by a general trauma model. Kendall-Tackett et al. (1993) go one step further in pointing out that PTSD is not the universal reaction to CSA, is not specific to CSA, and because much CSA lacks the defining characteristics of trauma, a general trauma model based on PTSD cannot explain the effects of CSA.

Specific CSA Trauma Models

Specific trauma models, which have been presented in an effort to understand the processes and mechanisms involved in the development of problems in victims of CSA, have focused on both the unique characteristics of the abuse and the developmental age of the traumatized victim. In these models some of the same processes (e.g., conditioning, challenges to cognitive structures) are proposed to operate in response to the experience of CSA.

For example, in an effort to explain how children might not have a memory for intrafamilial sexual abuse, Freyd (1996) focuses on the unique characteristics of incest. She points out that incest involves a parent or other adult who has power and authority over a child, and who the child needs to trust in order to survive. The resultant *Betrayal Trauma* is used to explain how it is that children will not remember what happened to them (i.e., not knowing or remembering the abuse is necessary for the children's survival).

Trickett and Putnam's (1993) psychobiological model attempts to understand the long-term impact of sexual abuse by emphasizing the fact that the CSA trauma interferes with the psychological and biological processes of pubertal development. Specifically, CSA occurring prior to puberty is believed to result in psychological stress. The increased stress due to the trauma of CSA has physiological concomitants that affect the developing child, thus leading to long-term problems. Puberty is viewed as an important developmental period, one where there are important challenges (i.e., developmental and physical changes). CSA adds to the adjustment challenges and likely problems because of the nature of the trauma (sexual) and the added stress. That is, the physiological effects of the sexual trauma (stimulation of the hypothalamic-pituitary-adrenal and hypothalamic-pituitary-gonadal, HPA and HPG axes) may result in faster maturation and result in even greater stress.

Recognizing the complexity of CSA, Finkelhor and his colleagues (e.g., Browne & Finkelhor, 1986; Kendall-Tackett et al., 1993) propose a multifaceted trauma model, Traumagenic Mechanisms, which attempts to account for the variety of outcomes or effects observed. The Traumagenic Mechanisms include (1) traumatic sexualization, (2) betrayal, (3) stigmatization, and (4) powerlessness. Specific characteristics of the CSA experienced (e.g., use of force, relationship of perpetrator, response of others to disclosure, chronicity) will determine to what extent a particular mechanism will be activated that leads to an observed outcome.

A Self-Trauma Model proposed by Briere (1996a, 1996b) attempts to integrate trauma theory within the developmental perspective. Briere proposes that the core effects of abuse (other-directedness, chronic perception of danger, negative self-perception, negative specialness, conditional reality, heightened ability to avoid distress, impaired self-functioning, and posttraumatic intrusion) result from disruptions in development caused by the abuse. These disruptions include: (1) alterations in early childhood attachment dynamics; (2) effects of early posttraumatic stress; (3) development of primitive coping strategies; and (4) distortions of the child's cognitive understanding of self, others, and the future. Through these disruptions of attachment, increased stress, the automatic use of primitive coping strategies (e.g., dissociation), and disturbed cognitions, self-capacities (e.g., identity, boundary, and affect regulation) fail to develop in the abused child. The result is a survivor who is chronically dissociated, experiences intrusive symptoms, and evidences characterological difficulties associated with identity, boundaries, and affect regulation problems.

While these specific CSA trauma models have been proposed in an attempt to move our understanding of the dynamics of CSA beyond what the general trauma models provide, we are still left with general propositions that have, for the most part, not been empirically tested (Briere, 1996a; Kendall-Tackett et al., 1993). Feiring et al. (1996) call for the development of middle-range theories that can be examined empirically. For example, they utilized the Traumagenic Mechanisms Model, specifically the traumagenic effect of stigmatization, in constructing and testing a model that related CSA to attributions and resultant feelings of shame (Feiring et al. 1996). Similarly, Epstein, Saunders, Kilpatrick, and Resnick (1998) conducted a path analytic study with two assessments one year apart that suggested that PTSD mediates the relationship between CSA and alcohol abuse. That is, CSA produces emotional distress that results in attempts at tension reduction, including alcohol use, which is a form of self-medication. While more general conceptualizations can lead to general treatment approaches, such middle-range theories and empirical studies have the potential to specifically inform our treatments.

Approaches to Understanding Mechanisms/Processes: Relations

The other broad, general approach to understanding problems of CSA survivors views CSA as occurring as a result of, or at least in the context of, family dysfunction. This dysfunction then interferes with the normal development of relationships (e.g., attachment, object relations), which has a direct impact on subsequent problems that have been attributed to CSA alone.

Attachment

Alexander and her colleagues (Alexander & Anderson, 1994; Alexander, Anderson, Brand, Schaeffer, Grelling, & Kretz, 1998) recognize that PTSD and abuse-specific trauma models may be useful in understanding the incest survivor, but argue that other experiences (i.e., the family context associated with the abuse) may explain even more long-term effects than the abuse itself. Specifically, they adhere to an attachment perspective that views the bond between child and caregiver as a biologically based drive that assures the survival and protection of a child. The attachment that results in childhood is determined by the caregiving environment. And this early attachment is related to later adult attachment (i.e., secure, fearful, dismissing, or preoccupied), which not only influences subsequent intimate relationships but also results in distress and personality problems. Thus, from this perspective the caregiving environment and attachment problems that result can explain (1) the individual and family dysfunction that led to the incest, (2) the way the abuse is experienced, and (3) patterns of outcomes in survivors (Alexander et al., 1998).

Empirical support for the claimed relationship between attachment and subsequent distress and personality problems was obtained in a study examining 92 incest survivors (Alexander et al., 1998). Specifically, individuals with fearful attachments showed more avoidant behaviors, those with preoccupied attachments evidenced more dependent behavior, and both presented with more self-defeating behaviors and borderline tendencies than individuals with secure or dismissing attachments. In addition, the authors reported that characteristics of the intrafamilial abuse (e.g., age of onset, severity, threats, etc.) were related to symptoms of PTSD (e.g., avoidance, intrusive thoughts, etc.). Alexander et al. conclude that ". . . this study has demonstrated the propensity for insecure attachment among incest survivors as well as the relationship between attachment and current functioning. Sexual abuse severity and attachment have significant but distinct effects on long-term outcome. Attachment theory would thus appear to be useful and relevant to the prediction of long-term effects and to the eventual therapeutic resolution of a traumatic abuse history in adults" (p. 58).

Object Relations

Psychoanalytic approaches to understanding the impact of intrafamilial sexual abuse have only recently emerged. As Scharff and Scharff (1994) confess, most clinicians who were working with incest survivors were feeling traumatized themselves. That is, they had no theory to support what they were encountering (i.e., actual versus fantasized molesting), were oftentimes viewed as an abuse object because of client transference, and had doubts about their ability to work with incest survivors (i.e., feelings of anguish, guilt, and helplessness due to countertransference). Finally, the culture of the psychoanalytic perspective was one which believed that memories of incest were to be interpreted as fantastic distortions of reality (e.g., Barnard, Hankins, & Robbins, 1992; Goodwin, 1993; Scharff & Scharff, 1994).

In the last decade, psychoanalytic formulations have moved from an exclusive reliance on drive discharge as an explanation of psychological development to those that include continuity of relationships (Barnard et al., 1992). For example, the object relations theory proposes that children experience those around them as part of the self in early life. Whole object relatedness is achieved when children come to see self and others as separate, and they recognize that both self and others can be at one time loving and somewhat destructive. Resolution of this split (between self and others, and between all good and all bad) is viewed as crucial for development. This development includes the formation of object relation units that are used to construct personalities (i.e., how to relate to self, others, and the world at large). When children are raised by abusive caregivers, the object relation units that develop are likely to be unhealthy. As a result, the cohesiveness of the self can be threatened from within, thus leading to observable character problems (i.e., personality disorders).

It is also the case that more traditional psychoanalytic formulations are beginning to focus less on whether the alleged abuse was real or is fantasy, and more on how the experience of intrafamilial abuse can (1) impact psychological development and (2) be treated (see Diamond, 1997; Steele, 1987). The trauma of childhood sexual abuse is seen as impacting the child's attachments, identity formation, and developing psychic functioning (Steele, 1987). This external trauma and excitation combine with intrapsychically generated stimulation to overwhelm the ego. The shock and state of helplessness leads to fears of ego collapse and annihilation (e.g., falling apart, going crazy), due in part to the undeveloped ego. When overwhelmed, the immature psychic structures of the child fail to elaborate or absorb the trauma, but instead register and express it somatically (i.e., implicit memory). Because the event is not represented in explicit memory (i.e., language-based or symbolic), verbal recall of the trauma is not likely. The differentiation or splitting of event memories, affect, etc. further supports the use of dissociation as the primary ego defense, protecting the victim from traumatic overstimulation and excitation (Diamond, 1997).

Common Themes for Treatment

This brief review of proposed explanations for understanding how CSA can lead to observed long-term problems in survivors was undertaken with the aim of identifying common targets for our treatments. It is interesting to note that though a variety of approaches to psychopathology (e.g., behavioral, cognitive, psychoanalytic, attachment) have identified very different mechanisms to explain the development of disorders (e.g., learning, processing of information, interpersonal, and intrapersonal) in response to CSA, there are some common themes. These common themes are most likely due to the fact that we are interested in the impact of an external event (i.e., risk factor) on an individual. This event, whether considered to be traumatic or a correlate of another dysfunction, must necessarily be the focal point of all conceptual explanations. Thus, unlike explanations for psychological disorders that begin with a focus on a specific ecological level (e.g., intrapersonal, interpersonal, superordinate, organic; see Wenar, 1994) that is predetermined by a given perspective, the sexual abuse itself is the initial focus for all perspectives. Other common explanatory themes that emerge after considering the characteristics of the abuse include (1) distress or anxiety that results from the external event, (2) disruption in the development of social rela-

tions, and (3) attempts to cope with or understand the event that led to changes in how the individuals interpret or perceive their inner and outer world. These common themes have in turn resulted in the identification of a number of general treatment targets or objectives: (1) exposure to the traumatic event (e.g., *in vivo*, imaginal, reenactment); (2) processing of the event (e.g., reinterpretation, reintegration); and (3) development of interpersonal attachment (e.g., trust, social skills) (Alexander et al., 1998; Briggs & Joyce, 1997; Foa & Meadows, 1997; Gelinas, 1993; Goodwin, 1993: Hartman & Burgess, 1993; Jaycox et al., 1997; Johnson & Williams-Keeler, 1998; Loewenstein, 1993; Roth & Newman, 1993).

A number of retrospective studies suggest that those survivors of CSA who disclosed, discussed, and re-appraised what happened to them were better adjusted than those who did not (Arata, 1998; Himelein & McElrath, 1996; Varia, Abidin, & Dass, 1996). In addition, we have recently completed follow-up interviews with parents and children who had participated in an evidentiary exam because of suspected molestation (Jinich & Litrownik, 1999). We are finding that both short- and long-term effects of CSA are related to how others, specifically caregivers, responded (e.g., support, belief, attributions) to disclosure of the abuse by the victim.

Thus, our review of explanatory approaches has yielded a number of common treatment themes. These themes (or factors) have in turn been found to be related to short- and long-term outcomes in CSA survivors (i.e., they appear to be related to adaptive coping). In addition, there is substantial anecdotal evidence suggesting that a variety of treatment approaches based on these conceptual models are effective with sexual abuse survivors (e.g., Corder, Haizlip, & DeBoer, 1990; Grammer & Shannon, 1992; Sturkie, 1983). In the following section we attempt to move from this first step in developing treatment approaches for incest survivors to one where the efficacy of these treatments is evaluated.

Empirical Evidence

One of the problems that we encountered as we began searching for empirical studies that evaluate treatments for CSA or incest survivors was that we could not find many. Because trauma models have been utilized to conceptualize child sexual abuse, we decided to review the empirical treatment outcome literature for other similar traumatized populations. In addition, we felt that the efficacy of interventions designed for child victims of CSA would also inform treatments targeted to adult CSA survivors. Thus, in this section we examine treatment outcome studies and reviews for children who have been sexually abused, adult trauma victims (e.g., rape/sexual assault, combat), and adult survivors of CSA. Our objective is to determine whether consistent patterns emerge in treatment efficacy across these different trauma-exposed populations.

Treatment of CSA Survivors

Recent qualitative (Finkelhor & Berliner, 1995; O'Donohue & Elliott, 1992) and meta-analytic (Reeker, Ensing, & Elliott, 1997) reviews have examined both published and unpublished reports of treatment effects with sexually abused children. The meta-analytic review identified 15 studies that examined the impact of group treatments (13 published and 2 unpublished). In order to be included in the meta-analyses, the studies had to have used empirical measures rather than clinical impressions or unstructured interviews with parents, and they had to have had sufficient information about the outcomes to allow for the calculation of effect sizes. The core outcomes examined included (1) general psychological distress, (2) internalizing symptoms (depression, anxiety, fears), (3) externalizing symptoms, (4) sexual behaviors, (5) self-esteem, and (6) knowledge of sexual abuse/prevention.

Reeker et al. (1997) reported a mean pre–post effect size of .79 (based on 49 measures overall) for the 15 identified studies. Unfortunately, as this meta-analysis was based on pre–post designs, conclusions that can be drawn about the effectiveness of group interventions for sexually abused youths are necessarily limited. That is, we cannot know if the improvements observed in these studies were due to the treatment provided or to the passage of time.

Finkelhor and Berliner (1995) conducted a more comprehensive and informative review of treatment outcome studies that targeted sexually abused children. Seventeen studies with pre–post, five with quasi-experimental, and seven with true experimental designs (i.e., equivalent group comparisons) were reviewed. In general, Finkelhor and Berliner report similar findings for pre–post design studies (many of the studies reviewed were the same as those included in Reeker et al., 1997), and somewhat less favorable results for quasi-experimental design studies (i.e., they found no

relationship between treatment and outcome in three of five studies). For the experimental design studies they found that three studies comparing randomly assigned treatment versus waiting-list control groups showed treatment-related reductions in depression, anxiety, sexual abuse fear, and internalizing symptoms in sexually abused children. In only one of the remaining studies that compared outcomes for different treatments was there an observed treatment effect. Specifically, Cohen and Mannarino (1996) found a greater reduction in symptoms (i.e., behavior problems and internalizing symptoms) for sexually abused preschool children who were treated in a structured, cognitive-behavioral, abuse-specific group as opposed to an unstructured, interpersonal support group.

As is evident by the limited number of true experimental studies in these recent reviews, the process of empirically validating treatments for sexually abused children is just beginning. Of the studies reviewed, few employed control groups (reportedly for ethical reasons), random assignment was not used, treatments were generally multimodal and unstandardized, and sample sizes were small. These limitations have begun to be addressed in some more recent studies. For example, continuing their work with sexually abused preschool children, Cohen and Mannarino have conducted several studies (1996, 1997) in which a two-group randomized design has been used to examine comparative treatment efficacy in abuse-specific cognitive-behavioral therapy groups and nondirective supportive groups. The results of these studies indicate that a cognitive-behavioral approach is more effective than a nondirective supportive approach. Children and their parents were randomly assigned to treatment groups, standardized assessments were utilized to evaluate outcomes, and assessments were conducted over time (pretreatment, posttreatment, and one-year follow-up).

In their most recent study, Cohen and Mannarino (1998) report on the efficacy of the abuse-specific cognitive-behavioral intervention delivered individually to school-aged children (7 to 14 years of age) compared to individual nondirective supportive therapy. Children and their nonoffending parents were provided 12 individual therapy sessions. As with the child abuse-specific group treatment for the younger preschool-aged children, the individual cognitive-behavioral treatment targeted symptoms of depression, anxiety, and behaviors related to these, while parent treatment aimed at decreasing emotional distress, enhancing parental support for the child, and managing child behavioral difficulties related to abuse (i.e., increasing parents' problem-solving skills). The nondirective supportive therapy was unstructured and provided a supportive, noncognitive-nonbehavioral treatment. Cohen and Mannarino (1998) found that children and parents receiving the cognitive-behavioral treatment evidenced less depression and greater social competence on standardized assessments over time than those in the nondirective supportive group.

In another recent study, Berliner and Saunders (1996) examined whether the addition of abuse-specific interventions targeting fear and anxiety (commonly found symptoms in sexually abused children) to a standard treatment protocol would lead to greater symptom reduction in children 4 to 13 years of age. Eighty sexually abused children were randomly assigned to either a 10-week index or comparison group. Both included typical components of conventional sexual abuse treatment; however, treatment for the index group also included stress inoculation training and gradual exposure treatment procedures. Children in the index group were, therefore, required to discuss their own sexual abuse experiences while children in the comparison group were not. Child and parent assessments were taken pre- and immediately posttreatment and again at one- and two-year follow-up time points. While significant improvements over time on most of the outcome measures were found for both intervention groups, additional hypothesized gains (e.g., fear and anxiety symptoms) for the enhanced group were not observed (Berliner & Saunders, 1996).

Finally, Deblinger, Lippman, and Steer (1996) examined the efficacy of an abuse-focused cognitive-behavioral treatment group for sexually abused children, and involvement of nonoffending parents in the treatment of their children. One hundred participating families were randomly assigned to one of three sexual abuse-focused cognitive behavioral treatment groups (mother only, child only, mother and child), or to a community control condition. Children's behavior problems, anxiety, depression, and post-traumatic stress disorder (PTSD) symptoms as well as parenting practices were assessed at pre- and posttreatment, using standardized instruments. Deblinger and her colleagues report that inclusion of the child in treatment (i.e., child only, parent and child) resulted in significantly fewer PTSD symptoms. Inclusion of the parent in treatment (i.e., mother only, mother and child) resulted in parents reporting greater improvements in their children's externalizing symptoms, increases in their use of effective parenting skills, and in children reporting significantly less depression posttreatment. These findings not only highlight the effectiveness of abuse-focused cognitive behavioral interventions, but also the positive impact of involving important support figures in therapy with the traumatized individual.

Thus, there is an emerging convergence of empirical findings that support the efficacy of cognitive-behavioral treatments (including involvement of nonoffending parents) for children who have been sexually abused. The evidence comes from three different research groups, including random assignment to treatment conditions, standardized assessments, and long-term follow-up in two of the studies (i.e., all criteria used to determine whether treatments have been empirically supported; see Chambless & Hollon, 1998). Some of the specific components of the abuse-focused cognitive-behavioral approaches found in these outcome studies were (1) gradual exposure to the abuse, (2) identifying and expressing feelings, (3) coping and social skills training, and (4) involvement of a significant person in the child's life (i.e., nonoffending parents who experienced many of the same components and were shown how to support their child) (Berliner & Saunders, 1996; Cohen & Mannarino, 1996, 1997, 1998; Deblinger et al., 1996).

Treatment of PTSD

Two recent qualitative reviews (see DeRubeis & Crits-Christoph, 1998; Foa & Meadows, 1997) utilized rigorous criteria (e.g., clearly defined target symptoms, reliable and valid measures, use of blind evaluators, assessor training, specific replicable treatment programs, unbiased assignment to treatment, and treatment adherence) in reviewing treatment efficacy for PTSD. Almost all of the studies reviewed targeted populations of rape victims and combat veterans. Foa and Meadows (1997) summarized the findings for each of a number of psychosocial treatments (e.g., hypnotherapy, psychodynamic treatments, and cognitive-behavioral treatments). The DeRubeis and Crits-Christoph (1998) review was included within a broader review of efficacious treatments for adult disorders, and only presented examples of outcome studies that were used to identify specific treatments as efficacious. A third review

(Frueh, Turner, & Beidel, 1995) took a critical look at the evidence for the efficacy of exposure therapy targeted specifically to combat-related PTSD.

The reviews were consistent in mentioning that most of the treatment outcome studies have examined cognitive-behavioral treatments, and that the approaches to treatment with the most empirical support are exposure and stress inoculation. These two cognitive-behavioral treatments include a variety of specific techniques. For example, exposure-based treatments vary along a number of dimensions (e.g., from prolonged to graduated, imaginal to *in vivo*, exposure to trauma-related cues only to psychodynamically hypothesized cues) and have been identified as distinct techniques (e.g., implosion, flooding, desensitization, eye movement desensitization, and reprocessing; see Frueh et al., 1995; Foa & Jaycox, in press). Stress inoculation approaches include behavioral anxiety management and coping techniques as well as cognitive restructuring (DeRubeis & Crits-Christoph, 1998). In addition, Foa and Meadows (1997) point out that some more rigorous recent studies examining the efficacy of psychodynamically oriented approaches (e.g., interpersonal process group therapy) hold some promise. At the same time they note that suggested components of this approach (e.g., dosing of the traumatic experience and encouraging expression) are similar to those coming from the cognitive-behavioral perspective. This, of course, is not unexpected given our discussion of the conceptual frameworks that generate suggested treatment techniques, and the common themes that result.

One additional review (Chard, 1995) was completed as part of a dissertation project. Specifically, a meta-analysis of 14 empirical treatment outcome studies of sexually abused women was conducted. The studies varied from pre–post and quasi-experimental to experimental designs with female rape, abuse, and/or battery survivors diagnosed with PTSD. Chard categorized the studies based on the type of design utilized, treatment modality (individual or group), and identified intervention approach (e.g., cognitive, cognitive-behavioral, supportive, psychodynamic, or mixed-model), and looked at differences in effect sizes. While this was an interesting and much needed look at interventions that have targeted sexually abused women, the project suffers from a number of problems. For example, there were a small number of studies and a large number of intervention categories, categorization of interventions was unique, effect size comparisons were made across single group pre–post and control group designs, and an adolescent group treatment study was included. Nevertheless, the findings appear to be consistent with the previous reviews. For example, the overall treatment effect size was large, and the components of the interventions (i.e., cognitive, psychodynamic) that contributed to this effect size had a number of common features (e.g., exposure, re-framing/reintegration of trauma, and interpersonal transaction). In addition, Chard (1995) reported that individual therapy appeared to be more beneficial than group therapy approaches. In summarizing her findings, Chard noted that she had a difficult time trying to determine treatment efficacy given the fact that most of the studies included in the meta-analytic review utilized multiple treatment approaches, lacked specific treatment protocols, and did not use randomized control group designs.

Treatment of Adult CSA Survivors

Included in the reviews noted previously (i.e., Chard, 1995; Foa & Meadows, 1997) were five studies (four published and one presentation) that specifically targeted adult women who had been sexually abused as children (Alexander, Neimeyer, Follette, Moore, & Harter, 1989; Carver, Stalker, Stewart, & Abraham, 1989; Jehu, 1989; Roberts & Lie, 1989; Scarvalone, Cloitre, & Difede, 1995). Two of the studies (Alexander et al., Scarvalone et al.) included a comparison group (i.e., wait-list control), while the remaining three examined pre–post differences in their treatment group only. Scarvalone et al. compared an interpersonal process group therapy (IPGT) with a naturally occurring wait-list control in a sample of 43 female CSA survivors. Reduced symptomatology was observed in both groups on several outcomes, with significantly fewer (39%) participants in the IPGT group who met criteria for PTSD at posttreatment compared to 83% of the control group. In addition, whereas both groups reported fewer symptoms of depression and dissociation at posttreatment, subjects in the IPGT group reported a greater reduction of intrusive symptoms than the control group. Unfortunately, not all patients were assessed by independent evaluators at posttreatment. Thus, it is difficult to determine to what extent experimenter expectancy may have accounted for positive findings.

Alexander et al. (1989) randomly assigned 65 women survivors of intrafamilial sexual abuse to either one of two 10-week treatment groups (i.e., interpersonal transaction or process group) or a wait-list condition. Analyses of changes from pre- to posttreatment suggested that the two treatment groups were effective, relative to the wait-list control group, in reducing depression, fearfulness, and general distress, while improving social adjustment.

In addition to these comparison group studies that examined the efficacy of group interventions with female survivors of CSA, two of the reviewed studies (Carver et al., 1989; Roberts & Lie, 1989) and two additional studies (Donaldson & Cordes-Green, 1994; Paddison, Einbinder, Maker, & Strain, 1993) report positive effects of group treatments for female survivors based on single group pre–post designs.

Finally, Westbury and Tutty (1999) attempted to assess the impact of group treatment for CSA survivors over and above the individual treatment they were receiving. Using a quasi-experimental design (i.e., nonrandom assignment to group or wait-list for the group), they found that both individual therapy and individual therapy plus group treatment resulted in decreased depression and trauma symptoms. And those who participated in the group showed significantly greater decreases in depression and anxiety than those who remained on a wait-list for participation in the group. All of the groups evaluated in these studies, as well as those developed by Alexander et al. (1989) and Scarvalone et al. (1995) were time-limited, included a focus on developing trust, required disclosure of the trauma, included some processing of feelings and beliefs related to the trauma, and targeted the development of interpersonal skills. While the specific format of the groups varied (i.e., number of sessions, time of sessions, order in which targeted sessions were presented), all of the authors attempted to take advantage of the major curative factors inherent in group treatment identified by Yalom (1995). Some of these factors, which are believed to be especially relevant for survivors of CSA (and incest specifically) are group cohesiveness (facilitating trust and disclosure), universality (recognition that they are not alone), and socialization (development of new healthier behaviors).

Still, the evidence for the efficacy of group treatments for survivors of CSA is minimal (only two published studies that included a control group with only one utilizing random assignment), whereas there is even less evidence supporting the efficacy of individual therapy (only one pre–post design study published; Jehu, 1989). It is hoped that two recently published studies (i.e., Freedman & Enright, 1996; Zlotnick, Shea, Rosen, Simpson, Mulrenin, Begin, & Pearlstein, 1997) that utilized randomized assignment to treatment and control conditions in an effort to evaluate the outcome of individual and group treatments, respectively, portend what the future holds. First, Zlotnick et al. compared the effectiveness of an affect-management treatment group (AMT) to a wait-list control condition. A total of 48 female survivors of childhood sexual abuse with PTSD were randomly assigned to either the 15-week treatment group or a wait list. Women in the treatment group also received both individual psychotherapy and pharmacotherapy for the duration of the study. The AMT program was developed, in part, because of the assumption that trauma-focused treatment (i.e., flooding and prolonged exposure) is contraindicated for survivors of sexual abuse in the early stages. This assumption is based on the expected pattern of emotional dysregulation found in CSA survivors (see Herman, 1992; Briere, 1996a). As a result, the treatment protocol consisted of homework assignments and their review, psychoeducational presentations (on topics such as PTSD, dissociation, flashbacks, identification of emotions, crisis planning, anger management, and techniques for distraction, self-soothing, and relaxation), skill building; and application of skills. Group materials were taken from Linehan's Dialectical Behavior Therapy (Linehan, 1993) and Matsakis's Treatment Guide for Post-Traumatic Stress Disorder (Matsakis, 1994).

Controlling for pretreatment scores, Zlotnick et al. (1997) found that patients who completed the AMT group reported significantly fewer posttreatment symptoms of PTSD and dissociation than those in the wait-list control group. The authors concluded that affect-management group treatment can serve as a beneficial adjunct to individual psychotherapy and pharmacotherapy for survivors of CSA with PTSD. In addition, as this treatment targeted dissociative symptoms, they noted that it can be particularly beneficial in reducing negative PTSD symptoms related to numbing experiences, which purportedly are most resistant to change. Unfortunately, information on maintenance of symptom change was lacking, and we cannot determine the efficacy of AMT because it was delivered in conjunction with individual psychotherapy and pharmacotherapy.

The second study (Freedman & Enright, 1996) reports on the efficacy of an intervention that attempts to promote forgiveness by the incest survivor for the actions of her abuser. Twelve female incest survivors were randomly assigned to an experimental group (receiving the forgiveness intervention immediately) or a wait-list control group (receiving the intervention when their matched experimental counterpart finished the intervention). Each participant met individually with the therapist once per week. A process model of forgiveness was used as the focus of intervention requiring that the participant progress through each of 17 units, e.g., examination of psychological defenses, confront anger, admit shame and guilt, cognitive rehearsal of offense, reframing, acceptance, absorption of the pain, and emotional release. The average length of the intervention (i.e., time required to complete the 17 units) for the 12 participants was 14.3 months. Dependent variables included measures of forgiveness, self-esteem, hope, psychological depression, and state-trait anxiety. Following the intervention, the experimental group evidenced significant gains relative to the control group in forgiveness and hope and decreased anxiety and depression. When the control group completed the treatment program, they evidenced similar patterns of change relative to their prior functioning. In addition, the experimental participants continued to report decreased depression up to one year after the intervention had ended.

Summary of Empirical Evidence

A number of qualitative and meta-analytic reviews of interventions targeted to adults who have a history of CSA, adults with PTSD who have experienced similar traumas (e.g., sexual assault or rape, combat), and children who have been sexually abused suggest that any treatment is better than no treatment. At the same time, it has been noted that most of the empirical studies have examined the efficacy of cognitive-behavioral interventions with the result being that this approach has received the most support. What is most interesting is that all the treatments evaluated that have demonstrated some effect seem to have a number of components in common. That is, regardless of the theoretical approach used in developing a specific intervention (e.g., psychoana-

lytic, cognitive-behavioral) and the mechanisms proposed to explain the problems experienced by victims (e.g., conditioning, failure to process the trauma, disruption of self systems or interpersonal relations), the same techniques have been applied. These techniques include attention to interpersonal relations (e.g., support from a significant other), some re-exposure to the trauma, and processing of the trauma experience (e.g., cognitive restructuring, resolution). Again, this is not surprising given the common themes for targeted treatments that result following a review of the various conceptual approaches used to understand the impact of CSA (see Figure 24.1 for a summary).

Even though only three controlled outcome studies have been conducted with CSA survivors, there may be some justification for claiming that possibly efficacious interventions for this population have been identified. Specifically, these three studies assessed different interventions, but they all contained similar features, as did the more numerous quasi-experimental reports. In addition, these same features or components have been demonstrated to be efficacious in treating children who have been sexually abused as well as adults who have experienced the trauma of sexual assault and combat. Thus, we may be at a stage in the development of our interventions for CSA survivors where we can begin to look at how we can move from efficacy to effectiveness studies, and to eventual application in community settings.

At this stage our task should be one of identifying the specifics of the treatment components (e.g., timing and type of exposure) that are best suited for a particular client. For example, Foa and her colleagues (Foa & Jaycox, in press; Foa & Meadows, 1997) have suggested that prolonged exposure is most effective for PTSD clients. Yet they and others (e.g., Dye & Roth, 1991; Ehlers, Clarke, Dunmore, Jaycox et al., 1998; McFarlane & van der Kolk, 1996; Zlotnick et al., 1997) have cautioned that it may not be appropriate for all sexual assault victims, much less for individuals who have experienced CSA. Similarly, Herman (1992) has suggested that trauma-focused therapy (i.e., treatment that facilitates the disclosure of sexual abuse experiences) may be detrimental for survivors of CSA in the early stages of recovery. Similarly, Zlotnick et al. (1997) point out that flooding techniques have little effect on PTSD symptoms that relate to emotional numbing and avoidance—symptoms that are frequently

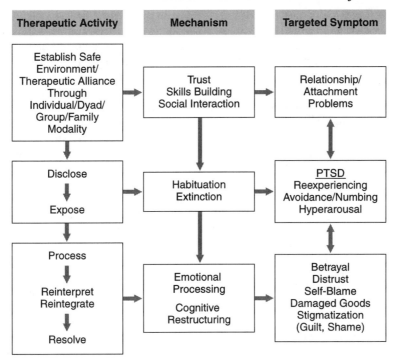

Figure 24.1   Schematic Summary of Empirical Findings.

found among survivors of CSA. In fact, Dye and Roth (1991) indicate that engaging in intense interactions focused on memories of abuse can be dangerous if a client (1) has a low tolerance for anxiety; and (2) does not have intimate relationships upon which she can rely. Thus, the treatment outcome studies that were utilized to identify efficacious treatments for sexual assault and combat-related PTSD may not be directly generalizable to survivors of CSA.

This caution has implications for assumptions that we might make about the appropriateness of treatments for male and female victims. That is, we are not aware of any empirical report of the efficacy of a treatment for male survivors of CSA. At the same time, most of the evaluations of treatment for combat-related PTSD have targeted males, while almost all of those targeting sexual assault victims have included females. Though we may not be able to generalize treatments designed for these populations (male combat and adult female sexual assault) to female (and male) CSA survivors, there is reason to assume that treatments for female CSA survivors can be generalized to male CSA survivors.

Specifically, there is evidence that the characteristics of CSA are similar across the genders (Gold et al., 1998), as are the effects (e.g., PTSD). And because males and females with PTSD (i.e., combat-related and sexual assault, respectively) respond favorably to similar interventions, it is logical to assume that approaches to treatment with female CSA survivors should be appropriate for male survivors. Of course, evidence to support this assumption must come from much needed treatment outcome studies that examine the impact of suggested treatments as well as the characteristics of survivors and the abuse that they experienced.

PRACTICE ISSUES AND RECOMMENDATIONS FOR THE FUTURE

The confluence of theoretical and empirical support for treatment approaches that involve exposure to the trauma of incest, cognitive restructuring, and a reliance on establishing a trusting supportive relationship clearly points to the need for evaluating these approaches in well-controlled outcome (i.e., efficacy) studies with survivors of CSA. This should include a determination of any differential effects attributable to the relationship of the perpetrator to the victim (i.e., intrafamilial versus extrafamilial abuse). In addition, a number of other factors need to be addressed as we evaluate these approaches when applied by practitioners in the community for patients entering community clinics and offices of private practitioners (i.e., effectiveness and practice issues). A number of these issues or factors are discussed in the following sections.

CSA Incest Survivors: Unique Characteristics

In their review of efficacious treatments for PTSD, Foa and Meadows (1997) conclude by discussing treatment issues that should be considered as a function of the specific trauma experienced. They point out that PTSD represents a change in the individual from pretrauma functioning. This is difficult to ascertain in cases where the trauma occurred when the individual was much younger (i.e., CSA or incest survivor). Thus, the link between the trauma and presenting problems may not be as clear in these cases (i.e., changes in the client's developmental course and/or subsequent factors could be responsible for current problems). Similarly, McFarlane and van der Kolk (1996) point out that the ability of a victim to adapt to a specific traumatic experience is related to the victim's developmental level (i.e., capabilities). They claim that there is now evidence to suggest that trauma occurring at an early age can affect the development of systems that regulate biological processes.

Briere's (1996a, 1996b) theoretical approach (i.e., self-trauma model) addresses this issue in greater detail. Specifically, he points out that the early trauma of sexual abuse can interfere with the normal development of self-capacities (e.g., identity, boundary, and self-regulation). As a result, the victim does not learn to modulate or tolerate affect, and is likely to develop enduring negative schemata (e.g., self as helpless, inadequate, loathsome). When faced with emotionally laden material in therapy (i.e., exposure to CSA history) the incest survivor who has not developed these self-capacities is likely to be overwhelmed, resorting to the use of the same primitive avoidance strategies used initially (e.g., dissociation). Briere cautions that while exposure to the trauma is necessary for treatment, it must be accomplished in a gradual fashion, and only as the client develops self-resources that can be utilized to cope with

the exposure to aspects of the trauma. These resources (e.g., self-awareness, positive identity, affect regulation) can be developed within a context of safety and support as the client learns to deal with aspects of the trauma. Thus, survivors of CSA trauma are seen as being quite different from other trauma victims (e.g., adult survivors of rape and those exposed to battle). Not only do incest survivors evidence arrested social/cognitive development, but they also have a distinctively different experience (e.g., betrayal by family member, response to disclosure) and history (period of time between trauma and when adult therapy begins). Therefore, "abuse-focused" therapy not only needs to include exposure to the trauma and the development of a supportive therapeutic relationship but also to encourage the expression of abuse-related feelings (e.g., anger, ambivalence, fear), clarify erroneous beliefs that might lead to negative attributions about self or others (e.g., self-blame), teach abuse prevention skills, and diminish the sense of stigma and isolation through reassurance or exposure to other victims (e.g., group therapy).

Assessment

The cornerstone for good therapeutic practice is an appropriate assessment. Alexander et al. (1998) suggest that assessments of CSA survivors should include gathering information about current relationships (including how past relationships contribute to the maintenance of current internal working models and problems). Though one of the suggested treatment components for CSA survivors involves exposure to the trauma, it is not clear that detailed information about the sexual abuse history needs to be obtained before treatment plans can be established. The objective should be one of gathering enough information to indicate that the client experienced sexual abuse. This is not always as easy as it might appear.

For example, Courtois (1995) identifies four ways in which a history of CSA or incest might be indicated by a client: (1) The client presents with relatively continuous memory of sexual abuse as a child, and if previously in therapy, the treatment has either not focused on this history or it has not had an impact (most common). (2) The client has some of the major symptoms of CSA and a partial or vague memory that something happened. (3) The client has some of the major symptoms of abuse, but no recall or memory of sexual abuse. And (4) the client requests that the therapist help in uncovering a history of abuse (i.e., the client believes the memory has been repressed). The latter two types of presentations are particularly problematic, the last one because of the danger of manufacturing or developing accounts of events that did not happen (e.g., Loftus, 1993), and the third because there is no indication by the client that there is a history of incest.

Some (e.g., Courtois, 1995; Fish, 1998) point out that the majority of clients who come to therapy with a positive history of abuse either do not disclose or disguise this history upon presentation. A variety of reasons have been proposed (e.g., amount of time passed, extreme shame and stigmatization, fear and terror, loyalty to perpetrator, previous negative experience when tried to disclose, fear of ridicule or abandonment). As a result, most clients who have a history of CSA are not identified because the majority of therapists do not ask about CSA histories, and few survivors volunteer information without being asked (Fish, 1998). We agree with Courtois who suggests that good practice now requires that therapists routinely ask about sexual abuse experiences as part of their overall clinical assessment. The therapist must walk a fine line (i.e., not be suggestive, avoid emotionally charged words such as *molest* or *incest*).

Nevertheless, therapists do need to ask their clients about this sensitive issue, as they ask about other behaviors or experiences that might be emotionally charged (e.g., substance use). In fact, Trotter (1995) suggests that sexual trauma should be addressed by therapists in the same manner they address substance use. That is, it should be questioned in a matter-of-fact manner during the routine psychosocial assessment. Trotter cautions that therapists also need to be aware that, like alcoholics, survivors of CSA tend to deny, repress, or avoid disclosing an abuse history. Thus, it is suggested that the therapist: (1) normalize the experience (e.g., "Many people who come to therapy report . . ."); (2) be specific in describing possible experiences (e.g., "Did anyone older than you ever touch your genitalia, or have you touch theirs when you didn't want to?"); (3) be available to follow up on a disclosure if the client is distressed; and (4) allow the assessment to unfold over time. Given the reported prevalence estimates of CSA in adult clinical populations, it is likely that such assessments will lead to even more clients being identified as having a sexual abuse history. This presents an additional dilemma for the therapist, i.e., how to treat the client who presents with a particular disorder (or problems) and a history of CSA. While there is some question about what problem or problems the therapist should focus on first, there is not a question about the need for additional assessment. Given our discussion about the unique character of the CSA survivor (e.g., disrupted development of self-capacities, danger of overwhelming them with trauma exposure) it is obvious that their ability to moderate affect, self-perceptions, etc. needs to be determined before proceeding with recommended treatment approaches (e.g., prolonged exposure).

Treatment Approaches: Moving from Efficacy to Practice

As we have suggested, the typical client presenting for therapy who has a history of CSA will most likely be seeking treatment because of other presenting problems. Thus, the clinician must make some decisions about how to approach treatment when there are multiple problems or issues. This requires some consideration of whether all or only some of the problems need to be treated, and if multiple problems are to be addressed should they be treated simultaneously or sequentially. If the decision is to treat the problems simultaneously, it may be necessary to adapt or adjust the application of an efficacious intervention when it is applied to persons who present with multiple problems. On the other hand, sequential approaches to treating multiple problems requires that decisions be made about which problem or problems need to be dealt with initially.

Two common problems associated with a history of CSA that are likely to be evidenced in survivors who present with PTSD are substance use and sexual problems. As Johnson and Williams-Keeler (1998) note, these can interfere with success of treatment if they are not integrated into the treatment plan. For example, there is some suggestion that substance abusers with PTSD who have completed treatment are at greater risk of relapsing than those without PTSD (Brown & Wolfe, 1994). While it is difficult to disentangle the cause–effect relationship between PTSD that might be a result of CSA versus substance use, it is likely that the two may operate in the individual's current environment to support each other. That is, when PTSD and the arousal or tension associated with the trauma are dealt with through self-medication (e.g., general tension reduction), both problems are maintained (e.g., reinforcement of substance use and the association between the trauma and PTSD). Similarly, PTSD that is associated with intrafamilial molestation has been related to problems in sexual desire or to the arousal phase (Douglas, Matson, & Hunger, 1989). As a result, Douglas et al. suggest that a detailed knowledge of abuse is needed in order to understand idiosyncratic phobic responses. It is only after this information is obtained that efficacious approaches to sexual dysfunctions can be modified to address the specific fears of a client.

In fact, we would suggest that as we move from efficacy to practice, our approach to treatment must necessarily become more flexible. Specifically, in practice settings the clinician should be assessing clients to determine presenting problems that need to be addressed, conceiving efficacious treatments for identified problems, and applying these treatments in a well-planned order to maximize desired outcome. Various treatment modalities (e.g., individual, couple, group) should be among the options available to the clinician in designing the treatment plan. These different treatment modalities may provide opportunities to address relationship issues in addition to trauma-related problems. For example, Johnson and Williams-Keeler (1998) describe a promising approach to treatment for couples when one or both have experienced trauma. While recognizing the need for individual therapy that targets the trauma, they argue that attachment issues (i.e., distance, defense, and distrust) can best be addressed in couples therapy. Though there haven't been any empirical studies demonstrating the efficacy of involving spouses in the treatment of CSA survivors, there is considerable support for involving parents in the treatment of children who have experienced CSA (e.g., Cohen & Mannarino, 1996, 1997, 1998; Deblinger et al., 1996).

CASE EXAMPLE—INITIAL THERAPIST

In this section we will present the case of Cindy, a 31-year-old Caucasian female client at the university outpatient psychology clinic with which both authors are affiliated. Background information will be provided on the client, followed by a summary of the case and a discussion of some specific issues that illustrate the treatment stages and conceptual issues we have discussed in the chapter thus far.

Client Characteristics and Initial Assessment

Cindy was a single mother (5- and 9-year-old daughters) who was in her senior year at the university. Her initial contact with the clinic occurred when she brought her 9-year-old in because of behavioral problems and her inability to manage them. After talking with Cindy, the therapist suggested that she too might benefit from individual therapy. Cindy agreed, indicating at her intake that she was seeking therapy for "stress and personal problems" while identifying specific difficulties with anger management, loneliness, parenting, depression, stress, fears, and relationships. While reporting that she had received psychological therapy two years earlier for "childhood issues, rape, abuse, and a split with the children's father," Cindy did not indicate that these issues were of current concern.

A personality assessment in the second week of treatment using the MMPI-II revealed a 2, 6 profile indicative of difficulties with depression and trust that are common among individuals who have experienced trauma. Cindy's MCMI-II profile was also representative of individuals who have been traumatized, indicating problems with suspiciousness and mistrust and a number of characteristics associated with personality disorders. Finally, Cindy obtained a score of 15 on the Beck Depression Inventory (BDI), indicating difficulties with sadness, failure, guilt, self-loathing, self-criticism, suicidal ideation, tearfulness, irritability, low energy, sleep problems, tiredness, and decreased libido.

Family and Social History

Cindy reported that she experienced a chaotic and traumatic childhood. It was marked by (1) a younger mentally retarded sister who spent much of her life in a residential treatment program, (2) a divorce that occurred when Cindy was 3-years of age, (3) a spiteful mother who prevented the father from seeing her, and (4) a troubled relationship with her mother (i.e., Cindy described her mother as a ". . . neglectful, and physically and emotionally abusive parent"). According to Cindy, her mother's moods were very unpredictable and she described being under a constant state of tension, "as though I was always walking on eggshells." When her mother would become angry and frustrated with her, she would beat Cindy with a metal hanger. Cindy married at age 21, in her words, "solely to get out of my mother's house." Her husband also turned out to be physically, verbally, and emotionally abusive. At the time of her intake, Cindy had been divorced for several years and had been dating and living with Bob for the past three years.

Initial Treatment

Cindy was initially seen for 17 sessions by a student therapist in training who had not previously worked with CSA survivors. During these sessions the therapist focused on the problems presented through parent training, stress management training (progressive muscle relaxation), and increasing interpersonal and communication skills. It was not until the final session with this therapist, who was moving to another placement, that Cindy mentioned problems in her current relationship with Bob and her past molestation.

CASE EXAMPLE— SUBSEQUENT THERAPIST

Initial Trust and Skill Building

In the initial session Cindy and the new therapist (Idalia Castillo-Cañez) reviewed Cindy's past history and the work she had done with the previous therapist. Though indicating dissatisfaction with her current relationship, Cindy indicated that she wanted to continue working on difficulties with assertion. In the beginning stages the therapist not only focused on building a therapeutic alliance but also explored trust issues related to both early and current attachment figures in her life (e.g., her mother and boyfriend).

During this initial phase Cindy revealed that she had a great deal of anger that was directed at Bob as well as a sense of hopelessness about expressing her feelings. Her approach in attempting to deal with this anger and the situation that led to it was to repress her feelings and avoid confrontation—a coping pattern she found had worked well in the past with her mother. Assertive skills and problem solving training (i.e., identifying and expressing feelings, identifying potential solutions) was presented in an effort to develop more adaptive coping responses.

As part of this focus, a couples session with Cindy and Bob was conducted after two months of individual sessions with Cindy. Common relationship difficulties experienced by trauma victims (e.g., need for control, mistrust, and repressed emotions) were identified and the expected course of Cindy's treatment was shared. Shortly after this, Cindy volunteered in an individual session

that she had started having a craving for drugs again. Exploration of the reason for her current cravings led Cindy to the realization that drugs had in the past provided her with a means to avoid and escape the pain of her reality (i.e., relationship with mother). She identified her dissatisfaction with her current relationship and her desire to avoid confronting Bob (and herself) with these painful issues. In an effort to help Cindy develop more appropriate alternative coping strategies to deal with this stress, progressive relaxation training was reinstituted. Cindy was prompted to develop and implement an exercise plan, and she was instructed to keep a record of (i.e., to monitor) her automatic thoughts that resulted when she was feeling stressed. In addition, she was taught to replace these maladaptive automatic thoughts with more positive, adaptive ones (e.g., "I am a good person, I can handle this"). Cindy reported that she implemented this in her day-to-day activities, and that she (with Bob's help) put a new discipline program for her children into practice.

Disclosure/Exposure

By the end of the third month of therapy an excellent therapeutic alliance between Cindy and the therapist had developed. In addition to the establishment of this trusting relationship, Cindy had developed a number of skills and was feeling that she had some control over her life. It was at this time that she finally appeared comfortable and ready to bring up details of her molestation history. During the disclosure/exposure stage of treatment, the therapist continued to work with Cindy on building adaptive coping skills and increasing self-worth. This included the use of role-play, positive affirmations, and identification and owning of positive qualities in herself.

As she revealed the details of her molestation Cindy often referred to it as "rape." She reported that she was 8-years-old when her mother's boyfriend began molesting her. The molestation included incidents of fondling, vaginal penetration, and forced oral copulation. In allowing Cindy to disclose incidents as she recalled or chose, it was possible for her to begin with those that were less traumatic. As the disclosures progressed, the therapist encouraged Cindy to identify her responses to and feelings about the incidents. During this exposure, Cindy described dissociative episodes when she recalled repeatedly asking the perpetrator to stop because she was in pain, but he would not. She said she would then repeat to herself, "Just put up with it—eventually it'll be over," and she would feel herself staring off at a wall and having a sense of leaving her body. Cindy said she had often found herself repeating this phrase when she had been abused by her ex-husband and at times in the present. Cindy said she learned from these experiences (in addition to earlier and later experiences with her mother and ex-husband) that it was pointless to express her feelings because they simply did not matter.

The most intense exposure sessions with Cindy were two in which she described, with a great deal of shame, incidents in which the perpetrator had forced her to perform oral sex on him. It was during these sessions that Cindy also expressed her greatest feelings of self-blame and guilt because, she said, he had not used physical force to restrain her and she believed that if she had tried, she could somehow have gotten away from him.

Reinterpretation/Reintegration

Interwoven with the disclosure/exposure stage of treatment, was the reinterpretation/reintegration and resolution of these traumatic experiences. This work was accomplished through emotional processing and cognitive restructuring of these experiences. For example, the therapist related the ways that perpetrators typically groom their victims so they do not resist, as had happened to Cindy. Specifically, the perpetrator had manipulated Cindy by recognizing her need for love and attention and protection from her abusive mother, which he provided. He also used fear tactics, threatening to tell her mother that Cindy had started the sexual relationship. Fearful of her mother, Cindy kept silent for the five years that the molestation continued.

During this phase of treatment, the therapist required that Cindy continue to identify, express, and interpret the anger she still felt toward her mother for not protecting her from the abuse, and toward the perpetrator. Cindy composed a letter to the perpetrator (although it was not meant to be sent), and scenarios in which she expressed her feelings to the perpetrator and to her mother were role-played. As Cindy came to recognize the manipulation that had taken place, processed the events emotionally, and re-enacted (e.g., role-played) molestation scenarios, she was able to reinterpret these events and finally acknowledge that any young child in these circumstances would have responded in the same manner. That is, she would have been vulnerable, confused, very frightened, and most importantly not responsible in any way for the abuse.

Changes Observed During Treatment Stages

During the early phase of the exposure stage of treatment, Cindy reported that the memories of the molestation had begun to interfere in her intimate relationship with Bob. As the exposure stage continued into the mid-phase, she reported increased difficulties with intimacy, increased triggering of memories and flashbacks of the perpetrator's face, and increased feelings of anger toward her mother. She also indicated the exposure sessions were having an overall negative affect on her sexual responsiveness. To help Cindy (and Bob) cope with the effects of the exposure/reprocessing stage of therapy, and to ensure her continued engagement in the process, the rationale for continued exposure to these incidents was provided (as was reading material to share with Bob related to posttraumatic stress symptoms).

Throughout the treatment the therapist noted positive changes in Cindy's appearance and behavior. For example, by the beginning of the disclosure/exposure stage Cindy had been slowly and progressively losing weight, was paying greater attention to her grooming, and appeared more interested in her appearance (i.e., she began styling her hair and wearing light makeup). Though re-experiencing some posttraumatic stress symptoms during the exposure/processing stages, Cindy also reported feeling more positive about herself and exhibited more assertive behavior. She began to find her voice and to express the opinion that she had a right to expect something of life, and she informed Bob that if he expected to continue living in her home, she expected him to help out with household chores, parenting duties, and financial matters.

At the most intense phase of exposure, Cindy had achieved a level of self-worth where she was able to acknowledge that she was worthy of expecting and receiving love and respect from others. For the first time, she came to a session with a clear agenda of topics she wanted to discuss, all related to Bob. She indicated she was no longer satisfied with putting up with relationships in which she believed others were taking advantage of her, and this included Bob. Toward the end of treatment Cindy appeared much more relaxed and in control of her emotions when discussing stressful events (e.g., molestation incidents, problems in her relationship with Bob, and feelings about her mother). This was consistent with her BDI score of 2. Cindy indicated that the most helpful part of therapy for her had been the homework assignments (i.e., recording of automatic thoughts and substituting positive affirmations).

Commentary

This case illustrates a number of typical patterns observed in CSA survivors who present for treatment. First of all, Cindy initially sought treatment for problems that she was having with her daughter. Her daughter was 9 years old, about the same age that Cindy was when she was first molested. When the therapist suggested that she might benefit from treatment, Cindy responded by indicating that she had already received treatment for her molestation and was now seeking help with more general problems. And finally, she evidenced a history of problems (e.g., substance abuse, use of dissociative coping strategies, relationship problems, inability or unwillingness to identify or express feelings, and posttraumatic stress symptoms) typically observed in CSA survivors (see Kendall-Tackett et al., 1993; Neumann et al., 1996). Although having this pattern of past and current problems along with information about Cindy's CSA history, the first therapist focused her assessment and treatment on a number of specific presenting problems rather than approaching this case as one that needed to address the history of CSA.

The second therapist, who was experienced in treating CSA survivors, conceptualized the case quite differently. While the initial focus of treatment was on establishing a trusting relationship, the therapist also attempted to assess current relationship problems, including self-defeating interpretations of the world (e.g., negative self-schemas), and to develop self-resources that prepared Cindy for later techniques of exposure and reprocessing (see Briere, 1996a, 1996b; Herman, 1993; Foa & Jaycox, in press; Zlotnick et al., 1997).

This focus not only led to the development of resources (e.g., disruption of automatic thoughts, positive affirmations, identification and expression of feelings, relaxation) that Cindy could use in dealing with stresses she was currently experiencing in her life, but also could be helpful when re-experiencing and reintegrating the CSA trauma. The exposure or reexperiencing of the trauma did not take the form of prolonged exposure that is typically utilized with PTSD clients who experienced sexual assault or combat-related trauma. Rather, exposure was gradual as

Cindy identified or disclosed memories that she could cope with first, followed by those that were more traumatic. Along with the gradual exposure of CSA incidents, Cindy's thoughts and feelings associated with these incidents were explored. Attempts to reintegrate or reinterpret these thoughts and feelings as well as the maladaptive understandings of the world and her relationship to it (i.e., feelings of powerlessness, self-blame) were made through cognitive-restructuring (e.g., provision of information and challenging conceptualizations and conclusions).

It is interesting to note that during the course of the exposure and reintegration treatment (i.e., emotional processing), Cindy reported a number of posttraumatic stress symptoms as well as a craving for drugs. These experiences are not only common in those who are processing traumatic events but also can be quite beneficial in treatment. Specifically, the therapist was able to assist Cindy as she attempted to cope with these symptoms that in the past had led to feelings of powerlessness as well as maladaptive responses. The therapist helped Cindy to identify alternative, more adaptive methods of resolving the problems that she was now facing. Utilizing skills that she had acquired (e.g., interruption of automatic responses, substitution of positive affirmations, relaxation), Cindy was able to meet this challenge adaptively. Thus, she was now more likely to be able to respond adaptively to other challenges that she might face outside of the therapy situation (i.e., this was an example of stress inoculation).

SUMMARY AND RECOMMENDATIONS

In the previous sections we have made a number of recommendations for treatment, some of which are demonstrated in the case of Cindy. While feeling comfortable enough to make such recommendations at this point in time, we recognize that much remains to be done. As we noted previously, most of our initial efforts to deal with the problem of CSA focused on detailing its consequences while also providing some relief for those who experience it. After three decades of work we are now at a point where new research questions are beginning to be asked. That is, we know what kinds of problems result for many who experience CSA but need to know how it is that these problems develop and why they are observed in some and not others. In addition, there are many treatments that have been suggested for survivors of CSA, but there is not only an absence of empirical evidence for the efficacy of any treatment but also little systematic concern for the effectiveness of treatments in clinical settings.

In an effort to help direct these much needed future efforts, we have reviewed the theoretical and empirical literature. The result was the identification of a number of common themes for understanding how CSA impacts individuals as well as some evidence of efficacious approaches to intervention based on these themes. That is, interventions that target exposure to the CSA trauma, the processing of information related to this trauma, and development of trusting relationships seem to hold the most promise.

In addition to these and other specific treatment suggestions that we have made, we make the obvious (and obligatory) recommendation that more research is needed. Specifically, research is needed to identify the processes or mechanisms that are involved in translating CSA into the problems that we observe. This will help in our attempts to develop effective treatments. And finally, the efficacy and effectiveness of current treatments as well as those that result from our research on mechanisms need to be evaluated. Our efforts to evaluate efficacy as well as effectiveness of such treatments should be informed by the issues that arise when we consider how to provide treatment in practice (see Burns, in press; Hoagwood et al., 1995).

REFERENCES

Alexander, P. C., & Anderson, C. L. (1994). An attachment approach to psychotherapy with the incest survivor. *Psychotherapy, 31*, 665–675.

Alexander, P. C., Anderson, C. L., Brand, B., Schaeffer, C. M., Grelling, B. Z., & Kretz, L. (1998). Adult attachment and long-term effects in survivors of incest. *Child Abuse and Neglect, 22*, 45–61.

Alexander, P. C., Neimeyer, R. A., Follette, V. M., Moore, M. K., & Harter. (1989). A comparison of group treatments of women sexually abused. *Journal of Consulting and Clinical Psychology, 57*, 479–483.

American Psychiatric Association. (1994). *Diagnostic and statistical manual of mental disorders* (4th ed.). Washington, D.C.: Author.

Arata, C. M. (1998). To tell or not to tell: Current functioning of child sexual abuse survivors who disclosed their victimization. *Child Maltreatment, 3*, 63–71.

Barnard, B. W., Hankins, G. C., & Robbins, L. (1992). Prior life trauma, post-traumatic stress symptoms, sexual disorders, and character traits in sex offenders: An exploratory study. *Journal of Traumatic Stress, 5*, 393–420.

Baynard, V. L. (1997). The impact of childhood sexual abuse and family functioning on four dimensions of women's later parenting. *Child Abuse and Neglect, 21*, 1095–1107.

Beitchman, J. H., Zucker, K. J., Hood, J. E., DaCosta, G. A., & Akman, D. (1992). A review of the short-term effects of child sexual abuse. *Child Abuse and Neglect, 15*, 537–556.

Beitchman, J. H., Zucker, K. J., Hood, J. E., DaCosta, G. A., Akman, D., & Cassavia, E. Z. (1992). A review of the long-term effects of child sexual abuse. *Child Abuse and Neglect, 16*, 101–118.

Berliner, L., & Saunders, B. (1996). Treating fear and anxiety in sexually abused children: Results of a controlled 2-year follow-up study. *Child Maltreatment, 1*(4), 294–309.

Briere, J. (1996a). A self-trauma model for treating adult survivors of severe child abuse. In J. Briere, L. Berliner, J. A. Bulkley, C. Jenny, & T. Reid (Eds.), *The APSAC handbook on child maltreatment* (pp. 140–157). Thousand Oaks, CA: Sage.

Briere, J. (1996b). *Therapy for adults molested as children: Beyond Survival* (2nd ed.) New York: Springer.

Briggs, L., & Joyce, P. R. (1997). What determines Post-Traumatic Stress Disorder symptomatology for survivors of childhood sexual abuse? *Child Abuse and Neglect, 21*, 575–582.

Brown, P. J., & Wolfe, J. (1994). Substance abuse and post-traumatic stress disorder comorbidity. *Drug and Alcohol Dependence, 35*, 51–59.

Browne, A., & Finkelhor, D. (1986). Impact of child sexual abuse: A review of the research. *Psychological Bulletin, 99*, 66–77.

Burns, B. J. (in press). A call for a mental health services research agenda for youth with serious emotional disturbance. *Mental Health Services Research*.

Carlson, E. G., Furby, L. Armstrong, J., & Shlaes, J. (1997). A conceptual framework for the long-term psychological effects of traumatic childhood abuse. *Child Maltreatment, 2*, 272–295.

Carver, C. M., Stalker, C., Stewart, E., & Abraham, B. (1989). The impact of group therapy for adult survivors of childhood sexual abuse. *Canadian Journal of Psychiatry, 34*, 753–758.

Chambless, D. L., & Hollon, S. D. (1998). Defining empirically supported therapies. *Journal of Consulting and Clinical Psychology, 66*, 7–18.

Chard, K. M. (1995). A meta-analysis of posttraumatic stress disorder treatment outcome studies of sexually victimized women. Unpublished doctoral dissertation, Indiana University, Bloomington.

Cohen, J. A., & Mannarino, A. P. (1996). A treatment outcome study for sexually abused preschool children: Initial findings. *Journal of the American Academy of Child and Adolescent Psychiatry, 35*, 42–50.

Cohen, J. A., & Mannarino, A. P. (1997). A treatment study for sexually abused preschool children: Outcome during a one year follow-up. *Journal of the American Academy of Child and Adolescent Psychiatry, 36*(9), 1228–1235.

Cohen, J. A., & Mannarino, A. P. (1998). Interventions for sexually abused children: Initial treatment outcome findings. *Child Maltreatment, 3*, 17–26.

Corder, B., Haizlip, T., & DeBoer, P. (1990). A pilot study for a structured, time-limited therapy group for sexually abused pre-adolescent children. *Child Abuse and Neglect, 14*, 243–251.

Courtois, C. A. (1995). Assessment and diagnosis. In C. Classen (Ed.), *Treating women molested in childhood* (pp. 1–34). San Francisco: Jossey-Bass.

Crosson-Tower, C. (1999). *Understanding child abuse and neglect*, (4th ed). Boston: Allyn & Bacon.

Daro, D. (1996). Preventing child abuse and neglect. In J. Briere, L. Berliner, J. A. Bulkley, C. Jenny & T. Reid (Eds.), *The APSAC handbook on child maltreatment* (pp. 343–358). Thousand Oaks, CA: Sage.

Deblinger, E., Lippman, J., & Steer, R. (1996). Sexually abused children suffering posttraumatic stress symptoms: Initial treatment outcome findings. *Child Maltreatment, 1*(4), 310–321.

DeRubeis, R. J., & Crits-Christoph, P. (1998). Empirically supported individual and group psychological treatments for adult mental disorders. *Journal of Consulting and Clinical Psychology, 66*, 37–52.

Diamond, M. J. (1997). The unbearable agony of being: Interpreting tormented states of mind in the psychoanalysis of sexually traumatized patients. *Bulletin of the Menninger Clinic, 61*, 495–519.

Donaldson, M. A., & Cordes-Green, S. (1994). *Group treatment of adult incest survivors*. Thousand Oaks, CA: Sage.

Douglas, A. R., Matson, I. C., & Hunger, S. (1989). Sex therapy for women incestuously abused as children. *Sexual and Marital Therapy, 4*, 143–158.

Dye, E., & Roth, S. (1991). Psychotherapy with Vietnam veterans and rape and incest survivors. *Psychotherapy, 28*, 103–120.

Ehlers, A., Clarke, D. M., Dunmore, E., Jaycox, L. et al. (1998). Predicting response to exposure treatment in PTSD: The role of mental defeat and alienation. *Journal of Traumatic Stress, 11*, 457–471.

Epstein, J. N., Saunders, B. E., Kilpatrick, D. G., & Resnick, H. S. (1998). PTSD as a mediator between childhood rape and alcohol use in adult women. *Child Abuse and Neglect, 22*, 223–234.

Feiring, C., Taska, L., & Lewis, M. (1996). A process model for understanding adaptation to sexual abuse: The role of shame in defining stigmatization. *Child Abuse and Neglect, 20*, 767–782.

Finkelhor, D. (1986). Sexual abuse: Beyond the family systems approach. *Journal of Psychotherapy & the Family, 2*, 53–65.

Finkelhor, D., & Berliner, L. (1995). Research on the treatment of sexually abused children: A review and recommendations. *Journal of the American Academy of Child and Adolescent Psychiatry, 34*, 1408–1423.

Fish, V. (1998). The delayed memory controversy in an epidemiological framework. *Child Maltreatment, 3*, 204–223.

Fischer, D. G., & McDonald, W. L. (1998). Characteristics of intrafamilial and extrafamilial child sexual abuse. *Child Abuse and Neglect, 22*, 915–929.

Foa, E. G., & Jaycox, L. H. (in press). Cognitive-behavioral treatment for PTSD: Theory and practice. In D. Spiegel (Ed.), *The practice of psychotherapy*. Washington, D. C.: American Psychiatric Press.

Foa, E. B., & Meadows, E. A. (1997). Psychosocial treatments for posttraumatic stress disorder: A critical review. *Annual Review of Psychology, 48*, 449–480.

Freedman, S. R., & Enright, R. D. (1996). Forgiveness as an intervention goal with incest survivors. *Journal of Consulting and Clinical Psychology, 64*, 983–992.

Freyd, J. J. (1996). *Betrayal trauma: The logic of forgetting childhood abuse*. Cambridge, MA: Harvard University Press.

Frueh, B. C., Turner, S. M., & Beidel, D. C. (1995). Exposure therapy for combat-related PTSD: A critical review. *Clinical Psychology Review, 15*, 799–817.

Gelinas, D. J. (1993). Relational patterns in incestuous families, malevolent variations, and specific interventions with the adult survivor. In P. L Paddison (Ed.), *Treatment of adult survivors of incest* (pp. 1–34). Washington, D.C.: American Psychiatric Press.

Gold, S. N., Elhai, J. D., Lucenko, B. A., Swingle, J. M., & Hughes, D. M. (1998). Abuse characteristics among childhood sexual abuse survivors in therapy: A gender comparison. *Child Abuse and Neglect, 22*, 1005–1012.

Goodwin, J. M. (1993). The seduction hypothesis 100 years after. In P. L. Paddison (Ed.), *Treatment of adult survivors of incest* (pp. 136–142). Washington, D.C.: American Psychiatric Press.

Gorey, K. M., & Leslie, D. R. (1997). The prevalence of child sexual abuse: Integrative review adjustment for potential response and measurement biases. *Child Abuse and Neglect, 21*, 391–398.

Grammer, H., & Shannon, J. (1992). Survivor's group: Clinical intervention for the sexually abused child in treatment foster care. *Community Alternatives: International Journal of Family Care, 4*, 19–32.

Hartman, C. R., & Burgess, A. W. (1993).

Information processing of trauma. *Child Abuse and Neglect, 17,* 47–58.

Heggen, C. H. (1996). Religious beliefs and abuse. In C. C. Kroeger & J. R. Beck (Eds.), *Women, abuse, and the Bible: How scripture can be used to hurt or to heal* (pp. 15–27). Grand Rapids, MI: Baker.

Herman, J. L. (1992). *Trauma and recovery.* New York: Basic Books.

Himelein, M. J., & McElrath, J. V. (1996). Resilient child sexual abuse survivors: Cognitive coping and illusion. *Child Abuse and Neglect, 20,* 747–758.

Hoagwood, K., Hibbs, E., Brent, D., & Jensen, P. (1995). Introduction to the special section: Efficacy and effectiveness in studies of child and adolescent psychotherapy. *Journal of Consulting and Clinical Psychology, 63,* 683–687.

Jaycox, L. H., Zoellner, L., & Foa, E. G. (1997). Cognitive behavior therapy for PTSD in rape survivors. *In Session: Psychotherapy in Practice, 3,* 43–58.

Jehu, D. (1989). Mood disturbances among women clients sexually abused as children. *Journal of Interpersonal Violence, 4*(2), 164–184.

Jinich, S., & Litrownik, A. J. (1999). Coping with sexual abuse: Development and evaluation of a brief videotape intervention for nonoffending parents. *Child Abuse and Neglect, 23,* 175–190.

Jinich, S., Paul, J. P., Stall, R., Acree, M., Kegeles, S., Hoff, C., & Coates, T. J. (1998). Childhood sexual abuse and HIV risk-taking behavior among gay and bisexual men. *AIDS and Behavior, 2,* 41–51.

Johnson, S. M., & Williams-Keeler, L. (1998). Creating healing relationships for couples dealing with trauma: The use of emotionally focused marital therapy. *Journal of Marital and Family Therapy, 24,* 25–40.

Kendall-Tackett, K. A., Williams, L. M., & Finkelhor, D. (1993). Impact of sexual abuse on children: A review and synthesis of recent empirical studies. *Psychological Bulletin, 113,* 164–180.

Krugman, R., & Jones, D. P. H. (1987). Incest and other forms of sexual abuse. In R. E. Helfer & R. S. Kempe (Eds.). *The battered child* (4th ed., pp. 286–300). Chicago: University of Chicago Press.

Lipovsky, J. A., Swenson, C. C., Ralston, M. E., & Saunders, B. E. (1998). The abuse clarification process in the treatment of intrafamilial child abuse. *Child Abuse and Neglect, 22,* 729–741.

Linehan, M. (1993). *Cognitive-behavioral treatment of borderline personality disorder.* New York: Guilford Press.

Loewenstein, R. J. (1993). Aspects of the treatment of dissociative disorders in survivors of incest. In P. L. Paddison (Ed.), *Treatment of adult survivors of incest* (pp. 77–99). Washington, D.C.: American Psychiatric Press.

Loftus, E. F. (1993). The reality of repressed memories. *American Psychologist, 48,* 518–537.

Lynskey, M. T., & Fergusson, D. M. (1997). Factors protecting against the development of adjustment difficulties in young adults exposed to childhood sexual abuse. *Child Abuse and Neglect, 21,* 1177–1190.

Matsakis, A. (1994). *Post-traumatic stress disorder: A complete treatment guide.* Oakland, CA: New Harbinger Publications.

McCann, I. L., Sakheim, D. K., & Abrahamson, D. J. (1988). Trauma and victimization: A model of psychological adaptation. *The Counseling Psychologist, 16,* 531–594.

McFarlane, A. C., & van der Kolk, B. (1996). Conclusions and future directions. In B. A. van der Kolk, A. C. McFarlane, & L. Weisaeth (Eds.), *Traumatic stress* (pp. 559–575). New York: Guilford.

Morris, L. A. (1995). The need for a multidimensional approach to the treatment of male sexual abuse survivors. In M. Hunter (Ed.), *Adult survivors of sexual abuse: Treatment innovations* (pp. 154–186). Thousand Oaks, CA: Sage.

National Research Council (1993). *Understanding child abuse and neglect.* Washington, D.C.: National Academy Press.

Neumann, D. A., Jousekamp, B. M., Pollock, V. E., & Briere, J. (1996). The long-term sequelae of childhood sexual abuse in women: A meta-analytic review. *Child Maltreatment, 1,* 6–16.

O'Donohue, W., & Elliott, A. (1992). Treatment of the sexually abused child: A review. *Journal of Clinical Child Psychology, 21,* 218–228.

Offord, D. R., Kraemer, H. C., Kazdin, A. E., Jensen, P. S., & Harrington, R. (1998). Lowering the burden of suffering from child psychiatric disorder: Trade-offs among clinical, targeted, and universal interventions. *Journal of the American Academy of Child and Adolescent Psychiatry, 37,* 686–694.

Paddison, P. L., Einbinder, R. G., Maker, E., & Strain, J. J. (1993). Title. In P. L Paddison (Ed.), *Treatment of adult survivors of incest* (pp. 35–53). Washington, D. C.: American Psychiatric Press.

Reeker, J., Ensing, D., & Elliott, R. (1997). A meta-analytic investigation of group treatment outcomes for sexually abused children. *Child Abuse and Neglect, 21,* 669–690.

Roberts, L., & Lie, G.-W. (1989). A group therapy approach to the treatment of incest. *Social Work with Groups, 12,* 77–90.

Roth, S., & Newman, E. (1993). The process of coping with incest for adult survivors: Measurement and implications for treatment and research. *Journal of Interpersonal Violence, 8,* 363–377.

Roy, R. (1998). *Childhood abuse and chronic pain: A curious relationship?* Toronto: University of Toronto Press.

Scarvalone, P., Cloitre, M., & Difede, J. (1995).

Interpersonal process therapy for incest survivors: Preliminary outcome data. Presented at a meeting of the Society of Psychotherapy Research, Vancouver, Canada.

Scharff, J. S., & Scharff, D. E. (1994). *Object relations therapy of physical and sexual trauma*. Northvale, NJ: Jason Aronson.

Sturkie, K. (1983). Structured group treatment for sexually abused children. *Health Social Work, 8*, 299–308.

Steele, B. (1987). Psychodynamic factors in child abuse. In R. E. Helfer and R. S. Kempe (Eds.), *The battered child* (4th ed., pp. 81–114). Chicago: The University of Chicago Press.

Taussig, H. N., & Litrownik, A. J. (1997). Self- and other-directed destructive behaviors: Assessment and relationship to type of abuse. *Child Maltreatment, 2*, 172–182.

Trickett, P. K., & Putnam, F. W. (1993). Impact of child sexual abuse on females: Toward a developmental, psychobiological integration. *Psychological Science, 4*, 81–87.

Trotter, C. (1995). Stages of recovery and relapse prevention for the chemically dependent adult sexual trauma survivor. In M. Hunter (Ed.). *Adult survivors of sexual abuse: Treatment innovations* (pp. 98–135). Thousand Oaks, CA: Sage.

U.S. Department of Health and Human Services, Children's Bureau. (1998). *Child maltreatment 1996: Reports from the states to the national child abuse and neglect data system*. Washington, D.C.: U.S. Government Printing Office.

van der Kolk, B., Weisaeth, L., & van der Hart, O. (1996). History of trauma in psychiatry. In B. A. van der Kolk, A. C. McFarlane, & L. Weisaeth (Eds.), *Traumatic stress* (pp. 47–74). New York: Guilford.

Varia, R., Abidin, R. R., & Dass, P. (1996). Perceptions of abuse: Effects on adult psychological and social adjustment. *Child Abuse and Neglect, 20*, 511–526.

Wenan, C. (1994). *Developmental psychopathology*. New York: McGraw-Hill.

Westbury, E., & Tutty, L. M. (1999). The efficacy of group treatment for survivors of childhood abuse. *Child Abuse and Neglect, 23*, 31–44.

Yalom, I. D. (1995). *The theory and practice of group psychotherapy* (4th ed.). New York: Basic Books.

Zlotnick, C., Shea, T. M., Rosen, K., Simpson, E., Mulrenin, K., Begin, A., & Pearlstein, T. (1997). An affect-management group for women with posttraumatic stress disorder and histories of childhood sexual abuse. *Journal of Traumatic Stress, 10*, 425–436.

CHAPTER 25

BRIEF COGNITIVE-DYNAMIC TREATMENT OF STRESS RESPONSE SYNDROMES

MARDI J. HOROWITZ
University of California, San Francisco

This chapter is primarily about the psychotherapy of Posttraumatic Stress Disorder (PTSD), related stress response syndromes such as complicated grief reactions, and some adjustment disorders. It begins with a general introduction of a bio-psycho-social model, and moves on to emphasize the importance of individualized case formulations in knowing how to plan treatment. Treatment is then reviewed as a series of phases. In the initial phase of providing support, social and biological interventions may be prominent features. In the phases that explore meanings and improve coping, the emphasis is on psychological information processing. Biological and social interventions are understood within this psychological framework.

Stress response syndromes often follow major, negative life events that include other people. If so, they occur in social as well as environmental contexts. They also occur in the context of pre-existing personality configurations. Such personality configurations involve traits of both temperament and character. Temperament includes biological vulnerabilities such as a low threshold for fear arousal; character includes habitual coping styles, core beliefs, and long range intentions and values. Treatment is best planned after formulating interactive causes and connections.

Cardinal symptoms in stress response syndromes include emotional pangs of distressing intensity coupled with intrusive images and ideas. To avoid these dreaded states of mind, people inhibit information processing that would otherwise lead toward a more complete understanding of the meanings of the stressor event to the self. This inhibition results in states with signs of denial, numbing, and avoidance. The balance between over- and undermodulated states shifts over time, making formulation complex. Helping people often means struggling to find a way through defensive obstacles.

The goal of treatment is to help the person work through both intrusive memories and excessive defenses, so that he or she is neither blunted nor emotionally flooded, and is restored to a pre-event level of functioning. Sometimes, however, additional efforts at character integration are indicated. In general, therapists use case formulations to plan how to help people achieve the following:

1. Restoration of equilibrium in emotion and action
2. Optimum skills in decision making
3. Ability to engage in adaptive coping
4. A realistic sense of self as stable, coherent, competent, and worthwhile
5. A rational preparation for the future

These goals include plans for how to protect the patient from dangers, some of which include accidents (from inattention and slowed reaction time); inappropriate decisions (made on the basis of erroneous beliefs); social stigmatization (as the consequences of loss, injury, culpability, or victimization); demoralization or suicide (due to impaired sense of identity and meaning); disruption of chemophysiology (from prolonged arousal, fatigue, substance abuse, or unnecessarily prolonged or intensified use of medication).

FORMULATION

Meeting the goals of symptom reduction and enhancement of coping skills requires planning that must go beyond diagnoses to formulation. Diagnosis alone is often too static, actuarial, and descriptive, while formulation is dynamic, individualized, and etiologically focused. Formulation helps clinicians see what topics should be addressed in therapy and to work through the stressor experiences to a point of completion.

One structure for formulation is called configurational analysis (Horowitz, 1997a), which is summarized in Table 25.1. Such an approach begins by selecting the key symptoms and problems that need to be explained. These phenomena often include both intrusive and omitted experiences and actions. The second step is to describe states in which such unwelcome or avoidant phenomena occur and then to contrast them with states in which symptoms are less intense or absent. This will often involve a contrast between dreaded states of horror and less distressing states of denial and numbing as well as desired states of restored equilibrium. In the third step the clini-

cian notes the topics most associated with problematic and dreaded states, and the patient's defensive inhibitions and distortions when talking about them. The fourth step adds self–other beliefs and person schemas that color emotional reactivity, motivate defensiveness, and organize problematic states. Pathogenic stress-induced shifts into roles such as degraded, incompetent, abandoned, shamed, scorned, abused, and unworthy are identified. The fifth step integrates the symptoms, states, defenses, and beliefs into a tentative but more comprehensive explanation and set of treatment plans. This integration includes a linkage between states, unresolved topics, and core relational models for each state. It also includes inferences about how defenses may shift schemas of self and other to alter emotionality. Ways of leading the patient away from irrational beliefs and ways to handle conundrums, dilemmas, and conflicts are devised.

A partial case example will clarify some of these steps. (This example is discussed in detail in *Stress Response Syndromes*, Horowitz, 1997a). Harry (fictitious name), a truck driver, picked up a female hitchhiker who was subsequently killed

TABLE 25.1   Steps of Formulation for Stress Response Syndromes: Configurational Analysis Method

1. PHENOMENA
Select the symptoms and problems that need to be explained, and describe the stressor events that precipitated them.

2. STATES OF MIND
Describe states in which the symptoms and problems do and do not occur. Indicate triggers to problematic or dreaded states. Include states of avoidance and impairments in achieving positive states of mind. Describe any maladaptive cycles of states.

3. TOPICS OF CONCERN AND DEFENSIVE CONTROL PROCESSES
Describe unresolved stress-related topics and how they evolve to problematic states. Indicate persisting dysfunctional beliefs. Describe how expression and contemplation is obscured. Infer how avoidant states ward off dreaded states.

4. IDENTITY AND RELATIONSHIPS
For each recurrent state, formulate organizing roles and schematized transactions between self and others. Describe desired and dreaded role relationship models. Infer how compromise role relationship models ward off dangers. Formulate configurations activated during recurring state cycles.

5. THERAPY PLANNING
Consider problematic bio-psycho-social interactions and how to ameliorate situations. Explain how schemas of self and others lead to problematic states, and how any pathogenic defenses prevent resolution of topics of concern. From this formulation predict what can change and how to facilitate that change. Plan how to stabilize working states and prevent pathologically impulsive actions; consider how and when to alter dysfunctional beliefs and how and when to advance biological, social, and psychological capacities.

Source: Horowitz (1997a).

while with him. Harry's truck ran off the road and a load of pipes lurched forward, piercing the un-armored section of the cab where the passenger was riding.

Phenomena to Explain

Four weeks after the accident Harry had a night-mare in which mangled bodies appeared; he awoke with an anxiety attack. Throughout the following days he had recurrent, intense, and in-trusive images of the dead woman's body. These images, together with ruminations about the woman, were accompanied by anxiety attacks of growing severity. Harry also developed a phobia about driving. His regular habits of weekend drinking increased to a nightly excessive use of al-cohol. He had temper outbursts over minor frus-trations and difficulty concentrating at work.

States of Mind

These phenomena occurred in a dreaded state of horror (Harry's guilt and shame), a problematic state of rage, and a defensive state where re-minders of the traumatic event were avoided. The state of horror occurred intrusively, and was hard to expel. The state of rage was also intrusive, even explosive, and therefore problematic. An avoidant, numb state was preferable for defensive reasons.

Themes and Defenses

The topics that led to dreaded states were the ac-cident, the death of the passenger, and the loss of his sense of self-control. To avoid these topics, Harry did not think about the event. He used al-cohol to blot out ideas and feelings about what had happened and to stifle the present and future implications to his life. This avoidance increased his risk of having another traumatic event because it altered his attention, reaction times, and ability to adapt. Yet he felt beleaguered, frustrated, and thus was vulnerable to rage rather than irri-tation when demands were made of him. His sense of self-control over expressed emotion was markedly reduced even though he inhibited the processing of information related to the stressor. Shock mastery did not occur in a progressive manner.

Self–Other Beliefs

In the dreaded and problematic states, important self–other beliefs were contained in thoughts about his nightmare of mangled bodies and his daytime, recurrent, unbidden images of the

woman's body. He felt he was either an aggres-sor—by causing the death—or a victim. The vic-tim role was intensified by Harry being stigma-tized as a person who broke the rules in picking up a female hitchhiker, by driving carelessly and causing the accident, and by being bad for feeling glad that he survived.

Explanation and Treatment Plan

Harry used alcohol to defensively ward off his in-trusive preoccupations, and he inhibited thoughts about the accident because he could not tolerate the shame, guilt, and horror of the memories and their implications. He felt too out of control and desperate. The first goal of treatment was to sta-bilize his state of mind. This meant reducing in-toxication, sleep deprivation, fatigue, and anxiety. An expert-helping relationship and a focus on dose-by-dose coping was enough to accomplish these aims; the therapeutic situation was expected to rapidly counteract demoralization. If this did not happen, short-term use of antianxiety med-ications could be contemplated. Once state stabi-lization occurred, his defensive avoidance of key topics was countered. Then the core beliefs with each topic were explored and modified. Once self-confidence and control were restored, a time of termination was set.

TREATMENT

Real treatment is seamless; however, a didactic division of it into phases helps indicate how tech-niques may usefully change over time. The fol-lowing five phases will be discussed:

1. Initial support
2. Exploration of meanings
3. Improving coping
4. Working through
5. Terminating

These five phases are presented in Table 25.2, and discussed more fully next. This theory of therapy is an integration of other approaches (Horowitz, 1997b, in press). It uses techniques of brief and focal therapy described by many in-cluding Basch (1980), Beck (1976), Foa and Kozak (1988), Klerman and Weissman (1993), Luborsky (1984), Malan (1979), Mann (1973), Sifneos (1972), Strupp and Binder (1984), and may also use special imagery techniques as de-scribed by Singer and Pope (1978) and Horowitz (1995).

TABLE 25.2 Phases of Treatment for Stress Response Syndromes

Approximate Phases	Therapeutic Alliance	Patient Activity	Therapist Activity
1. **Initial Support**	Initial hope fostered by expertise and empathy.	Patient tells story of traumatic event and focuses on how to cope with current stress.	Therapist obtains history, makes diagnoses, and early formulations. He or she acts to stabilize states if indicated, and establishes a preliminary focus (the traumatic event and its meaning to self).
2. **Exploration of Meanings**	Therapeutic alliance deepened by experience of safety. Patient may test therapist to see if fears of what may happen are justified, e.g., fear of emotional overload.	Patient expands on meaning to the self of the trauma and its sequelae.	Therapist realigns focus as he or she arrives at later formulations. If avoidance is maladaptive, he or she counteracts or interprets defensive and warded off contents. He or she clarifies how intrusive and warded-off emotions and ideas are linked to stressor events and the patient's appraisals of them.
3. **Improving Coping**	Deeper expression of usually private thoughts and emotions.	Work on themes previously avoided.	The therapist acts to encourage desensitization of triggers to emotional reactions and helps the patient to modify dysfunctional beliefs.
4. **Working Through**	Projections and transference reactions are confronted and clarified in relation to the actualities.	Reschematizes current inner cognitive maps.	Helps patient modify structure of beliefs (reschematization).
5. **Terminating**	Emphasis on safe separation.	Considers gains and unfinished issues as well as how to cope with loss of the therapy.	Clarifies gains and any unfinished issues for the future. Interprets and differentiates any links between termination experiences and stressor event experiences.

Initial Support

Patients often present weeks or months after a traumatic event, when they still have symptoms and an intuitive sense that they are not recovering. Usually these symptoms occur in an under-modulated state of mind characterized by intrusive experiences, dangerous impulses, or a sense of loss of control. If so, state stabilization through initial supportive measures is indicated. At the biological level this may include prescription of medications, restored nutrition, and more rest. At the social level, supportive measures include time structuring. At the psychological level, supportive measures involve the establishment of a therapeutic relationship and a plan for treatment. The patient gains hope for recovery after perceiving empathy, expertise, and a readiness to provide care from the clinician.

Biological Intervention: Initial Support Phase

Many biological systems shift under stress. One system involves catecholamine chemistry. Changes affect neural networks that connect the limbic, frontal cortical, basal ganglia, and hypothalamic structures. Disturbances in electrochemical physiology of these networks can disturb arousal control and alter capacity to regulate emotional responses (as in increased frequency of fright and rage). The amygdala may alter its danger recognition set points, the hippocampus may alter its memory-encoding properties, and the medial prefrontal cortex may alter its abilities to establish or reduce (desensitize) associational connections.

A prominent catecholamine in the physiologic reaction to stress may be dopamine, which is concentrated in the norepinephrine-rich areas of the brain such as the locus ceruleous and frontal cortex. These brain regions are connected to the emotional arousal regulating functions of the amygdala. The chemicals may be involved in heightening biological propensities for hyperarousal, for hypervigilence, and for sudden alarm reactions to trigger stimuli. Repeated alarms can lead to fatigue and further dysregulation of cognitive–emotional functioning (Southwick, Krystal, Morgan et al., 1993). Stress can affect many neurotransmitters, the autonomic nervous system, and hormonal functions, as well as their interactive processes. For example, serotonin subtypes and their receptors probably regulate complex brain activities, and are also involved in the production of stress hormones. Trauma-induced alterations in this chemistry could also lead to fight–flight arousals of the autonomic nervous system or even to hibernating-withdrawals.

Antianxiety and *affect-dampening medications* are sometimes used to prevent extremes of fatigue, emotional flooding, agitation, and racing thoughts. These agents can often be used in a single dose or as a night-by-night sedation. Transient use of benzodiazepines has sometimes been effective as a way of reducing explosive entry into extremely undermodulated states. Medications that reduce autonomic nervous system arousal, such as the beta-adrenergic blockers, have also been tried.

A variety of *antidepressant medications* has been used not just for depressive disorders exacerbated or precipitated by stressor events but also for specific symptoms of PTSD (or as panic attacks following traumatic events). Selective serotonin reuptake inhibitors, tricyclics, and monoamine oxidase inhibitors have all been tried with some reported successes. New research has also shown that some recurrent schizophrenic episodes may be precipitated by life events. At such times prescriptions of *antipsychotic medications* (or adjustment of dosage) may be indicated.

No specific drug treatment for PTSD has emerged. Medications are best selected according to the symptoms and biological formulation of each individual patient. Prescriptions should be carefully considered in terms of the length of trial for each agent used.

Social Intervention: Initial Support Phase

Persons who are exposed to traumatic events often feel overwhelmed. Interventions may consist of advice given to social companions who are less overwhelmed. This general advice is listed as follows:

1. The victim may need to be transiently protected from excessive stimulation. Structuring time following a disaster should emphasize short-range activities that effect reality.

2. Provide the patient with opportunities for communication and a sense of positive connection to others. Discussion of events with others may be useful because it clarifies differences between realistic and unrealistic interpretations.

3. Giving time lines for dose-by-dose coping can restore a sense of personal efficacy to a

bewildered or overwhelmed victim. The Scarlett O'Hara approach of "I'll think of that tomorrow" can be adaptive if not prolonged.

4. Activities should include time for respite. It is important for the person to feel that it is all right to rest, use humor, or change to non-coping activities for a period of restoration.

5. Give the person something active to do in the role of helping self or others. Sometimes membership in a mutual support group can serve this purpose.

6. Remember that the more the person has been traumatized, the longer it will take for symptoms to subside. This may contrast with the expectation in some work environments that the traumatized person will return to a normal functional level within a week. The workplace provides sustaining interest and social support; the victim should not be isolated from it, but neither should the person have to meet excessive expectations.

7. Children may see repetitious film clips of a disaster on TV and believe that the depicted event is really happening, over and over again. They need adult explanations to reassure them that they are safe.

8. Because sleep disruption is common, the victim may associate efforts to sleep with episodes of unpleasant imagery. It is helpful to increase a sense of safety. This can include leaving lights on or sleeping with a pet. Children may be allowed to sleep with a parent although that is not the usual domestic arrangement. In extreme cases, telling the victim that a companion will stay awake and watch over him or her during sleep can encourage rest.

9. The person may be more at risk for having an accident while driving or operating machinery. For these reasons, keeping the victim from driving unnecessarily or doing hazardous work tasks may be advisable for a time. It must be done tactfully to avoid incompetent self-concepts.

10. Right after a traumatic event, the victim's relatives and friends cluster around and want to know all about it. The victim recounts the story again and again. Later in time, companions may tire of hearing about it but the victim may still feel the need to review what happened. At these later stages, listening is still useful.

Psychological Intervention: Initial Support Phase

The therapist can provide some of the relationship support discussed under social interventions. Establishing a diagnosis and formulation can be quite reassuring. Conveying facts can reduce secondary anxieties. Some people may, for example, presume that intrusive symptoms represent such a high degree of lowered control over mental contents and interpersonal emotional expressions, that they are losing their mind. The therapist can reduce the patient's fears by giving accurate information about the prevalence of such posttraumatic responses in the population as well as the usual course of improvement (rather than deterioration) in such symptoms.

Establishing a commitment to care, by scheduling appointments and giving a plan for what will be done, provides both empathy for the patient's level of current distress and hope for change. Such initial support can lead to a sharp reduction in symptoms. The patient can then move rapidly toward exploring meanings, improving coping, and working through in the ensuing phases of psychotherapy.

Exploration of Meanings

Once the patient is capable of working states in which intense, unpleasant emotions can be tolerated, the meaning of the stressor to the self can be examined. That is why intense feelings are sanctioned within a therapeutic alliance and overwhelming feelings are divided into dose-by-dose experiences. The goal is to achieve a process of explanation aimed at reaching conclusions about the stressor events.

When the clinician discovers a block to working through reactions, he or she may help the patient by clarifying differences between realistic and fantasy-based beliefs. In doing so, the clinician allows the patient to learn by identification. The clinician represents a person who is not overwhelmed by thinking about the implications of illness, injury, or loss. The presence of the clinician as a compassionate and empathic person, thinking logically, is reassuring.

To maintain a safe situation, patients may be urged to take a one-dose-at-a-time approach, contemplating the most immediate consequences of what has happened and putting off long-range considerations for a period of time. This reassurance indicates to patients how to tolerate what has seemed intolerable.

Various phases of response to the stressor event will affect what meanings a patient can explore in a current state. A generalized prototype of phases of response to a trauma is summarized in Figure 25.1. Sometimes it helps patients to know of these phases.

The *outcry phase* is usually over after the phase of initial support. But patients fear recurrence of the horror of this phase. Certain unanswered questions involving the past ("Why me?") and the future ("How will I be happy again?") threaten to evoke horror, even during the phase of denial and numbing of emotions that may follow.

In such *phases of denial*, attention may be focused on topics postponed during the outcry phase. It is sometimes necessary to confront inhibitions that are maladaptively prolonged. In addition to explaining how and why defensive control processes have been used, the clinician may interpret warded-off views of self and others.

In the *intrusive phase*, the gradual telling and restructuring of the disastrous events occurs, as the therapist helps the patient to differentiate reality from fantasy. By placing each concept into a time frame and sequence, the therapist facilitates a sense of reality and integration about what has happened. Magical conjectures about what might have caused the catastrophic event can be counteracted by rational interpretation. The therapist may also bolster the patient's realistic attributes that lead to a sense of competence and worth.

In the *working through phase*, further desensitization of emotional associations and restructuring of beliefs occur. Larger frameworks of meaning are explored. Previous conflicts activated by the stressor life event and/or by the work of reacting to the stressor event are dealt with; the topics may include memories and fantasies of earlier traumas. The self-concepts may involve activation of degraded self-schemas once latent before the trauma. For example, in mourning the loss of a loved one, the issue is not only *what* was lost but also *who* the self becomes in current reality, without the deceased. Concepts of self such as worthless, incompetent, bad, shamed, guilty, or weak are challenged.

In this period of the exploration of meanings the aim is to achieve shock mastery and a bolstering of stable states of mind. Later on, the focus adds more emphasis on reschematization. The therapist hopes to gradually increase the patient's capacity to tolerate emotions as he or she contemplates the ideas and implications to self, as they are associated with the stressor event. This process of contemplation and new behavioral practices leads to a change in cognitive maps.

The major areas of focus include the trauma itself and its association with other meanings, such as beliefs, attitudes, expectations, and intentions. It also includes discussion of how to restore functional capacity in the future. Shock mastery and reschematization processes are encouraged (1) by focusing on links between traumatic memories and personal meanings, and (2) by focusing on links between trauma responses and activated maladaptive personality traits.

Improving Coping

After a reformulation on the basis of explored meanings, the therapist can plan how to help a patient improve future coping style. Attitudes that lead to unnecessary avoidances are inter-

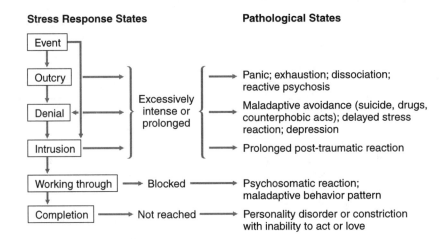

FIGURE 25.1 States induced by trauma.

TABLE 25.3   Obstacles to Therapy with People Who Habitually Inhibit Ideas

Defensive Style	Therapeutic Counter
Global or selective inattention with impressionistic rather than accurate discourse about the events.	Encourage talk and provide verbal labels. Ask for details, then construct cause-and-effect sequences.
Limited disclosure due to inhibitions of ideas.	Encourage verbal production through clarifications.
Short circuit to erroneous conclusions.	Keep the topic open and emphasize step-by-step decision making.
Misinterpretations based on past stereotypes of self and others.	Interpret what is realistically likely, and differentiate that from what is most dreaded, and what is ideally desired. Differentiate reality from fantasy; clarify time frames, distinguishing past from possible futures.

Source: Horowitz (1997a).

preted: this usually entails explaining why a person is inhibiting thought. A dose-by-dose approach is again encouraged, which means the patient will be encouraged to think the unthinkable in tolerable amounts, using volitionally specific rather than unconsciously global inhibitions of topics. This will lead to negative emotions but these will be within tolerable limits. If not, additional desensitization procedures such as relaxation exercises, stretching, biofeedback, systematic body movement, guided imagery, or somatic patterning re-training (as in yoga, breathing, and meditation) might be considered.

Coping can be improved by replacing pathogenic defensiveness with more adaptive conscious controls. To avoid dreaded states of mind, some people develop habitual styles of warding off unresolved and highly emotional themes. Obstacles to working through may stem from their automatic avoidances and unconscious distortions. Therapists may observe these defenses by noting how a patient minimizes, partially confronts and partially avoids, or dismisses specific topics. These defensive controls should be tactfully counteracted. Some techniques for use with people who habitually inhibit ideas are presented in Table 25.3, who avoid emotion in Table 25.4, or who distort reality for self-enhancement in Table 25.5.

Working Through

In persons who have enduring signs of psychopathology, further working-through is indi-

TABLE 25.4   Obstacles to Therapy with People Who Habitually Avoid Emotion

Defensive Style	Therapeutic Style
Excessively detailed but peripheral approach to talking about emotional stressors.	Ask for personal impressions and meanings.
Avoid disclosure of emotion.	Interpret linkage of emotional meanings to ideational meanings. Focus attention on mental images, emotions, and felt reactions.
Juggle opposing sets of meanings, back and forth.	Hold discussions on one valence of a topic. Interpret defensive shifting and meanings it conceals.
Endless rumination without reaching decisions about how to act.	Interpret reasons for warding off reaching decisions, and how impulsive actions can relate to indecision. Encourage action planning in relation to imagined outcomes.

Source: Horowitz (1997a).

TABLE 25.5   Obstacles to Therapy with People
Who Distort for Self-Enhancement

Defensive Style	Therapeutic Counter
Focuses on praise and blame and is deceitful.	Avoid being provoked into either praising or blaming, and do not accuse of lying.
Denial of "wounding" information.	Use tactful timing and wording to counteract denials and deceits.
Slides meanings about implications of the event to personal acts and intentions.	Consistently redefine meanings and encourage realistic appraisals while bolstering against shame.
Excessive attention to finding routes to self-enhancement.	Cautiously deflate grandiose meanings while emphasizing realistic skills and capacities.
Dislocates attributes of self to another.	Clarify who is who in terms of acts, intentions, and expectations.
Excessively quick forgiveness of self for culpability in stressors.	Support self-esteem by genuine interest while working toward an appropriate sense of responsibility. Help patient plan for realistic acts of remorse without excessive shame in instances of realistic "guilt."

Source: Horowitz (1997b).

cated. This usually involves exploration of prior personality-based beliefs and their association with the beliefs that were processed about the traumatic event. This configuration often involves activation of the following themes:

1. Excessive expectation and fear of victimization
2. Enduring and irrational shame over vulnerability or incompetence
3. Unusually intense anger and impulses for revenge
4. Exquisite sensitivity to guilt
5. Low threshold for despair

The *fear of victimization* has to do with the fear that either the self or loved ones will suffer torments and horrors. During a disaster, the person might have felt relief for having survived; that relief might later be remembered with shame or guilt because others suffered terribly. There may also be a fear of merger with victims, of being dead or maimed like them. A current trauma with self as victim can be associated with past traumas or fantasies of self as victim, intensifying emotional reactions and making cognitive processing more complex.

Shame or vulnerability and incompetence during a disaster can be associated with childhood views of the self as weak and lacking in sufficient skills or in courageous values. Anger, in which others are blamed, can be a defensive lid on such dreaded roles.

Anger at the source of a trauma and a thirst for revenge upon the aggressor persons (or displacement figures) is also a common but conflicted theme. It may serve as a self-strengthening defensive shift away from shame. Irrational attitudes may hold innocent others as the aggressors. Such rage can activate previously latent role relationship models, with a scenario of other as the aggressor or unreliable caretaker, followed by a sense of guilt at having been too angry and vengeful. The conflict between expressing and stifling hostility is re-activated by rage at the loss and injury or fright from the stressor event. The prior vulnerability schemas make normal rage more intense. Sometimes rage is directed at those who did not suffer, as did the self. This may awaken previously conflicted, but relatively latent, personal themes of envy.

Guilt may be a vulnerability. The person may have self-concepts (as bad, wicked, sinful, selfish, or irresponsible) that are latent, long-standing, and re-activated by traumas. After a stressor event such themes may be associated with memories at feeling relief that others and not the self suffered the most (survivor guilt). Inhibiting guilty themes can prevent working through.

Low thresholds for states of despair and depression can be crossed when events lead to loss. Loss may include loss of bodily functions and loss of comfort, as in chronic post-accident pain syndromes. In the case of loss of others, or body parts, a mourning process usually takes place, partially resolving the grief. But unresolved grief is more likely to occur in people who have been too frightened of sadness to allow grief-work to occur (and depression is more likely in those with biological or psychological vulnerabilities to such states).

During the working-through phase the therapist will deepen the focus of joint attention. This deepening involves interpretation of what has been warded off. Table 25.6 illustrates more surface and also deeper levels of interpretations. The therapist aims for the depth required to restore equilibrium. In most cases, attention is focused at levels 1–5, which can often be accomplished in a brief therapy to work through a trauma. Sometimes, however, focus at the deeper levels of 6–8 is necessary. This enables more reschematization and may require a longer time in therapy. An example follows.

Sally, a young woman in her early twenties, had a complex fracture of her femur, having fallen from a ladder while helping her father paint his house. A partial paralysis resulted from nerve damage that complicated matters; it disrupted her plans to accept a teaching position after graduating from college. She came for therapy with a diagnoses of Major Depressive Disorder and Adjustment Disorder precipitated by her accident and its sequelae.

One theme activated by her injury was hostility toward her father for not taking good care of her. The relevant ideas about the stress event were that her father had given her a rickety, second-class wooden ladder while he used his safer aluminum one. Awareness of her anger was partially warded off by defensive inhibitions of contemplating this theme at the time of treatment onset.

During an early treatment hour, she expressed signs of anger at the therapist because he would not prescribe sleeping pills for her insomnia. Though the therapist was able to see the non-verbal signs of this emotion, it was not expressed clearly in verbal form by the patient. The therapist considered possible statements he might make. He could say "I think you may be angry with me but are afraid to say so," or he could link the exploration of the transference anger to the object-relations meanings embedded in reactions to the recent stress event, worded as follows:

"I think you may be getting angry with me right now because I am not meeting your need for a sleeping pill, just as you may be angry with your father because you feel he took poor care of you by giving you a lousy stepladder."

This type of wording links transference reactions in the therapy situation to a relationship aspect of the current stressor situation. It maintains the focus of treatment on resolving reactions to recent events, but it also allows for a clarification of precursor themes. By raising unconscious sources of emotional arousal (her anger in therapy) to conscious recognition, contemplation can lead to revised views of the motives of others, and a clearer sense of one's own identity.

Terminating

Termination of the treatment threatens re-enactment of the patient's personal vulnerability as experienced during the recent stressor events. Therapists should introduce plans for terminating several sessions before the final one. This time, a loss can be faced gradually, actively rather than passively, and within a communicative relationship.

CASE EXAMPLES

Frank

Frank was a 25-year-old male lifeguard at a neighborhood pool. On one busy summer day, the pool accommodated a large crowd of children and adolescents. There were many people in the pool and unruly episodes on the deck. Frank was quite busy and realized that he was so overloaded with demands for his attention that he could not be sure that everyone was safe. Frank blew his whistle and ordered the pool cleared.

To his horror there was an inert body at the bottom of the pool. He dove in at once and brought a small, limp, non-breathing figure to the deck. Frank began cardiopulmonary resuscitation. This failed to revive the small boy, who was later pronounced dead. Overcome with remorse, Frank went to the funeral of the deceased child. He was greeted with many angry scowls and became upset by the grief-stricken faces of the child's parents.

Phenomena to Explain

Frank went through turbulent periods of remorse, insomnia, attacks of anxiety, guilt, shame, and developed a dread of dying. He quit his job; had difficulty concentrating; and avoided pools,

TABLE 25.6 Levels of Interpretation

Level	Content Areas	Current Situation	Therapy Situation	Past
1	Stressors and stress responses	Intentions of how to respond to stressors	Expectations of treatment	Relevant previous stress events
2	Conscious scenarios of pending coping choices	Conflicting plans of how to respond to stressors	Focus on what to deal with first	Long-standing goals and dilemmas
3	Avoidance of adaptive challenges	Defensive postures against threats	Resistance to work on important topics	History of self-impairing avoidance
4	Dreaded states of mind	Triggers to entry into symptomatic states	States of therapeutic work (and nonwork)	Habitual problematic and dreaded states
5	Systems with irrational beliefs	Differentiation of realistic from fantastic appraisals	Reasonable expectations versus fantastic hopes	Origin of unrealistic expectations
6	Maladaptive interpersonal patterns	Interpersonal problems and self-esteem	Difference between transferences and therapeutic alliances	Relation of current problems to past patterns
7	Identity and role relationships	Beliefs about self and others	Confrontations and challenges of irrational attitudes	Development of role relationship models
8	Life plans and future possible identities	Opportunities and social/biological contexts	Harmonizing conflicted beliefs	Development of valued goals, and intentions

Source: Horowitz (1997a).

children, and the neighborhood where he had worked as a lifeguard.

Six months after the event, Frank began having frightening nightmares, with visual images of a dead body in a pool, a blurred face of a child, and angry faces of adults. He was preoccupied with feelings of remorse, which disrupted his concentration at his new job. He had outbursts of anger with companions. These intrusions occurred despite his efforts to avoid them.

States of Mind

Frank could not sustain interest in his career or recreational activities. A desired state of productive working or focused concentration could seldom be stabilized. Instead, in a defensive but problematic state, he felt that everything in his world was cloaked in gray. At times he had a dreaded and undermodulated state that bordered on panic—he felt that he was about to die. These states were different from his usual amiability and enthusiasm before the boy's drowning.

Themes and Defensive Avoidances

Frank was remote and apathetic when pressed for details about his current feelings. It was hard to clarify those subjects that seemed to cause his most dreaded states. This was ameliorated as the therapist indicated empathic and compassionate recognition of his suffering. Frank was then able to move toward an exploration of the topic that seemed important: he had entangled realistic and fantastic aspects of his responsibility as a lifeguard for the safety of everyone in the pool. He felt terribly guilty and it was necessary to get beyond his surface statements that he had already worked through this issue. He used warding off and rationalizations: it was the fault of others.

Beliefs About Self and Others

Frank viewed himself in antithetical sets of self concepts. His worst sense of identity was as an irresponsible, careless, self-centered caretaker. He desired to regard himself as truly caring, and competent at protecting others. To shed guilt, he externalized blame onto pool directors who did not care enough to hire additional lifeguards, or to control the number of people allowed to use the pool.

Treatment Plan

In the phase of *improving coping*, Frank was encouraged to stop avoiding the neighborhood. In the phase of *working through*, the therapist asked Frank how much remorse he had to have.

Therapy Process

Frank did not require much *initial support*, which was provided sufficiently by *exploring meanings*. He quickly entered a phase of working-through processes that had other themes. One topic was his rage at the pool managers for putting him in an overly demanding situation. This then led to a negative reaction toward the therapist, including rage that the therapist was expecting too much of him. A warded-off but emergent feeling that "recovery was too good for him" was clarified. Linkages between themes were contemplated and clarified his continuing sense of guilt. He then reviewed past memories of how he, at age five, had piled toys onto his unwanted two-year-old brother in an effort to get rid of him. This past memory added intensity to his guilt. Frank was then able to explore the question of "how much remorse." Frank decided to volunteer his services in teaching drowning prevention to schoolchildren even though it made him tense and anxious. He saw how he could be constructive; this differed from a need to be self-punitive—as in seeking to fail in his current career efforts.

In the termination phase, Frank became frightened that his improvement was due to being dependent on the therapist. He feared relapse after the treatment ended. By the next-to-last session he felt that he could stop at the appointed time, provided he could return for booster visits as needed.

Connie

The second case example, to illustrate therapy processes, is about a young woman in her mid-twenties. Connie had completed college and was moving about in temporary employments. She also was frequently changing intimate attachments, which did not trouble her. But her life felt suddenly shattered after the unexpected death of her father. She had felt closer to him than to her mother, who was still alive. Her siblings grieved but she was far more distraught.

Phenomena to Explain

Connie was first seen, at her request, six weeks after the death of her father. She felt confused, intensely sad, and had a loss of initiative since the unexpected death. She faltered badly in her career activities, and felt as if her intimate relationships had come unglued.

States of Mind

Her dreaded state was one of being flooded with grief and being seen by others when she was out of control. She had a problematic compromise state of inert sitting, waiting, and feeling depressed. Her first aim was to retain control by entering into a somewhat rigidly defensive compromise state of seeming composure; this only imitated her desired state of well-modulated and poised spontaneity in relationships.

Themes and Defenses

Her central concern was her unresolved personal responses to her father's death. She puzzled over whether he had really loved her since he had ignored her concerns during the two years before he died. She inhibited thoughts on these topics, although she had intrusive memories of how she had not related well to him during that time.

Self-Other Beliefs

She emphasized an idealized, positive relationship with her father, but this was contrasted with contradictory beliefs. She felt like a disgustingly wailing and vulnerable waif who had been abandoned by an irresponsible caretaker during her more dreaded states. During her problematic depressive states she felt personally aimless without him.

Explanation and Treatment Plan

Connie seemed to have an early sense of being unable to go through a grieving process alone. The treatment plan was to facilitate such mourning by establishing a safe but time-limited relationship and to explore how, and then why, she warded off certain topics of grief. The older male therapist anticipated that her father–self role relationship models might lead to periodic transference reactions. In the course of the treatment, the aim was to clarify her varied beliefs and to help her integrate and harmonize contradictions in her memories and fantasies about her father and her own possible future identity.

Phases of Treatment

Initial support was provided by listening to her story in the first two sessions. After these sessions, Connie felt that she had regained control and could feel pangs of sadness without entering flooded, overwhelmed, or dazed states. She began to wonder what she might further accomplish in the therapy, and if any more sessions would be worthwhile. The focus then shifted from recounting the story of her father's death to understanding her past—and current inner—relationship with her father.

The therapy focused, for a time, on *exploring beliefs* that she was somehow degraded by her father, that she was too weak, or that she was too evil and vengeful. The focus of therapy became analysis of these meanings, defined as her vulnerability for entering into states organized by defective, weak, and evil views of self. The evil views of self were activated as she realized feelings of anger at her father for his perceived betrayals of her.

These degraded self-concepts related to feelings that her father had scorned her in recent years because she had not lived up to his ideals. He died before she could accomplish her goal of reestablishing a mutual relationship of admiration and respect. Her plan was to convince him that her own modified career line and lifestyle would lead to many worthwhile accomplishments. In this phase of exploring meanings, the role relationship model of formulation was amplified.

This image of herself as bad and defective was matched by a complementary image of her father as scornful of her. In brief transference reactions, she also anticipated derision from the therapist. Connie felt ashamed of herself and angry with her father for not confirming her as worthwhile. In this role relationship model, she held him to be strong, even omnipotent, and in a magical way she saw his death as his deliberate desertion of her. These ideas had been warded off because of the intense humiliation and rage that occurred when they were clearly represented. But contemplation of such ideas, in the phase of therapy for *improving coping*, allowed her to review and reappraise them, thus revising her view of herself and of him.

Every person has multiple self-schemas and role relationship models. They may be integrated or dissociated to various degrees. Connie, in some states of mind, viewed herself as a person too weak to tolerate being without a strong father. After she returned from her father's funeral, she turned to her lover for consolation and sympathy. But Connie had selected a lover who, like her father, was superior, cool, and remote. When she searched for an ideal of a strong, supportive figure, he was unable to provide what she wanted. Moreover, he was repelled by her sorrow and dependency and left her.

Clarification of these themes occurred in a *working-through* phase. Thematic linkages were examined in stories about her current life (lover), past life (father), and transference life with the therapist. Objectivity led to better coping with both her grief and her current situation. *Terminating* was at hand. The therapeutic alliance provided much needed support, but its termination threatened her once again with the loss of what she saw as an ideal transference relationship with a powerful, kind, and sustaining figure. In a further working-through process to improve coping, it was necessary to focus on weak self-concepts associated with attitudes of idealized yearning. She needed to mourn the loss of her fantasy of finding an ideal father. She also needed to increase her clarity of the real pros and cons of her relationship with her father and bolster realistic concepts of herself as capable of independent and interdependent relationships, rather than only dependent ones.

In later therapy sessions, the focus became more on her self-concepts as related to future plans. This included bolstering realistically competent, rather than dependently weak, beliefs about her ability to become skillful and accomplished. Finally, the focus shifted to the aim of working through and accepting termination.

EFFICACY: RESULTS OF THIS TYPE OF PSYCHOTHERAPY FOR STRESS RESPONSE SYNDROMES

Colleagues and I developed useful measures for assessing the levels of distress, subject predispositions, therapist techniques, and therapy outcomes. These measures include the Impact of Event Scale (self-report, Horowitz, Wilner, & Alvarez, 1979; Zilberg, Weiss, & Horowitz, 1982); the Stress Response Rating Scale (clinician's assessment; Horowitz, 1976; Weiss, Horowitz, & Wilner, 1984); the Patterns of Individualized Change Scales, which assess work, intimacy, caretaking, and other life functions (Kaltreider, DeWitt, Weiss, & Horowitz, 1981; DeWitt, Kaltreider, Weiss, & Horowitz, 1983; Weiss, DeWitt, Kaltreider, & Horowitz, 1985); assessments of the therapeutic alliance (Marmar, Horowitz, Weiss, & Marziali, 1986; Marziali, Marmar, & Krupnik, 1981), therapist actions (Hoyt, 1980; Hoyt, Marmar, Horowitz, & Alvarez, 1981), and patients' motivations (Rosenbaum & Horowitz, 1983). The dispositions measure of most importance was the *organizational level of self and other* schematization (Horowitz,

1979, 1997a, 1998; Horowitz, Marmar, Weiss, DeWitt, & Rosenbaum, 1984).

Using all of these measures in the study of 52 cases of pathological grief reactions after the death of a family member, we examined the results of a 12-session, time-limited therapy of the kind just described (as reported in detail in Horowitz, Marmar, Weiss, et al., 1984). Before treatment, this sample had levels of symptoms comparable with those of other psychiatric outpatient samples studied in treatment research: intake on the Symptom Checklist-90 (SCL-90) (general psychiatric symptoms rated by self-report; Derogatis, Rickels, & Rock, 1976) for the sample was 1.19 (SD = .59). This level is almost identical with the figure of 1.25 (SD = .39) reported by Derogatis et al. (1976) for a sample of 209 symptomatic outpatients. The mean depression subscale score in our sample at intake was 1.81, and in the Derogatis et al. study it was 1.87. The scores for anxiety were also comparable: 1.39 in our sample and 1.49 in the sample of Derogatis et al.

A significant improvement was seen in all symptomatic outcome variables when pretherapy scores were compared with follow-up levels. Our results can be expressed in terms of the standardized mean difference effect size coefficient recommended by Cohen (1979) for presenting before–after treatment data. He defined a large effect as 0.80 or greater. Our large effect sizes were in the domain of symptoms and ranged from 0.71 to 1.21. Changes in work, interpersonal functioning, and capacity for intimacy on the patterns of Individualized Change Scales indicated improvements that were more moderate (Horowitz, 1986).

This synthesized cognitive-psychodynamic approach, as recently reported in Horowitz (1997b), was effective in studies by other investigators in other institutions. It did as well as behavioral therapy in treatment of PTSD in the Netherlands (Brom, Kleber, & Defaris, 1989), and as well as behavioral-cognitive in brief treatment of Major Depressive Disorders (Thompson, Gallagher-Thompson, & Breckenridge, 1987; Thompson, Gallagher-Thompson, Fullerman, & Gilewski, 1991). In both studies, the psychotherapy groups did better than wait-list controls. As reviewed in meta-analyses of equivalent studies this cognitive-psychodynamic approach was one of the effective treatments (Crits-Christoph, Luborsky, Dahl, Popp, Mellon, & Mark 1988).

The synthesis of cognitive-psychodynamic theory involved is reported elsewhere (Horowitz, 1998), as is a systematic method of formulation (Horowitz, 1997b).

SUMMARY

The approach described is brief and focused. It aims at restoration of equilibrium by completing reactions to the external stressor event. Biological and social interventions, if and when made, are contained within a cognitive-psychodynamic central theory of case formulation.

Stress response syndromes tend to respond well to treatment. They may even reach resolution without treatment. Nonetheless, the course of improvement is not necessarily linear, and spontaneous remission of symptoms may not occur. Cases are sometimes complex, and it is important to formulate in a way that addresses such complexity. In formulation it is also important to consider what phase of response is current. Equilibrium apparently may be restored but then abruptly lost, only to return and fluctuate again. That is why taking a states-of-mind approach to case formulation is valuable.

States of mind are recognized by their emotional and regulatory qualities. Some are intense, others dull in affect. Some are undermodulated, others excessively controlled or overmodulated. Attributes of a state affect a person's sense of identity within that state: The person may feel in- or out-of-control, and have a variety of secondary anxieties or fears about one's volitility. Self-concepts, and unconscious-person schemas also organize the recurrent experiences and expressions of a state. These personal beliefs are often best conceptualized as aspects of emotional patterns with other people: formulating role relationship models for specific states helps in providing clarity during psychotherapy.

Adding attention to defensive operations and adding concepts of multiple and even contradictory self-schemas to theories about emotional conditioning, information processing, and cognitive schemas are central features of this cognitive-dynamic approach. Whereas it is more complex than some other approaches, it allows for inferences about why some people find it hard to recover on their own. And it provides for an understanding of how to facilitate both shock mastery and reschematization.

REFERENCES

Basch, M. (1980). *Doing psychotherapy*. New York: Basic Books.

Beck, A. (1976). *Cognitive therapy and emotional disorders*. New York: International Universities Press.

Brom, D., Kleber, R. J., & Defares, P. B. (1989). Brief psychotherapy for traumatic stress disorders. *Journal of Consulting and Clinical Psychology, 57*, 607–612.

Cohen, J. (1979). *Power analyses for the social and behavioral sciences*. New York: Academic Press.

Crits-Christoph, P., Luborsky, L. Dahl, L., Popp, C., Mellon, J., & Mark, D. (1988). Clinicians can agree in assessing relationship patterns in psychotherapy: The core conflictual relationship theme method. *Archives of General Psychiatry, 45*, 1001–1004.

Derogatis, L. R., Rickels, K., & Rock, A. (1976). The SCL-90 and the MMPI: A step in the validation of a new self-report scale. *British Journal of Psychiatry, 128*, 280–289.

DeWitt, K. N., Kaltreider, N. B., Weiss, D. S., & Horowitz, M. J. (1983). Judging change in psychotherapy: Reliability of clinical formulations. *Archives of General Psychiatry, 40*, 1121–1128.

Foa, E. B., & Kozak, M. J. (1988). Emotional processing of fear: Exposure to corrective information. *Psychological Bulletin, 99*, 20–35.

Horowitz, M. J. (In Press). *Essential papers on post traumatic stress disorders*. New York: New York University Press.

Horowitz, M. J. (1979). Depressive disorders in response to loss. In I. G. Sarason & C. D. Spielberger (Eds.), *Stress and anxiety* (pp. 235–255). New York: Hemisphere Publishing Co.

Horowitz, M. J. (1986). Stress-response syndromes: A review of post-traumatic and adjustment disorders. *Hospital and Community Psychiatry, 37*, 241–249.

Horowitz, M. J. (1995). Histrionic personality disorder. In G. Gabbard (Ed.), *Treatment of psychiatric disorders* (2nd ed., pp. 2311–2326). Washington D.C.: American Psychiatric Press Inc.

Horowitz, M. J. (1997a, 1976). *Stress response syndromes* (1st and 3rd eds.). Northvale, NJ: Aronson.

Horowitz, M. J. (1997b). *Formulation as a basis for planning psychotherapy*. American Psychiatric Press. Washington, D.C.

Horowitz, M. J. (1998). *Cognitive psychodynamics: From conflict to character*. New York: John Wiley & Sons, Inc.

Horowitz, M. J., Marmar, C., Weiss, D. S., DeWitt, K., & Rosenbaum, R. (1984). Brief psychotherapy of bereavement reactions: The relationship of process to outcome. *Archives of General Psychiatry, 41*, 438–448.

Horowitz, M. J., Wilner, N., & Alvarez, W. (1979). The Impact of Event Scale: A measure of subjective stress. *Psychosomatic Medicine, 41*(3), 209–218.

Hoyt, M. (1980). Therapist and patient actions in "good" psychotherapy sessions. *Archives of General Psychiatry, 37*, 159–161.

Hoyt, M., Marmar, C., Horowitz, M. J., & Alvarez, W. (1981). The therapist action scale and the patient action scale: Instruments for the assessment of activities during dynamic psychotherapy. *Psychotherapy, Therapy, Research, and Practice, 18*, 109–116.

Kaltreider, N. B., DeWitt, K., Weiss, D., & Horowitz, M. J. (1981). Patterns of individualized change scales. *Archives of General Psychiatry, 38*, 1263–1269.

Klerman, G., & Weissman, M. (Eds.). (1993). *New applications of interpersonal psychotherapy*. Washington, D.C.: American Psychiatric Press.

Luborsky, L. (1984). *Principles of psychoanalytic psychotherapy: A manual for supportive expressive treatment*. New York: Basic Books.

Malan, D. H. (1979). *Individual psychotherapy and the science of psychodynamics*. London: Butterworth.

Mann, J. (1973). *Time-limited psychotherapy*. Cambridge, MA: Harvard University Press.

Marmar, C. R., Horowitz, M. J., Weiss, D. S., & Marziali, E. (1986). The development of the Therapeutic Alliance Rating System. In L. S. Greenberg, W. M. Pinsof et al. (Eds.), *The psychotherapeutic process: A research handbook* (pp. 367–390). New York: Guilford Press.

Marziali, E., Marmar, C., & Krupnick, J. (1981). Therapeutic alliance scales: Development and relationship to therapeutic outcome. *American Journal of Psychiatry, 138*, 361–364.

Rosenbaum, R., & Horowitz, M. J. (1983). Motivation for psychotherapy: A factorial and conceptual analysis. *Psychotherapy: Theory, Research, and Practice, 20*, 346–354.

Sifneos, P. E. (1972). *Short-term psychotherapy and emotional crisis*. Cambridge, MA: Harvard University Press.

Singer, J. L., & Pope, K. S. (1978). *The power of the human imagination: New approaches in psychotherapy*. New York: Plenum Press.

Southwick, S. M., Krystal, J. H., Morgan, C. A., Johnson, D., Nagy, L. M., Nicolaou, A., Heninger, G. R., & Charney, D. S. (1993). Abnormal noradrenergic function in posttraumatic stress disorder. *Archives of General Psychiatry, 50*, 266–274.

Strupp, H. H., & Binder, J. L. (1984). *Psychotherapy in a new key: A guide to time-limited dynamic psychotherapy*. New York: Basic Books.

Thompson, L. W., Gallagher, D., & Breckenridge, J. S. (1987). Comparative effectiveness of psychotherapies for depressed elders. *Journal of Geriatric Psychiatry, 21*, 133–146.

Thompson, L., Gallagher-Thompson, D., Fullerman, A., Gilewski, M. J., et al. (1991). The effects of late-life spousal bereavement over a 30-month interval. *Psychology and Aging, 6*(3), 434–441.

Weiss, D., DeWitt, K., Kaltreider, N., & Horowitz, M. J. (1985). A proposed method for measuring change beyond symptoms. *Archives of General Psychiatry, 42*, 703–708.

Zilberg, N., Weiss, D., & Horowitz, M. J. (1982). Impact of Event Scale: A cross-validation study and some empirical evidence. *Journal of Consulting and Clinical Psychology, 50*, 407–414.

CHAPTER 26

HEALTH PSYCHOLOGY

TIMOTHY W. SMITH, JILL B. NEALEY, AND HEIDI A. HAMANN
University of Utah

INTRODUCTION

Since the early descriptions of the field over twenty years ago (Stone, Cohen, & Adler, 1979), health psychology has grown and matured. The emergence of the field was virtually necessitated by changing patterns of health and illness in the latter part of the 20th century. Advances in public health and medicine (e.g., sanitation, vaccines, antibiotics) have dramatically reduced the infectious illnesses that had been the leading causes of morbidity and mortality in industrialized nations. Other advances in medical technology have extended the life expectancy of individuals suffering from many, once lethal, conditions. Chronic diseases such as coronary heart disease and cancer have now become the leading threats to public health. Like the more recently emerging problem of HIV infection and AIDS, the development and course of these conditions are influenced by behavior, and these chronic illnesses have a strong impact on psychological adjustment. Therefore, the prevention and management of our most pressing health problems now require behavior change.

The field can be segmented into three general issues (Smith & Ruiz, 1999). The first—*health behavior and prevention*—examines the impact of daily habits and other potentially modifiable characteristics on subsequent health, as well as the efficacy and benefits of interventions intended to modify these behaviors. The prototypical example of this component of health psychology is the study of the health effects of smoking and the efficacy of smoking cessation interventions (Shiffman, Mason, & Henningfield, 1998). The second general issue—*stress and illness*, or *psy-*

chosomatics—addresses more direct psychobiologic effects of psychological processes on health (Lovallo, 1997). This component of the field includes epidemiologic investigations that identify psychosocial predictors of important health outcomes, as well as studies of the psychobiologic mechanisms linking these risk factors to the development and progression of disease. For example, depressive symptoms and disorders are associated with an increased risk of serious illness and premature mortality (Wulsin, Valiant, & Wells, 1999), perhaps because this risk factor is also associated with alterations in autonomic and immune system functioning (Herbert & Cohen, 1993; Sloan, Shapiro, Bagiella, Myers, & Gorman, 1999). The third area—*psychosocial impact and management of medical illness*—addresses the emotional and social impact of illness and medical care, as well as the potential benefits of adding psychological interventions to routine medical or surgical treatments. Examples of this component of health psychology include psychological preparations to reduce the emotional distress and physical discomfort following surgery (Auerbach, 1989) and behavioral interventions for the management of chronic pain (Gatchel & Turk, 1999).

The literature on interventions in health psychology includes many studies from each of these three areas. Studies of the feasibility and benefits of modifying behavioral risk factors have long been a central and essential focus of the field. This is true not only for risk factors identified decades ago, such as smoking and physical inactivity, but also for new behavioral risk factors, such as the sexual behaviors related to HIV transmission. Interventions derived from the study of stress and illness could include both attempts to prevent the initial occurrence of disease as well as adjuncts to traditional medical and surgical care of patients with established illnesses. However, very few studies have been conducted to assess the preventive effects among healthy persons of modifying psychosocial risk factors or the stress mechanisms presumed to link them to subsequent disease. Hence, most of the literature on the health benefits of stress management and related interventions can be grouped with intervention research from the third category, psychological adjuncts to traditional care. In this category, a very broad range of interventions has been applied to an equally broad range of medical conditions. In each case, the effects of such interventions on emotional and social functioning, subjective symptoms, adherence to medical care, and objective indicators of illness severity have been examined.

In this chapter, we provide a brief overview of the intervention research in the field, and discuss its implications for clinical practice and future research. We then discuss ongoing challenges in applied health psychology, including the impact of evolving medical technologies, the role of diversity in the field, and the practical issues encountered when psychological change methods are applied in health care settings and to advance public health. Before doing so, however, we first address critical conceptual and methodological considerations in health psychology interventions.

THE BIOPSYCHOSOCIAL MODEL IN HEALTH PSYCHOLOGY

Throughout its history, health psychology has reflected the biopsychosocial model of physical health and illness (Engel, 1977). In contrast to the traditional biomedical model that views physical illness as resulting from aberrations in biochemistry or physiology, the biopsychosocial model views health and illness as reflecting the reciprocal influences among biological, psychological, and social/environmental processes. Rather than reducing health and illness to basic biological causes and manifestations, the biopsychosocial approach is based on systems theory (von Bertalanffy, 1968). This broad conceptual framework, depicted in Figure 26.1, conceptualizes natural phenomena as reflecting hierarchically arranged levels of analysis, ranging in complexity from small, simpler units such as cells to large,

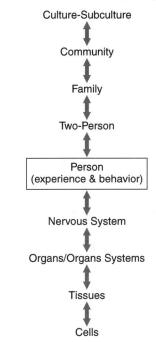

Figure 26.1 Systems hierarchy (levels of organization).

complex, and superordinate processes such as social communities and cultures. Each level of analysis has its own conceptual models, methods, and organization, but each system both influences and is influenced by adjacent levels. Therefore, any specific process cannot be fully understood without placing it in the context of the levels of analysis both above and below in the hierarchy.

The implications of this general conceptual framework for health psychology are clear. The traditional biomedical understanding of a disease—such as cancer—as reflecting aberrations at the level of cells and the biochemical events that influence them is incomplete. Even when the cellular abnormalities are placed in the context of the tissues and organ systems they disrupt, the understanding of the disease is still incomplete. It is only when the disease is considered in the context of the specific individual and that individual is in turn considered in the context of his or her surrounding social, environmental, and cultural context that the conceptualization becomes more complete; for example, a person's characteristics influence the occurrence and progression of cancer (e.g., smoking, participation in cancer screening), yet the disease influences other characteristics of the individual (e.g., emotional adjustment).

The development and progression of the illness both influence and are influenced by the individual's social relationships, and most aspects of the illness and its impact are influenced by broad environmental factors, such as socioeconomic status. This overarching conceptual approach guides both the basic research and applied intervention agendas in health psychology and behavioral medicine (Schwartz, 1982).

This general view of the reciprocal association between behavior and medical illness is also reflected in current psychiatric nosology (American Psychiatric Association, 1994). The DSM-IV diagnosis of Psychological Factors Affecting Medical Condition (i.e., DSM-IV Code No. 316) explicitly identifies a variety of ways in which psychological or behavioral processes can influence a medical condition (see Table 26.1). Mental disorders, psychological symptoms, personality traits and coping styles, maladaptive health behaviors, and stress-related physiological responses are all discussed as possible psychosocial influences on risk of disease, its course, the extent and impact of symptoms, and the adequacy of traditional medical-surgical treatment. This diagnostic category is rather general, as it does not specify how these various categories of influence operate. Nonetheless, a variety of direct, indirect or mediating, and moderating effects of psychosocial factors on illness have been identified in health psychology research (Smith & Nicassio, 1995). These models and the research supporting them guide the intervention research and practice we review in this chapter.

This DSM diagnosis is primarily concerned with psychosocial influences on health and illness. The other path in the reciprocal connection between psychosocial processes and health identified by the biopsychosocial model—health and illness as influences on psychological and social functioning—is included elsewhere in the current nosology. For example, Adjustment Disorders and Mental Disorders Due to a Medical Condition are categories of diagnoses that explicitly acknowledge the potential impact of physical illness on emotional well-being (American Psychiatric Association, 1994).

The application of the general biopsychosocial perspective in health psychology interventions obviously requires consideration of a variety of factors. The levels of analysis depicted in Figure 26.1 and the types of influences described in the DSM-IV language suggest several categories to be considered, as well as specific elements within categories (Smith & Nicassio, 1995), which are outlined in Table 26.2. This outline is most relevant to interventions for a specific illness or disorder (e.g., cancer, arthritis, etc.), but with minimal modification it is relevant to interventions intended to modify high-risk behaviors or characteristics (e.g., smoking and obesity). The outline is not procedural, but rather organizes the consideration of multiple levels of analysis or systems needed for a comprehensive understanding of the necessary targets of change, possible impediments to change, and the range of approaches that might be useful.

The illness or condition to be addressed is an obviously important consideration. The health psychologist must understand the underlying pathophysiology and likely prognosis of the illness or condition, as well as the usual medical and surgical approaches to the problem. These features of the condition are central determinants of

TABLE 26.1 DSM-IV Criteria for Psychological Factors Affecting Medical Condition

A. The presence of a general medical condition (coded on Axis III).

B. Psychological factors affect the general medical condition in at least one of the following ways:

1. The factors have influenced the course of the medical condition as shown by a close temporal association between the development, exacerbation, or delayed recovery from the general medical condition;

2. The factors interfere with treatment of the general medical condition;

3. The factors constitute additional health risks for the individual;

4. Stress-related physiological responses precipitate or exacerbate symptoms of a general medical condition.

Source: From *Diagnostic and Statistical Manual of Mental Disorders* (Washington, D.C.: American Psychiatric Association, 1994), 4th ed., p. 678. Copyright © 1994 by the American Psychiatric Association. Adapted with permission.

TABLE 26.2 Outline for Assessment and Intervention in the Clinical Application of the Biopsychosocial Model

I. The illness
  A. Pathophysiology
  B. Risk factors
  C. Prognosis
  D. Diagnostic procedures
  E. Treatment procedures
II. The patient
  A. DSM Axis I conditions
  B. Disease history
  C. Personality traits and coping styles or mechanisms
  D. Conceptualization of disease and treatment
  E. Educational and vocational status
  F. Impact of illness on subjective distress, social functioning, activity level, self-care, and overall quality of life
III. Social, family, and cultural contexts
  A. Quality of marital and family relationships
  B. Use and efficacy of social support
  C. Patient–physician relationship
  D. Patient's cultural background
IV. The health care system
  A. Medical organization, setting, and culture
  B. Insurance coverage for diagnostic and treatment procedures
  C. Geographical, social, and psychological barriers to accessing health services
  D. Existence of disability benefits for medical condition

the patient's experience, and identify critical targets for psychological interventions. Psychologists are naturally more familiar with the list of characteristics of the individual that are necessary considerations in the selection and implementation of interventions, such as emotional disorders, coping styles, and personality traits. A less familiar consideration is the patient's understanding of the condition and its management. This set of cognitive factors is a key determinant of the patient's ability and inclination to profit from both traditional medical care and psychological adjuncts (Leventhal, Diefenbach, & Leventhal, 1992). Simply put, patients with an accurate understanding of the nature of their condition and the related treatment are more likely to adhere to

and participate effectively in treatment. Finally, a variety of social, environmental, and cultural/organizational issues are relevant to the selection and implementation of interventions. For example, an overweight and sedentary spouse, subcultural acceptance of obesity, limited access to facilities for regular exercise, and lack of health insurance coverage of risk factor reduction treatments are all factors that can undermine an individual patient's weight loss efforts.

The limitations of the traditional biomedical model are apparent following even a brief review of the elements listed in Table 26.2. For example, two patients with the same objective medical condition, coronary heart disease, require different adjunctive psychological interventions depending on their particular individual, social, and environmental contexts. Adequate participation in cardiac rehabilitation poses very different challenges for a depressed, socially isolated patient with minimal health care coverage than it does for a more adjusted, upper socioeconomic status individual with a concerned and supportive spouse.

METHODOLOGICAL CONSIDERATIONS

Because of the influence of the biopsychosocial model and its multiple levels of analysis, health psychology lies at the intersection of several different biomedical, behavioral, and social sciences. This necessitates the integration of a variety of methodological traditions and techniques, as well as the related quantitative approaches. For example, methodological approaches from epidemiology, physiology, and psychology are central in most areas of health psychology research, and increasing attention has been paid in recent years to fields addressing lower (e.g., biochemistry, genetics) and higher levels of analysis (sociology, anthropology). Despite the complexity inherent in this plurality of approaches, several methodological issues familiar to clinical and counseling psychologists are central in the design and evaluation of intervention research in health psychology. Of course, the application of these principles to the specific context of physical health and illness requires thoughtful translation (Smith & Ruiz, 1999).

The Value of Conceptual Models

In all areas of psychological research, clear conceptual definitions of hypothetical constructs and the relationships among them are essential (Cook

& Campbell, 1979; Meehl, 1978). Despite the fact that most research on the determinants of health-relevant behavior and related interventions are well grounded in conceptual models, several areas of health psychology suffer from conceptual ambiguities (e.g., Coyne & Gottlieb, 1996; Weinstein, 1993; Weinstein, Rothman, & Sutton 1998). The importance and difficulty of achieving conceptual clarity and precision is heightened by the fact that the models guiding health psychological research contain biomedical elements. That is, the biopsychosocial perspective already discussed requires that the psychological level of analysis be supplemented by appropriate biological level processes and interactions between these levels. For example, studies of the benefits of stress management in the treatment of coronary heart disease (Blumenthal, Jiang, Babyak, & Krantz, 1997) should be based on an understanding of appropriate indicators of the illness, as well as a model of how stress reduction could impact the disease (Kamarck & Jennings, 1991; Smith & Gallo, 1994). In the specific context of theory-driven intervention research, these models provide the opportunity to evaluate simultaneously both the efficacy and mechanisms of health psychology treatments. For example, one can evaluate not only whether or not coping skills training improves activity levels in chronic pain patients but also whether or not such beneficial changes are mediated through the mechanism of increases in self-efficacy. This potential synergy between process and outcome research on health psychology interventions holds considerable promise for the refinement of clinical science and practice.

Measurement

Several areas of health psychology contain limitations stemming from inadequate measurement of key constructs. This is true for studies of psychosocial influences on health (Smith & Gallo, in press), and for studies of adjustment to illness and stressful medical care (Auerbach, 1989; Suls & Wan, 1989). For example, depressive symptoms and disorders are common occurrences in several chronic disease populations, but the somatic symptoms included in traditional depression measures can lead to an over-estimate of emotional distress when seriously ill patients simply describe the symptoms of their illness (Clark, Cook, & Snow, 1998; Peck, Smith, Ward, & Milano, 1989). In intervention research, common measurement problems can be particularly troublesome. For example, because some health-relevant behaviors are socially undesirable (e.g., poor diet, physical inactivity, smoking), the demand characteristics inherent in health behavior interventions can produce inflated estimates of treatment effects when self-reports are used as primary outcome assessments. In some intervention research, medical variables are the primary outcomes of interest. In such instances, health psychology researchers assess illness outcomes that are heavily influenced by illness behavior, rather than simply illness itself. For example, self-reports of physical symptoms, sick days, and visits to physicians in part reflect actual illness, but these measures also reflect strictly psychological processes independent of actual illness, such as a dimension of stoicism versus excessive somatic complaint. This measurement ambiguity creates uncertainty as to whether interventions are altering illness itself or the patient's response to an otherwise unmodified illness. Given the complexity of many medical outcome variables, the sophistication of assessments within a particular illness, and disease-specific criteria for diagnosis and quantification, outcome assessment often requires interdisciplinary collaborations.

Design

Experimental designs are essential in the evaluation of interventions in health psychology. The specific experimental conditions to be compared depends on the state of the literature in a given area. For example, simple comparisons between an additional psychosocial intervention and standard medical care are appropriate for initial evaluations of a treatment. However, expectancy, attention, and placebo effects are well documented in many health contexts (Turner, Deyo, & Lowser, 1994), creating the need for appropriate controls in order to identify the effects of specific interventions (Compas, Haaga, Keefe, Leitenberg, & Williams, 1998). Many research areas have evolved to a point where questions of relative effectiveness, active ingredients within multicomponent interventions, mechanisms of effects, and moderators of treatment outcome are the most pressing concerns. Such questions are best addressed through the use of carefully selected comparison groups and analytic methods (Chambless & Hollon, 1998; Kendall, Flannery-Schroeder, & Ford, 1999). In nearly all areas of intervention research in health psychology, the stability of intervention effects is a critical consideration. In some areas, such as smoking cessation and weight loss interventions, persistence of treatment effects is arguably the most important research issue (Brownell, Marlatt, Lichtensteing, & Wilson, 1986; Curry & McBride, 1994). Therefore, adequate follow-up intervals are a critical design feature. However, in the case of some adjunctive interventions in medical care, even brief effects are important, such as psychological interventions to reduce pain during the acute care of serious burns (Patterson & Ptacek, 1997). Thus, the length of follow-up and other elements of intervention research design must be carefully tailored to the specific context.

Sampling

In clinical intervention research in health psychology, participants often are enrolled after a complex process of access to health care, physician referral patterns, and response to traditional medical or surgical treatment. This selection process makes it extremely difficult to define the population to which treatment outcome results can be generalized. For example, Turk and Rudy (1990) argue that patients participating in clinical studies of chronic pain are quite unrepresentative of the general chronic pain population, given these multiple steps in sample construction. For researchers, care must be taken in describing the sample recruitment process and the resulting participant characteristics. For clinicians using research to guide practice, care must be taken in the implicit extrapolation of such findings.

Analysis

In traditional treatment outcome research in clinical and counseling psychology, clinical or practical significance—as opposed to simple statistical significance—has long been identified as an important component of quantitative analysis and interpretation of intervention effects (Jacobson & Traux, 1991). Although any effect of a psychological intervention on the occurrence or course of a physical disease has conceptual importance, the practical significance of such findings must be evaluated by other means. In some research areas, standards for evaluating clinical significance have been established through prior research (e.g., Blanchard & Malamood, 1996). Some outcome assessments are standardized, permitting post-treatment comparisons to normative groups (Jacobson & Traux, 1991; Kendall & Grove, 1988). Given the current, wide-spread interest in reducing health care expenditures, cost-benefit analysis of adjunctive psychological interventions

can be an important source of information about practical significance (Kaplan, 1994; Yates, 1994). However, the benefits of adjunctive and risk reduction interventions must be weighed not only against the cost of the intervention but also the potential cost of shifting causes of morbidity and mortality from one disease to another (Friedman, Subel, Meyers, Caudill, & Benson, 1995). Finally, the size of treatment effects in many health psychology studies may appear small by conventional standards. However, given the scope (i.e., prevalence) and cost of some diseases, even small effects can have significant public health and economic benefits.

BEHAVIORAL RISK REDUCTION

Daily habits exert strong effects on the risk of developing any and dying from each of the major health threats in industrialized nations. Tobacco use, low levels of physical activity, and a diet high in saturated fat clearly contribute to coronary heart disease, stroke, and some cancers (Adler & Matthews, 1994). These same behaviors also influence the development of conditions that independently confer additional risk to these and other sources of morbidity and premature mortality (e.g., diabetes, high blood pressure, obesity). Health behavior mechanisms are now responsible for risk of HIV infection as well (St. Lawrence & McFarlane, 1999). Other behaviors, such as driving under the influence of alcohol and seat belt use, profoundly alter the risk of accidental injury and death. Finally, participation in medical screening (e.g., mammography, blood pressure screening) may increase the likelihood that otherwise life-threatening illness can be detected at earlier, more treatable stages. The identification of this variety of behavioral influences on health, and the implication that behavior change therefore holds great promise for health promotion and disease prevention, has been a driving force throughout the history of health psychology (Matarazzo, 1980). In what follows, we review the general findings of the most well-developed areas of health behavior change research.

Smoking Cessation

Cigarette smoking is the leading cause of preventable illness, premature death, and health care expenditure in the United States (United States Department of Health and Human Services [USDHHS], 1994). An estimated 400,000 lives are cut short each year due to the effect of smoking on coronary heart disease, stroke, cancer, and lung disease. Despite several decades of progress in reducing the prevalence of smoking in this country, about a quarter of the adult population smokes (USDHHS, 1994). More worrisome is the fact that while adult smoking rate have remained stable for the past several years, the rate among adolescents has risen steadily (Shiffman et al., 1998). The prevention of adolescent smoking is an increasing focus of health psychology and public health research (Lynagh, Schofield, & Sanson-Fisher, 1997; Lynch & Bonnie, 1994), but is beyond our present scope. Rather, we focus on the value of behavioral interventions for smoking cessation.

The benefits of smoking cessation are well established, and include a significantly reduced likelihood of each of the causes of serious illness and death otherwise linked to smoking (USDHHS, 1990). Most smokers who quit successfully do so without professional assistance (Fiore, Novotny, Pierce et al., 1990), but relapse rates in this population and for those receiving help are extremely high. Each year, about one-third of the 50 million smokers in the United States try to quit, but only about 6 percent of those who try actually achieve long-term cessation (CDC, 1994). Thus, health psychology interventions increasingly address long-term smokers with a history of failed cessation attempts and a high likelihood of relapse (Lichtensteinn & Glasgow, 1992; Shiffman et al., 1998).

The current consensus of the efficacy of organized smoking cessation programs is that multicomponent behavioral interventions are effective, at least in producing important improvements to long-term cessation (Compas et al., 1998). Regrettably, even these more effective interventions do not achieve even 50% long-term success rates. So, the modal outcome is failure. Nonetheless, given the consequence of continued smoking, even modest effects on long-term rates have profound public health consequences. These multicomponent behavioral interventions are typically psycho-educational in orientation and are delivered in small group formats. Typical components include information about the benefits and feasibility of quitting; instruction in stimulus control techniques, such as reducing exposure to environmental cues (e.g., ashtrays, tobacco advertising) that evoke smoking urges; commitment to a quit date; relaxation and other stress management techniques to manage negative emotions and smoking urges; and specific training in re-

lapse prevention. Studies that control for nonspecific factors (e.g., therapist contact, encouragement to quit, etc.) with a minimum of one-year follow-up indicate significant and maintained treatment effects (e.g., Hill, Rigdon, & Johnson, 1993). The relapse prevention component, in which participants make specific plans for managing high-risk situations and possible "slips," has been found to have beneficial effects on long-term smoking rates (e.g., Curry & McBride, 1994; Stevens & Hollis, 1989). Most effective smoking cessation programs include several of these behavior change approaches.

Consistent with the general biopsychosocial approach, in recent years nicotine replacement therapy (NRT) has been added to smoking cessation programs in an effort to manage more directly the addictive process. NRT comes in the form of nicotine gum, the transdermal nicotine patch, intranasal nicotine, and nicotine inhalers. The results of several large and appropriately controlled trials provide clear evidence that NRT is effective in smoking cessation (Shiffman et al., 1998). Although most smokers still fail to quit and remain abstinent, NRT certainly improves their chances of success. However, the poor long-term success rates with NRT can be improved when it is combined with the multicomponent approach described previously (Fisher, Lichtenstein, Haire-Joshu, Morgan, & Rehberg, 1993; Hughes, 1991). This combined approach is consistent with the biopsychosocial approach in health psychology and addictions treatment (Shiffman et al., 1998). Recent evidence suggests that the newer antidepressant medications, such as the seratonin reuptake inhibitor bupropion, are effective alternatives or additions to NRT (e.g., Jorenby, Leischow, Nides, et al., 1999).

Given the high prevalence of smoking, the costs of formal behavioral treatment, and the difficulty in referral to and entry into formal treatment among patients in a primary medical care setting, lower cost combinations of NRT and self-help methods (e.g., bibliotherapy) have been evaluated. Although, this approach is clearly less effective than NRT plus multicomponent behavioral interventions (e.g., Killen, Fortmann, Davis, & Varady, 1997), newer approaches of low-cost, self-help interventions hold promise. For example, a computer-based interactive system in which self-help information is tailored to the individual's readiness or stage of change (DiClemente, Prochaska, Fairhurst, Velicer, Valesquez, & Rossi,

1991) has been found to produce increased cessation and maintenance (Velicer, Prochaska, Fava, Laforge, & Rossi, 1999).

Another approach to increasing cessation rates involves low-cost interventions delivered to smokers when they encounter the health care system. Physicians and other health care workers encounter approximately 70% of all smokers each year (Ockene, 1993). The delivery of even limited physician advice and encouragement can increase one-year abstinence rates, and more involved physician interventions can produce still higher cessation rates (Klesges, Ward, & DeBon, 1996; Lindsay, Ockene, Hymowitz, Giffen, Berger, & Pomrehn, 1994). Although the effects of these interventions are modest in comparison with multi-component behavioral interventions, the opportunity to deliver an even modestly effective low-cost intervention to a greatly increased number of smokers could have a large impact on public health. When smokers are hospitalized, brief bedside interventions can be offered along with physician encouragement. These programs have been found to produce one-year abstinence rates of 30% or above, compared to 10% or even lower among hospitalized smokers receiving usual care (Houston Miller, Smith, DeBusk, Sobel, & Taylor, 1997; Taylor, Houston Miller, Herman et al., 1996). Thus, taking advantage of the environmental and motivational features of hospitalization may be useful in smoking cessation efforts. Systematic practice guidelines have been developed for use when smokers encounter health care professionals; they reflect tailoring of the specific approach to patient readiness for change and the integration of NRT and cognitive behavioral methods described above (Fiore, Jorenby, & Baker, 1997).

Consideration of special populations of smokers also holds promise for improving cessation rates and long-term effectiveness, as well as simply engaging more smokers in the change process. Pregnant smokers are one such population. Although 40 percent of smoking women stop during pregnancy, postpartum relapse is high (Fingerhut, Kleinman, & Kendrick, 1990). Although special interventions directed to this population have produced mixed results (Gielen, Windsor, Faden, O'Campo, Repke, & Davis, 1997), tailoring interventions to the needs of women during this "teachable moment" may prove useful (Chesney & Nealey, 1996). For example, partners' smoking status and support for the mothers' smoking cessation efforts predict smoking outcomes in this group (McBride, Curry, Grothaus, Nelson, Lando, & Pirie, 1998), suggesting that cessation interventions for expectant fathers or couples may be valuable.

Given the rising proportion of women smokers, additional attention to the unique influences on smoking and cessation success in this population is important. The role of weight concerns and postcessation weight gain is one example of work of this type. For both men and women, concern that smoking cessation will lead to weight gain is often cited as a barrier to quitting, but this may be more true for women smokers (Camp, Klesges, & Relyes, 1993). The research on the effects of weight concerns on initial quit attempts, cessation, and maintenance provides mixed evidence of the importance of this factor (e.g., Jeffery, Boles, Strycker, & Glasgow, 1997; Meyers, Klesges, Winders, Ward, Peterson, & Eck, 1997), as does the research on the actual amount of weight gain following cessation (Klesges, Winders, Meyers et al., 1997; Klesges, Ward, Ray et al., 1998). Nonetheless, identification of potentially modifiable mediators of the effects of weight concerns and weight changes on smoking cessation attempts and success (e.g., disinhibited eating, negative affect; Suchanek-Hudman, Gritz, Clayton, & Nisenbaum, 1999) is an important avenue for research on women's smoking, as is the development of related interventions (Borrelli, Spring, Niaura, Kristeller, Ockene, & Keuthen, 1999).

In addition to the techniques for the management of nicotine addiction already described, the basic biomedical level of analysis has recently identified additional avenues for behavior change efforts. A variety of behavioral genetic designs have provided evidence of a genetic contribution to the likelihood of initiating smoking and difficulty quitting (Pomerleau & Kardia, 1999). Recent research has indicated that genetic influences on specific neurotransmitter functions may account for these genetic effects (Lerman, Caporaso, Audrain et al., 1999; Sabol, Hovell, Fisher et al., 1999). This suggests that it may be possible to identify subgroups of smokers for whom specific psychobiological mechanisms would be important targets for intervention (e.g., Lerman, Caporaso, Main et al., 1998).

Weight Loss

Over one-third of adult Americans are classified as overweight, as defined by a body weight at least 20% above an ideal based on height (Kuczmarski,

Flegel, Campbell, & Johnson, 1994; Williamson, Champagne, Jackman, & Varnado, 1996). In some minority populations, obesity is even more prevalent, affecting over 50% of African-American and Mexican-American women, for example (Wing & Klem, 1997). Obesity is associated with increased risk of high blood pressure, coronary heart disease, stroke (Eckel, 1997), Type II diabetes (Meigs, Nathan, Wilson, Cupples, & Singer, 1998), and premature mortality (Pi-Sunyer, 1993; Sjostrom, 1993). Thus, obesity is a prevalent and serious public health concern (Bray, 1996; Flegal, Carroll, Kuczmarski, & Johnson, 1998). Regrettably, obesity has proven to be difficult to treat, especially when maintenance of weight loss is appropriately included in the definition of intervention success. Across the wide variety of professional, commercial, and self-help interventions evaluated to date, initial weight loss during active treatment often only averages 10% to 20% of initial body weight, with regain of most—if not all—of the initial loss the most common outcome at one year (Brownell & Wadden, 1992; Foreyt & Goodrick, 1994; Wilson, 1994; Wing & Klem, 1997). Thus, obesity is also appropriately considered a refractory disorder (Brownell & Wadden, 1992).

Studies relevant to the etiology of obesity converge to suggest that it is best considered a biopsychosocial phenomenon. For example, both twin and adoption studies indicate that genetic factors appear to account for up to 70% of adult variability in adiposity, or body fatness (e.g. Stunkard, Harris, Pederson, & McClearn, 1990). Genetic influences have been identified for several of the physiological substrates of adiposity, including resting metabolic rate, fat cell number and size, and distribution of fat across body sites (Bouchard, Trembley, Despres et al., 1989; Bouchard, Trembley, & Nadeau, 1990). The location or distribution of excess body fat is important because abdominal adiposity appears to confer a greater health risk than do other sites (e.g., hips; Sjostrom, 1993). Original descriptions of psychological contributions of obesity as involving passive and neurotic personality characteristics have not been supported by controlled research (Plante & Rodin, 1990). However, there is some evidence to suggest that chronic dieting (i.e., restrained eating; Herman, 1987) is associated with heightened vulnerability to excessive food consumption, especially in response to stressful events and negative emotions (Heatherton, Herman, & Polivy, 1991, 1992).

Perhaps the most important behavioral influences on obesity that operate at the individual level of analysis are excess caloric consumption and decreased physical activity (Brownell & Wadden, 1992; Lichtman, Pisarka, Berman et al., 1992); the simple energy balance model of weight control suggests that weight gain occurs when energy consumed exceeds energy expended. For a subset of overweight persons, excessive eating may be especially problematic. Binge eating disorder (Spritzer, Devlin, Walsh et al., 1992) may complicate weight loss interventions, requiring some consideration of alternative approaches (Freidman & Brownell, 1995; Gladis, Wadden, Vogt, Foster, Kuehnel, & Bartlett, 1998). Finally, at the level of broader social, cultural, and environmental contributions to obesity, increased access to and reliance on high fat foods and decreases in energy expenditure at work, home, and in leisure activities are likely to play a role in the prevalence of the disorder (Friedman & Brownell, 1995).

Pharmacological interventions have been found to be somewhat effective, although side effects—especially in the context of long-term treatments—are the source of some concern (National Task Force on the Prevention and Treatment of Obesity, 1996). More recently developed pharmacological treatments that inhibit fat absorption hold some promise for improving weight loss outcome and producing positive changes on related metabolic risk factors for cardiovascular disease (Davidson, Hauptman, DiGirolamo et al., 1999). However, pharmacological interventions, even when combined with behavioral treatments, are only modestly successful.

Most psychosocial interventions for obesity share a common set of behavioral elements, including self-monitoring of food intake; reductions in exposure to cues that prompt an urge to eat excessively (i.e., stimulus control techniques); instruction in changing eating behavior, such as eating more slowly; exercise instruction; nutritional instruction; cultivation of social support for behavioral changes; and relapse prevention training (Clark & Goldstein, 1995; Freidman & Brownell, 1996). The current literature on efficacy has reached several tentative conclusions. As noted, whereas this basic form of intervention can produce initial weight loss, weight regain is common. Thus, strategies for long-term maintenance are an essential component of any intervention (Battle & Brownell, 1996; Foster & Kendall, 1994). Appropriate dietary recommendations and goals focus on shifting the balance of energy consumption from culturally common, high fat patterns to diets characterized by low fat levels, high carbohydrate and fiber, and a general intake of approximately 1,800 calories per day. This type of diet produces weight loss of 1 to 1.5 lbs per week, but long-term maintenance is limited (Brownell & Wadden, 1992). Diets of less than 800 calories per day (i.e., VLCDs [Very Low Calorie Diets]) produce more rapid and severe initial weight loss, but long-term maintenance remains problematic and the risk of side effects is increased with VLCDs (Wadden, Stunkard, & Liebschutz, 1988; Wadden, Van Italie, & Blackburn, 1990). The importance of exercise interventions is suggested by the results of several studies in which addition of regular exercise programs to other dietary and multicomponent interventions results in larger initial weight loss and improved maintenance (Skender, Goodrick, Del Junco et al., 1996; Wing, Epstein, Paternostro-Bayles, Kriska, Norwalk, & Gooding, 1988), though not all controlled trials of the addition of an exercise component have produced positive results (Wadden, Vogt, Anderson et al., 1997; Wadden, Vogt, Foster, & Anderson, 1998).

Efforts to improve long-term outcomes have found encouraging effects of increasing social support (Wing & Jeffery, 1999), more intensive maintenance phase interventions (Perri et al., 1988), and home-based or lifestyle activity interventions as alternatives to the traditional structured exercise interventions (Andersen, Wadden, Bartlett, Zemel, Verde, & Franckowiak, 1999; Perri, Martin, Leermakers, Sears, & Notelovitz, 1997). However, although these refinements hold promise, intervention outcomes remain modest at best for most individuals and quite discouraging for many (Brownell, 1991; Foster & Kendall, 1994; Wilson, 1994). This emerging conclusion has been the source of additional suggestions that smaller weight loss goals might not only be more realistic but also less likely to lead to the iatrogenic distress from treatment failures (Brownell & Rodin, 1994). Further, failure to meet initial, unrealistic weight loss goals could lead to discouragement, and ultimately to failure to maintain smaller but still beneficial losses. Therefore, it has been suggested that interventions include counseling obese patients in setting more attainable goals (Foster, Wadden, & Vogt, 1997). To the extent that patients achieving such partial successes remain dissatisfied with their body image (Foster et al., 1997; Sarwer, Wadden, & Foster, 1998), additional cognitive therapies could be employed to reduce this specific source of distress (Rosen, Orosan, & Reiter, 1995). Though improved body image and satisfaction are beneficial outcomes, there is little evidence that more realistic, attainable weight loss goals are associated with improved maintenance or psychological well-being (Jeffery, Wing, & Mayor, 1998). A second, highly promising response to the emerging consensus on the limited success of obesity interventions in adulthood is increased attention to the prevention of the condition, as well as treatments for overweight children compared to the effects of behavioral interventions for overweight adults. The prevention and early intervention approach has produced much more impressive results (e.g., Epstein, Valoski, Wing, & McCurley, 1994).

Exercise and Activity Level

Independent of the association with obesity, daily levels of physical activity and exercise are important influences on health and illness (Miller, Balady, & Fletcher, 1997; Paffenbarger, Hyde, Wing, & Hsieh, 1986). Sedentary adults are at increased risk of cardiovascular disease (Blair, Kohl, & Paffenbarger, 1989), Type II diabetes (Helmrich, Ragland, Leung, & Paffenbarger, 1991; Lynch, Helmrich, & Lakka, 1996), and some forms of cancer (Lee, 1994). Further, even modest increases in physical activity levels are associated with substantial reductions in risk of serious illness and death (Blair et al., 1995). In the elderly, a low level of physical activity is a risk factor for decreases in functional activity and loss of independence over time (Buchner, Beresford, Larson, LaCroix, & Wagner, 1992). Despite these well-established and widely known health benefits, fewer than one in five U.S. adults regularly engages in sustained aerobic exercise (USDHHS, 1996).

Improvements in exercise and physical activity have long been a major focus in health psychology and behavioral medicine (Martin & Dubbert, 1982). As in the case of other risk factor changes, a variety of behavioral interventions have proven to be useful in initial improvements in activity level (Dishman & Sallis, 1994; Dubbert, 1992), but maintenance of these changes over longer follow-up periods has been much more difficult to achieve (Sallis, Hovell, Hofstetter et al., 1990). The interventions found to produce initial increases in physical activity and regular exercise include behavioral contracting and goal setting, incentives (e.g., participation in lottery drawings), self-monitoring, and training in distraction during aerobic exercise (Dubbert & Stetson, 1995).

A variety of approaches have been used with some success to produce improved maintenance of increases in activity levels. Use of the stages of change approach (see Prochaska chapter) to tailor interventions to the individual's level of initial involvement in exercise appears to be beneficial (Calfas, Long, Sallis et al., 1996; Marcus, Banspach, Lefebvre et al., 1992). Given that lack of time, disruptions in routine, and limited access to exercise facilities are common barriers to maintenance, home based (King, Haskell, Young et al., 1995) and lifestyle approaches (Dunn, Marcus, Kampert et al., 1999) have been developed as alternatives to traditional structured programs. The home and lifestyle approaches attempt to increase physical activity levels in daily routines, leisure and recreational activities, and other elements of the usual daily schedule of sedentary individuals. This integration of exercise and increased activity into daily routines and leisure activities has also been found to be beneficial to children (Epstein et al., 1985, 1994).

Exercise interventions are a valuable component of the weight management programs described above, and are useful in the treatment of several chronic illnesses and serious conditions. As we discuss below, exercise interventions are used in cardiac rehabilitation, and are also useful adjuncts to the traditional care of heart transplant patients (Kobashigawa, Leaf, Lee et al., 1999), heart failure (Belardinelli, Georgiou, Cianci, & Purcaro, 1999), and chronic obstructive pulmonary disease (Emery et al., 1998).

HIV Infection Prevention

AIDS is currently the leading cause of death in the United States among adults aged 25–44 (CDC, 1996). Approximately 600,000 individuals are currently living with AIDS, and 1.5 million are believed to be HIV positive. In the two decades since its appearance, the face of HIV infection has changed. Though it first flourished among gay men, currently only about 25% of new infections are due to homosexual contact, whereas 50% occur among injection drug users and 25% occur as a result of heterosexual contact (Merson, 1996). Across these groups, women and minorities are at disproportionate risk, and women are the fastest growing group of new infections (CDC, 1996).

Health psychologists have primarily been involved in HIV prevention through interventions intended to modify sexual transmission of the disease (Kalichman, 1998). Early HIV prevention efforts focused on education and HIV testing. These approaches had beneficial effects on knowledge, but very limited impact on high risk behaviors (Higgins, Galavotti, O'Reilly et al., 1991; Ickovics, Morrill, Beren, & Walsh, 1994; Ross & Rosser, 1989). In contrast, more involved psycho-educational programs whose intentions are to modify the motivation and behavioral skills underpinning safer sexual practices have been found to be more effective (Kalichman, Carey, & Johnson, 1996). Key components of these individual and small group-based interventions include information about safer sexual practices, motivation-enhancing procedures (e.g., motivational interviewing), role-playing and other procedures to enhance necessary skills (e.g., assertion in sexual encounters), cognitive restructuring about related interpersonal beliefs (e.g., safer sexual practices as indications of level of trust and intimacy), enhancement of self-efficacy through guided practice and corrective feedback, awareness and modification of related high risk behaviors (e.g., alcohol and drug use), and development of social support for behavior changes. These multicomponent interventions have been found to be successful in changing sexual practices (e.g., frequency of unprotected intercourse), but the impact on HIV infection rates is difficult to assess given the small size of the trials (Kalichman et al., 1996). These positive results have been demonstrated in gay and bisexual men (e.g., Kelly, St. Lawrence, Hood, & Brasfield, 1989; Valdiserri, Lyter, Leviton et al., 1989), minority gay populations (Peterson, Coates, Catania et al., 1995), and heterosexual women (Hobfoll, Jackson, Lavin, Britton, & Shepherd, 1994; Kelly, Murphy, Washington et al., 1994).

Recently, interventions of this type have been undertaken with the more specific, emerging high risk groups, with encouraging results. Minority adolescents (St. Lawrence, Brasfield, & Jefferson, 1995), drug abusing women (Eldridge, St. Lawrence, Little et al., 1997), inner city heterosexual men (Kalichman, Rompa, & Coley, 1997), incarcerated women (St. Lawrence, Eldridge, Shelby et al., 1997), economically disadvantaged urban women (Carey, Maisto, Kalichman et al., 1997), and women with chronic mental illness (Weinhardt, Carey, Carey, & Verdecias, 1998) have shown positive response to this general type of intervention that addresses skills and motivation. Given that individual and small group interventions are inherently limited in the numbers of at risk individuals that can be contacted, community-based approaches have also been evaluated, with favorable outcomes. For example, identification and training of popular members of at risk communities (e.g., gay men) in local settings (e.g., gay bars, social events) have been found to have a beneficial effect on sexual practices in the local community (Kelly et al., 1991; Kelly, Murphy, Sikkema et al. 1997; Kegeles, Hays, & Coates, 1996).

General Issues

There are two central issues that are common to each of the four areas of health behavior change discussed. First, it is clear that health behavior change is best conceptualized as a process, with influences on change and optimal interventions varying across time. This general view is the foundation of the Stages of Change model of Prochaska and his colleagues (Prochaska & Di-Clemente, 1982; see Prochaska chapter in this volume). The optimal interventionsfor individuals uninterested in health behavior changes or even simply considering them are very different from individuals currently undertaking lifestyle modifications or attempting to maintain them. Thus, the design, selection, implementation, and evaluation of health behaviorinterventions must be guided by the notion of unfolding—and perhaps recurring—change processes over time. In each of the specific health behaviors discussed in this chapter, the stability of change is a critical concern. As a result, relapse prevention (Collier & Marlatt, 1995; Marlatt & Gordon, 1985) and continuing adherence to risk factor change programs (Burke, Dunbar-Jacob, & Hill, 1997) have become particularly important conceptual and practical issues in health behavior change. Explicit attention to these concerns has become a critical component in most areas of research and practice.

The second issue cutting across each of the topics discussed is the level targeted for intervention. Most of the treatments described are delivered to individuals or small groups. Given the prevalence of smoking, obesity, sedentary lifestyles, and unsafe sexual practices, interventions targeted to individuals and small groups cannot possibly reach all of the individuals who might profit from them. Increased dissemination of health behavior change interventions can be achieved through traditional health care settings

and services, as in the case of treatments for hospitalized smokers outlined in that section of this chapter. However, barriers to the delivery of behavior change interventions in health care settings and inadequate access to health care would still prevent the delivery of these interventions to many individuals who would otherwise benefit.

The potential public health impact and economic savings of more broadly focused interventions have spurred the development of community, worksite, and school-based programs (Sorensen, Emmons, Hunt, & Johnston 1998). Community level interventions involve a variety of components including advertising and public awareness campaigns, training of indigenous paraprofessionals, community organizing, and educational programs administered through existing organizations. Trials of this approach have produced mixed results; some programs have produced positive changes in health behavior and related risk factors (Puska, Salonen, Nissinen, Tuomilehto et al., 1983; Fortmann, Williams, Hulley, Haskell, & Farquhar, 1981; Hoffmeister, Mensink, Stolzenberg et al., 1996; Winkleby, Taylor, Jatulis, & Fortmann, 1996), whereas others have produced only small, fleeting, or variable effects (Carleton, Lasater, Assaf et al., 1995; COMMIT Research Group, 1995; Luepker, Murray, Jacobs et al., 1994). Worksite and school-based programs are similar intervention strategies, but within a more delineated group. Trials of these approaches have produced more consistent positive effects, but these effects are also small and somewhat inconsistent across studies (Sorensen et al., 1998). Nonetheless, even small risk factor changes in large populations can have large effects on prevalent conditions. Also, given the substantial costs associated with the major diseases such behavior change efforts are attempting to prevent, interventions with small effects can still be quite cost-effective (e.g., Tosteson, Weinstein, Hunink et al., 1997). Thus, in addition to the individual, family, and small group interventions familiar to clinical and counseling psychologists, the behavior change methods familiar to organizational and community psychologists are clearly relevant in health psychology.

PSYCHOLOGICAL ADJUNCTS TO MEDICAL CARE

Even if the prevention efforts described already prove to be highly successful, people will still require medical and surgical care. The second major intervention focus of health psychology evaluates the utility of adding psychological treatments to routine medical and surgical care. In what follows, we provide a brief overview of the most central health psychology applications of this type.

Stress Reduction and Medical Crises

It has long been recognized that psychological processes influence the outcome of acute medical care (Janis, 1958; Kiecolt-Glaser, Page, Marucha et al., 1998). The basic hypothesis that emotional distress prior to a potentially stressful medical or surgical procedure can lead to heightened pain and discomfort, increased risk of complications, and delayed recovery has been supported by several decades of research (Kiecolt-Glaser et al., 1998; Webne, 1995). Stress can delay the physical process of wound healing (Kiecolt-Glaser, Marucha, Malarkey et al., 1995; Marucha et al., 1998), most likely through the inhibition of the immune process involved in wound repair (Kiecolt-Glaser et al., 1995; Marucha et al., 1998). The intervention implication of this work is that stress management interventions could lead to reduced pain and suffering, fewer complications, and more rapid recovery. Both qualitative and quantitative reviews of the large amount of literature on the topic have supported this conclusion (Contrada, Leventhal, & Anderson, 1994; Johnston & Vogel, 1993; Suls & Wan, 1989; Webne, 1995).

The interventions that have been found effective include preoperative delivery of sensory or procedural information, observation of models who cope successfully with the medical stressor, distraction, hypnosis, relaxation training, social support, and supportive therapy. Benefits of these brief and simple interventions have been found in the context of invasive diagnostic procedures (e.g., Kendall, Williams, Pechacek et al., 1979), intensive care hospitalization (e.g., Gruen, 1975), major surgery (Anderson, 1987; Leserman, Stuart, Mamish, & Benson, 1989; Mahler & Kulik, 1998), aversive medical treatments (Meyer & Mark, 1995), and childbirth (Leventhal, Leventhal, Shacham, & Esterling, 1989). Thus, across a broad range of clinical problems, low cost interventions are a useful addition to routine care. The cost-effectiveness of these interventions are clear; a recent quantitative review found that interventions with an average duration of 30 minutes produced a mean reduction in length of hospitalization of 1.5 days (Devine, 1992). In some situations, such as pediatric surgery, preoperative psychological preparations (e.g., modeling, play therapy, hospital visits, preparation of parents) have become standard care.

Three clinical issues guide the implementation of these interventions. First, there is considerable evidence of individual differences in responses to these interventions. For example, some individuals benefit from additional information prior to surgery or invasive tests, whereas others respond negatively to such information—perhaps reflecting individual differences in preference for information. Thus, the individualization of interventions is important, and can be accomplished easily by discussion with patients (Webne, 1995). Second, these interventions do not require a psychologist, and in fact in many settings are the responsibility of the nursing service. Thus, the psychologist's role in these interventions might be either a direct service provider or a consultant responsible for training and evaluation. Finally, with the increasing use of outpatient surgery and home recovery, interventions must be tailored to fit a changing health care environment in which hospital stays are brief and patient care involves family members.

Cancer

Cancer is the second leading cause of death in the United States, but continual advances in oncology have resulted in dramatic improvements in cancer survival (American Cancer Society, 1998). This increased life expectancy, however, often comes at the cost of pain, emotional distress, loss of function, and side effects of treatment (Neal & Hoskin, 1997). The emotional sequelae of cancer and its treatment include symptoms of anxiety, depression, and even posttraumatic stress disorder (Andrykowski, Cordova, Studts, & Miller, 1998; Glanz & Lerman, 1992; McDaniel, Musselman, Porter et al., 1995; Vinokur, Threatt, Caplan, & Zimmerman, 1989). Side effects of treatment include conditioned nausea in response to chemotherapy (Carey & Burish, 1988), the impact of surgery on physical appearance and body image, and other aspects of social and sexual functioning. The type and extent of the psychosocial impact of cancer and related treatments is a function of the type of cancer, its stage or progression, and the nature of the medical and surgical treatment (Andersen, 1992).

Psychosocial interventions for cancer patients have two general goals: reduction of acute distress and discomfort during active treatment, and enhancement of longer-term social and emotional functioning. A wide variety of interventions have been found to be effective in managing the acute distress associated with active treatment, including relaxation therapy, coping skills training, distraction, hypnosis, and systematic desensitization (Compas et al., 1998; Meyer & Mark, 1995). For longer-term adjustment, both cognitive-behavioral group therapy (e.g., Fawzy, Cousins, Fawzy et al., 1990; Telch & Telch, 1986) and supportive-expressive group therapy (e.g., Speigel, Bloom, & Yalom, 1981) have been effective in improving emotional and social functioning (see Compas et al., 1998; Fawzy & Fawzy, 1998, for reviews). Although these two intervention approaches share many common components, cognitive-behavioral group therapy involves more emphasis on instruction and practice of specific skills, such as relaxation, cognitive coping with distress, and restructuring of dysfunctional beliefs. In contrast, supportive-expressive group interventions place more emphasis on the identification, expression, and resolution of the emotional impact of the illness and its treatment, with explicit attention to the interpersonal context of these emotions.

One of the most dramatic intervention effects reported in the recent history of behavioral medicine and clinical health psychology is the finding that seriously ill cancer patients undergoing group therapy (in addition to standard medical care) have better survival rates relative to controls receiving standard medical care alone (Fawzy et al., 1993; Spiegel, Bloom, Kraemer, & Gottheil, 1989). It is important to note that even though the results are biologically plausible (Andersen, Kiecolt-Glaser, & Glaser, 1994; Cohen & Rabin, 1998) and the studies well controlled, they are based on small samples of patients. As a result, group therapy is presently best considered useful in the management of emotional and social consequences of cancer.

Coronary Heart Disease

Coronary heart disease is the leading cause of death in the United States and most industrialized countries. Studies previously described demonstrate that brief psychological interventions are useful additions to the traditional medical and surgical management of coronary disease. For example, brief interventions improve emotional adjustment, physical discomfort, and medical outcomes for invasive diagnostic tests for coronary disease (Kendall et al., 1979), coronary

bypass surgery (Anderson, 1987; Mahler & Kulick, 1998; Smith & Dimsdale, 1989), and acute hospitalization in the coronary care unit (Gruen, 1975). Thus, behavioral interventions are useful additions to several aspects or phases of the acute care of coronary patients. The spouse of the cardiac patient is also often sufficiently distressed during this acute period that brief supportive interventions are useful (Delon, 1996). This approach to spousal involvement can also facilitate their participation in later stages of cardiac care, such as lifestyle modification after discharge.

Following acute care, behavior change becomes even more important for coronary patients. Smoking cessation, adoption of a low fat diet, participation in regular aerobic exercise, and adherence to medication regimens are behavioral cornerstones in the long-term management of coronary disease. For example, quantitative reviews of controlled trials of exercise for coronary patients indicate that these programs reduce mortality by 20% to 25% over three years (O'Connor, Buring, Yusuf et al., 1989; Oldridge, Guyatt, Fisher, & Rimm, 1988). Furthermore, these interventions have a beneficial effect on subsequent health care costs, with savings that far exceed the costs of such interventions (Ades, Huang, & Weaver, 1992; Bondestam, Breikles, & Hartford, 1995). In one particularly noteworthy study, a program of strict low fat diet, regular exercise, and stress management produced actual reductions in the severity of angiographically assessed coronary artery disease; control patients receiving standard medical care displayed worsening disease over the follow-up period (Ornish, Brown, Scherwitz et al., 1990).

A growing body of research has examined the effects of stress management in the treatment of coronary disease. This work is based on the clearly established effects of stress on this condition. Stress can accelerate the progression of the underlying disease process (i.e., coronary artery disease) and stress can contribute to the precipitation of acute indications of the disease (e.g., angina, myocardial ischemia, myocardial infarction; for a review, see Kamarck & Jennings, 1991; Smith & Gallo, 1994). Although some failures to replicate have been reported (e.g., Frasure-Smith, Lesperance, Prince et al., 1997), the majority of controlled trials reports beneficial effects of stress management on coronary disease outcomes, including recurrent coronary events and coronary death (Blumenthal et al., 1997; Linden, Stossel,

& Maurice, 1996). The interventions found to be useful are mostly multicomponent programs consisting of relaxation training, cognitive restructuring, and related techniques.

HIV/AIDS

Due to advances in medical care, HIV infected individuals can expect to live for many years. This is also increasingly true of individuals with symptomatic AIDS. Therefore, the condition can be appropriately construed as a serious chronic disease, rather than necessarily an acute medical condition. Of course, the HIV+ population is a particularly important group for the transmission prevention interventions described. However, the increased life expectancy of individuals with HIV/AIDS has clearly increased the already substantial need for adjunctive psychosocial interventions, similar to those employed with cancer and coronary patients.

Controlled intervention trials have found beneficial effects of stress management on the acute emotional distress surrounding HIV testing (e.g., Antoni, Baggett, Ironson et al., 1991). Similar stress management interventions have been found to be effective in improving emotional adjustment, coping skills, and social support (Lutgendorf et al., 1997; 1998). Coping skills training has been found to have similar beneficial effects (Chesney, Folkman, & Chambers, 1996; Kelly et al., 1993). Recent reviews of this literature have called for extension of such interventions to other consequences of advanced HIV infection, such as sleep disturbance, pain, and other aspects of quality of life (Kelly, 1998; Sikkema & Kelly, 1996). To date, there have been no controlled trials demonstrating effectiveness of psychosocial interventions on HIV progression.

Recent advances in the medical treatment of HIV/AIDS have raised additional concerns possibly requiring psychosocial intervention. For example, the positive outcomes obtained with protease inhibitors may influence some at-risk individuals to relax their safer sexual practices, if they assume that infection is now a less serious concern (Kalichman, Nachimson, Cherry, & Williams, 1998; Kelly, Otto-Salaj, Sikkema, Pinkerton, & Bloom, 1998). Further, the new regimens involve highly complex medication schedules. This makes adherence more difficult to achieve, perhaps requiring additional psychosocial intervention (Kelly et al., 1998). Adherence to the newer regimens may also be important for public health considerations, as

inconsistent adherence to these powerful combination therapies has the potential to facilitate emergence of more treatment-resistant strains of the virus (Kelly et al., 1998).

Chronic Pain

Most individuals with chronic pain have failed to respond adequately to traditional medical and surgical care, and as a result have a continuing need for symptomatic relief. These individuals pose health economic concerns, as chronic pain is a major source of health care expenditures and lost productivity. Over twenty years ago, these issues prompted the development of behavioral alternatives to traditional approaches (Fordyce, 1976), and a substantial body of literature now supports the utility of such interventions in a variety of chronic pain conditions.

The original operant approach to chronic pain conceptualized it as an overt behavior (verbal reports, limitations in movement, etc.) under the same sort of environmental control as other behaviors. The goal of the approach is the progressive reinforcement of "well" or "nonpain" behaviors, as well as the extinction of pain behaviors. A variety of controlled studies have demonstrated the effectiveness of the operant approach, especially with chronic low back pain and other benign conditions of musculoskeletal origin (Linton & Gotestam, 1984; Nicholas, Wilson, & Goyen, 1991; Turner, Clancy, McQuade, & Cardenas, 1990).

Cognitive-behavioral approaches to chronic pain are based on a broader conceptual model of the determinants and consequences of chronic pain. This multicomponent approach includes relaxation training, coping skills training, scheduled physical activities, and cognitive restructuring. Direct comparisons with operant treatments have demonstrated some advantages of the latter approach in the treatment of low back pain (Nicholas et al., 1991; Turner & Clancy, 1988). The cognitive-behavioral approach has also proven to be useful with a wide variety of chronic pain conditions (Compas et al., 1998), including chronic back pain (Jensen & Bodin, 1998; Turner, 1982) and rheumatoid arthritis (Bradely et al., 1987; Parker, Smarr, Buckelew et al., 1995).

Ongoing research is evaluating the effectiveness of pain management interventions in the treatment of other conditions, identifying predictors of treatment response, developing low cost versions of these treatments, and extending the range of clinical outcomes. For example, minimally supervised fitness training and education apparently have lasting benefits in the treatment of low back pain (Frost, Lamb, Moffett, Fairbank, & Moser, 1998). Other research indicates that cognitive behavioral treatment for rheumatoid arthritis pain results in reduced health care utilization (Young, Bradley, & Turner, 1995). Finally, inclusion of the patient's spouse in treatment may enhance the effects of cognitive-behavioral interventions (Keefe, Caldwell, Baucom, Salley, & Robinson, 1996; Radojevic, Nicassio, & Weisman, 1992).

Diabetes

Approximately 12 million Americans have diabetes, and the condition places them at increased risk of serious illness and premature death. Type I, or insulin-dependent diabetes, is caused by the destruction of the insulin-producing cells of the pancreas, and its management requires an extensive program of blood glucose monitoring and insulin administration (usually by injection). Type II, or noninsulin-dependent, diabetes is primarily caused by insulin resistence (often due to excess body weight). In both cases, poor control of blood glucose levels can lead to greater risk of coronary heart disease, kidney disease, peripheral vascular disease, and blindness. In both cases, the automatic physiological regulation of blood glucose is replaced by a behavioral self-regulation process through which the individual monitors blood sugar and makes adjustments in medication, diet, and activity accordingly. In the medical management of diabetes, this essential self-care is also often accompanied by encouragement of weight loss and other long-term behavioral changes.

Behavioral interventions in diabetes address a variety of factors. Good control of blood glucose greatly reduces the diabetic's risk of medical complications of the disorder (DCCT Research Group, 1993). Therefore, adherence to blood glucose monitoring, diet, activity, and insulin administration elements of the medical regimen is a primary focus of intervention efforts (Cox & Gonder-Frederick, 1992; Goetsch & Wiebe, 1995). Education, problem solving training, and social support interventions have been found to improve adherence among diabetics (Brown, 1992). Given the role of obesity in Type II diabetes, the lifestyle modifications (i.e., weight loss, exercise) discussed have also been found to produce improved glucose control. Finally, there is mixed evidence that stress management can improve glucose control among Type II, though perhaps not Type I, diabetics (Goetsch & Wiebe, 1995).

Given the complex behavioral self-regulation regimen required of diabetics and the medical importance of adherence, additional research has addressed potentially modifiable influences on poor self-regulation. For example, negative affect may lead patients to misattribute unrelated physical symptoms to variations in blood glucose levels. Such misattributions may lead, in turn, to poor behavioral self-regulation and poor metabolic control (Wiebe, Alderfer, Palmer, Lindsay, & Jarret, 1994). Thus, psychological adjuncts may improve diabetic care by facilitating emotional adjustment.

General Issues

Several problems and goals are common to the clinical applications we have discussed. As noted previously, consideration of the patient's specific biomedical context (i.e., diagnosis, prognosis, demands and effects of likely treatments) is an essential initial step in the identification and implementation of interventions. Across nearly all conditions, facilitating the patient's adherence to medical treatment (Dunbar-Jacobs, Burke, & Puczynski, 1995) and minimizing the distress of medical/surgical treatments are important targets for behavioral interventions. Psychological interventions for pain and symptom reduction are often highly useful adjuncts to traditional care. Further, the impact of illness on levels of functioning may be remediated, at least in part, by directly targeting functional activities for psychosocial intervention, rather than assuming that such behavior (i.e., level of disability) responds directly to improvements in medical status (Turk & Salovey, 1995). Finally, the general stress and coping paradigm (Lazarus & Folkman, 1984) guides much research and practice in medical conditions and, as a result, stress managment interventions are a mainstay of applied work (Parker, 1995). However, the impact of stress on disease processes and the impact of disease-related stress on adjustment are both likely to involve the patient's surrounding context. Therefore, clinical conceptualization, assessment, and interventions should include consideration of interpersonal processes.

ADDITIONAL CONSIDERATIONS

In closing, we discuss three general issues that shape intervention research and practice in health psychology. As we noted at the outset, the emergence of the field and the specific topics it now addresses were determined in large part by the evolution of medical science. That influence will continue, and the immediate future can be gleaned from current issues and opportunities created by recent medical advances. However, the future of research and practice must include attention to the demographic variables that are currently understudied. Finally, the challenges inherent in this work can be personally and professionally daunting because they require approaches and practices beyond the usual roles of clinical and counseling psychologists.

Advances in Medicine: The Example of Genetic Testing

The potential role of health psychology interventions in medical care is influenced by developments in medical science. As new treatments improve some types of care, adjunctive interventions may become less important, or may identify new ways in which the biopsychosocial model is relevant. For example, the recent discovery that peptic ulcer disease involves infectious agents does not eliminate the potential value of considering psychosocial influences on the illness and the utility of behavioral adjuncts to treatment. Rather, this innovation in medical science identifies new psychobiological models of the disease and its treatment (Levenstein, Ackerman, Kiecolt-Glaser, & Dubois, 1999). New treatments may also highlight the importance of long-standing issues, as in the case of the critical role of patient adherence in the highly complex but effective pharmacological protocols for the treatment of HIV infection and AIDS. Still other developments create the need for new areas of research, as in the case of genetic testing. We use this example to illustrate the dynamic relationship between changes in medical science and the research and practice agendas in health psychology.

The accelerating pace of genetic research has created the technology to detect mutations that predispose individuals to several serious medical conditions, including Huntington disease, neurofibromatosis, cystic fibrosis, some types of Parkinson's disease and Alzheimer's disease, and most recently some forms of cancer (Lerman, 1997). Decisions about whether to undergo the available genetic testing are complex, difficult, and possibly quite emotionally taxing (Croyle & Lerman, 1995). These patient and family decisions are potentially influenced by a variety of psychological factors (Baum, Friedman, & Zakowski, 1997; Lerman, Biesecker, Benkendorf et al., 1997), and the outcome of testing can have similarly far-reaching impacts on emotional and social functioning (Codori, Slavney, Young, Miglioretti, & Brandt, 1997; Croyle, Smith, Botkin, Baty, & Nash, 1997; Lynch, Lemon, Durham et al., 1997; Marteau, Dundas, & Axworthy, 1997; Tibben, Timman, Banninck, & Duivenvoorden, 1997). The few available controlled trials of psychological interventions prior to genetic testing suggest that brief counseling can reduce distress, facilitate acquisition of relevant knowledge, and produce more balanced evaluations of the test procedure (Lerman, Schwartz, Miller et al., 1996; Lerman, Biesecker, & Benkendorf, 1997).

Advances in genetic testing also impact other intervention goals in health psychology. For example, genetic research on smoking may help identify subgroups of smokers at varying degrees or sources of genetic resistence to smoking cessation, thereby permitting the concentration or individualization of intervention resources. This rapidly advancing area is likely to raise additional important biopsychosocial issues, as will other developements in medical science. In each case, developments create new potential impacts—both positive and negative—of medical care on psychological well-being, and also create the need for new types of psychological adjunctive care.

Diversity

Medical research has been accurately criticized for inadequate representation of women, minorities, and the economically disadvantaged in basic and clinical research samples (Anderson, 1989; Anderson & Armstead, 1995; Stanton, 1995). Despite the obvious place of sex, ethnicity, and socioeconomic status in the general systems and biopsychosocial models that are the foundation of the field, health psychology intervention research has only recently demonstrated increasing attention to this limitation (Park, Adams, & Lynch, 1998). There are sex, ethnic, and socioeconomic differences in the risk of many diseases, and in the prognoses of a given disease (Adler, Boyce, Chesney et al., 1993; Dries, Exner, Gersh et al., 1999). Risk factor modification is likely to be more successful to the extent that it takes these differences into account. Similarly, the unique adaptive challenges posed by illness, and hence the optimal targets of adjunctive interventions, are also likely to vary as a function of these demographic factors. It is even possible that these demographic factors influence physicians' decisions about medical tests and treatments (e.g., Schulman, Berlin, Harless et al., 1999). Thus, diversity is also an important agenda item for psychologists consulting with health care organizations. In each of these research areas and types of intervention, consideration of diversity is a key component of a comprehensive, biopsychosocial approach.

Professional Issues and Challenges

The potentially daunting array of health psychology interventions can be organized by considering two broad dimensions: the level of intervention and the stage in disease development (Winett, 1995). As depicted in Table 26.3, health psychology interventions can address any level from the individual to larger institutions. Further, interventions can be directed at any stage, from attempts to prevent the development of risk factors to efforts to manage the impact of established

disease. The variety of interventions relevant to coronary heart disease provide an illustration of these dimensions (Smith & Leon, 1992). Because the underlying medical condition—coronary atherosclerosis—begins in childhood and adolescence (Strong, Malcolm, McMahon et al., 1999) and because many risk factors are acquired in this period (e.g., smoking, diet and exercise habits), primary preventions directed toward individuals, families, schools, and communities are potentially quite valuable ways of reducing the initial development of risk factors or modifying them early in life. Later, in adulthood but well before the clinical onset of symptomatic coronary disease, individual, group, and community/organizational interventions can be useful in promoting smoking cessation, weight loss, and physical activity. Finally, we reviewed a variety of psychological interventions that are helpful in the care of coronary patients, including stress management and exercise-based rehabilitation.

Interventions in health psychology require

TABLE 26.3   Level and phase dimensions of health physiology interventions

Level	Phase		
	Primary	**Secondary**	**Tertiary**
Individual	Self-instruction guide on HIV prevention for noninfected lower risk individuals	Screening and early intervention for hypertension	Designing a very low-fat vegetarian diet for an individual with heart disease
Group	Parents' group to gain skills to communicate better with teens about risk behaviors	Supervised exercise program for lower SES individuals with higher risk of heart disease	Cardiac rehabilitation program for groups of heart disease patients
Organization	Worksite dietary change program focusing on altering vending machine and cafeteria offerings	Worksite incentive program to eliminate employee smoking	Extending leave benefits so employees can care for elderly/ill parent
Community	Focused media campaign to promote exercise in minority population segments	Developing support networks for recently widowed individuals	Providing better access for disabled individuals to all recreational facilities
Institution	Enforcing laws banning the sale of cigarettes to minors	Substantially increasing insurance rates for smokers	Mandating a course of treatment to facilitate recovery of stroke victims

Source: Adapted from Winnett (1995).

nearly all of the traditional skills of clinical and counseling psychology. However, unique features of specific intervention levels, phases, and goals require a different role and perspective for the clinical health psychologist than is typical of traditional mental health services and settings (Belar & Deardorff, 1995). For example, psychologists interested in primary prevention and behavioral health promotion are just as likely to need the skills of community organizers and activists as they are the skills of conventional assessment and treatment (Hancock, Sanson-Fisher, & Redman, 1997). In delivering psychological services to the medically ill, interdisciplinary teams, clinic and hospital environments, and various forms of service delivery and financing can require major departures from traditional mental health practices (Belar & Deardorff, 1995). Rather than transposing music to a new key, the application of psychological interventions to problems of physical health resembles jazz arrangements of classical melodies. Although not all clinicians are optimally suited for such work, those who are find it highly stimulating and gratifying. Given the behavioral origins and consequences of our current medical afflictions, health psychologists can play an essential part in improving the public health.

REFERENCES

Ades, P. A., Huang, D., & Weaver, S. O. (1992). Cardiac rehabilitation participation predicts lower rehospitalization costs. *American Heart Journal, 123*, 916–921.

Adler, N., Boyce, W. T., Chesney, M., Folkman, S., & Syme, S. L. (1993). Socioeconomic inequalities in health. *Journal of the American Medical Association, 269*, 3140–3145.

Adler, N., & Matthews, K. (1994). Health psychology: Why do some people get sick and some stay well? *Annual Review of Psychology, 45*, 229–259.

American Cancer Society (1998). *Cancer facts and figures: 1998.* Atlanta, GA: Author.

American Psychiatric Association (1994). *Diagnostic and Statistical Manual of Mental Disorders.* (DSM-IV). Washington, D.C., APA. 4th ed.

Andersen, B. L. (1992). Psychological interventions for cancer patients to enhance the quality of life. *Journal of Consulting and Clinical Psychology, 60*, 552–568.

Andersen, B. L., Kiecolt-Glaser, J. K., & Glaser, R. (1994). A biobehavioral model of cancer stress and disease course. *American Psychologist, 49*, 389–404.

Andersen, R. E., Wadden, T. A., Bartlett, S. J.,

Zemel., B., Verde, T. J., & Franckowiak, S. C. (1999). Effects of lifestyle activity vs. structured aerobic exercise in obese women. *Journal of the American Medical Association, 281*, 335–340.

Anderson, E. (1987). Preoperative preparation facilitates recovery, reduces psychological distress, and reduces the incidence of acute postoperative hypertension. *Journal of Consulting and Clinical Psychology, 55*, 513–520.

Anderson, N. B. (1989). Racial differences in stress-induced cardiovascular reactivity and hypertension: Current status and substantive issues. *Psychological Bulletin, 105*, 89–105.

Anderson, N. B., & Armstead, C. A. (1995). Toward understanding the association of socioeconomic status and health: A new challenge for the biopsychosocial approach. *Psychosomatic Medicine, 57*, 213–225.

Andrykowski, M. A., Cordova, M. J., Studts, J. L., & Miller, T. W. (1998). Posttraumatic stress disorder after treatment for breast cancer: Prevalence of diagnosis and use of the PTSD Checklist—Civilian Version (PCL-C) as a screening instrument. *Journal of Consulting and Clinical Psychology, 66*, 586–590.

Antoni, M., Baggett, L., Ironson, G., LaPierre, A., August, S., Klimas, N., Schneiderman, N., & Fletcher, M. A. (1991). Cognitive-behavioral stress management intervention buffers distress responses and immunologic changes following notification of HIV-1 seropositivity. *Journal of Consulting and Clinical Psychology, 59*, 906–915.

Auerbach, S. M. (1989). Stress management and coping research in the health care setting: An overview and methodological commentary. *Journal of Consulting and Clinical Psychology, 57*, 388–395.

Battle, E. K., & Brownell, K. D. (1996). Confronting a rising tide of eating disorders and obesity: Treatment vs. prevention and policy. *Addictive Behaviors, 21*, 755–765.

Baum, A., Friedman, A. L., & Zakowski, S. G. (1997). Stress and genetic testing for disease risk. *Health Psychology, 16*, 8–19.

Belar, C. D., & Deardorff, W. W. (1995). *Clinical health psychology in medical settings.* Washington, D.C:. American Psychological Association.

Belardinelli, R., Georgiou, D., Cianci, G., & Purcaro, A. (1999). Randomized, controlled trial of long-term moderate exercise on functional capacity, quality of life, and clinical outcome. *Circulation, 99*, 1173–1182.

Blanchard, E. B., & Malamood, H. S. (1996). Psychological treatment of irritable bowel syndrome. *Professional Psychology: Research and Practice, 27*, 241–244.

Blumenthal, J. A., Jiang, W., Babyak, M. A., Krantz, D. S., Frid, D. J., Coleman, R. E., Waugh, R., Hanson, M., Appelbaum, M., O'Connor, C., &

Morris, J. J. (1997). Stress management and exercise training in cardiac patients with myocardial ischemia. *Archives of Internal Medicine, 157,* 2213–2223.

Bondestam, E., Breikks, A., & Hartford, M. (1995). Effects of early rehabilitation on consumption of medical care during the first year after acute myocardial infarction in patients ≥65 years of age. *American Journal of Cardiology, 75,* 767–771.

Borrelli, B., Spring, B., Niaura, R., Kristeller, J., Ockene, J. K., & Keuthen, N. (1999). Weight suppression and weight rebound in ex-smokers treated with fluoxetine. *Journal of Consulting and Clinical Psychology, 67,* 124–131.

Bouchard, C., Trembley, A., Despres, J. P., Nadeau, A., Lupien, P., Theriault, G., Dussalt, J., Moorjani, S., Pinault, S., & Fournier, G. (1990). The response to long-term overfeeding in identical twins. *New England Journal of Medicine, 322,* 1477–1482.

Bouchard, C., Trembley, A., Nadeau, A., Depres, J. P., Theriault, G., Boulay, M. R., Lortie, G., Leblanc, C., & Fournier, G. (1989). Genetic effect in resting and exercise metabolic rates. *Metabolism, 38,* 364–370.

Bray, G. A. (1996). Health hazards of obesity. *Endocrinological and Metabolic Clinics of North America, 25,* 907–919.

Brown, S. A. (1992). Meta-analysis of diabetes patient education research: Variations in intervention effects across studies. *Research in Nursing and Health, 15,* 409–419.

Brownell, K. D. (1991). Dieting and the search for the perfect body: Where physiology and culture collide. *Behavior Therapy, 22,* 1–12.

Brownell, K. D., Marlatt, G. A., Lichtenstein, E., & Wilson, G. T. (1986). Understanding and preventing relapse. *American Psychologist, 41,* 765–782.

Brownell, K. D., & Rodin, J. (1994). The dieting maelstrom: Is it possible and advisable to lose weight? *American Psychologist, 49,* 781–791.

Brownell, K. D., & Wadden, T. A. (1992). Etiology and treatment of obesity: Understanding a serious, prevalent, and refractory disorder. *Journal of Consulting and Clinical Psychology, 60,* 505–517.

Buchner, D. M., Beresford, S. A. A., Larson, E. B., LaCroix, A. Z., & Wagner, E. H. (1992). Effects of physical activity on health status in older adults. *Annual Review of Public Health, 13,* 469–488.

Burke, L. E., Dunbar-Jacob, J. M., & Hill, M. N. (1997). Compliance with cardiovascular disease prevention strategies: A review of the research. *Annals of Behavioral Medicine, 19,* 239–263.

Calfas, K. J., Long, B. J., Sallis, J. F., Wooten, W. J., Pratt, M., & Patrick, K. (1996). A controlled trial of physician counseling to promote the adoption of physical activity. *Preventive Medicine, 25,* 225–233.

Camp, D. E., Klesges, R. C., & Relyes, G. (1993). The relationship between body weight concerns and adolescent smoking. *Health Psychology, 12,* 24–32.

Carey, M. P., & Burish, T. G. (1988). Etiology and treatment of the psychological side effects associated with cancer chemotherapy: A critical review and discussion. *Psychological Bulletin, 104,* 307–325.

Carey, M. P., Maisto, S. A., Kalichman, S. C., Forsyth, A. D., Wright, E. M., & Johnson, B. T. (1997). Enhancing motivation to reduce the risk of HIV infection for economically disadvantaged urban women. *Journal of Consulting and Clinical Psychology, 65,* 531–541.

Carleton, R. A., Lasater, T. M., Assaf, A. R., Feldman, H. A., & McKinlay, S. (1995). The Pawtucket Heart Health Program: Community changes in cardiovascular risk factors and projected disease risk. *American Journal of Public Health, 85,* 777–785.

Centers for Disease Control (1996, August 30). *Morbidity and Mortality Weekly Report, 45,* 729–733.

Centers for Disease Control and Prevention (1994). Trends and recent patterns in selected tobacco-use behaviors—United States, 1990–1994. *Morbidity and Mortality Weekly Report CDC Surveillance Summaries, 43,* 925–930.

Chambless, D. L., & Hollon, S. D., (1998). Defining empirically supported therapies. *Journal of Consulting and Clinical Psychology, 66,* 7–18.

Chesney, M. A., Folkman, S., & Chambers, D. (1996). Coping effectiveness training for men living with HIV: Preliminary findings. *International Journal of STD and AIDS, 7,* 75–82.

Chesney, M. A., & Nealey, J. B. (1996). Smoking and cardiovascular disease risk in women: Issues for prevention and women's health. In P. M. Kato & T. Mann (Eds.), *Handbook of diversity issues in health psychology* (pp. 199–218). New York: Plenum.

Clark, D. A., Cook, A., & Snow, D. (1998). Depressive symptom differences in hospitalized, medically ill, depressed psychiatric inpatients, and nonmedical controls. *Journal of Abnormal Psychology, 107,* 38–48.

Clark, M. M., & Goldstein, M. G. (1995). Obesity: A health psychology perspective. In A. J. Goreczny (Ed.), *Handbook of health and rehabilitation psychology* (pp. 151–173). New York: Plenum.

Codori, A. M., Slavney, P. R., Young, C., Miglioretti, D. L., & Brandt, J. (1997). Predictors of psychological adjustment to genetic testing for Huntington's disease. *Health Psychology, 16,* 36–50.

Cohen, S., & Rabin, B. S. (1998). Psychologic stress, immunity, and cancer. *Journal of the National Cancer Institute, 90,* 3–4.

Collier, C. W., & Marlatt, G. A. (1995). Relapse prevention. In A. J. Goreczny (Ed.), *Handbook of health and rehabilitation psychology. Plenum series in rehabilitation and health* (pp. 307–321). New York: Plenum.

COMMIT Research Group (1995). Community Intervention Trial for Smoking Cessation (COMMIT): I. Cohort results from a four year community intervention. *American Journal of Public Health, 85,* 183–192.

Compas, B. E., Haaga, D. A., Keefe, F. J., Leitenberg, H., & Wiliams, D. A. (1998). Sampling of empirically supported psychological treatments from health psychology: Smoking, chronic pain, cancer, and bulimia nervosa. *Journal of Consulting and Clinical Psychology, 66,* 89–112.

Contrada, R. J., Leventhal, E. A., & Anderson, J. R. (1994). Psychological preparation for surgery: Marshaling individual and social resources to optimize self-regulation. In S. Maes, H. Leventhal, & M. Johnson (Eds.), *International review of health psychology* (Vol. 3, pp. 219–266). New York: John Wiley, and Sons.

Cook, T. D., & Campbell, D. T. (1979). *Quasi-experimentation: Design and analysis issues for field settings.* Chicago: Rand McNally.

Cox, D. J., & Gonder-Frederick, L. (1992). Major developments in behavioral diabetes research. *Journal of Consulting and Clinical Psychology, 60,* 628–638.

Coyne, J. C., & Gottlieb, B. H. (1996). The mismeasure of coping by checklist. *Journal of Personality, 64,* 959–991.

Croyle, R. T., & Lerman, C. (1995). Psychological impact of genetic testing. In R. T. Croyle (Ed.), *Psychosocial effects of screening for disease prevention and detection* (pp. 11–38). New York: Oxford University Press.

Croyle, R. T., Smith, K. R., Botkin, J. R., Baty, B., & Nash, J. (1997). Psychological responses to BRCA1 mutation testing: Preliminary findings. *Health Psychology, 16,* 63–72.

Curry, S. J., & McBride, C. M. (1994). Relapse prevention for smoking cessation: Review and evaluation of concepts and interventions. *Annual Review of Public Health, 15,* 345–366.

Davidson, M. H., Hauptman, J., DiGirolamo, M., Foreyt, J. P., Halsted, C. H., Heber, D., Robbins, D. C., & Heymsfield, S. B. (1999). Weight control and risk factor reduction in obese subjects treated for 2 years with Orlistat: A randomized controlled trial. *Journal of the American Medical Association, 281,* 235–242.

Delon, M. (1996). The patient in the CCU waiting room: In-hospital treatment of the cardiac spouse. In R. Allan & S. Scheidt (Eds.), *Heart and mind: The practice of cardiac psychology* (pp. 421–432). Washington, DC: American Psychological Association.

Devine, E. C. (1992). Effects of psychoeducational care for adult surgical patients: A meta-analysis of 191 studies. *Patient Education and Counseling, 19,* 129–142.

DiClemente, C. C., Prochaska, J. O., Fairhurst, S. K., Velicer, W. F., Valesquez, M. M., & Rossi, J. S. (1991). The processes of smoking cessation: An analysis of precontemplation, contemplation, and preparation stages of change. *Journal of Consulting and Clinical Psychology, 59,* 295–304.

Dishman, R. K., & Sallis, J. F. (1994). Determinants and interventions for physical activity and exercise. In C. Bouchard, R. J., Shephard, & T. Stephens (Eds.), *Physical activity, fitness, and health* (pp. 214–238). Champaign, IL: Human Kinetics Press.

Dries, D. L., Exner, D. V., Gersh, B. J., Cooper, H. A., Carson, P. E., & Domanski, M. J. (1999). Racial differences in the outcome of left ventricular dysfunction. *New England Journal of Medicine, 340,* 609–616.

Dubbert, P. M. (1992). Exercise in behavioral medicine. *Journal of Consulting and Clinical Psychology, 60,* 613–618.

Dubbert, P. M., & Stetson, B. A. (1995). Exercise and physical activity. In A. Goreczny (Ed.), *Handbook of health and rehabilitation psychology* (pp. 255–274). New York: Plenum.

Dunbar-Jacobs, J., Burke, L. E., & Puczynski, S. (1995). Clinical assessment and management of adherence to medical regimens. In P. M. Nicassio & T. W. Smith (Eds.), *Managing chronic illness: A biopsychosocial perspective* (pp. 313–350). Washington DC: American Psychological Association.

Dunn, A. L., Marcus, B. H., Kampert, J. B., Garcia, M. E., Kohl, H. W., III, & Blair, S. N. (1999). Comparison of lifestyle and structured interventions to increase physical activity and cardiorespiratory fitness: A randomized trial. *Journal of the American Medical Association, 281,* 327–334.

Eckel, R. H. (1997). Obesity and heart disease. *Circulation, 96,* 3248–3250.

Eldridge, G. D., St. Lawrence, J. S., Little, C. E., Shelby, M. C., Brasfield, T. L., Service, J. W., & Sly, K. (1997). Evaluation of an HIV risk reduction intervention for women entering inpatient substance abuse treatment. *AIDS Education and Prevention, 9,* 62–76.

Engel, G. L. (1977). The need for a new medical model: A challenge for biomedicine. *Science, 196,* 129–136.

Epstein, L. H., Valoski, A., Wing, R. R., & McCurley, J. (1994). Ten-year outcomes of behavioral family-based treatment for childhood obesity. *Health Psychology, 13,* 373–383.

Epstein, L. H., Wing, R. R., Koeske, R., & Valoski, A. (1985). A comparison of lifestyle exercise, aerobic exercise, and calisthenics on weight loss in obese children. *Behavior Therapy, 16,* 345–356.

Fawzy, F. I., Cousins, N., Fawzy, N. S., Kemeny, M. E., Elashoff, R., & Morton, D. (1990). A structured psychiatric intervention for cancer patients: I. Changes over time in methods of coping and affective disturbance. *Archives of General Psychiatry, 47,* 720–725.

Fawzy, F. I., & Fawzy, N. S. (1998). Group therapy in the cancer setting. *Journal of Psychosomatic Research, 45,* 191–200.

Fawzy, F. I., Fawzy, N. S., Hyun, C. S., Elashoff, R., Guthrie, D., Fahey, J. L., & Morton, D. (1993). Malignant melanoma: Effects of an early structured psychiatric intervention, coping, and affective state on recurrence and survival 6 years later. *Archives of General Psychiatry, 47,* 729–735.

Fingerhut, L. A., Kleinman, J. C., & Kendrick, J. S. (1990). Smoking before, during, and after pregnancy. *American Journal of Public Health, 80,* 541–544.

Fiore, M. C., Jorenby, D. E., & Baker, T. (1997). Smoking cessation: Principles and practice based upon the AHCPR guideline, 1996. *Annals of Behavioral Medicine, 19,* 213–219.

Fiore, M. C., Novotny, T. F., Pierce, J. P., Giovino, G. A., Hatziandreu, E. J., Newcomb, P. A., Surawicz, T. S., & Davis, R. M. (1990). Methods used to quit smoking in the United States: Do cessation programs help? *Journal of the American Medical Association, 263,* 2760–2765.

Fisher, E. B., Jr., Lichtenstein, E., Haire-Joshu, D., Morgan, G. D., & Rehberg, H. R. (1993). Methods, successes, and failures of smoking cessation programs. *Annual Review of Medicine, 44,* 481–513.

Flegal, K., Carroll, M., Kuczmarski, R., & Johnson, C. (1998). Overweight and obesity in the United States. *International Journal of Obesity and Related Metabolic Disorders, 22,* 28–47.

Fordyce, W. E. (1976). *Behavioral methods in chronic pain and illness.* St. Louis, MO: Mosby.

Foreyt, J. P., & Goodrick, G. K. (1994). Impact of behavior therapy on weight loss. *American Journal of Health Promotion, 8,* 466–468.

Fortmann, S. P., Williams, P. T., Hulley, S. B., Haskell, W. L., & Farquhar, J. W. (1981). Effect of health education on dietary behavior: The Stanford three community study. *American Journal of Clinical Nutrition, 34,* 2030–2038.

Foster, G. D., & Kendall, P. C. (1994). The realistic treatment of obesity: Changing the scales of success. *Clinical Psychology Review, 14,* 701–730.

Frasure-Smith, N., Lesperance, F., Prince, R. H., Verrier, R. A., Garber, R. A., et al. (1997). Randomized trial of home-based psychosocial nursing intervention for patients recovering from myocardial infarction. *Lancet, 350,* 473–479.

Friedman, M. A., & Brownell, K. D. (1995). Psychological correlates of obesity: Moving to the next generation of research. *Psychological Bulletin, 117,* 3–20.

Friedman, M. A., & Brownell, K. D. (1996). A comprehensive treatment manual for the management of obesity. In V. B. Van Hasselt & M. Hersen (Eds.), *Sourcebook of psychological treatment manuals for adult disorders* (pp. 375–422). New York: Plenum Press.

Friedman, R., Subel, D., Meyers, P., Caudill, M., & Benson, H. (1995). Behavioral medicine, clinical health psychology, and cost offset. *Health Psychology, 14,* 509–518.

Frost, H., Lamb, S. E., Moffett, J. A., Fairbank, J. C., & Moser, J. S. (1998). A fitness programme for patients with chronic low back pain: 2-year follow-up of a randomized controlled trial. *Pain, 75,* 273–279.

Gatchel, R. C., & Turk, D. C. (Eds.). (1999). *Psychosocial factors in pain.* New York: Guilford Press.

Gielen, A. C., Windsor, R., Faden, R. R., O'Campo, P., Repke, J., & Davis, M. (1997). Evaluation of a smoking cessation intervention for pregnant women in an urban prenatal clinic. *Health Education Research, 12,* 247–254.

Gladis, M. M., Wadden, T. A., Vogt, R., Foster, G., Kuehnel, R. H., & Bartlett, S. J. (1998). Behavioral treatment of obese binge eaters: Do they need different care? *Journal of Psychosomatic Research, 44,* 375–384.

Glanz, K., & Lerman, C. (1992). Psychosocial impact of breast cancer: A critical review. *Annals of Behavioral Medicine, 14,* 204–212.

Goetsch, V. L., & Wiebe, D. L. (1995). Diabetes mellitus: Considerations of the influence of stress. In A. J. Goreczny (Ed.), *Handbook of health and rehabilitation psychology.* (pp. 513–533). New York: Plenum.

Gruen, W. (1975). Effects of brief psychotherapy during the hospitalization period on the recovery process in heart attacks. *Journal of Consulting and Clinical Psychology, 42,* 223–232.

Hancock, L., Sanson-Fisher, R. W., & Redman, S. (1997). Community action for health promotion: A review of methods and outcomes 1990–1995. *American Journal of Preventive Medicine, 13,* 229–239.

Heatherton, T. F., Herman, C. P., & Polivy, J. (1991). Effects of physical threat and ego threat on eating behavior. *Journal of Personality and Social Psychology, 60,* 138–143.

Heatherton, T. F., Herman, C. P., & Polivy, J. (1992). Effects of distress on eating: The importance of ego-involvement. *Journal of Personality and Social Psychology, 62,* 801–803.

Helmrich, S. P., Ragland, D. R., Leung, R. W., & Paffenbarger, R. S., Jr., (1991). Physical activity and reduced occurence of non-insulin dependent diabetes mellitus in women. *New England Journal of Medicine, 325,* 147–152.

Herbert, T. B., & Cohen, S. (1993). Depression and immunity: A meta-analytic review. *Psychological Bulletin, 113,* 472–486.

Herman, C. P. (1987). Social and psychological factors in obesity: What we don't know. In H. Weiner & A. Baum (Eds.), *Perspectives in behavioral medicine: Eating regulation and discontrol* (pp. 175–187). Hillsdale, NJ: Erlbaum.

Higgins, D. L., Galavotti, C., O'Reilly, K. R., Schnell, D. J., Moore, M. , Rugg, D. L., & Johnson, R. (1991). Evidence for the effects of HIV antibody counseling and testing on risk behaviors. *Journal of the American Medical Association, 266,* 2419–2429.

Hill, R. D., Rigdon, M., & Johnson, S. (1993). Behavioral smoking cessation treatment for older chronic smokers. *Behavior Therapy, 24,* 321–329.

Hobfoll, S. E., Jackson, A. P., Lavin, J., Britton, P. J., & Shepherd, J. B. (1994). Reducing inner-city women's AIDS risk activities. *Health Psychology, 13,* 397–403.

Hoffmeister, H., Mensink, G. B. M., Stolzenberg, H., Hoeltz, J., Kreuter, H., Nussel, E., Hullemann, K. D., & Trosche, J. V. (1996). Reduction of coronary heart disease risk factors in the German Cardiovascular Prevention study. *Preventive Medicine, 25,* 135–145.

Houston Miller, N., Smith, P. M., DeBusk, R. F., Sobel, D. S., & Taylor, C. B. (1997). Smoking cessation in hospitalized patients: Results of a randomized trial. *Archives of Internal Medicine, 157,* 409–415.

Hughes, J. R. (1991). Combined psychological and nicotine gum treatment for smoking: A critical review. *Journal of Substance Abuse, 3,* 337–350.

Ickovics, J. R., Morrill, A. C., Beren, S. E., Walsh., U., Walsh, S., & Rodin, J. (1994). Limited effects of HIV counseling and testing for women: A prospective study of behavioral and psychological consequences. *Journal of the American Medical Association, 272,* 443–448.

Jacobson, N. S., & Traux, P. (1991). Clinical significance: A statistical approach to defining meaningful change in psychotherapy research. *Journal of Consulting and Clinical Psychology, 59,* 12–19.

Janis, I. L. (1958). *Psychological stress: Psychoanalytic and behavioral studies of surgical patients.* New York: John Wiley and Sons.

Jeffery, R. W., Boles, S. M., Strycker, L. A., & Glasgow, R. E. (1997). Smoking-specific weight gain concerns and smoking cessation in a working population. *Health Psychology, 16,* 487–489.

Jeffery, R. W., Wing, R. R., & Mayer, R. R. (1998). Are smaller weight losses or more achievable weight loss goals better in the long term for obese patients? *Journal of Consulting and Clinical Psychology, 66,* 641–645.

Jensen, I. B., & Bodin, L. (1998). Multimodal cognitive-behavioral treatment for workers with chronic spinal pain: A matched cohort study with an 18-month follow-up. *Pain, 76,* 35–44.

Johnston, M., & Vogel, C. (1993). Benefits of psychological preparation for surgery: A meta-analysis. *Annals of Behavioral Medicine, 15,* 245–256.

Jorenby, D. E., Leischow, S. J., Nides, M. A., Rennard, S. I., Johnston, J. A., Huges, A. R., Smith, S., Muramoto, M. L., Daughton, D. M., Doan, K., Fiore, M. C., & Baker, T. B. (1999). A controlled trial of sustained-release bupropion, a nicotine patch, or both for smoking cessation. *New England Journal of Medicine, 340,* 685–691.

Kalichman, S. C. (1998). *Preventing AIDS: A sourcebook for behavioral interventions.* Mahwah, NJ: Lawrence Erlbaum Associates.

Kalichman, S. C., Carey, M. P., & Johnson, B. T. (1996). Prevention of sexually transmitted HIV infection: A meta-analytic review of the behavioral outcome literature. *Annals of Behavioral Medicine, 18,* 6–15.

Kalichman, S. C., Nachimson, D., Cherry, C., & Williams, E. (1998). AIDS treatment advances and behavioral prevention setbacks: Preliminary assessment of reduced perceived threat of HIV-AIDS. *Health Psychology, 17,* 546–550.

Kalichman, S. C., Rompa, D., & Coley, B. (1997). Lack of positive outcomes from a cognitive-behavioral HIV and AIDS prevention intervention for inner-city men: Lessons from a controlled pilot study. *AIDS Education and Prevention, 9,* 299–313.

Kamarck, T. W., & Jennings, J. J. (1991). Biobehavioral factors in sudden cardiac death. *Psychological Bulletin, 109,* 42–75.

Kaplan, R. M. (1994). The Ziggy theorem: Toward an outcomes-focused health psychology. *Health Psychology, 13,* 451–460.

Keefe, F. J., Caldwell, D. S., Baucom, D., Salley, A., Robinson, E., et al. (1996). Spouse-assisted coping skills training in the management of osteoarthritic knee pain. *Arthritis Care and Research, 9,* 279–291.

Kegeles, S. M., Hays, R., & Coates, T. J. (1996). The MPowerment project: A community-level HIV prevention intervention for young gay men. *American Journal of Public Health, 86,* 1129–1136.

Kelly, J. A. (1998). Group psychotherapy for persons with HIV and AIDS-related illnesses. *International Journal of Group Psychotherapy, 48,* 143–162.

Kelly, J. A., Murphy, D. A., Sikkema, K. J., McAuliffe, T. L., Roffman, R. A., Solomon, L., Winett, R. A., Kalichman, S. C., & the Community HIV Prevention Reseach Collaborative (1997).

Randomized, controlled, community-level HIV-prevention intervention for sexual-risk behavior among homosexual men in US cities. *Lancet, 350,* 1500–1505.

Kelly, J. A., Murphy, D., Washington, C., Wilson, T. S., Koob, J. J., Davis, D. R., Ledezma, G., & Davantes, B. (1994). Effects of HIV/AIDS prevention groups for high-risk women in urban primary health care clinics. *American Journal of Public Health, 84,* 1918–1922.

Kelly, J. A., Otto-Salaj, Sikkema, K. J., Pinkerton, S. D., & Bloom, F. R. (1998). Implications of HIV treatment advances for behavioral research on AIDS: Protease inhibitors and new challenges in HIV secondary prevention. *Health Psychology, 17,* 310–319.

Kelly, J. A., St. Lawrence, J. S., Diaz, Y. E., Stevenson, L. Y., Hauth, A. C., Brasfield, T. L., Kalichman, S. C., Smith, J. E., & Andrews, M. E. (1991). HIV risk behavior reduction following intervention with key opinion leaders of a population: An experimental community-level analysis. *American Journal of Public Health, 81,* 168–171.

Kelly, J. A., St. Lawrence, J. S., Hood, H. V., & Brasfield, T. L. (1989). Behavioral intervention to reduce AIDS risk activities. *Journal of Consulting and Clinical Psychology, 57,* 60–67.

Kendall, P. C., & Grove, W. (1988). Normative comparisons in therapy outcome. *Behavioral Assessment, 10,* 147–158.

Kendall, P. C., Flannery-Schroeder, E. C., & Ford, J. D. (1999). Therapy outcome research methods. In P. C. Kendall, J. N. Butcher, & G. N. Holmbeck (Eds.), *Handbook of research methods in clinical psychology* (2nd ed., pp. 330–363). New York: John Wiley & Sons.

Kendall, P. C., Williams, L., Pechacek, T. F., Graham, L. E., Shisslak, C., & Herzoff, N. (1979). Cognitive–behavioral and patient education interventions in cardiac catheterization procedures: The Palo Alto Medical Psychology Project. *Journal of Consulting and Clinical Psychology, 47,* 49–58.

Kiecolt-Glaser, J. K., Marucha, P. T., Malarkey, W. B., Mercado, A. M., & Glaser, R. (1995). Slowing of wound healing by psychological stress. *Lancet, 346,* 1194–1196.

Kiecolt-Glaser, J. K., Page, G. G., Marucha, P. T., MacCallum, R. C., & Glaser, R. (1998). Psychological influences on surgical recovery: Perspectives from psychoneuroimmunology. *American Psychologist, 53,* 1209–1218.

King, A. C., Haskell, W. L., Young, D. R., Oka, R. K., & Stefanick, M. L. (1995). Long-term effects of varying intensities and formats of physical activity on participation rates, fitness, and lipoproteins in men and women aged 50 to 65 years. *Circulation, 91,* 2596–2604.

Klesges, R. C., Winders, S. E., Meyers, A. W., Eck, L. H., Ward, K. D., Hultquist, C. M., Ray, J. W., & Shadish, W. R. (1997). How much weight gain occurs following smoking cessation? A comparison of weight gain using both continuous and point prevalence abstinence. *Journal of Consulting and Clinical Psychology, 65,* 286–291.

Klesges, R. C., Ward, K. D., & DeBon, M. (1996). Smoking cessation: A successful behavioral/pharmacologic interface. *Clinical Psychology Review, 16,* 479–496.

Klesges, R. C., Ward, K. D., Ray, J. W., Cutter, G., Jacobs, D. R., Jr, & Wagenknecht, L. E. (1998). The prospective relationships between smoking and weight in a young, biracial cohort: The coronary artery risk development in young adults study. *Journal of Consulting and Clinical Psychology, 66,* 987–993.

Kobashigawa, J. A., Leaf, D. A., Lee, N., Gleeson, M. P., HongHu, L., Hamilton, M. A., Moriguchi, J. D., Einhorn, K., Herlihy, E., & Laks, H. (1999). A controlled trial of exercise rehabilitation after heart transplantion. *New England Journal of Medicine, 340,* 272–277.

Kuczmarski, R., Flegel, K., Campbell, S., & Johnson, C. (1994). Increasing prevalence of overweight among U.S. adults. *Journal of the American Medical Association, 272,* 205–211.

Lazarus, R. S., & Folkman, S. (1984). *Stress, appraisal, and coping.* New York: Springer.

Lee, I. M. (1994). Physical activity, fitness, and cancer. In C. Bouchard & R. Shephard (Eds.), *Physical activity, fitness, and health: International proceedings and consensus statement* (pp. 814–831). Champaign, IL: Human Kinetics Publishers.

Lerman, C. (1997). Psychological aspects of genetic testing. *Health Psychology, 16,* 3–7.

Lerman, C., Biesecker, B., Benkendorf, J. L., Kerner, J., Gomez-Caminero, A., Hughes, C., & Reed, M. M. (1997). Controlled trial of pretest education approaches to enhance informed decision-making for BRCA1 gene testing. *Journal of the National Cancer Institute, 89,* 148–157.

Lerman, C., Caporaso, N. E., Audrain, J., Main, D., Bowman, E. D., Lockshin, B., Boyd, N. R., & Shields, P. G. (1999). Evidence suggesting the role of specific genetic factors in cigarette smoking. *Health Psychology, 18,* 14–20.

Lerman, C., Caporaso, N., Main, D., Audrain, J., Boyd, N. R., Bowman, E. D., & Shields, P. G. (1998). Depression and self-medication with nicotine: The modifying influence of dopamine D4 receptor gene. *Health Psychology, 17,* 56–62.

Lerman, C., Schwartz, M. D., Miller, S. M., Daly, M., Sands, C., & Rimer, B. K. (1996). A randomized trial of breast cancer risk counseling: Interacting effects of counseling, educational level, and coping style. *Health Psychology, 15,* 75–83.

Leserman, J., Stuart, E. M., Mamish, M. E., &

Benson, H., (1989). The efficacy of the relaxation response in preparing for cardiac surgery. *Behavioral Medicine, 2,* 111–117.

Levenstein, S., Ackerman, S., Kiecolt-Glaser, J. K., & Dubois, A. (1999). Stress and peptic ulcer disease. *Journal of the American Medical Association, 281,* 10–11.

Leventhal, H. S., Diefenbach, M., & Leventhal, E. A. (1992). Illness cognition: Using common sense to understand treatment adherence and affect cognitive interactions. *Cognitive Therapy and Research, 16,* 143–163.

Leventhal, E. A., Leventhal, H., Shacham, S., & Esterling, D. V. (1989). Active coping reduces reports of pain from childbirth. *Journal of Consulting and Clinical Psychology, 57,* 365–371.

Lichtenstein, E., & Glasgow, R. E. (1992). Smoking cessation: What have we learned over the past decade. *Journal of Consulting and Clinical Psychology, 60,* 518–527.

Lichtman, S. W., Pisarka, K., Berman, E. R., Pestone, M., Dowling, H., Offenbacher, E., Weisel, H., Heschka, S., Matthews, D. E., & Heymsfield, S. B. (1992). Discrepancy between self-reported and actual caloric intake and exercise in obese subjects. *New England Journal of Medicine, 327,* 1893–1898.

Linden, W., Stossel, C., & Maurice, J. (1996). Psychosocial interventions for patients with coronary artery disease: A meta-analysis. *Archives of Internal Medicine, 156,* 745–752.

Lindsay, E. A., Ockene, J. K., Hymowitz, N., Giffen, C., Berger, L., & Pomrehn, P. (1994). Physicians and smoking cessation. *Archives of Family Medicine, 3,* 341–348.

Linton, S. J., & Gotestam, K. G. (1984). A controlled study of the effects of applied relaxation and applied relaxation plus operant procedures in the regulation of chronic pain. *British Journal of Clinical Psychology, 23,* 291–299.

Luepker, R. V., Murray, D. M., Jacobs, D. R., Mittelmark, M. B., Bracht, N. et al. (1994). Community education for cardiovascular disease prevention: Risk factor changes in the Minnesota Heart Health Program. *American Journal of Public Health, 84,* 1383–1393.

Lovallo, W. (1997). *Stress and health.* Thousand Oaks, CA: Sage.

Lutgendorf, S. K., Antoni, M. H., Ironson, G., Klimas, N., Kumar, M., Starr, K., McCabe, P., Cleven, K., Fletcher, M. A., & Schneiderman, N. (1997). Cognitive behavioral stress management intervention decreases dysphoria and herplex simplex virus-Type 2 antibody titers in symptomatic HIV seropositive gay men. *Journal of Consulting and Clinical Psychology, 65,* 23–31.

Lutgendorf, S. K., Antoni, M. H., Ironson, G., Starr, K., Costello, N., Zuckerman, M., Klimas, N.,

Fletcher, M. A., & Schneiderman, N. (1998). Changes in cognitive coping skills and social support during cognitive behavioral stress management intervention and distress outcomes in symptomatic human immunodeficiency virus (HIV)-seropositive gay men. *Psychosomatic Medicine, 60,* 204–214.

Lynagh, M., Schofield, M. J., & Sanson-Fisher, R. W. (1997). School health promotion programs over the past decade: A review of the smoking, alcohol and solar protection literature. *Health Promotion International, 12,* 43–60.

Lynch, B. S., & Bonnie, R. J. (1994). *Growing up tobacco free: Preventing nicotine addiction in children and youths.* Washington, D.C.: National Academic Press.

Lynch, J., Helmrich, S. P., & Lakka, T. A. (1996). Moderately intense physical activities and high levels of cardiorespiratory fitness reduce the risk of non-insulin-dependent diabetes mellitus in middle-aged men. *Archives of Internal Medicine, 156,* 1307–1314.

Lynch, H. T., Lemon, S. J., Durham, C., Tinley, S. T., Connolly, C., Lynch, J. F., Surdam, J., Orinion, E., Slomanski-Caster, S., Watson, P., Lerman, C., Tonin, P., Lenoir, G., Serova, O., & Narod, S. (1997). A descriptive study of BRCA1 testing and reactions to disclosure of test results. *Cancer, 79,* 2219–2228.

Mahler, H. I., & Kulik, J. (1998). Effects of preparatory videotapes on self-efficacy beliefs and recovery from coronary bypass surgery. *Annals of Behavioral Medicine, 20,* 39–46.

Marcus, B. H., Banspach, S. W., Lefebvre, R. C., Rossi, J. S., Carleton, R. A., & Abrams, D. (1992). Increasing the adoption of physical activity among community participants. *American Journal of Health Promotion, 6,* 424–429.

Marlatt, G. A., & Gordon, J. J. (1985). *Relapse prevention.* New York: Guilford Press.

Marteau, T. M., Dundas, R., & Axworthy, D. (1997). Long-term cognitive and emotional impact of genetic testing for carriers of cystic fibrosis: The effects of test result and gender. *Health Psychology, 16,* 51–62.

Martin, J. E., & Dubbert, P. M. (1982). Exercise applications and promotion in behavioral medicine: Current status and future directions. *Journal of Consulting and Clinical Psychology, 50,* 1004–1017.

Matarazzo, J. D. (1980). Behavioral health and behavioral medicine: Frontiers for a new health psychology. *American Psychologist, 35,* 807–817.

McBride, C. M., Curry, S. J., Grothaus, L. C., Nelson, J. C., Lando, H., & Pirie, P. L. (1998). Partner smoking status and pregnant smoker's perceptions of support for and likelihood of smoking cessation. *Health Psychology, 17,* 63–69.

McDaniel, J. S., Musselman, D. L., Porter, M. R., Reed, D. A., & Nemeroff, C. B. (1995). Depression in patients with cancer. *Archives of General Psychiatry, 52,* 89–99.

Meehl, P. E. (1978). Theoretical risks and tabular asterisks: Sir Karl, Sir Ronald, and the slow progress of soft psychology. *Journal of Consulting and Clinical Psychology, 46,* 806–834.

Meigs, J., Nathan, D., Wilson, P., Cupples, L., & Singer, D. (1998). Metabolic risk factors worsen continuously across the spectrum of nondiabetic glucose tolerance. *Annals of Internal Medicine, 128,* 524–533.

Merson, M. H. (1996). Returning home: Reflections on the USE's response to the HIV/AIDS epidemic. *Lancet, 327,* 1673–1677.

Meyer, T. J., & Mark, M. M. (1995). Effects of psychosocial interventions with adult cancer patients: A meta-analysis of randomized experiments. *Health Psychology, 14,* 101–108.

Meyers, A. W., Klesges, R. C., Winders, S. E., Ward, K. D., Peterson, B. A., & Eck, L. H. (1997). Are weight concerns predictive of smoking cessation? A prospective analysis. *Journal of Consulting and Clinical Psychology, 65,* 448–452.

Miller, T. D., Balady, G. J., & Fletcher, G. F. (1997). Exercise and its role in the prevention and rehabilitation of cardiovascular disease. *Annals of Behavioral Medicine, 19,* 220–229.

National Task Force on the Prevention and Treatment of Obesity. (1996). Long-term pharmacotherapy in the management of obesity. *Journal of the American Medical Association, 276,* 1907–1915.

Neal, A. J., & Hoskin, P. J. (1997). *Clinical oncology: basic principles and practice* (2nd ed.). London: Oxford University Press.

Nicholas, M. K., Wilson, P. H., & Goyen, J. (1991). Operant-behavioral and cognitive-behavioral treatment for chronic low back pain. *Behaviour Research and Therapy, 29,* 235–238.

Ockene, J. (1993). Smoking among women across the life span: Prevalence, interventions, and implications for cessation research. *Annals of Behavioral Medicine, 15,* 135–148.

O'Connor, G. T., Buring, J. E., Yusuf, S., Goldhaber, S. Z., Olmstead, E. M., Paffenbarger, R. S., Jr., & Hennekens, C. H. (1989). An overview of randomized trials of rehabilitation with exercise after myocardial infarction. *Circulation, 80,* 234–244.

Oldridge, N. B., Guyatt, G. H., Fisher, M. E., & Rimm, A. A. (1988). Cardiac rehabilitation after myocardial infarction. Combined experience of randomized clinical trials. *Journal of the American Medicial Association, 260,* 945–950.

Ornish, D., Brown, S. E., Scherwitz, L. W., Billings, J. H., Armstrong, W. T., Ports, T. A., Melanahan, S. M., Kirkeeide, R. L., Brand, R. J. & Gould, K. L. (1990). Can lifestyle changes reverse coronary heart disease? *Lancet, 336,* 129–133.

Paffenbarger, R. S., Jr., Hyde, R. T., Wing, A. L., & Hsieh, C. C. (1986). Physical activity, all-cause mortality, and longevity of college alumni. *New England Journal of Medicine, 314,* 605–613.

Park, T. L., Adams, S. G., & Lynch, J. (1998). Sociodemographic factors in health psychology research: 12 years in review. *Health Psychology, 17,* 381–383.

Parker, J. C. (1995). Stress management. In P. M. Nicassio & T. W. Smith (Eds.), *Managing chronic illness: A biopsychosocial perspective* (pp. 285–312). Washington D.C.: American Psychological Association.

Parker, J. C., Smarr, K. L., Buckelew, S. P., Stucky-Ropp, R. C., Hewett, J. E., Johnson, J. C., Wright, G. E., Irvin, W. S., & Walker, S. E. (1995). Effects of stress management on clinical outcomes in rheumatoid arthritis. *Arthritis and Rheumatism, 38,* 1807–1818.

Patterson, D. R., & Ptacek, J. T. (1997). Baseline pain as a moderator of hypnotic analgesia for burn injury treatment. *Journal of Consulting and Clinical Psychology, 65,* 60–67.

Peck, J., Smith, T. W., Ward, J. J., & Milano, R. (1989). Disability and depression in rheumatoid arthritis: A multi-trait, multi-method investigation. *Arthritis and Rheumatism, 32,* 1100–1106.

Perri, M. G., Martin, A. D., Leermakers, E., Sears, S. F., & Notelovitz, M. (1997). Effects of group-versus home-based exercise in the treatment of obesity. *Journal of Consulting and Clinical Psychology, 65,* 278–285.

Perri, M., McAllister, D., Gange, J., Jordan, R., McAdoo, W., & Nezu, A. (1988). Effects of four maintenance programs on the long term management of obesity. *Journal of Consulting and Clinical Psychology, 56,* 529–534.

Peterson, J. L., Coates, T. J., Catania, J., Hauck, W. L., Acree, M., Daigle, D., Hillard, B., Middleton, L., & Hearst, N. (1996). Evaluation of and HIV risk reduction intervention among African-American homosexual and bisexual men. *AIDS, 10,* 319–325.

Pi-Sunyer, F. X. (1993). Medical hazards of obesity. *Annals of Internal Medicine, 19,* 655–660.

Plante, T. G., & Rodin, J. (1990). Physical fitness and enhanced psychological health. *Current Psychology: Research and Reviews, 9,* 3–24.

Pomerleau, O. F., & Kardia, S. L. (1999). Introduction to the featured section: Genetic research on smoking. *Health Psychology, 18,* 3–6.

Prochaska, J. O., & DiClemente, C. C. (1982). Transtheoretical therapy: Toward a more integrative model of change. *Psychotherapy: Theory, Research, and Practice, 19,* 276–288.

Prochaska, J. O., & DiClemente, C. C. (1984). *The transtheoretical approach: Crossing traditional boundaries of therapy.* Chicago: Dow Jones/Irwin.

Puska, P., Salonen, J. T., Nissinen, A., Tuomilehto, J., Vartianinen, E., et al. (1983). Change in risk factors for coronary heart disease during 10 years of a community intervention programme (North Karelia project). *British Medical Journal, 287*, 1840–1844.

Radojevic, V., Nicassio, P. M., & Weisman, M. H. (1992). Behavioral intervention with and without family support for rheumatoid arthritis. *Behavior Therapy, 23*, 13–30.

Rosen, J. C., Orosan, P., & Reiter, J. (1995). Cognitive behavior therapy for negative body image in obese women. *Behavior Therapy, 26*, 25–42.

Ross, M. W., & Rosser, B. S. (1989). Education and AIDS risks: A review. *Health Education Research, 4*, 273–284.

Sabol, S. Z., Nelson, M. L., Fisher, C., Gunzerath, L., Brody, C. L., Hu, S., Sirota, L. A., Marcus, S. E., Greenberg, B. D., Lucas, F. R., IV, et al. (1999). A genetic association for cigarette smoking behavior. *Health Psychology, 18*, 7–13.

Sallis, J. F., Hovell, M. F., Hofstetter, C. R., Elder, J. P., Faucher, P., Spry, V. M., Barrington, E., & Hackley, M. (1990). Lifetime history of relapse from exercise. *Addictive Behaviors, 15*, 573–579.

Sarwer, D. B., Wadden, T. A., & Foster, G. D. (1998). Assessment of body image dissatisfaction in obese women: Specificity, severity, and clinical significance. *Journal of Consulting and Clinical Psychology, 66*, 651–654.

Schulman, K. A., Berlin, J. A., Harless, W., Kerner, J., Sistrunk, S., Gersh, B. J., Dube, R., Taleghani, C., Burke, J. E., Williams, S., Eisenberg, J. M., & Escarce, J. J. (1999). The effect of race and sex on physician's recommendations for cardiac catheterization. *New England Journal of Medicine, 340*, 618–626.

Schwartz, G. E. (1982). Testing the biopsychosocial model: The ultimate challenge facing behavioral medicine? *Journal of Consulting and Clinical Psychology, 50*, 1040–1053.

Shiffman, S., Mason, K. M., & Henningfield, J. E. (1998). Tobacco dependence treatments: Review and prospectus. *Annual Review of Public Health, 16*, 335–358.

Sikkema, K. J., & Kelly, J. A. (1996). Behavioral medicine interventions can improve the quality-of-life and health of persons with HIV disease. *Annals of Behavioral Medicine, 18*, 40–48.

Sjostrom, L. (1993). Impacts of body weight, body composition, and adipose tissue distribution on morbidity and mortality. In A. J. Stunkard & T. A. Wadden (Eds.), *Obesity: Theory and therapy* (pp. 13–41). New York: Raven.

Skender, M. L., Goodrick, K., Del Junco, O. J., Reeves, R. S., Darnell, L., Gotto, A. M., & Foreyt, J. P. (1996). Comparison of 2 year weight loss trends in behavioral treatment of obesity: Diet, exercise, & combination interventions.

Journal of the American Dietetic Association, 96, 342–346.

Sloan, R. P., Shapiro, P. A., Bagiella, E., Myers, M. M., & Gorman, J. M. (1999). Cardiac autonomic control buffers blood pressure variability responses to challenge: A psychophysiologic model of coronary artery disease. *Psychosomatic Medicine, 61*, 58–68.

Smith, L. W., & Dimsdale, J. E. (1989). Postcardiotomy delirium: Conclusions after 25 years? *American Journal of Psychiatry, 146*, 452–458.

Smith, T. W., & Gallo, L. C. (1994). Psychological influences on coronary heart disease. *Irish Journal of Psychology, 15*, 8–26.

Smith, T. W., & Gallo, L. C. (In press). Personality traits as risk factors for physical illness. In A. Baum, T. Revenson, & J. Singer (Eds.), *Handbook of health psychology*. Hillsdale, N J: Erlbaum.

Smith, T. W., & Leon, A. S. (1992). *Coronary heart disease: A behavioral perspective*. Champaign-Urbana, IL: Research Press.

Smith, T. W., & Nicassio, P. (1995). Psychosocial practice in chronic medical illness: Clinical application of the biopsychosocial model. In P. C. Nicassio & T. W. Smith (Eds.), *Managing chronic illness: A biopsychosocial perspective* (pp. 1–32). Washington, D.C.: American Psychological Association.

Smith, T. W., & Ruiz, J. M. (1999). Methodological issues in adult health psychology. In P. C. Kendall, J. N., Butcher, & G. N. Holmbeck (Eds.), *Handbook of research methods in clinical psychology*. (2nd ed., pp. 499–536). New York: John Wiley & Sons.

Sorensen, G., Emmons, K., Hunt, M. K., & Johnston, D. (1998). Implications of the results of community intervention trials. *Annual Review of Public Health, 19*, 379–416.

Spiegel, D., Bloom, J. R., Kraemer, H. C., & Gottheil, E. (1989). Effect of psychosocial treatment on survival of patients with metastatic breast cancer. *Lancet*, 888–891.

Spiegel, D., Bloom, J. R., & Yalom, I. (1981). Group support for patients with metastatic cancer: A randomized outcome study. *Archives of General Psychiatry, 38*, 527–533.

Spritzer, R. L., Devlin, M. J., Walsh, B. T., Hasin, D., Wing, R., Marcus, M., Stunkard, A. J., Wadden, T., Yanovski, S., Agras, W. S., Mitchell, J., & Nonas, C. (1992). Binge eating disorder: A multisite field trial of the diagnostic criteria. *International Journal of Eating Disorders, 11*, 191–204.

Stanton, A. (1995). Psychology of women's health: Barriers and pathways to knowledge. In A. L. Stanton & S. J. Gallant (Eds.), *The psychology of women's health* (pp. 3–21). Washington DC: American Psychological Association.

Stevens, V. J., & Hollis, J. F. (1989). Preventing

smoking relapse, using an individually tailored skills-training technique. *Journal of Consulting and Clinical Psychology, 57*, 420–424.

St. Lawrence, J. S., Brasfield, T. J., & Jefferson, K. W. (1995). Cognitive-behavioral intervention to reduce African-American adolescents' risk for HIV infection. *Journal of Consulting and Clinical Psychology, 63*, 221–237.

St. Lawrence, J. S., Eldridge, G. D., Shelby, M. C., Little, C. E., Brasfield, T. L., & O'Bannon, R. E., III (1997). HIV risk reduction for incarcerated women: A comparison of brief interventions based on two theoretical models. *Journal of Consulting and Clinical Psychology, 65*, 504–509.

St. Lawrence, J. S., & McFarlane, M. (1999). Research methods in the study of sexual behavior. In P. C. Kendall, J. N. Butcher, & G. N. Holmbeck (Eds.), *Handbook of research methods in clinical psychology.* (2nd ed., pp. 584–615). New York: John Wiley & Sons.

Stone, G. C., Cohen, F., & Adler, N. E. (1979). *Health psychology.* San Francisco: Jossey-Bass.

Strong, J. P., Malcom, G. T., McMahan, C. A., Tracy, R. E., Newman, W. P., Herderick, E. E., Cornhill, J. F., & the Pathobiological Determinants of Atherosclerosis in Youth Research Group (1999). Prevalence and extent of atherosclerosis in adolescents and young adults: Implications for prevention from the pathobiological determinants of atherosclerosis in youth study. *Journal of the American Medical Association, 281*, 727–735.

Stunkard, A. J., Harris, J. R., Pedersen, N. L., & McClearn, G. E. (1990). A separated twin study of the body mass index. *New England Journal of Medicine, 322*, 1483–1487.

Suchanek Hudmon, K., Gritz, E. R., Clayton, S., & Nisenbaum, R. (1999). Eating orientation, postcessation weight gain, continued abstinence among female smokers receiving an unsolicited smoking cessation intervention. *Health Psychology, 18*, 29–36.

Suls, J., & Wan, C. K. (1989). Effects of sensory and procedural information on coping with stressful medical procedures and pain: A meta-analysis. *Journal of Consulting and Clinical Psychology, 57*, 372–379.

Taylor, C. B., Houston Miller, N., Herman, S., Smith, P. M., Sobel, D., Fisher, L., & DeBusk, R. F. (1996). A nurse-managed smoking cessation program for hospitalized smokers. *American Journal of Public Health, 86*, 1561–1569.

Telch, C. F., & Telch, M. J. (1986). Group coping skills instruction and supportive group therapy for cancer patients: A comparison of strategies. *Journal of Consulting and Clinical Psychology, 54*, 802–808.

Tibben, A., Timman, R., Banninck, E. C., &

Duivenvoorden, H. J. (1997). Three-year follow-up after presymptomatic testing for Huntington's disease in tested individuals and partners. *Health Psychology, 16*, 20–35.

Tosteson, A. N. A., Weinstein, M. C., Hunink, M. G. M., Mittleman, M. A., Williams, L. W., Goldman, P. A., & Goldman, L. (1997). Cost-effectiveness of population-wide educational approaches to reduce serum cholesterol levels. *Circulation, 95*, 24–30.

Turk, D. C., & Rudy, T. E. (1990). Neglected factors in chronic pain treatment outcome studies— referral patterns, failure to enter treatment, and attrition. *Pain, 43*, 7–21.

Turk, D. C., & Salovey, P. (1995). Cognitive-behavioral treatment of illness behavior. In P. M. Nicassio & T. W. Smith (Eds.), *Managing chronic illness: A biopsychosocial perspective* (pp. 245–284). Washington, D.C.: American Psychological Association.

Turner, J. A., Deyo, R. A., & Lowser, J. D. (1994). The importance of placebo effects in pain treatment and research. *Journal of the American Medical Association, 271*, 1609–1614.

Turner, J. A. (1982). Comparison of group progressive-relaxation training and cognitive-behavioral group therapy for chronic low back pain. *Journal of Consulting and Clinical Psychology, 50*, 757–765.

Turner, J. A., & Clancy, S. (1988). Comparison of operant behavioral and cognitive-behavioral group treatment for chronic low back pain. *Journal of Consulting and Clinical Psychology, 56*, 261–266.

Turner, J. A., Clancy, J. A., McQuade, K. J., & Cardenas, D. D. (1990). Effectiveness of behavioral therapy for chronic low back pain: A component analysis. *Journal of Consulting and Clinical Psychology, 58*, 573–579.

United States Department of Health and Human Services (1990). *Health benefits of smoking cessation.* Report of the United States Surgeon General, Washington, D.C.: United States Government Printing Office, DHHS publication No. (CDC) 90–8416.

United States Department of Health and Human Services (1994). Cigarette smoking among adults—United States 1993. *Morbidity and Mortality Weekly Report, 43*, 925–930.

United States Department of Health and Human Services, Center for Disease Control and Prevention, National Center for Chronic Disease Prevention and Health Promotion (1996). *Physical Activity and Health: A Report of the Surgeon General.* Atlanta, GA: Centers for Disease Control and Prevention.

Valdiserri, R. O., Lyter, D. W., Leviton, L. C., Callahan, C. M., Kingley, L. A., & Rinaldo, C. R. (1989). AIDS prevention in homosexual and bisexual men: Results of a randomized trial evaluating two risk reduction interventions. *AIDS, 3,* 21–26.

Velicer, W. F., Prochaska, J. O., Fava, J. L., Laforge, R. G., & Rossi, J. S. (1999). Interactive versus noninteractive interventions and dose-response relationships for stage matched smoking cessation programs in a managed care setting. *Health Psychology, 18,* 21–28.

Vinokur, A. D., Threatt, B. A., Caplan, R. D., & Zimmerman, B. L. (1989). Physical and psychosocial functioning and adjustment to breast cancer: Long-term follow-up of a screening population. *Cancer, 63,* 394–405.

von Bertalanffy, L. (1968). *General systems theory.* New York: Braziller.

Wadden, T. A., Stunkard, A. J., & Liebschutz, J. (1988). Three-year follow-up of the treatment of obesity by very low calorie diet, behavior therapy, and their combination. *Journal of Consulting and Clinical Psychology, 56,* 925–928.

Wadden, T. A., Van Italie, T. B., & Blackburn, G. L. (1990). Responsible and irresponsible use of very-low-calorie diets in the treatment of obesity. *Journal of the American Medical Association, 263,* 83–85.

Wadden, T. A., Vogt, R. A., Andersen, R. E., Bartlett, S. J., Foster, G. D., Kuehnel, R. H., Wilk, J., Weinstock, R., Buckenmeyer, P., Berkowitz, R. I., & Steen, S. N. (1997). Exercise in the treatment of obesity: Effects of four interventions on body composition, resting energy expenditure, appetite, and mood. *Journal of Consulting and Clinical Psychology, 65,* 269–277.

Wadden, T. A., Vogt, R. A., Foster, G. D., & Andersen, R. E. (1998). Exercise and the maintenance of weight loss: 1-year follow-up of a controlled clinical trial. *Journal of Consulting and Clinical Psychology, 66,* 429–433.

Webne, S. (1995). Preparation for surgery. In A. Goreczny (Ed.), *Handbook of health and rehabilitation psychology.* (pp. 291–306). New York: Plenum.

Weinhardt, L. S., Carey, M. P., Carey, K. B., & Verdecias, R. N. (1998). Increasing assertiveness skills to reduce HIV risk among women living with a severe and persistent mental illness. *Journal of Consulting and Clinical Psychology, 66,* 680–684.

Weinstein, N. D. (1993). Testing four competing theories of health-protective behavior. *Health Psychology, 12,* 324–333.

Weinstein, N. D., Rothman, A. J., & Sutton, S. R. (1998). Stage theories of health behavior. *Health Psychology, 17,* 211–213.

Wiebe, D. J., Alderfer, M. A., Palmer, S. C., Lindsay, R., & Jarret, L. (1994). Behavioral self-regulation in adolescents with Type I diabetes: Negative affectivity and blood glucose symptom perception. *Journal of Consulting and Clinical Psychology, 62,* 1204–1212.

Williamson, D. A., Champagne, C. M., Jackman, L. P., & Varnado, P. J. (1996). Lifestyle change. In V. B. Van Hasselt, & M. Hersen (Eds.), *Sourcebook of psychological treatment manuals for adult disorders* (pp. 423–488). New York: Plenum Press.

Wilson, G. T. (1994). Behavioral treatment of obesity: Thirty years and counting. *Advances in Behavioral Research and Therapy, 16,* 31–75.

Winett, R. A. (1995). A framework for health promotion and disease prevention programs. *American Psychologist, 50,* 341–350.

Wing, R. R., Epstein, L. H., Paternostro-Bayles, M., Kriska, A., Norwalk, M. P., & Gooding, W. (1988). Exercise in a behavioral weight control programme for obese patients with type 2 (non-insulin-dependent) diabetes. *Diabetologia, 31,* 902–909.

Wing, R. R., & Jeffery, R. W. (1999). Benefits of recruiting participants with friends and increasing social support for weight loss and maintenance. *Journal of Consulting and Clinical Psychology, 67,* 132–138.

Wing, R. R., & Klem, M. L. (1997). In S. Gallant, G. P. Keita, & R. Royak-Schaler (Eds.), *Health care for women: Psychological, social, and behavioral influences* (pp. 85–116). Washington, D.C.: American Psychological Association.

Winkleby, M. A., Taylor, B., Jatulis, D., & Fortmann, S. P. (1996). The long-term effects of a cardiovascular disease prevention trial: The Stanford Five-City project. *American Journal of Public Health, 86,* 1773–1779.

Wulsin, L. R., Valiant, G. E., & Wells, V. E. (1999). A systematic review of the mortality of depression. *Psychosomatic Medicine, 61,* 6–17.

Yates, B. T. (1994). Toward the incorporation of costs, cost-effectiveness analysis, and cost-benefit analysis into clinical research. *Journal of Consulting and Clinical Psychology, 62,* 729–736.

Young, L. D., Bradley, L., & Turner, R. A. (1995). Decreases in health care resource utilization in patients with rheumatoid arthritis following a cognitive behavioral intervention. *Biofeedback and Self-Regulation, 20,* 259–268.

CHAPTER 27

RACE AND ETHNICITY
IN PSYCHOTHERAPY RESEARCH

BERNADETTE GRAY-LITTLE AND DANIELLE KAPLAN
University of North Carolina, Chapel Hill

In response to the accelerating ethnic diversity in American society and to calls for action by members of minority and mental health communities, there has been increased attention to the availability and effectiveness of psychological interventions for racial and ethnic minorities. Investigators who conduct research relevant to race and ethnicity typically report substantial similarity between majority and ethnic minority groups and routinely note that intragroup variation in psychological processes exceeds intergroup differences. It is not uncommon, however, to find reliable differences between majority and minority groups, as well as among ethnic minorities in research on personality (e.g., Gray-Little & Hafdahl, in press), psychopathology (Castillo, 1996), and psychotherapy (Chambless & Williams, 1995). With regard to ethnicity and psychotherapy, an ideal research program would encompass programmatic research on the effectiveness of therapy for members of ethnic minority groups, exploration of the efficacy of specific types of intervention, and research comparing effectiveness across different groups. An important next step might entail identifying variables that account for any differences found, and examining the association of those variables to therapeutic processes and outcomes in all groups. For example, if we determined that perceived discrimination and outcome were related, we might then examine their covariation in members of both minority and majority groups. A research program of this type would be doubly beneficial, first by enhancing our understanding of fundamental psychotherapeutic processes and, second, through aiding the development of effective interventions for specific groups. Existing research, however, is not fully adequate to either goal.

Numerous publications theorize about the importance of specific issues or strategies in therapy with particular groups (e.g., Boyd-Franklin, 1984, on African-American families; Rosado & Elias, 1993, with Hispanic clients; LaFromboise, Trimble, & Mohatt, 1990, and Renfrey, 1992, on Native Americans) or on ethnic minority persons more generally (e.g., Hays, 1995; Wood & Mallinckrodt, 1990). Such papers are often very thoughtful, offering a conceptual framework for psychotherapy with the target population or recommending a design for the treatment of particular clinical problems; however, controlled empirical investigations are far less common. There are also frequent appeals for the development of new culturally sensitive treatments for ethnic minority clients. Research programs are beginning to show that some culturally tailored treatments are effective (e.g., Malgady, Rogler, & Constantino, 1990). Without such evidence, however, the use of culturally sensitive treatments that are unproven with any population seems a dubious alternative to interventions that have been empirically supported with some population. Hence the existence of culturally sensitive treatments does not forestall the need for rigorous research (Schulte, Kunzel, Pepping, & Schulte-Bahrenberg, 1992).

The primary groups to which we refer as ethnic minorities are African Americans (Blacks), Asian Americans, Hispanics (Latinos), and Native Americans. Although the average socioeconomic status (SES) of American Whites exceeds that of most ethnic minority groups, there is a range of economic, educational, and cultural heterogeneity for each group according to the 1990 U.S. census. Furthermore, the average characteristics of ethnic minority groups may differ from one another as much as they do from the average characteristics of Whites, and substantial cultural variation exists within each ethnic group. For example, there are more than 200 tribal and language groups among Native Americans, a sizeable minority of whom (22%) live on reservations and trust lands (Norton & Manson, 1996). Lifelong residence on a reservation may itself constitute an important element in psychotherapy utilization and outcome. Similarly, the distribution of Hispanic groups is not uniform across the United States: Thus, the pioneering research on family therapy conducted with Latinos at the Family Studies Center in Miami initially included largely Cuban Americans (Szapocznik, Scopetta, Aranalde, & Kurtines, 1978); however, the Latinos included in Sue, Fujino, Hu, Takeuchi, and Zane's (1991) research in Los Angeles were Mexican Americans. For these reasons, whether we contrast majority and minority groups on a single dimension or on a complex process such as psychotherapy, we are not contrasting discrete, homogeneous groups. Further, the ethnic groups to which we refer also constitute numerical and social minority groups and to varying degrees endure the consequences of minority status. Finally, the over-representation of some ethnic minorities (e.g., Puerto Ricans and African-Americans) in lower income groups means that unless SES is controlled in comparative research, ethnic minority status will often be confounded with SES. This is a vitally important consideration in view of the consistent association between SES and psychotherapy process and outcome variables (Lorion & Felner, 1986; Sutton & Kessler, 1986).

We begin our review with a cautious conclusion that echoes previous reviews on this topic. When a receptive client and a receptive, competent provider are engaged in therapy of adequate or typical intensity and duration, psychotherapy can be effective with members of ethnic minority groups. This *everything-being-equal* conclusion contains several assumptions that might be viewed as the conditions of treatment. The conditions are important in all psychotherapy and may be especially critical in examining the effectiveness of psychotherapy with minority clients. The first condition is that the ethnic minority client will have attitudes conducive to seeking and accepting psychological treatment and that competent services are available. Another condition is that the client's distress and potential to benefit from psychotherapy will be evaluated on grounds

other than ethnicity or socioeconomic status. Third, neither the ethnic minority client nor the therapist will terminate treatment prematurely. In the sections to follow we review the literature bearing on these conditions and on the outcomes of individual, group, marital, and family therapy with members of ethnic minority groups.

Pathways and Barriers to Psychotherapy
Who Seeks Psychotherapy?

According to the 1990 U.S. census, ethnic minorities constitute approximately 30% of the population of the United States; however, they comprise only about 10% of psychotherapy clients (Vessey & Howard, 1993), and an even smaller percentage of participants in psychotherapy research (Miranda, 1996). Thus in comparison with their numbers in the population, ethnic minority clients are infrequently seen for psychotherapy and rarely studied in psychotherapy research. As an exhaustive analysis of pathways and barriers to psychotherapy is beyond the scope of this review, our discussion will be illustrative. Andersen and Newman (1971) provided a useful model for examining three levels of factors related to seeking psychotherapy. *Predisposing factors* include attitudes toward mental health services and the types of help that are sought. *Enabling factors* encompass such practical considerations as financial resources and accessibility, among others. *Need considerations* comprise such factors as problem severity and perceived need.

With regard to *predisposing factors*, the attitudes of ethnic minority groups seem relatively less conducive than those of Whites to seeking psychotherapy. McKinley (1987) cites a pattern of differences—relating to authority figures, somatization of physical illness, and views regarding time—that may make therapy less familiar and less inviting to potential Hispanic clients than majority culture Whites. Neighbors (1985, 1988) suggested that at times of emotional distress African Americans are more likely than Caucasians to seek help from a general physician, minister, or hospital emergency room rather than a mental health professional. When mental health treatment is sought by African Americans, it is more likely to be from a mental health center or private psychotherapist than from a university or medical center where research might be conducted (Miranda, 1996). Fear of hospitalization has also been a factor affecting the attitudes toward mental health services among

African Americans (Pavkov, Lewis, & Lyons, 1989; Sussman, Robins, & Earls, 1987). Sue and Morishima (1982) argued that because of the stronger stigma associated with mental illness among Asian-American populations, members of that group are less likely than Caucasians to seek psychotherapy for the treatment of emotional distress.

Enabling factors are also relevant to the use of mental health services by ethnic minority persons, if for no other reason than the frequent association between poverty and minority status. Lack of insurance coverage and inability to pay out-of-pocket may limit access to private therapeutic services, while lack of reliable transportation or time to pursue treatment may impede access to otherwise affordable services. For clients who are not fluent in or fully comfortable speaking English, language may also present a practical barrier.

Finally, the *perception of need* for psychological services is associated with utilization. It stands to reason that the need is as great among ethnic minorities as among Whites; however, the perception of need and of psychological services as an appropriate remedy may differ. For example, there is substantial consistency in findings that Latinos are inclined to somatize personal distress and to first seek medical rather than psychological remedies (McKinley, 1987; Rosado & Elias, 1993). Furthermore, Dohrenwend (1973) found that only 50% of African Americans, but 70% of other groups, reported a stressful event during the preceding year. In view of the relatively unfavorable living conditions for African-American participants in their study, the difference in perception is likely to reflect a tolerance for stress and psychopathology that is often associated with chronic exposure to stressful situations and would be associated with reduced utilization of mental health services. Taken together, nonconducive attitudes, fewer resources, and lower perceived need may reduce minority clients' access to and utilization of psychotherapy service and may also lead them to seek treatment at a point of greater symptom severity than Whites (Sussman et al., 1987).

Several studies have specifically examined mental health service utilization rates (e.g., Snowden & Cheung, 1990). The general findings from such studies, however, can give a misleading impression with regard to psychotherapy services. For example, some reviews have indicated over-utilization of inpatient and outpatient services by Native Americans and African Americans in comparison to Caucasians and underutilization by Asian Americans and, to some extent, Hispanic Americans (Sue et al., 1991; see Sue, Zane, & Young, 1994 for a discussion). Other studies, however, also show underutilization by African Americans for even serious personal distress (Neighbors, 1985; Sussman et al., 1987). Similarly LaFromboise (1988) reported that Native Americans underutilize services. Hu, Snowden, Jerrel, and Nguyen (1991) conducted a finer-grained analysis of utilization rates, from which a more differentiated picture emerged. In that study, African Americans had a higher utilization rate for emergency services, but lower rates for case management and individual outpatient services, which are most likely to include psychotherapy. By comparison, Asian American and Latino clients used fewer emergency services and more outpatient services. Thus, patterns of mental health utilization vary among ethnic minority groups; nonetheless, available evidence indicates that ethnic minority persons are underrepresented among persons treated with psychotherapy (Vessey & Howard, 1993). Their additional absence from psychotherapy research creates a further disadvantage because it limits identification of the most effective interventions (Miranda, 1996).

Diagnosis

Once a client presents for treatment, the attitudes of the staff toward the patient as an individual or as the representative of a group may interact with the symptom picture to influence diagnostic judgments and treatment recommendations. A substantial body of evidence from both clinical and analogue studies indicates that diagnostic judgments are sometimes related to the patients' race and ethnicity (see reviews by Dana, 1993; Gray-Little, 1995; Gray-Little & Kaplan, 1998; Okazaki & Sue, 1995; Velasquez, 1995). Associations between ethnicity and diagnosis can be understood both in terms of variations in the expression of distress by members of different ethnic groups, and also with regard to diagnostician biases that appear to be independent of the client's symptoms. Cultural or ethnic variations in the expression of distress can be seen in the finding that among both Asian Americans and Hispanics, in comparison to Caucasians, psychological distress, especially depression, is often accompanied by extensive somatic symptoms (e.g., Greene, 1987; McKinley, 1987; Sue &

Morishima, 1982). The communication of personal distress in somatic rather than psychological complaints will typically make patients seem less suitable for psychotherapy. African-American and Hispanic patients with bipolar disorder apparently are more likely to experience hallucinations than Caucasians with the same diagnosis, and thus their accurate diagnosis may require more sophistication (Lawson, 1986).

Clinical and analogue studies of diagnosis also reveal that ethnicity can be associated with diagnosis, independent of symptoms (Loring & Powell, 1987; Strakowski, Lonczak, Sax et al., 1995). Research on African Americans, for example, reveals consistent evidence of overdiagnosis of schizophrenia and perhaps an underdiagnosis of personality disorders and depression in comparison to Caucasians (Lawson, 1986; Pavkov, Lewis, & Lyons, 1989; Strakowski et al., 1995). Mukherjee, Shukla, Woodle, Rosen, and Olarte (1983) found that ethnicity was a significant predictor of schizophrenia for both Hispanic and African-American patients. Friedman, Paradis, and Hatch (1994) also reported that anxiety-disordered African-American patients were more likely to have had prior inaccurate diagnoses of severe pathology and to have been inappropriately hospitalized more often than anxiety-disordered Caucasian patients. Whether stemming from bias on the part of the diagnostician or variations in the expression of distress, however, the over diagnosis of severe pathology in some minority patients, like the more frequent somatic presentation by others, may mean that they are less likely to be seen as appropriate candidates for psychotherapy.

Psychotherapy Dropouts

After being accepted for psychotherapy, a patient must decide whether to make a commitment to the recommended treatment. Although there is debate about the typical number of psychotherapy sessions that patients receive, most estimates place the median below ten sessions and closer to six (Garfield, 1994). The distribution of treatment sessions is often positively skewed: A small number of patients receives a large number of sessions, but most receive relatively few. Moreover, it is commonly accepted that a substantial percentage of the clients who begin psychotherapy terminate earlier than the therapist believes is advisable; many drop out after only one or two sessions. Premature termination and dropping out are thus widespread, with a negative impact

on both practice and research in psychotherapy. Two general findings are important here. First, therapeutic effects are related positively to the duration of treatment (Orlinsky, Grawe, & Parks, 1994). Second, a large number of studies suggests an association between ethnic minority status and premature termination and treatment dropout.

In our discussion of treatment duration among ethnic minorities, we will refer briefly to four narrative summaries of research published prior to 1992 and then review research not included in those reviews. Baekeland and Lundwald (1975) conducted a comprehensive narrative review of research on dropouts from psychotherapy, and from pharmacotherapy, among children and adults. They found that the therapist's low level of experience and client's social status, including minority status and low education, were predictive of dropout. Narrative reviews by Sattler (1977) and Garfield (1986, 1994) also revealed a frequent, but not invariant, relationship between dropout and lower SES. Garfield's work showed that minority clients, especially African Americans, were more likely to drop out and that those who remained past the intake continued for fewer sessions than Caucasians. Garfield cautioned that the findings regarding race and SES were confounded in many of the studies reviewed. Wierzbicki and Pekarik (1993) conducted a meta-analytic review of psychotherapy dropout in 125 clinical studies published prior to June 1990. Their analysis, which encompassed many of the studies from previous reviews, examined the association of six demographic variables—sex, age, race, education, SES, and marital status—to dropout rates. Three variables, African-American (or other minority) race, education, and SES, were significantly related to dropout, with effect sizes (ESs) ranging from .23 to .37. Unfortunately, due to missing data, it was not possible to examine ethnicity independent of social class. Wierzbicki and Pekarik noted, however, that the relationship between termination and ethnicity needs to be examined in studies controlling both social class and expectations regarding treatment duration because such controls may attenuate the relationship of race and social class to dropout (Pekarik, 1991; Pekarik & Wierzbicki, 1986; Sledge, Moras, Hartley, & Levine, 1990).

Richmond (1992) reviewed dropout patterns (termination without therapist agreement) for 624 primarily lower income clients seen in individual, dynamically oriented adult psychotherapy at a nonprofit private clinic. The mean age for clients was 32.9. Whites comprised 77.4% of the sample; Blacks, 12.3%; Hispanics, 4.2%; and Asians, 3.8%. Therapists were White, predoctoral psychology interns with masters' degrees. The distribution of sessions was quite skewed; the median number of sessions was seven, with a mean of sixteen sessions. Nearly 40% of the clients terminated by the end of the third session. Richmond examined rates of dropout during three phases: intake (after one session), evaluation (session two or three), and therapy proper. Although being a member of an ethnic minority group was related to dropout at each phase, the strength of this relationship was especially strong during the evaluation phase, where minority status was a stronger predictor of dropout than overall level of functioning (Axis V rating) or education. Dropouts at the evaluation stage were most distinguished by having been a focus of treatment more associated with domestic problems and less to personal adjustment or personal distress. As anticipated there were differences in client characteristics associated with dropout at each of the three phases; however, the four variables that were associated across all phases—higher tension level, racial minority, low education, and lower guilt feelings—suggest that dropouts differ from the preferred psychotherapy patient (Schofield, 1984). Therapists may have more difficulty establishing credibility and rapport with such patients, which would further hinder formation of a working alliance and agreement on the goals of therapy (Bordin, 1979).

Kazdin and Mazurick (1994) examined therapy dropout rates for 257 oppositional, aggressive, and antisocial children aged 3–14. Sixty percent of the sample was from the two lowest classes of the Hollingshead scale. All but one of the 12 master's level psychologists who served as therapists were White. Treatment completion and the expected duration of treatment, 7–8 months, were discussed with families prior to and during the initial visit. Although African Americans comprised 34% of those beginning treatment, they were only 24% of the completers. Other minority groups, primarily Hispanic and Asian, comprised approximately 4% of the original group and of the completers. The greatest discrepancy in dropout for African Americans and Whites occurred at the early termination phase (prior to the sixth session); minority status was not predictive of late termination (sessions 7–14). The authors speculate that for African-American patients, a poorer match between clinic and family expecta-tions may account for the association of minority status to attrition; however, this relationship was not investigated. In a related publication, the authors (Kazdin, Mazurick, & Siegel, 1994) also showed that dropouts had poorer treatment outcomes.

Atlas (1992) studied 80 patients applying for services at an urban mental health center. Dropouts and continuers did not differ in sex, social class, previous treatment experience, or level of symptomatology, but the rate of dropout for Hispanic patients was disproportionately high, despite the fact that they reported the highest symptom levels. Instruments administered early in treatment indicated that early terminators, in comparison with continuers, expected therapists to be more directive, whereas continuers reported that their therapists had greater depth. Lin (1994) studied attendance patterns for 145 Chinese-American outpatients. The distribution of sessions was skewed, but the median number of sessions ($Mdn = 8$; $M = 12$) was comparable to that for the general public. Lin's results are consistent with those of Sue et al. (1991), who investigated termination patterns (average number of sessions and termination after the first session) in a large sample of patients treated in the Los Angeles County Mental Health System (LACMHS). The average number of sessions for Asian patients (6) was significantly higher than the average for Caucasian and Hispanic (5) or African-American patients (4). Dropout rates after the first session ranged from 10.7% for Asian Americans to 19.4% for African Americans.

Because few studies have examined the role of ethnicity with a controlled social class, it is not possible to eliminate entirely SES as an explanation for variations in dropout rates between majority and minority groups or among ethnic minority groups. On the average, dropout rates and treatment duration for Asian Americans and Caucasians appear to be similar; however, dropout rates for Hispanics appear higher and may vary with the particular Hispanic group studied. Although there is less recent research on Native Americans, excess dropout appears to be a significant problem for this group (BigFoot-Sipes, Dauphinais, LaFromboise, & Bennett, 1992). Finally, past and recent research show premature termination to be a more severe problem for African Americans than for either Caucasians or the general population.

Acosta (1980) examined the reasons for early termination (prior to the completion of six sessions) in 79 patients, who were divided almost evenly among African Americans, Anglo Americans, and Mexican Americans, and had been seen for outpatient, dynamically oriented therapy. The primary reasons given by all groups were negative attitudes toward the therapist and the perception that therapy had no benefits. Practical considerations were also important, as was the patient's belief that improvement had already occurred. These impressions were partially confirmed in a later study by Beckman (1992), who studied dropouts from individual outpatient psychotherapy at a mental health center. The 31 dropouts in that study differed from the 24 continuers in rating the therapist as less warm, empathic, or genuine on the Barrett Lennard Relationship Inventory. Thus, for all groups, rapport achieved during the first one or two sessions seems critical to continuing in therapy. Although both the therapist and the client are essential players in establishing the therapeutic relationship, most research on dropout among minority clients has investigated attitudes and preferences of clients, with less research devoted to corresponding processes in the therapists. We next review recent literature on the relationship of client attitudes and preferences to dropout and then briefly consider literature addressing therapists' reactions that might be related to dropout among ethnic minority clients.

Client-Therapist Ethnic Similarity

A substantial portion of psychotherapy research with minority clients has been devoted to the question of whether ethnic similarity between the client and the counselor leads to better therapeutic outcomes. The justification for so much attention to this issue is the assumption that therapist–client ethnic matching may enhance the therapeutic or working alliance, which is often considered critical to success in psychotherapy (Gaston, 1990). The quality of the alliance rests on the client's beliefs that the therapist is competent and trustworthy, the setting is safe for self-disclosure, and treatment will be effective. Other things being equal, demographic similarity may reduce the social distance between therapist and client and enhance the likelihood of shared beliefs and experiences. In this way, an ethnically similar client and therapist may have an advantage in establishing a working alliance, in maintaining the therapy contact, and in having a successful outcome.

In an early review of archival, analogue, field diagnostic, questionnaire, and interview preference studies on client–therapist matching, Sattler (1977) concluded that there were no significant differences in length of treatment, treatment outcome, or client satisfaction for Black clients treated by either Black or White therapists. Several years later, the same data were reviewed by Abramowitz and Murray (1983), who also incorporated findings from studies conducted in the years since the publication of Sattler's original review. Interestingly, the latter authors drew somewhat different conclusions. Suggesting that Sattler may have been predisposed to give selective weight to studies that demonstrated no bias for or against Black clients matched with White therapists, Abramowitz and Murray concluded that the process and outcome of diagnosis and therapy with Black clients were indeed different when clients were seen by Black and White therapists. They were quick to note, however, that the prevalence of analogue studies and the absence of any clear evidence supporting or refuting bias precluded their drawing definitive conclusions about the effects of client–therapist matching (see also the review by Sue et al., 1994). More recent research on client–therapist matching addresses two related topics: client preference for an ethnically similar counselor; and treatment outcomes for clients with ethnically similar versus dissimilar therapists.

Client Preferences

Information on minority clients' preference for ethnically similar therapists is derived largely from analogue studies and has yielded mixed results. Studies with Native-American adolescents and college students (e.g., BigFoot-Sipes et al., 1992; Johnson & Lashley, 1989), Mexican-American college students (Sanchez & Atkinson, 1983), and Asian-American adults (Atkinson & Gim, 1991) support the hypothesis that clients view ethnically similar therapists as more desirable, trustworthy, and credible. Parallel findings indicate that African-American clients prefer ethnically similar therapists (Atkinson, 1983; Atkinson & Schein, 1986; Sue, 1988). Notably, however, findings from the last three studies failed to support a preference for ethnically similar counselors among Asian-American, Native-American, and Latino clients. In addition, Flaskerud (1990) reviewed the literature on client–therapist matching by ethnicity, gender, and language for Asian-

American clients, and did not find any overall differences in client preference or perceived counselor credibility.

Lopez, Lopez, and Fong (1991) identified two major research protocols in analogue research on therapist preference among Mexican-American college students. The first, the *judgment*, or perception protocol, asks participants to evaluate the trustworthiness, credibility, or competence of fictional counselors whose race and ethnicity are varied. Preferences are then inferred from differences in the ratings given by participants. The second predominant research design is the *choice*, or preference protocol, in which clients are presented with information about several counselors who vary on race or ethnicity, and then choose one of them as the most preferred. Lopez and his colleagues found a consistent difference in the results obtained with the two types of protocol. Whereas participants in choice protocol studies consistently reported a preference, the judgment method consistently yielded findings of "no preference" for ethnically similar counselors. However, Coleman, Wampold, and Casali's meta-analysis (1995) of 42 effect sizes (ESs) from research on participants from various ethnic groups strongly supported the hypothesis that minority individuals show a preference for ethnically similar counselors, with an average ES of .51. They also found, however, that studies using the choice protocol yielded a significantly larger average ES (.73) than those using the judgment protocol (.20). Interestingly, the authors also determined that ESs for studies published before 1985 were smaller than those published after 1985, suggesting that current clients are more sensitized to therapist ethnicity than was true in the past.

It should be noted that the distinction between the choice and judgment methods parallels the difference between forced-choice and rating-scale response formats. In the choice paradigm a dissimilarity response is required; the feature that determines the choice is the difference between the options (i.e., ethnic identity). In using rating scales (perception or judgment) all the features of each option can be considered and all can be judged meritorious (Payne, 1982). Thus, as noted by Coleman et al., "As the freedom to show no preference was restricted, the tendency to state a preference for an ethnically similar counselor increased" (1995, p. 60). Several studies suggest that judgment is distinguishable from choice (see,

for example, Tinsley & Westcot, 1990). A telling example of the distinction can be seen in research by Langley (1994) in which Black male clients chose or preferred a White counselor although they rated the Black counselor as more credible. Langley's findings suggest that current research procedures may often fail to assess the critical dimensions on which preferences are based (Speight & Vera, 1997).

Inconsistent findings regarding client preferences for ethnically similar counselors have led researchers to consider other characteristics that might influence clients' attitudes toward mental health service providers. One of the earliest systematic explorations of this topic came in the work of Helms and her associates. In early studies, Helms (1984; see also Helms & Carter, 1991; Parham & Helms, 1981) explored the relationship between the client's stage of racial identity development and preference for an ethnically similar counselor. These studies suggest a relationship far more complex than simple ethnic matching. For example, clients whose attitudes toward their own and the other ethnic groups most closely approximate that of the dominant culture (i.e., highly acculturated clients) are least likely to prefer an ethnically similar counselor.

It is possible that the most influential characteristics in clients' choices and preferences may be only indirectly related to therapist ethnicity. LaFromboise and Dixon (1981) found that Native-American students rated counselors more highly when the counselors, in a simulated interview, enacted "trustworthy roles," regardless of their ethnicity. Pomales, Claiborn, and LaFromboise (1986) also found that Black students perceived White counselors who openly acknowledged issues of race, racism, and culture to be more trustworthy, expert, and attractive than those who did not. Finally, in a study by Atkinson, Furlong, and Williams (1986), participants rated ethnic similarity fifth on a list of preferred counselor characteristics on which similar attitudes, values, and personalities were ranked more highly.

Taken in conjunction, these studies suggest that it is not ethnic matching per se, but clients' perception of the therapist as trustworthy and competent, that enhances the therapeutic relationship. Clients use a kind of schematic information processing in which demographic characteristics are perceived to convey probabilistic information about beliefs and attitudes of therapists. At times, therapists of the same ethnicity may be preferred because they are perceived as most likely to possess the desired qualities. However, when information more germane to those qualities is available, it is used instead of ethnicity or other demographic characteristics (Coleman et al., 1995).

Matching and Therapeutic Outcome

The critical question in client–therapist matching is the implication of matching for such outcomes as dropout rates, length of treatment, and clinical improvement. Much of the research on client–therapist matching has been conducted through analogue studies and only a few studies provide direct evidence of clinical outcomes for clients matched with an ethnically similar counselor. Flaskerud and Liu (1990) found better therapeutic outcomes on the Global Assessment Scale (GAS) for Southeast-Asian clients who had been treated by an ethnically similar counselor than for those who had engaged in treatment with a Caucasian therapist. In a study controlling for seriousness of the presenting disorder and Medi Cal status (eligibility for government subsidized health services), Yeh, Eastman, and Cheung (1994) found that ethnic matching was a significant predictor of outcome for adolescents (ages 12–17), but not for children (ages 6–11) from the LACMHS. Adolescents who were seen by therapists of the same ethnicity had significantly higher posttreatment GAS scores than those who were not matched. Results varied for specific ethnic groups; for example, matching was not a significant predictor of clinical improvement or treatment length for Caucasian adolescents. In research with adults from the same mental health system, Sue et al. (1991) found a relationship between ethnic match and GAS for only Mexican-American adults and not for other ethnic groups.

Evidence of an indirect link between matching and positive outcomes was offered by Flaskerud and Liu (1991), who found that utilization of mental health services by Asian-American clients increased with increased availability of Asian-American therapists, particularly those who spoke the clients' native languages. Yeh et al. (1994) also reported both reduced dropout and increased treatment duration for Asian and Latino adolescents who were matched with ethnically similar therapists; matching was associated with reduced dropout only for African Americans. Ethnic matching was unrelated to either variable for Caucasian adolescents and children

between the ages of 6 and 11. In a study of ethnic-specific mental health services, Sue et al. (1991) determined that the length of therapy for minority clients increased when clients and therapists were matched for ethnicity. Such findings have also been reported by O'Sullivan, Peterson, Cox, and Kirkeby (1989); Takeuchi, Sue, and Yeh (1995), and Yeh, Takeuchi, and Sue (1994). O'Sullivan and Lasso (1992) found that Hispanic clients matched with a Hispanic staff member had a lower rate of dropout after the first session (6.9%) than clients seen by a non-Hispanic staff member (17.9%); furthermore, among continuers, matched clients attended a significantly greater number of sessions.

Two general statements are warranted regarding client–therapist matching. The first is that in the absence of information pertinent to therapists' personal and political values, minority clients often, but not invariably, express a preference for ethnically similar therapists. Second, ethnic matching is not consistently related to improved clinical outcomes for those clients who continue in treatment. However, because treatment outcomes have been shown to be positively correlated with the number of sessions in treatment (Orlinsky et al., 1994), evidence that minority clients often stay in treatment longer when matched with an ethnically similar service provider suggests an indirect, nontrivial link between client–therapist match and positive therapeutic outcomes.

Research is needed to examine the specific values and attitudes that clients assume to be conveyed by a therapist's ethnicity. For example, does ethnic matching enhance perception of the therapists as trustworthy or as potentially more effective? To date, little or no research has been done on the question of whether the concept of *matching* extends beyond matching from specific ethnic membership to shared minority status between client and therapist. That is, in the absence of knowledge about a therapist's attitudes and personality, is it shared minority status, shared ethnic membership, or another characteristic that is important to clients? In view of the logistical problems associated with universal ethnic matching, we need to know which therapist behaviors will facilitate the development of therapeutic alliance with ethnic minority clients and what training will develop the requisite skills. There are other, more intricate issues associated with this body of research as well. For example, a number of investigators have highlighted minority clients' appreciation of a directive style in the therapist (Atlas, 1992; Szapocznik et al., 1978), and yet traditionally, therapist directness has had, at best, an equivocal relation to outcome in individual therapy (Luborsky, McLellan, Diguer, Woody, & Seligman, 1997). Similarly, the implicit assumption in much of this work is that clients prefer therapists who are similar in attitudes and values. However similarity may impede progress as well as facilitate it (Garfield, 1994). Empirically based responses to these and other questions would enhance our understanding of the manner in which client perceptions are related to therapy outcomes.

Therapist Attitudes and Preferences

Therapist characteristics have sometimes been called the neglected variable in psychotherapy research (Garfield, 1997). At the same time it is commonly understood that such therapist qualities as the ability to fashion a collaborative alliance with the client, commitment to being helpful, and general level of expertise are critical to therapeutic outcome (Luborsky et al., 1997). Furthermore, Beutler, Machado, and Neufeldt (1994) noted that "personal beliefs arising from developmental experience provide the cognitive elements that underwrite one's professional striving" (p. 239). Thus, as therapists are not blank slates and have personal beliefs and values that may influence their effectiveness in establishing a collaborative alliance, it is reasonable to ask, "How do therapists' attitudes influence their treatment of ethnic minority clients?"

Relevant research mostly concerns the attitudes of the majority of therapists toward minority group members, but studies including ethnic minority therapists illustrate the complexity of this issue. Sattler's (1977) review gave an inconsistent picture of White therapists' attitudes toward minority clients. Whereas several studies suggested White therapists had less favorable attitudes and less comfort in treating Black clients as well as stereotypes about other ethnic minority groups, other research indicated similar outcomes for clients who were retained in treatment. More recent studies devoted to this topic also suggest substantial ambivalence in therapists' reactions to patient ethnicity as well as relatively unfavorable attitudes toward clients of lower social status. The literature is fairly consistent in showing that therapists have less favorable attitudes toward lower income clients (Lorion & Felner, 1986). For example, Sutton and Kessler's (1986) ana-

logue study of 242 members of Division 12 showed that psychologists were less interested in treating an indigent client than treating clinically identical clients who were described as working or middle class. When professional psychotherapy was chosen for the indigent client, it was unlikely to be insight-oriented therapy. Interestingly, the indigent client was also rated as less severe and as less likely to need referral for medication. However, therapist experience and social class did not influence client ratings.

Franklin's (1985) survey of the attitudes of 183 masters and doctoral-level social workers toward Black and White clients of two different SES levels indicated that responses to race and social class are not identical. Therapists of both races felt the lower income client had a poorer prognosis, and White therapists also reported significantly less enthusiasm for working with the low income client. Interestingly, the Black client was rated just as favorably as the White client by White therapists and more favorably by Black therapists. Strickland, Jenkins, Myers, and Adams (1988) found a complex mix of attitudes in research with Black and White doctoral psychology students who viewed videotapes of White or Black and normal, neurotic, or psychotic patients. Although no race or psychopathology main effects were found, Black clients were rated as having less verbal facility than White clients by White respondents, even though the actors portrayed on the videotapes worked from verbatim transcripts. Black clients were seen as less appropriate for psychotherapy by Black respondents, although these clients were also given a higher rating on likelihood for success. The 62 White, experienced therapists in Jenkins-Hall and Sacco's (1991) research felt they would be equally comfortable working with patients presented in videotaped interviews as Black or White, depressed or nondepressed; however, their ratings of the Black depressed patients were more negative than their ratings of the other three patients.

Therapists' reactions to ethnicity can also be reflected in the minimization of symptoms. Allen (1992) found that White therapist ($n = 174$) assigned a more severe diagnosis to a vignette when the client was described as White rather than as Native American or no information about ethnicity was given. Analogous results were seen in the responses of 40 doctoral level psychologists who considered aggressive, delinquent behavior as less clinically significant when the patient was described as Black rather than White (Martin,

1993). Rieger (1996) showed that the basis for rating Black and White clients may differ: White therapists gave more favorable ratings to a Black client than to an identically described White client. Rieger found that cognitive complexity was more influential than egalitarianism in predicting attitudes toward the White patient, whereas, the reverse was true with regard to the Black patient.

In a rare clinical study relevant to this topic, Zane, Enomoto, and Chun (1994) examined the attitudes of both therapists and clients (65 White and 20 English-proficient Asian-American outpatients) being seen in individual psychotherapy. All Asian and most White (68%) clients were seen by Asian-American therapists. The two patient groups did not differ in their pretreatment attitudes toward psychotherapy and therapists did not differ in their liking for the two groups of clients at the end of the first session. However, Asian clients were seen as less suitable for treatment than Whites, and high SES clients were seen as more suitable than low SES clients. In analyses controlled for SES and pretreatment severity of symptoms, Asian Americans were found to experience worse outcomes with regard to clinical symptomatology and their attitudes toward treatment. The association of outcome to therapists' ratings of appropriateness for treatment was not reported, but this study illustrates the complexity in understanding the import of therapists' attitudes. For example, to what extent does a demographic marker such as ethnicity convey valid clinical information, independent of therapists' biases, discomfort, or lack of preparation to work with a nontraditional therapy client? When is the therapist's attitude (e.g., judgment of suitability) an independent determinant of outcome? In rating Asian clients as less suitable for psychotherapy, to what were the therapists, all of whom were Asian, responding? How could treatment and therapist training be tailored to address the relevant variable?

The one general statement that can be made about these disparate studies is that therapists who vary in experience, ethnicity, and disciplinary affiliation appear to be attuned to clients' ethnicity and social status in a way that may influence the kind of treatment for which a client is recommended. Because information concerning race and ethnicity is highly reactive, it is reasonable to assume that therapists' responses, especially in recent analogue studies, may be influenced by desire to appear unprejudiced. However, it is unclear what an unprejudiced response might be. Furthermore, most research in this area has examined therapists' impressions based on a written case study or videotaped interviews, and it is not known to what extent initial reactions to ethnicity abate or intensify during the treatment process. Research examining the effects of both the client's and therapist's attitudes over the course of treatment are sorely needed (see Gregory & Leslie, 1996).

Treatment Outcome

In this section we review recent research on the effectiveness of psychotherapy with minority clients. Navarro's (1993) attempt to conduct a meta-analysis on the effectiveness of psychotherapy with Latinos is indicative of the unfortunate state of psychotherapy research with ethnic minority populations. The author identified 123 studies published between 1970 and 1989; 103 were eliminated because they used single case study designs; an additional five were restatements of previous work. The 15 nonredundant, empirical studies suggested positive outcomes (ESs from 0 to 2.75), but were not easily interpretable because they included research on individual, family, and group therapy and most were focused on children and adolescents with behavioral or drug abuse problems. We have chosen to discuss the outcome of four treatment modalities—individual, group, family, and couple's therapy. Not all four modalities have been examined for every ethnic minority group, and due to the paucity of research, we were unable to make further distinctions, such as the theoretical orientation or brief versus long-term treatment, in the four approaches.

Individual Psychotherapy

In 1977, Sattler reviewed analogue and clinical studies of individual therapy and concluded that there were no differences in the benefits of psychotherapy for Blacks and Whites. Abramowitz and Murray (1983) addressed the general question of race effects (again focused on Black–White comparisons) in psychotherapy and concluded that no final conclusions were warranted. In their 1994 review, Sue et al. reviewed two additional empirical studies of clinical outcomes for ethnic minority clients treated with individual psychotherapy. One of these was unpublished at the time and the other was the large scale study from the LACMHS system, conducted by Sue et al. in 1991. The latter study examined therapist-rated treatment effectiveness for thousands of individuals for several racial/ethnic groups. The precise types of individual therapy were not known or controlled, nor were patients assigned randomly to treatment. Using the Global Assessment Scale (GAS), a therapist rating of overall functioning as the outcome measure, Sue et al. found improvement for Asian-American, Caucasian, Mexican-American, and African-American clients. Treatment duration was longest for Asian Americans and they had the best outcome, whereas African Americans received the briefest treatment and showed least improvement. Since that time, surprisingly little empirical research has been addressed to the general effectiveness of individual psychotherapy, to the efficacy of specific interventions with particular ethnic populations, or to comparisons of outcomes across ethnic-racial groups.

Our review of research published since 1991 revealed two empirical studies focused on general clinical outcomes for Asian-American clients treated in outpatient clinics and two studies examining treatment for agoraphobia in African-American patients. Zane, Hatanaka, Park, and Akutsu (1994) conducted a retrospective comparison of clinical outcomes for several Asian groups (186 Chinese, 124 Japanese, 71 Filipino, 150 Korean, 84 Lao or Cambodian, 190 Vietnamese) and 80 Caucasians who were treated at an Asian Pacific Counseling and Treatment Center in Los Angeles County. Patients had a wide variety of diagnostic labels. Therapists were from varied backgrounds, but all had some training in brief psychodynamic intervention and an introduction to cognitive behavioral intervention. There were no significant differences among the groups in premature treatment duration, nor in GAS scores, after controlling for initial scores. In a second study, Zane, Enomoto, and Chun (1994) examined the effectiveness of outpatient individual psychotherapy with 20 Asian and 65 White Americans, 35 years old or younger, in the San Francisco area. The treatment consisted mostly of short-term psychodynamically oriented therapy; some therapists also used cognitive-behavioral interventions. Treatment was provided by professionals and trainees in a variety of mental health fields. All Asian-American clients and most Caucasian clients were seen by Asian-American therapists. An assessment of outcome after four sessions revealed that, with SES and pretreatment symptom severity controlled, Asian-American clients experienced more clinical symptoms (SCL-90) and were less satisfied with aspects of their treatment than Caucasians. Asian clients also felt more hostility, depression, and anxiety after four sessions; however, on therapist-rated outcomes, there were no significant differences. Both studies by Zane and associates, like that by Sue et al. (1991), indicate that psychotherapy programs offered at mental health centers can be equally effective for Asian-American and Caucasian patients when outcome is assessed with therapist ratings. However, Asian patients had poorer outcomes (Zane, Hatanaka, Park, & Akutsu, 1994) on self-report instruments and were less satisfied with treatment, despite the fact that all were matched with ethnically similar therapists.

In a study of therapy for agoraphobia in Black patients, Friedman and Paradis (1991) compared outcomes for 15 Black and 15 White agoraphobic clients, aged 18–62 years, treated at the Downstate Medical Center in New York. Clients were matched for SES, and all were either indigent or working poor. There were no pretreatment differences on symptom severity; however, more Black patients had been misdiagnosed and inappropriately hospitalized on prior occasions. Patients were treated with *in vivo* exposure and tricyclic antidepressants. Using unspecified criteria, independent judges rated patient charts. Black patients were seen as less improved than Whites; 66% of Blacks but only 16% of Whites dropped out or were considered to have poor outcomes. The authors later reported similar differences in an enlarged sample including 43 Black patients and 100 White patients (Friedman, Paradis, & Hatch, 1994).

In a type of controlled study that is rare in this literature, Chambless and Williams (1995) conducted a prospective study of 18 Black and 57 White, mostly female, agoraphobic patients, who sought treatment at a university anxiety treatment program. Only two of the 20 therapists were Black and assignment of patients to therapists was not random. Most therapists (18 graduate students and 1 master's level social worker) were relatively inexperienced, but the one experienced therapist treated a disproportionate number (16) of the clients. Both groups of patients were comparable on depression, fear of fear, and frequency of panic attacks, but Black clients indicated significantly more avoidance behavior. White clients were of significantly higher SES. All patients received at least 10 sessions of treatment, consisting of therapist-assisted, *in vivo* exposure and a variety of panic management techniques. Both client groups improved significantly on most outcome measures, which consisted of objective self-report instruments; however, Blacks improved less than Whites. Racial differences were reduced, but not eliminated, when SES and initial symptomatology were controlled. Among the White patients, 44% met the criterion for clinically significant change at the end of treatment, but this was true for only 8% of Black patients. At 6-month follow-up, with SES controlled, Black patients continued to show more avoidance behaviors. The authors suggested that SES is not an adequate index of the different level of stressors to which Black and White patients in their study were exposed, and thus may not provide adequate control for environmental factors. It is unclear from this research what changes, for example, modifying the intervention techniques or expanding the length of treatment, should be made to improve effectiveness for Black clients.

Certainly no firm conclusions can be drawn from these recent studies alone. In conjunction with previous research, the current review suggests that individual psychotherapy is effective with Asian-American and African-American clients in that statistically significant changes can be demonstrated at posttreatment. Research with Asian-Americans clients does not give a clear picture about the overall effectiveness for this group in comparison with Caucasians. Research by Chambless and Williams (1995) indicates that behavioral intervention for panic and agoraphobia is less effective for African Americans than for Caucasians. Together with the work of Sue et al. (1991), these findings call into question Sattler's (1977) conclusion that individual psychotherapy is equally effective for African Americans and Caucasians. Additional basic research is needed on the effectiveness of different interventions with a variety of disorders in both Asian- and African-American populations as well as for Latinos and Native Americans. We identified no empirical, published studies of individual psychotherapy with the two latter groups since Sue et al.'s 1994 review.

Group Therapy

When discussing group therapy for ethnic minorities, it is useful to distinguish between groups composed entirely of members of a particular minority group and those in which minority group members participate in a mixed-ethnicity setting. Yalom (1985) was an early proponent of the idea

that mixed-ethnicity groups would be beneficial in helping participants adjust to a pluralistic society. In the several decades since this argument was first proposed, the U.S. population has become increasingly diverse, and it is anticipated that the proportion of White Americans will decrease further. Intuitively, then, the validity of Yalom's argument would appear to have been strengthened, but the research findings on the experiences of minorities in mixed-ethnicity groups seem to contradict this.

In a study of the rate of participation by members of various ethnic groups in therapeutic group discussions, Shen, Sanchez, and Huang (1984) found that White Americans had a significantly higher rate of verbal participation in group processes than did Mexican Americans and Native Americans of comparable educational backgrounds. Similarly, Tsui (1997) reported that Asian-American clients in mixed-ethnicity groups reported less satisfaction with therapy than either Whites in the same groups or Asian-American clients in homogeneous groups, and were more likely to question the value of their involvement. Because higher levels of verbal participation may reduce attrition (Oei & Kamierczak, 1997) and yield greater positive change in self-concept (Corey, 1990), lower participation by ethnic minorities has troubling implications for eventual therapeutic outcomes.

Due to the many conceptual articles suggesting that minority group members may feel uncomfortable disclosing personal information in mixed-ethnicity groups (Acosta & Yamamoto, 1984; Chu & Sue, 1984; Ho, 1984; Fenster, 1996), and due to a limited empirical study of such groups, we will concentrate primarily on the experiences of minority group members in single-ethnicity groups. The reader is cautioned not to assume that the single-ethnicity groups discussed here are culturally, linguistically, or socioeconomically homogeneous, and is referred to the original studies for a more thorough description of participant characteristics. Over the past several decades, researchers have reported findings suggesting the efficacy of group work with minority clients across several domains. Successful outcomes have been reported for Mexican Americans in support groups for parents of children with mental illness (Medvene, Mendoza, Lin, Harris, & Miller, 1995), Puerto Rican women in cognitive or behavioral group therapy for depression (Comas-Díaz, 1981), Southeast Asian refugees with Posttraumatic Stress Disorder (Kinzie, Leung, Bui et al., 1988), Mexican-American women in assertiveness training groups (Boulette, 1976), and African-American women in groups designed to aid in the development of self-exploration and insight (Boyd-Franklin, 1987). Successful outcomes have also been reported for Vietnamese adolescents (Tsui & Sammons, 1988), and for Native-American adolescents in substance abuse prevention programs (Schinke, Orlandi, Botvin, & Gilchrist, 1988).

These findings are largely based on data gathered from single groups, and it is difficult to draw any general conclusions about the effectiveness of group intervention from these data alone. Nonetheless, this literature suggests two primary areas of positive change common to group therapy with minority clients; the first is improvement in the overall self-concept of group participants. In his work with Native-American elementary school-aged girls, Mitchum (1989) reported increases in self-esteem after a group intervention that incorporated Native-American cultural values into the group structure and process. Guanipa, Talley, and Rapagna (1997) reported a similar improvement in Latina immigrants' self-concept as measured by the Tennessee Self-Concept Scale after a time-limited, structured group intervention designed to address issues of low self-esteem and adjustment. In a content analysis of themes discussed in a women's group for depression, Comas-Díaz (1984) reported moderate or sustained discussion of issues relating to culture shock in 40% of the sessions. Both this group and that discussed by Guanipa et al. were comprised of women who had recently relocated from their places of origin, with the former group having migrated to the mainland United States from Puerto Rico and the latter having emigrated to Canada. Both sets of authors report that involvement in group interventions was positively correlated with adaptation to the immigration experience.

The second major benefit suggested by the literature is an increase in ethnic identification for minorities engaged in group therapy. In their discussion of a comprehensive therapeutic program for gang-involved Mexican-American adolescents, Belitz and Valdez (1997) report that group work helped the adolescents to clarify issues of personal, ethnic, and cultural identity, and to distinguish positive from negative internalized messages about their ethnicity. Malgady, Rogler, and Costantino (1990) also found an increase in ethnic identification among male adolescents in father-absent families after a culture-specific group intervention designed to address anxiety and behavior problems. Finally, Edwards and Edwards (1984) suggest that groups designed to increase awareness of Native-American values and customs and identification with Native Americans may be of particular value for children and adolescents, particularly those raised outside of the extended family or tribe. It is notable that although the treatment benefits we've discussed were at times derived from therapeutic approaches specifically designed to address questions of adjustment and ethnic identity, similar benefits were derived from single-ethnicity groups that had not been formed specifically to address these issues. It is possible, therefore, that exposure to and support from ethnically similar group members with common backgrounds and goals may in itself be sufficient to increase clients' feelings of belongingness.

Malgady, Rogler, and Costantino (1990) designed a program of ethnic-specific group therapy for Puerto Rican children and adolescents. Their treatment program involves the incorporation of ethnic-specific folk tales, or *cuentos*, into therapy with children, and of stories of Puerto Rican heroes and heroines into their work with adolescents. The authors report a significant reduction of anxiety levels as measured by the State-Trait Anxiety Inventory and an increase in social judgment as measured by the Comprehension subtest of the WISC-R for participants in the *cuento* groups. Notably, however, these findings did not differ significantly at follow-up from findings for children participating in nonculture specific treatment. Findings for the adolescent group were mixed, with the primary gains at posttest made in ethnic identification for adolescents in father-absent households. The research program of Malgady and his associates is unique in that it clearly outlines the components of therapy that are culture-specific. Additional research of this type is needed to determine whether culture-specific group interventions do indeed represent an improvement over standard group interventions for the treatment of social and emotional dysfunction.

The literature on group work with minority clients would also benefit from attempts to systematically distinguish among groups conducted for different purposes. Drum and Lawler (1988, in Vasquez & Han, 1995) identified three primary purposes of group work. *Psychotherapeutic* groups are designed to help members resolve long-standing problems and traumas, and to deal with recurring social or emotional crises. *Developmental* groups, which may place a greater emphasis on skills training and short-term crisis intervention, are designed to help participants successfully negotiate normal development. Finally, *preventive* groups operate with the goal of forestalling future negative consequences by increasing participants' ability to act in their own behalf. The diversity of needs, political and economic histories, and current concerns of minority populations suggest that each of these types of groups may be potentially helpful in affecting change. It would therefore be useful for researchers to systematically examine the experiences of minority group members in each of these types of groups, with the goal of improving services for a range of presenting issues.

As a final note, an issue that remains to be resolved is the often-stated belief that group therapy may be an unsuitable treatment modality for Asian-American clients. Many authors (Ahn Toupin, 1980; Ching & Prosen, 1980; Leong, 1986) cite the cultural proscriptions against sharing personal information outside the family as an impediment to successful group work with this population. There is a small but growing body of clinical evidence, however, (e.g., Kinzie et al., 1988; Tsui, 1997) to suggest that Asian-American clients may benefit from culturally sensitive group therapy approaches. These findings are promising, as they suggest that a treatment modality that has heretofore been dismissed as ineffective and culturally dystonic for an entire group may in fact be employed with positive results.

Family Therapy

There is a prevailing assumption in the conceptual literature that family therapy may be the modality of choice for many minority clients. Kim Berg and Jaya (1993) point out that many Asian languages have no word to describe the concept of individual privacy, perhaps because of the cultural belief that individual problems and issues lie within the purview of the family. Similarly, the concept of *familismo* within many Latino cultures (Bernal & Shapiro, 1996; Falicov, 1996) speaks to the centrality of the family in both everyday functioning and problem solving. In spite of the almost universal belief that family therapy is an effective and culture-syntonic therapeutic modality for minority clients, there is limited research to support this claim. Both

process and outcome research on family therapy are often difficult to conduct and interpret. Many schools of family therapy advocate an integrative, flexible approach to conducting treatment with individual families. Such flexibility in even standardized therapy protocols allows for a good deal of therapist choice and modification from one session to the next, at times to the extent of varying the number and combination of family members who may be included in a particular session (Alexander, Holtzworth-Munroe, & Jameson, 1994). Although this approach has the advantage of tailoring services to the needs of particular families in the hopes of achieving better outcomes, the inconsistency in service delivery within even standardized protocols makes it difficult to conduct meaningful outcome research on particular therapeutic approaches.

Research on the process and outcome of therapy with minority families is vulnerable to all the challenges and shortcomings of the field in general, but presents the researcher with unique factors to consider as well. First, minority families are far more likely than White, European-American families to confront intergenerational differences in levels of acculturation, which combine with standard intergenerational differences to produce familial discord (Santisteban, Coatsworth, Perez-Vidal, Mitrani, Jean-Giles, & Szapocznik, 1997). Outcome research may also be complicated by the inapplicability of existing measures of family functioning to certain aspects of minority family life. For example, members of the extended family play a crucial role in daily family functioning in many cultures, and this may be especially true in ethnic minority families in the United States (McGoldrick, Giordano, & Pearce, 1996). Grandparents, godparents, and live-in friends and relatives may all be integral to the everyday workings of the system. Standard family therapy protocols may not provide a framework within which to conceptualize and measure the impact of extended family members' contributions to the system. Similarly, when the cultural strengths of a particular family are viewed under the lens of European-American family functioning, they may be misinterpreted as deviant. Boyd-Franklin (1984) has often cited role flexibility as one of the cultural strengths of Black families, suggesting that it is beneficial rather than dysfunctional for family members, including children, to be able to temporarily assume the duties of parents or caretakers when resources are overtaxed by current circumstances. It is unsurprising, then, that in spite of the easy availability of volumes dedicated to family therapy with minority families (e.g., McGoldrick, Giordano, & Pearce, 1996; Saba, Karrer, & Hardy, 1995), empirical data on this topic are scarce.

In lieu of presenting a detailed review of the limited empirical research in this area, we will discuss a model program of therapeutic outcome research that concentrates on work with Latino families. We will then present suggestions for future research directions, using some of the major conceptual issues that have emerged in the literature as a basis for our recommendations. Szapocznik and his colleagues have developed an extensive program of treatment outcome research designed to improve the engagement, retention rates, and outcomes for Latino families. The authors suggest that the therapeutic approach most closely matching the value orientation espoused by Latino clients is active, directive, and present-oriented, with the therapist in a leadership role (Szapocznik et al., 1978). This basic principle has informed the development and empirical validation of a series of interventions based on Minuchin's Structural Family Therapy (SFT) work with inner-city, low-income adolescents and their families. Specifically, Brief Structural Family Therapy (BSFT) utilizes the principles of joining with the family, identifying the family-specific maladaptive patterns that lead both to overall family malfunctioning and reluctance to engage in treatment, and modifying family interactions and individual roles of family members (Santisteban et al., 1997). In an early treatment outcome study comparing the efficacy of individual, conjoint family, and family ecological therapy for Hispanic families with drug-abusing adolescents, the authors found that their BSFT approach was most effective and most easily adaptable to work with Hispanic families (Scopetta, Szapocznik, King, Ladner, Alegre, & Tillman, 1977). Furthermore, BSFT was found to be more effective in improving both individual child behavior problems and overall family functioning than either child psychodynamic therapy or a recreation control group (Szapocznik, Rio, Murray et al., 1989). The principles behind SFT have also been used to recruit and retain difficult-to-engage families in therapy through a process known as Strategic Structural Systems Engagement (Szapocznik, Perez-Vidal, Hervis, Brickman, & Kurtines, 1990).

An innovative approach to family therapy with positive implications for families in which one or more members are difficult to engage in treatment is One-Person Family Therapy, or FamUno (Szapocznik, Kurtines, Perez-Vidal, Hervis, & Foote, 1990). One-Person Family Therapy is based on Minuchin and Fishman's (1981) principle of complimentarity; the idea that changes in one family member result in corresponding changes in the remaining members of the family. In a program of research with drug-abusing Hispanic adolescents, Szapocznik and his colleagues trained participants to modify their behavior in ways that would result in corresponding positive change from parents and siblings. The results of these studies indicate that this approach is as effective as conjoint brief strategic family therapy in improving family functioning and decreasing the adolescent's level of substance abuse. Notably, participants in the individual therapy control groups in these studies demonstrated reduced levels of substance abuse, but showed no improvement in overall family functioning.

Szapocznik's family therapy research program has promising implications for work with minority families. Originally conducted exclusively with Cuban-American families, recent updates to the SFT engagement research have been expanded to include Latinos of varying national origins (Santisteban, Szapocznik, Perez-Vidal, Kurtines, Murray, & LaPerriere, 1996). Furthermore, BSFT has been shown to decrease the incidence of behavior problems and improve family functioning for both Latino and African-American high-risk adolescents (Santisteban et al., 1997). Thus, this research program has begun to refine ethnic-specific models of family therapy, and explore their adaptability to families of varying ethnic and cultural origins.

As is the case with the literature on group therapy for clients of color, there is a need to move beyond the theoretical to include greater numbers of empirical studies. Much of the conceptual literature written about family therapy with minority families could potentially form the basis for substantive empirical research. Inclán (1990), for example, has developed an 18-module curriculum to increase clinicians' knowledge about issues of relevance to poor Latino and Puerto Rican migrant families, and to improve clinicians' effectiveness in working with such clients. Training modules include discussion of the life cycle of Hispanic families, the impact of religion, promoting institutional change, and the therapist's use of self. Inclán (1990) reports feedback from seminar participants indicating that the curriculum is applicable to work with many lower-SES minority groups, and noted the improvement in family therapy skills and therapeutic effectiveness among participants in the training. Such anecdotal findings are ripe for confirmatory empirical research. Similarly, the work of Boyd-Franklin (1984, 1987; see also Hines & Boyd-Franklin, 1996) on the characteristics, ecology, and strengths of Black families could easily be used to generate relevant research hypotheses about culturally sensitive treatment for Black couples and families.

Couples Therapy

In their comprehensive review of research on empirically supported couple and family interventions, Baucom, Shoham, Mueser, Daiuto, and Stickle (1998) reported no research on interventions with ethnic minority couples. We also found no empirical research addressed either to the efficacy of specific interventions with ethnic minority couples or to the general effectiveness of marital interventions with ethnic minority samples. However, a few studies have addressed the association of race or ethnicity with the assessment of marital satisfaction or specific aspects of marital interaction. For example, Negy and Snyder (1997) found that 75 Mexican-American and 66 White couples did not differ in marital satisfaction when such demographic characteristics as education and income were controlled. Their results are similar to those of Casas and Ortiz (1985), using the Dyadic Adjustment Scale. Fowers and Olson (1989) examined responses of 5039 married couples in a project designed to assess the clinical utility of the ENRICH Marital Inventory, a multidimensional diagnostic instrument designed for therapists and researcher. In a comparison that was uncontrolled for other demographic characteristics, they found Black couples to be significantly lower in overall marital satisfaction than White couples. In neither this study nor that of Negy and Snyder were the scores of ethnic minority participants linked to external criterion ratings of marital adjustment. Of particular interest in the Negy and Snyder study, however, was their examination of the association of marital distress to acculturation—the degree to which the individual adopts the beliefs, attitudes, and behaviors of the dominant culture. Acculturation was assessed with the Acculturation

Rating Scale for Mexican Americans (ARSMA; Cuellar, Harris, & Jasso, 1980). They found no relationship for men, but for wives, acculturation was positively associated with greater dissatisfaction on the subscales of Conventionalization, Time Together, and Sexual Dissatisfaction. It is unclear whether increased acculturation as measured by ARSMA is related to rising expectations that lead to increased dissatisfaction for women or is linked to a generally higher level of stress that negatively impacts their marital adjustment.

Oggins, Veroff, and Leber (1993) examined perceived interaction in six areas in a sample of 199 Black and 174 White couples. In general, there was substantial overlap in findings for the two groups, as well as consistency in the relationship of the marital interaction variables to marital satisfaction, but some differences were noted. In comparison to Whites, Blacks reported more self-disclosing communication but were also more likely to find it easiest to talk with a person other than their spouses. The two groups did not differ in perceived conflict, but Blacks had conflicts over a narrower range of areas and were more likely to avoid conflict by leaving the scene and trying to be calm. It is interesting to note that although the perception of the spouse as affirming was related to marital satisfaction for both Blacks and Whites, the association was stronger for Blacks. The reasons for the racial differences in communication, handling conflict, and affirmation from the spouse were not obvious; however, the authors attributed the difference to unspecified experiences associated with cultural values and history of racial discrimination. Although this study did not involve intervention, it does point to the potential need for different emphases in interventions that involve couple communications, problem solving, and emotional expression.

A small number of studies have attempted to explore directly the link between the experience of ethnic minority status and marital distress. Taylor and Zhang (1990) found that the endorsement of race stereotypic items (mostly items suggesting cognitive inferiority or greater sexual primitiveness and prowess) was more common in distressed than in nondistressed married couples who were matched for SES. Kelly and Floyd (1997) examined the association of stereotype endorsement (internalized racism) and ethnic identity (Afrocentricity) to marital satisfaction in 73 dating and married couples. They found the expected negative relationship between internalized racism and marital satisfaction; however, contrary to prediction, Afrocentricity was also negatively related to marital satisfaction.

The research of Negy and Snyder and of Kelly and Floyd underscores the complexity in conceptualizing and measuring constructs such as acculturation, internalized racism, and ethnic identity. For example, acculturation may be a double-edged sword in that higher levels may be associated with a better fit with majority culture, but acculturation may occur at a price. With regard to ethnic identity, it seems to be extremely important to clarify what constructs are measured by the instrument selected. The instrument used by Kelly and Floyd—the Bell African Self-Consciousness Scale (ASC)—contains items that seem to assess ethnocentrism and a feeling of victimization. Other measures of ethnic identity are focused on an internalized sense of identity and belongingness, without the rejection of other groups implied by some items from the ASC. The relationship of ethnic identity to marital adjustment may be quite different with the two types of instruments. The work of Taylor and Zhang as well as Kelly and Floyd suggests the need to assess spouses' ethnic identification and perceived discrimination. Discrimination may affect clients either by increasing external stressors that must be addressed or by leading to internalization of ethnic-specific stereotypes about gender roles or couple interactions that negatively impact the relationship.

As noted, empirical work on couples' intervention is already quite extensive (Baucom et al., 1998), and several empirically supported intervention strategies have been identified. However, there are no data-based demonstrations to support the efficacy of these approaches with ethnic minority couples or to direct therapists to desired modifications of existing interventions. In view of the range and maturity of the research literature on marital intervention, the field is ripe to assess how well existing treatment approaches generalize to ethnic minority couples.

CONCLUSIONS

Although there continue to be many unanswered questions regarding the processes and outcomes of psychotherapy, considerable research progress has been made in the past two decades. Progress can be seen both in the refinement of interventions and in accumulating support for their effectiveness. See, for example, special issues of *Clinical Psychology*, 1995, *2*(1); 1997, *4*(1) and the *Journal of Consulting and Clinical Psychology*, 1998, *66*(1). By contrast, the research specifically relevant to psychotherapy with members of ethnic minority groups is less well developed. The delayed progress seems to stem from both practical and conceptual impediments.

The practical obstacles to progress are fundamental: First, on the average, members of ethnic minority groups are infrequently seen as patients in psychotherapy. The remedies to this situation are probably beyond the purview of the typical psychotherapy researcher and require the use of public health strategies by national and local entities. These organizations need to encourage and support psychotherapy utilization by members of minority communities, as well as the training of providers in both public and private settings to encourage referrals of minority clients for psychotherapy and to retain them in treatment. The absence of minority persons in psychotherapy contributes to a second, associated dilemma: members of ethnic minorities are rarely participants in psychotherapy research trials. A psychotherapy investigator whose participants include a small number of ethnic minority members may confront the following alternatives: eliminating data from minority participants if discrepant; analyzing the data along with the majority group if not obviously discrepant; or simply deciding not to include minority participants so that the problem of what to do with the data never arises. Each option results in no information regarding treatment effectiveness with ethnic minority populations. The NIH Guidelines on the Inclusion of Women and Minorities in Clinical Research (1994) addressed this issue by requiring that NIH-funded projects include the target populations in a manner that will allow conclusions about the differential effectiveness of the treatment. This requirement will often necessitate oversampling, a challenging prospect in view of the fact that ethnic minority persons currently are not recruited in numbers proportionate to their representation in the general population. (For detailed discussion of this issue and of strategies for recruiting ethnic minority populations for psychotherapy research, see the special section of the *Journal of Consulting and Clinical Psychology*, 1996, *64*.) Until there is more extensive research participation by ethnic minority clients, however, no progress can be made in assessing general or differential effectiveness of various treatment approaches with different groups.

Conceptual obstacles to research progress in this area include difficulties in defining and measuring race and ethnicity and revealing their significance for psychotherapy research. Substantial attention has been focused on this question recently (Alvidrez, Azocar, & Miranda, 1996; Gray-Little & Hafdahl, in press; Phinney, 1996). It has become relatively common to decry the use of the word *race* as having excess biological implications and to embrace the term *ethnicity* as less likely to offend; however, the term *ethnicity* represents a mere substitution when used as a basis for self-labeling or assignment to a category by others. A potential response to this dilemma entails identifying the psychological processes associated with ethnicity. Definitions of ethnicity often refer to a sense of affiliation or belongingness to a particular group. From this perspective, both the person who is highly identified with Chinese Americans and one highly identified with African Americans can be described as high in ethnic identification; however, the entities to which they belong are quite different and the common label does not imply similarity to one another. An alternative strategy is to view acculturation to dominant societal values and attitudes as the operative process. If a generally accepted acculturation instrument existed, it might offer a common reference so that persons who are described as highly acculturated would be assumed to have common characteristics. Ethnicity can also be conceptualized as the experience that results from being a member of a social minority. Viewed in this way, the sense of being socially identifiable, of enduring social prejudice, and of internalizing negative stereotypes would be important considerations in research on therapy with members of ethnic minority groups. Acculturation, ethnic identification, and experience of prejudice are just three of the concepts that might profitably be clarified and studied for their relation to psychotherapy process and outcome.

If we were to create a list of suggested research directions, that list might easily recommend a duplication of the best of psychotherapy research for the past two decades, but with a focus on ethnic minority participants. Our review has left us feeling like the dinner guest who remarked that the food was disappointing and "such small portions." There are, however, several bright spots. For example, the conceptual clarification provided by Lopez et al. (1991) and the empirical work of Coleman et al. (1995) elucidate what is substantive and what might be artifactual in the extensive literature on ethnic matching. Research by Chambless and Williams (1995) provides a model for the type of controlled study that is needed to explore the effectiveness of specific interventions with members of ethnic minority groups. Research by Sue and Zane and their associates has laid the foundation for a much needed literature on the general effectiveness of psychotherapy with Asian Americans, while Szapocznik and colleagues have developed a research program on culturally sensitive therapy with Cuban Americans and other ethnic minority families. It is our hope and expectation that these and other programs of research will continue to develop and to help refine models of effective treatment for persons of varying ethnic and cultural origins.

References

Abramowitz, S. I., & Murray, J. (1983). Race effects in psychotherapy. In J. Murray & P. R. Abramson (Eds.), *Bias in psychotherapy* (pp. 215–255). New York: Praeger.

Acosta, F. X. (1980). Self-described reasons for premature termination of psychotherapy by Mexican-American, Black-American, and Anglo-American patients. *Psychological Reports, 47*(2), 435–443.

Acosta, F. X., & Yamamoto, J. (1984). The utility of group work practice for Hispanic Americans. *Social Work with Groups, 7*, 63–73.

Ahn Toupin, E. S. (1980). Counseling Asians: Psychotherapy in the context of racism and Asian-American history. *American Journal of Orthopsychiatry, 50*, 76–86.

Alexander, J. F., Holtzworth-Munroe, A., & Jameson, P. B. (1994). The process and outcome of marital and family therapy: Research review and evaluation. In A. E. Bergin & S. L. Garfield (Eds.), *Handbook of Psychotherapy and Behavior Change* (4th ed., pp. 595–630). New York: John Wiley & Sons.

Allen, A. M. (1992). Effects of race and gender on diagnostic judgments with the DSM-III-R. (Doctoral dissertation, University of South Dakota, 1992). *Dissertation Abstracts International, 53/05–A*, 1395.

Alvidrez, J., Azocar, F., & Miranda, J. (1996). Demystifying the concept of ethnicity for psychotherapy researchers. *Journal of Consulting and Clinical Psychology, 64*(5), 903–908.

Andersen, P., & Newman, J. F. (1971). Societal and individual determinants of medical care utilization in the United States. *Milbank Memorial Fund Quarterly, 51*, 95–124.

Atkinson, D. R. (1983). Ethnic similarity and

counseling psychology. *Counseling Psychologist, 2,* 79–92.

Atkinson, D. R., Furlong, M. J., & Williams, W. C. (1986). Afro-American preferences for counselor characteristics, *Journal of Counseling Psychology, 33,* 326–330.

Atkinson, D. R., & Gim, R. H. (1989). Asian-American cultural identity and attitudes towards mental health services. *Journal of Counseling Psychology, 36,* 209–212.

Atkinson, D. R., & Schein, S. (1986). Similarity in counseling. *Counseling Psychologist, 14,* 319–452.

Atlas, B. D. (1992). Premature termination in psychotherapy: The role of patient expectations and the intake interview (Doctoral dissertation, St John's, University, 1992). *Dissertation Abstract International,* 54/09B, 2186.

Baekeland, F., & Lundwald, L. (1975). Dropping out of treatment: A critical review. *Psychological Bulletin, 82*(5), 738–783.

Baucom, D. H., Shoham, V., Mueser, K. T., Daiuto, A. D., & Stickle, T. R. (1998). Empirically supported couple and family interventions for marital distress and adult mental health problems. *Journal of Counseling and Clinical Psychology, 66*(1), 53–88.

Beckham, E. E. (1992). Predicting patient dropout in psychotherapy. *Psychotherapy, 29*(2), 177–182.

Belitz, J., & Valdez, D. M. (1997). A sociocultural context for understanding gang involvement among Mexican-American male youth. In J. G. Garcia and M. C. Zea (Eds.), *Psychological interventions and research with Latino populations* (pp. 56–72). Needham Heights, MA: Allyn and Bacon.

Bernal, G., & Shapiro, E. (1996). Cuban families. In M. McGoldrick, J. Giordano, & J. K. Pearce (Eds.), *Ethnicity and family therapy* (2nd ed., pp. 155–168). New York: Guilford Press.

Beutler, L. E., Machado, P. P. P., & Neufeldt, S. A. (1994). In A. E. Bergin & S. L. Garfield (Eds.). *Handbook of psychotherapy and behavior change* (4th ed., pp. 229–269). New York: John Wiley & Sons, Inc.

BigFoot-Sipes, D., Dauphinais, P., LaFromboise, T., Bennett, S., et al. (1992). American Indian secondary school students' preferences for counselors. *Journal of Multicultural Counseling and Development, 20,* 113–122.

Boulette, R. T. (1976). Assertive training with low-income Mexican American women. In M. R. Miranda (Ed.), *Psychotherapy with the Spanish-speaking: Issues in research and service delivery* (Monograph 3, pp. 73–84). Los Angeles: Spanish Speaking Mental Health Research Center, University of California.

Boyd-Franklin, N. (1984). Issues in family therapy with Black families. *The Clinical Psychologist, 37*(2), 54–58.

Boyd-Franklin, N. (1987). Group therapy for Black women: A therapeutic support model. *American Journal of Orthopsychiatry, 57*(3), 394–401.

Casas, J. M., & Ortiz, S. (1985). Exploring the applicability of the Dyadic Adjustment Scale for assessing level of marital adjustment with Mexican-Americans. *Journal of Marriage and the Family, 47,* 1023–1027.

Castillo, R. J. (1996). *Culture and mental illness.* Pacific Grove, CA: Brooks/Cole.

Chambless, D. L., & Williams, K. E. (1995). A preliminary study of African Americans with agoraphobia: Symptom severity and outcome of treatment with in vivo exposure. *Behavior Therapy, 26,* 501–515.

Ching, W., & Prosen, S. S. (1980). Asian Americans in group counseling: A case of cultural dissonance. *Journal of Specialists in Group Work, 5,* 228–232.

Chu, J., & Sue, S. (1984). Asian/Pacific-Americans and group practice. *Social Work with Groups, 7,* 23–35.

Coleman, H. L. K., Wampold, B. E., & Casali, S. L. (1995). Ethnic minorities' ratings of ethnically similar and European American counselors: A meta-analysis. *Journal of Counseling Psychology, 42,* 55–64.

Comas-Díaz, L. (1981). Effects of cognitive and behavioral group treatment on the depressive symptomatology of Puerto Rican women. *Journal of Consulting and Clinical Psychology, 49,* 627–632.

Corey, G. (1990). *Theory and practice of group counseling* (3rd ed.). Pacific Grove, CA: Brooks/Cole.

Cuellar, I., Harris, L. C., & Jasso, R. (1980). An acculturation scale for Mexican American normal and clinical populations. *Hispanic Journal of Behavioral Sciences, 2,* 199–217.

Dana, R. H. (1993). *Multicultural assessment perspectives for professional psychology.* Boston: Allyn & Bacon.

Dohrenwend, B. S. (1973). Social status and stressful life events. *Journal of Personality and Social Psychology, 28,* 225–235.

Edwards, E. D., & Edwards, M. E. (1984). Group work practice with American Indians. *Social Work with Groups, 7,* 7–21.

Falicov, C. J. (1996). Mexican families. In M. McGoldrick, J. Giordano, & J. K. Pearce (Eds.), *Ethnicity and family therapy* (2nd ed., pp. 169–182). New York: Guilford Press.

Fenster, A. (1996). Group therapy as an effective treatment modality for people of color. *International Journal of Group Psychotherapy, 46*(3), 399–416.

Flaskerud, J. H. (1990). Matching client and therapist ethnicity, language, and gender: A review of the research. *Issues in Mental Health Nursing, 11,* 321–336.

Flaskerud, J. H., & Liu, P. Y. (1990). Influence of therapy ethnicity and language on therapy outcomes of Southeast Asian clients. *International Journal of Social Psychiatry, 36,* 18–29.

Fowers, B. J., & Olson, D. H. (1989). Enrich marital inventory: A discriminant validity and cross-validation assessment. *Journal of Marital and Family Therapy, 15*(1), 65–79.

Franklin, D. L. (1985, March). Differential clinical assessments: The influence of class and race. *Social Service Review,* 44–61.

Friedman, S., & Paradis, C. (1991). African American patients with panic disorder and agoraphobia. *Journal of Anxiety Disorders, 5*(1), 35–41.

Friedman, S., Paradis, C. M., & Hatch, M. (1994). Characteristics of African-American and White patients with panic disorder and agoraphobia. *Hospital and Community Psychiatry, 45*(8), 798–803.

Garfield, S. L. (1986).Research on client variables in psychotherapy. In S. Garfield & A. E. Bergin (Eds.), *Handbook of psychotherapy and behavior change* (3rd ed., pp. 157–211). New York: John Wiley & Sons, Inc.

Garfield, S. L. (1994). Research on client variables in psychotherapy. In A. E. Bergin & S. L. Garfield (Eds.), *Handbook of psychotherapy and behavior change* (4th ed., pp. 191–228). New York: John Wiley & Sons, Inc.

Garfield, S. L. (1997). The therapist as a neglected variable in psychotherapy research. *Clinical Psychology, 4*(1) 40–43.

Gaston, L. (1990). The concept of alliance and its role in psychotherapy: Theoretical and empirical considerations. *Psychotherapy, 27,* 143–153.

Gray-Little, B. (1995). The assessment of psychopathology in racial and ethnic minorities. In J. N. Butcher (Ed.), *Clinical personality assessment: Practical approaches* (pp. 140–157). New York: Oxford University Press.

Gray-Little, B., & Hafdahl, A. R. (in press). Factors influencing racial comparisons of self-esteem: A quantitative review. *Psychological Bulletin.*

Gray-Little, B., & Kaplan, D. A. (1998). Interpretation of psychological tests in clinical and forensic evaluations. In J. H. Sandoval, C. Frisby, K. Geisinger, J. Scheuneman, & J. R. Grenier (Eds.), *Test interpretation for diverse individuals* (pp. 141–178). Washington D.C.: APA Publications.

Greene, R. (1987). Ethnicity and MMPI performance: A review. *Journal of Consulting and Clinical Psychology, 55,* 497–512.

Gregory, M. A., & Leslie, L. A. (1996). Different lenses: Variations in clients' perception of family therapy by race and gender. *Journal of Marital and Family Therapy, 22*(2), 239–251.

Guanipa, C., Talley, W., & Rapagna, S. (1997). Enhancing Latin American women's self-concept: A group intervention. *International Journal of Group Psychotherapy, 47*(3), 355–372.

Hays, P. A. (1995). Multicultural applications of cognitive-behavior therapy. *Professional Psychology: Research and Practice, 26*(3), 309–315.

Helms, J. (1984). Toward a theoretical explanation of the effects of race on counseling: A Black and white model. *The Counseling Psychologist, 12,* 153–165.

Helms, J. E., & Carter, R. T. (1991). Relationship of White and Black racial identity attitudes and demographic similarity to counselor preferences. *Journal of Counseling Psychology, 38,* 446–457.

Hines, P. M., & Boyd-Franklin, N. (1996). African American families. In M. McGoldrick, J. Giordano, & J. K. Pearce (Eds.), *Ethnicity and family therapy* (2nd ed., pp. 64–84). New York: Guilford Press.

Ho, M. K. (1984). Social group work with Asian/Pacific-Americans. *Social Work with Groups, 7,* 49–61.

Hu, H. T., Snowden, L. R., Jerrel, J. M., & Nguyen, T. D. (1991). Ethnic populations in public mental health: Services choice and level of use. *American Journal of Public Health, 81,* 1429–1434.

Inclán, J. (1990). Understanding Hispanic families: A curriculum outline. *Journal of Strategic and Systemic Therapies, 9,* 64–82.

Jenkins-Hall, K., & Sacco, W. P. (1991). Effect of client race and depression on evaluations by White therapists. *Journal of Social and Clinical Psychology, 10*(3), 322–333.

Johnson, M., & Lashley, K. (1989). Influence of Native Americans' cultural commitment on preferences for counselor ethnicity and expectations about counseling. *Journal of Multicultural Counseling and Development, 17,* 115–122.

Kazdin, A. E., & Mazurick, J. L. (1994). Dropping out of child psychotherapy: Distinguishing early and late dropouts over the course of treatment. *Journal of Consulting and Clinical Psychology, 62*(5), 1069–1074.

Kazdin, A. E., Mazurick, J. L., & Siegel, T. C. (1994). Treatment outcome among children with externalizing disorder who terminate prematurely versus those who complete psychotherapy. *Journal of the American Academy of Child and Adolescent Psychiatry, 33*(4), 549–557.

Kelly, S., & Floyd, F. J. (1997). *The effects of negative racial stereotypes and Afrocentricity on trust and relationship quality within black couples.* Unpublished manuscript.

Kim Berg, I., & Jaya, A. (1993). Different and same: Family therapy with Asian American families. *Journal of Marital and Family Therapy, 19,* 31–38.

Kinzie, J. D., Leung, P., Bui, A., Ben, R., Keopraseuth, K. G., Riley, C., Fleck, J., & Ades, M. (1988). Group therapy with Southeast Asian refugees. *Community Mental Health Journal, 24,* 157–166.

LaFromboise, T. D., & Dixon, D. (1981). American Indian perceptions of trustworthiness in a counseling interview. *Journal of Counseling Psychology, 28*(2), 135–139.

LaFromboise, T. D., Trimble, J. E., & Mohatt, G. V.

(1990). Counseling intervention and American Indian tradition: An integrative approach. *The Counseling Psychologist, 18*(4), 628–654.

Langley, M. (1994). Effects of cultural/racial identity, cultural commitment, and counseling approach on African American males' perceptions of therapist credibility and utility. Summary. *Psychological Discourse, 25*(4), 7–9.

Lawson, W. B. (1986). Race and ethnic factors in psychiatric research. *Hospital and Community Psychiatry, 37,* 50–54.

Leong, F. T. L. (1986). Counseling and psychotherapy with Asian-Americans: Review of the literature. *Journal of Counseling Psychology, 33*(2), 196–206.

Lin, J. C. H. (1994). How long do Chinese Americans stay in psychotherapy? *Journal of Counseling Psychology, 41*(3), 288–291.

Lopez, S. R., Lopez, A. A., & Fong, K. T. (1991). Mexican Americans' initial preferences for counselors: The role of ethnic factors. *Journal of Counseling Psychology, 38,* 487–496.

Loring, M., & Powell, B. (1987). Gender, race, and the DSM: A study of the objectivity of psychiatric diagnostic behavior. *Journal of Health and Social Behavior, 29,* 1–22.

Lorion, R. P., & Felner, R. D. (1986). Research on mental health interventions with the disadvantaged. In S. L. Garfield & A. E. Bergin (Eds.), *Handbook of psychotherapy and behavior change* (3rd ed., pp. 739–775). New York: John Wiley & Sons.

Luborsky, L., McLellan, A. T., Diguer, L., Woody, G., & Seligman, D. A. (1997). The psychotherapist matters: Comparison of outcomes across twenty-two therapists and seven patient samples. *Clinical Psychology 4*(1), 53–65.

Malgady, R. G., Rogler, L. H., & Costantino, G. (1990). Culturally sensitive psychotherapy for Puerto Rican children and adolescents: A program of treatment outcome research. *Journal of Consulting and Clinical Psychology, 58*(6), 704–712.

Martin, T. W. (1993). White therapist's differing perceptions of Black and White adolescents. *Adolescence, 28,* 281–289.

McGoldrick, M., Giordano, J., & Pearce, J. K. (Eds.). (1996). *Ethnicity and family therapy* (2nd ed.). New York: Guilford Press

McKinley, V. (1987). Group therapy as a treatment modality of special value for Hispanic patients. *Internal Journal of Group Psychotherapy, 37,* 255–267.

Medvene, L. J., Mendoza, R., Lin, K.-M., Harris, N., & Miller, M. (1995). Increasing Mexican American attendance of support groups for parents of the mentally ill: Organizational and psychological factors. *Journal of Community Psychology, 23,* 307–325.

Minuchin, S., & Fishman, H. C. (1981). *Family therapy techniques.* Cambridge: Harvard University Press.

Miranda, J. (1996). Recruiting and retaining minorities in psychotherapy research (special section). *Journal of Consulting and Clinical Psychology, 64,* 848–903.

Mitchum, N. (1989). Increasing self esteem in Native American children. *Elementary School Guidance and Counseling, 23,* 266–271.

Mukherjee, S., Shukla, S. S., Woodle, J., Rosen, A. M., & Olarte, S. (1983). Misdiagnosis of schizophrenia in bipolar patients: A multiethnic comparison. *American Journal of Psychiatry, 140,* 1571–1574.

National Institutes of Health (1994). NIH guidelines on the inclusion of women and minorities as subjects in clinical research. Federal Regulation 14508–14513 (Document No. 94-5435). Washington D.C.: U.S. Department of Health and Human Services.

Navarro, A. M. (1993). Efectividad de las psicoterapias con Latinos en Los Estados Unidos: Una revision meta-analitica. *Revista Interamericana de Psicologia/ Interamerican Journal of Psychology, 27*(2), 131–146.

Negy, C., & Snyder, D. K. (1997). Ethnicity and acculturation: Assessing Mexican American couples' relationships using the Marital Satisfaction Inventory—revised. *Psychological Assessment, 9*(4), 414–421.

Neighbors, H. W. (1985). Seeking help for personal problems: Black Americans' use of health and mental health services. *Community Mental Health Journal, 21,* 156–166.

Neighbors, H. W. (1988). The help-seeking behavior of Black Americans. *Journal of the National Medical Association, 80,* 1009–1012.

Norton, I. M., & Manson, S. M. (1996). Research in American Indian and Alaska Native communities. *Journal of Consulting and Clinical Psychology, 64*(5), 856–860.

Oei, T. P. S., & Kazmierczak, T. (1997). Factors associated with dropout in a group cognitive behavior therapy for mood disorders. *Behavior Research and Therapy, 35*(11), 1025–1030.

Oggins, J., Veroff, J., & Leber, D. (1993). Perceptions of marital interaction among black and white newlyweds. *Journal of Personality and Social Psychology, 65*(3), 494–511.

Okazaki, S., & Sue, S. (1995). Cultural considerations in psychological assessment of Asian-Americans. In J. N. Butcher (Ed.), *Clinical personality assessment: Practical approaches* (pp. 107–119). New York: Oxford University Press.

Orlinsky, D. E., Grawe, K., & Parks, B. K. (1994). Process and outcome in psychotherapy—*Noch einmal.* In A. E. Bergin & S. L. Garfield (Eds.), *Handbook of psychotherapy and behavior change* (4th ed., pp. 270–376). New York: John Wiley & Sons, Inc.

O'Sullivan, M. J., & Lasso, B. (1992). Community

mental health services for Hispanics: A test of the culture compatibility hypothesis. *Hispanic Journal of Behavioral Sciences, 14,* 455–468.

O'Sullivan, M. J., Peterson, P. D., Cox, G. B., & Kirkeby, J. (1989). Ethnic populations: Community mental health services ten years later. *American Journal of Community Psychology, 17,* 17–30.

Paniagua, F. A. (1994). *Assessing and treating culturally diverse groups: A practical guide.* Newbury Park, CA: Sage.

Parham, T. A., & Helms, J. E. (1981). The influence of Black students' racial identity attitudes on preference for counselor's race. *Journal of Counseling Psychology, 28,* 250–257.

Pavkov, T. W., Lewis, D. A., & Lyons, J. S. (1989). Psychiatric diagnosis and racial bias: An empirical investigation. *Professional Psychology: Research and Practice, 29,* 364–368.

Payne, J. W. (1982). Contingent decision behavior. *Psychological Bulletin, 92,* 382–402.

Pekarik, G. (1991). Relationship of expected and actual treatment duration for child and adult clients. *Journal of Child Clinical Psychology, 20,* 121–125.

Pekarik, G., & Wierzbicki, M. (1986). The relationship between expected and actual psychotherapy treatment duration. *Psychotherapy, 23,* 532–534.

Phinney, J. S. (1996). When we talk about American ethnic groups, what do we mean? *American Psychologist, 51,* 918–927.

Pomales, J., Claiborn, C. D., & LaFromboise, T. D. (1986). Effects of Black students' racial identity on perceptions of White counselors varying in cultural sensitivity. *Journal of Counseling Psychology, 33,* 57–61.

Renfrey, G. S. (1992). Cognitive-behavior therapy and the Native American client. *Behavior Therapy, 23,* 321–340.

Richmond, R. (1992). Discriminating variables among psychotherapy dropouts from a psychological training clinic. *Professional Psychology: Research and Practice, 23*(2), 123–130.

Rieger, B. P. (1996). Client race and achievement, therapist cognitive complexity and egalitarianism, and white therapists' attitudes (Doctoral dissertation, Fordham University, 1996). *Dissertation Abstracts International, 57–10B,* pp. 6589–6722.

Rosado, J. W., Jr., & Elias, M. J. (1993). Ecological and psychocultural mediators in the delivery of services for urban, culturally diverse Hispanic clients. *Professional Psychology: Research and Practice, 24*(4), 450–459.

Saba, G. W., Karrer, B. M., & Hardy, K. V. (Eds.). (1995). *Minorities and family therapy.* New York: Haworth Press.

Sanchez, A. R., & Atkinson, D. R. (1983). Mexican-American cultural commitment, preference for counselor ethnicity, and willingness to use counseling. *Journal of Counseling Psychology, 30,* 215–220.

Santisteban, D. A., Coatsworth, J. D., Perez-Vidal, A., Mitrani, V., Jean-Gilles, M., & Szapocznik, J. (1997). Brief structural/strategic family therapy with African American and Hispanic high-risk youth. *Journal of Community Psychology, 25*(5), 453–471.

Santisteban, D. A., Szapocznik., J., Perez-Vidal, A., Kurtines, W. M., Murray, E. J., & LaPerriere, A. (1996). Efficacy of intervention for engaging youth and families into treatment and some variables that may contribute to differential effectiveness. *Journal of Family Psychology, 10*(1), 35–44.

Sattler, J. M. (1977). The effects of therapist-client racial similarity. In A. S. Gurman & A. M. Razin (Eds.), *Effective psychotherapy: A handbook of research* (pp. 252–290). New York: Pergamon Press.

Schinke, S. P., Orlandi, M. A., Botvin, G. J., Gilchrist, L. D., Trimble, J. E., & Locklear, H. H. (1988). Preventing substance abuse among American-Indian adolescents: A bicultural competence skills approach. *Journal of Counseling Psychology, 35*(1), 87–90.

Schofield, W. (1984). *Psychotherapy: The purchase of friendship* (2nd ed.). New Brunswick, N.J.: Transaction Books.

Schulte, D., Kunzel, R., Pepping, G., & Schulte-Bahrenberg, T. (1992). Tailor-make versus standardized therapy of phobic patients. *Advances in Behaviour Research and Therapy, 14,* 67–92.

Scopetta, M. A., Szapocznik, J., King, O. E., Ladner, R., Alegre, C., & Tillman, M. S. (1977). *Final report: The Spanish drug rehabilitation research project* (NIDA Grant #HB1 DAO1696). Miami: University of Miami, Spanish Family Guidance Center.

Shen, W. W., Sanchez, A. M., & Huang, T. (1984). Verbal participation in group therapy: A comparative study on New Mexico ethnic groups. *Hispanic Journal of Behavioral Sciences, 6,* 277–284.

Sledge, W. H., Moras, K., Hartley, D., & Levine, M. (1990). Effect of time-limited psychotherapy on patient dropout rates. *American Journal of Psychiatry, 147*(10), 1341–1347.

Snowden, L. R., & Cheung, F. K. (1990). Use of inpatient mental health services by members of ethnic minority groups. *American Psychologist, 45*(3), 347–355.

Speight, S. L., & Vera, E. M. (1997). Similarity and difference in multicultural counseling: Considering the attraction and repulsion hypotheses. *The Counseling Psychologist, 25*(2), 280–298.

Strakowski, S. M., Lonczak, H. S., Sax, K. W., West,

S. A., Crist, A., Mehta, R., & Thienhaus, O. J. (1995). The effects of race on diagnosis and disposition from a psychiatric emergency service. *Clinical Psychiatry, 56*(3), 101–107.

Strickland, T. L., Jenkins, J. O., Myers, H. F., & Adams, H. E. (1988). Diagnostic judgments as a function of client and therapist race. *Journal of Psychopathology and Behavioral Assessment, 10,* 141–152.

Sue, D. W. (1990). Culture-specific strategies in counseling: A conceptual framework. *Professional Psychology: Research and Practice, 21*(6), 424–433.

Sue, S. (1988). Psychotherapeutic services for ethnic minorities. *American Psychologist, 43,* 301–308.

Sue, S., Fujino, D. C., Hu, L.-t., Takeuchi, D. T., & Zane, N. W. S. (1991). Community mental health services for ethnic minority groups: A test of the cultural responsiveness hypothesis. *Journal of Consulting and Clinical Psychology, 59*(4), 533–540.

Sue, S., & Morishima, J. K. (1982). *The mental health of Asian Americans.* San Francisco: Jossey-Bass.

Sue, S., Zane, N., & Young, K. (1994). In A. E. Bergin & S. L. Garfield (Eds.), *Handbook of psychotherapy and behavior change* (4th ed., pp. 783–830). New York: John Wiley & Sons.

Sussman, L. K., Robins, L. N., & Earls, F. (1987). Treatment-seeking for depression by Black and White Americans. *Social Science and Medicine, 24*(3), 187–196.

Sutton, R., G. & Kessler, M. (1986). National study of the effects of client's socioeconomic status on clinical psychologists' professional judgments. *Journal of Consulting and Clinical Psychology, 54*(2), 275–276.

Szapocznik, J., & Kurtines, W. (1989). *Breakthroughs in family treatment.* New York: Springer.

Szapocznik, J., Kurtines, W., Perez-Vidal, A., Hervis, O., and Foote, F. (1990). One person family therapy. In R. A. Wells & V. A. Gianetti (Eds.), *Handbook of brief psychotherapies* (pp. 493–510). New York: Plenum Press.

Szapocznik, J., Perez-Vidal, A., Hervis, O., Brickman, A. L., & Kurtines, W. (1990). Innovations in family therapy: Overcoming resistance to treatment. In R. A. Wells & V. A. Gianetti (Eds.), *Handbook of brief psychotherapy* (pp. 93–114). New York: Plenum Press.

Szapocznik, J., Rio, A., Murray, E., Cohen, R., Scopetta, M., Rivas-Vasquez, A., Hervis, O., Posada, V., & Kurtines, W. (1989). Structural family versus psychodynamic child therapy for problematic Hispanic boys. *Journal of Consulting and Clinical Psychology, 57,* 571–578.

Szapocznik, J., Scopetta, M. A., Aranalde, M. A., & Kurtines, W. (1978). Cuban value structure: Clinical implications. *Journal of Consulting and Clinical Psychology, 46,* 961–970.

Takeuchi, D. T., Sue, S., & Yeh, M. (1995). Return rates and outcomes from ethnicity-specific mental health programs in Los Angeles. *American Journal of Public Health, 85*(5), 638–643.

Taylor, J., & Zhang, X. (1990). Cultural identity in maritally distressed and nondistressed black couples. *The Western Journal of Black Studies, 14*(4), 205–213.

Tinsley, H. E. A., & Westcot, A. M. (1990). Analysis of the cognitions stimulated by the items on the Expectations About Counseling-Brief form: An analysis of construct validity. *Journal of Counseling Psychology, 37,* 223–226.

Tsui, A. M., & Sammons, M. T. (1988). Group intervention with adolescent Vietnamese refugees. *Journal for Specialists in Group Work, 13,* 90–95.

Tsui, P. (1997). The dynamics of cultural and power relations in group therapy. In F. Lee (Ed.), *Working with Asian Americans* (pp. 354–363). New York: Guilford Press.

Vasquez, M. J. T., & Han, A. L. (1995). Group interventions and treatment with ethnic minorities. In J. F. Aponte, R. Y. Rivers, & J. Wohl (Eds.), *Psychological interventions and cultural diversity* (pp. 109–127). Boston, MA: Allyn and Bacon.

Velasquez, R. J. (1995). Personality assessment of Hispanic clients. In J. N. Butcher (Ed.), *Clinical personality assessment: Practical approaches* (pp. 120–139). New York: Oxford University Press.

Vessey, J. T., & Howard, K. I. (1993). Who seeks psychotherapy? *Psychotherapy, 30*(4), 546–553.

Wierzbicki, M., & Pekarik, G. (1993). A meta-analysis of psychotherapy dropout. *Professional Psychology: Research and Practice, 24*(2), 190–195.

Wood, P. S., & Mallinckrodt, B. (1990). Culturally sensitive assertiveness training for ethnic minority clients. *Professional Psychology: Research and Practice, 21*(1), 5–11.

Yalom, I. (1985). *The theory and practice of group psychotherapy* (3rd ed.). New York: Basic Books.

Yeh, M., Eastman, K., & Cheung, M. K. (1994). Children and adolescents in community mental health centers: Does the ethnicity or the language of the therapist matter? *Journal of Community Psychology, 22,* 153–163.

Yeh, M., Takeuchi, D. T., & Sue, S. (1994). Asian American children in the mental health system: A comparison of parallel and mainstream outpatient service centers. *Journal of Clinical Child Psychology, 23,* 5–12.

Zane, N., Enomoto, K., & Chun, C.-A. (1994). Treatment outcomes of Asian- and White-American clients in outpatient therapy. *Journal of Community Psychology, 22,* 177–191.

Zane, N., Hatanaka, H., Park, S. S., & Akutsu, P. (1994). Ethnic-specific mental health services: Evaluation of the parallel approach for Asian-American clients. *Journal of Community Psychology, 22,* 68–81.

CHAPTER 28

PSYCHOTHERAPY

WITH

OLDER

ADULTS

DOLORES GALLAGHER-THOMPSON
Older Adult and Family Research and Resource Center
Geriatric Research, Education, and Clinical Center
VA Palo Alto Health Care System
Stanford University School of Medicine
CHRISTINE MCKIBBIN
DARRELLE KOONCE-VOLWILER
ANA MENENDEZ
DOUGLAS STEWART
Older Adult and Family Research and Resource Center
Geriatric Research, Education, and Clinical Center
VA Palo Alto Health Care System
LARRY W. THOMPSON
Pacific Graduate School of Psychology

THE GRAYING OF AMERICA

Our nation's age structure is shifting. The aged, who once reflected a small proportion of our populace, are the fastest growing segment of society and represent a virtual population explosion. According the Bureau of the Census, the number of persons 65 and over increased from 3.1 million in 1900 to 33.2 million in 1994. Among these elderly living in 1994, 18.7 million were 65–74 years of age, 11 million were aged 75–84, and 3.5 million were 85 or older. These population statistics become even more staggering when population estimates are projected to the next several decades. By the middle of the next century, it is expected that the number of persons 65 and over will more than double (80 million) and even the oldest old, which is the fastest growing age group (Blazer, 1989), are expected to number approxi-

mately 19 million persons. This means that 1 in 8 Americans were elderly in 1994 and 1 in 5 could be elderly in the year 2030 (Bureau of the Census, 1996).

This *age wave* of older adults has been precipitated by a few demographic trends. First, the baby boomers who represent over 75 million births between 1946 and 1964 are reaching geriatric age. Second, the birthrate has declined and, therefore, there are fewer young persons represented in population statistics. Third, mortality rates have declined as people are living longer because of better nutrition, better health behaviors, increased accessibility of in-home care, and advances in medical care. Finally, the rapid

Preparation of this chapter was supported in part by grants #AG13289 and MH1910.

rate of population growth among the oldest old is largely due to medical advances, which have prolonged survival at the end of the age spectrum. This substantial growth in the number of elderly persons is expected to place a strain on services and programs available in the United States (American Association of Retired Persons, 1990).

Health and mental health care are two of several domains that will be tapped by current and future cohorts of older adults in the United States. Currently, there is a need for mental health services that target the elderly. Approximately, 15% of the 65 and over population are in need of mental health service and 20% of all suicides are committed by individuals age 65 or over (Butler, 1985). The need for mental health care is even greater among individuals with chronic illness or other psychosocial impairments. According to the National Institute of Mental Health Facility Survey and National Nursing Home Survey, almost 70% of nursing home residents have mental health needs (Burns, Larson, Goldstrom et al., 1988). Given the rapid increase in the numbers of surviving elderly, one could reasonably estimate that an inordinate number of older individuals will be in need of mental health services in the future. Therefore, it has become increasingly important to update our knowledge about the psychology of aging and mental health, in order to meet the growing needs of this population.

The purpose of this chapter is to review what is currently understood about effective mental health care for older adults. Specifically, we will review patterns of mental health access, issues pertaining to assessment of older adults presenting with physical and psychological symptomatology, preparation of older adults for psychotherapy (including barriers to treatment access or engagement), efficacy of different forms or models of psychotherapy with older adults, and limitations of our current knowledge so that future clinicians and researchers may begin to address these gaps and ultimately enhance quality of care for the coming wave of older Americans.

WHAT BRINGS OLDER ADULTS INTO TREATMENT?

It is generally not the case that an older adult will pursue psychotherapy as treatment in the same manner as do younger adults. This is due to the fact that many symptoms of psychological problems are comorbid with concrete medical symptoms; thus the general health care sector is the principal source for initial treatment. In most medical settings, older persons consult with a physician rather than a mental health professional, and are generally in search of a medical diagnosis for their symptoms (Haley, 1996). In fact, recently analyzed data show that more than 55% of older persons who used mental health care received this care from primary care physicians. In contrast, less than 3% of older individuals report having received outpatient treatment from mental health professionals (Olfson & Pincus, 1996). The result of this tendency to seek a medical explanation for psychological symptoms includes an increase in physician visits, medication use, emergency room visits, and outpatient charges (Callahan, Hui, Nienaber et al., 1994; Cooper-Patrick, Crumb, & Ford, 1994).

Older adults may present to their physicians with a myriad of symptoms that may either mimic or occur comorbidly with physical illness. Some of the more common of these symptoms involve those associated with the diagnoses of depression and anxiety, including complaints of poor memory or forgetfulness, physical fatigue or exhaustion, sleep disturbance, gastrointestinal complaints, and physical aches and pains (Newman, Enright, Manolio et al., 1997). Complaints such as these may be taken at face value and explored or treated as physical problems. However, many of these symptoms may reflect an underlying mental health issue in need of evaluation and treatment. At the same time we do not want to overlook the fact that many elders who are physically ill or frail are *also* clinically depressed (Haley, 1996) and therefore in need of treatment for both conditions.

Other factors also conspire to make mental health symptoms underdiagnosed and undertreated. Individual health care professionals often conclude that psychological symptoms experienced by older adults are a normal consequence of their physical illnesses and/or social and economic problems; this same attitude may be shared by the patients themselves (Lebowitz, Pearson, Schneider et al., 1997). Another explanation is that health professionals may perceive physical and cognitive symptoms as a normal part of the aging process, and therefore not inquire about the psychological issues that may have created the physical and/or cognitive complaints (Hendrie &

Crossett, 1990). The recognition of the role that psychological and social factors play in determining older adult symptom presentation is critical, given that the impact of untreated mental illness is significant, and often takes both a physical and financial toll. Older adults left untreated may experience further decreases in functional abilities, which ultimately can result in such negative outcomes as increased health care costs (Simon, Ormel, VonKorff, & Barlow, 1995; Wells, Stewart, Hays et al., 1989) or premature death due to suicide or other factors (DeVries & Gallagher-Thompson, 1994; Osgood, 1985).

ASSESSMENT ISSUES

It can be difficult to diagnose depression in older persons. First, older adults themselves tend not to label or describe their negative feelings as depressed but often report symptoms that are metaphors for depression such as complaints of worthlessness, demoralization, hopelessness, or despair (Blazer, 1994). Second, it is not always clear how to interpret behavioral and somatic symptoms of which older persons may complain. For instance, common behavioral symptoms (e.g., low energy, psychomotor retardation, and decreased pleasure in activities that were previously enjoyable) and somatic problems (e.g. difficulty sleeping, decreased appetite, and loss of libido) usually associated with depression may be due to undetected medical problems, or to chronic illnesses for which individuals are undergoing treatment, or to depression itself, or to some combination of these (Dick & Gallagher-Thompson, 1996; Futterman, Thompson, Gallagher-Thompson & Ferris, 1995). Given that the most common illnesses among older adults are chronic conditions such as heart disease, cancer, diabetes, and arthritis, which can in themselves sap energy, cause restless and disturbed sleep, and appetite problems, it is understandable that the symptom overlap can cause diagnostic confusion. Another complicating factor is the amount of either prescribed or over-the-counter medications that the elderly take, which can cause the same kind of depressive-like symptoms previously noted (Salzman, 1994). Given that the elderly have the highest overall rate of drug intake compared to other age groups, and that they commonly take two or more prescription medications at once (typically, cardiovascular drugs, analgesics, and antianxiety medications), it is not surprising that unintended adverse effects occur frequently,

including development of symptoms that mimic either depression or cognitive impairment (Schaie & Willis, 1996). In order to sort out what is actually occurring (and what is contributing to what), it is necessary for mental health professionals working with older adults to obtain written informed consent to communicate with the primary care physician, and often also with other specialists involved. While this may also be needed with younger patients, it is often optional or not really necessary; in contrast, it is an essential part of the assessment process with older adults.

Third, we and others have noted that, emotionally, older adults may present with a depressed tone that may be quite obvious to an interviewer, but will often be denied by the patient (Dick & Gallagher-Thompson, 1996). Unfortunately, the majority of older adults who are either clinically depressed or who have significant depressive symptoms (not accounted for by their physical health status) are not referred for treatment. This seems to reflect confusion about what constitutes an accurate diagnosis, as well as confusion of these symptoms with normal aging. Finally, the diagnostic process is further complicated by the fact that most of the present standards for diagnosis of depressive disorders were developed without considering the specifics of late-life depression. In our opinion and that of others in the field (e.g., Blazer, 1994), the current standard criteria for diagnosing mood disorders—namely, the Diagnostic and Statistical Manual of Mental Disorders (DSM-IV) (American Psychiatric Association, 1994)—are an imperfect fit to the characteristics of depression in older adults. This volume of the DSM has recently updated the DSM-III-R (American Psychiatric Association, 1987) with an expansion of the description and the range of Mood Disorders, but still with little attention to how these disorders present themselves in later life (e.g., dysthymic disorder, which is very common in older adults; Blazer, 1989). A similar point has been made regarding anxiety disorders by Palmer, Jeste and Sheikh (1997). More detailed discussion of this issue and specific recommendations for how to best assess late life depression can be found in Futterman et al. (1995) and in Pachana, Thompson, and Gallagher-Thompson (1994).

This omission of the specifics of these disorders in late life almost surely leads to underdiagnosis of geriatric depression, which in turn results in fewer patients being treated appropriately, despite the fact that a range of effective treatments does exist at the present time. This has led to a public health problem of considerable magnitude in that the most severe outcome of undiagnosed depression is suicide: suicide rates are the highest among older, Caucasian men, particularly those with chronic or terminal health problems (Salzman, 1994). Thus, mental health professionals serving older people need to ask directly about suicidal thoughts, wishes, and/or plans. A useful practitioners' guide to the assessment instruments available, as well as other methods for diagnosis of suicidal ideation and intent in the elderly, has been provided by Osgood (1985). In addition, Richman's (1993) volume on individual, group, and family therapy with suicidal elders provides a wealth of useful treatment information.

In this chapter we will focus our discussion on the topic of psychotherapy for later life depression, for several reasons. First, depression is the most common psychiatric disorder of later life. According to Blazer (1989, 1994), depression is the "common cold" of the mental life of older adults. While some studies have reported the prevalence of major depressive disorder to be under 5%, these epidemiological studies have been criticized for their lack of sensitivity to age-related issues that affect responses to a structured interview. These include unacknowledged sensory problems and/or cognitive deficits, difficulty admitting to depressive symptoms, and/or lack of adequate rapport established by the interviewer (Futterman et al., 1995). Blazer has shown that, in fact, subsyndromal depression (i.e., presence of significant depressive symptoms but not at a level to warrant a diagnosis of major depression) is far more common, being present in up to 40% of older persons (depending on what definition is used). Thus, depression is the most likely reason for an older adult to seek mental health services. The second reason we are focusing on depression here is because the interventions to be described are generally considered relevant and appropriate for the treatment of other mental health problems of later life, such as anxiety disorders and substance abuse, as well as depression. Finally, due to space limitations, we are unable to go into depth about these less common problems. The interested reader is referred to other sources for more detailed information, such as (1) anxiety disorders: Alexopoulos (1991), Beck and Stanley (1997), and Hersen and VanHasselt (1992); (2) substance abuse (alcohol and drug problems):

Dupree and Schonfeld (1996) and Liberto, Oslin, and Ruskin (1996); and (3) severe mental health problems such as schizophrenia: Marengo and Westermeyer (1996).

Returning now to a discussion of more typical assessment procedures for late-life depression, we will briefly describe several measures that we have found useful. It is crucial to begin with an assessment of cognitive functioning in order to screen for dementing disorders, and to evaluate whether or not the client has the cognitive capacity to participate in psychotherapy. We generally recommend administration of a brief evaluation of cognitive status such as the Mini-Mental State Examination (MMSE; Folstein, Folstein, & McHugh, 1975). This is a 20-item screening tool that offers general information about a patient's cognitive function and is both quick to administer and portable. Patients can score a maximum of 30 points based on their performance in a variety of areas of functioning including orientation, attention, concentration, recall memory, and ability to follow a 3-step command. Errors in any of these areas may indicate cognitive deficits, and suggest the need for further neuropsychological testing. Often depressed patients have memory complaints that mimic symptoms of dementia (discussed later in more detail); thus the administration of the MMSE can help in making a differential diagnosis. Furthermore, a treatment plan can be better designed within the framework of an older person's cognitive capabilities. The MMSE is generally regarded as a reliable and valid way to screen for cognitive impairment in older people (Braekhus, Laake, & Engedal, 1992). Recent research has shown that use of a single, standard cut-off score for all older patients causes problems with both the sensitivity and specificity of the measure. To address this concern, Crum, Anthony, Bassett, and Folstein (1993) have published population-based norms for the MMSE based on the patient's age and educational level; use of these corrected norms is recommended. A more psychometrically sound alternative to the MMSE is the Dementia Rating Scale (DRS; Mattis, 1988), which has a number of subscales that provide a more detailed picture of cognitive function. Although mental status screening can be helpful to develop a treatment program, at times it is necessary to obtain a more comprehensive cognitive assessment, as discussed next.

To assess depression itself, many mental health practicioners use the Hamilton Rating Scale for Depression (HAM-D; Hamilton, 1967).

Unfortunately, its use may be problematic with older adults, for several reasons. First, 9 of its 17 items are somatic in nature; as we have already pointed out, such complaints may be present because of actual (known or undetected) physical illnesses and/or may be side effects of commonly used medications, as well as truly be indicative of depression. Unless one is quite familiar with the patient's medical history and current status, as well as his or her medication regimen, responses to these items can be difficult to interpret (Thompson, Futterman, & Gallagher, 1988). Second, the original HAM-D contained no specific instructions for how questions were to be asked, which resulted in a lack of standardization in administration of the measure (Pachana et al., 1994). This shortcoming was addressed by Williams (1988), who developed a structured interview guide that provides specific wording for all the questions, thus leading to increased reliability and validity for psychiatric patients in general. Unfortunately, no studies could be found that demonstrate improvement in these areas when using the HAM-D with older adults (particularly the medically frail elderly). Finally, there are no norms for older persons (Futterman et al., 1995). For all of these reasons, we recommend its use with caution, and would suggest that a more comprehensive structured interview, such as the Structured Clinical Interview for DSM-III-R (SCID; Spitzer, Williams, Gibbons, & First, 1992) be considered for use with older adults. While it is true that there are no formal published data on the reliability and validity of the SCID for establishing psychiatric diagnoses in older adults, a number of clinical reports indicate that it can be used successfully and is well tolerated by older adults, particularly when choice is exercised in which diagnostic modules to administer (Pachana et al., 1994) so that the patient does not become overly fatigued from the SCID.

In addition to using a structured interview to assist in establishing diagnoses, we also recommend use of one or more self-report measures of depression. The Beck Depression Inventory (BDI; Beck, Ward, Mendelson, Mock, & Erbaugh, 1961) is probably the most widely used scale for this purpose. It consists of items assessing 21 (or 13, on the short form) different areas representing common complaints indicative of depression. Each area contains four statement of varying intensity, rated on a 4-point scale (from 0 to 3). Patients are asked to select which statement best reflects their belief about that area during the

past week. For example, the question about sad mood includes the following statements: (0) "I do not feel sad," (1) "I feel sad," (2) "I am sad all the time and I can't snap out of it," and (3) "I am so sad or unhappy I can't stand it." Advantages of the BDI include the ability to classify a person's score within varying ranges of the severity of depression, as well as the opportunity to track responses on each item over time, in order to assess progress. Also, the BDI directly asks about suicidal ideation so that assessment can be made quickly of possible suicide potential (Thompson et al., 1988). However, the BDI is not without its problems when used with older adults. First, it can be difficult for older patients to retain the four statements within each domain long enough in their memory so that they are responding properly. Second, older adults with low educational attainment may not really comprehend the meaning of all the items. Third, older adults with mild to moderate cognitive impairment may find that there are too many choices, and become confused and agitated. Despite these possible shortcomings, the BDI is reported to be a reliable and valid measure of depressive symptoms in older adults (Gallagher, 1986).

Many mental health professionals working with the elderly prefer to use the Geriatric Depression Scale (GDS; Yesavage, Brink, & Rose, 1983) as their self-report index. This 30-item (long form) or 15-item (short form) measure was developed partially in response to the difficulties of using the BDI and other similar, complex self-report scales with older people (Yesavage et al., 1983). Older adults can respond more easily to the GDS's yes/no format than to the forced-choice format of most other scales. In addition, the GDS focuses on the cognitive, behavioral, and affective components of depression, with deliberate omission of the usual somatic items. Items such as "Do you feel your life is empty?" or "Do you enjoy getting up in the morning?" dominate the scale. This measure is well tolerated by older adults who seem to appreciate its obvious face valildity. The GDS is regarded as a reliable and valid measure of depressive symptoms in older adults, and has been shown to be sensitive to improvement over time (Futterman et al., 1995). It has been effectively used to assess depression in persons with mild to moderate cognitive impairment, including individuals residing in nursing homes and in other types of institutional placements (Parmelee, Katz, & Lawton, 1992). Finally, the 15-item short form (Sheikh & Yesavage, 1986) has adequate reliability and validity as well, and is preferred in situations where limited time is available. Other psychometric properties of the short-form GDS are reviewed in Lesher and Berryhill (1994).

Regardless of their value, these assessment measures must not be used as the sole source of information. Assessment of depression in older adults must be an interactive and interdisciplinary endeavor, carried out within the context of at least one face-to-face interview that inquires about a variety of pertinent topics, including (minimally) the individual's educational, employment, and social history; his or her prior experiences with depression (or other mental health problems) and how they were coped with in the past; current social network and social supports; and of course, current medical situation and medication regimen. Suggested formats and questions to guide the conduct of such an interview can be found in Edelstein and Semenchuk (1996) and Zarit and Zarit (1998).

ADDITIONAL ISSUES IN DIFFERENTIAL DIAGNOSIS

As noted above, geriatric depression needs to be differentiated from conditions that often share common symptoms, such as health complaints and problems, medication side effects, cognitive disturbances, and grief reactions (Dick & Gallagher-Thompson, 1996). We have already indicated that many chronic health difficulties (e.g., heart disease, arthritis, stroke, or cancer) and a variety of commonly used medications may produce weight and sleep changes, somatic concerns, or depressed mood that may be either concurrent with the medical disorder or secondary to it (Ruegg, Zisook, & Swerdlow, 1988; Salzman, 1994). The interested reader is referred to Rapp, Parisi, Walsh, and Wallace (1988) for more detailed information on how to adequately assess the relative contribution of these particular factors to the presenting problem.

Symptoms of cognitive impairment (such as memory complaints and/or actual memory problems) may also accompany depression, both in the presence and absence of a true dementia. For example, a markedly depressed older adult's unresponsiveness and apathy during an assessment interview or a testing session often is viewed as evidence of cognitive decline when in fact that may not be the case (Kazniak, 1996). It can be helpful to observe the patient's style of respond-

ing to questions to assist in evaluating the responses. Depressed older adults will often respond with "I don't know" or will not try to complete an item or answer a given question, whereas demented patients will try to respond, although their responses will be incorrect (Wells, 1980). At other times, difficulties in concentration and memory may actually reflect a dementing process.

The assessment of dementia is a complex process. Mental health practitioners must be careful to not allow biases to operate here, and just assume that mild cognitive confusion indicates a dementing disorder; rather they must assess further (usually in collaboration with a neuropsychologist) in order to either rule out or rule in the presence of serious cognitive impairment (Albert, 1994). In addition, information regarding the course of the disorder, as well as the duration and progression of symptoms, can be useful in differential diagnosis. For example, most dementias are characterized by an insidious onset and a slow progressive deterioration, whereas depression often comes on more abruptly, with a distinct change from the individual's typical self (Wells, 1980). Depression is known to be common during the early stages of dementia—often as a reaction to the experience of cognitive changes—but it does tend to diminish as the dementia progresses. Because the assessment of both depression and dementia (when present simultaneously) requires skill, the reader is referred to other sources that provide more guidelines on this subject (Albert, 1994; Kazniak, 1996; Teri & Logsdon, 1994).

Recently bereaved individuals may also experience common symptoms of depression such as frequent, intense sadness; sleep and appetite disturbances; lack of interest in usual activities; and social and emotional withdrawal. Should these be considered indicative of a clinical level of depression that needs specialized treatment? Or are they part and parcel of normal grief, in which case they probably would resolve with the passage of time and adequate social support, in the absence of any specialized treatment for depression? This is also not a simple question to answer, and a full discussion is considerably beyond the scope of this chapter. The interested reader is referred to a comprehensive handbook on the topic of bereavement that includes several chapters on late-life issues (Stroebe, Stroebe, & Hansson, 1993). A few empirical studies also have attempted to address this issue. Breckenridge, Gallagher,

Thompson, and Peterson (1986) found that certain very specific symptoms distinguished between normal grief and depression in older adults (based on responses to the BDI and measures of grief intensity). Depressives were self-deprecating, generally guilty, and evidenced a strong negative image of themselves, whereas those who were simply experiencing grief did not endorse these particular symptoms. They more strongly endorsed feeling sad, having sleep and appetite difficulties, and being withdrawn from usual activities, but still basically having a positive self-image. Further research by this group found that when spousally bereaved older adults were followed for 30-months post loss, their responses to similar measures indicated that symptoms of depression abated over time, whereas symptoms specific to grief (e.g., thinking about the deceased, searching for meaning in the death, and reviewing past memories of that person) were still very common at that time (Thompson, Gallagher-Thompson, Futterman, & Peterson, 1991). Thus, older adults who have had a recent significant loss (such as death of a spouse or close family relative) should be assessed for *both* grief and depression. If both are present, it seems clinically prudent to treat the depression first, and then to encourage the individual to continue in the normal grief process. On the other hand, if the diagnosis is that of a normal grief reaction, then the individual may benefit more from self-help groups (e.g., Widow to Widow programs) and other programs specifically addressing those concerns. Unfortunately, there is very little empirical research on how depressed elders who are also bereaved respond to treatment over time. A recent study by Pasternak, Prigerson, Hall et al. (1997) followed bereaved elders who were also depressed and who were treated successfully for their depression. They found that symptoms of grief remained (despite improvement in depression), suggesting that these really are independent processes in older adults. More information on these and related issues can be found in a comprehensive book by Worden (1991).

To ensure that information about all of these different conditions that may affect an older person's affective status are interpreted accurately, we recommend that psychologists (and other nonmedical mental health care providers) work collaboratively with the older person's physician and other medical care providers (Campbell & Cole, 1987). Although this may seem like a great deal of extra effort, it is time well spent because there often are complex interactions present between medical and psychosocial factors that need to be understood adequately so that appropriate treatment(s) can be initiated. As Haley (1996) has so persuasively argued, psychologists need to become sensitive to the medical context within which much of the psychotherapy with older adults occurs. Until we move out of the traditional office and into the clinic, we often will not be able to provide optimal psychological services to older patients.

PREPARING OLDER ADULTS FOR PSYCHOTHERAPY

In the process of conducting psychotherapy with older adults, an important and often overlooked initial step is that of careful preparation for the overall therapeutic process that is to come (Gallagher-Thompson & Thompson, 1996; Zarit & Zarit, 1998). Older adults often may experience many unexpected barriers to their initiation and follow through with psychotherapeutic treatments. Identifying and addressing these barriers in a systematic way will help older adults prepare for the process of psychotherapy (Zeiss & Steffen, 1996b). Identifying and circumventing barriers is particularly important with older adult clients who often experience a complex array of obstacles that do not necessarily exist for younger patients. Attention to these obstacles is critical because, when left unidentified, they may result in missed mental health appointments, poor treatment compliance, and increased health care costs. In order to effectively ameliorate these negative outcomes, practitioners must watch for barriers that emerge from several domains including the older adult, the overarching structure of mental health care, the community, and the individual practitioner's attitudes or beliefs about the ability of older persons to benefit from psychotherapy (Knight, 1996).

Many barriers that prevent the individual and family from engaging in outpatient treatment are obvious and of a practical nature. These problems include financial restraints, which have been shown to lower attendance at both psychiatric and medical outpatient treatment; travel difficulties, especially for elderly and rural patients; and physical limitations. If an older adult with multiple medical problems is of low income and lives in a suburban or rural area, he or she will likely have difficulty mustering the energy to take a bus into the city and walk a block to get to his or her therapy appointment. In order to reduce these barriers, the practitioner must be prepared to go beyond traditional beliefs regarding therapy process and structure. The practitioner in this case may choose to secure transportation for the prospective client or consider traveling to the older adult's home to provide services. A report by Banerjee, Shamash, Macdonald, and Mann (1996) describes in-home delivery of therapeutic care to elders with depression. It is one of the only reports of its kind, yet in-home psychotherapy may be appropriate to consider for the truly medically frail elderly.

For many older adults, there is a stigma attached to seeking mental health treatment. It is quite common for older adults to have concerns about what engaging in psychotherapy might mean about them as a person. Many anticipate feelings of shame and embarrassment because they cannot solve their own problems and must rely on others for help. These feelings often co-exist with a lack of knowledge about what constitutes a mental disorder as well as what are the effective treatments available (Turner, 1992). The older adults may also carry prejudices and stereotypes about their own limitations due to their age. This ageism can add to the difficulty of seeking psychotherapy that is based on learning new coping skills and self-management techniques (Niederehe, 1994).

Finally, structural barriers within the mental health system may also keep an older adult from receiving appropriate treatment. These include both a lack of adequate reimbursement for psychotherapy services for older adults as well as a lack of programs designed specifically for the elderly, such as outreach programs and in-home services (Rosen, Pancake, & Rickards, 1995). In addition, a lack of interest and training in working specifically with the elderly can also be a barrier. Many mental health care providers do not have any kind of formal training in gerontology and geropsychiatry/geropsychology. Because psychologists are not ethically permitted to practice beyond the bounds of their professional competence, we have a bit of a *catch-22* situation in which more training is clearly needed first, so that practicioners can become adequately prepared in this field.

FRAIL ELDERLY CLIENTS

A special category of patients who experience multiple barriers to seeking and completing psychotherapy are the frail elderly. They have been defined generally as elderly persons (usually over the age of 75) who present with multiple physical and/or mental disabilities that interfere with their ability to function independently. It often is assumed that such clients are unable to benefit from psychotherapy of any kind. Recent studies have indicated that this perceived inability to benefit from psychotherapy is a myth and that certain types of psychotherapy, specifically cognitive-behavioral therapy (CBT), are effective treatments for depression and other affective disorders of the frail elderly (Grant & Casey, 1995). Grant and Casey also proposed in their review of recent literature that CBT is especially useful when medications are contraindicated for depression. This is often true in the frail elderly in order to avoid unwanted medication side effects (Rybarczyk, Gallagher-Thompson, Rodman et al., 1992).

Reminiscence therapy about family coping can be used to help elderly clients, even those with chronic illnesses. Reminiscence therapy is a form of life review in which positive aspects of one's earlier life are brought up for discussion, such as marriage and family, job accomplishments, or special occasions that were celebrated. These are used to promote positive affect and to help the frail older adult realize his or her many contributions throughout the lifespan. Because many people are now living longer with chronic illnesses, in-home therapy for the frail elderly and their families may be necessary, and may grow more common in the future. More and more studies have recently addressed the need of in-home psychiatric care, and are testing programs to establish their effectiveness. Banerjee et al. (1996) found that in-home psychiatric treatment was significantly more effective than primary medical care alone in treating the frail elderly. They recommended that practitioners abandon the notion that the frail elderly cannot benefit from treatment for depression. Palmer et al. (1997) reinforced this notion in regard to treating the elderly for anxiety disorders. Working with the frail elderly may involve more family involvement in psychotherapy as well as coordination of care. A number of studies have established the central role played by family members in coping with the frail elderly who have chronic illnesses (Rankin & Weekes, 1989). This will be a growing area of practice in the future.

In summary, in order to address the multifaceted needs of the elderly, a broadly conceptualized biopsychosocial model for both assessment and treatment is advantageous and often necessary (Knight, 1996). This approach becomes more or less comprehensive, depending upon the needs of the patient, and requires the individual mental health provider to rely on the perspectives and skills of professionals from a variety of disciplines, including general medicine, nursing, psychiatry, psychology, social work, and physical or occupational therapy. Moreover, this collaboration among professionals may take place in hospitals, psychiatric settings, and nursing homes; among providers in the community; or in any combination of these settings. For example, a mental health provider in a local county hospital may rely on a social work professional within or outside of that setting to conduct an in-home needs assessment with a particular client who would likely benefit from in-home services (Zeiss & Steffen, 1996a). Coordination of care among these varying professionals holds several advantages for mental health professionals and for their elderly clients. First, it may help ameliorate the stigma of mental health care because patients may be able to receive mental health services in the same location that they receive primary medical care. Second, mental health and other nonmedical professionals may be able to quickly and conveniently access needed medical information (e.g., health history, symptom patterns, or service utilization) by placing a telephone call to the physician or staff that may help in diagnosis and management of psychological problems. Third, mental health providers may also keep themselves apprised of changes in the medical treatment regimen that may impact their own treatment plans for the elderly patients. Each of these benefits contributes to the overarching goal, increased quality of patient care for our older adults. Following is a brief case study that illustrates some of the practical problem solving and coordination among professionals that is often required in order to engage older adults successfully in any form of psychotherapy.

CASE EXAMPLE

Mrs. G. is a 71-year-old Caucasian female who lives with husband, Mr. G., in a small coastal community. He is an 84-year-old Caucasian male in the later stages of Alzheimer's disease and also suffers from diabetes mellitus. Mrs. G. was initially referred for cognitive-behavioral group therapy for caregivers offered by trained mental health professionals in a community caregiver resource center. She was contacted regarding her participation, and although she seemed very open to the idea, she was unable to see past the many obstacles in her path. She presented to the clinician a total of four barriers that were preventing her from agreeing to attend group therapy. These barriers included no transportation (Mrs. G. didn't drive), no one to care for Mr. G. while she was gone, a lack of funds to pay for home care, and her fear/resistance in leaving him with a stranger whom she didn't know or trust.

Over the course of a few months, the psychologist running the group helped Mrs. G. address the barriers to treatment through a series of brief individual sessions and phone contacts. Through coordination with the social worker at the caregiver resource center, the psychologist arranged transportation that was affordable for Mrs. G. and was able to offer her money from a grant to fund in-home respite care for four hours on the days she was to attend the two-hour group sessions. With permission from Mrs. G., the psychologist coordinated directly with a home care agency to not only provide the care to Mr. G. but also to come out to the home for a pre-visit in order to allow Mrs. G. to get to know the agency worker who would be caring for her husband. This gave her the opportunity to directly address her fears about leaving Mr. G. home with a stranger. The psychologist also helped Mrs. G. enroll her husband in the medical clinic where she worked, so coordination with Mr. G.'s primary care physician could be facilitated as well.

Mrs. G. attended every one of the 10 sessions provided in this group. She also continues to meet informally with some women from the same group of caregivers, without the structure created by the psychologist. She now raves about the group and tells everyone she knows that he or she should attend as well. She also tells her story to others about how she was resistant and how the psychologist helped her by coordinating with other care providers to overcome the many barriers that prevented her from obtaining adequate help.

EFFICACY OF PSYCHOTHERAPIES FOR LATE-LIFE DEPRESSION

In this section we will describe several widely used theoretical approaches to psychotherapy and show how they have been applied to the most common presenting problems of later life (namely, the affective disorders). Included will be cognitive-behavioral therapy (CBT), psychodynamic therapy (PDT), and interpersonal therapy (IPT). We will emphasize CBT in this chapter because it is the modality with which we have had the most experience and the greatest success in our particular practice.

Cognitive-Behavioral Therapy (CBT)

As is well known, this category includes a variety of interventions ranging from the classic cognitively focused work of Beck and colleagues (Beck, Rush, Shaw, & Emery, 1979) to the very behaviorally oriented work of Lewinsohn (Lewinsohn, Biglan, & Zeiss, 1976). The perspective in most common use at present blends behavioral and cognitive aspects (in different proportions, according to individual clinical need). A particular variant, which we developed and modified, has been thoroughly described and researched by our group in a series of papers based on four different controlled clinical trials (and numerous published case studies) conducted over the past 10 years, with approximately 500 outpatients. These patients were primarily over age 60 and diagnosed with major depressive disorder, dysthymic disorder, or *double-depression*. They were seen as outpatients in a clinical research center in Palo Alto, California. Our results will be summarized below, following a brief description of the type of CBT that we use.

Conceptually, our approach took as its starting point a model first presented about a decade ago by Lewinsohn (Lewinsohn, Hoberman, Teri, & Hautzinger, 1985). This model integrates predisposing personality characteristics with current cognitive appraisals, reinforcement contingencies, and affective and behavioral responses, to explain the development and maintenance of depression. While it was not at all age-specific, it lent itself well to application with the elderly because of its emphasis on the interrelationship of events, thoughts, feelings, and behaviors. At the same time, Beck's basic theoretical approach was being refined and expanded. While he, too, recognizes these same reciprocal relationships, he places more emphasis on the role of cognitive appraisal and reprocessing (Beck, 1993), including the detection of biases in how information about oneself and one's world is evaluated, and the development of alternative points of view. Recently, Beck and colleagues have focused on the theoretical and clinical importance of linking specific dysfunctional beliefs to their underlying schemata, so that long standing personality patterns may be altered as well (Beck, Freeman, & Associates, 1990). Given the fact that the elderly typically experience so many unchangeable negative events (e.g., loss of spouse and friends; older children being too preoccupied to spend much time with them; and decline in income, health, and functional abilities), the emphasis on developing a more adaptive view of oneself and one's situation seems particularly appropriate. Of course, behavioral changes are usually needed as well, but these should always be processed cognitively so that their meaning and value can be ascertained.

The type of CBT that we do places primacy on the modification of dysfunctional beliefs, along with development of behavior patterns that will give maximum positive reinforcement. A number of specific content and process issues that are unique to employing this therapy with the elderly are discussed in the following sources: Coon, Rider, Gallagher-Thompson, and Thompson (in press); Dick, Gallagher-Thompson, and Thompson (1996); Florsheim and Gallagher-Thompson (1990); Florsheim, Leavesley, Hanley-Peterson, and Gallagher-Thompson (1991); Gantz, Gallagher-Thompson, and Rodman (1992); Rodman, Gantz, Schneider, and Gallagher-Thompson (1991); and Thompson, Davies, Gallagher, and Krantz (1986). A succinct presentation of adaptations needed to successfully use CBT with the elderly can be found in Thompson (1996). Note also that CBT treatment manuals for both therapist and client have been developed and describe this approach in great detail, based on a 16- to 20-session model of individual treatment. Both the therapist manual (Dick, Gallagher-Thompson, & Thompson, 1996) and the patient manual (Dick, Gallagher-Thompson, Coon, Powers, & Thompson, 1996) are available from the authors upon request. Finally, lengthy case reports can be found in Dick and Gallagher-Thompson (1995) and Gallagher-Thompson and Thompson (1992).

Briefly, several factors seem critical for maximizing the likelihood that CBT will be effective with the elderly. First, the older client needs to be socialized into therapy, meaning that the roles and expectations of both client and therapist need to be articulated, as well as incorrect expectancies elicited, so that a working contract can be established. Second, the therapist needs to recognize sensory problems (particularly vision and hearing loss) and cognitive changes (however minor) that can make it difficult for older adults to communicate in the therapy sessions, and tend to affect homework compliance as well. Third, the pace of therapy tends to be slower, as more time is often needed to learn and practice the specific techniques. In most other respects, CBT proceeds in a similar manner to what is done with adults in general. The high activity level of the therapist, the types of techniques used (e.g., recording dysfunctional thoughts, doing role-plays, and figuring out ways to challenge unhelpful thinking patterns), and the development of a maintenance plan for relapse prevention are done with older clients just as they are with younger adults.

A brief description follows of the results from four separate outcome studies we have conducted with adults over the age of 60, who were diagnosed with Major Depressive Disorder and no concurrent dementia. All four were randomized clinical trials, with therapy conducted according to specific protocols, with independent assessments done at specific intervals over time, and with therapy conducted by experts trained in the particular modality. The first study used a small sample ($n = 30$) comparing cognitive therapy with behavioral therapy and a relationship-oriented therapy. We found that there was highly significant pre–post change in all three conditions; however, those who received cognitive or behavioral therapy maintained their gains more at one year follow-up (Gallagher & Thompson, 1982, 1983; Thompson & Gallagher, 1984).

In the second study ($n = 109$), cognitive and behavioral therapy were again compared, but brief psychodynamic therapy (following Horowitz's model: Horowitz & Kaltreider, 1979) was used as the third condition. In the first part of this study, the active treatments were compared to a six-week delayed treatment control condition. We found that little change occurred in the latter over the waiting period, whereas those in the active treatment conditions had already begun to improve on various symptom measures by that point. In the second part of that study, the three types of therapy were compared, and results were similar to the earlier research in that patients changed to a similar extent in all three, based on pre–post assessments. This pattern held true for both one- and two-year follow-up data as well (Thompson, Gallagher & Breckenridge, 1987; Gallagher-Thompson, Hanley-Peterson, & Thompson, 1990). However, some differences emerged in the results, depending on whether or not a concurrent personality disorder was present

(see Thompson, Gallagher, & Czirr, 1988, for more details about the impact of personality disorders on CBT outcome in this particular study).

In the next study, CBT was used (representing a blend of the best features of each modality) in comparison with the antidepressant medication Desipramine, which was selected because of fewer anticholinergic side effects for the elderly (thus promoting compliance with its use). The two modalities were used alone or in combination in this three-group design ($n = 102$). Results were complex but, simply put, the combined condition showed some advantages over CBT alone, which in turn was superior to the drug-alone condition (Thompson & Gallagher-Thompson, 1991, 1993; Thompson, Gallagher-Thompson & Koin, under editorial review). Again, the presence of a personality disorder influenced results; see Gradman, Thompson, and Gallagher-Thompson (in press) for a more detailed presentation of these findings.

The fourth study focused on treating depression in family members who were self-identified as primary caregivers for demented older adults ($n = 66$). In this study we compared brief psychodynamic therapy with CBT (done individually) in an effort to determine which was more efficacious in the earlier versus later stages of the caregiving process. We hypothesized that CBT would be more effective in the earlier stages of the process, when family members are mobilizing resources and learning about dementia, and that the psychodynamic therapy would be more effective in the later stages, when grief and separation were key themes. Findings indicated just the opposite: short-term caregivers (empirically determined as those in the role for 44 months or less) responded better to the dynamic approach, while longer-term caregivers responded better to CBT—both in terms of short-term and longer-term (1-year follow-up) results. Interviews with participants after completion of follow-up revealed that later stage caregivers appreciated the coping focus of CBT. It gave them hope that there were still ways they could help themselves, despite the ongoing deterioration of their loved one due to dementia (Gallagher-Thompson & Steffen, 1994). Results from this study are among the first to empirically demonstrate that certain individual difference variables may be usefully integrated into a model to assist the clinician in treatment selection for future clients (Beutler & Clarkin, 1990).

Next, we will review data on the use of CBT

in a *group* format. Although the basic theoretical and technical aspects of CBT would appear to lend themselves to utilization in a group therapy mode (see, for example, Ellis, 1992), much less controlled research has been conducted on group as compared to individual CBT. Few reports could be found, in either the clinical or empirical literatures, about group CBT with older adults, with the exception of the work of Beutler and colleagues. The clinical aspects of selecting group members, doing pretherapy preparation, organizing time in sessions, dealing with homework problems, and dealing with alliance and termination issues are well presented in a book by Yost, Beutler, Corbishley, and Allender (1986). Results of a controlled clinical trial in which this method was used with 56 elderly individuals with major depression were reported in Beutler, Scogin, Kirkish et al. (1987). Briefly, they evaluated four conditions: cognitive therapy was used in combination with either placebo or Alprazolam compared to either placebo or Alprazolam alone. Patients who received group cognitive therapy reported significantly more improvement on a self-report measure of depression relative to non-group-therapy subjects, for both pre–post comparisons and at the three-month follow-up. Also, they were less likely than their counterparts to terminate therapy prematurely. From these effects, Beutler et al. (1987) concluded that group cognitive therapy can be effective in ameliorating subjective depressive symptoms. Recently our group prepared a review chapter on this topic, to which the reader is referred for more information (Thompson, Powers, Coon et al., in press).

Finally, we will close this section by mentioning several psychoeducational approaches that we developed, based on the CBT model, that we have chosen to implement in a group format. Although sometimes we refer to them as *group therapy*, they are just as frequently described as classes or workshops designed to teach specific cognitive and behavioral skills that are targeted for a specific problem, such as depressed mood or caregiving stress. Lewinsohn and colleagues pioneered this work with development of the "Coping with Depression" course for adults experiencing a unipolar depressive episode. It is available in manualized form and has been studied empirically by that group in several different investigations (though none focused specifically on the elderly). This class format was so well received by consumers that modifications were developed for special populations such as high school adolescents and Native Americans. In our center we developed a "Coping with Depression" class for mildly to moderately depressed elders (Thompson, Gallagher, Nies, & Epstein, 1983). We have since renamed it the "Increasing Life Satisfaction" class in order to highlight that we are focusing on the development of positive affect as well as the reduction of negative affect. We have developed both leaders' and participants' manuals for this class (Thompson, Gallagher, & Lovett, 1992) and have obtained feedback from many older adults who report that the manual is quite useful and user-friendly for their needs.

Recently, we have used this approach in several research programs focusing on the treatment of psychologically distressed family caregivers. Many report elevated levels of anxiety and frustration in addition to depression, yet are unlikely to use traditional mental health services because of the associated stigma. Further information about the rationale for use of a psychoeducational approach with this particular population can be found in Gallagher-Thompson (1994), and preliminary outcome data on its effectiveness can be found in Lovett and Gallagher (1988). In short, we found this particular class to be more effective than a 12-week waiting-list control condition, both for reduction of depression and improvement in life satisfaction, in a sample of both men and women older adult caregivers. Final results of the research, involving about 175 persons, can be found in Gallagher-Thompson, Lovett, Rose, Futterman, McKibbin, and Thompson (under editorial review). In general, a similar pattern was obtained, along with an increase in the use of adaptive (rather than avoidant) coping skills from pre- to post-intervention. A serendipitous finding of that research program was the observation that it was not feelings of depression, but rather feelings of anger (and angry behavior), that were quite prevalent in the participants. Thus, a new class was developed to address this issue, called the "Anger Management" class. We have just completed a controlled outcome study in which the "Increasing Life Satisfaction" and "Anger Management" classes were compared to each other, and to a waiting-list control condition, for their efficacy in reducing psychological distress in a sample of 169 wives or daughters caring for a relative with Alzheimer's disease or a related form of cognitive impairment. Preliminary analyses of these data indicate that participants in both class conditions showed marked reduction in angry, depressive, and anxious feelings from pre- to post-intervention (compared to the waiting-list group), along with an increase in positive affect and reduction of the perceived burdens of caregiving. Again, both leaders' and participants' manuals have been developed for the "Anger Management" class, and are available upon request.

A related interest of our group was in evaluating whether or not psychoeducational approaches (i.e., CBT in a group format) would prove to be both relevant and useful to family caregivers of various ethnic and cultural backgrounds. Because of our geographic location in California, and the particular interests of our staff, we chose to focus on Hispanic individuals as our first target group. We extended our caregiving research efforts to include Hispanic/Latino caregivers caring for an elderly relative with dementia or severe memory loss. Two studies have been done to date: one is completed and the other is ongoing at the time of this writing. Overall, we found that psychoeducational approaches are both well received and quite effective in improving the psychological well-being of Hispanic family caregivers. A review of the rationale and development of these programs can be found in Gallagher-Thompson, Leary, Ossinalde et al. (1997), and a clinically oriented discussion of our experiences can be found in Gallagher-Thompson, Talamantes, Ramirez, and Valverde (1996). Final analyses are being completed on the research data and will be available soon.

Returning now to the more general topic of the efficacy of CBT for the treatment of late-life depression, we would like to inform the reader about five separate review papers' of which we are currently aware that have documented the efficacy of CBT compared to a variety of comparison and control conditions for the treatment of affective distress in older adults. The first two reviews were done by Teri, Curtis, Gallagher-Thompson, and Thompson, and also Niederehe; both were published in 1994. That same year, a meta-analysis by Scogin and McElreath was published that reported a mean effect size of .78 for psychosocial treatments for depression (most of which were CBT or some variant), based on data from 17 published studies.

The next review and critique was done by Engels and Vermey (1997). Their work was a second meta-analysis of psychosocial treatments for late-life depression, based on 17 studies, of which only 10 overlapped with the studies used by Scogin and McElreath (1994). Using a more conservative statistical approach, they reported a lower mean effect size (.63) but did conclude that treatment was superior to either placebo or no treatment. Again, most of the studies included used CBT in some form as their active intervention. Engels and Vermey also concluded that individual psychotherapy was superior to group in terms of effects, though this conclusion was based on a very small number of studies.

The fifth and final review was done by Gatz, Fisk, Fox et al. (1998) and is extremely comprehensive and thoughtful, overall. The interested reader is referred to that publication for details of the studies included and the specific criteria used for their decision making. In brief, the goal of their investigation was to describe those treatments that can be regarded as either *well established* or *probably efficacious* for the treatment of various late-life problems (including depression). They based this on comparison of the extant data with the criteria developed recently by the American Psychological Association for documenting effective psychosocial interventions. For the purpose of this chapter, we will limit discussion of results to the topic at hand, and report, in a nutshell, that Gatz et al. (1998) found that cognitive, behavioral, and brief psychodynamic therapy met criteria for *probably efficacious* for the treatment of late-life depression. Neither one was superior to the others, and CBT as such (referring to a blend of cognitive and behavioral theories and methods) was not specifically cited. Nevertheless, these findings are quite promising and, taken together with the other reviews cited here, certainly support the conclusion that CBT will often be very helpful to older depressed people.

Psychodynamic Psychotherapy (PD)

Having their origins in the psychoanalytic formulations of Freud and his colleagues, there are many forms of PD that have been developed over the years. One of the first mental health professionals to describe PD therapy for older adults was Myers (1984). A few years later, Newton, Brauer, Gutmann, and Grunes (1986) published a review of PD therapy with older adults that pointed out a variety of different theoretical models that were being used at the time, within the overall psychodynamic framework. They pointed out that these models of PD therapy all shared some common features. All emphasized the importance of internal psychological processes in coping with stressful problems. Success in dealing with late-life challenges is dependent primarily on how early developmental issues were resolved.

And unresolved developmental features leading to early conflicts increase the likelihood of poor coping in late-life stressful situations.

It is noteworthy that, despite early beliefs that the elderly could not benefit from PD therapy, over the years a substantial number of psychodynamically oriented therapists have developed modifications in traditional models to render them more effective to treat common psychological problems of later life, such as depression (Myers, 1991). At present, the following are generally agreed-upon principles for doing PD with older adults.

First, most therapists who work within this framework argue that treatment objectives are different for older patients than for young adults, due in large part to the kind of problems confronting the older adult, such as numerous losses, fear of physical illness and pain, pronounced disability, and death. Second, the use of supportive strategies are readily accepted to help patients shore up defenses and improve self-esteem so that treatment as called for in the dynamic tradition can progress. Third, therapists often feel a need to take a more active role in the therapy process than they would in working with younger individuals, with a particular emphasis on attention to the solution of concrete, age-related problems that the patients are experiencing. Fourth, therapists emphasize the importance of focusing on the relationship to build a strong alliance, which in turn facilitates the reappearance of more self-perceptions in the patient. Fifth, parental transference issues are emphasized less to allow for focus on other transference issues, such as spouse, adult children, and other significant individuals. Countertransference issues more commonly involve therapists' unresolved problems with their own parents, fears of their own aging and death, and cultural stereotypes of the elderly. Sixth, therapists in this modality need to be more flexible than they are when working with younger individuals. For example, they may need to change therapy duration or time of meetings, and increase contacts with other family members who are involved with the patient. These and other modifications are elaborated in Curtis and Silberschatz (1986) and Curtis, Silberschatz, Sampson et al. (1988). The latter is a particularly helpful reference that describes how case formulations are arrived at when doing PD with older adults.

Typically, PD therapies for the elderly are usually 10 to 20 sessions, but this can be interrupted due to acute life crises (e.g., illnesses). These require the therapist to shift into a more supportive and problem-solving mode until the patient has successfully handled the problem and reasonably intact internal resources are again in evidence. As therapy progresses, most therapists place emphasis on the development of the patient–therapist relationship as a primary goal (Newton et al., 1986).

Clinical studies have reported techniques in this framework to be quite effective, but few empirical studies are available. As noted earlier, Thompson et al. (1987) compared one brief psychodynamic variant to cognitive and behavioral therapy in a randomized clinical trial of the effectiveness of psychotherapies for depression, and found that all three were equally effective in the treatment of major depressive disorder in elderly outpatients. Several case studies and empirical studies have been reported by Silberschatz and Curtis (1986; 1991), Lazarus, Groves, Gutmann et al. (1987), and Lazarus, Groves, Newton et al. (1984). In the studies by Lazarus and colleagues, very small samples of depressed outpatients over age 60 were seen for individual PD therapy, although no control or comparison conditions were included. Patients improved, as evaluated by independent observers. In both the 1986 and 1991 reports by Silberschatz and Curtis, outpatients without the concurrent presence of personality disorders responded well to their variant of PD, called control mastery therapy, after about 16 individual sessions. These authors concluded that although elderly patients may present initially in therapy as more rigid and defensive than younger patients, the severity of these characteristics is not so great as to preclude the attainment of substantial gains (Silberschatz & Curtis, 1991).

One particular movement emanating from the general PD approach to conceptualizing psychotherapy has received considerable attention for dealing with certain late-life problems. It is based on Erikson's theoretical perspective (1982), which provides a therapeutic strategy particularly suited to work with older adults. Erikson was perhaps the first psychodynamically oriented clinician to describe developmental tasks of later life. The final developmental stage in his model involves conflict between ego integrity and despair: individuals who attain ego integrity are those who have no major regrets, who are able to accept their lives as they were, and who are able to find meaning in their lives in the present, despite difficult circumstances or repeated challenges. Using this perspective, Butler developed the life review process (1963) as a form of psychotherapy that would enable the goal of ego integrity to be achieved. This strategy enables the patient to bring old, unresolved conflicts to consciousness that can be surveyed and re-integrated. Individuals can then take stock of themselves with the perspective of time, and come to terms with choices they have made in their past. This sets the stage for working through a process of self-forgiveness and forgiveness of others for past misdeeds. Life review can be accomplished in a variety of ways: through imagery, systematic recall of decades or events, and writing or telling one's life story. As one goes through this process, various positive and negative emotions may be experienced. Negative emotions can be worked through with the assistance of the therapist; positive emotions can be used to increase positive self-perceptions and to encourage the therapeutic work to continue.

Over the past three decades, this technique has received considerable attention, particularly as a tool to work with higher functioning elderly individuals. However, the Life Review method has not been widely used to treat mental illnesses such as depression, although its applicability seems evident. Typically, Life Review is conducted in a group rather than individual setting. Older persons share their stories with receptive peers who lend their support to reinforce the re-integrative process. One variation of this approach is the development of *autobiography groups*. These are often offered in senior centers or senior housing communities and are most often attended by the well elderly who want to gain perspective on their lives, but who are not necessarily suffering from any particular disorder. These and other variants are described in Disch (1988), who also provides a review of published studies indicating the effectiveness of the Life Review process for improving mood and morale. Results were generally positive, although few controlled empirical studies have been completed. One exception to this is the work of Haight who did complete a controlled empirical study with one-year follow-up (1988, 1992). He found a positive impact of Life Review on self-esteem, but no differential effects on depression. More empirical studies are clearly needed to draw firm conclusions about the effectiveness of this technique, particularly with elders who are in distress and seeking help.

Thus, in general the number of clinical studies supporting the efficacy of various psychodynamic therapies in the treatment of late-life emotional problems is steadily increasing, although randomized clinical trials are still needed for empirical validation. Continued outcome research may provide stronger endorsements for these therapies.

Interpersonal Therapy (IPT)

IPT emphasizes the role of interpersonal and social factors in the development and perpetuation of psychopathology. This approach was initially based on the work of Harry Stack Sullivan (1953), who held that mental illness resulted from inadequate interpersonal communication, that communication having been interfered with by anxiety. Current interpersonal theory recognizes not only how disturbances in interpersonal interactions can serve as the conduit through which psychological symptomatology develops but also how mental illness can impair an individual's ability to form interpersonal connections.

Derived from this broader perspective, IPT is a time-limited, present, and problem-focused, psychological intervention designed specifically to treat depression (Gotlib & Schraedley, this volume; Klerman, Weissman, Rounsaville, & Chevron, 1984). Given the significance of interpersonal factors in the lives of older adults (Hinrichsen & Hernandez, 1993; Hinrichsen & Zweig, 1994), IPT is well suited for the treatment of depression in later life.

IPT is conducted for approximately 12 to 16 sessions, each lasting about one hour. The goal of the initial sessions is to review the depressive symptoms, provide a diagnosis within a medical model, give the patient the sick role, and examine the patient's depressive symptomotology in an interpersonal context. Current and past interpersonal relationships are explored only as they relate to current depressive illness. This interpersonal inventory is aimed at identifying and examining (a) the nature of the patient's interaction with significant others, (b) expectations held for and by these significant others and whether these were fulfilled, (c) satisfying and unsatisfying aspects of the relationships, and (d) changes the patient wants in the relationships (Klerman et al., 1984).

General techniques used in IPT include the exploration of options, encouragement of affect, clarification, communication analysis, use of the therapeutic relationship, and behavior change techniques, including psychoeducation, direct suggestions, modeling, and role playing. However, specific strategies and goals for the intermediate sessions depend on the chosen problem area. Because IPT is a short-term treatment, it usually is focused on one or two of the following problem areas: (a) grief, (b) interpersonal disputes, (c) role transitions, and (d) interpersonal deficits.

Although the death of loved ones is experienced at all stages of the life cycle, it is more common in later life (Knight & McCallum, 1998). Grief becomes the chosen problem area of IPT when there has been a failure to progress through the various phases of the normal mourning process (Klerman et al., 1984). The goals of the intermediate sessions, therefore, are to facilitate the mourning process and to help the patient establish interests and relationships to substitute for what has been lost (Klerman et al., 1984).

An interpersonal dispute refers to a situation where the patient and at least one other significant person in his or her life have nonreciprocal expectations about the relationship (Klerman et al., 1984, p. 104). For older adults, conflict most often occurs with an adult child or spouse, with the potential for family conflict increasing dramatically when an older adult becomes a caregiver for a spouse that is chronically ill (Smith, Smith & Toseland, 1991; Stuifbergen, 1990). There are three ways that treatment of depression secondary to interpersonal disputes can progress. If it is apparent that the dispute is currently being negotiated, therapy focuses on calming down the participants to facilitate resolution. If the dispute is at an impasse, therapy focuses on reopening lines of communication. If it is determined that the relationship in question is irrevocably dissolved, therapy focuses on assisting the patient with mourning the loss of this relationship and in establishing new interpersonal connections.

Depression associated with role transitions occurs when an individual experiences difficulty in adjusting to a life change that also requires a role change (Klerman et al., 1984). This problem area is particularly common among depressed elders, many of whom have difficulty adjusting to changes brought on by retirement or compromised physical health (Miller, Wolfson, Frank et al., 1997). Goals for treatment are to (a) facilitate the mourning and acceptance of the role loss, (b) help the patient regard the new role more positively, and (3) help the patient restore self-esteem by developing a sense of mastery regarding the demands of the new roles (Klerman et al., 1984).

Positive and negative aspects of both the old and new roles are reviewed and feelings about the loss and subsequent changes are explored. Appropriate release of affect is encouraged, as is the development of skills appropriate for the new role.

Interpersonal deficits are chosen as the focus of treatment when a patient presents with marked deficiencies in social skills and a history of inadequate or unfulfilling interpersonal relationships (Klerman et al., 1984). This is both the least reported problem area among depressed older adults and also the most difficult to treat (Miller et al., 1997). Goals are to reduce social isolation and encourage formation of new relationships. Reviewing negative and positive aspects of past relationships is particularly significant, as is utilizing the patient–therapist relationship to identify and explore repetitive interpersonal patterns. Regardless of which problem area is chosen, termination of ITP always involves an explicit discussion of the end of treatment, acknowledgement that termination can be a time of grieving, and facilitation of the patient's recognition of his or her competence (Klerman et al., 1984).

Evidence from controlled clinical trials suggests that IPT is an effective treatment for both the acute and maintenance phases of late-life depression. Miller et al. (1997) reported a significant reduction of depressive symptoms in 81% of patients receiving IPT in combination with antidepressant medication. Mossey, Knott, Higgins, and Talerico (1996) found IPT to be an effective short-term intervention for treatment of subsyndromal depression in the medically ill elderly, reporting both symptom reduction and improvement in self-rated health. Reynolds et al. (1999) reported IPT to be highly efficacious when given on a monthly basis as maintenance therapy. At one-year follow-up, 50% of patients receiving IPT and a placebo medication continued to show absence of major depression as compared to 20% of patients receiving the placebo alone. Taken together, these studies support the growing body of literature on the efficacy of IPT for depression in later life.

SUMMARY, CONCLUSIONS, AND LIMITATIONS OF CURRENT KNOWLEDGE

It is our hope that these sections, reviewing three frequently employed forms of psychotherapy for late-life depression, have shown that efficacy data are in fact accumulating at a rapid rate. A variety of studies supports the conclusion that at least these forms of psychotherapy can be effective (in both the short and long term) when administered by trained clinicians, and when compared to other interventions such as placebo medications or wait-list control conditions. This should be very encouraging to the readers of this chapter and hopefully will stimulate additional research, using other modalities and more complex patient populations, such as the medically frail elderly and those with several comorbid conditions.

Despite this enthusiastic conclusion, there is still a great deal that is not known about older adults' responsiveness to psychotherapy. Some critical issues that remain to be addressed in the new millenium include the following: first, the development and careful evaluation of psychotherapies to treat distress among members of intergenerational families living together with at least one older adult included. This is becoming more of a concern for society as we see shifts in the composition of families, changing values about elder care, changing economic priorities, and increased incidents of family violence (Schaie & Willis, 1996; Zarit & Zarit, 1998).

Second, and perhaps most importantly, we must begin to address the psychological needs of an increasingly ethnically diverse population in this country. Within that issue is the related fact of continually increasing diversity of our older population, due to such factors as increased migration, variations in patterns of acculturation among different ethnic elderly groups, and the historical reality of racism and economic disadvantage for many minorities. These realities pose particular challenges to the psychotherapist—particularly one who is seriously attempting to work with elderly clients of various ethnic, sociocultural, and racial backgrounds. Although the literature on this topic is virtually nonexistent at the present time, the increasing ethnic diversity of the older population in the United States is a constant reminder of a variety of important facts that should no longer be ignored. According to the U.S. Bureau of the Census (1993), by the year 2020, ethnic minority elders, including American Indian/Alaska Native, Asian/Pacific Islander, Black, and Hispanic, are projected to make up more than 22% of the older American population. This will be particularly noticeable in states such as California, where the projections are even higher. The lack of systematic research that is oriented to the study of different ethnic elderly groups, and subsequently the growing concern among health care providers serving these populations, clearly indicate the need for culturally and linguistically sensitive tools and techniques for the appropriate assessment of their psychosocial needs and for more competent professional services and therapeutic interventions.

If we now focus on the literature that exists about assessment and treatment of depression in ethnic minority elders, we find very few studies. Arean and Miranda (1996) reported on treatment outcome among disadvantaged elderly seen in a large public hospital. Treatment consisted of individual or group CBT; although patients were not randomly assigned to treatments, they were reassessed after 16 weeks. Many were Spanish speaking, and some were monolingual, requiring services to be administered in Spanish. This was possible at that facility because of the nature of the available staff there. The authors found that substantial improvement occurred in self-reported depression for patients in both treatment conditions. Furthermore, they found no differences in responsiveness by ethnicity (about 25% of the patients were White, 25% were Black, and about 40% were Hispanic, of the total sample of 182 participants). The authors concluded that their findings demonstrate that depression in medically ill, elderly minority patients can be effectively treated with psychosocial interventions based on CBT.

Besides treatment of late-life depression, clinical researchers who work in the field of geropsychology or geropsychiatry are very interested in evaluating the efficacy of interventions (including different forms of psychotherapy) to assist dementia victims and their family caregivers. Based on invited presentations at a regional conference held several years ago, Yeo and Gallagher-Thompson (1996) edited a volume on ethnicity and the dementias that included a good deal of clinical material useful for working with patients and families of different ethnic backgrounds who are confronted with a dementing disorder. However, few of the chapters reported any empirical studies or controlled outcome research. This paucity of research is astonishing, given the public health implications of increasing rates of dementia as older adults live longer—including ethnic elders, whose lifespans are generally increasing.

Part of the difficulty lies in recruiting and retaining ethnic elders in clinical research. Arean and Gallagher-Thompson (1996) describe numerous barriers to research participation for ethnic elders and their family members. Besides some of the more obvious ones, such as language and educational differences that may make it difficult for the older adult to appropriately participate in either psychological assessment or any kind of psychotherapy, there are other, more subtle barriers, such as lack of trust in health care professionals and their methods of healing. Landrine and Klonoff (1992) were among the first psychologists to write about how health beliefs and practices vary across cultures, and how these beliefs in turn influence behavior—particularly help-seeking behavior. Their paper is valuable in that it is a clear reminder of the dangers of assuming that one's worldview about mental health problems and their treatment is held the same by patients of substantially different ethnic and cultural backgrounds. Clearly, considerably more clinically based and clinically relevant research is needed on these and related topics, so that we as clinicians will become better prepared to treat the mental health needs of the ever-growing population of older adults in this country in the 21st century.

REFERENCES

Albert, M. (1994). Brief assessments of cognitive function in the elderly. In M. P. Lawton & J. Teresi (Eds.), *Annual review of gerontology and geriatrics* (Vol. 14, pp. 93–106). New York: Springer.

Alexopoulos, G. S. (1991). Anxiety and depression in the elderly. In C. Salzman & B. D. Lebowitz (Eds.), *Anxiety in the elderly* (pp. 63–77). New York: Springer.

American Association of Retired Persons (1990). *A profile of older Americans*. Washington, D.C.: Author.

American Psychiatric Association (1987). *Diagnostic and statistical manual of mental disorders-III-R* (3rd ed., rev.). Washington, D.C.: Author.

American Psychiatric Association (1994). *Diagnostic and statistical manual of mental disorders-IV* (4th ed., rev.). Washington, D. C.: Author.

Arean, P., & Gallagher-Thompson, D. (1996). Issues and recommendation for the recruitment and retention of older ethnic minority adults into clinical research. *Journal of Consulting and Clinical Psychology, 64*, 875–880.

Arean, P., & Miranda, J. (1996). The treatment of depression in elderly primary care patients: A naturalistic study. *Journal of Clinical Geropsychology, 2*, 153–160.

Banerjee, S., Shamash, K., Macdonald, A. J., & Mann, A. H. (1996). Randomized controlled trial of effect of intervention by psychogeriatric team on depression in frail elderly people at home. *British Medical Journal, 313*, 1058–1061.

Beck, A. T. (1993). Cognitive therapy: Past, present and future. *Journal of Consulting and Clinical Psychology, 61*, 194–198.

Beck, A. T., Freeman, A. and Associates (1990). *Cognitive therapy of personality disorders*. New York: Guilford Press.

Beck, A. T., Rush, J., Shaw, B., & Emery, G. (1979). *Cognitive therapy of depression*. New York: Guilford Press.

Beck, A. T., Ward, C. H., Mendelson, M., Mock, J., & Erbaugh, J. (1961). An inventory for measuring depression. *Archives of General Psychiatry, 4*, 561–571.

Beck, J. G., & Stanley, M. A. (1997). Anxiety disorders in the elderly: The emerging role of behavior therapy. *Behavior Therapy, 28*, 83–100.

Beutler, L. E., & Clarkin, J. F. (1990). *Systematic treatment selection: Toward targeted therapeutic interventions*. New York: Brunner/Mazel.

Beutler, L. E., Scogin, F., Kirkish, P., Schretlen, D., Corbishley, A., Hamblin, D., Meredith, K., Potter, R., Bamford, C. R., & Levenson, A. I. (1987). Group cognitive therapy and Alprazolam in the treatment of depression in older adults. *Journal of Consulting and Clinical Psychology, 55*, 550–556.

Blazer, D. (1989). The epidemiology of psychiatric disorders in late life. In E. W. Busse & D. G. Blazer (Eds.), *Geriatric psychiatry* (pp. 235–260). Washington D.C.: American Psychiatric Association Press.

Blazer, D. (1994). Epidemiology of late-life depression. In L. Schneider, C. F. Reynolds, B. Lebowitz, & A. Friedhoff (Eds.), *Diagnosis and treatment of depression in late life* (pp. 9–19). Washington, D.C.: American Psychiatric Association. Press.

Braekhus, A., Laake, K., & Engedal, K. (1987). The Mini-Mental State Examination: Identifying the most efficient variables for detecting cognitive impairment in the elderly. *Journal of the American Geriatric Society, 40*, 1139–1145.

Breckenridge, J. N., Gallagher, D., Thompson, L. W., & Peterson, J. (1986). Characteristic depressive symptoms of elder bereaved. *Journal of Gerontology, 41*, 163–168.

Bureau of the Census (1996). U.S. Department of Commerce, Economics and Statistics Administration. *Sixty-five plus in the United States* (Current Population Reports, Special Studies P. 23–190). Washington, D.C.: U.S. Government Printing Office.

Burns, B., Larson, D., Goldstrom, I., Johnson, W.,

Taube, E., Miller, N., & Mathis, E. (1988). Mental disorder among nursing home patients: Preliminary findings form the National Nursing Home Survey Pretest. *International Journal of Geriatric Psychiatry, 3*, 27–35.

Butler, R. N. (1963). The life review: An interpretation of reminiscence in the aged. *Psychiatry, 26*, 65–76.

Butler, R. N. (1985). Geriatric psychiatry. In H. I. Kaplan & B. J. Saddock (Eds.), *Comprehensive textbook of psychiatry/IV.* (4th ed., pp. 1953–1959). Baltimore: Williams & Wilkins.

Callahan, C., Hui, S., Nienaber, N., Musick, B., & Tierney, W. (1994). Longitudinal study of depression and health services use among elderly primary care patients. *Journal of the American Geriatric Society, 42*, 833–838.

Campbell, L., & Cole, K. (1987). Geriatric assessment teams. *Clinical Geriatric Medicine, 3*, 99–110.

Coon, D., Rider, K., Gallagher-Thompson, D., & Thompson, L. W. (in press). Cognitive-behavioral therapy for late-life affective disorders. In M. Duffy (Ed.), *Handbook of psychotherapy with older adults*. New York: John Wiley & Sons.

Cooper-Patrick, L., Crum, R., & Ford, D. (1994). Characteristics of patients with major depression who receive care in medical and specialty health settings. *Medical Care, 32*, 15–24.

Crum, R. M., Anthony, J. C., Bassett, S. S., & Folstein, M. F. (1993). Population-based norms for the Mini-Mental State Examination by age and educational level. *Journal of the American Medical Association, 269*, 2386–2391.

Curtis, J. T., & Silberschatz, G. (1986). Clinical implications of research on brief dynamic psychotherapy: I. Formulating the patient's problems and goals. *Psychoanalytic Psychology, 3*, 13–25.

Curtis, J. T., Silberschatz, G., Sampson, H., Weiss, J., & Rosenberg, S. E. (1988). Developing reliable psychodynamic case formulations: An illustration of the planned diagnosis method. *Psychotherapy, 25*, 256–265.

DeVries, H., & Gallagher-Thompson, D. (1994). Crises with geriatric patients. In F. Dattilio & A. Freeman (Eds.), *Cognitive-behavior therapy and crisis intervention* (pp. 200–218). New York: Guilford Press.

Dick, L., & Gallagher-Thompson, D. (1995). Cognitive therapy with the core beliefs of a distressed lonely caregiver. *Journal of Cognitive Psychotherapy: An International Quarterly, 9*, 215–227.

Dick, L., & Gallagher-Thompson, D. (1996). Assessment and treatment of late-life depression. In M. Hersen & V. B. Van Hasselt (Eds.), *Psychological treatment of older adults: An introductory textbook* (pp. 181–208). New York: Plenum.

Dick, L., Gallagher-Thompson, D., Coon, D., Powers, D., & Thompson, L. W. (1996). *Cognitive-behavioral therapy for late-life depression: A patient's manual*. Stanford, CA: VA Palo Alto Health Care System and Stanford University.

Dick, L., Gallagher-Thompson, D., & Thompson, L. W. (1996). Cognitive-behavioral therapy for older adults. In B. Woods (Ed.), *Handbook of the clinical psychology of aging* (pp. 509–544). Chichester, England: John Wiley & Sons.

Disch, R. (Ed.). (1988). Twenty-five years of the life review: Theoretical and practical considerations (Special issue). *Journal of Gerontological Social Work, 12*, 1–148.

Dupree, L. W., & Schonfeld, L. (1996). Substance abuse. In M. Hersen & V. B. Van Hasselt (Eds.), *Psychological treatment of older adults: An introductory textbook* (pp. 281–297). New York: Plenum.

Edelstein, B. A., & Semenchuk, E. M. (1996). Interviewing older adults. In L. L. Carstensen, B. A. Edelstein, & L. Dornbrand (Eds.), *The practical handbook of clinical gerontology* (pp. 153–173). Thousand Oaks, CA: SAGE Publications.

Ellis, A. (1992). Group rationale-emotive and cognitive-behavior therapy. *International Journal of Group Psychotherapy, 42*, 63–80.

Engels, G. I., & Vermey, M. (1997). Efficacy of nonmedical treatments of depression in elders: A quantitative analysis. *Journal of Clinical Geropsychology, 3*, 17–35.

Erikson, E. H. (1982). *The life cycle completed: A review*. New York: Norton Publishing Co.

Folstein, M. F., Folstein, S. E., & McHugh, P. R. (1975). "Mini-mental state": A practical method for grading the cognitive state of patients for the clinician. *Journal of Psychiatric Research, 12*, 189–198.

Florsheim, M. J., & Gallagher-Thompson, D. (1990). Cognitive-behavioral treatment of atypical bereavement: A case study. *Clinical Gerontologist, 10*(2), 73–76.

Florsheim, M. J., Leavesley, G., Hanley-Petersen, P., & Gallagher-Thompson, D. (1991). An expansion of the A-B-C approach to cognitive/behavioral therapy. *Clinical Gerontologist, 10*(4), 65–69.

Futterman, A., Thompson, L. W., Gallagher-Thompson, D., & Ferris, R. (1995). Depression in later life. In E. Beckham & R. Leber (Eds.), *Handbook of depression: Treatment, assessment and research* (2nd ed., pp. 494–525). New York: Guilford Press.

Gallagher, D. (1986). The Beck Depression Inventory and older adults: Review of its development and utility. *Clinical Gerontologist, 5*, 149–163.

Gallagher, D., & Thompson, L. (1982). Treatment of major depressive disorder in older adult outpatients with brief psychotherapies. *Psychotherapy: Theory, Research and Practice, 19*, 482–490.

Gallagher, D., & Thompson, L. (1983). Effectiveness of psychotherapy for both endogenous and nonendogenous depression in older adult outpatients. *Journal of Gerontology, 38*(6), 707–712.

Gallagher-Thompson, D. (1994). Clinical intervention strategies for distressed family caregivers: Rationale and development of psychoeducational approaches. In E. Light, G. Niederele, & B. Lebowitz (Eds.), *Stress effects on family caregivers of Alzheimer's patients* (pp. 260–277). New York: Springer.

Gallagher-Thompson, D., Coon, D., Rivera, P., Powers, D., & Zeiss, A. (1998). Family caregiving: Stress, coping and intervention. In M. Hersen & V. B. Van Hasselt (Eds.), *Handbook of clinical geropsychology* (pp. 469–494). New York: Plenum Press.

Gallagher-Thompson, D., & DeVries, H. (1994). "Coping with Frustration" classes: Development and preliminary outcomes with women who care for relatives with dementia. *The Gerontologist: Practice Concepts Section, 34*, 548–552.

Gallagher-Thompson, D., Hanley-Peterson, P., & Thompson, L. W. (1990). Maintenance of gains versus relapse following brief psychotherapy for depression. *Journal of Consulting and Clinical Psychology, 58*, 371–374.

Gallagher-Thompson, D., Leary, M., Ossinalde, C., Romero, J. J., Wald, M., & Fernandez-Gamarra, E. (1997). Hispanic caregivers of older adults with dementia. Cultural issues in outreach and intervention. *Group: Journal of the Eastern Group Psychotherapy Society, 21*, 211–232.

Gallagher-Thompson, D., Lovett, S., Rose, J., Futterman, A., McKibbin, C., & Thompson, L. W. (under review). The impact of psychoeducational interventions on distressed family caregivers. *Journal of Clinical Gerontology*.

Gallagher-Thompson, D., & Steffen, A. (1994). Comparative effectiveness of cognitive-behavioral and brief psychodynamic psychotherapies for the treatment of depression in family caregivers. *Journal of Consulting and Clinical Psychology, 62*, 543–549.

Gallagher-Thompson, D., Talamantes, M., Ramirez, R., & Valverde, I. (1996). Service delivery issues and recommendations for working with Mexican American family caregivers. In G. Yeo & D. Gallagher-Thompson (Eds.), *Ethnicity and the dementias* (pp. 137–152). Washington, D.C.: Taylor & Francis Publishing Co.

Gallagher-Thompson, D., & Thompson, L. W. (1992). The older adult. In A. Freeman & F. Dattilio (Eds.), *Comprehensive casebook of cognitive-behavior therapy* (pp. 193–200). New York: Plenum Publishing Company.

Gallagher-Thompson, D., & Thompson, L. W. (1996). Applying cognitive behavior therapy to the common psychological problems of later life. In S. Zarit & B. Knight (Eds.), *Psychotherapy and aging: Effective interventions with older adults* (pp. 61–82). Washington, D.C.: American Psychological Association Press.

Gantz, F., Gallagher-Thompson, D., & Rodman, J. (1992). Cognitive-behavioral facilitation of inhibited grief. In A. Freeman and F. Dattilio (Eds.), *Comprehensive casebook of cognitive-behavior therapy* (pp. 201–207). New York: Plenum Publishing Company.

Gatz, M., Fiske, A., Fox, L., Kaskie, B., Kasl-Godley, J. E., McCallum, T. J., & Wetherell, J. E. (1998). Empirically validated psychological treatments for older adults. *Journal of Mental Health and Aging, 4*, 9–46.

Gradman, T. J., Thompson, L. W., & Gallagher-Thompson, D. (in press). Personality disorders and treatment outcome. In E. Rosowsky, R. Abrams, & R. Zweig (Eds.), *Personality in later life*. Hillsdale, NJ: Lawrence Erlbaum.

Grant, R. W., & Casey, D. A. (1995). Adapting cognitive-behavioral therapy for the frail elderly. *International Psychogeriatrics, 7*, 561–571.

Haight, B. K. (1988). The therapeutic role of a structured life review process in homebound elderly subjects. *Journal of Gerontology: Psychological Sciences Section, 43*, 40–44.

Haight, B. K. (1992). Long-term effects of a structured life review process. *Journal of Gerontology: Psychological Sciences Section, 47*, 312–315.

Haley, W. H. (1996). The medical context of psychotherapy with the elderly. In S. Zarit & B. Knight (Eds.), *Psychotherapy and aging: Effective interventions with older adults* (pp. 221–240). Washington, D.C.: American Psychological Association Press.

Hamilton, M. (1967). Development of a rating scale for primary depressive illness. *British Journal of Social and Clinical Psychology, 6*, 278–296.

Hendrie, H., & Crossett, J. (1990). An overview of depression in the elderly. *Psychiatric Annals, 20*, 64–69.

Hersen, M., & Van Hasselt, V. B. (1992). Behavioral assessment and treatment of anxiety in the elderly. *Clinical Psychology Review, 12*, 619–640.

Hinrichsen, G. A., & Hernandez, N. A. (1993). Factors associated with recovery from and relapse into major depressive disorder in the elderly. *American Journal of Psychiatry, 150*(12), 1820–1825.

Hinrichsen, G. A., & Zweig, R. A. (1994). Factors associated with suicide attempts by depressed older adults: A prospective study. *American Journal of Psychiatry, 150*(11), 1687–1692.

Horowitz, M., & Kaltreider, N. (1979). Brief therapy

of the stress response syndrome. *Psychiatric Clinics of North America, 2,* 365–377.

Kazniak, A. W. (1996). Techniques and instruments for assessment of the elderly. In S. Zarit & B. Knight (Eds.), *Psychotherapy and aging: Effective interventions with older adults* (pp. 163–220). Washington, D.C: American Psychological Association Press.

Klerman, G., Weissman, M. M., Rounsaville, B. J., & Chevron, E. S. (1984). *Interpersonal psychotherapy of depression.* Northvale, NJ: Jason Aronson.

Knight, B. G. (1996). Overview of psychotherapy with the elderly: The contextual, cohort-based, maturity-specific-challenge model. In S. Zarit & B. Knight (Eds.), *Psychotherapy and aging: Effective interventions with older adults* (pp. 17–34). Washington, D.C: American Psychological Association Press.

Knight, B. G., & McCallum, T. J. (1998). Psychotherapy with older adult families: The contextual, cohort-based maturity/specific challenge model. In I. H. Nordhus, G. R. VandenBos, S. Berg, & P. Fromholt (Eds.), *Clinical geropsychology* (pp. 313–328). Washington, D.C.: American Psychological Association.

Landrine, H., & Klonoff, E. A. (1992). Culture and health-related schemas: A review and proposal for interdisciplinary integration. *Health Psychology, 11,* 267–276.

Lazarus, L. W., Groves, L., Gutmann, D., Ripeckyj, A., Frankel, R., Newton, N., Grunes, J., & Havasy-Galloway, S. (1987). Brief psychotherapy with the elderly: A study of process and outcome. In J. Sadavoy & M. Leszcz (Eds.), *Treating the elderly with psychotherapy* (pp. 265–293). Madison, CT: International Universities Press.

Lazarus, L. W., Groves, L., Newton, N., Gutmann, D., Ripeckyj, A., Frankel, R., Grunes, J., & Havasy-Galloway, S. (1984). Brief psychotherapy with the elderly: A review and preliminary study of process and outcome. In L. W. Lazarus (Ed.), *Clinical approaches to psychotherapy with the elderly* (pp. 15–35). Washington, D.C.: American Psychiatric Press.

Lebowitz, B., Pearson, J., Schneider, L., Reynolds, C., Alexopoulos, G., Bruce, M., Conwell, Y., Katz, I., Meyers, M., Mossey, J., Niederehe, G., & Parmelee, P. (1997). Diagnosis and treatment of depression in late life. *Journal of the American Medical Association, 278,* 1186–1190.

Lesher, E., & Berryhill, S. (1994). Validation of the Geriatric Depression Scale short form among inpatients. *Journal of Clinical Psychology, 50,* 256–260.

Lewinsohn, P. M., Antonuccio, D. G., Steinmetz, J. L., & Teri, L. (1984). *The coping with depression course* (p. 213). Eugene, OR: Castalia Publishing Co.

Lewinsohn, P. M., Biglan, T., & Zeiss, A. (1976). Behavioral treatment of depression. In P. Davidson (Ed.), *Behavioral management of anxiety, depression, and pain* (pp. 91–146). New York: Brunner/Mazel.

Lewinsohn, P. M., Hoberman, H., Teri, L., & Hautzinger, M. (1985). An integrative theory of depression. In S. Reiss & R. R. Bootzin (Eds.), *Theoretical issues in behavior therapy* (pp. 331–359). New York: Academic Press.

Liberto, J. G., Oslin, D. W., & Ruskin, P. E. (1996). Alcoholism in the older population. In L. L. Carstensen, B. A. Edelstein, & L. Dornbrand (Eds.), *The practical handbook of clinical gerontology* (pp. 324–348). Thousand Oaks, CA: Sage Publications.

Lovett, S., & Gallagher, D. (1988). Psychoeducational interventions for family caregivers: Preliminary efficacy data. *Behavior Therapy, 19,* 321–330.

Marengo, J., & Westermeyer, J. F. (1996). Schizophrenia and delusional disorder. In L. L. Carstensen, B. A. Edelstein, & L. Dornbrand (Eds.), *The practical handbook of clinical gerontology* (pp. 255–273). Thousand Oaks, CA: Sage Publications.

Mattis, S. (1988). *Dementia Rating Scale: Professional manual.* Odessa, FL: Psychological Assessment Resources, Inc.

Miller, M. D., Wolfson, L., Frank, E., Cornes, C., Silberman, R., Ehrenpreis, L., Zaltman, J., Mallow, J., & Reynolds, C. F. (1997). Using interpersonal psychotherapy (IPT) in a combined psychotherapy/medication research protocol with depressed elders: A descriptive report with case vignettes. *Journal of Psychotherapy Practice and Research, 7*(1), 47–55.

Mossey, J. M., Knott, K. A., Higgins, M., & Talerico, K. (1996). Effectiveness of a psychosocial intervention, interpersonal counseling, for subdysthymic depression in medically ill elderly. *Journal of Gerontology, 51*(4), 172–178.

Myers, W. A. (1984). *Dynamic therapy of the older patient.* New York: Jason Aronson Pub. Co.

Myers, W., A. (Ed.). (1991). *New techniques in the psychotherapy of older patients.* Washington, D.C.: American Psychiatric Press.

Newman, A., Enright, P., Manolio, T., Haponik, E., & Wahl, P. (1997). Sleep disturbance, psychosocial correlates, and cardiovascular disease in 5201 older adults: The Cardiovascular Health Study. *The Journal of the American Geriatric Society, 45,* 1–7.

Newton, N. A., Brauer, D., Gutmann, D. L., & Grunes, J. (1986). Psychodynamic therapy with the aged: A review. *Clinical Gerontologist, 5,* 205–229.

Niederehe, G. (1994). Psychosocial therapies with depressed older adults. In L. S. Schneider, C. F.

Reynolds, B. D. Lebowitz, & A. J. Friedhoff (Eds.), *Diagnosis and treatment of depression in late life* (pp. 293–315). Washington, D.C.: American Psychiatric Press.

Olfson, M., & Pincus, H. A. (1996). Outpatient mental health care in non-hospital settings: Distribution of patients across provider groups. *American Journal of Psychiatry, 153*, 1353–1356.

Osgood, N. (1985). *Suicide in the elderly: A practitioners guide to diagnosis and mental health intervention*. Rockville, MD: Aspen Systems Corp.

Pachana, N., Thompson, L. W., & Gallagher-Thompson, D. (1994). Measurement of depression. In M. P. Lawton and J. Teresi (Eds.), *Annual review of gerontology and geriatrics* (Vol. 14; pp. 234–256). New York, NY: Springer Press.

Palmer, B. W., Jeste, D. V., & Sheikh, J. I. (1997). Anxiety disorders in the elderly: DSM-IV and other barriers to diagnosis and treatment. *Journal of Affective Disorders, 46*(3), 183–190.

Parmelee, P. A., Katz, I. R., & Lawton, M. P. (1992). Incidence of depression in long-term care settings. *Journals of Gerontology: Medical Science, 47*, M189–M196.

Pasternack, R. E., Prigerson, H., Hall, M., Miller, M. D., Fasiczka, A., Mazumdar, S., & Reynolds, C. F. (1977). The posttreatment illness course of depression in bereaved elders. *American Journal of Geriatric Psychiatry, 5*, 54–59.

Rankin, S. H., & Weekes, D. P. (1989). Life-span development: A review of theory and practice for families with chronically ill members. *Scholarly Inquiry for Nursing Practice, 3*(1), 3–22.

Rapp, S., Parisi, S. A., Walsh, D. A., & Wallace, C. E. (1988). Detecting depression in elderly medical inpatients. *Journal of Consulting and Clinical Psychology, 56*, 509–513.

Reynolds, C. F., Frank, E., Perel, J. M., Imber, S. D., Cornes, C., Miller, M. D., Mazumdar, S., Houck, P. R., Dew, M. A., Stack, J. A., Pollock, B. G., & Kupfer, D. J. (1999). Nortriptyline and interpersonal psychotherapy as maintenance therapies for recurrent major depression: A randomized controlled trial in patients older than 59 years. *Journal of the American Medical Association, 281*, 39–45.

Richman, J. (1993). *Preventing elderly suicide: Overcoming personal despair, professional neglect, and social bias*. New York: Springer.

Rodman, J., Gantz, F., Schneider, J., & Gallagher-Thompson, D. (1991). Short term treatment of endogenous depression using cognitive/behavioral therapy and pharmacotherapy. *Clinical Gerontologist, 10*(3), 81–84.

Rosen, A. L., Pancake, J. A., & Rickards, L. (1995). Mental health policy and older Americans:

Historical and current perspectives. In M. Gatz, (Ed.), *Emerging issues in mental health & aging* (pp. 1–18). Washington, D.C.: American Psychological Association.

Ruegg, R. G., Zisook, S., & Swerdlow, N. R. (1988). Depression in the aged: An overview. *Psychiatry Clinics of North America, 11*, 83–99.

Rybarczyk, B., Gallagher-Thompson, D., Rodman, J., Zeiss, A., Gantz, F., & Yesavage, J. (1992). Applying cognitive-behavioral psychotherapy to the chronically ill elderly: Treatment issues and case illustrations. *International Psychogeriatrics, 4*(1), 127–140.

Salzman, C. (1994). Pharmacological treatment of depression in elderly patients. In L. S. Schneider, C. F. Reynolds, B. D. Lebowitz, & A. J. Friedhoff (Eds.), *Diagnosis and treatment of depression in late life* (pp. 181–244). Washington, D.C.: American Psychiatric Press.

Schaie, K. W., & Willis, S. L. (1996). *Adult development and aging* (4th ed.). New York: HarperCollins.

Scogin, F., & McElreath, L. (1994). Efficacy of psychosocial treatment for geriatric depression: A quantitative review. *Journal of Consulting and Clinical Psychology, 62*(1), 69–74.

Sheikh, J. I., & Yesavage, J. A. (1986). Geriatric Depression Scale (GDS): Recent evidence and development of a shorter version. *Clinical Gerontologist, 5* (1-2), 165–173.

Silberschatz, G., & Curtis, J. T. (1986). Clinical implications of research on brief dynamic psychotherapy. II: How the therapist helps or hinders therapeutic progress. *Psychoanalytic Psychology, 3*, 27–37.

Silberschatz, G., & Curtis, J. T. (1991). Time-limited psychodynamic therapy with older adults. In W. Myers (Ed.), *New techniques in the psychotherapy of older patients* (pp. 95–108). Washington, D.C.: American Psychiatric Press.

Simon, G., Ormel, J., VonKorff, M., & Barlow W. (1995). Health care costs associated with depressive and anxiety disorders in primary care. *American Journal of Psychiatry, 152*, 352–357.

Smith, G. C., Smith, M. F., & Toseland, R. W. (1991). Problems identified by family caregivers in counseling. *The Gerontologist, 32*(5), 656–664.

Spitzer, R. L., Williams, J. B., Gibbon, M., & First, M. B. (1992). The Structured Clinical Interview for DSM-III-R (SCID). I: History, rationale, and description. *Archives of General Psychiatry, 49*, 624–629.

Stuifbergen, A. K. (1990). Patterns of functioning in families with chronically ill parent: An exploratory study. *Research in Nursing and Health, 13*, 35–44.

Stroebe, M., Stroebe, W., & Hansson, W. (Eds.). (1993). *Handbook of bereavement*. London: Cambridge University Press.

Sullivan, H. S. (1953). *The interpersonal theory of psychiatry*. New York: W. W. Norton and Company.

Teri, L., Curtis, J., Gallagher-Thompson, D., & Thompson, L. W. (1994). Cognitive-behavior therapy with depressed older adults. In L. S. Schneider, C. F. Reynolds, B. D. Lebowitz & A. Friedhoff (Eds.), *Diagnosis and treatment of depression in late-life: Results of the NIH consensus development conference* (pp. 279–291). Washington, D.C.: American Psychiatric Press, Inc.

Teri, L., & Logsdon, R. (1994). Assessment of behavioral disturbance in older adults. In M. P. Lawton & J. A. Teresi (Eds.), *Annual review of gerontology and geriatrics* (Vol. 14, pp. 107–124). New York: Springer Press.

Thompson, L. W. (1996). Cognitive-behavioral therapy and treatment for late-life depression. *Journal of Clinical Psychiatry, 57*(suppl. 5), 29–37.

Thompson, L. W., Davies, R., Gallagher, D., & Krantz, S. (1986). Cognitive therapy with older adults. *Clinical Gerontologist, 5*, 245–279.

Thompson, L. W., Futterman, A., & Gallagher, D. (1988). Assessment of late life depression. *Psychopharmacology Bulletin, 24*(4), 577–585.

Thompson, L. W., & Gallagher, D. (1984). Efficacy of psychotherapy in the treatment of late-life depression. *Advances in Behavior Research and Therapy, 6*, 127–139.

Thompson, L., Gallagher, D., & Breckenridge, J. S. (1987). Comparative effectiveness of psychotherapies for depressed elders. *Journal of Consulting and Clinical Psychology, 55*, 385–390.

Thompson, L. W., Gallagher, D., & Czirr, R. (1988). Personality disorder and outcome in the treatment of late-life depression. *Journal of Geriatric Psychiatry, 21*, 133–146.

Thompson, L., Gallagher, D., & Lovett, S. (1992). *Increasing life satisfaction class leaders' and participant manuals* (rev.). Palo Alto, CA: Dept. of Veterans Affairs Medical Center and Stanford University.

Thompson, L. W., Gallagher, D., Nies, G., & Epstein, D. (1983). Evaluation of the effectiveness of professionals and nonprofessionals as instructors of "Coping with Depression" classes for elders. *The Gerontologist, 23*, 390–396.

Thompson, L. W., & Gallagher-Thompson, D. (1991, November). *Comparison of Desipramine and cognitive-behavioral therapy in the treatment of late-life depression: A progress report*. Paper presented at the annual meeting of the Gerontological Society of America, San Francisco, CA.

Thompson, L. W., & Gallagher-Thompson, D. (1993). *Comparison of Desipramine and cognitive-behavioral therapy in the treatment of late-life depression: A progress report*. Paper presented at the 27th Annual American Association for Behavioral Therapy Convention, Atlanta, GA.

Thompson, L. W., Gallagher-Thompson, D., & Koin, D. (under review). Comparison of Desipramine and cognitive-behavioral therapy in the treatment of late-life depression.

Thompson, L. W., Gallagher-Thompson, D., & Dick, L. (1996). *Cognitive-behavioral therapy for late-life depression: A therapist's manual*. Stanford, CA: VA Palo Alto Health Care System and Stanford University.

Thompson, L. W., Gallagher-Thompson, D., Futterman, A., & Peterson, J. (1991). The effects of late-life spousal bereavement over a thirty-month interval. *Psychology and Aging, 6*, 434–441.

Thompson, L. W., Powers, D. V., Coon, D. W., Takagi, K., McKibbin, C., & Gallagher-Thompson, D. (in press). Group cognitive-behavioral therapy with older adults. In A. Freeman & J. White (Eds.), *Cognitive-behavioral group therapies*. New York: Guilford Press.

Turner, M. (1992). Individual psychodynamic psychotherapy with older adults: Perspectives from a nurse psychotherapist. *Archives of Psychiatric Nursing, 6*(5), 266–274.

U.S. Bureau of the Census & National Institute on Aging (1993, November). Racial and ethnic diversity of America's elderly population. *Profiles of America's Elderly, 3*(1).

Wells, C. E. (1980). The differential diagnosis of psychiatric disorders in the elderly. *Procedures of the Annual Meeting of the American Psychopathology Association, 69*, 19–35.

Wells, K. B., Stewart, A., Hays, R. D., Burnam, M. A., Rogers, W., Daniels, M., Greenfield, S., & Ware, S. (1989). The functioning and well-being of depressed patients: Results from the medical outcomes study. *Journal of the American Medical Association, 262*, 914–919.

Williams, J. B. W. (1988). A structured interview guide for the Hamilton Depression Rating Scale. *Archives of General Psychiatry, 45*, 742–747.

Worden, J. W. (1991). *Grief counseling and grief therapy* (2nd ed.). New York: Springer.

Yeo, G., & Gallagher-Thompson, D. (Eds). (1996). *Ethnicity and the dementias*. Washington, D.C.: Taylor & Francis.

Yesavage, J. A., Brink, T. L., & Rose, T. L. (1983). Development and validation of a geriatric depression scale: A preliminary report. *Journal of Psychiatric Residents, 17*, 37–49.

Yost, E., Beutler, L., Corbishley, A. M., & Allender, J. (1986). *Group cognitive therapy: A treatment approach for depressed older adults*. New York: Pergamon Press, Inc.

Zarit, S. H., & Zarit, J. M. (1998). *Mental disorders in older adults*. New York: Guilford Press.

Zeiss, A., & Steffen, A. M. (1996a). Interdisciplinary health care teams: The basic unit of geriatric care. In L. L. Carstensen, B. A. Edelstein, & L. Dornbrand (Eds.), *The practical handbook of clinical gerontology* (pp. 423–450). Thousand Oaks, CA: Sage Publications.

Zeiss, A. & Steffen, A. (1996b). Treatment issues with elderly clients. *Cognitive and Behavioral Practice, 3*, 371–389.

CHAPTER 29

THE ROLES OF FEMALE CLINICAL PSYCHOLOGISTS IN CHANGING THE FIELD OF PSYCHOTHERAPY

C. R. SNYDER, DIANE S. MCDERMOTT, RUTH Q. LEIBOWITZ, AND JEN CHEAVENS
The University of Kansas, Lawrence

WHY IS THIS TOPIC IMPORTANT?

A change with major implications for psychology's contribution to the field of psychotherapy has been taking place over the last four decades. Considering its magnitude, there has been little discourse about it. What is this change? We are not speaking of the movement to allow psychologists to prescribe medications. Likewise, we are not addressing empirically supported treatments, or the ebb and flow of popular interventions. Surely, then, we are addressing the role of applied clinicians in our national organization. Although all of these are important, the change we are talking about will influence, to some extent, these other issues. Who is behind this change? In brief, it is women. More specifically, there has been a dramatic increase in the number of women relative to men who are pursuing and obtaining doctoral degrees in clinical[1] psychology. Contrary to past years when roughly two-thirds of those in clinical psychology doctoral training programs were men, more recently the graduates have been *two females for every male*. If anything, this women-to-men ratio appears to be increasing.

How will this feminization impact the field of psychotherapy (Howard, 1987)? Many important possible sequelae are addressed in the present chapter. We first review the demographic changes pertaining to this influx of females, and explore the implications for the field of psychotherapy. Our central question is "Will women run things differently than men have in the past?" Our answer, in brief, is "Yes." We will base our detailed predictions on assumptions that women have predisposing characteristics that differ from those of men. In turn, these "feminine" characteristics should influence psychotherapy research, teaching, and practice. As such, our thesis is that the fe-

Authors' note: Thanks are extended to Rick E. Ingram and Rebecca Lee Snyder for comments on an earlier version of this article. This chapter is based, in part, on a paper by C. R. Snyder, D. S. McDermott, C. Cutter, & R. Q. Leibowitz titled "The Role of Women in Clinical Psychology: A Kinder and Gentler Look into the 21st Century," which was presented August 14, 1998, at the International Congress of Psychology, San Francisco.

[1] We use the term *clinical* in its generic sense so as to encapsulate the increasingly related fields of clinical and counseling. In wedding these fields into one term, we do not mean to give one field differential status. Furthermore, given our perception that counseling programs are placing more emphasis on training aimed at helping those with serious mental health problems over the last two decades, these two subfields actually are becoming increasingly similar.

male clinical psychologists will influence the living history of psychotherapy as it moves into the 21st century.

CLINICAL PSYCHOLOGY GENDER DEMOGRAPHICS: FEMALES > MALES

The American Psychological Association (APA) published the "Report of the Task Force on the Changing Genders Composition of Psychology" in 1995. This document, written by noted psychologists, vividly makes the case that women, by the force of their sheer numbers, will dominate clinical psychology in the future. Why has this change not gained more widespread attention? Our guess is that the slow rate of increase in the numbers of women with clinical psychology doctorates has made it difficult to discern changes at any one point in time.

Women were in the minority during the early years of psychology (13% of APA members in 1917; Furumoto, 1987); likewise, their influence in the field was minimal, and their efforts were marginalized (Furumoto, 1987). From 1920 through 1974, most women earned their doctorates in the developmental and school psychology specialties, with a mere 24.2% in clinical psychology specialties (Goodheart & Markham, 1992; Russo & Denmark, 1987). In response to continued marginalization, women psychologists formed the National Council of Women Psychologists in order to increase their impact in the wider field of psychology (Capshew & Laszlo, 1986) but their effort largely failed. This group changed its name to the International Council of Women Psychologists in 1947. This organization also did not prosper, and its attempts to join APA were thwarted (Task Force, 1995; Walsh, 1985). It was not until 1969 that the next formal organization of women, the Association for Women in Psychology, came into existence to fight sexism in the employment arenas. In response to the work of this group, APA initiated a Task Force on the Status of Women in Psychology, resulting in a progressive report on women's roles in psychology shortly thereafter (Astin, Bayton, Brackbill et al., 1973).

As these changes were taking place at the the organizational level, the previous male numerical domination began to reverse as more women pursued undergraduate psychology educations. In

1950 and 1960, respectively, women represented 36.8% and 41.0% of psychology students (National Science Foundation, 1982, 1983). By 1973, women and men were graduating in equal numbers with baccalaureate degrees in psychology. Over the ensuing years, the percentages of female psychology undergraduates obtaining degrees from colleges and universities steadily rose: 61.0% in 1975, 64.3% in 1980, 70.0% in 1985, and 71.9% in 1990 (Task Force, 1995). From 1970 to 1990, the undergraduate psychology degrees of males fell 17%, whereas those of females increased 73%.[2]

Because of these undergraduate trends, by 1979 there were roughly equal numbers of female and male psychology graduate students. The percentages of female graduate students thus continued to increase over subsequent years: 55.9% in 1981, 62.4% in 1985, and 63.9% in 1990 (Task Force, 1995). From 1970 to 1990, male graduate students decreased by 23%, whereas female graduate students increased by 84%. Looking only at clinical programs, the percentages of females admitted also increased over more recent years: 61.1% in 1988, 63.9% in 1990, 67.9% in 1992, and 68.7% in 1994 (Council of University Directors of Clinical Psychology, 1995).[3] If it were not for the occasional possible reverse discrimination wherein modern admissions committees gave preferential admission to males (perhaps in order to have some representation of this gender in their programs and training clinics, as well as to have a broad-based pool of therapists) (Goodheart & Markham, 1992), the percentages of women accepted into clinical programs might have been even higher.

If we follow this trend to examine the psychology doctorates granted, female psychology graduates equaled the number of males for the first time in 1984 (National Resource Council, 1974–1989; Ostertag & McNamara, 1991). After this 1984 crossover year, the percentages of female Ph.D. graduates continued to rise from

---

[2]The proportion of women entering graduate school in clinical psychology has not directly reflected the proportions garnering baccalaureate degrees, however, because a higher percentage of men go on to graduate educations (Howard, Pion, Gottsfredson et al., 1986).

[3]Goodheart, Markham, and Hannigan (1988) performed a survey showing similar percentages of women in clinical programs (58% to 77%).

54.1% in 1984, to 56.5% in 1988, and 58.5% in 1990. When clinical degrees (including clinical, counseling, and school psychology doctorates) are examined separately instead of collapsing across all psychology degrees, the percentages of female Ph.D. degrees rose from 26.5% in 1970, to 45.4% in 1981, and 64.0% in 1991 (Task Force, 1995). Thus, over recent years, the percentage of women has increased and the percentage of men has decreased. One final aspect of these trends is worth noting, namely, although the relative percentage of women has burgeoned in psychology generally, the increase has been especially marked for clinical psychology (from 1974 to 1989; Goodheart & Markham, 1992). These various increases across time are shown in Table 29.1.

To what degree has the swelling number of women in education impacted the labor force? In 1971, 21.3% of qualified women psychologists were in the professional labor pool, whereas this rose to 40.4% by 1991 (Task Force, 1995). Given that these data are almost a decade old, it is likely that female psychologists equal or exceed the number of males in the professional work force by now.

ASSUMED FEMALE CHARACTERISTICS

The numbers discussed so far give a vivid picture of how clinical psychology increasingly has become a female-dominated profession. Simply noting that more females are graduating, however, does not allow much insight into the potential changes for the psychotherapy field per se. To explore such changes, our approach is to make assumptions about women, and then apply these assumptions to yield predictions for the academic and applied arenas of the psychotherapy field.

Our assumptions admittedly create a stereotype of women. We do not hold that *all* women are similar; instead, we suggest that *many* women exhibit characteristics influenced by gender differences. As Spence (1985, p. 64) writes, "Gender is one of the earliest and most central components of the self-concept and serves as an organizing principle through which many experiences and perceptions . . . are filtered." That these sex differences repeatedly occur across many differing studies suggests that they are not small, unstable, and artifactual (for meta-analytic support, see Eagly, 1994, 1995). We also would note that

TABLE 29.1 Percentages of Women Within the Field of Psychology Throughout the 1900s

Year	Arena of Psychology			
	Undergraduate Majors	Graduate Students	Doctorates Granted	Clinical Doctorates Granted
1950	36.8			
1960	41.0			
1970				26.5
1973	50.0			
1975	61.0			
1980	64.3			
1981		55.9		45.4
1984			50.0	
1985	70.0	62.4		
1986			54.1	
1988			56.5	
1990	71.9	63.9	58.5	
1991				64.0
1992		67.9		
1994		68.7		

Source: The percentages in this table are taken from the National Resource Council Survey of Earned Doctorates (1974–1989), the National Science Foundation (1982), Ostertag & McNamara (1991), and the American Psychological Association Task Force (1995).

these assumptions have developed in the larger context of societal forces that have influenced the lives of women, and thus these female characteristics reflect covarying power and status differences of women and men (Unger, 1989, 1990). Finally, in response to the view that situational factors are more important than individual differences, we would echo the conclusions of recent reviews indicating that individual differences are robust predictors of human actions (Hogan, 1997; Snyder & Dinoff, 1999).

The study participants of the research we subsequently review typically are Caucasian women in their 20s and 30s. Although this hampers generalization to minorities and older women, it should be emphasized that the new clinical psychology doctorates overwhelmingly *are Caucasian women in their 20s and 30s.* Thus, the sex-characteristics research uses a population that matches the women who most imminently will be moving into the psychotherapy field, with one important exception—the research has not been conducted with female psychologists. Although the characteristics of female psychologists may differ some from those of women in general, we make the added supposition that the gender characteristics for women in general also apply to female clinical psychologists. Unfortunately, there is no research directly addressing the factors that shape professional female psychologists' lives.

Assumption 1: Ready Emotional Access

First, we suggest that women as compared to men have greater access to their emotions (Brooks-Gunn & Matthews, 1979; Tavris, 1992; Tavris & Offir, 1977), except for anger and other negative emotions (Persinger & Marecek, 1991). Women are both permitted and taught to exhibit their emotions, as well as to be gentle. Men, on the other hand, are rewarded for the stifling of their emotions in the service of a stoic and strong demeanor (Brooks-Gunn & Matthews, 1979; Mirowsky & Ross, 1995). How many little boys have learned to squelch their emotions as they are admonished to "be a man"? Indeed, research shows that men who reveal their emotions are regarded by both men and women as being feminine, weak, and poorly adjusted (Robertson & Fitzgerald, 1990). When men make it to therapy, therefore, it is not surprising that they find it hard to express their feelings. In the context of psychotherapy, however, women can more easily identify and discuss their emotional experiences.

In this latter regard, it follows that female-centered therapy focuses on the development and expression of emotions (Learner, 1988). Additional research on brief therapy reveals that female as compared to male therapists are "more accurate in the perception of . . . emotional states" (Jones, Krupnik, & Kerig, 1987, p. 346). These points thus support our first assumption regarding the relative ease with which women traffic in emotional matters.

Assumption 2: Not Confrontational

Second, women are less confrontational than men (Brooks-Gunn & Matthews, 1979; Tavris & Offir, 1977). Women are seen as being less self-assertive according to theoretical views (Bem, 1974; Spence, Helmreich, & Stapp, 1974), with empirical support for this assumption (Bridges, Sanderman, Breukers, Ranchor, & Arrindell, 1991; McBride, 1992). For example, college males perceive themselves as being more confrontational than their female counterparts, and college males are more assertive than females in expressing negative feelings (Persinger & Marecek, 1991). Consistent with this latter finding, women view assertion as being less socially desirable than do men (Buss, 1981). Furthermore, women are more likely than men to report avoiding confrontations (Gladue, 1991). They also are more likely to perceive that confrontation is not needed to solve problems.

That assertiveness training was popular for women during the 1980s is yet another social manifestation of their perceived need to rectify a tendency to subvert confrontation (Enns, 1993). Although the assertiveness training that was geared toward helping women to speak out for their needs is not as popular today as it was previously, it still remains a useful therapeutic technique for teaching appropriate confrontational skills to women (Wills-Brandon, 1990). Thus, learned submissiveness has been inherent in the traditional female sex role (Brooks-Gunn & Matthews, 1979). As such, much of what is called "feminine restraint" really may be related to this acquired reticence to confront.

Assumption 3: Communal and Other Awareness

The third assumption is that, relative to men, women are more communal and aware of others' needs (Bakan, 1966; Gilligan, 1982; Helgeson, 1994; Horney, 1923/1967; Miller, 1976; Spence, 1984). Through both childhood and adulthood, for example, females are taught to nurture others, and males are taught independence in their interactions (Conarton & Silverman, 1988). Instead of thinking about individuals, women tend to think in community or group terms. Therefore, while a Caucasian woman might focus on group support and networking (e.g., family or a circle of friends and coworkers), a Caucasian male would tend to emphasize the individual as the primary societal unit (Sue & Sue, 1990).

Some theoreticians have gone so far as to suggest that a woman's sense of self is based on her emotional connections and identifications with others (Kaplan & Surrey, 1984). Recent models of women's development posit that they, unlike men, grow through and toward relationships (Jordan, 1995). This latter theory suggests that women's style of connection is normal and different from (but not inferior to) that of men. As Chodorow (1978) puts it, "The basic feminine sense of self is connected to the world; the basic masculine sense of self is separate" (p. 169). Research supports this speculation in that women report being more connected (i.e., greater empathy and desire for intimacy), while men report more sense of separation (i.e., high self–other differentiation and independence) (Lang & Osterweil, 1992).

In a related vein, women appear to be more aware of others, they pay attention to the expressed needs of others, and they often base their actions on such perceptions. This may be seen as a natural part of "mothering," but it probably transcends that context. Sometimes, however, the awareness and attention to others may be problematic (McGowan & Hart, 1992), as revealed by self-help books offering to assist women in learning to "stop loving too much," "put themselves first," and "say no without guilt." Here, the sex role conditioning literature suggests that women are encouraged to be the caregivers for a wide range of people (children, males, parents, etc.) (Doress-Worters, 1994; Himes, 1994). Research consistently weighs in with support for females' greater nurturance and empathy in comparison with males (Whitehead & Nokes, 1990). Focusing on psychotherapy, people expect female therapists to be more nurturing and caring than male therapists (Dacy & Brodsky, 1992). To compound matters, nurturing behavior is perceived as atypical for men (Rane & Draper, 1995).

Assumption 4: Value Harmony and Relationships

Consistent with the third assumption is the fourth: Women value and work harder at preserving relationships than do men (Bakan, 1966; Cohler & Lieberman, 1980; Kessler & McLeod, 1984). Women's greater access to emotions, their capacity for emotional closeness, their awareness of and responsiveness to others, and their less confrontational demeanors all foster harmony in relationships more so than is the case for men. Indeed, women tend to subordinate their personal or self-related desires to their relationships (McGowan & Hart, 1992); moreover, women often base their identities on such relationships, while men's identities are more likely to be work-related (Schaef, 1985). As one example of this phenomenon, female APA members of the clinical psychology division reported that they were more likely than men to refuse a job that jeopardized a relationship, and to stay in an unsatisfying job because of loyalty to coworkers (McGowan & Hart, 1992). Likewise, a survey of approximately 1000 undergraduates at a liberal arts college revealed that, while women are conflicted about their career and family interests, they still are far more likely than their male counterparts to place family matters at the forefront (Novak & Novak, 1996).

Relative to men, women apparently perceive harmony in relationships as being more personally beneficial; also, women actually experience more harmony in their relationships. As such, women have rated social involvement and harmony as being more important to their health than men (Kenny, 1991). Men's relationships, on the other hand, are seen as being more competitive than women's. By preschool, boys are more competitive, more directive, and more controlling of others, whereas girls are more cooperative and collaborative (Atkins & Rohrbeck, 1993; Maccoby, 1990). Continuing this analysis into adulthood, women still value cooperation, whereas men develop competitive, exchange-like relationships (Clark & Mills, 1979; Mills & Clark, 1982). Turning to the therapy context, women therapists have reported harmony as being more typical of their work than men have reported (Parr, Bradley, Lan, & Gould, 1996).

The traditional sex roles appear to drive men and women in opposite directions. Namely, the *masculine* role of emphasizing autonomy, achievement, and emotional control makes men less likely to seek and obtain social support; conversely, the feminine role of emphasizing connection, nurturance, and emotional expressiveness makes it easier for women to give and receive social support. Again, research corroborates this hypothesis in that, relative to men, women both seek and obtain more social support (Sarason, Sarason, Hacker, & Basham, 1985; Shumaker & Hill, 1991; Turner, 1994).

Assumption 5: Egalitarian

The fifth assumption suggests that women are more willing to share power in relationships (Sturdivant, 1980) and, as such, are more egalitarian than men. The relationships of Caucasian males are described as being either *one-down* or *one-up*. Women, on the other hand, value perceived relationship equality (Schaef, 1985). Related research reveals that males prefer inequality and social dominance among social groups, whereas women prefer a higher degree of equality (Pratto et al., 1994). In this latter regard, women accentuate their similarities relative to others, and minimize differences and the appearance of superiority; men, however, focus more on status and use their perceived differences as a vehicle for such status pursuits (Tannen, 1990).

Feminist therapy highlights power sharing and egalitarianism principles in regard to the client–therapist relationship, and it has been suggested that these emphases differentiate this approach from therapies developed by males (Brown & Brodsky, 1992; Dambrot & Reep, 1993; Enns, 1993; Mowbray, 1995). Research supports this assertion that male therapists are more likely to influence therapy interactions by interrupting their clients; for example, in one study, they did so six times more frequently than female therapists (Cooke & Kipnis, 1986). Although women appear to be just as interested as men in possessing power (Stewart & Winter, 1976), through socialization women learn to manifest their power needs in a sharing or giving manner (Hirschowitz, 1987; Winter, 1988). Furthermore, women are likely to act modestly and not take credit for their successes (Gould & Slone, 1982). Accordingly, power among women becomes a means for enhancing their satisfying interpersonal relationships (McAdams, 1985).

Assumption 6: Understand Struggle and Social Inequality

Women have not had as much power as men in our society (Lips, 1991; Unger & Crawford, 1992), an observation that is buttressed by equal opportunity laws (one of many potential examples). This leads to the sixth assumption: Women are especially sensitive to struggle and social inequity. Women traditionally have crusaded for the rights of less fortunate others. As a case in point, feminist concerns about the health care needs of homeless, immigrant, and minority populations have helped to shape national health care policies (Travis, Gressley, & Crumpler, 1991). Indeed, women have been shown to be more willing than men to discuss special programs aimed at helping minorities (Snyder & Kendzierski, 1982). Although Caucasian women are more advantaged than women or men of color, they still are not as advantaged as Caucasian males in American society. It is from this underdog perspective that women identify more strongly with others lacking in power.

Assumption 7: Not Threatening

Women are perceived by both men and other women as being less threatening than men. This, at least partly, may reflect the fact that, on average, they are physically smaller than men. Furthermore, women historically have had less direct power in public and professional arenas to influence the lives of others (Unger & Crawford, 1992). Accordingly, their stations in life often have been less threatening to others. Because of their nonthreatening presence, women may seem more approachable and easier to interact with in a variety of situations. On this point, Tavris (1992) noted that both sexes find women easier to talk to, and feel better after talking with a woman than a man. Similarly, clients of female as compared to male counselors report less anxiety (Krippner & Hutchinson, 1990). Finally, the most common reason both sexes have given for preferring a female therapist is the expected comfort in speaking with a woman (Pikus & Heavey, 1996; see, however, Giles & Dryden, 1991, for data showing no differential fear ratings for female and male therapists).

Assumption 8: Contextual and Holistic Thought

The holistic approach of feminist therapists is said to emphasize the interconnections in the emotional, physical, and spiritual aspects of a client's life, along with perceiving clients' psychological distress in the social context in which that distress is experienced (Cammaert & Larsen, 1988). This relates to an earlier assumption that women are oriented toward community rather than individualistic matters. Practically, this means that women are more likely than men to attend to the family, community, and societal contexts in which problems are experienced (Marecek & Hare-Mustin, 1991; Mowbray, 1995). (Such holistic thinking not only characterizes women but also many persons in nonWestern cultures [Sue & Sue, 1990].) The holistic female thinker, however, is not necessarily less goal directed (i.e. instrumental, agentic) than her male counterpart (Snyder, 1994; Snyder, Harris, Anderson et al., 1991; Snyder, Hoza, Pelham et al., 1997). Although the goals of the two sexes may differ, with each pursuing goals that are socially expected and rewarded, both women and men actively seek their respective goals (many of which have been implicitly tapped via the assumptions in this chapter).

IMPLICATIONS OF FEMALE CHARACTERISTICS FOR PSYCHOTHERAPY IN ACADEMIA

The Influx of Women into Academia: Pros and Cons

Although more women have begun to enter academia, the programs and departments that train psychotherapy researchers and practitioners typically still have more male than female faculty members. The percentage of women in academia was 20% in 1973, and it had risen to 35% by 1991 (Task Force, 1995). For clinical psychology programs only, the percentages of female faculty increased from 25.8% to 32.4% in the period from 1988 to 1994 (Council of University Directors of Clinical Psychology, 1995). Many women probably are working their way through the professional ranks, with most still to be promoted to full professor. Large proportions of female faculty also have yet to advance to the leadership positions in their units. As recently as 1996, for example, only 28 of 154 (or 18.2%) directors of clinical psychology programs were women (Council of University Directors of Clinical Program, 1996).

Even as the number of women in academic settings that train psychotherapists has increased in proportion to men, *many of these gifted and capable female graduates avoid careers in academia.* This phenomenon, if our perception is accurate, will delay the rate at which women raise their proportionate ranks and influence in academia.

What are the possible reasons for this speculated avoidance of academic careers by women? One factor is that the academic psychotherapy arena is perceived by female graduate students as being extremely competitive. Based on workshops and feedback we have had from the female graduate students in our APA-approved counseling and clinical psychology programs, this perception is based, in part, on concerns that the female students have about being able to produce the required tenure-enhancing publications. Perhaps it is not that the female graduate students doubt their talents but question whether they can, or want to, produce while under publication pressure and time constraints. It also is the case that women, relative to men, have heavier demands outside of the workplace because of family commitments (Matusek, Nelson, & Quick, 1995). Contrary to males, female academicians frequently must take care of the children and the home, *as well as* doing the necessary research, teaching, and committee work (Ostertag & McNamara, 1991; Pizurka, Meija, Butter, & Ewart, 1987). This double day can be overwhelming, and seems too demanding to many female graduate students as they consider their career options. Clinical work, on the other hand, seems more desirable because it purportedly permits flexible hours and more freedom for women to attend to family-oriented activities. Perhaps this taps into our assumptions about women's foci on nurturing others.

Another factor inhibiting the influx of females into academia is that such positions are seen as paying relatively meager salaries. Indeed, many women in graduate school perceive that by working only part time, they can make as much or more money than would be the case if they worked full time in academia. Relatedly, there is the perception that when the practicing psychotherapist goes home, the work can be left behind, whereas in academia, the work never ends and the line between work and home is nonexistent.

Although we believe these perceptions are inaccurate, they nevertheless drive choices and make careers in academic psychotherapy seem quite unattractive to women. Let's look at some of these misconceptions more carefully.

With the increasing financial pressures and uncertain client loads of applied psychotherapists, it may well be that their incomes are not higher than those of academicians. Furthermore, the forces of the marketplace may lessen the financial remuneration for applied psychotherapists in the future. Academicians also have an advantage in terms of job security (assuming tenure has been attained), along with various guaranteed health and retirement benefits.

In regard to the applied clinician's "leaving

the job at the office," psychotherapists often think about their clients when away from the work setting, and they sometimes must deal with interruptions and emergencies at inopportune times. The double day probably is just as applicable to females working in the applied psychotherapy arenas as it has been to those women in academia. Also, the latitude that academicians have in setting their work schedules may not be readily apparent to female graduate students. In this latter regard, beyond the hours when academicians are in class teaching, advising, or in committee meetings, they are relatively free to set their agendas. On the issue of family-friendly policies, such arrangements already are in place at some universities, where there is available time-out from the tenure clock for family responsibilities, along with other programs that help the worker and her family (Norrell & Norrell, 1996).

Finally, some comments are warranted about the most disturbing misconception—that women somehow cannot do the same quality and/or quantity of research. Given their superb talents upon entering graduate school (e.g., high grades and entrance examination scores), one might expect women to excel in their research and scholarly production pertaining to psychotherapy. Female clinical psychology graduate students certainly have the requisite talents to do such research. Unless these inaccurate, albeit powerful, perceptions are changed, however, they will continue to dampen talented females from being drawn to the scientific exploration of psychotherapy (for related discussion, see APA, 1998). One force that may lessen such continued perceptions on the part of female graduate students is that more talented female academician role models should be available to dispel these misperceptions.

Women and Research

At present, the academic education of psychotherapists is mentored overwhelmingly by males. If and when women begin to achieve parity with men in the ranks of psychotherapy-focused academia, their preferred pattern of holistic thinking may become more acceptable. Currently, psychotherapy research methodology aims at isolating, controlling, and manipulating variables. This approach seeks to understand psychotherapy phenomena separated from their social and cultural contexts (Damarin, 1991). The centerpiece of this traditional male approach involves the manipulation of given independent variables, while controlling for other possible causes. The correct role of the researcher is seen as that of the objective scientist who is to maintain an objective distance from the research subjects. After the data are gathered, it is the objective researcher who interprets their meaning and importance. As more women begin to study psychotherapy, however, the emphasis may shift to the examination of people within their social, political, and relational contexts. This contextual approach to the scientific study of psychotherapy will have the advantage of being more ecologically valid than previous work.

Many feminist researchers already have moved away from the use of pure quantitative methodologies to use qualitative methodologies, or a combination of qualitative and quantitative methods, while focusing on the experiences of people within their contexts (Gilbert & Osipow, 1991). With this move to qualitative rather than pure quantitative designs, small samples and even n-of-1 designs are used. Another point of emphasis in qualitative research is the relationship between the observed and the observer. In a number of qualitative paradigms, for example, the researcher is not distant or objective, but rather involved in relation with participants and informants (versus subjects) who may be asked for their feedback on data interpretation and/or even be viewed as co-investigators or experts on the phenomenon being studied. There are a number of qualitative paradigms currently in use including participant action research, naturalistic inquiry, empowerment research, phenomenology, and grounded inquiry. (We are unable to provide details in the present context because of space constraints, but there are texts that address these qualitative approaches.) The participants are examined ideographically, placed in context, and viewed from several perspectives. These types of qualitative approaches reflect a holistic view of the client. Based on our assumptions, we would predict that such approaches should be embraced by women who value relationships and communication. While such research is gaining credibility in psychology, our sense is that it still is being greeted with considerable skepticism by many of the males involved in academic psychotherapy education and publishing. As more women use qualitative approaches to psychotherapy research, however, such methodologies should gain in respectability (for related points, see the chapters in this volume by Mahoney).

Women may choose to study psychotherapy

from humanistic and applied perspectives. Female researchers also may be more interested in examining the plights of disadvantaged client populations and finding efficacious ways to alleviate their suffering; this prediction is based on our assumption that women especially understand and identify with the struggle and inequities of others. Similarly, there should be more attention paid to the investigation of women's issues in the context of psychotherapy (for related reviews of the impact of the feminization, see Gilbert & Osipow, 1991; Marecek & Hare-Mustin, 1991; Ostertag & McNamara, 1991). Topics here would include the epidemiology, effects of, and treatment for physical and sexual abuse; sexual misconduct in therapy; sex-role socialization and sex bias in psychotherapy-related instruments and theories; sex-role stereotyping in assessment and therapy; and the influence of therapist and client gender on psychotherapy process and outcome. We foresee that female psychotherapy theorists and researchers will be less concerned with treatment outcome issues per se, which may run counter to the helping profession (medicine and mental health) accountability movement fostered by insurers and the public more generally. Because of their interpersonal predilections, we predict that the theory and research conducted by female academicians will be directed toward psychotherapy *process* issues. Further, given the shared social constructivist frameworks, we believe that feminist psychotherapy theorists will embrace narrative approaches to the helping process (see the Brown and the Neimeyer and Stewart chapters in this volume).

Female psychotherapy researchers may have special sensitivities about the rights of psychotherapy research participants. We base this on Gilligan's (1982) theory of women's moral development, as well as Peter and Gallop's (1994) findings that, in moral decision making, women attend more to the context and to the consequences of the decision (see previous discussion of females' attention to the process of psychotherapy), whereas men attend more to "universal" principles. Contrary to the previous patriarchal approach to psychotherapy research, it has been suggested that female researchers are guided more by a sense of personal responsibility and concerns about the consequences of the experimenter's actions (Damarin, 1991).

Any discussion of the feminization of psychotherapy research must address the difficult question of what will happen to the sheer output of experimentation. A previous study of the members of the APA Division of Psychotherapy found that men published significantly more articles than women (Norcross, Prochaska, & Farber, 1993); women spent a larger proportion of their time doing psychotherapy. The previous Norcross et al. paper does not provide information that would help to clarify lower publication numbers by females because the data are not broken into manuscripts submitted and accepted. On this point, it would be instructive to see whether female, as compared to male, scholars submit fewer manuscripts, have a higher rejection rate, or both.

Whether this tendency of women to not publish as frequently as men will continue as women form the majority of psychotherapists is critical because research on psychotherapy is a topic special to clinical psychology as a profession. Other disciplines have practitioners who engage in the delivery of psychotherapy, but psychotherapy research has been at the core of clinical psychology. Thus, female academicians simply must see that such research prospers. Part of the mentoring by both male and female supervisors should involve reinforcing women for submitting their psychotherapy research for publication consideration, as well as encouraging them to endure in the often difficult and critical review process.

Because of emotional, nurturance, relationship, egalitarian, and equality values, we also predict that female psychotherapists may provide the important and necessary increased attention to working with child populations. Because women traditionally have spent more time with children than have men, and because children require the nurturance that women (as a group) highly value, female psychotherapy researchers may have the interest, skills, and insights that will be needed to guide this subfield. Leadership also will be provided by women in psychotherapy with children. Likewise, women should be attracted to family systems approaches, as well as community-related issues. Furthermore, women scholars may embrace the potentially integrative interdisciplinary approach.

Women and Journals

Although women are beginning to make inroads in securing editorial positions in the journals of the psychotherapy field, it is still the case by far that most editorial positions are held by males. This issue is important because journal editors serve as important gatekeepers and, to some degree, set the scholarly agenda for the psychotherapy field.

One of the reasons that women have not become editors in psychotherapy-related journals is that they still are relatively junior in the profession, and such editorial positions are held by senior persons. A more serious and potentially enduring impediment to women serving in these important editorial roles, however, is that they prefer to be nurturing and supportive. As such, relative to men, they may feel less comfortable criticizing and rejecting works submitted by their colleagues. Thus, even when offered the opportunity to serve as editors, they may decline on the grounds that they find the manuscript decision-making process to be aversive and counter to their values. I, the senior author, experienced such reactions in 1988 when I became the editor of the *Journal of Social and Clinical Psychology*. My goal was to recruit leading female scholars as decision-making associate editors. In response to my requests, these renowned women declined because of their candid admissions that they would be disturbed by the prospect of having to reject the work of others. None of the males whom I approached expressed this concern.

As subsequent waves of female doctoral graduates are socialized by female and, importantly, supportive male faculty role models, this reticence to serve as editors may abate or disappear. Indeed, over the years, I have had more success in recruiting females to the editorial role. Nevertheless, the assumed female characteristics discussed in this chapter may slow the speed with which females undertake such editorial positions. For those persons who make decisions about editors and editorial boards, it will be essential to recruit females. In this arena, as well as in many others portending to the future of the psychotherapy field, males will have to play an activist educational role in making certain that female graduate students, as well as those females with doctorates, are disavowed of any unwarranted concerns that may keep them from participating in this important aspect of the field. For women to fully exercise their professional training about the scientific bases of the psychotherapy, they will need to be willing to make decisions about what will be published in scholarly and nonscholarly outlets. Part of this change would reflect women increasingly taking academic careers. It would be a paradox if the minority of present and future males continued to hold sway over the publications in the field of academic psychotherapy by virtue of their in-fluential academic and journal editor positions. This latter scenario is unlikely, however, given the overwhelming numbers of females pouring into the field. Furthermore, there is the possibility that male editors will become more open to alternate (e.g., less positivistic, more phenomenological) methods of research.

General Predictions

What changes in the psychotherapy field might we expect as women increasingly enter academia and gain positions of power? Our short answer to this crucial question is that the clinical training programs will become "kinder and gentler." Educational environments may become less competitive and feature more frequent and intense student and faculty interactions. Collaboration on psychotherapy research projects might become the norm. Daily activities of academia will take on a more communal and collegial flavor as women increasingly are mixed into the interactive milieu. Joint projects and authorships with shared credit will supplant the previous male approach of single authorships and the building of personal research empires. In the degree to which psychotherapy research involves the intense, cooperative efforts of many people working together, these developments will be productive; however, if a more communal approach delimits the positive motivational properties of psychotherapy researchers' needs for uniqueness (see Snyder & Fromkin, 1980), new psychotherapy theory and research may be lessened.

Women should further the cross-fertilization of disciplines and interactions across academic departments as a manifestation of their various communication-related values (see Dufort & Maheux, 1995, for a related research finding on women's interest in multidisciplinary activities with other health professionals in medicine). As women take control of education in psychotherapy, they may be expected to develop links to colleagues in other fields, including social work, anthropology, medicine, occupational therapy, and nursing. Health psychology, which may increasingly have ties to the psychotherapeutic processes (see Snyder, 1999), will offer another arena of influence for female clinical psychologists who are studying psychotherapy.

The emphasis on relationships already can be seen as women begin to take positions of influence in academia. Women in administrative psychotherapy education positions provide role models for the younger women who are coming through the system. Through mentoring, women will prepare their female protégés for faculty and administrative positions (see Gilbert, 1992; Knox & McGowan, 1988). Some of the inaccurate views that women in graduate training have held previously about academic positions may be addressed via such mentoring (see our previous discussion). In a critique of the views expressed in this paragraph, a reviewer suggested that the women who are being hired are really *proxy* males who will perpetuate the previous, purportedly uncaring mentoring styles of males. We disagree, first, because we have seen many past and present male mentors who cared deeply about the welfare of their students, and it is inaccurate to portray that all or even most male mentors as disinterested. Second, we observe that the new female academicians also take their mentoring roles very seriously and, indeed, such supportive behaviors are entirely consistent with the female characteristics that we have posited in this chapter.

Relative to men, women in academia are more sensitive to others who have not previously shared in power. As such, women may be more likely to teach those psychotherapy-related courses that are concerned with cultural diversity; moreover, it is likely that women will construct graduate training programs with more emphases on culturally diverse populations. As more women obtain power in the administrative hierarchy, they also will foster increased efforts to attract people of diverse ethnicities to the faculty and student body. Such efforts are particularly important for the field of psychotherapy because it often is construed as being the bastion of upper, middle-class Caucasian males. As we quickly approach that time in our American history where Caucasian, native-born Americans will themselves constitute a minority (see Norcross et al., 1993; see also the Snyder and Ingram chapter later in this volume), this attention to other populations by female psychotherapy educators is most timely.

Ethical Concerns

Sexual harassment charges are perhaps the most frequent complaints leveled in the academic field dominated by males. As female clinical psychologists fill more influential academic positions, we predict that the ethical concerns will move somewhat away from matters of sex and coercion (as a caveat, however, see subsequent discussion on sexual improprieties by women in the applied sec-

tor) to various problems related to the setting of standards, as well as the monitoring, remediating, and dismissing of students for not meeting performance standards. These predictions flow from our assumption that women are concerned with and work harder at maintaining harmonious relationships than men. Furthermore, based on our assumption that women are less confrontational than men, we predict that women may be more willing to give second chances, and to consider extenuating circumstances for poor performance. Dismissing a student can require a difficult, unpleasant confrontation. As such, women may prefer to attempt to work out other solutions to such thorny academic dilemmas.

The Rate of Change in Academic Psychotherapy

Although the changes we note already are being seen on a small scale, there may be a lag between the time when women become a majority in academic psychotherapy education and the time when these changes become more structural in institutions (Kanter, 1977; Novak & Novak, 1996). The previous years of Caucasian, male-engineered psychotherapy training may take some time to change. Although females in psychotherapy-related academic settings will encounter many male colleagues who are invested in sustaining the *status quo*, we also believe that significant numbers of male academicians will embrace female-induced changes. As the female majority of academic psychotherapists lingers long enough in the halls of academia, therefore, their values increasingly will impact all aspects of the formal and informal psychotherapy curriculum.

IMPLICATIONS OF FEMALE CHARACTERISTICS FOR THE PRACTICE OF PSYCHOTHERAPY

Motivated by their desires to help others, the majority of women receiving their doctorates probably will seek employment in an already oversubscribed applied job market. These female graduates will join female cohorts in seeking applied jobs in which they can use their psychotherapy training to help others. At the risk of stating the obvious, *the available positions in the applied marketplace will be pursued by women competing with other women.* Whether this market can be expanded so as to support all of these new female psychotherapists is debatable, and the reimbursement picture is rather uncertain. Using the present behavior of insurers to predict the future, for example, psychotherapists will be reimbursed only for a few sessions, and then only for a circumscribed set of diagnoses. This is not the most encouraging job picture for a hypothetical young woman who has just received her doctorate in clinical psychology. Against this backdrop, what other trends can we foresee in this applied marketplace populated mostly by women? We turn to these issues next.

Women and Underserved Client Populations

Based on our assumptions, as well as practice-building necessities, we would predict that female psychotherapists would attempt to reach out to previously underserved populations, particularly minority members and the poor. Research relevant to this issue, however, is inconclusive. Fenton, Robinowitz, and Leaf (1987) found that females treated more minority clients than males, but these women also were more likely to work in settings where minority clients present themselves (i.e., state- or federally funded institutions). Indeed, these gender differences disappeared when Fenton and colleagues focused only on those psychotherapists who were in private practice. Related to these findings, however, it may be that women psychotherapists were working in the more public-oriented institutions as a manifestation of their social values, rather than working principally for money. On this latter point, women have been shown to value money less than men (Lynn, 1993).

Assuming for the moment that female as compared to male psychotherapists may be more willing to work with minority clients, will such clients prefer them over male therapists? Although the evidence relevant to this question is limited, it appears that the race of the therapist is far more important than gender for ethnic minority clients (Bernstein, Wade, & Hofmann, 1987; Haviland, Horswell, O'Connell, & Dynneson, 1983; Kenney, 1994). Because the race of the therapist appears to be of greater importance for many clients than gender, ethnic minority psychotherapists (of both sexes) should be in especially high demand. Unfortunately, there are very few practicing minority psychotherapists of either gender. In a survey of members of the APA psychotherapy division, Norcross, Prochaska, and Farber (1993) concluded, "In terms of minority

representation, we have barely progressed from 3.2% in 1981 to 4.2% in 1991. Given the fact that native-born Caucasians will be the minority in America by the end of the next decade, our profession may be poorly prepared to meet the needs of what have traditionally been minority populations" (p. 697).

The research output on the gender of therapist *and* client ethnicity variables together is very small and inconsistent. For example, one study finds dramatic effects of ethnic and gender matching (Fujino, Akazaki, & Young, 1994), while another fails to find differences attributable to gender and ethnic matching (Gottheil, Sterling, Weinstein, & Kurtz, 1994). The relationship between therapist gender and client ethnicity appears to be very complex and, to compound matters, may not generalize between ethnic groups. Overall, therefore, the issue of female psychotherapists increasing their client base via the recruiting of minorities remains unclear.

We also expect the new waves of female psychotherapists to reach out in their practices to children (see the chapter in this volume by Roberts, Vernberg, and Jackson; see also earlier discussion as to why female academicians should be more likely to study children). Both clinical psychologists trained in general programs and those coming out of newer doctoral programs that focus expressly on psychotherapy with children will recruit children into their practices. Beyond the fact that work with children is an avenue for female clinicians to satisfy and reinforce their "female" characteristics, such work is consistent with the view that major societal improvements will come by helping more people in their formative developmental years. Additionally, working with children will have the financial advantage of widening a psychotherapist's client base.

Women and Male Clients

Would male clients consider treatment from female psychotherapists as readily as they would from male therapists? We turn to the relevant research for answers. Although a sizable proportion of potential minority clients expresses no preference, many prefer a same-sex therapist. This has been found for Asian Americans, Native Americans, and African Americans (Haviland et al., 1983; Kenney, 1994). Turning to Caucasian clients, female therapists tend to be preferred by both female and male potential clients (Dacy & Brodsky, 1992; Kaplan, 1996; Pikus & Heavey,

1996; Stamler, Christiansen, Staley & Macagno-Shang, 1991).[4] This latter conclusion must be tempered by the facts that (1) the majority of potential clients have no preference; (2) among both male and female subjects who express a preference, most, especially females, prefer a female therapist; and (3) the issue of gender appears secondary when compared with preferences for other variables such as experience, expertise, age, or ethnicity (e.g., DeHeer, Wampold, & Freund, 1992). What does this evidence suggest for the soon-to-be large female cohorts of psychotherapists? It appears that having large numbers of female psychotherapists will not compromise the choices available to male clients—at least Caucasian males. Women, however, prefer female therapists (Pikus & Heavey, 1996). Thus, in terms of initial therapy preference, it seems that women will be served better by the increased numbers of women psychotherapists.[5]

---

[4]Interestingly, this is not the case when one looks at literature going back several decades. When female therapists truly were in the minority numerically, the surveys generally found preferences for male therapists (see Stamler et al., 1991). Yet, as early as 1978, Walker and Stake already were contending that "recent sex role research suggests that previously held notions about the superior competence of male professionals are disappearing" (p. 1153).

[5]Regardless of a client's initial preference, the outcome research suggests that both sexes are equally effective (e.g., Bowman, 1993). We did not want to leave this topic without mentioning that while gender preference may be important to a particular client upon entering therapy, there is no evidence that the gender of therapist is, by itself, an important predictor of actual outcome (e.g., Bowman, 1993). Even those studies that did show small gender-related outcome differences did not centrally consider the issue of gender. For example, Jones, Krupnick, and Kerig (1987) reported that patients treated by female therapists reported more satisfaction with treatment and more symptomatic improvement than those treated by males; however, they cautioned that other variables such as age accounted for far more of the outcome variance. The literature pertaining primarily to ethnic minorities, however, has uncovered some potential evidence for the wisdom of gender matching under certain circumstances. For example, Fujino, Akazaki, and Young (1994) found that Asian female clients seeing therapists who were jointly matched for ethnicity and gender were 20 times less likely to drop out of treatment than those who were not afforded this match.

Women and Fees

We would predict that women psychotherapists will lower their fees in order to recruit and sustain their client bases. (We already have heard of examples of this occurring in large cities.) This potentially would reflect a natural market reaction to an over-supplied commodity. Insurance companies also may contribute to this phenomenon as they continue to limit the total dollars of psychotherapy for which they are willing to reimburse. Additionally, if the clientele of female psychotherapists are minorities and women, they only may be able to afford relatively small fees due to current socioeconomic disparities in this country.

The aforementioned considerations for lower fees are market based; as such, it is important to emphasize that these forces would apply equally to male psychotherapists. However, there is another, more troubling potential reason for lowering of fees: women may undervalue their work. The data relevant to this point suggest that, among male and female psychotherapists, females see less therapeutic value in the fees charged (Herrell, 1993). Another survey found that women value money and savings less than men do (Lynn, 1993). Female business and economics majors report that they expect to earn markedly lower starting salaries than their male counterparts (Martin, 1989), and women have been found to negotiate lower starting salaries than men (Steven, Bavetta, & Gist, 1993). Lastly, a random survey of psychotherapists' fee practices showed that men charged significantly more per session than women; moreover, the men more frequently ran their sessions for shorter time periods (Burnside, 1986). Therefore, the *male psychotherapists were charging more money for less time per session.*

A variety of historical factors and values may contribute to the phenomenon of female psychotherapists charging low fees. Burnside (1986, p. 52) writes, "As culturally conditioned and professionally prepared helpers, some women may be more attuned to being good helpers rather than making good money. The lower fees of women may be related to altruism as opposed to lowered self-esteem. Likewise, sympathetic understanding of the financial drain of psychotherapy may cause women to ask for somewhat less than men." Thus, the lowering of fees certainly is not all negative in that it may make treatment more attractive and affordable to some people. Instead of using the previous type of accounting that emphasized the financial repercussions of any transactions, women psychotherapists may adopt something more akin to a "social balance sheet" in which the benefits in terms of people are weighed along with the traditional monetary benefits.

Beyond their possible lowering of fees, women may be less likely than men to increase their fees as inflation occurs. Instead, women may gain their rewards from the interpersonal transaction of attempting to help others. Whether it is the actual lowering of fees or the unwillingness to increase fees with inflation, the swelling numbers of female clinicians may result in a relative decrease in remuneration for psychotherapy in comparison to other personal services. That women do not place the same positive emphasis on money and fees as do men is not necessarily a problem—labeling it as such may be another sexist example of unfairly applying male values to females. The issue potentially becomes more troubling, however, if the prediction made in the next section becomes accurate.

Professional Status

The arguments that we have made regarding women psychotherapists and fees are related to our status predictions. If it indeed is the case that the relative costs of psychotherapy will decrease as women form the majority, so too will the status of the profession decrease in the eyes of the public. The formula is a simple one: *lower fees charged = lower status*. Thus, our thesis is that the typical U.S. citizen assigns lower status to any professional activities that are relatively inexpensive and not covered by insurance. Furthermore, in an American society that still is under the forces of sexism, less status will be ascribed to a predominately female profession—psychotherapy. Again, the implication that the predicted lowering of status ascribed to psychotherapy is a negative outcome may reflect male biases that lower status is by necessity "bad." Indeed, for many women going into the practice of psychotherapy, the status ascribed to their work by society may be less important than the intrinsic rewards of the work itself. Even though they realize that society ascribes relatively low status to their work, therefore, many women may honor their own values that such work is very worthwhile.

The Practice of Psychotherapy

We see several changes resulting from the feminization of the psychotherapy process. As a beginning point, take the finding that female as compared to male psychotherapists perceive their clients as having more problematic spousal and offspring relationships (Jones & Zoppel, 1982). In this study, both male and female clients reported that their therapeutic alliances were more effective with the female as compared to the male therapists. Furthermore, the female therapists themselves reported better working relationships with their patients, and appeared to interact more often with their clients on a *feeling* level. Related research reveals that women comment more often on patients' feelings than do male therapists (Jones et al., 1987). In this same study, the female therapists also were more accurate in their perceptions of clients' emotions and ongoing therapeutic experiences. Although attention to feelings can be helpful, it also conceivably could be detrimental for clients who already focus too much on negative feelings to the exclusion of other ways of knowing themselves and the world.

Yet another prediction is that the female characteristics of psychotherapists will increase the probability of clients' self-disclosing (see Cozby, 1973), and inhibit clients' aggressive tendencies in the therapy setting (Eagly & Steffen, 1984). This latter effect presumably would occur because women are more supportive and less confronting of others; moreover, relative to males, they are less tolerant of aggression (Borden, 1975). On one hand, these predictions imply a positive therapeutic environment that is open, supportive, and nonconfronting. The implications are more negative, however, if important and difficult therapeutic issues are not addressed because the client does not feel comfortable revealing and exploring aggressive or confrontational content, or because of an unspoken rule that client and therapist always must be in accord with one another. We also foresee the possibility that female psychotherapists at times may be overly optimistic about the effects of their interventions because of seeing the good in their clients. Related research shows that female as compared to male therapists use more socially desirable adjectives to describe their clients (Jones & Zoppel, 1982). Moreover, although the female therapists rated their clients as experiencing more therapeutic change, the clients themselves did not report such differences.

Another related potential problem for female psychotherapists is that they may be reticent to terminate treatment at an appropriate point. Due to their desire to continue a connection with the client and their optimism regarding how much change has occurred, they may be slow to terminate treatment that is not working. Similarly, even when treatment has worked, female psychotherapists may not want to end the treatment sessions because they enjoy the interactive, relational process. In truth, however, the future economic necessity of retaining clients so as to maintain a viable practice may enhance the possibility that both female and male psychotherapists will retain their clients in treatment for longer periods of time than are necessitated by treatment considerations alone.

Yet another possible result of women's skills and propensities for interpersonal conversation is that they may be unwilling to try any new forms of treatment that do not feature the exchange of words. In this latter regard, the prescription rights for psychologists comes to mind, such that women might be relatively unwilling to prescribe drugs because they lessen the "talking" aspects of psychotherapy. Contrary to this perspective, however, it might be argued that women might be open to medications as an adjunctive approach to treatment because of their predispositions to more holistic, interdisciplinary ways of viewing reality.

The Research/Practice Interface

People receiving their doctorates in clinical psychology rarely publish after taking an applied position. One reason for this is that practicing psychotherapists cannot implement the large-n studies that typify the presently favored methodology by researchers. In the future, some improvement in this record may occur if n-of-1 and qualitative studies become more acceptable to the women who serve as journal editors and referees on submitted manuscripts. This would mean that the therapeutic methods and techniques being used by practitioners would be disseminated more readily to other professionals than has been the case in the past. Because of the economic necessity of maintaining high client loads, however, we are dubious that practicing psychotherapists (both women and men) will have any more time to do research than they do presently.

A related important issue involves the present gap between practitioners and researchers. These two groups traditionally have not communicated well, and each has behaved at times as if they "have all the answers." Women are more facile and dedicated to communication and, as such, female-applied and academic psychotherapists may lead any future rapprochement.

Ethics in Therapy

It can be postulated that the sexual and coercive ethical infractions of male psychotherapists have been related to their gender characteristics. In a similar fashion, what ethical problems will arise for females because of their gender characteristics? First, will female psychotherapists have problems in the area of sexual contact with their female (and male) clients, or are such improprieties only applicable to men? Surveys suggest that the percentage of sexual contact *by female psychotherapists* ranges from approximately 4% (Gartell, Herman, Olarte, Feldstein, & Localio, 1986; Holroyd & Brodsky, 1977; Lyn, 1990) to 7% (Friedeman, 1981, Russell, 1984; Schoener, Milgrom, & Gonsiorek, 1984). Although these surveys sometimes recruited psychotherapists trained in other professions besides clinical psychology (e.g., psychiatry), the results suggest that *sexual contacts with clients will not go away even when the number of women psychotherapists far surpasses the number of men.*

Another point about future female psychotherapists is that, because of their strong desires to communicate, they may be prone to talk somewhat freely about their clients. As such, client confidentiality occasionally may be compromised. Similarly, therapeutic boundaries may need attention in that women psychotherapists may naturally interact with their clients outside of the therapy arenas. We would emphasize, however, that both of these potential "concerns" ironically stem from the strengths that women have in establishing truly caring relationships with others. Finally, and consistent with our previous discussion of women and their fees charged for psychotherapy services as well as their lesser tendency to be confrontational, we believe that female psychotherapists may tend to avoid dealing with nonpayment as a therapeutic issue (see Herrell, 1993).

WRITING WOMEN INTO THE FUTURE OF PSYCHOTHERAPY

We have presented various forms of this chapter to our colleagues and, without fail, it has elicited strong reactions in both directions—agreement and disagreement. Likewise, the contents have stirred debates among the authors of this chapter. Although we have attempted to build our predictions on what we perceive to be the characteristics of women and men in American society presently, the benefits of our predictions do not rest solely on their veracity. Rather, we would suggest that this chapter's major usefulness would be to inspire further discussion in the psychotherapy field about the implications of the successive waves of new female clinical psychologists.

In this chapter, we have suggested that women have many assets that will change the face of psychotherapy in the academic and applied arenas. These same strengths, however, at times may pose problems for the psychotherapy enterprise in upcoming years. The female characteristics we have discussed are not passive descriptors. Rather, they are characteristics that will produce profound changes in the psychotherapy field. Unfortunately, in the field of psychology and beyond, women often have not been recognized for their consequential roles. As such, there is merit in the bumper-sticker slogan "Write women back into history." We had best give more attention to the activities of female psychologists whose insights and values will have a tremendous impact on the psychotherapy field in the 21st century.

REFERENCES

American Psychological Association (APA). (1998). *Surviving and thriving in academia: A guide for women and ethnic minorities*. Washington, D.C.: APA.

Astin, H. S., Bayton, J. A., Brackbill, Y., Cumming, T., David, H. P., Fields, R. M., Keigger, M. G., Maccoby, E. E., McKeachie, W. J., & Rubinstein, E. A. (1973). Report of the task force on the status of women of psychology. *American Psychologist, 28*, 611–616.

Atkins, M., & Rohrbeck, C. A. (1993). Gender effects in self-management training. Individual versus cooperative institutions. *Psychology in the Schools, 30*, 362–368.

Bakan, D. (1966). *The duality of human existence*. Chicago: Rand McNally.

Bem, S. L. (1974). The measurement of psychological androgyny. *Journal of Consulting and Clinical Psychology, 42*, 155–162.

Bernstein, B. L., Wade, P., & Hofmann, B. (1987, April). Students' race and preferences for counselor race, sex, age, and experience. *Journal of Multicultural Counseling and Development*, pp. 60–70.

Borden, R. J. (1975). Witnessed aggression: Influence of an observer's sex and values on aggressive responses. *Journal of Personality and Social Psychology, 31*, 567–573.

Bowman, D. (1993). Effects of therapist sex on the outcome of therapy. *Psychotherapy, 30*, 678–684.

Bridges, K. R., Sanderman, R., Breukers, P., Ranchor, A., & Arrindell, W. A. (1991). Sex differences in assertiveness on the US version of the scale for interpersonal behavior. *Personality and Individual Differences, 12*, 1239–1243.

Brooks-Gunn, J., & Matthews, W. (1979). *He & she: How children develop their sex role identity*. Englewood Cliffs, NJ: Prentice-Hall.

Brown, L. S., & Brodsky, A. M. (1992). The future of feminist therapy. *Psychotherapy, 29*, 51–57.

Burnside, M. A. (1986). Fee practices of male and female therapists. In D. W. Krueger (Ed.), *The last taboo: Money as symbol and reality in psychotherapy and psychoanalysis* (pp. 48–54). New York: Brunner/Mazel.

Buss, D. M. (1981). Sex differences in the evaluation and performance of dominant acts. *Journal of Personality and Social Psychology, 40*, 147–154.

Cammaert, L. P., & Larsen, C. C. (1988). Feminist frameworks of psychotherapy. In M. A. Dutton-Douglas & L. E. Walker (Eds.), *Feminist psychotherapies: Integration of therapeutic and feminist systems* (pp. 12–36). Norwood, NJ: Ablex Publishing Company.

Capshew, J. H., & Laszlo, A. C. (1986). We would not take no for an answer: Women psychologists and gender politics during World War II. *Journal of Social Issues, 42*, 157–180.

Chodorow, N. (1978). *The reproduction of mothering: Psychoanalysis and the sociology of gender*. Berkeley, CA: University of California Press.

Clark, M. S., & Mills, J. (1979). Interpersonal attraction in exchange and communal relationships. *Journal of Personality and Social Psychology, 37*, 12–24.

Cohler, B. J., & Lieberman, M. A. (1980). Social relations and mental health. *Research on Aging, 2*, 445–469.

Conarton, S., & Silverman, L. K. (1988). Feminine development through the life cycle. In M. A. Dutton-Douglas & L. E. Walker (Eds.), *Feminist psychotherapies: Integration of therapeutic and feminist systems* (pp. 37–67). Norwood, NJ: Ablex Publishing Company.

Cooke, M., & Kipnis, D. (1986). Influence tactics in psychotherapy. *Journal of Consulting and Clinical Psychology, 54*, 22–26.

Council of University Directors of Clinical Psychology. (1995). *Summary of biennial questionnaire*. Blacksburg, VA: Virginia Polytechnic Institute and State University.

Council of University Directors of Clinical Program. (1996, February). *List of members*.

Cozby, F. (1973). Self-disclosure: A literature review. *Psychological Bulletin, 79*, 73–91.

Dacy, J. M., & Brodsky, S. L. (1992). Effects of therapist attire and gender. *Psychotherapy, 29*, 486–490.

Damarin, S. K. (1991). Rethinking science and mathematics curriculum and instruction:

Feminist perspectives in the computer era. *Journal of Education, 173*, 107–123.

Dambrot, F., & Reep, D. C. (1993). Overview of feminist therapy: A treatment choice for contemporary women. *Journal of Training and Practice in Professional Psychology, 7*, 10–25.

DeHeer, N. D., Wampold, B. E., & Freund, R. D. (1992). Do androgynous subjects prefer counselors on the basis of gender or effectiveness? They prefer the best. *Journal of Counseling Psychology, 39*(2), 175–184.

Doress-Worters, P. B. (1994). Adding elder care to women's multiple roles: A critical review of the caregiver stress and multiple roles literature. *Sex Roles, 31*, 597–616.

Dufort, B., & Maheux, B. (1995). When female medical students are the majority: Do numbers really make a difference? *Journal of the American Medical Women's Association, 50*(1), 4–6.

Eagly, A. H. (1994). On comparing men and women. *Feminism and Psychology, 4*(4), 513–522.

Eagly, A. H. (1995). The science and politics of comparing women and men. *American Psychologist, 50*(3), 145–158.

Eagly, A. H., & Steffen, V. (1984). Gender stereotypes stem from the distribution of women and men in social roles. *Journal of Personality and Social Psychology, 46*, 735–754.

Enns, C. Z. (1993). Twenty years of feminist counseling and therapy: From naming biases to implementing multifaceted practice. *Counseling Psychologist, 21*, 3–87.

Fenton, W. S., Robinowitz, C. B., & Leaf, P. J. (1987). Male and female psychiatrists and their patients. *American Journal of Psychiatry, 144*, 358–361.

Friedeman, S. D. (1981). *The effects of sexual contact between therapist and client on psychotherapy outcome.* University Microfilms International (No. 8309699), Ann Arbor, MI.

Fujino, D. C., Akazaki, S., & Young, K. (1994). Asian-American women in the mental health system: An examination of ethnic and gender match between therapist and client. *Journal of Community Psychology, 22*(2), 164–176.

Furumoto, L. (1987). On the margin: Women and the professionalization of psychology in the United States, 1890–1940. In M. G. Ash & W. R. Woodward (Eds.), *Psychology in twentieth century thought and society* (pp. 93–113). Cambridge, MA: Cambridge University Press.

Gartell, N., Herman, J., Olarte, S., Feldstein, M., & Localio, R. (1986). Psychiatrist–patient sexual contact: Results of a national survey, I: Prevalence. *American Journal of Psychiatry, 143*, 1126–1131.

Gilbert, L. A. (1992). Gender and the mentoring process of women: Implications for professional development. *Professional Psychology: Research and Practice, 23*(3), 233–238.

Gilbert, L. A., & Osipow, S. H. (1991). Feminist contributions to counseling psychology. *Psychology of Women Quarterly, 15*, 537–547.

Giles, S., & Dryden, W. (1991). Fears about seeking therapeutic help: The effect of sex of subject, sex of professional, and the title of the professional. *British Journal of Guidance and Counseling, 19*, 81–92.

Gilligan, C. (1982). *In a different voice: Psychological theory and women's development.* Cambridge, MA: Harvard University Press.

Gladue, B. A. (1991). Qualitative and quantitative sex differences in self-reported aggressive behavioral characteristics. *Psychological Reports, 68*, 675–684.

Goodheart, C. D., & Markham, B. (1992). The feminization of psychology: Implications for psychotherapy. *Psychotherapy, 29*, 130–138.

Goodheart, C. D., Markham, B., & Hannigan, P. (1988, August). *The feminization of psychology.* Paper presented at the 96th annual convention of the American Psychological Association, Atlanta, Georgia.

Gottheil, E., Sterling, R. C., Weinstein, S. P., & Kurtz, J. W. (1994). Therapist/patient matching and early treatment dropout. *Journal of Addictive Diseases, 13*(4), 169–176.

Gould, R. J., & Slone, C. G. (1982). The "feminine modesty" effect: A self-presentational interpretation of sex differences in causal attributions. *Personality and Social Psychology Bulletin, 8*, 477–485.

Haviland, M., Horswell, R., O'Connell, J., & Dynneson, V. (1983). Native American college students' preference for counselor race and sex and the likelihood of their use in a counseling center. *Journal of Counseling Psychology, 30*, 267–270.

Helgeson, V. S. (1994). Relation of agency and communion to well-being: Evidence and potential explanations. *Psychological Bulletin, 116*, 412–428.

Herrell, J. M. (1993). The therapeutic value of fees: What do practitioners believe? *Journal of Mental Health Administration, 20*, 270–277.

Himes, C. L. (1994). Parental caregiving by adult women: A demographic perspective. *Research on Aging, 16*, 191–211.

Hirschowitz, R. (1987). Behavioral and personality correlates of a need for power in a group of English-speaking South African women. *Journal of Psychology, 121*, 575–590.

Hogan, R. (1997). Personality matters. *Journal of Social and Clinical Psychology, 17*, 1–10.

Holroyd, J., & Brodsky, A. (1977). Psychologists' attitudes toward and practices regarding erotic and non-erotic physical contact with patients. *American Psychologist, 32*, 843–849.

Horney, K. (1967). *Feminine psychology.* New York: Norton. (Originally published in 1923).

Howard, A. (1987, May). The pendulum swings. *APA Monitor*, p. 40.

Howard, A., Pion, G. M., Gottsfredson, G. D., Flattau, P. E., Oskamp, S., Pfafflin, S. M., Bray, D. W., & Burstein, A. G. (1986). The changing face of American psychology: A report from the Committee on Employment and Human Resources. *American Psychologist, 41*, 1311–1317.

Jones, E. E., Krupnik, J. L., & Kerig, P. K. (1987). Some gender effects in a brief psychotherapy. *Psychotherapy, 24*, 336–352.

Jones, E. E., & Zoppel, C. L. (1982). Impact of client and therapist gender on psychotherapy process and outcome. *Journal of Consulting and Clinical Psychology, 50*, 259–272.

Jordan, J. V. (1995). A relational approach to psychotherapy. *Women and Therapy, 16*, 51–61.

Kanter, R. M. (1977). Some effects of proportions on group life: Skewed sex ratios and responses to token women. *American Journal of Sociology, 82*(5),965–990.

Kaplan, A. G., & Surrey, J. L. (1984). The relational self in women: Developmental theory and public policy. In L. E. Walker (Ed.), *Women and mental health policy* (pp. 79–84). Beverly Hills, CA: Sage Publications.

Kaplan, M. (1996). Patients' preferences for sex of therapist. *American Journal of Psychiatry, 153*, 136–137.

Kenney, G. E. (1994). Multicultural investigation of counseling expectations and preferences. *Journal of College Student Psychotherapy, 9*(1), 21–38.

Kenny, J. W. (1991). Perceptions of health among lay consumers. *Perceptual and Motor Skills, 73*, 427–432.

Kessler, R. C., & McLeod, J. D. (1984). Sex differences in vulnerability to undesirable life events. *American Sociological Review, 49*, 620–631.

Knox, P. L., & McGowan, T. V. (1988). Mentoring women in academia. *Teaching of Psychology, 15*(1), 39–41.

Krippner, K. M., & Hutchinson, R. L. (1990). Effects of a brief intake interview on clients' anxiety and depression: Follow-up. *International Journal of Short-Term Psychotherapy, 5*, 121–130.

Lang, T. E., & Osterweil, Z. (1992). Separateness and connectedness: Differences between the genders. *Sex Roles, 27*, 277–289.

Learner, H. (1988). *Women in therapy*. New York: Harper & Row.

Lips, H. M. (1991). *Women, men, and power*. Mountain View, CA: Mayfield.

Lyn, L. (1990). *Life in the fishbowl: Lesbian and gay therapists' social interactions with their clients*. Unpublished master's thesis, Southern Illinois University, Carbondale, Illinois.

Lynn, R. (1993). Sex differences in competitiveness and the valuation of money in twenty countries. *Journal of Social Psychology, 133*(4), 507–511.

Maccoby, E. E. (1990). Gender and relationships: A developmental account. *American Psychologist, 45*, 513–520.

Marecek, J., & Hare-Mustin, R. T. (1991). A short history of the future: Feminism and clinical psychology. *Psychology of Women Quarterly, 15*, 521–536.

Martin, B. A. (1989). Gender differences in salary expectations when current salary information is provided. *Psychology of Women Quarterly, 13*, 87–96.

Matusek, P., Nelson, D., & Quick, J. C. (1995). Gender differences in distress: Are we asking all the right questions? Gender in the workplace. *Journal of Social Behavior and Personality, 10*(6), 121–134.

McAdams, D. P. (1985). *Power, intimacy, and the life story: Personological inquiries into identity*. Homewood, IL: Dorsey Press.

McBride, M. (1992). Gender issues in graduate students in counseling and student development services. *College Student Journal, 26*(4), 491–496.

McGowan, K. R., & Hart, L. E. (1992). Exploring the contributions of gender identity to differences in career experiences. *Psychological Reports, 70*, 723–737.

Miller, J. B. (1976). *Toward a new psychology of women*. Boston: Beacon Press.

Mills, J., & Clark, M. S. (1982). Exchange and communal relationships. In L. Wheeler (Ed.), *Review of personality and social psychology* (pp. 121–144). Beverly Hills, CA: Sage.

Mirowsky, J., & Ross, C. E. (1995). Sex differences in distress: Real or artifact. *American Sociological Review, 60*, 449–468.

Mowbray, C. T. (1995). Nonsexist therapy: Is it? *Women and Therapy, 16*, 9–30.

National Resource Council Survey of Earned Doctorates. (1974–1989). Unpublished data, Washington, D.C..

National Science Foundation. (1982). *Science and engineering degrees: 1950–80* (NSF Publication No. 82–307). Washington, D.C.: U. S. Government Printing Office.

National Science Foundation. (1983). *Science and engineering doctorates: 1960–82* (NSF Publication No. 83–328). Washington, D.C.: U. S. Government Printing Office.

Norcross, J. C., Prochaska, J. O., & Farber, J. A. (1993). Psychologists conducting psychotherapy—New findings and historical comparisons of the psychotherapy division membership. *Psychotherapy, 30*(4), 692–697.

Norrell, J. E., & Norrell, T. H. (1996). Faculty and family policies in higher education. *Journal of Family Issues, 17*, 204–226.

Novak, L. L., & Novak, D. R. (1996). Being female in the eighties and nineties: Conflicts between new opportunities and traditional expectations among white, middle class, heterosexual college women. *Sex Roles, 35*(12), 57–77.

Ostertag, P. A., & McNamara, J. R. (1991). "Feminization" of psychology: The changing sex ratio and its implications for the profession. *Psychology of Women Quarterly, 15,* 349–369.

Parr, G. D., Bradley, L. J., Lan, W. Y., & Gould, L. J. (1996). The career satisfaction of the Association for Counselor Education and Supervision members. *Journal of Employment Counseling, 33,* 20–28.

Persinger, M. A., & Marecek, K. (1991). Psychometric differentiation of men and women by the Personal Philosophy Inventory. *Personality and Individual Differences, 12,* 1267–1271.

Peter, E., & Gallop, R. (1994). The ethic of care: A comparison of nursing and medical students. *IMAGE: Journal of Nursing Scholarship, 26,* 47–51.

Pikus, C. F., & Heavey, C. L. (1996). Client preferences for therapist gender. *Journal of College Student Psychotherapy, 10,* 35–43.

Pizurka, H., Meija, A., Butter, I., & Ewart, L. (1987). *Women as providers of health care.* Geneva: World Health Organization.

Pratto, F., Sidanius, J., Stallworth, L. M., & Malle, B. F. (1994). Social dominance orientation: A personality variable predicting social and political attitudes. *Journal of Personality and Social Psychology, 67,* 741–763.

Rane, T. R., & Draper, T. W. (1995). Negative evaluations of men's nurturant touching of young children. *Psychological Reports, 76,* 811–818.

Robertson, J., & Fitzgerald, L. F. (1990). The (mis)treatment of men: Effects of client gender role and life-style on diagnosis and attribution of pathology. *Journal of Counseling Psychology, 37,* 3–9.

Russell, R. (1984). *Social workers' awareness of and response to the problem of sexual contact between clients and helping professionals.* Unpublished master's thesis, University of Washington, Seattle.

Russo, N. F., & Denmark, F. (1987). Contributions of women to psychology. *Annual Review of Psychology, 38,* 279–298.

Sarason, B. R., Sarason, I. G., Hacker, T. A., & Basham, R. B. (1985). Concomitants of social support: Social skills, physical attractiveness, and gender. *Journal of Personality and Social Psychology, 49,* 469–480.

Schaef, A. W. (1985). *Women's reality: An emerging female system in a white male society.* San Francisco: Harper & Row.

Schoener, G. R., Milgrom, J. H., & Gonsiorek, J. (1984). Sexual exploitation of clients by therapists. *Women & Therapy, 3,* 63–69.

Shumaker, S. A., & Hill, D. R. (1991). Gender differences in social support and physical health. *Health Psychology, 10,* 102–111.

Snyder, C. R. (1994). *The psychology of hope: You can get there from here.* New York: Free Press.

Snyder, C. R. (1999). Coping: Where are you going? In C. R. Snyder (Ed.), *Coping: The psychology of what works* (pp. 324–333). New York: Oxford University Press.

Snyder, C. R., & Dinoff, B. (1999). Coping: Where have you been? In C. R. Snyder (Ed.), *Coping: The psychology of what works* (pp. 3–17). New York: Oxford University Press.

Snyder, C. R., & Fromkin, H. L (1980). *Uniqueness: The human pursuit of difference.* New York: Plenum.

Snyder, C. R., Harris, C., Anderson, J. R., Holleran, S. A., Irving, L. M., Sigmon, S. T., Yoshinobu, L., Gibb, J., Langelle, C., & Harney, P. (1991). The will and the ways: Development and validation of an individual differences measure of hope. *Journal of Personality and Social Psychology, 60,* 570–585.

Snyder, C. R., Hoza, B., Pelham, W. E., Rapoff, M., Ware, L., Danovsky, M., Highberger, L., Rubinstein, H, & Stahl, K. (1997). The development and validation of the Children's Hope Scale. *Journal of Pediatric Psychology, 22*(3), 399–421.

Snyder, M., & Kendzierski, D. (1982). Choosing social situations: Investigating the origins of correspondences between attitudes and behavior. *Journal of Personality, 50,* 280–295.

Spence, J. T. (1984). Masculinity, femininity, and gender-related traits: A conceptual analysis and critique of current research. In B. A. Maher & W. B. Maher (Eds.), *Progress in experimental personality research* (Vol. 13, pp. 1–97). San Diego, CA: Academic Press.

Spence, J. T. (1985). Gender identity and its implications for concepts of masculinity and femininity. In T. Sondregger (Ed.), *Nebraska Symposium on Motivation* (pp. 59–75). Lincoln: University of Nebraska Press.

Spence, J. T., Helmreich, R. L., & Stapp, J. (1974). The Personal Attributes Questionnaire: A measure of sex role stereotypes and masculinity-femininity. *JSAS Catalog of Selected Documents in Psychology, 4,* 43 (Ms. No. 617).

Stamler, V. L., Christiansen, M. D., Staley, K. H., & Macagno-Shang, L. (1991). Client preferences for counselor gender. *Psychology of Women Quarterly, 15,* 317–321.

Steven, C. K., Bavetta, A. G., & Gist, M. E. (1993). Gender differences in the acquisition of salary negotiation skills: The role of goals, self-efficacy, and perceived control. *Journal of Applied Psychology, 78,* 723–735.

Stewart, A. J., & Winter, D. G. (1976). Arousal of the power motive in women. *Journal of Consulting and Clinical Psychology, 44,* 495–496.

Sturdivant, S. (1980). *Therapy with women.* New York: Springer.

Sue, D. W., & Sue, D. (1990). *Counseling the culturally different: Theory and practice*. New York: Wiley.

Tannen, D. (1990). *You just don't understand*. New York: William Morrow.

Task Force. (1995). *Report of the task force on the changing genders composition of psychology*. Washington, D.C.: American Psychological Association.

Tavris, C. (1992). *The mismeasure of woman*. New York: Simon & Schuster.

Tavris, C., & Offir, C. (1977). *The longest war*. New York: Harcourt Brace Jovanovich.

Travis, C. B., Gressley, D. L., & Crumpler, C. A. (1991). Feminist contributions to health psychology. *Psychology of Women Quarterly, 15,* 557–566.

Turner, H. A. (1994). Gender and social support: Taking the bad with the good? *Sex Roles, 30,* 521–541.

Unger, R. K. (Ed.). (1989). *Representations: Social constructions of gender*. Amityville, NY: Baywood.

Unger, R. K. (1990). Imperfect reflections of reality. In R. I. Hare-Mustin & J. Marecek (Eds.), *Making a difference: Psychology and the construction of gender* (pp. 102–149). New Haven: Yale University Press.

Unger, R. K., & Crawford, M. (1992). *Women & gender: Feminist psychology*. New York: McGraw-Hill.

Walker, E. F., & Stake, J. E. (1978). Changes in preferences for male and female counselors. *Journal of Consulting and Clinical Psychology, 46,* 1153–1154.

Walsh, M. R. (1985). Academic professional women organizing for change: The struggle in psychology. *Journal of Social Issues, 41,* 17–28.

Whitehead, M. M., & Nokes, K. M. (1990). An examination of demographic variables, nurturance, and empathy among homosexual and heterosexual Big Brother/Big Sister volunteers. *Journal of Homosexuality, 19,* 89–101.

Wills-Brandon, C. (1990). *Learning to say no*. Deerfield Beach, FL: Health Communications, Inc.

Winter, D. G. (1988). The power motive in women—and men. *Journal of Personality and Social Psychology, 54,* 510–519.

CHAPTER 30

FUTURE DIRECTIONS FOR PREVENTION SCIENCE: FROM RESEARCH TO ADOPTION

KENNETH HELLER, MARY F. WYMAN, AND SEAN M. ALLEN
Indiana University

In a recent president's column in the *APA Monitor*, Seligman (1998) noted that psychology had become sidetracked by its exclusive focus on weakness and damage. National priorities after World War II pushed psychology toward the study of psychological disabilities, and "practicing psychologists found that they could make a living treating mental illness." But the downside was to create a psychology that focused on the study of weakness and damage and "fixing what was broken." By spotlighting prevention, Seligman hoped to turn psychology's attention toward the study of strength, resilience, and health.

Whereas prevention may have been ignored by mainstream psychology, it has had a distinguished history in public health medicine. The goals of prevention in public health are to identify and reduce disease-causing agents in the environment and to inoculate and strengthen individuals against disease. So, for example, public health antismoking campaigns might focus on reducing or eliminating tobacco advertising directed toward young people while at the same time teaching them how to resist peer pressure to smoke. But how is this straightforward concept operationalized in mental health? In the psychological sphere, what can be done to reduce environmental risks or strengthen resistance resources? We still need to know more about how environmental factors contribute to psychological risks and what factors protect or strengthen individuals and decrease their risk vulnerability. This is why the National Institute of Mental Health (NIMH) is sponsoring efforts in psychological *prevention science* that are based on the systematic study of risk and protective factors.

Risk factors are variables associated with the increased probability of problem onset, severity, or duration. Protective factors, on the other hand, refer to variables that decrease vulnerability to environmental risks (Coie et al., 1993). Ideally, prevention programs should be designed to address risk and protective factors before dysfunction has the opportunity to develop (primary prevention). However, there are several reasons why this goal can be difficult to achieve. One major impediment is that the relationship between risk factors and ultimate disorders is difficult to determine and is rarely straightforward. For example, specific disorders are usually associated with multiple risks, so targeting risk factors one at a time is not likely to lead to improvement by itself. Furthermore, there is usually a considerable time delay between the presence of risks and the eventual appearance of the disorder, so it is hard to assess the potency and importance of particular antecedent risk and protective factors.

Early critics of prevention argued that prevention programs were premature because the causes of psychological and psychiatric disorders were not known. The problem with this criticism is that the same charge could be leveled against the entire treatment enterprise in psychology. Should one expect to successfully treat disorders when their etiology remains uncertain? Yet, over the years, treatment activities flourished despite the ambiguities about causation. In many ways, prevention and treatment specialists are both faced with a similar dilemma—deriving preventive or therapeutic procedures from the existing literature on risk factors even though *full* etiological knowledge is still unknown for most psychological disorders.

A second criticism of prevention is a concern that the field does not rest on a firm empirical foundation. It is true that the concept of prevention has been discussed in the literature for over thirty years, and in its early days there was a great deal of rhetoric but little empirical work. Early prevention reviewers were sometimes bemused by reporting that prevention seemed to have as many different meanings as there were people writing about it (Cowen, 1997). It is only in recent years that an empirical literature has emerged on which specific prevention activities could be built.

The NIMH
Prevention Intervention Research Cycle

The approach to prevention research that we have just described can be illustrated by the Preventive Intervention Research Cycle (Figure 30.1), advocated by the NIMH Prevention Research Branch (Mrazek & Haggerty, 1994).

The first two steps of the cycle involve collecting epidemiological information about the extent of disorder and the risk and protective factors that are likely to influence its development. Prevention trials are built on this more basic knowledge of risk and protective factors and are initially

tested in pilot studies before large-scale prevention trials are implemented. The final step involves the disseminating of knowledge from formal intervention trials and providing support for communities as they try to implement model programs. The entire process is considered to be cyclical and iterative in that prevention trials provide information not only about the efficacy of specific interventions but also about the theoretical assumptions that were derived from the more basic research on risk and protective factors.

The recent distinction in the psychotherapy research literature between "efficacy" and "effectiveness" evaluation research (Jacobson & Cristensen, 1996; Mintz, Drake, & Crits-Christoph, 1996) is also relevant to discussions of prevention. The large-scale prevention trials that have been funded by NIMH in the last decade are similar in concept to efficacy research in that programs are controlled and administered by researchers who test interventions in randomized control-group designs. The dissemination of these findings to the community to determine what works best in the field (effectiveness) is a separate and often neglected step in the research process. As is highlighted at the end of this chapter, we know little about how to facilitate community adoption of efficacious prevention programs.

Prevention Definitions and Goals

A distinction is usually made among primary, secondary, and tertiary prevention. The goal of primary prevention is to reduce the incidence of dysfunction by decreasing the impact of

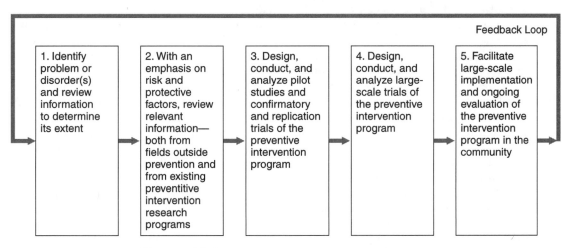

Figure 30.1 **Preventive intervention research cycle**

environmental risks or by increasing resistance resources (Antonovsky, 1974). Secondary prevention efforts are intended to identify incipient cases of disorder so they can be treated at the earliest possible moment, thus decreasing the severity and duration of dysfunction. Tertiary prevention, which focuses on reducing impairment levels in cases in which disorder has already occurred, is generally seen to be similar to the goals of therapy and is rarely discussed in the prevention literature. Whereas primary prevention might be oriented toward groups who have risk factors for disability but have no symptoms (e.g., children entering kindergarten from disruptive families or children with alcoholic parents), secondary prevention focuses on those already showing early stages of dysfunction (e.g., shy children or heavy-drinking teenagers).

Preventionists also distinguish between universal, or community-wide, prevention programs that target an entire population and high-risk programs that target only vulnerable groups (Bloom, 1968). Media campaigns that are accessible to all citizens are examples of relatively inexpensive universal programs. They have the advantage of not singling out or labeling particular persons as being in need of help. They also are democratic because every citizen is eligible to receive the program's benefits. However, they have the potential for being wasteful because most people who would receive a universal program do not actually need it. Furthermore, those who benefit most from universal programs are sometimes the most competent—those who need it the least. For example, television programs that teach school readiness skills (e.g., "Sesame Street") are watched more consistently by children from educationally advantaged homes than by children from disadvantaged homes—the group they were originally designed to help. High-risk programs, on the other hand, can be specific and targeted to those who are more likely to benefit from them. They have the advantage of being more cost-efficient as long as they can be structured to avoid the potential negative effects of labeling essentially symptom-free individuals as "in need of help."

The discussion thus far has emphasized types of prevention programs and their goals but has not focused on the design or content of such programs. A missing element in these definitions of prevention is the specification of how prevention goals are to be achieved. For example, how does one design a program to reduce the incidence of academic failure in the elementary grades, and would it contain the same elements as a program to reduce the incidence of classroom disruption? Would a program to reduce teenage drinking be similar in design to a program whose goal was to reduce the incidence of teen pregnancy? When we confront practical prevention questions such as these, we begin to recognize the difficulties in operationalizing prevention definitions, as well as the broad knowledge base and clear theory required for the design of actual prevention programs.

DISTINCTIONS BETWEEN PREVENTION AND PSYCHOTHERAPY

Because this is a book about psychotherapy processes, it would be instructive to take a moment to highlight some distinctions between psychotherapy and prevention. Therapists sometimes claim that they already "do prevention" by helping their clients deal with future life stresses. So, for example, the technique of "relapse prevention" (Marlatt & Gordon, 1985) refers to specific procedures utilized with alcohol-abusing clients to help them anticipate and cope with drink-eliciting situations. If successful, such procedures do indeed have the potential for reducing the severity and/or the duration of future disability.

However, the term *prevention*, as commonly understood in both public health and community psychology, refers to reduced incidence and prevalence of disorder in defined *populations*. The population and not the individual is the unit of concern, and preventionists look for ways to reduce disability and promote well-being in populations. Thus, although individual therapists might help prevent relapse in individual clients, that activity is not likely to have an impact on community rates of disorder. Prevention at the community level means putting programs in place to reduce the likelihood that individuals will become mental health clients in the first place.

Are prevention programs similar in content to that which occurs in therapy? Although the locus of activity might be different—a school, work setting, or community organization instead of a therapist's office—and whereas prevention occurs earlier, before patienthood is achieved, is prevention simply early "therapy" applied to groups of normal children and/or adults? This question is actually more complex than it may initially appear and requires a greater explication and contrast of the assumptions that underlie both prevention and therapeutic procedures.

Preventionists are likely to adopt an ecological orientation that focuses on the joint role of environmental and personal factors in shaping behavior. Although such an interactionist view is not new to clinical psychology and can be found in various "diathesis-stress" models concerned with the development of psychopathology (e.g., Davison & Neale, 1994), the locus of intervention in clinical psychology is almost always individual change. Individuals are expected to change their behavior to accommodate environmental circumstances. This might mean, for example, learning to change their attitudes or beliefs or learning better ways of dealing with environmental stress. The idea that environments can be changed to become more growth-enhancing is rarely considered, except perhaps in family therapy. Even in this instance, families are expected to change as a function of the attitudes and behaviors of individual family members. The role that broader environmental factors might play in the etiology of the family's problem is rarely considered to be subject to modification. So, for example, the role that community institutions might play in a family's adjustment to the sudden unemployment of the family's principal breadwinner is rarely discussed. Nor would there be any consideration given to what organized communities might do to reduce community unemployment levels.

A common theme that can be found in both prevention work and in cognitive-behavioral therapies is an emphasis on building strengths and competencies. Whereas many dynamic therapies focus on uncovering conflicts and expressing repressed emotions that such conflicts engender, behavioral interventions are usually more oriented toward the present, helping clients learn cognitive and interpersonal skills to resolve current problems. This emphasis on strengths and competencies can also be found in prevention work. Preventionists share the assumption that people can learn better means of coping with environmental stress, and they often teach these skills to children and adults. A problem-solving attitude and problem-solving skills are relevant in overcoming a wide range of individual and community-level problems.

Why have a chapter about prevention in a book about therapeutic change? As has become obvious throughout this volume, practice in psychology is changing drastically. The practice of psychotherapy is quite different today from 25 years ago, and the field will continue to evolve as psychologists are called on to address pressing problems of the day. To meet the future requests of community members, we should be thinking of our work not just as techniques for helping distressed individuals but also as principles of change that can be applied to a wide variety of problems. Preventionists address social concerns by analyzing problems in terms of needs and resources and then develop programs to meet these needs by strengthening individual competencies and community resources. This is an important way for psychologists in general to conceptualize their work, and it is the reason we believe that regardless of their orientation, psychologists should know something about the field of prevention.

COMPONENTS OF A SUCCESSFUL PREVENTION PROGRAM

The general steps that typically need to be considered in constructing a prevention program can be described as follows. The reader should look for these components in the prevention research that is described later in the chapter.

1. Provide knowledge to citizens concerning risk behavior.
2. Increase the attractiveness and motivation to perform desired behaviors while decreasing motivation that maintains undesirable behaviors.
3. Teach and reinforce component problem-solving skills, as well as skills in resisting pressure to return to previous behaviors.
4. Assess social and environmental factors contributing to the continuance of problem behaviors and find ways of reducing these negative influences. Possibilities for environmental modification include working to change group norms and developing social structures that support behavioral change.
5. Evaluate the program to provide data that show the public what can be accomplished by the program.

Community education that describes risk behaviors is a first step in a prevention program but is rarely sufficient by itself. For example, public health messages concerning the dangers of smoking rarely change behavior; most smokers know the health risks of smoking but continue to smoke nonetheless. Although people need to understand the nature of a problem before they will act, other components focused on attitudes, motivation, behavioral change, and social reinforcement of these changes are important as well. People need motivation to give up old behavioral habits, they need the necessary skills to initiate changes in their lives, and they need social approval that supports the changes that they institute.

New behaviors are not likely to be adopted unless people want to do them and believe they have the ability to do so. For example, teenagers will not turn away from smoking as long as that behavior is seen as "cool." Similarly, a major impediment in the adoption of diet and exercise programs by obese individuals is their pessimistic belief that they will be unable to follow the prescribed program (Heller, King, Arroyo, & Polk, 1997).

An important goal for prevention research is to set in place group norms and social structures that support individual efforts to adopt new behaviors. There is a limit to what individuals can do on their own without group support, particularly when environmental pressures push them toward deviant behavior. For example, it is difficult for teenagers to resist pressures to drink or smoke when they are bombarded by media that glorify these activities and when they receive similar pressure from peers. Successful prevention programs address these social pressures by getting groups, institutions, and communities involved. Examples of activities at each of these levels include working with peer and parent groups; involving personnel in schools, churches, and recreational centers; and working to develop community-wide initiatives and events.

Finally, it is important to remember that programs should be properly evaluated. Lack of clear evidence can perpetuate misinformation and slow the adoption of effective programs. For example, there is a fairly prevalent belief among school administrators that antismoking and antidrinking prevention campaigns have either not been effective or have served to increase, rather than decrease, these behaviors. This erroneous conclusion occurs for two main reasons. First, a wide variety of prevention programs is advocated in the popular press without much empirical evidence available to support their efficacy. Without knowing the data, it is difficult for a school administrator to distinguish among the effectiveness of a "Just say no" program; a program that

provides education about the dangers of substance use; and a more empirically supported program that deals with knowledge, motivation, social skills, and group reinforcement (e.g., Botvin & Tortu, 1988). A second problem is the lack of control-group comparisons. Because the base rate for substance use generally increases from early to late adolescence, a program without a control or comparison group will look ineffective. Rates of substance use may be generally increasing, but a good program can lower the incidence or amount of substance use compared to rates observed in a no-intervention control group.

IS PREVENTION EFFECTIVE?

The primary prevention literature has been growing exponentially in the last two decades, and periodic reviews are available that capture both the accomplishments and problems associated with this new field (Albee & Gullotta, 1997; Durlak, 1995; Heller, 1990; Kessler & Goldston, 1986; Mrazek & Haggerty, 1994; Price, Cowen, Lorion, & Ramos-McKay, 1988; Yoshikawa, 1994). In a meta-analysis of 177 primary prevention programs designed to reduce behavioral and social problems in children and adolescents, Durlak and Wells (1997) concluded that on the average the prevention programs for children that they reviewed produced outcomes similar or better than those obtained in medical prevention or treatment programs (e.g., heart bypass surgery and cancer chemotherapy). In their review, the average prevention program participant surpassed the performance of between 59% and 82% of control-group participants. Interventions produced improvements in multiple domains of adjustment—both in increasing competencies and in reducing problem behaviors—and these gains did not diminish over time (p. 135).

Although meta-analyses can provide a useful benchmark for a field's progress, they are limited by the quality and scope of the research that is reviewed. For example, in the Durlak and Wells (1997) review, only studies published before 1991 that had children's mental health outcomes were covered. Studies directed toward academic achievement, substance abuse, smoking, or delinquency prevention were not reviewed. Thus, the finding that parent-training programs focused on improving parents' child-rearing skills "was the only type of intervention that did not achieve significant positive mean effects" (p. 142) must be interpreted cautiously and may be a function of the outcomes examined. Parent training may not affect scores on mental health inventories but may be important for other academic or social behaviors not covered by the review. It is also important to recognize that this review covered only individual outcomes—that is, changes that were noted in the children's adjustment. Other outcomes that may have occurred in either the setting or in other persons were not reported (e.g., changes in a school's atmosphere or in the behavior of teachers or parents). This is an important omission because there is reason to believe that effective interventions require changes in institutional practices, as well as changes in people (Weissberg & Bell, 1997). Also absent were data on the ethnic composition of the study samples (Trickett, 1997), an issue that we return to later.

In this chapter, we review some of the exemplar studies discussed by Durlak and Wells (1997), but we describe other important prevention studies as well. Prevention activities with adults are receiving increased attention, as is work with ethnic minorities. Also, research on health and well-being outcomes, academic or job performance, and changes in organizational and community-level variables are at least as important as outcomes focused on individual psychological adjustment.

EXEMPLAR PRIMARY PREVENTION PROGRAMS

Head Start: A Political Response to Social and Educational Inequity

When the Head Start program was first initiated as part of the 1960s' War on Poverty, much of the research to support the value of early intervention had not yet been conducted. Head Start is a service program that was launched as a political response to growing public alarm about the quality of public education. Deficiencies in the U.S. educational system had become a concern when the Soviets developed the scientific technology to launch their Sputnik space satellite before the United States. Worry about lagging behind was further reinforced by popular press accounts of undereducation and cognitive delay associated with poverty. What had initially been seen as a racial problem now took on greater urgency, with articles featuring the plight of children in poor, white Appalachia (Ramey & Ramey, 1998). As part of the Johnson administration's War on Poverty, the Head Start program sought to raise academic achievement by igniting a spark of hope among low-income citizens and empowering them to work with teachers to raise the level of education of their children. Academic achievement was seen as a major route toward overcoming socioeconomic inequity.

The basic idea behind the Head Start program was to provide economically disadvantaged children with the same school readiness and social development training that more affluent children were receiving in privately run preschool programs. Over time, as other problems of economically disadvantaged children became evident, Head Start grew to include a number of additional elements, such as early medical screening and treatment, nutritionally balanced meals, and parent education. These components were added not on the basis of research findings but because they seemed important at the time. Teaching child-rearing and educational skills to parents was particularly popular and was supported by later prevention research. The research found that parent training was a way for parents at home to supplement what was being taught in preschool, and it set the stage for younger children, not yet of preschool age, to benefit from improved parenting skills.

The reviews of the effectiveness of Head Start have produced mixed results, in part because the program has been evolving over the more than thirty years of its existence. Variations in quality across sites have also been produced by uneven and insufficient funding and by variations in the quality of trained personnel (Zigler & Styfco, 1994). Research has also demonstrated that program intensity, duration, and breadth are crucially important. Programs that engaged children early, provided at least a three-day-a-week program, involved both children and parents, had at least a two-year duration, and were willing to help families deal with multiple problems (e.g., health, transportation, nutrition, and assistance with problems of daily living) were more likely to produce lasting academic and social benefits (Ramey & Ramey, 1998). What seems clear from the evaluation research is that preschool education as represented by Head Start should not be considered a one-time inoculation against all manner of noxious environmental elements. While Head Start could provide a foundation for academic and social competencies, there is now a growing body of research demonstrating the value of competency training at a number of different developmental milestones.

Research on Competency Training

Research on competency training has been evolving over the years. The early work initiated by Shure and Spivack (Shure, 1979; Shure & Spivack, 1988; Spivack & Shure, 1974) demonstrated that disturbed children and adults who had difficulties in solving interpersonal problems were more likely to use impulsive solutions to psychological problems or to withdraw from them. This observation led to the development of formal programs to train young children in problem-solving skills as a primary prevention strategy (Spivack & Shure, 1974). Their basic program, which is oriented toward teaching children "how to think, not what to think," involves teaching children how to develop alternative solutions to interpersonal problems and then how to weigh the consequences of these solutions before acting.

Spivack and Shure believed that their approach involved teaching a generalized problem-solving strategy that would be applicable across a wide variety of situations, but generalization from the classroom to other settings has sometimes been problematic (Heller, Price, Reinharz, Riger, & Wandersman, 1984). More recent uses of problem-solving training in prevention programs have treated it as a situation-specific skill whose components can be shaped to fit specific situations (Levine & Perkins, 1997). Thus, problem-solving training can now be found as a component of programs to ease the transition to middle school (Elias, Gara, Ubriaco, Rothbaum, Clabby, & Schuyler, 1986); improve the adjustment of children experiencing parental divorce (Pedro-Carroll, 1997); and decrease substance use (Botvin & Tortu, 1988), teen pregnancy (Weissberg, Barton, & Shriver, 1997), and HIV risk behaviors (Jemmott, Jemmott, & Fong, 1992) in teens. In each of these programs, problem-solving training is an important component but not the sole ingredient.

The substance abuse prevention program developed by Gilbert Botvin can be used as an illustration. The components of this program include providing knowledge and correcting myths about the effects of drugs on the body; developing decision-making strategies and understanding the media's role in influencing decisions about substance use; discussing how self-images are formed and how one's view of oneself can be improved; and teaching techniques for coping with anxiety,

skills in communicating and relating to members of the opposite sex, and assertion skills for resisting peer pressure to use tobacco, alcohol, and drugs (Botvin & Tortu, 1988). For each of these topics, experiential exercises were developed to teach youths how to identify particularly difficult tasks and then how to think of and evaluate alternative solutions to these problems.

Community and Ecological Influences on Competency Development

Competency skills learned in classrooms can be eroded if environmental forces continue to pull for deviant behavior. Levine (1998) warns that competency skills will dissipate over time unless there are changes in the social climate that support and reinforce the newly learned behaviors. What is needed are changes in group attitudes and norms, and prevention programs need design features that address the social context in which behavior is imbedded. For example, this problem was noted by Biglan, Ary, Koehn, Levings, Smith, Wright, James, and Henderson (1996) concerning influences on adolescent tobacco use. Classroom-based antismoking campaigns can be undermined by parent and peer smoking and by tobacco marketing that targets youths and glamorizes tobacco use. Given these societal influences, it is not surprising that school-based tobacco prevention programs have produced only modest reductions in smoking prevalence rates (Rooney & Murray, 1996). A more effective approach developed by Biglan, Ary, Yudelson, Duncan, Hood, James, Koehn, Wright, Black, Levings, Smith, and Gaiser (1996) added components to increase active involvement by youths in antismoking activities outside the classroom (e.g., poster competitions, games, and T-shirt giveaways), increased family communication about tobacco (pamphlets to parents and student quizzes of their parents about tobacco use), and target stores that sell tobacco by publicizing and rewarding store clerks who refuse to sell it to minors. We can see by these examples that prevention programming needs to address significant others in the individual's social environment in ways that produce changes in group attitudes and norms.

A second illustration of this point can be seen in a program developed by Hingson, McGovern, Howland, Heeren, Winter, and Zakocs (1996) to reduce traffic injuries and deaths associated with alcohol-impaired driving. The Saving Lives program, conducted in six Massachusetts communities, was made up of multiple components oriented toward reducing speeding and drunk driving. Included were media campaigns, speeding and drunk-driving awareness days, information programs for businesses, speed-watch telephone hotlines for citizens to report speeders in their neighborhoods, police training, increased surveillance of liquor outlets, and peer education programs in high schools and colleges. High school students were targeted with such programs as developing chapters of Students Against Drunk Driving and the promotion of alcohol-free prom nights. Over the five years of this multipronged program, there was a significant 39% reduction in fatal crashes involving drivers aged 15 to 25 in the program communities compared to the rest of Massachusetts. There also was a 43% greater decline in speeding and a 17% greater increase in seat-belt use compared to the rest of the state. These improvements were produced not by a single element alone but by changes in behavioral norms that were reinforced community-wide. Designing program elements that address social norms, then, is a crucial element in the success of prevention programming.

The Design of Culturally Appropriate Prevention Programs

Designing prevention programs so they address community norms also means being aware of cultural, geographic, and ethnic variations in standards of behavior. Prevention programs cannot be administered with the expectation that "one size fits all." Variations in cultural standards mean that program elements have to be adapted to local conditions. This was the problem faced by the Fast Track Program, a school-based, multicomponent program for children at risk for conduct disorders. The program included curriculum components that focused on prosocial and friendship skills, emotional understanding and self-control skills, communication and conflict resolution skills, and problem-solving skills taught in grades 1–5. In addition, the program included extra training sessions for students identified as being at risk for future conduct problems. Bierman (1997) describes the modifications that were needed to adapt this program, originally developed for urban schools, to a rural area in Pennsylvania. Rural life is frequently characterized by homogeneous populations who are geographically dispersed across the area, have traditional religious and social values, distrust outsiders, and

have limited access to social and recreational services. The researchers found that both parents and teachers were initially wary of participation, so the introduction of the program spanned a two-year period and included both informal contacts and meetings with school personnel, as well as home visits to parents. Parents were invited to enroll their children in the program only after first responding to a telephone survey, a personal home interview, and a dessert party held in their local school building. Many parents were concerned about the potential negative effects of participating in a program for "problem" children. Concerns about the reputation of one's family are more acute in rural areas, where personal privacy can be limited. The program, therefore, was described as building educational competencies as opposed to remediating deficits. The program also had to be modified to gain acceptance by the teachers. For example, the program developers found that teachers in rural areas were more likely to emphasize order and obedience in the classroom and so felt less need for consultation in the management of classroom disruption. However, acting-out behavior that was suppressed in the classroom blossomed in less structured situations, such as recess and the lunchroom. Teachers' interest in the program was maintained by discussing aggressive behavior that occurred in these nonclassroom settings.

The literature is still rather sparse concerning what needs to be done to adapt prevention programs to meet the needs of ethnic minority groups. Alvy (1988) described how he modified standard parent-training programs to fit the values of Black parents, and some of his suggestions resemble those of Bierman (1997). As was true for low-income, rural Whites, Black parents in Alvy's groups emphasized obedience and discipline. However, Black parents were also achievement-oriented and wanted their children to acquire better study skills, self-discipline, and cultural pride. These elements were then incorporated into a parent-training program that emphasized that children's success in meeting their life goals rested on a foundation of family support, encouragement, and reinforcement of positive habits (called the Pyramid of Success for Black Children). What is important about Alvy's work is not only the content of the program but also the methods his group used to ascertain what modifications were needed for the design of a culturally appropriate prevention program. Alvy started with a multiracial staff and then assembled a consultant group of Black mental health, child development, and educational experts. However, because Black communities can be quite heterogeneous along socioeconomic, educational and cultural lines, equally important were preliminary interviews with local Black parents.

This was also the strategy adopted by Johnson and his colleagues in designing a parent-training program for low-income Mexican-American mothers in Houston (Johnson, 1988; Johnson & Breckenridge, 1982; Johnson & Walker, 1987). His staff first conducted door-to-door surveys in the Houston neighborhoods to focus on parental goals for their children and to increase parental motivation and awareness of the importance of child education. Ideas from indigenous families were supplemented with opinions of Mexican-American professionals and parental advisory councils that were set up in local neighborhoods. These various sources helped determine the structure and content of the program. For example, informants suggested that there were cultural taboos to Mexican-American women leaving their homes to participate in a public program. Thus, the first year of the program was designed to be completely home-based, with staff serving as in-home educators and counselors.

A similar strategy is to use culturally appropriate focus groups to help shape program procedures. Hughes and DuMont (1994) offer some useful tips about how the task of focus groups should be structured. For example, in their experience, homogeneous groups of 6 to 12 participants are ideal. Homogeneity within groups is important in facilitating ease of communication, and broader sampling of different segments of the community can be obtained by using more than one group. They also note that the questions that the group addresses should be fairly structured so that comparisons among groups can be made, but it is important to have open discussion time to allow group cohesion and consensus to emerge.

We can see, then, that several procedures are available for determining the social values of targeted groups and that this information can be used to develop more culturally sensitive prevention programs. For example, it is important for the program design to determine whether participants have cultural values that are antithetical to the program's goals. An illustration can be found in the program developed by David Olds (1988, 1997) to teach parenting skills to first-time teenage mothers. The program's goals were to improve infant health and reduce subsequent teen pregnancy and child abuse. The vehicle for carrying out these goals was home visits by trained nurses. The researchers found that, at times, parents held cultural views that were counter to the practices advocated by the nurses. For example, parents sometimes believed that picking up and soothing a crying child would "spoil" it, or cultural practices might involve the frequent use of physical punishment. Some mothers were also involved in behaviors that were deleterious to their health, such as smoking and drinking, but that were being reinforced by others in the mother's social circle. Although nurses generally accepted culturally defined behaviors, they could not do so if the mother's or child's health was being compromised. Recognizing that positive child-rearing and health practices could be undermined by significant others, mothers were urged to invite the most influential member of their social network to the home visits. In this way, resistance to the nurses' messages could be dealt with on the spot by attempting to enlist the cooperation of these significant others. Even though these efforts were not always successful in changing deeply entrenched attitudes (e.g., a few parents continued to apologize for not spanking their children enough), overall the project was remarkably successful in improving the children's and parents' health, encouraging parental employment, and reducing welfare dependency.

Should Prevention Programs Adopt a Disorder or a Stressor Focus?

It may not be immediately apparent, but there is a choice of how the focus of prevention should be conceptualized. A common view is to orient prevention programs to particular disorders. So, for example, there are several interesting illustrations of depression prevention or alcohol and drug abuse prevention programs in the literature. The general prevention strategy employed is to offer a program to persons at risk for the disorder in question but who are not yet symptomatic. In the areas of substance abuse and sexual practices, programs often adopt a harm reduction philosophy, which focuses on reducing harmful consequences of behavior even when unhealthy practices cannot be totally eliminated. Another, very different strategy is to focus on environmental stressors that research suggests can lead to a number of deleterious mental health outcomes. By reducing the stressors' negative effects, the expectation is that there will be a lowered incidence of several disorders. For example, if unemployment can trigger the increased likelihood of depression, alcohol abuse, spousal abuse, and so on, rates of these disorders could be lowered by programs to maintain community employment or by teaching people how to cope with the stress of unemployment when economic retrenchment becomes unavoidable. Both strategies are represented in the literature, so examples of each are presented here.

Depression Prevention Programs

Gillham, Reivich, Jaycox, and Seligman (1995) administered depression- and parental conflict–screening questionnaires to fifth- and sixth-grade students and then offered a 12-week depression prevention program to those who revealed distress in both of these scales. A matched group of distressed children served as controls. The intervention program had two components. A cognitive component taught children to identify negative beliefs, to examine the evidence for and against them, and then to generate more realistic alternative beliefs. Children were also provided with explanatory style training, in which they were taught to identify pessimistic explanations and to generate more optimistic and realistic alternatives. A second program component taught more adequate social problem–solving skills.

The results of the study indicated that those children receiving the prevention program reported fewer depressive symptoms through the two-year period of follow-up and that the effects of the program in distinguishing between program children and controls increased over time. The results seem to be due to increases in depression scores in members of the control group as students moved from elementary school through middle school, with its increased potential for academic stress and social rejection. Another finding was that program effects were mediated by changes in explanatory styles toward less pessimistic attributions for events.

Similar findings were reported by Clarke, Hawkins, Murphy, Sheeber, Lewinsohn, and Seeley (1995). Participants in this study were high school adolescents screened for elevated depressive symptoms, using the Center for Epidemiologic Studies Depression Scale, or CES-D (Radloff, 1977). Students with high CES-D scores were invited to participate in the prevention trial if they did not meet diagnostic criteria for major depression or dysthymia (those who did meet the criteria for a current psychiatric depressive diagnosis were referred to community treat-

ment sources). Adolescents were randomly assigned to intervention or control groups. The intervention was a Coping with Stress course, which consisted of 15 sessions in which participants were taught cognitive techniques to identify and challenge negative or irrational thoughts through group discussions, cartoons, or role-play participation. After a 12-month follow-up, the incidence of unipolar depression in the program group was half that of the control group. Even so, program adolescents still had higher depression rates than not-at-risk community samples of adolescents. The authors speculate that better maintenance of preventive effects would have been achieved if they had included "booster sessions" at periodic intervals, as has been found in therapy research.

Depression prevention programs have also been developed for adult primary-care patients (Munoz et al., 1995). In this study, participants were recruited for a depression prevention course from primary care clinics serving primarily low-income, minority populations. They were randomly assigned to intervention or control groups and were followed for one year. (Again, persons who met diagnostic criteria for a current psychiatric disorder were referred for treatment and were excluded from the prevention trial.) The course was based on cognitive-behavioral methods to control one's mood, previously described by Lewinsohn, Munoz, Youngren, and Zeiss (1986).

Over the one-year follow-up, participants who attended the course showed a greater reduction in depressive symptoms, which appeared to be mediated by increases in positive thoughts and decreases in negative thoughts. These results are worthy of attention because primary-care patients do not always conceptualize their difficulties in mental health terms and are less likely to consider using mental health treatment services.

Harm Reduction Approaches to Prevention: Reducing Binge Drinking and HIV Risk

Harm reduction is a public health concept that was developed abroad as an approach to controlling the negative consequences of addictive behavior. It is a pragmatic approach that recognizes the difficulty of getting drug users to "just say no" and stop drug use completely. Rather, the goal is to lower the damage to both user and society that continued high levels of substance use can cause (Marlatt, 1996). This approach to addiction, which was pioneered in the Netherlands, has taken on new urgency with the spread of the AIDS epidemic. Public health officials throughout the world, in countries as diverse as Thailand and Australia, have come to recognize that punitive attempts to curb both drug addiction and the sex trade drive these problems underground, where they are even more difficult to control. Government-sanctioned needle exchange programs are one example of a harm reduction philosophy in action. Although an ultimate goal might be to curb drug addiction completely, given the enormity of that task a worthwhile, practical, feasible, and immediate goal is to decrease the rate of infection produced by the sharing of unsanitary needles. Encouraging condom use in sexually active groups and discouraging binge drinking among college students are two examples of prevention research that have focused on reducing harmful consequences rather than expecting abstinence.

In a number of research reports, Marlatt and colleagues at the University of Washington have illustrated the utility of a harm reduction approach in students' binge drinking (Marlatt, Baer, & Larimer, 1995). Binge drinking is defined as drinking five or more drinks on a single occasion. Rates of binge drinking among freshmen have been found to vary from 31% to 56%, with lower rates for women than for men (Marlatt et al., 1995). Whereas heavy drinking declines with age and students begin to assume adult responsibilities, binge drinking during the college years is associated with a number of dangerous consequences such as unplanned and unprotected sexual intercourse, property damage, personal injury, and driving while under the influence of alcohol. In a survey of alcohol-related problems of fraternity men, 42% reported getting into fights, 53% reported neglecting responsibilities, 58% reported missing school or work, 31% reported blackouts, and 42% reported increased tolerance (Marlatt et al., 1995).

In a series of studies, Marlatt et al. (1995) developed and tested an educational program that described the effects of drinking and provided training in a number of coping behaviors to reduce harmful consequences. Exercises included dealing with high-risk drinking situations, assertiveness training and drink refusal skills, and relapse prevention strategies to maintain changes in drinking behavior. Participants in a six-week discussion group covering these points successfully reduced their self-reported drinking and

maintained these changes over a two-year period. But so did a single, nonconfrontive, motivational interview with a staff member (Baer, Marlatt, Kivlahan, Fromme, Larimer, & Williams, 1992). The brief, single-session motivational interview was also successful in reducing drinking rates and harmful consequences for freshmen who were judged to be at risk because of their drinking patterns during their senior year of high school (Marlatt et al., 1998).

Another example of harm reduction comes from research focused on encouraging safe sex practices. Although high-risk sexual activity has been a major factor in the initially high rates of AIDS among gay men, the incidence of AIDS has been declining in large cities with organized gay communities. Norms toward sexual activity have been slowly changing in these communities because of media attention and the availability of good, informal communication opportunities among community members. These changes in community norms have been important in discouraging risky practices and encouraging the adoption of precautionary measures (Kelly et al., 1992). However, in small towns and rural communities, less media attention is given to safe sex practices and there is less opportunity for informal discussion and the development of new subgroup norms. Kelly et al. confronted this problem in their research on the gay communities of three small Southern towns. They asked bartenders in predominately gay bars to nominate "opinion leaders," whom they then recruited and trained to publicize safe sex practices.

The design of the Kelly et al. (1992) research involved the sequential introduction of the intervention in three comparable small cities. After an initial baseline survey, the intervention was sequentially introduced in each city, followed by an assessment period in all three cities before moving on to the next intervention city, until finally all of the cities received the intervention. Anonymous surveys covering sexual practices and attitudes were completed by participants as they entered the bars. The intervention involved training opinion leaders in procedures to correct others' misconceptions about the AIDS risk, in recommending risk reduction strategies, and in teaching how to assertively refuse unsafe sexual coercion. Opinion leaders were also asked to personally endorse the benefits, importance, and social acceptability of precautionary behaviors.

Results indicated that the intervention produced systematic and significant reductions in high-risk behavior, with the pattern of results sequentially replicated in all three cities. The importance of this study is in its procedures for changing group norms through the cooperation and endorsement of opinion leaders. This is an important step in prevention research. Without community support for new behaviors, individual efforts to change behavior may dissipate over time.

Stressor-focused Prevention: Reducing the Stresses Associated with Unemployment

Loss of employment as a stressful life event has been shown to be associated with a number of deleterious outcomes, such as increases in rates of depression, alcohol abuse, suicide, marital disruption, and spousal abuse (Caplan, Vinokur, & Price, 1997). Research has indicated that the key mediating variable seems to be the financial strain associated with job loss, which exacerbates the effects of other negative life events (Kessler, Turner, & House, 1988). Furthermore, it seems clear that these negative effects are due to unemployment and its associated financial strain because they are not present for previously unemployed men who become reemployed (Kessler, Turner, & House, 1987).

The JOBS program developed by Richard Price and his colleagues at the Michigan Prevention Research Center (Caplan, Vinokur, & Price, 1997) was designed to promote the reemployment of workers who had recently lost their jobs by training them in job search skills in a supportive workshop format that emphasized active learning, role playing, and practice. Participants were recruited from regional unemployment offices and were then randomly assigned to intervention or control conditions. Because this was a primary prevention program, respondents with high scores on a depression-screening instrument were excluded from the study. The components of the program can be seen in Table 30.1.

As the table shows, each component was first discussed with participants in an active-learning framework and then was modeled by the trainers before participants were asked to practice the skill themselves in a role-playing format. For example, in discussing how to use the telephone for networking, that is, talking to people who might know of job openings, the trainers first modeled an ineffective way of conducting such a telephone conversation and then asked the participants to critique their role playing. The trainers followed the participants' suggestions, role-played better interview techniques, and then asked participants to role-play and practice these skills themselves. Using participant suggestions increases motivation and confidence by demonstrating that participants already have a fair amount of implicit knowledge that could be used and refined.

The results of the research indicated that participants in the program were more likely to be reemployed earlier than control workers and at better-paying jobs (Vinokur, van Ryn, Gramlich, & Price, 1991). Following the intervention, there also were lower levels of depressive symptomatology among program participants than among their counterparts in the control group (Caplan, Vinokur, Price, & van Ryn, 1989). The two variables that were found to mediate effective reemployment and reduction in depressive symptoms were an enhanced sense of mastery produced by the program and the "inoculation against setbacks" program component, which was found to protect those individuals who lost a job a second time after having temporarily regained one (Vinokur & Schul, 1997).

In the JOBS program, depression reduction was secondary to stress mastery—participants were less depressed because they had acquired job search skills that resulted in their more rapid return to employment. What if the focus of the program had been on correcting pessimistic attributional cognitions of unemployed workers (as in Clark et al., 1995, and Munoz et al., 1995) rather than on teaching job skills? A comparative test between these two different approaches has not been conducted, so we have no data that can resolve this question. However, we believe that the advantage would go to the more direct approach of teaching skills to overcome the stress of unemployment rather than to a program focused on the secondary emotional fallout from unemployment. Our belief is based on two interesting findings from the JOBS program. First, structural equation modeling revealed that financial strain contributed to the job seeker's depression, but the reverse path from initial depression to subsequent financial strain was not significant (Vinokur, Price, & Caplan, 1996). Second, cost-benefit analyses indicated clear financial benefits to participants that would be difficult for a program not focused on reemployment to duplicate. Not all participants improved their financial status, and there was a substantial group who did not attend a significant number of sessions and so did not show a financial benefit. Still, across all program

TABLE 30.1 Components of the JOBS Program and the Processes by Which Components Were Implemented

Goals	Active Learning (All elements in this table are examples of active learning)	Processes		Reinforcement of Self-efficacy and Role Taking
		Social Modeling	Graded Exposure	
Recruit participants	Elicit reasons why participation would be beneficial (vs. tell participants why)	Present examples of similar others participating	Indicate that the participant can make a final decision after trying out the first session	Indicate that participation in seminar is part of job-seeker role and that the participant has the capacity to overcome potential barriers to participation
Establish and maintain trust and social influence of trainers and peers	As a form of moderate self-disclosure, ask participants to interview one another and present each other to the group (vs. let acquaintance happen informally or give everyone a prepared list of participant name and interests)	Have trainers demonstrate how to engage in moderate self-disclosure by interviewing each other	Have trainers self-disclose before participants do	Have trainers praise participants for how well they introduced one another, noting that these are exactly the skills that are important in interviewing for a job

Enhance motivation to cope	Engage participants in identifying how the *trainers* can improve a role play of a poor approach to coping such as interviewing for a job (vs. tell the participants the best way to interview)	Have trainers model the suggestions made by the participants	Have participants observe the trainers role-play, then role-play, and then enact outside of the seminar	Have peers as well as trainers provide efficacy-building feedback to the participants on their role performances and contributions
Enhance procedural knowledge and skills	Engage participants in generating this knowledge (vs. give them a handout, a lecture, or a video)	Have trainers model the suggestions made by the participants	Have trainers model, followed by participants role-playing the application of the same principles and then trying them out outside the seminar	Have peers as well as trainers provide efficacy-building feedback to the participants on their role performances and contributions
Promote transfer, inoculation against setbacks, and coping with barriers	Engage participants in considering what might go wrong when they try new coping behaviors	Have trainers model the suggestions made by the participants	Have trainers model, followed by participants role-playing the application of the same principles and then trying them out outside the seminar	Have peers as well as trainers provide efficacy-building feedback to the participants on their role performances and contributions

Source: R. D. Caplan, A. D. Vinokur, & R. H. Price. (1997). From job loss to reemployment: Field experiments in prevention-focused coping. In G. W. Albee & T. P. Gullotta (Eds.), *Primary prevention works* (pp. 356–357). Thousand Oaks, CA: Sage,

participants, there was a significant increase in reemployment at higher paying jobs so that within three years after the program, there was a financial gain to the average participant of more than $5,000. At that rate, by the time they reached age 60, participants would have accrued an additional $48,151 each in lifetime earnings than control-group participants. The program also more than paid for itself with the federal and state taxes that would be due on this additional income (Vinokur et al., 1991).

We have seen thus far that prevention programs can be oriented toward disorders (e.g., depression or alcoholism) or toward teaching groups how to overcome the negative effects of environmental stressors (e.g., unemployment). A third approach is to consider the needs of various population groups and to design programs that maximize their well-being. This approach can be illustrated by our discussion of research on intervention programs for older adults.

PREVENTION ACTIVITIES FOR OLDER ADULTS

Given the predicted increases in the number of older adults in the general population in the next 30 years, it is surprising how few formally evaluated prevention programs have been targeted to this age group. Estimates are that by the year 2025, 20% of the population of North America will be over the age of 65. Yet, although there are notable exceptions (e.g., see the Chapter 28 in this volume), most psychologists do not have training in gerontology and many rarely see older adults in practice (Gatz & Smyer, 1992). Perhaps preventionists also neglect older adults because of the tendency to think of prevention in terms of work with young people to prevent later dysfunctions. The conceptual bias among many psychologists is to see older adults as already impaired, and from this perspective it might seem reasonable to question whether resources should be devoted to attempts to prevent what is seen as an inevitable decline.

Despite these ageist stereotypes, most gerontologists recognize the heterogeneous nature of the older adult population (Konnert, Gatz, & Hertzsprung, in press). Age does not eradicate sex, race, or socioeconomic distinctions or differences in personality and temperament that occur in this age group. In addition, there are major differences between the "young-old" (those under 74 years of age) and the "old-old" (those over 75).

Most older adults are not institutionalized and manage to live meaningful and relatively independent existences. So from a prevention standpoint, the question is whether anything is needed to support their continued health, vitality, and well-being (Heller, 1993). The approach to any particular group should involve these same questions: are there particular risk factors for this group, and are there protective factors or resources that can be strengthened by intervention?

Prevention as it is applied to older adults can focus on different risk and protective factors (Gatz, 1995; Konnert et al., in press). Some researchers focus on the prevention of physical decline and institutionalization. This might mean, for example, the advocacy of lifestyle changes that emphasize exercise or early health screening to detect the onset of chronic diseases while they are still treatable (Ory & Cox, 1994). Helping older adults check their homes for physical hazards is another example of how independent living can be supported and institutionalization prevented (Stevens, Hornbrook, Wingfield, Hollis, Greenlick, & Ory, 1992).

Another type of prevention activity with older adults emphasizes the maintenance of useful social roles. With age, individuals lose social roles that are important sources of identity maintenance—for example, involuntary retirement or loss of homemaker roles (Rosow, 1985). As Price (1985) has noted, "For many of us, the kind of work we have—or don't have—is an eloquent, if silent, statement of who we think we are and what is meaningful to us" (p. 2). Because individuals vary in their attachment to the work role, we are not suggesting that retirement is a major stressor for all workers. For some, work is not particularly meaningful or important, whereas for others work provides a sense of identity and support that is not available in other aspects of their lives. For this latter group, opportunities for part-time work may be important to their continued adjustment (Heller, 1993). Volunteer activities by older adults can serve this same function of identity maintenance (Payne, 1977), as long as the activity is not construed as busy work that has no social usefulness. An example of an interesting intergenerational prevention program run by volunteers, called Grandma Please, links older adults with latchkey children by telephone. Children are encouraged to call the seniors when they come home from school and would otherwise be alone (Szendre & Jose, 1996).

Prevention research with older adults is still very much in a fledgling state. Occasional negative findings illustrate why further descriptive or ethnographic research to determine risk and protective factors is important before expensive intervention studies are attempted. For example, in previous research Seligman and colleagues found that pessimistic attributional styles were generally predictive of later depressive symptoms. Among older adults, however, optimistic participants who had experienced a major life event showed a higher level of depressive symptoms than those with a more pessimistic explanatory style (Isaacowitz & Seligman, 1998). The authors speculate that because the death of a loved one is a frequent life event in old age, perpetual optimists may have a harder time dealing with the reality of shrinking social networks. A similar counter-intuitive finding was reported by Zautra (1996), who found that network encouragement of independence was associated with less depression in relatively healthy, older arthritis patients. But patients with more severe illness were more depressed when their network members continued to emphasize independence in the face of their increasing debility.

Similar ambiguous findings were reported in two studies directed at increasing the social networks of older adults. Heller, Thompson, Trueba, Hogg, and Vlachos-Weber (1991) found that linking lonely older women to similar others in telephone-calling dyads did not improve the participants' mental health. In the group studied, ties to family members were more important than spending telephone time with new friends (Thompson & Heller, 1990). Baumgarten, Thomas, Poulin de Courval, and Infante-Rivard (1988) also found disappointing results in attempting to establish a mutual aid network among older adult members of an age-restricted apartment house. Older adults who volunteered to help their frail neighbors became more, not less, depressed over the course of the study. Two possible explanations can be offered for this counterintuitive finding. Perhaps it was too demoralizing for older adults to increase their contact with frail peers. Or the problem may have been due to ethnic and language differences among the residents. Participant pairs were assigned randomly, yet there were significant numbers of two distinct ethnic groups in the apartment unit—French-speaking Catholics and Yiddish-speaking Jews. Perhaps pairings of residents should have been done within ethnic groups. In all of these examples we see the importance of age-specific ethnographic research to

more thoroughly understand the population with whom prevention research is to be attempted.

CONCLUSIONS AND FUTURE DIRECTIONS

It should be apparent from the research reviewed in this chapter that a great deal has been accomplished in prevention science in the last decade. Before 1980, prevention was a much discussed ideal with only limited empirical support (Cowen, 1982; Felner, Jason, Moritsugu, & Farber, 1983). Systematic research on controlled prevention trials began in earnest in 1982 with the establishment of the Center for Prevention Research at NIMH, later to become the Prevention Research Branch, which supported many of the studies highlighted in this chapter.

However, the impressive results of prevention research in the last decade should be seen as only the initial phase of what will require a sustained national effort, partly because there are fewer resources available to support the local adoption of programs than for demonstration projects. Research on factors to facilitate program adoption and dissemination should receive greater emphasis and should appear earlier in the prevention intervention research cycle, when projects are still in the planning stage.

The question for the field now is how to move from the successful demonstration projects supported by NIMH to widespread dissemination and community adoption. Unfortunately, the history of federal demonstration projects is that generally, with rare exceptions, they tend to disappear, are not adopted, or are subverted once the demonstration period is over and federal funds are withdrawn. Heller (1996a) argues that there are multiple impediments to community adoption and that these problems have not received sufficient attention in the NIMH Prevention Intervention Research Cycle (see Figure 30.1). Examples of impediments to adoption include the following: researchers not starting their projects with a clear adoption plan and not considering changes that may be needed to adapt programs to local conditions; the absence of community structures to facilitate adoption; an intervention that advocates practices counter to existing community attitudes and traditions; and a failure to articulate the costs, as well as the benefits, of an intervention. Thus, it seems reasonable that community adoption strategies should be considered at the start of projects, not as an afterthought when projects are winding down.

There is now a growing literature on the dissemination of innovation and the development of community coalitions to facilitate adoption (Blakey et al., 1987; Butterfoss, Goodman, & Wandersman, 1993; Dennis, Soderstrom, Koncinski, & Cavanaugh, 1990; Glaser, Abelson, & Garrison, 1983; Wandersman, Goodman, & Butterfoss, 1997). Heller (1996b) summarized the recommendations that could be gleaned from this literature and offered the following suggestions for the dissemination and adoption of prevention programs:

1. Begin by assessing the values and traditions of various stakeholder and community groups to determine how to develop a supportive constituency group. Consider interviewing key informants to solicit membership nominations. Learn about the needs of potential coalition members and how your project will affect them.

2. Discuss the problems that the intervention will address in order to build a consensus that an action plan is needed.

3. Discuss alternative intervention possibilities and the benefits and liabilities of the proposed program. Be honest in defining your objectives and do not promise more than can be delivered.

4. Determine who will host the intervention after the termination of the program's empirical test. Do not proceed with your program if a strong, supportive, working group cannot be established and if the majority of involved stakeholders prefer an alternative intervention.

5. Once the project is underway, establish a socially cohesive organizational structure for project participants. Clearly define the roles, duties, and responsibilities of participants and provide opportunities and social structures for participants to discuss their progress.

6. Encourage the open discussion of program impediments and how they might be overcome. Encourage the transmission of grievances but also provide opportunities for and model positive feedback and the transmission of rapport-building messages.

7. Provide formative evaluation feedback to constituency groups and consider their suggestions for program modification before embarking on final outcome evaluations.

It is also important to recognize that in real life, adoption and diffusion of new ideas or procedures are usually guided by informal interactions. Innovations are given a try, not just because they are good ideas, but also because trusted friends and associates vouch for them. Prevention researchers should not wait until they have something to sell, but early on they should become part of ongoing community life—and the kinds of activities around which trusted relationships are built.

In summary, although a great deal is known about prevention research, there is still much to be learned. Like other forms of psychological intervention, prevention activities should start with a "theory of the problem" (i.e., a theory that specifies the factors thought to be important in the etiology of the problem), as well as a "theory of the intervention" (i.e., a theory that specifies how targeted behaviors are best modified) (R. H., Price, personal communication). The theory of the problem describes the risk factors that contribute to problem development and maintenance and the extent to which they might be modifiable. The theory of the intervention describes strengths and competencies within communities, organizations, and individuals and how these factors might be developed and harnessed in a positive growth cycle. Because most psychologists are generally clearer about factors leading to the development of disordered behavior than they are about psychological strengths and competencies (see Cowen, 1994, for a notable exception), prevention researchers are also clearer about risk factors they hope to address than they are about how individuals, organizations, and communities are mobilized to engage in a sustained prevention effort.

Like psychotherapists, preventionists hope to change knowledge, attitudes, motivation, and behaviors in prosocial directions. But because they are aware of the social embeddedness of behavior, preventionists try to use the power of group and community processes to reinforce, maintain, and strengthen individual efforts. By recruiting community groups and understanding their traditions and values, preventionists increase the odds that their programs are more likely to be adopted initially and, in addition, are more likely to survive by becoming part of ongoing community life.

REFERENCES

Albee, G. W., & Gullotta, T. P. (Eds.). (1997). *Primary prevention works*. Thousand Oaks, CA: Sage.

Alvy, K. T. (1988). Parenting programs for black parents. In L. A. Bond & B. M. Wagner (Eds.), *Families in transition: Primary prevention programs that work* (pp. 135–169). Newbury Park, CA: Sage.

Antonovsky, A. (1974). Conceptual and methodological problems in the study of resistance resources and stressful life events. In B. S. Dohrenwend & B. P. Dohrenwend (Eds.), *Stressful life events: Their nature and effects* (pp. 245–258). New York: Wiley.

Baer, J. S., Marlatt, G. A., Kivlahan, D. R., Fromme, K., Larimer, M. E., & Williams, E. (1992). An experimental test of three methods of alcohol risk reduction with young adults. *Journal of Consulting and Clinical Psychology, 60,* 974–979.

Baumgarten, M., Thomas, D., Poulin de Courval, L., & Infante-Rivard, C. (1988). Evaluation of a mutual help network for the elderly residents of planned housing. *Psychology and Aging, 3,* 393–398.

Bierman, K. L. (1997). Implementing a comprehensive program for the prevention of conduct problems in rural communities: The Fast Track experience. *American Journal of Community Psychology, 25,* 493–514.

Biglan, A., Ary, D., Koehn, V., Levings, D., Smith, S., Wright, Z., James, L., & Henderson, J. (1996). Mobilizing positive reinforcement in communities to reduce youth access to tobacco. *American Journal of Community Psychology, 24,* 625–638.

Biglan, A., Ary, D., Yudelson, H., Duncan, T. E., Hood, D., James, L., Koehn, V., Wright, Z., Black, C., Levings, D., Smith, S., & Gaiser, E. (1996). Experimental evaluation of a modular approach to mobilizing antitobacco influences of peers and parents. *American Journal of Community Psychology, 24,* 311–339.

Blakey, C. H., Mayer, J. P., Gottschalk, R. G., Schmitt, N., Davidson, W. S., Roitman, D. B., & Emshoff, J. G. (1987). The fidelity-adaptation debate: Implications for the implementation of public sector social programs. *American Journal of Community Psychology, 15,* 253–268.

Bloom, B. L. (1968). The evaluation of primary prevention programs. In L. M. Roberts, N. S. Greenfield, & M. H. Miller (Eds.), *Comprehensive mental health: The challenge of evaluation* (pp. 117–135). Madison: University of Wisconsin Press.

Botvin, G. J., & Tortu, S. (1988). Preventing adolescent substance abuse through life skills training. In R. H. Price, E. L. Cowen, R. P. Lorion, & J. Ramos-McKay (Eds.), *Fourteen ounces of prevention: A casebook for practitioners* (pp. 98–110). Washington, DC: American Psychological Association.

Butterfoss, F. D., Goodman, R. M., & Wandersman, A. (1993). Community coalitions for prevention and health promotion. *Health Education Research: Theory and Practice, 8,* 315–330.

Caplan, R. D., Vinokur, A. D., & Price, R. H. (1997). From job loss to reemployment: Field experiments in prevention-focused coping. In G. W. Albee & T. P. Gullotta (Eds.), *Primary prevention works* (pp. 341–379). Thousand Oaks, CA: Sage.

Caplan, R. D., Vinokur, A. D., Price, R. H., & van Ryn, M. (1989). Job seeking, reemployment, and mental health: A randomized field experiment in coping with job loss. *Journal of Applied Psychology, 74,* 759–769.

Clarke, G. N., Hawkins, W., Murphy, M., Sheeber, L. B., Lewinsohn, P. M., & Seeley, M. S. (1995). Targeted prevention of unipolar depressive disorder in an at-risk sample of high school adolescents: A randomized trial of a group cognitive intervention. *Journal of the American Academy of Child and Adolescent Psychiatry, 34,* 312–321.

Coie, J. D., Watt, N. F., West, S. G., Hawkins, J. D., Asarnow, J. R., Markman, H. J., Ramey, S. L., Shure, M. B., & Long, B. (1993). The science of prevention: A conceptual framework and some directions for a national research program. *American Psychologist, 48,* 1013–1022.

Cowen, E. L. (1982). Research in primary prevention in mental health. *American Journal of Community Psychology* (Special issue), *10*(3).

Cowen, E. L. (1994). The enhancement of psychological wellness: Challenges and opportunities. *American Journal of Community Psychology, 22,* 149–179.

Cowen, E. L. (1997). On the semantics and operations of primary prevention (Or will the real primary prevention please stand up?). *American Journal of Community Psychology, 25,* 245–255.

Davison, G. C., & Neale, J. M. (1994). *Abnormal psychology* (6th ed.). New York: Wiley.

Dennis, M. L., Soderstrom, E. J., Koncinski, W. S., & Cavanaugh, B. (1990). Effective dissemination of energy-related information: Applying social psychology and evaluation research. *American Psychologist, 45,* 109–117.

Durlak, J. A. (1995). *School-based prevention programs for children and adolescents*. Newbury Park, CA: Sage.

Durlak, J. A., & Wells, A. M. (1997). Primary prevention mental health programs for children and adolescents: A meta-analytic review. *American Journal of Community Psychology, 25,* 115–152.

Elias, M. J., Gara, M., Ubriaco, M., Rothbaum, P. A., Clabby, J. F., & Schuyler, T. (1986). Impact of a preventive social problem solving intervention on children's coping with middle-school stressors. *American Journal of Community Psychology, 14,* 259–275.

Felner, R. D., Jason, L. A., Moritsugu, J. N., & Farber, S. S. (1983). *Preventive psychology: Theory, research and practice.* New York: Pergamon.

Gatz, M., (1995). Questions that aging puts to preventionists. In L. A. Bond, S. J. Cutler, & A. Grams (Eds.), *Promoting successful and productive aging* (pp. 36–50). Thousand Oaks, CA: Sage.

Gatz, M., & Smyer, M. A. (1992). The mental health system and older adults in the 1990s. *American Psychologist, 47,* 741–751.

Gillham, J. E., Reivich, K. J., Jaycox, L. H., & Seligman, M. E. P. (1995). *Psychological Science, 6,* 343–351.

Glaser, E. M., Abelson, H. H., & Garrison, K. N. (1983). *Putting knowledge to use: Facilitating the diffusion of knowledge and the implementation of planned change.* San Francisco: Jossey-Bass.

Heller, K. (1990). Social and community intervention. *Annual Review of Psychology, 41,* 141–168.

Heller, K. (1993). Prevention activities for older adults: Social structures and personal competencies that maintain useful social roles. *Journal of Counseling and Development, 72,* 124–130.

Heller, K. (1996a). The coming of age of prevention science: Comments on the 1994 National Institute of Mental health—Institute of Medicine prevention reports. *American Psychologist, 11,* 1123–1127.

Heller, K. (1996b). *Models of community adoption in prevention research.* Paper presented at the Fifth National Conference on Prevention Research, sponsored by NIMH, Tysons Corner, VA. (Abstract published in *Conference Proceedings,* pp. 65–66.)

Heller, K., King, C. M., Arroyo, A. M., & Polk, D. E. (1997). Community-based health interventions. In A. Baum, C. McManus, S. Newman, S. Weinman, & R. West (Eds.), *Cambridge handbook of psychology, health and medicine* (pp. 203–206). Cambridge: Cambridge University Press.

Heller, K., Price, R. H., Reinharz, S., Riger, S., & Wandersman, A. (l984). *Psychology and community change* (2nd ed.). Pacific Grove, CA: Brooks/Cole.

Heller, K., Thompson, M. G., Trueba, P. E., Hogg, J. R., & Vlachos-Weber, I. (1991). Peer support telephone dyads for elderly women: Was this the wrong intervention? *American Journal of Community Psychology, 19,* 53–74.

Hingson, R., McGovern, T., Howland, J., Heeren, T., Winter, M., & Zakocs, R. (1996). Reducing alcohol-impaired driving in Massachusetts: The Saving Lives Program. *American Journal of Public Health, 86,* 791–796.

Hughes, D., & DuMont, K. (1994). Using focus groups to facilitate culturally anchored research. *American Journal of Community Psychology, 21,* 775–806.

Isaacowitz, D. M., & Seligman, M. E. P. (1998, August). *Prevention of depression in older adults: Theory, methodology and pitfalls.* Paper presented at the meeting of the American Psychological Association, San Francisco.

Jacobson, N. S., & Christensen, A. (1996). Studying the effectiveness of psychotherapy: How well can clinical trials do the job. *American Psychologist, 51,* 1031–1039.

Jemmott, J. B., Jemmott, L. S., & Fong, G. T. (1992). Reductions in HIV risk-associated sexual behaviors among black male adolescents: Effects of an AIDS prevention intervention. *American Journal of Public Health, 82,* 372–377.

Johnson, D. L. (1988). Primary prevention of behavior problems in young children: The Houston Parent-Child Development Center. In R. H. Price, E. Cowen, R. Lorion, & J. Ramos-McKay (Eds.), *Fourteen ounces of prevention: A casebook for practitioners* (pp. 44–52). Washington, DC: American Psychological Association.

Johnson, D. L., & Breckenridge, J. N. (1982). The Houston Parent-Child Development Center and the primary prevention of behavior problems in young children. *American Journal of Community Psychology, 10,* 305–316.

Johnson, D. L., & Walker, T. (1987). Primary prevention of behavior problems in Mexican-American children. *American Journal of Community Psychology, 15,* 375–385.

Kelly, J. A., St. Lawrence, J. S., Stevenson, L. Y., Hauth, A. C., Kalichman, S. C., Diaz, Y. E., Brasfield, T. L., Koob, J. J., & Morgan, M. G. (1992). Community AIDS/HIV risk reduction: The effects of endorsement by popular people in three cities. *American Journal of Public Health, 82,* 1483–1489.

Kessler, M., & Goldston, S. E. (Eds.). (1986). *A decade of progress in primary prevention.* Hanover, NH: University Press of New England.

Kessler, R. C., Turner, J. B., & House, J. S. (1987). Intervening processes in the relationship between unemployment and health. *Psychological Medicine, 17,* 949–961.

Kessler, R. C., Turner, J. B., & House, J. S. (1988). The effects of unemployment on health in a community survey: Main, modifying and mediating effects. *Journal of Social Issues, 44,* 69–86.

Konnert, C., Gatz, M., & Hertzsprung, E. (in press). Preventive interventions for older adults. In M. Duffy (Ed.), *The handbook of counseling and psychotherapy with older adults.* New York: Wiley.

Levine, M. (1998). Prevention and community. *American Journal of Community Psychology, 26,* 189–206.

Levine, M., & Perkins, D. V. (1997). *Principles of community psychology* (2nd ed.). New York: Oxford University Press.

Lewinsohn, P. M., Munoz, R. F., Youngren, M. A., & Zeiss, A. M. (1986). *Control your depression* (rev. ed.). New York: Prentice Hall.

Marlatt, G. A. (1996). Harm reduction: Come as you are. *Addictive Behaviors, 21*, 779–788.

Marlatt, G. A., Baer, J. S., Kivlahan, D. R., Dimeff, L. A., Larimer, M. E., Quigley, L. A., Somers, J. M., & Williams, E. (1998). Screening and brief intervention for high-risk college student drinkers: Results from a 2-year follow-up assessment. *Journal of Consulting and Clinical Psychology, 66*, 604–615.

Marlatt, G. A., Baer, J. S., & Larimer, M. (1995). Preventing alcohol abuse in college students: A harm reduction approach. In G. M. Boyd, J. Howard, & R. A. Zucker (Eds.), *Alcohol problems among adolescents: Current directions in prevention research* (pp. 147–172). Northvale, NJ: Erlbaum.

Marlatt, G. A., & Gordon, J. R. (Eds.). (1985). *Relapse prevention*. New York: Guilford.

Mintz, J., Drake, R. E., & Crits-Christoph, P. (1996). Efficacy and effectiveness of psychotherapy: Two paradigms, one science. *American Psychologist, 10*, 1084–1085.

Mrazek, P. J., & Haggerty, R. J. (Eds.). (1994). *Reducing risks for mental disorders: Frontiers for preventive intervention research*. Washington, DC: National Academy Press.

Munoz, R. F., Ying, Y. W., Bernal, G., Perez-Stable, E. J., Eliseo, J., Hargreaves, W. A., Miranda, J., & Miller, L. S. (1995). Prevention of depression with primary care patients: A randomized controlled trial. *American Journal of Community Psychology, 23*, 199–222.

Olds, D. L. (1988). The prenatal/early infancy project. In R. H. Price, E. Cowen, R. Lorion, & J. Ramos-McKay (Eds.), *Fourteen ounces of prevention: A casebook for practitioners* (pp. 9–23). Washington, DC: American Psychological Association.

Olds, D. (1997). The prenatal/early infancy project: Fifteen years later. In G. W. Albee & T. P. Gullotta (Eds.), *Primary prevention works* (pp. 41–67). Thousand Oaks, CA: Sage.

Ory, M. G., & Cox, M. (1994). Forging ahead: Linking health and behavior to improve quality of life in older people. *Social Indicator Research, 33*, 89–120.

Payne, B. P. (1977). The older volunteer: Social role continuity and development. *The Gerontologist, 29*, 710–711.

Pedro-Carroll, J. (1997). The children of divorce intervention program: Fostering resilient outcomes for school-aged children. In G. W. Albee & T. P. Gullotta (Eds.), *Primary prevention works* (pp. 213–238). Thousand Oaks, CA: Sage.

Price, R. H. (1985). Work and community. *American Journal of Community Psychology, 13*, 1–12.

Price, R. H., Cowen, E. L., Lorion, R. P., & Ramos-McKay, J. (Eds.) (1988). *Fourteen ounces of prevention: A casebook for practitioners*. Washington, DC: American Psychological Association.

Radloff, L. (1977). The CES-D scale: A self-report depression scale for research in the general population. *Applied Psychological Measurement, 1*, 385–401.

Ramey, C. T., & Ramey, S. L. (1998). Early intervention and early experience. *American Psychologist, 53*, 109–120.

Rooney, B. L., & Murray, D. M. (1996). A meta-analysis of smoking prevention programs after adjustment for errors in the unit of analysis. *Health Education Quarterly, 23*, 48–64.

Rosow, I. (1985). Status and role change through the life cycle. In R. Binstock and E. Shanas (Eds.), *Handbook of aging and the social sciences* (pp. 62–93). New York: Van Nostrand Reinhold.

Seligman, M. E. P. (1998). President's column. *APA Monitor, 29*, 1, 2.

Shure, M. B. (1979). Training children to solve interpersonal problems: A preventive mental health program. In R. F. Munoz, L. R. Snowden, & J. G. Kelly (Eds.), *Social and psychological research in community settings* (pp. 30–68). San Francisco: Jossey-Bass.

Shure, M. B., & Spivack, G. (1988). Interpersonal cognitive problem solving. In R. H. Price, E. L. Cowen, R. P. Lorion, & J. Ramos-McKay (Eds.), *Fourteen ounces of prevention: A casebook for practitioners* (pp. 69–82). Washington, DC: American Psychological Association.

Spivack, G., & Shure, M. B. (1974). *Social adjustment of young children*. San Francisco: Jossey-Bass.

Stevens, V., Hornbrook, M., Wingfield, D., Hollis, J., Greenlick, M., & Ory, M. (1992). Design and implementation of a falls prevention intervention for community-dwelling older persons. *Behavior, Health and Aging, 2*, 57–73.

Szendre, E. N., & Jose, J. E. (1996). Telephone support by elderly volunteers to inner-city childdren. *Journal of Community Psychology, 24*, 87–96.

Thompson, M. G., & Heller, K. (1990). Facets of support related to well-being: Quantitative social isolation and perceived family support in a sample of elderly women. *Psychology and Aging, 5*, 535–544.

Trickett, E. J. (1997). Ecology and primary prevention: Reflections on a meta-analysis. *American Journal of Community Psychology, 25*, 197–205.

Vinokur, A. D., Price, R. H., & Caplan, R. D. (1996). Hard times and hurtful partners: How financial strain affects depression and relationship satisfaction of unemployed persons and their spouses. *Journal of Personality and Social Psychology, 71*, 166–179.

Vinokur, A. D., & Schul, Y. (1997). Mastery and inoculation against setbacks as active ingredients in the JOBS intervention for the unemployed. *Journal of Consulting and Clinical Psychology, 65,* 867–877.

Vinokur, A. D., van Ryn, M., Gramlich, E. M., & Price, R. H. (1991). Long-term follow-up and benefit-cost analysis of the JOBS program: A preventive intervention for the unemployed. *Journal of Applied Psychology, 76,* 213–219.

Wandersman, A., Goodman, R. M., & Butterfoss, F. D. (1997). Understanding coalitions and how they operate: An "open systems" organizational framework. In M. Minkler (Ed.), *Community organizing and community building for health* (pp. 261–277). New Brunswick, NJ: Rutgers University Press.

Weissberg, R. P., Barton, H. A., & Shriver, T. P. (1997). The social-competence promotion program for young adolescents. In G. W. Albee & T. P. Gullotta (Eds.), *Primary prevention works* (pp. 268–290). Thousand Oaks, CA: Sage.

Weissberg, R. P., & Bell, D. N. (1997). A meta-analytic review of primary prevention programs for children and adolescents: Contributions and caveats. *American Journal of Community Psychology, 25,* 207–214.

Yoshikawa, H. (1994). Prevention as cumulative protection: Effects of early family support and education on chronic delinquency and its risks. *Psychological Bulletin, 115,* 28–54.

Zautra, A. J. (1996). Investigations of the ongoing stressful situations among those with chronic illness. *American Journal of Community Psychology, 24,* 697–717.

Zigler, E., & Styfco, S. J. (1994). Head Start: Criticisms in a constructive context. *American Psychologist, 49,* 127–132.

CHAPTER 31

NATIONAL
MENTAL
HEALTH
ISSUES

CHARLES A. KIESLER
University of Missouri, Columbia

NATIONAL MENTAL HEALTH ISSUES

More than ever before, any discussion of the future of psychotherapy needs to be placed in the broader context of the problems and pressures of the *system* of health and mental health care in the United States. It is a system that has undergone wrenching change, especially in the last decade, although the changes have been increasingly fast-paced for 30 years.

As one outcome of the last decade of change, the importance of psychotherapy—whether considered to be a technique, a mode of delivering mental health services, a mental health service itself, or a process of ameliorative change—has declined. Certainly, psychologists' income from therapy has declined. A not unlikely scenario for the future is that these declines will continue, perhaps even precipitously.

Indeed, one possible future (some would say, the most likely one) for psychotherapy is that it will exist but essentially no one will be willing to pay for it, or at least third-party payors won't. If no one will pay, people will not be trained in psychotherapy (the traditional model anyway) and graduate departments will no longer teach it. Ethical considerations alone would argue against maintaining a five-year (more or less) doctoral program, the completion of which would not allow one to make a living. A recent article in the *APA Monitor* about doctoral students incurring increasing debt included laments by recent doctorates that they could not make a decent living, let alone repay sizable student loans.

In short, one can't discuss the future of psychotherapy in isolation, as if it were separate from the overwhelming forces of systematic change in health and mental health care. The field of psychotherapy, at least that part of it for which reimbursement is received, does not control its own future. The future must be discussed in the context of managed care.

The history of current managed care has its primary roots in the public's disgust with health care costs rising at a rate of 15% or so a year, thereby doubling and redoubling every five years. Health care costs 30 years ago had a share of gross domestic product (GDP) equal to that of education, but will soon cost twice what we spend on education.

The so called *health care revolution* was initiated mostly by large corporations, such as Chrysler and Honeywell, who by virtue of their size were allowed to insure the health costs of their own employees, without some of the legal restrictions placed on insurance companies. Chrysler, in particular, under the direction of Joe Califano (the former Secretary of Health, Education and Welfare, now HHS), was especially active (see Kiesler & Morton, 1988). Califano had noted that the standard treatment for back pain, for example, involved a week of inpatient care in one city and no inpatient care in another.

Chrysler hired physicians to be *utilization reviewers* and to move from a standard of reasonable and justifiable treatment for reimbursement to best practice.

At the same time, the passages of Medicare and Medicaid (1965) and legislation promoting HMOs (1974) laid the groundwork for possible rapid change. The development of hospital chains further facilitated change. This phenomenon, dating to the 1960s, emphasized a variety of cost-saving measures within hospitals through various means, including economies of scale and not duplicating expensive equipment across hospitals of the same ownership. Large corporations were allowed to directly insure health costs (without going through insurance companies), whereas other organizations and corporations could not. Insurance companies such as Blue Cross/Blue Shield tended to operate on a *cost-plus* basis with minimal risk.

The combination of developments led to the establishment of corporations willing to bid on the delivery of health services at a set cost per subscriber, thereby assuming risks formerly dumped on corporations and their employees (certainly risk across years, if not always within years).

HMOs were the initial providers of such *risk-free* guarantees of health services (risk-free, at least to the corporations and their employees). Soon, other acronyms popped up such as PPOs (Preferred Provider Organizations) and IPOs (Independent Provider Organizations). A superordinate term was also developed—Managed Care Organizations (MCO). Today, corporations and other organizations develop a potential contract specifying the array of health services they wish to insure for their employees. This list of services (and the conditions of offering them) could be based on previous corporate experience, or be affected by negotiations with the union, less formal discussions with employees, or any combination of influences. Because tax law now forbids special treatment of highly compensated employees, the contract might be strongly influenced by what the CEO wants for him- or herself.

Managed Care Organizations now are requested to bid on the contract, including offering proposed changes in extent or type of service. MCO #1 might propose $75.00 per month per covered "soul" (a typical term), but also limiting psychiatric inpatient care to 27 days per year, perhaps, and psychiatric outpatient visits to ten per episode and 40 total per year. MCO #2 might propose $70.00 per month per capita and no limitation on mental health, but also propose not paying for any medication. As one can imagine, the negotiations can quickly become very complex, with proposals difficult to compare in terms of actual costs and extent of services. Bidding on an overall contract of providing all health (and/or mental health) services on a per-person or per-capita basis is called capitation. I personally do not believe that mental health services can be offered on a cost effective basis without being capitated.

In turn, the MCO may be subcontracting out various aspects of its proposal. Such subcontracting might include tests that require very expensive equipment or all health treatment in rural areas or, more to the point here, various aspects of or even all mental health care. If the MCO contracts out all mental health services as a package, that is typically called *carving out mental health services* or simply *a carve-out*. If the organization (the MCO) keeps the mental health services in-house, but hires someone else to manage it, that is regarded as a *carve-in*, but also with mental health as an *at-risk contract* (because the MCO bears the cost of any over care). If one carves out at a capitated rate, that is a *risk-bearing* contract. In a 1997 survey of HMOs (Scheffler & Ivey, 1998), two-thirds of the HMOs negotiated subcontracts for which they were not at risk (whoever wins the subcontract bears the risk accordingly).

I will return to more detailed discussion of the implications of carve-ins and carve-outs for psychology and for psychotherapy later in this chapter. I also will return to the issue of MCOs and capitated care and their effects.

The trick, dear reader, to understanding all this and its implications is to be able to put yourself into the role of the MCO. If you can do that successfully, you will begin to understand—indeed be able to intuit or infer—not only what is going on today, but probably most of what will go on in the near-term future.

These are not new issues. In 1979, Kiesler, Cummings, and VandenBos edited a book called *Psychology and National Health Insurance*. In part of it, we outlined a number of the proposals for national health insurance then being considered in Congress (at one point there were about 20). Looking at that volume again recently, I discovered that many of those proposals are very relevant today. They had died at the time because Presidents Ford, Reagan, and Bush were opposed to national health insurance. In 1980 (Kiesler, 1980), I tried to interest psychology in starting a subfield called Mental Health Policy. Later (Kiesler, 1985; Kiesler & Teru, 1987), I showed that, contrary to our intentions, the country spent 70% of the mental health dollar on in-patient care, but that outpatient care for the severely mentally ill was both more effective and less expensive. In spite of that, we showed (Kiesler & Sibulkin, 1987; and Kiesler & Simpkins, 1993) that inpatient care was increasing in the United States. In 1988, Kiesler and Morton described the health care revolution, where it was going, and its probable impact on psychology. Later, I argued (Kiesler, 1993) that a national mental health policy was doomed to fail because it attempted to mimic health policy, which, obviously, was going to fail (and it did, to be replaced by managed care). The list of other investigators involved in raising the red flags on this concern is too long to describe in the space allocated, but Pat De Leon comes to mind and George Albee (in this volume) and the first one to ring many of these bells, Nicholas Cummings.

If one can successfully see the world as the leadership of Managed Care Organizations must do, many things becomes clearer. Organizations must put out contracts because they need to control costs better; many have no choice. For example, when I was a university chancellor working on a five-year plan for the campus, I concluded that our health care cost—absent of dramatic action on our part—would increase by $25,000,000 by the fifth year. Indeed in year seven in this scenario, our health cost for the employees of the university would exceed the total income received from undergraduate tuition. Obviously, we went to managed care. We had to.

Organizations, in my opinion, do want to give their employees first-rate and sufficient health care. Employees obviously want it, too. Remember that most employees share the cost of health care with employers. The rising cost was hurting them, as well as employers. The employees have not typically fought the switches to managed care as much as many had anticipated. That is not to say, however, they haven't fought many of the details of managed care.

Competitive biddings require a very sharp pencil. Bidders are encouraged to come in with a bid as low as possible, of course. However, the in-terpretation that the decision of which MCO will be approved will be based on dollars per capita alone leads to several problems that could have and perhaps should have been anticipated.

(1) Marginal companies, that is, those with insufficient funding backing them, sometimes made bids that were too risky. That is, the health care they promised to deliver cost more than they predicted, which left some to try to reduce their costs later in ways that involved borderline ethics, or worse. As readers know from following the news, MCOs have been accused of raising barriers to care (making it more difficult to receive needed care), trying too hard to avoid elective surgery, trying to exclude from the contract a variety of chronic care (or to receive special compensation outside the contract for this care), and so forth. When very much of this sort of thing occurs, consumers become infuriated. Many of them, in their frustration, have turned to Congress to obtain special legislation, such as that dealing with a patients' Bill of Rights and the like.

(2) The financial position of some of the under-funded MCOs became so precarious that they were themselves victims of hostile takeovers or went bankrupt in the middle of a contract. Some argue bankruptcy laws have become too lenient so the company can too easily declare bankruptcy as a strategy to reduce debt. These antics can be especially difficult for health care consumers to endure. One only has to consider cases of people with expensive and life-threatening conditions caught in the middle of such "strategies" to understand the anger of consumers about many of these issues.

As Chancellor of The University of Missouri, Columbia, I was in the unusual position of being both the employer of the faculty and staff and the owner of the hospital for which income was needed. When we established an HMO to better control costs, we kept the above considerations in mind, and took a number of actions that helped make the new health plan a success. It may be educational to consider some of the actions.

First, we held extensive open meetings with faculty and staff, both to hear their concerns and to better inform medical planners of ways in which our group had special needs.

Second, we also established a *consumer council* (of faculty and staff) to have an easier impact on the system and to keep it constantly evolving. This also provided an easy channel for consumers to bring their problems to their peers. This council then wrote a monthly report on complaints, which was published in the campus newspaper.

Third, we established a feedback loop on all services by requesting anonymous completion of patient satisfaction forms for every contact with the health system, and then published a statistical summary of them. At the end of the first month, for example, we published approval ratings of over 92% for every aspect of health delivery but two: time spent in the waiting room, and time taken after initial contact to the dates of the actual appointment.

Feedback was enormously helpful to patients and service providers alike. For example, as a result of the first patient satisfaction ratings, we hired as an outside consultant an expert in Queuing Theory to bring down the time between request, appointment, and the subsequent time spent in the waiting room. For the patients, the published ratings allowed them to put their own impressions and criticisms of the system into perspective. That is, one could see in print if the negative and/or positive experiences one had were typical or unusual.

I said at the beginning of this chapter that we had to put psychotherapy in the context of the current system of health and mental health care. *System* is the key word here and several connotations of it are important to the future of psychotherapy in the 21st century. One connotation of system is its singularity: things that affect the system as a whole are considered most important. The first stage of the concept by an MCO is the successful bidding on and implementation of a contract. The key aspect (but not the only determinate) of that success is cost. When considering how to cut costs without affecting quality, I suspect certain rules of thumb (drawn from the literature) would come to mind. Consider the following from health practice:

1. Seventy percent of the health dollar is spent on 15% of the insurees.
2. Specialists cost more than generalists, but are overused.
3. Every hospital is in a very competitive situation regarding expensive equipment (MRIs and the like) and perquisites for physicians. For example, some states have more MRI machines than does the country of Canada. We are overly equipped in the most expensive way possible.
4. For every dollar of prenatal care, we save $8.00 in subsequent health care costs.
5. Emergency room care is the most expensive, yet is used (especially in the evenings and weekends) for routine treatment.
6. There is no evidence that the health problems of the people who visit physicians are any worse than the ones who don't (Mechanic, 1994).

For the purposes of this discussion, let's not argue about the veracity of these statements. We only need assume that the manager of the system believes them to be true. Let us also assume that the manager of the system wants to preserve needed health care while decreasing costs, decreasing it perhaps to the point of providing some new kinds of care. What would he or she do? It's fairly obvious.

Utilization review is an obvious step. We would find in further investigation that the small number of patients accounting for the majority of health care costs tends to have ill-defined health problems that lead them to wander from specialist to specialist with each patient always ending with (from the patient's point of view) unsatisfactory care. Each specialist is typically unaware of the other treatment, and when becoming aware of it, often sends the patient to a psychiatrist.

Utilization review also increases the proportion of care given by a generalist, who is less expensive but still very well trained to handle most problems. Utilization review, if handled correctly, could deflect routine care from the emergency room to the generalist during non-prime hours.

Number three in the list might impel the system to acquire more than one hospital to decrease the duplication of the most expensive technology, which was one of the first emphases of the budding hospital corporate chains. Number four would suggest an aggressive outreach campaign to reach insurees for whom preventive services would be the most effective (free condoms and free pregnancy tests come under this general rubric).

Who uses a physician and why suggests a program of active research and follow-up. It might also suggest initiating a thorough checkup when entering the plan (much as Kaiser Permanente has been doing for decades, meeting the goal of prevention as well).

Suppose we agree to all that. What rules of thumb might our system planner come up with when considering mental health? Some obvious, but data-based, ones follow:

1. Seventy percent of the mental health dollar goes for inpatient care.
2. In mental health care there is no evidence of the Ph.D. therapist being more effective than a non-Ph.D. therapist.
3. There is no *best practice* model through which the therapist and the client can agree on what the problem is and what the goals of therapy should be.
4. Inpatient treatment for alcoholism is no more effective than outpatient treatment and can be ten times as expensive, but the typical treatment is inpatient.
5. No data indicate that long-term psychotherapy is more effective than short-term, but some data do show short-term to be more effective under certain conditions. In both instances, short-term would be the more cost effective.
6. There is controversy in the literature as to whether it is more effective for psychotherapy to treat the overt problem or its presumed latent roots.
7. We can treat most of the seriously mentally ill in the community, but the proper programs either do not exist or are underfunded.
8. There are no data indicating which psychological problems are more amenable to psychotherapy and which are more likely to be ameliorated without formal treatment.

With these rules of thumb, obviously the system would require some active means of deflecting patients away from inpatient care, certainly for serious mental illness and alcoholism. This will require some increased flexibility of funding and some enhanced support of, say, Aggressive Community Treatment (ACT) programs. Some MCOs have done exactly this (and surprisingly, some of the early flexible programs involved Medicaid).

Utilization review would be emphasized in mental health as well as in physical health, although the issues become much more complicated regarding privacy and confidentiality. Issues regarding underutilization of needed care arise as well.

The data suggest therapy can drift on and on. Clearly the system would emphasize mutually agreed-upon goals and short-term therapy (see the Bloom chapter in this volume).

One suspects that MCOs have thought about the issue of substitutability of therapists. There is some hint that psychiatrists have been reduced in number at HMOs in favor of psychologists, and that apparently clinical social workers are now being substituted for psychologists. It is not clear that any of these people were actually doing therapy because the numbers are aggregate figures. However, no profit-minded organization tries to avoid the problem of appropriate pay for a given task. None tries to overpay, or use a specialist when a generalist would do.

Therapists need to provide, gather, or instigate the data base necessary to show what they are able to accomplish and what the cost benefit and cost effectiveness of their efforts are. It may be necessary to suggest who should pay for it. For example, Medicaid and Medicare are funded by public monies (Medicaid completely by public monies; individuals contribute to the Medicare dollars, with some copayment as well). A given treatment may well have positive effect but still provoke the question, "Should the public pay for it?"

The for-profit corporation can ask "It may be good for our employees and desired by them, but should we pay for it?" Mohl (1998) describes this issue very well: "I tell my patients their insurance company believes they contracted for treatment of their depression, including minimizing risk of relapse, but not to help them relate better to their mates, raise baseline self-esteem, or be more qualified at work. These last improvements are on the patient's nickel" (p. 1391).

The question of "Who pays?" in health and mental health is one that perhaps will not go away in the near-term future of service provision, nor should it. There is a certain moral and ethical underpinning to this question that glib responses should not be allowed to deflect. It is a question well worth continuing to ask in the long run, however uncomfortable it may make some of us in the short run.

The flip side of "Who pays?" for the promising economist is "Who gains?", and many therapists and other service providers have seemed more shocked (and annoyed) with this question than the former one. The shock is only partly due to public acknowledgement of the fact that most therapists clearly do gain financially from therapy. More central to their horror at the question being asked (or its answer being readily assumed) is that it undercuts, perhaps besmirches, their long-term permanent roles as benevolent caregiver and expert. In the United States we have gone through a period of over 80 years in which the physician (and later the therapist) defined who should receive care, what care was needed, what should it cost, and implicitly who should pay for it. The assertion that they gain from the service implies a mixed motive and a notion that therefore they are not to be completely trusted in answering all these questions. The professionals have in essence been ruled out of many important discussions in which their expertise and experience would have been very helpful, if not perhaps dominating.

We have rapidly gone from a setting with too much authority granted to professionals to too little. Physicians' anger with this path has spread to their patients (no coincidence, by the way) and one suspects that the implicit system will soon correct itself to a more moderate and defensible position. However, we'll never return to the overdependence on professional judgement of the past.

There is a good deal of research activity relating to health outcomes: What are they? What should they be? How do we measure them (especially changes in health outcomes)? There has not yet been major fallout from this effort to the mental health area, although surely there soon will be.

One of the concepts routinely accepted in health services that is now appearing in mental health discussions is that of *good enough*. That is, one cannot expect the health insurance program, particularly a capitated one, to maintain one in excellent health, or when a problem occurs, to restore one to excellent condition. So one does not ask in terms of a specific treatment, "Was the outcome excellent?" That may be impossible or simply too expensive. Instead, one asks, "Was it good enough?"

Good enough for what? Well, good enough to return to work is what the employer (who is likely to be the payor) legitimately asks. That's what therapist Mohl (1998) was implying in our previous quote. The employer was interested in the employee returning to work. If the patients were more interested in enhanced self-esteem and gratification at work, they had to consider paying for that themselves.

The treatment of alcoholism might be another instance in which the employer wants the employee to be at work, on time, and capable and willing to perform his or her job. How the employee feels about him or herself and how they relate to their families may not be of primary interest to the employer, who may be unwilling to pay for it.

The combination of capitation and competitive bidding almost inevitably leads to such considerations. They are complicated issues, partly because they are continual and multidimensional. In the future in mental health, any episode involving such concepts as, for example, addiction, self-esteem, interpersonal relationships, pain management, conduct disorders, and even serious mental disorders will provoke discussions of the treatments as being *good enough*. It goes without saying that therapists will not enjoy these conversations. It is critical, though, that they learn to deal with them.

Further, the same kind of considerations inevitably lead the system toward short-term therapy (or other treatment), with explicit sets of goals. The goals themselves will be reviewed with respect to the *good enough* to *ideal* dimensions, and at each request to renew or continue treatment, one will be asked if the patient hasn't reached the *good enough* stage yet. The relationship of *good enough* to recurrence of the problems will be raised, but is essentially an unresearched issue. This issue deserves considerable work in the future.

SOME ISSUES FOR PSYCHOTHERAPY IN THE NEAR-TERM FUTURE

Many issues revolve around the fact that mental health service providers became players in health care reform rather late in a process of very rapid change. They were startled to find their product was not highly valued. As Glazer (1998) says, "Had we been able to clearly demonstrate the value of our treatment early in the managed care era, we would never have been subjected to the current level of intrusion from forces purchased by payors. Ultimately, we will have to demonstrate that we are delivering best practices" (p. 1013). One near-term issue, then, is to define best practices.

In defining best practices, it will surely be important not to lean heavily on the concepts of *medical necessity* and *standards of practice*. MCOs have raised a skeptical eyebrow toward both concepts, saying in essence that they represent traditional practices rather than demonstrated practices. MCOs have changed many traditional practices without noticeably negative results, turning the concepts of medical necessity and standards of practice into moving targets under constant revision. It will take empirical data to convincingly define best practices and perhaps some ingenuity in devising how appropriate data bases may be accumulated across, perhaps, otherwise unconnected caregivers.

Meanwhile, income is decreasing. Williams, Kohout, and Wickerski (1998), as part of a larger survey of the American Psychological Association, report that 57% of independent practitioners reported decreases in income (an average decrease of 17%) in 1997 (53% reported such decreases in 1995) and that 57% of those in group practice reported decreases as well. Practitioners overwhelmingly attributed the negative change to health care reform. It's interesting to note that while only 5% of practitioners reported increases in income in 1997, their average increase was 24%. Those who solved the problems in dealing with systems do very well indeed.

While these issues are dominating the professional lives of service providers, it is difficult to see much change in the training system to accommodate these pressures. I see little or no attempt to start courses on mental health policy or managed care organizations, nor an attempt to deal with the concepts of best practice, good enough, and long- versus short-term care.

Any number of ways of tackling the objective problems imposed by managed care could be developed. For example, one could imagine a service offered on contract to deliver psychological services to people before, during, and after surgery, with the goal being to reduce the number of cancelled surgeries, the average number of inpatient days spent in the hospital, and difficulties (including recurrence) experienced after discharge. I could imagine such a service being very successful and, therefore, highly sought by MCOs. There are services needed that could be much better delivered by clinical psychologists than perhaps by anyone else.

One issue that recurs in MCO planning and implementation is that people want to choose their own physician and therapist; PPOs have an easier time of dealing with this than HMOs, but it still can be an important problem. Aside from the expense of convincing people to go along with the plan, the cost of choice of therapists probably continues. For example, it's been found that patients with a good relationship with their physician were less likely to use very expensive emergency room treatment during the evenings and weekends. Mutual self-presentations of doctor and patient surely have important subsequent ramifications for both cost and patient satisfaction. This is a fertile area for empirical investigation, and corporate development.

THE UNINSURED

The number of people without health insurance continues to rise. Although difficult to count (for many of the same reasons the Census Bureau has difficulty counting the whole population), the most sophisticated guess is that around 65 million people are without health insurance at least sometime during a given year. There have been promising experiments and programs in both Medicaid and Medicare on this issue. The former expands the number of people in its care and the latter expands the services that lowers the cost of the individual.

Although one reads much about the elderly in the press, the group without medical insurance that is most rapidly growing is composed of those aged 55 to 64. This is an age when many chronic conditions develop as well. People age 60 and over average 2.2 chronic conditions each. Some are early retirees trying to mark time until Medicare kicks in; others are forced retirees, victims of corporate downsizing or bankruptcies in the very competitive international marketplace. The group 55 to 64 years of age is one that desperately needs new public policy.

HEALTH AND MENTAL HEALTH TIERS

We used to say (with regret) that we had a two-tiered mental health delivery system: those with private insurance and those forced to lesser quality care in the overworked public system. Now we seem to be moving toward a third tier: those who have health insurance, but who are also wealthy enough to pay privately for desired aspects of health care that competition has reduced in managed care, such as choice of physician, an emphasis on excellence rather than good enough, and using nongeneric drugs. The federal government has taken a hands-off or even an encouraging attitude toward the development of managed care in the private sector. It has done so for a wide variety of reasons, of which two are reducing the percentage of gross domestic product going to health care and using the developed system principle in the public sector. Now there are dozens of bills in Congress on health dealing with regulating the current system: increasing patients' choices, allowing patients to sue, introducing ombudsmen, and the like. Although some regulation is needed, we would hope it would be avoided if it substantially increases cost.

A similar public policy problem concerns underfunded corporations that promise more than they can deliver. Midcontract bankruptcy or draconian changes in services provided or cost-sharing arrangements can wreak havoc in the covered population, particularly if it is not affluent. We need some kind of legislation or regulation about who can get into this game and when, at the same time without bringing back the old regulations governing insurance companies.

It is clear that problems will continue to grow rapidly regarding issues of chronicity in long-term care, especially when one recalls the growing number of uninsured in the age range of 55 to 64. Tack on the number of aging baby boomers and one can anticipate, absent clear action, a substantial mess in health care. Furthermore, add in the existing health care system in which acute care, rather than chronic care, was the centerpiece all this century and the probability of a mess increases substantially.

There are many opportunities for inventive and/or policy oriented caregivers in the coming confusion. Telemedicine, I believe, can play a central role in handling these problems (as well as in the rest of health practice), building on inexpensive video cameras for PCs already available, and inexpensive (non-PC) access to the Internet in such areas as personalizing interaction and enhancing medical compliance.

The last public policy issue I want to raise is diversity, a topic that has received insufficient attention in the health care revolution. We know that minorities are less likely to receive care; that when received, it is less intensive; that among the seriously mentally ill, they are more likely to receive old-fashioned inpatient care; and that they disproportionately do not have health insurance. Recent immigrants, especially the illegal ones, have exacerbated problems. Add to those the trauma already experienced by many recent immigrants in such places as Central and South America, Southeast Asia, Middle Europe, and the Near East, and one has a major national crisis receiving very insufficient attention.

The issues of psychotherapy in the 21st century are here now and are complicated. One must place psychotherapy in a broad definition, in a broad context that already exists, and be prepared to argue what it adds, at what cost, and with what easily measurable outcomes. Steven Shortell said that "Managed care has enormous potential for both benefit and harm" (1997, p. 557). Managed care is here to stay. To have it produce more benefit than harm, professionals who care deeply about the outcomes of their services need to become intimately involved in these issues.

REFERENCES

Glazer, W. H. (1998). Best practices: Defining best practices: A prescription for greater autonomy. *Psychiatric Services, 49*(8), 1013, 1016.

Kiesler, C. A. (1980). Mental health policy as a field of inquiry for psychology. *American Psychologist, 35,* 1066–1080.

Kiesler, C. A. (1985). Psychology and public policy. In E. M. Altmaier & M. E. Meyer (Eds.), *Applied specialties in psychology* (pp. 375–390). New York: Random House.

Kiesler, C. A. (1993). U.S. Mental health policy: Doomed to fail. *American Psychologist, 47*(9), 1077–1082.

Kiesler, C. A., Cummings, N. A., & VandenBos, G. (Eds.). (1979). *Psychology and national health insurance: A sourcebook.* Washington, D. C.: American Psychological Association.

Kiesler, C. A., & Morton, T. L. (1988). Psychology and public policy in the health care revolution. *American Psychologist, 43,* 993–1003.

Kiesler, C. A., & Sibulkin, A. E. (1987). *Mental hospitalization: Myths and facts about a national crisis.* Beverly Hills, CA: Sage Publications.

Kiesler, C. A., & Simpkins, C. (1993). *The unnoticed majority in psychiatric inpatient care.* New York: Plenum.

Kiesler, C. A., & Teru, M. (1987). Responsible public policy in a rapidly changing world. *Clinical Psychologist, 40,* 28–32.

Mechanic, D. (1994). *Inescapable decisions: The imperatives of health reform.* New Brunswick, N. J.: Transaction Pub.

Mohl, P. C. (1998). Medical necessity: A moving target. *Psychiatric Services, 49*(11), 1391.

Scheffler, R., & Ivey, S. L. (1998). Mental health staffing in managed care organizations: A case study. *Psychiatric Services, 49*(10), 1303–1308.

Shortell, S. M. (1997). Managed care: Achieving the benefits, negating the harm. *HSR: Health Services Research, 32*(5), 557–560.

Williams, S., Kohout, J. L., & Wickerski, H. (1998). Data points: Changes in salaries of independent practitioners of psychology. *Psychiatric Services, 49*(8), 1020.

CHAPTER 32

CRITIQUE OF PSYCHOTHERAPY IN AMERICAN SOCIETY

GEORGE W. ALBEE
Professor Emeritus, University of Vermont, and Courtesy Professor, Florida Mental Health Institute

THE BENEFITS OF PSYCHOTHERAPY

At the outset, it is important to recognize that there is sound evidence that often psychotherapy does help people deal with their problems (see the Ingram, Hayes, and Scott chapter in this volume). By now the research literature is quite clear. More often than not people feel better, have more energy for living, and enjoy better self-esteem after therapy. Even severe mental disorders have been shown to improve with psychotherapy (Albee, 1990a; Saxe, 1980).

Author's note: I have been writing about the importance of primary prevention and the problems of individual psychotherapy for 40 years. In this chapter I have used short excerpts from a few earlier articles. These include an article, "Overview of Primary Prevention" (with K. Ryan), that appeared in the *Journal of Counseling and Human Development* (1993), *72*, 115–123; reprinted with permission of the American Counseling Association. I have used, and revised, some paragraphs from my article "The Fourth Mental Health Revolution" that appeared in the *Journal of Prevention* (now the *Journal of Primary Prevention*) (1980), *1*(2, 67–70); reprinted with permission of Plenum Press. I have used a few scattered paragraphs, revised and updated, from chapters I wrote in the volumes published by the Vermont Conference on the Primary Prevention of Psychopathology, for which the copyright owner graciously gave permission. I have used a part of an op-ed page article "Quality Child Care Can Be Had Without Orphanages," that appeared in The *Sarasota Herald-Tribune*, August 20, 1995; permission was obtained and appreciated.

The demonstration by psychotherapists of the *reversibility* of patterns of disturbed behavior in their clients—the disappearance of uncontrolled or overcontrolled behavior, and the development of more positive interpersonal relationships—is of enormous theoretical value to the mental/emotional field of study. Not all therapists, nor all forms of therapy, are equally successful, of course. Most psychotherapy is good enough to show clearly that many of the so-called *mental illnesses* are not irreversible as the current organicists claim. In this regard, there is a long-standing division between the organicists who say, "all mental illness is a medical disease" that results from bad genes, bad brain chemistry, or other organic causes, and those nonorganicists who argue that people learn to be emotionally disturbed in pathological, stressful social environments. The psychotherapy findings on reversibility support the learning explanation (Mowrer, 1950). Psychotherapy and a learning model are strongly opposed by the organic psychiatrists who control the system.

Psychotherapeutic experiences also weaken drastically another position of the organicists who argue that there are specific and discrete mental illnesses (American Psychiatric Association, 1988). Again, clinical experience shows that most mental disorders are on a continuum, and that they often blend into a complex pattern that is not appropriate for a single diagnostic label (Mirowsky & Ross, 1989).

Also, a related issue involves competence promotion as a therapeutic and preventive strategy. Both clinical and controlled studies support the value of competence promotion (Cowen, 1991). Psychotherapy often provides a source of needed social support, improved self-esteem, social skills, and feelings of competence. As a consequence, the individual is more resistant to stress. In many cases the therapist becomes a substitute parent who eventually may replace the damaging real parents whose original painful lives with resulting neglect/abuse/rejection were the basis for the client's disturbance. An insightful book explaining why children (and wives or women partners) keep returning to their batterer is Celani's (1995) *The Illusion of Love*. This is the kind of major contribution to theory and effective prevention that can be made by psychotherapists.

Of what additional value is individual psychotherapy? Clearly it is a window that gives a view of the damage that sometimes is done to children by uncaring or hurting parents who are themselves damaged by our uncaring society. It also allows a view of the damage done by factors in the social system based on mindless competition that measures the value of persons or families by their abilities to consume expensive manufactured goods. This point of view implicitly embraces the philosophy of Social Darwinism: Let the fittest survive, and don't level the playing field for those who are handicapped at playing the game. Therapy often reveals the human effects of failures of an economic system that goes boom and bust periodically, produces jobs of incredible boredom and meaninglessness, periodically throws people out of work, eliminates jobs for people who want to work, and also often prevents the employment of people who are seeking to work. Economic problems are often at the root of the stresses that lead to anxiety, depression, and bad parenting (Albee, 1996).

THE CHILD IS PARENT OF THE ADULT

One of the many important contributions of the interventions by clinical, community, and developmental psychologists is the clear delineation of parenting as a critically important contributor to the later adjustment of the child and adult. There are many empirical sources of support for this relationship. These range from life history research (Roff & Ricks, 1970), to individual case study (Celani, 1995), to follow-up of children with early positive and negative emotional experiences (Skodak, 1992). To survive, the human infant requires constant care. Ordinarily, the care includes bonding with caregivers, affection, and social interaction.

Infants who are born unwanted (David, Dytrych, Matejcek et al., 1988), or who are deemed to be below average at birth by their mothers (Broussard, 1976), are seriously disturbed when followed up many years later. Careful laboratory follow-up studies of the effects of inadequate mothering in infant monkeys showed distorted emotional development, especially in sexual behavior, in later life. And adult female monkeys who were themselves deprived of adequate maternal care became *Monster Mothers*, rejecting or damaging physically their own infants (Harlow, 1958, 1962; Harlow & Harlow, 1966). These infants grow up to be disturbed adults and inadequate parents. So the cycle may repeat itself.

One of the most dramatic examples of the long-term effects of the early childhood emotional environment is the following (see Albee, 1995; Skodak, 1984, 1992; Skodak & Skeels, 1949):

> More than a half a century ago a psychologist, Harold Skeels at the University of Iowa, made a dramatic observation. Back in that distant past many children were placed in orphanages. These were babies born "out of wedlock" or to mentally retarded mothers, or in other circumstances that made them wards of the state. Life in the orphanages was dreadful, replete with neglect and often with abuse. Few of these unwanted and/or retarded children were ever adopted or left the orphanage for any reason.
>
> Skeels, a psychologist at the University of Iowa's Child Welfare Research Station, observed two scrawny, underdeveloped and apathetic infants in a state orphanage. One was just over a year old and the other a couple months older than that. Both had estimated IQs and developmental delays that placed them in the "imbecile range" (25–50 IQ). He decided that they should be transferred from the orphanage to the state institution for mentally retarded because clearly they would always be mentally retarded. Because the institution for retardates had no arrangement to take care of infants, they were placed on a ward of mentally retarded women.

Six months later, Skeels stopped by to see how they were doing and found, to his complete surprise, that both infants were alert, responsive and exceedingly active. Both had shown, on retesting, major improvements of their developmental quotient, improvements so dramatic that they were both now within the normal range.

Startled by this change, he observed how they were treated on the ward. He found that several of the "older and brighter girls" spent much of the day fussing over them, talking to them, and playing with them. Also, the ward attendants often took them along on trips to the store or brought them toys and books, and even took them into their homes on their days off.

Skeels was struck with an outlandish idea. Why not put several mentally retarded infants, under the age of two, into this institution to see whether living with the "feeble-minded girls" might make the infants more normal? He transferred 13 infants, all ranging from seven months to 30 months of age, to such wards.

This was not a carefully done experiment. Some of the infants were evaluated after seven months and some after four years. Whenever they were evaluated however, they all had made significant gains in alertness and development. A dozen other infants, most of them "normal" in development, who had been left at the orphanage were also tested after various periods of time; and all but one of these showed a significant decrease in developmental quotients.

The differences in the two kinds of social-environmental experience were exceedingly great. Skeels' colleague, Marie Skodak (1992), followed up these children 25 years later. With a great deal of effort and detective work, all of them were found and interviewed, and their children were seen and tested. Eleven of the 13 who had been placed in the institution with the mentally retarded "foster mothers" had been adopted as children because they were so "attractive." None of the ones left in the orphanage was adopted.

The 11 "retarded infants" who got the loving attention from the retarded foster mothers were found by Skodak to be doing unbelievably well a quarter-century later. They were all self-supporting and their median educational attainment was 12th grade. Four of the 11 had attended college and one had earned a doctorate at a major university!

Most of them had married and had children of their own. Their 28 children had a mean IQ of 104 and were doing well in school.

The 12 children who had been classed as "normal infants" but who, for a variety of reasons, had been left in the orphanage, had IQs averaging 66 in first grade. Ten of the 12 spent all, or nearly all, of the next 25 years in state institutions (Albee, 1995)

With all of the evidence of negative childhood experiences leading to many adult mental disorders and, conversely, the evidence for the beneficial adult consequences of positive social experiences in infancy and early childhood, why is there so much opposition to this knowledge?

The answer comes from two sources. First, groups of parents of disturbed young adults have banded together (the National Alliance for the Mentally Ill, NAMI), for example, to use economic and political strategies to argue that parents are not to blame for the mental/emotional disturbances of their children. Most of these problems of mental illness, NAMI argues, are the result of a brain disease (or other biochemical defect). Members of NAMI are mostly white and upper-middle (or higher) class. They have the political clout of a large affluent group. They command respect from politicians and bureaucrats.

No new director of the U.S. National Institute of Mental Health (NIMH) is appointed without NAMI's scrutiny and approval. These powerful bureaucrats, for the past 20 years, have been organically oriented psychiatrists who insist that "all mental illness is a medical illness." The childhood learning model is a threat to the organic viewpoint. The conservative bureaucrats deny the evidence that mental disorders often have their origins in negative interpersonal experiences in childhood, and that the learned patterns of distress lead to later disorders. If mental disorders are learned, perhaps they can be unlearned, and even prevented. The bureaucrats and NAMI prefer to treat victims with drugs. In this context, psychotherapy is a threat. But as one old psychiatrist told me: Drugs cannot help someone play the violin nor can they teach social skills to a schizophrenic.

WHY THE CURRENT CURTAILMENT OF PSYCHOTHERAPY?

Psychotherapy is dangerous to the evolving medical model that explains most mental disorders as the consequences of disturbed brain chemistry and/or physical/genetic defects. Therapists using psychoanalysis or psychodynamic derivatives are a major threat to the organicists in psychiatry because their successes with clients are contradictory to the organic disease model. How can mental conditions be caused by brain malfunction if they can be eliminated or greatly reduced by talking with a psychotherapist? The equally positive results of behavior therapy also support a learning-unlearning model of most mental disorders. Why are these psychotherapeutic successes such a threat that there is an active effort to suppress or eliminate them? The issue is fairly simple. Most mental conditions are not real diseases. A real disease has an objective marker that can be identified in a lab. But the organicists are a wily lot. Their strategies include, first, getting rid of psychoanalytically oriented faculty members at psychiatric departments in medical schools; second, setting such unreasonably short limits for interventions supported by Health Maintenance Organizations (HMOs) and Managed Care (MC) programs that the clients do not improve and the psychotherapists income is cut to the bone; and third, teaching new psychiatric residents what to prescribe from the fast-growing number of psychotropic drugs. The pharmaceutical companies help, even taking tomorrow's psychiatrists (and their spouses or guests) to tropical retreats where they must listen, an hour or so a day, to lectures on drug therapy.

Relative to traditional psychotherapy approaches, drug therapy is much less costly to HMOs and MC programs. While drugs do not reduce or eliminate the underlying social problem, they often do hide the symptoms. And because of the very large number of people suffering from mental problems, drug companies have enormous profits, and enormous power to call the tune.

Since 1980 when the United States turned sharply to the right politically, NIMH has stopped supporting research on social and familial causes of mental disorders; NIMH now focuses on organic brain research, genetics, and chemical imbalances. The current director of NIMH, Steve Hyman (1998), (a *wet brain* devotee), states with certainty that "We can now diagnose mental disorders with as much (or more) certainty with the same accuracy as we can many other forms of illness" (p. 5). Someone should ask Dr. Hyman why NIMH epidemiological studies must still rely on a two-hour interview for diagnosis. Clearly there is no objective marker for a large majority of mental disorders; diagnosis is a judgment call. The American Psychiatric Association's (1988) Diagnostic and Statistical Manual IV (DSM-IV) is an unreliable (and therefore invalid) instrument, as discussed later in this chapter.

A few months before NIMH Director Hyman's (1998) reassurance that we now have scientifically certain treatments for reliably diagnosed mental diseases, there appeared in the same NMHA publication, *The Bell*, an article by Altshuler (1997), who listed by name 14 new mind-altering drugs, soon-to-be released "to our therapeutic arsenal" (p. 7). The newly developed "psychiatric drugs" include: clozapine, sestraline, carbamazepine, divalpoex, sodium venlafaxine, fluroxamine, nifazadone, clonepezil, mirtazapine, resperidone, olangapine, quetiapine, serindole, and gabapentin. The task now, Altshuler said, is to define which medications "best suit particular symptoms." Apparently he does not see the irony in discovering and patenting medications that will later be tried for effectiveness on unreliable conditions that are not yet even specified. Altschuler goes on to question whether doctors will know how to use the 14 new drugs, what size doses are to be prescribed, what are their contraindications, when to seek blood levels, and what combinations of drugs can be used, etc. Altschuler is a distinguished professor of psychiatry at the University of Texas Southwestern Medical College at Dallas. He is helping develop a large-scale research project that will eventually "show what medications should be employed when" (p. 7). Sometime in the future, he hopes, a computerized system of algorithms will tell doctors what drugs and how much of them to prescribe and when. But "the computer application is only a hope at present" (p. 7). Costs of new drugs and expensive office visits "is a major problem, especially in consistently underfunded public systems." (One can imagine that the problems will be larger in Third World countries.) Kleinman (1997) points out that half of the leading causes of disability in the world are mental health problems. Of these, half are preventable or treatable, but they are neither presently diagnosed nor responded to effectively.

THE THREATS TO PSYCHOTHERAPY

Clinical psychologists and other psychotherapists face a bleak future. While there is clear evidence that therapy is often effective in resolving client problems, the process is often long and expensive. Now U.S. "health care" has become industrialized and its emphasis is on making money. This means greatly reducing treatment costs so less money is spent, while more is collected (the difference is called profits). Decisions about how many visits a client can make to the psychotherapist rest with gatekeepers employed by the Health Maintenance Organization, (HMO) or Managed Care (MC) companies. These decision-makers, often nurses or masters-level persons, generally know little about psychotherapy. They must rely largely on therapists' descriptions of the clients' problems and make an assigned diagnosis chosen currently from The American Psychiatric Association's *Diagnostic and Statistical Manual IV* (1988), the latest in a never-ending series of revisions. With each revision, more categories of "mental illness" are added. The reason is clear. Professionals cannot be reimbursed for their treatment unless they are treating a genuine illness. So smoking addiction, unruly children and adolescents, school learning problems—the list goes on and on—all become reimbursable mental conditions (Albee 1977a, 1977b).

One of the many bizarre consequences of the steadily changing and expanding list of mental disorders is the lack of reliability of judgments about diagnosis. Kutchins and Kirk (1997) have taken a careful, sophisticated look at DSM-IV (and earlier versions) and concluded that diagnoses never have been demonstrated to be reliable. As everyone who has studied statistics knows: There can be no validity in the absence of reliability. So, decisions about the number of sessions of psychotherapy that will be allowed are made by junior personnel, and often are based on an unreliable and invalid diagnostic system. But the outcome is determined: a few sessions for modest pay—not enough in most instances to make a real change. Psychotherapists are being starved out of the health system. Instead of rejecting the whole unreliable, invalid, profit-driven medical model of mental disorder, a great many psychotherapists (and their national organization, the American Psychological Association) search frantically for ways to be included. One of the strategies is the fight for parity. Another is the quest for the right to prescribe drugs. Parity is impossible and drug prescription privileges is a sell-out to the invalid medical model. Either effort is doomed.

Psychotropic drugs do not cure mental disorders. They blunt, dampen, and suppress behavior produced by stress and anxiety. Many real diseases (with objective, reliable markers) are cured by medicines, which the patient can stop. Not so with drugs for mental disorder.

The idea of parity (i.e., we must spend as much on treatment of mental disorders as we do on other real diseases) is bizarre. With 300 mental disorders listed in DSM-IV, and a third of American adults suffering from mental disorders, the idea of parity is illogical and impossible.

Long ago, I showed (Albee, 1959) that the gap between the number of disturbed people lining up for therapy and the number of therapists available was unbridgeable. This is even more true today.

THE THERAPISTS ARE WHITE MALES

The numbers of African-American, Asian-American, and Hispanic-American psychotherapists are extremely small because of unequal and poor schools and long-existing barriers to higher education for ethnic minority group members. This bias was particularly acute in the graduate programs in psychology that were long closed to members of ethnic minority groups. Between 1879 and 1920, of ten thousand doctorates awarded in psychology, only eleven were earned by Black scholars in America. Between 1920 and 1966, the ten most prestigious departments of psychology awarded a grand total of eight doctorates to African-American candidates, while granting a total of 3,767 Ph.D.s during this period (Albee, 1969). Women applicants to graduate study also were long discriminated against, even though the majority of therapy clients is female (Albee, 1969, 1981; Mays & Albee, 1992). Now White women graduate students outnumber men and soon will be a majority (see Snyder and colleagues chapter in this volume).

Similar problems were faced by Hispanic young people seeking graduate studies in psychology. Carlos Albizu-Miranda, a giant in Puerto Rican psychology, returned to his native island after completing a doctorate on the mainland. He opened his own school to train Puerto Rican clinical psychologists. A large majority of Puerto Rican psychotherapists have done their graduate work at the school he founded in San Juan. In recent years, graduate education for minorities has been partly opened in the United States largely as a result of the protest movements of minority groups and women.

In addition to the small number of minority psychotherapists, there are further problems affecting the availability of help for members of minority groups. Thirty years ago the American Medical Association often was quoted as saying the country did not need more physicians because no American lived more than 10 miles from the nearest doctor. This was small comfort to the residents of Harlem who, though they lived only five miles from Park Avenue, might as well have lived five light years away for all the help they might receive. On this point, a majority of psychotherapists practice and live in the affluent suburbs of urban centers in five states (Mays & Albee, 1992).

Clearly, psychotherapy can be considered a social luxury used by societies that are industrialized and by subgroups who are relatively affluent (Albee, 1975). Papers at the 1990 Vermont Conference on the Primary Prevention of Psychopathology (Albee, Bond, & Monsey, 1991) by Sefa-Dedeh of Ghana and El-Mouelly of Egypt, as well as reports by psychologists and psychiatrists from Pakistan (Arshad), India (Sonty), and Eastern Europe (Sek), all present a picture of massive human social/mental problems that are untouched by psychotherapy. In spite of the impossibility of reaching more than a handful of the billions of people who live in Third World countries in Africa, Asia, Latin America, and elsewhere, however, many university psychology departments in countries of the Third World are busily training psychotherapists.

HOW MANY PEOPLE ARE EMOTIONALLY DISTURBED?

There are many, often conflicting answers to this question. One of the oldest American psychiatric texts in my library (Rosanoff, 1905) describes eight types of mental illness. By the 1950s, the number of mental disorders listed in the *Diagnostic and Statistical Manual* (DSM) of the American Psychiatric Association (1952) had increased to 60. DSM-II (1968) expanded this number to 145, and DSM-III (1980) listed 230. The most recently published DSM-IV (1990) lists 300 *psychiatric disorders*. At this rate we will have more diagnosable disorders than people!

One clear implication is that the more mental disorders identified, the more likely it is that therapists would be reimbursed to treat them. There is something wrong with a diagnostic system that varies so widely over time in a society and differs so much cross-culturally.

Clinical (and community) psychology should have been protesting for years the lack of reliability and validity of psychiatric diagnosis. Psychologists are trained in statistics and know that poor reliability means poor validity. But psychotherapists were benefiting from high and continuing fees paid for using the medical model. Why complain? Instead, there was a long-term major effort to train more and more professional psychotherapists, often in new professional schools granting the Psy.D.'s (Doctor of Psychology). The whole character of American psychology was tilted by the influx of aspiring therapists.

REVISING THE DSM

Over the years, psychology has had to accept many changes in the DSM. The changes illustrate the unreliability of the systems, and the problem of counting cases.

In 1973, the American Psychiatric Association's board voted to remove homosexuality from the DSM-III. Subsequently, against protests from psychoanalysts, a majority of the membership voted in 1974 to uphold the board's decision. As a result, millions of gay and lesbian Americans who had been "mentally ill" suddenly were restored to "health". At the same time, millions in other countries continued to be "mentally ill" because the International Classification of Disease of the World Health Organization (1989) continued to list homosexuality as a disease. DSM-III (1980), while dropping homosexuality as a disease, added a detailed description of a new *Ego Dystonic Homosexuality* for those gays and lesbians who allegedly wanted help in changing their sexual orientation. In 1987, with DSM-III-R, this category was quietly dropped. The other major change was the elimination of the neuroses in DSM-III. In one stroke, millions of neurotics were no longer anxious, depressed, hysterical, obsessive, compulsive, neurasthenic, or hypochrondriacal!

With the loss of the neuroses and homosexuality, it might seem that the size of the DSM would shrink. But this ignores the creative ability of the committee in charge of writing new diagnoses. A major addition was the Posttraumatic Stress Disorder. The veterans of recent American wars insisted on being included in the Manual so they could have a justification for demanding prepaid treatment and other compensation. And Posttraumatic Stress Syndrome also has come to include the later problems of spouse abuse victims and child abuse victims. Millions more to include in counts of the mentally ill! And it has turned out that drug abuse, alcoholism, compulsive gambling, and sex addiction are all (genetically caused) mental illnesses. Add new children's problems like Attention Deficit Disorder, Arithmetic Learning Problems, Adolescent Rebellion Disorder, and millions more are included. Smoking addiction is now a mental disorder. It seems as if almost everyone has a psychiatric disorder, treatable with drugs to be paid for by health insurance (forty million people without health coverage excepted).

The latest political demand is for treatment parity for mental cases. Many Managed Care programs exclude mental problems—they "trade dental for mental," or have high copayments and sharply limit the number of therapy visits. Why, it is asked indignantly, should people with mental diseases not have the same rights to treatment without limits as people with physical ills? The current director of the National Institute of Mental Health (Hyman, 1998) says, "There is absolutely no scientific or medical justification for policies that treat mental disorders as if they are in any way less real or less deserving of treatment than other illnesses" (p. 5). Hyman, an organically oriented biologist, is perhaps the least knowledgeable in a series of recent directors of NIMH. He is fixated on genes and *wet brains* and knows little about the social history of the field. He keeps making vague statements about recent discoveries and new research to "diagnose mental disorders with as much (or more) certainty as we can diagnose many other illnesses" (p. 5). This is nonsense, of course. The confusion and unreliability of the Diagnostic Manuals make any kind of certainty unattainable. And he ought to know that medications cannot "return sufferers of serious mental illnesses to full health and function" (p. 5).

WHAT ABOUT REAL BRAIN DISEASES?

There is no question that some mental problems are organic. But the current strident voices from psychiatry insist that brain diseases are the causes of mental problems. The implication here is that only physicians are competent to deal with these people suffering from organic brain disorder. The curious problem is that genuine brain disorders are neglected by psychiatrists.

There are a few million people at risk for real organic mental disorders, but they are low priority for medicine and psychiatry. About one-half million persons suffer from a cerebrovascular stroke each year in the United States. Of these, about 150,000 die shortly after the stroke and approximately 350,000 survive. While the length of life expectancy of stroke survivors has a wide range, it is safe to estimate that at any time there are between 750,000 and a million stroke victims alive. There is at least an equal number of caregivers. Often the spouse or child or other family member must provide help and support for the stroke victim. This means that there are another million or so persons in the United States under the continuing stress of providing round-the-clock assistance. Being mildly to severely incapacitated as a result of a cerebrovascular stroke is an organic brain disease. Few receive (or are eligible) for psychotherapy.

The fate of the stroke victim is illustrative of many of the problems of American business-oriented-for-profit health care. Many stroke victims could benefit from extended rehabilitation programs, but hospitals discourage such a long-term stay because reimbursement from insurance policies, MCs, and HMOs does not cover such rehabilitation efforts. They are prohibitively expensive in the current health scheme. Because it is not often that an individual family is able to fund such care, the result is insufficient and inadequate rehabilitation. This puts more stress on both the patient and the caretaker, of course. But there are other problems as well.

One and a half million people in the United States reportedly are now positive for the virus that subsequently develops into AIDS. The percentage of persons positive for the virus who subsequently develops AIDS keeps increasing as time passes, and large numbers of people harbor the virus for extended periods of time. If 50 percent of the HIV-positive people actually develop AIDS (a modest estimate), this would mean 750,000 people at a given time with the disease. Clearly, the for-profit medical/hospital system of the United States is not prepared to deal with these awesome numbers of victims, particularly inasmuch as persons who are likely to develop the disease are not spread uniformly across the country, but are more likely to live in a few places like the cities of California and in New York City and Miami. Just as hospitals are reluctant to care for stroke victims because their periods of rehabilitation extend over a significantly long time, so too are hospitals even more resistant to caring for AIDS patients whose period of suffering may extend for months and end in death. Further, health care workers are often fearful about caring for AIDS patients because of the alleged possibility of infection. To compound matters, few psychotherapists can collect for caring for AIDS clients despite the clear need.

Still a third group of chronically disabled (and relatively hopeless organic patients) are those who develop Alzheimer's disease. The number keeps increasing as our population ages. This degenerative brain condition results in nearly total dementia in a majority of cases. It is now the fourth leading cause of death and currently affects two to three million people in the United States. The patient becomes demented, helpless, incontinent, and a serious problem for nursing care. The cost of care is astronomical and Medicare contributes nothing. The number of Alzheimer's patients keeps increasing as the number of elderly persons in the U.S. population also increases. The Alzheimer's patient is not acutely ill, in most cases, but requires nursing and custodial care. The medical health insurance system (Medicaid) in the United States does not provide care for Alzheimer's victims until their financial resources have been exhausted. Because of the very high cost of nursing home care for Alzheimer's patients, none of which is covered by Medicare, the patient (or the patient's family) must spend itself into pauperism before Medicaid kicks in. Much has been written about the tragedy of Alzheimer's on the family and other loved ones. Clearly the caretakers are under great stress and could benefit from counseling, but rarely is it available. It is too expensive.

AM I MY SIBLINGS' KEEPER?

Another critical fault of the psychotherapeutic enterprises is its neglect of large groups of disturbed children and adults. Some of this neglect

is a result of an insufficient supply of therapists trying to cope with an excessive number of persons with emotional problems. There is the further problem of social class biases. Psychotherapy clients, as a general rule, come from the educated upper-class groups, are verbally sophisticated and insight-seeking. Poor people are less likely to want to talk about their emotional problems that often are rooted in real stresses like poverty, involuntary unemployment, bad housing, and poor education. If one considers this issue carefully, what may we conclude about whose needs are being met? It appears that those of the psychotherapists take precedence.

POVERTY

The number of children living in poverty-stricken urban families in America has increased substantially, partly as a product of urbanization since World War II. The current proportion of six-year-olds living in poverty in the United States is estimated at 24% (Kramer, 1992). This figure is particularly striking given that the birthrate of children to impoverished women has been decreasing. Working-class families with ethnic minority status increasingly are at risk for poverty. Nearly half of African-American children live in poverty, and more than one-third of Latin American parents are poor. Children born in poverty have increased levels of prematurity, low birth weight, malnutrition, and resulting mental retardation. They are more likely to be abused or neglected. Children have replaced the aged as the poorest age group. And while the aged are now a major political force, children, especially poor children, are not an organized force—and they do not vote (Mays & Albee, 1992).

A LITTLE EPIDEMIOLOGY

Epidemiological studies have shown that emotional disorders (usually called mental illnesses) are much more common among the poor, the lowest social classes, and the exploited (see for examples, Albee, Bond, & Monsey, 1991; Dohrenwend, 1990; Hollingshead & Redlich, 1955; Perry, 1996; President's Commission on Mental Health, 1977). Mirowski and Ross (1989) showed clearly that 85% of all stress occurs in the lower economic half of the population. If it is stress that is largely responsible for mental/emotional disorders, then the choice for intervention is easy: level the economic playing field. Indeed, the evidence is clear. Wilkinson (1996) has shown that those societies that have the smallest gap between rich and poor have the greatest social cohesiveness, the lowest crime rate, the best health, and the best longevity.

It is no mystery that the reasons for psychiatric rejection of this socioeconomic causation model of mental disorder are those that protect the *status quo*. We have long known that the ruling ideas of a society are those that protect the ruling class.

A major problem in studying the epidemiology of most mental conditions is the inability to find a conclusive marker to establish the presence of the alleged disorder. Real illnesses always have distinctive markers such as the presence of specific organisms (microbes or viruses), the presence of sugar in the urine and blood, cancerous growths, blockage of blood vessels, skin rashes, kidney stones—the list is long. A diagnosis of a specific disease is objective. It is based on identification and observation of the marker. There are sometimes ambiguities (like Alzheimer's, which must await autopsy). But a correct diagnosis often leads to corrective treatment, to an accurate prognosis, and sometimes suggests a way to prevent the disease (lead poisoning, for example).

This is not the case for most mental disorders. These conditions are diagnosed by observing the unusual behavior of the individual or by interpreting the thoughts and feelings of the person who may report fears, anxieties, delusions, odd ideas, and strange feelings. The presence of a mental disorder is not based on objective laboratory findings, but rather on inferences from behavioral and ideational observation. One important result is that the presence or absence of a disorder depends on what kinds of behavior are acceptable or unacceptable by the culture as well as the interpreter of the culture who is making the diagnosis. An example is sexual behavior that is considered abnormal in some cultures and not in others. For many years, behaviors listed as perversions in abnormal textbooks are now considered acceptable. *The startling possibility is that mental conditions are not real diseases but rather learned patterns of behavior that are socially disapproved.*

Many responsible voices add to the chorus intoning the high risk of being poor. David Hamburg (1990), recently retired president of the Carnegie Corporation, writes about the importance of "A decent start: Promoting healthy child development in the first three years of life." Hamburg cites many of the problems of poverty.

Poor women with little formal education tend to be the heaviest smokers, are more likely to be heavy alcohol users, and crack cocaine abusers. Women at the lowest socioeconomic levels need prenatal medical care, increased social support, better information about nutrition, and more access to quality day care. They lack medical care for their own health and the health of their children. Fathers are little help—many are absent. Hamburg points out that fewer than half of poor and ethnic minority children under age four are immunized fully against preventable infections. They are at greater risk for injuries, which is the leading cause of death and disability among children, as well as for stress and, according to Hamburg, the need for "comprehensive child development programs for economically disadvantaged children" (p. 9). He stresses the positive consequences of home visiting programs to help with more effective child rearing in disadvantaged families. Again and again, he emphasizes the devastating consequences of poverty. Psychotherapists rarely see the poor and they are silent about a society that tolerates injustice. Poverty is the result of a system based on selfish individualism (a condition that affects many psychotherapists).

SUBSTANCE ABUSE

Infants of mothers addicted to alcohol have high rates of physical and mental abnormalities. The most severe consequence of maternal alcohol addiction is Fetal Alcohol Syndrome (FAS). Mothers who smoke cigarettes heavily during pregnancy tend to have at-risk infants with lower birth weight. Children born with low birth weight often have a range of visual–motor coordination difficulties, together with more serious later social and learning problems. The incidence of fetal and infant death is also more common among the poor and the exploited.

HOW MANY THERAPISTS ARE THERE?

The public is regularly misinformed by the mass media about the availability of psychotherapy. Ann Landers, and other popular advisors, suggest counseling and psychotherapy as the solution to individual problems described in letters from readers. The implication is that therapy is available. Even as scientifically sophisticated a writer as Jane Brody (1981) can be misinformed, and thereby misinform her readers, about the availability of help. In her *New York Times* article she stated that 34 million Americans are in psychotherapy. She was wrong. Probably no more than 1 million are actually in therapy at any given time. To treat 34 million clients would require a 20-fold increase in the currently existing number of therapists. No foreseeable increase of this magnitude is in prospect, especially with the withdrawal of adequate funding by HMOs and MC programs.

How many psychotherapists actually are available for the vast sea of troubled people? Kiesler and Sibulkin (1987, p. 812) have calculated the total number of (full-time equivalent) psychotherapists in the United States to be about 45,000. This may be a conservative estimate, but even if we add to this figure the unlicensed and unregulated personal counselors, yoga instructors, teachers of meditation, pastoral counselors, and school guidance personnel, we have only doubled or tripled the total number of qualified, licensed, and unlicensed interventionists for people with personal problems. So one conventional argument for the futility of psychotherapy is the unbridgeable gap between need and available resources. Enormous sums of money spent on treating the few might be better spent on other interventions affecting more people. Self-help groups, for example, reach many times the number seen in individual therapy. (See Surgeon General's [Koop] Workshop on Self-Help and Public Health, 1987, for optimistic examples of groups of people helping each other in support groups). But we must remind ourselves that even if there were twenty times as many psychotherapists, there would be no reduction in the incidence of problems, a majority of which are caused by poverty, powerlessness, exploitation and social injustice (Albee, 1977a, 1977b; Joffe, 1981).

Our American fixation on high technology, individual medical treatment is as irrelevant and as tragic as is our fixation on individual psychotherapy. It is simply not credible to suggest that spare parts of bodies (from organ donors) and mechanical body organ devices (artificial hearts) are the most promising medical treatments of the future in a world in which millions die of the infectious diseases of childhood and the specter of mass starvation haunts much of humankind. Fifteen million of the world's children die each year of preventable conditions like infant diarrhea from polluted water, infectious diseases, and starvation. Four hundred million women live in regions where the soil is deficient in iodine and as a result give birth to a high number of retarded children. The rate of epilepsy is high in the Third World from too much lead and too little iron (Musarrat, 1988). Millions of children live with preventable handicaps—underdeveloped, malnourished bodies and minds. Little or no help is available to them.

Often women do not receive appropriate care in the mental health system. Neither do persons who live in rural America, in small towns, or in the poor sections of American cities. Neither do 10 million persons with alcohol-related problems, nor an unspecified but growing number of persons who misuse psychoactive drugs, nor the large number of family members involved in child abuse, nor 5 million children with learning disabilities, nor 40 million physically handicapped Americans, nor 6 million persons who are mentally retarded.

THE FUTURE IS WORSE

Kramer (1983, 1992) has raised some important and alarming questions about what he calls "the rising pandemic of mental disorders" throughout the world. He points out that the United States faces, in the decades immediately ahead, a steadily increasing prevalence rate of serious mental disorders, as well as diseases and disabilities involving hypertension and cerebrovascular strokes. The growth in frequency of all these conditions will result from the large increase in the numbers of persons in those age groups who are at higher risk for their occurrence, as well as the steadily increasing duration of such chronic conditions directly resulting from the development of effective techniques of prolonging the lives of affected individuals. In brief, more people, in the United States and throughout the world, are living into middle and old age, and the chronic mental and physical conditions that are more likely with advancing years are not only occurring but are being treated in ways that prolong their duration.

Among the "failures of success" we note effective medical techniques for prolonging the lives of the severely retarded, and for intervening successfully with severely premature and underweight infants and infants with severe handicaps and complications, all resulting in a subsequent increase in the prevalence of mentally and physically handicapped persons. Before the development of antibiotics, the life expectancy of severely retarded crib cases and other institutionalized retardates was comparatively short because of the prevalence of infectious diseases in institutions. The use of antibiotics and deinstitutionalization policies have resulted in many severely handicapped individuals having a longer life expectancy. The deinstitutionalization of persons labeled schizophrenic has increased the number of pregnancies in schizophrenic women, for example, and therefore the number of children born with the risk of being reared with an alleged genetic handicap and/or with a schizophrenic mother. Infants born with phenylketonuria (PKU) are being identified through routine lab tests and are being treated with a special diet, allowing them to live into adult childbearing years, with the resulting increase in genetic carriers and mentally retarded offspring.

Kramer is not suggesting that we turn back the clock on all these medical advances, but that we be aware of the serious problems these changes will cause. The mechanisms he discusses are occurring worldwide, including in the less developed regions. Indeed, as Kramer points out, there will be further aggravation of the problem of chronic conditions as developing countries industrialize, as their populations move from rural agrarian to urban industrial areas, and as the pattern of living in extended families shifts to a more nuclear family structure. Kramer sees one of the few hopes to be effective research emphasizing the prevention of chronic disease. He points to the current increases in the prevalence rate of schizophrenia and the growing rate of admission and readmission to mental health facilities and prisons, also admission rates to homes for the aged and to nursing homes continue to rise. Kramer (1992) suggests that prevention is the only logical solution.

> . . . extraordinary increases . . . can be expected in the number of persons who will be affected by major problems of disease and disability that are of concern to mental health. This includes persons in every age group, from the youngest to the oldest. Prevalence rates of mental disorders, Down's Syndrome, hypertensive disease, cerebrovascular disease, cirrhosis of the liver, diabetes, visual and hearing impairments, and other chronic conditions are increasing throughout the world. This worldwide increase in the prevalence of mental disorders and chronic disease may be best characterized as a rising chronic disease pandemic. . . . the number of cases of mental disorder will continue to increase until effective methods are discovered for preventing their occurrence and equally effective and practical methods are found for their application. It is, therefore, particularly important that our policy makers give the highest priority to the support of research and research training directed toward discovering the preventable causes of those conditions that are increasing in prevalence. (pp. 27, 28, 31)

Is There a Solution to the Need for Help?

There are ironic aspects to this bleak picture. Back in the early 1960s in response to the final report *Action for Mental Health* (1960) of the Joint Commission on Mental Illness and Health, a bold new federal mental health program was launched. The centerpiece of this new program was the establishment of community mental health centers designed to intercept persons headed for the state mental hospitals and to provide early and intensive treatment in the community for persons at highest risk for mental hospitalization. Some 2,000 community mental health centers were to be built with federal funds (Kiesler & Sibulkin, 1987). These centers would function in ways that gradually would reduce to an absolute minimum the need for beds in public mental hospitals.

Community mental health centers receive only about 5% of the total mental health expenditures in the nation, while in-patient services at state hospitals, general hospitals, and nursing homes continue to expend some 70% of available funds. In recent years, there has been a dramatic increase in the number of "mental patients" hospitalized for short periods in general hospitals, including facilities without separate psychiatric units. Most such admissions are for intensive, profitable diagnostic study, not treatment.

Klerman (1977) argued that mental health workers, particularly psychiatrists, should limit their professional concern to the treatment of the 15% who constitute America's 2–3 million "hard core mentally ill." He has suggested that other medical personnel, especially family care physicians, should be prepared to deal with the vast number of others seeking professional support for emotional disturbances resulting from crises. However, Klerman's solution appears beyond realization.

How many persons who suffer from emotional disturbances and life crises are actually seen each year in the mental health system in the United States? If we add up all the persons seen in the private offices of mental health professionals, in community mental health centers, in public and private mental hospitals, and on psychiatric wards of general hospitals, we arrive at a grand total of seven million persons (Kiesler & Sibulkin, 1988). Obviously, not even one person in eight (of those identified in the Regier, 1984, and Robins & Regier, 1991, reports) is being seen. A large proportion of those persons receiving therapy is not hard core, but is suffering from various life crises. Not being seen is a large proportion of the impoverished, the exploited, the children, and the aged.

WHO WILL HELP THE HAVE-NOTS?

Even with third-party insurance coverage, psychotherapy has a limited clientele. Psychotherapy has not been a source of support for the poor. This has long been true in America (Albee, 1990a), and it is true in most countries. It is especially true in the Third World where real diseases have a much higher priority for intervention; there are few psychotherapists in poor countries.

It is an incontrovertible fact that the groups with the most prevalent mental health problems are those least likely to avail themselves of psychotherapy. The group in the United States with the highest rate of emotional disturbances is the five million migrant farm workers (Task Panel on Migrant and Seasonal Farm Workers, 1978). It was found that as a group, migrant workers had significantly higher rates of reported child abuse than the general population or even nonimmigrant groups of the same socioeconomic status. Indeed, a body of research suggests that exposure to abject conditions such as chronic poverty, social isolation, inadequate education, and weak cultural ties, especially affecting exploited groups such as migrant farm workers, increases the risk of all forms of illness and psychopathology. Therapeutic intervention can do little to alleviate the effects of these stressors, and it will never reduce the incidence of psychopathology in this and other have-not groups (such as inner-city minorities, including African Americans, Native Americans, Alaskan natives, and Hispanics). In fact, it is misleading to speak of the efficacy of therapeutic intervention when these groups simply are not covered for treatment despite their high levels of emotional distress. Two surveys (Albee & Ryan,

1993; Mays & Albee, 1992) make clear the unavailability of treatment for most minority groups (the same can be said of millions of poverty-level Anglo-Saxon people living in Appalachia and other *loci* of poverty).

Availability of individual treatment also is influenced by the fact that more than half of the total number of psychiatrists and psychologists are to be found in five states and the District of Columbia. There are large regions of the United States where few mental health professionals are available. This is particularly true of such rare groups as child psychiatrists and professionals speaking Spanish, Aleut, and Navajo.

SEARCHING FOR THE MAGIC MARKER

A hundred years hence, around the year 2100, the history of psychology will recognize a major intellectual breakthrough that occurred in the second half of the twentieth century. It is the conclusive insight that *most mental disorders are learned in a social context*. They are not diseases like any other. *Mental disorders are problems in interpersonal (or intrapersonal) relations*. Psychotherapy has discovered this truth, often without recognizing its implication.

Elsewhere (Albee, 1990b), I have written at length about those things that distinguish real illnesses from mental/emotional disorders. The major difference is the presence of an *objective marker* for a real illness and the absence of an objective marker for most mental conditions.

Then there is also *cultural relativity*. In the 1920s, 1930s and 1940s, beginning in part with the work of Ruth Benedict, Margaret Mead, Franz Boas, and Otto Klineberg, social scientists became aware of the *cultural relativity* of diagnoses of disturbed behavior. For example, Benedict's (1934) book, *Patterns of Culture*, and Mead's (1928) *Coming of Age in Samoa* illuminated the fact that behaviors we label abnormal (like hallucinations, ideas of reference, group cooperation, or teen-age sexual freedom) may be regarded as normal in other cultures, and vice versa; patterns considered to be abnormal in other cultures (like competitiveness) are considered to be normal in our own. A range of sexual behavior is considered normal or abnormal depending on the culture and religion. No such cultural relativity exists for physical illnesses.

Science thrives on criticism. Often, in hard sciences, like astronomy or physics, disagreements concern the interpretation of facts, or the implications of measurements or new experiments. This is not often the case in the field of psychiatry. Human behavior is subject to a range of interpretations depending on the social context and on the biases of the observer. For example, no interpretation can be certain about the implication to be made from observing a person talking aloud in the absence of a listener. We must know whether the person is praying, rehearsing a speech or a part in a play, reciting a poem, speaking back to imaginary voices, talking to the devil, etc. The same objective behavior can mean very different things. Understanding the relevance of social context, different cities, different cultures, and different value systems all may influence judgments about behavior. One of the clearest examples here is the interpretation of sexual behavior. Many fundamentalists in the Bible belt have a narrow view of what is acceptable public and private sexual behavior. Two same-sex persons kissing and fondling each other in public are in danger of being arrested in some places and are ignored in San Francisco. Women selling sex by posing in street-side windows in Amsterdam are protected by city police and provided regular physical exams by city health clinics. Women who engage in extramarital sex in Muslim countries are in danger of violent punishment. The beaches of Sicily in December are filled with near-naked bikini-clad Swedes, but no Sicilian peasant woman would don a bathing suit. Normal and abnormal are culturally relative.

Our society reacts strongly to the sexual abuse of children, and major efforts are being made to reduce and eliminate child pornography and the abuse of children by adults. Abusive adults (nearly always male) are adjudged to be emotionally disturbed, often called sociopathic. But it is illuminating to point out (*not* to justify) that, in many cultures around the world, young girls are sold by dealers to adult males with the purchase price as child brides, as child sex objects, or as servants. The patriarchal state does not object and even condones the practice. The World Federation for Mental Health (WFMH) has a Committee on Child Sexual Exploitation (1990) that is transacting with governments where girls are purchased from their impoverished families by traders for resale on the slave market. The WFMH tries to negotiate with governments of countries where these girls are sold as prostitutes, sex toys, or household slaves. One of the many findings of this committee is that often the male-dominated, patriarchal governments fail to see how such long-standing practices are subject to disapproval. If (little-valued) girls are the property of their fathers, then they can be sold like other chattel in a patriarchal society.

HOW CLEAR IS THE PROGNOSIS, ONSET, END?

For most medical real diseases there is a reasonably good prognosis. Ever since Virchow instructed medicine in the late 19th century about the existence of separate diseases, each with a separate cause and treatment, and each with a relatively clear prognosis, it has been possible to make a fairly accurate predictive statement for most physical conditions. Whether a person has a cold, a strep throat, appendicitis, or gonorrhea, predictions can be made as to the severity of the condition, its duration, and its probable outcome, with or without treatment. The *prognosis* for mental disorders is mostly uncertain.

It is also usually clear when real illnesses strike that the onsets follow exposures to pathogens, organ malfunctions, or accidents. On the contrary, with mental disorders, we do not know when they begin nor when they end.

VOLUNTARY OR INVOLUNTARY TREATMENT?

John Stuart Mill (1937), in his widely quoted *Essay on Liberty* said, in effect, that control over one's own body is sovereign. Others may entreat, request, or urge a person to do or not do something with his or her body, but over one's body the person is in charge and free to choose. In the case of nearly all physical illnesses, one may freely choose to seek professional help, and to follow or to ignore the prescriptions and recommendations of medical authorities. Even in cases where to refuse medicine or surgery may be life threatening, the individual is still free to choose not to be treated. Increasingly popular are living wills in which individuals may indicate that in the event that they are incapacitated and unable to make decisions about their own care, certain kinds of treatment are unwanted and rejected in advance.

In the case of mental conditions, the responsibility of the individual for choosing or rejecting treatment is considerably less clear. The topic of involuntary treatment of mental cases has been widely discussed and debated in recent years. *Psychiatric survivors* (former mental patients) strongly reject, for the most part, the use of involuntary treatment with drugs, electric shock, lobotomy, and other major interventions. On the other hand, citizens' groups like NAMI urge involuntary treatment and even involuntary mental hospitalization. Arguments for (Torrey, 1997) and against this psychiatric totalitarianism (Szasz, 1963, 1990) would never occur over real medical illness where the patient is free to decide to refuse treatment or accept it.

RESPONSIBILITY

The insanity defense often is considered as a way to absolve persons for criminal behavior, the excuse being that those persons were not in control of their behaviors because of the presence of mental illness. Beginning with the M'Naughton Rule, promulgated by a special committee of the House of Lords in England during the last century, various alternative legal criteria have been drafted to try to define ways in which "mental illness" can be used to justify a lack of responsibility for a criminal act. M'Naughton, a decorated British soldier who had been wounded in the head in defense of the Empire, developed delusions about the prime minister and attempted to shoot him. The prime minister's secretary was hit and killed by the bullet. Normally this kind of assassination would have led quickly to hanging, but because of M'Naughton's heroic background, a special committee of the House of Lords, which was appointed to wrestle with the question of responsibility, recommended that he be placed in a mental hospital rather than hanged. Since that time there have been numerous other attempts (the Durham Rule, the American Law Institute recommendations, etc.) to define the mental conditions absolving the guilt of a person committing a crime. The argument arises out of the belief that some people commit crimes when they do not know why, or what, they are doing. The problem, of course, is to determine the presence of insanity in the absence of an objective marker.

WHAT IS TO BE DONE?

As two distinguished 19th-century sociologists (Marx & Engels, 1859) often pointed out, the ruling ideas of a particular society are those that support the ruling class. Our American ruling class does not want to build a more just, equalitarian, and nonexploitative society. It likes things the way

they are. The wealthy establishment has no personal interest in improving the lives of the disadvantaged and oppressed, and it refuses to face the probability that many people become emotionally disturbed and mentally disordered as a result of social injustices. Elsewhere, I have written extensively about the evidence supporting a social-environmental model (Albee, 1990). People suffer from poverty, child abuse and neglect, exploitation, and low self-esteem—the list of environmentally caused problems is extensive. Surely the psychotherapists are aware of this relationship. But they remain silent and even seek prescription privileges for themselves, further attesting to the value of the medical model.

WHAT DOES IT MATTER?

Does it really matter whether mental disorders are or are not viewed as illnesses? Are there not advantages to calling these people sick? Does this not reduce the stigma long associated with mental problems?

At the heart of these questions is a major political issue. What are the major causes of mental disorders? Are the basic causes to be found in the biology of the individual affected—in his or her genes, brain chemistry, physiology, etc.? Or are the causes to be found in social-environmental stresses like poverty and powerlessness; involuntary unemployment; and the painful experiences of being a woman in a patriarchal society, of being a minority person in a rejecting society, of being an outsider—gay, physically handicapped, aged, or with low self-esteem?

The answer to this question is crucial because it determines the possibility of eventually preventing or greatly reducing the problem of mental disorder. If, as most political conservatives contend, all mental disorders are brain diseases, then not much can be done to prevent them. There is a flavor of Calvinism to this view; one is doomed or saved even before one's birth. This model is also consistent with Social Darwinism: Genes determine who will survive and succeed and who will fail and disappear (Albee, 1996). On the other hand, if mental disorders are caused by preventable social pathology—bad parenting, prejudice, exploitation, social injustice—then a reduction in rate is possible with the development of a more just, equalitarian society. Conservatives strongly oppose social change because this means redistributing power, and so they favor the disease explanation. It is cheaper.

No Disease or Disorder Has Ever Been Treated Out of Existence

One of the major lessons to be learned from public health research is that individual treatment does not change incidence. Public health focuses on prevention. It is the only hope for reducing incidence. The field of public health began, as a specific discipline, in the middle of the 19th century when scholars, mostly MDs, discovered clear causes of widespread plagues and ways of interpreting them or preventing their spread. One of the most important first steps in public health strategy is careful examination of the distribution of the condition in the population. Who is most at risk? Who least? This is the heart of epidimiology.

An example: The incidence of cholera in London was observed to be a function of the source of drinking water. Different water companies often served different houses on the same street. Some water companies drew water from the Thames River from upstream, above the city. The incidence of cholera in homes so served was low or nonexistent. On the other hand, companies drawing water from downstream of the city served homes where the incidence of cholera was high. Clearly something dumped into the water as it passed through the city was causing the disease. Other observations confirmed the waterborne source of cholera. People using certain wells were at high risk. Other wells carried no risk. John Snow, a young physician, observed that the well at the corner of Broad and Water streets was used by impoverished people at high risk. In the most famous act in the history of public health, he removed the handle of the pump to this well and halted a localized epidemic of cholera. (For a fascinating account of public health success and challenges, see Garrett, 1994.)

Psychotherapists must become politically active. They must admit the hopelessness of one-to-one intervention, but ally with those struggling for a just and equitable world.

The Truth Will Make Us Free

On the early NBC evening news, July 7, 1998, Rosalynn Carter was interviewed about her long-standing interest in the field of mental health/illness. She made the same incorrect statement so common today: "We now know that mental illnesses are due to problems in the brain. We can treat brain diseases."

This is the current politically correct (PC) statement that is generated by the biological bureaucrats at NIMH who insist on the fiction that all mental illness is medical (biological). Gullible but well-meaning citizens like Ms. Carter, Tipper Gore, Elizabeth Dole, and National Public Radio all parrot the organic line. We should not be too hard on them: they are simply repeating what they have been told by authorities who should know. But these authorities are not chosen for their knowledge; They are selected for their ideological support of a medical–organic–biological model of causation favored by the drug industry and conservatives.

Psychologists-psychotherapists know better. Psychoanalysts know better. Adlerians know better. Marxists know better. But left-leaning liberal therapists lack courage. They know a great deal about the causes of mental disorder, but speaking out would be a threat to their livelihood. They who pay the piper call the tune.

Most importantly, this must change. Our own attitudes toward causation must shift away from an individualistic and individual organic pathology model, and toward a more socially oriented and community-oriented approach to causation, to intervention, and to prevention. Before this change to a social-causation model can occur, there must be prior revolution.

First, for a revolution to begin there must be widespread injustice. This is clearly the case today. The Report of the President's Commission on Mental Health (1978) and more recent surveys (Albee & Ryan, 1993; Kramer, 1990) identified 32–40 million persons with serious mental and emotional problems—especially children, minorities, and elderly people (who were repeatedly identified in the Report of the President's Commission as unserved groups). According to the President's Commission, only seven million persons were being seen annually by our whole mental health system, reflecting a gap that will only get wider and never will be closed. We are neglecting the elderly and children, as well as minorities, the rural poor, the urban poor, and the handicapped. So injustice is a condition that widely prevails.

Second, a revolution always calls for an *overt challenge to authority*. The number of voices criticizing medical hegemony in dealing with people's emotional problems must become a large chorus. We are beginning to converge in our theories in the various human service professions that the defect model that sees personal taint and genetic or biochemical defect as the causes of all mental problems is an invalid model. This insight should lead us to demand that there should be changes focused on obtaining a more just and equitable society and world.

Third, a revolution needs a *clear-cut political position* that everyone can understand. The position: "Mass disorder afflicting humankind has never been eliminated through one-to-one intervention but only as a result of successful prevention." Related to this position is the recognition that *powerlessness* and stress are the major causes of emotional distress, and that the only resolution for powerlessness is a redistribution of power. So the revolutionary political position is that the aged, the poor, the minorities, children and youth, women, and other powerless groups must benefit from a redistribution of power through political and even revolutionary social action.

Fourth, revolutions need a core of *dedicated leaders* with a clear vision of the goals. We have learned a great deal from our brothers and sisters doing one-to-one casework and psychotherapy. People involved in attempting to help individually distressed and disturbed persons have given us a great deal of insight into the social origins of their clients' problems. From these one-to-one interventionists we need to recruit a cadre of leaders who will dedicate themselves to the cause of prevention through redistribution of power.

Fifth, we need to anticipate and be prepared for strong *resistance* from those whose power would be reduced or usurped by our efforts at social change. The Establishment (including the pharmaceutical industry) is ruthless in its defense of the defect (illness) model. Enormous power and resources are at stake in this struggle. We can expect continued resistance from the mental health establishment to any suggestion that the cause of distress is not a number of separate and discrete biological mental illnesses, each with an individual cause and cure. The suggestion that most human stress results from the injustice and unfairness of the present international cartel and corporate economic system will result in a powerful counterattack from them. We already see that federal funds available for prevention are going to relatively meaningless and trivial projects including prevention of recurrence. It is clear that a great deal of noise will be made about the importance of prevention to cover the fact that little

significant work in this area is being supported by the establishment.

Finally, revolutions occur when there is an unstable *power structure*. Psychiatry is decreasing in its power and control largely because it is unable to recruit bright young people into residency training. Forty years ago when I wrote a book on the nation's mental health manpower (Albee, 1959), psychiatry was recruiting some nine to ten percent of medical school graduates into its residency programs, and even then the numbers were insufficient to satisfy the need. Recent studies indicate that psychiatry is now recruiting only about three percent of medical school graduates and its popularity continues to decline.

In short, conditions are ripe for revolution. Back in the days when the world was a much simpler place, a great many of us held firmly to the belief that scientific judgments were based on facts, and that social policy changed with accumulating knowledge. Now, it is clear, power, especially economic power, rules.

If we are serious about the role of psychology in the promotion of human welfare, we will find ourselves engaging in political and social action in roles and in places where we least expected to be (see Albee, Joffe, & Dusenbury, 1988). A society that is truly oriented toward human welfare rather than toward the ever-increasing output of goods or the maximization of profits on capital needs to change the structure and content of its power and educational systems (Prilleltensky, 1994, 1997). Education will have to promote values and attitudes that ultimately lead to the dismantling of patriarchy and international corporate capitalism, and to the creation of a humanistic, democratic socialism governed primarily from the local level and pervading all aspects of economic and social life. Let the revolution begin!

REFERENCES

Action for mental health. (1960). Final Report of the Joint Commission on Mental Illness and Health. New York: Basic Books.

Albee, G. W. (1959). *Mental health manpower trends*. New York: Basic Books.

Albee, G. W. (1969). A conference on recruitment of black and other minority students and faculty. *American Psychologist, 24,* 720–723.

Albee, G. W. (1975). To thine own self be true: Comments on insurance reimbursement. *American Psychologist, 30,* 1156–1158.

Albee, G. W. (1977a). Does including psychotherapy in health insurance represent a subsidy to the rich from the poor? *American Psychologist, 32,* 719–721.

Albee, G. W. (1977b). Problems in living are not sickness: Psychotherapy should not be included under national health insurance. *The Clinical Psychologist, 30,* 3–5, 6–8, 13.

Albee, G. W. (1981). The prevention of sexism. *Professional Psychology, 12,* 20–28.

Albee, G. W. (1990a). The answer is prevention. In N. P. Chance & T. G. Harris (Eds.), *The best of Psychology Today* (pp. 60–62). New York: McGraw-Hill.

Albee, G. W. (1990b). The futility of psychotherapy. *Journal of Mind and Behavior, 11*(34).

Albee, G. W. (1995, August 20). Quality child care can be had without orphanages. *Sarasota-Herald Tribune,* op. ed. p.

Albee, G. W. (1996). Social Darwinism and political models of mental/emotional problems. *Journal of Primary Prevention, 17*(1).

Albee, G. W. (1996). The psychological origins of the white male patriarchy. In G. W. Albee (Ed.), Social Darwinism and political models of mental/emotional problems, *Journal of Primary prevention 17*(1), 75–97.

Albee, G. W., Bond, L. A., & Monsey, T. V. C. (1992). *Improving children's lives: Global perspectives on prevention.* Newbury Park, CA, London, & New Delhi: Sage.

Albee, G. W., Joffe, J. M., & Dusenbury, L. (Eds.). (1988). *Prevention, powerless and politics: Reading in social change and political action as prevention.* Newbury Park, CA: Sage.

Albee, G. W., & Ryan K. (1993). An overview of primary prevention. *Journal of Counseling and Development, 72*(2), 115–123.

Altshuler, K. (1997, December). Newer medicine: Opportunity and challenge. *The Bell,* Newsletter of the National Mental Health Association, p. 7.

American Psychiatric Association. (1952). *Mental disorders: Diagnostic and statistical manual* Washington, D.C.: Author.

American Psychiatric Association. (1988). *Diagnostic and statistical manual of mental disorders* (4th ed.). Washington, D.C.: Author.

Benedict, R. (1934). *Patterns of culture.* New York: Houghton Mifflin Co.

Brody, J. (1981, October 28). Guide through the magic of psychotherapies. *The New York Times,* pp. C3–C8.

Broussard, E. (1976). Neonatal prediction and outcome at 10/11 years. *Child Psychiatry and Human Development, 7,* 85–93.

Celani, D. (1995). *The illusion of love.* New York: Columbia University Press.

Cowen, E. L. (1991). In pursuit of wellness. *American Psychologist, 46*(4), 404–408.

David, H., Dytrych, Z., Matejcek, Z., & Schüller, S. (Eds.). (1988). *Born unwanted.* New York: Springer Publishing Co., & Prague: Avicenum, Czechoslovak Medical Press.

Dohrenwend, B. P. (1990). Socioeconomic status (SES) and psychiatric disorders. *Social Psychiatry and Psychiatric Epidemiology, 25,* 41–47.

Garrett, L. (1994). *The coming plague: Newly emerging diseases in a world out of balance.* New York: Farrar, Straus & Giroux.

Hamburg, D. (1990, Spring). A decent start: Promoting healthy child development in the first three years of life. *Carnegie Quarterly.*

Harlow, H. F. (1958). The nature of love. *American Psychologist, 13,* 673–685

Harlow, H. F. (1962). Social deprivation in monkeys. *Scientific American, 207,* 136–146.

Harlow, H. F., & Harlow, M. K. (1966). Learning to love. *American Scientist, 54,* 244–272.

Hollingshead, A. B., & Redlich, F. C. (1958). *Social class and mental illness.* New York: John Wiley & Sons.

Hyman, S. (1998, April). Research clearly shows parity is important and just. *The Bell,* Newsletter of the National Mental Health Association, p. 5.

Joffe, J. (1988). The cause of the causes. In G. Albee, J. Joffe, & L. Dusenbury (Eds.). *Prevention, powerlessness, and politics: Reading on social change* (pp. 57–79). Newbury Park, CA: Sage.

Kiesler, C. A., & Sibulkin, A. E (1987). *Mental hospitalization. Myths and facts about a national crises.* Newbury Park, CA: Sage.

Kleinman, A. (1997, July 11). The burden and the scandal. *Meeting of the International Women Leaders for Mental Health.* Helsinki, Finland. Published by The Carter Center and the World Federation for Mental Health (with support from Janssen-Cilag-Organon and Eli Lilly and Co. Foundation).

Klerman, G. (1997). Mental illness, the medical model, and psychiatry. *The Journal of Medicine and Philosophy, 2,* 220–243.

Kramer, M. (1983). The continuing challenges: The rising prevalence of mental disorders, associated chronic diseases and disabling conditions. *American Journal of Social Psychiatry, 3,* 13–24.

Kramer, M. (1992). Barriers to the primary prevention of mental, neurological, and psychosocial disorders of children: A global perspective. In G. W. Albee, L. A. Bond, & T. V. Cook Monsey (Eds.), *Improving children's lives: Global perspectives on prevention* (pp. 3–36). Newbury Park, CA: Sage.

Kutchins, H., & Kirk, S. A. (1997). *Making us crazy. DSM: The psychiatric bible and the creation of mental disorders.* New York: The Free Press.

Marx, K., & Engels, F. (1959). Manifesto of the Communist Party. Section II. In K. Marx, *Selected*

Works (Vol. 1). New York: International Publishers.

Mays, V. M., & Albee, G. W. (1992). Psychotherapy and ethnic minorities. In D. K. Freedheim, H. J. Freudenberger et al. (Eds.) *History of psychotherapy; A century of change* (pp. 552–570). Washington, D.C.: American Psychological Association.

Mead, M. (1928). *Coming of age in Samoa*. New York: W. Morrow Co.

Mill, J. S. (1937). *Autobiography and essay on liberty*. New York: Collier.

Mirowsky, J., & Ross, C. E. (1989). *Social causes of psychological distress*. New York: Adeline de Gruyter.

Mowrer, O. H. (1950). *Learning theory and personality dynamics*. New York: Routledge.

Musarrat, H. (1988, December). *Community mental health in Pakistan*. Paper presented at the 7th International Conference in Psychiatry, Karachi, Pakistan.

Perry, M. J. (1996). The relationship between social class and mental disorder. In G. W. Albee (Ed.). *Social Darwinism and political models of mental/emotional problems* (pp. 17–30).

President's Commission on Mental Health (1978). *Report to the President*. Washington, D.C.: U.S. Printing Government Office.

Prilleltensky, I. (1997). Values, assumptions, and practices: Assessing the moral implications of psychological discourse and action. *American Psychologist, 47,* 517–535.

Prilleltensky, I. (1994). *The morals and politics of psychology: Psychological discourse and the status quo*. Albany, NY: State University of New York Press.

Regier, D. A. (1984). The NIMH Epidemiologic Catchment Area program. Historical context, major objectives, and study population characteristics. *Archives of General Psychiatry, 41,* 934–941.

Report to the President. (1978). President's Commission on Mental Health. Washington, D.C.: Superintendent of Documents, U.S. Government Printing Office.

Robins, L. N., & Regier, D. A. (1991). *Psychiatric disorders in America: The Epidemiologic Catchment Area study*. New York: Free Press.

Roff, M., & Ricks, D. (Eds.), (1970). *Life history research in psychopathology*. Minneapolis, MN: University of Minnesota Press.

Rosanoff, A. J. (Ed.). (1905). *Manual of psychiatry*. New York: John Wiley & Sons, Inc.

Saxe, L. (1980). *The efficacy and cost-effectiveness of psychotherapy*. Office of Technology Assessment, Congress. Washington, D.C.: U.S. Government Printing Office.

Skodak, M. (1984). Prevention in retrospect: Adoption follow-up. In J. M. Joffe, G. W. Albee, & L. D. Kelly (Eds.), *Reading in primary prevention: Basic concepts* (pp. 348–361). Hanover, NH: University Press of New England.

Skodak (Crissey), M. (1992). Some research revisited. In M. Kessler, S. E. Goldstron, & J. M. Joffe (Eds.), *The present and future of prevention* (pp. 41–54). Newbury Park, CA: Sage.

Skodak, M., & Skeels, H. M. (1949). A final follow-up study of one hundred adopted children. *Journal of Genetic Psychology, 66,* 21–58.

Surgeon General's Workshop on Self-help and Public Health. (1987). Washington, D.C.: United States Department of Health and Human Services, Public Health Service.

Szasz, T. S. (1963). *Law, liberty and psychiatry*. New York: Macmillan.

Szasz, T. S. (1990). Law and psychiatry: The problems that will not go away. *The Journal of Mind and Behavior, 11,* 557–563.

Task Panel on Migrant and Seasonal Farmworkers. (1978). The President's Commission on Mental Health. Washington, D.C.: U.S. Government Printing Office.

Torrey, E. F. (1997). *Out of the shadows: Confronting America's mental illness crisis*. New York: Wiley.

Wilkinson, R. G. (1996). *Unhealthy societies: The afflictions of inequality*. London & New York: Routledge.

World Federation for Mental Health, Committee on commercial sexual exploitation of children (1990–1995) Annual reports in Newsletter.

CHAPTER 33

PSYCHOTHERAPY: QUESTIONS FOR AN EVOLVING FIELD

C. R. SNYDER
The University of Kansas-Lawrence
RICK E. INGRAM
San Diego State University

WHERE ARE WE GOING?

For as long as people have been living together in groups, there have been persons recognized as *therapists* by those around them. Indeed, as we increasingly discover the effective components of psychotherapy, we also acknowledge that these processes have been around in varying forms for centuries. Thus, as the door to the 21st century opens, we are witnessing an exciting time of change in regard to scientific and applied psychotherapeutic activities. In this chapter, we will raise questions that strike us as being crucial for the continued evolution of the science and practice of psychotherapy. For the questions for which we do not have answers, we will raise other questions or point to possible directions for finding the answers. For many of the issues we raise, however, we at least have educated guesses, and will share them. Of course, our views may not reflect what you, the reader, believe. On this point, we would suggest that the questions raised are far more important than any answers that we attempt. For purposes of exposition, we have grouped our questions into five categories: Training for Psychotherapy-Related Careers; the Science of Psychotherapy; the Practice of Psychotherapy; the Science and Practice Interface; and the Public and Psychotherapy.

Authors' note Thanks are extended to Ruth Q. Leibowitz for comments on an earlier version of this chapter.

TRAINING FOR PSYCHOTHERAPY-RELATED CAREERS

Do We Know How Many Professional Psychotherapists There Are, and How Many Are Needed?

To make systematic estimates of the need for psychotherapy services in the ensuing years, we first need to refine the means of ascertaining how many psychotherapists of differing orientations there are in various settings. This is part of the supply and demand issue that any profession should examine so as to make decisions about the training of new persons entering into the field. The present prevailing approach is a *laissez-fare* "the market will correct itself." This approach has at least two difficulties—either an under- or oversupply of psychotherapists may be trained. Should there be an oversupply, educational programs need to face the ethical question of whether they are explicitly or implicitly falsely suggesting available jobs for their students upon graduation (see Kiesler chapter in this volume). Within the field of psychology, professional schools have been criticized for flooding the applied marketplace with too many graduates. In fairness, all clinical psychology doctoral programs are open to similar criticisms. It is the case, however, that in response to a perceived shrinking of available jobs for their graduates, many Ph.D. clinical psychology programs have cut back the number of students accepted in the 1990s. We encourage all programs, including the free-standing professional schools and the university-based ones, to consider carefully the ethical implications of potentially training more students than the market will bear (for an important exception, see our subsequent discussion regarding the need for therapists from traditionally underrepresented ethnic and racial groups).

Examining the supply issue from a more global perspective, there are shortages of psychotherapists in many countries (see, for example, the Albee chapter in this volume). Typically, this supply issue has been equated with the applied side of the field, but there is an equally important need to find out how many psychotherapy researchers are needed. As noted in the chapter by Snyder, McDermott, and colleagues in this volume, the overwhelming majority of persons receiving their doctorates in clinical and counseling psychology are women. As such, women will be called upon to fill the needs in the psychotherapy field for practitioners and researchers.

Initiatives taken by the major national organizations in psychology, psychiatry, and social work to ascertain the numbers of psychotherapy students in training within their professions would help to clarify the supply issue. Moreover, these organizations could spearhead careful projections about the present and future needs for applied and research psychotherapists. Possible arguments that we have heard for not estimating the needs are twofold. First, some hold that such surveys would be very difficult to conduct, and second, yet others suggest that the needs for psychotherapists are fluid in a quickly evolving and entrepreneurial society. Changing insurance companies' coverage, as well as mental health legislation, also clouds our ability to make estimates. Likewise, as societal misunderstandings and stigmas associated with psychotherapy change in the 21st century, the demand for services also will vary. What we can say for certain, however, is that many new clinical and counseling psychology doctorates trained to do psychotherapy currently cannot obtain appropriate work in the major urban centers of the United States.

Training for the Science of Psychotherapy, the Practice of Psychotherapy, or Both?

As we noted previously, the data are sparse in regard to the needs for persons with doctorates who can deliver psychotherapy and conduct psy-

chotherapy research. Beyond this numbers issue, there are questions within the field about the best forms for such education. Since the 1940s the traditional norm for the doctorate in psychology has been the Boulder model (see for history Korchin, 1983). At the first of many conferences, the participants agreed that the scientist–practitioner model for clinical psychologists should be based on scientific measurements of people, along with how to effect positive changes in their lives. At a subsequent Vail conference in 1973, the idea of a professional doctorate was approved and added to the traditional Ph.D. *Boulder Model*. This legitimized the professional doctorate and gave rise to the establishment of Psy.D. degrees in which applied psychotherapy educational activities were emphasized; moreover, many Ph.D. programs also have emphasized applied psychotherapy education. In the context of recent developments, the psychotherapy field should weigh these two educational approaches in relation to the current and projected needs.

Beyond the decisions that are made because of marketplace demands, the judgments about the best educational approaches need to be made with an eye toward the education that ensures maximally effective psychotherapy delivery. In order to deliver excellent care, psychotherapists should be well trained in the scientific bases of the change process; moreover, this scientific foundation should help practitioners keep up with the latest information in the psychotherapy field. The drift away from an understanding of the scientific foundations of the change process is counterproductive and potentially unethical in terms of jeopardizing the very best in psychotherapy treatments. Both Ph.D. and Psy.D. degree programs have lessened the scientific aspects of psychotherapy education and have accentuated the delivery of services. As an example, consider the recent move by the credentialing body of the American Psychological Association *to allow programs to attain accreditation as long as they are doing what they espouse in their particular model of training*. There should be core scientific requirements that simply cannot be omitted no matter what the training model of a given program might be. This recent change in accreditation standards will serve only to increase the flow away from those difficult and intensive educational experiences that relate to understanding the science of psychotherapy.

Part of such required scientific education would include how to stay open to new developments and how to continually renew one's education throughout the subsequent stages of a career. We, the editors of this volume, have spent the bulk of our professional careers trying to see that the students in our respective doctoral programs acquire this scientific foundation and respect for the science of psychotherapy, and that they remain open to such an inquiry. It is not that we disdain the notion of psychotherapy as *art;* on the contrary, the experiential and intuitive aspects of the helping process always have and always will play an important role in effective psychotherapy (for an informative interchange between the emphasis on empirically supported treatments as compared to an emphasis on relationships, see Perez, 1999 and Schneider, 1998, 1999). An aggregating, cumulative body of scientific information must be imparted to all students of psychotherapy. Equally important, students must acquire a respect for the scientific approach to the psychotherapy endeavor. Whatever individuals, educational institutions, and accrediting bodies can do to keep the science of psychotherapy at the forefront of our field will help to produce not only more effective psychotherapists for today, but for the many tomorrows that follow. Interestingly, the very insurance companies that often are assailed for their sparse payments for psychotherapy may help to highlight the importance of the scientific approaches to psychotherapy because they have espoused the necessity of empirically verified treatment.

What Are the Characteristics of a "Good" and Competent Psychotherapist, and How Can These Be Imparted in the Educational Sequence?

Therapist variables should be understood better, especially as they relate to successful outcomes (see the chapter in this volume by Ingram, Hayes, and Scott, as well as the chapter by Teyber and McClure). Just as we increasingly come to understand more fully the workings of successful psychotherapy processes and practices, so too shall we begin to have a clearer understanding of the successful psychotherapist. Learning to do psychotherapy involves incremental increases in the requisite skills shown to be effective. Beyond those particular skills, we have been impressed with the power of the therapist's ability to establish and maintain a helping alliance with the client. Similarly, all forms of successful psychotherapy involve, to some degree, effective interpersonal communications. The ability to establish an alliance and to communicate with ease and trust seem to be essential for effective psychotherapists.

Research into the psychotherapists' skills that foster improvement and growth in clients should be at the forefront of our research activities. Given their importance, we are surprised at the relatively scant attention that has been paid to the issues of what constitutes the good and competent psychotherapist. On this point, we would call upon our clinical educational and research institutions not only to formalize what it is that we know about the good and competent therapists but also to greatly expand our future efforts on this crucial issue. Likewise, this is an absolutely essential area for granting agencies to take the lead and to support more research. To find the characteristics of good therapists is a logical parallel to finding efficacious psychotherapies. The field will profit enormously as we learn about and agree upon such psychotherapist competencies.

For most psychotherapy training programs in clinical psychology, the curricula focus on the knowledge base of the discipline, along with giving feedback to trainees about their psychotherapy activities (i.e., practica and internships). Based on such curricular content, we would infer that psychotherapy competency must be related to such activities. As we come to understand these psychotherapy competencies more fully, presumably our training programs will tailor their curricula to impart the knowledge and experiential bases of such competencies. As such, we would advocate approaches aimed at maximizing the acquisition of such competencies. To do otherwise not only would be wasting the trainees' time but also would neglect the educational mission of psychotherapy training programs. Although these suggestions may seem rigid, we would add that we believe there are also many very *human* qualities and interpersonal characteristics that will emerge as being necessary for being a competent psychotherapist (see the final Mahoney chapter in this volume for excellent exemplars).

What Are the Contributions of Informal or Formal Education?

Another training-related issue involves the degree to which formal training is necessary for delivering efficacious psychotherapy. We may have heard stories of miraculously effective psychotherapists who have no formal education in the psychological change process. At the other end of the spectrum, we also may know someone who has had years of graduate and postgraduate education and is seemingly a woeful therapist.

Certainly it would be preposterous to deny that, in the course of their childhood experiences, some people are trained naturally in the very scientific-based principles that facilitate positive change. Still, this does not negate the importance of formal training, which can broaden and improve the abilities of both the *natural* psychotherapist and the therapist who requires more formal instruction. Given the accumulating evidence that certain psychotherapeutic techniques are particularly helpful, it follows that our student psychotherapists should be trained in the very latest technologies related to such science-based knowledge. To not promulgate this science-based knowledge would not only be irresponsible but also unethical.

As can be seen in Figure 33.1, there are four possibilities in regard to psychotherapeutic education. For the potential therapist in cell #1, neither natural life experiences and talent nor formal education has been obtained. Such a person would be the least effective therapist and may even do harm to clients. In cell #2, we see the naturally talented person who has obtained the psychotherapeutic education from life experience, but not from formal education. We would expect such persons, in varying degrees, to be effective in their psychological helping of others. In cell #3, we find the person who has obtained formal psychotherapeutic education, but who had no psychotherapeutic education from life experiences; such a person, in varying degrees, can become effective in his or her psychotherapeutic work. The type of person in cell #3 may be familiar to those who educate psychotherapists; such students can learn to *do therapy*, but they do not seem to have a basic affinity for these activities because of their relative lack of earlier experi-

ences. Finally, in cell #4, we see the person who has obtained the psychotherapeutic experiences in both natural life experiences *and* formal education; such persons should be especially effective in their work. Again, for those who educate psychotherapists, this cell #4 type of person may seem readily able to understand the lessons being taught in the context of more formal psychotherapy education.

This informal versus formal framework would apply to any of those common or shared psychotherapeutic processes that are related to good psychotherapy (hope, interpersonal trust, therapeutic alliance, etc.). Furthermore, this informal versus formal distinction may apply to the particular skills that are imparted in specific psychotherapy interventions.

In summary, we offer this informal versus formal matrix as a means of understanding the genesis of psychotherapeutic skills. Instead of being pulled into the potentially unproductive debate regarding the relative efficacy of nonprofessional versus professionally trained psychotherapists, we suggest that it may be more useful to ascertain how psychotherapeutic characteristics and skills are obtained in both training arenas.

Can We Make Effective Judgments About the Best Students To Be Admitted into Psychotherapy Training Programs?

At present, we are not aware of data that illustrate the characteristics or qualifications of the best students to be admitted to our psychotherapy graduate education programs (see Ingram, 1983). Perhaps this is the case because we just now are beginning to understand what competence means in our field, as well as what the characteristics of a good psychotherapist might be.

The traditional information examined by admissions committees in clinical psychology programs have included grades, letters of recommendation, coursework, publications, presentations, Graduate Record Examination scores, and personal statements (Ingram & Zurawski, 1981). Although clinical psychology program directors have talked among themselves for years about which of these factors should be weighted more heavily, there does not appear to be much clarity or agreement about which are the important factors. This has been the case when performance in the program (typically tapped by grades, with

Informal

		No	Yes
No		#1	#2
Formal			
Yes		#3	#4

FIGURE 33.1 Informal and Formal Sources of Psychotherapy Education.

very little variability between students) is the criterion variable. One can speculate about what factors might be weighted more heavily once we begin to operationalize psychotherapeutic competency. Might we actually want to begin to test for such characteristics as part of our admissions procedures? To complicate matters further, what applicant qualifications would be important if we want to train the next generation of psychotherapy researchers and scholars? Does this involve a different criterion? Different predictors? On these latter two questions, we believe that different predictors probably will emerge.

It is important to make the best decisions about those applicants who will undergo extensive psychotherapy training because this process is expensive in terms of the resources involved, and the persons selected eventually will be serving other people in crucial psychotherapist or researcher roles. As such, much more attention needs to be given to all the questions that surround this selection issue.

What Are the Genders and Ethnic Backgrounds of Psychotherapists in Training?

As noted previously in the chapter by Snyder, McDermott, and colleagues in this volume, clinical and counseling psychology will be sending predominately female cohorts into the psychotherapy applied and scientific fields during the next few decades. We would refer the reader to that chapter for the potential positive and negative effects of this feminizing of the psychotherapy field. Women soon will form the overwhelming majority of practicing psychotherapists, and perhaps the researchers also.

The applied and scientific branches of psychotherapy presently have very few members of under-represented groups. Moreover, given the small numbers of under-represented students who are in the pipeline or entering psychotherapy graduate education, increases are not projected. At the risk of stating the obvious, we need to recruit more ethnically diverse cohorts into the psychotherapy field. The United States in the 21st century will have a population in which Caucasians will constitute a plurality rather than a numerical majority. Through the forces of immigration and birthrate, non-Caucasian ethnic groups are increasing their relative percentages in American society (Sue & Sue, 1999), and it is estimated that somewhere between the years 2030 and 2050, persons of varying ethnic backgrounds (e.g., African-American, Hispanic, Native-American, and Asian-American) will constitute a numerical majority (U.S. Census Bureau, 1992). In some large states such as California, Texas, and Florida, these changes will occur even sooner. Overall, the United States is clearly becoming a much more visibly multiethnic, multicultural society, and our psychotherapy field must change to reflect this factor and avoid a widening gulf between psychotherapists and their potential clients. Psychotherapy already is seen by many people as an option primarily available to the Caucasian middle and upper classes.

How can more individuals from ethnically and culturally diverse backgrounds be attracted to the psychotherapy field? As Gray-Little and Kaplan (this volume) have pointed out, ethnic minority clients are underrepresented as participants in both psychotherapy and psychotherapy research. Our sense is that ethnic minority individuals tend not to pursue psychotherapy careers because they do not see psychotherapy as particularly relevant to their lives. Researchers and practitioners alike could remedy this by making ethnic groups more of a focus in their work (see Gray-Little & Kaplan, this volume). For example, researchers could embrace mental health issues that are important to various ethnic groups. Practitioners could reach out with more *pro bono* work aimed at helping African-, Asian-, Hispanic-, and Native-American clients; likewise, more talks and interactions could be initiated with agencies or institutions serving these populations. Also, if we do more work in the area of prevention, individuals from all ethnic and cultural backgrounds may view psychotherapy as an option.

Additionally, funding agencies could earmark grant priorities for minority-related issues. On this point, the National Institute of Health already is mandating that investigators consider diverse populations in their research. Government at the national and local levels, as well as psychotherapy organizations large and small, could initiate more public education outreach aimed at making psychotherapy a viable option for an ethnically and culturally diverse population. In short, there needs to be more outreach to persons of all ethnic backgrounds. Psychotherapy has much to offer people, and more students of various ethnicities who are moving through grade school, junior high, high school, and college need to be progressively recruited into the field. In summary, we need more outreach—*psychotherapy is not just for the few, but for the many.*

What Should We Do to Ensure Competence Throughout Psychotherapists' Careers?

Given that many changes and new science-based psychotherapy approaches will be discovered or refined after a person completes his or her psychotherapy graduate education, what can we do to ensure more of a lifelong learning model? More specifically, what should be done in terms of the credentialing and continued evaluation of practicing psychotherapists? On this point, we advocate rigorous continuing education requirements in order to maintain licensure. Most states already have moved to some form of required continuing education, and the major psychotherapy-related organizations of psychology, social work, and psychiatry have become involved in such ventures. We applaud such initiatives, and would note again that by focusing reimbursement on empirically supported treatments insurance companies implicitly may have reinforced practicing psychotherapists for staying up-to-date with the latest science-based interventions.

Part of the credentialing, full-career education process also should address those instances where practicing psychotherapists become impaired. For example, some mechanism is needed to help psychotherapists who become burned out. As the literature shows, such burnout occurs among the very helpers who were filled with energy at the beginning of their careers (Snyder, 1994). These psychotherapists invest so much in their helping endeavors that they do not take care of their own selves. Accordingly, more acknowledgment should be given to the stress endured by psychotherapists. Likewise, explicit mechanisms should be put into place for seeing that assistance is given to the psychotherapists. One possibility here is that faculty members of the various doctoral training programs across the United States and Canada could offer free psychotherapy to their applied colleagues, with the respective national organizations serving as an informational source for such referrals. Conversely, some set of applied psychotherapists could provide *pro bono* help to their applied colleagues, as well as to any academician psychotherapists needing aid. Such two-way helping also would diminish the potential frictions between applied and academic psychotherapists. Relatedly, some attention should be given to these stress and burnout issues in the training phases of psychotherapists so that they can construct their practices and professional activities in order to protect themselves from such burnout. For psychotherapists who are impaired for other reasons, such as psychological or drug problems, similar local support services could be established. A principle that we advocate here is that *those of us in the psychotherapy field should take care of our own.*

What Do Scientific- and Practice-Oriented Psychotherapists Owe Because of Their Education?

Many people who have been trained for either applied or academic/research careers were supported for a large portion (sometimes all) of their educational expenses by federal, state, or local money. For many graduate students, their tuition, books, and even stipends for living expenses were provided as part of their training. Such support often lasted for four and five years, or perhaps more. The editors of this handbook, for example, were supported by both federal and state money for our entire graduate educations. Of course, we know that some graduates have accrued huge personal debts for their graduate education to become psychotherapists, but most recent students also have been the recipients of scholarships in one form or another. Do those of us who have been so kindly and generously supported by state and federal money, along with the efforts of our mentors and graduate school faculty members, have an obligation to repay these gifts in some manner? *We strongly believe that we do.*

How can a graduate repay such a debt? We would like to describe some things that we have done. We would hasten to note, however, that it is not that we are particularly virtuous—many readers of this volume probably have done far more. We simply would like to illustrate some ways in which we have attempted to give back to those who provided for our education. For example, we donate money to our graduate school departments, and we are thankful and proud of what they provided us. We believe that such donations are important inasmuch as many graduate psychotherapy education programs today are experiencing severe financial hardships in their ability to support their students. Our experience has been that such gifts will be appreciated greatly; readers may wish to contact the director of their particular graduate program and ask if there is a development fund to which they could make a donation. In addition, while you will find that the director will be delighted to learn of your donation, she or he also will be pleased just to hear from you. If you cannot afford a donation, merely write or call one or more of the faculty members at your graduate program who made a positive difference for you. Tell them that you appreciate what they did on your behalf. Again, in our experiences, we have found that the "old" mentors loved to hear what we were doing.

There are, of course, other ways to give back for the education that one has received. For example, we both have undertaken careers in educating graduate students in psychotherapy, and regard this as part of our payback. Other ways include providing services on a free or reduced fee basis; the senior editor does *pro bono* psychotherapy, and runs a graduate student support group to help students from various other departments who are having difficulties in completing their theses or dissertations.

These are but some of the things that we have tried, and no doubt the reader can imagine other possible activities that can fulfill the payback function. For many of you, the simple fact of assisting others in your daily job can be an ongoing thank you for the support that you were given during your training days. Helping, like psychotherapy, is a carousel; what has been given to you, you can give back, and the cycle goes on.

THE SCIENCE OF PSYCHOTHERAPY

Do We Understand the Interplay Between Stability and Change?

Increased focus is needed in the academic/scholarly community on the issues of stability and change. In many ways, people seem to have an affinity toward both constancy *and* transformations. At a theoretical level, we would suggest that the field of psychotherapy could profit by considering the roles that consistency and constancy play in the lives of people (for an analysis of the role of change in the lives of people, see Silka, 1989). The unfolding of human life always starts with a base from which both natural growth and psychotherapy-induced transformations evolve.

The psychotherapy field would benefit from attending more to the core of thoughts, feelings, and behaviors that people seek to maintain as they navigate their lives (Costa & McCrae, 1980). This becomes important because a key issue for any person who seeks psychotherapy is that which must be preserved. Change always must be in relation to some comparison base, and an essential task for both the person helped and the person helping is to ferret out what works and requires no transformation, what is not as valued or not working and needs to be changed as part of the restructuring of the person seeking treatment.

A core issue here, and one that often is shoved inappropriately into the background, is the measurement of the person as a whole. That is to say, in addressing what the nature of any given person may be, we must tackle the thorny issue of the diagnosis of areas of potential improvement and change and strengths (see Wright, 1991). To embark on a joint venture at helping a person to change, we must take seriously the task of forming a reasonably thorough understanding of that individual in his or her context. For example, for a given client, what seem to be the recurring themes of thoughts, feelings, and behaviors, *along with the contexts in which these occur?* To undertake this task is to map the person with sufficient depth and breadth of measurement so that we can feel comfortable in then moving onto the task of helping that person to make changes in particular aspects of his or her "self." As the readers of this volume know quite well, diagnosis in and of itself has become an enormous topic, with the DSM-(Roman numeral increasing to reflect the latest edition) being the most common charting device.

One principal weakness of the DSM manual is that it is used to label a person who may need or want help to change psychologically, but it does not have much to do with the actual interventions that the person will receive. Over the years, *diagnosis and treatment have become separated,* and diagnosis has lost much of its usefulness for the change process. Diagnostic information should fit hand in glove with the intervention aimed to yield change, as well as with those subsequent measurements aimed at examining the direction and degree of that change. Thus, psychotherapy theorists and researchers either should alter the presently available diagnostic approaches or produce new diagnostic approaches that truly are useful for charting the type of intervention to be used, as well as the degree to which change has occurred. To develop such a diagnostic system would enable us to understand the enduring aspects of the person, some of which are to be valued and preserved, and others of which are not desired and need to be changed. In this sense, *measurement and change form a dialectic that is at the very core of the psychotherapy endeavor.*

There is a lack of communication, shared concepts, and goals among different groups of researchers. As one prime example, researchers examining the present diagnostic categories rarely are interested in psychotherapy outcomes, but rather typically focus on exploring how the person is manifesting thoughts, feelings, and actions that are consistent with a label (Barone, Maddux, & Snyder, 1997). Psychotherapy researchers who examine the change that accompanies psychological intervention typically use instruments that differ from those developed by the researchers who assess the various features of psychotherapy. Coping and personality researchers generally are interested in individual differences as predictors of various outcomes, especially cognitive performance and health—but not psychotherapy (Snyder, 1999). What is needed is a diagnostic system that provides suggestions about the interventions that should be implemented, along with statelike indexes that are appropriate to follow the course of those changes.

Once we have systems of charting personhood that clearly translate into related change mechanisms, we can embark on a more lucid exploration of what change means for individuals and people more generally. Just as people are motivated to have a degree of stability in their lives, it also is the case that incremental, slow change is a natural part of our existence. Such cumulative, incremental change is similar to what Kuhn (1962) has described as an "additive theory of change," and Watzlawick, Weakland, and Fish (1974) have called "first-order change."

Perhaps through evolutionary processes, we also are equipped to alter our thoughts, feelings, and actions when the circumstances so demand. Indeed, the history of our species is a tale about a creature with splendid capacities for change over time. When and how we can tap into the natural transformational potentials of people forms a research agenda that is truly worthy of scientific psychotherapy. So too, however, can we use the evolutionary lever that we have been given as a species—our "big" and convoluted brains—to uncover the many forms for helping people to induce changes in their lives. In such a search, we should abandon any contemporary smugness and be fully willing to learn from historical precedents about when and where particular change mechanisms can and do work.

In this section, we have suggested that the psychotherapy process taps into a fundamental human dialectic, perhaps even *the* basic dialectic, between constancy and transformation. We humans may want both ends of this dialectic, and indeed at times we may achieve it via psychother-

apy. But, for the science of psychotherapy, we need to return and carefully describe the anchors of the dialectic, the core person and that part (or parts) selected for change.

Should Our Theories of Change Reflect Principles That Are Applicable Just to "Troubled" People?

We would be well advised to try to make our theories of change as widely applicable as possible, and such theories should have as their goals the empowerment of all people to achieve maximal functioning and satisfaction in society. To embrace this approach is to view all forms of human thoughts and actions within the "normal" spectrum of principles that apply to most people. The principles that apply in such theories of change would be just as applicable to persons with problems in the "neurotic" or the "psychotic" range— the issue thus becomes a matter of degree (Barone, Maddux, & Snyder, 1997). This viewpoint has emerged from the interface of social and clinical psychology, where it has been proposed that we should use the same explanatory mechanisms for understanding the actions of people in general (for a counterpoint view, see Coyne, 1994). Problems in living and, more importantly, *the principles that undergird these*, are similar whether the target person lives in a state mental hospital, university dorm, urban apartment, or house in the suburbs. This perspective is captured succinctly in the opening words of Ullman and Krasner (1969) in their book on treating abnormal behavior, "The central tenet of this book is that the behaviors traditionally called abnormal are no different, either quantitatively or qualitatively, in their development and maintenance from other learned behaviors" (p. 1).

A major potential advantage of this approach is that it leaves the highest potential functioning as the change goal for all participants. With the caveat that persons with subnormal cognitive capacities may not as readily undertake change processes, it nevertheless is the case that they too are capable of some impressive alterations in their lives. Devising powerful explanatory systems of change applicable to all people will place a burden on theorists, but the potential benefits for including a wider spectrum of people are well worth the efforts. In abandoning the theories that are specific to circumscribed populations of "problem" persons, we would move toward simplified and yet more elegant and powerful models of change.

This essentially is what the behavioral interpretation attempted. Perhaps it may not be possible to develop one such overriding theory of change, but at the very least, we should attempt maximally inclusive theories. The psychotherapy field can do better than the present proliferation of countless mini-theories. It is not that such specialized theories do not have a role, but rather that we have not balanced them with wider theories. Optimal theorization in the psychotherapy field should include both the overarching theoretical perspectives, as well as the more specified mini-theories.

What Is the Status of Present Research on the Efficacy of Drug-Based Interventions?

With the enormous amounts of money that have been poured into the examination of drug-based psychotherapy effects, what can be concluded? We have both positive and negative reactions to such research. Our favorable observation is that pharmacological interventions do produce positive changes of the same magnitude as placebo effects (see Fisher & Greenberg, 1997). As has been argued elsewhere in this handbook (see chapter by Snyder and colleagues on hope), the placebo-like belief that one will improve is powerful in instilling actual positive changes. The other side of this issue, however, is that the use of many drugs can be questioned when their effects are of the same magnitude as psychologically induced placebo-like states (that are less expensive and without possible physical side effects).

Perhaps it may be useful to describe briefly how the efficacy of a medication is tested in order to provide a context for our next concern. This paradigm typically involves some version of a double-blind methodology wherein both the psychotherapist and the drug recipient supposedly are unaware of whether the recipient is receiving the new, active medication or an inert sugar-pill comparison. The problem in this paradigm is that the double-blind procedure does not work. That is to say, the bodily sensations produced by the new, active drugs are so strong that both the recipients and the researchers know that the new drug is being received rather than the inert sugar-pill. What is needed in this paradigm are placebo medications that yield at least similar bodily sensations to those elicited by the particular psychiatric drugs. This would give a true test of the efficacy of the new medications for producing improvements. In the present methodology of

drug research, it is all the more notable that those persons in the placebo conditions have done just as well as their active drug-ingesting counterparts. If the placebo actually matched the side effects of the psychiatric drug, the pure placebo effects might be even more powerful in relation to those resulting from the psychiatric drugs.

Even if one ignores this fundamental design problem, another problem with the results regarding psychiatric drugs is that evidence generally is lacking in linking the parameters of the drugs to their associated effectiveness. For example, in the majority of cases, neither dose sizes nor blood plasma levels have been related differentially to psychotherapy outcomes.

Another troubling possibility is related to the fact that the drug companies are directing huge amounts of money into testing their new psychiatric pharmaceuticals. Given our already discussed concern that the seemingly naive researchers come to know that certain of their drug recipients are receiving the active, new psychiatric medication, how can we ignore possible experimenter biases? Even if researchers are not aware of sending differential cues to the recipients of the "real psychiatric drug" as compared to the placebo drug, the experimenter expectancy literature informs us clearly that they subtly can influence psychiatric drug outcomes in the desired positive directions.

It is not that we cannot see real and meaningful potential uses for psychiatric drugs in helping people with various psychological problems (for counterpoint, however, see the Albee chapter in this volume). Potentially there is a very important role for psychiatric drugs. Whatever the psychotherapeutic change agents may be, however, we need to apply the very best of scientific methodologies to test and demonstrate their efficacies. This is true for traditional *talk-based* forms of psychotherapy, and as we are suggesting here, it also applies to pharmaceutical approaches. Our projection is that the 21st century will witness a further refinement of the methodologies used to test the effectiveness of such pharmaceuticals and, in doing so, provide further clarification of the contribution of medications to the psychotherapy process.

What Do We Really Know About the Potency of Psychotherapy?

"It works" is the short answer to the question that leads this section. Across a wide variety of approaches differing in their foci, operations, and temporal (short- to long-term) perspectives for engendering change; as applied by practitioners of varying age, gender, ethnicity, and amounts of experience; as delivered to a wide range of clientele varying in age, ethnicity, diagnostic label, and chronicity of problems, psychotherapy enables people to increase their personal satisfaction, interpersonal effectiveness, job and school performance, adaptive physiological responding to aversive circumstances, and a myriad of other behaviors in the human repertoire. Furthermore, the effects for psychotherapy appear to be as robust as those for educational interventions or medical procedures (see the Ingram, Hayes, & Scott chapter in this volume for a review of related issues).

The results of a poll (*Consumer Reports*, 1995; Seligman, 1995) showing that clients are quite satisfied with psychotherapy can be interpreted as further support for the efficacy of psychotherapy. We would caution researchers, however, to be mindful of parallel findings that emerged from an earlier acceptance of feedback literature (sometimes also called the Barnum effect). More specifically, the recipients of personal feedback from psychologists highly accept such feedback and have equally high praise for the tester and the psychological instruments on which the feedback was based (see Snyder, Shenkel, & Lowery, 1977, for review). Unfortunately, rather than tapping the accuracy of the feedback *per se*, such acceptance often reflects the recipients' reactions to the high status of the interpreter, the favorability and ambiguity of the feedback itself, as well as other factors in the situation and in the recipients themselves. As several investigators have suggested (see the Ingram et al. chapter in this volume), although it certainly is good for the psychotherapy profession that our consumers are quite satisfied, *we cannot infer anything about the actual efficacy of our efforts from such praise.* In a related vein, we applaud the skepticism inherent in the Karoly and Anderson chapter in this volume *about the many things that we do not know about the impact of psychotherapy.* We would refer the reader to that chapter for a more sobering view of the effectiveness of psychotherapy, along with the key questions needing to be asked in the future science of psychotherapy outcome research.

One other issue that is worth highlighting in this section on the effectiveness of psychotherapy pertains to what we know about its long-term effects. Although there are some notable exceptions

(see Hollon, Evans, & DeRubeis, 1990), there is too much of a *snapshot* mentality in psychotherapy research. Much more is needed in the way of long-term follow-ups of psychotherapy interventions. This research is both time-consuming and labor-intensive, and young investigators may be wary of such paradigms because they need quicker publications that help enable them to attain tenure. Therefore, we would call upon tenured investigators to launch studies of long duration. Furthermore, we would encourage funding agencies to make such long-term studies a priority.

Also, beyond the fundamental question of how the progress on target symptoms is maintained over time, it also will be important to explore the degree to which the principles that are taught to clients in psychotherapy generalize to arenas beyond those that were the focus in the original sessions. As such, we would encourage psychotherapy researchers to embrace not only the previous *repair* model in which specified problematic symptoms are alleviated but also a *growth* model in which people are taught how to transcend their present problems *and* possible future related ones.

Though some forms of psychotherapy espouse the need for booster sessions, another question that is worthy of attention is whether such boosters can and should become a routine part of all psychotherapy interventions. Perhaps at six-month or yearly intervals for a period of three years after the ending of the first phase of treatment, the impact of such booster sessions could be tested. These sessions might take on a *continuing education* perspective in which the recipients learn how to keep their recently acquired coping skills viable and flexible in response to any new and differing impediments that they may encounter.

What Is the Future of the Empirically Supported Psychotherapy Movement?

With the emergence of the empirically validated psychotherapy movement, what can we say about those treatments that have not been validated? Is it that they are invalid? The answer to this latter question probably is not so much that they are invalid, *per se, but rather that they have not been tested yet.* As such, we would encourage psychotherapy researchers to submit more treatment approaches to their empirical scrutiny. It may be that some approaches are not judged to be efficacious, but it is more likely that a version of the Dodo's Verdict (Luborsky, Singer, & Luborsky, 1975) will result in that many approaches will prove to be winners.

If this latter prediction holds true, how important will empirical validation be when most approaches meet this gold standard? Empirical validation always will be a key issue for new psychotherapy approaches that, by necessity, must undergo such analyses. Because successive, different approaches to psychotherapy have been supported via empirical validation, a logical next move would be a more cooperative search for the common factors across several empirically validated treatments (see Ingram et al. chapter in this volume).

There are some obstacles to this goal, however. For example, uniqueness presently is emphasized in individual theory and outcome research, and this hampers the potential aggregation of the cumulative body of knowledge about those shared factors that facilitate change. We would encourage researchers to try to reach agreement on some of the common outcome markers that are important in ascertaining whether a treatment works. The empirical validation movement eventually should lead to such crucial questions about core psychotherapy processes; the field would profit by having more researchers focus on such common factors. Moreover, granting agencies could provide a needed impetus to this natural evolution by underwriting psychotherapy research on common factors. Some incentives may be needed here because theory-based psychotherapy researchers manifest strong biases to validate the working processes that supposedly are special only to their approaches.

What Role Does the New "Positive Psychology" Movement Have to Play Regarding Psychotherapy?

The 1998 president of the American Psychological Association, Martin Seligman, has advocated a new approach for psychology that focuses on the positive aspects of human functioning (Seligman, 1998). In the psychotherapy arena, new models of change also are needed so as to focus upon the strengths rather than the weaknesses or deficiencies of people (e.g., the previous pathology or medical models). Furthermore, psychotherapy researchers may do well to attend more to prevention modes of intervention. What can we do to prevent people from having to endure some of the needless suffering and perfor-

mance deficits? Perhaps such prevention research can learn from the recent positive psychology movement (McCullough & Snyder, in press; Snyder & McCullough, in press), and understand the strengths of people in order to construct familial, educational, and governmental environments that simultaneously inoculate people against problematic behaviors and promote adaptive outcomes.

Although we see considerable utility in embracing the positive psychology perspective within the context of prevention, we also believe that this new perspective could become part of the typical problem amelioration paradigm. More specifically, in order to help people to deal better with those problematic areas of their lives, psychotherapy researchers might explore ways to expand the already strong or adaptive thought and behavioral repertoire. Or, at the very least, the strengths of the client can be used to lessen the overgeneralization of negative self-referential thoughts and feelings.

Will Biological or Environmental Factors Predominate in the 21st Century as the Primary Change Mechanisms?

The battle within the psychotherapy field as to the primacy of biological versus environmental factors needs to end. It is important to realize that the supposedly pure biological effects always translate into behaviors and, conversely, that the supposedly pure environmental effects always have their bases in neurochemical functioning. Accordingly, more attention should be given to interactive models that embrace multiple perspectives. Or, at minimum, the one-sided rhetoric by the proponents of the biological or environmental perspectives should tone down. Such polar attitudes and interactions have done nothing to profit the psychotherapy research field.

Individual or Group Psychotherapy?

We predict that psychotherapy theorists and researchers increasingly will attend to interpersonal factors as being conducive to productive and positive psychotherapy outcomes. Whether the actual context is one of individual or group psychotherapy, recognition of interpersonal factors will play a pivotal role. Thus, even for the person in individual treatment, researchers will find that interpersonal matters are important (see the Gotlib & Schraedley and the Forsyth &

Corazzini chapters in this volume). Likewise, those who conduct research on the etiology of problems also may conclude that most have an interpersonal origin (see also Ingram, Miranda, & Segal, 1998). In turn, psychotherapy theorists and researchers will develop and test interventions with interpersonal foci.

What Emphasis Should Be Placed on Psychotherapy Research with Children?

We need more psychotherapy research of both the preventative and remediational nature for children. That is, for our psychotherapy research to have its strongest influences, we need to place more emphasis on children (see the chapter by Roberts, Vernberg, & Jackson in this volume). This means that more researchers will need to be trained to do such research on children, and that present investigators who focus on adult samples should consider also examining the change processes with samples of children. Likewise, granting agencies need to fund more psychotherapy research on child and adolescent populations. In this process, it will be interesting to see if the present adult models can be applied to children, or whether new models are needed. Consistent with our views cited earlier in this chapter about deriving change characteristics for the full range of people, we believe that there are theoretical change principles applicable to children and adults.

What Emphasis Should Be Placed on Psychotherapy Research with the Elderly?

Two separate trends in society guarantee an increased population of citizens 65 years of age and over in the upcoming decades. First, the baby boomers are aging. Second, life expectancy is increasing. The growing numbers of seniors will have needs for psychological treatments. As such, we should increase our efforts at studying those interventions that are most effective for the elderly. Perhaps as today's middle-aged psychotherapy researchers age into their senior years, they naturally will be drawn to investigate psychotherapy for the elderly. Just as we argued for the training of psychotherapy researchers for children, we also would suggest that training programs turn some of their attentions and resources to instructing students to do psychotherapy research with seniors.

What Emphasis Should Be Placed on Psychotherapy Research with Gay Men and Lesbian Women?

To assert that gay men and lesbian women have been marginalized in the area of psychotherapy research is an understatement. Indeed, we are almost silent when it comes to understanding the change processes as they may apply to these two sizable groups of people. It has been estimated that anywhere from 4% to 10% of the U.S. population are homosexual (Norton, 1995)—potentially 25 million Americans as we start the 21st century. In addition to the other stressors encountered by all people, lesbian women and gay men are faced with three issues that are particularly troubling—identity, coming out, and loss of support because of prejudice (Sue & Sue, 1999). These and other issues need to be examined so as to find the most efficacious psychotherapy approaches for individuals who are homosexual. The present lack of psychotherapy research with homosexual clients may reflect the unfortunate and sad residue of 20th-century biases against such persons. Homosexual individuals have suffered enough because of their sexual orientation; the 21st century offers psychotherapy researchers a chance to rectify this unfortunate reality by increasing the amount of research with populations of gay men and lesbian women. Granting agencies and philanthropists also could facilitate this process by contributing funds that are specially earmarked for psychotherapy research with lesbian women and gay men. Likewise, educational institutions could train the next generation of psychotherapy researchers to focus at least some of their work on homosexual populations.

What Technology-Based Additions Could Be Made to the Science of Psychotherapy?

There could be a large bank of shared data regarding psychotherapy sessions (including outcomes) that is accessible to researchers. Such a data set could be stored on a central computer (perhaps funded by a large philanthropic organization), and made available over the Internet to interested persons (much as other data bases currently operate). This would help to facilitate the examination of common factors as discussed previously. Another suggestion is that a granting organization could fund the archiving of videotapes of the major 20th-century psychotherapy theorists (Hans Strupp, Donald Meichenbaum, Aaron

Beck, etc.), demonstrating how they conduct psychotherapy, perhaps with some commentary on the part of each expert. Such an archival project would benefit future generations of psychotherapists well into the 21st century, but it would need to start soon.

To What Degree Should Granting Agencies Support Psychotherapy Research?

The level of funding for psychotherapy research of all kinds should be increased dramatically. This has been explicit in many of our suggestions regarding the other issues in this section on the science of psychotherapy. The benefits for a happier and more productive citizenry would more than outweigh any potential costs using traditional monetary accounting principles. We should embrace something that is more akin to a social accounting approach wherein we calculate the cost/benefits ratio not only with an eye toward the traditional monetary returns but also toward the net effects of our investments for the welfare of people. With this perspective, psychotherapy research is a truly wise investment.

THE PRACTICE OF PSYCHOTHERAPY

Do Psychotherapists Use Diagnostic Information in Tailoring Interventions?

The answer to the lead question of this section is "Occasionally." As we argued in the section on the science of psychotherapy, we need more theory and research aimed at increasing the relationship between diagnosis and subsequent treatment. Presently in applied settings, diagnosis typically is a separate activity conducted by a different person from the one who delivers the treatment. Behavioral approaches in which the assessment of behaviors to be shaped is inextricably linked to the subsequent treatments constitute one general exception to this point.

Assuming that more attention is paid to research on developing and testing assessment approaches that logically are tied to later interventions, it is likely that the applied psychotherapists would embrace this change. Graduate education institutions would do well to teach future psychotherapists how to conduct diagnoses that truly would inform the subsequent intervention processes. Likewise, applied agencies could facilitate this assessment and intervention linkage by ensuring that the diagnostic workups are performed by the same professional who delivers the treatment. Such a process would promote a natural tendency to make the diagnostic workup more relevant to the actual psychotherapy. Furthermore, insurance companies could facilitate this process by remunerating diagnoses that are linked to therapy processes, and are perhaps even conducted by the same mental health professional. Staff meetings at diagnostic/treatment centers also could be implemented so as always to ask what the diagnostic workup has to say about the subsequently delivered intervention.

What Will Be the Typical Length of Interventions?

Brief psychotherapy is truly here to stay (see the Bloom chapter in this volume). This is not to suggest that longer-term interventions will disappear, but rather that brief interventions will maintain their popularity. This should happen for several reasons. First, data suggest that brief interventions work for a variety of different problems. Second, empirical validation of brief treatments will grow rapidly, making more of them available to practitioners. Third, insurance companies will continue to favor brief treatments because of their cost and outcome effectiveness. Fourth, we foresee more emphasis being placed on brief interventions in the various graduate education programs of psychotherapists. Accordingly, persons trained to do brief psychotherapy will be predisposed to use this approach as they take applied positions. Fifth, and perhaps less obvious, brief interventions may be well suited to the preferences of psychotherapy consumers in the 21st century. That is to say, with many people living fast, action-oriented lives, the pace and length of brief psychotherapies may provide a good match, especially in the United States.

For all of these reasons, we predict that the average length of psychotherapy will diminish in the 21st as compared to the 20th century. As a seeming paradox, however, the net effect of this change toward brief therapies is that people may become more likely to undertake several such brief psychotherapies at differing points in their lives, as well as for varying problems that they face. Likewise, assuming that the stigma for seeking psychotherapy continues to diminish in the 21st century, short-term psychotherapies will be perceived as a natural and useful part of the normal life activities of people.

What Is the Future of Individual and Group Psychotherapy?

If our speculations that the forthcoming increased interest among psychotherapy theorists and researchers in interpersonal matters will be crucial for the change process are accurate, then practitioners also will advocate interpersonal frameworks. Both individual and group therapies will continue to be popular, with even more marked increase in groups of various types. We are beginning to see the emergence of groups as being attractive for clientele who may be going through common experiences (single parenthood, drug dependencies, cancer treatment, etc.). People are drawn to the shared experiences with other people, and the list of such *theme* groups is long. Thus, there will be a growing market of people who will seek psychotherapy experience in both individual and group contexts. Psychotherapists and clients alike will favor explanatory and change mechanisms that emphasize inherent interpersonal linkages among people.

What Will Insurance Companies Cover and How Will They Influence the Psychotherapy Field?

So as to maintain the viability of the applied side of the field, we should continue to work to ensure that a wide range of psychotherapy is reimbursed via insurance companies. People need and deserve more power in determining their mental health care. Too often throughout the 1990s, the typical client was deprived of rights in regard to choice about the type of treatment, as well as the sheer amount of such treatment (see Shore, 1996). Eventually, as we move further into the 21st century, however, our guess is that public sentiment will dictate that mental health services be mandated by law as part of insurance packages. Beneficial possible effects of such insurance would include financial savings in terms of lowered physical health problems, as well as improved attendance and performance in work settings. Once these beneficial realities are understood, mental health coverage should be widely implemented.

Having made this prediction about the future, we would warn against assuming easy victories in this process of garnering increased mental health coverage. Indeed, it will be important to keep local, state, and national political representatives sensitized to the importance of psychotherapy. *It is our perception that psychotherapists are passive when it comes to purveying the advantages of their work to the societies in which they live.* The 21st century is no time to refrain from legitimate publicizing of the benefits that flow from psychotherapy. Just as individual psychotherapists must keep making the case publicly for their work, so too should the national organizations in psychology, psychiatry, and social work allocate sufficient money, personnel, attention, and time to making certain that all the segments of the population understand how psychotherapy contributes to the welfare of people. Psychotherapy can be promoted through national and local radio and television spots. Likewise, individual psychotherapists can speak at local functions or write columns in community newspapers to make our case. *It simply will not work to assume that people, without some special collective efforts on the part of those of us in the field, will understand the benefits of psychotherapy.*

What Should We Do About Applied Prevention Activities?

Just as more scientific attention should be directed to prevention, so too those in the applied sector should use knowledge about prevention to help keep people from developing psychological problems. More broadly, prevention efforts should encompass: (a) reducing the risk of developing problems, or perhaps at least delaying their onset; (b) decreasing the course and severity of disorders; and (c) preventing the recurrence or relapse of problems. One vehicle for increasing the attention paid to prevention would be for graduate psychotherapy training programs to expand the amount of formal coursework and practica on prevention-related activities. Subsequent students then will use the prevention-related knowledge and skills they have been taught in graduate school (see the Heller, Wyman, and Allen chapter in this volume).

One of the forces that dampens prevention activities is that the public may not believe that bad things can happen to them. Indeed, people often have an "illusion of uniqueness" in which they assume that bad things are less likely to happen to them than to other people (Snyder, 1997c; Snyder & Fromkin, 1980). One thing that can be done to increase public awareness of the fact that one may encounter problems is to deliver actuarial data in regard to the prevalence of such problems, thereby making it more "normal" to have a problem and to even seek help before it looms large in one's life (for an empirical example, see Snyder & Ingram, 1983). Television spots to describe the ubiquity of given problems, perhaps even with a celebrity disclosing that she or he has the problem, can help people to seek help long before the problem becomes less manageable.

Yet another force that diminishes applied psychotherapists' likelihood of engaging in prevention is that there typically is no remuneration for such activities. Because prevention by definition means that we are giving something to people before they have a marked psychological problem (indeed, it is to prevent such problems), they naturally are not identified as clients and, as noted in the previous paragraph, often do not see the need for it. Likewise, such persons lack a diagnosis and therefore cannot receive insurance reimbursement. So, whom in this scenario should fund prevention-related psychotherapy ventures? The answer is that government agencies, or perhaps granting institutions, should underwrite them. Furthermore, once local city and business organizations can see the direct payoffs of such prevention in terms of lessening the overall money that must be directed to their constituencies, they too would find prevention to be worth the investment. This latter approach would mean that the psychotherapist who wants to explore prevention activities may have to become quite entrepreneurial, but the efforts potentially can be very valuable in terms of the positive outcomes for the clientele.

What Emphasis Should Be Placed on Psychotherapy for Children and the Elderly?

Paralleling our observations about the necessity of enhanced psychotherapy research efforts aimed at children and the elderly, applied psychotherapists would be well advised to attend to these two pivotal groups of citizens (see the chapter by Roberts, Vernberg, & Jackson regarding psychotherapy with children, and the chapter by Gallagher-Thompson, McKibbin, Koonce-Volwiler et al. for insights into psychotherapy with older adults). To invest in psychotherapy for children is to invest in our collective futures, whereas the treatment of the elderly enables them to feel better and to continue contributing to our society.

Which Psychotherapists Will Be Allowed to Prescribe Medication?

How are we going to incorporate medications (or not) into our psychotherapy approaches? (For a balanced review of the pros and cons of psychologist prescription privileges, see Guttierez and Silk, 1998.) Of course, some professionals already are prescribing medications (i.e., psychiatrists). Should this prescription privilege be expanded to include psychotherapists other than just those with psychiatry training? We, the authors, have resisted this idea for clinical psychologists, but given our previous logic in regard to the need to examine both the biological and environmental contributors to change, we can see how a case could be made for more psychotherapists, including psychologists, being allowed to prescribe as part of an integrated treatment approach. As long as psychotherapists undertake a thorough program of study in psychopharmacological issues, approaches, and current knowledge, there is no reason that they would not be qualified to prescribe adjunctive therapeutic medications. Furthermore, if psychologists are to become involved in the rigorous testing of the efficacy of psychiatric drugs, then it follows that they too should be able to prescribe them when the particular client and circumstances call for this.

Demonstrated competence in terms of educational training and related testing about drug knowledge should be absolutely mandatory before a nonpsychiatrist is allowed to prescribe. Moreover, continuing education and readministered competence tests for psychopharmacological drugs should be required. Related to these points, the recommendations of the American Psychological Association Task Force on the psychopharmacological training of psychologists suggests three levels of education (APA, 1992). Level 1 would be a comprehensive course in psychopharmacology that would be required in all American Psychological Association accredited programs (clinical, counseling, and school), or via continuing education. Level 2 would be for collaborative practice, with persons who previously have earned doctorates, and would include specific training in "psychodiagnostics, pathophysiology, therapeutics, emergency treatment, substance abuse treatment, developmental psychopharmacology, psychopharmacology research, and supervised clinical experience" (APA, 1992, pp. 63–64). Level 3 would prepare the psychologist for independent prescribing, and it would require graduate courses in psychopharmacology, biochemistry, pharmacology, physiology, biological bases of behavior, behavior pharmacology, clinical pharmacology, and professional pharmacology, as well as a specialized internship in psychopharmacology. This three-level approach would allow practitioners to step into the appropriate level of prescribing for medications that are used in conjunction with psychotherapeutic interventions.

Some psychotherapists may not wish to undergo extensive education in psychopharmacological issues, or for theoretical (e.g., those who are behaviorally oriented) or other reasons may wish to emphasize the psychologically based change processes; as such, we anticipate that many psychotherapists will *not* want to include prescription privileges as part of their practices.

What Role Will Computers Play in the Practice of Psychotherapy?

Computers already have had important impacts on many aspects of our society. The same potential exists for the practice of psychotherapy. One possibility would be a national system (perhaps via the Internet, located at local libraries) implemented so as to allow clients to input their psychological problems or symptoms, and thereafter receive a printout of the local professional mental health psychotherapists with the appropriate expertise. Similarly, the practicing psychotherapist could have the latest therapeutic advances available by computer. For difficult cases, or perhaps just to verify one's professional judgments, computer programs could become available so that the therapist could enter key diagnostic indicators and thereafter receive suggestions for interventions that are based on the latest empirical psychotherapy outcome research. Likewise, the Internet could become a major source for acquiring continuing education by practicing psychotherapists. Some psychotherapists already have started chat rooms for their clients so they might share similar experiences. Perhaps similar chat rooms also could be established for psychotherapists to offer ideas and insights regarding clients to one another. Virtual reality paradigms also might be quite helpful for some problems. For example, phobic situations could be simulated in these paradigms so as to produce treatments in sensory contexts that are similar to the actual fearful situations. Obviously, computers can make many exciting contributions to both the client seeking psychotherapeutic help and the professional administering it.

Are there also potential problems that should be anticipated? With networked computer files, what safeguards will there be for protecting the privacy of client records? Relatedly, what will happen legally to confidentiality issues? Confidentiality is a bedrock notion for the conduct of psychotherapy. As computers increasingly become linked via networks, some safeguards are needed to ensure this. Practicing psychotherapists also will need to monitor the inappropriate use of computer-scored psychological tests that are part of the diagnostic process prior to, during, and after psychotherapy. The professional training that goes along with the appropriate interpretation of psychological tests may be of little concern to those persons selling computer-scored tests. The profession will need to monitor its own constituency and watch for untrained persons using computer-based psychological test analyses.

THE SCIENCE AND PRACTICE INTERFACE

Attention needs to be given to translating psychotherapy research into the practitioners' actual activities. One way to understand this relationship is to examine what practitioners and academician/researchers do with their time. Many practitioners spend their time in activities necessary to sustain their practices, with relatively little opportunity to read journals and keep up with the latest empirically based approaches. The academician's job, however, can be devoted to conducting research on, and teaching about, the advances in psychotherapy that appear in the latest journals. These faculty members also are guided by a model mixing the science and practice of psychotherapy. Also, they have the time and are more likely to read journals and to think about this area.

These are the players in this real-life drama. If we follow their activities further, we may derive other insights about their different perspectives. Academicians may give lip service to the fact that the science and the practice of psychotherapy go hand in hand, but their time typically is devoted to research. Practitioners, on the other hand, must attend to applied considerations related to keeping a professional business going. Academicians may not fully understand the time pressures faced by practicing psychologists, nor do academicians comprehend that practitioners are not rewarded for reading journals. Thus, while the academicians read and contribute research to psychotherapy journals, and assume that these activities are crucial, such activities may be viewed by practitioners as unavailable extravagances.

In many cases, practitioners may use the psychotherapy techniques learned in graduate school, and have little time available for acquiring new skills. When clients appear satisfied, and they generally get better, this approach is reinforced. Of course, for some proportion of academicians, similar scenarios may result as they essentially recycle ideas learned in graduate school (Snyder, 1997a, 1997b).

If these descriptions have some accuracy for both academicians and practitioners, the breach between them represents a serious problem. Indeed, researcher-practitioner conflicts consistently have been voiced at meetings of the American Psychological Association (APA), and can be seen in the breaking off of a number of researchers who were displeased by the domination of APA by practitioners and started the American Psychological Society. Instead of there being much in the way of a connection (as implied in the title of this section), divisiveness and acrimony characterize many of the interactions.

Yet other forces must be added to this equation to understand the potential interactions of those who research, teach, and practice psychotherapy. Consider the role of managed care, which undoubtedly will be with us into the 21st century. It is likely that insurers will limit the number of sessions for which they will pay. Also, there is a growing movement to make the applied sector more accountable in terms of documenting the efficacy of its interventions. We thus will see more scientifically supported treatments being mandated, and any reliance on client satisfaction will no longer succeed as the sole criterion for acceptable psychotherapy (Snyder, 1997a, 1997b). With the ascent of scientifically based interventions, insurers also may ask that these interventions be delivered in a cost-efficient manner (i.e., persons trained at the masters level). All of these changes will occur in the context of psychotherapy becoming a female-dominated profession in the 21st century (see the Snyder, McDermott, and colleagues chapter in this volume).

Crises sometimes can bring people together, and we hope that both academicians and practitioners will resonate to the issues raised in this section. In the 21st century, there will be many problems encountered by the psychotherapy field, and here is a simple and productive beginning point: *we need each other*. When constituents are at war with each other, it is difficult to reach agreement, to share ideas, information, and resources. This point seems so basic, but somehow those of us who collectively are involved in the field of psychotherapy must accept and act upon it. We often tout insight as being crucial for our

clients. Perhaps we should adopt this same view about our within-discipline disagreements. We also must cease the criticism between academicians and practitioners. The psychotherapy field deserves better; it warrants our shared nurturance. We owe this to our clients who deserve the very best in psychotherapeutic care that comes from the joint efforts of practitioners and academicians.

THE PUBLIC AND PSYCHOTHERAPY

Can We Do a Better Job of Informing the Public About Our Field?

We should continue our serious efforts to measure the power and strength of psychotherapy, and be more entrepreneurial in conveying these facts to the public. In the process, we should be careful not to be too grandiose or too cautious in describing the impact and potential benefits of psychotherapy. We can and must do a better job of informing the public, and this leads to the next question.

How Will Psychotherapists Be Viewed by the Public?

In the coming decades, how will psychotherapists be viewed by our society? What status will be associated with being a psychotherapist? Will psychotherapists be remunerated at levels commensurate with similar professionals? What role will the media play in shaping the public's impression of psychotherapists? Will the Bob Newharts and Frasier Cranes in American television comedies be the norm, with psychotherapy as the inadvertent butt of the jokes? Or, will cinematic portrayals of psychotherapists acting on countertransferent sexual and romantic desires paint a picture of helpers as being in need of treatment as much as or more than their clients (Bram, 1997; Gabbard & Gabbard, 1987)? These questions are critical because public perception will influence the influx of young people into our profession, support for the education of future cohorts of students, funding of psychotherapy research, payment for psychotherapy by insurers, public policy relative to mental health (Knapp & Kamin, 1993; Pallak & Kilburg, 1986), the willingness of people to seek treatment (Furnham & Wardley, 1990; Wong, 1994), beginning clients' expectations and persistence in treatment (Goldstein & Higginbotham, 1991), and a myriad of other related issues. To be unconcerned about how we are perceived is to be unconcerned with how we will be treated as a profession and as individuals whose careers are dedicated to that profession.

Should Psychotherapy Become Involved in Self-Help Approaches?

It is our impression that self-help approaches are held in some disdain by psychotherapy researchers, whereas many practitioners are more positively disposed toward them. Two separate studies have revealed that 88% of practitioners supplement their treatments with self-help books (Marx, Royalty, Gyorky, & Stren, 1992; Starker, 1988). The source of prejudicial attitudes on the part of researchers may be the pop-psychology books with their brightly colored covers and equally beaming claims regarding the potency of the points made within their pages. Although we do not condone the popularized change books that are *not* based on valid, research-based approaches, our view is that self-help needs to be brought into the mainstream of psychotherapy research and treatments. We have several reasons for advocating this position.

The essence of self-help is that the person—him- or herself—is the author of lasting changes. Surely, this premise would be embraced by even the most rabid anti-self-help mental health professionals. More specifically, within the context of regular psychotherapy interventions, the theories are aimed at having the person become the author of improved coping skills. In the degree to which a sense of personal empowerment happens, people not only will improve initially but will become more likely to maintain and generalize their changes. Indeed, self-help principles are at the heart of psychotherapy change and maintenance. Interestingly, recent meta-analyses reveal that bibliotherapies made up of self-help books significantly augment outcomes beyond appropriate comparison conditions (Cuijpers, 1997; Marrs, 1995). Thus, instead of automatically distancing ourselves from self-help approaches, psychotherapy researchers need to better understand how personal empowerment can be attained in the context of psychotherapy.

When self-help processes are better understood, psychotherapy professionals rightfully may want to build a scientifically based self-help literature that can be made available to people who normally would not seek professional help. Furthermore, autobiographies can be very useful additions to normal treatments.

Related to the points made in this section, we would argue strongly that *the adaptive, teachable processes of psychotherapy should be for the many rather than just the few*. For too long, psychotherapy has been for the select people who could afford it and who were educated as to its usefulness. One means of changing this unfortunate usage pattern is to make self-help part of our domain. In the degree to which such self-help literature can be based on the latest scientifically based change principles, then the use of such books will have the added advantage of helping many people to lessen their reservations about seeking professional psychotherapy treatment. In summary, there are many benefits that follow from researchers and professional psychotherapists embracing the use of self-help literature. It is informative to note that our view about the increased use of self-help techniques is echoed by a poll taken of psychotherapists (see Neimeyer & Norcross, 1997). Of the various techniques that are in the armamentarium of psychotherapists (cognitive restructuring, problem solving, social skills training, hypnosis, relaxation, etc.), self-help approaches were rated as evidencing the greatest increase in recent years.

How Can We Do a Better Job of Getting Treatment to People?

As wonderful as advances in psychotherapy may be in the 21st century, and as well prepared as the practitioners of psychotherapy may become, if people do not make contact to begin treatment, then such progress is not very meaningful. This surely is an issue on which scientists and practitioners can join together so as to improve our collective positive impact on society. We know that a typical pattern for seeking help for psychological problems follows a usual sequence of self → friend → clergy → physicians → professional mental health persons (Wills & DePaulo, 1991). Perhaps there are ways to facilitate persons moving through this cycle more quickly, or even skipping certain steps. Perhaps public information programs about the frequency of various problems would make it seem more natural to visit a psychotherapist. If psychotherapists were in settings that people visit often, such as shopping malls, then people may become more likely to cross the threshold and see them. Whatever we can do to enhance the seeking of help from professional psychotherapists should be a first priority on practitioners' and scientists' agendas. It is tragic when people whose suffering and overall welfare could be improved by psychotherapy do not avail themselves of it. As long as many of those people who need psychological help do not get it, then psychotherapy will be for the few rather than the many. We can do better, and the 21st century will ask that those of us in the psychotherapy field do precisely that.

REFERENCES

American Psychological Association. (1992, July). *Report of the Ad Hoc Task Force on Psychopharmacology of the American Psychological Association.* Washington, D.C.: Author.

Barone, D. F., Maddux, J. E., & Snyder, C. R. (1997). *Social cognitive psychology: History and current domains.* New York: Plenum.

Bram, A. D. (1997). Perceptions of psychotherapy and psychotherapists: Implications from a study of undergraduates. *Professional Psychology: Research and Practice, 28*(2), 170–178.

Consumer Reports. (1995, November). Mental health: Does therapy help? 734–739.

Costa, P. T., Jr., & McCrae, R. R. (1980). Still stable after all these years: Personality as a key to some issues of aging. In P. B. Baltes & O. G. Brim, Jr. (Eds.), *Life-span development and behaviors* (Vol. 3, pp. 66–102). New York: Academic Press.

Coyne, J. C. (1994). Self-reported distress: Analog or ersatz depression? *Psychological Bulletin, 116,* 29–45.

Cuijpers, P. (1997). Bibliotherapy in unipolar depression: A meta-analysis. *Journal of Behavior Therapy & Experimental Psychiatry, 28,* 139–147.

Fisher, S., & Greenberg, R. P. (Eds.). (1997). *From placebo to panacea: Putting psychiatric drugs to the test.* New York: Wiley.

Furnham, A., & Wardley, Z. (1990). Lay theories of psychotherapy: 1. Attitudes toward and beliefs about psychotherapy and therapists. *Journal of Clinical Psychology, 46,* 878–890.

Gabbard, K., & Gabbard, G. O. (1987). *Psychiatry and the cinema.* Chicago: University of Chicago Press.

Goldstein, A. P., & Higginbotham, H. N. (1991). Relationship-enhancement methods. In F. H. Kanfer & A. P. Goldstein (Eds.), *Helping people change* (pp. 20–69). Elmsford, NY: Pergamon.

Guttierez, P. M., & Silk, K. R. (1998). Prescription privileges for psychologists: A review of the psychological literature. *Professional Psychology: Research and Practice, 29*(3), 213–222.

Hollon, S. D., Evans, M. D., & DeRubeis, R. J. (1990). Cognitive mediation of relapse prevention following treatment for depression: Implications of differential risk. In R. E. Ingram (Ed.), *Contemporary psychological approaches to depression: Theory, research, and practice* (pp. 117–136). New York: Plenum.

Ingram, R. E. (1983). The GRE in the graduate admissions process: Is how it is used justified by the evidence of its validity? *Professional Psychology: Research and Practice, 14,* 711–714.

Ingram, R. E., Miranda, J., & Segal, Z. V. (1998). *Cognitive vulnerability to depression.* New York: Guilford Press

Ingram, R. E., & Zurawski, R. M. (1981). Choosing clinical psychologists: An examination of the utilization of admissions criteria. *Professional Psychology, 12,* 684–689.

Knapp, H. D., & Kamin, J. (1993, December). Therapy's value [Letter to the editor]. *APA Monitor,* p. 3.

Korchin, S. (1983). The history of clinical psychology: A personal view. In M. Hersen, A. E. Kazdin, & A. S. Bellack (Eds.), *The clinical psychology handbook* (pp. 5–19). New York: Pergamon.

Kuhn, T. S. (1962). *The structure of scientific revolutions.* Chicago: University of Chicago Press.

Luborsky, L., Singer, B., & Luborsky, L. (1975). Comparative studies of psychotherapies. Is it true that "everyone has won and all must have prizes"? *Archives of General Psychiatry, 32,* 995–1008.

Marrs, R. W. (1995). A meta-analysis of bibliotherapy studies. *American Journal of Community Psychology, 23,* 843–870.

Marx, J. A., Royalty, G. M., Gyorky, Z. K., & Stern, T. E. (1992). Use of self-help books in psychotherapy. *Professional Psychology: Research and Practice, 23,* 300–305.

McCullough, M. E., & Snyder, C. R. (in press). Classical sources of human strength: Revisiting an old home and building a new one. *Journal of Social and Clinical Psychology.*

Neimeyer, G. J., & Norcross, J. C. (1997). The future of psychotherapy and counseling psychology in the USA: Delphi data and beyond. In S. Palmer & V. Varma (Eds.), *The future of counseling and psychotherapy* (pp. 64–81). London: Sage Publications Inc.

Norton, J. L. (1995). The gay, lesbian, bisexual populations. In N. A. Vacc, S. B. DeVaney, & J. Wittmer (Eds.), *Experiencing and counseling multicultural and diverse populations* (3rd ed., pp. 147–177). Bristol, PA: Accelerated Development.

Pallak, M. S., & Kilburg, R. R. (1986). Psychology, public affairs, and public policy: A strategy and review. *American Psychologist, 41,* 933–940.

Perez, J. E. (1999). Clients deserve empirically supported treatments, not romanticism. *American Psychologist, 54,* 205–206.

Schneider, K. J. (1998). Toward a science of the heart: Romanticism and the revival of psychology. *American Psychologist, 53,* 277–289.

Schneider, K. J. (1999). Clients deserve relationships, not merely "treatments." *American Psychologist, 54,* 206–207.

Seligman, M.E.P. (1995). Effectiveness of

psychotherapy: The *Consumer Reports* study. *American Psychologist, 50,* 965–974.

Seligman, M.E.P. (1998). Positive social science. *APA Monitor, 29,* 2.

Shore, K. (1996). An alternative view. *Professional Psychology: Research and Practice, 27,* 324.

Silka, L. (1989). *Intuitive judgments of change.* New York: Springer-Verlag.

Snyder, C. R. (1994). *The psychology of hope: You can get there from here.* New York: Free Press.

Snyder, C. R. (1997a). I've led three lives, but is there a life for the interface? *The Counseling Psychologist, 25*(2), 256–265.

Snyder, C. R. (1997b). The state of the interface. *Journal of Social and Clinical Psychology, 16*(3), 1–13.

Snyder, C. R. (1997c). Unique invulnerability: A classroom demonstration in estimating personal mortality. *Teaching of Psychology, 24,* 197–198.

Snyder, C. R. (1999). Coping: Where are you going? In C. R. Snyder (Ed.), *Coping: The psychology of what works* (pp. 324–333). New York: Oxford University Press.

Snyder, C. R., & Fromkin, H. L. (1980). *Uniqueness: The human pursuit of difference.* New York: Plenum.

Snyder, C. R., & Ingram, R. E. (1983). "Company motivates the miserable": The impact of consensus information upon help-seeking for psychological problems. *Journal of Personality and Social Psychology, 45,* 1118–1126.

Snyder, C. R. , & McCullough, M. E. (in press). A positive psychology field of dreams: "If you build it, they will come. . . ." *Journal of Social and Clinical Psychology.*

Snyder, C. R., Shenkel, R. J., & Lowery, C. R. (1977). Acceptance of personality interpretations: The "Barnum Effect" and beyond. *Journal of Consulting and Clinical Psychology, 45,* 104–114.

Starker, S. (1988). Psychologists and self-help books: Attitudes and prescriptive practices of clinicians. *American Journal of Psychotherapy, 42,* 448–455.

Sue, D. W., & Sue, D. (1999). *Counseling the culturally different: Theory and practice* (3rd ed.). New York: John Wiley and Sons.

Ullman, L. P., & Krasner, L. (1969). *A psychological approach to abnormal behavior.* Englewood Cliffs, NJ: Prentice-Hall.

U.S. Census Bureau. (1992). *Statistical abstract of the United States: The national data book* (112th ed.). Washington, D.C.: Bureau of the Census.

Watzlawick, P., Weakland, J., & Fish, R. (1974). *Change: Principles of problem formation and problem resolution.* New York: Norton.

Wills, T. A., & DePaulo, B. M. (1991). Interpersonal analysis of the help-seeking process. In C. R. Snyder & D. R. Forsyth (Eds.), *Handbook of social and clinical psychology: The health perspective* (pp. 350–375). New York: Pergamon.

Wong, J. L. (1994). Lay theories of psychotherapy and perceptions of therapists: A replication and extension of Furnham and Wardley. *Journal of Clinical Psychology, 50,* 624–632.

Wright, B. A. (1991). Labeling: The need for greater person-environment individuation. In C. R. Snyder & D. R. Forsyth (Eds.), *Handbook of social and clinical psychology: The health perspective* (pp. 469–487). New York: Pergamon.

CHAPTER 34

TRAINING
FUTURE
PSYCHOTHERAPISTS

MICHAEL J. MAHONEY
University of North Texas

INTRODUCTION

In this concluding chapter of a volume devoted to our understandings of human change, my goal is to focus on themes that are, in my opinion, essential to the training of future psychotherapists. These themes are *above and beyond*, but also *below and within*, the operational recommendations of the American Psychiatric Association, the American Psychological Association, the European and World Councils for Psychotherapy, and a variety of other organizations that have made valuable efforts to define the essentials of psychotherapist training. In my opinion, essentials of training cannot be separated from essentials of practice and essentials of professional being. I do not assume that the themes listed here are complete, but I hope that they complement other guides to essential themes in professional training.

ESSENTIAL THEMES IN THE TRAINING OF PSYCHOTHERAPISTS

Being a psychotherapist is a complex challenge. The training of psychotherapists is an even more complex undertaking. Teaching people to help other people may sound like a simple and straightforward endeavor, but it is not. It requires many considerations that we do not understand

Author's note This chapter draws from in-press materials from M. J. Mahoney, *Constructive Psychotherapy: Exploring Principles and Practices* (New York: Guilford).

fully, and it demands a dynamic and flexible balance of theory, research, and practical applications. Like psychotherapy itself, the training of psychotherapists is often a mixture of perplexing, inspiring, and humbling experiences.

In this chapter, I attempt to distill some of the essential themes in psychotherapist training. I do not deal with the complexities of selecting psychotherapy trainees or the particulars of an imaginary ideal curriculum. Nor do I comment upon the current and evolving recommendations for training being made by a variety of professional organizations. The extensive literatures on this topic are not reviewed here. Rather, my focus is on general themes and a rhetorical voice that is more common in clinical supervision than in technical volumes.

Any discussion of essentials, and hence the essence of therapist training, necessarily must invoke and reflect an image of the good therapist. It also implies judgments about methods of teaching and the apprenticeship experience. Such images and judgments will pervade what follows. I will conclude with a brief consolidation of my best imaginings of the good therapist and the good training program. My remarks are organized around seven themes: (1) self-knowledge, (2) human relatedness, (3) compassion, (4) philosophy, (5) survival and coping skills, (6) values issues, and (7) lifespan development.

Self-Knowledge

Self-knowledge should pervade all other aspects of the training of a psychotherapist (Mahoney, in press a, in press b). To be optimally helpful to her clients, a psychotherapist must be at least minimally aware of her inner life. He must know what he is thinking, feeling, and doing. She must know what her biases, issues, and sensitivities may be. And he must know how his wishes and needs affect perceptions of and exchanges with other people, particularly clients. Knowledge of self facilitates knowledge of others, and this relationship is a reciprocal one. With some important and noteworthy exceptions, however, most training programs for psychotherapists generally have avoided or minimized the importance of this dimension in the preparation of professional service providers.

Self-knowledge is not a simple phenomenon, and its pursuit involves more of a process than a finished product. To the extent that such a pursuit can be divided further into sub-processes, some of the most important themes for psychotherapists have to do with developmental history, present-moment emotional experiencing, and life purpose. These sub-themes parallel the dimensions of personal past, present, and future. To help clients in making sense of life experiences, a therapist often must encourage the viewing of present activities in the historical context of family of origin and the associated developmental challenges. Helping clients to make peace with their past generally is easier when the therapist too has made such peace. This holds also for emotional awareness and regulation. Many clients are frightened and disorganized by their feelings. Helping them to persevere, to function responsibly, and to develop psychologically often requires attending to their emotions. The therapist who is relatively more aware of and dialectically engaged with his own feelings is in a better position to guide and comfort another person in such explorations. Because psychotherapy often involves a "restoration of morale" (Frank, 1961), it entails issues of life purpose and personal meaning. These existential dimensions are expressed concretely in hopes and fears about the future. The therapist who is aware of her own hopes and fears is more likely to succeed in fostering such awareness in her clients (see the chapter on hope by Snyder and colleagues in this volume).

Of course, there are limits to the degree of self-awareness. No one can achieve exhaustive self-knowledge, no matter how long, hard, or wisely one searches. This lifelong limitation on self-awareness deserves continuing reflection throughout a psychotherapist's training. Combined with the appreciation that self-awareness is essential for psychological service providers, this second realization leads to the psychotherapist's lifelong commitment to personal reflection (Skovholt & Rønnestad, 1992). Ideally, however, such reflection should foster more than just self-awareness. It also should encourage self-appreciation (or self-love)[1] and a quest for lifelong psychological development. The therapists who wish to help clients become less self-critical, more forgiving, and more satisfied with self and other relations must be actively engaged in those same quests in their own lives.

How can this theme of self-knowledge be incorporated into training experiences? There is a variety of possible methods (Carlson & Shield, 1989; Goleman, 1988). The value of self-study processes can be taught at the abstract level in courses, and it also can be modeled by mentors. Trainees can be encouraged to reflect actively on their personal experiences during their apprenticeships. Peer support groups and personal therapy can be encouraged.[2] Episodic retreats aimed at the elaboration and consolidation of self-knowledge can be organized. Whatever the method, the goal is an enrichment of self-relating processes. Familiarity with and skills in these processes can be invaluable to the quality of therapists' personal lives and to the quality of their professional services.

Human Relatedness and Personal Knowing

A second essential feature in the training of psychotherapists is focused on the social realm. It includes interpersonal sensitivity, communication skills, and sociality, but none of these concepts accommodates the full range of human relatedness and the complex challenges of knowing another person. Furthermore, I would emphasize that

---

[1]For a classic discussion of the "heresy of self-love" and its deprecation as narcissism in Western civilization, see Zweig (1980).

[2]Clinical trainees have ranked their work with clients, their personal therapy, and their supervision, in that order, as more valuable to their training than academic coursework or outside readings (Kaslow & Friedman, 1984). Complications can arise, however, when counseling center faculty have close relations with a training program. Some practitioners in the community will offer *pro bono* brief therapy to trainees. In areas where there is more than one training program, faculty can develop a reciprocity that allows trainees to experience personal therapy without risking dual-role relationships or confidentiality.

self-awareness and human relatedness *go together* in selecting and shaping the kind of person who can help other human beings.

Human relatedness means more than having read the theories and research on the social bases of human activity. There is a wide gap between thinking about something and experiencing it. Indeed, that gap repeatedly needs to be bridged in the training process. Self-awareness is not automatically enhanced by successful mastery of the formidable literatures on self psychology. Communication skills are not adequately developed by the rote imitation of experts' patterns of asking questions, making eye contact, and so on. Human relatedness, like all of the other themes discussed here, is grounded in an emotional epistemology, a kind of knowing that is thoroughly, subtly, and powerfully emotional.

More will be said about epistemology in my later discussion of philosophy as a theme in psychotherapists' training. At this point, however, it is worth noting that this emotionally felt knowing is being championed by numerous representatives of feminist theory in psychology. It is a kind of knowing that involves a connected rather than separated process of relating to self and to others (Belenky, Clinchy, Goldberger, & Tarule, 1986, 1997). The quest for objectivity is supplanted by a quest for intersubjectivity, or *interbeing*, with the latter being recognized as the foundational context for human knowing (Bowlby, 1979, 1985, 1988; Schore, 1994; Stolorow & Atwood, 1992; Watkins, 1990). Likewise, a primary psychotherapist task is not one of achieving aseptic distance from the client, but rather that of elaborating an emotional relationship to aid the client's adaptation and development (Kahn, 1991).

Most would agree that good therapists get to know their clients. Another widely held view is that therapists' knowledge of clients serves important roles in their services to those persons. These accepted and obvious views become much more elusive, however, when examined at deeper levels. How do we come to *know* another person? How does our knowing of others influence our knowledge of ourselves? Because our knowledge of others as well as of self is always incomplete, how should we act in our moments with our clients? I shall not presume to suggest simple or final answers to such complex questions. I shall suggest, however, that optimal psychotherapist training involves an ever-deepening appreciation for the importance of these and related questions. That appreciation also extends to the *oneness* (uniqueness) of each person seeking our professional services, as well as to the fundamental connectedness of human experience (see Snyder & Fromkin, 1980). As the existentialists remind us, the English word *alone* is an ancient contraction of *all one*. We cannot completely know another and, as such, our constructions of and actions toward that person are excursions into the unknown (Buber, 1958; Tillich, 1952). This means that psychotherapy training should include an emphasis on individual diversity, the uniqueness of life challenges, *along with* the importance of human relations in personal phenomenology.

To summarize, I believe that being a good psychotherapist requires an interest and ability in knowing the other. In turn, such knowing requires an ability to listen to and sense what it is like to be that other. Learning to develop such interests and abilities may be served by the study of developmental histories, theory and methods of applied phenomenology, and diversity in the samples of persons whom we seek to help. Such learning is best accomplished in training environments that honor the dynamics of individuality, social and cultural contexts, and personal history. It also is facilitated by mentors who are themselves humanly related and who convey a respectful fascination with the infinite diversities of human experience.

Compassion

A good psychotherapist is compassionate. As with self-knowledge and human relatedness, professional training fosters such compassion through the experiential process. The development of compassion is not equivalent to abstract knowledge of current theory and research on human emotionality. It also involves a capacity to feel *with* (and not simply *for*) others. In this regard, it is worth mentioning that the literal meaning of the word *compassion* is with feeling. Of course, there are differences of opinion as to how a therapist should feel with clients. In traditional objectivist perspectives, psychotherapists' feelings are impediments to their therapeutic effectiveness. In the sciences more generally (Forman, 1995a, 1995b), and psychotherapy in particular (Kahn, 1991), the feasibility and wisdom of such perspectives have been challenged. Increasingly, the consensus is that compassion lies at the heart of this human activity that we call psychotherapy. When compassion is lacking, the quality of the relationship suffers, as do the range and power of its possible effects.

There is an important difference between viewing compassion as a capacity for empathic affect or as help rendered in the presence of pain (Ram Dass & Gordon, 1985). The ability to feel and to feel deeply is essential to both, as is the ability to imagine and approximate another's pain. But a sensitive individual also can be frightened, immobilized, and overwhelmed by the intensity of that pain. Practicing compassion thus involves an elusive but invaluable skill of *working in the presence of that pain*. The forms of such work are diverse, but they share some basic characteristics. Namely, compassionate helping does not deny or diminish the importance of pain. At the same time, however, it is not preoccupied solely with the suffering. When intense feelings have been denied or suppressed, it may be critically important to encourage and witness their expressions. Accordingly, therapists should be comfortable with and skilled in facilitating emotionality. Moreover, therapists need to encourage clients to *harvest* the lessons of their pains (often including appreciations for their resiliencies and capacities to endure difficult times). Also, helpers need to teach clients how to be more compassionate with themselves (e.g., patience, gentleness, and a fidelity to self), along with encouraging responsible and self-caring actions.

Even though not tapped in most examinations required of applicants, our selection criteria for psychotherapy apprentices somehow need to grant priority to the heart as being at the core of human helping. Compassion also can be taught and learned, but there are related, underlying individual differences. Willingly, of course, we are all lifelong students of such lessons.

Reflective and Experimental Philosophy

Good psychotherapists, like good scientists, are insatiable inquirers. They move with remarkable flexibility between their conceptual maps and the complex terrain of lived experience. At times they may feel overwhelmed by the magnitude of the tasks they have undertaken, and often they may feel privileged to have had the opportunity to make such ventures. These feelings and their dialectical dynamics were expressed well in the near-final words of philosopher Bertrand Russell:

> Three passions, simple but overwhelmingly strong, have governed my life: the longing for love, the search for knowledge, and unbearable pity for the suffering of mankind. These passions, like great winds, have blown me hither and thither, in a wayward course, over a deep ocean of anguish, reaching to the very verge of despair.
>
> I have sought love, first, because it brings ecstasy—ecstasy so great that I would often have sacrificed all the rest of life for a few hours of this joy. I have sought it, next, because it relieves loneliness—that terrible loneliness in which one shivering consciousness looks over the rim of the world into the cold unfathomable lifeless abyss. I have sought it, finally, because in the union of love I have seen, in a mystic miniature, the prefiguring vision of the heaven that saints and poets have imagined. This is what I sought, and though it might seem too good for human life, this is what—at last—I have found.
>
> With equal passion I have sought knowledge. I have wished to understand the hearts of men. I have wished to know why the stars shine. And I have tried to apprehend the Pythagorean power by which number holds sway above the flux. A little of this, but not much, I have achieved.
>
> Love and knowledge, so far as they were possible, led upward toward the heavens. But always pity brought me back to earth. Echoes of cries of pain reverberate in my heart. Children in famine, victims tortured by oppressors, helpless old people a hated burden to their sons, and the whole world of loneliness, poverty, and pain make a mockery of what human life should be. I long to alleviate the evil, but I cannot, and I too suffer.
>
> This has been my life. I have found it worth living, and would gladly live it again if the chance were offered to me. (1967, pp. 3–4)

This fundamental spirit of passionate and compassionate inquiry is an important force in the psychotherapist's lifelong development. Ours is a profession located strategically at the crux between theory and practice, an area of tension that has plagued Western philosophies and health practice for centuries. Epistemology is that domain of inquiry focused on knowledge and knowing processes. What do we know? How do we know? How shall our knowledge be applied? How do we foster the development of what we know? And how do we foster the knowing, the well-being, and the development of our clients?

The above questions are central to the practice of psychotherapy. Hence, the well-trained psychotherapist is an applied philosopher in the noblest sense of this term. He is a lifelong student of histories and systems, ideas, contemporary theories, and research. She reads, reflects, and—most importantly—inquires. They pursue courses and opportunities for dialogue that will elaborate and challenge their past assumptions of fact and possibility. They follow the fires within them that burn a very personal path of life-seeking questions and quests, both from and toward the heart of human consciousness. And they strive to respect that parallel spirit of seeking in their clients. There is an intrinsic openness in their activities, an openness that reflects a lifelong respect for the possibilities of learning and, increasingly, sharing.

Experimental philosophy is an exercise in both *what if* and *as if*. The *what if* part is the heart of science as a developmental form of human inquiry. Francis Bacon's publication of "The New Instrument" (*Novum Organum*) in 1620 generally is considered the seminal document of the scientific revolution in Western cultures. In contrast to Aristotle's "The Instrument" (*Organon*) and its canonization of logical deduction, Bacon argued for the value of systematic observation and induction. Experimentation was a creative and participatory form of observation—an excursion into the general question, "What happens if I do this?" A systematic philosophy of possibility was formally proposed by Immanuel Kant and elaborated by the Kantian scholar Hans Vaihinger—the man whose dissertation on "the philosophy of as if" formatively shaped the theories and psychotherapies of Alfred Adler and George Kelly.

How can philosophy be integrated into the training of psychotherapists? To begin, it requires readings in the history of ideas. But there is much more to philosophy than a passive reading of ideas proposed by long-dead thinkers. Its essence, like that of its scientific offspring, is a never-ending process of searching. This process is most effectively taught by means of live dialogue and examples. It therefore is facilitated by mentors who model and encourage questioning processes. Such activities recognize education and professional training as endeavors that value the reciprocity between mentors and apprentices. Unfortunately, the structures and traditions that dominate many psychotherapy training programs are not conducive to such dialogue. Classes and

practica have an authoritarian structure wherein teachers possess the knowledge that is transmitted to students. Many questions go unasked or unanswered, and too many answers go unquestioned. More importantly, the essential and developmental dialectic reciprocity between questioning and answering goes unrecognized. Questions are considered only preludes to answers, and the answer allegedly is where the action is. The implication is that without answers there can be no action. The inveterate questioner is caricatured as lost in thought, while the answering agent is portrayed as a practical person of action. But reflection and questioning also are forms of action, and they need not stop simply because a life decision must be made. The essential tension among question, questioning, and acting in response to answers, or to acting in response to tentative answers to those questions, forms a continuous dynamic process.

Psychotherapy trainees, like the clients they wish to serve, often are impatient for simple answers to complex questions, and important themes in their development therefore are likely to include patience and a respectful tolerance of ambiguity and complexity. Indeed, one of the most important skills to be learned by the trainee is that many crucial decisions in life must be made in the face of incomplete information, very limited control, and unfinished answers. It therefore follows that psychotherapists report substantially increased tolerance for ambiguity as their career experience accumulates (Mahoney & Fernandez-Alvarez, 1995).

Survival and Coping Skills

Good therapists are more than self-aware, interpersonally attuned, compassionate, and inquiring. They also must know how to assess and teach basic skills in survival; they must be grounded in the real demands of life support and adaptation. Crisis management, coping skills, problem solving, health maintenance, and skills in living are demanding practicalities that come up repeatedly for the psychological service provider. While some clients may be functioning well in their search for greater well-being, others are desperately struggling to survive a day or week at a time. For them, help takes on concrete meaning at the more basic levels of human needs: safety, life support, and caring companionship.

Another way of saying this, perhaps more crudely, is that a good therapist has enough common sense to ask what's for dinner. If the client's next meal or overnight shelter are unknowns, then he or she is seeking a more basic level of services than one who seeks counsel on chronic depression or an unsatisfying intimate relationship. It is important for psychotherapists to work at clients' different levels of needs, with accompanying insight that such needs often are mixed and changeable. This is not to imply that all therapists can serve all clients equally well, but it emphasizes the importance of flexibility in service skills. Some clients want and need highly structured assistance in basic survival, many want comfort and reassurance, all need to be respected and encouraged, some need to be challenged *while* they are comforted, and so on. The point is that the well-trained therapist has developed a sensitivity to assessing the priorities of such needs and wants. Moreover, such a therapist is at least minimally *world-wise*. She or he knows about community agencies and support sources. They know that some clients are in more danger than others, and they know that some clients present dangers to themselves and possibly others.

Philosophers sometimes distinguish between "knowing that" and "knowing how." This distinction is particularly apt in the realm of survival and coping skills. The best way to teach such skills to the psychotherapy trainee is experientially. Training to be a therapist is itself a formidable challenge associated with considerable personal stress (Guy, 1987; Mahoney, 1991; Skovholt & Rønnestad, 1992). Skills that are useful for clients also are useful for therapists. In supervision and clinical practica, trainees can be involved in live demonstrations of such skills, which they can then practice in coping with the everyday challenges of their personal lives. As they elaborate these skills, trainees then can be supervised in teaching them to clients. An important corollary of this process is that such teaching is facilitated by the therapist's familiarity with and adeptness at the skill involved. The beginning trainee can recite the words of a relaxation protocol, for example, without their having much effect on a client. When that same trainee is able to embody those words in a personal relaxation response, however, the effects on the client are markedly different.

Ethics and Value Issues

All forms of inquiry and application are necessarily value-laden. This is nowhere more apparent than in the field of psychological services. To even offer those services is itself a value judgment (Cushman, 1993). The human interactions involved in rendering those services also are value-laden, and the well-trained psychotherapist is well aware of this inevitability. This awareness allows therapists to maintain both humility and existential homage in the enactment of psychotherapy. The humility is multiply generated by awarenesses about the limitations of knowing, the constraints on knowing an other, and the overall complexities of individual lives with their infinitely unique processes of self-maintenance and self-knowledge. The existential homage comes from a fundamental realization that it is the client, more than the therapist, who must live out the consequences of his or her life choices. Many of those consequences will have been unanticipated. Most of those choices will have been based on very partial information and very limited control. As our training and reflections in experimental philosophy continue to teach us, we do not know many things for sure. We can, with clear conscience, rarely claim to be certain about what is best for our clients. And they are the ones who ultimately are choosing—often suffering until and even when they do. Can or should they change jobs? Relationships? Selves? As therapists, we must guard against presuming to know the unequivocal answers to such questions. Likewise, it is important that we appreciate that our counsel often sways the courses of lives. We need to be personally prepared to accept the existential responsibilities for such influence.

Issues such as these encourage diverse professional reactions. At one extreme are therapists who refuse to ever offer a clear opinion, suggestion, or directive. These are the *radical noninterventionists* who believe it is possible to assume the role of a professional helper and yet refrain from having more than a catalytic influence on clients. At the other extreme are the *radical interventionists* who proclaim that service is action and that all clients need to be strategically changed according to an explicit and generic plan. These are the *doers* who presume that all clients need to be trained, educated, or otherwise modified. Most therapists are probably complex mixtures of these extremes, and the mixture may vary from client to client and moment to moment.

More important than the dynamics of one's therapeutic style, however, is an awareness that everything a psychotherapist has done and said, as well *not* done and said, is necessarily a choice that reflects values. Some of those deeds and omissions will turn out to be more important for the experience and development of the client. A good therapist repeatedly needs to understand that values permeate practice. The goal is not to become obsessed with evaluative micro moments in sessions. Rather, a meaningful goal is to foster a deeper self-awareness and development in the direction of familiarity with, and respect for, the infinite diversity and complexity of human lives.

Training in ethics therefore should involve more than a memorization of national and state documents on professional ethics. Being an ethical therapist requires more than knowing what one legally must do under specified circumstances. An ethical consciousness minimally should include a history of axiology (theories of values); readings of representative opinions from classical, multicultural, and postmodern ethics; a respectful survey of world religions; and substantial reflection on the rights and responsibilities of being culturally defined as a helping professional. I believe that such reflections necessarily bring the therapist back to the realm of self-awareness and the complexities of knowing.

Therapists' Lifespan Development

The seventh and final theme that is essential in the training of psychotherapists spirals back over all the others. It involves the recognition that a career in psychotherapy has effects on the personal life of the practitioner. One cannot be emotionally involved in clients' lives without its having an impact on one's own. People who seek psychotherapy often are in the throes of major life difficulties. Many of those difficulties are related to extremely painful experiences such as cruelty and abuse, loss, neglect, rejection, and trauma. The daily life of the psychotherapy practitioner is filled with people who are unhappy, many of whom are tortured by experiences of intense anger, anxiety, confusion, depression, and guilt. Their anguish is difficult to witness. Also difficult to hear are their individual stories of endured accidents, cruelties, and injustices. And although their stories always are uniquely theirs, their requests converge on common themes: they want to be heard and known; they want to be comforted and encouraged; and they want to be helped in their private struggles to survive and prosper.

The psychotherapist in training needs and deserves to know that being a therapist is not easy. He or she needs to be prepared sometimes to feel overwhelmed by clients' pain, or by the perplexities of not being able to help as much or as quickly as desired (by helper or helpee). The trainee also needs to know that his or her experienced difficulties with the responsibilities of the profession are common and natural. They need to know that they, too, are human, and will struggle with their own unpredictable challenges. Finally, and most importantly, they deserve to know that the burdens of their professional responsibilities can be counterbalanced by a variety of blessings. Central among these are the lessons taught by clients: inspiring human perseverance and resilience, the importance of human relationships, and the diversity of paths in life journeys.

Research on the personal lives of psychotherapists and their psychological development during their careers is just now reaching a critical mass (Guy, 1987; Mahoney, 1991; Skovholt & Rønnestad, 1992). Overall, that research suggests that psychotherapy practitioners generally are satisfied and often enriched by their work, although they do experience unique and substantial stressors, and they report their share of personal problems. They also report accelerated psychological development and a variety of beneficial effects attributed to their work as therapists. Some evidence also suggests that therapists' epistemological styles may be related to their relative risks of career stagnation and burnout. In general, therapists who maintain an open and flexible orientation toward their work appear to be less at risk than those who are more closed and rigid (Skovholt & Rønnestad, 1992).

There are at least two important implications of our current knowledge about the personal lives of psychotherapists that bear on training. The first is that practicing therapy is likely to force the practitioner into a variety of challenges and stressors that are unique to the profession. The second is that the practitioner is therefore well advised to be aware of these stressors and to prioritize self-care activities. The commendable priorities of the profession—which are to serve others in their pursuit of well-being—should be balanced with a priority of taking good care of the serving self. Such balance is warranted not only by its positive effects on the quality of professional services offered to clients but also by its recognition that the therapist is a human being who has taken on a uniquely stressful role. During their apprenticeship, psychotherapy trainees should be encouraged to explore the balance in their lives and to establish meaningful routines of self-care.

CONCLUDING REMARKS

The foregoing remarks have implied both a caricature of the good therapist and recommendations for the apprenticeship experience. That caricature and those recommendations are here consolidated. The good therapist implied in this chapter emerges as a person who exhibits: a commitment to knowing self; an appreciation for the complex social fabric of modern existence; a genuine respect for and celebration of human diversity; a capacity to feel deeply, to imagine what others might be feeling, and to use those capacities in the service of others; an enduring fascination with ideas and inquiries into the mysteries of being; a capacity to explore, pretend, and experiment; an ability to cope and adapt; an ability to teach and to learn in the process; a sensitivity to value judgments and their powerful subtlety; and an appreciation for the individual dynamics of lifespan psychological development, especially their own. These are not easy achievements. In fact, they are never completely achieved by anyone—a fact that often is repeated in the preceding pages. Like the clients they serve, good therapists are lifelong processes.

The good training program implied here is one that values the characteristics of the good therapist. It consciously selects trainees with those characteristics in mind, and it provides a learning environment that nurtures their continuing elaboration in individual trainees. Critically important to such a program are its human context and its atmosphere. These include faculty with diverse training and experience who express and exemplify mutual respect, openness, and a commitment to service. Such faculty should themselves be good therapists and good supervisors. They should also be willing to be seen in action by their apprentices—not simply on edited training tapes but in live work with real clients. Training program staff also are important as part of its human context. Staff often serve as the intermediaries between faculty and students, as well as liasons with clients and community agencies. They play an important role in humanizing a clinic and program.

Students are perhaps the most central figures in the human context of a training program, and even though they rotate through, they represent the main focus of the program itself. It is therefore important that they be provided with facilities and support conducive to their difficult and commendable undertaking. Psychotherapy trainees should be challenged and disciplined, to be sure, but such interactions should be embedded in a professional mentoring relationship. Trainees should have the opportunity to observe and to consult with a wide variety of clients. Their hours of experience as a service provider should be considerable during training. More important than the absolute number of client contact hours, however, are their opportunities to reflect upon and dialogue about their experiences as a therapist. Because of the stresses of training and the profession itself, trainees also should be encouraged to prioritize their own health, emotional nurturance, recreation, relaxation, and rest.

These are my current reflections on what it means to be a psychotherapist and how our professional responsibilities shape the essential themes in our training. These themes are not easily translated into a specific or simple curriculum. They entail an experiential style of training more than any particular contents. Moreover, they reflect the complexity of the endeavor to which we aspire as professionals, and therefore the complexity of elucidating the processes of optimal preparation. Central to these themes is a respect for the human context of helping and the lifelong process of learning.

REFERENCES

Belenky, M. F., Clinchy, B. M., Goldberger, N. R., & Tarule, J. M. (1986). *Women's ways of knowing: The development of self, voice, and mind.* New York: Basic Books. (Reprinted 1997)

Bowlby, J. (1979). *The making and breaking of affectional bonds.* London: Tavistock.

Bowlby, J. (1985). The role of childhood experience in cognitive disturbance. In M. J. Mahoney & A. Freeman (Eds.), *Cognition and psychotherapy* (pp. 181–199). New York: Plenum.

Bowlby, J. (1988). *A secure base.* New York: Basic Books.

Buber, M. (1958). *I and thou.* New York: Macmillan.

Carlson, R., & Shield, B. (Eds.). (1989). *Healers on healing.* Los Angeles: Tarcher.

Cushman, P. (1993). Psychotherapy as moral discourse. *Journal of Theoretical and Philosophical Psychology, 13,* 103–113.

Forman, P. (1995a). Truth and objectivity, part 1: Irony. *Science, 269,* 565–567.

Forman, P. (1995b). Truth and objectivity, part 2: Trust. *Science, 269,* 707–710.

Frank, J. D. (1961). *Persuasion and healing.* Baltimore, MD: Johns Hopkins University Press.

Goleman, D. (1988). *The meditative mind: The varieties of meditative experience.* Los Angeles: Tarcher.

Guy, J. D. (1987). *The personal life of the psychotherapist.* New York: John Wiley and Sons.

Kahn, M. (1991). *Between therapist and client: The new relationship.* New York: Freeman.

Kaslow, N. J., & Friedman, D. (1984). The interface of personal treatment and clinical training for psychotherapist trainees. In F. W. Kaslow (Ed.), *Psychotherapy with psychotherapists* (pp. 33–57). New York: Haworth.

Mahoney, M. J. (1991). *Human change processes: The scientific foundations of psychotherapy.* New York: Basic Books.

Mahoney, M. J. (in press a). *Constructive psychotherapy: Principles and practice.* New York: Guilford.

Mahoney, M. J. (in press b). Ways of knowing in psychotherapy: Facilitating developments in personal epistemologies. In N. Goldberger, M. Belenky, B. Clinchy, & J. Tarule (Eds.), *Women's ways of knowing revisited.* New York: Basic Books.

Mahoney, M. J., & Fernandez-Alvarez, H. (1995). *The personal life of the psychotherapist.* Unpublished manuscript.

Ram Dass & Gordon, P. (1985). *How can I help?* New York: Knopf.

Russell, B. (1967). *The autobiography of Bertrand Russell: 1872–1914.* Boston: Little, Brown.

Schore, A. N. (1994). *Affect regulation and the origin of the self.* Hillsdale, NJ: Erlbaum.

Skovholt, T. M., & Rønnestad, M. H. (1992). *The evolving professional self: Stages and themes in therapist and counselor development.* New York: John Wiley and Sons.

Snyder, C. R., & Fromkin, H. L. (1980). *Uniqueness: The human pursuit of difference.* New York: Plenum.

Stolorow, R. D., & Atwood, G. E. (1992). *Contexts of being: The intersubjective foundations of psychological life.* Hillsdale, NJ: Analytic Press.

Tillich, P. (1952). *The courage to be.* New Haven, CT: Yale University Press.

Watkins, M. (1990). *Invisible guests: The development of imaginal dialogues.* Boston: Sigo Press.

Zweig, P. (1980). *The heresy of self-love: A study of subversive individualism.* Princeton, NJ: Princeton University Press.

AUTHOR INDEX

SUBJECT INDEX